KT-151-970

WITHDRAWN

This Book
was Donated To

LRC Stoke Park

Date: 3|1|07

HEALTH PSYCHOLOGY

Biopsychosocial Interactions

To my mother and in memory of my father.
They gave me life, loved and nurtured me,
and helped me be healthy.

PREFACE

"The first wealth is health," wrote the poet/philosopher Ralph Waldo Emerson in the 19th century. Although people have probably always valued good health, they are becoming increasingly health conscious. This heightened consciousness generally reflects two beliefs: that we can do things to protect our health and that being sick is unpleasant. As Emerson put it, "Sickness is poor-spirited, and cannot serve anyone." Serious health problems can be quite distressing to the patient and his or her family and friends. These beliefs underlie psychologists' interests in helping people behave in ways that promote wellness, adjust to health problems that develop, and participate effectively in treatment and rehabilitation programs. I wrote this book because I share these interests.

Since 1987 when I began writing the first edition of this text, my goal for each edition has been to create a teaching instrument that draws from the research and theory of many disciplines to describe how psychology and health are interconnected. The resulting book is a comprehensive text that is appropriate for several courses, especially those entitled either Health Psychology or Behavioral Medicine. Two objectives were central regarding the likely audience in these courses. First, I aimed to make the content appropriate for upper-division students—mainly juniors. But the straightforward writing style also makes the material accessible to most sophomores. The content assumes that the reader has already had at least an introductory psychology course. Second, I tried to make the material relevant and interesting to students from diverse disciplines—particularly psychology, of course, but also fields such as sociology, medicine, allied health, and health and physical education. Training in health psychology has developed rapidly and can play an important role in helping students from many disciplines understand the interplay of biological, psychological, and social factors in people's health.

The field of health psychology is enormously exciting, partly because of its relevance to the lives of those who study it and individuals the students know or will work with in the future. The field is also exciting because it is so new, and researchers from many different disciplines are finding fascinating and important relationships between psychology and health every day. Keeping up to date in each area of such a complex field presents quite a challenge. After culling through thousands of abstracts, I examined more than 1,000 new articles and books for the current revision. Most of the more than 2,500 references cited in this edition were published within the last 10 years, and about 450 were published since the last edition of this book went to press in 1997.

NEW TO THIS EDITION

Although this edition retains the overall organization, pedagogy, and varieties of boxed material that students and instructors have praised in the last edition, important changes have been made. Every chapter was updated with new information, and I substantially revised or expanded the coverage of the following topics:

- Psychoneuroimmunology
- Coping with acute and chronic stress
- AIDS prevention
- Smoking cessation
- Weight control
- Alternative medicine
- Medical and psychosocial interventions for chronic illnesses
- Age and gender differences in health and health promotion
- Sociocultural differences in health and health promotion

Throughout the text, I endeavored to *internationalize* the content by searching for and citing information about health and health-related behavior of people around the world. I also added boxed material that focuses on *clinical methods and issues*.

THEMES

A phrase we often hear in psychology is that we need to understand the "whole person." In approaching this goal, this book adopts the *biopsychosocial model* as the basic explanatory theme. I have tried to convey a sense that the components of this model interrelate in a dynamic and continuous fashion, consistent with the concept of *systems*. The psychological research cited reflects an eclectic orientation and supports a variety of behavioral, physiological, cognitive, and social–personality viewpoints. In addition, *gender and sociocultural differences* in health and related behaviors are addressed at many points in the book. In these ways, this book presents a balanced view of health psychology that is squarely in the mainstream of current thinking in the field.

One additional theme makes this book unique. I have integrated a focus on *life-span development* in health and illness throughout the book, and each chapter contains information dealing with development. For example, the book discusses how health and health-related behavior change with age and describes health care issues and examples that pertain to pediatric and elderly patients. Sometimes this information is organized as a separate unit, as with the sections "Development and Health-Related Behavior," "When the Hospitalized Patient Is a Child," "Assessing Pain in Children," and "Alzheimer's Disease."

ORGANIZATION

This text examines the major topics and problem areas in health psychology by using an overall organization that progresses in main focus across chapters from *primary*, to *secondary*, to *tertiary* prevention and care. As the table of contents shows, the book is divided into 15 chapters in the following seven parts:

● **Part I.** Chapter 1 presents the history and focus of health psychology and introduces the major concepts and research methods used in the field. Chapter 2 describes physical systems of the body in an engaging manner a reviewer called "a pleasant surprise." Three reasons guided my decision to have a chapter on body systems, rather than introducing the needed physiological principles as they became relevant. First, this approach allows students to see how the various systems interrelate, as in the section entitled "The Endocrine and Nervous Systems Working Together." Second, each body system is mentioned at many points in the book, and students have a single place to refer back to if needed, such as when reading about the neural transmission of pain signals in Chapter 11. Third, the next three chapters of the book rely on the reader's firm knowledge of almost all body systems and discuss them in connection with people's experience of stress.

● **Part II.** Chapters 3, 4, and 5 discuss stress, its relation to illness, and methods for coping with and reducing it. The material on body systems in Chapter 2 connects directly to discussions in Chapters 3 and 4, particularly the sections entitled "Biological Aspects of Stress," "Physiological Arousal," "Stress, Physiology, and Illness," and "Psychoneuroimmunology." This connection is one of the reasons why stress is covered early in the book. A reviewer recognized a second reason and wrote: "The issue of stress permeates all of the other topics, and it would be useful to have the students read about this first." Chapter 5 includes information on psychosocial methods psychologists use in helping people cope better.

● **Part III.** The third part of the book examines issues involved in enhancing health and preventing illness. Chapters 6, 7, and 8 discuss how health-related behaviors develop and are maintained, can affect health, and can be changed via psychosocial and public health efforts. Chapter 7 gives special attention to the topics of tobacco, alcohol, and drug use, and Chapter 8 discusses nutrition, weight control, exercise, and safety. The role of stress in health behaviors and decision-making is considered in these chapters. The book up to this point focuses mainly on primary prevention.

● **Part IV.** In Chapter 9, the main focus shifts to secondary prevention by describing the kinds of health services that are available and considering why people use, do not use, and delay using these services. This chapter also examines patients' relationships to practitioners and problems in adhering to medical regimens. Chapter 10 discusses the hospital setting and personnel, how people react to being hospitalized and cope with stressful medical procedures, and the role psychologists play in helping patients cope with their illnesses and medical treatments.

● **Part V.** Chapters 11 and 12 explore the physical and psychological nature of pain, ways to assess patients' discomfort, the psychosocial impact pain, and methods for managing and controlling pain.

● **Part VI.** The two chapters in this part of the book emphasize tertiary prevention. They examine different chronic health problems, their impact on patients and their families, and medical and psychosocial treatment approaches. The chapters separate illnesses on the basis of mortality rates. Chapter 13 focuses on health conditions, such as diabetes and arthritis, that have either very low or moderate rates of mortality and may lead to other health problems

TO THE STUDENT

"I wish I could help my father stop smoking," a student in my health psychology course said. Maybe she did help—he quit by the end of the semester. This example points out two things that will probably make health psychology interesting to you: (1) the material is *personally relevant* and (2) many of the things you learn can actually be *applied* in your everyday life. Studying health psychology will also help you answer important questions you may have considered about health and psychology in the past. Does the mind affect our health—and if so, how? What effect does stress have on health and recovery from illness? What can be done to help people lead more healthful lives than they do? Why don't patients follow their doctors' advice, and what can health care workers do to help? What special needs do children have as patients, and how can parents and health care workers address these needs? How can families, friends, and health care workers help patients adjust to disabling or life-threatening health problems?

As these questions indicate, a knowledge of health psychology can be relevant both now and later when you enter *your future career*. This is so whether you are studying to be a psychologist, medical social worker, nurse or physician, physical or occupational therapist, public health worker, or health educator. You will learn in this course that the relationship between the person's health and psychology involves a "two-way street"—each affects the other. Psychological factors go hand in hand with medical approaches in preventing and treating illness and in helping patients adjust to the health problems they develop.

To help you master the material and remember it longer, the book includes the following learning aids:

- **Chapter Contents and Prologue.** Each chapter begins with a contents list that outlines the major topics in the order in which they are covered. The prologue then introduces the chapter with a vignette that is relevant to the material ahead and gives an overview of the basic ideas you will read about.

- **Illustrations.** The many figures, tables, and photographs in each chapter are designed to clarify concepts and research findings and help them stick in your mind.

- **Boxed material.** Four types of boxed material are included in the chapters. Each type of box has a special icon that is used in "Go to . . ." instructions, prompting you to read the appropriate box at the right point in the text.

- **Summary and Key Terms.** Each chapter closes with two features: (1) the summary, which presents the most important ideas covered, and (2) the key terms—a list of the most important terms in the chapter, arranged in order of their appearance.

- **Glossary.** The glossary at the back of the book gives definitions of important terms and concepts, along with pronunciation keys for the most difficult words. It will be useful when you are studying or reading and are not sure of the exact meaning or pronunciation of a term.

THE BOOK

This book was designed for you, the reader. First and foremost, it provides a thorough and up-to-date presentation of the major issues, theories, concepts, and research in health psychology. Throughout the book, the major point of view is "biopsychosocial"—that is, that health and illness influence and result from the interplay of biological, psychological, and social aspects of people's lives. Because integrating these aspects involves complex concepts and technical material, I have made special efforts to write in a straightforward, clear, and engaging fashion.

STUDY HINTS

There are many ways you can use the features of this book to learn and study well, and you may want to "experiment" to find the best way for you. I will describe one method that works well for many students.

Survey the chapter first. Read the contents list and browse through the chapter, examining the figures, tables, and photographs. Some students also find it useful to read the summary first, even though it contains terms they may not yet understand. Then read the prologue. As you begin each new section of the chapter, look at its title and turn it into a *question*. Thus, the heading early in Chapter 1, "An Illness/Wellness Continuum," might become "What is an illness/wellness continuum?" Doing this helps you focus on your reading. After reading the section, *reflect* on what you have just read. Can you answer the question you asked when you reworded the title?

When you have finished the body of the chapter, *review* what you have read by reading the summary and trying to define the items in the list of key terms. If there is something you do not understand, look it up in the chapter or glossary. Last, *reread* the chapter at least once, concentrating on the important concepts or ideas. You may find it helpful to underline or highlight selected material now that you have a good idea of what is important. If your exam will consist of "objective" questions, such as multiple choice, using this approach intensively should be effective. If your exam will have essay items, you will probably find it helpful to develop a list of likely questions and write an outline or a complete answer for each one.

I hope that you enjoy this book, that you learn a great deal from it, and that you will share my enthusiasm and fascination for health psychology by the time you finish the course.

Edward P. Sarafino

BRIEF CONTENTS

CONTENTS

PART I

AN INTRODUCTION: BASIC ISSUES AND PROCESSES

1

AN OVERVIEW OF PSYCHOLOGY AND HEALTH

"Wide load!" the boys shouted as they pressed themselves against the walls of the hallway at school. They were "making room" for a very overweight girl named Ana to pass through. Lunch time in the cafeteria was even more degrading for Ana because when she sat down to eat, her schoolmates would stop eating, stare at her every move, and make pig noises. "Kids can be cruel," her parents would say to console her. One of Ana's aunts told her that she "inherited a glandular problem, and you can't do anything about it," and another aunt said, "You'll lose weight easily in a couple of years when you start getting interested in boys." Is either aunt right?

Ana's parents are concerned about her weight because they know that overweight people often have social problems and face special health risks, particularly for high blood pressure and heart disease. But her parents are not sure why she is so heavy or how to help her. Although her father is a bit overweight, her mother is very heavy, was heavy as a child, and did not lose weight when she became interested in boys. This could support the idea of an inherited cause of her being overweight. On the other hand, they know Ana eats a lot of fattening foods and gets very little exercise, a combination that often causes weight gains. As part of their effort to change these two behaviors, they encouraged her to join a recreation program, where she will be involved in many physical activities.

This story about Ana illustrates important issues related to health. For instance, being overweight is associated with the development of specific health problems and may affect the individual's social relations. Also, weight problems can result from a person's inheritance and his or her behavior. In this book, we will examine the relationships between health and a wide variety of biological, psychological, and social factors in people's lives.

This chapter introduces a relatively new and very exciting field of study called *health psychology*. We look at its scope, its history, its research methods, and how it draws on and supports other sciences. As we study these topics, you will begin to see how health psychologists would answer such questions as: Does the mind affect our health? What role does the cultural background of individuals play in their health? Does the age of a person affect how he or she deals with issues of health and illness? But first let's begin with a definition of health.

WHAT IS HEALTH?

You know what health is, don't you? How would you define it? You would probably mention something about health being a state of feeling well and not being sick. We commonly think about health in terms of an absence of (1) objective *signs* that the body is not functioning properly, such as measured high blood pressure, or (2) subjective *symptoms* of disease or injury, such as pain or nausea (Birren & Zarit, 1985; Thoresen, 1984). Dictionaries define health in this way, too. But there is a problem with this definition of health. Let's see why.

AN ILLNESS/WELLNESS CONTINUUM

Consider Ana, the overweight girl in the opening story. You've surely heard people say, "It's not healthy to be overweight." Is Ana healthy? What about someone who feels fine but whose lungs are being damaged from smoking cigarettes or whose arteries are becoming clogged from eating foods that are high in saturated fats? These are all signs of improper body functioning. Are people with these signs healthy? We probably would say they are not "sick"—they are just *less* healthy than they would be without the unhealthful conditions.

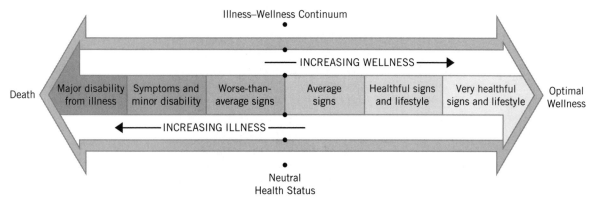

Figure 1–1 An illness/wellness continuum to represent people's differing health statuses. Starting at the center (neutral level) of the diagram, a person's health status is shown as progressively worse to the left and progressively healthful as it moves to the right. The segments in the central band describe dominant features that usually characterize different health statuses, based on the person's *physical condition*—that is, his or her signs (such as blood pressure), symptoms, and disability—and *lifestyle*, such as his or her amount of regular exercise, cholesterol consumption, and cigarette smoking. Medical treatment typically begins at a health status to the left of the neutral level and intensifies as the physical condition worsens. Medical treatment can bring the person's health status back to the mid-range of the continuum, but healthful lifestyles can help, too. Increasing wellness beyond the mid-range can be achieved through lifestyle improvements. (Based on information in Antonovsky, 1987; Bradley, 1993; Ryan & Travis, 1981.)

This means health and sickness are not entirely separate concepts—they overlap. There are degrees of wellness and of illness. Medical sociologist Aaron Antonovsky (1979, 1987) has suggested that we consider these concepts as ends of a continuum, noting that "We are all terminal cases. And we all are, so long as there is a breath of life in us, in some measure healthy" (1987, p. 3). He also proposed that we revise our focus, giving more attention to what enables people to stay well than to what causes people to become ill. Figure 1–1 presents a diagram of an **illness/wellness continuum,** with *death* at one end and *optimal wellness* at the other.

We will use the term **health** to mean a positive state of physical, mental, and social wellbeing—not simply the absence of injury or disease—that varies over time along a continuum. At the wellness end of the continuum, health is the dominant state. At the other end of the continuum, the dominant state is illness or injury, in which destructive processes produce characteristic signs, symptoms, or disabilities.

ILLNESS TODAY AND IN THE PAST

People in the United States and other developed, industrialized nations live longer, on the average, than

they did in the past, and they suffer from a different pattern of illnesses. During the 17th, 18th, and 19th centuries, people in North America suffered and died chiefly from two types of illness: dietary and infectious (Grob, 1983). **Dietary diseases** result from malnutrition—for example, beriberi is caused by a lack of vitamin B₁ and is characterized by anemia, paralysis, and wasting away. **Infectious diseases** are acute illnesses caused by harmful matter or microorganisms, such as bacteria or viruses, in the body. In most of the world today, infectious diseases continue to be the main causes of death (WHO, 1999c).

A good example of the way illness patterns have changed in developed nations comes from the history of diseases in the United States. From the early colonial days in America through the 18th century, colonists experienced periodic epidemics of many infectious diseases, especially smallpox, diphtheria, yellow fever, measles, and influenza. It was not unusual for hundreds, and sometimes thousands, of people to die in a single epidemic. Children were particularly hard hit. Two other infectious diseases, malaria and dysentery, were widespread and presented an even greater threat. Although these two diseases generally did not kill people directly, they weakened their victims and reduced the ability to

Epidemics of deadly infectious diseases have occured throughout the world. Before the 20th century, there were no effective methods for prevention or treatment of the plague, for instance, which is the disease illustrated in this engraving.

resist other fatal diseases. Most, if not all, of these diseases did not exist in North America before the European settlers arrived—the settlers brought the infections with them—and the death toll among Native Americans was extremely high. This high death rate occurred for two reasons. First, the native population had never been exposed to these new microorganisms, and thus lacked the natural immunity that our bodies develop after lengthy exposure to most diseases (Grob, 1983). Second, Native Americans' immune functions were probably limited by a low degree of genetic variation among these people (Black, 1992).

In the 19th century, infectious diseases were still the greatest threat to the health of Americans. The illnesses of the colonial era continued to claim many lives, but new diseases began to appear. The most significant of these diseases was tuberculosis, or "consumption," as it was often called. In 1842, for example, consumption was listed as the cause for 22% of all deaths in the state of Massachusetts (Grob, 1983). But by the end of the 19th century, deaths from infectious diseases had decreased sharply. For instance, the death rate from tuberculosis declined by about 60% in a 25-year period around the turn of the century.

Did this decrease result mostly from advances in medical treatment? Although medical advances helped to some degree, the decrease occurred long before effective vaccines and medications were introduced. This was the case for most of the major diseases we've discussed, including tuberculosis, diphtheria, measles, and influenza (Grob, 1983; Leventhal, Prohaska, & Hirschman, 1985). It appears that the decline resulted chiefly from *preventive* measures such as improved personal hygiene, greater resistance to diseases (owing to better nutrition), and public health innovations, such as building water purification and sewage treatment facilities. Many people had become concerned about their health, and began to heed the advice of health reformers like William Alcott, an advocate of moderation in diet and sexual behavior (Leventhal, Prohaska, & Hirschman, 1985). Fewer deaths occurred from diseases because fewer people contracted them.

The 20th century has seen great changes in the patterns of illness afflicting people, particularly in developed nations where advances in preventive measures and medical care have reduced the death rate from life-threatening infectious diseases (WHO, 1999c). At the same time, the average life expectancy

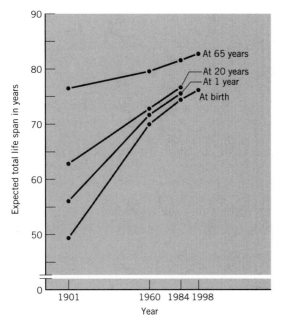

Figure 1–2 Expected total life span for people in the United States at various years since 1900 who were born in the specified year or had reached 1 year, 20 years, or 65 years of age. (Data from USDHHS, 1987, p. 2, for years 1900–1902, 1959–1961, and 1984; USBC, 1999, for 1998.)

of people has increased dramatically. At the turn of the century in the United States, the life expectancy of babies at birth was about 48 years (USDHHS, 1987); today it is 76 years (USBC, 1999). Figure 1–2 shows this change and an important reason for it: the death rate among children was very high many years ago. Babies who survived their first year in 1900 could be expected to live to about 56 years of age. Surviving that first year added seven years to their expected total life span. Moreover, people in 1900 who had reached the age of 20 years could expect to live to almost 63 years of age. Today the death rate for American children is much lower, and only a small difference exists in the expected total life span for newborns and 20-year-olds.

Death is still inevitable, of course, but people die at later ages now and from different causes. The main health problems and causes of death in developed countries today are **chronic diseases**—that is, degenerative illnesses that develop or persist over a long period of time. About two-thirds of all deaths in developed nations are caused by three chronic diseases: heart disease, cancer, and stroke (WHO,

1999c). These diseases are not new, but they were responsible for a much smaller proportion of deaths before the 20th century. Why? One reason is that people's lives are different today. For example, the growth of industrialization increased people's stress and exposure to harmful chemicals. In addition, more people today survive to old age, and chronic diseases are more likely to afflict the elderly than younger individuals. Thus, another reason for the current prominence of chronic diseases is that more people are living to the age when they are at high risk for contracting them (USDHHS, 1982).

Are the main causes of death in childhood and adolescence different from those in adulthood? Yes. In the United States, for example, the leading cause of death in children and adolescents, by far, is not an illness, but accidental injury (USBC, 1999). Nearly 40% of child and adolescent deaths result from accidents, frequently involving automobiles. In childhood, the next two most frequent causes of death are cancer and congenital abnormalities; in adolescence, they are homicide and suicide (USBC, 1999). Clearly, the role of disease in death differs greatly at different points in the life span.

VIEWPOINTS FROM HISTORY: PHYSIOLOGY, DISEASE PROCESSES, AND THE MIND

Is illness a purely physical condition? Does a person's mind play a role in becoming ill and getting well? People have wondered about these questions for thousands of years, and the answers they have arrived at have changed over time.

EARLY CULTURES

Although we do not know for certain, it appears that the best educated people thousands of years ago believed physical and mental illness were caused by mystical forces, such as evil spirits (Stone, 1979). Why do we think this? Researchers found ancient skulls in several areas of the world with coin-size circular holes in them that could not have been battle wounds. These holes were probably made with sharp stone tools in a procedure called *trephination*. This procedure was done presumably for superstitious reasons—for instance, to allow illness-causing demons to leave the head. Unfortunately, we can only speculate about the reasons for these holes because there are no written records from those times.

ANCIENT GREECE AND ROME

The philosophers of ancient Greece produced the earliest written ideas about physiology, disease processes, and the mind between 500 and 300 B.C. Hippocrates, often called "the Father of Medicine," proposed a *humoral theory* to explain why people get sick. According to this theory, the body contains four fluids called *humors* (in biology, the term humor refers to any plant or animal fluid). When the mixture of these humors is harmonious or balanced, we are in a state of health. Disease occurs when the mixture is faulty (Stone, 1979). Hippocrates recommended eating a good diet and avoiding excesses to help achieve humoral balance.

Greek philosophers, especially Plato, were among the first to propose that the mind and the body are separate entities (Marx & Hillix, 1963; Schneider &

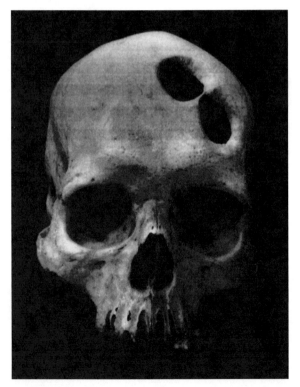

A skull with holes probably produced by trephination. This person probably survived several of these procedures.

Tarshis, 1975). This view is reflected in the humoral theory: people get sick because of an imbalance in body fluids. The mind was considered to have little or no relationship to the body and its state of health. This remained the dominant view of writers and philosophers for more than a thousand years.

Many people today still speak about the body and the mind as if they were separate. The *body* refers to our physical being, including our skin, muscles, bones, heart, and brain. The *mind* refers to an abstract process that includes our thoughts, perceptions, and feelings. Although we can distinguish between the mind and the body conceptually, an important issue is whether they also function independently. The question of their relationship is called the **mind/body problem.**

Galen was a famous and highly respected physician and writer of the 2nd century A.D. who was born in Greece and practiced in Rome. Although he believed generally in the humoral theory and the mind/body split, he made many innovations. For example, he "dissected animals of many species (but probably never a human), and made important discoveries about the brain, circulatory system, and kidneys" (Stone, 1979, p. 4). From this work, he became aware that illnesses can be localized, with pathology in specific parts of the body, and that different diseases have different effects. Galen's ideas became widely accepted.

THE MIDDLE AGES

After the collapse of the Roman Empire in the 5th century A.D., much of the Western world was in disarray. The advancement of knowledge and culture slowed sharply in Europe and remained stunted during the Middle Ages, which lasted almost a thousand years. Galen's views dominated ideas about physiology and disease processes for most of this time.

The influence of the Church in slowing the development of medical knowledge during the Middle Ages was enormous. According to historians, in the eyes of the Church the human being

was regarded as a creature with a soul, possessed of a free will which set him apart from ordinary natural laws, subject only to his own willfulness and perhaps the will of God. Such a creature, being free-willed, could not be an object of scientific investigation. Even the body of man was regarded as sacrosanct, and dissection was dangerous for the dissector. These strictures against observation hindered the development of anatomy and medicine for centuries. (Marx & Hillix, 1963, p. 24)

The prohibition against dissection extended to animals as well, since they were thought to have souls, too.

People's ideas about the cause of illness took on pronounced religious overtones, and the belief in demons became strong again (Sarason & Sarason, 1984). Sickness was seen as God's punishment for doing evil things. As a result, the Church came to control the practice of medicine, and priests became increasingly involved in treating the ill, often by torturing the body to drive out evil spirits.

It was not until the 13th century that new ideas about the mind/body problem began to emerge. The Italian philosopher St. Thomas Aquinas rejected the view that the mind and body are separate. He saw them as an interrelated unit that forms the whole person (Leahey, 1987). Although his position did not have as great an impact as others had had, it renewed interest in the issue and influenced later philosophers.

THE RENAISSANCE AND AFTER

The word *renaissance* means rebirth—a fitting name for the 14th and 15th centuries. During this period in history, Europe saw a rebirth of inquiry, culture, and politics. Scholars became more "human-centered" than "God-centered" in their search for truth and "believed that truth can be seen in many ways, from many individual perspectives" (Leahey, 1987, p. 80). These ideas set the stage for important changes in philosophy once the scientific revolution began after 1600.

The 17th-century French philosopher and mathematician Rene Descartes probably had the greatest influence on scientific thought of any philosopher in history (Schneider & Tarshis, 1975). Like the Greeks, he regarded the mind and body as separate entities, but he introduced three important innovations. First, he conceived of the body as a machine and described the mechanics of how action and sensation occurred. For example, Figure 1–3 shows his concept of how we experience pain. Second, he proposed that the mind and body, although separate, could *communicate* through the pineal gland, an organ in the brain (Leahey, 1987). Third, he believed that animals have no soul and that the soul in humans leaves the body at death (Marx & Hillix, 1963). This belief meant

Figure 1–3   Descartes' concept of the pain pathway. Descartes used this drawing to illustrate the mechanisms by which people experience and respond to pain: The heat of the fire (at A) sends tiny particles to the foot (B) that pull on a thread that courses from the foot to the head. This action opens a pore (*de*), releasing spirits from a cavity (F) that travel to the parts of the body that respond (e.g., the leg moves away). (From Descartes, 1664, Figure 7.)

that dissection could be an acceptable method of study—a point the Church was now ready to concede (Engel, 1977).

In the 18th and 19th centuries, knowledge in science and medicine grew quickly, helped greatly by the development of the microscope and the use of dissection in autopsies. Once scientists learned the basics of how the body functioned and discovered that microorganisms cause certain diseases, they were able to reject the humoral theory of illness and propose new theories. The field of surgery flourished after antiseptic techniques and anesthesia were introduced in the mid-19th century (Stone, 1979). Before that time, hospitals were "notorious places, more likely to spread diseases than cure them" (Easterbrook, 1987, p. 42). Over time, the reputation of physicians and hospitals began to improve, and people's trust in the ability of doctors to heal increased.

These advances, coupled with the continuing belief that the mind and body are separate, laid the foundation for a new approach, or model, for conceptualizing health and illness. This approach—called the **biomedical model**—proposes that all diseases or physical disorders can be explained by disturbances in physiological processes, which result from injury, biochemical imbalances, bacterial or viral infection, and the like (Engel, 1977; Leventhal, Prohaska, & Hirschman, 1985). The biomedical model assumes that disease is an affliction of the body and is separate from the psychological and social processes of the mind. This viewpoint became widely accepted during the 19th and 20th centuries and still represents the dominant view in medicine today.

SEEING A NEED: PSYCHOLOGY'S ROLE IN HEALTH

The biomedical model has been very useful. Using it as a guide, researchers have made enormous achievements. They conquered many infectious diseases, such as polio and measles, through the development of vaccines. They also developed antibiotics, which made it possible to cure illnesses caused by bacterial infection. Despite these great advances, the biomedical model needs improvement. Let's see why.

PROBLEMS IN THE HEALTH CARE SYSTEM

Scarcely a week goes by when we don't hear through the mass media that health care costs are rising rapidly, particularly for prescription drugs and for hospital and nursing home care. Countries worldwide have been facing escalating costs in health care (WHO, 1999c). For example, between 1960 and 1983, there was a tenfold increase in the amount of money spent per capita on health care in the United States (USBC, 1995). The burden of health costs on the economy increased sharply during that same period: health care spending amounted to 5.3% of the gross domestic product in 1960, and 10.5% in 1983. Since 1983, these costs have continued to rise faster than the overall rate of inflation. By 1997, health care spending doubled to $3,900 per capita per year and equaled 13.5% of the gross domestic product (NCHS, 2000). Because medical costs continue to rise rapidly,

we need to consider new approaches for improving people's health.

We saw earlier that the patterns of illness affecting people have changed, particularly in developed nations where the main health problems now are chronic diseases. Although a great deal of progress is being made in understanding the causes of chronic diseases, improvements in techniques for treating them have been modest. For example, gains in cancer survival rates since 1950 have resulted more from earlier detection of the disease than from improved treatments (Boffey, 1987). Although detection occurs earlier today partly because diagnostic methods and technology have improved, another part of the reason is that *people* have changed. Many individuals are more aware of signs and symptoms of illness, more motivated to take care of their health, and better able to afford visits to physicians than they were in the past. These factors are clearly important and relate to psychological and social aspects of the person. But *the person* as a unique individual is not included in the biomedical model (Engel, 1977, 1980).

"THE PERSON" IN HEALTH AND ILLNESS

Have you ever noticed how some people are "always sick"—they get illnesses more frequently than most people do and get well more slowly? These differences between people can result from biomedical sources, such as variations in physiological processes and exposure to harmful microorganisms. But psychological and social factors also play a role. Let's look briefly at two of these factors: the lifestyle and personality of the person. (Go to 🍎—as described in the Preface, this instruction prompts you to read the nearby boxed material that has the same icon.)

Lifestyle and Illness

Earlier we saw that the occurrence of infectious diseases declined sharply in the late 19th century chiefly because of such preventive measures as improving nutrition and personal hygiene. These measures involved changes in people's *lifestyles*—their everyday patterns of behavior, such as in preparing and eating better balanced meals. The chief health problems in technological societies today are chronic diseases. People can reduce these, too, by making changes in their lives. Let's see how.

ASSESS YOURSELF

What's Your Lifestyle Like?

At various points in this book, you'll find brief self-assessment surveys like this one that you should try to fill out as accurately as you can. These surveys relate to the nearby content of the chapter, and most of them can be completed in less than a minute or two.

This survey assesses seven aspects of your *usual* lifestyle. For each of the listed practices, put a check mark in the preceding space if it describes your usual situation.

_____ I sleep 7 or 8 hours a day.

_____ I eat breakfast almost every day.

_____ I rarely eat between meals.

_____ I am at or near the appropriate weight (see Table 8.1 on page 245)

_____ I never smoke cigarettes.

_____ I drink alcohol rarely or moderately.

_____ I regularly get vigorous physical activity.

Count the check marks—six or seven is quite good. The more of these situations that describe your lifestyle now and in the future, the better your health is likely to be, particularly after the age of 50.

Characteristics or conditions that are associated with the development of a disease or injury are called **risk factors** for that health problem. Although some risk factors are *biological*, such as having inherited certain genes, others are *behavioral*. For example, it is well known that people who smoke cigarettes face a much higher risk of developing cancer and other illnesses than nonsmokers do. Other risk factors for cancer include eating diets high in saturated fat and having a family history of the disease. People who "do more" or "have more" of these characteristics or conditions are more likely to contract cancer than people who "do less" or "have less" of these factors. Keep in mind that a risk factor is *associated* with a health problem—it does not necessarily *cause* the problem. For example, being poor is a risk factor for cancer (Levy, 1985), but it does not cause the disease—at least, not directly.

Many risk factors result from the way people live or behave, such as smoking cigarettes and eating unhealthful diets. Some behavioral risk factors associated with the five leading causes of death are:

1. *Heart disease*—smoking, high dietary cholesterol, and lack of exercise.

2. *Cancer*—smoking, high alcohol use, and diet.

3. *Stroke*—smoking, high dietary cholesterol, and lack of exercise.

4. COPD (chronic lung diseases, e.g., emphysema)—smoking.

5. *Accidents* (including motor vehicle)—alcohol/drug use, driving vehicles too fast, and not using seat belts. (Sources: McGinnis, 1994; USBC, 1999)

Many of the people who are the victims of these illnesses and accidents live for at least a short while and either recover or eventually succumb. Part of today's high medical costs result from people's lifestyles that contribute to their health problems, and most health care efforts and funds are directed toward treating illness, not preventing it. Society, not the individual, often bears the burden of medical costs through public and private health insurance programs.

"Why don't people do what's good for them?" There's no simple answer to that question—there are many reasons. One reason is that less healthful behaviors often bring immediate pleasure, as when the person has a "good-tasting" cigarette or ice cream. Long-range negative consequences seem remote, both in time and in likelihood. Another reason is that people sometimes feel social pressures to engage in unhealthful behavior, as when an adolescent begins to use cigarettes, alcohol, or drugs. Also, some behaviors can become very strong habits, perhaps involving a physical addiction or psychological dependency, as happens with drugs and cigarettes. Quitting them becomes very difficult. Lastly, sometimes people are simply not aware of the dangers involved or how to change their behavior. These people need information about ways to protect their health. (Go to 🕮.)

FOCUS ON RESEARCH

Health and Lifestyles

In 1965, Nedra Belloc and Lester Breslow began a project to study the importance of personal lifestyles on people's health. The researchers surveyed nearly 7,000 adults who ranged in age from about 20 to over 75, and asked them two sets of questions. One set asked about the health of these people over the previous 12 months—for instance, whether illness had prevented them from working for a long time, forced them to cut down on other activities, impaired their continued activities, or reduced their energy level. The second set of questions asked about seven aspects of their lifestyles: sleeping, eating breakfast, eating between meals, maintaining an appropriate weight, smoking cigarettes, drinking alcohol, and getting physical activity. The questions you answered above are similar to those in this research.

How important were these lifestyle factors? When the researchers compared the data for subjects in different age groups, they found that at each age health was typically better as the number of healthful practices increased. The impact of these lifestyle practices is suggested by the finding that the health of those who "reported following all seven good health practices was consistently about the same as those 30 years younger who followed few or none of these practices" (Belloc & Breslow, 1972, p. 419).

Were these health practices important in the future health of these people? Very much so. Breslow (1983) has described later studies of the same group of subjects. One study determined which people had died in the 9½ years after the original survey. These data were then separated according to the age, sex, and number of healthful behaviors the people reported practicing in the original survey. Figure 1F–1 presents the results of this analysis for the men. The important finding was that the percentage

dying generally decreased with increases in the number of healthful behaviors practiced, and this impact was greater for older people than for younger ones. The results for the female subjects were similar, but the impact of these health practices was not as strong.

These findings suggest that people's practicing healthful behaviors can reduce their risk of illness and early death substantially. These lifestyle factors appear to be more critical for the health of men than women, and are particularly important as individuals get older.

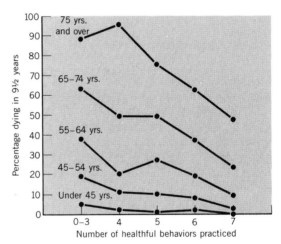

Figure 1F-1 Percentage of male adults who died within 9½ years as a function of the number of healthful behaviors they reported practicing and of their ages (at the start of the study, in 1965). The findings for women were similar, but the decreases in deaths associated with increasing numbers of healthful behaviors were not as sharp. (Data from Breslow, 1983, Table 3.6.)

Personality and Illness

Do you believe, as many do, that people who suffer from ulcers tend to be worriers or "workaholics"? Or that people who have migraine headaches are highly anxious? If you do, then you believe there is a link

between personality and illness. The term **personality** refers to a person's cognitive, affective, or behavioral tendencies that are fairly stable across time and situations.

Researchers have found evidence linking personality traits and health. For example, low levels of *conscientiousness* in childhood and *poor mental health* in adulthood are associated with dying at earlier ages from diseases such as heart disease and cancer (Friedman, Tucker et al., 1995). In addition, people whose personalities include high levels of *anxiety, depression, anger/hostility,* or *pessimism* seem to be at risk for developing a variety of illnesses, particularly heart disease (Everson et al., 1996; Friedman & Booth-Kewley, 1987; Scheier & Bridges, 1995). These four emotions are reactions that often occur when people experience stress, such as when they have more work to do than they think they can finish or when a tragedy happens.

People differ in the way they deal with stressful situations. Many people approach these situations with relatively positive emotions. Their outlook is more optimistic than pessimistic, more hopeful than desperate. These people are not only less likely to become ill than are people with less positive personalities, but when they do, they tend to recover more quickly (Reker & Wong, 1985; Scheier & Carver, in press). A dramatic and well-known anecdotal example of the role of this optimistic and hopeful outlook is the case of Norman Cousins, the former editor of *Saturday Review*, who developed an incurable and painful illness. His strong knowledge of medicine allowed him to react to his doctors' prognosis by becoming actively involved in decisions regarding his medical treatment. He decided to stop taking massive doses of painkillers, supplement his treatment with high doses of vitamin C, and try to reduce his pain with lots of laughter, which he got by watching comic films like those of Groucho Marx and Laurel and Hardy. As his condition began to improve, he came to believe he was recovering because his optimism enabled him to mobilize his body's resources to fight the disease (Cousins, 1979).

The link between personality and illness is not a one-way street: illness can affect one's personality, too (Cohen & Rodriguez, 1995). People who suffer from serious illness and disability often experience feelings of anxiety, depression, anger, and hopelessness. But as psychologists Irwin and Barbara Sarason (1984) have pointed out, even minor health problems, such as the flu or a toothache, produce temporary negative thoughts and feelings. People who are ill and overcome their negative thoughts and feelings can speed their recovery. We will examine this relationship in more detail later in this book.

Our glimpse at the relationships of the person's lifestyle and personality in illness demonstrates why it is important to consider psychological and social factors in health and illness. Next we will see how this recognition came about.

HOW THE ROLE OF PSYCHOLOGY EMERGED

The idea that medicine and psychology are somehow connected has a long history, dating back at least to ancient Greece. It became somewhat more formalized early in the 20th century in the work of Sigmund Freud, who was trained as a physician. He noticed that some patients showed symptoms of physical illness without any organic disorder. Using principles from his *psychoanalytic theory*, Freud proposed that these symptoms were "converted" from unconscious emotional conflicts (Alexander, 1950; Davison & Neale, 1998). He called this condition *conversion hysteria.*

What symptoms do patients with conversion hysteria show? The symptoms can include paralysis, deafness, blindness, and the loss of sensation in part of the body, such as the hand. This last symptom is called *glove anesthesia* because only the hand has no feeling. When a loss of sensation in the body is inconsistent with the relevant nerve pathways, it probably does not have an organic cause (Davison & Neale, 1998). These forms of conversion hysteria occur less frequently in urban than in backwoods areas, perhaps because urbanites realize that medical tests can generally determine if an organic disorder exists (Rosenhan & Seligman, 1984). The need to understand conditions such as conversion hysteria led professionals to develop the first field dedicated to studying the interplay between emotional life and bodily processes.

Psychosomatic Medicine

The field called **psychosomatic medicine** was formed in the 1930s in association with the National Research Council, which began publishing the journal *Psychosomatic Medicine* (Alexander, 1950). Its founders were primarily researchers trained in medicine, and their leaders included the psychoanalyst Franz Alexander and the psychiatrist Flanders Dunbar. Four years later the field was organized as a society now called the American Psychosomatic Society.

The term *psychosomatic* does not mean a person's symptoms are "imaginary"; it means that the mind and body are both involved. Until the 1960s or so, research in psychosomatic medicine focused on psychoanalytic interpretations for specific, real health problems, including ulcers, high blood pressure, asthma, migraine headaches, and rheumatoid arthritis. We can see this approach in the case study of a 23-year-old man who had developed a bleeding ulcer. According to his therapist (Alexander, 1950, pp. 113–114),

- This patient's "most conspicuous personality trait was his extreme casualness," which served as his defense against feelings of insecurity and dependence that resulted from his mother's exaggerated expectations. These conflicting feelings caused his ulcers.

- This casualness prevented him from becoming emotionally involved with women. He had had casual sexual relationships, but ended each one when he thought the woman was personally interested in him.

- Through therapy, the man overcame his dependency, adopted a mature attitude, and eventually fell in love and married. His stomach complaints decreased, and he could consume a normal diet.

In the 1960s, psychosomatic medicine began to focus on new approaches and theories (Totman, 1982). It is currently a broader field concerned with the interrelationships among psychological and social factors, biological and physiological functions, and the development and course of illness (Lipowski, 1986).

Behavioral Medicine and Health Psychology

Two new fields emerged in the 1970s to study the role of psychology in illness: one is called behavioral medicine, and the other is called health psychology.

The field of **behavioral medicine** was launched in association with the National Academy of Sciences; the *Journal of Behavioral Medicine* was established, and the Society of Behavioral Medicine was founded. This field has two defining characteristics (Gentry, 1984): First, its membership is *interdisciplinary*, coming from a wide variety of fields, including psychology, sociology, and various areas of medicine. Second, it grew out of the perspective in psychology called *behaviorism*, which proposed that people's behavior results from two types of learning:

- *Classical (or respondent) conditioning*, in which a stimulus (the conditioned stimulus) gains the ability to elicit a response through association with a stimu-

lus (the unconditioned stimulus) that already elicits that response.

- *Operant conditioning*, in which behavior is changed because of its consequences: *reinforcement* (reward) strengthens the behavior; *punishment* suppresses it.

Conditioning methods had shown a good deal of success as therapeutic approaches in helping people modify problem *behaviors*, such as overeating, and *emotions*, such as anxiety and fear (Sarafino, 2001). By the 1970s, physiological psychologists had clearly shown that psychological events—particularly emotions—influence bodily functions, such as blood pressure. And researchers had demonstrated that people can learn to control various physiological systems if they are given *feedback* as to what the systems are doing (Miller, 1978).

Why were these findings important? They revealed that the link between the mind and the body is more direct and pervasive than was previously thought. Soon they led to an important therapeutic technique called *biofeedback*, whereby a person's physiological processes, such as blood pressure, are monitored by the person so that he or she can gain voluntary control over them. The feedback serves as a consequence of operant conditioning. As we shall see in later chapters, biofeedback has proven to be useful in treating a variety of health problems, such as headaches.

Behaviorism also served as an important foundation for **health psychology,** a field that is principally within the discipline of psychology. The American Psychological Association has many divisions, or subfields; the Division of Health Psychology was introduced in 1978 (Wallston, 1993). The journal *Health Psychology* began publication 4 years later as the official journal of this division. Joseph Matarazzo (1982), the first president of the Division, outlined four goals of health psychology. Let's look at these goals and some ways psychologists can contribute to them.

- *To promote and maintain health.* Psychologists study such topics as why people do and do not smoke cigarettes, use safety belts in cars, drink alcohol, and eat particular diets. As a result, health psychologists can help in the design of school health education programs and media campaigns to encourage healthful lifestyles and behaviors.

- To *prevent and treat illness*. Psychological principles have been applied effectively in preventing illness, such as in reducing high blood pressure and, therefore, the risk of heart disease and stroke. For those people who become seriously ill, psychologists with clinical training can help them adjust to their current condition, rehabilitation program, and future prospects, such as reduced work or sexual activity.

- To *identify the causes and diagnostic correlates of health, illness, and related dysfunction*. Psychologists study the causes of disease; the research we saw earlier showing the importance of personality factors in the development of illness is an example of the work toward this goal. Psychologists also study physiological and perceptual processes, which affect people's experience of physical symptoms.

- To *analyze and improve health care systems and health policy*. Psychologists contribute toward this goal by studying how characteristics or functions of hospitals, nursing homes, medical personnel, and medical costs affect patients. The resulting knowledge enables them to make recommendations for improvement, suggesting ways to help physicians and nurses become more sensitive and responsive to the needs of patients and to make the system more accessible to individuals who fail to seek treatment.

Psychologists work to achieve these goals in a variety of ways, some of which involve applying techniques that were derived from behaviorism. (Go to 🌲.)

An Integration

By now you may be wondering, "Aren't psychosomatic medicine, behavioral medicine, and health psychology basically the same?" In a sense they are. In large measure, the three fields have very similar goals, study similar topics, and share the same knowledge. Perhaps the main distinction among them is the degree to which their membership is interdisciplinary. Behavioral medicine has the most diverse membership, drawing knowledge directly from a wide variety of disciplines. Psychosomatic medicine continues to be closely allied with medical disciplines, especially psychiatry. And health psychology is a subfield of psychology—almost all of its members are psychologists—and draws directly on the many other subfields within the discipline: clinical, developmental, experimental, physiological, and social psychology. Even though the focus of this book is mainly on health psychology, we should keep in mind the overlap with and contributions of the fields of psychosomatic medicine and behavioral medicine.

CLINICAL METHODS AND ISSUES

Behaviorism's Legacy: Progress in Health Psychology's Goals

The perspective of behaviorism led to the development of *behavior modification* techniques, which use principles of learning and cognition to understand and change people's behavior (Sarafino, 2001). These techniques can be grouped into two categories: **Behavioral methods** apply mainly principles of operant and classical conditioning to change behavior. **Cognitive methods** are geared toward changing people's feelings and thought processes, such as by helping individuals identify and alter problematic beliefs; most cognitive methods were developed since the mid-1960s.

How can professionals use behavioral and cognitive methods to promote and maintain people's health and to prevent and treat illness? Let's consider two examples. Using behavioral methods, psychologists reduced work-related injuries at worksites with high accident rates by applying a program of reinforcement for safety behaviors (Fox, Hopkins, & Anger, 1987). In an example that used cognitive methods with patients suffering from chronic back pain, a psychologist reduced their degree of pain, depression, and disability by providing training in ways to relax and think differently about the pain (Turner, 1982).

It is important to realize also that these three fields are separate mainly in an organizational sense. Many professionals are members of all three organizations. Although the fields have slightly different perspectives, they share the view that health and illness result from the interplay of biological, psychological, and social forces. As this suggests, these fields are interested in knowledge from a wide variety of disciplines and are engaged in a cooperative effort to enhance wellness and reduce illness.

HEALTH PSYCHOLOGY: THE PROFESSION

Because the field of health psychology is so new, the profession is developing. Most health psychologists work in hospitals, clinics, and academic departments of colleges and universities. In these positions, they either provide direct help to patients or give indirect help through research, teaching, and consulting activities.

The direct help health psychologists provide generally relates to the patient's psychological adjustment to and management of health problems. Health psychologists with clinical training can provide therapy for emotional and social adjustment problems that being ill or disabled can produce—for example, in reducing the patient's feelings of depression. They can also help patients manage the health problem by, for instance, teaching them psychological methods, such as biofeedback, to control pain.

Health psychologists provide indirect help, too. Their research provides information about lifestyle and personality factors in illness and injury. They can apply this and other knowledge to design programs that help people lead more healthful lifestyles, such as by preventing or quitting cigarette smoking. They can also educate physicians and the other health care workers we have discussed toward a fuller understanding of the psychosocial needs of patients.

The qualifications for becoming a health psychologist include completion of the doctoral degree in psychology (Belar, 1997). Additional study may be needed if the doctoral program contained little training in health psychology. *Clinical health psychology* is an accredited specialty of the American Psychological Association. State licensing is required to practice clinical techniques, and board certification is available (Deardorff, 1996).

CURRENT PERSPECTIVES ON HEALTH AND ILLNESS

Once we add the person to the biomedical model, we have a different and broader picture of how health and illness come about. This new perspective, called the **biopsychosocial model,** expands the biomedical view by adding to *biological* factors the influence of *psychological* and *social* factors (Engel, 1977, 1980; Schwartz, 1982). This new model proposes that all three factors *affect* and *are affected by* the person's health.

THE BIOPSYCHOSOCIAL PERSPECTIVE

We can see elements of the biopsychosocial perspective in the story about Ana at the beginning of the chapter. A possible biological contribution to her becoming overweight might be her inheritance, since her mother is overweight and was heavy as a child. Psychological factors are probably important, as shown in Ana's behavior—she eats too much fattening food and gets little exercise. And, although the story did not describe how social factors play a role in her weight problem, they are probably there—for example, if she imitates her mother's dietary and exercise habits. But we *did* see social factors relating to Ana's condition when her schoolmates taunted her and her parents expressed concern and urged her to join a recreation program. Let's look at the elements of the biopsychosocial model in more detail.

The Role of Biological Factors

What is included in the term *biological factors*? This term includes the genetic materials and processes by which we inherit characteristics from our parents. It also includes aspects of the person's physiological functioning—for example, whether the body (1) contains structural defects, such as a malformed heart valve or some damage in the brain, that impair the operation of these organs; (2) responds effectively in protecting itself, such as by fighting infection; and (3) overreacts sometimes in the protective function, as happens in many allergic reactions to harmless substances, such as pollen or dust.

The body is made up of enormously complex physical systems. For instance, it has organs, bones, and nerves, and these are composed of tissues, which in turn consist of cells, molecules, and atoms. The efficient, effective, and healthful functioning of these systems depends on the way these components operate and interact with each other.

The Role of Psychological Factors

When we discussed the role of lifestyle and personality in health and illness earlier, we were describing behavior and mental processes, in other words, psychological factors. Behavior and mental processes are the focus of psychology, and they involve cognition, emotion, and motivation.

Cognition is a mental activity that encompasses perceiving, learning, remembering, thinking, interpreting, believing, and problem solving. How do these cognitive factors affect health and illness? Suppose, for instance, you strongly believe, "Life is not worth living without the things I enjoy." If you enjoy smoking cigarettes, would you quit to reduce your risk of getting cancer or heart disease? Probably not. Or suppose you develop a pain in your abdomen and you remember having had a similar symptom in the past that disappeared in a couple of days. Would you seek treatment? Again, probably not. These examples are just two of the countless ways cognition plays a role in health and illness.

Emotion is a subjective feeling that affects and is affected by our thoughts, behavior, and physiology. Some emotions are positive or pleasant, such as joy and affection, and others are negative, such as anger, fear, and sadness. Emotions relate to health and illness in many ways. For instance, people whose emotions are relatively positive are less disease-prone and more likely to take good care of their health and to recover quickly from an illness than are people whose emotions are relatively negative. We considered these relationships when we discussed the role of personality in illness. Emotions can also be important in people's decisions about seeking treatment. People who are frightened of doctors and dentists may avoid getting the health care they need.

Motivation is a term applied to explanations of why people behave the way they do—why they start some

activity, choose its direction, and persist in it. A person who is motivated to feel and look better might begin an exercise program, choose the goals to be reached, and stick with it. Many people are motivated to do what important people in their lives want them to do. Parents who quit smoking because their children plead with them to protect their health are an example.

The Role of Social Factors

People live in a social world. We have relationships with individual people—an acquaintance, a friend, or a family member—and with groups. As we interact with people, we affect them and they affect us. But our social world is larger than just the people we know or meet, and it contains levels of social spheres, such as our community and our family, and each level affects the others.

On a fairly broad level, our *society* affects the health of individuals by promoting certain values of our culture. One of these values is that being fit and healthy is good. Often the mass media—television, newspapers, and so on—reflect these values by setting good examples and urging us to eat well, not to use drugs, and not to drink and drive. The mass media can do much to promote health. But sometimes these media encourage unhealthful behavior, such as when we observe celebrities on television smoking cigarettes or drinking excessively. Can individuals affect society's values? Yes. As part of the society, we can affect its values by writing our opinions to the mass media, selecting which television shows and movies to watch, and buying healthful products, for example.

Our *community* consists of individuals who live fairly near one another, such as in the same town or county. These people influence and are influenced by each other. This influence can be seen in the research finding that communities differ in the extent to which their members practice certain health-related behaviors, such as smoking cigarettes or consuming fatty diets (Diehr et al., 1993). These differences may develop in many ways. For instance, adolescents often start smoking cigarettes and drinking alcohol as a result of peer pressure (Jessor, 1984). Sometimes simply observing other teenagers engaged in these behaviors can encourage adolescents to smoke and drink. They want very much to be popular and to look "cool" or "tough" to others in their community. These examples

Society can help prevent disease or injury in many ways, such as through advertisements against drunk driving.

involve clear and powerful motivational elements that are social in nature.

The closest and most continuous social relationships for most people occur within the *family*, which can include nonrelatives who live together and share a strong emotional bond. As individuals grow and develop in early childhood, the family has an especially strong influence (Sarafino & Armstrong, 1986). Children learn many health-related behaviors, attitudes, and beliefs from their parents, brothers, and sisters. For instance, parents can set good examples for healthful behavior by using seat belts, serving and eating nutritious meals, exercising, not smoking, and so on. Families can also encourage children to perform healthful behaviors and praise them when they do. Moreover, as we have said, an individual can influence the larger social unit. A family may stop eating certain nutritious foods, such as brussels sprouts or fish, because one of the children has a tantrum when these foods are served.

The role of biological, psychological, and social factors in health and illness is not hard to see. What is more difficult to understand is how health is affected by the *interplay* of these components, as the biopsychosocial model proposes. The next section deals with this interplay.

"LORETTA'S DRIVING BECAUSE I'M DRINKING, AND I'M DRINKING BECAUSE SHE'S DRIVING."

Reprinted courtesy of Bunny Hoest.

The Concept of "Systems"

The whole person—as in the sentence, "We need to understand the whole person"—is a phrase we often hear. It reflects our recognition that people and the reasons for their behavior are very complex. Many health professionals strive to consider the impact of all aspects of a person's life as a total entity in understanding health and illness. This approach uses the biopsychosocial model and is sometimes called holistic. This term is derived from the Greek word *holos*, which means "whole" (Lipowski, 1986). But many people today use the term *holistic* to include a broad range of "alternative" approaches to promote health, such as treatments that use aromas and herbs to heal.

How can we conceptualize the whole person? George Engel (1980) has proposed that we can do this by applying the biological concept of "systems" (von Bertalanffy, 1968). A **system** is a dynamic entity with components that are continuously interrelated. By this definition, your body qualifies as a system— and it includes the immune and nervous systems, which consist of tissues and cells. Your family is a system, too, and so are your community and society. As systems, they are entities that are dynamic—or constantly changing—and they have components that interrelate, such as by exchanging energy, substances, and information.

As you can see in Figure 1–4, the systems concept places smaller, simpler systems within larger, more complex ones. There are levels of systems. Cells are within the person who is within a society, for instance. In the previous section of this chapter, we saw that a system at one level, such as a person, is affected by and can affect a system at another level, such as the family. Similarly, if we look at levels within the person, illness in one part of the body can have far-reaching effects: if you fell and seriously injured your leg, your internal systems would be automatically mobilized to help protect the body from further damage.

In addition, the discomfort and disability you might experience for days or weeks might affect your social relations with your family and community.

To illustrate how the systems concept can be useful, let's use it to explain how Ana's weight problem might have come about. Let's assume that she did inherit some factor that affects her weight. The nature of this factor might involve a preference for sweet foods, for instance (Rozin, 1989). When she was a toddler, her parents quieted her tantrums by giving her candy, which almost always calmed her. Ana's parents were not concerned that she was getting heavy because they believed a popular misconception: "A chubby baby is a healthy baby." The meals the family ate usually contained lots of high-fat, high-calorie foods and a sweet dessert. Because Ana was heavy, she was less agile and tired more easily than children who were not overweight. So she usually preferred to engage in sedentary activities, such as playing with dolls or watching television, rather than sports. She and her friends snacked on cookies while watching television. The commercials on most children's television shows made her weight problem worse, promoting high-fat, sweet breakfast and snack foods, which she got her parents to buy. This hypothetical account shows how different but interacting biopsychosocial systems can contribute to a person's weight problem.

Using the biopsychosocial model as a guide, researchers have discovered new and important findings and ways to promote people's health and recovery

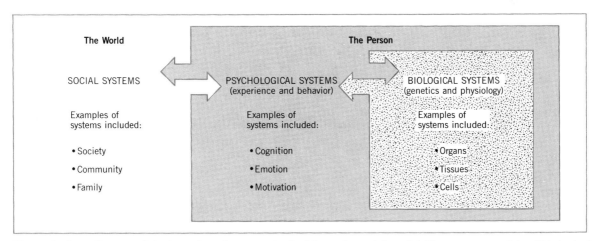

Figure 1–4   A diagram of the interplay of systems in the biopsychosocial model. The person consists of biological and psychological systems, which interrelate; and each of the systems includes component systems. The person interrelates with the social systems of his or her world. Each system can affect and be affected by any of the other systems.

from illness. Here is a sample of discoveries that we will discuss in later chapters:

- Using psychological methods to reduce anxiety of patients who are awaiting surgery enables them to recover more quickly and leave the hospital sooner.

- Programs that teach safer sex practices have dramatically reduced risky sexual behavior and the spread of HIV infection.

- People who have a high degree of social support from family and friends are healthier and live longer than people who do not.

- Stress impairs the functioning of the immune system.

- Appying psychological and educational programs for cancer patients reduces their feelings of depression, improves their immune system functioning, and enables them to live longer.

- Biofeedback and other psychological techniques can reduce the pain of people who suffer from chronic, severe headaches.

THE LIFE-SPAN PERSPECTIVE

People change over time through the process called development. As people develop, each portion of the life span is affected by happenings in earlier years, and each affects the happenings in years that will come. Throughout people's lives, health, illness, and the role of different biopsychosocial systems change. This is why it is important to keep the life-span perspective in mind when we examine health psychology.

In the **life-span perspective,** characteristics of a person are considered with respect to their prior development, current level, and likely development in the future. How do characteristics relating to health and illness vary with development? One way is that the kinds of illnesses people have tend to change with age. Compared with older individuals, children suffer from relatively few chronic diseases (USBC, 1999). Illnesses that keep children out of school tend to be short-term infectious diseases, such as colds or the flu. In contrast, many people in late adulthood and old age suffer from heart disease, cancer, and stroke.

How do the roles of different biopsychosocial systems change as we develop? Biological systems change in many ways. Virtually all systems of the body grow in size, strength, and efficiency during childhood

and decline in old age. The decline can be seen in the slowing down that older people notice in their physical abilities. They have less stamina because the heart and lungs function less efficiently and the muscles are weaker (Tortora & Grabowski, 2000). They also recover from illness and injury more slowly.

Changes occur in psychological systems, too— for example, in cognitive processes. Children's knowledge and ability to think are limited during the preschool years but grow rapidly during later childhood. Before children can assume responsibility for their health, they need to understand how their behavior can affect it. As children get older and their cognitive skills improve, they are more likely to engage in behaviors that promote their health and safety (Maddux, Roberts, Sledden, & Wright, 1986). They also become better able to understand the implications of their own illness when they are sick.

How do people's social relationships and social systems change with development? For one thing, there are some usual progressions: children usually become parents of their own families in adulthood, and grandparents in old age. As people develop, they progress through levels of education and employment, and retire in old age. Changes in social relationships also relate to health and illness. Children's health is largely the responsibility of adult caregivers—parents and teachers. During the teenage years, adolescents take on more and more of these responsibilities. At the same time, social relationships with age-mates in the community start to have a very powerful influence on adolescents. The strong need to be accepted by peers sometimes leads teens toward unhealthful or unsafe behavior. For example, an adolescent who has a chronic illness that can be controlled—as diabetes can—may neglect his or her medical care to avoid looking and feeling different from other adolescents (La Greca & Stone, 1985).

The life-span perspective adds an important dimension to the biopsychosocial perspective in our effort to understand how people deal with issues of health and illness.

RELATING HEALTH PSYCHOLOGY TO OTHER SCIENCE FIELDS

Knowledge in health psychology is greatly enriched by information from many other disciplines, including some disciplines within *psychology*, such as the clinical and social areas; *medicine*, including psychiatry and pediatrics; and *allied fields*, such as nursing, nutrition, pharmacology, biology, and social work. We will look at four fields that are especially important because they provide both information and a context for health psychology.

RELATED FIELDS

To understand health psychology fully, we need to know the context in which health and illness exist. The field of *epidemiology*—the scientific study of the distribution and frequency of disease and injury—provides part of this context. Researchers in this field determine the occurrence of illness in a given population and organize these data in terms of when the disease or injury occurred, where, and to which age, gender, and racial or cultural groups. Then they attempt to discover why specific illnesses are distributed as they are. You have probably seen the results of epidemiologists' work in the mass media. For example, news reports have described areas of the United States where Lyme disease, a tick-borne illness, occurs at high levels and where certain forms of cancer are linked to high levels of toxic substances in the environment.

Epidemiologists use several terms in describing aspects of their findings (Gerace & Vorp, 1985; Runyan, 1985). We will define five of these terms:

- **Mortality** means death, generally on a large scale. An epidemiologist might report a decrease in mortality from heart disease among women, for instance.

- **Morbidity** means illness, injury, or disability—basically any detectable departure from wellness.

- **Prevalence** refers to the number of cases, such as of a disease or of persons infected or at risk. It includes both continuing (previously reported) and new cases at a given moment in time—for example, the number of cases of asthma as of the first day of the current year.

- **Incidence** refers to the number of *new* cases, such as of illness, infection, or disability, reported during a period of time. An example is the number of tuberculosis cases in the previous year.

- **Epidemic** usually refers to the situation in which the incidence, generally of an infectious disease, has increased rapidly.

Some of these terms are used with the word *rate*, which adds relativity to the meaning. For instance, the mortality rate refers to the number of deaths per number of people in a given population during a specified period of time. An example might be a mortality rate of 6 babies per 1,000 births dying in their first year of life during the current year in Canada.

Another discipline of importance to health psychology is *public health*, the field concerned with protecting, maintaining, and improving health through organized effort in the community. People who work in public health do research and set up programs dealing with immunizations, sanitation, health education and awareness, and ways to provide community health services (Runyan, 1985). This field studies health and illness in the context of the community as a social system. The success of public health programs and the way individual people react to them are of interest to health psychologists.

Two other related fields are sociology and anthropology (Adler & Stone, 1979). *Sociology* focuses on human social life; it examines groups or communities of people and evaluates the impact of various social factors, such as the mass media, population growth, epidemics, and institutions. *Medical sociology* is a subfield that studies a wide range of issues related to health, including the impact of social relationships on the distribution of illness, social reactions to illness, socioeconomic factors of health care use, and the way hospital services and medical practices are organized. *Anthropology* includes the study of human cultures. Its subfield, *medical anthropology*, examines differences in health and health care across cultures: How do the nature and definition of illness vary across different cultures? How do people in these cultures react to illness, and what methods do they use to treat disease or injury? How do they structure health care systems? Without the knowledge from sociology and anthropology, health psychologists would have a very narrow view. Knowledge from sociology and anthropology gives us a broad social and cultural view of medical issues and allows us to consider different ways to interpret and treat illness.

The combined information health psychologists obtain from epidemiology, public health, sociology, and anthropology paints a broad picture for us. It describes the social systems in which health, illness, and the person exist and develop. (Go to .)

HIGHLIGHT ON ISSUES
Related Nonpsychology Careers

The process of providing care for a patient who is suffering from a chronic illness, serious injury, or disability involves a variety of professionals working together with physicians as a team. Each professional has specific training for a special role in the treatment or rehabilitation process. Most of them have some education in psychology. We've already seen how health psychologists can play a role. Let's look at some careers outside of psychology and the training they require in the United States.

Nurses and Physician Assistants

There are two overall categories of nurses: *registered nurses* (RNs) and *licensed practical nurses* (LPNs). RNs work in hospitals, community health clinics, physicians' offices, and industrial settings. They assess and record patients' symptoms and progress, conduct tests, administer medications, assist in rehabilitation, provide instructions for self-treatment, and instruct patients and their families in ways to improve or maintain their health. RNs often deal with mental and emotional aspects of the patient as well. All RNs throughout the United States must be licensed to practice, have graduated from an approved training program in nursing, and have passed a national examination (NLN, 2000). RN training programs vary in structure and length; college and university programs take 4 or 5 years and lead to a baccalaureate degree.

LPNs work in hospitals, clinics, physicians' offices, and patients' homes. They perform nursing activities that require less training than those performed by RNs. For example, they take and record temperatures and blood pressures, administer certain medications, change dressings, assist physicians or RNs, and help patients with personal hygiene. Like RNs, all LPNs in the United States must be licensed to practice, have graduated from an approved practical nursing program, and have passed a national examination. Training programs for LPNs take about a year to complete and are offered through various types of institutions, such as trade and vocational schools, community and junior colleges, and hospitals.

Physician assistants and *nurse practitioners* usually work closely with medical doctors, performing routine tasks that physicians ordinarily did in the past, such as examining patients with symptoms that do not appear serious and explaining treatment details (AANP, 2000; AAPA, 2000). Training involves a program of about 2 years of study; admission often requires that applicants have a relevant bachelor's degree, such as in nursing, and prior health care experience.

Dietitians

Dietitians study and apply knowledge about food and its effect on the body (ADietA, 2000). They do this in a variety of settings, such as hospitals, clinics, nursing homes, colleges, and schools. Some dietitians are administrators; other work directly with patients in assessing nutritional needs, implementing and evaluating dietary plans, and instructing patients and their families on ways to adhere to needed diets after discharge from the hospital. Some dietitians work for social service agencies in the community, where they counsel people on nutritional practices to help maintain health and speed recovery when they are ill.

Becoming a dietitian requires a bachelor's or master's degree specializing in nutrition sciences or institutional management. To become a Registered Dietitian, the individual must complete a supervised internship and pass an exam.

Physical Therapists

Many patients need help in restoring functional movement to parts of their body and relieving pain. If they have suffered a disabling injury or disease, treatment may be needed to prevent or limit permanent disability. *Physicial therapists* plan and apply treatment for these goals in rehabilitation (APTA, 2000).

To plan the treatment, physical therapists review the patient's records and perform tests or measurements of muscle strength, motor coordination, endurance, and range of motion of the injured body part. Treatment is designed to increase the strength and function of the injured part and aid in the patient's adaptation to having reduced physical abilities, which may be quite drastic. People who have suffered severe strokes are sometimes left partially paralyzed, for instance. The most universal technique used in physical therapy involves exercise, generally requiring little effort initially and becoming more and more challenging. Another technique involves electrical stimulation to move paralyzed muscles or reduce pain. Physical therapists also give instructions for carrying out everyday tasks, such as tying shoelaces or cooking meals. If the patient needs to use adaptive devices, such as crutches or a prosthesis (replacement limb), the therapist provides training.

All physical therapists throughout the United States must have a degree or certificate from an approved training program and be licensed by passing an exam. A bachelor's degree has been the minimum educational requirement to enter the profession, but a master's degree in physical therapy will be the minimum as of January 2002.

Occupational Therapists

Occupational therapists help physically, mentally, and emotionally disabled individuals gain skills needed for daily activities in a work setting, at school, in the community, and at home (AOTA, 2000). Their patients are often people who had these skills at one time, but lost them because of a spinal cord injury or a disease, such as muscular dystrophy. These professionals usually specialize in working with a particular age group, such as the elderly, and a type of disability—physical, for example. Based on the patient's age and the type and degree of disability, a program of educational, vocational, and recreational activities is designed and implemented. The program for a child, for instance, might involve academic tasks and crafts; for an adult, it might involve typing, driving a vehicle, and using hand and power tools.

Occupational therapists in the United States must have a degree or certificate from an approved training program and be licensed by passing an exam. Training requires completing a baccalaureate program plus either a certificate program or a master's degree in occupational therapy.

Social Workers

The field of *social work* is quite broad. Probably most social workers are employed in mental health programs, but many others work in hospitals, nursing homes, rehabilitation centers, and public health programs (NASW, 2000). When working with people who are physically ill or disabled, social workers help patients and their families make psychological and social adjustments to the illness and obtain needed community services, including income maintenance. Thus, social workers may arrange for needed nursing care at home after a patient leaves the hospital or refer a patient for vocational counseling and occupational therapy if the illness or disability requires a career change. These professionals are usually called medical social workers.

Training requires a bachelor's degree in a social science field, usually social work, but often a degree in psychology or sociology is sufficient. Most states mandate some form of licensing or certification. Many positions require an advanced degree, typically a master's in social work, the MSW degree.

HEALTH AND PSYCHOLOGY ACROSS CULTURES

Health and illness have changed across the history and cultures of the world, as the following excerpt shows:

Less than a hundred years ago the infant mortality rate in Europe and North America was as high as it is in the developing world now. In New York City in the year 1900, for example, the IMR [infant mortality rate] was approximately 140 per 1,000—about the same as in Bangladesh today. In the city of Birmingham, England a survey taken in 1906 revealed an IMR of almost 200 per 1,000—higher than almost any country in the world in the 1980s. A look behind these statistics also shows that the main causes of infant death in New York and Birmingham *then* were much the same as in the developing world *now*—diarrheal disease and malnutrition, respiratory infections, and whooping cough. (UNICEF, cited in Skolnick, 1986, p. 20)

The world view we get from historical–cultural comparisons can be quite dramatic. Each country's present culture is different from every other's and from the culture it had 200 years ago. Lifestyles have changed in each culture, and so has the pattern of illnesses that afflict its citizens.

Sociocultural Differences in Health

The term **sociocultural** means involving or relating to social and cultural factors, such as ethnic and income variations within and across nations. Epidemiologists have examined sociocultural differences in health and found, for instance, that certain forms of cancer, particularly stomach cancer, have far higher prevalence rates in Japan than in the United States today, but the reverse is true for breast (in females) and prostate (in males) cancers (Williams, 1990). Furthermore, large sociocultural differences exist in rates of specific cancers within the same country, too (Williams & Rucker, 1996). In the United States, for example, Chinese-Americans have far higher rates of liver cancer than Caucasians do. The differences we see in illness patterns between countries, regions, or ethnic groups result from many factors, including heredity, environmental pollution, economic barriers to health care, and cultural differences in people's diets, health-related beliefs, and values (Flack et al., 1995; Johnson et al., 1995). Although people around the world value good health, some people feel that maintaining health is more important than others do. It seems reasonable that the more people value their health, the more likely they are to take care of it.

Sociocultural Differences in Health Beliefs and Behavior

Differences across history and culture can also be seen in the ideas people have about the *causes* of illness. Recall our discussion of the widespread beliefs in the Middle Ages that evil spirits caused illness. Today, educated people in technological societies generally reject such ideas. But less sophisticated people often do not, as the following excerpt shows:

> I've heard of people with snakes in their body, how they got in there I don't know. And they take 'em someplace to a witch doctor and snakes come out. My sister, she had somethin', a snake that was in her arm. She was a young woman. I can remember her bein' sick, very sick, and someone told her about this healer in another little town. And I do know they taken her there. This thing was just runnin' up her arm, whatever it was, just runnin' up her arm. You could actually *see* it. (Snow, 1981, p. 86)

A disadvantaged person in the United States gave this account, which is typical of the level of knowledge generally found in people in underdeveloped regions or countries. This is important to recognize because the large majority of people in the world live in underdeveloped societies.

The United States has been described as a melting pot for immigrants from every corner of the world. Immigrants carry with them health ideas and customs from their former countries. For example, many Chinese immigrants have entered their new country with the belief that illness results from an imbalance of two opposing forces, *yin* and *yang*, within the body (Campbell & Chang, 1981). According to this view, too much *yin* causes colds and gastric disorders, for instance, and too much *yang* causes fever and dehydration. Practitioners of traditional Chinese medicine treat illnesses by prescribing special herbs and foods or by using *acupuncture*, in which fine needles are inserted under the skin at special locations of the body. These methods are intended to correct the balance of *yin* and *yang*. Immigrants and others with these beliefs who are sick will often use these methods instead of or as a supplement to treatment by an American physician. They may also pressure their children and grandchildren to do this, too. As an example, a pregnant Chinese woman who was a registered nurse "followed her obstetrician's orders, but at the same time, under pressure from her mother and mother-in-law, ate special herbs and foods to insure birth of a healthy baby" (Campbell & Chang, 1981, p. 164).

Religion is an aspect of culture. Many religions include beliefs that relate to health and illness. For instance, Jehovah's Witnesses reject the use of blood and blood products in medical treatment (Sacks & Koppes, 1986). Christian Scientists reject the use of medicine totally, believing that only mental processes in the sick person can cure the illness. As a result, sick persons need prayer and counsel as treatment to help these processes along (Henderson & Primeaux, 1981). These beliefs are controversial and have led to legal conflicts between members of these religions and health authorities in the United States, particularly when parents reject medical treatments for life-threatening illnesses for their children. In such cases, the physician and hospital can move quickly to seek an immediate judicial decision (Sacks & Koppes, 1986).

Some religions include specific beliefs that promote healthful lifestyles. Seventh-day Adventists, for example, believe that the body is the "temple of the Holy Spirit." They cite this belief as the reason people should take care of their bodies. Adventists abstain from using tobacco, alcohol, and nonmedically prescribed drugs. In addition, they promote in fellow members a concern for exercise and eating a healthful diet (Henderson & Primeaux, 1981). Although it is clear that cultural factors play a role in health, our knowledge about this role is meager and needs to be expanded through more research.

RESEARCH METHODS

Contemporary mass media constantly bombard us with scientific findings. Diets high in fiber and low in saturated fats are good for your health. Smoking is not. Dozens of toxic, or poisonous, chemicals appear to cause cancer. How do scientists discover these relationships? What methods do they use?

Scientists do research. Often their research is planned and conducted to test a **theory**—a *tentative explanation* of why and under what circumstances certain phenomena occur. For example, a leading theory of the cause of heart disease is that excess *cholesterol*, a fatty substance in the blood, is deposited on artery walls. Because this substance, like other saturated fats, is not water soluble, it builds up on the walls over time. This buildup hardens and narrows the diameter of the artery, thereby reducing the flow of blood and nutrients and causing tissue damage to the heart or arteries. Cholesterol comes from two sources. Most cholesterol in the blood is manufactured by the body; the rest of it comes from the foods we eat—especially red meats, egg yolks, butter, and most cheeses.

The cholesterol theory is one of several useful theories of heart disease. By useful we don't necessarily mean that it is correct. We mean that it:

1. Is clearly stated.
2. Brings together or organizes known facts.
3. Relates information that previously seemed unrelated.
4. Enables us to make predictions, such as what would happen if cholesterol levels were reduced.

Useful theories play an extremely important role in all sciences. Because theories provide predictions, they guide research programs by suggesting a "road map" of relationships to study.

As you think about the causes of heart disease, you will realize that both the illness and the theoretical cause—in this case, high levels of cholesterol—can change or vary from one time to another and from one individual to another. That is, the condition of the heart and arteries and the amount of cholesterol in the blood are not constant. Because these things *vary*, they are called *variables*. A **variable** is any measurable characteristic of people, objects, or events that may change. The variables studied in research are of two types: an *independent variable* is studied for its potential or expected influence, as in the case of cholesterol levels; a *dependent variable* is assessed because its value, such as the condition of the heart, is expected to "depend" on the independent variable.

Researchers who study heart disease use a variety of *experimental* and *nonexperimental* methods to examine variables like the ones we have discussed.

EXPERIMENTS

An **experiment** is a controlled study in which researchers manipulate an independent variable to study its effect on a dependent variable. In a well-designed experiment—which is often called a *trial* in health research—all other variables are controlled or held constant. The term *manipulate* means that the researchers produce or introduce the levels of the independent variable they are studying.

The Experimental Method: A Hypothetical Example

To illustrate the experimental method, let's see how researchers might test the cholesterol theory of heart disease. One prediction, or *hypothesis*, from the theory is that people's incidence of heart disease should decrease if they reduce their cholesterol levels. We could test this hypothesis by lowering some people's cholesterol levels and seeing if these people develop fewer heart attacks over a suitable period of time than they otherwise would. How can we lower their cholesterol levels? There are two ways to manipulate this independent variable, both of which would require including medical professionals in the research team. One way is to alter the subjects' diets, and the other is to have them take an anticholesterol drug regularly. We will use the latter approach and assume, for our example, that the drug is new and the only one available.

The first thing we need to do is to select a sample of subjects—preferably middle-aged people, because they have a relatively high risk of having a heart attack in the near future. Then we assign them *randomly* to the conditions or groups in the experiment. One way to assign them randomly is to put their names on cards in a bowl, mix up the cards, and draw the cards out one at a time. The first name drawn would be assigned to one group, the second name to another group, and so on. By doing this, we distribute other characteristics, such as their personality traits and genetic factors, fairly equally across the groups. As a result, these characteristics will have about the same impact on the dependent variable (heart attacks) for each of the groups.

To test the hypothesis, we will need two groups of subjects. One group receives the experimental treatment, the anticholesterol pills, and is called the *experimental group*. The other group receives their usual care without the drug, and is called the *control group* (or *comparison* group). By administering the drug to and lowering the cholesterol level of one group, but not the other, we are manipulating the independent variable. We then observe over several years the incidence of heart attacks. If the experimental group has fewer heart attacks than the control group, the hypothesis is supported.

You may be wondering, "Isn't it possible that a decrease in heart attacks for the experimental group could result *not* from the drug per se, but simply from taking *any* substance a medical person prescribes?" Sometimes people's beliefs or expectations can affect their health (Ader, 1997; Sobel, 1990). To control for this possibility, we would have a third group of subjects. This group would receive an inert, or inactive, substance or procedure—called a **placebo**—in the form of pills that look like medicine. The placebo

group would be given the same instructions as the experimental group, and both would have equal expectations about the effectiveness of the pills. Any influence the placebo has on the dependent variable is called a *placebo effect*.

One other control procedure is needed. Just as the subjects should not know which pills contain the active drug, neither should the person who distributes the pills. Why? This person could inadvertently bias the outcome of the experiment, such as by giving instructions offhandedly to the placebo group and emphatically and precisely to the experimental group. Being unaware of which individuals are getting the experimental treatment is called being *blind* as to the treatment. Since both the subjects and the person who distributes the pills are unaware, the method we are using is called the **double-blind** procedure.

Now that we have included these control procedures, let's look at the outcome of our hypothetical experiment. As Figure 1–5 shows, the experimental subjects had far fewer heart attacks than the subjects in the other groups. Thus we can conclude that lowering cholesterol levels in the blood causes a decrease in heart disease, as the theory predicts. Notice also in the graph that the subjects in the placebo group had somewhat fewer heart attacks than the control subjects. This suggests a placebo effect, with expectancy having some effect on heart disease, but not nearly as much as the active ingredient in the anticholesterol drug.

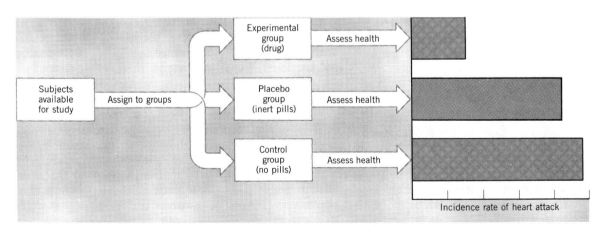

Figure 1–5 The left-hand portion of this diagram shows how the study would be carried out. Subjects are assigned to groups and, after a suitable period of time, the researcher checks whether they have had heart attacks. The right-hand portion illustrates how the results might appear on a graph: subjects who received the anticholesterol drug had far fewer heart attacks than subjects in the placebo group, who had somewhat fewer attacks than those in the control group.

You may have noticed that our conclusion used the word *causes*: lowering cholesterol "causes" a decrease in heart disease. To make a *cause-effect* conclusion, we must be able to see that three criteria have been met: (1) the levels of the independent and dependent variables corresponded or varied together, (2) the cause preceded the effect, and (3) all other plausible causes have been ruled out. Well-designed experiments meet these requirements because the researchers manipulate the independent variable while controlling variables that are not being studied. Other research approaches do not use experimental methods and do not provide the ability to determine what causes what.

Comparing Experimental and Nonexperimental Methods

Research always involves the study of variables, but in *nonexperimental methods*, the researchers *do not manipulate an independent variable*. In addition, there is frequently less opportunity for precise measurement and for control of variables not being studied. As a result, although nonexperimental methods may be used to point out relationships between variables, they do *not* provide direct and unambiguous tests of cause-effect relationships.

Nonexperimental methods are nevertheless very valuable and have some important advantages. Sometimes it is simply not possible or feasible to assign subjects randomly and manipulate the variable of interest. We cannot manipulate the past lifestyles of people, for instance; the past has already happened. Nor can we have individuals in one group of a study do harmful things they would ordinarily not do simply to test an important theory. For instance, it would be unethical to assign people of a sample to a group in which all subjects must smoke cigarettes for the next 5 years if some of these people do not smoke or want to quit. Even if it were ethical, nonsmokers might refuse to do it. What if we didn't randomly assign the subjects to groups? If we do not randomly assign subjects to groups, the groups are not likely to be equal at the start of the study with respect to characteristics, such as genetics or past lifestyle, that could affect the outcome of the research. In situations like this in which ethical considerations prevent the use of human subjects, animals are sometimes used.

In many cases, the aim of a research project requires only that an association between variables be demonstrated. We may want to know, for instance,

which individuals are at greatest risk for a disease so that we may help them avert it. Studies to determine risk factors are examples. This kind of research has revealed that people who are among the most likely to develop heart disease are male and/or over 50 years old (Susser, Hopper, & Richman, 1983). Researchers can determine this relationship without manipulating gender or age, and a nonexperimental method is, in fact, the most appropriate technique.

The remainder of our examination of research methods will focus on nonexperimental approaches in research relating to health psychology. We will continue to use the cholesterol theory of heart disease as the basis for research examples. Let's turn to correlational studies as the first of these methods.

CORRELATIONAL STUDIES

The term *correlation* refers to the *co* or joint relation that exists between variables—changes in one variable correspond with changes in another variable. Suppose, for example, we did a study of two variables: heart function and people's diets, particularly the amount of cholesterol they consume. A measure of heart function is *cardiac output*, the amount of blood the heart pumps per minute. Working with a physician, we recruit a sample of, say, 200 middle-aged adults. We contact the subjects and have them keep detailed records of their diets for the 2 weeks prior to the visit when the physician measures their cardiac output. We then calculate the amount of cholesterol consumed on the basis of their records.

Once we know the cardiac output and cholesterol intake of each of the subjects, we can assess the degree to which these variables are related. This is expressed statistically as a **correlation coefficient,** which can range from +1.00 through .00 to −1.00. The sign (+ or −) of the coefficient indicates the *direction* of the relationship. A plus sign means that the association is "positive": high scores on one variable, say, cardiac output, tend to be associated with high scores on another variable, such as blood pressure. Conversely, a minus sign means that the association is "negative": *high* scores on one variable tend to be associated with *low* scores on another variable. For example, high cardiac output is correlated with low concentrations of cells in the blood, because cells thicken the blood (Rhoades & Pflanzer, 1996). Thus, there is a negative correlation between cardiac output and concentration of blood cells.

Disregarding the sign of the correlation coefficient, the absolute value of the coefficient indicates the *strength* of association between variables. The higher the absolute value (that is, the closer to either +1.0 or −1.0), the stronger the correlation. As the absolute value decreases, the strength of the relationship declines. A coefficient approximating .00 means that the variables are not related. From the information we have just covered, we can now state a definition: **correlational studies** are nonexperimental investigations of the degree and direction of statistical association between two variables.

Let's suppose that our study revealed a strong negative correlation—a coefficient of −.72—between cardiac output and cholesterol intake. This would support the cholesterol theory, because low cholesterol intake should produce less fatty buildup to clog the arteries, thereby allowing the heart to pump more blood per minute. But we cannot say on the basis of our study that these events occurred, and we cannot conclude that low cholesterol intake *causes* high cardiac output. Why? Because we did not manipulate any variable—we simply measured what was there. It may be that some variable we did not measure was responsible for the correlation. For example, the people with low cholesterol intake may also have had low concentrations of blood cells, and it may have been this latter factor that was responsible for their high cardiac output. We don't know. We would only know for sure that the two variables have a strong negative relationship.

Although correlational studies typically cannot determine cause-effect relations, they are useful for examining existing relationships and variables that cannot be manipulated, developing hypotheses that may be tested experimentally, and generating predictive information, such as risk factors for health problems.

QUASI-EXPERIMENTAL STUDIES

Sometimes researchers conduct nonexperimental studies by selecting for or assessing an existing variable and then using it to categorize subjects into one of two or more groups, such as male or female, for example, or high, moderate, or low blood cholesterol levels. Investigations of this type are called **quasi-experimental studies**—they *look* like experiments because they have separate groups of subjects, but they are not: the variable—gender or cholesterol level—that defines the groups was *not manipulated*, and the subjects *cannot be randomly assigned* to the groups.

We could do a quasi-experimental study relating to the cholesterol theory of heart disease in the following way. Suppose we wanted to see if people's cholesterol level at the time of a heart attack is associated with the severity of the attack. For this study, we could just consult the medical records of heart disease patients, since it is standard practice to assess both variables. We could categorize the patients as having a high or low cholesterol level at the time they were admitted to the hospital. Then we would determine whether the attacks were more severe for one group than for the other.

If we found that the high-cholesterol patients had the more severe heart attacks, could we conclude that higher levels of cholesterol in the blood cause more severe attacks? No—for the same reasons we've discussed before. We cannot tell what caused what. In fact, this particular study could have been turned around. We could have categorized the patients on the basis of the severity of their attacks and then compared these groups for cholesterol levels. We would have found the same relationship: severe heart attacks are associated with a high level of cholesterol in the blood.

In general, the conclusions from quasi-experimental studies are basically correlational. The relationships they reveal do not become causal simply because we categorize subjects. There are many variations to the quasi-experimental method. We will look at a few of the more important ones, beginning with retrospective and prospective approaches.

Retrospective and Prospective Approaches

The prefix *retro* means "back" or "backward," and *spective* comes from the Latin word meaning "to look." Thus, the **retrospective approach** uses procedures that look back at the histories of subjects, such as individuals who do or do not have a particular disease. The purpose of this approach is to find commonalities in the people's histories that may suggest why they developed the disease.

How is the retrospective approach used in a quasi-experimental study? We might identify two groups of individuals. One group would consist of people who have already developed a particular illness, such as heart disease. They would be compared against a control group, consisting of similar people without the disease. We would then examine the two groups for characteristics of their histories that are common to one group, but not the other. We might find, for example, that the heart disease victims reported having eaten higher-cholesterol diets during the preceding 10 years than the control subjects did. Although the retrospective approach is relatively easy to implement, it has a potential shortcoming: when the procedures rely on people's memories, especially of long-past happenings, the likelihood of inaccurate reports increases.

The **prospective approach** uses procedures that look *forward* in the lives of people, by studying whether differences in a variable at one point in time are related to differences in another variable at a later time. We could do this to see whether certain characteristics or events in people's lives are associated with their eventual development of one or more diseases. In using the prospective approach, we would start by recruiting a large group of people—say, 2,000—who did not yet have the illness in question, heart disease. Periodically over several years we would interview them, have a physician examine them, and check their medical records. The interviews would inquire about various events and characteristics, such as cholesterol intake. Then we would categorize the subjects—for instance, as having or not having had a heart attack—and determine whether these groups differed in some earlier aspects of their lives.

What might our study show? We might find that, compared with people who did not have heart attacks, those who did had eaten diets that were much higher in cholesterol. We might also find that changes in people's diets, becoming higher or lower in cholesterol content over the years, corresponded with their suffering an attack. That is, those who consumed increasing amounts of cholesterol had more heart attacks than those whose cholesterol intake decreased. Because this is a quasi-experimental study, we cannot be certain that high-cholesterol diets caused the heart disease. But the prospective approach gives greater plausibility to a causal link than the retrospective approach would. This is because the diets, and changes in them, clearly preceded the heart attacks.

Retrospective and prospective approaches to study health were developed by epidemiologists. These approaches have been useful in identifying risk factors for specific illnesses.

Developmental Approaches

We saw earlier that the life-span perspective adds an important dimension to the study of health and illness. An essential research approach in studying life-span development is to examine and compare people at different ages. Of course, the age of the subjects cannot be manipulated; we can assign individuals to groups based on their age, but this assignment is not random. This approach is quasi-experimental, and, therefore, *age* itself cannot be viewed as a cause of health or behavior.

Two basic approaches are used for studying the age variable. In the **cross-sectional approach,** different individuals of different ages are observed at about the same time. The **longitudinal approach** involves the repeated observation of the *same* individuals over a long period of time. The longitudinal approach is like the prospective method, but it focuses specifically on age as a variable. Let's see how the cross-sectional and longitudinal approaches are used.

Suppose we were interested in examining age-related changes in dietary intake of cholesterol among middle-aged adults. If we use a *cross-sectional* approach, we might evaluate the diets of, say, 50 adults at each of three approximate ages—for example, 35, 45, and 55 years—during the current month. On the other hand, if we use a *longitudinal* approach to examine the same age range, we would evaluate the diets of 50 35-year-olds during the current month, and again when they are 45 and 55 years of age. This longitudinal study would take 20 years to complete.

Not all longitudinal studies take so long to do. Often a shorter span of ages—sometimes only a few months—is appropriate, depending on the question or issue the researcher wants to resolve. But the longitudinal approach, and the prospective approach in general, is typically more costly in time and money than the cross-sectional approach. Also the longer a study lasts, the greater the likelihood that subjects in the sample will be lost. Some will move away, others will lose interest in participating, and still others may die. Despite these difficulties, it is a valuable research approach that is unique in its ability to examine *change and stability in the lives of individuals* across time. For example, our longitudinal study could tell us whether individuals who eat a high-cholesterol diet at age 35 will generally continue to do so many years later. In contrast, a cross-sectional approach loses sight of stability and individual changes.

Now, let's suppose we did our cross-sectional study and found that the cholesterol content of adults' diets decreased with age. We would then like to know why this is so. One possible answer is that people change their diets as they get older because they feel more vulnerable to heart disease. So we asked the oldest group, using the retrospective approach, if they feel more vulnerable and eat less high-cholesterol food today than they used to. Sure enough, they said yes. But another reason for the current age differences in diet could be that the older adults never ate diets as high in cholesterol as those of the younger adults. So we asked the oldest group to describe the diets they ate 10 or 20 years ago. The diets they described contained less cholesterol than their current diets (which we already knew) *and* the current diets of the 35- and 45-year-olds in our study! This finding reflects the fact that the older subjects grew up at a different time, when food preferences or availability may have been different.

The influence of having been born and raised at a different time is called a **cohort effect.** The term *cohort* refers to a group of individuals who have a demographic factor, such as age or social class, in common. As a result, they share a set of experiences that are distinct from those of adjacent cohorts. In developmental approaches, the meaning of "cohort" is similar to "generation," but the amount of time separating adjacent cohorts can be much shorter than the time separating a generation. For example, suppose researchers at a high school planned to present a drug prevention program to all tenth-graders in a particular year. They might compare attitudes about drug use among the tenth-graders at the end of that year with those of two cohorts: tenth-graders 2 years before and 2 years after the program.

How can research methods take cohort effects into account? One way would be to combine the two developmental approaches to produce a *cross-sectional/longitudinal design* (Buss, 1973; Schaie, 1965). Looking back at our study with middle-aged adults, the combined approach could be carried out by selecting and testing 35-, 45-, and 55-year-olds initially. So far the study is cross-sectional, but we would follow most of these same adults longitudinally and add younger subjects along the way. By doing this in a planned and systematic way, we will have information about cross-sectional differences, changes within each cohort, and differences between cohorts.

Single-Subject Approaches

Sometimes studies are done with just one subject. One type of research that uses this approach is the **case study,** in which a trained researcher constructs a systematic biography from records of the person's history, interviews, and current observation. This kind of research is useful in describing, in depth, the development and treatment of an unusual medical or psychological problem. Earlier in this chapter we considered a case study of a young man who had developed an ulcer. Other types of research that use one subject are called **single-subject designs.** This approach is often used for demonstrating the usefulness of a new treatment method for a specific medical or psychological problem. In the simplest of these designs, the statuses of the patient's condition at the beginning and end of therapy are compared. Often, follow-up assessments are made weeks or months later to see if the patient's condition has regressed. Some single-subject designs have additional phases or features that enable them to provide strong evidence for cause-effect relationships.

The principal disadvantage of single-subject approaches is that information gained from only one subject, no matter how detailed it is, may not describe what would be found with other individuals. A major purpose of psychological research is to collect information that can be applied or generalized to other people. Nevertheless, studies using one subject stimulate the development of new treatment procedures and suggest topics for further research.

GENETICS RESEARCH

How do psychologists and other scientists determine whether hereditary factors influence people's health and illness? The methods are based on a distinction between two types of twins. *Monozygotic*, or identical, twins have exactly the same genetic inheritance because they result from the splitting of a single fertilized egg, called a zygote. *Dizygotic*, or fraternal, twins develop from two separate zygotes, each of which was fertilized by a separate sperm. As a result, they are no more genetically similar than any singly born siblings and may, of course, be of different sex.

Most of the research on hereditary factors has focused on the differences in characteristics shown in monozygotic (MZ) twins as compared with dizygotic (DZ) twins. Investigations using this approach are called **twin studies.** The rationale for making these comparisons, although statistically complex, is logically simple. Because the two individuals in an MZ pair are genetically identical, we can assume that differences between them are environmentally determined. Conversely, the greater the similarity between MZ twins, the more likely it is that the characteristic is genetically influenced. Differences between DZ twins, on the other hand, are due to both genetic and environmental factors, even when they are the same sex. If we could assume that both members of each MZ and same-sex DZ pair that we study have had equal environmental experiences, then we could measure genetic influence simply by subtracting the differences for MZs from the differences for DZs.

The assumption that both members of each MZ and DZ pair have had equal environmental experiences presents a problem for researchers. As you might expect, environments are more likely to differ for fraternal pairs than for identical pairs. For instance, MZ children more often dress alike, play together, and share the same friends than do same-sex fraternal twins (McClearn, 1968). When this kind of problem exists—and it is hard to avoid totally—it makes the influence of heredity less clear. But some studies have been able to take environmental similarity into account—and when they do, important genetic forces are still found (Scarr & Kidd, 1983).

Another way to examine hereditary influences is to study children adopted at very early ages. **Adoption studies** compare traits of adopted children with those of their natural parents and their adoptive parents. Why? Adoptive parents contribute greatly to the rearing environment, but are genetically unrelated to the children; the natural parents are genetically related to the children, but play little or no role in rearing them. So, if adopted children are more similar to their natural parents than to their adoptive parents, we then have evidence for heredity's influence.

What conclusions relevant to health psychology have come from twin and adoption studies? Let's look at four. First, heredity affects not only physical characteristics, such as height and weight, but also physiological functions, including heart rate and blood pressure (Ditto, 1993). Second, genetic disorders can produce very high levels of cholesterol in the blood, making their victims susceptible to heart disease at very early ages (AMA, 1989). Third, some evidence indicates that heredity has its greatest impact on people's health early in life, and by old age the role of habits and lifestyle become increasingly important (Harris et al., 1992). Fourth, although genetic factors affect people's risk of developing cancer, environ-

mental factors appear to play a stronger role for most people (Lichtenstein et al., 2000).

In this chapter, we have discussed a variety of research methods that are useful in health psychology. Which one is best? Some scientists might say that the experiment is best because it can uncover cause-effect relationships. But precise control and manipulation do not always yield results that help us understand real-life behavior. For example, studying behavior in experimental settings sometimes involves artificial conditions, such as precisely occurring events and special equipment. To the extent that these conditions are unlike the real world, the subjects' behavior may be influenced. As a result, when reading about an experiment, it is useful to keep two questions in mind: Does the experimental situation approximate anything the subjects might experience in real life? If the experimental situation is highly artificial, what specific effect might this have on the outcome of the experiment? A new methodology called *ecological momentary assessment* may avoid these and other problems in health psychology research by using devices, such as pagers, to cue and collect data on subjects periodically in their day-to-day living (Shiffman & Stone, 1998).

In a sense, all the research methods we discussed are "best," since the investigator must select the most suitable method(s) to answer the specific question(s) under study. This leads us to a final point: it is possible and desirable to use experimental and nonexperimental methods *simultaneously* in one study. Suppose, for instance, we wanted to find out whether reading information about the health effects of excessive cholesterol would induce people to modify their diets. Using experimental methods, we would manipulate the independent variable in the following way: the experimental group would read the cholesterol information and a control group might read some unrelated material. But isn't it possible that the success of this experiment might depend on a variable that cannot be manipulated, such as the subjects' age or gender? People who are 50 years of age might be more inclined to follow recommendations to lower their cholesterol levels than people who are 20, for example. We could examine both variables by testing experimental and control groups for each of the two ages. Note, however, that the kinds of conclusions yielded by each variable will differ; only the manipulated variable can yield unambiguous causal statements.

SUMMARY

Health and illness are overlapping concepts that exist along a continuum. One end of the continuum is dominated by health—a positive state of physical, mental, and social well-being that varies over time. The other end of the continuum is dominated by illness, which produces signs, symptoms, and disabilities. The patterns of illness affecting people have changed across history, especially in the 20th century. Compared with earlier times, today people die at later ages and from different causes. Infectious diseases are no longer the principal cause of death in technological societies around the world. Chronic illnesses now constitute the main health problem in developed nations.

Ideas about physiology, disease processes, and the mind have changed since the early cultures thousands of years ago, when people apparently believed that illness was caused by evil spirits and the like. Between the years 500 and 300 B.C., Greek philosophers produced the earliest written ideas about health and illness. They tried to explain how sickness happens and proposed that the mind and body are separate entities. During the Middle Ages, the Church had an enormous influence on ideas about illness, and the belief in mystical causes of disease became strong again. Philosophers and scientists from the 17th to the 20th centuries provided the foundation for the biomedical model as a way to conceptualize health and illness.

The biomedical model has been extremely useful, enabling researchers to make great advances in conquering many infectious diseases through the development of vaccines and treatments. But many researchers today have come to recognize that aspects of individual patients—their histories, social relationships, lifestyles, personalities, mental processes, and biological processes—must be included in a full conceptualization of health and illness. As a result, the biopsychosocial model has emerged as an alternative to the biomedical approach as the fields of psychosomatic medicine, behavioral medicine, and health psychology have developed. This new model proposes a constant interplay of biological, psychological, and social systems—each interrelated with and producing changes in the others. The life-span perspective adds an important dimension to this model by considering the role of the person's development in health and illness. Health psychology draws on knowledge from a variety of other subfields in psychology and several nonpsychology fields, such as medicine, biology, social work, epidemiology, public health, sociology, and anthropology.

The study of important variables in health psychology involves the use of experimental and nonexperimental research methods. Experimental methods usually involve rigorous control and manipulation of variables and lead to cause-effect conclusions. Nonexperimental methods focus on the study of relationships between variables. A correlation describes an association between variables but does not indicate whether it is a causal relation. Quasi-experimental approaches are useful in studying variables that cannot be manipulated, such as the subjects' history, age, and gender. To study people at different ages, researchers use cross-sectional and longitudinal approaches. The role of heredity in health and illness can be examined through twin and adoption studies.

KEY TERMS

illness/wellness continuum	behavioral medicine	incidence	quasi-experimental studies
health	health psychology	epidemic	retrospective approach
dietary diseases	behavioral methods	sociocultural	prospective approach
infectious diseases	cognitive methods	theory	cross-sectional approach
chronic diseases	biopsychosocial model	variable	longitudinal approach
mind/body problem	system	experiment	cohort effect
biomedical model	life-span perspective	placebo	case study
risk factors	mortality	double-blind	single-subject designs
personality	morbidity	correlation coefficient	twin studies
psychosomatic medicine	prevalence	correlational studies	adoption studies

2

THE BODY'S
PHYSICAL SYSTEMS

PROLOGUE

When Tom was born 20 years ago, his parents were thrilled. Here was their first child—a delightful baby with such promise for the future. He seemed to be healthy. His parents were pleased that he began to consume large amounts of milk, often without becoming satiated. They took this as a good sign. But, in this case, it wasn't.

As the weeks went by, Tom's parents noticed that he wasn't gaining as much weight as he should, especially since he was still consuming lots of milk. He started to cough and wheeze often and developed one respiratory infection after another. They became concerned, and so did his pediatrician. After a series of tests, the devastating diagnosis was clear: Tom had *cystic fibrosis*, a chronic, progressive, and eventually fatal disease. Cystic fibrosis is an inherited disease of the respiratory system for which there is no cure and no effective treatment.

Tom has had a difficult life, and so has his family. The respiratory infections he had in infancy were just the beginning. His disease causes thick, sticky secretions that constantly block airways, trap air in the lungs, and help bacteria to thrive. Other body systems also become affected, causing additional problems, such as insufficient absorption of food and vitamins. As a result, he was sick often and remained short, underweight, and weak compared with other children. His social relationships have always been limited and strained, and the burden of his illness has taken its toll on his parents.

When Tom was younger and people asked him, "What do you want to be when you grow up?" he would answer, "I'm going to be an angel when I grow up." What other plans could he have had, realistically? At 20, he has reached the age by which half of the victims of cystic fibrosis die. Physical complications, such as heart damage, that generally afflict several body systems in the last stages of this disease have begun to appear.

We can see in Tom's story that biological factors, such as heredity, can affect health; illness can alter social relationships; and all interrelated physiological systems of the body can be affected. In this chapter we outline the major physical systems of the body. Our discussion focuses on the normal functions of these systems, but we consider some important problems, too. What determines the degree of paralysis a person suffers after injury to the spine? How does stress affect our body systems? What is a heart attack, and what causes it?

THE NERVOUS SYSTEM

We all know that the nervous system, particularly the brain, in human beings and other animals controls the way we initiate behavior and respond to events in our world. The nervous system receives information about changes in the environment from sensory organs, including the eyes, ears, and nose, and it transmits directions that tell our muscles and other internal organs how to react. The brain also stores information—being a repository for our memory of past events—and provides our capability for thinking, reasoning, and creating.

HOW THE NERVOUS SYSTEM WORKS

The nervous system is constantly integrating the actions of our internal organs—although we are not generally aware of it. Many of these organs, such as the heart and digestive tract, are made of muscle tissues that respond to commands. The nervous system provides these commands through an intricate network of billions of specialized nerve cells, called **neurons.**

Although neurons in different parts of the nervous system have a variety of shapes and sizes, the diagram in Figure 2–1 shows their general features. Projecting from the *cell body* are clusters of branches called *dendrites*. Generally, dendrites function as receivers for

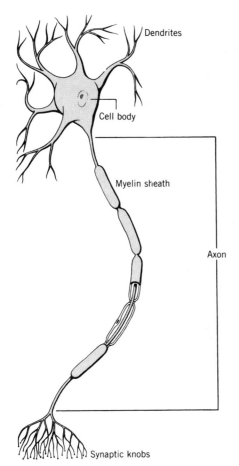

Figure 2–1   An idealized diagram of a neuron and some of its major parts. Electrochemical messages received by the dendrites are transmitted to the synaptic knobs. The myelin sheath covers the axon of most neurons.

messages from adjacent neurons. These messages then travel through a long, slender projection called the *axon*, which splits into branches at the far end. The tips of these branches have small swellings called *synaptic knobs* that connect to the dendrites of other neurons, usually through a fluid-filled gap. This junction is called a *synapse*. Messages from the knobs cross the gap to adjacent neurons, and in this way eventually reach their destination.

The messages neurons send consist of *electrochemical* activity. Within the neuron, the message begins with chemical changes that occur when a dendrite is stimulated. If these changes produce a sufficient concentration of electrically charged particles, called *ions*, an impulse of electrical potential is triggered. That

impulse travels through the axon and stimulates the synaptic knobs to release a chemical called a **neurotransmitter,** which travels to the dendrites of an adjacent neuron. Dozens of different neurotransmitters have been identified. Some of them tend to *excite* the receiving neuron, increasing the likelihood that an electrical impulse will be generated. Others tend to *inhibit* the neuron, making an impulse less likely. Some neurotransmitters can have either effect, depending on certain characteristics of the receiving neuron.

What changes occur in the nervous system as a person develops? By the time the typical baby is born, a basic structure has been formed for almost all the neurons this person will have. But the nervous system is still quite immature—for instance, the brain weighs only about 25% of the weight it will have when the child reaches adulthood (Sarafino & Armstrong, 1986). Most of the growth in brain size after birth results from an increase in the number of *glial cells* and the presence of a white fatty substance called *myelin*. The glial cells are thought to service and maintain the neurons. A myelin sheath surrounds the axons of most, but not all, neurons. This sheath is responsible for increasing the speed of nerve impulses and preventing them from being interfered with by adjacent nerve impulses, much the way insulation is used on electrical wiring. The importance of myelin can be seen in the disease called *multiple sclerosis*, which results when the myelin sheath degenerates and nerves become severed (Trapp, 1998). People afflicted with this disease have weak muscles that lack coordination and move spastically (AMA, 1989).

As the infant grows, the network of dendrites and synaptic knobs to carry messages to and from other neurons expands dramatically, as Figure 2–2 shows. The myelin sheath covering the neurons is better developed initially in the upper regions of the body than in the lower regions. During the first years of life, the progress in myelin growth spreads down the body—from the head to shoulders, to the arms and hands, to the upper chest and abdomen, and then the legs and feet. This sequence is reflected in the individual's motor development: the upper parts of the body are brought under control at earlier ages than the lower parts. Studies with animals have found that chronic poor nutrition early in life impairs brain growth by retarding the development of myelin, glial cells, and dendrites. Such impairment can produce long-lasting deficits in a child's motor and intellectual performance (Reinis & Goldman, 1980). Although

At birth At 1 month At 6 months At 2 years

Figure 2–2 Drawings showing the neural structure of a section of the human cortex at four different ages. Notice that the number of cell bodies (dark spots) does not change much, while the network of dendrites expands with age. (Drawings from Lenneberg, 1967, Figure 4.6, based on photographs from Conel, 1939–1963.)

researchers had thought that the brain forms few, if any, new neurons after birth, it is now known that new cells do form in some areas of the brain, but it is not yet clear how extensive this growth is (Eriksson et al., 1998).

Beginning in early adulthood, the brain slowly loses weight with age (Tortora & Grabowski, 2000). Although the number of brain cells does not change very much, the synapses do, leading to a decline in ability to send nerve impulses. These alterations in the brain are associated with the declines people often notice in their mental and physical functions after they reach 50 or 60 years of age.

The nervous system is enormously complex and basically has two major divisions—the central nervous system and the peripheral nervous system—that connect to each other. The **central nervous system** consists of the brain and spinal cord. The *peripheral nervous system* is composed of the remaining network of neurons throughout the body. Each of these major divisions consists of interconnected lower-order divisions or structures. We will examine the nervous system, beginning at the top and working our way down.

THE CENTRAL NERVOUS SYSTEM

People's brain and spinal cord race toward maturity early in life. For example, the brain weighs 75% of its adult weight at about 2 years of age, 90% at 5 years, and 95% at 10 years (Tanner, 1970, 1978). The brain may be divided into three parts: the *forebrain*, the *cere-*

bellum, and the *brainstem*. Each of these parts has special functions.

The Forebrain

The forebrain is the uppermost part of the brain. As Figure 2–3 shows, the forebrain has two main subdivisions: the *telencephalon*, which consists of the cerebrum and the limbic system, and the *diencephalon*, which includes the thalamus and hypothalamus. As a general rule, areas toward the top and outer regions of the brain are involved in our perceptual, motor, learning, and conceptual activities. Regions toward the center and bottom of the brain are involved mainly in controlling internal and automatic body functions and in transmitting information to and from the telencephalon.

The **cerebrum** is the upper and largest portion of the human brain and includes the *cerebral cortex*, its outermost layer. The cerebrum controls complex motor and mental activity. It develops rapidly in the first few years of life, becoming larger, thicker, and more convoluted. The cerebrum has two halves—the *left hemisphere* and the *right hemisphere*—each of which looks like the left hemispheres drawn in Figure 2–4.

Although the left and right hemispheres are physically alike, they control different types of processes. For one thing, the motor cortex (see Figure 2–4*b*) of each hemisphere controls motor movements on the opposite side of the body. This is why damage to the motor cortex on, say, the right side of the brain may leave part of the left side of the body paralyzed. The

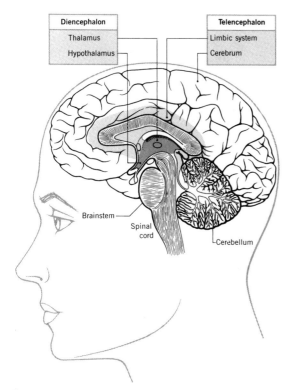

Figure 2–3   A side view of the human brain in cross section, sliced through the middle from front to back. The forebrain consists of the telencephalon (cerebrum and limbic system) and the diencephalon (thalamus and hypothalamus). The remaining divisions of the central nervous system—the cerebellum, the brainstem, and the spinal cord—are also labeled.

two hemispheres also control different aspects of cognitive and language processes. In most people, the left hemisphere contains the areas that handle language processes, including speech and writing. The right hemisphere usually processes such things as visual imagery, emotions, and the perception of patterns, such as melodies (Tortora & Grabowski, 2000).

You probably noticed in Figure 2–4 that each hemisphere is divided into a front part, called the frontal lobe, and three back parts: the temporal, occipital, and parietal lobes. The *frontal lobe* is involved in a variety of functions, one of which is motor activity. The back part of the frontal lobe contains the motor cortex, which controls the skeletal muscles of the body. If a patient who is undergoing brain surgery receives stimulation to the motor cortex, some part of

the body will move. The frontal lobe is also involved in important mental activities, such as the association of ideas, planning, self-awareness, and emotion. As a result, injury to areas of this lobe can produce personality and emotional reactions, like those described by the physician of Phineas P. Gage:

> He is fitful, irreverent, indulging in the grossest profanity (which was not previously his custom), manifesting but little deference to his fellows, impatient of restraint or advice when it conflicts with his desires, at times...obstinate, capricious, and vacillating.... His mind was radically changed, so that his friends said he was no longer Gage. (Cited in McClintic, 1985, p. 93.)

Phineas had survived a workplace accident in which a tamping iron was blown through the front of his head.

The *temporal lobe* is chiefly involved in hearing, but also in vision and memory. Damage to this region can impair the person's comprehension of speech and ability to determine the direction from which a sound is coming. The *occipital lobe* contains the principal visual area of the brain. Damage to the occipital lobe can produce blindness or the inability to recognize an object by sight. The *parietal lobe* is involved mainly in body sensations, such as of pain, cold, heat, touch, and body movement.

The second part of the telencephalon—called the **limbic system**—lies along the innermost edge of the cerebrum, and adjacent to the diencephalon (refer back to Figure 2–3). The limbic system is not well understood yet. It consists of several structures that seem to be important in the expression of emotions, such as fear, anger, and excitement. To the extent that heredity affects a person's emotions, it may do so by determining the structure and function of the limbic system (McClintic, 1985).

The diencephalon includes two structures—the thalamus and hypothalamus—that lie below and are partially encircled by the limbic system. The **thalamus** is a truly pivotal structure in the flow of information in the nervous system. It functions as the chief relay station for directing sensory messages, such as of pain or visual images, to appropriate points in the cerebrum, such as the occipital or parietal lobe. The thalamus also relays commands going out to the skeletal muscles from the motor cortex of the cerebrum.

The **hypothalamus,** a small structure just below the thalamus, plays an important role in people's

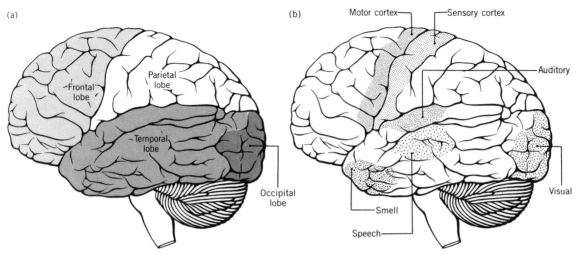

Figure 2–4   Two drawings of the surface of the left hemisphere of the cerebrum. The left drawing shows the four parts of the hemisphere, and the right drawing points out the areas associated with specific functions. The right hemisphere has the same four parts and functional areas.

emotions and motivation. Its function affects eating, drinking, and sexual activity, for instance (Tortora & Grabowski, 2000). For example, when the body lacks water or nutrients, the hypothalamus detects this and arouses the sensation of thirst or hunger, which is relieved when we consume water or food. Research with animals has shown that stimulation of specific areas of this structure can cause them to eat when they are full and stop eating when they are hungry. A rare disease that affects this structure can cause people to become overweight. Another important function of the hypothalamus is to maintain *homeostasis*—a state of balance or normal function among our body systems. Our normal body temperature and heart rate, which are characteristic of healthy individuals, are examples of homeostasis. When our bodies are cold, for instance, we shiver, thus producing heat. When we are very warm, we perspire, thus cooling the body. The hypothalamus controls these adjustments (McClintic, 1985). We will see later that the hypothalamus also plays an important role in our reaction to stress.

The Cerebellum

The **cerebellum** lies at the back of the brain, below the cerebrum. The main function of the cerebellum is in maintaining body balance and coordinating movement. This structure has nerve connections to

the motor cortex of the cerebrum and most sense organs of the body. When areas of the cerebrum initiate specific movements, the cerebellum makes our actions precise and well coordinated.

How does the cerebellum do this? There are at least two ways. First, it continuously compares our intent with our performance, ensuring that a movement goes in the right direction, at the proper rate, and with appropriate force. Second, it smoothes our movements. Because of the forces involved in movement, there is an underlying tendency for our motions to go quickly back and forth, like a tremor. The cerebellum damps this tendency (McClintic, 1985). When injury occurs to the cerebellum, the person's actions become jerky and uncoordinated—a condition called *ataxia*. Simple movements, such as walking or touching an object, become difficult and unsteady.

Figure 2–5 shows the location of the cerebellum relative to the brainstem, which is the next section of the brain we will discuss.

The Brainstem

The lowest portion of the brain—called the **brainstem**—has the form of an oddly shaped knob at the top of the spinal cord. The brainstem consists of four parts: midbrain, pons, reticular system, and medulla.

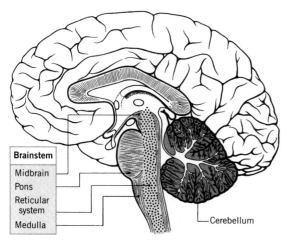

Brainstem

Midbrain

Pons

Reticular system

Medulla

Cerebellum

Figure 2–5 A side view of the human brain in cross section, showing the cerebellum and the brainstem, which includes the midbrain, pons, reticular system, and medulla.

The **midbrain** lies at the top of the brainstem. It connects directly to the thalamus above it, which relays messages to various parts of the forebrain. The midbrain receives information from the visual and auditory systems and is especially important in muscle movement. The disorder called *Parkinson's disease* results from degeneration of an area of the midbrain (Tortora & Grabowski, 2000). People severely afflicted with this disease have noticeable motor tremors, and their neck and trunk postures become rigid, so that they walk in a crouch. Sometimes the tremors are so continuous and vigorous that the victim becomes crippled.

The **reticular system** is a network of neurons that extends from the bottom to the top of the brainstem and into the thalamus. The reticular system plays an important role in controlling our states of sleep, arousal, and attention. When people suffer a coma, often it is this system that is injured or disordered (McClintic, 1985). *Epilepsy* a condition in which a victim may become unconscious and begin to convulse, seems to involve an abnormality in the reticular system. One type of epileptic seizure called *grand mal* may result from "reverberating cycles" in the reticular system:

That is, one portion of the system stimulates another portion, which stimulates a third portion, and this in turn restimulates the first portion,

causing a cycle that continues for 2 to 3 minutes, until the neurons of the system fatigue so greatly that the reverberation ceases. (Guyton, 1985, p. 356)

Following a grand mal seizure, the person often sleeps at least a few minutes and sometimes for hours.

The **pons** forms a large bulge at the front of the brainstem and is involved in eye movements, facial expressions, and chewing. At the bottom of the brainstem is the **medulla,** which contains vital centers that control breathing, heartbeat rate, and the diameter of blood vessels (which affects blood pressure). Because of the many vital functions it controls, damage to the medulla can be life threatening. *Polio*, a crippling disease that was once epidemic, sometimes damaged the center that controls breathing. Patients suffering such damage needed constant artificial respiration to breathe (McClintic, 1985).

The Spinal Cord

Extending down the spine from the brainstem is the **spinal cord,** a major neural pathway that transmits messages between the brain and various parts of the body. It contains neurons that carry impulses away from (the *efferent* direction) and toward (*afferent*) the brain. Efferent commands travel down the cord on their way to produce muscle action; afferent impulses come to the spinal cord from sense organs in all parts of the body.

The organization of the spinal cord parallels that of the body—that is, the higher the region of the cord, the higher the parts of the body to which it connects. Damage to the spinal cord results in impaired motor function or paralysis; the duration and extent of the impairment depends on the amount and location of damage. If the damage does not sever the cord, the impairment is less severe, and may be temporary. If the lower portion of the cord is severed, the lower areas of the body are paralyzed—a condition called *paraplegia*. If the upper portion of the spinal cord is severed, paralysis is more extensive. Paralysis of the legs and arms is called *quadriplegia*.

Figure 2–6 depicts the spinal cord and its relation to the brain and the branching network of afferent and efferent neurons throughout the body—the peripheral nervous system. (Go to ☙.)

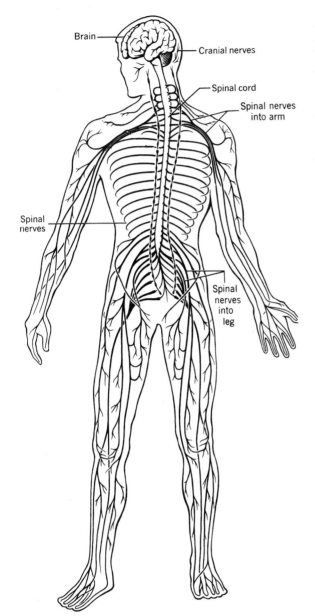

Figure 2–6 labels:

Brain

Cranial nerves

Spinal cord

Spinal nerves into arm

Spinal nerves

Spinal nerves into leg

Figure 2–6 Diagram showing the branching network between the spinal cord and the peripheral nervous system.

THE PERIPHERAL NERVOUS SYSTEM

The **peripheral nervous system** has two parts: the somatic nervous system and the autonomic nervous system. The **somatic nervous system** is involved in both sensory and motor functions, serving mainly the skin and skeletal muscles. The **autonomic nervous system** activates internal organs, such as the lungs and intestines, and reports to the brain the current state of activity of these organs.

In the somatic nervous system, afferent neurons carry messages from sense organs to the spinal cord, as Figure 2–7 diagrams. Efferent neurons carry messages to, and activate, *striated* (grooved) skeletal muscles, such as those in the face, arms, and legs, that we can move voluntarily. A disorder called *myasthenia gravis* can develop at the junction of these muscles and neurons, weakening muscle function of the head and neck. This produces characteristic symptoms—such as drooping eyelids, blurred vision, and difficulty swallowing and breathing—and can lead to paralysis and death. Although medical treatment is effective in restoring muscle function, some symptoms may recur when the person is under stress (AMA, 1989).

Figure 2–7 also shows that in the autonomic nervous system, neurons carry messages between the spinal cord and the *smooth* muscles of the internal organs, such as the heart, stomach, lungs, blood vessels, and glands. This system itself has two divisions, the sympathetic and parasympathetic, which often act in opposite ways, as Figure 2–8 diagrams. The **sympathetic nervous system** helps us mobilize and expend energy in responding to emergencies, expressing strong emotions, and performing strenuous activity. For instance, suppose you are crossing a street, notice a speeding car barreling toward you, and hear its brakes start to squeal. The sympathetic nervous system instantly moves into action, producing several simultaneous changes—for example, it speeds up the heart, dilates certain arteries to increase blood flow to the heart and skeletal muscles, constricts other arteries to decrease blood flow to the skin and digestive organs, decreases salivation, and increases perspiration. These changes, in general, enable you to mobilize energy, and you leap to safety out of the car's path. This system is called "sympathetic" because it acts in agreement with your current emotional state.

What does the parasympathetic division do? The prefix *para* means "alongside of"—this division acts alongside of, and often in opposition to, the sympathetic division. The **parasympathetic nervous system** regulates "quiet" or calming processes, helping our individual organ systems conserve and store energy. One example of parasympathetic activity can be

CLINICAL METHODS AND ISSUES
Biofeedback Treatment for Paralysis

Neuromuscular disorders, which impair the muscles and nerves that control movement, often involve paralysis resulting from a spinal cord injury or a stroke that damages the brain. Biofeedback, the operant conditioning method we described in Chapter 1, is a treatment that psychologists and physical therapists can apply successfully to improve muscle control if the spinal cord is not completely severed (Fogel, 1987). The procedure involves attaching sensors to the skin to detect tiny changes in the activity of an affected muscle, immediately reporting back to the person when the muscle has tensed a bit, and encouraging him or her to tense it more and more. One study found that two biofeedback sessions a week for 6 weeks improved muscle function substantially in patients who had suffered strokes years earlier (Burnside, Tobias, & Bursill, 1982). Biofeedback can also help people gain control over other body processes, enabling them to reduce their blood pressure or asthma attacks, for example.

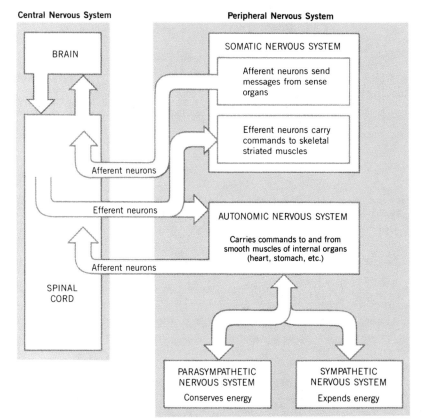

Figure 2–7 Illustration of the flow and function of nerve impulses among the major parts of the nervous system.

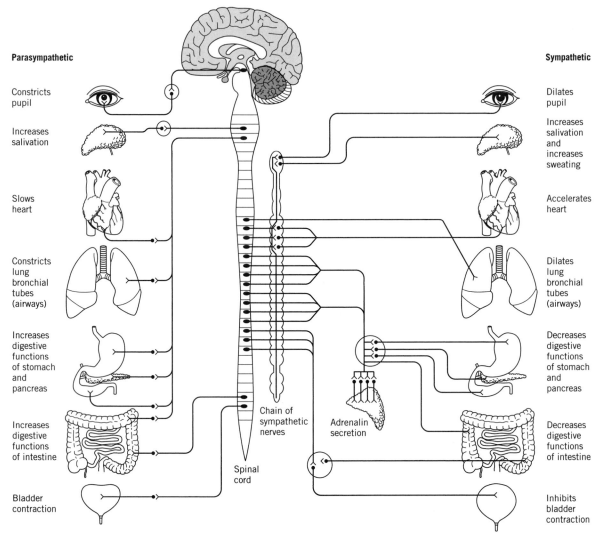

Figure 2–8   The autonomic nervous system and its interconnections between the spinal cord and various organs of the body. The function of the parasympathetic division in conserving energy is shown on the left side of the diagram. The function of the sympathetic division in expending energy is shown on the right side. Notice that each organ connects to both divisions.

seen in the digestion of food. When you eat a meal, the parasympathetic nervous system carries messages to regulate each step in the digestive process, such as by increasing salivation and stomach contractions. Another example can be seen in the course of emotional or emergency reactions—when an emergency has passed, the parasympathetic division helps restore your normal body state.

Communication within the peripheral nervous system is handled by 12 sets of *cranial nerves*, most of which originate in the brainstem. The *vagus nerve* extends from there to muscles of most major body organs, such as the airways, lungs, heart, and intestines, and is directly involved in the regulation of sympathetic and parasympathetic activity (Porges, 1992, 1995; Tortora & Grabowski, 2000). Efferent messages from the brain can target specific organs to increase or decrease their function.

As you now realize, the nervous system is connected to and regulates all of our other body systems, and the brain is the control center. The remainder of this chapter examines these other body systems, beginning with the endocrine system.

THE ENDOCRINE SYSTEM

The **endocrine system** consists of a set of glands that often work in close association with the autonomic nervous system. These systems share an important function: they communicate with various parts of the body. But they do this in somewhat different ways. Whereas the nervous system uses both electrical and chemical messages, the endocrine system communicates only with chemical substances, which are called **hormones.** Each endocrine gland secretes specific hormones directly into the bloodstream, which carries these chemicals to various parts of the body. Figure 2–9 shows where several important endocrine glands are located. Certain chemicals are produced by both the endocrine and nervous systems and function as both hormones and neurotransmitters.

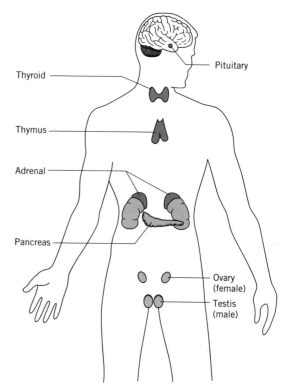

Figure 2–9   Some of the endocrine glands and their locations in the body.

THE ENDOCRINE AND NERVOUS SYSTEMS WORKING TOGETHER

How are the endocrine and nervous systems associated? The nervous system is linked to the endocrine system by connections between the hypothalamus (in the forebrain) and a gland that lies just below it— the **pituitary gland.** The hypothalamus sends chemical messages directly to the pituitary gland, causing it to release pituitary hormones into the blood. In turn, most of these hormones selectively stimulate the other endocrine glands to secrete chemicals. Because the pituitary gland controls the secretion of other endocrine glands, it is called the "master gland."

Researchers have identified dozens of different hormones that course through our veins and arteries. Each hormone has its own specific effects on cells and organs of the body, thereby directly or indirectly affecting psychological and physical functions. Some hormones, such as estrogens and testosterone, are

produced mainly in females' *ovaries* (where egg cells develop) and males' *testes* (where sperm develop). These hormones are especially important in the development and functioning of female and male reproductive systems. Other hormones affect blood pressure, general body growth, and the balance of various chemicals, such as calcium, in the body. Still other hormones help us react to specific situations we encounter in our lives.

We saw earlier that the autonomic nervous system plays an important role in our reaction to an emergency. So does the endocrine system through a process called the *hypothalamus–pituitary–adrenal axis* (Sternberg & Gold, 1997). Let's see how by returning to the incident in which you leaped out of the path of a speeding car. When the sympathetic nervous system reacts to your emergency, the hypothalamus immediately sends a hormone called corticotropin-releasing factor to the pituitary gland. This causes the pituitary to release ACTH (adrenocorticotropic hormone) into the blood. The ACTH then travels throughout the body and stimulates the release of a variety of hormones—especially those of the adrenal glands—that affect your reaction to the emergency.

ADRENAL GLANDS

The **adrenal glands** are located on top of the kidneys (see Figure 2–9). These glands release several important hormones in response to emergencies and stress (Tortora & Grabowski, 2000). One of these hormones, *cortisol*, helps control swelling when we are injured. If when you leaped to avoid being hit by the car you sprained your ankle, this hormone would help reduce swelling. But continued high levels of cortisol and similar hormones over a long time can be harmful to the body. They can lead to high blood pressure and the formation of ulcers, for example.

Two other important adrenal hormones are *epinephrine* and *norepinephrine* (also called adrenalin and noradrenalin). These hormones work in conjunction with the sympathetic nervous system to produce such bodily reactions as speeding up heart and respiration rates and increasing the liver's sugar output for quick energy. After the emergency has passed and sympathetic activity has subsided, some impact of the hormones may continue for a while because they are still in the bloodstream.

The impact of the nervous and endocrine systems' activities in emergency situations differs in the speed and persistence of their effect. The nervous system responds by sending messages that move instantly to specific locations; once they reach their destination, they become deactivated or dissipated. For example, the nervous system also produces and uses epinephrine and norepinephrine, but these chemicals function as neurotransmitters, relaying their commands from neuron to neuron and having a localized effect. The impact of the message stops quickly, and persists only if additional messages are sent. Hormones from the endocrine system move more slowly and broadly through the bloodstream, and their effects can be delayed and long-lasting.

OTHER GLANDS

Several other endocrine glands are also important. The *thyroid gland*, located in the neck, produces hormones, such as thyroxine, that regulate the body's general activity level and growth. Disorders in thyroid production are of two types: *hypothyroidism*, or insufficient secretion of thyroid hormones, and *hyperthyroidism*, or excessive thyroid secretion (AMA, 1989). Hypothyroidism leads to low activity levels and to weight gain. If the condition is congenital and untreated, dwarfism and mental retardation often result. The condition can be treated medically by having the person take hormone supplements orally. Hyperthyroidism leads to high activity levels, short attention spans, tremors, insomnia, and weight loss. Untreated people with a common form of this condition, called *Graves' disease*, act in a highly restless, irritable, and confused manner.

The *thymus gland*, which is located in the chest, is quite large in infancy and childhood but diminishes in size and efficiency after puberty (Tortora & Grabowski, 2000). The thymus plays an important role early in life in the development of antibodies and immunities against diseases.

Another endocrine gland is the *pancreas*, which is located below the stomach. Its main function is to regulate the level of blood sugar, or glucose. The pancreas does this by producing two hormones, *glucagon* and *insulin*, that act in opposition. Glucagon raises the concentration of glucose in the blood, and insulin lowers it (Tortora & Grabowski, 2000). The disorder called *diabetes mellitus* results when the pancreas does not produce sufficient insulin to balance the action of glucagon. This imbalance produces excess blood sugar levels—a condition called *hyperglycemia*. If this condition persists and is untreated, it may cause coma and death. Diabetes can be medically controlled, generally through diet and either medication or daily insulin injections (AMA, 1989; Kilo & Williamson, 1987) (Go to 💡.)

THE DIGESTIVE SYSTEM

Whether we eat an apple, drink some milk, or swallow a pill, our bodies respond in the same general way. The **digestive system** breaks down what we have ingested, converts much of it to chemicals the body can use, and excretes the rest. The chemicals the body uses are absorbed into the bloodstream, which transports them to all of our body cells. Chemical nutrients in the foods we eat provide energy to fuel our activity, body growth, and repair.

Highlight on Issues
Our Physiological Individuality

Think about some differences between two people you know. Probably the first things that come to mind are their physical and behavioral characteristics. One person is tall and has blond hair, blue eyes, and an outgoing personality; the other is short and has dark hair, dark eyes, and is shy. But what about their internal physiological structure and functions?

We don't usually think about internal physiological differences between people. This is partly because the pictures of internal organs we see in books are always the same. As a result, we get the impression that if you've seen one heart or stomach, you've seen them all. This impression is wrong. Our individuality exists not only in our external features, but in our internal organs and bodily chemistry as well. The aorta is a major blood vessel that arches, or curves, over and attaches to the heart. Examples of some of its structural variations are given in Figure 2H–1. The drawing on the left depicts the usual branching that forms at the arch of the aorta, and the other drawings show variations that occur, sometimes quite frequently. Major differences like these occur in virtually all organs (Skolnick, 1986).

Our physiological individuality can have major implications for health and behavior. How? One way is that people's reactions to medicines differ, sometimes quite substantially. Some people may require many times the normal dose of certain drugs before the desired effect occurs. A person's age, weight, and heredity contribute to this variability (Bennett, 1987; USDHHS, 1981). Heavy people usually require larger doses of a drug than other people do. Infants and the elderly seem to be particularly sensitive to the effects of drugs, and overdoses are a danger for them. Blood pressure medication in the elderly may overshoot and lower the pressure too far, for example.

There are gender differences in many organ systems, too. Males generally have larger hearts and lungs, and higher blood pressure, than females do. Their body systems also react to stress differently. We saw earlier that the adrenal glands respond to stress by secreting hormones—two of which are epinephrine and cortisol. When under stress, males secrete more of these hormones than females do (Collins & Frankenhaeuser, 1978; Pollack & Steklis, 1986).

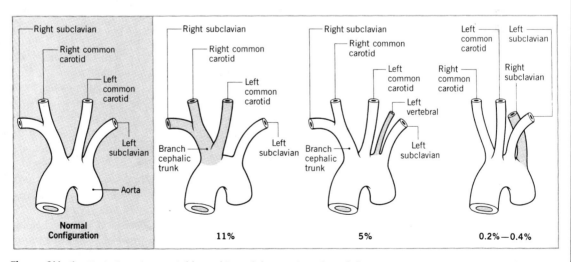

Figure 2H–1 Variations in arterial branching of the aortic arch and the approximate percentages of their occurrence. (Drawings of variations are from Grant, 1972, plate 446.4.)

FOOD'S JOURNEY THROUGH DIGESTIVE ORGANS

Think of the digestive system as a long hose—about 20 feet long—with stations along the way. The journey of food through this hose begins in the *mouth* and ends at the *rectum*. These digestive organs and the major organs in between are shown in Figure 2–10.

Digesting Food

How does this system break down food? One way is mechanical: for example, we grind food up when we chew it. Another way is chemical: by the action of **enzymes,** substances that act as catalysts in speeding up chemical reactions in cells. How do enzymes work? You can see the effect of an enzyme by doing the following experiment (Holum, 1994). Place a bit of liver in some hydrogen peroxide and watch what happens: An enzyme in liver called *catalase* causes the peroxide to decompose, frothing as oxygen is given off as a gas. This is the same reaction you see when you use peroxide to disinfect a wound.

In most cases, the names for enzymes end in the letters *-ase*, and the remainder of each name reflects the substance on which it acts. The following list gives some examples:

- *Carbohydrase* acts on carbohydrates.
- *Lactase* acts on lactose (milk).
- *Phosphatase* acts on phosphate compounds.
- *Sucrase* acts on sucrose (sugar).

As food is broken down into smaller and smaller units in the digestive tract, water molecules become attached to these units (Rhoades & Pflanzer, 1996).

When food is in the mouth, there is more digestive action going on than just chewing. Saliva moistens food and contains an enzyme that starts the process of breaking down starches. The salivary glands release saliva in response to commands from the brainstem, which responds primarily to sensory information from taste buds. Simply seeing, smelling, or even thinking about food can produce neural impulses that cause the mouth to water (Rhoades & Pflanzer, 1996).

The journey of food advances to the *esophagus,* a tube that is normally flattened when food is not passing through it. The esophagus pushes the food down to the stomach by wavelike muscle contractions called *peristalsis.* By the time food enters the esophagus, the stomach has already begun digestive activities by releasing small amounts of gastric juice even before food reaches it. Tasting, smelling, seeing, or thinking about food can initiate this process (Feldman & Richardson, 1986). Once food reaches the stomach, this organ amasses large amounts of gastric juices, including *hydrochloric acid* and *pepsin,* an enzyme that breaks down proteins. (This enzyme name is one of the few that does not end in *-ase.*) The stomach also produces a sticky mucus substance to protect its lining from the highly acidic gastric juices.

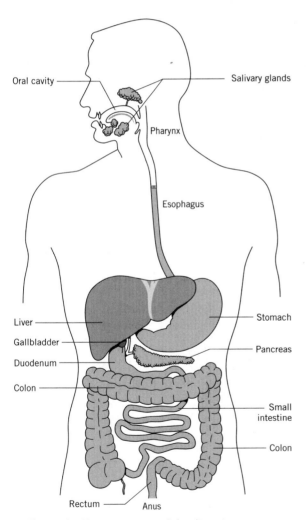

Figure 2–10 Major parts of the digestive system.

The muscular stomach walls produce a churning motion—that we are generally not aware of—which mixes the food particles with the gastric juices. This mixing continues for 3 or 4 hours, producing a semi-liquid mixture.

Peristalsis in the stomach then moves this mixture on, a little at a time, to the initial section of the small intestine called the *duodenum*. Important digestive processes occur in the small intestine (Rhoades & Pflanzer, 1996; Tortora & Grabowski, 2000). First, the highly acidic food mixture becomes chemically alkaline as a result of substances added from the pancreas, gallbladder, and wall of the small intestine. This is important because the linings of the small intestine and remainder of the digestive tract are not protected from high acidity, as the stomach is. Second, enzymes secreted by the pancreas into the duodenum break down carbohydrates, proteins, and fats further. Third, *absorption* increases. Because the stomach lining can absorb only a few substances, such as alcohol and aspirin, most materials we ingest are absorbed into the bloodstream through the lining of the small intestine (Tortora & Grabowski, 2000). If alcohol is consumed along with fatty foods, very little alcohol is absorbed until it reaches the small intestine. By the time food is ready to be absorbed through the intestine wall, nutrients have been broken down into molecules—carbohydrates are broken down into *simple sugars*, fats into *glycerol* and *fatty acids*, and proteins into *amino acids*.

How does absorption occur? The inside of the small intestine is made of a membrane that will allow molecules to pass through. To increase the absorbing surface, the intestine wall has many folds that contain projections, as pictured in Figure 2–11. Each of the many thousands of projections contains a network of structures that will accept the molecules and transport them away to other parts of the body. These structures include tiny blood vessels called *capillaries* and a tube called a *lacteal*. Capillaries absorb amino acids, simple sugars, and water; they also absorb some fatty acids, vitamins, and minerals. Lacteals accept glycerol and the remaining fatty acids and vitamins.

The remaining food material continues its journey to the large intestine, most of which is called the *colon*. Absorption, mainly of water, continues in the first half of the colon, and the remaining material is transported on. Bacterial action converts the material

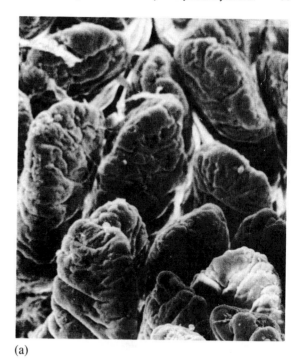

(a)

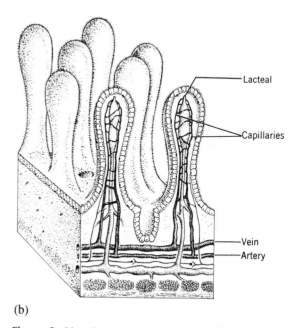

(b)

Figure 2–11   The interior wall of the small intestine. (a) The wall has many tiny projections, shown greatly magnified in the photograph. (b) The cross-sectional drawing shows the capillaries and lacteal of each projection.

into feces, which eventually reach the rectum, where they are stored until defecation occurs.

Disorders of the Digestive System

Judging from the many media advertisements for stomach and "irregularity" remedies, it seems that people have a good deal of trouble with their digestive processes. We will consider a few digestive problems.

One disorder of the digestive system is *peptic ulcers*, which are open sores in the lining of the stomach or intestine, usually in the duodenum. These sores appear to result from excess gastric juices chronically eroding the lining when there is little or no food in the stomach, but bacterial infection can play a role, too (Tortora & Grabowski, 2000). Abdominal pain is the chief symptom of the disorder. Although the victims of ulcers are mostly adults, the disorder also occurs in children, particularly boys (Whitehead, 1986). People who experience high levels of stress seem to be more susceptible to ulcers than people who do not.

Hepatitis is a class of several viral diseases in which the liver becomes inflamed and unable to function well. The first symptoms often are like those of flu. But the symptoms persist, and jaundice, a yellowing of the skin, generally follows. *Hepatitis* A appears to be transmitted through contaminated food, water, and utensils. *Hepatitis* B and C infections occur through sexual contact, transfusion of infected blood, and sharing of contaminated needles by drug addicts, but the modes of transmission may be broader. Some forms of hepatitis can lead to permanent liver damage (AMA, 1989; Tortora & Grabowski, 2000).

Another disease of the liver is called *cirrhosis*. In this disease, liver cells die off and are replaced by nonfunctional fibrous scar tissue. The scar tissue is permanent, and when it becomes extensive, the liver's normal functions are greatly impaired. As we will see later, the liver is not only important in the digestive process; it also cleanses and regulates the composition of the blood. Cirrhosis can result from several causes, including hepatitis infection and, particularly, alcohol abuse (AMA, 1989).

Cancer may occur in any part of the digestive tract, especially in the colon and rectum (AMA, 1989; Levy, 1985). People over 40 years of age have a higher prevalence for cancers of the digestive tract than do younger individuals. Early detection for many of these cancers is possible and greatly improves the person's chances of recovery.

USING NUTRIENTS IN METABOLISM

The term **metabolism** refers to all chemical reactions that occur in the body's cells (Holum, 1994; Tortora & Grabowski, 2000). Three principal outcomes of metabolism are:

1. *Synthesis* of new cell material from proteins and minerals to build and repair the body.
2. *Regulation* of body processes—by producing enzymes and hormones, for example—through the use of proteins, minerals, and vitamins.
3. *Energy* to heat the body and fuel its activities.

We will focus on the third outcome, energy production.

Metabolism takes place constantly in the cells of all living organisms. Without the energy it produces, all of our body systems would cease to function. The energy to fuel our internal functions and our physical actions comes mainly from the metabolism of carbohydrates and fats (Tortora & Grabowski, 2000). The amount of energy a food contains is measured in *calories*. One calorie is the amount of heat needed to raise one gram of water one degree Celsius. Nutrition researchers measure the calories contained in a given quantity of a food by burning it in a special apparatus.

How much energy do we use to support our basic bodily functions? The number of calories we burn up when our bodies are at rest—an index called the *basal metabolic rate*—depends on the size of the body (Tortora & Grabowski, 2000). For this reason, the basal metabolic rate is expressed in terms of calories per area of body surface (in square meters) per hour. A person who is 67 inches tall and weighs 132 pounds has a body surface area of about 1.7 square meters, for example. The basal metabolic rate also varies with the person's age and gender: the average rate is higher in males than in females and higher in younger people than in older people, as Figure 2–12 indicates.

What other factors affect the basal metabolic rate? People who are under stress, who live in cold climates, or whose hormone secretion by the thyroid gland is greater than normal tend to have high basal metabolic rates (McClintic, 1985; Tortora & Grabowski, 2000). Factors such as these account for the fact that

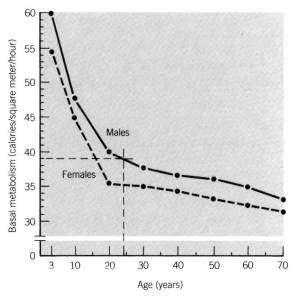

Figure 2–12 Normal basal metabolic rate for males and females at different ages in the life span. The dashed vertical and horizontal lines give an illustration: an average 24-year-old male's basic metabolism is 38.7 calories per square meter per hour. (Data from Hafen, 1981, Table 16.6.)

different people of the same size, age, and gender may have different metabolic rates.

Activity raises metabolism above the basal rate. Food materials that are not used up by metabolic processes are stored as body fat. This means that people become overweight generally because they regularly consume more calories than their body uses to fuel their internal functions and physical actions. To maintain normal body weight, people who do not metabolize all the calories they consume need to eat less, exercise more, or both. (Go to 🍎.)

THE RESPIRATORY SYSTEM

Breathing supplies the body with oxygen—but why do we need oxygen? The chemical reactions in metabolism require oxygen, some of which joins with carbon atoms from food to form *carbon dioxide* (CO_2) as a waste product. So breathing has another function— it lets us get rid of this waste product. We will begin our examination of the **respiratory system** by looking at its structures.

THE RESPIRATORY TRACT

After air enters the body through the nose or mouth, it travels past the *larynx*, down the *trachea* and *bronchial tubes*, and into the *lungs*. These organs are depicted in Figure 2–13. The bronchial tubes divide into smaller and smaller branches called *bronchioles* inside the lungs. These branches finally end in millions of tiny air sacs called *alveoli*. Each alveolus looks like a minute bubble made of a membrane that is thin enough to allow oxygen, CO_2, and other gases to pass through. Alveoli are enmeshed in beds of capillaries so that gases can be transferred to and from the bloodstream quickly and efficiently.

When we breathe, what makes the air go in and out? When we inhale, the rib muscles draw the ribs up and outward and the diaphragm—a horizontal sheet of muscle below the lungs (see Figure 2–13)— contracts, pulling downward on the bottom of the lungs. These actions pull air in and enlarge the lung chambers (Rhoades & Pflanzer, 1996). When we exhale, these muscles relax, and the elasticity of the lungs forces the air out, like a balloon.

RESPIRATORY FUNCTION AND DISORDERS

How do the muscles "know" when it's time to inhale and exhale? Our blood vessels contain sensors that monitor blood gases and send this information to the medulla of the brain, which directs actions of the muscles to cause us to inhale and exhale. When the CO_2 level is high, the medulla increases the breathing rate; when the level is low, breathing rate is decreased (Rhoades & Pflanzer, 1996).

Foreign matter, such as airborne particles and microorganisms, can readily enter the respiratory tract. The respiratory system therefore needs protective mechanisms to prevent foreign matter from reaching the lungs and entering the bloodstream. Two protective mechanisms are *reflexes*: (1) sneezing in response to irritation in nasal passages and (2) coughing in response to irritation in lower portions of the system. Another protective mechanism is the *mucociliary escalator*. How does this mechanism work? Most of the lining of the respiratory system is coated with a sticky mucus that traps foreign matter. Furthermore, the air passages leading from the mouth to the lungs are lined with tiny hairlike structures called *cilia* that

ASSESS YOURSELF

How Many Calories Do You Burn While Resting?

To figure out the number of calories your body probably burns while you are just resting, we need to estimate two factors:

1. *Your basal metabolic rate* (BMR). Although we cannot assess your BMR directly, we can use Figure 2–12 to estimate it by finding the average BMR for people of your age and gender. Do this by: (a) finding on the horizontal axis where your age would be, (b) drawing a vertical line from that point to the graph for your gender, and (c) drawing a horizontal line to the vertical axis. The value at this intersect is our estimate of your BMR, which you should enter in the formula (below, right).

2. *Your body surface area* (BSA). Estimates of BSA in square meters are usually made by plotting the person's height and weight on complex graphs. I have used one of these graphs (Hafen, 1981, Figure 16–5) to develop an alternative two-step method. First, start with a BSA score of 1.540 and adjust it based on your height by adding (or subtracting) .035 for *each inch* by which you

are taller (or shorter) than 60 inches. Thus, if you are 66 inches tall, your score at this point would be 1.750. Second, take your weight into account by adjusting your score in *one* of four ways: (a) If your body has a small frame and you are very slim, subtract .08 to get your BSA. (b) If you have a medium frame and an average weight, do nothing; your current score is your BSA. (c) If your frame is large and/or you are moderately heavy, add .08 to get your BSA.(d) If you are overweight by 20 pounds or more, add .15 to get your BSA.

Enter your BSA in the formula below and multiply it by your BMR to estimate the number of calories you burn per hour while sleeping or lying down.

_____ BMR × _____ BSA = _____ cal./hr.

When engaged in light activities, such as shopping or golfing, you burn 2 to 4 times that much, and when doing moderate or heavy activities, such as scrubbing floors or jogging, you burn 4 to 10 times that much.

---

move in such a way as to force the mucus coating up toward the mouth. Hence the name "mucociliary escalator." When the mucus reaches the back of the mouth, it is usually swallowed (McClintic, 1985). In this way, the respiratory system cleanses itself and protects the body from harmful matter that we inhale.

The opening story of this chapter is about a young man named Tom who is a victim of cystic fibrosis, a fatal disease of the respiratory system. We will look at several of the many other disorders that attack this system. Some of these disorders mainly affect the alveoli of the lungs, thereby impairing the normal exchange of CO_2 and oxygen. For instance, there are several types of *pneumonia*, which can be caused by either bacterial or viral infection (AMA, 1989). Although this disease often affects the bronchial tubes, the most serious types of pneumonia cause the alveoli to become inflamed and filled with fluid. In another respiratory disease called *emphysema* the walls between

alveoli are destroyed. This decreases the lungs' surface area for exchanging gases and their elasticity for exhaling CO_2 (Haas & Haas, 1990; Tortora & Grabowski, 2000). *Pneumoconiosis* is a disease that afflicts people who chronically inhale air containing high concentrations of dust—generally at their workplaces. The black lung disease of coal miners provides an example. Dust that is not removed by protective mechanisms accumulates as thick sheets around the alveoli and bronchioles, damaging these structures and blocking air exchange.

Other disorders of the respiratory system primarily affect the bronchial tubes, usually by narrowing the tubes and reducing airflow. *Asthma* is a disorder in which the bronchial airways narrow, because they become inflamed, develop spasms, and secrete too much mucus (ALA, 2000; AAFA, 2000). Attacks usually are temporary and occur in response to an irritant, such as an infection or something to which the victim

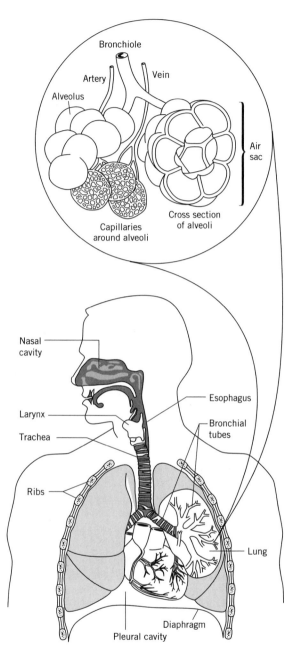

Figure 2–13 Major organs of the respiratory (also called pulmonary) system and closeup of alveoli. The organ shown between the lungs and the pleural cavity is the heart.

is allergic. Breathing becomes difficult and, in very serious attacks, portions of the lungs may collapse temporarily. In *chronic bronchitis,* inflammation and excess mucus occur in the bronchial tubes for an extended period. This condition may be permanent or occur several times a year, lasting 2 weeks or more each episode (Haas & Hass, 1990).

Lung cancer involves an unrestrained growth of cells that crowd out cells that aid respiration. This process usually begins in the bronchial tubes and spreads to the lungs (Tortora & Grabowski, 2000). In its final stages, the diseased cells enter the bloodstream through the capillaries and spread throughout the body. At this point death is almost always near. Many of the respiratory diseases we have discussed can be caused or worsened by smoking cigarettes. This risk factor is also important in diseases of the cardiovascular system.

THE CARDIOVASCULAR SYSTEM

The physical design of every complex organism has to deal with a basic problem: How can the body service its cells—supplying the substances they need to function properly and removing the wastes that metabolism produces? In humans and many other animals, this problem is solved by having a **cardiovascular system** to transport these materials. The blood circulates through blood vessels—capillaries, arteries, and veins—within a closed system, one in which the blood does not directly contact the cells and tissues it services (Tortora & Grabowski, 2000). All transfers of oxygen, nutrients, waste products, and other substances occur through membranes that are separated by fluid-filled spaces. The heart is the center of the cardiovascular system.

THE HEART AND BLOOD VESSELS

The *heart* is a fist-sized pump made of muscle that circulates the blood throughout the body. It "beats," or pumps, about 100,000 times a day (AHA, 1994). The muscular portion of the heart wall is called the *myocardium.* The interior of the heart has four chambers, as the drawing in Figure 2–14 illustrates. The two upper chambers are called atriums, and the two lower ones are called ventricles; the left and right sides are labeled from the body's perspective, not from ours.

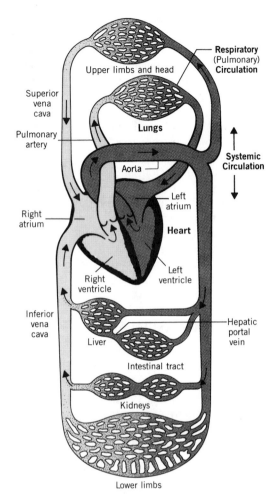

Figure 2–14 Blood circulation in the cardiovascular system. The heart pumps blood through two loops: *respiratory* (pulmonary) circulation and *systemic* (general) circulation. The respiratory loop allows blood to exchange CO_2 for oxygen; the systemic loop transports the blood to and from the rest of the body.

Looking at the drawing, we see several blood vessels that connect to the heart. How are arteries and veins different? A*rteries* carry blood *from* the heart, and *veins* carry blood *to* it. You will also notice in the drawing that the shading of some blood vessels is light, and in others the shading is dark. The vessels with light shading carry blood that is laden with CO_2 toward the lungs; the dark vessels carry blood away from the lungs after it has expelled CO_2 and received oxygen.

Now, let's follow the route of blood through the body. The blood that enters the *right atrium* of the heart is laden with waste products, such as CO_2, from our cells and is deficient in oxygen, which makes the blood bluish in color. After the atrium is filled, the blood passes through a valve to the *right ventricle*. The ventricles provide the main pumping force for circulation as the heart muscle contracts, and their valves prevent the blood from going back up to the atriums. From the right ventricle, the blood enters pulmonary circulation to the lungs, where it becomes oxygenated and, consequently, red in color. The oxygenated blood travels to the *left atrium* of the heart and is passed to the *left ventricle*, which pumps it out through the *aorta* into systemic circulation. It then goes to various parts of the body before returning to the heart and beginning the cycle again. The complete cycle takes about 1 minute in the resting person (Tortora & Grabowski, 2000).

Portions of each quantity of blood pumped by the heart travel through the liver and kidneys, where important functions take place (Guyton, 1985). The *kidneys* receive blood from the general circulatory system, cleanse it of waste products, and pass these wastes on to be eliminated in the urine. The *liver* receives blood from two sources: most of the blood comes from the intestinal tract, and the remainder comes from systemic circulation. What does the liver do to the blood? First, it cleanses the blood of harmful debris, such as bacteria. In fact, it is "so effective in removing bacteria that probably not one in a thousand escaps through the liver into the general circulation" (Guyton, 1985, p. 467). Second, the liver removes nutrients and stores them. The blood that comes from the intestinal tract after we consume a meal is rich in nutrients, such as simple sugars and amino acids. Large portions of these nutrients are retained in the liver until the body needs them. In this way, the ebbs and flows of nutrients in the blood are kept relatively even over time.

BLOOD PRESSURE

Imagine you are holding a long balloon that is filled with air. Its end is tied off. If you squeeze it in the middle, the rest of it expands. This is what happens when pressure is applied to a closed system. The cardiovascular system is also closed, and the myocardium does the squeezing when it pumps blood from the heart. Like the balloon, the cardiovascular system always has some pressure in it. The squeezing increases the pressure.

Our arteries are elastic—they expand when pressure is applied. **Blood pressure** is the force exerted by blood on the artery walls. The heart is at rest between myocardial contractions, while it fills with blood. The resting force in the arteries that occurs at this time is called *diastolic pressure*. When the heart pumps, each contraction produces a maximum force in the arteries, which is called *systolic pressure*. A person's blood pressure is expressed with two numbers: a larger number, representing systolic pressure, followed by a smaller number, representing diastolic pressure. Your physician might tell you that your blood pressure is "120 over 80," for example. Blood pressure readings are standardized in units of *mm Hg* to reflect the number of millimeters (mm) the pressure can raise a column of mercury (Hg).

Blood pressure varies. It changes from one moment to the next, it is higher in one part of the body than in another, and different people have different blood pressures. What determines blood pressure? We can answer this question in two ways—one involves the laws of fluid dynamics and the other involves factors in people's lives that affect these dynamics. We will start with the first approach and examine five aspects of fluid dynamics that affect blood pressure (McClintic, 1985).

1. *Cardiac output* is the volume of fluid being pumped per minute. Blood pressure increases as cardiac output rises.

2. *Blood volume* refers to the total amount of blood circulating in the system. The greater the volume, the higher the blood pressure needed to move it.

3. *Peripheral resistance* refers to the difficulty fluid encounters in passing through narrow tubes or openings. When you put a nozzle on a hose and turn on the water, the pressure is greater at the nozzle than in the hose. Arteries vary in diameter. *Arterioles* are small arteries that connect larger arteries to capillaries. Peripheral resistance is generally greater in arterioles than in larger arteries. Normally arterioles are highly elastic and can expand or contract readily in response to messages from the nervous and endocrine systems. After we eat a meal, extra blood is needed around the small intestine for the absorption of nutrients. Messages to the ar-

terioles in that region cause them to expand and accept more blood.

4. *Elasticity*, as we have seen, describes the ease in expanding and contracting. When blood vessels become less elastic, blood pressure—especially systolic pressure—rises.

5. *Viscosity* refers to the thickness of the fluid. The viscosity of blood depends on its composition, such as whether it contains high levels of red blood cells. Thicker blood flows less easily than thinner blood and requires more blood pressure for it to circulate through the cardiovascular system.

What factors in people's lives affect these dynamics? In our everyday lives we experience a variety of states that affect blood pressure. The *temperature* of our environment defines one of these states. When the temperature is high, the blood vessels in our skin enlarge and our cardiac output and diastolic pressure fall, which makes us feel drowsy. Low temperatures have the opposite effect. Another factor is *activity*. For example, exercise increases blood pressure during and after the activity. Simply changing posture can also affect blood pressure. When we go from a lying position to standing, blood flow in the veins that feed the heart slows down because of gravity. This causes a drop in cardiac output and blood pressure. As a result, blood flow to the brain drops, sometimes making us feel dizzy (McClintic, 1985). A third factor is *emotional experience*. When we experience stress, anger, or anxiety, the sympathetic nervous system is activated. This causes a variety of cardiovascular reactions, such as increased cardiac output. Both systolic and diastolic pressures increase when people are emotionally aroused (James et al., 1986).

High blood pressure strains the heart and arteries. Some people have high blood pressure consistently over a period of several weeks or more. This condition is called *hypertension*. How high is "high" blood pressure? People whose pressure is at or above 140 (systolic) over 90 (diastolic) are classified as hypertensive (AHA, 2000). When systolic pressure reaches 200, the danger is high that a rupture may occur in a blood vessel, particularly in the brain (McClintic, 1985). This is one way by which strokes occur. High diastolic pressure is troubling because the arteries are constantly being strained, even between heartbeats, when they should encounter little pressure.

There are several known risk factors for hypertension. For example, blood pressure shows a positive correlation with body weight, especially in early and middle adulthood (Alexander, 1984). Heavy people have more body mass to move when they are active than lighter people do, and they have a larger volume of blood for the heart to pump. Another factor is age—blood pressure generally rises with age. The percentage of individuals who are hypertensive is several times higher among the elderly than among young adults (NCHS, 2000). But aging per se may not be responsible for this relationship. Why? As adults get older, for instance, they tend to get heavier, at least in industrialized countries. In a number of primitive societies where adults do not show an increase in body weight as they get older, blood pressure does not seem to increase with age (Herd & Weiss, 1984).

Other risk factors for hypertension among Americans relate to gender, race, and family history (AHA, 1994; NCHS, 2000; USBC, 1999). Gender and racial differences in blood pressure do not show up before adulthood (Harlan, 1984). In adulthood, the prevalence rate for hypertension is higher for males than for females, particularly before about 50 years of age. Thereafter, this gender difference disappears. Black adults develop hypertension at a much higher rate than whites do. This is so for both sexes and at virtually every age in adulthood. Family history is important, too. People are more likely to become hypertensive if their parents had high blood pressure.

The reasons for these gender, race, and family history differences in hypertension are not fully clear. Evidence from twin studies suggests that genetics plays a role in blood pressure (Rose, 1986; Smith et al., 1987). Perhaps hereditary factors are responsible for these differences. Body weight may also be important: the percentage of adults who are overweight is greater for men than women, and much greater for black women than white women (NCHS, 2000). After 50 years of age, but not before, females are more likely than males to be overweight. In addition, there are racial differences in being overweight: blacks are more likely to be overweight than are whites, and this racial differences is quite pronounced among adult females at all ages (NCHS, 2000). Still other factors, such as stress, may play a role—and so may diet, as we will see in the next section.

BLOOD COMPOSITION

Blood is sometimes thought of as a "liquid tissue" because it consists of cells that are suspended in a liquid. The average adult's body contains about 5 liters of blood (Tortora & Grabowski, 2000). Because our bodies can replace blood quickly, we can donate half a liter of blood with no ill effects.

Blood composition can affect blood pressure. As we saw earlier, the thicker the blood, the more pressure is needed to circulate it. What is blood made of, and how does its composition change its thickness? Blood has two components, formed elements and plasma (Holum, 1994; Tortora & Grabowski, 2000). We will look at formed elements first.

Formed Elements

Formed elements are the cells and cell-like structures in the blood that constitute about 45% of our blood volume. There are three types of formed elements:

1. *Red blood cells* are the most abundant cells in the blood—there are about 5 million of them per cubic millimeter of blood. They are formed in the bone marrow and have a lifetime of about 3 months. Red blood cells are important mainly because they contain *hemoglobin*, a protein substance that attaches to oxygen and transports this element to body cells and tissues. *Anemia* is a condition in which the level of red blood cells or hemoglobin is below normal (AMA, 1989).

2. *Leukocytes* are white blood cells. Each of several types of leukocytes serves a special protective function—for example, some engulf or destroy bacteria. White blood cells are produced in the bone marrow and various organs in the body. Although there normally are several thousand leukocytes per cubic millimeter of an adult's blood, they are the least abundant type of formed element. *Leukemia* is a malignant disease in which abnormal white blood cells are produced in extremely high quantities, crowding out normal leukocytes, which fight infection, and red blood cells, which prevent anemia (ACS, 2000; AMA, 1989).

3. *Platelets* are granular fragments, produced by the bone marrow, that enable the body to prevent blood loss. They do this by plugging tiny wounds or helping the blood to clot when the wound

is larger. *Hemophilia* is a disease in which the platelets do not function properly, thereby impairing clotting, because the blood lacks a critical protein (AMA, 1989; Tortora & Grabowski, 2000).

How do formed elements affect the viscosity of blood? The higher the concentration of formed elements suspended in the plasma, the thicker the blood.

Plasma

Plasma is a liquid substance that comprises about 55% of our blood. About 90% of plasma is water, and the remainder consists of *plasma protein* and various other organic and inorganic elements (Holum, 1994; Tortora & Grabowski, 2000). Plasma protein consists of large molecules that are needed within the blood to help other substances pass through capillary walls. Plasma protein increases the thickness of the blood.

Although the remaining elements in plasma constitute only a small percentage of its volume, they are extremely important substances. They include hormones, enzymes, and waste products. They also include the nutrients we derive from digestion—vitamins, minerals, simple sugars, amino acids, and fatty materials.

Fatty materials make up the broad class of substances in the blood called **lipids.** Two of these fatty materials are triglycerides and cholesterol (Holum, 1994; Rhoades & Pflanzer, 1996). *Triglycerides* are the material we commonly think of as fat. Made of glycerol and fatty acids, they are the most abundant lipid in the body. Some of the fatty acids in triglycerides are fully hydrogenated—they cannot take up any more hydrogen—and are called *saturated* for that reason. They are usually solid at room temperature and are mostly derived from animal fat. Other fatty acids are *unsaturated* or *polyunsaturated*. They can take up more hydrogen, are usually liquid at room temperature, and are derived from plants.

Cholesterol is a fatty substance that builds up in patches on artery walls over time and narrows the artery (Ross & Glomset, 1976a, 1976b). Although the body manufactures most of the cholesterol in the blood, the rest comes from the foods we eat. Eating fats that are highly saturated tends to increase blood cholesterol levels. Let's see why is this a problem.

CARDIOVASCULAR DISORDERS

The accumulation of fatty patches, or plaques, on artery walls is called **atherosclerosis.** These plaques tend to harden. This is a common process by which the diameter and elasticity of arteries is reduced—a condition called **arteriosclerosis** (Tortora & Grabowski, 2000). The narrowing and hardening of arteries increase blood pressure. Although arteriosclerosis becomes an increasing problem as adults get older, plaque begins to form early in life (Clarkson, Manuck, & Kaplan, 1986). Autopsies on thousands of 15- to 34-year-old American males and females who died of other causes showed that atherosclerosis had begun in all subjects and worsened with age (Strong et al., 1999).

Of the many diseases of the heart and blood vessels, we will describe just a few. One of them is *myocardial infarction*, or "heart attack." Infarction refers to the death of tissue caused by an obstruction in the supply of blood to it. Thus, a myocardial infarction is the death of heart muscle (myocardium) tissue as a result of arterial blockage, usually resulting from atherosclerosis (Clarkson, Manuck, & Kaplan, 1986). Another form of heart disease is *congestive heart failure*, a condition in which an underlying problem, such as severe arteriosclerosis, has reduced the heart's pumping capacity permanently. This condition occurs most frequently in old age. Although its victims can live for years, they are quite disabled. A third form of heart disease is *angina pectoris*, in which the victim feels strong pain and tightness in the chest because of a brief obstruction in an artery, but little or no damage occurs. This kind of attack is often brought on by overexercise or stress.

One disorder of the blood vessels is an *aneurysm*, a bulge in a weakened section of an artery or vein. If the bulge is in a major blood vessel and it ruptures, the person may die (AMA, 1989). Another disorder of the blood vessels—a *stroke*—occurs when the blood supply to a portion of the brain is disrupted. This can be caused by a rupture in a cerebral artery, causing a hemorrhage in the brain, or by a blood clot, called a *thrombosis*, in a cerebral blood vessel. In either case, damage occurs to the brain. The effects of this damage depend on where it occurs and how extensive it is. It may cause paralysis or sensory impairments, for instance, or even death (AHA, 2000). Aneurysms and strokes can result from atherosclerosis and hypertension.

THE IMMUNE SYSTEM

You may not realize it, but wars are raging inside your body. They happen continuously, every day. Most of the time they are minor skirmishes, and you are unaware of them. When they become major battles, however, you are usually aware something's going on. The "good guys" are the organs and cells that make up your **immune system.** This system fights to defend the body against "foreign" invaders, such as bacteria and viruses.

The immune system is quite remarkable. Scientists knew little about this intricate and enormously important system until the 1970s. But it is now the subject of major research efforts, and new information about how the immune system functions is emerging rapidly. We know, for instance, that this system is highly sensitive to invasions by foreign matter and is able to distinguish between "self," or normal body constituents, and "not self"—friend and foe.

ANTIGENS

When the body recognizes something as a "not self" invader, the immune system mobilizes body resources and attacks. Any substance that can trigger an immune response is called an **antigen.** Bacteria and viruses are recognized as invaders by telltale aspects of their protein coats and DNA (Krieg et al., 1995).

What triggers an immune response? Some of the first antigens that come to mind are bacteria, fungi, protozoa, and viruses. *Bacteria* are microorganisms that exist in vast numbers throughout the environment—in rivers and oceans, in the air, on and in plants and animals, and in decaying organic matter. Billions of them may populate just one pound of rotting garbage. Because they help in breaking down organic matter into simpler units, their activities are essential to the life and growth of all living things. Some bacteria cause illnesses, such as tuberculosis, scarlet fever, and food poisoning. They do this by growing rapidly and competing with our cells for nutrients and by excreting *toxic*, or poisonous, substances that destroy our cells or impair their metabolic processes (AMA, 1989; Jaret, 1986). Although treatment

with antibiotics kills bacteria, these drugs are becoming less effective because they have been overused and bacteria are developing drug-resistant strains (Stolberg, 1998).

Fungi are organisms, such as molds and yeasts, that attach to an organic host and absorb nutrients from the host. Some of them can cause skin diseases through direct contact, as occurs in ringworm and athlete's foot, and internal diseases through inhalation of contaminated air. Other fungi are very beneficial—for example, penicillin is derived from molds (AMA, 1989). *Protozoa* are one-celled animals, such as amoebas, that live primarily in water and insects. Drinking water contaminated with protozoa can cause amoebic dysentery, an intestinal illness, and being bitten by an infected mosquito can cause malaria (AMA, 1989; Jaret, 1986).

The tiniest antigens are *viruses*, particles of protein and nucleic acid that are smaller than cells and, strictly speaking, may not even be alive. They consist of genetic information that allows them to reproduce. A virus functions by attaching to a cell, slipping inside, and taking over by issuing its own genetic instructions. The invaded cell abandons its own metabolic activities and becomes a "factory" for making viruses. In short order, enough viruses can be produced to rupture the cell and spread to infect other cells. Viruses can be quite devious, too, developing new strains and lying dormant in the body for periods of time before becoming infectious. They are responsible for a variety of diseases, including flu, herpes, measles, and polio (AMA, 1989; Jaret, 1986, 1994).

The immune system also tends to recognize the tissue of an organ transplant as "not self" and treat it as an antigen. This is what physicians mean when they say that the body "rejected" a transplant. There are two basic ways to encourage transplant acceptance. The first is to select the transplant carefully so that the tissues of the donor and the recipient are closely matched. The closer the genetic relationship between the two people, the better the match is likely to be. Identical twins provide the best match, of course. The second approach uses drugs to suppress the immune system so it won't mobilize and reject the organ. A drawback to this approach is that long-term suppression of immune function leaves the patient susceptible to disease.

For many people, the immune system mounts an attack against normally harmless substances, such as pollen, tree molds, poison ivy, animal dander, and particular foods. These people suffer from *allergies*; the specific substances that trigger their allergic reactions, such as sneezing and skin rashes, are called *allergens*. Most allergic people react to some, but not all, of the known allergens—someone with hay fever may not be allergic to poison ivy, for instance. Being allergic is partly determined by heredity (Hershey et al., 1997; Sarafino, 2000). Some allergies can be reduced by administering regular, small doses of the allergen, usually by injection (Benjamini, Sunshine, & Leskowitz, 1996).

THE ORGANS OF THE IMMUNE SYSTEM

The organs of the immune system are located throughout the body (Benjamini, Sunshine, & Leskowitz, 1996; Tortora & Grabowski, 2000). These organs are generally referred to as *lymphatic* or *lymphoid* organs because they have a primary role in the development and deployment of **lymphocytes,** specific white blood cells that are the key functionaries or "soldiers" in our body's defense against invasion by foreign matter. The main lymphatic organs include the bone marrow, thymus, lymph nodes and vessels, and spleen.

Lymphocytes originate in *bone marrow*, the soft tissue in the core of all bones in the body. Some of these cells migrate to one of two organs where they mature. One of these organs is the *thymus*, which, as we saw earlier in this chapter, is a gland that lies in the chest. The other organ is not known for certain, but it is thought to have the same function in maturing human lymphocytes that a structure called the "bursa" has in birds (Benjamini, Sunshine, & Leskowitz, 1996). Most of this processing of lymphocytes occurs before birth and in infancy.

The *lymph nodes* are bean-shaped masses of spongy tissue that are distributed throughout the body. Large clusters of them are found in the neck, armpits, abdomen, and groin. What do they do? Each lymph node contains filters that capture antigens and compartments that provide a home base for lymphocytes and other white blood cells. A network of *lymph vessels* that contains a clear fluid called *lymph* connects the lymph nodes. These vessels ultimately empty into the bloodstream. Although the lymph nodes and vessels play an important role in cleansing body cells of antigens, they can become a liability in some forms of cancer either by becoming infected with cancer or by distributing cancer cells to other parts of the body through the lymph and blood.

Lymphocytes and antigens that enter the blood are carried to the *spleen*, an organ in the upper left side of the person's abdomen. The spleen functions like an enormous lymph node except that blood, rather than lymph, travels through it. The spleen filters out antigens and serves as a home base for white blood cells. It also removes ineffective or worn-out red blood cells from the body. (Go to 💡.)

SOLDIERS OF THE IMMUNE SYSTEM

White blood cells play a key role in the immune system—they serve as soldiers in our counterattack against invading substances in the body. There are two types of white blood cells. Lymphocytes, as we have seen, are one type; phagocytes are the other.

> **Phagocytes** are scavengers that patrol the body and engulf and ingest antigens. They are not choosy. They will eat anything suspicious that they find in the bloodstream, tissues, or lymphatic system. In the lungs, for instance, they consume particles of dust and other pollutants that enter with each breath. They can cleanse lungs that have been blackened with the contaminants of cigarette smoke, provided the smoking stops. Too much cigarette smoking, over too long a time, destroys phagocytes faster than they can be replenished. (Jaret, 1986, p. 715)

There are two types of phagocytes: *macrophages* become attached to tissues and remain there, and *monocytes* circulate in the blood (Benjamini, Sunshine, & Leskowitz, 1996; Rhoades & Pflanzer, 1996). The fact that phagocytes "are not choosy" means that they are involved in *nonspecific immunity*—they respond to any kind of antigen.

Lymphocytes react in a more discriminating way, being tailored for attacks against specific antigens. The diagram in Figure 2–15 shows that, in addition to the process of nonspecific immunity, there are two types of *specific* immune processes: cell-mediated immunity and antibody-mediated "humoral" immunity (Benjamini, Sunshine, & Leskowitz, 1996; Borysenko, 1984; Braveman, 1987; Jaret, 1986; Rhoades & Pflanzer, 1996; Tortora & Grabowski, 2000). Let's examine these two specific immune processes and how they interrelate.

HIGHLIGHT ON ISSUES
When Immune Functions Are Absent

I can remember reading for the first time many years ago about a child who had to live in a large plastic "bubble" because he was born with virtually no major immune defenses. The condition he had is very rare and is called *severe combined immunodeficiency disease*. He lived in the bubble because it was germ free—exposure to microorganisms in the general environment would have been fatal. Transplants of healthy bone marrow tissue early in the child's life can cure this disorder (Benjamini, Sunshine, & Leskowitz, 1996). More common inborn immune deficiencies involve the absence of only part of the system and can sometimes be treated with injections.

Having little or no immune defense was almost unheard of prior to the 1970s, and people were not very concerned about immune processes. All that changed in the 1980s as people became aware of the disorder called *acquired immune deficiency syndrome* (AIDS). This disorder is not inborn—it results from an infection when a virus (*human immunodeficiency virus*, or HIV) from an infected person's body fluid, such as blood or semen, contacts the body fluid of an uninfected person. This occurs in three major ways: through sexual activity if the body fluids become exposed to each other, in intravenous drug use if syringes are shared, and from an infected mother to her baby (Insel & Roth, 1998). Receiving contaminated blood in a transfusion was once a major source of the virus, but in the United States and many other countries close monitoring of hospital blood supplies has sharply reduced this risk.

Although AIDS is a fatal disorder, it does not kill directly. It disables or destroys an extremely important component of the immune system—*helper T cells*—and leaves the victim defenseless against a variety of diseases, including pneumonia and a form of cancer called Kaposi's sarcoma (Insel & Roth, 1998;

Tortora & Grabowski, 2000). One of these diseases becomes the actual cause of death. Although researchers have made great progress in finding ways to prevent and treat AIDS, no fully successful methods exist yet.

AIDS is a worldwide epidemic: health agencies estimate that over 14 million people have died of AIDS since the epidemic began 20 years ago, over 33 million are currently infected with HIV, and 5.6 million are newly infected each year (WHO, 1999a). In the United States, nearly 690,000 people have been diagnosed with AIDS and over 410,000 have died from it; about 44,000 new infections occur each year (CDC, 2000). Developing countries have had the vast majority of HIV/AIDS cases, most of whom became infected through heterosexual contact. But in North America and Europe, infection has occurred mainly through sharing needles when injecting illicit drugs and practicing certain sexual acts, particularly anal intercourse. Prevention by changing high-risk behavior is essential, and studies of these changes have found encouraging results in developed countries. Gay males have shown substantial changes in their behavior, such as by avoiding sex with unfamiliar partners and using condoms and other methods to prevent the exchange of body fluids (Kalichman, Carey, & Johnson, 1996; Stall, Coates, & Hoff, 1988; Van Griensven, de Vroome, Goudsmit, & Coutinho, 1989). Many intravenous drug users have reduced their risks by decreasing drug use and using sterile or decontaminated (with bleach) needles (Des Jarlais, Friedman, & Casriel, 1990). But more progress in preventive efforts is needed in these high-risk groups and among people in the larger population, especially since most AIDS victims around the world have been neither gay nor drug users. We will discuss the topic of AIDS again in later chapters.

Cell-mediated immunity operates at the level of the cell. The soldiers in this process are lymphocytes called **T cells**—the name of these white blood cells reflects their having matured in the *thymus*. T cells are divided into several groups, each with its own important function:

- *Killer T cells* (also called (CD8 cells) directly attack and destroy three main targets: transplanted tissue that is recognized as foreign, cancerous cells, and cells of the body that have already been invaded by antigens, such as viruses.

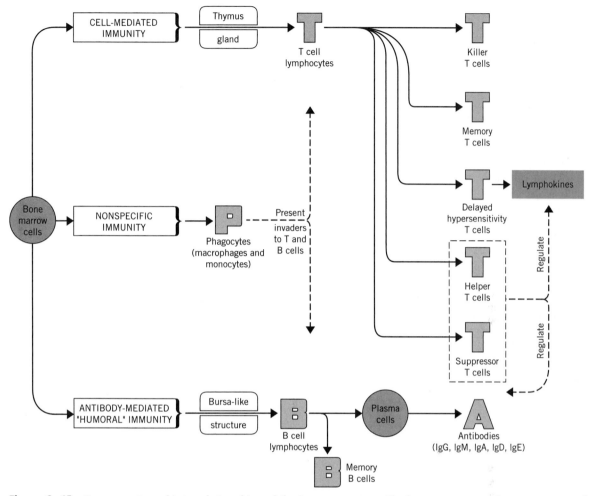

Figure 2–15 Components and interrelationships of the immune system. The bone marrow produces two types of white blood cells (leukocytes): *phagocytes* and *lymphocytes*. There are two kinds of lymphocytes: T *cells*, which are processed by the *thymus* gland; and B *cells*, which are processed by an as-yet-unknown *bursa*-like structure (B cells were first discovered in the "bursa of Fabricius" structure of birds). See text for description. (*Sources:* Benjamini, Sunshine, & Leskowitz, 1996; Borysenko, 1984; Braveman, 1987; Jaret, 1986; Rhoades & Pflanzer, 1996; Tortora & Grabowski, 2000.)

- *Memory* T *cells* "remember" previous invaders. At the time of an initial infection, such as with mumps, some T cells are imprinted with information for recognizing that specific kind of invader—the virus that causes mumps—in the future. Memory T cells and their offspring circulate in the blood or lymph for long periods of time—sometimes for decades—and enable the body to defend against subsequent invasions more quickly.

- *Delayed-hypersensitivity* T *cells* have two functions. They are involved in delayed immune reactions, particularly in allergies such as of poison ivy, in which tissue becomes inflamed. They also produce protein substances called *lymphokines* that stimulate other T cells to grow, reproduce, and attack an invader.

- *Helper* T *cells* (also called CD4 cells) receive reports of invasions from other white blood cells that patrol the body, rush to the spleen and lymph nodes, and stimulate lymphocytes to reproduce and attack. The lymphocytes they stimulate are from both the cell-mediated and the antibody-mediated immunity (also called "humoral" immunity) processes.

● *Suppressor T cells* operate in slowing down or stopping cell-mediated and antibody-mediated immunity processes as an infection diminishes or is conquered. Suppressor and helper T cells serve to regulate cell-mediated and antibody-mediated immune processes.

What is antibody-mediated immunity, and how is it different from the cell-mediated process? **Antibody-mediated immunity** attacks bacteria, fungi, protozoa, and viruses while they are still in body fluids and before they have invaded body cells. Unlike the cell-mediated process of attacking infected cells of the body, the antibody-mediated approach focuses on the antigens directly. The soldiers in this approach are lymphocytes called **B cells**. Figure 2–15 shows that B cells give rise to *plasma cells* that produce antibodies. This process is often induced by helper T cells or inhibited by suppressor T cells.

How are antibodies involved? **Antibodies** are protein molecules called *immunoglobulins* ("Ig") that attach to the surface of invaders and accomplish three results. First, they slow down the invader, making it an easier and more attractive target for phagocytes to destroy. Second, they recruit other protein substances that puncture the membrane of an invading microorganism, causing it to burst. Third, they find new invaders and form *memory B cells* that operate in the future like memory T cells. As you can see, antibodies are like sophisticated weapons in immune system wars. Researchers have identified five classes of antibodies—IgG, IgM, IgA, IgD, and IgE—each with its own special function and "territory" in the body. For example, IgA guards the entrances of the body in fluids, such as saliva, tears, and secretions of the respiratory tract.

DEFENDING THE BODY WITH AN IMMUNE RESPONSE

Now that we have seen the soldiers and weaponry of the immune system, let's see how all of this is orchestrated in defending your body. Protection from disease actually involves a series of defenses (Benjamini, Sunshine, & Leskowitz, 1996; Jaret, 1986; Rhoades & Pflanzer, 1996; Tortora & Grabowski, 2000). We will start at the beginning, as the invader tries to enter the body.

Your body's first line of defense is the skin and the mucous membranes that line the respiratory and digestive tracts. The skin serves as a barrier to entry, and mucous membranes are coated with fluids that contain antibodies and other antimicrobial substances. Even though these defenses are highly effective, large numbers of antigens get through, either by eluding the antibodies or by entering a wound in the skin or the mucous membrane.

Once an antigen penetrates this barrier, it encounters the second line of defense, which includes nonspecific and specific immune processes. Phagocytes in your blood and tissues attack and consume invading substances of all types. They also have another important function: They present the antigen to B cells and helper T cells, as if to say, "Here's the enemy. Go get 'em!" The B cells respond to this message and to stimulation from helper T cells by giving rise to plasma cells that produce the needed antibodies. The role of the phagocytes is especially important if the antigen is new and the body has no memory B cells for this substance. Antibodies in body fluids attach to microorganisms, thereby aiding the phagocytes and other protein substances that can kill the invaders.

Antigens that manage to get through and invade body cells encounter the third line of defense in which killer T cells destroy the invaded cells. Phagocytes often initiate this process by presenting antigens to T cells, as we have seen. Once again, this is especially important if the antigen is new to the cell-mediated system and the body has no memory T cells for the substance. As the invasion subsides, suppressor T cells slow down the cell-mediated and antibody-mediated immune responses. Memory B and T cells are left in the blood and lymph, ready to initiate the immune response if the same antigen invades the body again.

You may be thinking, "This is a wonderful and complex system that responds when there are antigens in the body, but killer T cells also attack cancer cells. Why? Aren't cancer cells basically normal cells that multiply out of control?" Cancer cells have antigens on their surface to which T cells respond (Benjamini, Sunshine, & Leskowitz, 1996). What scientists don't yet know is why some cancers escape destruction. One reason is that some cancer cells appear to release substances that suppress the immune response (Acevedo, Tong, & Hartsock, 1995; Mizoguchi et al., 1992). Another possibility is that the antigen is simply not easy for the immune system to recognize.

As a result, the immune response may not be strong enough to stop the cells from multiplying wildly. Some researchers are studying approaches for treating cancer that are designed to strengthen the patient's own immune processes. In one of these approaches, for example, researchers manufacture antibodies that are sensitive to and seek out a specific type of cancer cell. These approaches are not yet perfected, but they are very promising.

LESS-THAN-OPTIMAL DEFENSES

If our immune systems always functioned optimally, we would become sick much less often. Why and in what ways do our defenses function less than optimally?

The effectiveness of the immune system changes over the life span, becoming increasingly effective throughout childhood and declining in old age (Benjamini, Sunshine, & Leskowitz, 1996; Tortora & Grabowski, 2000). Newborns come into the world with relatively little immune defense. They have only one type of antibody (IgG), for example, which they receive prior to birth from their mothers through the placenta (the filterlike organ that permits the exchange of nutrients and certain other substances between the bloodstreams of the mother and baby). Infants who are nursed receive antibodies, particularly IgA, in their mother's milk (Ashburn, 1986).

In early infancy, children in technological societies generally begin a regular schedule of immunization through the use of vaccines. Most vaccines contain dead or disabled disease microorganisms that get the body to initiate an immune response and produce memory lymphocytes, but do not produce the full-blown disease (Benjamini, Sunshine, & Leskowitz, 1996; Insel & Roth, 1998). The efficiency and complexity of the immune system develop very rapidly in childhood. As a result, the incidence of illness serious enough to keep children home from school declines with age (Ashburn, 1986).

Throughout adolescence and much of adulthood, the immune system generally functions at a high level. Then, as people approach old age, the effectiveness of the system tends to decline (Braveman, 1987; Tortora & Grabowski, 2000). Although the overall numbers of T cells, B cells, and antibodies circulating in the blood do not decrease, their potency diminishes in old age. Compared with the T cells and B cells of younger adults, those of elderly people respond weakly to antigens and are less likely to generate the needed supply of lymphocytes and antibodies to fight an invasion.

Unhealthful lifestyles, such as smoking cigarettes and being sedentary, have been associated with impaired immune function (Kusaka, Kondou, & Morimoto, 1992). Poor nutrition can also lead to less-than-optimal immune function (Benjamini, Sunshine, & Leskowitz, 1996; Braveman, 1987). Diets deficient in vitamins seem to diminish the production of lymphocytes and antibodies, for example.

When your immune system functions optimally, it attacks foreign matter and protects the body. Sometimes this process goes awry, and the immune response is directed at parts of the body it was designed to protect. Several disorders result from this condition—they are called *autoimmune diseases*. One of these diseases is *rheumatoid arthritis*, in which the immune response is directed against tissues and bones at the joints. This causes swelling and pain and can leave the bones pitted. In *rheumatic fever*, the muscles of the heart are the target. This disease can damage the heart valves permanently. *Multiple sclerosis*, a disease we considered earlier, results when the immune system attacks the myelin sheath of neurons. Another autoimmune disease is *lupus erythematosus*, which affects various parts of the body, including the skin and kidneys. What causes autoimmune diseases? Although we are not certain of the causes, it is likely that heredity and immune responses to prior infections play important roles (Benjamini, Sunshine, & Leskowitz, 1996; Jaret, 1986). (Go to ✿.)

THE REPRODUCTIVE SYSTEM AND HEREDITY

At one time, many educated people believed that a miniature, completely formed, baby was passed on from a man to a woman during sexual intercourse. Then, in the 18th century, researchers disproved this and similar ideas and demonstrated that a *sperm* cell from a male had to combine with an egg cell—an *ovum*—from a female before development could begin.

Focus on Research
Stress and the Immune Response

Many people believe stress and illness often are related—and they are right. Research has confirmed this belief, showing, for instance, that the incidence of respiratory illnesses increases when people experience high levels of stress (Jemmott & Locke, 1984). Why is this so? One likely answer is that stress suppresses immune functions in some way, leaving the person open to infection.

Associations between stress and illness are provocative, but they do not show a direct link between stress and immune function. Psychologist Janice Kiecolt-Glaser and her colleagues from a variety of disciplines have done an impressive series of studies to examine this link. Let's look at one of their studies in detail (Kiecolt-Glaser et al., 1984). The researchers recruited 75 first-year medical students who were scheduled to take a series of highly stressful final examinations. The study assessed important variables in two sessions: the first session occurred at a time when examination stresses should be relatively low—1 month before the finals and 1 month after their last major exam. The second occurred when stresses should be high, just after the students had taken their first two exams during the final exam week.

In the first session, the researchers took a sample of blood from the students and had them fill out questionnaires that assessed their experience of loneliness and stress during the past year. In the second session, only a blood sample was taken. Both samples of blood were analyzed for the degree of killer-T-cell activity and concentrations of antibodies. The results showed that, although antibody concentrations were not consistently related to stress variables, killer-T-cell activity was. Killer-cell activity was considerably lower in the second (high stress) blood sample than in the first. Moreover, in both blood samples, killer-

cell activity was lower for students who scored high on the loneliness and stress questionnaires than for those who scored low.

In another study, Kiecolt-Glaser and her coworkers (1987) analyzed blood samples of married and separated or divorced women. Among the married women, those who reported less marital satisfaction showed weaker immune function than those who reported greater satisfaction. Among the separated or divorced women, those who refused to accept the fact of the separation or thought excessively about their ex-spouse had weaker immune function than those who did not. In addition, women who had been separated for relatively short amounts of time showed weaker immune function than married women and women separated for a longer time. The findings of these two investigations provide direct evidence of an association between stress and immune suppression.

Studies by other researchers support these results, finding, for example, that immune function is suppressed in individuals several weeks following the deaths of their spouses (Antoni, 1987; Jemmott & Locke, 1984). How does the suppression occur? One way is through the endocrine system. Earlier in this chapter we saw that stress causes the adrenal glands to produce epinephrine and cortisol. These substances affect immune cells (Antoni, 1987; Biondi & Pancheri, 1995). Epinephrine appears to increase suppressor T cells and decrease helper T cells in the blood, at least for a short while. Cortisol inhibits the function of phagocytes and lymphocytes—and if stress is chronic, cortisol causes important lymphoid tissues to wither away. The nervous system also can affect immune function: research has shown that chemicals secreted by nerves in the skin can suppress immune function in nearby cells (Hosoi et al., 1993).

CONCEPTION AND PRENATAL DEVELOPMENT

A human being begins to form at conception when a sperm cell unites with an ovum. The resulting single fertilized cell, called a *zygote*, starts to divide,

forming new cells. It soon attaches to the wall of the mother's uterus, and the *placenta* and umbilical cord develop. These structures allow nourishment, wastes, and other substances to be exchanged between the mother's and offspring's separate bloodstreams.

During the next few weeks, the offspring begins to develop all the body systems we have just examined. By the 9th week of prenatal development, for instance, the fetus has a tiny and incompletely formed heart that pumps blood through minute blood vessels, and the basic structures of the brain, liver, and kidneys have developed. The body systems undergo continuous improvement in organ structure and functioning during the remainder of gestation (Sarafino & Armstrong, 1986).

Pregnancy produces substantial alterations in the mother's anatomy and enormous additional demands on her body systems (Tortora & Grabowski, 2000). The most obvious changes result from the size and weight of the fetus and the accompanying structures and fluids. But other, less obvious changes also occur. The mother's blood volume increases by 30% or more, which places heavy demands on her heart. Furthermore, her usual dietary intake of iron is likely to be inadequate for meeting the combined needs of herself and the fetus. This condition can produce *iron deficiency anemia*—a general physical weakness—in both the mother and baby before and after birth unless she increases her iron intake. Added burdens are also placed on her respiratory and digestive systems.

GENETIC PROCESSES IN DEVELOPMENT AND HEALTH

Although researchers in the 19th century discovered that each person developed from the union of a sperm and an ovum, no one knew what forces or substances inside these cells directed the growth processes. Charles Darwin speculated that unseen particles called "gemmules" were present in the sperm and ovum. Darwin's concept of gemmules formed the basis for the search for genetic materials.

Genetic Materials and Transmission

What did this search yield? By the early 20th century, researchers discovered threadlike structures called **chromosomes** and proposed that these structures contained units called *genes*. Soon they determined the basic substance common to all genetic material—*deoxyribonucleic acid*, or DNA for short—and described its structure. Today we know that DNA determines our growth patterns and physical structures. We also know that genes are discrete particles of DNA and that strings of genes are organized into chromosomes.

In what form are these genetic materials passed on to the next generation? Each ovum and sperm contains 23 chromosomes. At conception, the 23 chromosomes of the ovum are paired with those of the sperm, yielding 46 chromosomes in the zygote. As the offspring grows, these 46 chromosomes are duplicated and passed on to each newly formed cell of the body. Sperm and ova, which are produced by the reproductive system, are the only cells in the human body that contain just 23 chromosomes. Thus, half of the genetic information contained in each of your body cells comes from each of your parents, and half of their genetic information comes from each of their parents.

Chromosomes can be identified by certain features. Photographs taken through a microscope can be arranged according to the size and shape of chromosome pairs. One pair is called the *sex chromosomes* because they carry the genes that will determine whether an individual will be female or male. The normal sex chromosomes for males consist of one large chromosome (called an X chromosome) and one small chromosome (called a Y chromosome); females have two X chromosomes. Since the mother can provide only an X sex chromosome to her offspring, the child's gender is determined by the information received from the father. If the sperm that fertilizes the ovum carries an X chromosome, the zygote will develop into a female. If the sperm carries a Y chromosome, the child will be a male.

As with chromosomes, genes come in pairs (Tortora & Grabowski, 2000). Some of a person's traits are determined by a single pair of genes. Furthermore, some traits occur in the presence of a single gene, with the paired gene making little or no contribution. Such genes are said to be *dominant*. In humans, dominant genes produce such characteristics as freckles and poor visual acuity. On the other hand, when a trait occurs only if two identical genes make up the pair, these genes are called *recessive*. Recessive characteristics include flat feet and albinism (lack of coloration in skin, hair, and eyes). When the pair consists of one dominant and one recessive gene—say, one gene for freckles and one for no freckles—the dominant trait appears. This is why it is important to distinguish between the trait we observe, which is called a *phenotype*, and the underlying genetic makeup, which is called the *genotype*.

Not surprisingly, geneticists have discovered that genetic transmission is often far more complicated than the process just described. First of all, paired genes can be *codominant* so that the phenotype will show the influence of both genes. This is the case for the ABO blood type. Also, some genes become dominant at different ages in the life span—changes in hair color and distribution, eruption and loss of teeth, and the production of sex hormones are but a few examples. Second, *mutations* occur that change the chemical or structural composition of a gene. Most mutations are harmful and can be passed on to an offspring as a recessive gene (Snustad & Simmons, 2000). Such alterations sometimes result from excessive exposure to environmental agents, such as X rays. In addition, it is likely that many behavioral traits, such as intelligence, are partially determined by the process of *polygenic inheritance*, involving the combined interaction of many gene pairs.

The Impact of Genetics on Development and Health

Researchers have determined that every human cell contains 30,000–40,000 genes and have identified and mapped almost all of the human system of genes (IHGSC, 2001). Genes control a vast number of traits, including more than 3,000 diseases. For some diseases, researchers have even pinpointed the exact gene locations. We will look at some of these traits and diseases.

Sickle-cell anemia is a hereditary disease whose victims are usually black people. In the United States, nearly 10% of the black population carry a recessive gene for this disease and do not have the disorder (Raphael, 1999). But when a person has two of these genes, the body manufactures large quantities of sickle-shaped red blood cells. Compared with normal blood cells, these defective cells carry little oxygen and tend to clump together in the bloodstream—often they cannot pass through capillaries. As a result, the oxygen supply to vital organs becomes inadequate, and tissue damage often occurs. The condition, which usually develops in childhood, produces painful episodes, progressive organ failure, and brain damage.

Another recessive disease is *phenylketonuria* (PKU). In this disease, which occurs more frequently among whites than other racial groups, the baby's body fails to produce a necessary enzyme for metabolizing phenylalanine, a toxic amino acid present in many common foods (Snustad & Simmons, 2000). If the disease is not treated, the amino acid builds up and

causes brain damage. Placing PKU babies on special diets as soon as possible after birth can prevent this. When the brain is more fully developed after about 5 years of age, many PKU children can switch to normal diets. PKU provides a good example of an inherited disease that can be controlled by modifying the victim's behavior.

The X chromosome has a special significance beyond determining a person's gender: it sometimes carries genes for dozens of disorders that are described as *sex-linked* (Snustad & Simmons, 2000). These disorders include *color blindness, hemophilia,* and *mitral stenosis,* a heart valve abnormality. For these disorders, if the child has only one X chromosome—as a boy does—and it carries the sex-linked gene, he will have the phenotype. If the child has two X chromosomes—as a girl does—*both* must carry the gene for the phenotype to show up. It is partly for this reason that females can be carriers of a sex-linked disorder but rarely show the phenotype.

Genetics researchers have made enormous progress in the last few decades in discovering the specific genes that cause certain diseases, such as the muscle-wasting disease called *Duchenne's muscular dystrophy,* and can test for the presence of each gene in a fetus early in pregnancy. This ability recently enabled researchers to discover a surprising finding about the genes for hereditary diseases: they can enlarge across generations. For example, the gene that causes the most common form of muscular dystrophy, *myotonic dystrophy,* grows larger each time it is inherited (Harley et al., 1992). Moreover, the bigger the gene, the more severe the illness. These findings contradict the long-held beliefs that genes are transmitted across generations essentially unchanged and that a gene is either normal or it is not.

Researchers are also closing in on certain *oncogenes,* which are genes that can cause cancer (Snustad & Simmons, 2000). Researchers have, for example, found oncogenes for certain types of cancers of the colon (Bodmer et al., 1987), breast (Chen et al., 1995; Wooster et al., 1995), skin (Hussussian et al., 1994), lung (Rodenhuis et al., 1987), and prostate (Lee et al., 1994). Oncogenes can be normal genes or mutations that may result from exposure to harmful environmental agents, such as tobacco smoke. Once the genes are isolated for hereditary disorders, it may be possible to treat the disorders by replacing the defective genes. But tests of this kind of "gene therapy" have not been successful (Snustad & Simmons, 2000).

Acromegaly is an inherited condition in which excess hormone production by the pituitary gland leads to a gradual thickening of the bones in the head, hands, and feet in adulthood. The photographs of this patient were taken when he was 24, 29, 37, and 42 years of age.

We know that oncogenes can cause cancer. One of the next steps in research will be to increase our knowledge regarding what causes genes to mutate into oncogenes. Assume for a moment that this mutation can result from engaging in certain behaviors, such as smoking cigarettes and eating diets that are high in fats and low in fiber. If this is true, as many researchers believe, we would have additional evidence that behavioral risk factors for cancer constitute major causal links in its development. The case for believing in biopsychosocial determinants of this disease is already strong; it would be ironclad with this evidence.

A biopsychosocial perspective in our examination of heredity is important in another way. Many researchers believe that we often inherit a predisposition or susceptibility—rather than a certainty—for developing a disease (Syme, 1984; Weiner, 1977). This might account in part for the observation that not everyone who is exposed to harmful substances and microorganisms in their environments become sick. People who inherit a high degree of susceptibility to a form of cancer and have relatively little exposure to relevant antigens may be just as likely to develop the illness as someone who has little genetic susceptibility but high antigen exposure. If physicians could determine whether a patient has a genetic predisposition to a specific disease, they could provide the person with instructions for taking early preventive action.

SUMMARY

To understand health psychology, we need to know how the body systems function. The nervous system provides a communications network for all systems of the body. The central nervous system consists of the brain and spinal cord and is the control center, sending and receiving electrochemical messages through neurons throughout the body. The brain is divided into the forebrain, the cerebellum, and the brainstem. The uppermost regions of the brain are involved in perceptual, motor, learning, and conceptual activities. Areas toward the center and bottom of the brain are important in controlling internal and automatic body functions and the flow of information to and from the brain. The spinal cord is the major neural pathway that connects the brain to the peripheral nervous system.

The peripheral nervous system is a branching network of afferent and efferent neurons throughout the body. It has two divisions, somatic and autonomic. The somatic nervous system is involved in sensory and motor functions. The autonomic nervous system carries messages between the spinal cord and various internal organs, and this system has two parts, sympathetic and parasympathetic. The sympathetic nervous system acts in agreement with our current emotional state and helps us mobilize and expend energy. The parasympathetic nervous system is involved in processes to conserve and store energy and in calming the body following sympathetic arousal.

The endocrine system also communicates with various parts of the body, but does so by sending chemical messages through the bloodstream. This system consists of several glands that secrete hormones. As the "master gland" in this system, the pituitary gland releases hormones that stimulate other glands to secrete. The adrenal glands secrete hormones such as cortisol and epinephrine (adrenaline), which are important in our response to emergencies and stress. Other glands are important in regulating such factors as general body growth and the level of blood sugar.

The digestive and respiratory systems provide the body with essential nutrients, oxygen, and other substances for energy, body growth, and repair. These systems are also involved in removing wastes from the body. The outcomes of chemical reactions called metabolism that occur in our body cells include the synthesis of new cells, the regulation of body processes, and the production of energy to heat the body and fuel its activity.

The cardiovascular system uses the heart to pump blood through an intricate network of blood vessels. The blood's circulation takes it to body cells, where it supplies oxygen and nutrients for metabolism and takes CO_2 and other waste materials away. Cardiac output, blood volume, peripheral resistance, elasticity, and viscosity affect systolic and diastolic blood pressure. Blood consists of plasma and formed elements.

The immune system responds to antigens by attacking and eliminating invading substances and microorganisms to protect us from infection and disease. It does this by using white blood cells, including phagocytes and two types of lymphocytes: B cells, which produce antibodies, and T cells. Stress, poor nutrition, and HIV infection impair the effectiveness of the immune system.

The reproductive system and heredity play an important role in development and health by producing a new generation of the species and transmitting genetic information from parents to their offspring. Genetic transmission occurs at conception, when a sperm from the father fertilizes an ovum from the mother. The sperm and ovum each contain 23 chromosomes, which are composed of genes. Each of the body systems that we have examined changes across the life span. In general, they are immature at birth, develop during childhood, function relatively effectively during adolescence and early adulthood, and decline in old age.

KEY TERMS

neurons	medulla	hormones	arteriosclerosis
neurotransmitter	spinal cord	pituitary gland	immune system
central nervous system	peripheral nervous system	adrenal glands	antigen
cerebrum	somatic nervous system	digestive system	lymphocytes
limbic system	autonomic nervous	enzymes	phagocytes
thalamus	system	metabolism	cell-mediated immunity
hypothalamus	sympathetic nervous	respiratory system	T cells
cerebellum	system	cardiovascular system	antibody-mediated immunity
brainstem	parasympathetic nervous	blood pressure	B cells
midbrain	system	lipids	antibodies
reticular system	endocrine system	atherosclerosis	chromosomes
pons			

PART II

STRESS, ILLNESS, AND COPING

3

Stress—Its Meaning, Impact, and Sources

"Tell me what's been happening in your life in the past several months, Vicki," the college counselor probed in the student's first visit to his office. A nurse suggested that Vicki talk to a counselor because she has been physically run down for the past few months, has been sleeping poorly, and has had several viral infections. During this visit, she described many problems she has experienced. For one thing, this is her first year in college and, although she goes home most weekends, she has never been away from her family, high school friends, and boyfriend Chris so long before—and she misses them.

Her relationship with Chris is a special problem. He decided to go to a college closer to home so that he could commute. They've been going together for 2 years, and he says he loves her, but Vicki isn't convinced. She feels a lot of jealousy, often imagining that he is seeing others on the side even though she has no evidence that he is. She calls him several times a week, saying she wants to hear his voice, but they both know deep down that she's calling to check up on him. They argue about her suspicions at least once a week. She says he's seeing others because, "He's so good looking and I'm so fat." Keeping her weight down is a constant struggle that, in her view, she always loses. Actually, her weight is within the recommended healthful range for her height.

Vicki has also had other difficulties. She worries that she's preparing for the wrong career, argues often with other students about the noise on her dormitory floor, and is overcommitted with schoolwork, club activities on campus, and a part-time job. On top of all this, her car keeps breaking down, she's running out of money to fix it, and her illnesses are compounding her problems.

Vicki's situation is not uncommon. We all experience stress in our everyday lives, probably more than we would like. It occurs in a wide variety of situations and settings—in the family, in school, and on the job, for example. Sometimes the stress experience is brief, and sometimes it continues for a long time. Sometimes it is intense, and sometimes it is mild. It varies across time in a particular person, and it varies between individuals. An experience that is stressful for one person—such as taking a difficult examination—may not be stressful for another, and may even be exciting or challenging for still another person.

In this chapter we discuss what stress is, where it comes from, and the impact it has. As we do, you will find answers to questions you may have about stress. What makes an event stressful? Why does a particular event produce more stress in one person than in another? How does stress affect our bodies and our behavior? Does the experience of stress change across the life span?

EXPERIENCING STRESS IN OUR LIVES

When you hear people say they are "under a lot of stress," you have some idea of what they mean. Usually the statement means they feel unable to deal with the demands of their environment, and they feel tense and uncomfortable. You understand the meaning because you have had similar experiences, which you labeled "stress." Because of the pervasiveness and commonality of these experiences in our lives, you might expect that defining the concept of stress would be simple. But it isn't. Let's see how psychologists have conceptualized stress and what the prevailing definition is today.

WHAT IS STRESS?

The condition of stress has two components: *physical*, involving direct material or bodily challenge, and *psychological*, involving how individuals perceive circumstances in their lives (Lovallo, 1997). These components can be examined in three ways (Baum, 1990; Coyne & Holroyd, 1982; Hobfoll, 1989). One approach focuses on the environment, describing stress as a *stimulus*. We see this in people's reference to the source or cause of their tension as being an event or set of circumstances—such as having "a high-stress job." Physically or psychologically challenging events or circumstances are called **stressors.** Researchers who follow this approach study the impact of a wide range of stressors, including (1) catastrophic events, such as tornadoes and earthquakes, (2) major life events, such as the loss of a loved one or a job, and (3) chronic circumstances, such as living with severe pain from arthritis.

The second approach treats stress as a *response*, focusing on people's reaction to stressors. We see an example of this approach when people use the word *stress* to refer to their state of tension, and when someone says, "I feel a lot of stress when I have to give a speech." Our responses can take two interrelated forms. Psychological responses involve behavior, thought patterns, and emotions, as when you "feel nervous." Physiological responses involve heightened bodily arousal—your heart pounds, your mouth goes dry, your stomach feels tight, and you perspire. The person's psychological and physiological response to a stressor is called **strain.**

The third approach describes stress as a *process* that includes stressors and strains, but adds an important dimension: the relationship between the person and the environment (Lazarus, 1999; Lazarus & Folkman, 1984a, 1984b). This process involves continuous interactions and adjustments—called **transactions**—with the person and environment each affecting and being affected by the other. According to this view, stress is not just a stimulus or a response, but rather a process in which the person is an active agent who can influence the impact of a stressor through behavioral, cognitive, and emotional strategies. People differ in the amount of strain they experience from the same stressor, such as being stuck in traffic or losing a job. One person who is stuck in traffic and late for an important appointment keeps looking at his watch, honking his horn, and getting angrier by the minute; another person in the same circumstances stays calm, turns on the radio, and listens to music.

We will define **stress** as the condition in which person–environment *transactions* lead to a *perceived discrepancy* between the physical or psychological *demands* of a situation and the *resources* of the individual's biological, psychological, or social systems (Lazarus & Folkman, 1984b; Lovallo, 1997; Singer & Davidson, 1986; Trumbull & Appley, 1986). Let's look at the four components of this definition, starting at the end.

1. Stress taxes the person's biopsychosocial resources for coping with difficult events or circumstances. These resources are limited, as we saw when Vicki had depleted her ability to cope with her problems, became ill, and sought counseling. Sometimes the impact is focused mainly on our biological system—for instance, when we tax our physical strength to lift something heavy. More typically, however, the strain has an impact on all three systems; in Vicki's stressful experience, her physical, psychological, and social resources were strained and became exhausted. Other stressful encounters that strain our biopsychosocial resources include participating in a competitive athletic event, being injured in an accident, or becoming nauseated before performing in a play.

2. The phrase *"demands* of a situation" refers to the amount of our resources the stressor appears to require. For instance, Vicki thought achieving the body weight she would need to keep Chris required tremendous willpower.

3. When there is a poor fit, or a mismatch, between the demands of the situation and the resources of the person, a *discrepancy* exists. This generally takes the form of the demands taxing or exceeding the resources, as in Vicki's belief that she did not have the willpower to keep her weight down. But the opposite discrepancy also occurs—that is, our resources may be underutilized—and this can be stressful, too. A worker who is bored by a lack of challenge in a job may find this situation stressful. An important point to keep in mind is that the discrepancy may be either *real* or just *believed* to exist. Suppose you had to take an exam and wanted to do well, but worried greatly that you would not. If you had procrastinated and did not prepare for the test, the discrepancy you see between the demands and your resources might be real. But if you had previously done well on similar exams, prepared thoroughly for this one, and scored well on a pretest in a study guide yet still thought you would not do well, the discrepancy you see would not reflect the true state of affairs. Stress often results from inaccurate perceptions of discrepancies between environmental demands and the actual resources. Stress is in the eye of the beholder.

4. In our *transactions* with the environment, we assess demands, resources, and discrepancies between them—as Vicki might do if she notices Chris looking at an attractive woman. These transactions are affected by many factors, including our prior experiences and aspects of the current situation. Suppose you are on a track team and are running in a race. Relevant transactions for this race actually began long before the race started, such as during your previous wins and losses, your recent training and fitness, and your knowledge of and experience with your competitors. In the race, these prior transactions have an impact on the continuous transactions that occur: you assess your strength and energy reserves, the position you are in relative to the other runners, and the likelihood that another runner will show a surge of speed toward the end of the race.

APPRAISING EVENTS AS STRESSFUL

Transactions in stress generally involve an assessment process that Richard Lazarus and his coworkers call **cognitive appraisal** (Cohen & Lazarus, 1983; Lazarus, 1999; Lazarus & Folkman, 1984b). Cognitive appraisal is a mental process by which people assess two factors: (1) whether a demand threatens their physical or psychological well-being and (2) the resources available for meeting the demand. These two factors distinguish two types of appraisal—primary and secondary.

Primary and Secondary Appraisal

When we encounter a potentially stressful event—for example, feeling symptoms of pain or nausea—we first try to assess the meaning of the situation for our well-being. This assessment process is called **primary appraisal.** In effect this appraisal seeks answers to such questions as, "What does this mean to me?" and "Will I be okay or in trouble?" Your primary appraisal regarding the pain or nausea could yield one of three judgments:

1. It *is irrelevant*—as you might decide if you had had similar symptoms before that lasted only a short while and were not followed by illness.

2. It *is good* (called "benign-positive")—which might be your appraisal if you wanted very much to skip work or have a college exam postponed.

3. It *is stressful*—as you might judge if you feared the symptoms were of a serious illness, such as botulism (a life-threatening type of food poisoning).

Events that we appraise as stressful receive further appraisal for three implications: harm-loss, threat, and challenge.

Harm-loss refers to the amount of damage that has already occurred, as when someone is incapacitated and in pain following a serious injury. Sometimes people who experience a relatively minor stressor think of it as a "disaster," thereby exaggerating its personal impact and increasing their feelings of stress (Ellis, 1987). *Threat* involves the expectation of future harm—for example, when hospitalized patients contemplate their medical bills, difficult rehabilitation, and loss of income. Stress appraisals seem to depend heavily on harm-loss and threat (Hobfoll, 1989). *Challenge* is the

This woman's face reveals that she appraises the pain in her chest as stressful.

opportunity to achieve growth, mastery, or profit by using more than routine resources to meet a demand. For instance, a worker might view an offer of a higher-level job as stressful, but see it as an opportunity to expand her skills, demonstrate her ability, and make more money.

Sometimes we experience stress even when the stressor does not relate to us directly—that is, the transaction is *vicarious*. If we see other people in stressful circumstances, such as suffering from pain or a life-threatening illness, we may empathize with their feelings and feel vulnerable ourselves. A classic experiment demonstrated empathic appraisal by showing college-student subjects a film called "Subincision" (Speisman, Lazarus, Mordkoff, & Davison, 1964). The film showed a rite of passage for young adolescent boys in a primitive society in which the underside of the penis is cut deeply from the tip to the scrotum, using a sharp stone. Before seeing the film, the subjects were divided into four groups, so that each group would see the film a different way. One of the groups saw the film with no sound track. Another group heard a sound track with a "trauma" narrative that emphasized the pain, danger, and primitiveness of the operation. A third group heard a "denial" narration that denied the pain and potential harm to the boys, describing them as willing participants in a joyful occasion who "look forward to the happy conclusion of the ceremony." The fourth group heard a "scientific" narration that encouraged the viewers to watch in a detached manner—for example, the narrator commented, "As you can see, the operation is formal and the surgical technique, while crude, is very carefully followed."

Did the different sound tracks affect the subjects' appraisals of stress? To evaluate this, the researchers used both physiological and self-report measures of stress. The physiological measures, such as heart rate, were taken continuously during the viewing of the film. The self-report measures were questionnaires that evaluated feelings of stress immediately after the film presentation. The results showed that, compared with the subjects who saw the film with no sound track, those who heard the trauma narration reacted with more stress, particularly during the film; those who heard the denial and scientific narration reacted with less stress. These results show that people can experience stress vicariously and that their reactions depend on the process of primary appraisal.

Secondary appraisal refers to our ongoing assessment of the resources we have available for cop-

ing. Although we generally engage in an assessment of our resources after we appraise an event as stressful, secondary appraisal "does not necessarily follow primary appraisal in time" (Cohen & Lazarus, 1983, p. 609). The two processes are highly interrelated, and sometimes our secondary appraisal of limited resources, or weakness, can lead to primary "appraisals of threat where they would not otherwise occur" (Coyne & Holroyd, 1982, p. 109). Nevertheless, we are probably more aware of secondary appraisal when we judge a situation as potentially stressful and try to determine whether our resources are sufficient to meet the harm, threat, or challenge we face. Examples of secondary appraisal judgments include:

- I can't do it—I know I'll fail.
- I'll try, but my chances are slim.
- I can do it if Ginny will help.
- If this method fails, I can try a few others.
- I can do it if I work hard.
- No problem—I can do it.

The condition of stress that we experience often depends on the outcome of the appraisals we make in our transactions with the environment. When we judge the fit between demands and resources to be close, we may experience little or no stress; but when our appraisals indicate a discrepancy, particularly if we appraise greater demands than resources, we may feel a great deal of stress.

Can stress occur without cognitive appraisals? According to some researchers, it can, particularly in emergency situations. Suppose you are in your car, stopped at a red light. In a split second you hear the squealing of brakes; your body tenses as you say, "Oh my God!"; and a car smashes yours in the rear. Your saying, "Oh my God!" is not really a cognitive appraisal—it's a reflexive response. But a stress reaction has already begun, as the tensing of your body indicates, and this is "*followed* by 'feelings' and appraisals" (Trumbull & Appley, 1986, p. 34). Often in serious emergencies the stress reaction includes a state of shock in which the person is stunned, dazed, or disoriented (Shontz, 1975). This state may last for minutes or hours, or much longer. Because cognitive functioning is impaired during shock, it is unlikely that appraisal processes play an important role in the stress experienced while in that state. In non-emergency situations, cognitive appraisals appear to precede stress reactions (Tomaka, Blascovich, Kibler, & Ernst, 1997).

What Factors Lead to Stressful Appraisals?

Appraising events as stressful depends on two types of factors—those that relate to the person and those that relate to the situation (Cohen & Lazarus, 1983; Lazarus & Folkman, 1984b). Let's begin by looking at how personal factors can affect appraisals of stress.

Personal factors include intellectual, motivational, and personality characteristics. One example is self-esteem: people who have high self-esteem are likely to believe they have the resources to meet demands that require the strengths they possess. If they perceive an event as stressful, they may interpret it as a challenge rather than a threat (Cohen & Lazarus, 1983). Another example relates to motivation: the more important a threatened goal, the more stress the person is likely to perceive (Paterson & Neufeld, 1987). One other example involves the person's belief system: as the psychologist Albert Ellis has noted, many people have irrational beliefs that increase their stress, for instance:

> "Because I strongly desire to have a safe, comfortable, and satisfying life, the conditions under which I live *absolutely must* be easy, convenient and gratifying (and it is *awful* and I *can't bear it* and *can't be happy at all* when they are unsafe and frustrating)!" (1987, p. 373)

A person who has such a belief is likely to appraise almost any sort of inconvenience as harmful or threatening.

What is it about situations that make them stressful? First, events that involve very *strong demands* and are *imminent* tend to be seen as stressful (Cohen & Lazarus, 1983; Paterson & Neufeld, 1987). Thus, patients who expect to undergo a physically uncomfortable or painful medical procedure, such as surgery, tomorrow are likely to view their situation as being more stressful than, say, expecting to have a blood pressure test next week.

Also, *life transitions* tend to be stressful (Moos & Schaefer, 1986; Sarason & Sarason, 1984). Life has many major events that mark the passing from one condition or phase to another, and they produce substantial changes and new demands in our lives. These events are called tansitions, and include starting day care or school, moving to a new community, entering a career, getting married, becoming a parent, losing a spouse through divorce or death, and retiring from a career. Becoming a parent, for instance, can be stressful before and after the birth (Miller & Sollie, 1986; Quadagno, Dixon, Denney, & Buck, 1986). The stressors before birth may include the physiological burden of pregnancy on the mother's body and concerns about the baby's and mother's health. After birth, the parents' stressors may involve being tied down, having a less orderly and predictable lifestyle, and having sleep interrupted often.

The *timing* of a life transition can affect the stress it produces. People expect some events, such as marriage or retirement, to occur at certain times in the life span (Neugarten & Neugarten, 1987). Deviations from the expected timetable are stressful. Why? For one thing, events that happen too early or too late often leave the person without the support of compatible peers, as a 40-year-old first-time mother might find (Lazarus & Folkman, 1984b). Also, the person may interpret being off schedule as a failure, and this is stressful. People who are "late" graduating college or advancing on the job may feel as if they have failed.

Ambiguity—a lack of clarity in a situation—can have an effect on stress appraisals. But the effect seems to depend on the type of ambiguity that exists. *Role ambiguity* occurs when the information about a person's function or task is unclear or confusing (Quick, Quick, Nelson, & Hurrell, 1997). In the workplace, for instance, this is reflected in unclear guidelines, standards for performance, and consequences for job-related activities. Role ambiguity often increases people's stress because they are uncertain about their actions and decisions. *Harm ambiguity* occurs when the likelihood of harm or the availability of resources to meet situational demands is unclear. With harm ambiguity, the effect on stress is variable and depends heavily on the person's personality, beliefs, and general experience (Lazarus & Folkman, 1984a, 1984b; Paterson & Neufeld, 1987). One person who is seriously ill and has unclear information about the chances of recovery may draw hope from this ambiguity; another person in the same situation may believe people are deliberately giving ambiguous information because the prognosis is so poor.

Another factor that influences stress appraisals is the *desirability* of the situation. Some events are typically undesirable to a person in most or all respects—losing your house in a fire is an example.

Other events, such as selling a house, are usually viewed as desirable. But either selling a house or losing it in a fire can be stressful because each produces demands that may tax or exceed the individual's resources. Stress can involve a wide variety of both desirable and undesirable situations, including the transitions we saw earlier, as well as less momentous circumstances, such as preparing to throw a party and getting a traffic ticket. In general, people are more likely to appraise undesirable events as stressful than desirable ones (McFarlane et al., 1980; Sandler & Guenther, 1985; Suls & Mullen, 1981).

One other aspect of the situation that affects stress appraisal is its *controllability*—that is, whether the person has the real or perceived ability to modify or terminate the stressor. People tend to appraise an uncontrollable event as being more stressful than a controllable event, even if they don't actually do anything to affect it (Miller, 1979; Suls & Mullen, 1981; Thompson, 1981). There are at least two types of control, behavioral and cognitive. In the case of *behavioral control*, we can affect the impact of the event by performing some action. Suppose, for example, you are experiencing intense pain from a headache. If you have the ability to reduce the pain, you are less likely to be stressed by the headache than if you do not have this ability. In the case of *cognitive control*, we can affect the impact of the event by using some mental strategy, such as by distracting our attention from the stressor or developing a plan to overcome a problem.

DIMENSIONS OF STRESS

Psychologists who study stress or perform therapy to help people manage it assume that the amount of stress a person experiences increases with stressor frequency, intensity, and duration (Cattanach & Rodin, 1988; Sarafino & Ewing, 1999). Evidence supports this assumption. Research has shown that stronger stressors produce greater physiological strain (Steptoe, Cropley, & Joekes, 2000). Many people experience *chronic stress*—that is, their stressors occur extremely often or last a long time (Gottlieb, 1997). Being under chronic stress makes people more susceptible to catching cold when exposed to infection (Cohen et al., 1998). (Go to 🌳.)

BIOPSYCHOSOCIAL ASPECTS OF STRESS

We've seen that stressors can produce strain in the person's biological, psychological, and social systems. Let's examine biopsychosocial reactions to stress more closely.

BIOLOGICAL ASPECTS OF STRESS

Anyone who has experienced a very frightening event, such as a near accident or other emergency, knows

CLINICAL METHODS AND ISSUES
Posttraumatic Stress Disorder

Experiencing an extremely severe stressor that creates intense fear and horror can lead to a psychiatric condition called *posttraumatic stress disorder*. This condition is marked by being highly aroused (with difficulty sleeping or concentrating), reliving the event often, and being unresponsive to other people (Davison & Neale, 1998). The disorder occurs frequently in people who have been injured in car accidents, exposed to war, forcibly raped, or subjected to intense, painful cancer treatment (Aaron, Zaglul, & Emery, 1999; Boscarino, 1997; Foa, 1998; Jacobsen et al., 1998). Being a victim of posttraumatic stress disorder may affect people's health: among Vietnam veterans, those who suffered from this disorder were more likely to develop various serious illnesses in the years after the war (Boscarino, 1997). Studies have demonstrated that behavior modification therapy with behavioral and cognitive methods is effective in preventing this disorder and helping people overcome it (Davison & Neale, 1998; Foa, 1998).

that there are physiological reactions to stress—for instance, our heartbeat and breathing rates increase immediately and, a little later, our skeletal muscles may tremble, especially in the arms and legs. The body is aroused and motivated to defend itself. As we saw in the preceding chapter, the sympathetic nervous system and the endocrine system cause this arousal to happen. After the emergency has passed, the arousal subsides. The physiological portion of the response to a stressor—or strain—is called **reactivity,** which researchers measure by comparison against a baseline, or "resting," level of arousal (Matthews, 1986). People who are under chronic stress show heightened reactivity when a stressor occurs, and their arousal takes more time to return to baseline levels (Gump & Matthews, 1999).

Many years ago the distinguished physiologist Walter Cannon (1929) provided a basic description of how the body reacts to emergencies. He was interested in the physiological reaction people and animals make in response to a perceived danger. This reaction has been called the *fight-or-flight* response because it prepares the organism to attack the threat or to flee. In the fight-or-flight response, the perception of danger causes the sympathetic nervous system to stimulate the adrenal glands of the endocrine system to secrete epinephrine, which arouses the body. Cannon proposed that this arousal could have both positive and negative effects: the fight-or-flight response is adaptive because it mobilizes the organism to respond quickly to danger, but the state of high arousal can be harmful to health if it is prolonged.

General Adaptation Syndrome

What happens to the body when high stress levels are prolonged? Hans Selye studied this issue by subjecting laboratory animals to a variety of stressors—such as very high or low environmental temperatures,

X rays, insulin injections, and exercise—over a long period of time. He also observed people who experienced stress from being ill. Through this research, he discovered that the fight-or-flight response is only the first in a series of reactions the body makes when stress is long-lasting (Selye, 1956, 1976, 1985). Selye called this series of physiological reactions the **general adaptation syndrome** (GAS). As Figure 3–1 shows, the GAS consists of three stages:

1. **Alarm reaction.** The first stage of the GAS is like the fight-or-flight response to an emergency—its function is to mobilize the body's resources. At the very beginning of the alarm reaction, arousal—as measured by blood pressure, for example—drops below normal for a moment, but then rapidly rises to above normal. This fast-increasing arousal results from activation of the *hypothalamus–pituitary–adrenal axis:* the hypothalamus triggers the pituitary gland to secrete ACTH, which causes the adrenal glands to release epinephrine, norepinephrine, and cortisol into the bloodstream. By the end of this stage in the GAS, the body is fully mobilized to resist the stressor strongly. But the body cannot maintain this intense arousal for very long. Some organisms that have experienced a continuous and unrelieved alarm reaction to an extremely intense stressor have died within hours or days.

2. **Stage of resistance.** If a strong stressor continues but is not severe enough to cause death, the physiological reaction enters the stage of resistance. In this stage, the body tries to adapt to the stressor. Physiological arousal declines somewhat but remains higher than normal, and the body replenishes the hormones released by the adrenal glands. Despite this continuous physiological arousal, the organism may show few outward signs of stress. But the ability to resist new stressors may be impaired for long periods of time. According to Selye, one outcome of this

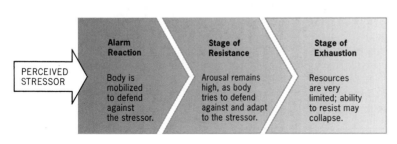

Figure 3–1   General adaptation syndrome.

impairment is that the organism becomes increasingly vulnerable to health problems he called *diseases of adaptation*. These health problems include ulcers, high blood pressure, asthma, and illnesses that result from impaired immune function.

   3.   Stage of exhaustion. Prolonged physiological arousal produced by severe long-term or repeated stress is costly. It weakens the immune system and depletes the body's energy reserves until resistance is very limited. At this point, the stage of exhaustion begins. If the stress continues, disease and damage to internal organs are likely, and death may occur.

   Two lines of evidence support the long-term effects the GAS describes. First, people who experience chronically high levels of stress show greater reactivity to stressors they encounter: compared with other people, individuals under chronic stress respond to a stressor with greater increases in blood pressure and decrements in immune function (Lepore, Miles, & Levy, 1997; Pike et al., 1997). Second, having to adapt repeatedly to intense stressors may take a high physiologic toll that accumulates over time in a process called *allostatic load* (McEwen & Stellar, 1993). Studies of chronic stress have confirmed that high levels of allostatic load are related to poor health in children and the elderly (Johnston-Brooks, Lewis, Evans, & Whalen, 1998; Seeman et al., 1997).

Do All Stressors Produce the Same Physical Reactions?

Many studies have demonstrated that stressors of various types increase the secretion of hormones by the adrenal glands (Baum, Grunberg, & Singer, 1982; Ciaranello, 1983). These stressors include cold temperatures, noise, pain, athletic competition, failure, taking examinations, flying in an airplane, and being in crowded situations.

   Selye (1956) believed that the GAS is *nonspecific* with regard to the type of stressor. That is, the series of physiological reactions the GAS describes will occur regardless of whether the stress results from very cold temperature, physical exercise, illness, or the death of a loved one. However, although various stressors increase the secretion of adrenal hormones, the notion of nonspecificity does not take important psychosocial processes into account. There are at least two reasons why this is a problem.

   One reason is that some stressors elicit a stronger *emotional* response than others do. This is important because the amount of hormone released in reaction

Physical exertion, such as in athletic competition, is a stressor that produces strain in the body.

to a stressor that involves a strong emotional response, as a *sudden* increase in environmental temperature might produce, appears to be different from the amount released with a less emotional stressor, such as a *gradual* increase in temperature. After conducting extensive studies of various stressors and hormones, John Mason concluded that he and his colleagues "have not found evidence that any single hormone responds to *all* stimuli in *absolutely* nonspecific fashion" (1975, p. 27). For instance, some stressors led to increases in epinephrine, norepinephrine, and cortisol, but other stressors increased only two of these hormones. He also pointed out that research conducted since Selye first described the GAS has shown that stressors are most likely to trigger the release of large amounts of all three of these hormones if the individual's response includes a strong element of emotion.

The second reason is that cognitive appraisal processes appear to play a role in people's physiological reaction to stressors. This role is suggested by the results of a study by Katherine Tennes and Maria Kreye (1985). The researchers assessed elementary school children's cortisol levels in urine samples taken on regular school days and on days when achievement tests were given. The expected increase in cortisol on test days was found, but not for all children—their intelligence was an important factor. Intelligence test scores were obtained from school records. Cortisol levels increased on test days for children with above-average intelligence, but not for children with low to average intelligence. The influence of intelligence suggests that the brighter children were more concerned about academic achievement and, as a result, appraised the tests as more threatening than did the other children.

To summarize, the basic structure of the GAS appears to be valid, but it incorrectly assumes that all stressors produce the same physiological reactions and fails to include the role of psychosocial factors in stress.

PSYCHOSOCIAL ASPECTS OF STRESS

At this juncture, we can begin to see how interwoven our biological, psychological, and social systems are in the experience of stress. Stressors produce physiological changes, but psychosocial factors also play a role. To give a more complete picture of the interplay among these systems, we will now examine the impact of stress on people's cognitive, emotional, and social systems.

Cognition and Stress

Many students have had this experience: While taking a particularly stressful exam in school, they may neglect or misinterpret important information in a question or have difficulty remembering an answer they had studied well the night before. It is infuriating to know that an answer is "on the tip of your tongue," especially since you will probably remember it after the test is over. High levels of stress affect people's memory and attention. Let's see how.

Stress can impair cognitive functioning, often by distracting our attention. Noise can be a stressor, which can be chronic for people who live in noisy environments, such as next to train tracks or highways (Lepore, 1997). How does chronic noise affect people's cognitive performance? Many people try to deal with this kind of stress by changing the focus of their attention from the noise to relevant aspects of a cognitive task—they "tune out" the noise. Research evidence suggests that children who try to tune out chronic noise may develop generalized cognitive deficits because they have difficulty knowing which sounds to attend to and which to tune out (Cohen, Evans, Stokols, & Krantz, 1986).

But stress can also enhance our attention, particularly toward the stressor. For instance, researchers had people watch a series of pictures while listening to a story about a boy and his mother who go to a hospital (Cahill, Prins, Weber, & McGaugh, 1994). For some subjects, the story was emotional: the boy had a terrible accident, his feet were severed, and surgeons reattached the feet. For other subjects, the story was neutral: the boy went to the hospital to watch activities there. Before this experience, the subjects with each type of story received an injection of either a placebo or a drug that stops the action of epinephrine and norepinephrine. When tested a week later, the subjects who heard the emotional story remembered more details of it if they had gotten the placebo rather than the drug. But the drug had no effect on subjects' memory of the neutral story. These findings suggest that epinephrine and norepinephrine enhance the memory of stressors we experience.

Not only can stress affect cognition, but the reverse is true, too. In the opening story about Vicki, she kept imagining that her boyfriend was seeing other women, which was very distressing for her. Her thinking was making the stress chronic. Andrew Baum (1990) has studied this kind of thinking in individuals who were living near the Three Mile Island nuclear power plant in Pennsylvania when a major nuclear accident occurred. He found that some of these people still experienced stress from the incident years later, but others did not. One of the main factors differentiating these people was that those who continued to feel this stress had trouble keeping thoughts about the accident and their fears out of their minds. It seems likely that these thoughts perpetuated their stress and made it chronic.

Emotions and Stress

Long before infants can talk, they display what they feel by their motor, vocal, and facial expressions. You can test this with a little experiment: place a bit of a bitter food, such as unsweetened chocolate, in a newborn's mouth and watch the baby's face—the eyes squint, brows drop and draw together, the mouth opens, and tongue juts out. This is the facial expression for the emotion of disgust. Each emotion has a specific facial pattern.

According to researcher Carroll Izard (1979), newborn babies do not display all the emotional expressions they will develop, but they do express several emotions, such as disgust, distress, and interest. Using procedures like the one with bitter food, he and his colleagues studied 2- to 19-month-old infants' emotional reactions to the stress of receiving their regular inoculations (Izard, Hembree, Dougherty, & Spizzirri, 1983). The facial expressions following needle penetration were mainly of distress and anger, but the younger infants' principal emotion was distress, and the older infants' immediate and dominant emotion was anger. As babies develop, they become more able to try to act for themselves, such as by pushing at the nurse's hand. Anger spurs this kind of defensive action; distress merely signals the need for help.

Emotions tend to accompany stress, and people often use their emotional states to evaluate their stress. Cognitive appraisal processes can influence both the stress and the emotional experience (Lazarus, 1999; Schachter & Singer, 1962; Scherer, 1986). For example, you might experience stress and fear if you came across a snake while walking in the woods, particularly if you recognized it as poisonous. Your emotion would not be joy or excitement, unless you were studying snakes and were looking for this particular type. Both situations would involve stress, but you might experience fear if your appraisal was one of threat, and excitement if your appraisal was one of challenge.

Fear is a common emotional reaction that includes psychological discomfort and physical arousal when we feel threatened. Of the various types and intensities of fears people experience in everyday life, psychologists classify many into two categories: phobias and anxiety. *Phobias* are intense and irrational fears that are directly associated with specific events and situations. Some people are afraid of being enclosed in small rooms, for instance, and are described as claustrophobic. *Anxiety* is a vague feeling of uneasiness or apprehension—a gloomy anticipation of impending doom—that often involves a relatively uncertain or unspecific threat. That is, the person may not be aware either of the situations that seem to arouse anxiety or of exactly what the "doom" entails. Patients awaiting surgery or the outcome of diagnostic tests generally experience high levels of anxiety. In other situations, anxiety may result from appraisals of low self-worth and the anticipation of a loss of either self-esteem or the esteem of others.

The things children fear tend to become *less* concrete or tangible and *more* abstract and social as they get older (Graziano, DeGiovanni, & Garcia, 1979; Sarafino, 1986). In early childhood, many children develop fears of concrete things, such as animals, doctors, and dentists, often because of negative experiences with these things. Cognition can also play a role in these fears. A study of children's fears of dental treatment found that the most fearful children were those who had *not* experienced invasive procedures, such as having a tooth pulled, during the prior few years (Murray, Liddell, & Donohue, 1989). Not having had these experiences probably allowed the children to imagine that invasive procedures are worse than they are. Later in childhood, concrete fears tend to decline while anxieties relating to school, individual competence, and social relations become pronounced. Children who see themselves as less able than their age-mates are likely to appraise their own resources as insufficient to meet the demands of stressors.

Stress can also lead to feelings of sadness or *depression*. We all feel depressed at times, although we may call the feeling something else, like "sad," or "blue," or "unhappy." These feelings are a normal part of life for children and adults (Davison & Neale, 1998; Quay & La Greca, 1986). The difference between normal depression and depression as a serious *disorder* is a matter of degree. Depression becomes a psychological disorder when it is severe, frequent, and long-lasting. People with this disorder tend to:

- Have a mostly sad mood nearly every day
- Appear listless, with loss of energy, pleasure, and interest
- Show poor appetite and sleeping habits
- Have thoughts of suicide, feeling hopeless about the future
- Have low self-esteem, often blaming themselves for their troubles (Davison & Neale, 1998)

Having long-term disabling health problems, such as being paralyzed by a stroke, often leads to depressive disorders.

Another common emotional reaction to stress is *anger*, particularly when the person perceives the situation as harmful or frustrating. You can see this in the angry response often shown by children whose favorite toy was taken away and by adults who are stuck in a traffic jam. Anger has important social ramifications—it can produce aggressive behavior, for instance.

Social Behavior and Stress

Stress changes people's behavior toward one another. In some stressful situations, such as train crashes, earthquakes, and other disasters, many people may work together to help each other survive. Perhaps they do this because they have a common goal that requires cooperative effort (Sherif & Sherif, 1953). In other stressful situations, people may become less sociable or caring and more hostile and insensitive toward other individuals.

When stress and anger join, negative social behaviors often increase. Research has shown that stress-produced anger increases aggressive behavior, and these negative effects continue after the stressful event is over (Donnerstein & Wilson, 1976). This increased aggressive behavior has important implications in real life, outside the laboratory. Child abuse is a major social problem that poses a serious threat to children's health, physical development, and psychological adjustment. Studies have found a connection between parental stress and child abuse (Kempe,

1976; Kolbe et al., 1986). Prior to an act of battering, frequently the parent has experienced a stressful crisis, such as the loss of a job. A parent under high levels of stress is at risk of losing control. If, for example, the child runs around the house making a racket, a stressed parent may become very angry, lose control, and start beating the child.

Stress also affects helping behavior. This was shown in an experiment conducted in a shopping center (Cohen & Spacapan, 1978). After each subject completed either a difficult shopping task or an easy one in either a crowded or uncrowded shopping center, he or she walked through a deserted hallway to meet with the researcher. In the hallway, the subject encountered a woman who feigned dropping a contact lens—a situation in which the subject could provide help. Those subjects who had just experienced the most stress, having completed the difficult shopping task in crowded conditions, helped less often and for less time than those who had completed the easy task in uncrowded conditions.

Gender and Sociocultural Differences in Stress

Does the experience of stress depend on a person's gender and sociocultural group membership? Apparently it does. Women generally report having experienced a greater number of major and minor stressors than men do (Davis, Matthews, & Twamley, 1999). Although this difference may result partly from women's greater willingness to say they experienced stress, it probably also reflects real variations in experiences. Because in today's two-income households, mothers still do most of the chores at home, they often have heavier daily workloads than men and greater physiological strain than women without children (Luecken et al., 1997; Lundberg & Frankenhaeuser, 1999).

Being a member of a minority group or being poor appears to increase the stressors people experience (Clark, Anderson, Clark, & Williams, 1999; Johnson et al., 1995). Research in the United States has shown that individuals with these sociocultural statuses report having experienced a disproportionately large number of major stressors (Gottlieb & Green, 1987). For example, black Americans report far more stressors than Hispanics, who report more stressors than do nonminority people.

There appear to be gender and sociocultural differences in physiological strain from stressors, too.

Many studies have found that men show more reactivity than females when psychologically stressed (Collins & Frankenhaeuser, 1978; Kirschbaum, Wüst, & Hellhammer, 1992; Kudielka et al., 1998; Ratliff-Crain & Baum, 1990). Men also seem to take longer for their physiological arousal to return to baseline levels after the stressor has ended (Earle, Linden, & Weinberg, 1999). But some evidence suggests that men and women differ in the events they find stressful, and the strength of reactivity compared with that of the opposite sex may be greater when the stressor is relevant to the person's gender (Weidner & Messina, 1998). For instance, men show greater reactivity than women do when their competence is challenged, and women show greater reactivity than men when their friendship or love is challenged (Smith et al., 1998).

Regarding sociocultural differences, some studies in the United States have found that blacks show greater reactivity than whites when under stress (Calhoun et al., 1993; McAdoo et al., 1990; Miller et al., 1995). And a study found that black siblings were more similar to each other in their degree of reactivity than white siblings were, which suggests that heredity may play a role (Wilson, Holmes, Arheart, & Alpert, 1995). But the outcomes of other studies suggest that differences between blacks and whites vary depending on the stressor and the subjects' gender (Saab et al., 1997; Sherwood, May, Siegel, & Blumenthal, 1995).

We have seen that the effects of stress are wide-ranging and involve an interplay among our biological, psychological, and social systems. Even when the stressor is no longer present, the impact of the stress experience can continue. Some people experience more stress than others do, but we all find stress somewhere in our lives. Stress arises from a countless variety of sources.

SOURCES OF STRESS THROUGHOUT LIFE

Babies, children, and adults all experience stress. The sources of stress may change as people develop, but the condition of stress can occur at any time throughout life. Where does stress come from, and what are its sources? To answer this question, we will examine sources that arise within the *person*, in the *family*, and in the *community* and *society*.

SOURCES WITHIN THE PERSON

Sometimes the source of stress is within the person. *Illness* is one way stress arises from within the individual. Being ill creates physical and psychological demands on the person, and the degree of stress these demands produce depends on the seriousness of the illness and the age of the individual, among other things. Why is the person's age important? For one thing, the ability of the body to fight disease normally improves in childhood and declines in old age (Benjamini, Sunshine, & Leskowitz, 1996). Another reason is that the meaning of a serious illness for the individual changes with age. For example, young children have a limited understanding of disease and death. Because of this, their appraisal of stress that arises from their illness is likely to focus on current, rather than future, concerns—such as how well they feel at the moment and whether their activities are impaired (La Greca & Stone, 1985). Stress appraisals by ill adults typically include both current difficulties and concerns for the future, such as whether they may be disabled or may die.

Another way stress arises within the person is through the appraisal of opposing motivational forces, when a state of *conflict* exists. Suppose you are registering for next semester and find that two courses that you need meet at the same time. You can take only one. Which will you choose? You have a conflict—you are being pushed and pulled in two directions. Many conflicts are more momentous than this one. We may need to choose between two or more job offers, or different medical treatments, or houses we are thinking of buying, for instance. Conflict is a major source of stress.

The pushes and pulls of conflict produce two opposing tendencies: *approach* and *avoidance*. These two tendencies characterize three basic types of conflict (Lewin, 1935; Miller, 1959):

    1. *Approach/approach conflict* arises when we are attracted toward two appealing goals that are incompatible. For example, people who are trying to lose weight to improve either their health or their appearance experience frequent conflicts when delicious, fattening foods are available. Although individuals generally resolve an approach/approach conflict fairly easily, the more important they perceive the decision to be, the greater the stress it is likely to produce.

2. *Avoidance/avoidance conflict* occurs when we are faced with a choice between two undesirable situations. For example, patients with serious illnesses may be faced with a choice between two treatments that will control or cure the disease, but have very undesirable side effects. People in avoidance/avoidance conflicts usually try to postpone or escape from the decision: a patient might delay or discontinue treatment or change physicians in the hope of getting choices that are more appealing. When delaying or escaping is not possible, people often vacillate between the two alternatives, changing their minds repeatedly. Sometimes they get someone else to make the decision for them. People generally find avoidance/avoidance conflicts difficult to resolve and very stressful.

3. *Approach/avoidance conflict* arises when we see attractive and unattractive features in a single goal or situation. This type of conflict can be stressful and difficult to resolve. Consider, for instance, individuals who smoke cigarettes and want to quit. They may be torn between wanting to improve their health and wanting to avoid the weight gain and cravings they believe will occur.

As you may realize, conflicts can be more complicated than the examples we have considered. People often have to choose between two or more alternatives, recognizing that each has multiple attractive and unattractive features, as in buying a new house or car. In general, people are likely to find conflict stressful when the choices involve many features, when opposing motivational forces have fairly equal strength, and when the "wrong" choice can lead to very negative and permanent consequences. These conditions often apply when people face major decisions about their health.

SOURCES IN THE FAMILY

The behavior, needs, and personality of each member of a family have an impact on and interact with those of the other members of the family system, sometimes producing stress. Interpersonal conflict can arise from financial problems, from inconsiderate behavior, or from opposing goals, such as which television program to watch. Living in an overcrowded household increases conflict over privacy and the use of family resources, such as the bathroom. Of the many sources of stress in the family, we will focus on three: adding a new family member, divorce, and illness and death in the family.

An Addition to the Family

A new child in the family is a joyful event, but it also brings stress—particularly to the mother, of course, during pregnancy and after the birth. But an addition to the family is stressful to other family members, too. For instance, the father may worry about the health of his wife and baby or fear that his relationship with his wife may deteriorate, and both parents may feel the need to earn more money.

After the baby is born, parents experience stress from their new responsibilities in caring for the child. An important factor in parental stress relates to the child's personality. Each baby comes into the world with certain personality dispositions, which are called **temperaments** (Buss & Plomin, 1975; Thomas, Chess, & Birch, 1970). Pediatric nurses and physicians, well aware of the unique combinations of temperaments that babies show right from birth, describe infants broadly as "easy" babies and "difficult" ones. These terms do, in fact, capture the general dispositions of most infants fairly accurately on the basis of differences in the way babies react to feeding, cuddling, bathing, and dressing and undressing.

Temperamentally difficult babies tend to cry a great deal—often very loudly—and efforts to soothe them do not seem to work very well. They resist being introduced to new foods, routines, and people, and their patterns of sleep, hunger, and bowel movements are hard to predict from day to day. Although only about 10% of babies are classified as "difficult," displaying most or all of these traits fairly consistently, many others show some of these traits at least occasionally. A child who reacts in a very negative manner to minor irritations is very stressful to parents (Cutrona & Troutman, 1986). Although children's temperaments are fairly stable across time, with aspects of these traits continuing for many years, many difficult children show changes toward the development of easy traits (Carey & McDevitt, 1978; Thomas, Chess, & Birch, 1970).

The arrival of a new baby can also be stressful to other children in the family (Honig, 1987; Rutter, 1983). This stress seems to be particularly strong among children who are very young, say, 2 or 3 years old, and who may not want to share their parents with the new brother or sister. After the baby arrives, these children may show increased clinging to the mother, as well as increased sleeping and toileting problems. If the children are older, they are less likely to view the baby as a rival for their parents' attention, and their stress seems to relate to changes in family behavior and rules, such as not making noise when the baby is asleep.

Divorce

A divorce produces many stressful transitions for all members of the family as they deal with changes in their social, residential, and financial circumstances. In the case of the children, they may move to a new neighborhood, be left with new sitters, or have to take on new chores at home. The custodial parent may not be very available to the children because of work or other preoccupations. According to psychologist Judith Wallerstein (1983, 1986), the way children react to the stress of divorce depends in part on their age. Very young children may feel responsible for the divorce, worry that the custodial parent will also leave, and develop sleep disturbances. Older children and adolescents tend to react with anger, often siding with one parent and blaming the other. Adapting to divorce usually takes several years, and some family members may never adjust fully. Parents can do several things to enhance their children's adjustment to a divorce (Sarafino & Armstrong, 1986). They can maintain a loving, secure home life and:

- Tell the children in advance of the impending separation.

- Encourage open communication and answer the children's questions truthfully, but sensitively.

- Gear information to the children's levels of understanding, with concrete and accurate explanations of what will happen to all members of the family.

- Recruit help and advice from others, such as relatives, parent organizations, counselors, and the children's school personnel.

- Encourage the children to have contact with both parents.

Family Illness, Disability, and Death

The following is a familiar story to many parents: In the middle of a frantic day at work, the parent receives a call from the school nurse, who says, "Your child is

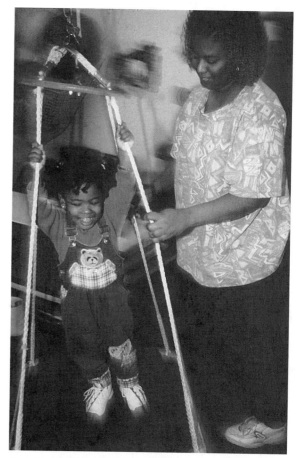

A mother helping her child with cerebral palsy to do exercises. Family stressors increase when children require special attention.

sick. You'll have to come and pick him up." Having a sick child adds to the stress in an already stressful day.

When children have a serious chronic illness, their families must adapt to unique and long-term stresses (Johnson, 1985; Leventhal, Leventhal, & Van Nguyen, 1985; Quittner et al., 1998). Part of the stress stems from the amount of time needed to care for the child and from the reduced freedom family members have in their schedules. For example, children with the respiratory disease called cystic fibrosis generally need physiotherapy two or three times a day to reduce the mucus that collects in their lungs (Burroughs & Dieterle, 1985). The family also faces many difficult decisions and must learn about the illness and how to care for the child. The medical needs of chronically ill children are expensive, and this burden adds to the family's stress. Relationships between family members may also suffer. The parents are likely to feel that having a chronically ill child reduces the time they have to devote to each other. In addition, other children in the family may feel isolated and deprived of parental attention.

Adult illness or disability is another source of family stress. The strain on their financial resources is especially severe if the sick adult is a principal breadwinner. Having a physically ill or disabled adult in the family restricts the family's time and personal freedom and produces very important changes in interpersonal relationships (Leventhal, Leventhal, & Van Nguyen, 1985; Michela, 1987; Skelton & Dominian, 1973). For example, suppose a man has a heart attack. His spouse may experience stress from fears that he may have another attack and changes in his behavior, such as being more irritable and dependent. Although the couple may show increased affection for one another during convalescence, their sexual relations are generally curtailed—often because of fears that sex could induce another attack. And the roles of family members change: the healthy spouse and the children who are old enough take on many of the responsibilities and tasks of the recovering spouse. As the convalescing adult begins to show good physical recovery, the stress generally diminishes in the family.

Does the stress a family experiences when an adult is seriously ill depend on the sick person's age? Often it does. For instance, advanced cancer in an elderly person has a very different meaning than the same illness in someone at 30 years of age, especially if the young adult has one or more children. In the latter case, the disease is inconsistent with the person's roles and threatens the family unit. Chronic illness is likely to produce intense frustration, distress, and anger if it is out of step with expectations and needs for the future (Leventhal, Leventhal, & Van Nguyen, 1985). But if an elderly person who is ill or disabled must live with and be cared for by relatives, the stress for all those in the household can be severe, especially if the person requires constant care and shows mental deterioration (Robinson & Thurnher, 1986). Elderly spouses who provide care for such individuals are often emotionally distressed and show heightened physiological strain, making them more susceptible to infectious disease (Vedhara et al., 1999).

Age is also an important factor in the experience of stress when a family member dies. Some children suffer the loss of a parent during the childhood years—one of the most traumatic events a child can face. Children under about 5 years of age seem to grieve for the lost parent less strongly and for a shorter time than older children and adolescents do (Garmezy, 1983; Rutter, 1983). This age difference probably results from their different levels of understanding about the nature of death. Children's concept of death changes between 4 and 8 years of age (Lonetto, 1980; Speece & Brent, 1984). Young children often think death is reversible: the person is simply living somewhere else—such as underground—and can come back. By about 8 years of age, most children understand that death is final and involves an absence of bodily functions.

An adult whose child or spouse dies suffers a tremendous loss (Kastenbaum & Costa, 1977; Kosten, Jacobs, & Kasl, 1985). Losing a child creates other losses—for example, bereaved mothers reported that they had lost important hopes and expectations for the future (Edelstein, 1984). Parents who lose their only child lose their identity and role as mothers and fathers, too. When a spouse dies, the surviving spouse also loses important hopes, expectations, and roles—as well as the one companion who made him or her feel loved, wanted, special, and safe. Although the loss of a spouse is difficult at any age, it appears to be especially stressful in early adulthood (Ball, 1976–77). (Go to 💡.)

SOURCES IN THE COMMUNITY AND SOCIETY

Interpersonal contacts people make outside the family provide many sources of stress. For instance, children experience stress at school and in competitive events, such as in sports and band performances (Passer, 1982; Sears & Milburn, 1990). Much of the stress adults experience is associated with their occupations, and a variety of environmental situations can be stressful. We will focus on how people's jobs and environments can be sources of stress.

Jobs and Stress

Almost all people at some time in their lives experience stress that relates to their occupations. Often these stressful situations are minor and brief and have little impact on the person. But for many people, the stress is intense and continues for long periods of time. What factors make jobs stressful?

HIGHLIGHT ON ISSUES
Gender Differences in Caregiving?

If I mentioned to you that an elderly friend was receiving care at home from family members, would you picture most of those caregivers as women? Probably most people would. Although many studies have found that women are more likely than men to be caregivers, not all have. And some researchers have questioned the societal image of women being the main caregivers among family members.

To examine this issue, Baila Miller and Lynda Cafasso (1992) did a **meta-analysis,** a statistical research method that pools the results of prior studies to create an integrated overview of their findings. No new data are collected. The prefix *meta* means "after" or "among"—thus, researchers apply this method *after* a series of studies has been done and assess the overall relationships these studies found *among* relevant variables. Meta-analysis is a useful technique for revealing patterns in relationships and clarifying what has been found, *especially* when some studies found different results than others. This meta-analysis was based on 14 published studies that had investigated gender differences in caregiving for elderly individuals.

Miller and Cafasso decided to examine the data from these studies for gender differences in several aspects of the caregiving experience. These analyses revealed that female caregivers were somewhat more likely than males to:

- Carry out personal care activities, such as dressing, bathing, and grooming the elderly person.
- Do the household chores in the elderly person's dwelling.
- Report experiencing greater degrees of stress from the caregiving.

But these differences were not very great, and no gender differences were found for any of the other aspects of caregiving, including:

- The degree of caregiving involvement, which was based on the number of tasks the caregiver had to do, the extent of assistance the elderly person needed to perform tasks, and the number of hours spent in caregiving.
- The extent to which the elderly person was functionally impaired, or unable to carry out activities of daily living.
- The caregiver's involvement in managing the elderly person's finances.

The researchers concluded that their results contradict gender-role stereotypes of Western societies and indicate that females and males are fairly similar in the degree to which they provide care for elderly relatives, the types of caregiving tasks they do, and the stress they experience from caregiving.

The *demands of the task* can produce stress in two ways. First, the workload may be too high. Some people work very hard for long hours over long periods of time because they feel required to do so—for example, if they need the money or think their bosses would be unhappy if they did not. Studies have found that excessive workloads are associated with increased rates of accidents and health problems (Mackay & Cox, 1978; Quick, Quick, Nelson, & Hurrell, 1997). Second, some kinds of job activities are more stressful than others. For example, repetitive manual action, as in cashier work, can be stressful and is linked to physical symptoms, such as neck and shoulder pain (Lundberg et al., 1999). Also, jobs that underutilize the

worker's abilities can produce stress. As one worker put it:

> I sit by these machines and wait for one to go wrong, then I turn it off, and go and get the supervisor. They don't go wrong very much. Sometimes I think I'd like them to keep going wrong, just to have something to do. . . . It's bloody monotonous. (Mackay & Cox, 1978, p. 159)

Another kind of activity that can produce stress is the evaluation of an employee's job performance—a process that can be difficult for both the supervisor and the employee.

Firefighters have stressful jobs, partly because of their responsibility for people's lives.

Jobs that involve a *responsibility for people's lives* can be very stressful. Medical personnel have heavy workloads and must deal with life or death situations frequently. Making a mistake can have dire consequences. In an intensive care unit of a hospital, emergency situations are common; decisions must be made instantly and carried out immediately and accurately. As part of the job,

> the nurse must reassure and comfort the man who is dying of cancer; she must change the dressings of a decomposing, gangrenous limb; she must calm the awakening disturbed "overdose" patient. . . .It is hard to imagine any other situation that involves such intimacy with the frightening, repulsive, and forbidden. . . .To all this is added the repetitive contact with death. (Hay & Oken, 1985, p. 108)

These and other conditions of jobs in the health professions take their toll, often leading to feelings of emotional exhaustion (Maslach & Jackson, 1982). Similar stressors exist in the jobs of police and fire personnel.

Several other aspects of jobs can increase workers' stress (Cottington & House, 1987; Hepburn, Loughlin, & Barling, 1997; Mackay & Cox, 1978; Quick, Quick, Nelson, & Hurrell, 1997). For example, stress can result from:

● *The physical environment* of the job. Stress increases when the job involves extreme levels of noise, temperature, humidity, or illumination.

● *Perceived insufficient control* over aspects of the job. People experience stress when they have little influence over work procedures or the pace of the work, such as when a machine feeds work to them at a predetermined speed (Steptoe, Fieldman, Evans, & Perry, 1993).

● *Poor interpersonal relationships.* People's stress on the job increases when their boss or a co-worker is socially abrasive, being insensitive to the needs of others or condescending and overly critical of the work other individuals do.

● *Perceived inadequate recognition or advancement.* Workers feel stress when they do not get the recognition or promotions they believe they deserve.

● *Job loss.* People experience stress when they lose their jobs or think their jobs are threatened. Workers who believe they are likely to be fired or laid off feel a sense of *job insecurity*—and this is stressful, particularly if they have little prospect of finding another job. Studies have shown that *unemployment* is associated with psychological and physiological signs of stress, such as in people's loss of self-esteem and heightened blood pressure (Olafsson & Svensson, 1986).

Research has linked these aspects of jobs to physiological strain—particularly for high blood pressure and heart rate (Melin, Lundberg, Söderlund, & Granqvist, 1999; Schnall et al., 1998; Steptoe, Cropley, & Joekes, 2000)—and eventual development of heart disease (Bosma, Peter, Siegrist, & Marmot, 1998).

Many elderly people approach *retirement* with expectations of blissful freedom and leisure. But it does not always turn out that way. Retirees often find that they have lost opportunities for social interaction and an important part of their identity. They may miss the power and influence they once had, the structure and routines of a job, and the feeling of being useful and competent (Bohm & Rodin, 1985; Bradford, 1986). The stress from these circumstances can affect not only the retirees, but their spouses, too. What's more, many retirees have the added problem that their income is not sufficient for their needs.

Environmental Stress

Have you ever been at a big noisy event with thousands of people jammed into an arena and felt physiologically aroused, tense, and uncomfortable? Events like these can be stressful because of the noise and the crowded conditions (Karlin, Epstein, & Aiello, 1978). Crowded conditions reduce your control over interpersonal interaction and restrict your ability to move about freely or obtain resources, such as seats. Also, you may feel that other people are physically closer than you usually prefer people to be— they are intruding into your *personal space* (Sarafino, 1987a).

Some environmental conditions are intensely stressful—imagine how you would react to learning that a hazardous substance has seeped into the water supply where you live. How much of it have you and your family already drunk? Has it damaged your bodies already? Will you develop serious illnesses because of it in the future? Can the substance be removed? And after it is, will you believe there is no more danger? Can you sell your house now without suffering a great financial loss? Many people who are exposed to hazardous substances or other continuous threats in their environment worry for years about what will happen to them (Baum, 1988; Bland et al., 1996; Specter, 1996). Natural disasters, such as earthquakes, have the added difficulty of long-term disruptions in social relationships, which worsen the stress (Bland et al., 1997).

In the late 1970s, attention was focused on this type of situation at Love Canal in New York State, where a chemical dump site had contaminated a residential community. In many ways this situation is more stressful than a natural disaster—at least a tornado ends quickly, its damage can be assessed, and much of the damage can be repaired in time. At Love Canal, however, "the nightmare goes on and on" (Holden, 1980). Another example of the psychological effects of living in a hazardous environment comes from the nuclear accident at the Three Mile Island power plant in Pennsylvania. More than a year after the accident, researchers compared the stress of nearby residents to that of people who lived near a different nuclear facility that had not had an accident. This comparison revealed greater psychological and physiological evidence of stress among the residents around Three Mile Island than among those near the other facility (Fleming, Baum, Gisriel, & Gatchel, 1982).

So far in this chapter we have seen that stress involves biopsychosocial reactions, and that all sorts of events or circumstances can be stressors, including extreme temperatures, noise, taking an exam, being stuck in a traffic jam, having a painful medical test, getting married, and losing a job. The possible stimuli and reactions, and the appraisal processes that link them, make for an interesting question: If you were doing research and needed to know whether different people had experienced different amounts of stress, how could you assess this variable?

MEASURING STRESS

Researchers have used several different approaches for measuring stress. The three most commonly used approaches involve assessing people's physiological arousal, life events, and daily hassles.

PHYSIOLOGICAL AROUSAL

Stress produces physiological arousal, which is reflected in the functioning of many of our body systems. One way to assess arousal is to use electrical/mechanical equipment to take measurements of blood pressure, heart rate, respiration rate, or galvanic skin response (GSR). Each of these indexes of arousal can be measured separately, or they can all be measured and recorded simultaneously by one apparatus called the **polygraph** (Figure 3–2). Miniaturized versions of these devices are available with recording units that can fit in a pocket, thereby allowing assessments during the person's daily life at home, at work, or in a stressful situation, such as while flying in an airplane or receiving dental treatment (Carruthers, 1983). Using one of these devices, researchers have shown that paramedics' blood

(a)

(b)   (c)

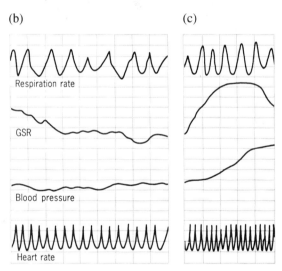

Figure 3–2 A typical polygraph (a) makes a graphical record of several indexes of arousal, including blood pressure, heart rate, respiration rate, and the galvanic skin response (the GSR measures skin conductance, which is affected by sweating). A comparison of the two graphs depicts the difference in arousal between someone who is calm (b) and someone who is under stress (c).

pressure is higher during ambulance runs and at the hospital than during other work situations or at home (Goldstein, Jamner, & Shapiro, 1992).

Another way to measure arousal is to do biochemical analyses of blood, urine, or saliva samples to assess the level of hormones that the adrenal glands secrete profusely during stress (Kirschbaum & Hellhammer, 1999; van Eck & Nicolson, 1994). Using this approach, researchers can test for two classes of hormones: **corticosteroids,** the most important of which is cortisol, and **catecholamines,** which include epinephrine and norepinephrine. A chemist does the analysis using special procedures and equipment.

There are several advantages to using measures of physiological arousal to assess stress (Baum, Grunberg, & Singer, 1982; Cacioppo, Petty, & Marshall-Goodell, 1985). Physiological measures are reasonably direct and objective, quite reliable, and easily quantified. But there are disadvantages as well. Assessing physiological arousal can be expensive, and the measurement technique may itself be stressful for some people, as may occur when blood is drawn or when electrical devices are attached to the body. Lastly, measures of physiological arousal are affected by the person's gender, body weight, activity prior to or during measurement, and consumption of various substances, such as caffeine. (Go to ♞.)

LIFE EVENTS

If you wanted to know whether people were feeling stress, you might simply ask them. Using a self-report method is easy to do. But in doing research, you would probably want to get a more precise answer than, "Yes, I am," or even, "Yes, I'm under a lot of stress." For this reason, a number of different scales have been developed to measure people's stress and assign it a numerical value.

The Social Readjustment Rating Scale

One approach many scales have used is to develop a list of **life events**—major happenings that can occur in a person's life that require some degree of psychological adjustment. The scale assigns each event a value that reflects its stressfulness. The most widely used scale of life events has been the *Social Readjustment Rating Scale* (SRRS) developed by Thomas Holmes and Richard Rahe (1967). To develop this scale, these researchers constructed a list of events they derived from clinical experience. Then they had hundreds of men and women of various ages and backgrounds rate the amount of adjustment each event would require, using the following instructions:

FOCUS ON RESEARCH

Stress and Measures of Physiological Arousal

Marianne Frankenhaeuser and her colleagues have conducted many studies of stress, using measures of physiological arousal. In one of their experiments, they studied male and female engineering students' reactions to stress (Collins & Frankenhaeuser, 1978). Each student was tested individually in an experimental (stress) and a control session—each of which lasted 100 minutes and occurred in the morning, a few days apart. The researchers had previously asked the subjects not to smoke or consume any drugs, coffee, or alcohol prior to participating. At the beginning of each session, the subjects gave a urine sample and then ate a light breakfast the researchers provided.

In the control condition, the subjects relaxed, read magazines and newspapers, and listened to the radio for an hour or so. In the stress condition, the subjects spent about an hour engaged in a difficult and increasingly stressful cognitive–perceptual task. Heart rate was measured for all subjects continuously during each session, and the subjects gave another urine sample at the end. The urine samples were later analyzed for catecholamine (epinephrine and norepinephrine) and corticosteroid (cortisol) concentrations per unit of body weight. The results revealed that heart rate and epinephrine levels increased in both males and females during stress, but other physiological reactions depended on the gender of the subjects.

The outcomes of this and many other studies have led Frankenhaeuser to propose that the pattern of physiological arousal under stress depends on two factors: effort and distress. *Effort* involves the person's interest, striving, and determination, and *distress* involves anxiety, uncertainty, boredom, and dissatisfaction. She has described that:

> *Effort with distress* tends to be accompanied by an increase of both catecholamine *and* cortisol excretion. This is the state typical of daily hassles. . . .In working life, it commonly occurs among people engaged in repetitive, machine-paced jobs on the assembly line or in highly routinized work as, for example, at a computer terminal.
>
> *Effort without distress* is a joyous state, characterized by active and successful coping, high job involvement, and a high degree of personal control. It is accompanied by increased catecholamine secretion, whereas cortisol secretion may be suppressed.
>
> *Distress without effort* implies feeling helpless, losing control, giving up. It is generally accompanied by increased cortisol secretion, but catecholamines may be elevated, too. This is the endocrine profile typical of depressed patients. (1986, p. 107)

Clearly, psychosocial processes play an important role in physiological reactions to stress.

Research on physiological reactions to stress has shown that it is important to measure more than one index of arousal and to examine psychological and social factors, too.

Use all of your experience in arriving at your answer. This means personal experience where it applies as well as what you have learned to be the case for others. Some persons accommodate to change more readily than others; some persons adjust with particular ease or difficulty to only certain events. Therefore, strive to give your opinion of the average degree of readjustment necessary for each event rather than the extreme. (p. 213)

The researchers used these ratings to assign values to each event and construct the scale shown in Table 3.1.

As you can see, the values for the life events in the SRRS range from 100 points for death of a spouse to 11 points for minor violations of the law. To measure the amount of stress people have experienced, respondents are given a survey form listing these life events and asked to check off the ones that happened to them during a given period of time, usually not more than the past 24 months. The researcher sums the values of the checked items to get a total stress score.

How commonly do life events like those in the SRRS occur? A study of nearly 2,800 adults

Table 3.1 *Social Readjustment Rating Scale*

Rank	Life Event	Mean Value
1	Death of spouse	100
2	Divorce	73
3	Marital separation	65
4	Jail term	63
5	Death of close family member	63
6	Personal injury or illness	53
7	Marriage	50
8	Fired at work	47
9	Marital reconciliation	45
10	Retirement	45
11	Change in health of family member	44
12	Pregnancy	40
13	Sex difficulties	39
14	Gain of new family member	39
15	Business readjustment	39
16	Change in financial state	38
17	Death of close friend	37
18	Change to different line of work	36
19	Change in number of arguments with spouse	35
20	Mortgage over $10,000	31
21	Foreclosure of mortgage or loan	30
22	Change in responsibilities at work	29
23	Son or daughter leaving home	29
24	Trouble with in-laws	29
25	Outstanding personal achievement	28
26	Wife begin or stop work	26
27	Begin or end school	26
28	Change in living conditions	25
29	Revision of personal habits	24
30	Trouble with boss	23
31	Change in work hours or conditions	20
32	Change in residence	20
33	Change in schools	20
34	Change in recreation	19
35	Change in church activities	19
36	Change in social activities	18
37	Mortgage or loan less than $10,000	17
38	Change in sleeping habits	16
39	Change in number of family get-togethers	15
40	Change in eating habits	15
41	Vacation	13
42	Christmas	12
43	Minor violations of the law	11

Source: From Holmes & Rahe (1967, Table 3).

used a modified version of the SRRS and found that 15% of the subjects reported having experienced none of the events during the prior year, and 18% reported five or more (Goldberg & Comstock, 1980). The three most frequent events reported were "took a vacation" (43%), "death of a loved one or other important person" (22%), and "illness or injury" (21%). The number of life events the subjects the reported *decreased* with age from early adulthood to old age and *increased* with the number of years of schooling. Single, separated, and divorced people reported larger numbers of events than did married and widowed individuals.

Strengths and Weaknesses of the SRRS

When you examined the list of life events included in the SRRS, you probably noticed that many of the events were ones we have already discussed as stressors, such as the death of a spouse, divorce, pregnancy, and occupational problems. One of the strengths of the SRRS is that the items it includes represent a fairly wide range of events that most people do, in fact, find stressful. Also, the values assigned to the events were carefully determined from the ratings of a broad sample of adults. These values provide an estimate of the relative impact of the events, distinguishing fairly well between such stressors as "death of a close family member" and "death of a close friend." Another strength of the SRRS is that the survey form can be filled out easily and quickly.

One of the main uses of the SRRS has been to relate stress and illness. Many studies have addressed this issue by using retrospective approaches—for example, by asking subjects to recall events and illnesses they experienced over the past year. Other studies have combined retrospective and prospective methods—for instance, by having subjects report recent life events and then checking their medical records over the next months. Studies using these approaches have generally found that people's illness and accident rates tend to increase following increases in stress (Holmes & Masuda, 1974; Johnson, 1986; Rahe, 1974, 1987; Rahe & Arthur, 1978). But the correlation between subjects' scores on the SRRS and illness is only about .30—which means that the relationship is not very strong (Dohrenwend & Dohrenwend, 1981). One reason that the relationship is not stronger is that people get sick and have accidents for many reasons other than stress. But another factor is that the SRRS has several weaknesses.

Some researchers have criticized items in the SRRS as being vague or ambiguous (Hough, Fairbank, & Garcia, 1976). For example, "change in responsibilities at work" fails to indicate how much change and whether it involves more or less responsibility. As a result, someone whose responsibility has decreased a little gets the same score as someone whose responsibility has increased sharply. Similarly, "personal injury or illness" does not indicate the seriousness of the illness—someone who had the flu gets the same score as someone who became paralyzed. Vague or ambiguous items reduce the precision of an instrument and the correlation it is likely to have with other variables (Anastasi, 1982).

Another criticism is that the scale does not consider the meaning or impact of an event for the individual (Cohen, Kamarck, & Mermelstein, 1983; Lazarus & Folkman, 1984b). For example, two people who each had a mortgage for $50,000 would get the same score for "mortgage over $10,000" even though one of them made ten times the income of the other. Similarly, the score people get for "death of spouse" is the same regardless of their age, dependence on the spouse, and the length and happiness of the marriage. These items do not take the person's subjective appraisal into account, and this may also reduce the precision of the instrument.

One other problem with the SRRS is that it does not distinguish between desirable and undesirable events. Most people view some events, such as "marriage" or "outstanding personal achievement," as desirable; but "sex difficulties" and "jail term" are undesirable. Other items could be either desirable or undesirable, for example, "change in financial state"; the score people get is the same regardless of whether their finances improved or worsened. This is important because studies have found that undesirable life events are correlated with illness, but desirable events are not (McFarlane, Norman, Streiner, & Roy, 1983; Sarason, Sarason, Potter, & Antoni, 1985).

Given the weaknesses of the SRRS, the correlations between its scores and illness may be considered all the more impressive. Because the overall approach it uses to measure stress is clearly useful, researchers have constructed other life event scales in an effort to develop more precise instruments.

Other Life Events Scales

Among the several life events scales that have attempted to improve on the method of the SRRS are the following:

1. The *Life Experiences Survey* (LES) contains 57 items that are stated relatively precisely, for exam-

ple, "major change in financial status (a lot better off or a lot worse off)." Subjects rate each event on a 7-point scale, ranging from extremely negative (-3) to extremely positive ($+3$). The items perceived as positive or as negative can be examined separately or combined for a total change score (Sarason, Johnson, & Siegel, 1978).

2. The PERI *Life-Events Scale* contains 102 items that describe events involving either a gain, a loss, or an ambiguous outcome. The items are stated clearly and organized into 11 topic areas, including work, finances, family, and health. For example, an item dealing with work is, "took on a greatly increased workload." Like the SRRS, each item has an assigned value, and the subject simply indicates which events occurred within a given time period (Dohrenwend, Krasnoff, Askenasy, & Dohrenwend, 1978).

3. The *Unpleasant Events Schedule* (UES) contains 320 items and takes an hour to complete (although a shorter, 53-item form is also available). The items are divided into a number of categories, such as sexual/marital/friendship and achievement/academic/job, and stated relatively precisely, for example, "being fired or laid off from work." The subjects rate each item on a 3-point scale twice, first for frequency and then for aversiveness. These two ratings are multiplied, and a total score is summed for the entire schedule (Lewinsohn, Mermelstein, Alexander, & MacPhillamy, 1985).

New scales such as these are being used extensively in research today. Through this research, we should be able to determine which scales are most useful as measures of stress.

The instruments we have discussed so far have been designed to measure stress mainly in adults. Other scales have been developed to measure stress in children and adolescents. The most widely used scale for children is the *Life Events Record*, which is very similar to the SRRS in its format and scoring (Coddington, 1972a, 1972b). The items are relevant to children, such as "divorce of parents" and "change to a different school," and are assigned separate values for children of different age groups. When children are not old enough to respond to the items themselves, their parents complete the scale for them. Because the Life Events Record has many of the same problems as the SRRS, other instruments for children have been developed (Johnson, 1986).

DAILY HASSLES

Not all of the stress we experience comes from major life events. Lesser events can also be stressful, as when we give a speech, misplace our keys during a busy day, or have our quiet disrupted by a loud party next door. These are called **daily hassles.** Some people experience more daily hassles than others do.

Richard Lazarus and his associates developed a scale to measure people's experiences with day-to-day unpleasant or potentially harmful events (Kanner, Coyne, Schaefer, & Lazarus, 1981). This instrument—called the *Hassles Scale*—lists 117 of these events that range from minor annoyances, such as "silly practical mistakes," to major problems or difficulties, such as "not enough money for food." Respondents indicate which hassles occurred in the past month and rate each event as "somewhat," "moderately," or "extremely" severe. These researchers tested 100 middle-aged adults monthly over a 9-month period. The half-dozen most frequent hassles reported were "concerns about weight," "health of a family member," "rising prices of common goods," "home maintenance," "too many things to do," and "misplacing or losing things."

© 1988 King Features Syndicate, Inc. World rights reserved   10-16

"I JUST READ THAT A CERTAIN AMOUNT OF STRESS IS GOOD FOR YOU."

Reprinted courtesy of Bunny Hoest.

Because the researchers felt that having *desirable* experiences may make hassles more bearable and reduce their impact on health, they also developed the *Uplifts Scale,* which lists 135 events that bring peace, satisfaction, or joy. The respondents who filled out the Hassles Scale completed this scale, too. Some of the most frequently occurring uplifts were "relating well to your spouse or lover," "completing a task," and "feeling healthy."

Are hassles and uplifts related to health? Studies have examined this issue. One study tested middle-aged adults, using four instruments: (1) the Hassles Scale; (2) the Uplifts Scale; (3) a life events scale that includes no desirable items; and (4) the Health Status Questionnaire, which contains questions regarding a wide variety of bodily symptoms and overall health (DeLongis et al., 1982). Hassles scores and life events scores were associated with health status—both correlations were weak, but hassles were more strongly associated with health than life events were. Uplifts scores had virtually no association with health status. Other studies generally support these findings regarding the relationship of hassles and uplifts to health (Gortmaker, Eckenrode, & Gore, 1982; Holahan, Holahan, & Belk, 1984; Weinberger, Hiner, & Tierney, 1987; Zarski, 1984).

In general, most available measures of stress either have shortcomings or have not been sufficiently tested to know how accurate they are. Researchers have found that self-report measures of life events may be unreliable: A study had subjects fill out a scale regarding life events they experienced during the prior year and then fill out the same scale each month during the next year. The extent to which their later reports agreed with the first measurement declined sharply over time (Raphael, Cloitre, & Dohrenwend, 1991). Stress is a difficult concept to define, and it is even more difficult to measure. Still, judging from the evidence that exists, stress seems to have a consistent but moderate relationship to health. Stress is one of many factors that contribute to the development of illness. (Go to 🍎.)

CAN STRESS BE GOOD FOR YOU?

Another reason why measures of stress do not correlate very highly with illness may be that not all stress is unhealthy. Is it possible that some types or amounts

ASSESS YOURSELF
Hassles in Your Life

Table 3A.1 gives a list of common events you may sometimes find unpleasant because they make you irritated, frustrated, or anxious. The list was taken from the Hassles Assessment Scale for Students in College, which has respondents rate the *frequency* and *unpleasantness* of and *dwelling* on each event.

For this exercise, rate only the *frequency* of each event. Beside each item estimate how often it oc-

curred during the past month, using the scale:

0 = never, **1** = rarely, **2** = occasionally, **3** = often, **4** = very often, **5** = extremely often. Then add all of the ratings for a total score. You can evaluate your relative hassles with the following schedule: compared to the stress other college students have from hassles, a total score of 105 is about average, 135 indicates much more stress, and 75 indicates much less stress.

Table 3A.1   *Hassles Assessment Scale for Students in College* (HASS/Col)

_____ Annoying social behavior of others (e.g., rude, inconsiderate, sexist/racist)

_____ Annoying behavior of self (e.g., habits, temper)

_____ Appearance of self (e.g., noticing unattractive features, grooming)

_____ Accidents/clumsiness/mistakes of self (e.g., spilling beverage, tripping)

_____ Athletic activities of self (e.g., aspects of own performance, time demands)

_____ Bills/overspending: seeing evidence of

_____ Boredom (e.g., nothing to do, current activity uninteresting)

_____ Car problems (e.g., breaking down, repairs)

_____ Crowds/large social groups (e.g., at parties, while shopping)

_____ Dating (e.g., noticing lack of, uninteresting partner)

_____ Environment (e.g., noticing physical living or working conditions)

_____ Extracurricular groups (e.g., activities, responsibilities)

_____ Exams (e.g., preparing for, taking)

_____ Exercising (e.g., unpleasant routines, time to do)

_____ Facilities/resources unavailable (e.g., library materials, computers)

_____ Family: obligations or activities

_____ Family: relationship issues, annoyances

_____ Fears of physical safety (e.g., while walking alone, being on a plane or in a car)

_____ Fitness: noticing inadequate physical condition

_____ Food (e.g., unappealing or unhealthful meals)

_____ Forgetting to do things (e.g., to tape TV show, send cards, do homework)

_____ Friends/peers: relationship issues, annoyances

_____ Future plans (e.g., career or marital decisions)

_____ Getting up early (e.g., for class or work)

_____ Girl/boy-friend: relationship issues, annoyances

_____ Goals/tasks: not completing enough

_____ Grades (e.g., getting a low grade)

_____ Health/physical symptoms of self (e.g., flu, PMS, allergies, headaches)

_____ Schoolwork (e.g., working on term papers, reading tedious/hard material, low motivation)

_____ Housing: finding/getting or moving

_____ Injustice: seeing examples or being a victim of

_____ Job: searching for or interviews

_____ Job/work issues (e.g., demands or annoying aspects of)

_____ Lateness of self (e.g., for appointment or class)

_____ Losing or misplacing things (e.g., keys, books)

_____ Medical/dental treatment (e.g., unpleasant, time demands)

_____ Money: noticing lack of

_____ New experiences or challenges: engaging in

_____ Noise of other people or animals

_____ Oral presentations/public speaking

_____ Parking problems (e.g., on campus, at work, at home)

_____ Privacy: noticing lack of

_____ Professors/coaches (e.g., unfairness, demands of, unavailability)

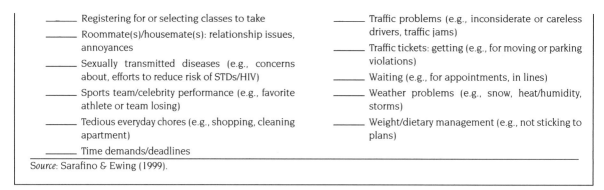

_____ Registering for or selecting classes to take	_____ Traffic problems (e.g., inconsiderate or careless drivers, traffic jams)
_____ Roommate(s)/housemate(s): relationship issues, annoyances	_____ Traffic tickets: getting (e.g., for moving or parking violations)
_____ Sexually transmitted diseases (e.g., concerns about, efforts to reduce risk of STDs/HIV)	_____ Waiting (e.g., for appointments, in lines)
_____ Sports team/celebrity performance (e.g., favorite athlete or team losing)	_____ Weather problems (e.g., snow, heat/humidity, storms)
_____ Tedious everyday chores (e.g., shopping, cleaning apartment)	_____ Weight/dietary management (e.g., not sticking to plans)
_____ Time demands/deadlines	

Source: Sarafino & Ewing (1999).

of stress are neutral or, perhaps, _good_ for you? There is reason to believe that this is the case (McGuigan, 1999).

How much stress may be good for people? Some theories of motivation and arousal propose that people function best, and feel best, at what is, _for them_, an optimal level of arousal (Fiske & Maddi, 1961; Hebb, 1955). People differ in the amount of arousal that is optimal, but too much or too little arousal impairs their functioning. Figure 3–3 gives an illustration of how stress, as a form of arousal, relates to the quality of functioning. Let's consider an example of how dif-

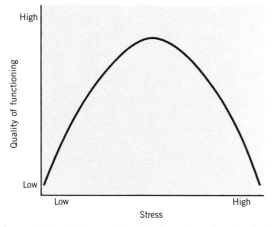

Figure 3–3 Quality of functioning at varying levels of stress. Functioning is poor at very low and very high levels of stress, but is best at some moderate, "optimal" level. (Based on material in Hebb, 1955.)

ferent levels of stress affect functioning. Imagine that you are in class one day and your instructor passes around a surprise test. If the test would not be collected or count toward your final grade, you might be underaroused and answer the questions carelessly or not at all. But if it were to count as 10% of your grade, you might be under enough stress to perform well. And if it counted a lot, you might be overwhelmed by the stress and do poorly.

Are some types of stress better than others for people? Three prominent researchers on stress have taken very similar positions on this question, claiming that there are at least two kinds of stress that differ in their impact. Selye (1974, 1985), for instance, claimed one kind of stress is harmful and damaging, and is called _distress;_ another kind is beneficial or constructive, and is called _eustress_ (from the Greek _eu_, which means "good"). Similarly, as we saw earlier, Frankenhaeuser (1986) has described two components of stress: _distress_ and _effort_. Distress with or without effort is probably more damaging than effort without distress. And Lazarus has described three types of stress appraisals—_harm-loss, threat,_ and _challenge_—and noted:

> Challenged persons are more likely to have better morale, because to be challenged means feeling positive about demanding encounters, as reflected in the pleasurable emotions accompanying challenge. The quality of functioning is apt to be better in challenge because the person feels more confident, less emotionally overwhelmed, and more capable of drawing on available resources than the person who is inhibited or blocked. Finally, it

is possible that the physiological stress response to challenge is different from that of threat, so that diseases of adaptation are less likely to occur. (Lazarus & Folkman, 1984b, p. 34)

There is a commonality to these three positions: to state it in its simplest form, there is good stress and bad stress—bad stress generally involves a strong negative emotional component. Cognitive appraisal processes play an important role in determining which kind of stress we experience.

Finally, in discussing whether stress is harmful, one other point should be made: individuals seem to differ in their susceptibility to the effects of stress. John Mason (1975) has proposed that these differences are like those that people show to the effects of viruses and bacteria. That is, not all people who are exposed to a disease-causing antigen, such as a flu virus, develop the illness—some individuals are more susceptible than others. Susceptibility to the effects of antigens and to stress varies from one person to the next and within the same individual across time. These differences result from biological variations within and between individuals, and from psychosocial variations, as we will see in the next chapter.

SUMMARY

Researchers have conceptualized stress in three ways. In one approach, stress is seen as a stimulus, and studies focus on the impact of stressors. Another approach treats stress as a response and examines the physical and psychological strains that stressors produce. The third approach proposes that stress is a process that involves continuous interactions and adjustments—or transactions—between the person and the environment. These three views lead to a definition of stress: the condition that results when person–environment transactions lead to a perceived discrepancy between the demands of a situation and the resources of the person's biological, psychological, and social systems.

Transactions that lead to the condition of stress generally involve a process of cognitive appraisal, which takes two forms. One type of appraisal, called primary appraisal, focuses on whether a demand threatens the person's well-being. It produces one of three judgments: the demand is irrelevant, it is good, or it is stressful. A stressful appraisal receives further assessment for the amount of harm or loss, the threat of future harm, and the degree of challenge the demand presents. The other type of appraisal, called secondary appraisal, assesses the resources available for meeting the demand. When primary and secondary appraisals indicate that the fit between demands and resources is close, we may experience little stress. But when we appraise a discrepancy—especially if the demands seem greater than our resources—we may feel a substantial amount of stress.

Whether people appraise events as stressful depends on factors that relate to the person and to the situation. Factors of the person include intellectual, motivational, and personality characteristics, such as the person's self-esteem and belief system. With regard to situational factors, events tend to be appraised as stressful if they involve strong demands, are imminent, are undesirable and uncontrollable, involve major life transitions, or occur at an unexpected time in the life span.

Stressors produce strain in the person's biological, psychological, and social systems. Emergency situations evoke a physiological fight-or-flight reaction, by which the organism prepares to attack the threat or flee. When stress is strong and prolonged, the physiological reaction goes through three stages: the alarm reaction, the stage of resistance, and the stage of exhaustion. This series of reactions is called the general adaptation syndrome. According to Selye, continuous high levels of stress can make the person vulnerable to diseases of adaptation, including ulcers and high blood pressure. Psychosocial factors influence reactivity, the physiological reaction to stressors.

Stress is linked to psychosocial processes. It can impair momentary cognitive functioning and may lead to cognitive deficits in children. Various emotions can accompany stress—these emotions include fear, anxiety, depression, and anger. When stress is accompanied by anger, aggressive behavior tends to increase and remain at a relatively high level even after the stressful experience is over. Stress also reduces people's helping behavior. Although the sources of stress may change as people develop, the condition of stress can occur at any time in the life span. Sometimes stress arises from within the person, such as when the person is ill or experiences conflict. Other sources of stress include the family, such as if one of its members is seriously ill or dies and if there is a new baby who has a difficult temperament, as well as the community and society—for example, from problems related to people's jobs or environmental hazards.

Researchers measure stress in three ways. One way involves assessing physiological arousal. Blood pressure, heart rate, respiration rate, and galvanic skin response can be measured with an apparatus called the polygraph. Biochemical analyses of blood or urine samples can test for corticosteroids (for example, cortisol) and catecholamines (for example, epinephrine and norepinephrine). Another method of measuring stress uses a survey of people's life events, such as the Social Readjustment Rating Scale and newer instruments. The third method for measuring stress involves assessing the daily hassles people experience. Although stress can contribute to the development of illness, many psychologists believe that not all stress is harmful.

KEY TERMS

stressors	primary appraisal	alarm reaction	polygraph
strain	secondary appraisal	stage of resistance	corticosteroids
transactions	reactivity	stage of exhaustion	catecholamines
stress	general adaptation	temperaments	life events
cognitive appraisal	syndrome	meta-analysis	daily hassles

4

STRESS, BIOPSYCHOSOCIAL FACTORS, AND ILLNESS

Psychosocial Modifiers of Stress
Social Support
A Sense of Personal Control
A Hardy Personality
Type A and Type B Behavior Patterns

How Stress Affects Health
Stress, Behavior, and Illness
Stress, Physiology, and Illness
Psychoneuroimmunology

Psychophysiological Disorders
Digestive System Diseases
Asthma
Recurrent Headache
Other Disorders

Stress and Cardiovascular Disorders
Hypertension
Coronary Heart Disease

Stress and Cancer

PROLOGUE

They were best friends, Joan and Sally, on their way to an art museum a year ago when a car accident ended their lives. Their husbands, Bob and Walt, were devastated, not only by their individual losses but also for each other's. These men were also friends—both worked as engineers for the same company and shared hobbies and other interests. The four of them used to double date often, leaving the kids with one babysitter. How did the terrible loss of their wives affect these men?

The initial impact of their loss was similar, but the amounts of stress that followed were different. Bob's stress was not as severe as Walt's. One thing that helped Bob was that he had an extended family that lived nearby. They provided consolation for his grief, a place to go to get out of the house and to socialize, and help in caring for his children. After school, the kids would go to either Bob's or Joan's parents' house, and Bob would pick them up on his way home from work. Sometimes he and the children would stay there for dinner. This helped save him time and money—both of which were in short supply. How was Bob doing a year later? He had made a good adjustment, had a good relationship with his children, was starting to date, and was in good health.

Walt was not so fortunate. For one thing, he had no nearby family to rely on. Compared to Bob, Walt had little emotional support in his grief, and being a single parent made his workload and financial situation very difficult. Walt had little time or money for socializing, and virtually all of his adult contacts were at work. Although he and Bob often had lunch together, their interests were drifting apart. Unlike Bob, Walt had never been very outgoing, and he felt awkward and insecure in meeting women. A year after Sally died, he was isolated and lonely. His relationship with his children was deteriorating, and so was his health. He had developed migraine headaches, neck problems, and high blood pressure. The stress in Walt's life was taking its toll.

This chapter examines the effects of stress on health. We begin by looking at psychosocial factors that can modify the stress people experience. Then we consider how stress affects health and the development of specific illnesses. And in this chapter we address many questions about stress and illness that are of great concern today. Why can some people experience one traumatic event after another without ill effects, but others cannot? Are hard-driving people more likely to have a heart attack than people who are easygoing? Can people actually "die of a broken heart"? Can stress retard people's recovery from illness?

PSYCHOSOCIAL MODIFIERS OF STRESS

People's reactions to stress vary from one person to the next and from time to time for the same person. These variations often result from psychological and social factors that seem to *modify* the impact of stressors on the individual. Let's look at some of these modifiers, beginning with the role of social support.

SOCIAL SUPPORT

We saw in the bereavement experiences of Bob and Walt how important social ties and relationships can be during troubled times. The social support Bob got from his family tempered the impact of his stressful loss and probably helped him adjust. **Social support** refers to the perceived comfort, caring, esteem, or help a person receives from other people or groups (Cobb, 1976; Gentry & Kobasa, 1984; Wallston, Alagna, DeVellis, & DeVellis, 1983; Wills, 1984). This support can come from many different sources—the person's spouse or lover, family, friends, coworkers, physician, or community organizations. According to researcher Sidney Cobb (1976), people with social support believe they are loved and cared for, esteemed and valued, and part of a social network, such as a family or community organization, that can provide goods, services, and mutual defense in times of need or danger.

Types of Social Support

What specifically does social support provide to the person? To answer this question, researchers have tried to classify various types of support (Cohen & McKay, 1984; Cutrona & Russell, 1990; House, 1984; Schaefer, Coyne, & Lazarus, 1981; Wills, 1984). These classifications suggest that there are five basic types of social support:

1. *Emotional support* involves the expression of empathy, caring, and concern toward the person. It provides the person with a sense of comfort, reassurance, belongingness, and being loved in times of stress. We saw earlier how Bob's family gave him emotional support after the death of his wife.

2. *Esteem support* occurs through people's expression of positive regard for the person, encouragement or agreement with the individual's ideas or feelings, and positive comparison of the person with others, such as people who are less able or worse off. This kind of support serves to build the individual's feeling of self-worth, competence, and being valued. Esteem support is especially useful during the appraisal of stress, such as when the person assesses whether the demands exceed his or her personal resources.

3. *Tangible or instrumental support* involves direct assistance, as when people give or lend the person money or help out with chores in times of stress. Bob's family helped with childcare, for example, which reduced the demands on his time and finances.

4. *Informational support* includes giving advice, directions, suggestions, or feedback about how the person is doing. For example, a person who is ill might get information from family or a physician on how to treat the illness. Or someone who is faced with a very difficult decision on the job might receive suggestions or feedback about his or her ideas from coworkers.

A patient receiving informational support from her physician.

5. *Network support* provides a feeling of membership in a group of people who share interests and social activities.

The type of support a person receives and needs depends on the stressful circumstances (Wortman & Dunkel-Schetter, 1987). For instance, Figure 4–1 shows that cancer patients find emotional and esteem support to be especially helpful, but patients with less serious chronic illnesses find the different types of support equally helpful (Martin et al., 1994).

What type of support do people generally get? Carolyn Cutrona (1986) studied this issue by having college students fill out a questionnaire, rating the degree to which their current relationships provided them with different types of support, and then keep a daily record of their stress and social experiences for 2 weeks. The daily records revealed that most of

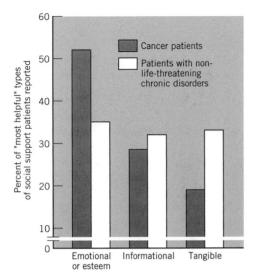

Figure 4–1 Percentage of patients with cancer and with non-life-threatening disorders (chronic headache or irritable bowel syndrome) whose reports of the "most helpful" social support they received described the emotional/esteem, instrumental, or tangible types of support. Notice that the cancer patients found emotional or esteem support especially helpful. (Data from Martin et al., 1994, Figure 1.)

the stressors were relatively minor, such as having car trouble or an argument with a roommate, but one-fifth of the students reported a severe event, such as a parent's diagnosis of cancer or the ending of a long-term romantic relationship. As you might expect, the subjects received more social support following stressful events than at less stressful times, and those who initially perceived themselves as having high levels of social support reported receiving more support during the 2 weeks. Tangible support occurred very infrequently, but emotional, informational, and esteem support occurred often. Students who received more frequent esteem support tended to report less depression following stressful experiences, suggesting that esteem may protect people from negative emotional consequences of stress.

Who Gets Social Support?

Not everyone gets the social support they need. Many factors determine whether people receive support (Broadhead et al., 1983; Connell & D'Augelli, 1990; Wortman & Dunkel-Schetter, 1987). Some factors

relate to the potential *recipients* of support. People are unlikely to receive support if they are unsociable, don't help others, and don't let others know that they need help. Some people are not assertive enough to ask for help, or feel that they should be independent or not burden others, or feel uncomfortable confiding in others, or don't know whom to ask. Other factors relate to the potential *providers* of support. For instance, they may not have the resources needed, or may be under stress and in need of help themselves, or may simply be insensitive to the needs of others.

Whether people receive social support also depends on the composition and structure of their **social network**—that is, the linkages they have with people in their family and community (Mitchell, 1969; Schaefer, Coyne, & Lazarus, 1981). The linkages we have vary in *size*—the number of people with whom we have regular contact; *frequency of contact*—how often we see these people; *composition*—whether these people are family, friends, coworkers, and so on; and *intimacy*—the closeness of individual relationships and mutual willingness to confide in each other.

People's need for, sources of, and ability to provide social support change throughout the life span (Antonucci, 1985; Broadhead et al., 1983; Bruhn & Phillips, 1987; Sarafino & Armstrong, 1986). For example, most young children readily ask for and receive help from older people, but their immature cognitive and social skills hamper their ability to recognize other people's needs easily and provide effective help themselves. As children's social contacts expand outside the family, their peers become an increasingly important source of both stress and social support, particularly during the adolescent years. Although teenagers generally have strong cognitive and social skills and can provide very effective support, many are reluctant to ask for help or confide in others. Adulthood is a time for taking on increasing levels of responsibility in a family, on the job, and in the community. The intimacy and caring that usually characterize adult loving relationships, such as in marriage, give adults the opportunity for a continuous source of support. Old age is a time when social support sometimes declines. Although people's social networks do not get smaller in old age, the elderly exchange less support, perhaps because of the loss of a spouse or because they may feel reluctant to ask for help if they become unable to reciprocate.

How can we assess people's social support, given the different types of support and the complex

Assess Yourself

How Much Emotional Support Do You Get?

Think of the ten people to whom you feel closest. For some of them, you may not feel a strong bond—but they are still among the closest ten people in your life. Write their initials in the following spaces:

— — — — — — — — — —

In the *corresponding* spaces below each of the following four questions, rate each person on a 5-point scale, where **1** = "not at all" and **5** = "extremely."

• How reliable is this person; is this person there when you need him or her?

— — — — — — — — — —

• How much does this person boost your spirits when you feel low?

— — — — — — — — — —

• How much does this person make you feel he or she cares about you?

— — — — — — — — — —

• How much do feel you can confide in this person?

— — — — — — — — — —

Add together all of the ratings you gave across all of the people and questions. A total score between 120 and 150 is fairly typical and suggests that you can get a reasonably good level of emotional support when you need it. (*Source:* Based on material in Schaefer, Coyne, and Lazarus, 1981.)

relationships that are involved? Questionnaires have been developed, but none provides a strong measure of all aspects of social support (Heitzmann & Kaplan, 1988; Wortman & Dunkel-Schetter, 1987). One of the more highly regarded instruments is the *Social Support Questionnaire*, which consists of 27 items, such as, "Who helps you feel that you truly have something positive to contribute to others?" (Sarason et al., 1983). For each item, the respondents list the people they can rely on and then indicate their overall degree of satisfaction with the support available. Using this instrument, these researchers have found that some people report high levels of satisfaction with support from a small number of close friends and relatives, but others seem to need a large social network. (Go to .)

Gender and Sociocultural Differences in Receiving Support

The amount of social support individuals receive appears to depend on their gender and sociocultural group membership. Some evidence suggests that women receive less support from their spouses than men do and seem to rely heavily on women friends for social support (Greenglass & Noguchi, 1996). These gender differences may result from the greater intimacy that seems to exist in the friendships of females

than males and may reflect mainly differences in the emotional and esteem support males and females seek out and give (Heller, Price, & Hogg, 1990). Research on social networks in the United States has revealed interesting gender and sociocultural relationships (Gottlieb & Green, 1987): Black Americans have smaller social networks than whites and Hispanics, and men's networks are larger than women's among black and Hispanic groups but not among nonminority people. Hispanics tend to focus mainly on extended families as their networks, whites have broader networks of friends and coworkers, and blacks focus on family and church groups.

Social Support, Stress, and Health

A fortune cookie I received said, "Friendship is to people what sunshine is to flowers." What benefits do we get from the social support of friends, relatives, and other people? To answer this question, we will look at how social support relates to stress and health.

Research findings suggest that social support may reduce the stress people experience. One study examined the relationship between job stress and social support in over 2,000 men in a variety of white- and blue-collar occupations (LaRocco, House, & French, 1980). The data revealed that the greater the social support available to the employees, the lower the psychological strain they reported. Although lower job stress was linked to social support from home, it was more strongly related to the support the employees received from their supervisors and coworkers. Similar associations between social support and reduced job stress have been found in several other studies (Constable & Russell, 1986; Cottington & House, 1987). Social support has also been associated with reduced stress from a variety of other sources, such as living near the damaged nuclear power plant at Three Mile Island (Fleming, Baum, Gisriel, & Gatchel, 1982).

Experiments have assessed people's physiological strain while they were engaged in a stressful activity (giving a speech) either alone or in the presence of one or more other people. Strain was typically assessed as *cardiovascular reactivity*—that is, an increase in blood pressure and/or heart rate from a baseline level. These studies have yielded three main findings. First, while giving a speech, people show much less reactivity if a supportive person is present than if speaking alone (Lepore, Allen, & Evans, 1993; Uchino & Garvey, 1997). Second, reactivity is lower with a friend present than with a supportive stranger (Christenfeld et al., 1997). Third, reactivity in male and female speakers is lower in the presence of a supportive female than a supportive male (Glynn, Christenfeld, & Gerin, 1999). Other research findings suggest that the benefits of social support on reactivity depend on the person's gender and the type of support: when instrumental support is given, males show less reactivity than females; when emotional support is given, females show less reactivity than males (Wilson et al., 1999).

Having social support also seems to benefit people's health (Berkman, 1995). This has been shown in the death rates for people who have different amounts of social support. Lisa Berkman and S. Leonard Syme (1979) conducted a prospective study of more than 4,700 men and women between 30 and 69 years of age. The subjects reported data on four aspects of social support: marital status, contacts with family and friends, church membership, and formal and informal group associations. Mortality data collected over the next 9 years revealed that the greater the degree of social support the subjects had, the lower the likelihood of their dying during the period of the study. Figure 4–2 shows an example of these findings. In each age category, individuals who had few contacts with friends and relatives had higher mortality rates than

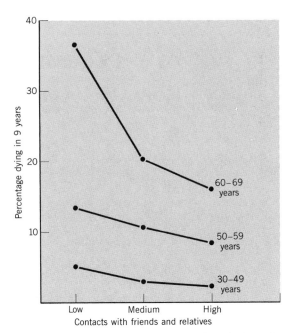

Figure 4–2 Percentage of adults who died within 9 years as a function of the number of contacts with friends and relatives and the subjects' ages at the start of the study, in 1965. (Data from Berkman & Syme, 1979, Table 2.)

those with many contacts. In addition, social support was not only associated with deaths from all causes, but also with mortality from several specific diseases, including cancer and heart disease.

The relationship between social support and mortality in these studies is correlational. How do we know whether social support leads to better health and lower mortality or whether the influence is the other way around? That is, could the people who had less social support be less active socially because they were already sick at the start of the study? Berkman and Syme provided some evidence that this was not the case. For instance, the subjects had been asked about past illnesses at the initial interview, and those with high levels of social support did not differ from those with low levels of support. But better evidence comes from a similar study of more than 2,700 adults (House, Robbins, & Metzner, 1982). The subjects in this study were medically examined at the start of the research. These researchers found essentially the same relationship between social support and mortality as Berkman and Syme did, and the initial health of the subjects with low social support was the same as that of those with high support.

Researchers have also studied the association between social support and the likelihood that people will develop illnesses and recover quickly when they do. Some early studies found an association between support and illness or recovery, but others did not (Wallston, Alagna, DeVellis, & DeVellis, 1983). These inconsistencies probably occurred because of variations in research methodology, such as in the way support was defined and measured (Friis & Taff, 1986; Wortman & Dunkel-Schetter, 1987). Newer research has produced more consistently positive results, showing, for example, that heart disease and surgery patients with high levels of social support recover more quickly than comparable patients with less support (Berkman, 1995; Fontana, Kerns, Rosenberg, & Colonese, 1989; Kulik & Mahler, 1989; Reifman, 1995). Although these findings suggest that social support reduces the likelihood of illness and speeds recovery, the connection between social support and health is not always very strong, probably because support is only one of many factors that are involved (Kobasa, Maddi, Puccetti, & Zola, 1985; Smith et al., 1994). Social support appears to have a strong impact on the health of some individuals, and a weak influence on the health of others. For instance, some evidence indicates that the recovery of many patients who believe they can cope with the emotional demands of their illness does not benefit from social support (Wilcox, Kasl, & Berkman, 1994).

How May Social Support Affect Health?

To explain how social support may influence health and well-being, researchers have proposed two theories: the "buffering" and the "direct effects" hypotheses. Studies have found evidence consistent with both theories (Cohen & Wills, 1985; Payne & Jones, 1987; Thoits, 1982; Wortman & Dunkel-Schetter, 1987). We will begin with the buffering hypothesis.

We have seen that prolonged exposure to high levels of stress can lead to illness. According to the **buffering hypothesis,** social support affects health by *protecting* the person against these negative effects of high stress. A graphical illustration of the buffering hypothesis appears in Figure 4–3*a*. As the graph shows, this protective function is effective only or mainly when the person encounters a strong stressor. Under low-stress conditions, little or no buffering occurs.

How does buffering work? There are at least two ways (Cohen & Wills, 1985). First, when people encounter a strong stressor, such as a major financial crisis, those who have high levels of social support may be less likely to appraise the situation as stressful than those with low levels of support. Individuals with high social support may expect that someone they know will help them, such as by lending money or giving advice on how to get it. As a result, they judge that they can meet the demands and decide that the situation is not very stressful (Peirce, Frone, Russell, & Cooper,

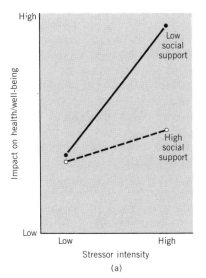
(a)

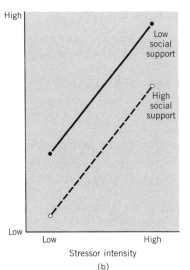
(b)

Figure 4–3 Illustration of two ways social support may benefit health and well-being. Graph (a) illustrates the buffering hypothesis, which proposes that social support modifies the negative health effects of high levels of stress. Graph (b) depicts the direct effects hypothesis, which proposes that the health benefits of social support occur irrespective of stress.

1996). Second, social support may modify people's response to a stressor after the initial appraisal. For instance, people with high social support might have someone provide a solution to the problem, convince them that the problem is not very important, or cheer them on to "look on the bright side" or "count their blessings." People with little social support are much less likely to have any of these advantages—so the negative impact of the stress is greater for them than for those with high levels of support.

The **direct effects hypothesis** maintains that social support benefits health and well-being regardless of the amount of stress people experience. According to this hypothesis, the beneficial effects of social support are similar under high and low stressor intensities, as depicted in Figure 4–3*b*. There are several ways by which direct effects may work (Cohen & Wills, 1985; Wortman & Dunkel-Schetter, 1987). For example, people with high levels of social support may have strong feelings of belongingness and self-esteem. The positive outlook this produces could be beneficial to health independently of stress experiences: studies have found lower blood pressures in daily life and in laboratory tests among middle-aged and younger adults with higher levels of social support (Carels, Blumenthal, & Sherwood, 1998; Uchino et al., 1999). Other evidence suggests that high levels of support may encourage people to lead healthful lifestyles (Broman, 1993; Peirce et al., 2000). People with social support may feel, for example, that because others care about them and need them, they should exercise, eat well, and not smoke or drink heavily.

Does Social Support Always Help?

Social support does not always reduce stress and benefit health. Why? For one thing, although support may be offered or available to us, we may not *perceive* it as supportive (Dunkel-Schetter & Bennett, 1990; Wilcox, Kasl, & Berkman, 1994). This may happen because the help is insufficient or we may not want help or are too emotionally distraught to notice it, for instance. When we do not perceive help as supportive, it is less likely to reduce our stress.

Another reason why social support does not always help is that the type of support we receive may not *match* the needs that the stressor has produced. For example, if your car broke down, your passenger's emotional consolation probably would not reduce your stress very much. Carolyn Cutrona and Daniel

Russell (1990) have outlined a pattern for matching support with need. Instrumental support is particularly valuable for stressful events that are *controllable*—that is, we can do something to achieve a goal or prevent the situation from becoming worse, such as when we feel ill. Emotional support is especially important for *uncontrollable* stressful events, such as when a loved one dies. But other types of support may also be needed—for instance, if the uncontrollable event involved losing your job, esteem and tangible support might help, too.

Marriage is often thought to convey a protective health benefit to people by providing social support. Consistent with this idea, studies have found that married people live longer than divorced and never-married individuals (Berkman & Syme, 1979; House, Robbins, & Metzner, 1982). James Lynch (1990) has argued that being lonely or having a "broken heart" is a risk factor for heart disease because widowed, divorced, and never-married individuals have higher death rates from heart disease than married people do. But newer research has found that individuals who had not married by midlife were not at greater risk of dying before 80 years of age and that differences in death rates for married and divorced people result in part from differences in their personality characteristics (Tucker, Friedman, Wingard, & Schwartz, 1996). Marriage by itself probably does not protect people's health.

Lastly, there are many circumstances in which social ties with people can harm an individual's health (Burg & Seeman, 1994; Kaplan & Toshima, 1990; Suls, 1982). One circumstance is when people set a bad example for the person, as when smoking and drinking behavior by friends and family lead an adolescent to engage in these behaviors. Friends and family can also set bad examples by *not* engaging in healthful behaviors, such as using seat belts, eating a balanced diet, or exercising. Other circumstances in which social support can be harmful arise when the person has developed a health problem. For instance, someone who is overweight and has high blood pressure may be encouraged by family to eat prohibited foods. They may say, "Doctors don't know everything," or, "A little more cheesecake can't hurt," or, "You can make up for it by dieting next week." Also, when someone suffers a long and serious illness, such as heart disease, families may be overprotective and discourage the patient's desire to become more active or to go back to work. This can interfere with a program of

CLINICAL METHODS AND ISSUES
Social Support, Therapy, and Cognitive Processes

Years ago, a reporter asked actress Melina Mercouri about psychotherapy in her native country, and she replied that in Greece people don't need therapists, they have friends. Although her view oversimplifies the therapy process, therapy does include two features friends can provide: social support and the opportunity to *express* negative experiences and feelings. James Pennebaker and other researchers have found that people's talking or writing about traumatic or very emotional experiences for a few 15–30-minute sessions has beneficial effects that last for months. It reduces their stress and negative feelings and seems

to improve their health, as reflected in the number of physician visits and episodes of chronic illness symptoms (Pennebaker, 1990, 1997; Smyth, Stone, Hurewitz, & Kaell, 1999). Other research has shown that less upsetting procedures, such as describing the benefits gained from traumatic events or the success in managing one's stress, can have similar effects (King & Miner, 2000; Leake, Friend, & Wadhwa, 1999). It may be that expressing these feelings allows people to reconceptualize and cope better with very stressful experiences.

rehabilitation and make the patient increasingly dependent and disabled.

In summary, people receive various types of support from friends, family, and others in their lives. Social support usually tends to reduce people's stress and benefit their health. (Go to 🌳.)

A SENSE OF PERSONAL CONTROL

Another psychosocial factor that modifies the stress people experience is the degree of control people feel they have in their lives. People generally like the feeling of having some measure of control over the things that happen to them, and they take individual action when they want to influence events directly. In doing these things, people strive for a sense of **personal control**—the feeling that they can make decisions and take effective action to produce desirable outcomes and avoid undesirable ones (Rodin, 1986). Studies have found that people who have a strong sense of personal control report experiencing less strain from stressors (McFarlane, Norman, Streiner, & Roy, 1983; Suls & Mullen, 1981).

Types of Control

How can feelings of personal control reduce the stress people experience? Let's see by considering the process of giving birth—a stressful event. Women who

attend natural childbirth classes learn many techniques that enhance their personal control in the birth process. They, like other people in stressful situations, can influence events in their lives and reduce the stress they experience in many ways. These ways include four types of control (Averill, 1973; Cohen, Evans, Stokols, & Krantz, 1986; Miller, 1979; Thompson, 1981):

1. **Behavioral control** involves the ability to take concrete action to reduce the impact of a stressor. This action might reduce the intensity of the event or shorten its duration. During childbirth, for example, the mother can use special breathing techniques that reduce the pain of labor.

2. **Cognitive control** is the ability to use thought processes or strategies to modify the impact of a stressor. These strategies can include thinking about the event differently or focusing on a pleasant or neutral thought or sensation. While giving birth, for instance, the mother might think about the event differently by going over in her mind the positive meanings the baby will give to her life. Or she could focus her attention on the sensation of the baby's movements or on an image, such as a pleasant day at the beach.

3. **Decisional control** is the opportunity to choose between alternative procedures or courses of action. The mother and father have many choices to

make about the birth process before it occurs. For many of these decisions, the mother usually has the final word—such as in the choice of the obstetrician, whether to use conventional or natural childbirth methods, and whether the birth will occur in a hospital, at home, or at an alternative birth center. In other medical situations, the patient may be given a choice regarding which treatment procedure to use, when the treatment will occur, and so on.

4. Informational control involves the opportunity to get knowledge about a stressful event—what will happen, why, and what the consequences are likely to be. For example, a pregnant woman may get information about the sensations she will experience during labor and delivery, the procedures she can expect to happen, and the range of time the process generally takes. Informational control can help reduce stress by increasing the person's ability to predict and be prepared for what will happen and by decreasing the fear people often have of the unknown.

Each of these types of control can reduce stress, but one of them—cognitive control—seems to have the most consistently beneficial effect (Cohen, Evans, Stokols, & Krantz, 1986; Thompson, 1981).

Beliefs About Oneself and Control

People differ in the degree to which they believe they have control over their lives. Some people believe they have a great deal of control, and others think they have almost none. The latter is shown in the case study of a chronically unemployed man named Karl, who was referred to therapy by the Veterans Administration with

> an almost total lack of social and interpersonal skills. . . . After much coaching and discussion, Karl applied for a job and got it. But this did not raise his expectancies of being able to get another job should he have to do so. Indeed, he attributed his success entirely to good fortune. He believed that the employer probably was partial to veterans or just happened to be in a good mood that day. . . . After several comparable episodes, it began to dawn upon the therapist that here was a person who believed that the occurrence of reinforcement was outside his own personal control. (Phares, 1984, pp. 505–506)

People who believe they have control over their successes and failures are described as possessing an *internal* **locus of control.** That is, the control for these events lies within themselves—they are responsible.

Other people, like Karl, who believe that their lives are controlled by forces outside themselves, for example, by luck, have an *external* locus of control (Phares, 1987; Rotter, 1966).

Certainly it is unrealistic for people to assume everything in their lives is under their control. But the degree to which they attribute responsibility to themselves, versus other forces, determines their locus of control. Julian Rotter (1966) has developed the I-E *Scale,* a test that is used for measuring the degree of internality or externality of a person's beliefs about personal control. This scale presents a series of paired items, such as: "The average citizen can have an influence in government decisions," and, "This world is run by a few people in power, and there is not much the little guy can do about it." For each pair of internal–external items, the respondent selects the one with which he or she most agrees. Most people have moderate beliefs regarding the influence they have on events in their lives. Their locus of control falls in the midrange between being highly internal or highly external.

Another important aspect of personal control is our sense of **self-efficacy**—the belief that we can succeed at a specific activity we want to do (Bandura, 1977, 1986). People estimate their chances of success in an activity, such as quitting smoking or running a mile, on the basis of their prior observations of themselves and others. They decide whether to attempt the activity according to their expectations that (1) the behavior, if properly carried out, would lead to a favorable outcome, and (2) they can perform the behavior properly. For example, you may know that by taking and doing well in a series of college honors courses you can graduate with recognition of that accomplishment, such as a special diploma or certificate. But if you estimate the likelihood of achieving that feat as "zilch," you are not likely to try. For people engaged in a stressful activity, those with strong self-efficacy for the activity show less psychological and physiological strain than do those with a weak sense of efficacy (Bandura, Reese, & Adams, 1982; Bandura et al., 1985; Holahan, Holahan, & Belk, 1984).

Determinants and Development of Personal Control

On what basis do people judge that they have control over things that happen in their lives? We make these assessments by using information we gain from our experiences throughout life (Bandura, 1986; Phares, 1987; Rodin, 1987a; Schunk & Carbonari, 1984). One of the most important information sources is our own performance—the successes and failures we perceive in the activities we attempt. Infants begin to learn about personal control as they coordinate sensory experiences with their motor activity—for example, learning that they can make a noise with a rattle by shaking it.

Throughout the life span, we assess our personal control through the process of *social learning*, in which we learn by observing the behavior of others (Bandura, 1969, 1986). During early childhood, the family is particularly important in this process, with members serving as models of behavior, agents of reinforcement, and standards for comparison. Parents who are caring, encouraging, and consistent in their standards for behavior tend to have children who develop an internal locus of control and a sense of efficacy for a variety of activities (Harter, 1983). School and other social experiences in childhood and adolescence become increasingly important factors in developing personal control. In old age, people tend to be relatively external in locus of control—that is, beliefs that chance and powerful others affect their lives are greater in the elderly than in younger adults (Lachman, 1986). So, among adults who develop serious illnesses, those who are elderly are more inclined to prefer having professionals make health-related decisions for them (Woodward & Wallston, 1987).

You may have noticed that the information people use in determining their personal control is usually retrospective, can be very complex, and is not always clear-cut. As a result, the judgments we make about our control are not always very objective or based on fact. We sometimes develop what Ellen Langer (1975) calls an *illusion of control*—a belief in our control over an event that is really determined by chance. An experiment demonstrated this illusion by finding that individuals often claim they have control in winning a game of chance if they are given the opportunity to perform part of the activity in the game, even though their actions obviously do not influence the outcome (Wortman, 1975).

Gender and Sociocultural Differences in Personal Control

Gender and sociocultural differences in personal control often develop, depending on the social expe-

riences individuals have. Sometimes parents and teachers inadvertently lead girls more than boys toward beliefs in external control and in low self-efficacy for certain activities (Dweck & Elliott, 1983). This socialization may carry over to old age: among elderly cardiac patients, men report greater self-efficacy than women for being able to walk various distances, a common rehabilitation behavior (Jenkins & Gortner, 1998). Because minority groups and poor people generally have limited access to power and economic advancement, they tend to have external locus of control beliefs (Lundin, 1987).

When People Lack Personal Control

What happens to people who experience high levels of stress over a long period of time and feel that nothing they do matters? They feel helpless—trapped and unable to avoid negative outcomes. A worker who cannot seem to please her boss no matter what she does, a student who cannot perform well on exams, or a patient who is unable to relieve his severe low back pain—each of these situations can produce apathy. As a result, these people may stop striving for these goals, come to believe they have no control over these and other events in their lives, and fail to exert control even when they could succeed. This is the condition Martin Seligman (1975) has called **learned helplessness**—which he describes as a principal characteristic of depression.

An experiment showed how people can learn to be helpless by being in uncontrollable situations that lead to repeated failure (Hiroto & Seligman, 1975). The researchers assigned college students to one of three training groups that experienced an unpleasant loud noise. In one group, the *controllable-noise* condition, the students were told that a noise would come on from time to time and "there is something you can do to stop it." They were given an opportunity to discover that pressing a button on an apparatus would stop it, which they did. The *uncontrollable-noise* group had the same instructions and apparatus, but nothing they did affected the presence of the noise. Students in a *comparison* group were simply told to sit and listen to a tone they would hear from time to time. All subjects were tested later for helplessness in a uniform way: they were told that a noise would come on and off and that "there is something you can do to stop it." The apparatus was new—it had a sliding knob that, when manipulated correctly, would stop the noise. In this test,

This homeless woman probably sees little personal control in her life and feels very helpless.

students in the uncontrollable-noise group performed much more poorly than those in the controllable-noise and comparison groups. Learning that the noise is uncontrollable with the push-button apparatus impaired the individuals' discovering how to control the noise with the knob apparatus.

Seligman and his colleagues have extended the theory of learned helplessness to explain two important observations (Abramson, Seligman, & Teasdale, 1978). First, being exposed to uncontrollable negative events does not always lead to learned helplessness. Second, depressed people often report feeling a loss in self-esteem. The theory needed to answer the question of why people would blame themselves for negative events that are beyond their control. The revised theory proposes that when people experience uncontrollable negative events, they ask themselves, "Why am I unable to affect these events, and how long will they continue?" They answer this question through the cognitive process called **attribution,** in which people try to arrive at causes or judgments regarding events, such as their own or others' actions, motives, feelings, or intentions.

How does attribution work? When uncontrollable negative events happen, people consider possible judgments and causes by assessing three dimensions of the situation:

1. *Internal–external.* People who feel trapped and unable to control negative events assess whether this situation results from their own personal inability to control outcomes or whether it is due to external causes that are beyond anyone's control. For example, suppose a boy receives physical therapy for a serious injury but cannot seem to meet the goals each week. He might attribute this failure either to his own lack of fortitude or to the rehabilitation program the physical therapist designed. Both judgments may make him stop trying. He is likely to suffer a loss of self-esteem if he attributes the difficulty to a lack of personal strength, but not if he attributes the difficulty to external causes.

2. *Stable–unstable.* Individuals who experience uncontrollable negative events assess whether the situation results from a cause that is long-lasting (stable) or temporary (unstable). If they determine that it is long-lasting, as when people develop a chronic and disabling disease, they are more likely to feel helpless and depressed than if they think their condition is temporary.

3. *Global–specific.* People in unpleasant situations that they cannot control try to assess whether these events result from factors that have global and wide-ranging effects or specific and narrow effects.

Someone who is unable to stop smoking cigarettes and arrives at a global judgment—for example, "I'm totally no good and weak-willed"—is more likely to feel helpless and depressed than a similar individual who makes a specific judgment, such as "I'm not good at controlling this part of my life."

Thus, people who tend to attribute negative events in their lives to *stable* and *global* causes are at high risk for feeling helpless and depressed. If their judgments are also *internal*, their depressive thinking is likely to include a loss of self-esteem as well. People who believe bad events result from internal, stable, and global factors while good events result from external, unstable, and specific factors have a very *pessimistic* view of life (Kamen & Seligman, 1989).

How does the lack of personal control affect people in real-life stressful conditions? Some studies have examined this question by testing students in college dormitories (Baum, Aiello, & Calesnick, 1978; Baum & Gatchel, 1981; Rodin & Baum, 1978). Stress and control were defined on the basis of differences in crowding that result from different dormitory floor plans. Surveys of dormitory residents have shown that those who live in crowded floors report more stress and less ability to control unwanted social interaction than those in uncrowded floors. Moreover, these differences are related to helplessness. When tested in social situations, students who live in crowded floors show more evidence of helplessness than those who live in uncrowded floors—for example, residents from crowded floors initiate fewer conversations with strangers and show less cooperation and a greater tendency to give up in competitive games.

Carol Dweck and her associates have examined attributions and learned helplessness in schoolchildren. In one study, fifth-graders were given multicolored blocks and asked to arrange the blocks to match a pictured design (Dweck & Repucci, 1973). The task was actually impossible—the design could not be made with the blocks given. Children who attributed their failure to stable, uncontrollable factors, such as their own lack of ability, showed poorer performance on subsequent problems than those who attributed failure to unstable, modifiable factors, such as a lack of effort. Thus, the children's attributions were linked to their feelings of helplessness. Another study found evidence that some teachers provide feedback that leads girls to feel more helpless than boys (Dweck,

Davidson, Nelson, & Enna, 1978). Children's experiences often lead them to acquire feelings of helplessness.

Personal Control and Health

There are two ways in which personal control and health may be related. First, people who have a strong sense of personal control may be more likely or able to maintain their health and prevent illness than those who have a weak sense of control. Second, once people become seriously ill, those who have a strong sense of control may adjust to the illness and promote their own rehabilitation better than those who have a weak sense of control. Both types of relationships have been examined.

To study these relationships, researchers have used several approaches to measure people's personal control. For instance, some researchers have constructed questionnaires or interviews to assess the degree to which people use specific types of control— such as cognitive, behavioral, or informational control. Others have examined people's locus of control, either by applying the I-E Scale or by using scales developed to assess specifically health-related control. One of the best-developed health-related measures today is called the *Multidimensional Health Locus of Control Scales* (Wallston, Wallston, & DeVellis, 1978). This instrument contains 18 statements; the person responds to each item with ratings ranging from "strongly agree" to "strongly disagree." These statements are divided into three scales:

1. *Internal health locus of control.* This scale measures how internal the person's beliefs are with items such as, "The main thing which affects my health is what I myself do."
2. *Powerful-others' health locus of control*, which assesses the belief that one's health is controlled by other people, such as physicians. One item to measure this is, "Whenever I don't feel well, I should consult a medically trained professional."
3. *Chance locus of control.* This scale measures the belief that luck or fate controls health, using items such as, "Luck plays a big part in determining how soon I will recover from an illness."

As you can see, the powerful-others and chance scales are directed toward assessing the degree to which people believe important external sources have control over their health.

Does a sense of personal control influence people's health? Studies have shown that pessimistic people—those who believe they have little control—have poorer health habits, have more illnesses, and are less likely to take active steps to treat their illness than are people with a greater sense of control (Kamen & Seligman, 1989; Lin & Peterson, 1990). A strong sense of control also appears to help people adjust to becoming seriously ill and promote their recovery (Thompson & Kyle, in press). Patients with illnesses such as kidney failure or cancer who score high on either internal or powerful-others' health locus of control suffer less depression than those with strong beliefs in the role of chance (Devins et al., 1981; Marks, Richardson, Graham, & Levine, 1986). The belief that either they or someone else can influence the course of their illness allows patients to be hopeful about their future. Moreover, patients with strong internal locus of control beliefs probably realize they have effective ways for controlling their stress.

Some types of control may be more effective than others in helping people adjust to serious illness. One study investigated the relationship between women's adjustment to breast cancer and their use of different types of control, three of which were cognitive, behavioral, and informational (Taylor, Lichtman, & Wood, 1984). Adjustment was most strongly associated with the women's use of cognitive control, such as by thinking about their lives differently and taking life more easily. Also, women who used behavioral control—for example, by exercising more than before—showed better adjustment than those who did not. But adjustment was not related to their use of informational control, such as by reading books on cancer. It may be that seeking information about the illness either leads the patients to materials that increase their fears or simply has little influence if the patients have no cognitive or behavioral possibilities for control.

Personal control also affects the efforts patients make toward their own rehabilitation; in particular, feelings of self-efficacy enhance their efforts. A study demonstrated this with older adult patients who had serious respiratory diseases, such as chronic bronchitis and emphysema (Kaplan, Atkins, & Reinsch, 1984). The patients were examined at a clinic and given individualized prescriptions for exercise, based on their performance on a treadmill exercise test. They also rated on a questionnaire their exercise self-efficacy—that is, their belief in their ability to perform specific physical activities, such as walking different distances, lifting objects of various weights, and climbing stairs. Correlational analyses revealed that the greater the patients' self-efficacy for doing physical activity, the more likely they were to adhere to the exercise prescription.

Health and Personal Control in Old Age

Here are two things we know about elderly people who live in nursing homes: first, they often show declines in their activity and health after they begin living in nursing homes. Second, residents of nursing homes frequently have few responsibilities or opportunities to influence their everyday lives. Could it be that the declines in activity and health among nursing-home residents result in part from their dependency and loss of personal control that the nursing home procedures seem to encourage?

Ellen Langer and Judith Rodin (1976) studied this issue by manipulating the amount of responsibility allowed residents of two floors of a modern, high-quality nursing home. The residents on the two floors were similar in physical and psychological health and prior socioeconomic status. On one floor, the residents were given opportunities to have responsibilities—for example, they were given small plants to care for and encouraged to make decisions about participating in activities and rearranging furniture. In comparison, the residents of the other floor continued to have little personal control. For example, they were assigned to various activities without choice, and when they were given plants, they were told that the staff would take care of them. Measures of the activity and happiness of the residents revealed that the residents who were given more responsibility became happier and more active and alert than the residents who had little control. A year and a half later the residents who were given responsibility were still happier and more active than those who had little control (Rodin & Langer, 1977). Moreover, comparisons of health data for the residents of the two floors during these 18 months showed that the residents with responsibility were healthier and had half the rate of mortality.

Other research with residents of a retirement home also demonstrated the importance of personal control for physical and psychological well-being and showed that withdrawing opportunities for personal control may impair people's health (Schulz, 1976; Schulz & Hanusa, 1978). The results of these studies suggest two important conclusions. First, personal control—even over relatively simple or minor events—can have a powerful effect on people's health and psychological condition. Second, healthcare workers and researchers need to consider the nature of the personal control they introduce and what the impact will be if it is removed.

To summarize the material on personal control, people differ in the degree to which they believe they have control over the things that happen in their lives. People who experience prolonged, high levels of stress and lack a sense of personal control tend to feel helpless. Having a strong sense of control seems to benefit people's health and help them adjust to becoming seriously ill. A sense of personal control contributes to people's hardiness, which is the next psychosocial modifier of stress we will examine.

A HARDY PERSONALITY

According to researchers Suzanne Kobasa and Salvatore Maddi, individual differences in personal control provide only part of the reason why some people who are under stress get sick whereas others do not. They have proposed that a broader array of personality characteristics—called **hardiness**—differentiates people who do and do not get sick under stress (Kobasa, 1979, 1986; Kobasa & Maddi, 1977; Maddi, 1998). Hardiness includes three characteristics: (1) *Control* refers to people's belief that they can influence events in their lives—that is, a sense of personal control. (2) *Commitment* is people's sense of purpose or involvement in the events, activities, and people in their lives. For instance, people with a strong sense of commitment tend to look forward to starting each day's projects and enjoy getting close to people. (3) *Challenge* refers to the tendency to view changes as incentives or opportunities for growth rather than threats to security.

Hardiness, Coherence, and Resilience

Other researchers have described similar personality traits that, like hardiness, might protect people from the effects of stress. Aaron Antonovsky (1979, 1987) has described the *sense of coherence*, which involves the tendency of people to see their worlds as comprehensible, manageable, and meaningful. People's low sense of coherence has been linked to heightened stress and illness symptoms (Jorgensen, Frankowski, & Carey, 1999).

Another trait—*resilience*—seems to include high levels of three components: self-esteem, personal control, and optimism (Major et al., 1998). Resilient people appraise negative events as less stressful; they bounce back from life's adversities and recover their strength and spirit. For example, resilient children develop into competent, well-adjusted individuals despite growing up under extremely difficult conditions (Garmezy, 1983; Werner & Smith, 1982). The following case shows what this means:

> In the slums of Minneapolis...is a 10-year-old boy who lives in a dilapidated apartment with his father, an ex-convict now dying of cancer, his illiterate mother, and seven brothers and sisters, two of whom are mentally retarded. Yet his teachers describe him as an unusually competent child who does well in his studies and is loved by almost everyone in the school. (Pines, 1979, p. 53)

Other cases have been described of children who flourished or were well-adjusted despite being abused by their parents, or growing up in concentration camps, or living in societies with civil strife and wars (Garmezy, 1983; Hartup, 1983; Werner, 1987).

Optimism—which may be part of resilience—is the point of view that good things are likely to happen. Optimists tend to experience life's difficulties with less distress than do pessimists (Scheier, Carver, & Bridges, 2000). They also tend to have better mental and physical health than pessimists have, and they recover more quickly when they become ill (Carver, 1998).

Why are some individuals resilient and others not? Part of the answer may lie in their genetic endowments. Resilient people may have inherited traits, such as relatively easy temperaments, that enable them to cope better with stress and turmoil. Another part lies in their experiences. Resilient people who overcome a history of stressful events often have compensating experiences and circumstances in their lives, such as special talents or interests that absorb them and give them confidence, and close relationships with friends or relatives. Hardiness, resilience, and coherence have a great deal in common and may be basically the same thing.

Hardiness and Health

Kobasa (1979) has proposed that hardy people will remain healthier when under stress than those whose personalities are less hardy because they are better able to deal with stressors and are less likely to become anxious and aroused by these events. As a result, the spiraling process that can lead from stress to illness never takes hold.

The results of some studies support this prediction. For instance, retrospective and prospective research has found that hardy individuals report having developed fewer illnesses during extended stressful periods than less hardy people (Kobasa, 1979; Kobasa, Maddi, & Puccetti, 1982; Kobasa, Maddi, Puccetti, & Zola, 1985). Other studies have found that people who are high in hardiness tend to deal more effectively with stressful situations than low-hardiness people do—for example, by working through problems or transforming negative situations into positive ones (Holahan & Moos, 1985; Williams, Wiebe, & Smith, 1992). In addition, hardy people show less physiological strain when under stress than less hardy individuals (Contrada, 1989). But other studies have found conflicting results, and some evidence indicates that tests used in assessing hardiness may simply be measuring negative affect, such as the tendency to be anxious, depressed, or hostile (Funk, 1992; Hull, Van Treuren, & Virnelli, 1987). We saw in Chapter 1 that people with these personality characteristics are at risk for developing heart disease and other illnesses.

Although the status of the concept and measurement of hardiness is uncertain at this time, related aspects of personality are clearly involved in maintaining health. Future research will need to clarify what these personality variables are and how they operate.

Hardiness in Old Age

As individuals develop, they learn to deal with change by trying and succeeding, failing, or compromising. Old age is a time when some very difficult life events occur, particularly those that involve reduced income, failing health and disability, and the loss of one's spouse and close friends. What are hardy people like in old age, and how did they get that way?

Elizabeth Colerick (1985) studied 70- to 80-year-old men and women for the quality she called *stamina*, which is similar to hardiness. This research was un-

dertaken to determine how people who do and do not have stamina in later life deal with setbacks, such as the loss of a loved one. By using questionnaires and interviews, she was able to identify two groups: one with high stamina and one with low stamina. She found that stamina in old age is characterized by "a triumphant, positive outlook during periods of adversity," as illustrated by the following interview excerpts from two different high-stamina people:

> The key to dealing with loss is not obvious. One must take the problem, the void, the loneliness, the sorrow and put it on the *back* of your neck and use it as a driving force. Don't let such problems sit out there in front of you, blocking your vision. . . . Use hardships in a positive way. (p. 999)
>
> I realize that setbacks are a part of the game. I've had 'em, I have them now, and I've got plenty more ahead of me. Seeing this—the big picture—puts it all into perspective, no matter how bad things get. (p. 999)

In contrast, low-stamina people described a negative outlook and feelings of helplessness and hopelessness in the face of changes they experienced in old age. One woman who had undergone surgery for colon cancer said:

> I was certain that I would die on the table . . . never wake up. . . . I felt sure it was the end. Then I woke up with a colostomy and figured I have to stay inside the house the rest of my life. Now I'm afraid to go back to the doctor's and keep putting off my checkups. (p. 999)

There is little research available that bears directly on the question of how people become hardy, but the study by Colerick found some interesting relationships. Compared with low-stamina individuals, those with high stamina reported healthier pasts, more years of schooling, and more activities in their current lives involving social service and personal growth, for example, visiting museums and traveling. More research is needed on a variety of biopsychosocial factors that are likely to shape hardy personalities.

In summary, people with a high degree of hardiness, coherence, or resilience—or some related personality traits—may have some protection against the harmful effects of stress on health. The last psychosocial modifier of stress we will consider is people's tendency toward the Type A or B behavioral and emotional style.

TYPE A AND TYPE B BEHAVIOR PATTERNS

The history of science has many stories about researchers accidently coming upon an idea that changed their focus and led to major discoveries. Such was the case for bacteriologist Alexander Fleming, for instance. When the bacteria cultures he was studying developed unwanted molds, he happened to notice some properties of the molds that led to the discovery of penicillin. Serendipity also led to the discovery of the "Type A" behavior pattern by cardiologists Meyer Friedman and Ray Rosenman. They were studying dietary differences in cholesterol intake between male heart disease victims and their wives when one of the wives exclaimed: "If you really want to know what is giving our husbands heart attacks, I'll tell you. It's stress, the stress they receive in their work, that's what's doing it" (Friedman & Rosenman, 1974, p. 56). These researchers began to study this possibility by looking at differences between heart disease patients and similar individuals who were healthy, focusing on the people's stress and related behavioral characteristics. This comparison revealed differences in behavioral and emotional style: the patients were more likely than the nonpatients to display a pattern of behavior we now refer to as Type A.

What is the Type A behavioral and emotional style? The **Type A behavior pattern** consists of three characteristics (Chesney, Frautschi, & Rosenman, 1985; Friedman & Rosenman, 1974):

1. *Competitive achievement orientation*. Type A individuals tend to be very self-critical and to strive toward goals without feeling a sense of joy in their efforts or accomplishments.

2. *Time urgency*. Type A people seem to be in a constant struggle against the clock. Often, they quickly become impatient with delays and unproductive time, schedule commitments too tightly, and try to do more than one thing at a time, such as reading while eating or watching TV.

3. *Anger/hostility*. Type A individuals tend to be easily aroused to anger or hostility, which they may or may not express overtly.

In contrast, the **Type B behavior pattern** consists of low levels of competitiveness, time urgency, and hostility. People with the Type B pattern tend to be more easygoing and "philosophical" about life—they are more likely to "stop and smell the roses."

Measuring Type A and Type B Behavior Patterns

Researchers measure people's Type A and Type B behavior either by using a standard interview procedure or by having people fill out questionnaires. The most widely used interview procedure is called the *Structured Interview*: a trained interviewer asks individuals a standard series of questions about their behavioral and emotional styles, particularly regarding their competitiveness, impatience, and hostility (Chesney, Eagleston, & Rosenman, 1980; Rosenman, 1978; Rosenman, Swan, & Carmelli, 1988; Tallmer et al., 1990). For instance, the interviewer asks, "When you play games with people your own age, do you play for the fun of it, or are you really in there to win?" Although the specific answers people give to these questions contribute to the assessment of their behavior pattern, their style of interaction with the interviewer also contributes. Some features of the interview are designed to encourage Type A behaviors, such as interrupting and talking fast and loudly. For example, the interviewer asks slowly and with hesitations, "Most people who work have to get up fairly early in the morning. In your particular case, uh, what time, uh, do you, uh, ordinarily, uh-uh-uh, get up?" (You can imagine the Type A person saying, "Six o'clock!" at the second "uh.") The interviewer also tries to annoy or challenge the person, encouraging Type A behavior, by interrupting the subjects often and asking for clarifications in a harsh manner—asking, for instance, "What do you mean by that?" rather than, "Could you tell me a bit more about that?"

Structured Interview sessions are audiotaped or videotaped and scored by a trained rater who knows nothing about the subjects beyond what the tapes present. In the scoring process, the rater considers specific answers given to questions, speech characteristics, and a variety of behaviors that suggest annoyance, for example, sighing frequently or attempting to hurry the interviewer. Videotapes allow the rater to consider other behavioral features also, such as facial expressions, sitting on the edge of the chair, and fidgeting. The rater's overall scores for subjects determine their classification as Type A or B.

The questions used in the Structured Interview have been adapted to construct a 52-item self-report questionnaire called the *Jenkins Activity Survey* (Jenkins, Zyzanski, & Rosenman, 1979). Some items inquire about the person's usual way of responding to situations that can produce stress as a result of, for example, competition, time pressure, or frustration. A sample question is: "Would people who know you well agree that you tend to do most things in a hurry?" Other questions ask about the person's speed of eating, tendency to hurry someone who talks slowly, and work habits. This questionnaire was designed to test adults, but versions have also been developed for college students (Yarnold, Bryant, & Grimm, 1987). Another questionnaire for measuring the Type A and B behavior patterns is the *Framingham Type A Scale* (Haynes et al., 1978). It contains only 10 items and has slightly different versions for testing students, housewives, and people who are employed (Powell, 1987). Researchers have also developed instruments by which adults can rate Type A and B behavior patterns in children. Probably the most widely used of these methods is the *Matthews Youth Test for Health* (Matthews & Angulo, 1980).

Is one approach for measuring Type A and B behaviors better than the others? Each approach has its own strengths and weaknesses (Carver, Diamond, & Humphries, 1985; Matthews, 1982; O'Rourke, Houston, Harris, & Snyder, 1988; Powell, 1984, 1987). The Structured Interview has two important strengths. Its assessment of behavior patterns seems to involve all three Type A characteristics: competitiveness, time urgency, and anger/hostility. In addition, Type A classification using this method has been associated fairly consistently with health outcomes, particularly heart disease. But the Structured Interview is time-consuming and expensive to use, and details of its procedure can affect the outcome (Tallmer et al., 1990). The strengths of self-report methods rest mainly in their time- and cost-efficiency. But they have three important weaknesses. First, the relationship between health outcomes and Type A classification with existing self-report methods appears to be weak and inconsistent. Second, people may underreport Type A tendencies, such as impatience and hostility, because they are socially undesirable. Third, Type A measurements with the Jenkins Activity Survey and Framingham Type A Scale rely very little on and provide poor measures of the anger/hostility dimension of the behavior pattern. Because of these problems, researchers generally favor the Structured Interview approach when studying connections between Type A behavior and illness.

Behavior Patterns and Stress

Individuals who exhibit the Type A behavior pattern react differently to stressors than do those with the Type B pattern. Type A individuals respond more quickly and strongly to stressors, often interpreting them as threats to their personal control (Carver, Diamond, & Humphries, 1985; Glass, 1977). The Type A behavior pattern may also perpetuate stress, increasing the person's likelihood of encountering stressful events (Byrne & Rosenman, 1986; Smith & Anderson, 1986). Why? Type A individuals tend to seek out demanding situations in their lives. What's more, people who are often in a hurry and impatient with delays—as is the case for Type A individuals—tend to have more accidents than people who are more easygoing (Suls & Sanders, 1988). In these ways people's Type A and B patterns can affect their environmental transactions and modify the stress they experience in their lives.

We have seen that people's response to a stressor—or strain—includes a physiological component called *reactivity*, such as increased blood pressure or cortisol levels compared against baseline levels. Do Type A individuals show greater reactivity to stressors than Type Bs? In general, yes. One study examined the reactivity of men who each competed in a video game against an individual who was a confederate of the researchers (Glass et al., 1980). Although the instructions indicated that the winner would receive a prize, the game was rigged so that a subject could never win. The men were assigned to two groups, Type A or Type B, on the basis of their performance in the Structured Interview. Half of the men in each group played the game while being harassed and insulted by the confederate; for the remaining subjects, the confederate was silent. Several physiological measures were used, including blood pressure, heart rate, and plasma catecholamine levels. Although both Type A and Type B subjects showed substantial and equal increases in physiological arousal in the absence of harassment, the Type A subjects showed greater reactivity than the Type Bs in the harassment condition.

Some research suggests the intriguing possibility that people's Type A behavior may, in part, be caused by their physiological responses to stress (Contrada, Krantz, & Hill, 1988; Krantz & Durel, 1983; Krantz, Lundberg, & Frankenhaeuser, 1987). For example, researchers conducted a study with Type A patients who were either taking or not taking a type of medication called *beta-blockers*, which dampen sympathetic nervous system transmission. This research demonstrated that Type A patients who were taking a beta-blocker exhibited less Type A behavior in the Structured Interview than those who were not taking the drug (Krantz et al., 1982). This suggests that physiological reactions to stressors may influence Type A behavior.

Gender and Sociocultural Differences in Type A Behavior

Is Type A behavior more common among males than females or among different ethnic groups? Studies on these issues have produced inconsistent results (Thoresen & Pattillo, 1988). We may never have a definitive answer to these questions because the prevalence of Type A behavior depends on specific characteristics of the population tested, such as the community in which they live and the type of work they do (Friedman, 1996).

However, reactivity differences between Type A and Type B people seem to depend on the subjects' gender. Although the results have not always been consistent, most studies have found greater reactivity among Type A individuals, especially males (Carver, Diamond, & Humphries, 1985; Contrada & Krantz, 1988; Houston, 1986). These studies have used a variety of stressors and ways to measure behavior patterns. Other researchers have examined reactivity in Type A and Type B boys and girls and found results similar to those found with adults (Lawler, Allen, Critcher, & Standard, 1981; Lundberg, 1986; Matthews & Jennings, 1984; Thoresen & Pattillo, 1988). These findings suggest that the tendency of Type A individuals to be highly reactive is greater in males than females and may begin in childhood. Sociocultural and gender differences in Type A behavior are important because of the relationships researchers have found between reactivity and health, such as in the development of heart disease.

Type A Behavior and Health

How are people's health and behavior patterns related? To answer this question, researchers have used two approaches. First, studies have examined whether Type A individuals are at greater risk than Type Bs for becoming sick with any of a wide variety of illnesses. One study, for instance, found that Type A people

reported having experienced more respiratory symptoms, such as asthma attacks and coughing spells, and more gastrointestinal symptoms, such as ulcers, indigestion, and nausea (Woods & Burns, 1984). Although several other studies have found similar results, the overall evidence for a link between Type A and B behaviors and general illnesses is weak and inconsistent (Orfutt & Lacroix, 1988; Suls & Sanders, 1988).

The second approach has focused on the Type A pattern as a risk factor for **coronary heart disease** (CHD)—illnesses that result from the narrowing or blocking of the coronary arteries, which supply blood to the heart muscle. These illnesses include *angina*, *arteriosclerosis*, and *myocardial infarction* (commonly called "heart attack"). Dozens of studies have been done to assess the link between Type A behavior and CHD, and most studies have confirmed the link when behavior patterns were evaluated *with the Structured Interview* (Booth-Kewley & Friedman, 1987; Haynes & Matthews, 1988; Matthews, 1988). Type A women and men, particularly white-collar workers, have a much greater chance of developing CHD than Type B adults do.

A good example of the evidence for this link comes from a large-scale prospective study of healthy men. The Western Collaborative Group Study determined the health status and behavior patterns (using the Structured Interview) of over 3,000 39- to 59-year-old employed men, most of whom had white-collar jobs (Rosenman et al., 1975; Rosenman, Brand, Sholtz, & Friedman, 1976). A follow-up on these men 8½ years later showed that the Type A subjects were twice as likely as Type Bs to have developed CHD and to have died of CHD. Because of these and similar results, Type A behavior has been called "coronary-prone behavior."

But some studies assessed behavior patterns with the Structured Interview and did *not* confirm the link to CHD (see, for example, Ragland & Brand, 1988; Shekelle et al., 1985). Why? Karen Matthews (1988) has noted that these studies generally used subjects who either were at *high risk* for developing heart disease or were *already coronary patients*. She then suggested several convincing reasons why the studies didn't find the expected association between behavior patterns and CHD. We'll consider two of these reasons: (1) Type A high-risk and CHD subjects may have been misclassified as Type Bs in the studies if they were taking certain medications, such as beta-blockers, or trying to change their stress-related behavior. (2) For subjects who were coronary patients, the main cause of the CHD may have been different for Type A and Type B subjects. If the Type Bs' CHD resulted mainly from atherosclerosis, their risk of a recurrent heart attack or death might be fairly high. As we saw in Chapter 2, this condition involves the buildup of fatty patches on artery walls. And if the Type A subjects' CHD resulted from an acute precipitating factor, such as coronary spasms, their risk of recurrent attacks might be fairly low. This would be the case if Type A behavior is linked more closely to developing acute precipitating factors than to atherosclerosis.

Why is the Type A behavior pattern linked to CHD? Part of the answer seems to involve the relatively high physiological reactivity of Type A people (Carver, Diamond, & Humphries, 1985; Krantz, Lundberg, & Frankenhaeuser, 1987; Wright, 1988). Frequent episodes of high arousal produce a lot of wear and tear on the cardiovascular system. One way this may occur is through the hormones that are released during arousal. Research has shown that chronically high levels of certain hormones, such as epinephrine and norepinephrine, can injure the heart and blood vessels. Another way wear and tear may lead to CHD in Type A people is through blood pressure. Studies have recorded higher blood pressure reactivity among Type A individuals—particularly those who score high on measures of anger and hostility—than among Type Bs during stressful situations (Diamond, 1982; Diamond et al., 1984; Spiga, 1986). High blood pressure strains the heart and arteries.

Three behavioral factors may also contribute to the link between Type A behavior and CHD. First, Type A individuals drink much more alcohol than Type Bs do (Carmargo, Vranizan, Thoresen, & Wood, 1986). Excessive alcohol use is associated with CHD Second, of adults who smoke, Type A people inhale the smoke for a much longer time than Type Bs do, which provides more time for the lungs to absorb the harmful elements of smoke (Lombardo & Carreno, 1987). Type A individuals also have more difficulty quitting smoking than Type Bs do (Caplan, Cobb, & French, 1975). Smoking is an important risk factor for CHD. Third, compared with Type Bs, Type A individuals are more likely to drive themselves far beyond the point when they should slow down (Carver, De-Gregorio, & Gillis, 1981; Weidner & Matthews, 1978). Their frequent physical exhaustion may lead to ill-

ness, such as CHD (Carver, Diamond, & Humphries, 1985).

Type A's "Deadly Emotion"

As we have seen, the Type A behavior pattern consists of three components. Is one component more damaging than the others? Redford Williams (1989; Williams & Barefoot, 1988) has argued that the anger/hostility component is the most important factor. One of several studies that support this idea examined the records of 255 men (Barefoot, Dahlstrom, & Williams, 1983). These men were physicians who had taken a psychological test that included a scale for hostility while they were in medical school 25 years earlier. For the physicians with high scores on the hostility scale, the rates of both CHD and overall mortality during the intervening years were several times higher than for those with low hostility scores. Several other studies have examined the hostility–CHD connection and, although a few studies have not confirmed the link, most have (Smith, 1992). Hostility seems to be a deadly emotion that may be especially damaging to cardiovascular health when it is expressed outwardly and when it involves a cynical or suspicious mistrust of others (Everson et al., 1999; Knox et al., 1998; Siegman, 1993; Williams, 1989; Williams et al., 1980).

A person's tendency toward hostility can be assessed in several ways, including the Structured Interview and various self-report questionnaires. The Cook–Medley Hostility Scale has 50 true/false items, such as "It is safer to trust nobody" and "Some of my family have habits that bother and annoy me very much" (Cook & Medley, 1954). This scale measures anger, as well as cynicism, suspiciousness, and other negative traits (Friedman, Tucker, & Reise, 1995). By using such measures to identify hostile and nonhostile people, researchers have discovered physiological differences that help account for the CHD link with hostility. For instance, hostile individuals have higher resting blood pressure and serum cholesterol levels; and when harrassed or stressed, they show poorer heart pumping efficiency and higher heart rate, blood pressure, and blood platelet activity (Everson, McKey, & Lovallo, 1995; Ironson et al., 1992; Markovitz, Matthews, Kiss, & Smitherman, 1996; Powch & Houston, 1996; Suarez, Bates, & Harralson, 1998; Suls, Wan, & Costa, 1995; Vitaliano et al., 1993). The role of hostility is particularly important with social stressors. Research results suggest that hostility may be more closely associated with reactivity to interpersonal stressors in men than women (Guyll & Contrada, 1998; Smith & Gallo, 1999; Suarez et al., 1998).

These factors form only part of the process linking hostility to CHD. As psychologist Timothy Smith (1992) has pointed out, a person with cynical and suspicious beliefs about and behaviors toward other people is likely to provoke and worsen social conflicts and undermine his or her social support. A vicious circle emerges: as the social environment becomes less supportive and more stressful, the person's hostility and reactivity are maintained or increased. Research on college students confirmed this scenario, finding that hostile individuals tend to experience excessive anger in many situations and not to seek or accept social support (Houston & Vavak, 1991).

Behavior Patterns and Development

Do people's behavior patterns change over the life span? Longitudinal studies have found that although people's behavior patterns often change over time, many individuals exhibit the same pattern across many years. This has been shown for both children and adults (Bergman & Magnusson, 1986; Carmelli, Dame, Swan, & Rosenman, 1991; Carmelli, Rosenman, & Chesney, 1987; Visintainer & Matthews, 1987). Also, cross-sectional studies have found that the Type A behavior pattern among Americans becomes more prevalent with age from childhood through middle age or so and then declines (Amos et al., 1987; Moss et al., 1986; Powell, 1987). But the decline in prevalence in old age could be result of Type A individuals dying at earlier ages than Type Bs.

Other studies have been conducted to determine the origins of the Type A pattern and factors that influence its development. One approach for determining the origins of Type A behavior is to study how its development relates to the early *temperaments* of children. Behavior patterns and temperaments involve some similar characteristics, such as the impulsiveness and intensity with which the person reacts and his or her ease in adjusting to changes in the environment. One longitudinal study found that temperament ratings taken in early childhood were related to measures of Type A behavior taken 20 years later (Steinberg, 1985). Another longitudinal study examined this relationship in adults and found an association between measures of temperament and Type A behavior both at the

beginning of the study and 10 years later (Carmelli, Rosenman, & Chesney, 1987). Thus, adult Type A behavior may have roots in the person's early temperament, which remains influential over time in at least some individuals.

Biopsychosocial Factors in Type A Behavior

Do both biological and psychosocial factors affect the development of Type A and B behavior patterns? It appears that they do. Research with identical (monozygotic) and fraternal (dizygotic) twins has demonstrated a genetic contribution in the development of temperament (Buss & Plomin, 1975, 1986) and of Type A behavior (Carmelli, Rosenman, & Chesney, 1987; Matthews et al., 1984; Pedersen et al., 1989). That is, identical twins are more similar to each other in temperament and behavior patterns than are fraternal twins. And they are much more similar than fraternal twins in their reactivity to stressors, too (Ditto, 1993; Turner & Hewitt, 1992).

Research has also examined the influence of various psychosocial factors on Type A behavior. We'll consider several findings. First, children's behavior patterns are related to the parenting styles they experience. For example, compared with Type Bs, Type A boys who are working on a task receive less praise from their mothers and more statements to strive for improvement, such as, "That was fine, but next time try harder" (Krantz, Lundberg, & Frankenhaeuser, 1987; Matthews & Woodall, 1988). Second, hostile subjects report that their parents were less accepting, more punitive, and more interfering with the subjects' desires during childhood (Houston & Vavak, 1991). Third, social support tends to reduce people's reactivity, but not if they are cynically hostile (Kamarck, Manuck, & Jennings, 1990; Lepore, 1995).

Fourth, the behavior patterns of employed adults relate to the stress they experience at work. For instance, Type A individuals work longer hours and have less supportive relationships with coworkers than Type Bs do (Sorensen et al., 1987). And a longitudinal study found that workers exhibit less Type A behavior a year after retirement than they did shortly before retiring (Howard, Rechnitzer, Cunningham, & Donner, 1986). It should be clear that a wide variety of environmental factors influence people's development of Type A behavior. The relationships between psychosocial factors and Type A behavior are very complex and seem to involve multiple levels of human experience.

Table 4.1   *Levels of Relationships Between Psychosocial Factors and Type A Behavior*

The many psychosocial factors that can affect Type A behavior may operate at four levels (Margolis, McLeroy, Runyan, & Kaplan, 1983):
- *Intrapersonal*: within the person, Type A behavior is linked to many psychological factors, such as personal control. Type A behavior seems to represent an effort by individuals to control stressful experiences in their lives (Glass, 1977; Matthews, 1982).
- *Interpersonal*: social processes and Type A behavior affect each other. Studies have tested this by having pairs of Type A or of Type B individuals engage in tasks together. For example, in tests with children or college students who could either cooperate or compete in a game, Type A pairs showed more competitive behavior and less cooperation than Type B pairs (Spiga, 1986; Van Egeren, Sniderman, & Roggelin, 1982). Similarly, a study of married couples found that Type A pairs showed more hostile and dominant behavior than Type Bs when discussing a marital conflict (Sanders, Smith, & Alexander, 1991). In general, people who display Type A behavior tend to elicit reactions from others that create more demands and stimulate more Type A behavior (Smith & Anderson, 1986).
- *Institutional*, which includes people's experiences in educational and occupational settings. One way these experiences can foster Type A behavior involves reward structures that promote aggressive competition, as can happen when many individuals are vying for a small number of rewards, such as job promotions or high grades. Another way involves time or work demands by a boss or teacher that encourage the feeling of time urgency. For example, employees with high scores on the Jenkins Activity Survey for Type A behavior have longer work hours and less supportive relationships with coworkers than Type B workers do (Sorensen et al., 1987).
- *Cultural*: some cultures place great emphasis on the work ethic, getting ahead, status, and accumulating goods that reflect status. People in cultures that emphasize these values are likely to display more Type A behavior than those who live in cultures that do not.

Table 4.1 describes four "ecological" levels in which these relationships operate.

As a summary of the role of psychosocial modifiers of stress, we have seen that social support, personal control, hardiness, and the Type A and B behavior patterns are factors that can modify the impact of stress on health. High levels of social support, personal control, and hardiness are generally associated with reduced stress and resulting illnesses; Type A behavior is associated with increased stress and illness. The remainder of this chapter focuses on health problems that are affected by people's experience of stress. We begin by considering how stress leads to illness.

HOW STRESS AFFECTS HEALTH

Researchers conducted an interesting experiment: they gave subjects nasal drops that contained a "common cold" virus or a placebo solution and then quarantined them to check for infection and cold symptoms (Cohen, Tyrrell, & Smith, 1991). Before the nasal drops were administered, the subjects had filled out questionnaires to assess their stress. Of these subjects, 47% of those with high stress and 27% of those with low stress developed colds. Other studies have produced two related findings. First, people who are under chronic, severe stress are especially vulnerable to infection (Cohen et al., 1998). Second, people

who show high reactivity to stress are at greater risk to respiratory infections when stressed than less reactive people (Bulcourf, Unrod, & Adams, 1996). What is it about stress that leads to illness? The causal sequence between stress and illness can involve either of two routes: (1) a direct route, resulting from the changes stress produces in the body's *physiology*, or (2) an indirect route, affecting health through the person's *behavior*. Let's look first at the behavioral route.

STRESS, BEHAVIOR, AND ILLNESS

Stress can affect behavior, which, in turn, can lead to illness or worsen an existing condition (Baum, 1994). We can see the behavioral links between stress and illness in many stressful situations, such as when a family undergoes a divorce. In many cases during the first year following the separation, the parent who has the children is less available and responsive to them than she or he was before—a situation described as "diminished parenting" (Wallerstein, 1983). Behavioral changes during stressful times often make conditions for all family members less healthful, with haphazard meals, less regular bedtimes, delays in getting medical attention, and failures to follow physicians' recommendations, for example.

Research has shown that people who experience high levels of stress tend to perform behaviors that increase their chances of becoming ill or injured

(Weidner, Kohlmann, Dotzauer, & Burns, 1996; Wiebe & McCallum, 1986). For instance, they consume more alcohol, cigarettes, and coffee than people who experience less stress (Baer et al., 1987; Conway, Vickers, Ward, & Rahe, 1981). Consumption of these substances has been associated with the development of various illnesses. In addition, behavioral factors, such as alcohol use and carelessness, probably play a role in the relatively high accident rates of people under stress. Studies have found that children and adults who experience high levels of stress are more likely to suffer accidental injuries at home, in sports activities, on the job, and while driving a car than individuals under less stress (Johnson, 1986; Quick, Quick, Nelson, & Hurrell, 1997).

STRESS, PHYSIOLOGY, AND ILLNESS

Stress produces many physiological changes in the body that can affect health, especially when stress is chronic and severe. In Chapter 3, we discussed the concept of *allostatic load* in which the strain involved in adapting repeatedly to intense stressors produces wear and tear on body systems that accumulate over time and lead to illness (McEwen & Stellar, 1993). Clear connections have been found between illness and the degree of reactivity people show in their cardiovascular, endocrine, and immune systems when stressed.

Cardiovascular System Reactivity and Illness

Cardiovascular reactivity includes any physiological change that occurs in the heart, blood vessels, and blood in response to stressors. People's degree of cardiovascular reactivity is very stable, showing little change when retested with the same stressors years later (Sherwood et al., 1997; Veit, Brody, & Rau, 1997).

Research has demonstrated links between chronically high cardiovascular reactivity and the development of CHD and hypertension (Manuck, 1994; Sherwood & Turner, 1995). For example, high levels of job stress are associated with high blood pressure and abnormally enlarged hearts (Schnall et al., 1990), and people's laboratory reactivity to stress in early adulthood is associated with their later development of high blood pressure (Menkes et al., 1989). The heightened blood pressure reactivity that people display in

laboratory tests appears to reflect their reactivity in daily life (Turner et al., 1994).

Stress produces several cardiovascular changes that relate to the development of CHD. For instance, the blood of people who are under stress contains high concentrations of activated platelets (Malkoff, Muldoon, Zeigler, & Manuck, 1993; Patterson et al., 1994) and unfavorable levels of lipids, such as cholesterol (Patterson, Matthews, Allen, & Owens, 1995; Vitaliano, Russo, & Niaura, 1995). These changes in blood composition tend to promote atherosclerosis—the growth of plaques (fatty patches) on artery walls. As these plaques build up, they narrow and harden the arteries, thereby increasing blood pressure and the likelihood of a heart attack or stroke. Prospective studies have found that people who display high cardiovascular reactivity to stressors show faster progression of atherosclerosis than those with lower reactivity, especially if they experience chronic, severe stress in their lives (Everson et al., 1997; Lynch et al., 1998; Matthews et al., 1998). (Go to 💡.)

Endocrine System Reactivity and Illness

Part of reactivity involves activation of the *hypothalamus–pituitary–adrenal axis*, which releases endocrine hormones—particularly catecholamines and corticosteroids—during stress (Lundberg, 1999; Sternberg & Gold, 1997). The increased endocrine reactivity that people display in these tests appears to reflect their reactivity in daily life (Williams et al., 1991). One way in which high levels of these hormones can lead to illness involves their effects on the cardiovascular system. For example, an intense episode of stress with extremely high levels of these hormones can cause the heart to beat erratically and may lead to sudden death. In addition, chronically high levels of catecholamines and corticosteroids appear to increase atherosclerosis.

Stephen Manuck and his colleagues (1988, 1995) have demonstrated this link between stress and atherosclerosis in research with monkeys. In one study, some of the subjects were relocated periodically to different living groups, thereby requiring stressful social and psychological adjustments to retain their dominant social status; the remaining subjects stayed in stable groups. Regardless of whether the monkeys' diets had high or low levels of cholesterol, the stressed subjects who had to retain their dominant status developed greater atherosclerosis

HIGHLIGHT ON ISSUES

Sudden "Voodoo" Death

Can a person die from extreme psychological distress? It seems so, at least on the basis of anecdotal evidence, as seen in the following case study:

In 1967 a distraught woman, pleading for help, entered the Baltimore City Hospital a few days before her 23rd birthday. She and two other girls had been born of different mothers assisted by the same midwife in the Okefenokee Swamp on a Friday the 13th. The midwife cursed all three babies, saying one would die before her 16th birthday, another before her 21st birthday, and the third before her 23rd birthday. The first had died in a car crash during her 15th year; the second was accidentally shot to death in a nightclub fight on the evening of her 21st birthday. Now she, the third, waited in terror for her death. The hospital somewhat skeptically admitted her for observation. The next morning, two days before her 23rd birthday, she was found dead in her hospital bed—physical cause unknown. (Seligman, cited in Rosenhan & Seligman, 1984, p. 292.)

This woman died of **sudden death**—the abrupt death from cardiac dysfunction of a seemingly healthy person (AHA, 2000). Sudden death was orginally called "voodoo death" (Cannon, 1942), perhaps because many of the cases described were from primitive cultures.

Sudden death usually results from cardiac failure of some sort and frequently involves two factors: a preexisting cardiovascular disorder and a severe physical or psychological stressor, such as extreme anger or fear (Allan & Scheidt, 1990; Kop, 1999; Mittleman et al., 1995; Möller et al., 1999). Type A individuals seem to be at high risk for sudden death (Perini et al., 1993). The underlying cardiovascular disorder may take two forms (Kop, 1999; Verrier, DeSilva, & Lown, 1983). First, the disorder may involve damage to the myocardium caused by high levels of catecholamines in the blood. Second, the disorder typically involves the occurrence of *cardiac arrhythmia*—an abnormal rhythm of the heart's functioning. Arrhythmias can take the form of an extremely high heart rate, called *flutter*, or of uncoordinated heartbeats, called *fibrillation* (Tortora & Grabowski, 2000).

---

than the subjects in the low stress condition. This effect of stress is probably very similar in humans. Disruptions of soldiers' social status in boot camp affect endocrine reactivity (Hellhammer, Buchtal, Gutberlet, & Kirshbaum, 1997). And as we saw earlier, people with chronically high stress are more likely to develop atherosclerosis than those with less stress. But social support may help: people with high levels of social support tend to exhibit lower endocrine reactivity than people with less support (Seeman & McEwen, 1996).

Immune System Reactivity and Illness

The release of catecholamines and corticosteroids during arousal affects health in another way: some of these hormones impair the functioning of the immune system (Jemmott & Locke, 1984; Rozlog et al., 1999; Sternberg & Gold, 1997). For example, increases in cortisol and epinephrine are associated with de-

creased activity of T cells and B cells against antigens. This decrease in lymphocyte activity appears to be important in the development and progression of a variety of infectious diseases and cancer (Kiecolt-Glaser & Glaser, 1995; Vedhara et al., 1999). Among women diagnosed with breast cancer, those with high levels of killer-T-cell activity exhibit less spread of the cancer to surrounding tissue than those with low levels of lymphocyte activity (Levy et al., 1985).

Immune processes also protect the body against cancers that result from excessive exposure to harmful chemical or physical agents called **carcinogens,** which include radiation (nuclear, X, and ultraviolet types), tobacco tars, and asbestos (AMA, 1989). Carcinogens can damage the DNA in body cells, which may then develop into mutant cells and spread. Fortunately, people's exposure to carcinogens is generally at low levels and for short periods of time, and most DNA changes probably do not lead to cancer

(Glaser et al., 1985). When mutant cells develop, the immune system attacks them with killer T cells. Actually, the body begins to defend itself against cancer even before a cell mutates by using enzymes to destroy chemical carcinogens or to repair damaged DNA. Research has shown that high levels of stress, however, reduce the production of these enzymes and the repair of damaged DNA (Glaser et al., 1985; Kiecolt-Glaser & Glaser, 1986; Kiecolt-Glaser et al., 1985).

PSYCHONEUROIMMUNOLOGY

We have seen in this and earlier chapters that psychological and biological systems are interrelated—as one system changes, the others are often affected. The recognition of this interdependence and its connection to health and illness led researchers to form a new field of study called **psychoneuroimmunology.** This field focuses on the relationships between psychosocial processes and the activities of the nervous, endocrine, and immune systems (Ader & Cohen, 1985; Dunn, 1995; Maier, Watkins, & Fleshner, 1994). These systems form a *feedback loop*: the nervous and endocrine systems send chemical messages in the form of neurotransmitters and hormones that increase or decrease immune function, and cells of the immune system produce chemicals, such as ACTH, that feed information back to the brain. The brain appears to serve as a control center to maintain a balance in immune function, since too little immune activity leaves the individual open to infection and too much activity may produce autoimmune diseases.

Emotions and Immune Function

People's emotions—both positive and negative—play a critical role in the balance of immune functions. Research has shown that pessimism, depression, and stress from major and minor events are related to impaired immune function (Biondi & Pancheri, 1995; Dunn, 1995; Leonard, 1995; Levy & Heiden, 1991; Zautra et al., 1989). For example, studies have compared immune variables of caregiver spouses of Alzheimer's disease patients with matched control subjects. One study found that the caregivers had lower immune function and reported more days of illness over the course of about a year (Kiecolt-Glaser et al., 1991). Other studies have confirmed caregivers' reduced immune function and found that men's immune systems are more vulnerable than women's to caregiving stress (Scanlan et al., 1998) and that caregiving does not seem to impair immune responses when new brief stressors occur (Cacioppo et al., 1998).

Positive emotions can also affect immune function, giving it a boost (Futterman, Kemeny, Shapiro, & Fahey, 1994; Stone, Neale et al., 1994). In the study by Arthur Stone and his coworkers, adult men kept daily logs of positive and negative events and gave saliva samples for analyses of antibody content. Negative events were associated with reduced antibodies only for the day the events occurred, but positive events enhanced antibody content for the day of occurrence and the next two.

Some stressful situations start with a crisis, and the ensuing emotional states tend to continue and suppress immune processes over an extended period of time. This was demonstrated with healthy elderly individuals who were taking part in a longitudinal study of the aging process (Willis, Thomas, Garry, & Goodwin, 1987). The subjects were asked to contact the researchers as soon as they were able if they experienced any major crisis, such as the diagnosis of a serious illness in or the death of a spouse or child. Fifteen subjects did so. A month after the crisis, and again several months later, the researchers assessed the subjects' cortisol and lymphocyte blood concentrations, recent diets, weights, and psychological distress. Because the subjects were already participating in the longitudinal study, comparable data were available from a time prior to the crisis. Analysis of these data revealed that lymphocyte concentrations, caloric intake, and body weight decreased, and cortisol concentrations and psychological distress increased, soon after the crisis. By the time of the last assessment several months later, however, all of these measures had returned almost to the precrisis levels.

When people are reacting to short-term, minor events, such as doing difficult math problems under time pressure, changes in the number and activity of immune cells occur for fairly short periods of time—minutes or hours (Delahanty et al., 1996), and some measures even improve (Benschop et al., 1998). The degree of change seems to vary with the event's intensity, duration, and type—such as whether the event is interpersonal or nonsocial (Herbert & Cohen, 1993). Long-lasting and intense interpersonal events seem to produce especially large immune reductions. Of course, immune system reactivity varies from one person to the next, but a person's degree of response to a type of event seems to be much the

Reprinted with permission of United Features Syndicate, Inc.

same when tested weeks apart (Marsland et al., 1995). This suggests that an individual's reaction to specific stressors is fairly stable over time.

Psychosocial Modifiers of Immune System Reactivity

We saw earlier that psychosocial factors in people's lives may modify the stress they experience. Such factors seem to affect immune system responses, too. For instance, social support affects the immune function of people under long-term, intense stress. People who have strong social support have stronger immune systems and smaller immune impairments in response to stress than others with less support (Esterling, Kiecolt-Glaser, & Glaser, 1996; Kennedy, Kiecolt-Glaser, & Glaser, 1990; Kiecolt-Glaser et al., 1991; Levy et al., 1990). Research has also demonstrated that physical exercise and psychotherapy to reduce stress can enhance immune function in people infected with the AIDS virus (Antoni et al., 1990).

A related psychosocial modifier involves describing one's feelings about stressful events. An experiment with college student subjects examined the effect of expressing such feelings on blood concentrations of antibodies against the Epstein-Barr virus, a widespread virus that causes mononucleosis in many of those who are infected (Esterling et al., 1994). The students were randomly assigned to three conditions that met in three weekly 20-minute sessions when they either described *verbally* or *in writing* a highly stressful event they had experienced or wrote about a trivial (nonstress-related) topic, such as the contents of their bedrooms. The subjects in each condition had the same level of immune control against the virus

before the start of the study. But analysis of blood samples taken a week after the last session revealed that immune control improved substantially in the verbal condition, moderately in the written condition, and declined slightly in the control (trivial topic) condition, as Figure 4–4 depicts. Other research has found that describing feelings about stressful events is more effective in enhancing immune function in cynically hostile than in nonhostile individuals (Christensen et al., 1996).

The influence of optimism on immune function appears to depend on whether the stress is short-term or chronic. A study examined this issue with healthy women for 3 months (Cohen, Kearney et al.,

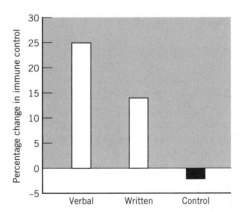

Figure 4–4   Percent change in immune control against the Epstein-Barr virus, as reflected in blood concentrations of specific antibodies, for subjects having sessions for verbal expression of stress feelings, written expression of stress feelings, or a control condition. (Based on data from Esterling et al., 1994, Figure 3.)

1999). The impact of optimism varied with the intensity of short-term stressors: immune function declined among pessimistic women, but not optimistic women, as stressor intensity increased. Perhaps the optimists appraised their stress in a more positive way. During chronic stressors, optimists showed progressive declines in immune function over time, but pessimists did not. It may be that the persistence of stress disconfirms optimists' beliefs that they can control negative events, which then makes the stress less bearable.

Lifestyles and Immune Function

Do people's lifestyles affect the functioning of their immune systems? Some evidence suggests that they do. People with generally healthful lifestyles—including exercising, getting enough sleep, eating balanced meals, and not smoking—show stronger immune functioning than those with less healthful lifestyles (Kusaka, Kondou, & Morimoto, 1992). Other studies have found that sleeping poorly impairs immune function the next day (Irwin et al., 1994) and people who smoke are more susceptible to catching colds (Cohen et al., 1993).

Conditioning Immune Function

Research on psychoneuroimmunology with animals has revealed that the influence of psychological processes on immune function is not limited to the effects of stress. The impact may be far more broad and pervasive. Robert Ader and Nicholas Cohen (1975, 1985) have described research showing that *immunosuppression can be conditioned.* In their original research, they were actually studying how animals learn to dislike certain tastes. The procedure used a single conditioning trial: the subjects (rats) received saccharin-flavored water to drink (which they seemed to like) and then got an injection of a drug that induces nausea. To see if the rats' subsequent dislike of the taste depended on its strength, some subjects received more saccharin flavoring than others in this conditioning trial. Over the next several weeks, the drug was *not* used, but the animals continued to receive saccharin-flavored water. During this time, the researchers noticed a curious thing: a number of rats had fallen ill and died—and these animals tended to be the ones that had consumed the greatest amount of saccharin in the conditioning trial.

How did these deaths relate to immunosuppression? Since the nausea-inducing drug used in the conditioning trial was also known to suppress immune function temporarily, Ader and Cohen hypothesized that the continued intake of saccharin water served as a conditioned stimulus, suppressing the ability of the rats to fight infection. Subsequent experiments by these researchers and others confirmed this hypothesis and demonstrated that conditioning can influence both antibody-mediated and cell-mediated immune processes (Ader & Cohen, 1985). Although the extent to which this kind of conditioning impairs immune function is fairly moderate, the effect is clear. Moreover, similar conditioning effects have been demonstrated in multiple sclerosis and cancer patients who receive medications that impair immune function (Giang et al., 1996; Lekander et al., 1995).

Psychoneuroimmunology is a very new and exciting field, and researchers are discovering fascinating connections between biological and psychosocial processes very quickly. And they are developing ways to apply this knowledge (Maier, Watkins, & Fleshner, 1994). For instance, Ader and Cohen (1982) demonstrated that conditioned immunosuppression may be useful in treating autoimmune diseases, in which the immune system attacks parts of the person's own body.

PSYCHOPHYSIOLOGICAL DISORDERS

The word *psychosomatic* has a long history, and was coined to refer to symptoms or illnesses that are caused or aggravated by psychological factors, mainly emotional stress (Lipowski, 1986). Although many professionals and the general public still use this term, the concept has undergone some changes and now has a new name: **psychophysiological disorders,** which refers to physical symptoms or illnesses that result from the interplay of psychosocial and physiological processes. This definition clearly uses a biopsychosocial perspective. We will discuss several illnesses traditionally classified as psychosomatic. Some of these illnesses will be examined in greater detail in later chapters.

DIGESTIVE SYSTEM DISEASES

Ulcers and **inflammatory bowel disease** are two illnesses that involve wounds in the digestive tract that may cause pain and bleeding (AMA, 1989). Ulcers are found in the stomach and the duodenum, or upper section of the small intestine. Inflammatory bowel disease, which includes disorders such as *colitis*, can occur in the colon (large intestine) and the small intestine. Although ulcers and inflammatory bowel disease afflict mostly adults, these illnesses also occur in childhood and adolescence (Schwartz & Blanchard, 1990; Whitehead, 1986). Another digestive system illness, **irritable bowel syndrome,** produces abdominal pain, diarrhea, and constipation without organic evidence of disease (AMA, 1989).

Researchers generally believe most ulcers are produced by a combination of excess gastric juices chronically eroding the lining of the stomach and duodenum that has been weakened by bacterial infection (Rhoades & Pflanzer, 1996). But stress plays a role, too (Levenstein, Ackerman, Kiecolt-Glaser, & Dubois, 1999). In a classic study, a patient (called Tom) agreed to cooperate in a lengthy and detailed examination of gastric function (Wolf & Wolff, 1947). Tom was unique in that many years earlier, at the age of 9, he had had a stomach operation that left an opening to the outside of the body. This opening, which provided the only way he could feed himself, was literally a window through which the inside of his stomach could be observed. When Tom was subjected to stressful situations, causing feelings of hostility and anxiety, his stomach-acid production greatly increased. When he was under emotional tension for several weeks, there was a pronounced reddening of the stomach lining. Another study reported similar effects with a 15-month-old girl, Monica, who had a temporary opening to her stomach. Her highest levels of acid secretion occurred when she experienced rage (Engel, Reichsman, & Segal, 1956).

The physical causes of inflammatory bowel disease and irritable bowel syndrome are not yet known (AMA, 1989). Most studies have found that flare-ups of these illnesses are related to stress, but some studies have not (Levy, Cain, Jarrett, & Heitkemper, 1997; Schwartz & Blanchard, 1990; Suls, Wan, & Blanchard, 1994; Traue & Kosarz, 1999). Although stress seems to influence these digestive system diseases in many patients, its specific role is currently unclear.

ASTHMA

Asthma is a respiratory disorder in which inflammation, spasms, and mucous obstruct the bronchial tubes and lead to difficulty breathing, with wheezing or coughing. This ailment is prevalent around the world—in the United States it afflicts nearly 6% of the population and is more common in children than in adults (ALA, 2000; AAFA, 2000). Asthma attacks appear to result from some combination of three factors: allergies, respiratory infections, and biopsychosocial arousal, such as from stress (AAFA, 2000; Wright, Rodriguez, & Cohen, 1998). In most cases, the cause of an attack is largely physical, but sometimes it may be largely psychosocial.

Professionals working with hospitalized children have noted an interesting phenomenon that suggests a role of psychosocial factors in asthma. About one-third of asthmatic children show reduced symptoms shortly after admission to the hospital even though their medication is not changed. When they return home, the symptoms reappear (Purcell, Weiss, & Hahn, 1972). Does this happen because the children are allergic to something in their own houses, such as dust, or because of other factors? This question was tested in an ingenious study with asthmatic children who were allergic to house dust (Long et al., 1958). Without the children knowing, the researchers vacuumed the children's homes and then sprayed the collected dust from each house into their individual hospital rooms. *None* of the children had respiratory difficulty when exposed to their home dust, which suggests that psychosocial factors may be involved. The results of other research indicate that stress can trigger asthma attacks (Miller & Wood, 1994; Sarafino & Goldfedder, 1995; Wright, Rodriguez, & Cohen, 1998).

RECURRENT HEADACHE

Many people suffer chronically from intense headaches. Although there are many types of recurrent headache, two of the most common are called tension-type and migraine headache (Andrasik, Blake, & McCarran, 1986; Lipton, Silberstein, & Stewart, 1994; Pothmann et al., 1994). **Tension-type** (or *muscle-contraction*) **headaches** seem to be caused by persistent contraction of the head and neck muscles, which is a typical feature of people's reaction to stressors (AMA, 1989). The pain it produces is a dull and steady ache that often feels like a tight band of pressure around the head. Recurrent tension-type headaches occur twice a week or more, and may last for hours, days, or weeks (Dalessio, 1994).

Figure 4–5 Drawing by 11-year-old Meghan of her experience of migraine headache pain. The lower left-hand corner has a self-portrait with a dramatic facial expression. When a headache begins, Meghan typically retreats to her bedroom "to ride out the storm," lying down in a darkened room. (From Andrasik, Blake, & McCarran, 1986, Figure 18.1.)

Migraine headaches seem to involve the dilation of blood vessels surrounding the brain (AMA, 1989). The pain often begins on one side of the head near the temple, is sharp and throbbing, and lasts for hours or, sometimes, days (Dalessio, 1994). One form of migraine either begins with or is preceded by an *aura*, a set of symptoms that signal an impending headache episode. These symptoms usually include sensory phenomena, such as seeing lines or shimmerings in the visual field. This may be accompanied by dizziness, nausea, and vomiting. Recurrent migraine is marked by periodic debilitating symptoms, which occur about once a month, with headache-free periods in between (Dalessio, 1994; Stewart, Shechter, & Lipton, 1994).

The great majority of adults and children have headaches at least occasionally, and frequent tension-type headaches are common (Andrasik, Blake, & McCarran, 1986; Lipton, Silberstein, & Stewart, 1994; Pothmann et al., 1994). The prevalence of migraine varies widely across cultures, but is about 10% overall, is far greater in females than males, and increases with age from childhood to middle age, and then declines (Stewart, Shechter, & Rasmussen, 1994). Many children experience their first headaches in the preschool

years, and chronic headaches have been reported in boys and girls as young as 6 years of age (Andrasik, Blake, & McCarran, 1986). Figure 4–5 presents a drawing by an 11-year-old girl named Meghan to describe her experience of migraine headache pain.

What triggers headaches? They often are brought on by weather changes, missing a meal, sunlight, sleeping poorly, and consuming certain substances, such as alcohol or chocolate. Research has also shown that stressors—particularly the hassles of everyday living—are among the most common triggers of migraine and tension-type headaches (Köhler & Haimerl, 1990; Martin & Seneviratne, 1997; Robbins, 1994; Wittrock & Myers, 1998). Yet some chronic-headache patients have attacks when they are not under great stress, and others fail to have headaches when they are under stress. Stress appears to be one of many factors that produce headaches, but the full nature of these causes is not yet known.

OTHER DISORDERS

There are several other psychophysiological disorders for which stress appears to be involved in triggering or aggravating episodes. One of these illnesses is *rheumatoid arthritis*—a chronic and very painful disease that produces inflammation and stiffness of the small joints, such as in the hands. It afflicts about 1% of the general population, and its victims are primarily women (AF, 2000; Anderson et al., 1985). Another disorder, called *dysmenorrhea*, affects millions of women. It is characterized by painful menstruation, which may be accompanied by nausea, headache, and dizziness (Calhoun & Burnette, 1983; Schuster, 1986). A third stress-related problem involves skin disorders, such as *hives*, *eczema*, and *psoriasis*, in which the skin develops rashes or becomes dry and flakes or cracks (Grossbart, 1982). In many cases, specific allergies are identified as contributing to episodes of these skin problems (Burg & Ingall, 1985).

Although current evidence implicates both biological and psychosocial causes for each of the psychophysiological disorders we have considered, the evidence is sketchy and the nature of the interplay of these factors is unclear. For the remainder of this chapter we will focus on the role of stress in the development of cardiovascular disorders and cancer.

STRESS AND CARDIOVASCULAR DISORDERS

Earlier in this chapter, we saw that psychosocial modifiers of stress can affect health—for instance, the risk of developing CHD is greater for people with the Type A than the Type B behavior pattern. Such findings indirectly implicate stress as a factor in the development of cardiovascular disorders, the number-one cause of death in the United States and many other countries. Is there more direct evidence for this link? A large body of evidence indicates that stress plays a role in the development of two types of cardiovascular disorders, hypertension and CHD.

HYPERTENSION

Hypertension—the condition of having high blood pressure consistently over several weeks or more—is a major risk factor for CHD, stroke, and kidney disease (AHA, 2000; NCHS, 2000; NKF, 2000). In the United States, about one-fourth of the adult population is classified as hypertensive, having blood pressures that consistently exceed 140 (systolic) over 90

(diastolic). The prevalence rates for hypertension increase in adulthood, particularly after about 40 years of age. Fortunately, the percentage of American adults with high blood pressure has markedly declined since 1980 (NCHS, 2000). Some cases of hypertension are caused by, or are *secondary* to, disorders of other body systems or organs, such as the kidneys or endocrine system. Secondary hypertension can usually be cured by medical procedures. But the vast majority—over 90%—of hypertensive cases are classified as *primary* or **essential hypertension,** in which the mechanisms causing the high blood pressure are unknown.

To say that the causes for essential hypertension are unknown is somewhat misleading. In cases of essential hypertension, physicians are unable to identify any biomedical causes, such as infectious agents or organ damage. But many risk factors are associated with the development of hypertension—and there is evidence now implicating several of these risk factors as determinants of hypertension (AHA, 2000; Shapiro & Goldstein, 1982). These determinants include:

- Obesity
- Dietary elements, such as salt, fats, and cholesterol
- Excessive alcohol use
- Physical inactivity
- Family history of hypertension
- Psychosocial factors

The psychosocial factors that have received the most research attention involve stress and emotional behaviors, such as anger and hostility. One interesting finding is that just the anxiety involved in having blood pressure tested can increase the reading in some individuals, leading to a false diagnosis of hypertension (McGrady & Higgins, 1990).

Stress, Emotions, and Hypertension

People's occupations provide sources of stress that can have an impact on their blood pressure. Traffic controllers at airports provide an example. Sidney Cobb and Robert Rose (1973) compared the medical records of thousands of men employed as air traffic controllers or as second-class airmen. Both occupations require yearly physical examinations for renewal of their licenses. The medical records were separated so that comparisons could be made for

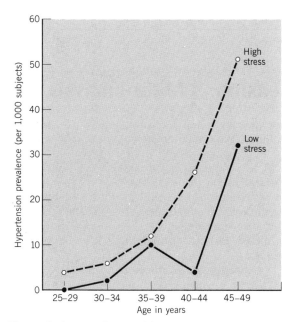

Figure 4–6 Prevalence of hypertension per 1,000 air traffic controllers as a function of stress and age. Hypertension rates increase with age and stress. (Data from Cobb & Rose, 1973, Table 3.)

different age groups, since blood pressure increases with age. These comparisons for each age group revealed prevalence rates of hypertension among the traffic controllers that were several times higher than those among airmen. The researchers also compared the records of traffic controllers who experienced high and low levels of stress, as measured by the traffic density at the air stations where they worked. Figure 4–6 depicts the results of this analysis: for each age group, prevalence rates of hypertension were higher for traffic controllers working at high-stress locations than for those at low-stress sites.

Aspects of social environments, such as crowding and aggression, are also linked to stress and hypertension. Experiments with animals have shown that living in crowded, aggressive conditions induces chronic hypertension (Henry et al., 1993). Research with humans compared cardiovascular reactivity among people who live in crowded and uncrowded neighborhoods to see if living in these conditions influences blood pressure (Fleming et al., 1987). The subjects from the two types of neighborhoods were similar in important characteristics, such as age, gender, and family income. While working on a stressful cognitive

task, residents from crowded neighborhoods showed greater increases in heart rate and systolic and diastolic pressure than those from uncrowded neighborhoods. Findings of other research indicate that high cardiovascular reactivity may be a risk factor for, or even a cause of, hypertension (Fredrikson & Matthews, 1990; Manuck, 1994; Menkes et al., 1989). Taken together, the evidence suggests that chronic stress plays an important role in the development of hypertension.

Research on psychosocial factors in the development of essential hypertension has also examined the roles of pessimism, anger, and hostility. Pessimistic individuals have higher blood pressure than optimistic people (Räikkönen et al., 1999). Some studies have found that hypertensives are more likely to be chronically hostile and resentful than are *normotensives*—that is, people who have normal blood pressure (Diamond, 1982). Other studies have shown that systolic and diastolic blood pressure increase more when people experience anger and hostility in their everyday lives than when they experience positive emotions, such as happiness (James et al., 1986; Southard et al., 1986). In some families, interpersonal conflicts among parents and children can be major sources of chronic anger, which may lead to hypertension (Ewart, 1991a). These findings indicate that chronically high levels of pessimism, anger, and hostility may contribute to the high blood pressure of many hypertensives. (Go to ✎.)

Stress and Sociocultural Differences in Hypertension

The impact of occupational and environmental stressors on hypertension may be particularly relevant for black people in the United States, who have a much higher prevalence rate of high blood pressure than whites do (NCHS, 2000). In a study of black and white people in Detroit, the highest blood pressure readings found were those of blacks living in high-stress areas of the city—neighborhoods that were crowded and had high crime rates and low incomes (Harburg et al., 1973). But blacks and whites who lived in low-stress areas had similar blood pressures. In addition, a study of occupational stressors among black men found that high blood pressure was associated with the subjects' perceptions of low job security, of lack of job success, and of being hindered in their chances of achieving

FOCUS ON RESEARCH

Reactivity and Hypertension: A Meta-analysis

We saw in Chapter 3 that *meta-analysis* is a statistical research method that pools the results of prior studies to create an integrated overview of their findings. Although the purpose of meta-analysis is fairly easy to understand, doing one can be very complex because decisions that can alter the outcome need to be made (Suls & Swain, 1993). For example, if you were doing a meta-analysis, would you use only studies that have been published? Will you want to restrict the included studies to only those that had control groups or tested people of certain ages or genders? How broadly will you define your variables—for instance, for the variable of fear, will you include anxieties and phobias?

Mats Fredrikson and Karen Matthews (1990) did a meta-analysis to clarify the connection between reactivity and hypertension. They knew that some studies had found greater reactivity to stressors in hypertensive people than in normotensives, but other studies had not. They decided to focus their meta-analysis on *cardiovascular* reactivity—blood pressure and heart rate—and to include only studies that, for instance, tested hypertensive patients who were

not currently taking antihypertensive drugs; had a normotensive control group; and measured reactivity in a laboratory with a psychological stressor, such as performing mental arithmetic or watching a stressful film, rather than a physical one, such as exercising. Then they searched the medical and psychological literature using the restrictions they had decided on, found dozens of studies that qualified, and analyzed relevant data with a computer program.

Fredrikson and Matthews organized the meta-analysis to examine several important issues. This analysis revealed two previously unknown patterns: (1) Patients with relatively mild hypertension exhibit heart rate and blood pressure reactivity mainly to psychological stressors that require them to be *active*, such as doing arithmetic, rather than *passive*, as in watching a stressful film. (2) Patients with more severe hypertension show reactivity to *all* types of psychological stressors. Many earlier studies had found no link between cardiovascular reactivity and hypertension because they tested mild hypertensives with passive stressors.

---

job success because they were black (James, LaCroix, Kleinbaum, & Strogatz, 1984). The role of racial discrimination in hypertension is suggested by the finding that blood pressure and darkness of skin color are correlated for black men and women of low socioeconomic status, but not for blacks with higher income or education. For lower-class black people, those with darker skin probably have fewer economic and social resources available, thereby worsening their stress (Klag et al., 1991).

Few, if any, cases of essential hypertension are likely to be caused by emotional factors alone (Schneiderman & Hammer, 1985). Most cases of high blood pressure probably involve several of the determinants listed earlier in this section.

CORONARY HEART DISEASE

Epidemiologists have studied the distribution and frequency of CHD over many decades in many differ-

ent cultures. The data they have collected suggest that CHD is, to some extent, a disease of modernized societies—that is, the incidence rate of heart disease is higher in technologically advanced countries than in other nations (Susser, Hopper, & Richman, 1983).

There are many reasons why modernized societies have higher rates of CHD. For one thing, people in technologically advanced societies live longer than people in less-developed countries—they are less likely to die of infectious diseases, such as malaria, for instance. As a result, people in advanced societies live long enough to become victims of CHD, which afflicts mainly older individuals. Also, people in modernized societies are more likely than those in less-developed countries to have certain risk factors for CHD, such as obesity and low levels of physical activity. Last, the psychosocial stressors of modernized societies are different from those in other societies and may be more conducive to the development of heart disease.

The link between stress and CHD has considerable support. For example, studies of occupational stress have shown that high workloads, job responsibility, and job dissatisfaction are associated with a high incidence of CHD (Cottington & House, 1987; Quick, Quick, Nelson, & Hurrell, 1997). Other research has examined the relationship between heart disease and major life stressors. Retrospective studies have found that victims of myocardial infarction tended to have high levels of life events in the months preceding the attack (Garrity & Marx, 1979). Prospective research has also supported the link between stress and CHD. For instance, researchers carried out periodic follow-up assessments over an 8-year period with patients who had recovered from their first myocardial infarctions (Theorell & Rahe, 1975). These patients were separated into two groups—those who did and those who did not have subsequent attacks. The group who suffered subsequent infarctions—some of whom died—had experienced a substantial buildup in life events over the year or so preceding the attacks. But the group who had no recurrence of heart attack reported no increase in life events during the study.

We have seen that stress increases catecholamine and corticosteroid release by the endocrine glands and that chronically high levels of these hormones can damage the arteries and heart, promote atherosclerosis, and lead to the development of hypertension and arteriosclerosis (hardening of the arteries). Stress can also produce cardiac arrhythmia, which can cause a cardiac episode and sudden death. These are some of the physiological connections between stress and CHD. There are behavioral connections, too. Stress is associated with cigarette smoking and high levels of alcohol use, for example, which are behavioral risk factors for CHD (Epstein & Jennings, 1986; Levenson, 1986). In later chapters we will examine in greater detail various risk factors and issues relating to CHD and the next stress-related illness, cancer.

STRESS AND CANCER

The idea that stress and other psychosocial factors contribute to the development of cancer has a long history. The physician Galen, who practiced in Rome during the second century A.D., believed that individuals who were sad and depressed, or "melancholy," were more likely to develop cancer than those who were happy, confident, and vigorous (Sklar & Anisman, 1981). Similar ideas have appeared in the writings of physicians in later eras.

Cancer is a term that refers to a broad class of disease in which cells multiply and grow in an unrestrained manner. As such, cancer does not refer to a single illness, but to dozens of disease forms that share this characteristic (ACS, 2000; Levy, 1985; Williams, 1990). It includes, for instance, *leukemias*, in which the bone marrow produces excessive numbers of white blood cells, and *carcinomas*, in which tumors form in the tissue of the skin and internal organ linings. Some cancers take longer to develop or follow more irregular courses in their development than others do. Because cancer appears in so many different forms, each with its own characteristics, it is very difficult to study its causes (Fox, 1978). Nevertheless, some evidence suggests that stress may play a role in the beginnings and progression of cancer.

Early evidence linking stress and cancer came from research using retrospective methods (Blaney, 1985; Sklar & Anisman, 1981). This research generally had cancer patients fill out life events questionnaires to assess the stress they experienced during the year or so preceding the diagnosis. A number of studies found that the appearance of several forms of cancer in children and adults was associated with their reports of high levels of prior stress. But there are problems with retrospective methods that cloud the interpretation of the results of these studies (Fox, 1978; Sklar & Anisman, 1981). For one thing, the cancer diagnosis is typically made years after—sometimes many years after—the disease process starts. As a result, the patients' cancers were probably present prior to and during the year for which they reported high levels of stress. Also, the patients' perceptions or recollections of prior stress may have been distorted by their knowledge that they have cancer. A better approach to assess the role of stress in the development of cancer would be to use prospective methods: measure or introduce psychosocial factors and follow up on the subjects' health over time. Some studies have used this approach, either by monitoring the incidence of cancer in individuals who were healthy at the start of the research or by following the progress of the disease in people who were already diagnosed with cancer.

An overview of findings from research on cancer and stress published since the mid-1970s suggests five conclusions. First, there is little connection between the experience of stress and later development of cancer (McKenna, Zevon, Corn, & Rounds, 1999;

Petticrew, Fraser, & Regan, 1999; Temoshok, 1990; Watson & Ramirez, 1991). Second, cancer patients who have relapses within a given time period, such as a year, tend to have experienced more stressful life events or received less social support during that time than those who do not have relapses (Rogentine et al., 1979; Sabbioni, 1991; Watson & Ramirez, 1991). Third, although cancer patients typically experience high levels of stress after diagnosis, their immune functions are less able to fight the cancer if their stress is very high (Andersen et al., 1998). Fourth, people who generally respond to stressors with appeasing, compliant, and unexpressive behaviors (sometimes called the Type C behavior pattern) seem more likely than others to develop cancer (Temoshok, 1990; Temoshok & Dreher, 1992). Fifth, some evidence indicates that cancer patients who receive therapy to reduce their stress live longer than those who do not (Kiecolt-Glaser & Glaser, 1995).

The effects of stress on cancer seem to be influenced by many factors, such as the stressor's source or type, whether it is chronic, the way the person reacts to it, and whether it is experienced before or after initiation of the carcinogen or tumor. If stress plays a causal role in the development of cancer, it probably does so by impairing the immune system's ability to combat the disease and by increasing behavioral risk factors, such as smoking cigarettes.

SUMMARY

Researchers have identified several psychosocial factors that modify the impact of stress on the individual. One of these factors is social support—the perceived comfort, caring, esteem, or help a person receives from other people or groups. There are five basic types of support: emotional, esteem, tangible or instrumental, informational, and network. Whether people receive social support depends on characteristics of the recipients and providers of support and on the composition and structure of the social network.

Social support appears to reduce the stress people experience and generally enhance their health. The greater the degrees of support people have, the lower their mortality rates and likelihood of becoming ill. These benefits seem to accrue in two ways. First, social support may buffer the person against the negative effects of high levels of stress. Second, social support may enhance health regardless of the level of stress by simply providing encouragement for leading healthful lifestyles, for instance.

Another psychosocial modifier of stress is people's sense of personal control over events in their lives. Personal control includes beliefs about one's locus of control—that is, whether control is internal or external to the person—and self-efficacy. People acquire a sense of personal control from their successes and failures and through the process of social learning. Individuals who experience prolonged, high levels of stress and have a weak sense of personal control tend to feel helpless. The cognitive process of attribution seems to be important in the development of learned helplessness. A strong sense of personal control tends to benefit people's health and help them adjust to a serious illness if it occurs. Hardiness is another psychosocial modifier of stress that may help people remain healthy when under stress.

One other psychosocial modifier of stress is people's tendency toward either the Type A or the Type B behavior pattern. The Type A behavior pattern consists of three characteristics: competitive achievement orientation, time urgency, and anger or hostility. Compared with Type Bs, Type A individuals respond more quickly and strongly to stressors both in their overt behaviors and in their physiological reactivity. The Type A pattern—particularly the anger/hostility component—is associated with the development of coronary heart disease (CHD) and hypertension. Both biological and psychosocial factors affect the development of the Type A and B behavior patterns.

Stress affects health in two ways. First, stress can affect health-related behaviors, such as alcohol and cigarette use. Second, it produces changes in the body's physical systems, as when the endocrine system releases catecholamines and corticosteroids, which can cause damage to the heart and blood vessels and impair immune system functioning. The physical effects of intense stress can even lead to sudden death. Psychoneuroimmunology is a new field of study that focuses on how psychosocial processes and the nervous, endocrine, and immune systems are interrelated. Stress also plays a role in many psychophysiological disorders, such as ulcers, asthma, tension-type and migraine headache, rheumatoid arthritis, and several skin disorders. In addition, stress is implicated in the development of hypertension, CHD, and cancer.

KEY TERMS

social support	informational control	coronary heart disease (CHD)	inflammatory bowel disease
social network	locus of control	sudden death	irritable bowel syndrome
buffering hypothesis	self-efficacy	carcinogens	asthma
direct effects hypothesis	learned helplessness	psychoneuroimmunology	tension-type headaches
personal control	attribution	psychophysiological disorders	migraine headaches
behavioral control	hardiness	ulcers	hypertension
cognitive control	Type A behavior pattern		essential hypertension
decisional control	Type B behavior pattern		

5

COPING WITH AND REDUCING STRESS

PROLOGUE

One morning while taking a shower, Cicely felt a small lump in her breast. She was sure it had not been there before. It didn't hurt, but she was momentarily alarmed—her mother had had breast cancer a few years before. "It could be a pimple or some other benign growth," she thought. Still, it was very worrisome. She decided not to tell her husband or her physician about it yet because as she thought, "it may not be anything." Over the next several days, she examined the lump daily. This was a very stressful time for her, and she slept poorly and seemed preoccupied. After a week without the lump changing, she decided to take action. She told her husband and made an appointment to see her physician.

Another woman, Beth, had a similar experience. Finding a lump on her breast alarmed her, but she didn't deal with the stress as rationally as Cicely did. Beth's initial fright led her to reexamine her breast just once, and in a cursory way. She told herself, "There isn't really a *lump* on my breast, it's just a rough spot." And she convinced herself that she should not touch it because, she thought, "That will only make it worse." During the next few months, Beth was quite worried about the "rough spot." She studiously avoided touching it, even while washing. She became increasingly moody, slept poorly, and developed many more headaches than usual. She also told her husband that she didn't like him to fondle her breasts in lovemaking. When he asked why she was acting so differently in recent weeks, she denied that anything was wrong. Beth finally mentioned the "rough spot" to a friend who convinced her to have her physician examine it.

People vary in the ways they deal with stress. Sometimes people confront a problem directly and rationally, as Cicely did, and sometimes they do not. For these two women, the way they dealt with their stress had the potential for affecting their health. Because Beth did not face up to the reality of the lump, she delayed seeking medical attention and experienced high levels of stress for a long time. If the lump were malignant, delaying treatment would allow the cancer to progress and spread. As we have seen, prolonged stress can have adverse health effects even in healthy people.

In this chapter we discuss the ways people can and do deal with stress. Through this discussion, you will find answers to questions you may have about the methods people use in handling stress. Are some methods for coping with stress more effective than others? How can people reduce the potential for stress in their lives? When people encounter a stressor, how can they reduce the strain it produces?

COPING WITH STRESS

Individuals of all ages experience stress and try to deal with it. During childhood years, people learn ways to manage feelings of stress that arise from the many fearful situations they experience (Sarafino, 1986). Many children fear thunderstorms. Psychologist Lois Murphy (1974, p. 76) has described the progress a little girl named Molly made in dealing with the terror she felt during thunderstorms. At 3 years of age, Molly's efforts to gain control of her fear during a storm were reflected in her trying to reassure herself and her baby brother by saying, "It's just noise and it really won't hurt you a bit." But a month later, she was again frightened by overhead noise, this time from a plane flying low, and later said, "I'm not scared of planes, only thunder."

At the age of 4, Molly's behavior during two storms, 4 months apart, showed that she was gaining substantial control over her fear. In the first storm, she awoke

from a nap during a thunderstorm, but remained quietly in bed. Afterward she said to her sister,

"There was lots of thunder, but I just snuggled in my bed and didn't cry a bit."

In the second storm, she

> showed no open fear herself during a storm, and comforted her frightened brother, saying, "I remember when I was a little baby and I was scared of thunder and I used to cry and cry every time it thundered."

Although Molly's progress had some setbacks, such as when the plane flew very low, she became better able to cope effectively with this stressor as she grew older. What's more, in the last steps of her progress she showed pride in having mastered her fear.

WHAT IS COPING?

Because the emotional and physical strain that accompanies stress is uncomfortable, people are motivated to do things to reduce their stress. These "things" are what is involved in coping.

What is coping? Several definitions of coping exist (Lazarus, 1987; Lazarus & Folkman, 1984b). We will use a definition that is consistent with the way we defined stress earlier. In Chapter 3 we saw that stress involves a *perceived discrepancy* between the demands of the situation and the resources of the person. Since people engage in coping in an effort to neutralize or reduce stress, coping activities are geared toward decreasing the person's appraisal of or concern for this discrepancy. Thus, **coping** is the process by which people try to *manage the perceived discrepancy* between the demands and resources they appraise in a stressful situation.

The word *manage* in this definition is important. It indicates that coping efforts can be quite varied and do not necessarily lead to a solution of the problem. Coping efforts can—and, some would argue, should—be aimed at correcting or mastering the problem. But they may also simply help the person alter his or her perception of a discrepancy, tolerate or accept the harm or threat, or escape or avoid the situation (Lazarus & Folkman, 1984b; Moos & Schaefer, 1986). For example, a child who faces a stressful exam in school might cope by feeling nauseated and staying home.

We cope with stress through our cognitive and behavioral transactions with the environment. Suppose you are overweight and smoke cigarettes,

and your physician has asked you to lose weight and stop smoking because several factors place you at very high risk for developing heart disease. You have a threat: you may become disabled or die. This is stressful, but you don't think you can change your behavior. How might you cope with this? Some people would cope by seeking information about ways to improve their ability to change. Other people would simply find another doctor who is not so directive. Others would attribute their health to fate or "the will of God," and leave the problem "in His hands." Still others would try to deaden this and other worries with alcohol, which would add to the risk. People use many different methods to try to manage the appraised discrepancy between the demands of the situation and their resources.

The coping process is not a single event. Because coping involves ongoing transactions with the environment, the process is best viewed as a dynamic series

> of continuous appraisals and reappraisals of the shifting person–environment relationships. Shifts may be the result of coping efforts directed at changing the environment, or coping directed inward that changes the meaning of the event or increases understanding. They may also be the result of changes in the environment that are independent of the person and his or her coping activity. Regardless of its source, any shift in the person–environment relationship will lead to a reevaluation of what is happening, its significance, and what can be done. The reevaluation process, or reappraisal, in turn influences subsequent coping efforts. (Lazarus & Folkman, 1984b, pp. 142–143)

And so, in coping with the threat of serious illness, people who make efforts to change their lifestyles may receive encouragement and better relationships with their physician and family. But individuals who ignore the problem are likely to experience worse and worse health and relations with these people. Each shift in one direction or the other is affected by the transactions that preceded it and affects subsequent transactions.

FUNCTIONS AND METHODS OF COPING

You have probably realized by now that people have an enormous number of ways for coping with stress. Because of this, researchers have attempted to

ASSESS YOURSELF

Your Focuses in Coping

Think about a very stressful personal crisis or life event you experienced in the last year—the more recent and stressful the event, the better for this exercise. How did you handle this situation and your stress? Some of the ways people handle stressful experiences are listed below. Mark an "X" in the space preceding each one you used.

_____ Tried to see a positive side to it

_____ Tried to step back from the situation and be more objective

_____ Prayed for guidance or strength

_____ Sometimes took it out on other people when I felt angry or depressed

_____ Got busy with other things to keep my mind off the problem

_____ Decided not to worry about it because I figured everything would work out fine

_____ Took things one step at a time

_____ Read relevant material for solutions and considered several alternatives

_____ Drew on my knowledge because I had a similar experience before

_____ Talked to a friend or relative to get advice on handling the problem

_____ Talked with a professional person (e.g., doctor, clergy, lawyer, teacher, counselor) about ways to improve the situation

_____ Took some action to improve the situation

Count how many of the first six ways you marked—these are examples of "emotion-focused" ways. How many of the second six—"problem-focused"—ways did you mark? When you read the upcoming text material entitled _Functions of Coping_, answer these questions: Did you use mostly emotion- or problem-focused methods? Why, and what functions did your methods serve? (_Source:_ Based on material in Billings and Moos, 1981.)

organize coping approaches on the basis of their functions and the methods they employ. (Go to 🍎.)

Functions of Coping

According to Richard Lazarus and his colleagues, coping can serve two main functions (Cohen & Lazarus, 1979; Lazarus, 1999; Lazarus & Folkman, 1984b). It can alter the _problem_ causing the stress or it can regulate the _emotional_ response to the problem.

Emotion-focused coping is aimed at controlling the emotional response to the stressful situation. People can regulate their emotional responses through _behavioral_ and _cognitive_ approaches. Examples of _behavioral_ approaches include using alcohol or drugs, seeking emotional social support from friends or relatives, and engaging in activities, such as sports or watching TV, that distract one's attention from the problem. _Cognitive_ approaches involve how people think about the stressful situation. In one cognitive approach, people change the meaning of the

situation—for example, by deciding, "There are worse things in life than having to change jobs because of my heart condition," or, "Now that my girlfriend has left me, I realize that I really didn't need her." Another cognitive approach involves denying unpleasant facts, as Beth did with the lump on her breast.

People tend to use emotion-focused approaches when they believe they can do nothing to change the stressful conditions (Lazarus & Folkman, 1984b). An example of this is when a loved one dies—in this situation, people often seek emotional support and distract themselves with funeral arrangements and chores at home or at work. Other examples can be seen in situations in which individuals believe their resources are not and cannot be adequate to meet the demands of the stressor. A child who tries very hard to be the "straight A" student his or her parents seem to want, but never succeeds, may reappraise the situation and decide, "I don't need their love."

Problem-focused coping is aimed at reducing the demands of the stressful situation or expanding the resources to deal with it. Everyday life provides many examples of problem-focused coping, including quitting a stressful job, negotiating an extension for paying some bills, devising a new schedule for studying (and sticking to it), choosing a different career to pursue, seeking medical or psychological treatment, and learning new skills. People tend to use problem-focused approaches when they believe their resources or the demands of the situation are changeable (Lazarus & Folkman, 1984b). For example, caregivers of terminally ill patients use problem-focused coping more in the months prior to the death than during bereavement (Moskowitz, Folkman, Collette, & Vittinghoff, 1996).

To what extent do people use problem-focused and emotion-focused approaches in coping with stress in their lives? Andrew Billings and Rudolf Moos (1981) studied this issue by having nearly 200 married couples fill out a survey. The respondents described a recent personal crisis or negative life event that happened to them and then answered questions that were very similar to the ones you answered in the self-assessment exercise. The outcomes of this research revealed some interesting relationships. Both the husbands and the wives used more problem-focused than emotion-focused methods to cope with the stressful event. But the wives reported using more emotion-focused approaches than the husbands did. People with higher incomes and educational levels reported greater use of problem-focused coping than those with less income and education. Last, individuals used much less problem-focused coping when the stress involved a death in the family than when it involved other kinds of problems, such as illness or economic difficulties.

Can problem-focused and emotion-focused coping be used together? Yes, and they often are—for instance, when people have painful medical conditions (Tennen, Affleck, Armeli, & Carney, 2000). We can see an example of using both in the case of a man who experienced stress when he was accused by a coworker of not sending out the appropriate letters for a job. In describing how he reacted to this accusation, he said:

> Well, it burned me up. . . . My immediate first reaction was to confirm . . . that what he was saying was not true, that everything [letters] had gone out. There's always a chance you might be wrong so I checked first. Then I told him. No, everything had gone out. My immediate reaction was to call him on the carpet first. He doesn't have any right to call me on something like this. Then I gave it a second thought and decided that that wouldn't help the situation. (Kahn et al., cited in Lazarus & Folkman, 1984b, p. 155)

This example shows problem-focused coping in confirming that the letters had gone out, and emotion-focused coping in controlling his angry impulse "to call him on the carpet."

Methods of Coping: Skills and Strategies

What types of skills and strategies do people use in altering the problem or regulating their emotional response when they experience stress? Table 5.1 describes several commonly used ways of coping that Susan Folkman, Richard Lazarus, and their colleagues (1986, 1988) identified from their research. The table labels the strategies as serving problem- or emotion-focused coping functions and gives examples of cognitive or behavioral efforts a hospital patient might make when using each strategy. Coping methods that focus on emotions are important because

"I COULD HAVE OPENED THE JAR THAT WAY!"

Reprinted courtesy of Bunny Hoest.
Sometimes people don't cope effectively with stress.

Table 5.1 *Ways of Coping with Stressful Situations*

- *Planful problem-solving* (problem-focused): analyzing the situation to arrive at solutions and then taking direct action to correct the problem. For instance, Roy, a hospital patient who needs to choose a specialist for a serious illness, might seek and study information about different specialists before choosing.
- *Confrontive coping* (problem-focused): taking assertive action, often involving anger or risk-taking, to change the situation. For example, if Roy's medical insurance balks at paying for a desired treatment, he might stand his ground and fight for payment.
- *Seeking social support* (can be problem- or emotion-focused): trying to acquire informational or emotional support. For instance, Roy might ask friends and nurses about different specialists (informational support with a problem-focused function) and describe his worries to get comfort and encouragement from people he loves (emotion-focused function).
- *Distancing* (emotion-focused): making cognitive efforts to detach oneself from the situation or create a positive outlook. As an example, Roy might try not to think about the health-related problems he's facing or try to make light of them.
- *Escape–avoidance* (emotion-focused): thinking wishfully about the situation or taking action to escape or avoid it. For instance, Roy might engage in fantasies of miracles or other external happenings that would make his problems go away, or he might try to avoid dealing with the problems by sleeping or using alcohol a lot.
- *Self-control* (emotion-focused): attempting to modulate one's own feelings or actions in relation to the problem. Roy might hide his feelings to prevent emotional interactions with others or slow down the pace of decision making to prevent impulsive choices.
- *Accepting responsibility* (emotion-focused): acknowledging one's own role in the problem while also trying to put things right. For example, Roy might lecture himself for not having gotten medical attention sooner and promise to respond to symptoms more promptly in the future.
- *Positive reappraisal* (emotion-focused): trying to create a positive meaning from the situation in terms of personal growth, sometimes with a religious tone. For instance, Roy might become a better or stronger person from the experience or feel that he has developed a stronger faith.

Source: Folkman & Lazarus, 1988; Folkman et al., 1986.

they sometimes interfere with getting medical treatment or involve unhealthful behaviors, such as using cigarettes, alcohol, and drugs to reduce tension. People often use these substances in their efforts toward emotion-focused coping (Wills, 1986).

Each of these strategies is quite broad and can be applied in many ways and situations. To clarify how people use emotion-focused methods, we can describe some variations on the strategies in the table. For instance, people may engage in a coping method called *emotional discharge*, which involves expressing or releasing their feelings about a stressful situation. This approach usually occurs in conjunction with seeking social support, such as with friends or family or in support groups, and can also involve using jokes or gallows humor (Moos & Schaefer, 1986). For instance, a man jokingly nicknamed himself "Semicolon" after part of his cancerous colon was removed. Humor can effectively reduce people's stress (Newman & Stone, 1996). Although using emotional discharge can help people cope, many people who suffer from chronic stress fail to express their feelings. Instead, they have *intrusive thoughts* and images that perpetuate their stress (Baum, 1990). For example, they may think repeatedly about how they or others are to blame for their problems or have "flashbacks" of painful or traumatic events. People who often have intrusive thoughts report having poorer health habits and health than individuals who seldom have such thoughts (Nowack, 1989).

Cognitive redefinition is a strategy whereby people try to put a good face on a bad situation, such as by noting that things could be worse, making comparisons with individuals who are less well off, or seeing something good growing out of the problem. We can see this approach in two statements of women with breast cancer (Taylor, 1983):

> What you do is put things into perspective. You find out that things like relationships are really the most important things you have—the people you know and your family—everything else is just way down the line. It's very strange that it takes something so serious to make you realize that. (p. 1163)

> The people I really feel sorry for are these young gals. To lose a breast when you're so young must be awful. I'm 73; what do I need a breast for? (p. 1166)

People who want to redefine a stressful situation can generally find a way to do it since there is almost always *some* aspect of one's life that can be viewed positively (Taylor, 1983). Optimistic individuals are more likely than pessimists to use problem-focused methods and to redefine their situation in a positive light

(Scheier, Carver, & Bridges, 2000). Cognitive redefinition may involve the distancing and positive reappraisal strategies described in Table 5.1.

Other coping processes include the cognitive strategies Freud called "defense mechanisms," which involve distorting memory or reality in some way (Cramer, 2000). For instance, when something is too painful to face, the person may deny that it exists. This defense mechanism is called *denial*. In medical situations, individuals who are diagnosed with terminal diseases often use this strategy and refuse to believe they are really ill. Another defense mechanism, called *intellectualization*, consists of dealing with or confronting a stressor on an abstract, intellectual level. Nurses and physicians who have to deal with enormous amounts of human suffering need some way to detach their emotions from these situations. They may intellectualize, for example, by referring to a patient dying of liver cancer as "the liver in 203." These approaches are similar to those of distancing and escape-avoidance described in the table.

You may have noticed that some coping methods tend to increase the *attention* people give to their stressful situations. Problem-focused methods generally do this. Other methods, particularly some emotion-focused methods, tend to promote *avoidance* of the problem. Both attention to and avoidance of a stressor can be beneficial under some circumstances. Avoidance-promoting approaches, such as distancing, are beneficial when there is little the person can do about the problem (Cohen & Lazarus, 1979; Lazarus, 1983). For instance, a study examined the coping strategies of women after they had undergone mastectomies for breast cancer. Patients who avoided thinking about cancer and minimized the impact of their illness showed less evidence of distress than those who did not use avoidance-promoting strategies (Meyerowitz, 1983). But if the person *can* do something about the problem, failing to give it attention can be more harmful than helpful, as we saw in Beth's denial of the lump in her breast at the beginning of the chapter.

The time frame for using strategies that promote attention to or avoidance of the problem is also important. Jerry Suls and Barbara Fletcher (1985) pooled the results of a large number of studies in a meta-analysis to clarify the effects of attention-promoting and avoidance-promoting strategies. Their analysis led to two conclusions. First, avoidance-promoting strategies can benefit coping mainly in the short run, such as during an early stage of a prolonged stress experience. This is the case for individuals who are diagnosed with a serious illness, for instance. Second, as time goes by, attention-promoting strategies become more effective than avoidance in the coping process. As a rule of thumb, the effectiveness of avoidance-promoting methods seems to be limited to the first couple of weeks of a prolonged stress experience. Thereafter, coping is better served by attention-promoting strategies.

The degree to which individuals rely on strategies that promote avoidance of the problem may have important health implications. A one-year prospective study compared people who differed in their reported use of avoidance-promoting approaches (Holahan & Moos, 1986). Of the people who experienced high levels of stress during the intervening year, those who had reported a greater tendency to use avoidance-promoting methods had, at the end of the study, more psychosomatic symptoms—for example, headaches and acid stomach.

Our discussion indicates that there is no one best method of coping. No single method is uniformly applied or effective with all stressful situations (Ilfeld, 1980; Pearlin & Schooler, 1978). Four issues about people's patterns in using different coping methods should be mentioned. First, individuals tend to be consistent in the way they cope with a particular type of stressor—that is, when faced with the same problem, people tend to use the same methods they used in the past (Stone & Neale, 1984). Second, people seldom use just one method to cope with a stressor. Their efforts typically involve a combination of strategies, such as planful problem-solving and denial (Holahan & Moos, 1985). Third, the methods people use in coping with short-term stressors may be different from those they use under long-term stress, such as from a serious chronic illness (Aldwin & Brustrom, 1997). Fourth, although the methods people use to cope with stress develop from the transactions they have in their lives, a genetic influence is suggested by the finding that identical twins are more similar than fraternal twins in the coping styles they use (Busjahn, Faulhaber, Freier, & Luft, 1999).

Developing Methods of Coping

Psychologists have long assumed that coping processes change across the life span. But the nature of these changes is unclear because there is little research, especially longitudinal studies, charting these changes (Aldwin & Brustrom, 1997; Lazarus & DeLongis, 1983; Lazarus & Folkman, 1984b).

Some aspects of the changes in coping that occur in the early years are known. Infants and toddlers do not cope very effectively with stress. For example, when being examined by their pediatricians, infants and toddlers often react by trying to stop the examination, and preschoolers tend to protest after it's over (Hyson, 1983). We saw earlier in the case of Molly that young children develop coping skills that enable them to overcome many of their fears. The skills she acquired often made use of her expanding cognitive abilities, such as in thinking logically and stating her ideas. Over the next several years, children come to rely increasingly on cognitive strategies for coping (Brown, O'Keeffe, Sanders, & Baker, 1986; Miller & Green, 1984). So, for example, they learn to think about something else to distract themselves from stress. More and more, they regulate their feelings with emotion-focused methods, such as cognitive redefinition—for instance, saying to themselves, "I can do it," while preparing to give a speech. In coping with their parents having a serious illness, such as cancer, children and adolescents rarely use problem-focused methods and rely more and more on emotion-focused methods, such as playing with toys or watching TV, as they develop (Compas, Worsham, Ey, & Howell, 1996).

Few studies have examined changes in methods of coping from adolescence to old age. One study used interviews and questionnaires to compare the daily hassles and coping methods of middle-aged and elderly men and women (Folkman, Lazarus, Pimley, & Novacek, 1987). The middle-aged men and women used more problem-focused forms of coping, whereas the elderly subjects used more emotion-focused approaches. For example, the middle-aged people were more likely to report coping with stress in a confrontive and planful manner—claiming such actions as, "Stood my ground and fought for what I wanted," and, "I made a plan of action and followed it." The elderly individuals were more likely to report passive, emotion-focused methods—claiming such approaches as, "Went on as if nothing happened," and, "Wished that the situation would go away or somehow be over with."

Why do adults use less problem-focused and more emotion-focused coping as they get older?

These changes probably result at least in part from differences in what people must cope with as they age. The elderly subjects in this study were retired from full-time work and reported more stress relating to health and home maintenance than the middle-aged people did; the middle-aged individuals reported more stress relating to work, finances, and family and friends. Planful and confrontive action are probably more effective strategies for coping with the kinds of stressors encountered by middle-aged than by elderly people. But there was also a difference in the outlook of the two age groups: regardless of the source of stress, the elderly people appraised their problems as *less* changeable than the middle-aged subjects did. As we saw earlier, people tend to use problem-focused approaches when they believe the situation is changeable, and rely on emotion-focused coping when they do not.

Gender and Sociocultural Differences in Coping

Studies of gender differences in coping have generally found that men are more likely to report using problem-focused strategies and women are more likely to report using emotion-focused strategies in dealing with stressful events. But when the men and women are similar in occupation and education, no gender differences are found (Greenglass & Noguchi, 1996). These results suggest that societal sex roles play an important role in the coping patterns of men and women.

Billings and Moos (1981) found that people with higher incomes and educational levels report greater use of problem-focused coping than those with less income and education. This finding suggests that the social experiences of disadvantaged people lead many of them to believe they have little control over events in their lives. In general, disadvantaged individuals—a category that typically includes disproportionately more minority group members—are more likely to experience stressful events and less likely to cope with them effectively than other people are (Gottlieb & Green, 1987).

We have examined many ways people cope with stress. Each method can be effective and adaptive for the individual if it neutralizes the current stressor and does not increase the likelihood of future stressful situations. Some ways of coping can reduce the potential impact of stressors. For instance, many people who receive a bill that has an error would appraise this situation as a hassle. But a person who often uses humor to cope may appraise this situation differently, perhaps finding it almost amusing (Folkman, Lazarus, Pimley, & Novacek, 1987). In the next section, we consider how people can reduce the potential for stress for themselves and for others.

REDUCING THE POTENTIAL FOR STRESS

Can people become "immune" to the impact of stress to some extent? Some aspects of people's lives can reduce the potential for stressors to develop and help individuals cope with problems when they occur. Prevention is the first line of defense against the impact of stress. We will look at several ways people can help themselves and others prevent and cope with stress. The first approach makes use of the beneficial effects of social support.

ENHANCING SOCIAL SUPPORT

We have all turned to others for help and comfort when under stress at some time in our lives. If you have ever had to endure troubled times on your own, you know how important social support can be. But social support is not only helpful after stressors appear, it also can help avert problems in the first place. Consider, for example, the tangible support newlyweds receive when they get married. The gifts they receive include many of the items they will need to set up a household, without which the couple would be saddled either with the financial burden of buying the items or with the hassles of not having them.

Although there are people in all walks of life who lack the social support they need, some segments of the population have less than others (Antonucci, 1985; Broadhead et al., 1983; Ratliff-Crain & Baum, 1990). For instance:

- Although men tend to have larger social networks than women, women seem to use theirs more effectively for support.
- Many elderly individuals live in isolated conditions and have few people on whom to rely.

- Network size is related to social prestige, income, and education: the lower the prestige, income, and education level of individuals, the smaller their social networks tend to be.

Furthermore, the networks of people from lower socioeconomic classes are usually less diverse than those of people from higher classes—that is, lower-class networks contain fewer nonkin members. In contemporary American society, the traditional sources of support have shifted to include greater reliance on individuals in social and helping organizations. This is partly because extended family members today have different functions and live farther apart than they did many decades ago (Pilisuk, 1982).

Social support is a dynamic process. People's needs for, giving of, and receipt of support change over time. Some factors within the individual determine whether he or she will receive or provide social support when it is needed (Broadhead et al., 1983; Wortman & Dunkel-Schetter, 1987). One factor is the person's temperament. People differ in their need for and interest in social contact and affiliation. Those persons who tend to seek interaction with others are more likely to give and receive support than those who do not. To some extent the experiences people have determine these tendencies. Children who grow up in caring families and have good relations with peers learn the social skills needed to seek help and give it when needed. But research has found that people who experience high levels of chronic stress, such as when their health declines severely, often find that their social support resources deteriorate at the same time (Kaplan et al., 1997; Lepore, 1997; Wortman & Dunkel-Schetter, 1987). These results are disheartening because they suggest that people whose need for social support is greatest may be unlikely to receive it.

Efforts to enhance people's ability to give and receive social support can begin in early childhood, particularly at school (Broadhead et al., 1983). Teachers can enhance children's giving social support by reading appropriate storybooks to the class and by having boys and girls engage in cooperative games that promote prolonged interactions with one another (Sapon-Shevin, 1980). These experiences can teach children how to talk nicely to and compliment others, share and take turns, include individuals who have been left out in activities, and help people who are injured or having difficulty.

Teachers can help enhance children's social support by having them work together.

In adulthood, people can enhance their ability to give and receive social support by joining community organizations, such as social, religious, special-interest, and self-help groups. These organizations have the advantage of bringing together individuals with similar problems and interests, which can become the basis for sharing, helping, and friendship. In the United States, there are many widely known self-help groups, including Alcoholics Anonymous and Parents without Partners, and special-interest groups, including the American Association of Retired People and support groups for people with specific illnesses, such as arthritis or AIDS. Individuals with serious illnesses are most likely to join a support group if they have an embarrassing or stigmatizing disorder, such as AIDS or breast cancer (Davison, Pennebaker, & Dickerson, 2000). Isolated people of all ages—especially the elderly—with all types of difficulties should be encouraged to join suitable organizations.

Communities can play a valuable role in enhancing people's resources for social support by creating programs to help individuals develop social networks (Taylor, Lam, Roppel, & Barter, 1984). Social support can also be encouraged in occupational settings (Quick, Quick, Nelson, & Hurrell, 1997). Employers can do this in many ways, such as by organizing workers in teams or work groups, providing facilities for recreation and fitness, arranging social events for workers and their families, and providing counseling services to help employees through troubled times. Some bosses get so caught up in the role of manager that they fail to give the personal support their employees need. A supportive boss discusses decisions and problems with employees, compliments and credits them for good work, and stands behind reasonable decisions they make (Kobasa, 1986). Less supportive bosses can make a conscious effort to improve these behaviors. Although social support is generally helpful and appreciated, it isn't always. As we saw in Chapter 4, well-meaning efforts by friends and relatives can undermine good health habits and impair the recovery of people who are ill. Social support can also be ineffective if the recipient interprets it as a sign of inadequacy, feels uncomfortable about not being able to reciprocate, or believes his or her personal control is limited by it (Cohen & McKay, 1984). Providing effective social support requires sensitivity and good judgment. (Go to 💡.)

IMPROVING ONE'S PERSONAL CONTROL

When life becomes stressful, people who lack a strong sense of personal control may stop trying, thinking, "Oh, what's the use." Instead of feeling they have

HIGHLIGHT ON ISSUES

The Amish Way of Social Support in Bereavement

The Amish people in North America form a conservative religious sect that settled in Pennsylvania in the 18th century. Amish families generally live in colonies that now exist in about 20 states and Canada. These families have a strongly religious orientation and a serious work ethic that revolves around farming. Their way of life is quite distinctive: they wear uniquely simple and uniform clothing; speak mainly a Pennsylvania-German dialect; and reject modern devices, using horse-driven buggies instead of automobiles, for example. Their social lives require their adherence to strict rules of conduct and obedience to patriarchal authority.

One feature of Amish life is that community members give assistance to one another in all times of need. Their way of dealing with death provides a good example, as Kathleen Bryer (1986) has studied and described. Before death, a person who is seriously ill receives care from his or her family. This almost always occurs at home, rather than in a hospital. The Amish not only expect to give this care, but see it as a positive opportunity. A married woman who was asked about caring for a dying relative replied, "Oh yes, we had the chance to take care of all four

of our old parents before they died. We are both so thankful for this" (p. 251). The experience of death typically occurs at home, in the presence of the family.

Upon someone's death, the Amish community swings into action. Close neighbors notify other members of the colony, and the community makes most of the funeral arrangements. The family receives visits of sympathy and support from other Amish families, some of whom come from other colonies far away and may not even know the bereaved family. In contrast to the social support most Americans receive in bereavement, Amish supportive efforts do not end shortly after the funeral—they continue at a high level for at least a year. Supportive activities include evening and Sunday visiting, making items and scrapbooks for the family, and organized quilting projects that create fellowship around a common task. Moreover, Amish individuals often give extraordinary help to bereaved family members. For instance, the sister of one widower came to live with him and care for his four children until he remarried. The community encourages widowed individuals to remarry in time, and they often do so.

The Amish provide social support to one another in many ways, as when they build a barn for a member of their colony.

power and control, they feel helpless and afraid that their efforts will lead to failure and embarrassment. For instance, people with painful, disabling, or life-threatening chronic illnesses may stop trying to improve their conditions. When seriously ill patients who feel little personal control face a new severe stressor, they show more emotional distress and, perhaps, less effective endocrine function than those who feel more control (Benight et al., 1997). The main psychological help such people need is to bolster their self-efficacy and reduce their passiveness and helplessness (Smith & Wallston, 1992). A pessimistic outlook increases people's potential for stress and can have a negative effect on their health.

How can a person's sense of control be enhanced? The process can begin very early. Parents, teachers, and other caregivers can show a child their love and respect, provide a stimulating environment, encourage and praise the child's accomplishments, and set reasonable standards of conduct and performance that he or she can regard as challenges, rather than threats. Doing these things is likely also to enhance the child's resilience or hardiness, and hardy individuals tend to use coping strategies that manage their stress effectively (Holahan & Moos, 1985; Kobasa, 1986; Williams, Wiebe, & Smith, 1992).

Adults' personal control can be enhanced, too. Employers can help by giving workers some degree of control over aspects of their jobs, allowing them input in decisions about the hours they work, which tasks to work on, and ways to improve the quality of their work (Quick, Quick, Nelson, Hurrell, 1997). Similarly, nursing homes and families can allow elderly individuals to do things for themselves and have responsibilities, such as in cleaning, cooking, and arranging social activities. One woman described the prospect of living with her children in the following way: "I couldn't stand to live with my children, as much as I love them, because they always want to take over my life" (Shupe, 1985). For people with serious chronic illnesses, health psychologists can help those with little control by training them in effective ways to cope with stress (Thompson & Kyle, in press).

ORGANIZING ONE'S WORLD BETTER

"Where did I put my keys?" you have surely heard someone ask frantically while running late to make an appointment. People often feel stress because they are running late or believe they don't have enough time to do the tasks of the day. They need to organize their worlds to make things happen efficiently. This can take the form of keeping an appointment calendar, designating certain places for certain items, or putting materials in alphabetized file folders, for instance. Organizing one's world reduces frustration, wasted time, and the potential for stress.

An important approach for organizing one's time is called **time management.** It consists of three elements (Lakein, 1973). The first element is to *set goals.* These goals should be reasonable or obtainable ones, and they should include long-term goals, such as getting a job promotion next year, and short-term ones, such as meeting a weekly sales quota. The second element involves making daily *To Do* lists with priorities indicated, keeping the goals in mind. These lists should be composed early each morning or late in the preceding day. Each list must be written—trying to keep the list in your head is unreliable and makes setting priorities difficult. The third element is to set up a *schedule* for the day, allocating estimated time periods to each item in the list. If an urgent new task arises during the day, the list should be adjusted to include it.

EXERCISING: LINKS TO STRESS AND HEALTH

You have probably heard from TV, radio, magazine, and newspaper reports that exercise and physical fitness can protect people from stress and its harmful effects on health. These reports cite a wide range of benefits of exercising from increased intellectual functioning and personal control to decreased anxiety, depression, hostility, and tension. Do exercise and fitness reduce the potential for stress and its effects on health?

Correlational and retrospective studies of this question have found that people who exercise or are physically fit often report less anxiety, depression, and tension in their lives than do people who do not exercise or are less fit (Abele & Brehm, 1993; Blumenthal & McCubbin, 1987; Dishman, 1986; Holmes, 1993). Although these results are consistent with the view that exercise and fitness reduce the potential for stress, there are two problems in interpreting them. First, some evidence indicates that part of the reduction in self-reported stress and emotion may have resulted from a placebo effect—that is, the subjects' expectations that psychological improvements would occur (Desharnais et al., 1993). Second, the results of correlational research do not tell us what causes what. Do exercise and fitness cause people to feel less stress? Or are people more likely to exercise and keep fit if they feel less stress and time pressures in their lives? Or are other factors involved? These questions cannot be answered using correlational or retrospective methods. Fortunately, there is stronger evidence for the beneficial effects of exercise and fitness on stress and health.

An experiment by Bram Goldwater and Martin Collis (1985) examined the effects of exercise on cardiovascular fitness and feelings of anxiety in healthy males between 19 and 30 years of age. The men were randomly assigned to one of two groups. In one group, the men worked out 5 days a week in a vigorous fitness program, including swimming and active sports, such as soccer. Subjects in the second group had a more moderate fitness program. They met twice a week and engaged in less demanding exercise activities, such as badminton. Both groups participated in their programs for 6 weeks and were tested for cardiovascular fitness and anxiety before and after participating. Compared with the subjects in the moderate program, those in the vigorous program showed greater gains in fitness and reductions in anxiety. Other experiments have shown similar beneficial effects of exercise on depression and anxiety with adults of various ages (Babyak et al., 2000; Blumenthal, Williams, Needels, & Wallace, 1982).

Research has also assessed the effects of exercise on blood pressure and heart rate. Most of the evidence is correlational, revealing that people who exercise or are physically fit show less cardiovascular reactivity to stressors and are less likely to be hypertensive than individuals who do not exercise or are less fit (Dimsdale, Alpert, & Schneiderman, 1986; Martin & Dubbert, 1985). But some studies have used experimental methods. Garry Jennings and his colleagues (1986) conducted an experiment with healthy 19- to 27-year-old individuals who had sedentary occupations and had not regularly engaged in vigorous physical activity in the previous year. Over the next 4 months, the subjects spent 1 month at each of four levels of activity: (1) their sedentary normal

activity; (2) below-normal activity, which included 2 weeks of rest in a hospital setting; (3) above-normal activity, which involved their normal activity plus three sessions of vigorous exercise weekly; and (4) much-above-normal activity, consisting of their normal activity plus daily vigorous exercise. Each exercise period lasted 40 minutes. Measurements of heart rate and blood pressure were taken after each month, when the subjects came into the laboratory and rested before beginning the next activity level. Compared with data for the sedentary activity level, the two exercise conditions reduced heart rate by 12% and systolic and diastolic blood pressure by 8% and 10%. Below-normal activity levels did not alter heart rate or blood pressure. Other researchers have found similar beneficial effects of exercise on blood pressure with normotensive elderly people (Braith et al., 1994).

We need to consider one more question in reviewing the protective effects of exercise and fitness against the impact of stress on health: Do exercise and fitness prevent people from developing stress-related illnesses? The results of two studies suggest they do. One of these studies used retrospective methods with men who reported having experienced either high or low levels of stress in the previous 3 years (Kobasa, Maddi, & Puccetti, 1982). Those men who scored higher on a survey of their exercise practices reported less illness during the 3-year period than those who had lower scores on exercise, and these protective effects were greater for subjects with high levels of stress than for those with less stress. The other study used prospective methods by first assessing the subjects' recent life events and fitness, and then having them keep records concerning their health over the next 9 weeks (Roth & Holmes, 1985). The results revealed that individuals who reported high levels of stress had poorer subsequent health if they were not fit; stress had little impact on the health of fit subjects.

The evidence that engaging in regular exercise can promote health by reducing stress is fairly strong. Does participating in sports games, such as tennis or soccer, have similar effects? Little evidence exists on this issue, but some research findings indicate that sports activities arouse emotions, especially before participation, and arouse anger and sadness for losers (Abele & Brehm, 1993). The health effects of these emotional experiences are not yet clear.

PREPARING FOR STRESSFUL EVENTS

In this and previous chapters we have discussed many types of stressful events, ranging from being stuck in traffic, to starting day care or school, being overloaded with work, going through a divorce, and experiencing a disaster. Preparing for these events often can reduce the potential for stress. For instance, parents can help prepare a child for starting day care by taking the child there in advance to see the place, meet the teacher, and play for a while (Sarafino, 1986).

Irving Janis (1958) pioneered the psychological study of the need to prepare people for stressful events, such as surgery. From his research findings, Janis proposed that some degree of worry in anticipation of a stressful event is adaptive because it motivates coping via the process he called the *work of worrying*. Too much or too little anxiety interferes with this process and leads to poor adjustment and recovery after surgery. Subsequent research confirmed part, but not all, of Janis's ideas. In particular, studies have shown that low levels of anxiety do not impair patients' success in coping with or recovery from surgery. The overall picture from this research indicates that the higher the patients' *preoperative* fear, the worse their *postoperative* adjustment and recovery tend to be (Anderson & Masur, 1983; Johnson, 1983). These postoperative outcomes have been shown for a variety of measures, including:

- The patient's self-reported pain
- The amount of medication taken to relieve pain
- Self-reported anxiety or depression
- The length of stay in the hospital after surgery
- Ratings by hospital staff of the patient's recovery or adjustment

These poorer postoperative outcomes of patients with high levels of anxiety suggest that helping patients cope with their preoperative concerns could enhance later adjustment and recovery.

Many studies have been done to determine what methods are effective in preparing people psychologically for surgery. The most clearly effective methods of preparing people for the stress of surgery are those designed to enhance the patients' feelings of *control* (Anderson & Masur, 1983; Mathews & Ridgeway, 1984). One approach attempts to improve patients' *behavioral control* by teaching them how to reduce discomfort or promote rehabilitation through specific actions they can take, such as by doing leg exercises to improve strength or deep breathing exercises to reduce pain. Another method is designed to enhance patients' *cognitive control*, for instance, by instructing them on ways to concentrate on the pleasant or beneficial aspects of the surgery, rather than the unpleasant aspects. One other method involves *informational control*, in which patients receive information about the procedures and/or sensations they will experience. Each of these and other control-enhancing methods is effective in promoting postoperative adjustment and recovery. (We will examine these methods in greater detail in Chapter 10, when we discuss hospital treatment.)

Although enhanced control can be helpful in reducing the potential for stress, these methods need to be carefully applied to prevent some possible negative effects. One consideration is that sometimes information that is meant to reassure people and reduce stress can have the opposite effect. As psychologist Suzanne Thompson has described:

> The Los Angeles City Council had placed cards in the city elevators assuring riders that they should stay calm, since "there is little danger of the car dropping uncontrollably or running out of air."...A year later the cards had to be removed because of complaints from elevator riders that the message made them anxious. Apparently most people had not worried about these dangers until they read the card meant to reassure them. (1981, p. 96)

Another consideration is whether a person can have *too much* control. There is some evidence that having too much information, for example, can be confusing and actually arouse fear. Young children often become more anxious when they receive a great deal of information about the medical procedures they will undergo (Miller & Green, 1984). With children in dental or medical settings, it is generally best not to give a lot of detail. Describing some sensory experiences to expect is especially helpful, such as the sounds of equipment or the tingly feeling from the dental anesthetic.

In summary, we have discussed several methods that are helpful in reducing the potential for stress and, thereby, benefiting health. These methods take advantage of the stress-moderating effects of social support, personal control, exercise, being well organized, and being prepared for an impending stressor. In the next section, we consider ways to reduce the reaction to stress once it has begun.

REDUCING STRESS REACTIONS: STRESS MANAGEMENT

People acquire coping skills through their experiences, which may involve strategies they have tried in the past or methods they have seen others use. But sometimes the skills they have learned are not adequate for a current stressor because it is so strong, novel, or unrelenting. In some cases, the approaches they have acquired reduces stress in the short run—as alcohol or drug use can do—but are not adaptive and increase stress in the long run. These problems in coping often arise in individuals whose potential for stress is high because of a lack of social support, personal control, and so on; but coping problems also happen among people whose potential for stress is relatively low. When people cannot cope effectively, they need help in learning new and adaptive ways of managing stress.

Many techniques are available to help individuals manage stress. These *stress management* techniques are mainly psychological, but *pharmacological* approaches are sometimes used under medical supervision.

MEDICATION

Of the many types of drugs physicians prescribe to help patients manage stress, we will consider two: benzodiazepines and beta-blockers. Both of these drugs reduce physiological arousal and feelings of anxiety (Priest, 1986; Shapiro, Krantz, & Grim, 1986). *Benzodiazepines*, which include drugs with the trade names Valium and Librium, appear to work by activating a neurotransmitter that decreases neural transmission in the central nervous system. *Beta-blockers*, such as Inderal, appear to block the activity of sympathetic neurons in the peripheral nervous system that are stimulated by epinephrine and norepinephrine. Beta-blockers cause less drowsiness than benzodiazepines, probably because they act on the periph-

eral rather than central nervous system. Using drugs to manage stress should be only a temporary measure, either to help during an acute crisis, such as in the week or two following the death of a loved one, or while the patient learns new psychological methods for coping. But more and more people are relying on drugs for long-term control of their stress and emotions (Begley, 1994).

BEHAVIORAL AND COGNITIVE METHODS

Psychologists have developed methods they can train people to use in coping with stress. Some of these techniques focus mainly on the person's behavior, and some emphasize the person's thinking processes. People who use these methods usually find them helpful.

Relaxation

The opposite of arousal is relaxation—so relaxing should be a good way to reduce stress. "Perhaps so," you say, "but when stress appears, relaxing is easier said than done." Actually, relaxing when under stress is not so hard to do when you know how. One technique people can learn to control their feelings of tension is called **progressive muscle relaxation** (or just *progressive relaxation*), in which they focus their attention on specific muscle groups while alternately tightening and relaxing these muscles (Sarafino, 2001).

The idea of teaching people to relax their skeletal muscles to reduce psychological stress was proposed many years ago by Edmund Jacobson (1938). He developed a device to measure electrical activity in muscle fibers. Using this device, he found that people would reduce the tension in their muscles when simply asked to "sit and relax." He later found that muscle tension could be reduced much more if the subjects were taught to pay attention to the sensations as they tense and relax individual groups of muscles. Research findings indicate that one reason muscle relaxation reduces psychological stress is that the technique tends to arouse pleasant thoughts in the person (Peveler & Johnston, 1986).

Although there are various versions of the progressive muscle relaxation technique, they each outline a particular sequence of muscle groups for the person to follow. For example, the sequence might begin with the person relaxing the hands, then the forehead, followed by the lower face, the neck, the stomach, and, finally, the legs. For each muscle group, the person first tenses the muscles for 7–10 seconds, and then relaxes them for about 15 seconds, paying attention to how the muscles feel. This is usually repeated for the same muscle group two or three times in a relaxation session, which generally lasts 20 or 30 minutes. The relaxation technique works best in a quiet, nondistracting setting with the person lying down or sitting on comfortable furniture.

Stress management has been applied mainly with adults, but children also experience stress without being able to cope effectively. Fortunately, many behavioral and cognitive methods are easy to learn and can be adapted so that an adult can teach a young child to use them (Siegel & Peterson, 1980). Relaxation exercises provide a good example. An adult could start by showing the child what relaxing is like by lifting and then releasing the arms and legs of a rag doll, allowing them to fall down. Then, the adult would follow a *protocol*, or script, giving instructions like those in Table 5.2. When children and adults first learn progressive muscle relaxation, they sometimes don't actually relax their muscles when told to do so. Instead of letting their arms and legs *fall* down, they *move* them down.

They also sometimes tense more muscles than they are asked to—for example, tightening facial muscles when they are supposed to tense only hand muscles. These errors should be pointed out and corrected.

Often, after individuals have thoroughly mastered the relaxation procedure, they can gradually shorten the procedure so they can apply a very quick version in times of stress, such as when they are about to give a speech (Sarafino, 2001). This quick version might have the following steps: (1) taking a deep breath, and letting it out; (2) saying to oneself, "Relax, feel nice and calm"; and (3) thinking about a pleasant thought for a few seconds. In this way, relaxation methods can be directly applied to help people cope with everyday stressful events.

Research has demonstrated that progressive muscle relaxation is highly effective in reducing stress (Carlson & Hoyle, 1993; Lichstein, 1988). What's more, people who receive training in relaxation show less cardiovascular reactivity to stressors and stronger immune function (Lucini et al., 1997; Sherman, Carlson, McCubbin, & Wilson, 1997).

Systematic Desensitization

Although relaxation is often successful by itself in helping people cope, it is frequently used in

---

Table 5.2 *Progressive Muscle Relaxation Protocol for Children*

1. "OK. Let's raise our arms and put them out in front. Now make a fist with both your hands, really hard. Hold the fist tight and you will see how your muscles in your hands and arms feel when they are tight." (hold for 7–10 seconds)
   "That's very good. Now when I say relax, I want the muscles in your hands and arms to become floppy, like the rag doll, and your arms will drop to your sides. OK, relax." (about 15 seconds)
2. "Let's raise our legs out in front of us. Now tighten the muscles in your feet and legs, really hard. Make the muscles really tight, and hold it." (7–10 seconds)
   "Very good. Now relax the muscles in your feet and legs, and let them drop to the floor. They feel so good. So calm and relaxed." (15 seconds)
3. "Now let's do our tummy muscles. Tighten your tummy, really hard—and hold it." (7–10 seconds)
   "OK. Relax your tummy, and feel how good it feels. So comfortable." (15 seconds)
4. "Leave your arms at your side, but tighten the muscles in your shoulders and neck. You can do this by moving your shoulders up toward your head. Hold the muscles very tightly in your shoulders and neck." (7–10 seconds)
   "Now relax those muscles so they are floppy, and see how good that feels." (15 seconds)
5. "Let's tighten the muscles in our faces. Scrunch up your whole face so that all of the muscles are tight—the muscles in your cheeks, and your mouth, and your nose, and your forehead. Really scrunch up your face, and hold it." (7–10 seconds)
   "Now relax all the muscles in your face—your cheeks, mouth, nose, and forehead. Feel how nice that is." (15 seconds)
6. "Now I want us to take a very, very deep breath—so deep that there's no more room inside for more air. Hold the air in. (use a shorter time: 6–8 seconds)
   "That's good. Now slowly let the air out. Very slowly, until it's all out. . . . And now breathe as you usually do." (15 seconds)

Source: From Sarafino (1986, pp. 112–113).

conjunction with **systematic desensitization,** a useful method for reducing fear and anxiety (Sarafino, 2001). This method is based on the view that fears are learned by *classical conditioning*—that is, by associating a situation or object with an unpleasant event. This can happen, for example, if a person associates visits to the dentist with pain, thereby becoming "sensitized" to dentists. Desensitization is a classical conditioning procedure that *reverses* this learning by pairing the feared object or situation with either pleasant or neutral events, as Figure 5–1 outlines. According to Joseph Wolpe (1958, 1973), an originator of the desensitization method, the reversal comes about through the process of *counterconditioning*, whereby the "calm" response gradually replaces the "fear" response. Desensitization has been used successfully in reducing a variety of children's and adults' fears, such as fear of dentists, animals, high places, public speaking, and taking tests (Lichstein, 1988; Morris & Kratochwill, 1983; Sarafino, 2001).

An important feature of the systematic desensitization method is that it uses a *stimulus hierarchy*—a graded sequence of approximations to the conditioned stimulus, the feared situation. The purpose of these approximations is to bring the person gradually in contact with the source of fear in about 10 or 15 steps. To see how a stimulus hierarchy might be constructed, we will look at the one in Table 5.3 that deals with the fear of dentists. The person would follow the instructions in each of the 14 steps. As you can see, some of the steps involve real-life, or *in vivo*, contacts with the feared situation, and some do not. Two types of non-real-life contacts, of varying degrees, can be included. One type uses *imaginal* situations, such as having the person think about calling the dentist. The other involves *symbolic* contacts, such as by showing pictures, films, or models of the feared situation.

The systematic desensitization procedure starts by having the person do relaxation exercises. Then the steps in a hierarchy are presented individually, while the person is relaxed and comfortable (Sarafino, 2001). The steps follow a sequence from the least to the most fearful for the individual. Each step may elicit some wariness or fear behavior, but the person is encouraged to relax. Once the wariness at one step has passed and the person is calm, the next step in the hierarchy can be introduced. Completing an entire stimulus hierarchy and reducing a fairly strong fear can

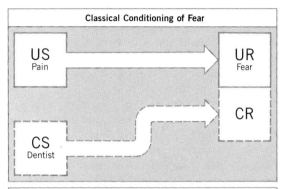

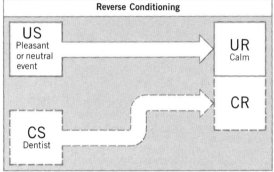

Figure 5–1   Classical conditioning in learning to fear dental visits and in reversing this learning. In conditioning the fear, the unconditioned stimulus (US) of pain elicits the unconditioned response (UR) of fear automatically. Learning occurs by pairing the dentist, the conditioned stimulus (CS), with the US so that the dentist begins to elicit fear. The reverse conditioning pairs the feared dentist with a US that elicits calm.

be achieved fairly quickly—it is likely to take several hours, divided into several separate sessions. In one study with dental-phobic adults who simply imagined each step in a hierarchy, the procedure successfully reduced their fear in six 1½-hour sessions (Gatchel, 1980). Individual sessions for reducing fears in children are usually much shorter than those used with adults, especially for a child who is very young and has a short attention span.

Biofeedback

Biofeedback is a technique in which an electromechanical device monitors the status of a person's physiological processes, such as heart rate or muscle

Table 5.3 *Example of a Stimulus Hierarchy for a Fear of Dentists*

1. Think about being in the dentist's waiting room, simply accompanying someone else who is there for an examination.
2. Look at a photograph of a smiling person seated in a dental chair.
3. Imagine this person calmly having a dental examination.
4. Think about calling the dentist for an appointment.
5. Actually call for the appointment.
6. Sit in a car outside the dentist's office without having an appointment.
7. Sit in the dentist's waiting room and hear the nurse say, "The hygienist is ready for you."
8. Sit in the examination room and hear the hygienist say, "I see one tooth the dentist will need to look at."
9. Hear and watch the drill run, without its being brought near the face.
10. Have the dentist pick at the tooth with an instrument, saying, "That doesn't look good."
11. See the dentist lay out the instruments, including a syringe to administer an anesthetic.
12. Feel the needle touch the gums.
13. Imagine having the tooth drilled.
14. Imagine having the tooth pulled.

tension, and immediately reports that information back to the individual. This information enables the person to gain voluntary control over these processes through operant conditioning. If, for instance, the person is trying to reduce neck-muscle tension and the device reports that the tension has just decreased, this information reinforces whatever efforts the individual made to accomplish this decrease.

Biofeedback has been used successfully in treating stress-related health problems. For example, an experiment was conducted with patients suffering from chronic muscle-contraction headaches (Budzynski, Stoyva, Adler, & Mullaney, 1973). Those who were given biofeedback regarding muscle tension in their foreheads later showed less tension in those muscles and reported having fewer headaches than subjects in control groups. What's more, these benefits continued at a follow-up after 3 months. Biofeedback seems to be about as effective as progressive muscle relaxation methods for treating headache

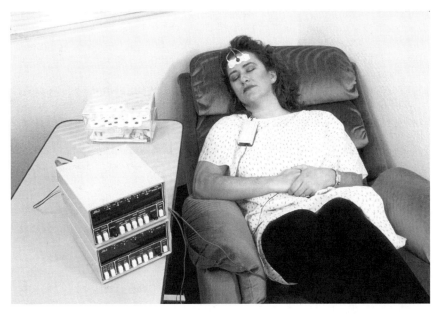

A biofeedback procedure for forehead muscle tension. One way to give feedback regarding the status of the muscles is with audio speakers, such as by sounding higher tones for higher levels of tension.

(Blanchard & Andrasik, 1985; Holroyd & Penzien, 1985). But research on approaches for reducing stress itself has found that biofeedback is no more effective than progressive muscle relaxation techniques, which are less expensive to use (Hatch, Gatchel, & Harrington, 1982). Still, some findings from research are encouraging and suggest that some individuals may benefit from biofeedback methods more than others.

According to Virginia Attanasio, Frank Andrasik, and their colleagues (1985), children may be better candidates for biofeedback treatment than adults. In treating recurrent headache with biofeedback, these researchers noticed that children seem to acquire biofeedback control faster and show better overall improvement than adults. Part of this observation has been confirmed in research: the headaches of children and adults improve with biofeedback, but children's headaches improve more (Sarafino & Goehring, 2000). Why? Attanasio and her coworkers have offered some reasons. First, although a small proportion of children are frightened initially by the equipment and procedures, most are more enthusiastic than adults, often regarding biofeedback as a game. In fact, some children become so interested and motivated in the game that their arousal interferes with relaxation if the therapist does not help them remain calm. Second, children are usually less skeptical about their ability to succeed in biofeedback training and to benefit from doing so. Adults often say, "Nothing else I've ever tried has worked, so why should biofeedback?" This difference in skepticism may reflect differences in experience: adults are likely to have had more failure experiences with other treatments than children. Third, children may be more likely than adults to practice their training at home, as they are instructed to do.

Although children have characteristics that make them well-suited to biofeedback methods, they also have some special difficulties (Attanasio et al., 1985). For one thing, children—particularly those below the age of 8—have shorter attention spans than adults. If biofeedback sessions last more than 20 minutes or so, it may be necessary to divide each session into smaller units with brief breaks in between. A related problem is that children sometimes perform disruptive behaviors during a session, disturbing the electrodes and wires or interrupting to talk about tangential topics, for instance. The therapist can reduce the likelihood of these unwanted behaviors, such as by providing rewards for being cooperative. Clearly, the difficulties some children have in biofeedback training can usually be overcome.

Modeling

People learn not just by doing, but also by observing. They see what others do and the consequences of the behavior these models perform. As a result, this kind of learning is called **modeling,** and sometimes "observational" or "social" learning.

People can learn fears and other stress-related behavior by observing fearful behavior in other individuals. In one study, children (with their parents' permission) watched a short film showing a 5-year-old boy's reaction to plastic figures of the cartoon characters Mickey Mouse and Donald Duck (Venn & Short, 1973). In the film when the boy's mother showed him the Mickey Mouse figure, he screamed and withdrew; but when she showed him the Donald Duck figure, he remained calm and displayed no distress. While the subjects watched the film, physiological measures of stress were taken, confirming that the children were more aroused while watching the episode with Mickey Mouse (fearful) than while watching the one with Donald Duck. After the children watched these scenes, they each participated in a task that involved the two figures from the film. At this time, they tended to avoid the Mickey Mouse figure (the stressful one) in favor of Donald Duck. This avoidance reaction was pronounced initially—but a day or two later, the children showed no avoidance or preference for either figure.

Since people can learn stressful reactions by observing these behaviors in others, modeling should be effective in reversing this learning and helping people cope with stressors, too. A large body of research has confirmed that it is (Sarafino, 2001; Thelen, Fry, Fehrenbach, & Frautschi, 1979). The therapeutic use of modeling is similar to the method of desensitization: the person relaxes while watching a model calmly perform a series of activities arranged as a stimulus hierarchy—that is, from least to most stressful. The modeling procedure can be presented *symbolically*, using films or videotapes, or *in vivo*, with real-life models and events. Using symbolic presentations, for example, Barbara Melamed and her coworkers have shown that modeling procedures can reduce the stress experienced by hospitalized 4- to 17-year-old children and

CLINICAL METHODS AND ISSUES

The Case of "Bear"

We've seen that people's thought processes can affect their stress. Appraisals of stress are often based on thoughts that are not rational. To illustrate how irrational thoughts can increase stress and lead to psychological problems, consider the case of a college baseball player, nicknamed "Bear," who

> was not hitting up to expectations, and was very depressed about his poor performance. In talking with Bear, it quickly became apparent that his own expectations were unrealistic. For instance, Bear wanted to hit the ball so hard that it would literally be bent out of shape (if someone happened to find it in the next county!). After a particularly bad batting session, he would go home and continue to practice until he was immobilized with exhaustion. Simply put, he

believed that if an athlete was not performing well, this could only mean he was not trying hard enough. (Rimm & Masters, 1979, p. 40)

Bear's therapy involved progressive muscle relaxation and cognitive methods to help him realize two important things: First, although motivation and desire do increase performance, they do so only up to a point, after which additional motivation impairs performance. Second, although hitting very well is "nice," hitting moderately well is not "terrible" or "intolerable." These realizations restructured Bear's thinking about his performance, and his batting average increased dramatically. Similar methods can help people reduce irrational thoughts that lead to their debilitating feelings of anxiety and depression (Sarafino, 2001).

---

improve their recovery from surgery (Melamed, Dearborn, & Hermecz, 1983; Melamed & Siegel, 1975). But the child's age and previous experience with surgery were also important factors in the results. Children under the age of 8 who had had previous surgery experienced increased anxiety rather than less. These children may benefit from other methods to reduce stress, such as activities that simply distract their attention. (Go to 👤.)

Approaches Focusing on Cognitive Processes

Because stress results from cognitive appraisals that are frequently based on a lack of information, misperceptions, or irrational beliefs, some approaches to modify people's behavior and thought patterns have been developed to help them cope better with the stress they experience. To achieve this goal, these methods guide people toward what Arnold Lazarus (1971) has called a "restructuring" of their thought patterns. **Cognitive restructuring** is a process by which stress-provoking thoughts or beliefs are replaced with

more constructive or realistic ones that reduce the person's appraisal of threat or harm.

A widely known approach that focuses on cognitive restructuring is **rational-emotive therapy** (RET), which was developed by Albert Ellis (1962, 1977, 1987). RET is based on the view that stress often arises from faulty or irrational ways of thinking. These ways of thinking affect stress appraisal processes, increasing the appraisal of threat or harm. According to Ellis, some commonly used irrational ways of thinking include:

- *Awfulizing*—for example, "It is *awful* if I get turned down when I ask for a date."

- *Can't-stand-itis*—as in, "I *can't stand* not doing well on a test."

- *Musterbating*—for instance, "People *must* like me, or I'm worthless."

These thoughts exaggerate the person's negative view of a situation and are upsetting. The purpose of RET is to change these thoughts and beliefs.

The procedures used in RET focus on several aspects or stages of the person's thought processes, using Ellis's (1977) A-B-C-D-E paradigm. Table 5.4

Table 5.4 *Illustration of Ellis's A-B-C-D-E Paradigm for Rational Emotive Therapy*

- **A** stands for the *activating* experience, the event Sue describes as having precipitated her upset: Her boss said, "I've warned you time and again about your lateness and sloppy work. I don't want you to work here anymore. You're fired."
- **B** refers to the *beliefs* and thoughts that go through the person's mind in response to A. These thoughts may be rational, as in, "I guess I deserved being fired. I need to be more responsible and careful about my work." But Sue focused on irrational beliefs, thinking, "I can't do anything right. I wish I had behaved better; that was a good job. I'm totally worthless and useless. I can't stand myself, and I can't bear facing people and telling them I was fired."
- **C** symbolizes the emotional and behavioral *consequences* of feelings of disappointment and a determination to improve in her next job. But Sue's consequences were inappropriate—she felt depressed, ashamed, and helpless, and has not tried to find a new job in the several months since she was fired.
- **D** refers to the *disputing* of irrational beliefs that goes on in therapy. It includes discriminating between true ideas, such as "I wish I had behaved better," and irrational ones, such as "I'm totally worthless." Irrational beliefs are critically and logically examined in RET so that they can be disproved.
- **E** stands for the therapy's *effect*, which consists of a restructured belief system and philosophy. With this effect, Sue should be able to cope with her world more sensibly in the future.

describes the basic outline of this paradigm by using the case of a woman we will call Sue, who is in therapy and is upset at having been fired from a job. An important feature of RET is that it uses homework assignments—the person might be asked to read some materials about irrational beliefs or do relaxation exercises, for instance. Research into the effectiveness of RET has found it successful in treating anxiety and depression (Engels, Garnefski, & Diekstra, 1993; Haaga & Davison, 1993). But the evidence is far from conclusive, and many questions remain as to why it works and whether improvements persist.

Another cognitive restructuring approach—called **cognitive therapy**—has been proposed by Aaron Beck (1976; Beck et al., 1990; Beck & Shaw, 1997). Its approach is similar to RET's in attempting to change maladaptive thought patterns. Although it was developed originally to treat psychological depression, it is also being applied in treating anxiety. Cognitive therapy attempts to help clients see that they are not responsible for all of the problems they encounter, the negative events they experience are usually not catastrophes, and their maladaptive beliefs are not logically valid. For instance, the following dialogue shows how a therapist tried to counter the negative beliefs a woman named Sharon had.

THERAPIST: ...what evidence do you have that all this is true? That you are ugly, awkward? Or that it is not true? What data do you have?

SHARON: Comparing myself to people that I consider to be extremely attractive and finding myself lacking.

THERAPIST: So if you look at that beautiful person, you're less?

SHARON: Yeah.

THERAPIST: Or if I look at that *perfect* person, I'm less. Is that what you're saying? . . .

SHARON: Yeah. I always pick out, of course, the most attractive person and probably a person who spends 3 hours a day on grooming and appearance.... I don't compare myself to the run-of-the-mill.... (Freeman, 1990, p. 83)

One technique cognitive therapy uses, called *hypothesis testing*, has the person treat an erroneous belief as a hypothesis and test it by looking for evidence for and against it in his or her everyday life. Research has shown that cognitive therapy is clearly effective in treating depression (Hollon, Shelton, & Davis, 1993; Robins & Hayes, 1993) and appears to be a very promising approach for treating anxieties (Chambless & Gillis, 1993).

Not all cognitive-based approaches to help people cope with stress have restructuring irrational thought patterns as the principal focus. Donald Meichenbaum and his colleagues have developed a procedure called **stress-inoculation training** that is designed to teach people skills for alleviating stress and achieving personal goals (Meichenbaum & Cameron, 1983; Meichenbaum & Turk, 1982). The training program involves three phases:

1. *Conceptualization.* In this phase, the person learns about the nature of stress and how people react to it. This learning occurs by considering the person's past stressful experiences. These discussions can be done on an individual basis or in groups, with each member contributing.

2. *Skills Acquisition and Rehearsal.* In the second phase, the person learns behavioral and cognitive skills to use in emotion-focused and problem-focused coping. Some of these skills are general ones that all individuals in the program would learn, such as skills in relaxation, desensitization, emotional discharge, seeking social support, and cognitive redefinition. Other skills may depend on the individual's circumstances and problems. Thus, one person might learn communication skills; another person might learn parenting techniques, or study skills, and so on. The person practices the skills he or she has learned under the therapist's supervision.

3. *Application and Follow-Through.* The last phase involves making the transition to using the learned coping skills in the real world. To achieve this transition, the person practices coping skills in response to actual or imagined stressors that are introduced in the therapy setting in a graded sequence, as in a stimulus hierarchy.

The methods used in stress-inoculation training are well thought out and include a number of well-established techniques, such as relaxation, desensitization, and modeling. Although research on the effectiveness of stress-inoculation training in alleviating stress has produced encouraging results, much more evidence is needed to demonstrate its value relative to other approaches (Meichenbaum & Deffenbacher, 1988).

One other cognitive approach is designed to help clients solve problems in their lives. By a "problem" we mean a life circumstance, such as being stuck in traffic or feeling a worrisome chest pain, that requires a response based on thinking and planning. People experience stress when they face a problem and don't know what to do or how to do it. **Problem-solving training** is an approach in which clients learn a strategy for identifying, discovering, or inventing effective or adaptive ways to address problems in everyday life (D'Zurilla, 1988; Nezu, Nezu, & Perri, 1989). In this approach, clients learn to watch for problems that can arise, define a problem clearly and concretely, generate a variety of possible solutions, and decide on the best course of action. Evidence indicates that problem-solving training reduces anxiety and other negative emotions (D'Zurilla, 1988).

Multidimensional Approaches

The coping difficulties individuals have are often multidimensional and multifaceted. As a result, one particular technique is not sufficient in helping that person, and the most effective approach usually draws upon many techniques. The method of stress-inoculation training provides an example of an approach that teaches people to use a variety of techniques. When designing a multidimensional approach, the program for helping an individual cope better with stress would be tailored to the person's specific problems (Sarafino, 2001). The program may make use of any of the methods we have considered, many methods that would take this discussion too far afield, and the methods we are about to examine.

MASSAGE, MEDITATION, AND HYPNOSIS

Three additional techniques have been used in stress management. The first two we will consider—massage and meditation—are often classified as relaxation methods. The third technique, hypnosis, seems to produce an *altered state of consciousness* in which mental functioning differs from its usual pattern of wakefulness. Some people believe that meditation and massage are other ways by which we can alter consciousness.

Massage

Massage has several forms that vary in the degree of pressure applied. Some forms of massage use soothing strokes with light pressure, others involve a rubbing motion with moderate force, and others use a kneading or pounding action. Infants seem to prefer light strokes, but adults prefer more force (Field, 1996). When seeking a massage therapist, it is a good idea to ask about licensing and certification.

Deep tissue massage uses enough pressure to penetrate deeply into muscles and joints. Studies of deep tissue massage have revealed several health psychology applications: it appears to be effective in reducing stress, some types of pain, and asthma symptoms, for example; and some evidence indicates that it can bolster immune function (Field, 1996, 1998).

Meditation

Transcendental meditation is a method in the practice of yoga that was promoted by Maharishi Mahesh Yogi as a means of improving physical and mental health and reducing stress (Benson, 1984, 1991; Nystul, 1987). Individuals using this procedure are instructed to practice it twice a day, sitting upright but comfortably relaxed with eyes closed, and mentally repeating a word or sound (such as "om"), called a *mantra*, to prevent distracting thoughts from occurring.

Psychologists and psychiatrists have advocated similar meditation methods for reducing stress. For example, Herbert Benson has recommended that the person:

> Sit quietly in a comfortable position and close your eyes. . . . Deeply relax all your muscles. . . . Become aware of your breathing. As you breathe out, say the word *one* silently to yourself. . . . Maintain a passive attitude and permit relaxation to occur at its own pace. Expect other thoughts. When these distracting thoughts occur, ignore them by thinking, "Oh well," and continue repeating, "One." (1984, p. 332)

The purpose of this procedure is to increase the person's ability in the face of a stressor to make a "relaxation response," which includes reduced physiological activity, as an alternative to a stress response. According to Benson, the relaxation response enhances health, such as by reducing blood pressure, and may be achieved in many different ways. For example, a religious person might find that a meditative prayer is the most effective method for bringing forth the relaxation response.

Although meditation helps people relax, it has a broader purpose: to develop a clear and *mindful awareness*, or "insight" regarding the essence of one's experiences, unencumbered by cognitive or emotional distortions (Hart, 1987; Solé-Leris, 1986). Jon Kabat-Zinn (1982; Kabat-Zinn, Lipworth, & Burney, 1985) has emphasized the mindful awareness component of meditation to help individuals who suffer from chronic pain to detach themselves from the cognitive and emotional distortions they have with their pain. The patients were trained to pay close attention to their pain and other sensations without reacting toward them in any way, thereby enabling the people to be aware of the pain itself, unembellished by thoughts or feelings about it. Using this technique led to a reduction in the patients' reports of physical and psychological discomfort.

Many people believe that meditation enables the person to reach a state of profound rest, as is claimed by popular self-help books (for example, Forem, 1974). Many quasi-experimental studies have examined this issue by measuring the physiological arousal of experienced meditators while they practiced meditation and of nonmeditators while they simply rested. Reviews of these studies do not support the view that meditation produces an uncommonly profound level of rest—that is, research has revealed no consistent differences in blood pressure, heart rate, or respiration rate between the meditating and the resting subjects (Holmes, 1984; Lichstein, 1988). But the quasi-experimental nature of these studies leaves open the possibility that the failure to find consistent differences in arousal may be due to other differences between indivduals who do and do not meditate. Two findings from research are important here. First, Buddhist monks in Southeast Asia can dramatically alter their body metabolism and their brain electrical activity through meditation (Benson et al., 1990). Second, people's blood pressure decreases while they meditate (Barnes et al., 1999).

Still, the main question of concern for stress management is whether meditation is a useful procedure for alleviating stress in daily life. Research has generally found that it is for many individuals (Kabat-Zinn, Massion, Hebert, & Rosenbaum, 1998; Lichstein, 1988; Shapiro, Schwartz, & Bonner, 1998).

Hypnosis

The modern history of hypnosis began with its being called "animal magnetism" and "Mesmerism" in the 18th and 19th centuries. The Austrian physician Franz Anton Mesmer popularized its use in treating patients who had symptoms of physical illness, such as paralysis, without a detectable underlying organic disorder. Today, *hypnosis* is considered to be an altered state of consciousness that is induced by special techniques of suggestion and leads to varying degrees of responsiveness to directions for changes in perception, memory, and behavior (Orne, 1989).

Not everyone can be hypnotized. People differ in their *suggestibility*, or the degree to which they can be hypnotized. Perhaps 15–30% of the general population is easily and deeply hypnotizable (Evans, 1987; Hilgard, 1967). Suggestibility appears to change with age, being particularly strong among children between the ages of about 7 and 14, and then declining in adolescence to a level that remains stable throughout adulthood (Hilgard, 1967; Place, 1984). People who are reasonably suggestible can often learn to induce a hypnotic state in themselves—a process called *self-hypnosis*. Usually they learn to do this after they have experienced hypnosis under the supervision of a skilled hypnotist.

Because individuals who have been hypnotized usually claim that it is a relaxing experience, some researchers have examined whether it can help in reducing stress. But there are two interwoven problems with doing therapy and research with hypnosis: most people are not highly suggestible, and the success of the treatment depends heavily on how suggestible the subjects are. Despite these problems, studies have found that hypnosis can be helpful in stress management, but it is not necessarily a more effective method than other relaxation techniques (Tapp, 1985; Wadden & Anderton, 1982).

In summary, we have seen that many different behavioral and cognitive methods, massage, meditation, and hypnosis offer useful therapeutic approaches for helping people cope with stress. Research is also revealing more and more clearly the important benefits of stress management in preventing illness. For instance, one study showed that immune and endocrine system reactions to a stressor depend on ways people cope with it (Olff et al., 1995). And the effects of stress management can be long-lasting—for example, a study by Angele McGrady and her colleagues (1992) found that people who received relaxation training showed stronger immune function than control subjects a month later.

USING STRESS MANAGEMENT TO REDUCE CORONARY RISK

Of the many risk factors that have been identified for CHD, a few of them—such as age and family history—are beyond the control of the individual. But many risk factors for CHD are directly linked to the person's experiences and behavior, which should be modifiable. One of these risk factors is stress. In the remainder of this chapter, we will consider how stress management techniques can be applied to reduce coronary risk.

MODIFYING TYPE A BEHAVIOR

When the Type A behavior pattern was established as a risk factor for CHD, researchers began to study ways to modify Type A behavior in an effort to reduce coronary risk (Roskies, 1983; Suinn, 1982). The task is a difficult one because we don't yet know for certain exactly what makes Type A individuals vulnerable to heart disease (Johnston, 1992).

Ethel Roskies and her colleagues (1978, 1979, 1986) began a research and therapy program in the 1970s to modify Type A behavior in healthy professional or managerial men. In the initial research (Roskies et al., 1978, 1979), Type A men were identified with the Structured Interview and randomly assigned to two types of therapy, each with weekly sessions for 14 weeks. One group received progressive muscle relaxation; the other had brief psychotherapy, in which a therapist discussed with the men how their childhood experiences may have led to their competitive, hard-driving behavior. The results showed that the groups improved during treatment with respect to their feelings of time pressure, blood cholesterol levels, and blood pressure. During a 6-month follow-up period, the men who received relaxation therapy maintained their improvements better than the psychotherapy group did.

Although these results were encouraging, Roskies and her coworkers decided they could increase the impact of the intervention by using a multidimensional approach (Roskies, 1983). They added a variety of cognitive and behavioral components, so that the revised program included progressive muscle relaxation and most aspects of RET and stress-inoculation training. Their rationale was to combat Type A individuals' *physical tension* through relaxation, *emotional outbursts* through RET, and *interpersonal friction* through stress-inoculation training in problem-solving and communication skills. They then tested the revised program with Type A men in managerial jobs (Roskies et al., 1986). The men were randomly assigned to either the revised program or to one of two physical exercise groups: an aerobic training (mostly jogging) and a weight-training program. After 10 weeks, the men were retested for Type A behavior (Structured Interview) and their cardiovascular reactivity (blood pressure and heart rate) to stressors, such as doing mental arithmetic, for comparison with measures taken earlier. Although none of the three treatments reduced the men's physiological reactivity, the multidimensional program was substantially more successful than either of the exercise programs in reducing the three components of Type A behavior. Its beneficial effect on the subjects' hostility, for example, can be seen in Figure 5–2. These benefits can be quite durable: a study found that improvements in Type A behavior with a similar intervention were maintained at a 2-year follow-up (Karlberg, Krakau, & Undén, 1998).

Raymond Novaco (1975, 1978) has demonstrated the usefulness of stress-inoculation training and relaxation in helping people control their anger. He trained individuals who were both self-identified and clinically assessed as having serious problems controlling anger. In this treatment program, the subjects first learned about the role of arousal and cognitive processes in feelings of anger. Then they learned muscle relaxation along with statements—like those in Table 5.5—they could say to themselves at different times in the course of angry episodes, such as at the point of "impact and confrontation." Finally, they practiced the techniques while imagining and role-playing realistic anger situations. The results showed that this treatment improved the subjects' ability to control anger, as measured by their self-reports and their blood pressure when provoked in the laboratory. Many studies have confirmed the success of interventions using cognitive and behavioral methods in decreasing anger (Beck & Fernandez, 1998), and a study has shown that such interventions reduce both hostility and diastolic (resting) blood pressure in patients

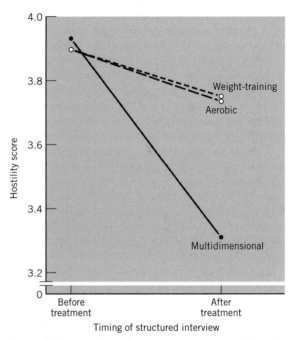

Figure 5-2 Hostility of Type A men measured by the Structured Interview method before and after a 10-week multidimensional, aerobic exercise, or weight-training treatment program. (Data from Roskies et al., 1986, Table 4.)

Table 5.5 *Examples of Anger Management Self-Statements Rehearsed in Stress-Inoculation Training*

Preparing for Provocation

This could be a rough situation; but I know how to deal with it. I can work out a plan to handle this. Easy does it. Remember, stick to the issues and don't take it personally. There won't be any need for an argument. I know what to do.

Impact and Confrontation

As long as I keep my cool, I'm in control of the situation. You don't need to prove yourself. Don't make more out of this than you have to. There is no point in getting mad. Think of what you have to do. Look for the positives and don't jump to conclusions.

Coping with Arousal

Muscles are getting tight. Relax and slow things down. Time to take a deep breath. Let's take the issue point by point. My anger is a signal of what I need to do. Time for problem solving. He probably wants me to get angry, but I'm going to deal with it constructively.

Subsequent Reflection

a. Conflict unresolved

Forget about the aggravation. Thinking about it only makes you upset. Try to shake it off. Don't let it interfere with your job. Remember relaxation. It's a lot better than anger. Don't take it personally. It's probably not so serious.

b. Conflict resolved

I handled that one pretty well. That's doing a good job. I could have gotten more upset than it was worth. My pride can get me into trouble, but I'm doing better at this all the time. I actually got through that without getting angry.

Source: From Novaco (1978, p. 150).

FOCUS ON RESEARCH

Effect of Changing Type A Behavior on CHD

Does decreasing Type A behavior with stress management techniques decrease the incidence of CHD? Meyer Friedman, Lynda Powell, and Carl Thoresen worked together and with other colleagues in an ambitious intervention program called the Recurrent Coronary Prevention Project to examine this question (Friedman et al., 1986; Powell, 1984; Powell & Friedman, 1986; Powell et al., 1984; Thoresen et al., 1985). The researchers recruited over 1,000 patients who had suffered a myocardial infarction and who agreed to participate in the study for 5 years. The subjects were primarily married, middle-aged males, and about half were college educated. They were *not* selected on the basis of their exhibiting Type A behavior, and they continued to be treated by their own physicians throughout the study. Over 860 of the subjects were randomly assigned to two intervention groups; the remaining people served as a control group, receiving no special intervention. The purpose of this study was to determine whether Type A behavior can be modified in a general sample of cardiac patients and whether this modification will lower their subsequent cardiac morbidity and mortality rates.

Subjects in one of the two intervention groups received a program of frequent *cardiac counseling*, which provided information about the causes of myocardial infarction; the importance of altering standard coronary risk factors, such as cigarette smoking (Type A behavior was not discussed); surgical and drug treatment of CHD; and the importance of avoiding activities, such as excessive physical exertion, that may precipitate another attack. The second group—called the *Type A/cardiac group*—had the same cardiac counseling, but also participated in a multidimensional program to modify Type A behavior. Type A modification sessions met frequently at first, and then met monthly for the remainder of the study. The multidimensional program included progressive muscle relaxation and cognitive restructuring techniques, as well as several other methods.

This research demonstrated the importance of modifying Type A behavior. The Type A/cardiac group showed a much larger decrease in Type A behavior (measured with Structured Interview and questionnaire methods) than those in the other groups and had substantially lower rates of cardiac morbidity and mortality (Friedman et al., 1986). For example, subsequent infarctions occurred in about 13% of the Type A/cardiac subjects, 21% of the cardiac counseling subjects, and 28% of the control subjects during the 4½-year follow-up.

with CHD and mild hypertension (Gidron, Davidson, & Bata, 1999; Larkin & Zayfert, 1996).

Some researchers have investigated the possibility of using pharmacological approaches to modify Type A behavior, particularly by prescribing beta-blockers. In one experiment, male hypertensive patients were randomly assigned to either a group treated with beta-blockers or a control group (Schmieder et al., 1983). The groups were equivalent in Type A behavior before treatment, but after treatment, the subjects treated with beta-blockers showed less Type A behavior and lower cardiovascular reactivity than the controls. Although the use of beta-blockers may not be the treatment of choice for most Type A individuals, it may be an appropriate alternative for people who are at coronary risk who do not respond to behavioral and cognitive interventions (Chesney, Frautschi, & Rosenman, 1985). (Go to ✂.)

TREATING HYPERTENSION

As we discussed in Chapter 4, essential hypertension is an important risk factor for CHD. Patients with diagnosed hypertension above the borderline level usually receive medical treatment that includes the use of prescription drugs, such as *diuretics*, which lower blood pressure by decreasing blood volume. In addition, physicians generally try to get all hypertensive patients to reduce their body weight, exercise regularly, and reduce their intake of sodium, cholesterol, caffeine, and alcohol (AHA, 2000; Herd & Weiss, 1984).

Sometimes physicians and others urge hypertensive patients "to try to relax" when hassles and pressure occur. But there is a danger in this advice: untrained people who make an effort to relax often end up increasing their blood pressure rather than decreasing it (Suls, Sanders, & Labrecque, 1986).

Because the development of essential hypertension has been linked to the amount of stress people experience, researchers have examined the utility of stress management techniques in treating high blood pressure. In general, studies have found that blood pressure can be reduced with certain stress management techniques, such as progressive muscle relaxation, biofeedback, and meditation (Johnston, 1992). Two outcomes of research are important here. First, using a single technique, such as relaxation, to lower blood pressure often provides only limited success, but stress management methods are more effective when combined in multidimensional programs (Larkin, Knowlton, & D'Alessandri, 1990; Spence et al., 1999). Second, a meta-analysis by Wolfgang Linden and Laura Chambers (1994) of dozens of studies found that multidimensional programs consisting of behavioral and cognitive methods for stress management are highly effective—as effective as diuretic drugs—in reducing blood pressure. It is now clear that psychological approaches have considerable value in treating hypertension, making effective treatment possible without drugs or with lower doses for most patients.

Other researchers have examined the usefulness of stress management methods in modifying cardiovascular reactivity. Recall from Chapter 4 that reactivity refers to the physiological response to a stressor, as when blood pressure rises during a confrontation, and that frequent and prolonged high reactivity may lead to CHD. Some studies have shown that biofeedback, progressive muscle relaxation, and cognitive restructuring methods can reduce reactivity,

but other studies have produced inconsistent or negative findings (Blanchard et al., 1988; Jacob & Chesney, 1986; Seraganian et al., 1987). Why are the outcomes of these studies so discrepant? The reason may involve differences in the studies' methodological details, such as the duration of the intervention training or therapy, the specific stressors used, and whether the participants liked or believed in the particular intervention they received (Seraganian et al., 1987). Even without intervention, people appear to adapt to repeated exposure to the same stressor, showing decreased reactivity over time (Frankish & Linden, 1991).

In an effort to improve the health of employees, many large companies have introduced voluntary stress management programs for their workers. Most studies of these programs have found that they produce improvements in measures of workers' psychological and physiological stress (Alderman, 1984; Sallis et al., 1987). Despite the success of stress management programs in reducing coronary risk by modifying Type A behavior and lowering blood pressure, they are not yet widely applied—partly because the evidence supporting the use of these programs is relatively new, and partly because they cost money to run. Other reasons relate to the participants: although people typically recognize the seriousness of heart disease, Type A individuals probably don't see any connection between CHD and their hard-driving lifestyles (Roskies, 1983). Also, people with high blood pressure either don't know they have it or say they "feel good anyway." For these and similar reasons, many people who could benefit from stress management programs don't join one when it is available. And many of those who do join drop out before completing the program or don't adhere closely to its recommendations, such as to practice relaxation techniques at home (Alderman, 1984; Hoelscher, Lichstein, & Rosenthal, 1986).

SUMMARY

Coping is the process by which people try to manage the real or perceived discrepancy between the demands and resources they appraise in stressful situations. We cope with stress through transactions with the environment that do not necessarily lead to solutions to the problems causing the stress.

Coping serves two types of functions. The function of emotion-focused coping is to regulate the person's emotional response to stress. This regulation occurs through the person's behavior, such as using alcohol or seeking social support, and through cognitive strategies, such as denying unpleasant facts. People tend to rely on emotion-focused coping when they believe they cannot change the stressful conditions. The function of problem-focused coping is to reduce the demands of the stressor or expand the resources to deal with it, such as by learning new skills. People tend to use problem-focused coping when they believe they can change the situation. Adults report using more problem-focused than emotion-focused coping approaches when they experience stress. People use a wide variety of strategies to cope with stress. Some of these methods tend to increase the attention the person gives to the problem, and other methods promote avoidance of the problem. There is no one best method of coping, and no method is uniformly applied or effective with all stressors. People tend to use a combination of methods in coping with a stressful situation.

Although coping changes across the life span, the exact nature of these changes is unclear. Young children's coping is limited by their cognitive abilities, which improve throughout childhood. During adulthood, a shift in coping function occurs as people approach old age—they rely less on problem-focused and more on emotion-focused coping. Elderly people seem to regard stressors as less changeable than middle-aged individuals do.

People can reduce the potential for stress in their lives and others' lives in several ways. First, they can increase the social support they give and receive by joining social, religious, and special-interest groups. Second, they can improve their own and others' sense of personal control and hardiness by giving and taking responsibility. Also, they can reduce frustration and waste less time by organizing their world better, such as through time management. And by exercising and keeping fit, they can reduce the experience of stress and the impact it has on their health. Last, they can prepare for stressful events, such as a medical procedure, by improving their behavioral, cognitive, and informational control.

Sometimes the coping skills individuals have learned are not adequate for dealing with a stressor that is very strong, novel, or unrelenting. A variety of stress management techniques is available to help people who are having trouble coping effectively. One technique is pharmacological, that is, using prescribed drugs, such as beta-blockers. Stress management methods include progressive muscle relaxation, systematic desensitization, biofeedback, modeling, and several cognitive approaches. Rational-emotive therapy (RET) and cognitive therapy attempt to modify stress-producing, irrational thought patterns through the process of cognitive restructuring. Stress-inoculation training and problem-solving training are designed to teach people skills to alleviate stress and achieve personal goals. Stress-inoculation training is an example of a multidimensional approach in that it uses a variety of techniques that are designed to reduce specific components of the person's problems. Beneficial effects on people's stress have been found for all of the behavioral and cognitive stress management methods, particularly relaxation. Massage, meditation, and hypnosis have shown promise for reducing stress, too. Stress management techniques can reduce coronary risk by modifying Type A behavior and by treating hypertension.

KEY TERMS

coping	progressive muscle	modeling	stress-inoculation
emotion-focused coping	relaxation	cognitive restructuring	training
problem-focused coping	systematic desensitization	rational-emotive therapy	problem-solving
time management	biofeedback	cognitive therapy	training

PART III

LIFESTYLES TO ENHANCE HEALTH AND PREVENT ILLNESS

6

HEALTH-RELATED BEHAVIOR AND HEALTH PROMOTION

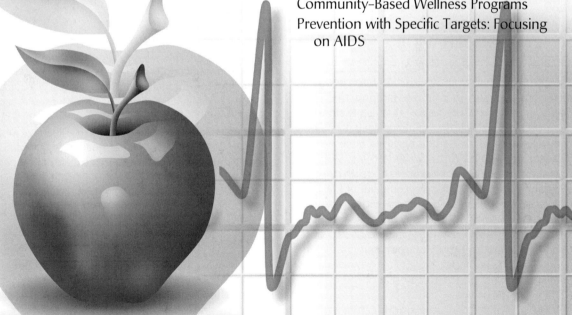

"It's getting worse—those health nuts are all over the place these days, telling me how to live my life," said Joshua between puffs on his cigarette. Things were not necessarily "worse," but they had changed. People were now much more health conscious. They were exercising more, eating more healthful diets, and using better hygiene. Does this story describe the contemporary scene in a technologically advanced country? It could, but it could also describe the mid-1800s. People of today are not the first to be interested in health and fitness.

In mid-1800s America, disease was widespread, epidemics were common, and physicians had few effective methods for preventing or treating illness. As a result, health reformers advocated that people change their lifestyles to protect their health (Collins, 1987; Leventhal, Prohaska, & Hirschman, 1985). These reformers were often imbued with patriotic or religious zeal. Some of them advocated vegetarian diets. Others proposed that people chew their food to a watery consistency, or stop smoking cigarettes and drinking, or get more exercise if they led sedentary lives. Often people who exercised wore loose-fitting gym suits and used a variety of apparatuses, such as rowing machines. It was a lot like today, wasn't it?

This chapter begins our examination of health enhancement and illness prevention. We first consider what health habits people practice and how their lifestyles affect their health. Then we turn our attention to factors that influence the health-related behaviors individuals adopt. The final section of this chapter discusses programs to help people lead more healthful lives. As we study these topics, you will find answers to questions you may have about health-related behavior and health promotion. Are people leading more healthful lives today than they did in the past? Why is it that some people take better care of themselves than others do? How effective are health-promotion programs that try to motivate healthful behavior through fear?

HEALTH AND BEHAVIOR

The role of behavior in health has been receiving increased attention in countries around the world because people's *health habits*—that is, their usual health-related behaviors—influence their likelihood of developing fatal and chronic diseases, such as heart disease, cancer, and AIDS (WHO, 1999c). Mortality from most of today's leading causes of death could be substantially reduced if people would adopt lifestyles that promote wellness, such as by eating healthful diets and not smoking. This knowledge led the U.S. Secretary of Health, Education and Welfare to state: "We are killing ourselves by our own careless habits" and permitting pollution, poverty, and ignorance to persist and harm our health and that of our children (Califano, 1979, p. viii).

The percentage of deaths resulting from any specific cause changes over time. Figure 6–1 depicts the pattern of changes in the United States that occurred since the late 1960s. These changes resulted partly from the modifications people made in their behavioral risk factors for major chronic diseases. Of course, making all of the lifestyle changes health experts recommend won't enable us to live forever. Even if researchers found cures for most of the leading fatal diseases, people's average life expectancy in technologically advanced countries would increase by perhaps a decade or so to its likely upper limit of about 85 years (Olshansky, Carnes, & Cassel, 1990).

LIFESTYLES, RISK FACTORS, AND HEALTH

The typical person's lifestyle includes many behaviors that are risk factors for illness and injury. For instance, millions of people in the United States smoke cigarettes, drink excessively, use drugs, eat high-fat and high-cholesterol diets, eat too much and become

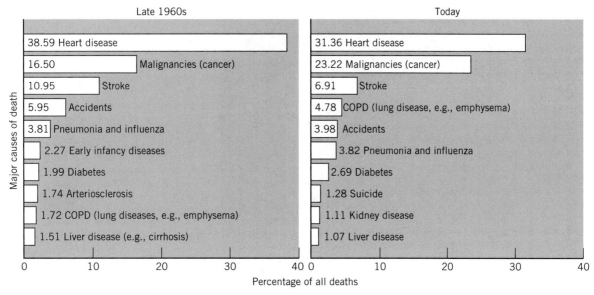

Figure 6–1 Percentage of all deaths caused by each of the ten leading causes of death in the United States in the *late* 1960s (1968) and *today*. Notice that cancer and COPD deaths increased markedly since 1968 (partly due to cigarette smoking); heart disease and stroke deaths declined (partly due to recent lifestyle changes, such as in diet); deaths from diseases of early infancy declined markedly and are no longer in the top ten. (Data from USBC, 1971, Table 77; USBC, 1999, Table 137.)

overweight, have too little physical activity, and behave in unsafe ways, such as by not using seat belts in automobiles. Many people realize these dangers and adjust their behavior to protect their health. Middle-aged men and women who do not smoke and have favorable blood pressure and cholesterol levels can expect to live 6 years longer than they would otherwise (Stamler et al., 1999).

Health Behavior

Health behavior is any activity people perform to maintain or improve their health, regardless of their perceived health status or whether the behavior actually achieves that goal. Researchers have noted that people's health status influences the type of health behavior they perform and their motivation to do it (Kasl & Cobb, 1966a, b; Parsons 1951, 1964). To illustrate these differences, we will consider examples of behaviors people perform when they are well, experience symptoms, and are clearly sick.

Well behavior is any activity people undertake to maintain or improve current good health and avoid illness. These activities can include healthy people's

exercising, eating healthful diets, having regular dental checkups, and getting vaccinations against diseases. But when people are well, they may not feel inclined to devote the effort and sacrifice that health behavior entails. They may take the view, "If it ain't broke, don't fix it." Thus, whether a person engages in health behavior depends heavily on motivational factors, particularly with regard to the individual's perception of a threat of disease, the value in the behavior in reducing this threat, and the attractiveness of the opposite behavior. Unhealthful behaviors, such as drinking or smoking, are often seen as pleasurable or the "in" thing to do. As a result, many individuals do not resist beginning unhealthful behaviors and may reject efforts or advice to get them to quit. Some people think health and pleasure are incompatible, feeling that a life that stresses health behavior is doomed to dullness and fear of illness.

Symptom-based behavior is any activity people who feel ill undertake to determine the problem and find a remedy. These activities usually include complaining about symptoms and seeking help or advice from relatives, friends, and medical practitioners. You would be showing symptom-based behaviors if you

People engage in health behaviors, such as jogging, to maintain or improve their health and avoid illness.

felt stomach pains and described them to a friend or made a doctor's appointment, for example. People do not always engage in symptom-based behavior when symptoms appear, and some people are more likely than others to complain and seek help (Kasl & Cobb, 1966a; Rosenstock & Kirscht, 1979). There are many reasons for these differences. For instance, some individuals may be more afraid than others of physicians, hospitals, or the serious illness a diagnosis may reveal. Some people are stoic or unconcerned about the aches and pains they experience, and some people do not seek medical care because they simply do not have the money to pay for it. Chapter 9 will examine these and other reasons why people do and do not use health care services.

Sick-role behavior refers to any activity people undertake to get well after deciding that they are ill and what the illness is. This behavior is based on the idea that sick people take on a special "role," making them exempt from their normal obligations and life tasks, such as going to work or school. You would be showing sick-role behaviors if you got a prescription filled, used it as the physician directed, stayed home from work to recover, and had someone else do your household chores. An obligation ordinarily accompanies this status—that of trying to get well. Unfortunately, many sick people do not follow the recommended treatment, particularly if it is inconvenient to do or is impersonally administered (Rosenstock & Kirscht, 1979). Other sick-role behaviors seem to serve

emotional functions, as when patients moan or sigh and receive sympathy as a result.

How people behave when they are sick depends in large measure on what they have learned. As an example, a study of female college students assessed whether they had been encouraged during adolescence to adopt the sick role for menstruation or had observed their mothers exhibit menstrual distress. Compared with students who did not have these experiences, those who *did* reported more menstrual symptoms, disability, and clinic visits for these symptoms as adults (Whitehead, Busch, Heller, & Costa, 1986). Other research has found that there are cultural differences in the way people respond to their symptoms and go about trying to get well (Chrisman & Kleinman, 1983; Zola, 1973). For example, studies in the United States have found differences among groups of immigrants in their willingness to tolerate pain, but these differences diminish in succeeding generations (Chapman & Brena, 1985). (Go to ♥.)

Practicing Health Behaviors

What health behaviors do people actually do? One study interviewed hundreds of adults from the general population in the Cleveland area and found that most of these people claimed to perform a wide range of health habits (Harris & Guten, 1979). But less than half claimed to practice regularly some very important behaviors, such as watching their weight, getting

HIGHLIGHT ON ISSUES

Two Health Behaviors: Breast and Testicular Examinations

Breast cancer is a leading cause of women's deaths around the world. For women in the United States, one of every eight is likely to develop breast cancer at some time in her life, especially after the age of 50, and breast cancer is the second most frequent cause of cancer death (ACS, 2000). Compared with breast cancer, *testicular cancer* is much less prevalent, but several thousand cases are diagnosed each year in American men, mainly between the ages of 15 and 35 (ACS, 2000; Rosella, 1994). Breast and testicular cancers are treated with some combination of radiation therapy, chemotherapy, and surgery, and both cancers have very high cure rates if treated early.

Individuals can detect cancer of the breast or testicles in its early stages by self-examination. Breast and testicular self-examinations are done with the fingers, searching mainly for abnormal lumps. For breast self-examination (BSE), the woman lies on her back and, before examining a breast, places the arm of the same side of the body as that breast behind her head. With her other hand, she presses the ends of the middle three fingers flatly against the breast tissue and moves them in dime-sized circular forms. Although women can choose from different search patterns to examine the region, one pattern that produces a thorough search has the hand follow a series of vertical strips to cover a somewhat square area that includes the breast (Atkins, Solomon, Worden, & Foster, 1991; Clarke & Savage, 1999). The method for testicular self-examination (TSE) is relatively simple. The man first locates the tubelike structures that extend behind the testicle. Then he rotates the entire surface of each testicle between the fingers and thumbs of both hands, looking for lumps.

Do people practice BSEs and TSEs? Most of what we know about the practice of these health behaviors comes from research on BSEs. Almost all American women know of BSE, and the great majority have tried it at least once. Yet less than half of them practice it at the recommended monthly frequency (Newcomb et al., 1991; Shepperd et al., 1990; USBC, 1995). This is disheartening because the procedure appears to be effective, and over 90% of breast cancers are detected by the women themselves. There are many reasons why women do not practice BSE regularly: they may lack the knowledge or confidence for doing it correctly, not know how important early detection can be, be afraid they will find a malignant lump, feel embarrassed or immodest by the method, or simply forget and have no reminders to do it (Alagna & Reddy, 1984; Champion, 1990; Craun & Deffenbacher, 1987; Shepperd et al., 1990). Similar factors seem to be involved in men's practice and nonpractice of TSE (Brubaker & Wickersham, 1990; Moore, Barling, & Hood, 1998; Rosella, 1994).

How can we encourage the practice of BSE and TSE? One way is through mass communication. Following news reports of breast cancer in prominent women, such as First Ladies Betty Ford and Nancy Reagan, increases in mammograms (breast X-ray tests) and women's concerns about the disease were reported in newspapers. Reports concerning breast and testicular cancer should note the very high cure rates (over 90%) when detected in early stages and that treatment for cancer is often less extensive and disfiguring in earlier than later stages. For example, breast cancer in its early stages can often be treated without removing the entire breast.

Another way to encourage these health behaviors is for health practitioners, such as physicians or nurses, to provide information and training through individual and group contacts, such as at colleges, worksites, and medical offices. TSE is easy to learn and can be taught effectively by peers with audiovisual aids (Best, Davis, Vaz, & Kaiser, 1996). BSE is harder to learn, and many women receive no training for it. Effective training in BSE can be presented by video and discussion or by having the women perform the examination on a synthetic model (the Betsi Breast model) that has lumps of different sizes and depths in the breasts (Clarke & Savage, 1999; Craun & Deffenbacher, 1987). Having reminders to do examinations increases the frequency with which they are done. It is especially important that men and women with family histories or other risk factors for cancer devise effective BSE or TSE reminders, such as by writing them in a calendar.

Table 6.1 *Percentages Reporting Selected Health-Related Behaviors or Characteristics*

Behavior	Men (%)	Women (%)
Eat breakfast almost every day	54.6	58.0
Rarely snack	25.6	25.4
Exercise or play sports regularly	44.0	37.3
Average two or more drinks per day	9.7	1.7
Smoke regularly	28.4	22.8
Overweight by at least 20%[a]	29.6	25.6

[a]Subjects reported height and weight data; researchers compared against standard recommendations for healthful weights.
Source: USBC (1995, Table 215).

enough exercise, limiting fats and coffee in their diets, and using seat belts. Table 6.1 presents the results of a more recent, national survey of American men and women that focused on a relatively limited set of clearly healthful behaviors. Although these data show important shortcomings in the health practices of people in the United States, data from other research reveal that most of these levels of health-related behavior represent clear improvements over the levels assessed about 10 years earlier (McGinnis & Lee, 1995).

Who practices healthful behavior and why? We are far from a complete answer to this question, but there are gender, sociocultural, and age differences in practicing health behaviors (Schoenborn, 1993; USBC, 1995). For instance, an international survey of adults in European countries found that women perform more healthful behaviors than men (Steptoe et al., 1994). One reason for such differences is that people seem to perform behaviors that are salient to them. A survey comparing licensed practical nurses (LPNs), high school teachers, and college students found that LPNs were the most likely to keep emergency numbers near the phone, the teachers were the most likely to watch their weight, and the students were the most likely to exercise (Turk, Rudy, & Salovey, 1984). Another study compared the lifestyles of medical and nonmedical students and found that the medical students exercised more and were much less likely to smoke cigarettes, drink alcohol excessively, and use drugs (Golding & Cornish, 1987).

You probably know some individuals who are highly health-conscious and others who display little concern about their health. Do individuals who practice certain behaviors that benefit their health also practice other healthful behaviors and continue to perform these behaviors over time? To some ex-

tent they do (Schoenborn, 1993). Many people lead very healthful lifestyles, and the number of health behaviors individuals practice remains fairly constant over many years. But many other people show little consistency in their health habits (Harris & Guten, 1979; Langlie, 1977; Mechanic, 1979). The results of research suggest three conclusions. First, although people's health habits are fairly stable, they often change over time. Second, particular health behaviors are not strongly tied to each other—that is, if we know a person practices one specific health habit, such as using seat belts, we cannot accurately predict that he or she practices another specific habit, such as exercising. Third, health behaviors do not seem to be governed in each person by a single set of attitudes or response tendencies. Thus, a girl who uses seat belts to protect herself from injury may watch her weight to be attractive and not smoke because she is allergic to it.

Why are health behaviors not more stable and strongly linked to each other? There are at least four reasons. First, different habits may serve different purposes. For example, people practice some habits, such as getting enough sleep and eating breakfast, to *promote health* but engage in other health behaviors, such as limiting their use of alcohol and cigarettes, to *avoid health risks* (Leventhal, Prohaska, & Hirschman, 1985). Second, various factors at any given time in people's lives may differentially affect different behaviors. For instance, a person may have lots of social encouragement to eat heartily ("You don't like my cooking?") and fatteningly, and, at the same time, to limit drinking and smoking. Third, people change as a result of experience. For example, many people did not avoid smoking until they learned that it is harmful. And fourth, people's life circumstances change. Thus, factors, such as peer pressure, that may have been important in initiating and maintaining exercising or smoking at one time may no longer be present, thereby increasing the likelihood that the habit will change (Leventhal, Prohaska, & Hirschman, 1985).

INTERDISCIPLINARY PERSPECTIVES ON PREVENTING ILLNESS

According to public health expert Lester Breslow, although medical science and technology have made great progress in treating disease, "the principal advances in health have come about through health promotion and disease prevention rather than through diagnosis and therapy" (1983, p. 50). Using tooth decay as an example, we can illustrate three preventive approaches:

- *Behavioral influence*, such as by encouraging and demonstrating good brushing and flossing techniques.
- *Environmental measures*, which can involve fluoridating water supplies.
- *Preventive medical efforts*, such as by removing calculus from teeth and repairing cavities.

Comprehensive and effective efforts for health promotion and disease prevention consist of some combination of these three approaches. In the world's industrialized nations, the greatest opportunity for health promotion probably lies in influencing behavior, such as by reducing cigarette smoking, excessive alcohol use, and unhealthful dietary practices (Breslow, 1983).

We usually think of prevention as occurring before an illness takes hold. Actually, there are three levels of prevention, only one of which applies before a disease or injury occurs (Leventhal, Prohaska, & Hirschman, 1985; Runyan, 1985; Sanson-Fisher, 1993). These levels are called *primary*, *secondary*, and *tertiary* prevention. Each level of prevention can include the efforts of oneself, one's social network, and professionals who are working to promote health. Preventive efforts can include our own well, symptom-based, and sick-role behaviors.

Primary Prevention

Primary prevention consists of actions taken to avoid disease or injury. In avoiding automobile injuries, for example, primary prevention activities might include our well behavior of using seat belts, a friend reminding us to use them, and public health reminders on TV to buckle up. Primary prevention can also be directed at improving people's diet, exercise, toothbrushing and flossing, and immunity against a contagious disease.

Primary prevention for an individual can begin before he or she is born, or even conceived. Today it is possible to estimate the risk of a child's inheriting a genetic disorder and, in some cases, to diagnose genetic abnormalities in the unborn fetus. Through **genetic counseling,** prospective and expectant parents may obtain information to help them make important family planning decisions (Emery & Pullen,

1986; Tortora & Grabowski, 2000). If the child has not yet been conceived, the counselor can use several types of information to estimate genetic risks. For some inherited diseases or defects, the incidence increases with the parent's ages; for others, there are biological tests for carriers of the gene (Tortora & Grabowski, 2000). If conception has already occurred, these same techniques may be used for determining whether biological tests on the fetus are warranted. These tests, *amniocentesis* and *chorionic villi sampling*, are expensive and may present some degree of risk of injury to the fetus. If the likelihood of the child inheriting a serious health problem greatly exceeds the risk of injury during the test, the procedure is usually recommended. Genetic counseling and biological tests can be applied to determine the risk of many serious and potentially fatal problems, such as the metabolic disorder *Tay-Sachs disease*, the red blood cell disorder *sickle-cell anemia*, and *Duchenne muscular dystrophy*. Clearly, the use of genetic counseling and biological tests on the fetus can play an important role in primary prevention. Physicians can help in selecting genetic counselors.

Another way parents can exercise primary prevention for children is by following medically recommended immunization schedules. Although many prevalent illnesses, such as pneumonia and the common cold, cannot be controlled through immunization, several diseases can. These diseases include diphtheria, tetanus, whooping cough, measles, rubella, mumps, and polio. Although immunization rates increased greatly in the last decades of the 20th century worldwide, they remain lower in poorer societies than richer ones (WHO, 1999c). In the United States, the percentage of preschool children who have full immunization from controllable diseases has increased to over 75%, but poor and nonwhite children have lower immunization rates (NCHS, 2000).

Two promising approaches to primary prevention exist. One involves having medical professionals give health-promotion advice to patients. Although physicians find it hard to incorporate this approach in their practices (Levine et al., 1992; Radecki & Brunton, 1992), perhaps other medical staff would be better able to do it. Interventions that remind practitioners to provide such advice with individual patients can improve these activities (Anderson, Janes, & Jenkins, 1998). The second approach helps people recognize the need for improvements in their health behaviors by using questionnaires to assess their risk factors (Weiss, 1984). You may have seen magazines with questionnaires to assess the reader's life expectancy or risk of disease by asking about the person's current health and lifestyle; family history of illness; and personal characteristics, such as age, weight, and sex. Other tests are more elaborate, are scored and analyzed by computer, and may need interpretation by a health professional.

Secondary Prevention

In **secondary prevention,** actions are taken to identify and treat an illness or injury early with the aim of stopping or reversing the problem. In the case of someone who has developed an ulcer, for example, secondary prevention activities include the person's symptom-based behavior of seeking medical care for abdominal pain, the physician's prescribing medication and dietary changes, and the patient's sick-role behavior of following the doctor's prescriptions. Instances of secondary prevention for other health problems can be found in many different settings: examination of the mouth and jaw regions for early cancer detection during dental visits, free blood pressure measurements at shopping malls, and assessments of children's vision and hearing at school, to cite a few.

Many physicians and adult patients practice secondary prevention through complete physical examinations each year. These checkups are costly in time and money—they consist of a medical history, examination of the body, assessment of vital signs (blood pressure, heart rate, etc.), and a variety of X-ray and laboratory tests. Because not all of these tests have proven useful in preventing illness, medical experts now recommend getting specific tests, each with recommended schedules ranging from 1 to 5 years, depending on the person's age (CU, 1998a). For instance, the American Cancer Society recommends that women should have *mammograms* (breast X ray) annually after the age of 40, but less frequently at younger ages (ACS, 2000). All adults over the age of 50 should have a *sigmoidoscopy* (colon inspection) every 5 years or so. Individuals who are not healthy or are considered to be at high risk—for example, because of past illnesses, family history, or hazardous work conditions—should be examined more often.

These medical examinations are recommended because they detect the disease earlier and save lives. In the case of mammograms, their accuracy in detecting breast cancer increased dramatically in the 1970s (Smart, 1994), and women who follow the recommended schedules for examinations after age 50 reduce their mortality rates by 26% in follow-ups of 10 years or so after diagnosis (Kerlikowske et al., 1995). But a national survey found that only about 60% of American women over 40 years of age had had a mammogram in the prior 2 years, and the rate was especially low for poor and less educated women (NCHS, 2000). Women whose family histories put them at relatively high risk of developing breast cancer do not have more mammograms than other women, unless their risk is explicitly described to them (Curry et al., 1993). Among elderly middle- and upper-middle-class women, the main reasons for not having mammograms are fears of pain and radiation (Fullerton, Kritz-Silverstein, Sadler, & Barrett-Connor, 1996).

Tertiary Prevention

When a serious injury occurs or a disease progresses beyond the early stages, the condition often leads to lasting or irreversible damage. **Tertiary prevention** involves actions to contain or retard this damage, prevent disability or recurrence, and rehabilitate the patient. For patients with severe arthritis, for instance, tertiary prevention includes doing exercises for physical therapy and taking medication to control inflammation and pain. In the treatment of incurable forms of cancer, the goal may be simply to keep the patient reasonably comfortable and the disease in remission as long as possible. And people who suffer disabling injuries may undergo intensive long-term physical therapy to regain the use of their limbs or develop other means for independent functioning.

PROBLEMS IN PROMOTING WELLNESS

The process of preventing illness and injury can be thought of as operating as a *system*, in which the individual, his or her family, health professionals, and the community each play a role. According to health psychologist Craig Ewart (1991b), many interrelated factors and problems can impair the effectiveness of each component in the system, and each component affects each other. Let's look at some of these factors, beginning with those within the individual.

Factors Within the Individual

People who consider ways to promote their own health often face an uphill battle with themselves. One problem is that many healthful behaviors are less pleasurable than their unhealthful alternatives, which may produce a state of conflict. Many people deal with this conflict by maintaining a balance in their lives, setting reasonable limits on the unhealthful behaviors they perform. But most people probably do not—they opt too frequently in favor of pleasure, sometimes vowing to change in the future: "I'll go on a diet next week," for example. On the other hand, some people become obsessed with illness prevention, sometimes doing more harm than good (Brownell, 1991).

Another problem is that adopting wellness lifestyles may require individuals to change longstanding behaviors that have become habitual and may involve addictions, as in cigarette smoking. Habitual and addictive behaviors are very difficult to modify. A third problem is that people who are currently healthy often have little immediate incentive to practice healthful behavior, particularly if the behavior is unappealing or inconvenient. The desirable consequences of well behavior—such as being healthier and more fit—are not immediate, and the undesirable consequences of not practicing health behavior—that is, developing a serious illness—may never materialize. Moreover, even when individuals know they have health problems, all too frequently they drop out of treatment or fail to follow some of the recommendations of their physician (DiMatteo & DiNicola, 1982; Rosenstock & Kirscht, 1979).

Several other factors within the individual are also important. For one thing, people need to have certain cognitive resources, such as the knowledge and skills, to know what health behaviors to adopt, to make plans for changing existing behavior, and to overcome obstacles to change, such as having little time or no place to exercise. In addition, individuals need sufficient self-efficacy regarding their ability to carry out the change. Without self-efficacy, their motivation to change will be impaired. Also, being sick or taking certain drugs can affect people's moods and energy levels, which may affect their cognitive resources and motivation.

Interpersonal Factors

Many social factors influence people's likelihood to adopt health behaviors. These factors include whether they have friends or family who model the behaviors and receive social support and encouragement for trying to change their lifestyles.

People living in a family system may encounter problems in their efforts to promote wellness. Some problems come about because the family is composed of individuals, each with his or her own motivations

"ENOUGH, LORETTA! YOU MUST BE HALFWAY TO ENGLAND BY NOW!"

Reprinted courtesy of Bunny Hoest.

and habits. Suppose, for instance, that a member of a family wants to consume less cholesterol, but no one else is willing to stop eating high-cholesterol foods, such as butter, eggs, and red meats. Or suppose the person has begun exercising three times a week, but this disrupts the daily routine of another family member. The interpersonal conflicts that circumstances like these can create in the family may undermine preventive efforts that the majority of family members support. Similar interpersonal conflicts can undermine prevention efforts among friends, classmates at school or college, and fellow employees at work.

Factors in the Community

People are more likely to adopt health behaviors if these behaviors are promoted or encouraged by community organizations, such as governmental agencies and the health care system.

Health professionals face unique problems in trying to promote wellness. One problem is that their knowledge regarding their patients' health-related behavior comes mainly from the patients, whose reports may be distorted (Beach & Mayer, 1990). Second, the knowledge professionals need to help people lead more healthful lives is incomplete—they need more information to know when and how to intervene to change unhealthful behaviors effectively. Also, medical practitioners have traditionally focused their attention on treating, rather than preventing, illness and injury. But this focus has begun to change, and physicians are becoming increasingly interested in prevention (Radecki & Brunton, 1992).

Finally, the larger community faces an enormous array of problems in trying to prevent illness and injury. These problems include having insufficient funds for public health projects and research, needing to adjust to and communicate with individuals of very different ages and sociocultural backgrounds, and providing health care for those who need it most. Also, people's health insurance may not cover preventive medical services. Among the most difficult problems communities face is trying to balance public health and economic priorities. For example, in some industries, workers are subjected to potentially unhealthful conditions, such as toxic substances, which may also pose a threat to the community as a whole. Suppose a company with these conditions exists in a town that depends heavily on that industry for jobs and tax revenue, and that the cost of reducing the potential for harm would force the company out of business. What should the community do? Many dilemmas of this type exist in most societies throughout the world.

WHAT DETERMINES PEOPLE'S HEALTH-RELATED BEHAVIOR?

If people were all like Mr. Spock of the TV show *Star Trek*, the answer to the question of what determines people's health-related behavior would be simple: facts and logic, for the most part. These people would have no conflicting motivations in adopting wellness lifestyles to become as healthy as they can be. In this section we examine the complex factors that affect health-related behavior.

GENERAL FACTORS IN HEALTH-RELATED BEHAVIOR

The "average" person can describe healthful behaviors and generate a fairly complete list: "Don't smoke," "Don't drink too much, and don't drive if you do," "Eat balanced meals, and don't overeat," "Get regular exercise," and so on. But practicing these acts is another matter. Several processes affect people's health habits, and one factor is *heredity*. Genetic factors influence some health-related behaviors, and excessive alcohol use provides a good example. Twin studies and adoption studies have confirmed that heredity plays a role in the development of alcoholism (Ciraulo & Renner, 1991; Schuckit, 1985). As we will see in Chapter 7,

the exact nature of this role and the relative degree to which genetic and psychosocial factors are involved are unknown.

Learning

People also learn health-related behavior, particularly by way of *operant conditioning*, whereby behavior changes because of its consequences (Sarafino, 2001). Three types of consequences are important:

- **Reinforcement.** When we do something that brings a pleasant, wanted, or satisfying consequence, the tendency to repeat that behavior is increased or *reinforced*. A child who receives something she wants, such as a nickel, for brushing her teeth at bedtime is more likely to brush again the following night. The nickel in this example is a positive reinforcer partly because it was wanted and partly because it was *added* to the situation. But reinforcement can also occur in a different way. Suppose you have a headache, you take aspirin, and the headache goes away. In this case, your headache was unpleasant and your behavior of taking aspirin *removed* it from the situation. The headache is called a "negative" reinforcer because it was *unwanted* or *unpleasant* and it was *taken away* from the situation. In both cases of reinforcement, the end result is a desirable state of affairs from the person's point of view.

- **Extinction.** If the consequences that maintain a behavior are eliminated, the response tendency gradually weakens. The process or procedure of extinction exists only if no alternative maintaining stimuli (reinforcers) for the behavior have supplemented or taken the place of the original consequences. In the above example of toothbrushing behavior, if the money is no longer given, the child may continue brushing if another reinforcer exists, such as praise from her parents or her own satisfaction with the appearance of her teeth.

- **Punishment.** When we do something that brings an unpleasant consequence, the behavior tends to be suppressed. A child who gets a scolding from his parents for playing with matches is less likely to repeat that behavior, especially if his parents might see him. The influence of punishment on future behavior depends on whether the person expects the behavior will lead to punishment again. Take, for example, people who injure themselves (punishment) jogging—those who think they could be injured again are less likely to resume jogging than those who do not.

We have seen before that people can learn by observing the behavior of others—a process called *modeling*. In this kind of learning, the consequences the model receives affect the behavior of the observer (Bandura, 1965a, 1965b). If a teenager sees people enjoying and receiving social attention for smoking cigarettes, these people serve as powerful models and increase the likelihood that the teenager will begin smoking, too. But if models receive punishment for smoking, such as being avoided by classmates at school, the teenager may be less likely to smoke. In general, people are more likely to perform the behavior they observe if the model is *similar to themselves*—that is, of the same sex, age, or race—and is a *high-status person*, such as a physically attractive individual, movie star, or well-known athlete (Bandura, 1969, 1986). Advertisers of products such as alcoholic beverages know these facts and use them in their commercials.

If a behavior becomes firmly established, it tends to be *habitual*, that is, the person often performs it automatically and without awareness. For example, a man who smokes and has a head cold might be engaged in an activity and "respond to the sight of an open pack of cigarettes by automatically reaching out, taking one, and starting to smoke without at all being aware of what he has done. Only when the irritation produced in his nose and throat … by the smoke 'captures his attention' is he likely to disengage in smoking behavior" (Hunt, Matarazzo, Weiss, & Gentry, 1979, p. 115). Even though the behavior may have been learned because it was reinforced by positive consequences, it is now less dependent on consequences and more dependent on antecedent cues (seeing a pack of cigarettes) with which it has been linked in the past (Sarafino, 2001). A *ntecedents* are internal or external stimuli that precede and set the occasion for a behavior. A smoker who says, "I have to have a cigarette with my coffee after breakfast," is pointing out an antecedent. Behaviors that become habitual can be very difficult to change.

Because habitual behaviors are hard to change, people need to develop well behaviors as early as possible and eliminate unhealthful activities as soon as they appear. Families play a major role in children's learning of health-related behaviors (Baranowski &

Nader, 1985). Children observe, for example, the dietary, exercise, and smoking habits of other family members and often receive encouragement to behave in similar ways. Children who observe and receive encouragement for healthful behavior at home are more likely than others to develop good health habits.

Social, Personality, and Emotional Factors

Many health-related behaviors are affected by *social* factors (Baranowski & Nader, 1985; Kirscht, 1983). One of these factors is the degree of support or encouragement individuals receive from other people for health-related behaviors, such as smoking and exercising. Friends and family promote or discourage a health behavior by providing consequences, such as praise or complaints, for it, modeling it, and conveying a value for good health (Burg & Seeman, 1994; Weiss, Larsen, & Baker, 1996). These processes probably also lead to gender differences, such as the greater physical activity of American boys than girls. Although this difference may be determined partly by biology, right from birth, many parents' perceptions of their newborn son or daughter seem to be biased (Rubin, Provenzano, & Luria, 1974). Even when male and female babies are matched for size, weight, and general health, fathers and mothers rate sons as firmer, stronger, better coordinated, and alert. These perceptions tend to continue and seem to affect how parents treat boys and girls, such as by playing more roughly and vigorously with their sons than with their daughters (Block, 1983; Huston, 1983). Very different patterns of encouragement may lead boys more than girls toward healthful physical activity.

Two other factors that are linked to health-related behavior are the person's *personality* and *emotional state*, particularly stress. One personality characteristic that is associated with practicing health behavior is conscientiousness. People who score high on a test of conscientiousness are more likely to take prescribed medications and follow the recommended schedule for getting mammograms than those who score low on this trait (Christensen & Smith, 1995; Siegler, Feaganes, & Rimer, 1995). The role of emotions can be seen in two ways. First, among women who have a close relative with breast cancer and are low in conscientiousness, those who are very distressed about cancer are especially unlikely to have a mammogram (Schwartz et al., 1999). A brief cognitive intervention to enhance coping skills can reduce cancer distress among women who have a close relative with cancer and substantially improve their preventive behavior (Audrain et al., 1999). Second, people who experience high levels of stress consume more alcohol, cigarettes, and coffee than those who experience less stress (Baer et al., 1987; Conway, Vickers, Ward, & Rahe, 1981). If you ask people why they smoke, they often will say, "To relieve tension." Many people cite coping with stress as their most important reason for continuing to smoke (Gottlieb, 1983).

Perception and Cognition

People's *perceived symptoms* also influence their health-related behaviors. The way people react varies from ignoring the problem to seeking immediate professional care. Certainly when the symptoms are severe—as with excruciating pain, obvious bone fractures, profuse bleeding, or very high fever—almost everyone who has access to a health care system will decide to use it (Rosenstock & Kirscht, 1979). How do symptoms affect behavior when they are not so severe? People who are ill report performing more health behavior, such as limiting certain foods and not drinking, than people who are healthy (Harris & Guten, 1979). Many people react to illness in reasonable ways, adjusting their health habits to meet the needs of their health problems.

Cognitive factors play an important role in the health behaviors people perform. As we saw earlier, people must have correct knowledge about the health issue and the ability to solve problems that arise when trying to implement healthful behavior, such as how to fit an exercise routine into their busy schedules. People also make many judgments that have an impact on their health. They assess the general condition of their health: Is it good or bad? They also make decisions about other questions, such as: Should I cut back on the salt in my diet? Should I begin an exercise program? And, will I stick with these health behaviors if I start them?

But these answers are sometimes based on misconceptions, as when hypertensive patients overestimate their ability to know intuitively when their blood pressure is high (Baumann & Leventhal, 1985; Brondolo, Rosen, Kostis, & Schwartz, 1999; Pennebaker & Watson, 1988). Hypertensive patients generally report that they can tell when their blood pressure is up, citing symptoms such as headache,

warmth or flushing face, dizziness, and nervousness. But research has shown that these symptoms are poor estimators of blood pressure. When hypertensive and normotensive individuals are asked to assess their blood pressure, their assessments often correlate with their symptoms and moods, but not with their actual blood pressure. The potential harm in their erroneous beliefs is that patients often alter their medication-taking behavior, and sometimes drop out of treatment, on the basis of their subjective assessments of their blood pressure. Clearly, beliefs are important determinants of health behavior. The next section examines the role of beliefs in people's health.

THE ROLE OF BELIEFS AND INTENTIONS

Suppose your friend believed in *reflexology*, a "healing" method that involves massaging specific areas of the feet to treat illnesses. The belief that underlies this method is that each area of the foot connects to a specific area of the body—the toes connect to the head, for instance, and the middle of the arch links to certain endocrine glands (Livermore, 1991). For a patient with a head tumor, a reflexologist's treatment might include massaging the toes. Your friend would probably try ways to prevent and treat illness that are different from those most other people would try.

People's thinking may affect how they feel. Researchers conducted an experiment to determine how women's beliefs about premenstrual symptoms affect how they feel during the premenstrual period (Fradkin & Firestone, 1986). The women were assigned to three informational groups: a *control* group, which received no information, and two experimental groups. Both experimental groups received information on premenstrual tension by reading an article on the topic, seeing a videotape of a gynecologist discussing it, and taking part in a discussion group. Each experimental group received information with a different orientation—either biological or psychological. The information women in the *biological* group received focused on the physiological causes of the "universal, unavoidable fluctuations in mood" they experience. In contrast, the *psychological* group received information arguing that premenstrual symptoms have no biological basis and result from "self-fulfilling expectations" perpetuated by societal myths. The symptoms the women reported in a questionnaire were equivalent for the three groups initially, and remained the same for the control and biological groups after receiving the information. But the women in the psychological group reported a dramatic decline in their symptoms during the month after getting the information. The information may have changed their beliefs and reduced the symptoms they experienced.

Researchers have also been interested in the role of health beliefs in people's practice and nonpractice of health behaviors. The most widely researched and accepted theory of why people do and do not practice these behaviors is called the health belief model (Becker, 1979; Becker et al., 1977; Becker & Rosenstock, 1984; Rosenstock, 1966). Let's see what this theory proposes.

The Health Belief Model

According to the **health belief model,** the likelihood that a person will take *preventive action*—that is, perform some health behavior—depends directly on the outcome of two assessments he or she makes. One assessment pertains to the *threat* the person feels regarding a health problem, and the other weighs the *pros and cons* of taking the action. What factors go into these assessments?

Figure 6–2 shows that several factors can influence people's *perceived threat*—that is, the degree to which they feel threatened or worried by the prospect of a particular health problem. These factors include:

● *Perceived seriousness* of the health problem. People consider how severe the organic and social consequences are likely to be if they develop the problem or leave it untreated. The more serious they believe its effects will be, the more likely they are to perceive it as a threat and take preventive action.

● *Perceived susceptibility* to the health problem. People evaluate the likelihood of their developing the problem. The more vulnerable they perceive themselves to be, the more likely they are to perceive it as a threat and take action.

● *Cues to action.* Being reminded or alerted about a potential health problem increases the likelihood

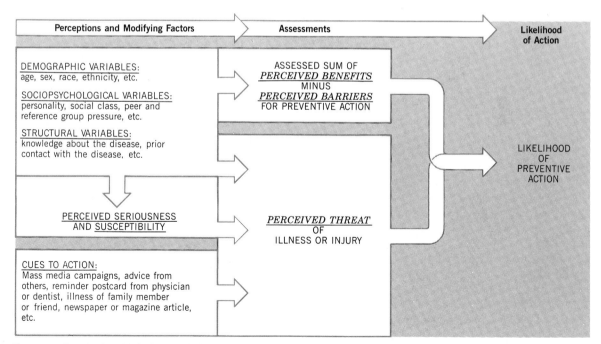

Figure 6–2 The health belief model. People's likelihood of taking preventive action is determined by two assessments they make: their perceived threat of the health problem and the sum of pros and cons they perceive in taking action. Many factors contribute to these assessments. (Adapted from Becker & Rosenstock, 1984, Figure 2.)

of perceiving a threat and taking action. Cues to action can take many forms, such as a public service announcement of a dangerous storm approaching or a reminder phone call for an upcoming dental appointment.

In addition, three other factors are implicated in people's perceived threat of illness or injury. These factors are: *demographic variables*, which include age, sex, race, and ethnic background; *sociopsychological variables*, including personality traits, social class, and social pressure; and *structural variables*, such as knowledge about or prior contact with the health problem. Thus, for example, elderly individuals whose close friends have developed severe cases of cancer or heart disease are more likely to perceive a personal threat of illness than young adults whose friends are in good health.

In weighing the pros and cons of taking preventive action, people assess the *benefits*—such as being healthier or reducing health risks—and the *barriers* or costs they *perceive* in taking action. What barriers might people see in preventive action? For the health behavior of getting a periodic physical checkup, the barriers might include financial considerations ("Can I afford the bills?"), psychosocial consequences ("People will think I'm getting old if I start having checkups"), and physical considerations ("My doctor's office is across town, and I don't have a car"). As these examples suggest, demographic, sociopsychological, and structural variables can affect people's assessments. Thus, for instance, individuals from lower economic classes are more likely than people from higher classes to feel that affording the bills or getting to the doctor's office is very difficult. The connection between these factors and the assessment process can be seen in Figure 6–2. The outcome of weighing the benefits against the barriers is an assessed *sum*: the extent to which taking the action is more beneficial for them than not taking the action.

The perceived threat of illness or injury combines with the assessed sum of perceived benefits and barriers to determine the likelihood of preventive action. Thus, for the health behavior of having a medical checkup, people who feel threatened by an illness and believe the benefits of having a checkup outweigh the barriers are likely to go ahead with it, taking action for primary prevention. But people who do not feel threatened or assess that the barriers are too strong are unlikely to have the checkup. According to the health

belief model, the processes we described for primary prevention also determine people's symptom-based behavior in secondary prevention, such as going to the doctor when sick, and sick-role behavior in tertiary prevention, such as sticking with a rehabilitation program following a stroke.

Has research generally supported the health belief model's explanation of health-related behavior? The model has generated a great deal of research, much of which has upheld its predictions (Becker, 1979; Becker & Rosenstock, 1984; Curry & Emmons, 1994; Kirscht, 1983; Rosenstock & Kirscht, 1979). Let's consider the case of primary prevention. Studies have found that compared to people who do *not* get vaccinations, have regular dental visits, get regular breast and cervical cancer tests, or take part in exercise programs, those who *do* are more likely to believe that they are susceptible to the related health problem, that developing the problem would have very serious effects, and that the benefits of preventive action outweigh the barriers. Similar relationships have been found for secondary and tertiary prevention. That is, compared to people who do not take medication as directed or do not stick with prescribed dietary and weight loss programs, those who do are more likely to believe they are susceptible to a worsening of their health, that the resulting illness would have serious effects, and that the benefits of protective action exceed the costs. Furthermore, studies have shown that cues to action, such as reminders to perform breast self-examinations (Clarke & Savage, 1999; Craun & Deffenbacher, 1987), and demographic and sociopsychological variables (Becker, 1979) influence people's practice of preventive measures.

Despite the success that the health belief model has had, it has some shortcomings. One shortcoming is that it does not account for health-related behaviors people perform habitually, such as tooth brushing—behaviors that probably originated and have continued without the person's considering health threats, benefits, and costs. Another problem is that there is no standard way of measuring its components, such as perceived susceptibility and seriousness. Different studies have used different questionnaires to measure the same factors, thereby making it difficult to compare the results across studies. These problems do not mean the theory is wrong, but that it is incomplete. We now turn to another theory that focuses on the role of people's beliefs on their practice of health-related behavior. (Go to 🔎.)

FOCUS ON RESEARCH
Pollyannas about Health

"Compared to other people your age and sex, are your chances of getting lung cancer greater than, less than, or about the same as theirs?" This is the kind of question Neil Weinstein used in his research to examine how optimistically people view their future health. Through this research, he has shown that people tend to be Pollyannas—or *unrealistically optimistic*—about their health.

In one of these studies, Weinstein (1982) had students fill out a questionnaire with a long list of health problems. The subjects were asked to indicate their own risk for developing each problem, relative to other students of the same sex at the university, using a 7-point scale ranging from "much below average" to "much above average." The results revealed that the students believed they were less likely than others to develop three-quarters of the health problems listed, including:

- Alcoholism
- Arteriosclerosis
- Diabetes
- Drug addiction
- Heart attack
- Lung cancer
- Overweight by 40 pounds
- Skin cancer
- Venereal disease

They believed they were more susceptible than other students to only one of the health problems, that of ulcers.

In a later study, Weinstein (1987) used very similar questions in a mailed survey with 18- to 65-year-old adults in the general population. These people also believed they were less likely to develop over three-quarters of the listed health problems, as compared with other adults of their own age and sex. Furthermore, they did not believe they were more susceptible than others for developing any of the problems. What is it about people's thinking that makes them so optimistic? This study found four cognitive factors that affect people's optimism:

(1) the belief that if the problem has not yet appeared, one is exempt from future risk; (2) the perception that the problem is preventable by individual action; (3) the perception that the hazard is infrequent; and (4) lack of experience with the hazard. If a hazard had such characteristics, people had a strong tendency to conclude that their own risk was less than the risk faced by their peers. (Weinstein, 1987, p. 496).

Note that the thinking described by these factors is not very logical. For instance, the frequency with which a health problem occurs does not affect one's risk relative to that of others.

Do people remain optimistic about their health when they are sick or when a threat of illness is clear? Evidently not. Using a procedure similar to Weinstein's, a study found that university students who were waiting for treatment at the student health center were less optimistic about their future health than were healthy students in a psychology course (Kulik & Mahler, 1987b). Another study was conducted with students in Poland, just after the radioactive cloud reached their community from the explosion of the atomic power plant at Chernobyl in the Soviet Union (Dolinski, Gromski, & Zawisza, 1987). Although these people believed they were less likely than others to have a heart attack or be injured in an accident, they believed they were equally likely to develop cancer and *more* likely than others to suffer illness effects of the radiation over the next several years. Thus, in the face of a real threat, they showed "unrealistic pessimism" regarding their health.

Other studies have revealed similar biases in children and teenagers, indicating that feelings of invulnerability are not a unique feature of adolescence (Cohn, Macfarlane, Yanez, & Imai, 1995; Whalen et al., 1994). Clearly, people's beliefs play a powerful role in their perceptions of health risks, and their beliefs are not always logical. Studies of optimistic and pessimistic beliefs are important because people who practice health behaviors tend to feel they would otherwise be at risk for associated health problems (Becker & Rosenstock, 1984).

The Theory of Planned Behavior

Suppose you are having dinner at a restaurant with Dan, a friend who is overweight, and you wonder whether he will order dessert. How could you predict his behavior? That's simple—you could ask what he *intends* to do. According to the **theory of planned behavior** (Ajzen, 1985), an expanded version of the *theory of reasoned action* (Ajzen & Fishbein, 1980), people decide their intention in advance of most voluntary behaviors, and intentions are the best predictors of what people will do.

What determines people's intentions to perform a behavior? The theory indicates that three judgments determine a person's intention, which we'll illustrate with a girl named Ellie who has decided to start exercising:

- *Attitude regarding the behavior*, which is basically a judgment of whether or not the behavior is a good thing to do. Ellie has decided that exercising "would be a good thing for me to do." This judgment is based on two expectations: the likely *outcome* of the behavior (such as, "If I exercise, I will be healthier and more attractive") and whether the outcome would be *rewarding* (for example, "Being healthy and good looking will be satisfying and pleasant").
- *Subjective norm*. This judgment reflects the impact of social pressure or influence on the behavior's acceptability or appropriateness. Ellie has decided that exercising "is a socially appropriate thing for me to do." This decision is based on her beliefs regarding *others' opinions* about the behavior (such as, "My family and friends think I should exercise") and her *motivation to comply* with those opinions (as in, "I want to do what they want").
- *Perceived behavioral control*, or the person's expectation of success in performing the contemplated behavior (which is very similar to the concept of self-efficacy). Ellie thinks she can do the exercises and stick to the program.

The theory of planned behavior proposes that these factors combine to produce an intention, which leads to performance of the behavior. Suppose Ellie's decisions were different because she had the following beliefs:

- "Exercising is inconvenient and uncomfortable, and can cause injury."

- "I suffer enough inconvenience and discomfort in my life without having to exercise."
- "Nobody I know seems to want me to exercise, and they don't exercise either."
- "I value the opinion of my friends and family and want to be like them."
- "I'll never find the time to exercise."

With these beliefs, Ellie almost certainly would not generate an intention to exercise, and thus would not do so.

Studies have found support for aspects of the theory in explaining several health-related behaviors. A study by Richard Bagozzi (1981), for example, examined the attitudes, intentions, and behavior of adults regarding donating blood during an annual Red Cross blood drive. In the week prior to the drive, the possible donors filled out a questionnaire that asked them to rate the strength of their intentions and their attitudes, such as the degree of pleasantness or unpleasantness, toward giving blood. The Red Cross provided information on whether they actually gave blood. As the theory predicts, attitudes about giving blood related to the actual behavior through their impact on the individuals' intentions. Other studies have found that people's attitudes and intentions influence their quitting smoking cigarettes (Norman, Conner, & Bell, 1999), exercising (Wurtele & Maddux, 1987), losing weight (Schifter & Ajzen, 1985), using condoms for safer sex (Sutton, McVey, & Glanz, 1999), and practicing testicular self-examinations (Brubaker & Wickersham, 1990; Moore, Barling, & Hood, 1998).

What shortcomings does the theory of planned behavior have? One problem is that intentions and behavior are only moderately related—people do not always do what they plan (or *claim* they plan) to do. And people's attitudes seem to predict some health-related behaviors, such as alcohol use, but not others, such as smoking and drunk driving (Stacy, Bentler, & Flay, 1994). Another problem is that the theory is incomplete; it does not include, for example, the important role of people's prior experience with the behavior. In the blood donation study described, the subjects were also asked about their past behavior in donating or not donating blood (Bagozzi, 1981). Of those subjects who said they intended to give blood, those who had given before were more likely actually to give than those who had not donated in the past. Similarly, other studies have found that people's history of performing a health-related behavior, such as exercising, using alcohol or drugs, or using condoms is a strong predictor of their future practice of that behavior (Bentler & Speckart, 1979; Godin, Valois, Shephard, & Desharnais, 1987; Sutton, McVey, & Glanz, 1999). Thus, for example, compared to adults who have engaged in little exercise in the past, those who have exercised are much more likely to carry out their promises to exercise in the future.

The health belief model and the theory of planned behavior both provide valid explanations for parts of the process that determines people's practice of health-related behavior. At their core, both theories assume people weigh perceived benefits and costs and behave according to the outcome of their analysis. But neither approach is sufficient and both have limitations (Janis, 1984; Kirscht, 1983; Weinstein, 1988). One weakness in these theories is that they assume people think about risks in a detailed fashion, knowing what diseases are associated with different behaviors and estimating the likelihood of becoming seriously ill. In reality, people may modify their lifestyles, such as reducing coffee consumption, for very vague reasons, such as, "My doctor says coffee is bad for you." People appear to be especially inaccurate in estimating the degree of increased risk when the risks of illness, such as cancer, increase beyond moderate levels—for example, when individuals smoke more than 15 cigarettes a day (Sastre, Mullet, & Sorum, 1999; Weinstein, 2000).

Beliefs in Personal Control

In Chapter 4 we examined how a sense of personal control can modify the stress people experience. In this section, we will consider how people's health-related behavior relates to their beliefs in two aspects of personal control: *locus of control* and *self-efficacy*.

You might expect that people whose health locus of control is strongly *internal*—as measured by a locus of control scale—would tend to practice behaviors that prevent illness and promote their health. Because these individuals believe they can influence their health, they should practice more healthful behavior than those who score high on external control. This seems to be so. Compared to people who score high on external control beliefs, those who score high on internal control tend to perform more health behaviors, such as getting physical examinations and dieting for health reasons (Seeman & Seeman, 1983). They

also tend to be more successful in reducing cigarette smoking and seek out more information on some health issues, such as high blood pressure (Strickland, 1978; Wallston, & Walls 1982). A meta-analysis has revealed that these relationships are fairly strong, particularly for individuals from the middle and upper social classes (Reisch, Wiehl, & Tinsley, 1994). Other findings indicate that the belief in internal control appears to have a greater impact on the behavior of people who place a high value on their health than on that of those who do not (Lau, Hartman, & Ware, 1986).

In some cases, performing a healthful behavior is hard to do, for instance, it may be strenuous or complicated. Therefore, people's belief that they can succeed at something they want to do—or self efficacy—may be an important determinant of whether they choose to practice specific behaviors (Bandura, 1986). Individuals acquire a sense of efficacy through their own successes and failures, observations of others' experiences, and assessments of their abilities that other people communicate (McAuley, Talbot, & Martinez, 1999). When deciding to practice a health behavior, people appraise their efficacy on the basis of the effort required, complexity of the task, and other aspects of the situation, such as whether they are likely to receive help from other people (Schunk & Carbonari, 1984).

Research has found that self-efficacy does influence people's health behavior. Cigarette smokers who believe they are incapable of kicking the habit typically don't try, but smokers who believe they can succeed in quitting often break the habit (DiClemente, Prochaska, & Gilbertini, 1985). Similarly, individuals who believe they can succeed in losing weight are more likely to try and to succeed than those who do not (Schifter & Ajzen, 1985). Moreover, patients recovering from serious illnesses, such as heart or respiratory disease, who believe they can perform a progressive program of recovery behaviors, such as walking various distances, are more likely to adhere to the program than those who have less self-efficacy (Jenkins & Gortner, 1998; Kaplan, Atkins, & Reinsch, 1984).

The Stages of Change Model

A wife's letter in an Ann Landers newspaper column once described her worry about her husband, who had suffered a heart attack but hadn't tried to lose weight or exercise as his doctor recommended. This situation is not uncommon. Although there are probably many reasons why this man hadn't changed his behavior, one may be that he wasn't "ready." Readiness to change is the main focus of a theory called the **stages of change model** (also called the *transtheoretical model* because it includes factors described in other theories) (DiClemente et al., 1991; Prochaska & DiClemente, 1984; Prochaska, DiClemente, & Norcross, 1992). The model outlines five *stages* of intentional behavior change:

1. *Precontemplation.* People in this stage are not considering changing, at least during the next several months or so. These people may have decided against changing or just never thought about it.

2. *Contemplation.* During this stage, people are aware a problem exists and are seriously considering changing to a healthier behavior within the next several months. But they are not yet ready to make a commitment to take action.

3. *Preparation.* At this stage, individuals are ready to try to change and plan to pursue a behavioral goal, such as stopping smoking, in the next month. They may have tried to reach that goal in the past year without being fully successful. For instance, these people might have reduced their smoking by half, but did not yet quit completely.

4. *Action.* This stage spans a period of time, usually 6 months, from the start of people's successful and active efforts to change a behavior.

5. *Maintenance.* People in this stage work to maintain the successful behavioral changes they achieved. Although this stage can last indefinitely, researchers often define its length as, say, 6 months, for follow-up assessment.

According to the stages of change model, people who are currently in one stage show different psychosocial characteristics from people in other stages. For instance, people in the precontemplation stage regarding an unhealthy behavior, such as eating a high-cholesterol diet, are likely to have less self-efficacy and see more barriers than benefits for changing that behavior than people in the more advanced stages. Efforts of their own or of others to change the behavior are not likely to succeed until these individuals advance through the stages. Is it possible to help them advance? One of the values of the stages of change model is that it enables an intervention to *match* useful strategies with important characteristics of people

at each stage to help them advance to the next stage (Oldenburg, 1994; Patrick, Sallis et al., 1994; Perz, DiClemente, & Carbonari, 1996; Prochaska, DiClemente, & Norcross, 1992).

Let's consider an example of matching. Suppose you are a nurse providing care to an elderly woman with heart disease who doesn't exercise, even though her physician advised her to do so. If she is at the precontemplation stage, you might talk with her about why exercise would help her physically, for instance, and have her generate ways this would improve her general functioning. The goal at this point is just to get the person to consider changing the behavior. If she is at the contemplation stage, the goal might be to help her decide to change soon. Discussing the benefits and barriers she perceives in exercising, finding ways to overcome barriers, and showing her that she can do the physical activities would help.

The stages of change model is a very useful theory. Studies have confirmed that people at higher stages are more likely to succeed at adopting healthful behaviors, such as quitting smoking (DiClemente et al., 1991), getting breast cancer testing (Rakowski et al., 1992), and using safer sex practices (Bowen & Trotter, 1995). But research has not yet demonstrated consistently that matching an intervention to people's stage of readiness improves its success in helping to change unhealthful behaviors (see Dijkstra, De Vries, Roijackers, & van Breukelen, 1998; Quinlan & McCaul, 2000; Velicer et al., 1999).

In the preceding sections, we have examined many aspects of people's beliefs and intentions that appear to influence their health-related behavior. These aspects include people's perceived susceptibility to illness, perceived barriers and benefits to changing unhealthy behavior, ideas about what behaviors are socially acceptable and encouraged by family and friends, self-efficacy beliefs, and readiness to change. But these factors do not adequately account for *irrational* decisions people often make about their health. For instance, these theories do

> not provide an adequate explanation for the widespread tendency of patients who have painful heart attacks to delay obtaining medical aid .... Typically, when the afflicted person thinks of the possibility that it might be a heart attack, he or she assumes that "it couldn't be happening to me." The patients' delay of treatment is not attributable to unavailability of medical aid or transportation

delays; approximately 75% of the delay time elapses before a patient decides to contact a physician. (Janis, 1984, pp. 331–332)

Thus, theories that focus on rational processes do not specify or examine conditions that can override logical decision-making. The next section considers how nonrational processes, such as illogical thinking and stress, affect people's likelihood of taking preventive action.

THE ROLE OF NONRATIONAL PROCESSES

Although body builders generally know that using anabolic steroids can harm their health, some may try to justify using these substances to build muscles with statements like, "Experts have told us almost everything is bad for us and later found out lots of things aren't." Why are the decisions people make regarding health-related behavior not more rational? Nonrational motivational and emotional factors can influence cognitive processes.

Motivational Factors in Beliefs

Research findings indicate that people's desires and preferences influence the judgments they make of the validity and utility of new information, through a process called **motivated reasoning** (Kunda, 1990). In one form of motivated reasoning, individuals who prefer to reach a particular conclusion, such as to continue to eat fatty foods or smoke cigarettes, tend to use biased processes: they search for reasons to accept supportive information and discount disconfirming information. The reasons they choose seem "reasonable" to them, even if the logic is actually faulty. People's tendency to use biased reasoning processes appears to be fairly stable and consistent across a variety of situations (Sarafino, Groff, & DePaulo, 2000).

Studies have demonstrated nonrational thought processes in several types of health-related decisions. First, people with a chronic illness, such as diabetes, who tend to use illogical thought patterns in health-related situations tend not to follow medical advice for managing their illness (Christensen, Moran, & Weibe, 1999). Second, people who use defense mechanisms a lot to cope with stressful information are more likely than other individuals to deny that they are at risk for AIDS, especially if their risk of infection is high (Gladis, Michela, Walter, & Vaughan, 1992).

Perhaps their high feeling of threat motivates their use of denial. Similarly, individuals seem to use irrelevant information, such as a sexual partner's attractiveness, to judge the risks in having sex with that person (Blanton & Gerrard, 1997; Gold & Skinner, 1996). Third, people who smoke cigarettes give lower ratings of risk than nonsmokers do when asked to rate their own risk of developing smoking-related diseases, such as lung cancer (Lee, 1989; McCoy et al., 1992). Beliefs like these appear very resistant to change (Kreuter & Strecher, 1995; Weinstein & Klein, 1995).

Emotional Factors in Beliefs

Stress also affects the cognitive processes people use in making decisions. **Conflict theory** presents a model to account for both rational and irrational decision-making, and stress is an important factor in this model (Janis, 1984; Janis & Mann, 1977). The model describes the cognitive sequence by which people make important decisions, including health-related decisions. According to conflict theory, the cognitive sequence people use in arriving at a stable decision starts when an event challenges their current course of action or lifestyle. The challenge can be either a *threat*, such as a symptom of illness or a news story about the dangers of smoking, or an *opportunity*, such as the chance to join a free program at work to quit smoking. The first step in the cognitive sequence involves *appraising the challenge*, basically answering the question, "Are the risks serious if I don't change?" If the judgment is "no," the behavior stays the same and the decision-making process ends; but if the answer is "yes," the process continues—for instance, with a survey of alternatives for dealing with the challenge.

Conflict theory proposes that people experience stress with all major decisions, particularly those relating to health, because of conflicts about what to do. According to Irving Janis (1984, p. 335), these individuals may "realize that whichever course of action or inaction they choose could lead to serious material or social losses, such as becoming physically incapacitated or losing the esteem of loved ones." Thus, the way people cope with stress may play an important role in their health behavior.

What determines how effectively individuals deal with health-related decisions? Conflict theory indicates that people's coping with decisional conflict depends on their perceptions of the presence or absence of three factors: *risks, hope,* and *adequate time*. Different combinations of these three factors produce different coping patterns, two of which are:

- *Hypervigilance.* People sometimes see serious risks in their current behavior *and* those alternatives they have considered. If they believe they may still find a better solution *but* think they are fast running out of time, they experience high stress. These people tend to search frantically for a solution—and may choose an alternative hastily, especially if it promises immediate relief.

- *Vigilance.* People who perceive serious risks in all possibilities they have considered *but* believe they may find a better alternative and have the time to search experience only moderate levels of stress. Under these conditions, people tend to search thoroughly and make rational choices.

Conflict theory proposes that vigilant coping is the only consistently adaptive pattern for decision making. When the challenge consists of a physician's warning or obvious symptoms of illness, other coping patterns can be highly maladaptive. Although the conflict theory model was developed on the basis of an existing and extensive body of research, studies have not yet directly tested its predictions to the point that its strengths and weaknesses are clear. Still, there is little question that the impact of stress is an important determinant of preventive action, particularly in people's symptom-based and sick-role behavior.

We have examined how each of many different psychological and social factors can affect people's health behavior. But these factors constitute only part of the picture, and a full understanding of all relevant biopsychosocial factors and the way they interact with one another as a *system* is needed. We next examine the relationships that exist between individuals' lifestyles and three factors—age, sex, and sociocultural background.

DEVELOPMENTAL, GENDER, AND SOCIOCULTURAL FACTORS IN HEALTH

It comes as no surprise that people's health changes across the life span, that women and men have some differences in health risks and needs, and that variations in preventive behavior occur between individuals of different social classes and ethnic backgrounds.

What are some of these changes and differences, and why do they exist? Let's examine these health issues, starting with the role of development.

DEVELOPMENT AND HEALTH-RELATED BEHAVIOR

The biological, psychological, and social factors that affect people's health change throughout the life span, causing individuals to face different health risks and problems as they develop. For instance, adolescents and young adults are at relatively high risk for injury from automobile accidents, but older adults are at relatively high risk for hypertension and heart disease. As a result, people's preventive needs and goals change with age. Table 6.2 presents main preventive goals for each period in the life span. During the beginning of the life span, and sometimes toward the end, the individual may lack the ability to take preventive action, and other people assume that responsibility.

During Gestation and Infancy

Each year millions of babies around the world are born with birth defects—in the United States alone, there are 150,000, or 3.8 out of every 100 births annually (MDBDF, 2000). These defects range from relatively minor physical or mental abnormalities to gross deformities; some are not apparent until months or years later, and some are fatal. Birth defects result from genetic abnormalities and harmful factors in the fetal environment.

A mother can control much of the fetal environment through her behavior. Early in gestation, a *placenta* and *umbilical cord* develop and begin to transmit substances to the fetus from the mother's bloodstream. These substances typically consist mostly of nourishment, but they can also include hazardous microorganisms and chemicals that happen to be in her blood. We will consider three main hazards. First, the mother may be malnourished, because of inadequate food supplies or knowledge of nutritional needs. Babies born to malnourished mothers tend to have low birth weights, poorly developed immune and central nervous systems, and a high risk of mortality in the first weeks after birth (Chandra, 1991; Huffman & del Carmen, 1990; Pillitteri, 1981; Smart, 1991).

Second, certain infections the mother may contract during pregnancy can also attack her gestating baby, sometimes causing permanent injury or death

Table 6.2 *Prevention Goals over the Life Span*

Health Goals of Gestation and Infancy

- To provide the mother a healthy, full-term pregnancy and rapid recovery after a normal delivery.
- To facilitate the live birth of a normal baby, free of congenital or developmental damage.
- To help both mother and father achieve the knowledge and capacity to provide for the physical, emotional, and social needs of the baby.
- To establish immunity against specified infectious diseases.
- To detect and prevent certain other diseases and problems before irreparable damage occurs.

Health Goals of Childhood and Adolescence

- To facilitate the child's optimal physical, emotional, and social growth and development.
- To establish healthy behavioral patterns (in children) for nutrition, exercise, study, recreation, and family life, as a foundation for a healthy lifetime lifestyle.
- To reinforce healthy behavior patterns (in adolescents), and discourage negative ones, in physical fitness, nutrition, exercise, study, work, recreation, sex, individual relations, driving, smoking, alcohol, and drugs.

Health Goals of Adulthood

- To prolong the period of maximum physical energy and to develop full mental, emotional, and social potential.
- To anticipate and guard against the onset of chronic disease through good health habits and early detection and treatment where effective.
- To detect as early as possible any of the major chronic diseases, including hypertension, heart disease, diabetes, and cancer, as well as vision, hearing, and dental impairments.

Health Goals in Old Age

- To minimize handicapping and discomfort from the onset of chronic conditions.
- To prepare in advance for retirement.
- To prolong the period of effective activity and ability to live independently, and avoid institutionalization so far as possible.
- When illness is terminal, to assure as little physical and mental stress as possible and to provide emotional support to patient and family.

Source: Based on Breslow & Somers (1977).

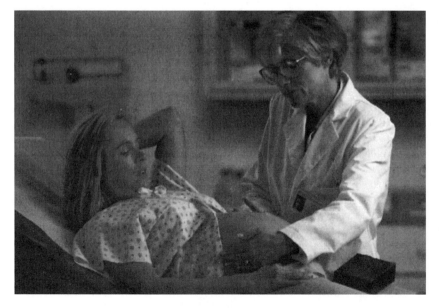

Women who receive and follow medical advice during pregnancy can enhance the healthfulness of their baby's prenatal environment.

(LaBarba, 1984; Moore, 1983). For example, *rubella* (German measles) in the first several weeks of pregnancy may cause the baby to die or be severely malformed, and *toxoplasmosis* can cause brain damage or death. Pregnant women can protect the fetus from rubella through vaccination and from toxoplasmosis by avoiding contact with major sources of infection (cats, cat litter, and undercooked meats).

Third, various substances the mother uses may enter her bloodstream and harm the baby (Cook, Petersen, & Moore, 1990; LaBarba, 1984). Babies exposed prenatally to addictive drugs, such as cocaine and heroin, are far more likely than others to die in infancy or be born with very low weights or malformations, such as of the heart (Lindenberg et al., 1991; MDBDF, 2000). Also, cigarette smoke exposure from the mother's smoking or from her environment—for instance, if the father smokes—is associated with low birth weight and other health problems in babies (DiFranza & Lew, 1995; Eliopoulos et al., 1994; Martinez et al., 1994). And drinking alcohol excessively has been linked to the birth of babies with *fetal alcohol syndrome*, which has several symptoms: (1) low birth weight and retarded subsequent growth, (2) subnormal intelligence, and (3) certain facial characteristics, such as small eye openings (Burns & Arnold, 1990; NIAAA, 1993). Ideally, expectant mothers should use *none* of these substances. Health education for pregnant women can help, such as by getting those who smoke to quit (Windsor et al., 1993).

Birth catapults the newborn into a new world, where risks continue. The rate of infant mortality in some developing countries is extremely high, greater than 100 per 1,000 live births for the first year of life (WHO, 1999c). Although infant mortality is greater in the United States than in many other industrialized countries, its rate has declined since 1980 from 12.6 to 7.1 per 1,000 live births (USBC, 1999). Out of these, approximately half die within the first week. In early infancy, the baby's immunity to disease depends largely on the white blood cells and antibodies passed on by the mother prenatally and in her milk if she breast-feeds (Moore, 1983). Because of the immunity it gives to the baby, breast milk is sometimes called "nature's vaccine." Parents should arrange for the baby to begin a vaccination program early in infancy for such diseases as diphtheria, whooping cough, and polio.

Childhood and Adolescence

In the second year of life, toddlers are walking and beginning to "get into everything." Although children's advancements in motor development are important, they place children at increasing health risk for injury around the house, such as with sharp objects and chemicals, and outdoors in automobile, swimming, and skateboarding mishaps. In the United States, accidental injury is the leading cause of death during childhood and adolescence (Cataldo et al., 1986; USBC, 1999). Parents, teachers, and other caregivers can reduce the likelihood of injury by teaching children safety behaviors, supervising them when possible, and decreasing their access to dangerous situations, such as by keeping chemicals out of reach.

The role of cognitive processes in the practice of health-related behavior has important implications here, since cognitive abilities are immature in early childhood and become increasingly sophisticated as children get older. With these advances, children are more able to make decisions and assume responsibility for promoting their own health and safety (Burbach & Peterson, 1986; Maddux, Roberts, Sledden, & Wright, 1986). As part of this ability, children need to understand the relationship between behavior and health. This understanding develops gradually, often progressing through the six stages outlined in Table 6.3. Caregivers and health professionals need to adjust their explanations and expectations for preventive action to match the cognitive limitations of children and the progress they make as they get older (Burbach & Peterson, 1986). As individuals enter adolescence, they become more aware of the complex interaction of internal and external factors in health, illness, and recovery (La Greca & Stone, 1985).

Adolescence is a particularly critical time in the development of preventive behavior. Although teenagers have the cognitive ability to make the logical decisions leading to healthful behavior, they face many temptations and forces—especially peer pressure—that lead them in other directions (Jessor, 1984; La Greca & Stone, 1985; Leffert & Petersen, 1998). This is the time when they stand the greatest chance of starting to smoke, drink, use drugs, and have sexual relations. These risky behaviors are interrelated: teens who smoke and drink are more

Table 6.3 *Six Stages in Children's Understanding of Relationships Between Health and Behavior*

1. *Phenomenism*. In children's earliest understanding of the relationship between health and behavior, they tend to define an illness in terms of a single symptom they associate with it. The cause they cite for the illness is likely to be remote; for example, a 3-year-old might say the sun causes heart attacks.
2. *Contagion*. At this stage, children continue to describe an illness in terms of a single symptom, but they know a little more about its cause. They attribute a person's sickness to the proximity of a person or object that is its source—without understanding how nearness is important. If a child at this stage says that "you get measles from people," and you ask how, he or she might simply answer, "When you walk near them."
3. *Contamination*. Children at this stage define an illness with multiple symptoms and understand still more about its cause. Most children progress this far by 7 years of age. They state that contact with dirt or germs causes illness, and they recognize that behavior can play a role, saying that people catch colds from "taking your jacket off outside." But they also say that just doing something "bad" can cause illness.
4. *Internalization*. At this stage, children conceptualize illness in terms of a problem inside the body. They also know that the problem can result from contaminants getting inside when the person swallows or inhales. And they realize the direct effect that behavior can have, such as that people get heart attacks "from lifting heavy stuff and working too hard." Children now view themselves as being able to prevent illness through proper care.
5. *Physiological*. By about 11 years of age, most children can define illness in terms of specific body organs, giving details of how internal functions break down and citing multiple physical causes. They might say, for example, "Cancer is when cells grow too fast. It happens because of air pollution or chemicals."
6. *Psychophysiological*. In the last stage, children realize that illness can result from both physiological and psychological sources. They may say, for instance, that people get headaches "from problems and aggravation."

Source: Based on Bibace & Walsh (1979).

likely to use marijuana and have unsafe sex (Duncan, Strycker, & Duncan, 1999). Teens also learn to drive, and too often combine this new skill with drinking and using drugs. The large majority of teenage deaths in industrialized countries result from accidents and violence. In the United States, the death rates for accidents and violence rise sharply during the teenage years and are 4½ times as high for 15- to 24-year-olds as for younger age groups (USBC, 1999). All these newly acquired behaviors involve substantial health risks, which teenagers are highly susceptible to taking. In performing these behaviors, the immediate experience and impressing peers seem to be more important to adolescents than the possible long-term consequences.

Adulthood and Aging

When people reach adulthood, they become less likely than they were in adolescence to adopt new behavioral risks to their health. In general, older adults are more likely than younger ones to engage in various health behaviors, such as eating healthful diets and getting medical checkups (Belloc & Breslow, 1972; Leventhal, Prohaska, & Hirschman, 1985).

Do these age-related improvements in health behavior indicate that adults become more concerned about health habits as they get older? Probably, but this is not clear for two reasons. First, developmental research on the practice of health behavior has generally used cross-sectional methods. Age-related increases in the percentages of individuals who practice healthful behaviors may simply reflect an increased rate of survival of people who engage in these habits. Second, older and younger adults have very similar beliefs regarding the effectiveness of these behaviors in preventing such chronic illnesses as high blood pressure, heart attacks, and cancer (Leventhal, Prohaska, & Hirschman, 1985). Still, older adults are likely to perceive themselves as more vulnerable to these illnesses than younger adults, and may engage in preventive acts for that reason.

Old age is not what it used to be. Older people in industrialized countries are living longer and are in better financial and physical condition than in the past (Horn & Meer, 1987). One health behavior that generally declines as adults get older is regular substantial exercise (Leventhal, Prohaska, & Hirschman, 1985). Many elderly people avoid physical exercise because they tend to exaggerate the danger that exertion poses to their health, underestimate their physical capabilities, and feel embarrassed by their performance of these activities (Woods & Birren, 1984).

GENDER AND HEALTH-RELATED BEHAVIOR

At birth worldwide, an average female's expected life span is about 4 years longer than a male's (WHO, 1999c). In developed countries the gap in life expectancy at birth is wider: females can expect to outlive males by about 8 years in Europe and 7 years in the United States (WHO, 1999c). For people in the United States who survive to 65 years of age, women's remaining life expectancy is 3.3 years longer than men's (NCHS, 2000). Why is this so? The answer involves both biological and behavioral factors (Cataldo et al., 1986; Greenglass & Noguchi, 1996; Reddy, Fleming, & Adesso, 1992; Verbrugge, 1985). Some of these factors are:

- Physiological reactivity, such as blood pressure and catecholamine release, when under stress is greater in men than women, which may make men more likely to develop cardiovascular disease.

- Males have shorter life expectancies in almost all countries of the world, and boys have higher death rates than girls even in infancy. Biological factors may underlie part of these gender differences in mortality.

- Behavioral factors are implicated in the fact that boys have far higher rates of injury than girls— such as from drowning, bicycling, and pedestrian traffic accidents.

- In adolescence and adulthood, males have far higher rates of injury and death from automobile accidents than females do.

- Men smoke more and drink more than women do, thereby making men more susceptible to cardiovascular and respiratory diseases, some forms of cancer, and cirrhosis of the liver.

- It may be that men's jobs, household work, and leisure activities pose greater health hazards than women's, but little or no research has been done on these issues.

One of the few behavioral advantages men have is that they get more strenuous exercise than women do. The practice of many other health-related behaviors is similar for men and women.

Women's longer lives do not mean that they have fewer health problems than men. Actually, the opposite is true (NCHS, 2000; Reddy, Fleming, & Adesso, 1992; Verbrugge, 1985). For example, American women have much higher rates than men of acute illnesses, such as respiratory and digestive ailments, and nonfatal chronic diseases, such as varicose veins, arthritis, anemia, and headache. They also use medical drugs and services much more than men, even when pregnancy and other reproductive conditions are not counted.

SOCIOCULTURAL FACTORS AND HEALTH-RELATED BEHAVIOR

Although people's health has been improving in many parts of the world (WHO, 1999c), there have been sharp declines in others, particularly in Eastern and Central European countries with high levels of environmental pollution and of tobacco and alcohol use (Little, 1998). Have people's health behaviors been improving in other countries? A survey on improvements in health behaviors across 2 years found that the percentage of people who reported having increased exercising and decreased alcohol and red meat intake was much greater among Americans than Britons, whose percentage was greater than that of the French (Retchin, Wells, Valleron, & Albrecht, 1992). People's health behaviors are improving in industrialized nations, but the rates vary across cultures.

Cultural differences also exist within nations. Most Americans feel they are in pretty good health— for instance, a national survey of males and females of all ages and backgrounds found that fewer than 10% claimed to be in only "fair" to "poor" health (NCHS, 2000). But this was not true for all segments of the population. Compared with the population as a whole, people were much more likely to rate their health as "fair" or "poor" if they were over 45 years of age, or from the lower social classes, or of African American or American Indian background. As it turns out, these lower assessments reflect real health problems of the individuals these groups comprise.

Social Class and Minority Group Background

The concept of *social class*, or *socioeconomic status*, describes differences in people's resources, prestige, and power within a society (Filsinger, 1987; Williams & Rucker, 1996). These differences are reflected in three main characteristics: income, occupational prestige, and education. The lowest social classes in industrialized societies contain people who live in poverty or are homeless. By almost any gauge of wellness, health correlates with social class (Adler et al., 1994; Anderson & Armstead, 1995; Marmot, Kogevinas, & Elston, 1987; Ostrove, Feldman, & Adler, 1999). Individuals from lower classes are more likely than those from higher classes to:

● Be born with very low birth weight

● Die in infancy or in childhood

● Die in adulthood before age 65

● Have poorer overall health and develop a long-standing illness in adulthood

● Experience days of restricted activity because of illness

Not coincidentally, individuals from the lower classes have poorer health habits and attitudes than those from higher classes. For instance, they smoke more, participate less in vigorous exercise, and are less likely to feel that people can actively promote their own health (Adler et al., 1994; Marmot, Kogevinas, & Elston, 1987; Williams & Rucker, 1996). Research has also shown that people from the lower classes have less knowledge about risk factors for disease. They are less likely than individuals from upper classes to receive health information from the mass media (Ribisl, Winkleby, Fortmann, & Flora, 1998). And they are less likely to know, for example, that people can reduce their cardiovascular risk by controlling their blood pressure, stopping smoking, and eating a low cholesterol diet (Hossack & Leff, 1987). You probably realize that members of minority groups usually are disproportionately represented in the lower social classes.

Minority group background is an important risk factor for poor health. Today a baby born in Cuba stands a better chance of reaching the age of one than the average African American newborn in the United States (NCHS, 2000; WHO, 1999c). The rate of infant mortality in America is twice as high for blacks as it is for whites. Among babies who survive the first year, the life expectancy for an African American baby is about 6 years shorter than that for a white baby in America (USBC, 1999). Moreover, regardless of that African American baby's gender, he or she is far more likely than a same-sex white baby to develop a major chronic disease in its lifetime and to die of that

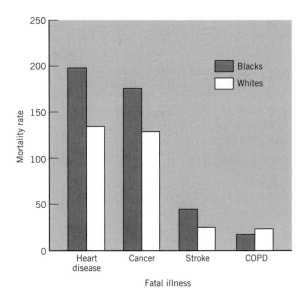

Figure 6–3 Death rates (per 100,000 individuals in the population) for whites and blacks in the United States, resulting from four leading chronic diseases (COPD is chronic obstructive lung disease). The rates are averaged for males and females and age-adjusted to take into account that mortality rates increase with age and that the average age of blacks is less than that of whites. (Data from USBC, 1991, Table 118.)

disease. Figure 6–3 compares racial mortality data for four major causes of death and shows that the death rates for the three most deadly diseases are far higher for blacks than whites. Although American racial differences in health were much larger decades ago, they are still substantial and remain a dilemma and a national disgrace.

Three minority groups that have high levels of health problems and risks in the United States are blacks, American Indians, and Hispanics. In general, the health problems and risk factors of Hispanics are intermediate, being neither as negative as those of blacks and American Indians nor as positive as those of whites (NCHS, 2000). Many individuals in these minority groups live in environments that do not encourage the practice of health behavior (Johnson et al., 1995; Schinke, 1996). African Americans and Hispanics also share a vulnerability to three health problems: substance abuse, AIDS, and injury or death from violence (Myers et al., 1995; Yee et al., 1995). These individuals are more likely than whites to smoke, use drugs, and practice unsafe sex. And African

Americans and Hispanics—especially young males—are several times more likely than their white counterparts to become victims of homicide. These problems are disturbing, and correcting them will take a great deal of time, effort, and social change.

Promoting Health with Diverse Populations

How can societies help their diverse populations live healthful lives? Part of the solution would involve broad programs to reduce poverty. Because communities contain people of different ages, genders, and sociocultural backgrounds, professionals who are trying to prevent and treat illness need to take a biopsychosocial perspective (Flack et al., 1995; Johnson et al., 1995; Young & Zane, 1995). Let's see what this means by focusing on sociocultural differences to illustrate factors of three types that professionals need to consider:

- *Biological factors.* Sociocultural groups can differ in their physiological processes, as reflected in African Americans' high risk of developing the genetic blood disease of sickle-cell anemia. Some evidence also indicates that black people metabolize a carcinogen in tobacco smoke less efficiently than whites, which may partly explain why they are more likely to develop cancer (Blakeslee, 1994). This metabolic difference may result from hereditary or environmental factors, such as diet.

- *Cognitive and linguistic factors.* People of different sociocultural groups seem to have different ideas about the causes of illness, give different degrees of attention to their body sensations, such as pain, and interpret symptoms differently. Hispanic Americans often believe in using "folk healing" practices, such as actions to drive away evil spirits (Suarez, Raffaelli, & O'Leary, 1996). Professionals who try to refute these beliefs may drive their patients away (Belluck, 1996). Language differences between professionals and the people they serve impair their ability to communicate with each other.

- *Social and emotional factors.* Sociocultural groups differ in the amount of stress they experience, their physiological reactivity to it, and the ways they cope with it. They also differ in their amount and use of social support.

These examples describe some issues that can be incorporated in culturally sensitive health-promotion services. Ideally, programs to promote minority health would use a grassroots, culturally relevant approach with trained health leaders from the community (Castro, Cota, & Vega, 1999). An example program, called *Por La Vita*, increased breast and cervical cancer testing in Hispanic women by identifying and training respected women of their community to provide weekly educational sessions on cancer prevention (Navarro et al., 1998). The remainder of this chapter focuses on techniques and program designs for enhancing health and preventing illness.

PROGRAMS FOR HEALTH PROMOTION

In 1982, fast-food chains in New Orleans began using a gimmick to reverse a dangerous trend: more and more parents were not having their children vaccinated. The gimmick involved offering discount coupons for meals to parents who had their children immunized before the end of the summer. Other creative approaches by public health agencies have been used in other communities for the same purpose. We will begin our discussion of programs for health promotion by looking at some of the methods they use.

METHODS FOR PROMOTING HEALTH

Interventions to promote health try to encourage the practice of healthful behavior by teaching individuals what these behaviors are and how to perform them, and by persuading people to change their current unhealthful habits. An important step in this effort is motivating individuals to *want* to change, and this often requires modifying their health beliefs and attitudes. What methods do these programs use to encourage health behavior?

Providing Information

People who want to lead healthful lives need information—they need to know what to do and when, where, and how to do it. In reducing dietary cholesterol, people need to know what cholesterol is and that it can clog blood vessels, which can produce heart disease. They also need to know where they can have their blood tested for cholesterol level, what levels are high, how much cholesterol is in the foods they currently eat, which foods might be good substitutes for ones they should eliminate from their diets, and how to prepare these foods. There are several sources for information to promote health.

One source for health information is the *mass media*. Television, radio, newspapers, and magazines can play a useful role in promoting health by presenting warnings and providing information, such as to help people avoid or stop smoking (Flay, 1987). One such approach simply provides information to the general population about the *negative consequences* of an activity—smoking, for instance—as public service advertisements often do. This approach has had limited success in changing behavior (Flay, 1987; Lau et al., 1980). One reason for the limited success is that people often misunderstand the health reports they encounter (Yeaton, Smith, & Rogers, 1990). Another reason may be that they just don't want to change the behavior at issue: a noted newspaper columnist who did not want to change his diet railed against warnings, writing,

> Cholesterol, shmolesterol!...Almost everything [experts] say is good for you will turn out bad for you if you hang around long enough, and almost everything they say is bad for you will turn out not to matter. (Baker, 1989, p. A31)

This quote is a good example of motivated reasoning.

Other approaches the mass media have used focus on people who already want to stop an unhealthful habit. For example, programs conducted on TV have been effective in getting smokers to take the first steps in quitting by offering free printed materials or kits with hints on how to stop and contact persons at a community agency (Flay, 1987; Freels et al., 1999). A more comprehensive program on TV, called Cable Quit, was successful in helping people stop smoking by showing them how to prepare to quit, helping them through the day they quit, describing ways to maintain their success, and giving them opportunities to call for advice (Valois, Adams, & Kammermann, 1996). Of those who started the program, 17% continued to abstain from smoking a year later.

Another source of health promotion information is the *computer*, particularly via the Internet. People anywhere in the world who are already interested in promoting their health and have access to the Internet can contact a wide variety of websites. Some are huge databases with information on all aspects of health promotion, and others provide detailed information on specific illnesses, such as cancer and arthritis, or support groups for health problems. People can learn how to avoid health problems and, if they become ill, what the illness is and how it can be treated.

A third source of health promotion information is *medical settings*, particularly physicians' offices. There are advantages and disadvantages in using medical settings as sources of health information. Two advantages are that many individuals visit a physician at least once a year, and they respect health care workers as experts. Two disadvantages are that these efforts take up time in already busy practices and medical personnel may not know how to help people overcome problems they have in following prevention recommendations (Radecki & Brunton, 1992). Because of the problem of time in busy practices, researchers have developed 5- to 10-minute counseling programs that medical staff can be trained to give in person or on the telephone. Having an office system that cues the staff to deliver the program increases its delivery (Adams, Ockene, Wheeler, & Hurley, 1998). These programs are effective in helping individuals get cancer screening (Rimer, 1998) and to stop smoking, to reduce drinking, and to reduce their fat intake and weight (Lichtenstein et al., 1996; Ockene, Adams et al., 1999; Ockene, Hebert et al., 1999). Unfortunately, medical staff do not provide enough health promotion advice. For example, less than half of patients who smoke report in surveys that their physician ever advised them to quit (Frank et al., 1991; Thorndike, Rigotti, Stafford, & Singer, 1998).

Medical professionals now have another avenue for providing health promotion information. They can offer individuals who are at risk for inherited illnesses, such as some forms of cancer, estimates of their chances of getting the disease and opportunities to undergo tests, such as periodic examinations and genetic testing. But even when genetic testing is offered at no cost, less than half of individuals request the testing and results (Lerman et al., 1996, Lerman, Hughes et al., 1999). Are there psychological risks for people who receive this advice and undergo the tests? Making the decision to have genetic testing can be very agonizing because of the possibility that it will reveal a genetic risk and the conflicts that arise among family members who do and do not want the information. In breast cancer testing, for example, although most women who receive the opportunity and have the test do not show adverse psychological effects, women who were already very anxious about health threats before receiving the opportunity often become more distressed (Lerman, Audrain, & Croyle, 1994). More research is needed on ways to prevent these adverse effects and how best to provide all types of information for health promotion. (Go to .)

Features of Information to Enhance Motivation

Individuals do not necessarily follow advice and warnings on ways to promote their health. How can the information they receive enhance their motivation to adopt health behavior?

One approach to enhance people's motivation to follow health promotion advice is to use *tailored content*—that is, the advice delivered in person, in print, or on the telephone is designed for a specific individual, based on characteristics of that person. For example, the message would refer to the person by name and might include personal or behavioral details, such as the person's age or smoking history, and a message geared to the person's readiness to adopt the proposed health behavior, such as stopping smoking, scheduling a mammogram, or losing weight. Tailoring the content appears to enhance the success of health promotion information (Kreuter, Strecher, & Glassman, 1999; Rimer et al., 1999; Skinner et al., 1999).

Another approach to enhance motivation is based on a concept called *message framing*, which refers to whether the information emphasizes the benefits

---

CLINICAL METHODS AND ISSUES
Dialogues to Help People Stop Smoking

Patients who smoke tend to express many common rationalizations for not quitting that their medical or psychological practitioner can discuss with them. Each of the following rationalizations has a reply the practitioner can give (Adapted from USDHHS, 1986a).

PATIENT: *I am under a lot of stress, and smoking relaxes me.*

STAFF (practitioner): Your body has become accustomed to nicotine, so you naturally feel more relaxed when you get the nicotine you have come to depend on. But nicotine is actually a stimulant that temporarily raises heart rate, blood pressure, and adrenaline level. After a few weeks of not smoking, most ex-smokers feel less nervous.

PATIENT: *Smoking stimulates me and helps me to be more effective in my work.*

STAFF: Difficulty in concentrating can be a symptom of nicotine withdrawal, but it is a short-term effect. Over time, the body and brain function more efficiently when you don't smoke, because carbon monoxide from cigarettes is displaced by oxygen in the bloodstream.

PATIENT: *I have already cut down to a safe level.*

STAFF: Cutting down is a good step toward quitting. But smoking at any level increases the risk of illness. And some smokers who cut back inhale more often and more deeply, thus maintaining nicotine dependence. It is best to quit smoking completely.

PATIENT: *I only smoke safe, low-tar/low-nicotine cigarettes.*

STAFF: Low-tar cigarettes still contain harmful substances. Many smokers inhale more often or more deeply and thus maintain their nicotine levels. Carbon monoxide intake often increases with a switch to low-tar cigarettes.

PATIENT: *I don't have the willpower to give up smoking.*

STAFF: It can be hard for some people to give up smoking, but for others it is much easier than they expect. Millions of people quit every year. It may take more than one attempt for you to succeed, and you may need to try different methods of quitting. I will give you all the support I can.

Similar dialogues can help people change other health-related behaviors, too.

(gains) or costs (losses) associated with a behavior or decision. For a health behavior, a gain-framed message would focus on attaining desirable consequences or avoiding negative ones; it might state, for example, "If you exercise, you will become more fit and less likely to develop heart disease." A loss-framed message would focus on getting undesirable consequences and avoiding positive ones; for instance, "If you do not get your blood pressure checked, you could increase your chances of having a heart attack or stroke, and you will not know that your blood pressure is good." A large body of evidence indicates that the best type of framing to use depends on the type of health behavior (Rothman & Salovey, 1997; Salovey, Schneider, & Apanovitch, in press). Gain-framed messages seem to work best for motivating behaviors that serve to prevent or recover from illness or injury; two such behaviors are using condoms and performing physical therapy. Loss-framed messages work best for behaviors that serve to detect a health problem early, as getting a mammogram can do.

A special case of loss-framed messages is when information arouses fear. According to the health belief model, people are likely to practice healthful behavior if they believe that by not doing so they are susceptible to serious health problems. In other words, they are motivated by fear to protect their health. Studies have found that fear-arousing warnings can motivate people to adopt a variety of more healthful attitudes and behavior, such as regarding dental health, safe driving, and smoking cigarettes (Sutton, 1982; Sutton & Hallett, 1988). But two issues about using fear are unclear. First, given the role of message framing, it may be that fearful warnings, as loss-framed messages, may work better for early detection behaviors than for illness prevention behaviors. Second, it is not clear how much fear the message should generate to be most successful. Irving Janis (1967, 1984) has argued that too much fear may stimulate the person to use avoidance coping processes—ignoring, minimizing, or denying the threat. This seems most likely to happen when warnings become personally and directly threatening (Lee, 1989). Although some studies of warnings support this view, others do not, sometimes finding that very upsetting appeals are more likely to induce people to change their attitudes than weaker appeals are (Janis, 1984; Sutton, 1982). More research is needed to identify conditions under which fear appeals work best.

What can be done to make fear messages more effective? A study by Carol Self and Ronald Rogers (1990) found that self-efficacy is a crucial factor. Highly threatening appeals were associated with strong intentions to change an unhealthful behavior only if the subjects received information indicating that they could perform the healthful behavior, such as exercising, and succeed in protecting their health. People who received highly threatening appeals with information that minimized their ability to protect their health tended to use avoidance processes to cope with the threat. Other research has shown that fear appeals are more effective with adolescents and adults than children (Sturges & Rogers, 1996) and if they emphasize the organic and social consequences—that is, the perceived seriousness—of developing the health problem (Banks et al., 1995; Kalichman & Coley, 1995; Klohn & Rogers, 1991).

An important problem with using fear-arousing warnings is that the attitude changes they produce often do not lead to behavioral changes. Programs to change unhealthful behavior are more likely to be successful if they provide specific instructions for performing the behavior and if they help bolster people's self-confidence before urging them to begin the plan (Sutton, 1982).

Behavioral Methods

Behavioral methods focus directly on enhancing people's performance of the preventive act itself by altering its antecedents and consequences. We can alter antecedents to promote healthful behavior in many ways, such as by providing specific instructions or training for performing the behavior, calendars to indicate when to perform infrequent preventive actions, and reminders of appointments. Research has shown that these techniques enhance the effectiveness of programs for health promotion (Sarafino, 2001).

To encourage healthful behavior by manipulating its consequences, we can provide reinforcers when the behavior occurs. Although reinforcers can be useful for increasing health behavior, such as practicing good dental hygiene, the effectiveness of this method depends on many factors. These factors include the types of reward used, the age and sociocultural background of the individual, and the person's interest in performing the activity (Lund & Kegeles, 1984; Sarafino, 1987b, 2001; Suls, 1984). For instance, people differ in their reward preferences—

tickets for a Sting concert might be very enjoyable for you, but your friend might prefer hearing a symphony performed by the Philadelphia Orchestra; and attending either of these events might be very unpleasant for someone else. The consequences need to be matched to the person. There is also some evidence that reward preferences change with age: kindergarten children tend to prefer material rewards (a charm, money, candy) over social rewards such as praise, but this preference seems to reverse by third grade (Witryol, 1971). For adults, monetary rewards seem to be particularly effective in encouraging health behaviors, such as breast self-examination (Solomon et al., 1998). Programs for health promotion need to consider the point of view of the individual with regard to the preventive action and any consequences that the program introduces to enhance performance of that behavior.

Maintaining Healthy Behaviors

When people adopt a new behavior in place of one they performed for a long time, their success usually has some setbacks, or lapses (Sarafino, 2001). A *lapse* is an instance of backsliding—for instance, a person who quits smoking might have a cigarette one day. Lapses should be expected; they do not indicate failure. A more serious setback is a **relapse,** or falling back to one's original pattern of the undesirable behavior. Relapses are very common when people try to change long-standing habits, such as their eating and smoking behaviors.

Psychologists G. Alan Marlatt and Judith Gordon (1980) have proposed that for many individuals who quit a behavior, such as smoking, experiencing a lapse can destroy their confidence in remaining abstinent and precipitate a full relapse. This is called the **abstinence-violation effect.** Because these people are committed to total abstinence, they tend to feel guilty about any lapses, even with just one cigarette, and see their violation as a sign of a personal failure. They might think, for instance, "I don't have any willpower at all and I cannot change." In programs to change behavior, relapses can be reduced by training individuals to cope with lapses and maintain self-efficacy about the behavior and by providing "booster" sessions or contacts (Curry & McBride, 1994; Irvin, Bowers, Dunn, & Wang, 1999). Contacts, even by phone, can reduce relapses substantially by providing counseling on dealing with difficult situations that could lead to lapses (Zhu et al., 1996).

Many types of programs have been carried out to promote health in different settings and with a variety of goals, methods, and populations. We will examine different types of interventions, beginning with health education efforts that are designed to reach children and adolescents in schools and establish healthful habits at early ages.

PROMOTING HEALTH IN THE SCHOOLS

Public and private schools have a unique opportunity to promote health. In developed nations, they have access to virtually all individuals during the years that are probably most critical in the development of health-related behavior. Effective school-based health education teaches children what healthful and unhealthful behaviors are and the consequences of practicing them. This can produce two benefits. First, children may avoid developing unhealthful habits at the

Schools can use awards to encourage fitness, as these proud winners show.

time when they are most vulnerable to these behaviors taking hold. Second, children may acquire health behaviors that become established or habitual aspects of their beliefs and lifestyles that may stay with them throughout their lives.

Are school programs effective? Some have been. An experiment in 22 American elementary schools introduced a carefully designed curriculum with emphasis on nutrition and physical fitness (Walter et al., 1985). The schools were randomly assigned so that their students either participated in the program or served as a control group for that year. Relative to the control subjects, the children who participated in the program showed improvements in their blood pressure and cholesterol levels. Another study found that more children practiced safety behavior if they were taught about health and safety in a 4-year program than if they were not (Parcel, Bruhn, & Cerreto, 1986). But many schools do not provide health education at all, or their programs are poorly designed and funded and taught by teachers whose interests and training are in other areas (Kolbe & Iverson, 1984).

WORKSITE WELLNESS PROGRAMS

There is a new "epidemic" in the health field—wellness programs are spreading rapidly in workplaces in industrialized countries. A survey of more than 1,300 American work sites with 50 or more employees found that nearly two-thirds offered some form of health promotion activity, such as for fitness and weight control (Fielding & Piserchia, 1989). Some programs use incentives, such as prizes or bonuses for losing weight, stopping smoking, or staying well. By doing this, employers are helping their workers and saving a great deal of money. Workers with poor health habits in the United States cost employers substantially more in health benefits and other costs of absenteeism than those with good habits. These savings offset and often exceed the expense of running a wellness program (Winett, King, & Altman, 1989). Psychologists who study or administer such programs are called *occupational health psychologists* (Quick, 1999).

Worksite wellness programs vary in their aims, but usually address some or all of the following risk factors: hypertension, cigarette smoking, unhealthful diets and overweight, poor physical fitness, alcohol abuse, and high levels of stress. These risk factors do not seem to be equally changeable. For exam-

ple, worksite programs seem to achieve more healthful changes in dietary and exercise behaviors than in smoking (Biener et al., 1999; Emmons et al., 1999). Housing these interventions in workplaces has several advantages. Worksite programs are convenient to attend, are fairly inexpensive for employees, can provide participants with reinforcement from the employer and coworkers, and can structure the environment to encourage healthful behavior, such as by making healthy food available in the cafeteria (Cohen, 1985). Unfortunately, worksite programs don't always attract high levels of participation, and employees who do not participate are often the ones who need it most—those who report having poor health and fitness (Alexy, 1991). We will look at two model interventions and how effective they are.

Johnson & Johnson's "Live for Life" Program

Johnson & Johnson, America's largest producer of health care products, began the *Live for Life* program in 1978. The program covers tens of thousands of employees and is one of the most effective worksite programs yet developed (Fielding, 1990; Nathan, 1984). The program is designed to improve employees' health knowledge, stress management, and efforts to exercise, stop smoking, and control their weight.

For each participating employee, Live for Life begins with a *health screen*—a detailed assessment of the person's current health and health-related behavior, which is shared with the individual later. After taking part in a lifestyle seminar, the employee joins *action groups* for specific areas of improvement, such as quitting smoking or controlling weight. Professionals lead sessions of these action groups, focusing on how the employees can alter their lifestyle and maintain these improvements permanently. Follow-up contacts are made with each participant during the subsequent year. The company also provides a work environment that supports and encourages healthful behavior: it has designated no-smoking areas, established exercise facilities, and made nutritious foods available in the cafeteria, for example.

Evaluation of Live for Life involves ongoing studies, using quasi-experimental research methods. These studies generally compare the health and behavior of employees from different Johnson & Johnson companies that either did or did not offer the Live for Life program (Fielding, 1990; Nathan, 1984; Quick,

1999). All the employees studied completed a health screen in the initial year and then again in later years. Compared with the employees at the companies where Live for Life was not offered, those where it *was* have shown greater improvements in their physical activity, weight, smoking behavior, ability to handle job stress, absenteeism, and hospital medical claims.

Control Data's "StayWell" Program

Control Data Corporation is a major computer manufacturer. This company introduced the *StayWell* worksite program in 1979 and offers it to thousands of employees (Jose & Anderson, 1990; Naditch, 1984). The program has enrolled a large majority of these employees, particularly workers who are women, have higher levels of education, and do not travel a great deal. The goals of this intervention are very similar to those of Live for Life.

Each StayWell participant completes a *health screening*, receives a resulting confidential health risk profile, and attends a workshop that focuses on interpreting the profile. The person can then join courses taught by professionals that provide information about lifestyle and health and teach the skills needed to change unhealthful behaviors. There are courses in physical fitness, nutrition, weight control, stopping smoking, and stress management. The individual can also join *action teams* that focus on two things: (1) making the work environment more healthful, such as by suggesting more nutritious foods for vending machines or organizing hiking or aerobic dance activities, and (2) forming support groups whereby members help one another in changing their behavior.

Evaluation of the StayWell program uses two approaches. First, because the program was not offered at some locations of Control Data, the health behaviors of workers at these sites could be compared against employee behavior at sites offering the program, using quasi-experimental methods. Second, at worksites with the StayWell program, comparisons could be made of health behaviors practiced by employees with different levels of participation, ranging from not participating at all to enrolling in courses to change unhealthful behaviors. Evaluations of StayWell using these approaches indicate that the program has been successful in reducing absenteeism and health insurance claims and in improving employees' health behaviors in weight control, exercise,

smoking, nutrition, and stress management (Jose & Anderson, 1990; Naditch, 1984).

COMMUNITY-BASED WELLNESS PROGRAMS

Community-based programs for health promotion are designed to reach large numbers of people and improve their knowledge and performance of preventive behavior (Israel, Schulz, Parker, & Becker, 1998). These interventions may use any or all of the methods we have considered. They may, for instance, use a media blitz to warn people of the dangers of drinking and driving, or provide information regarding free blood pressure testing, or offer people a chance to win a prize for stopping smoking or getting vaccinations. We will look at large-scale programs that were designed to improve people's health behavior and evaluate the effectiveness of the methods used.

The Three Community Study

In the early 1970s, researchers began the Stanford Heart Disease Prevention Program—an ambitious community-based effort to get people to change their behavior and reduce their risk of cardiovascular disease.

One of the program's earliest and best-known projects is called the *Three Community Study* (Farquhar et al., 1977; Meyer et al., 1980). For this study, the investigators selected three very similar towns in northern California. Two of these towns, which shared the same TV and radio stations, were chosen to receive an extensive mass-media campaign. The third town received no campaign and served as a control community because it was relatively distant and isolated from media in the other towns. The media campaign lasted for 2 years and consisted of warnings and information concerning smoking, diet, and exercise. The media included TV, radio, newspapers, posters, and materials sent through the mail.

To evaluate the success of the campaign, the researchers randomly selected several hundred men and women from each community and interviewed them annually. At each interview, the researchers took measurements of blood variables, recent health behavior, and knowledge about risk factors for heart disease. They used these data to calculate each person's *overall risk* of cardiovascular disease by combining data on age, blood pressure, blood cholesterol levels, weight, smoking behavior, and so on. Some individuals at high cardiovascular risk received face-to-face health counseling. Analyses found that people's overall risk increased somewhat in the control community and decreased moderately in the two campaign towns. Face-to-face counseling was particularly effective in getting people to stop smoking. Subsequent follow-up research revealed that the program's long-term success was greatest with older people and lowest with individuals who were much younger, had little education, and were from the lower socioeconomic classes (Winkleby, Flora, & Kraemer, 1994).

At about the time that the Three Community Study occurred, other researchers did a similar study in Finland and found similar results (Salonen, Heinonen, Kottke, & Puska, 1981). Although the magnitudes of risk factor improvement were not dramatic in either study, they showed that community-based programs offer promising approaches for health promotion (Farquhar, Maccoby, & Solomon, 1984).

Integrated Community–Based Programs

The success of the Three Community Study has led researchers in different areas of the United States to undertake larger-scale, longer-term projects with more advanced methods for reducing cardiovascular risk factors (Blackburn et al., 1984; Farquhar, Maccoby, & Solomon, 1984; Lasater et al., 1984; Stunkard, Felix, & Cohen, 1985). Each program involves communities with hundreds of thousands of people and spans several years. The interventions include media campaigns and the extensive participation and integration of community organizations, such as schools, religious groups, and businesses, to provide health-promotion activities. Periodic assessments have revealed favorable outcomes. In one project in California, for example, people's blood pressure showed greater declines in the campaign cities than in the control cities (Fortmann et al., 1990). (Go to 🐾.)

PREVENTION WITH SPECIFIC TARGETS: FOCUSING ON AIDS

Sometimes prevention programs focus on reducing people's risk of developing a specific health problem and center these efforts on specific segments of the population. One example of this approach is the Multiple Risk Factor Intervention Trial (MRFIT), a project that recruited and provided health promotion

programs for thousands of men across the United States who were at substantial risk for heart disease (Caggiula et al., 1981; Shekelle et al., 1985). Another example involves efforts to reduce the spread of *acquired immune deficiency syndrome* (AIDS), an incurable and usually fatal disease. We will focus this section on efforts to prevent infection with the *human immunodeficiency virus* (HIV), which causes AIDS.

HIV Infection

The magnitude of the AIDS threat is astounding—the World Health Organization has estimated that 47 million people around the world had been infected with HIV by the year 2000, and over 14 million had died of AIDS (WHO, 1999a). Over 160 countries have reported cases of AIDS, but the infection is unevenly distributed worldwide. The largest concentration of infections continues to be in sub-Saharan Africa, where the outlook is cataclysmic: more than 12 million women and 10 million men are currently infected and millions of new infections occur each year. The incidence is also high in many Asian and South American countries. But the rate of infection in the world's industrialized countries has been declining steadily since the mid-1990s (WHO, 1999b). Over 1 million people have been infected in the United States and 44,000 new infections occur each year (CDC, 2000). Although new medical treatments can extend the lives of victims, AIDS is still a fatal disease that kills the large majority of those who develop it (WHO, 1999a).

There is no vaccine against the HIV virus, and there is not likely to be one in the near future. The virus spreads to an uninfected person only through contact of his or her body fluids with those of an infected person, generally either through sexual practices or when intravenous drug users share needles. The likelihood of infection increases if the person has wounds or inflammation from other sexually transmitted diseases, such as syphilis, herpes, or chlamydia (Peterman, 1990). Infected mothers sometimes transmit the virus to their babies during gestation, delivery, and later during breast-feeding (European Collaborative Study, 1991; Fathalla, 1990). Changing people's behavior is virtually the only means of reducing the risk of infection, and worldwide public health efforts for prevention have concentrated on using fear-arousing warnings and providing information.

These efforts also try to correct misconceptions about HIV transmission—for instance, that AIDS can

ASSESS YOURSELF
Your Knowledge about AIDS

Answer the following true-false items by circling the T or F for each one.

T   F   1. People who develop AIDS usually die within a couple of years.

T   F   2. Blood tests can usually tell within a week after infection whether someone has received the AIDS virus.

T   F   3. People do not get AIDS from using swimming pools or rest rooms after someone with AIDS does.

T   F   4. Some people have contracted AIDS from insects, such as mosquitoes, that have previously bitten someone with AIDS.

T   F   5. AIDS can now be prevented with a vaccine and cured if treated early.

T   F   6. People who have the AIDS virus can look and feel well.

T   F   7. Gay women (lesbians) get AIDS much more often than heterosexual women, but not as often as gay men.

T   F   8. Health workers have a high risk of getting AIDS from or spreading the virus to their patients.

T   F   9. Kissing or touching someone who has AIDS can give you the disease.

T   F   10. AIDS is less contagious than measles.

Check your answers against the key below that is printed upside down—a score of 8 items correct is good, 9 is very good, and 10 is excellent. (*Sources:* Carey, Morrison-Beedy, & Johnson, 1998; DiClemente, Zorn, & Temoshok, 1987; Vener & Krupka, 1990).

Answer:

1. T; 2. F; 3. T; 4. F; 5. F; 6. T; 7. F; 8. F; 9. F; 10. T

---

only happen to homosexuals and drug users, that all gay men are infected, that mosquitoes can spread the virus, or that the virus can be transmitted through casual contact, such as by touching or hugging infected individuals or by sharing office equipment they have used (DiClemente, Zorn, & Temoshok, 1987). Many people also believe that health care personnel are usually at high risk of becoming infected when working with AIDS patients, but research has disconfirmed this. Health care workers' becoming infected is rare even when they are accidently stuck with a needle that had been used on an AIDS patient (Clever & LeGuyader, 1995; Henderson et al., 1990).

A large proportion of AIDS victims in the United States and other industrialized countries have been gay men. This is probably because many gay men have tended to be very promiscuous and have engaged regularly in certain sexual practices, especially anal intercouse, that involve a high risk of transmission (Kalichman, 1998). But many other gay men do not lead high-risk lifestyles, lesbians have a very low prevalence of AIDS, and the vast majority of victims in Africa are heterosexuals. A person's sexual orientation is not a guarantee of high or low risk—as many peo-

ple came to realize in 1991 when basketball star Magic Johnson announced that he had the virus. Today in the United States, sexual contact between men no longer accounts for the majority of AIDS cases (NCHS, 2000).

Why do people continue to engage in unsafe sex? Although ignorance and a lack of availability of protection are the main reasons in many developing countries, other factors are more influential in other cultures. One factor is that people are much more likely to have very unsafe sex if they are promiscuous or have sex while under the influence of alcohol or drugs (Cooper, Peirce, & Huselid, 1994; Leigh, 1990; Lowry et al., 1994). In men, intoxication seems to increase negative attitudes and decrease self-efficacy about using condoms and to increase the willingness to have unsafe sex when they are sexually aroused (Gordon & Carey, 1996; MacDonald et al., 2000). Second, unmarried partners are less likely to use condoms if they perceive their relationship to be close or serious (Cooper & Orcutt, 2000; Misovich, Fisher, & Fisher, 1997). Third, decision making in sexual situations is often subject to nonrational processes, such as denial or wishful thinking (Blanton & Gerrard,

1997; Gold, Skinner, & Hinchy, 1999; Thompson, Kent, Thomas, & Vrungos, 1999). Fourth, many individuals have maladaptive beliefs about their own low self-efficacy to use condoms and the effect that doing so would have on sexual pleasure and spontaneity (Kelly et al., 1991, 1995; Wulfert, Wan, & Backus, 1996). Fifth, some people appear to gain greater reinforcement from sex when it involves risky behavior (Kelly & Kalichman, 1998). Sixth, the advent of medical treatments that lower viral load and prolong life has led to overoptimism in many individuals, leading them to think that protection is not so necessary anymore (Halkitis & Wilton, 1999). People's maladaptive beliefs are often clear when they recognize their behavior contradicts what experts say, so they add qualifiers, such as, "I know that's what they say but . . ." or, "but in my case . . ." (Maticka-Tyndale, 1991).

Basic Messages to Prevent HIV Infection

Major efforts have been introduced in most countries around the world to prevent HIV infection by having the mass media and health organizations provide information about several basic behaviors (Carey, 1999; Kalichman, 1998). First, people should avoid or reduce having sex outside of long-term monogamous relationships or, otherwise, to use "safer sex" practices with new partners. Safer sex involves selecting sexual partners carefully, avoiding practices that may injure body tissues, and using condoms in all forms of sexual intercourse. Second, not all people who have the virus know they do, and not all of those who know they do tell their sexual partners (Marks, Richardson, & Maldonado, 1991; Simoni et al., 1995). Third, drug users should not share a needle or syringe; if they do, they should be sure it is sterile. Fourth, women who could have been exposed to the virus should have their blood tested for the HIV antibody before becoming pregnant and, if the test is positive, avoid pregnancy. Much of this information has been designed to arouse fear, and it has in many people.

Do informational efforts change people's HIV knowledge and behavior? In the United States, public health programs have been directed toward youth in the general population, intravenous drug users and their sexual partners, and gays and bisexuals. Adolescents and young adults of the general population are vulnerable to infection because of their relatively high levels of sexual promiscuity and drug use. Providing information to teens has increased their knowledge about AIDS (Dorman & Rienzo, 1988; Holtzman et al.,

1994), but most sexually experienced teenagers and young adults do not seem to take the precautions they should (Hernandez & Smith, 1990; Ku, Sonenstein, & Pleck, 1993; Liegh, Morrison, Trocki, & Temple, 1994). Informational programs that focus on getting adolescents to abstain from or reduce the frequency of sexual activity can help, but efforts to promote condom use are more effective for teens who are sexually experienced (Jemmott, Jemmott, & Fong, 1999).

Providing information about HIV has also reduced risk behaviors of intravenous drug users. The vast majority of drug users in the United States learned that sharing needles can transmit AIDS, and most of these people then began to use sterile needles, reduce their drug use, or use drugs in other ways, such as by inhaling (Des Jarlais & Friedman, 1988; Des Jarlais, Friedman, & Casriel, 1990). The risk of HIV infection among drug users appears to decrease if they can buy needles legally or exchange used needles for new ones (Groseclose et al., 1995; Leary, 1995). But drug users' caution is not extending as readily into their sexual behavior. Few drug users and their sexual partners use condoms (Krajick, 1988). Most drug users are heterosexual men, and their sexual partners often are women who know about the risks but feel powerless and are willing to go along with having unprotected sex (Fullilove, Fullilove, Haynes, & Gross, 1990).

Perhaps the best-organized efforts to change sexual practices have been directed at gay men, particularly in gay communities in large cities. This is partly because many gay social, political, and religious organizations existed before the AIDS epidemic began, and these groups have become actively involved in public health campaigns to prevent the spread of the disease. Studies have found that these efforts have had a substantial impact on gay sexual behavior across the United States—such as in Chicago (Joseph et al., 1987), New York City (Martin, 1990), and San Francisco (Catania et al., 1991; Coates, 1990). In San Francisco, for instance, gay and bisexual men significantly reduced several high-risk patterns of sexual behavior between 1982 and 1986, and this greatly decreased the spread of the virus: incidence rates of infection declined during that period from over 13% to about 1% per year. Today, only about a third of new infections in the United States are in gay men (NCHS, 2000). Similar changes in gay men's behavior and rates of infection have also occurred in other parts of the world, such as Amsterdam, Holland (Van Griensven, de Vroome, Goudsmit, & Coutinho, 1989).

AIDS education and prevention campaigns with gay and bisexual men have produced "the most profound modifications of personal health-related behaviors ever recorded" (Stall, Coates, & Hoff, 1988, p. 878). Ominous trends appeared in the mid-1990s and suggested that young gays were engaging more in unsafe sex, but new infections in young people showed a decrease in later years (CDC, 2000).

Focusing on Sociocultural Groups and Women

Although more needs to be done to reduce HIV risk in urban gay men and intravenous drug users around the world, efforts must be intensified among heterosexual women and disadvantaged sociocultural groups (Coates, 1990; Mays & Cochran, 1988; Peterson & Marin, 1988). For minority groups in the United States, particularly African Americans and Hispanics, there can be added problems of lesser knowledge about risky behavior and suspicions concerning information from health care systems they believe have treated them badly (Dula, 1994; Lollis, Johnson, Antoni, & Hinkle, 1996; Rodrigue, Tercyak, & Lescano, 1997). Women are often vulnerable to HIV infection when they are with a male partner who resists using condoms, are socially or economically dependent on the man, and have less power in their relationships (Sikkema, 1998). A woman's ability to protect herself from infection by asking for condom use under these circumstances is especially difficult if the man has violent tendencies and interprets such requests

negatively—for example, that she doesn't care about him or thinks he has been unfaithful (Neighbors, O'Leary, & Labouvie, 1999).

Interventions have been tested with large numbers of Hispanic and African American women who met in small group sessions to enhance their motivation and interpersonal skills for adopting safer sex practices. Comparisons were made during subsequent months with women in control groups. Women who received the interventions were more likely to report using safer sex practices and to use coupons to redeem free condoms (Carey et al., 2000; Sikkema et al., 2000); they were also less likely to develop STDs (chlamydia or gonorrhea) over the next year (Shain et al., 1999).

Making HIV Prevention More Effective

Many interventions provide individual counseling and testing to prevent HIV infection (Carey, 1999; Kalichman, 1998). Although these methods are moderately effective in decreasing risky behavior (Kalichman, Carey, & Johnson, 1996), their success is mainly with men and women who are already infected (Weinhardt, Carey, Johnson, & Bickham, 1999). Uninfected people who should reduce their risky sexual behavior often do not, and the reasons they don't seem to be similar for homosexual and heterosexual individuals. We need to keep in mind that the vast majority of today's new infections worldwide are in individuals who are neither gay nor intravenous drug users (WHO, 1999a).

Efforts to prevent the spread of AIDS include using billboards to reach teenagers.

How can programs to reduce the spread of HIV infection be made more effective? Prevention programs must provide information about HIV transmission and prevention, use techniques to enhance people's motivation to avoid unsafe sex, and teach the skills needed to perform preventive acts (Fisher et al., 1996; Kalichman, 1998). Some ways to incorporate these features include:

- Tailoring the program to meet the needs of the sociocultural group being addressed (Kalichman et al., 1993).

- Giving strong emphasis to training in the actual skills individuals will need to resist having unsafe sex (Kalichman, Rompa, & Coley, 1996; St. Lawrence et al., 1995; St. Lawrence, Jefferson, Alleyne, & Brasfield, 1995).

- Making sure the training is geared toward bolstering self-efficacy and advancing the individuals through the stages of change (Galavotti et al., 1995).

- Making use of respected or popular individuals as leaders to endorse the program and promote its acceptance by the group being addressed (Kelly et al., 1997).

- Encouraging infected individuals to disclose their HIV status to prospective sexual partners (Kalichman & Nachimson, 1999).

- Using techniques to reduce nonrational influences in sexual decisions. For example, having people give advice publicly that contradicts their own behavior can reduce their future use of denial (Eitel & Friend, 1999).

SUMMARY

People's behavior has an important impact on their health. Mortality from today's leading causes of death could be markedly reduced if people would adopt a few health behaviors, such as not smoking, not drinking excessively, eating healthful diets, and exercising regularly. Although some individuals are fairly consistent in their practice of health-related behaviors, these behaviors can be quite changeable over time. Practicing one habit is not strongly related to practicing other habits. A person's practice of health behaviors does not seem to be governed by a single set of attitudes or response tendencies. Health-related behaviors that become well established tend to become habitual, or automatically performed.

Health problems can be averted through three levels of prevention, one of which applies before a disease or injury occurs. Each level can involve efforts by the individual and by his or her social network, physician, and other health professionals. Primary prevention consists of actions taken to avoid illness or injury. It can include public service announcements, genetic counseling, and a wide variety of health behaviors, such as using seat belts and performing breast or testicular self-examinations. Secondary prevention involves actions taken to identify and stop or reverse a health problem. It includes tests and treatments health professionals may conduct, as well as people's visiting a physician when ill and taking medication as prescribed. Tertiary prevention consists of actions taken to contain or retard damage from a serious injury or advanced disease, prevent disability, and rehabilitate the patient.

People acquire health-related behaviors through modeling and through operant conditioning, whereby behavior changes because of its consequences: reinforcement, extinction, and punishment. Other determinants of these behaviors include genetic, social, emotional, and cognitive factors. Errors in symptom perception and ideas people have about illnesses can lead to health problems. People's thinking about health and illness is not always logical—it often includes motivated reasoning and unrealistic optimism about their health.

Some theories focus on the role of health beliefs to account for people's performance of health-related behavior. The health belief model proposes that people take preventive action on the basis of their assessments of the threat of a health problem and the pros and cons of taking the action. Threat perceptions are based mainly on the person's perceived seriousness of and susceptibility to the health problem. Assessing the pros and cons of the action involves weighing its perceived benefits and barriers. These assessments combine to determine the likelihood of preventive action. The theory of planned behavior proposes that people's health-related behaviors are determined by their intentions, which are a function of their attitudes regarding the behaviors (for example, "Is it a good thing to do?"), subjective norms, and self-efficacy. The stages of change model focuses on people's readiness to modify their behavior, and other approaches include focusing on the role of stress (conflict theory), personal control, and nonrational thought processes.

People's age, sex, and sociocultural background also affect health-related behavior and need to be considered in programs for health promotion. Efforts to promote healthful behavior use information, fear-arousing warnings, and behavioral methods. But changes in behavior can be temporary; relapses can occur, partly via the abstinence-violation effect. Programs for health promotion can be effective in the schools and in worksites. Community-based wellness programs are designed to reach large numbers of people and improve their knowledge and practice of preventive behavior. The Three Community Study demonstrated that media campaigns can promote health, and subsequent research has also integrated extensive efforts by community organizations toward improving people's preventive actions, such as in stemming the spread of AIDS.

KEY TERMS

health behavior	tertiary prevention	health belief model	conflict theory
primary prevention	reinforcement	theory of planned behavior	relapse
genetic counseling	extinction	stages of change model	abstinence-violation effect
secondary prevention	punishment	motivated reasoning	

7

REDUCING SUBSTANCE USE AND ABUSE

PROLOGUE

The stakes were high when Jim signed an agreement to quit smoking for a year, beginning January 2nd. The contract was with a worksite wellness program at the large company where he was employed as a vice president. It called for money to be given to charity by either Jim or the company, depending on how well he abstained from smoking. For every day he did not smoke, the company would give $10 to the charity; and for each cigarette Jim smoked, he would give $25, with a maximum of $100 for any day.

Jim knew stopping smoking would not be easy for him—he had smoked more than a pack a day for the last 20 years, and he had tried to quit a couple of times before. In the contract, the company could have required that he submit to medical tests to verify that he did in fact abstain but were willing to trust his word and that of his family, friends, and coworkers. These people were committed to helping him quit, and they agreed to be contacted by someone from the program weekly and give honest reports. Did he succeed? Yes, but he had a few "lapses" that cost him $325. By the end of the year, Jim had not smoked for 8 months continuously.

People voluntarily use many different substances that can harm their health. This chapter focuses on people's use of three of the most common of these substances: tobacco, alcohol, and drugs. For each substance, we examine who uses it and why, how the substance can affect health, and what can be done to help prevent people from using it and abusing it once they start. And we address questions of concern to people who want to enhance their own and others' health. Do people smoke tobacco, drink alcohol, and use drugs more than in the past? Why do people start to smoke, or drink excessively, or use drugs? Why is it so difficult to quit these behaviors? If individuals succeed in stopping smoking, will they gain weight?

SUBSTANCE ABUSE

"I just can't get started in the morning without a cup of coffee and a cigarette—I must be addicted," you may have heard someone say. The term *addicted* used to have a very limited meaning, referring mainly to the excessive use of alcohol and drugs. It was common knowledge that these chemical substances have *psychoactive effects*: they alter the person's mood, cognition, or behavior. We now know that other substances, such as nicotine and caffeine, have psychoactive effects, too—but people are commonly said to be "addicted" also to eating, gambling, buying, and many other things. How shall we define addiction?

Addiction is a condition, produced by repeated consumption of a natural or synthetic substance, in which the person has become physically and psychologically dependent on the substance. **Physical dependence** exists when the body has adjusted to a substance and incorporated it into the "normal" functioning of the body's tissues. For instance, the

structure and function of brain cells and chemistry change (Torres & Horowitz, 1999). This state has two characteristics:

- **Tolerance** is the process by which the body increasingly adapts to a substance and requires larger and larger doses of it to achieve the same effect. At some point, these increases reach a plateau.

- **Withdrawal** refers to unpleasant physical and psychological symptoms people experience when they discontinue or markedly reduce using a substance on which the body has become physically dependent. The symptoms experienced depend on the particular substance used, and can include anxiety, irritability, intense cravings for the substance, hallucinations, nausea, headache, and tremors.

Different substances appear to have different degrees of *potential* for producing physical dependence: the potential is very high for heroin but appears to be lower for other substances, such as LSD (NCADI, 2000; Schuster & Kilbey, 1992).

Psychological dependence is a state in which individuals feel compelled to use a substance for the pleasant effect it produces, without necessarily being physically dependent on it. They rely heavily on it—often to help them adjust to life and feel good—and they center many activities on obtaining and using it. People learn to depend on substances through repeated use (Cunningham, 1998). Users who are not physically dependent on a substance experience less tolerance and withdrawal (Schuckit et al., 1999). Those who become addicted usually become psychologically dependent on the substance first; later they become physically dependent as their bodies develop a tolerance for it. The potential for producing psychological dependence differs from one substance to another—it seems to be high for heroin and cocaine, moderate for marijuana, and lower for LSD (NCADI, 2000; Schuster & Kilbey, 1992).

Classifying a person as *abusing* a substance depends on the extent and impact of the use. Psychiatrists and clinical psychologists are concerned mainly with the psychosocial functioning of the person. They diagnose **substance abuse** on the basis of two criteria (Davison & Neale, 1998). First, the person shows a *clear and persistent pattern of pathological use*, such as heavy daily use and an inability to stop or decrease using the substance. Second, the *abuse has produced at least one of the following problems*:

● Failing to fulfill important obligations, such as in repeatedly neglecting a child or being absent from work.

● Putting oneself or others at risk for physical injury, for instance, by driving while intoxicated.

● Having legal difficulties, such as being arrested for disorderly conduct.

● Having serious social or interpersonal problems, for instance, repeated arguments with family or coworkers.

These four problems clearly apply to alcohol and drug use, but not tobacco use.

Psychologists in general share a concern about people's psychosocial functioning, but health psychologists give special emphasis to the impact of substance use on illness and injury. As a result, we might want to add the issue of increased risk factors for illness to the second problem, which would then read: "Putting oneself or others at risk for physical injury *or for illness*..." Individuals who meet the criteria, as revised, would be considered "substance abusers" from a health psychology point of view. Smoking cigarettes on a regular basis would qualify as abuse.

SMOKING TOBACCO

When Columbus explored the Western Hemisphere, he recorded in his journal that the inhabitants would set fire to leaves—rolled up or in pipes—and draw in the smoke through their mouths (Ashton & Stepney, 1982). The leaves these people used were tobacco, of course. Other early explorers tried smoking and, probably because they liked it, took tobacco leaves back to Europe in the early 1500s, where tobacco was used mainly for "medicinal purposes." Smoking for pleasure spread among American colonists and in Europe later in that century. In the 1600s, pipe smoking became popular, and the French introduced *snuff*, powdered tobacco that people consumed chiefly by inserting it in the nose and sniffing strongly. After inventors made a machine for mass-producing cigarettes and growers developed mellower tobacco in the early 1900s for easier inhaling, the popularity of smoking grew rapidly over the next 50 years.

Today there are about 1.1 billion smokers in the world (WHO, 1998). In the United States, cigarette smoking reached its greatest popularity in the mid-1960s, when about 53% of adult males and 34% of adult females smoked regularly (Shopland & Brown, 1985). Among adults between 20 and 45 years of age, smoking was even more prevalent: about 60% of the men and 40% of the women smoked regularly. Before that time, people generally didn't know about the serious health effects of smoking. But in 1964 the Surgeon General issued a report describing these health effects, and warnings against smoking began to appear in the American media and on cigarette packages. Since that time, the prevalence of adult smokers has dropped steadily, and today about 27% of the men and 23% of the women in the United States smoke (NCHS, 2000).

Do these trends mean cigarette manufacturers are on the verge of bankruptcy? Not at all—their profits are still quite high! In the United States, there are still about 45 million smokers, the retail price of cigarettes has increased, and manufacturers have sharply increased sales to foreign countries. At the same time that smoking has declined in many industrialized countries, it has been increasing in developing nations, such as in Asia and Africa (Fiore, Newcomb, & McBride, 1993; WHO, 1999c).

WHO SMOKES?

Although huge numbers of people in the world smoke, most do not. In the United States, the adolescent and adult populations have about three times as many nonsmokers as smokers. Are some people more likely to smoke than others?

Age and Gender Differences in Smoking

Smoking varies with age. For example, few Americans begin to smoke regularly before 12 years of age (NCHS, 2000). But the great majority of people who will ever become regular smokers begin the habit before the age of 20 or so (Matarazzo, 1982; McGinnis, Shopland, & Brown, 1987). The habit generally develops gradually, and several years may pass before an individual's rate of smoking reaches its eventual adult level (Pechacek et al., 1984). The percentage of adults in the American population who smoke reaches its highest level among individuals between 35 and 45 years of age and declines among older individuals (NCHS, 2000). Many people stop smoking in adulthood (McGinnis, Shopland, & Brown, 1987). About one-quarter of American adults are *former* smokers.

Gender differences in smoking are quite large in some parts of the world: worldwide, 47% of men and 12% of women smoke (WHO, 1998). Among Americans, the prevalence of smoking had always been far greater among males than females before the 1970s, but this gender gap has narrowed considerably for two reasons (McGinnis, Shopland, & Brown, 1987). First, much larger numbers of men than women stopped smoking after starting. Second, although the percentage of individuals who started smoking declined until 1990, it decreased more sharply for males than for females. In every year from the mid-1970s to about 1990, the percentage of high-school senior girls who smoked daily exceeded that of boys (Johnston, O'Malley, & Bachman, 2000). Cigarette advertising targeted at one gender or the other, such as by creating clever brand names and slogans, played a major part in these gender-related shifts in smoking (Pierce

& Gilpin, 1995). A slogan designed to induce young females to smoke is:

> "You've come a long way, baby," with its strong but still subtle appeal to the women's liberation movement. The "Virginia Slims" brand name artfully takes advantage of the increasingly well-documented research finding that, for many female (and male) smokers, quitting the habit is associated with gaining weight. (Matarazzo, 1982, p. 6)

Since 1990, these trends have changed; smoking prevalence is again higher among young males than females (Johnston, O'Malley, & Bachman, 2000). There is an important and hopeful point to keep in mind about the changes we have described in smoking behavior: they demonstrate that people can be persuaded to avoid or quit smoking.

Sociocultural Differences in Smoking

Large variations in smoking occur across and within countries (WHO, 1998). Nearly three-quarters of the world's smokers live in developing countries, where 48% of the men and 7% of the women smoke. Although smoking declined in developed nations in the late 1900s, 42% of men and 24% of women in these countries still smoke.

In the United States, ethnic groups differ in smoking rates (NCHS, 2000). Although the percentages of blacks and whites who smoke regularly have declined substantially since the 1960s, these percentages are still higher among African American than white men and women who are over 35 years of age. But for individuals under age 25, the percentage of smokers is much lower for blacks than whites, with Hispanics being intermediate. Differences in smoking rates are also related to social class (McGinnis, Shopland, & Brown, 1987). The percentage of people who smoke tends to decline with increases in education, income, and job prestige. Thus, the highest rates of smoking are likely to be found among adults who did not graduate from high school, have low incomes, and have blue-collar occupations, such as carpentry, maintenance work, and truck driving.

HOW MUCH SMOKERS SMOKE

An examination of cigarette sales figures in the United States in the two decades after the mid-1960s reveals

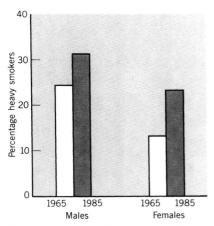

Figure 7–1   Percentage of American adult male and female smokers in 1965 and 1985 who were heavy smokers, consuming 25 or more cigarettes a day. (Data from McGinnis, Shopland, & Brown, 1987, Table 5.)

two curiously contrasting trends (Shopland & Brown, 1985). First, the number of cigarettes sold per adult person decreased sharply, which corresponds with the decline in the percentage of smokers. Second, the total cigarette consumption in America *increased* considerably during most of that period. These trends seem inconsistent, but they are not.

There are two reasons why total cigarette consumption increased in that time period. One reason is that the number of adults in the population increased, thereby offsetting the effect of the decline in the percentage of adults who smoke. The other reason is that the proportion of smokers who smoke *heavily* increased (McGinnis, Shopland, & Brown, 1987). Figure 7–1 shows how the percentages of male and female smokers who smoked heavily increased from 1965 to 1985. During that period, the percentages of male and female smokers who were moderate smokers remained fairly stable and the percentages who were light smokers decreased. What this means, of course, is that the people who continued to smoke after the 1960s are the ones who needed to quit the most.

WHY PEOPLE SMOKE

Cigarette smoking is a strange phenomenon in some respects. If you ever tried to smoke, chances are you coughed the first time or two, found the taste unpleasant, and, perhaps, even experienced nausea. This is not the kind of outcome that usually makes people

want to try something again. But many teenagers do, even though most teens say that smoking harms people's health (Johnston, O'Malley, & Bachman, 2000). Given these circumstances, we might wonder why people start to smoke and why they continue.

Starting to Smoke

Smoking usually starts during the teenage years, and psychosocial factors provide the primary forces that lead adolescents to begin. Several aspects of the social environment are influential in shaping teenagers' attitudes, beliefs, and intentions about smoking. For instance, studies have found that adolescents are more likely to begin smoking if their parents and friends smoke (Conrad, Flay, & Hill, 1992; Epstein, Botvin, & Diaz, 1999; Hansen et al., 1987; Killen et al., 1997; Robinson & Klesges, 1997). Teens who try their first cigarette typically smoke it in the company of peers and with their encouragement (Leventhal, Prohaska, & Hirschman, 1985). And adolescents are more likely to start smoking if their favorite movie stars smoke on or off screen (Distefan, Gilpin, Sargent, & Pierce, 1999). Thus, modeling and peer pressure are important determinants of smoking.

Personal characteristics, such as being rebellious and a risk-taker, seem to influence whether adolescents begin to smoke (Conrad, Flay, & Hill, 1992; Griffin et al., 1999; Robinson & Klesges, 1997). As psychologists Howard Leventhal and Paul Cleary have suggested, teenagers

> who are less successful in school ..., more rebellious, and doing less well in meeting expectations of parents and traditional authorities ... are more likely to be attracted to smoking at an early age and begin using cigarettes as a means of defining themselves as tough, cool, and independent of authority. (1980, p. 384)

Many teens also believe that smoking can enhance their image (Robinson & Klesges, 1997). Studies have found that boys and girls between the ages of 11 and 15 often associate smoking with being attractive to and interested in the opposite sex, looking mature, and being "glamorous" and "exciting" (Barton, Chassin, Presson, & Sherman, 1982; Dinh, Sarason, Peterson, & Onstad, 1995). Teenagers who are very concerned with how others view them do not easily overlook social images, models, and peer pressure. How the psychosocial factors we've considered impact on smoking seems to depend on the person's gender and sociocultural background. In the United States, for example, smoking by peers and family members is more closely linked to smoking in girls than boys and in white than black teenagers (Flay, Hu, & Richardson, 1998; Robinson & Klesges, 1997).

Becoming a Regular Smoker

There is a rule of thumb about beginning to smoke that seems to have some validity: individuals who smoke their *fourth* cigarette are very likely to become regular smokers (Leventhal & Cleary, 1980). Although the vast majority of youngsters try at least one cigarette, most of them never get to the fourth one and don't go on to smoke regularly. Becoming a habitual smoker generally develops slowly, often taking a few years (Ary & Biglan, 1988; Chassin et al., 2000).

Why is it that some people continue smoking after the first tries, and others don't? Part of the answer lies in the psychosocial influences that got them to start in the first place. Two longitudinal studies examined the role of psychosocial factors in the development of smoking by having thousands of adolescents fill out questionnaires in at least two different years (Chassin, Presson, Sherman, & Edwards, 1991; Murray, Swan, Johnson, & Bewley, 1983). The responses for the different years were then examined to determine whether the teenagers' social environments and beliefs about smoking were related to changes in their smoking behavior. Smoking tended to continue or increase if the subjects:

● Had at least one parent who smoked.

● Perceived their parents as unconcerned or even encouraging about their smoking.

● Had siblings or friends who smoked.

● Socialized with friends very often.

● Felt peer pressure to smoke, for example, reporting, "Others make fun of you if you don't smoke," and, "You have to smoke when you're with friends who smoke."

● Held positive attitudes about smoking, such as, "Smoking is very enjoyable," and, "Smoking can help people when they feel nervous or embarrassed."

● Did not believe smoking would harm their health, for instance, feeling, "Smoking is dangerous only to older people," and, "Smoking is only bad for you if you have been smoking for many years."

Other research has shown that teenagers usually smoke in the presence of other people, especially peers, and that smokers consume more cigarettes when in the company of someone who smokes at a high rate rather than a low rate (Antonuccio & Lichtenstein, 1980; Biglan et al., 1984). Adolescents who smoke also receive many more offers of cigarettes from friends than nonsmokers do (Ary & Biglan, 1988).

Psychologist Silvan Tomkins (1966, 1968) has outlined four psychological reasons why people who begin to smoke on a regular basis continue to smoke. One reason focuses on achieving a *positive affect*—smoking for stimulation, relaxation, or pleasure. Another reason centers on reducing *negative affect*, such as to relieve anxiety or tension. The third explanation is that smoking may become a *habitual* or automatic behavior that the person performs without awareness. Fourth, a person may develop a *psychological dependence* (which he called "addiction") on smoking to regulate positive and negative emotional states. According to Tomkins, one or another of these reasons is the chief controlling factor in a particular person's smoking behavior. As a result, the person can be categorized as a "positive affect smoker" or a "habitual smoker," and so on. Research has generally supported this model, finding that people can be classified according to the chief controlling reason they express for smoking and that this reason affects their smoking behavior (Leventhal & Cleary, 1980). For example, people who feel that the taste of cigarettes is the main reason for smoking smoke less than other smokers when their cigarettes are altered to taste less pleasant.

Findings of other research also indicate that people use smoking as a means of coping with stress. One study found that smoking among adolescents is related to the amount of stress in their lives—the greater the stress, the more likely they are to smoke (Wills, 1986). Another study found that adult smokers reported less anxiety and greater ability to express their opinions if they smoked during stressful social interactions than if they did not smoke (Gilbert & Spielberger, 1987). But even if smokers perform better and feel more relaxed in stressful situations when they are allowed to smoke than when they are not, they do not necessarily perform better or feel more relaxed than nonsmokers do (Schachter, 1980). Three other findings are important: smokers appear to have heightened stress between cigarettes that is reduced while they smoke, new smokers report increases in stress levels as their smoking increases and they become regular smokers, and former smokers report experiencing less stress than people who continue smoking (Parrott, 1999). These findings suggest that smoking may reduce stress temporarily, but may increase it in the long run.

Biological factors are also involved in sustaining smoking behavior. The fact that adolescent smoking is strongly associated with parental and sibling smoking shows that smoking runs in families. Certainly part of this relationship results from social learning processes. And some evidence suggests that nicotine passed on by a smoking mother to her baby in pregnancy may make the child more susceptible to the addictive effects of nicotine (Kandel, Wu, & Davies, 1994). Does heredity also play a role? Twin and adoption studies have demonstrated that genetic factors influence people's acquisition and maintenance of smoking (Hughes, 1986). What's more, researchers have identified a specific gene pattern that affects smoking: individuals with this gene pattern are less likely to become smokers and more able to quit after starting (Lerman, Caporaso et al., 1999).

How do genetic factors influence smoking? Some routes are indirect: for example, it may be that heredity affects people's taste preferences for tobacco or personality traits, such as rebelliousness, that are associated with smoking. One study found that the gene pattern we just discussed is associated with a low need for novelty (Sabol et al., 1999). Other routes are more direct: evidence indicates that heredity affects how easily and strongly a person becomes physically dependent on tobacco (Pomerleau, Collins, Shiffman, & Pomerleau, 1993). For instance, as people become regular smokers, they generally show the phenomenon of tolerance, using increasing amounts of tobacco; and if smokers try to quit, they often suffer withdrawal symptoms, such as irritability and difficulty concentrating (Jarvik & Henningfield, 1993; Shadel et al., 2000). Also, a study found that a specific gene may affect the rate at which the body metabolizes nicotine (Pianezza, Sellers, & Tyndale, 1998).

The Role of Nicotine

People become physically dependent on tobacco because of the chemical substances their bodies take in when they use it. A person who smokes a pack a day takes more than 50,000 puffs a year, with each puff delivering chemicals into the lungs and bloodstream (Pechacek, Fox, Murray, & Luepker, 1984; USDHHS, 1986c). These chemicals include carbon monoxide, tars, and nicotine. Cigarette smoke has high concentrations of **carbon monoxide,** a gas that is readily absorbed by the bloodstream and rapidly affects the person's physiological functioning, such as by reducing the oxygen-carrying capacity of the blood. It is possible that these physiological changes influence whether people like or dislike smoking. **Tars** exist as minute particles of residue, suspended in smoke. Although tars have important health effects, there is no evidence that they affect people's desire to smoke. **Nicotine** is the addictive chemical in cigarette smoke and clearly produces rapid and powerful physiological effects.

Nicotine is a substance that occurs only in tobacco. When a person smokes, nicotine penetrates cell membranes of the mouth and nose on the way to the lungs, where alveoli quickly absorb it and transmit it to the blood (Henningfield, Cohen, & Pickworth, 1993; Pechacek, Fox, Murray, & Luepker, 1984; Shadel et al., 2000). In a matter of seconds the blood carries the nicotine to the brain, where it leads to the release of various chemicals that activate both the central and sympathetic nervous systems. One effect of these changes is to arouse the body, increasing the person's alertness, heart rate, and blood pressure. While the person is smoking a cigarette, nicotine accumulates very rapidly in the blood. But it soon decreases through metabolism—in about 2 hours, half of the nicotine inhaled from a cigarette has decayed.

Biological explanations of people's continued cigarette smoking have focused chiefly on the role of nicotine. One prominent explanation, called the **nicotine regulation model,** is based on the addictive quality of nicotine. According to this model, established smokers continue to smoke to maintain a certain level of nicotine in their bodies and to avoid withdrawal symptoms. Stanley Schachter and his associates (1977) provided evidence for this model in an ingenious series of studies with adult smokers. In one study, the researchers had subjects smoke low-nicotine cigarettes during one week and high-nicotine cigarettes during another week. As the model predicts, the subjects smoked more low- than high-nicotine cigarettes. This effect was especially strong for heavy smokers, who smoked 25% more of the low- than high-nicotine cigarettes. Consistent with these results, other researchers have found that people who regularly smoke ultralow-nicotine cigarettes do not consume less nicotine than those who smoke other cigarettes—ultralow smokers simply smoke more cigarettes (Maron & Fortmann, 1987).

Although the nicotine regulation model has received research support, there are reasons to think it provides only part of the explanation for people's smoking behavior (Leventhal & Cleary, 1980). One reason is that people who quit smoking typically continue to crave it, and often return to smoking, long after all the nicotine is gone from their bodies. Another reason is that some people who smoke regularly for years don't become addicted. These people, called "chippers," smoke a few cigarettes a day, don't show the tolerance and withdrawal characteristics of addiction, and absorb as much nicotine from a cigarette as heavier smokers do (Shiffman, Fischer, Zettler-Segal, & Benowitz, 1990; Shiffman et al., 1995). Why do chippers continue to smoke? One explanation may be that nicotine has reinforcing effects (Donny et al., 1998; Shadel et al., 2000).

The **biobehavioral model** of Ovide and Cynthia Pomerleau (1989) proposes that people continue to smoke and often have a hard time quitting because they use and come to depend on the effects of nicotine to regulate their cognitive and emotional states. As we saw earlier, nicotine quickly reaches the brain and leads to the release of chemicals that activate body systems. These chemicals include *acetylcholine* and *norepinephrine*, which, independent of smoking, do two things: they (1) *increase* alertness, concentration, memory, and feelings of pleasure and (2) *decrease* symptoms of nicotine withdrawal and feelings of anxiety, tension, and pain. These very desirable, reinforcing effects begin very soon after the first puff of a cigarette and are temporary (McGehee et al., 1995). Nicotine also seems to reduce anger episodes in people who test high in hostility (Jamner, Shapiro, & Jarvik, 1999). According to the biobehavioral model, smokers learn to use nicotine to supplement or fine-tune the other coping processes they use to regulate these states. Habitual smokers have trouble quitting partly because they have come to rely on nicotine to help them cope.

Researchers today generally recognize that a complete explanation of the development and maintenance of smoking behavior involves the interplay of biological, psychological, and social factors (Fisher, Lichtenstein, & Haire-Joshu, 1993; Shadel et al., 2000). An example of this interplay is seen in the finding that among depressed smokers, those with a specific gene rely more on smoking to cope than those without that gene (Lerman et al., 1998).

SMOKING AND HEALTH

"Warning: The Surgeon General has determined that cigarette smoking is dangerous to your health," states a cigarette pack sold in the United States. At the end of the 20th century, deaths from smoking-related illnesses had risen to 4 million a year worldwide, and projections indicated that this rate would rise to 10 million a year by 2030 (WHO, 1999c). Smoking reduces people's life expectancy by several years and increases their risk of many illnesses, particularly cancer and cardiovascular diseases (Thun et al., 1995). No other single behavior takes such a toll. To what extent do your odds of dying of lung cancer or heart disease increase if you smoke? Figure 7–2 shows that the odds increase greatly, especially for lung cancer (Mattson, Pollack, & Cullen, 1987). The more you smoke, the worse your odds become—and if you quit, your odds improve steadily, in about 15 years becoming similar to those of people who never smoked (LaCroix et al.,

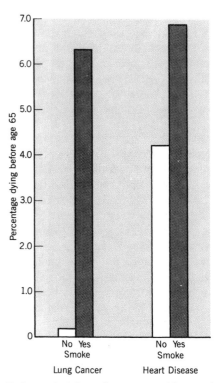

Figure 7–2 Probability of a 35-year-old man dying of lung cancer or heart disease before age 65 as a function of smoking heavily or not smoking. Data for women were less complete, but probably would reveal similar risk increases. (Data from Mattson, Pollack, & Cullen, 1987, p. 427.)

1991; WHO, 1998). Smoking and, specifically, nicotine also impair immune function (McAllister-Sistilli et al., 1998).

Cancer

In the late 1930s, two important studies were done that clearly linked smoking and cancer for the first time (Ashton & Stepney, 1982). One study presented statistics showing that nonsmokers live longer than smokers. In the other study, researchers produced cancer in laboratory animals by administering cigarette tar. By producing cancer with experimental methods, these researchers demonstrated a causal link between cancer and a chemical in tobacco smoke and identified tar as a likely *carcinogen*. The evidence now is overwhelming that tobacco tars and probably other byproducts of tobacco smoke cause cancer (Denissenko, Pao, Tang, & Pfeifer, 1996; USDHHS, 1986c, 1989).

Hundreds of retrospective and prospective studies have consistently demonstrated the link between tobacco use and cancer in humans. Prospective research provides strong evidence for a causal relationship because smokers and nonsmokers are identified and then followed over a long period of time to see if they develop cancer. Many large-scale prospective studies have linked smoking with cancers of various body sites, including the lung, mouth, esophagus, bladder, and kidney (Levy, 1985; Shopland & Burns, 1993). The latter two may result because carcinogenic chemicals in tobacco smoke are absorbed into the blood and conveyed to the urine. Cancers of the mouth and esophagus can also result from using smokeless tobacco—chewing tobacco or snuff (Severson, 1993; USDHHS, 1989). Thus, carcinogenic substances exist not only in smoke, but in tobacco itself.

As recently as the 1930s, lung cancer in America was quite uncommon and much less prevalent than many other forms of cancer, such as cancer of the breast, stomach, and prostate (ACS, 2000). Deaths from lung cancer at that time occurred at an annual rate of about 5 per 100,000 people in the population, whereas mortality rates for breast and stomach cancer were more than five times that high. Over the years, the mortality rates for most forms of cancer have either declined or remained fairly constant, but not for lung cancer. The annual death rate per 100,000 population for lung cancer has risen sharply; it is now about 70 for men and 34 for women. It is the deadli-est form of cancer, being responsible for nearly three times more deaths yearly than cancer of the colon or rectum, the second most deadly form. Lung cancer claims almost 159,000 lives in the United States each year. Over 90% of these deaths are related to smoking (WHO, 1999c).

The correspondence between the rises in lung cancer deaths and in smoking prevalence since the 1930s is quite striking (McGinnis, Shopland, & Brown, 1987; Shopland & Burns, 1993). The rate of mortality from lung cancer began to rise about 15 or 20 years after the rate of smoking started to rise, and these rates have paralleled each other ever since. During this time, the rates of smoking and of lung cancer were higher for males than for females, but since the mid-1960s, important gender-related changes have occurred. Smoking has decreased among men and increased among women, thus narrowing the gender gap—and corresponding changes in the incidence of lung cancer are now evident. Among men, incidence rates of lung cancer have declined steadily since the mid-1980s, but the rates have increased alarmingly among women (NCHS, 2000).

How does smoking harm the lungs? When smoke recurrently passes through the bronchial tubes, the lining of the tubes begins to react to the irritation by increasing the number of cells just below the surface. Then,

> the fine, hairlike growths, or cilia, along the surface of the lining, whose function is to clear the lungs of foreign particles, begin to slow or stop their movement. In time, the cilia may disappear altogether, and as a consequence carcinogenic substances remain in contact with sensitive cells in the lining of the bronchi instead of being removed in the mucus. . . . At this stage, a *smoker's cough* may develop. It is a feeble attempt by the body to clear the lungs of foreign particles in the absence of functioning cilia. (La Place, 1984, p. 326)

Lung cancer usually originates in the bronchial tubes. In most cases, it probably develops because of the continual contact of carcinogens with the bronchial lining.

Smoking is a major risk factor for all forms of cancer, but its role is more direct and powerful in lung cancer than in other cancers. People's environments contain many other carcinogens, and smoking is not the only cause of these diseases. (Go to 🔦.)

HIGHLIGHT ON ISSUES

Does Someone Else's Smoking Affect Your Health?

"What do you mean I can't smoke on this plane! I paid for my ticket, and it isn't anybody else's business what I do to my body," a passenger said indignantly to a flight attendant. Some customers of airlines and other businesses have reacted strongly to smoking bans in a variety of public places. Why were these regulations introduced?

Not all tobacco smoke goes into the smoker's body, and much of that which does comes back out. All this excess smoke gets into the environment for others to consume and is called *secondhand smoke* or *environmental tobacco smoke*. Breathing secondhand smoke is called **passive smoking** or involuntary smoking. In the mid-1980s, the United States Surgeon General issued a report on the effects of passive smoking, based on a careful examination of available evidence by dozens of physicians and scientists. This examination led to three conclusions:

1. Involuntary smoking is a cause of disease, including lung cancer, in healthy nonsmokers.

2. Compared with the children of nonsmoking parents, children of parents who smoke have a higher frequency of respiratory infections, increased respiratory symptoms, and slightly smaller rates of increase in lung function as the lungs mature.

3. The simple separation of smokers and nonsmokers within the same air space may reduce, but does not eliminate, the exposure of nonsmokers to environmental tobacco smoke. (USDHHS, 1986c, p.7)

The smoke that comes from the burning tip of a cigarette—or *sidestream smoke*—makes up most of environmental tobacco smoke and contains high concentrations of known carcinogens (Eriksen, LeMaistre, & Newell, 1988). High levels of sidestream smoke are found in public places, such as worksites, when smoking is permitted (Hammond, Sorenson, Youngstrom, & Ockene, 1995).

Evidence of the harmful effects of secondhand smoke is quite substantial. Some of the strongest evidence has linked passive smoking to lung cancer (Erikson, LeMaistre, & Newell, 1988; USDHHS, 1986c). Many studies of this relationship in various countries around the world have examined the development of cancer in nonsmokers who had spouses who smoked. These studies have typically found that passive smokers' risk of lung cancer increases, and sometimes doubles or triples. Studies attempting to relate passive smoking to other cancers have produced mixed or inconclusive results so far. But research has found a higher risk of cardiovascular disease in nonsmoking spouses of smokers than nonsmokers (Humble et al., 1990).

Passive smoking also has other health effects. For instance, an experiment with animals showed that being exposed to sidestream smoke accelerates the development of atherosclerosis (Penn & Snyder, 1993). What's more, for people with existing cardiovascular conditions, such as angina, and respiratory problems, such as asthma and hay fever, environmental tobacco smoke can bring on attacks or aggravate acute symptoms (Eriksen, LeMaistre, & Newell, 1988). Increasingly, people are becoming aware of the health effects of secondhand smoke and making efforts to have smoke-free environments.

Cardiovascular Disease

Cardiovascular disease—including coronary heart disease (CHD) and stroke—is the leading cause of death by far worldwide (WHO, 1999c). In the United States, it is responsible for over 40% of all deaths each year and claims more lives than cancer, accidents, and several other causes combined (USBC, 1999). When you point out these facts to some smokers, they say, "Well you have to die of *something*." Of course, that's true—but *when* you will die is the real issue. Cardiovascular disease takes many lives early: one in seven people it kills are under 65 years of age.

Many millions of Americans suffer from CHD and stroke. The risk of having a heart attack is about twice as high for smokers as for nonsmokers (AHA, 2000;

USDHHS, 1989). A prospective study examined the impact of smoking on the incidence of CHD across $8\frac{1}{2}$ years (Rosenman, Brand, Sholtz, & Friedman, 1976). Over 3,000 men participated in the research, beginning when they were 39 to 59 years of age. Compared to nonsmokers, the incidence of CHD was more than 50% higher for men who smoked about a pack a day and over twice as high for those who smoked more than a pack a day. These higher risks for smokers also depend on, or interact with, several other factors (Epstein & Jennings, 1986; Khaw & Barrett-Connor, 1986; Perkins, 1985). In general, the risks that smoking presents for developing CHD are especially strong for people who:

- Are males.
- Are 45 to 55 years of age, rather than older.
- Have a family history of heart disease.
- Have high levels of cholesterol in their blood.
- Have high blood pressure.

Two other points are important in the link between smoking and CHD. First, the greater risks for CHD among smokers than among nonsmokers may be aggravated by stress, since smoking increases when people are under stress. Second, smokers tend to have lifestyles that include other risk factors for CHD, such as being physically inactive (Castro, Newcomb, McCreary, & Baezconde-Garbanati, 1989).

How does smoking cause cardiovascular disease? Researchers generally believe the disease process involves several effects that the nicotine and carbon monoxide in cigarette smoke have on cardiovascular functioning (USDHHS, 1986a). Nicotine constricts blood vessels and increases heart rate, cardiac output, and both systolic and diastolic blood pressure. Carbon monoxide reduces the availability of oxygen to the heart, which may cause damage and lead to atherosclerosis. Studies have found that the more cigarettes people smoke per day the greater their level of serum cholesterol and size of plaques on artery walls (Haapanen et al., 1989; Muscat, Harris, Haley, & Wynder, 1991; Tell et al., 1994). Exposure to secondhand smoke also increases atherosclerosis (Howard et al., 1998). The risk of heart attack or stroke declines greatly in the first few years after stopping smoking (Kawachi et al., 1993; Negri et al., 1994).

Other Illnesses

Smoking can lead to a wide variety of other illnesses—particularly emphysema and chronic bronchitis—which are classified together as *chronic obstructive pulmonary disease* (COPD) (ALA, 2000; Haas & Haas, 1990). People with COPD experience permanently reduced airflow, which is especially evident when they try to exhale with force. Over 80% of cases of COPD in the United States are related to smoking (Parker, 1985; USDHHS, 1986a). As we saw earlier, recurrent smoking irritates and damages respiratory organs. Research has shown that more damage occurs from smoking high-tar than low-tar cigarettes and that regularly smoking nontobacco (marijuana) cigarettes also damages the respiratory system (Bloom et al., 1987; Paoletti, Camilli, Holberg, & Lebowitz, 1985). COPD can incapacitate its victims, often forcing relatively young individuals to retire from work. It causes over 2 million deaths each year worldwide, particularly among its victims who smoke (WHO, 1999c).

Smoking may also increase acute respiratory infections. This has been shown in two ways. First, studies have found that children of smokers are more likely to develop pneumonia than are children of nonsmokers (USDHHS, 1986c). Second, when exposed to common cold viruses, smokers are much more likely to catch cold than nonsmokers, probably because their immune functions are impaired (Cohen et al., 1993).

PREVENTING SMOKING

How can we prevent people from smoking? Effective public health approaches include increasing the price of cigarettes through taxation and restricting the advertisement and purchase of cigarettes, such as by underage adolescents (Altman et al., 1999; Kaplan, Orleans, Perkins, & Pierce, 1995). Other approaches try to help people avoid beginning to smoke. To do this effectively, prevention programs need to consider two important factors: *when* and *why* individuals start to smoke. The first factor is straightforward and easily addressed by prevention programs. Because people's likelihood of starting to smoke rises during the junior high school years, increases sharply in the high school years, and is very low in adulthood, prevention programs should begin early (Evans, 1984). Programs to prevent smoking are often conducted in schools before children reach the age of 12 or so.

School programs to prevent smoking focused originally on giving fear-arousing warnings of the health consequences of smoking (Evans, 1984). These programs did not take into account the past social experiences and current psychosocial forces that exert very strong influences on teenage behavior. Although knowing the health consequences can change children's beliefs and attitudes about smoking, it is usually not sufficient to stop them from starting to smoke (Bruvold, 1993; Flay, 1985). This failure points out the need of smoking-prevention programs to consider more fully *why* youth begin to smoke.

As we saw earlier, researchers have identified several psychosocial reasons why young people start to smoke. Social influences and associated social skills appear to have stronger effects on teenage smoking than long-range health consequences that seem remote, both in time and in likelihood. Recognizing this, Richard Evans and his colleagues designed and tested a school-based program to deter teenage smoking by addressing psychosocial factors (Evans, 1976, 1984; Evans et al., 1978). The program focused on the immediate consequences of smoking, such as how much it costs and its physiological effects. Films with same-age peers as narrators gave information to help students understand how modeling, peer pressure, and cigarette advertising influence their willingness to smoke and to teach them how to resist these forces. The purpose of the program was to provide the knowledge and skills to "immunize" teenagers against forces that lead to smoking. This psychosocial approach produced very encouraging results and has since served as the basis for developing increasingly effective methods for deterring smoking (Best et al., 1988; Botvin & Epstein, 1999; Flay, 1985).

The psychosocial perspective became the foundation for two types of smoking prevention efforts:

- *Social influence approaches* focus on training skills to help individuals resist social pressures to smoke. They include (1) discussions and films regarding how peers, family members, and the media influence smoking by teenagers, (2) modeling and role-playing of specific refusal skills, such as saying, "No thank you, I don't smoke," and (3) requiring that each student decide his or her intention regarding whether or not to smoke and announce that decision publicly to classmates (Flay et al., 1985).

- *Life skills training approaches* address general social, cognitive, and coping skills. Because many individuals who begin smoking seem to lack these general skills, this approach focuses on improving (1) personal skills, including critical thinking for making decisions, techniques for coping with anxiety, and basic principles for changing their own behavior and (2) general social skills, including methods for being assertive and making conversation (Botvin, Renick, & Baker, 1983; Botvin & Wills, 1985).

Longitudinal studies have tested these approaches for smoking prevention for 1 to 6 years. Although the exact procedures varied somewhat from one study to the next, they were fairly similar. Most of the programs began when the children were in sixth or seventh grade (about age 12). They used a large number of schools, which were assigned to *program* or *control* groups in ways to assure comparability of the schools' size and social class across conditions. The programs gave information about the short- and long-term health and social consequences of smoking. And the subjects' self-reports of their smoking were verified, using biochemical analyses of saliva or breath samples.

Were these approaches successful? Compared with the control subjects, children who received each type of program were less likely to begin to smoke during the next couple of years or so (Bruvold, 1993). In the case of social influence programs, these benefits were found at assessments after 1 to 3 years (Best et al., 1988; Flay et al., 1985; Johnson, Hansen, Collins, & Graham, 1986; Murray et al., 1988; Murray, Richards, Luepker, & Johnson, 1987). The life skills approaches showed these benefits in several junior high schools over a 2-year period (Botvin, Renick, & Baker, 1983; Botvin & Wills, 1985).

Not all studies have found encouraging results of these psychosocial approaches to prevent smoking. Some long-term follow-up studies of teens in social influence programs found that the programs' beneficial effects do not last beyond 4 years or so (Flay et al., 1989; Murray, Pirie, Leupker, & Pallonen, 1989). In the junior or senior high school year, a surge in smoking occurred among program subjects, wiping out their earlier advantages over the controls. And some psychosocial programs have been unsuccessful and have had high attrition rates, particularly among smokers and those at high risk of becoming smokers (Ary et al., 1990; Biglan et al., 1987). In some cases, failures may have resulted from deficiencies in the programs. Interventions should be long enough (at least five sessions) to have an impact, be administered correctly and fully, and have "booster" sessions every year or two (Botvin & Epstein, 1999). Psychosocial programs with these features are much more likely to produce long-lasting smoking prevention.

Research findings suggest other ways to improve psychosocial approaches to prevent smoking. First, programs should assess and provide special components for psychosocial characteristics that put each child at risk for smoking. For example, students who already smoke occasionally at the start of the program may require special efforts because they are especially likely to become regular smokers. Second, programs may need to start before the fifth grade and focus on attitudes about smokers. A study found that by the time children enter fifth grade many already have positive attitudes about smokers, and having these attitudes at that time was associated with beginning to smoke by the ninth grade (Dinh, Sarason, Peterson, & Onstad, 1995). Third, getting parents involved may also be useful. For example, if parents smoke, their children will be much less likely to smoke if the parents quit, especially if quitting occurs before the child is 9 years old (Farkas et al., 1999). The successes psychosocial programs have had suggest that these approaches should be applied in schools more widely to prevent smoking.

QUITTING SMOKING

People are finding that cigarette smoking is not only harmful to their health, but it has negative social effects, too. Smoking has become something like a deviant behavior in some cultures—many nonsmokers resent people smoking in their presence, and many smokers feel guilty when they smoke because they know it offends others and believe it is unhealthy, irrational behavior. Smokers today probably want to quit more than smokers ever did before. What methods do they use to quit, and which ones work?

Stopping on One's Own

You probably know people who were smokers—perhaps heavy smokers—who have quit. Chances are they quit without any sort of professional help. Millions of people around the world stop smoking each year, and the vast majority do it on their own. But only

An advertisement by the American Cancer Society that may motivate people to avoid starting or to quit smoking.

a small percentage of individuals who begin smoking in adolescence quit in the next 20 years (Chassin et al., 2000). Are people effective at stopping on their own, and does it take enormous effort?

Stanley Schachter (1982) interviewed 16- to 79-year-old men and women about their experience in stopping smoking if they had ever smoked cigarettes regularly. Of these people, 94 had been or were currently smokers—73 were classified as heavy smokers (smoking at least three-quarters of a pack a day), and the remainder were classified as light smokers. These interviews revealed that over 60% of the smokers who tried to quit eventually succeeded—virtually all had not smoked in the last 3 months, and the average length of abstinence was more than 7 years. Was it harder for the heavy smokers to quit than the light smokers? Yes, much harder. Nearly half of the heavy smokers who quit reported severe withdrawal symptoms, such as intense cravings, irritability, sleeplessness, and cold sweats; less than 30% reported having no difficulties. In contrast, almost all of the light smokers said quitting had been easy, even if they had failed!

A similar study conducted by researchers at another university found very similar results (Rzewnicki & Forgays, 1987).

The results of these studies suggest that most people can stop smoking on their own, even if they smoke heavily. Other studies have clarified the process of quitting on one's own: most people do not succeed in one attempt, but eventually succeed after several tries, and certain factors differentiate those people who do and don't succeed (Carey et al., 1993; Cohen et al., 1989; Curry, Wagner, & Grothaus, 1990; DiClemente et al., 1991; Gritz, Carr, & Marcus, 1991; Pallonen et al., 1990; Rose, Chassin, Presson, & Sherman, 1996). Compared to smokers who do not succeed in quitting, those who do are likely to:

● Have decided that they want and are ready to quit.

● Feel confident that they can succeed.

● Have smoked less than a pack a day.

● Experience less stress.

● Feel less nicotine dependence and experience less craving for tobacco and fewer and less-severe withdrawal symptoms, such as restlessness and tension.

● Be highly motivated to quit. Although being motivated by *extrinsic* factors, such as financial incentives, can help, people are more likely to succeed if they are motivated by *intrinsic* factors, such as a feeling of self-control or a concern about their health.

● Be willing to try again if they don't succeed. Many people fail the first few times they try, but learn from their mistakes.

Many people decide to quit when rules restricting smoking are introduced at work, especially if the worksite offers a program to help them stop; these same factors seem to affect their success, too (Fielding, 1991; Grunberg, 1991; Klesges, Haddock, Lando, & Talcott, 1999).

What methods do smokers use when trying to quit? To answer this question, researchers interviewed participants in a month-long communitywide stop-smoking contest that had a grand prize of a trip to Disney World (Glasgow, Klesges, Mizes, & Pechacek, 1985). These interviews revealed that:

● The vast majority of the men and women attempted to quit cold turkey rather than trying to reduce their smoking gradually before the contest began.

● Most participants used oral substitutes, such as candy or mints, in place of cigarettes.

● Most tried to go it alone, without involving other people, but many others used a buddy system or made bets with others.

● Most used cognitive strategies, such as telling themselves, "I don't need a cigarette," or reminding themselves of the health risks in smoking, the commitment they made to quit, or the possibility of winning a prize.

● A minority of individuals provided themselves with material rewards for sticking with quitting or punishment for backsliding.

Fifty-five participants—about 40%—remained abstinent throughout the month (which was verified through biochemical saliva or breath analyses). Some methods were more strongly related to successful quitting than others. Although some of the strategies were probably effective in helping particular individuals quit, only a few methods stood out as being effective for many participants. Compared to individuals who failed, those who succeeded tended to quit cold turkey rather than gradually, provide themselves with rewards for abstaining, and use positive cognitive statements to themselves (for example, "Think of the example I'll set by stopping smoking") rather than negative ones (for example, "Think how weak I'll be if I give in and smoke").

Women seem to be less successful at quitting smoking than men (Wetter et al., 1999). Although the reasons for this are unclear, research has found that women experience heightened withdrawal if quitting begins toward the end of the menstrual cycle (Perkins et al.,2000). What about smokers who cannot seem to succeed in stopping on their own even after many attempts? Many of them stop trying to quit and continue to smoke, of course. Many others seek professional help in trying to stop.

Treatment for Stopping Smoking

Of the smokers who are willing to try to stop smoking, the ones who seek help are likely to be psychologically and physically very dependent on smoking, decreasing the chances that they will succeed. Therapists in clinics can design programs that use a variety of methods to help.

One approach therapists have tried involves the use of *drugs* that might combat the conditions that maintain or increase smoking behavior (Jarvik & Henningfield, 1993; Kozlowski, 1984). People report many reasons for smoking, including wanting to become aroused or to reduce tension. As a result, therapists have tried using tranquilizers and stimulants to reduce people's smoking, but these drugs have not been effective. The most useful drug approach involves having the smoker take nicotine directly, such as by chewing *nicotine-containing gum* or wearing a *nicotine patch* on the skin. The nicotine dose is gradually tapered off across a few months. Using nicotine in this way decreases withdrawal symptoms, such as sleeplessness, and helps in achieving short-term and long-term quitting success (Cepeda-Benito, 1993; Fiore, Smith, Jorenby, & Baker, 1994; Wetter, Fiore, Baker, & Young, 1995).

Therapists also use many *behavioral methods* for helping smokers quit. These behavior modification methods can be classified into two categories, aversion strategies and self-management strategies, that include several techniques (Kamarck & Lichtenstein, 1985; Lichtenstein & Mermelstein, 1984; Sarafino, 2001). **Aversion strategies** involve the use of unpleasant stimuli to discourage behavior—in this case, smoking. Therapists have tried three main types of unpleasant stimuli: electric shock, imagined negative scenes, and cigarette smoke itself. When *electric shock* is used in aversion methods, the level of shock is usually predetermined by increasing it from a low level until the person feels that it is uncomfortable or somewhat painful. The shock is then paired with smoking situations. Using *imagined negative scenes* involves having the person think about a sequence of events, such as getting ready to smoke but becoming nauseated and vomiting. Cigarette smoke can be made into an unpleasant stimulus in several ways. One way, called *satiation*, has the person double or triple his or her usual smoking rate at home for some period of time. Using cigarette smoke as an aversion strategy for controlling smoking appears to be more effective than imagined scenes or electric shock (Kamarck & Lichtenstein, 1985; Lichtenstein & Mermelstein, 1984). For some smokers, aversion strategies may be useful as a first step in a treatment program for quitting.

Self-management strategies involve techniques a therapist teaches people to help them gain control over environmental conditions that sustain an undesirable behavior, such as smoking (Lichtenstein & Mermelstein, 1984; Sarafino, 2001). These strategies are based on the recognition that behavior modification requires changing the *behavior itself* and its *antecedents* and *consequences*. For example, the consequences can be changed by introducing rewards for not smoking and penalties for smoking, as occurred for Jim at the start of this chapter. Although self-management methods are each useful in changing behavior, such as smoking, they are most effective when combined and used together (Sarafino, 2001; USDHHS, 1989). A recent addition to these techniques that shows great promise involves a *scheduled reduction* in the number of cigarettes smoked. The program begins by having the person smoke the usual number of cigarettes, but they must be smoked at specified regular intervals, such as on the half-hour during waking hours. Then the schedule is changed to fewer and fewer cigarettes with longer and longer intervals. In a test of this technique, all smokers used a self-management program (Cinciripini et al., 1995). But of those who used the scheduled reduction method, 44% were still abstaining a year later; of those who quit "cold turkey," only 22% were still abstinent. Quitting smoking by gradual reductions seems to work best for people who smoked at least fairly heavily before cutting back and who can maintain a low level of smoking for a while before trying to quit entirely (Farkas, 1999).

Several other therapy techniques have been tested, sometimes receiving a great deal of media attention. But research has not demonstrated that they are clearly more effective than control conditions (Glasgow & Lichtenstein, 1987; Hunt & Matarazzo, 1982). These techniques include *hypnosis, systematic desensitization*, and *Restricted Environmental Stimulation Therapy* (REST). In the REST technique, the smoker lies on a bed for a 24-hour period in a very dark and quiet chamber, with no objects or stimulation available, but is allowed to eat, drink, and use the toilet freely (Suedfeld & Ikard, 1974; Suedfeld, 1990).

Research has shown that some of the drug methods, aversion strategies, and self-management strategies are useful in controlling smoking, but none is highly effective *alone* (USDHHS, 1989). As a result, they are usually combined in a *multidimensional program* to improve their effectiveness (Lando, 1993; Shiffman, 1993). For instance, studies have found that programs combining behavioral methods with the nicotine patch are far more effective than using either approach alone (Cinciripini et al., 1996;

Laforge, Willey, Prochaska, & Levesque, 1995). Three other features should be considered when designing multidimensional programs to stop smoking. First, using biochemical analyses to verify self-reports of smoking and demonstrating these verification procedures at the *beginning* of treatment enhances the success of a program (Glynn, Gruder, & Jegerski, 1986). Second, a brief daily telephone call to the smokers improves their performance of certain procedures, such as keeping records of smoking (McConnell, Biglan, & Severson, 1984). Third, physician involvement helps. People are more likely to try to quit smoking and stick with it if they are advised to stop by their physician,

receive a prescription for nicotine, are shown on an apparatus how impaired their respiratory system is, and have been diagnosed with a serious smoking-related disease. (Fiore, Jorenby, & Baker, 1997; Ockene et al., 1991, 1994; Risser & Belcher, 1990; USDHHS, 1986a). (Go to 🐾.)

Succeeding at Quitting and Abstaining for Good

Quitting smoking is one thing—staying quit is another. As Mark Twain noted: "To cease smoking is the easiest thing I ever did; I ought to know because I've

---

CLINICAL METHODS AND ISSUES

Behavioral Methods: Applications for Stopping Smoking

Psychologists often provide training in behavior modification techniques that clients can apply as self-management strategies (Sarafino, 2001). In designing a multidimensional program to help clients quit smoking, four behavioral methods can be used.

- *Self-monitoring* is a procedure in which people record information pertaining to their problem behavior, such as how often they smoked and the circumstances, place, and time of each instance. To encourage self-monitoring, a pencil and paper can be kept with the smokers' cigarettes. Although this technique by itself can produce a temporary decrease in smoking, its utility is mainly in gathering information to be used in other techniques.

- *Stimulus control* procedures address the antecedents by altering elements of the environment that serve as cues and lead a person to perform the problem behavior. Many smokers report that they regularly have (and "*need* to have") a cigarette in certain situations, such as after meals, or with coffee or alcohol, or when talking on the phone, or while sitting in a favorite chair watching TV. Elements of these environments can be altered in many ways, for example, by removing smoking cues such as ashtrays and matches or by restricting the time spent watching TV

or sitting at the table after meals. Stimulus control procedures by themselves are moderately effective in reducing smoking and are very useful when combined with other techniques.

- *Response substitution* involves replacing a problem behavior with an alternative response, particularly one that is incompatible with or not likely to be performed at the same time as the problem behavior. A smoker who "has to have a cigarette with coffee after breakfast" could skip coffee and take a shower right after breakfast. People are not likely to smoke in the shower (but some smokers do!).

- *Behavioral contracting* is a technique whereby certain conditions and consequences regarding the problem behavior are spelled out in a contract. Behavioral contracts usually indicate the conditions under which the behavior may or may not occur and specify what reinforcing and punishing consequences will be applied, and when. Contracts for quitting smoking often have the person deposit a substantial sum of money, which is then meted out if he or she meets certain goals. This technique seems to be effective in controlling smoking, but only while the contingencies are in effect.

These methods can also help people to change many other health-related behaviors (Sarafino, 2001).

done it a thousand times" (Grunberg & Bowen, 1985). The methods we have considered work well in helping people stop smoking, but preventing backsliding is a major problem.

Regardless of how smokers quit, their likelihood of *relapse*—that is, returning to the full-blown pattern of behavior—is very high in the first weeks and months after stopping. Most people who quit smoking start again within a year, and most relapses occur in the first 3 months (Ockene et al., 2000). Estimates of relapse rates vary from 50 to 80%, depending on many factors, including the methods used in quitting, how heavily the person smoked, and characteristics of the individual and his or her environment (Curry & McBride, 1994; Ossip-Klein et al., 1986). Withdrawal symptoms probably contribute strongly to immediate relapses, but these symptoms decline sharply in the first week or so after stopping (Gritz, Carr, & Marcus, 1991; Killen & Fortmann, 1994; Piasecki et al., 1997). Smokers who are trying to quit need to be reassured that their cravings and negative feelings will diminish greatly in less than a month. What other factors lead people to return to smoking?

One important factor in smoking relapse is *stress*: people who experience high levels of stress are more likely to start smoking again than those who experience less stress (Caplan, Cobb, & French, 1975; Lichtenstein et al., 1986; Shiffman et al., 1996). Ex-smokers who go back to smoking often report that acute episodes of anxiety or frustration at work or at home led to their relapse (Shiffman, 1986). Sheldon Cohen and Edward Lichtenstein (1990) examined the role of stress in relapse longitudinally among smokers who had decided to quit. The subjects were interviewed before quitting and at 1, 3, and 6 months after their quit date regarding their recent stress levels and smoking status, with biochemical verification. Those subjects who remained continuously abstinent over the full 6 months reported less and less stress at each interview, but those who relapsed early reported high levels of stress throughout. Some evidence also suggested that the abstinent subjects' reduced stress not only helped them succeed but may have resulted partly from succeeding, such as by increasing their feelings of self-efficacy and self-esteem. People who get treatment for stopping smoking need to receive training in ways to cope with stress without relying on smoking as a coping strategy (Shadel & Mermelstein, 1993).

Another factor in smoking relapse is *social support*. High levels of positive social support can prevent individuals from backsliding by buffering them against stress, as we saw in Chapter 4. Also, social support can prevent relapse if people in the ex-smoker's social network encourage the person not to smoke (Colletti & Brownell, 1983; Nides et al., 1995). Encouragement can come from the person's family, friends, and coworkers, as well as from buddy systems in self-help support groups. But not all social contacts help prevent a relapse. Some social situations often encourage a relapse, particularly when the ex-smoker is in a restaurant or bar (Shiffman, 1986). Unfortunately, many people who quit smoking do not have the kind of support they need, and may even be explicitly *discouraged* from abstinence by others offering them cigarettes or expressing doubt that they will remain abstinent (Sorensen, Pechacek, & Pallonen, 1986).

People's beliefs and attributions about themselves can also affect whether they return to smoking. Research has shown that people with high levels of *self-efficacy* for quitting and remaining abstinent are less likely to relapse than individuals with less self-efficacy (Baer, Holt, & Lichtenstein, 1986; Curry & McBride, 1994). Maintaining a sense of self-efficacy for remaining abstinent is not always easy. As we saw in Chapter 6, people who quit a behavior and experience a lapse may lose their confidence in remaining abstinent. Their commitment to total abstinence makes them feel guilty about any lapses, even with just one cigarette, and see their violation as a sign of a personal failure. These events can lead to a full relapse through the process called the *abstinence-violation effect* (Marlatt & Gordon, 1980). Research has shown that self-efficacy during quitting is dynamic: it remains fairly high before a lapse and drops after the lapse; the sharper the drop, the more likely a relapse will occur (Shiffman et al., 2000). Relapses can be reduced if treatment programs provide training on ways to cope with lapses and maintain self-efficacy and provide "booster" sessions or contacts (Curry & McBride, 1994; Irvin, Bowers, Dunn, & Wang, 1999). Well-designed contacts, even by phone or mailings, can reduce relapses markedly by providing information on dealing with difficult situations that could lead to lapses (Brandon, Collins, Juliano, & Lazev, 2000; Zhu et al., 1996).

An interesting thing happens to smokers' beliefs when they relapse: they tend to lower their perceptions of the health risks of smoking. A study of people who relapsed after completing a treatment program to stop smoking found that they reported strong beliefs that smoking could harm their health when they entered the program, but after the relapse these beliefs decreased (Gibbons, McGovern, & Lando, 1991). Why? They probably used cognitive processes, such as motivated reasoning or denial, to cope with the fact that their attempt to quit smoking failed. This finding is important because it means people who relapse may not be ready to retry quitting until their beliefs change back again. Many smokers deny or minimize the health risks of smoking, thereby decreasing the likelihood that they will try to quit (Lee, 1989; Strecher, Kreuter, & Kobrin, 1995).

Some people who go back to smoking claim they did so because they were *gaining weight* (Jeffrey et al., 2000; Perkins, 1994). Smokers tend to weigh less than nonsmokers, and this difference is greater among middle-aged than younger individuals (Klesges, Zbikowski et al., 1998). When people stop smoking, most—but not all—do, in fact, tend to gain several pounds over the next few years (Klesges et al., 1997; Klesges, Ward et al., 1998; Williamson et al., 1991). There are two reasons why this is so (Klesges, Benowitz, & Meyers, 1991). First, ex-smokers often increase their caloric intake, sometimes by eating more fats and sweet-tasting carbohydrates. Second, the amount of energy they expend in metabolism declines, for at least a short time, after quitting. Thus both behavioral and physiological factors contribute to the changes in weight that ex-smokers experience. To prevent weight gain, many ex-smokers may need to control their diets, get more exercise, and perhaps use a nicotine supplement. Research has shown that ex-smokers who used nicotine gum during the weeks after quitting gained much less weight than controls who used a placebo gum (Doherty, Militello, Kinnunen, & Garvey, 1996; Perkins, 1994).

The factors that lead an ex-smoker to smoke again are very powerful; controlling them will be difficult. Some efforts to do this with behavioral methods have been tried, but have had mixed success (Brandon, Zelman, & Baker, 1987; Glasgow & Lichtenstein, 1987; Hall, Rugg, Tunstall, & Jones, 1984). As you might expect, these programs have been more successful with people who had been lighter smokers than with heavier smokers—the ones who are likely to need help the most. Combining behavioral and pharmacological

methods to prevent relapse may be the best approach (Klesges, Benowitz, & Meyers, 1991).

ALCOHOL USE AND ABUSE

People's use of alcoholic beverages has a very long history, beginning before the eras of ancient Egypt, Greece, and Rome, when using wine and beer was very common. Its popularity continued through the centuries and around the world—except in cultures that strongly prohibit its use, as in Islamic nations—and eventually reached America in the colonial period. Colonial Americans arrived with

> the drinking habits and attitudes of the places they left behind. Liquor was viewed as a panacea; even the Puritan minister Cotton Mather called it "the good creature of God." By all accounts, these people drank, and drank hard. (Critchlow, 1986, p. 752)

But the Puritans also realized that excessive drinking led to problems for society, so they condemned drunkenness as sinful and enforced laws against it.

Over the next two centuries, attitudes about alcohol changed in many cultures. In the United States, the *temperance* movement began in the 18th century and pressed for total abstinence from alcohol. By the mid-1800s, the use of alcohol had diminished sharply and so had its reputation: many Americans at that time believed alcohol destroyed morals and created crime and degenerate behavior (Critchlow, 1986). These attitudes persisted and helped bring about Prohibition, beginning in 1920, when the production, transport, and sale of alcohol became unlawful. After the repeal of Prohibition, the use of alcohol increased, of course, and attitudes about alcohol softened. Americans today believe alcohol has both good and bad effects. (Go to 🍎.)

WHO DRINKS, AND HOW MUCH?

The casualness of many young people's attitudes today about drinking is reflected in a college yearbook rendition of an alcoholic little Miss Muffet who sat on her tuffet and noticed:

> Along came a spider, and sat down beside her,
> Said she, "It's the D.T.s again."
> (Anonymous, cited in Kett, 1977, p. 261)

Women in the temperance movement were very assertive, and some went to saloons to keep records of who bought drinks.

The "D.T.s" is slang for *delirium tremens*, the withdrawal syndrome commonly seen when alcoholics stop drinking. The symptoms of withdrawal often include intense anxiety, tremors, and frightening hallucinations.

Age, Gender, and Alcohol Use

People's experience with drinking alcoholic beverages is influenced by age and gender in most societies.

ASSESS YOURSELF

What's True about Drinking?

Put a check mark in the space preceding each of the following statements you think is true.

_____ Alcohol is a stimulant that energizes the body.

_____ Having a few drinks enhances people's performance during sex.

_____ After drinking heavily, people usually sober up a lot when they need to, such as to drive home.

_____ Most people drive better after having a few beers to relax them.

_____ Drinking coffee, taking a cold shower, and getting fresh air help someone who is drunk to sober up.

_____ People are more likely to get drunk if they switch drinks, such as from wine to beer, during an evening rather than sticking with the same kind of drink.

_____ Five 12-ounce glasses of beer won't make someone as tipsy as four mixed drinks, such as highballs.

_____ People seldom get drunk if they have a full meal before drinking heavily.

_____ People can cure a hangover by any of several methods.

_____ Most people with drinking problems are either "skid row bums" or over 50 years of age.

Which statements did you think were true? They are wrong—all of the statements are false. (*Source:* Based on *Drinking Myths* distributed by the U.S. Jaycees.)

One reason for gender differences in drinking is that females experience more intoxication than males from the same amount of alcohol. This is because, even when body size is the same, females have smaller blood volume and metabolize alcohol less quickly than males (Tortora & Grabowski, 2000).

Drinking typically begins in adolescence, and sometimes in childhood. In a survey of thousands of students across the United States, high school seniors' answers indicated that 80% had consumed an alcoholic drink at some time in their lives, 51% had had a drink in the last month, 53% had been drunk in the past year, and 31% had drunk "five or more drinks in a row" (binge drinking) in the preceding 2 weeks (Johnston, O'Malley, & Bachman, 2000). Males reported more drinking than females. Nearly 44% of eighth graders reported having had a drink in the past year. Although young people sometimes have alcohol at home with the parents present, such as at special occasions, most teenage drinking occurs in different circumstances. Even when it is illegal for high school and college students to purchase alcohol and to drink without parental supervision, many do anyway. In adulthood, males continue to drink more than females (SAMHSA, 1999). Over 60% of young adult and middle-aged Americans drink, but the prevalence is lower in older groups.

Sociocultural Differences in Using Alcohol

Alcohol use varies widely across cultures around the world: people in Norway drink very little, and the French and Italians consume a great deal of alcohol, mainly wine, which they commonly have with meals (Criqui & Ringel, 1994). In the United States, sharp contrasts in drinking patterns can be made among its many different ethnic groups. The percentage of adults who drink is higher for white Americans than Hispanics, and higher for Hispanics than blacks—the respective percentages are about 55%, 45%, and 40% (SAMHSA, 1999). Drinking prevalence is very high for Native Americans overall, and very low for Asian Americans, especially those of Chinese origin (NIAAA, 1993). Of course, all ethnic groups consist of subgroups, and this is especially important to point out for Native Americans, whose tribes number over 300. Different tribes hold different views toward drinking and show different patterns of alcohol use, with some having very high rates of heavy drinking.

Problem Drinking

In the United States, 113 million individuals age 12 and over drink alcohol at least occasionally (SAMHSA, 1999). Most of these people are light-to-moderate drinkers, consuming fewer than, say, 60 drinks a month. Many people drink much more heavily, but not all of these drinkers meet the criteria for substance abuse we described earlier. One definition of heavy drinking is binge drinking—that is, consuming five or more drinks on a single occasion—on five or more days in a month. Using this definition, over 12 million Americans are heavy drinkers (SAMHSA, 1999). Binge drinking occurs at very high levels on college campuses, especially among fraternity and sorority members (Goldberg, 1998). Of those individuals who develop problems associated with drinking, most—but not all—do so within about 5 years of starting to drink regularly (Sarason & Sarason, 1984).

How many drinkers meet the criteria for substance abuse? Estimates have been made on the basis of the proportion of individuals at a given time who had ever experienced the problem. This statistic, called the *lifetime prevalence rate*, indicates that about 20% of men and 8% of women in the United States become alcohol abusers (Davison & Neale, 1998). People who abuse alcohol drink heavily on a regular basis, are psychologically dependent on it, and suffer social and occupational impairments. These people are called **problem drinkers.** They often get drunk, frequently drink alone, regularly drink during the day or go to work intoxicated, drive under the influence, and so on. Although alcohol abuse is far more common in males than females, it is most likely to develop between the ages of 18 and 29 for both sexes (McCrady, 1988; NIAAA, 1993). More than half of those who abuse alcohol are physically dependent on it, or addicted to it, and are classified as **alcoholics.** These people have developed a very high tolerance for alcohol and often have blackout periods or substantial memory losses; many experience delirium tremens when they stop drinking. Although alcoholics often drink the equivalent of a fifth of whiskey (about 25 ounces) a day, 8 ounces can sometimes be sufficient to produce addiction in humans (Davidson, 1985).

Who abuses alcohol? Many people have an image of the "typical" alcoholic as a scruffy looking, unemployed derelict with no family or friends. But this image is valid for only a small minority of people who abuse alcohol (Mayer, 1983; McCrady, 1988; USDHHS,

Drinking and celebrating often occur together, and this association conveys the message that drinking is fun.

1990). Most problem drinkers are married, living with their families, and employed. Many women who are problem drinkers are homemakers and are married to men who drink heavily. Although individuals from the lower social classes—especially homeless people—are at greater risk than those from higher classes for abusing alcohol, large numbers of problem drinkers come from the higher classes and hold high-status jobs. Problem drinking is very rare in childhood; its prevalence increases in adolescence, rises sharply in early adulthood, and gradually declines across ages thereafter (NIAAA, 1993). Alcohol abuse is a major social problem that affects substantial numbers of people from almost all segments of many societies around the world. (Go to 🍎.)

WHY PEOPLE USE AND ABUSE ALCOHOL

In examining why people use and abuse alcohol, we need to consider why individuals start to drink in the first place. The chief reasons for starting to drink involve social and cultural factors (Bandura, 1986; Jessor, 1984; NIAAA, 1993). Children and adolescents perceive through watching others that drinking is

"fun"—people who are drinking are often boisterous, laughing, and, perhaps, celebrating. These people are typically family members, friends, and celebrities on TV or in movies—all of whom are powerful models. Through social learning processes, such as by watching TV shows and advertisements, children and adolescents acquire *expectancies* about the positive effects of alcohol (Adesso, 1985; Dunn & Goldman, 1998; Grube & Wallack, 1994; Scheier & Botvin, 1997). Teenagers also perceive that drinking is "sociable" and "grown up," two things they generally want very much to be. As a result, when teens are offered a drink by their parents or friends, they are likely to see this as a very positive opportunity.

Adolescents continue drinking partly for the same reasons they started, but these factors intensify, and new ones come into play. For one thing, the role of peers increases. Although teenagers usually begin drinking under their parents' supervision, drinking at home tends to remain at about the same level throughout adolescence, while drinking with peers at parties or in cars increases steadily (NIAAA, 1974). A study of 14- to 17-year-olds found that as teens got older, they reported requiring more alcohol to "get a buzz," and more of them claimed to have friends who

ASSESS YOURSELF
Do You Abuse Alcohol?

Ask yourself the following questions about your drinking:

- Do you usually have more than 14 drinks a week (assume a drink is one mixed drink, 12 ounces of beer, or the equivalent)?
- Do you often think about how or when you are going to drink again?
- Is your job or academic performance suffering by your drinking?
- Has your health declined since you started drinking a lot?

- Do family or friends mention your drinking to you?
- Do you sometimes stop and start drinking to "test" yourself?
- Have you been stopped for drunk driving in the past year?

If you answered "yes" to the first question, consider changing your drinking pattern. If you answered "yes" to any additional questions, consult your college's counseling office for their advice or help. (*Sources*: Based on TSC, 1992; and USDHHS, 1995)

---

had used alcohol often; among the 17-year-olds, one-fourth reported that a close friend had been cited for driving while intoxicated (Schwartz, Hayden, Getson, & DiPaola, 1986). In late adolescence and early adulthood, drinkers drink frequently and almost always socially, with friends at parties or in bars. The social aspect is important in two ways (McCarty, 1985; NIAAA, 1993). First, in social drinking, modeling processes affect behavior—for example, people tend to adjust their drinking rates to match those of their companions. Second, drinking socially creates a subjective norm in individuals that the behavior is appropriate and desirable.

Operant conditioning is another process by which people continue or increase their drinking behavior through either positive or negative reinforcement (Cunningham, 1998; Davidson, 1985; NIAAA, 1993). Individuals may receive *positive* reinforcement for drinking if they like the taste of a drink or the feeling they get from it, or if they think that they succeeded in business deals or social relationships as a consequence of drinking. Having reinforcing experiences with drinking increases individuals' expectancies for desirable consequences when deciding to drink in the future (Adesso, 1985; Stacy, 1997). In the case of *negative* reinforcement—that is, the reduction of an unpleasant situation—people often use alco-

hol to reduce stress. Research has shown that people drink more when they experience higher levels, rather than lower levels, of stress (Baer et al., 1987; Marlatt, Kosturn, & Lang, 1975; Wills, 1986). Also, individuals drink to suppress their negative thoughts about themselves (Hull, Young, & Jouriles, 1986). But the effects of alcohol on people's anxiety and tension are not so simple. Although drinkers report that alcohol reduces tension and improves their mood, it seems to do so only with the first few drinks they consume in a series. After people consume many drinks, their anxiety and depression levels usually increase (Adesso, 1985; Davidson, 1985; Hull & Bond, 1986).

Why can most people drink in moderation, but others become problem drinkers? Part of the answer lies in psychosocial differences between these people. Compared to individuals who do not abuse alcohol, those who do are more likely to perceive fewer negative consequences for drinking (Hansen, Raynor, & Wolkenstein, 1991). They also tend to experience high levels of stress and live in environments that encourage drinking. For instance, adolescents who abuse alcohol are more likely to have experienced a major trauma, such as physical assault, and have family members who drink heavily (Kilpatrick et al., 2000). But a complete answer also includes biological factors

(NIAAA, 1993; Zucker & Gomberg, 1986). Dozens of twin and adoption studies, as well as research with animals, have clearly demonstrated a genetic influence in the development of drinking problems (Ciraulo & Renner, 1991; NIAAA, 1993; Prescott & Kendler, 1999; Schuckit, 1985). Twin studies in general have found that if one member of a same-sex twin pair is alcoholic, the risk of the other member being alcoholic is twice as great if the twins are identical rather than fraternal. Moreover, the results of adoption studies indicate that adopted children of alcoholics are about four times as likely to become problem drinkers than other adoptees, irrespective of the drinking habits of their adoptive parents. But the interplay of genetic and psychosocial factors seems to be very complex, and their relative impact depends on the person's gender and the timing and severity of alcohol abuse. For instance, heredity plays a much stronger role when the abuse begins before age 25 than after (Kranzler & Anton, 1994). (Go to 🔍.)

Focus on Research
How Does Heredity Lead to Alcohol Abuse?

It's one thing to know that heredity affects the development of alcohol abuse—as twin and adoption studies have shown—and another thing to know *how* it does. One way to understand how involves comparing individuals who are genetically at *high risk* for becoming alcoholic with those who are at *low risk*, where risk is determined by whether they have close relatives who abuse alcohol.

In these studies, the high-risk and low-risk subjects are matched on the basis of important variables, such as age, amount of alcohol consumed per week, race, and amount of education. A critical feature of these studies is that the participants are tested during the late adolescent or early adulthood years, *before* any of them actually develops a drinking problem. In the research, these people receive either an alcoholic drink or a placebo and are then tested for their reaction to the drink. The alcoholic drink is a pretty strong one—the equivalent of a few drinks—and the placebo looks, smells, and tastes like the alcoholic drink. The subjects in these studies have been males because menstrual cycles or using birth control pills may affect females' reactions to alcohol.

What kinds of reactions to alcohol have been studied in these people, and what was found? Marc Schuckit (1985) examined the subjective feeling of intoxication, as rated by the participants an hour or more after taking the drink. Of the individuals who had the alcoholic drink, those in the high-risk group reported less intoxication than those in the low-risk group, and both of these groups reported far higher intoxication levels than those who drank the placebo. David Newlin and James Thomson (1991) used a somewhat different approach. They administered alcohol to each high- and low-risk person on three separate days and took physiological measures, such as heart rate and skin conductance (GSR). On a fourth day, the participants got a placebo. The results revealed that the physiological reactions to alcohol were stronger among the high-risk than the low-risk individuals, and these differences increased across the tests with alcohol.

What do these findings suggest regarding how heredity may lead to alcohol abuse? Schuckit's findings suggest that people who are genetically prone to becoming problem drinkers may have an impaired ability to perceive alcohol's effects. As a result, they fail to notice the symptoms of drunkenness early enough to stop drinking. The physiological differences in Newlin and Thomson's study suggest a role of reinforcement: perhaps high-risk individuals find alcohol more rewarding each time they drink, but low-risk people do not. Other research has found that heavy drinkers develop heightened physiological reactions and positive feelings to alcohol-related stimuli, such as seeing or smelling liquor, especially when alcohol is available (Turkkan, McCaul, & Stitzer, 1989). Genetic factors seem to combine with operant and classical conditioning processes in the development of drinking problems.

DRINKING AND HEALTH

Drinking too much is associated with a wide range of health hazards for the drinker and for people he or she may harm. Drinkers can harm others in several ways. Pregnant women who drink more than two drinks a day place their babies at substantial risk for health problems, such as being born with low birth weight or *fetal alcohol syndrome*, which can involve serious cognitive and physical defects (Cooper, 1987; NIAAA, 1993). And drinking lesser amounts during pregnancy has been associated with impaired learning ability in the child. The safest advice to pregnant women is *not to drink at all*.

Drinking also increases the chance that individuals will harm themselves and others through accidents of various types, from unintentionally firing a gun to having a mishap while driving a car, boating, or skiing (Smith & Kraus, 1988). Drunk driving is a major cause of death in the United States: about 28% of the more than 42,000 traffic deaths each year are associated with alcohol use (DeJong & Hingson, 1998; USBC, 1999). Fortunately, the number of motor vehicle deaths and those related to alcohol use have declined greatly since the early 1980s. Consuming alcohol impairs cognitive, perceptual, and motor performance for several hours, particularly the first 2 or 3 hours after drinks are consumed. The degree of impairment individuals experience can vary widely from one person to the next and depends on the rate of drinking and the person's weight. Figure 7–3 gives the *average* impairment for driving—but for some people, one or two drinks may be too many to drive safely.

Many people have misconceptions about the effects of alcohol, believing that drinking on a full stomach prevents drunkenness, or thinking, "I'll be OK as soon as I get behind the wheel," for example. One study demonstrated sober college students' misconceptions by having them estimate the effects of alcohol in a variety of drinking scenarios (Jaccard & Turrisi, 1987). For instance, the students underestimated the impact that alcohol has 2 or 3 hours after drinking; thought that later drinks in a series have less impact than the first couple; and downplayed the effects of beer relative to wine, and wine relative to mixed drinks. Although beer contains a smaller percentage of alcohol than other liquors, many people seem to interpret this to mean "beer does not make you as drunk as hard liquor," which is false. Getting drunk just takes a greater volume of beer than straight hard liquor.

Long-term, heavy drinkers place themselves at risk for developing several health problems (NIAAA, 1993; Piette, Barnett, & Moos, 1998). One of the main risks is for a disease of the liver called *cirrhosis*. Heavy drinking over a long period can cause liver cells to die off and be replaced by permanent, nonfunctional scar tissue. When this scar tissue becomes extensive, the liver is less able to cleanse the blood and regulate its composition. Cirrhosis causes thousands of deaths each year. Heavy drinking also presents other health risks: it has been linked to the development of some forms of *cancer, high blood pressure,* and *heart* and *brain damage* (NIAAA, 1993). The brain damage many alcoholics develop can impair their perceptual and memory functions (Goldman, 1983; Parsons, 1986). These functions may recover gradually after the person stops

Drinks (Two-hour period)
1.2 ozs. 80-Proof Liquor or 12 ozs. Beer

Weight												
100	1	2	3	4	5	6	7	8	9	10	11	12
120	1	2	3	4	5	6	7	8	9	10	11	12
140	1	2	3	4	5	6	7	8	9	10	11	12
160	1	2	3	4	5	6	7	8	9	10	11	12
180	1	2	3	4	5	6	7	8	9	10	11	12
200	1	2	3	4	5	6	7	8	9	10	11	12
220	1	2	3	4	5	6	7	8	9	10	11	12
240	1	2	3	4	5	6	7	8	9	10	11	12

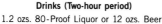

BE CAREFUL DRIVING   DRIVING IMPAIRED   DO NOT DRIVE
BAC TO .05%   .05%–.09%   .10% & UP
Source: NHTSA

Figure 7–3 Chart developed by the National Highway Traffic Safety Administration (NHTSA) showing the *average* effects of blood alcohol concentration (BAC) on driving. Although alcohol impairment varies from one person to the next, three drinks (the equivalent of three 12-ounce bottles of beer) in a 2-hour period will make most adults' driving unsafe.

drinking, but some impairments may persist for years or never disappear. As you might expect, long-term heavy drinkers have higher death rates than do other people (Bullock, Reed, & Grant, 1992; Thun et al., 1997). But if they quit, their mortality risk declines greatly in several years.

Some people believe that drinking in moderation—having, say, a drink or two each day—is *good* for their health, and they may be right. Long-term prospective studies of many thousands of people have found that individuals who drink light or moderate amounts of alcohol, especially wine, each month have lower morbidity and mortality rates than those who drink heavily or who do not drink at all (Friedman & Kimball, 1986; Grønbæk et al., 2000; Rimm et al., 1991; Sacco et al., 1999; Thun et al., 1997). Does moderate drinking cause better health? We cannot be sure because of the quasi-experimental nature of these studies. If it does, the greatest benefit may be in reducing coronary heart disease and stroke. Although the reason drinking may protect people from cardiovascular disease is not yet clear, there is evidence supporting two possibilities. First, alcohol affects the body's response to stress, reducing cardiovascular and endocrine (for example, catecholamine production) reactions (Levenson, 1986). Second, substances in alcoholic beverages, particularly wine, seem to improve blood cholesterol levels (Criqui & Ringel, 1994; Facchini, Chen, & Reaven, 1994; Gaziano et al., 1993; Stein et al., 1999). Still, not enough is known yet about the effects of alcohol to recommend its light use to reduce cardiovascular risk.

PREVENTING ALCOHOL ABUSE

Individuals and agencies concerned with public health around the world have tried many different approaches to prevent alcohol abuse. In the United States since the repeal of Prohibition in 1933, the most common methods have been of three types: public policy and legal approaches, health promotion and education, and early intervention approaches.

Public policy and legal approaches for preventing alcohol abuse are designed to reduce per-capita consumption of alcohol by creating barriers to drinking (Ashley & Rankin, 1988; NIAAA, 1993). These approaches include limiting the number of outlets where alcoholic beverages can be bought and restricting the times when they are on sale. These two methods do not seem to be very effective in reducing drinking. A more effective method is to prohibit underage individuals from buying or consuming alcohol. This method reduces alcohol consumption and related automobile accidents among individuals in the late adolescent and early adulthood years. One of the most effective methods for reducing per-capita alcohol consumption and preventing alcohol-related health problems is to increase the price of alcoholic beverages through taxation.

Health promotion and education approaches for preventing alcohol abuse provide information and training to help people avoid drinking heavily. Most of these programs have been directed at children and adolescents in schools and colleges. Unfortunately, the great majority of programs introduced before the late 1970s either were poorly conceived or did not provide a means for evaluating their success (Engstrom, 1984; Nathan, 1985; Pandina, 1986). More recent programs have demonstrated that *social influence* methods, like those we considered for preventing smoking, can reduce the amount of drinking among adolescents, and the effects may last 2 or 3 years (Kivlahan et al., 1990; Klepp, Kelder, & Perry, 1995; NIAAA, 1993).

Early intervention approaches try to identify people at high risk for alcohol abuse and then provide information to help reverse the individual's pattern of drinking (Ashley & Rankin, 1988; Engstrom, 1984). High-risk drinkers are usually identified on the basis of current drinking patterns or problems, such as being charged with drunk driving. For drunk drivers, a variety of interventions have yielded disappointing results. These efforts have been successful *only* with people who are relatively *light* drinkers; heavy drinkers often get *worse* after receiving an intervention (McGuire, 1982). But the picture is brighter for early interventions with most other people who are at high risk for abusing alcohol. If drinking problems are detected early, successful interventions may simply involve providing information and advice, and the individuals may be able to reduce their drinking to a pattern of moderation (Ashley & Rankin, 1988; NIAAA, 1993). Approaches that are more structured can also be used. For instance, individuals who responded to advertisements for help in controlling drinking received a computer software program that provided an interactive intervention that is like the social influence and life skills training approaches (Hester & Delaney, 1997). The intervention produced a substantial reduction in drinking that was maintained at a follow-up assessment 12 months later.

Early intervention approaches have been successful with high-risk drinkers identified at educational institutions, in medical settings, and at worksites. In college, for example, researchers used a questionnaire to identify high-risk drinkers among incoming freshmen and offered them a brief counseling intervention (Marlatt et al., 1998). Although the high-risk drinkers who received the intervention continued to drink more than other incoming freshmen, they showed reductions in drinking over the next 2 years. In medical settings, physicians identified high-risk drinkers by having patients fill out a health survey that included questions on drinking; some of these patients received information and advice on reducing their drinking (Fleming et al., 2000). Compared with high-risk drinkers who did not get the intervention, those who got the intervention incurred lower expenses for health care and for legal and motor vehicle events over the next year. In worksites, many employers and unions provide *employee assistance programs* (EAPs) to help individuals who have personal problems, such as with drinking or stress (USDHHS, 1990). EAPs can be helpful, but they usually don't identify high-risk drinkers until the problem is severe, and workers are not likely to use them at all if they worry that counselors will leak information back to their bosses. The worksite should be a good place for preventing alcohol abuse because most individuals who abuse alcohol have jobs, and drinking is often related to stresses on the job (Mayer, 1983). Worksite wellness programs should try to include specific efforts to reduce employee drinking.

TREATMENTS FOR ALCOHOL ABUSE

In psychology and medicine, the term *spontaneous remission* refers to the disappearance of symptoms or problems without the benefit of formal treatment. Many people who abuse alcohol stop or markedly reduce their drinking on their own, without treatment. What proportion of people who abuse alcohol recover on their own? The best estimates available are based on data from a small number of studies of treatment effectiveness in which some problem drinkers were randomly assigned to control groups that received no treatment. Using the data on the control subjects, William Miller and Reid Hester (1980) calculated that spontaneous remission—stopping or markedly

reducing drinking—occurs in about 19% of alcohol abuse cases. Compared with drinkers who do not quit on their own, those who do generally report having had social support from a spouse and changed the way they weighed the pros and cons of drinking—for example, realizing "I was sick and tired of it, really weary of it" (Sobel, Sobel, Toneatto, & Leo, 1993).

Alcohol abusers who quit drinking on their own and those who seek treatment often have an important thing in common: they want to change. We saw in Chapter 6 that the *stages of change model* is useful in describing people's readiness to modify health-related behaviors. A critical transition occurs when the person's stage of readiness moves from *contemplation*, or thinking about changing, to *preparation* and *action*. According to psychologist William Miller (1989a), this transition is like a door that opens for a period of time and closes if the alcohol abuser doesn't use it in that time; using it can be encouraged in several ways, such as:

- Giving the person clear advice about why and how to change.

- Removing important barriers for change.

- Introducing external consequences, such as rewards for changing or real threats (for example, of being fired) if no change occurs.

- Offering help and showing a helping attitude.

Family members, friends, coworkers, physicians, or therapists can use these and other approaches to increase the person's motivation to change. Family members who receive training in motivational methods can be very successful in getting problem drinkers to start therapy (Miller, Meyers, & Tonigan, 1999).

Because of the physical dependence alcoholics have when they enter treatment, the first step in their recovery is **detoxification**—the drying out process of getting an addicted person safely through the period of withdrawal from a substance. This is an essential step for all addicted drinkers before treatment can proceed. Because withdrawal symptoms can be very severe, sometimes even causing death, detoxification often takes place in hospitals under medical supervision, using medication to control the symptoms (Ciraulo & Renner, 1991; Miller & Hester, 1985). Improved assessment procedures and detoxification methods have reduced the need for direct medical supervision during alcohol withdrawal today. It is now possible to identify those alcoholics who are likely to need medical supervision and those who are not. About half of alcoholics who seek treatment can undergo detoxification at home if they receive careful assistance and support from trained individuals.

Where Should Treatment Occur, and What Should Be the Goals and Criteria for Success?

In designing a treatment program, one of the many decisions the treatment team needs to make is whether it should be carried out in a residential setting or on an outpatient basis. Is residential treatment more effective than nonresidential treatment? For most problem drinkers it is not, but strongly addicted drinkers appear to benefit more from inpatient than outpatient care (Finney & Moos, 1997; NIAAA, 1993; Rychtarik et al., 2000). In the United States, most problem drinkers who receive treatment do so as outpatients (USBC, 1999).

Ideally, treatment should "cure" the person's drinking problem forever, but at what point can the team expect that their assessments of the success of treatment are likely to reflect durable effects? On this issue, there is considerable agreement among researchers: They generally recommend and use a minimum follow-up interval of 12 to 18 months to determine the success of treatment (Emrick & Hansen, 1983; Nathan, 1986). Many programs today also attempt to verify self-reports of drinking behavior through other sources—through reports by the ex-drinker's spouse or through blood or breath tests, for instance—and measure other outcomes of treatment, such as physical health, employment status, and legal problems encountered.

Another decision the treatment team needs to make is whether the program should aim to have all of its problem drinkers become *permanently abstinent* or whether some can return gradually to *controlled drinking*. This distinction generated a bitter controversy in the 1980s (Marlatt, 1983; Peele, 1984). Research findings indicated to some researchers that some problem drinkers—including alcoholics—can learn to drink in moderation after first becoming abstinent, but other researchers strongly challenged this view. Although the controversy is not completely resolved, it does appear that *some* problem drinkers can learn through treatment to drink in moderation (Miller & Hester,

1980; Peele, 1984). Problem drinkers who have the best prospects for controlled drinking:

- Are relatively young.
- Are socially stable, that is, married or employed.
- Have had a relatively brief history of alcohol abuse.
- Have *not* suffered severe withdrawal symptoms while becoming abstinent.
- Prefer trying to drink in moderation, and have *not* made a personal commitment to abstinence as a goal.

In other words, the less severe the drinking problem, the better the chances of succeeding in controlled drinking. What's more, long-term alcoholics who choose abstinence as their goal have fewer drinking problems at 1-year follow-up than those who choose controlled drinking (Hodgins, Leigh, Milne, & Gerrish, 1997). For long-term alcoholics to pursue a goal of controlled drinking is unrealistic and probably not in their best interests (Nathan, 1986; Sandberg & Marlatt, 1991).

Alcoholics Anonymous

Alcoholics Anonymous (AA) is a widely known self-help program that was founded in the 1930s by people with drinking problems (Bean-Bayog, 1991; McCrady & Irvine, 1989). The program now has thousands of chapters throughout the United States and around the world and has set up organizations to help alcoholics' families, such as *Alateen* for their adolescent children and *Al-Anon* for adults in the family. The AA philosophy includes two basic views. First, people who abuse alcohol are alcoholics and remain alcoholics for life, even if they never take another drink. Second, taking one drink after becoming abstinent can be enough to set off an alcoholic binge and, therefore, must be avoided. As a result, AA is committed to the goal of permanent and total abstinence, and their approach is aimed at helping their members resist even one drink.

Because the AA philosophy has its roots in evangelical Protestantism, the program emphasizes the individual's needs for spiritual awakening, public confession, and contrition (McCrady & Irvine, 1989; Peele, 1984). This philosophy can be seen in the Twelve Steps AA uses to help drinkers quit—for example, one step is, "Admitted to God, to ourselves, and to another human being the exact nature of our wrongs." Members attend frequent AA meetings, which use the Twelve Steps to promote frank discussions about the members' experiences with alcohol and difficulties resisting drinking. An important feature of the AA approach is that its members develop friendships with other ex-drinkers and get encouragement from each other and from knowing individuals who have succeeded.

Does AA work, and is it more effective than other approaches for helping drinkers quit? AA claims a very high rate of success: for example, one AA report claimed that 75% of those "who really tried" became abstinent (Miller & Hester, 1980). But AA's overall effectiveness is actually unknown because its membership is anonymous and the organization does not keep systematic information about people who attend. One way to compare the AA program against other approaches would be to assign a pool of problem drinkers to different programs and a control group randomly, as one experiment did (Brandsma, Maultsby, & Welsh, 1980). The courts had referred most of the participants because of their drinking problems. The results revealed greater improvement among those who received treatment than those in a control group, and people in the AA program showed somewhat less improvement than those in other treatments. Two other studies compared the success of different methods conducted by professional therapists and found that treatments using the AA approach produced as much improvement as other treatments (Ouimette, Finney, & Moos, 1997; PMRG, 1998). Other studies of the effectiveness of AA have produced mixed findings (McCrady & Irvine, 1989). It may be that AA is the best approach for certain types of problem drinkers, particularly those who need an authoritarian structure and the intense social support of other problem drinkers (Miller & Hester, 1980). And AA is being used more and more as an approach to prevent relapse after other forms of treatment (NIAAA, 1993).

Insight Therapy

Many approaches to psychotherapy are designed to help the person achieve *insight*—an understanding of the roots of his or her problem. *Insight therapy* focuses on discovering these roots, especially when they involve underlying motivations. Although most types of psychotherapy try to help people understand why problem behaviors occur, insight, and not behavior change, is the main focus of insight therapy. This approach assumes that awareness of motivations will

lead to greater control of behaviors and emotions (Davison & Neale, 1998). Insight therapy approaches generally involve some form of counseling and share certain goals for treating people with drinking problems. These goals include helping drinkers accept that they need help, believe that they are worthwhile individuals, understand the factors that led them to drink heavily, and cope effectively with these factors. Insight therapy can be conducted with individual clients or with groups, and it appears to be modestly effective in treating drinking problems (Miller & Hester, 1980).

Behavioral and Cognitive Methods

Drinking excessively and smoking cigarettes heavily have a great deal in common—these behaviors can lead to addiction, and they are difficult to quit. As a result, variations of the methods we considered in the section on treatment for stopping smoking may apply to stopping drinking, too. Behavioral and cognitive methods are among the most effective approaches for treating problem drinking (Finney & Moos, 1997).

Aversion strategies—using unpleasant stimuli to discourage behavior—have been applied as treatments for alcohol abuse. One aversion strategy involves pairing drinking with electric shock, but this method has not been very successful in stopping people's problem drinking (Miller & Hester, 1980). A much more effective aversion strategy has been to have the person take an **emetic drug,** such as *emetine,* that induces nausea when alcohol is consumed. In a typical half-hour session, the person first receives an injection of emetine and then repeatedly drinks an alcoholic beverage, each time quickly becoming nauseated and vomiting (Miller & Hester, 1980). The person undergoes several of these sessions, typically as an inpatient in a hospital, and then receives booster sessions periodically after discharge. A study of hundreds of problem drinkers who received emetine therapy revealed that 63% of the men and women remained abstinent during the 12 months after treatment, and half of these individuals remained abstinent for the next 2 years (Wiens & Menustik, 1983). Other studies using emetine therapy have also demonstrated high rates of success (Miller & Hester, 1980).

Because *self-management strategies* are useful in helping people stop smoking, you might expect them to aid in quitting drinking—and they do (Hester & Miller, 1989; Lang & Marlatt, 1982). Successful treatment programs have used:

- Self-monitoring to help problem drinkers determine the situations that elicit and maintain drinking behavior.

- Stimulus control procedures to change or eliminate environmental cues that promote drinking, for example, by socializing with people who don't drink.

- Response substitution, such as finding someone to talk to instead of drinking when upset.

- Behavioral contracting to structure a set of rewards for abstinence and punishment for drinking. In addition, using a lottery with a variety of prizes (from $1 gift certificates to small TV sets) for passing breath tests for abstaining from alcohol greatly increases the likelihood that drinkers will stay in treatment and be abstinent by the end of the program (Petry, Martin, Cooney, & Kranzler, 2000).

The problem drinker's family can play an important role in self-management. Research has found that training family members, such as the alcoholic's spouse, in these strategies enables them to help rather than undermine the drinker's self-management efforts (Sisson & Azrin, 1986).

Two other methods seem to be useful in helping people quit drinking. One method involves training problem drinkers in *stress management* techniques (Stockwell & Town, 1989). This approach has value because feelings of anxiety and tension increase people's drinking behavior. The other method, called *cue exposure*, tries to counteract the classical conditioning that occurs with long-term drug use: stimuli associated with drinking, such as seeing the liquor bottle, gain the ability to produce internal conditioned responses like those that happen when the person is actually drinking. To reduce these internal reactions to conditioned stimuli, therapists expose problem drinkers repeatedly to alcohol-related stimuli, such as holding a beer can, while not allowing them to drink. This approach has had some success by itself and in combination with other behavioral methods (Blakey & Baker, 1980; Drummond & Glautier, 1994; Monti et al., 1993).

Chemical Therapies

Drugs are sometimes prescribed as a component of treatment for alcohol abuse. One approach uses an emetic drug called *disulfiram* (brand name Antabuse) that the person needs to take each day orally (Ciraulo

& Renner, 1991; Schuckit 1996). In addition to producing nausea if the person drinks, it has some important side effects that can preclude its use—it causes drowsiness, raises blood pressure, and has physiological effects that make it inappropriate for people with heart and liver diseases. For those who can use it, disulfiram can be an effective therapy, but getting them to take the drug consistently is often a problem. Several other chemicals appear promising for treating alcohol abuse, but their utility has not been sufficiently demonstrated (Schuckit, 1996).

Treatment Success and the Relapse Problem

Many different techniques can be effective in helping people overcome drinking problems. Which ones should be used? One consideration is cost: some of the most effective methods are among the least expensive to implement (Finney & Moos, 1997). Another concern is to *match* the techniques with the needs of the person (Miller, 1989b). Doing this requires two steps: (1) assessing the person's drinking problem, readiness to change, and beliefs and personality; and (2) negotiating with the person the goals of treatment and the amount and type of help to use. Although the idea of matching is intuitively reasonable, studies of treatment programs have yielded little evidence that matching improves success in reducing drinking (Finney & Moos, 1997; PMRG, 1998).

Who succeeds when treated for alcohol abuse? Generally speaking, problem drinkers who function the best at the start of treatment are the most likely ones to succeed (Nathan, 1986). Thus,

> high socioeconomic status, a stable marriage or relationship, a steady and supportive employment milieu, higher education (12 years or more), a stable residential setting, and no criminal record (or few convictions) have all been related to a good prognosis irrespective of the type of treatment employed. (Caddy & Block, 1985, p. 353)

But many people drop out of treatment for alcohol abuse—and of those who complete a program, less than a majority maintain their improvement in drinking behavior beyond the first year or so (Nathan, 1986).

The problem of *relapse* is at least as severe in efforts to stop drinking as it is in quitting smoking. Many of the more successful treatment approaches for alcohol abuse produce very high rates of success initially, but these rates decline sharply by the end of the first year and again during the next 2 years (Nathan, 1986). Studies of problem drinkers who relapsed have found that the circumstances preceding the relapse generally involve *negative emotional states*, such as depression or anxiety; *interpersonal conflict*, such as arguments with family members or coworkers; and *social pressure* to drink (Abrams et al., 1986; Hodgins, el-Guebaly, & Armstrong, 1995; Sandberg & Marlatt, 1991). Alcoholics often use these circumstances to justify a lapse, saying for instance, "With all these hassles, I *deserve* a couple of drinks." One way to help prevent relapses involves training drinkers to cope with lapses, maintain self-efficacy, and resist the urge to return to drinking in highly tempting situations, such as in a restaurant with friends who have drinks (Chaney, 1989; Chaney, O'Leary, & Marlatt, 1978; Irvin, Bowers, Dunn, & Wang, 1999). In addition, social support systems, like those in AA programs, are likely to help ex-drinkers avoid relapse (Colletti & Brownell, 1983). Discovering effective methods of preventing relapse among problem drinkers has become a major focus of research.

DRUG USE AND ABUSE

The word "drug" can refer to a wide variety of substances, including prescription and nonprescription medicine, that people may take into their bodies. We will limit the term *drug* to mean psychoactive substances other than nicotine and alcohol that can cause physical or psychological dependence. Like smoking and drinking, the use of drugs has a long history—for example, the Chinese evidently used marijuana 27 centuries B.C. In the United States, addiction to narcotics was widespread among people of all ages in the 19th century. Many "patent medicines" in those days contained opium and were sold without government regulation. As a result, large numbers of people became addicted at early ages (Kett, 1977). Laws were enacted in the early 1900s against the use of narcotics in America. (Go to ⚲.)

WHO USES DRUGS, AND WHY?

Drug use has become a serious problem in many countries of the world, especially in North America and Europe. Some individuals and segments of society are more likely than others to use drugs.

Age, Gender, and Sociocultural Differences in Drug Use

We have seen that smoking and drinking are more likely to begin in adolescence than at any other time in the life span. This developmental pattern is true for using most drugs, too. Two types of drugs that are exceptions to this pattern are tranquilizers and barbiturates: using these drugs commonly begins in adulthood, often with prescriptions from physicians (AMA, 1989; Ciraulo & Shader, 1991; Davison & Neale, 1998).

One of the most popular drugs in the United States is marijuana. Its use often begins by the eighth grade, and individuals who eventually try it are likely to do so before they reach the 11th grade (Johnston, O'Malley, & Bachman, 2000). Nearly half of American teenagers try it before they graduate high school. Teenagers' use of most other drugs tends to begin somewhat later and is much less prevalent—for instance, about 9% try cocaine before graduation. Drug use in the United States has fluctuated over time and has been decreasing in recent years. These changes have coincided with adolescents' beliefs about whether drugs are harmful, rather than changes in drug availability (Johnston, O'Malley, & Bachman, 2000). Drug use is far more prevalent in males than females at virtually all adolescent and adult ages and for almost all drug types, but the prevalence of drug use by different American ethnic groups varies with age and drug type (NCHS, 2000). For example, the prevalence of marijuana use by whites, blacks, and Hispanics is similar in the teen-age years, but is higher among whites and blacks than Hispanics in early adulthood. The prevalence of cocaine use is higher among whites and Hispanics than blacks in the teen-age years, but the gap narrows sharply in early adulthood.

Many individuals engage in *polysubstance abuse*, using more than one substance. Does using one substance lead to using another? The likelihood that individuals will progress from a less serious drug, such as marijuana, to a more serious drug, such as cocaine, is related to how heavily the earlier drug was used (Kandel & Faust, 1975; Newcomb & Bentler, 1986). Heavy users of a less serious drug are more likely to begin using more serious drugs than light users are. Similarly, smoking cigarettes and using alcohol has

HIGHLIGHT ON ISSUES
Types and Effects of Drugs

"Oh, I feel so light, like a feather," said Dolores, after taking several hits from a "joint." That lightness of feeling is a common effect people get from smoking a marijuana cigarette. Each drug has its own set of general psychological and physiological effects (Ciraulo & Shader, 1991; NCADI, 2000; Schuster & Kilbey, 1992). Some drugs are highly addictive, and others have little potential for producing physical dependence. Drugs are usually classified into four categories: stimulants, depressants, hallucinogens, and narcotics.

Stimulants are chemicals that produce physiological and psychological arousal, keeping the user awake and making the world seem to race by. This category of drugs includes *amphetamines, caffeine,* and *cocaine,* which can be inhaled, injected, or smoked ("crack"). Chronic use of stimulants can produce mental confusion, exhaustion, and weight loss—and can lead to psychological dependence. Physical dependence on amphetamines, cocaine, or caffeine can develop; the withdrawal symptoms often are subtle, but are still very influential on behavior.

Depressants decrease arousal and increase relaxation. People use these drugs to reduce anxiety and induce sleep. Depressants include various *tranquilizers* (such as Valium) and *barbiturates,* which are commonly called "downers." Excessive and chronic use of depressants interferes with motor and emotional stability and produces psychological dependence. Addiction can develop with long-term use of depressants and can occur rapidly for barbiturates.

Hallucinogens produce perceptual distortions, such as when the body or mind feels light. The most commonly used drug of this type is *marijuana,* which people use for the relaxation and intoxication it causes. Other hallucinogens, such as *mescaline,* LSD (lysergic acid diethylamide), and PCP (phencyclidine), often produce a feeling of exhilaration. Hallucinogens have a relatively low potential for causing physical dependence, but chronic use of these drugs can lead to psychological dependence.

Narcotics or *opiates* are sedatives that relieve pain. In many people, but not all, they produce a euphoric and relaxed feeling. The narcotics include *morphine, codeine,* and *heroin.* These drugs, especially heroin, generally cause intense physical *and* psychological dependence when used in large doses continually.

The effects of drugs can vary. The same dose of a drug may produce quite different reactions in different people and in the same person on different occasions (Bardo & Risner, 1985). Why? Physiological processes, such as metabolism and absorption by tissues, vary from one person to the next and within each individual over time. Partly because very young people and the elderly have lower rates of metabolism than others do, they tend to experience relatively strong reactions to drugs. Stress can also influence the effects of a drug. Being under stress causes physiological changes that may increase a drug's impact.

been linked to subsequent drug use (Petraitis et al., 1998).

Why Adolescents Use Drugs

Why do teens try marijuana and other drugs? They do so for many of the same reasons they start to drink or smoke cigarettes (Hansen et al., 1987; Stein, Newcomb, & Bentler, 1987). Two of the strongest factors in determining initial and early stages of drug use are availability and social learning. Teenagers see peers and important adults, such as parents and

celebrities, model behaviors and attitudes that promote drug use. Studies have shown that adolescents are more likely to use marijuana and other drugs if their parents and friends use mood-altering substances, such as alcohol and marijuana (Petraitis et al, 1998; Stein, Newcomb, & Bentler, 1987). Teenagers' marijuana use seems to be affected more by their friends' than their parents' substance use, and the first introduction of most youths to marijuana is through a friend (Kandel, 1974).

After people start using drugs, they tend to continue if they like the experience—that is, if the drug makes them "feel good" or helps them feel *better* than they felt before taking it (Barrett, 1985). Many people claim that taking drugs reduces their anxiety and tension. In other words, drugs have reinforcing effects. Then, with continued use, drug-related stimuli become conditioned to the drug's effects and can elicit physiological reactions like those the drug itself produces (Caggiula et al., 1992; Childress, 1996). Because people often use drugs in the presence of friends and other peers, social pressure and encouragement also tend to maintain and increase drug use.

Why do some individuals progress from drug use to *drug abuse*? Personality traits seem to be involved. Compared to individuals who use drugs occasionally, those who go on to abuse drugs tend to be *more* rebellious, impulsive, accepting of illegal behavior, and oriented toward sensation seeking; and they tend to be *less* socially conforming and less committed to a religion (Brook, Whiteman, Gordon, & Cohen, 1986; Cox, 1985; Newcomb, Maddahian, & Bentler, 1986; Stein, Newcomb, & Bentler, 1987).

DRUG USE AND HEALTH

The effects of drug use and abuse on people's health are not as well documented as those of drinking and cigarette smoking. This is because drug use did not become widespread until the 1960s, it is still much less prevalent than drinking and smoking, and many drug users are unwilling to admit to researchers that they use drugs—a criminal offense—for fear of being prosecuted. Nevertheless, some health effects are known. For example, drugs taken by women during pregnancy cross the placenta and may harm the fetus; and babies born to addicted mothers are likely to be addicted, too (Cook, Petersen, & Moore, 1990). Also, smoking marijuana damages the user's lungs (Bloom et al., 1987). Furthermore, drug use is implicated in many automobile accidents each year (Jessor, 1984).

The health effects of cocaine are becoming increasingly clear, particularly with regard to the cardiovascular system (Mittleman et al., 1999; Rowbotham & Lowenstein, 1990). Taking cocaine causes the person's blood vessels to constrict, heart rate to speed up, and blood pressure to increase suddenly. It can also trigger cardiac arrhythmia. These events can cause a stroke or myocardial infarction and can lead to death. Cocaine also produces many other health problems. For example, the more people use it in their mid-20s, the more

likely they will have neurological symptoms and poor general health 10 years later (Chen, Scheier, & Kandel, 1996). What's more, poor health leads to continued cocaine use.

PREVENTING AND STOPPING DRUG ABUSE

Two public health approaches can be used to prevent teenage drug abuse. One way is directed at children and adolescents through educational programs and campaigns in the schools and mass media. Before the 1980s, these efforts presented mainly information about the negative consequences of drug use and were not very successful (Des Jarlais, Friedman, Casriel, & Kott, 1987). Prevention today tends to focus

A demonstration against the use of drugs.

on teaching children and adolescents how to resist starting to use drugs, using programs based on the *social influence* and *life skills training* methods we considered in preventing smoking. These programs have effectively reduced the likelihood of using drugs, such as marijuana, in many individuals (Botvin & Wills, 1985; Chou et al., 1998). The second approach is directed at getting the parents more actively involved in supervising their children. A prospective study showed that children of parents who provide little monitoring, rules, and supervision are four times more likely to try drugs in the future than children with actively involved parents (Chilcoat, Dishion, & Anthony, 1995). An approach that does *not* seem to work is the widely publicized Project DARE, in which police officers lead sessions in school to prevent substance use (Lynam et al., 1999).

Drug abuse involves entrenched behaviors that are difficult to stop, particularly if physical dependence has developed. Most of the approaches that have been tried for treating drug abuse are similar to those we considered for stopping drinking. The outcomes of research on treating drug abuse seem to point to two conclusions (Maude-Griffin et al., 1998; Schuster & Kilbey, 1992; Tims, Fletcher, & Hubbard, 1991). First, the more effective treatments include behavioral and cognitive methods, such as self-management techniques. For example, studies have found that reinforcing abstinence increases the success of cocaine treatments (Higgins et al., 2000; Silverman et al., 1998). Second, for cases of narcotic addiction, effective treatment programs also use chemical agents to block the euphoric effects of heroin, morphine, or codeine. The most widely used agent is called **methadone,** a chemical that has physiological effects that are similar to those of opiates. However, methadone does not produce euphoria and, when taken regularly, it prevents euphoria from occurring if the person then takes an opiate (O'Brien, 1996). Methadone is usually taken orally.

Having a narcotics addict take methadone—or a similar agent, *levoalpha acetylmethadyl* (LAAM)—regularly as a substitute for the opiate is called *methadone maintenance*. Research has shown that treatment combining methadone and psychological treatment is far more effective than methadone alone (McClellan et al., 1993).

Although methadone maintenance can be very effective in reducing the addict's craving for opiates, preventing withdrawal symptoms, and enabling the person to function in society, it also has some drawbacks (Callahan, 1980; Sarason & Sarason, 1984). For one thing, methadone is a form of narcotic, too—and the person can become physically dependent on it. Taking methadone may also lead to weight gain and increased alcohol use, and sometimes produces involuntary muscle jerking. One other problem with methadone is that it does not stop addicts from using other drugs, such as cocaine, which is a nonnarcotic. But this problem seems to have been solved: programs often stipulate that before addicts get their next dose of methadone, they must submit to a urine test, which must show no evidence of drug taking. This approach is very effective in stopping methadone users from using nonnarcotic drugs (Callahan, 1980).

In our discussions of stopping smoking and drinking, we noted that relapse is a persistent and important problem. It is also a problem in stopping drug abuse, such as of marijuana (Stephens, Roffman, & Simpson, 1994). Methadone maintenance reduces relapse rates for ex-opiate users. To prevent people's relapse for tobacco, alcohol, and drug use, programs for quitting will need to enhance substance users' motivation, teach them critical skills for avoiding relapse, and have an aftercare program to monitor their behavior, provide helpful social support, and help them adjust to lifestyle changes (Brownell, Marlatt, Lichtenstein, & Wilson, 1986; Sandberg & Marlatt, 1991).

SUMMARY

People's use of tobacco, alcohol, or drugs can affect their health, particularly if the substance is abused. Addiction is a condition in which individuals have become psychologically and physically dependent on the substance.

People who are physically dependent on a substance have developed a tolerance for it and suffer withdrawal symptoms when they abruptly stop using it. Substance abuse exists when a person has shown a clear pattern of pathological use for at least a month with resulting problems in social and occupational functioning.

Smoking tobacco is a worldwide problem. In the United States it became popular after the early 1900s, reached its greatest popularity in the mid-1960s, and then declined after the United States Surgeon General released a report describing its harmful health effects. Most people who become cigarette smokers begin the habit in adolescence. Although a larger percentage of men than women smoke, this gap has decreased in recent years. Americans are more likely to smoke if they are from the lower rather than the higher social classes. Psychosocial factors influence whether individuals will start to smoke.

Whether people go on to smoke on a regular basis is determined by biopsychosocial factors. The likelihood of individuals becoming regular smokers increases if they have peer and adult models of smoking, experience peer pressure to smoke, and find that smoking helps them relax and have less tension. Cigarette smoke contains tars, carbon monoxide, and nicotine, a chemical that appears to produce physical dependence. Two theories describe why established smokers continue to smoke: (1) the nicotine regulation model proposes that they smoke to maintain a certain level of nicotine in their bodies and avoid withdrawal; and (2) the biobehavioral model proposes that they smoke to regulate their performance and mood. Research has shown that heredity also plays a role in people's becoming smokers. Smoking reduces the person's life expectancy and increases the risk of lung cancer, other cancers, cardiovascular disease, and chronic obstructive pulmonary disease. Breathing secondhand smoke is called passive smoking and is also harmful to one's health.

Programs to prevent smoking attempt to address relevant psychosocial factors by providing information and teaching important social skills. These programs teach children and adolescents about the immediate and long-term consequences of smoking, the ways modeling and peer pressure influence their tendency to smoke, and the ways they can resist these forces. Some programs also teach general social, cognitive, and coping skills. Once people become regular smokers, many are able to quit on their own, but many others are not, especially if they smoke heavily. For those who have trouble stopping, therapists use several approaches that help. These approaches include having the smoker take nicotine directly, using aversion strategies, and having the smoker learn and apply self-management strategies, such as self-monitoring and behavioral contracting. Combining effective methods in a multidimensional approach improves treatment success. Many people who quit eventually return to smoking. Relapse can result if the person experiences high levels of stress, little helpful social support, feelings of low self-efficacy, or an increase in body weight.

Alcohol use varies widely across cultures and time periods. Americans drank alcohol at extremely high rates prior to the mid-1800s, when the temperance movement changed people's views and eventually led to Prohibition. After the repeal of Prohibition, alcohol use began to increase gradually. Most American adults drink at least occasionally. Many of those who drink abuse alcohol and are classified as problem drinkers, and those who are physically dependent on alcohol are classified as alcoholics. People who are addicted to alcohol suffer withdrawal symptoms when they quit drinking. Psychosocial factors—such as modeling, social pressure, and reinforcement—have a very powerful influence on drinking. Heredity plays an important role in the development of alcohol abuse.

Heavy drinking is related to a variety of health problems, including fetal alcohol syndrome in babies of drinking mothers, automobile accidents, and such diseases as cirrhosis of the liver, cancer, high blood pressure, and brain damage. The most promising programs for preventing alcohol abuse involve public policy and legal approaches, health promotion and education approaches, and early intervention approaches. For people who become problem drinkers, the first step in their recovery is detoxification. Treatment approaches for stopping drinking include Alcoholics Anonymous, insight therapy, a variety of behavioral and cognitive methods, and using emetic drugs.

Many people use and abuse drugs that can be classified as stimulants, depressants, hallucinogens, and narcotics. Drugs differ in their potential for producing physical and psychological dependence. Drug abuse is related to a number of psychosocial factors, such as modeling, social pressure, reinforcement, and personality traits. The health effects of drug use and abuse are becoming increasingly clear. For example, using cocaine produces cardiovascular reactions that can cause a potentially fatal myocardial infarction. Prevention efforts today focus on social influence methods, like those used in preventing smoking and drinking. The most effective programs for treating drug abuse involve behavioral and cognitive methods; treatments for narcotic addiction often use drugs, such as methadone, that block the euphoric effects of opiates. Relapse is a critical problem in treatment programs for all of the substances discussed in this chapter.

KEY TERMS

addiction
physical dependence
tolerance
withdrawal
psychological dependence
substance abuse

carbon monoxide
tars
nicotine
nicotine regulation model
biobehavioral model
passive smoking

aversion strategies
self-management
    strategies
problem drinkers
alcoholics
detoxification

emetic drug
stimulants
depressants
hallucinogens
narcotics
methadone

8

IMPROVING NUTRITION, WEIGHT CONTROL AND DIET, EXERCISE, AND SAFETY

PROLOGUE

"Let's share something with each other," said the health expert to the members of a community workshop. "What excuses do we find ourselves using for not eating more healthfully, not exercising regularly, and not behaving in other ways that promote health, such as using seat belts? I'll start it off," she continued, "by confessing that I sometimes skip exercising because I run out of time. What excuses do you use?" The answers came quickly:

"I never seem to have the energy to exercise."

"My wife sprained her ankle jogging, and I know lots of other people who injured themselves exercising."

"I don't have the time to prepare healthful meals."

"My grandparents ate high-fat diets and lived past 85."

"My kids hate vegetables and my husband insists on having meat for dinner."

"Seat belts are uncomfortable to use and wrinkle my clothes."

"I've had my habits for so long—it's hard to change."

People cite many reasons for not leading more healthful lifestyles. Some of the obstacles they describe can be overcome fairly easily, but others are more difficult. In most cases, people could find ways to overcome obstacles to healthful behavior if they believed it was important and were motivated to do so.

In this chapter, we discuss how nutrition, weight control, exercise, and safety habits are important to people's health. We also examine what people do and do not do in these areas of their lifestyles, as well as why they behave as they do and how they can change unhealthful behaviors. As we study these topics, we will consider important questions and problems people have in leading healthy lives. Which foods are healthful, and which are not? What determines people's preferences for different foods, such as sweets? Why do overweight individuals have such a hard time losing weight and keeping it off? What kinds of exercise benefit health? What hazards exist in our environments, and how can we protect ourselves from them?

NUTRITION

"You are what you eat," as the saying goes. This saying has at least two meanings. Most commonly, it means that the quality of your diet can determine how you look, act, and feel. Another meaning is that

food and the human body are made up of the same classes of chemicals: water, carbohydrates, fats, proteins, vitamins, and minerals. ... Each of these classes makes identifiable contributions to the metabolic processes of all cells in the body. (Greenfield, 1985, pp. 293–294)

In this section, we will examine both meanings, beginning with the components of food and their importance in metabolic processes.

COMPONENTS OF FOOD

Healthful diets provide optimal amounts of all essential nutrients for the body's metabolic needs. In addition to water, food contains five types of chemical components that provide specific nutrients for body functioning (Greenfield, 1985; Holum, 1994; Insel & Roth, 1998). The five types of components and their roles in metabolism are as follows:

1. *Carbohydrates* include simple and complex sugars that constitute major sources of energy for the body. Simple sugars include *glucose*, which is found in foods made of animal products, and *fructose*, which is found in fruits and honey. Diets may also provide more complex sugars, such as *sucrose* (table sugar), *lactose* in milk products, and *starch* in many plants.

Reading labels informs the consumer of the food's content. Guidelines adopted in the 1990s for labeling packaged foods in the United States make nutritious choices easier for consumers.

2. *Lipids* or "fats" also provide energy for the body. Lipids include saturated and polyunsaturated fats, as well as cholesterol. Nutritionists recommend that diets contain not more than 30% of calories (nor less than 10%) from fat. To calculate a food's percent of calories from fat, you need to know its number of calories and grams of fat. Multiply the grams of fat by 9 (because a gram of fat has 9 calories), and divide that value by the number of calories.

3. *Proteins* are important mainly in the body's synthesis of new cell material. They are composed of organic molecules called *amino acids*; about half of the 20 or so known amino acids are essential for body development and functioning and must be provided by our diet.

4. *Vitamins* are organic chemicals that regulate metabolism and functions of the body. They are used in converting nutrients to energy, producing hormones, and breaking down waste products and toxins. Some vitamins (A, D, E, and K) are *fat-soluble*—they dissolve in fats and are stored in the body's fatty tissue.

The remaining vitamins (B and C) are *water-soluble*—the body stores very little of these vitamins and excretes excess quantities as waste.

5. *Minerals* are inorganic substances, such as calcium, phosphorus, potassium, sodium, iron, iodine, and zinc, each of which is important in body development and functioning. For example, calcium and phosphorus are components of bones and teeth, potassium and sodium are involved in nerve transmission, and iron is important in transporting oxygen in the blood.

Food also contains *fiber*, which is not considered a nutrient because it is not used in metabolism but is still needed in the process of digestion. People can get all the nutrients and fiber they need by eating diets that consist of a variety of foods from five basic groups: grains, fruits, vegetables, milk products, and meats and fish, as shown in Figure 8–1. Breads and cereals made of whole grains have more fiber than those made of grains that are "enriched" or "fortified" with nutrients.

Most people who eat healthfully do not need to supplement their diets with vitamins and other nutrients—one carrot, for instance, provides enough vitamin A to last 4 days. Women who are pregnant have greater needs of all nutrients; although most of the extra nutrients can come from adjustments in their diets, they should also take recommended supplements, such as of iron (Insel & Roth, 1998; St. Jeor, Sutnick, & Scott, 1988). Women who have a specific, detectable gene may need to take folic acid, a B vitamin, to prevent their babies from developing a severe birth defect called *spina bifida* (Whitehead et al., 1995). Some people who take supplements have an attitude of "the more the better." But one can overdo taking some nutrients, leading to a form of "poisoning" if they accumulate in the body. For example, too much of vitamins A and D can pose serious health hazards to the liver and kidneys, respectively. The value of taking vitamin C or E supplements daily is controversial (CU, 1994b).

Unprocessed foods are generally more healthful than processed foods, which often contain additives that benefit the food industry more than the consumer. Some additives lengthen the shelf life of the food, improve or maintain the texture of foods, or enhance the taste of foods, for example (Insel & Roth, 1998). Although most additives are not dangerous to people's health, some cause allergic reactions

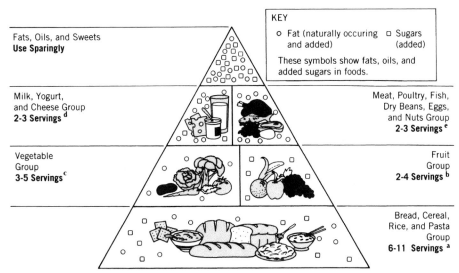

Figure 8–1   Food Guide Pyramid. A diagram indicating the relative amounts of different classes of foods a healthful diet should contain each day (USDA, 1995). Smaller amounts are recommended for foods in the upper levels than for those in the lower levels of the pyramid. *Serving-size guide:* [a] 1 slice of bread, 1 ounce of dry ready-to-eat cereal, or ½ cup of cooked cereal/rice/pasta; [b] 1 medium apple/orange/banana, ½ cup of small or diced fruit, or ¾ cup of fruit juice; [c] 1 cup of raw leafy vegetables, ½ cup of other vegetables, or ¾ cup of vegetable juice; [d] 1 cup of low-fat milk or yogurt, 1½ ounces of natural cheese, or 2 ounces of processed cheese; [e] 2–3 ounces of cooked lean meat/poultry/fish. (*Note:* can substitute for 1 ounce of meat with ¼ cup dry beans/peas/lentils, 1 egg, 2 tablespoons of peanut butter, or 6 tablespoons of nuts.)

or may be carcinogenic. For instance, some people are sensitive to monosodium glutamate (MSG, a flavor enhancer), experiencing heightened blood pressure and sweating when they consume it. Children may be especially vulnerable to the effects of additives because their body systems are still forming and maturing rapidly and, pound-for-pound, they eat more than adults.

WHAT PEOPLE EAT

Diets vary across cultural groups (Criqui & Ringel, 1994). For instance, Danish people consume 60% more animal fat than Americans, who consume twice as much as Israelis and Japanese. And Italians and Spaniards consume 40% more vegetables than Finnish and American people do. For most of the 20th century, American diets showed a fairly consistent trend: people consumed more and more sugar, animal fats, and animal proteins, while consuming less and less fiber (Winikoff, 1983). Their consumption of vegetables, fruits, and cereals declined while that of

meats and sugary foods, such as soft drinks and processed goods, increased. The way food is prepared also changed and affected people's diets. Consider the potato, for example. A baked or boiled potato by itself has few calories and almost no fat, but when french-fried or made into potato chips, its calorie and fat content skyrockets. Americans' increased use of processed and fast foods has contributed to the changes in their diets.

How healthful are people's diets in the United States today? One dimension of this question involves their consumption of sugars and animal fats, which is too high (USDA, 1999). Nutritionists and others concerned with people's health have been recommending that Americans reduce these components in their diets. Are Americans beginning to follow these recommendations? Yes, in some ways (USBC, 1999; USDA, 1999). Since 1980, people's consumption of red meats has declined, and they're eating more fish and poultry, cereals and grains, and fruits and vegetables. But they've also increased their intake of sugars, soft drinks, and fats and oils. Although most Americans at all ages consume sufficient amounts of the essential nutrients, many adults consume too little calcium, magnesium, vitamin B$_6$, vitamin E, and zinc (USDA, 1999). Some of these deficiencies are especially large among women and the elderly, and supplements of these nutrients may be warranted.

Why do people eat what they eat? Diets are determined by biopsychosocial factors (Logue, 1991; Rozin, 1989). Most people around the world—even newborn babies—like sweet tastes and avoid bitter tastes. These preferences appear to be inborn. Other evidence indicates that brain chemicals can lead people to eat fatty foods and activate their brain pleasure centers when they do (Azar, 1994). But people's diets also depend on their individual and social experiences (Hearn et al., 1998; Rozin, 1989; Schutz & Diaz-Knauf, 1989). Some foods are more available than others at home, work, or school. Children receive certain foods, but not others, depending on cultural and economic conditions—and simply being exposed to a food may increase their liking of it. They also observe in person and through TV commercials how other people respond to a food and tend to become more attracted to it if they see others eat it and like it. Through social experiences, people can develop ideas about foods they have never even tried: suppose you saw TV commericals for two new chocolate candies, one with "a special fruit filling" and the other filled with cockroaches. How would you feel about trying these products? Cockroaches are a great delicacy in some cultures.

Enormous numbers of children around the world simply do not have nutritious diets available to them for proper growth and development. Half or more children are stunted in growth from malnutrition in several countries, such as Ethiopia, Guatemala, and India (WHO, 1999c). A study of the average heights of children in different parts of the world revealed that the smallest children tend to live in highly impoverished areas, and the tallest in wealthier locations (Meredith, 1978). For example, children in the Netherlands, a prosperous, well-fed, and healthy nation, were nearly 20% taller than children in rural India and Thailand, where poverty, famine, and disease were common. The study also found contrasts between children from rich and poor families living in the same area: in Hong Kong, for instance, upper-class Chinese children were taller than their lower-class counterparts. But these same upper-class Chinese were shorter than upper-class children living in the Netherlands. Regional and social class differences in bodily growth result from many factors, including genetics, nutrition, and disease.

NUTRITION AND HEALTH

The mass media announce almost daily that many individuals eat diets that are not as healthful as they should be. Some people have responded by using foods and substances sold at health food stores. Although some of these products—such as whole

"...MAN. THE FDA IS REALLY CRACKING DOWN ON FOOD LABELING!....."

Reprinted by permission: Tribune Media Services.

grains—are clearly beneficial, many supplements and other products are of dubious worth (CU, 1994b, 1995a). Some people attempt to improve their diets by becoming *vegetarians*. There are degrees of vegetarianism, ranging from simply avoiding red meats to strictly using only plant foods and no animal products whatsoever. When people avoid all animal products, they must plan very carefully to assure that their diets, and especially their children's, contain a balance of proteins and sufficient amount of essential vitamins and minerals (Insel & Roth, 1998). In many nations of the world, dietary excesses are the main nutritional problem, especially in developing atherosclerosis, hypertension, and cancer.

Diet and Atherosclerosis

Cholesterol is the main dietary culprit in atherosclerosis, the deposit of fatty plaques in our blood vessels. As we saw in Chapter 2, cholesterol is a fatty substance. Our bodies produce most of the cholesterol in blood, and our diets provide the remainder. Whether cholesterol forms plaques in our blood vessels depends on the presence of different types of cholesterol-carrying proteins called **lipoproteins.** There are three types of lipoproteins: **Low-density lipoprotein** (LDL) and **very-low-density lipoprotein** (VLDL) are related to *increased* plaque deposits, but **high-density lipoprotein** (HDL) is linked to *decreased* likelihood of plaque buildup (AHA, 2000; Cooper, 1988). Cholesterol carried by LDL and VLDL is called "bad cholesterol" because it mixes with other substances to form plaques, whereas cholesterol carried by HDL is called "good cholesterol" because it seems to carry LDL away to be processed or removed by the liver. There are many other types of dietary fat, two of which are clearly linked to health. *Omega-3 fatty acids*, which occur at high levels in fish, appear to raise HDL; *trans fatty acids*, produced in processed oils, such as margarine, increase LDL (Insel & Roth, 1998).

How much cholesterol in the blood is too much? Normal levels of cholesterol increase with age in adulthood; they are measured in milligrams of cholesterol per 100 milliliters of blood serum. Americans between 20 and 34 years of age have average total cholesterol levels of about 185 mg, and those between 55 and 64 have about 225 mg (NCHS, 2000). A prospective study followed the health of over 350,000 middle-aged Americans for 6 years and found that, within any age group, the higher the subjects' cholesterol levels at the start of the study, the greater their risk of death from heart disease or stroke (Stamler et al., 1986). The risk for people with cholesterol levels over 245 mg was 3.4 times as high as for those with levels below 180. Although experts once thought that long-term total serum cholesterol levels above 240 mg put people at high risk for heart disease or stroke, they refined this view (EPDET, 2001). "Bad" cholesterol (LDL) is the real culprit, and its risk depends on five other risk factors: *age* (over 45 years for men, 55 for women); *family history* of early cardiovascular disease; and *cigarette smoking, high blood pressure,* and *low "good" cholesterol* (HDL less than 40 mg). To determine one's cardiovascular risk, count up the person's risk factors and subtract 1 if his or her HDL is high (60 mg or higher). People with scores of 0 or 1 are at *low risk* and should maintain LDL levels below 160 mg. People with higher scores or with related diseases, such as diabetes, should maintain much lower LDL levels.

People's cholesterol levels are determined partly by heredity and partly by their lifestyles (Hopkins, 1992; Rona et al., 1985). Some evidence suggests that smoking cigarettes may increase LDL and decrease HDL levels (Muscat, Harris, Haley, & Wynder, 1991). Diet is an important factor: some foods, such as eggs, many milk products, and fatty meats, contain very high concentrations of cholesterol. The intake of such foods showed gender and cultural variations in the last decades of the 20th century. In France, for example, cholesterol intake increased (Law & Wald, 1999). In the United States, people reduced their intake of fatty meats and eggs, but increased their intake of dairy products (NCHS, 2000). Average daily consumption of cholesterol for Americans is 331 mg for men and 213 mg for women (USDA, 1999).

People's daily cholesterol intake should not exceed 300 mg, and should be much lower than that for those at moderate or high risk for cardiovascular disease. Children after the preschool years should follow diets like those recommended for adults; those whose parents or grandparents had heart disease at early ages should have their cholesterol levels and diets assessed. Atherosclerosis can begin in childhood, and children need to develop good eating habits early so that they don't have entrenched habits to overcome later (Cooper, 1988; DISC, 1995). If dietary changes do not lower patients' high cholesterol levels enough, physicians may prescribe medication. *Statin* drugs (some brand names: Lipitor, Zocor) greatly reduce LDL but not HDL levels (CU, 1998; Maron, Fazio, & Linton, 2000).

Does lowering serum cholesterol reduce cardiovascular illness? Yes. Studies have demonstrated that large reductions in serum cholesterol, produced with combined dietary and drug treatment, retard and often *reverse* the development of atherosclerosis (Superko & Krauss, 1994). Other research has found that lowering cholesterol with statins greatly reduces the risk of heart attack among people with and without heart disease when they begin taking the drug (Maron, Fazio, & Linton, 2000). But there may be a caution about other health effects of lowering people's cholesterol: although current evidence is inconsistent and inconclusive, some studies have found that markedly reduced serum cholesterol is associated with non-illness deaths, such as from accidents, suicide, and violence (Muldoon & Manuck, 1992; Muldoon, Manuck, & Matthews, 1990). Studies have tested prospectively to see if lowering cholesterol might, perhaps, increase people's depression or aggressiveness in the following years and found that it does not (Bovbjerg et al., 1999; Weidner, Connor, Hollis, & Connor, 1992). (Go to .)

Diet and Hypertension

People with blood pressures exceeding 140 systolic/90 diastolic are classified as hypertensive. Nearly 700 million people around the world and one-fourth of American adults are hypertensive (NCHS, 2000; WHO, 1999c). Although medication can lower blood pressure, the first methods doctors advise usually involve lifestyle changes, especially losing weight and restricting certain foods in the patient's diet. People who are at risk for developing hypertension can effectively reduce their risk by making such changes (Stamler et al., 1989).

Of all the substances in people's diets that could affect blood pressure, *sodium*—such as in salt (sodium chloride)—may play the strongest role. Consuming high levels of sodium can increase people's blood pressure and reactivity in stressful situations (Denton et al., 1995; Falkner & Light, 1986; Kaplan, 1986). The body needs about 500 mg of sodium a day, and health experts recommend consuming less than 2300 mg, the amount in 1 teaspoon of salt (Insel & Roth, 1998; USDA, 1999). American adults consume an average of 3,270 mg of sodium daily in foods that contain sodium before eating or cooking, as do many processed meats, potato chips, and cereals, for example. And many people add salt to foods. Because sodium can elevate blood pressure, physicians often place hypertensive patients on low-sodium diets. Although some people are more sensitive to the effects of sodium than others (Sullivan, 1991), the evidence is now clear that reducing dietary sodium lowers blood pressure in hypertensives and normotensives alike (Law, Frost, & Wald, 1991). Salt-sensitive individuals can lower their blood pressure by reducing sodium intake or by increasing potassium intake, which counteracts sodium effects (West et al., 1999; Wilson, Sica, & Miller, 1999).

Caffeine is another dietary substance that can affect blood pressure. Most of the caffeine people consume generally comes from drinking caffeinated coffee, strong tea, and cola beverages. Caffeine increases people's reactivity to stress and raises their blood pressure at least temporarily (France & Ditto, 1988; Green & Suls, 1996; Lovallo et al., 1991, 1996). Does caffeine consumption lead to hypertension and coronary heart disease? Studies have found conflicting results (Grobbee et al., 1990; LeGrady et al., 1987; Salvaggio, Periti, Miano, & Zambelli, 1990). A meta-analysis of several studies found no link between the amount of caffeine consumption and heart disease (Kawachi, Colditz, & Stone, 1994). Habitual coffee drinkers do not appear to be at risk for cardiovascular disease.

Diet and Cancer

Diets high in saturated fat and low in fiber are associated with the development of cancer (ACS, 2000), particularly of the colon (Bristol, Emmett, Heaton, & Williamson, 1985) and prostate gland (Giovanucci et al., 1993; Wang et al., 1995). Dietary fats have also been linked to breast cancer (Wolk et al., 1998). By following the guidelines of the Food Guide Pyramid, consuming little of fatty meats and much of fruits, vegetables, and high-fiber breads and cereals, people could reduce their risk of cancer. In the United States, few people follow these guidelines closely (USBC, 1999, USDA, 1999).

Do vitamins protect people from cancer? Many fruits and vegetables are rich in *beta-carotene*, which the body converts to vitamin A. These foods are also good sources of vitamins C and E. Early studies yielded results suggesting that these vitamins may protect people from cancers, but newer research has

FOCUS ON RESEARCH

Interventions to Reduce Cholesterol Intake

Most people can lower their cholesterol intake markedly if they will modify their eating habits, sometimes by making very simple changes. For example, a person can lower cholesterol intake from 400 mg per day to under 300 mg by substituting low-cholesterol foods, such as cereals, for just four eggs per week—an egg contains over 200 mg of cholesterol. Other ways to reduce cholesterol intake include reducing the amounts and changing the types of meats in the diet, broiling or baking foods instead of frying, using low-cholesterol vegetable fats for cooking, and using low-fat dairy products. Most cereals, breads, fruits, nuts, and vegetables contain little or no cholesterol. But people should be wary of some processed foods that do not specify the kind of vegetable oil they use—these products often contain *saturated* fats (coconut or palm oils) rather than the more expensive polyunsaturated fats, such as corn or soybean oils. Oils that derive from certain plants, such as olives, consist of *monounsaturated* fats that contain no cholesterol and appear to *lower* serum LDL, but not HDL, cholesterol (Cooper, 1988; Insel & Roth, 1998).

Because most Americans consume too much cholesterol, researchers have tested intervention programs to help people lower their intake levels. One of these programs was part of the Multiple Risk Factor Intervention Trial (MRFIT) and was designed to modify the diets of thousands of men over a period of 6 years (Caggiula et al., 1981; Dolecek et al., 1986; Gorder et al., 1986). The subjects were between 35 and 57 years of age at the start of the study and were at risk of coronary heart disease because of high serum cholesterol levels, high blood pressure, and cigarette smoking. Before they entered the study, they had already made self-initiated changes to reduce saturated fats in their diets. The subjects were randomly assigned to two groups: half of the men participated in the intervention program and half were in a control group, receiving "usual care" from their physicians. All subjects returned periodically for medical examinations and to report the diets they consumed during the prior 24 hours. The men in the intervention received counseling each year, when they and

"their homemakers" participated in group meetings that provided information about the benefits of and methods for modifying their diets.

The MRFIT program was successful in modifying the men's diets substantially and lowering their serum cholesterol levels. The men who most needed to modify their diets tended to do so and achieved the greatest gains. Still, these improvements fell short of the guidelines of the American Heart Association. As a result, other studies have compared different methods. One study compared three methods with male and female adults from the general population—that is, they were *not* selected for being at high risk for health problems (Foreyt, Scott, Mitchell, & Gotto, 1979). The subjects were randomly assigned to three methods: one simply used a *booklet* describing a low-cholesterol diet; another provided a series of *nutrition education* classes; and the third used a *behavioral/education* program that combined the nutrition education classes with self-management training. Serum cholesterol levels were assessed at the start of the study and after 3, 6, and 12 months. The results showed that the behavioral/education program was the most effective approach, but that a follow-up program may be needed to maintain improved diets. The success of this approach is especially impressive because the subjects did not have very high serum cholesterol levels to begin with.

A meta-analysis of many studies found that programs to reduce high serum cholesterol help people improve their diets and reduce cardiovascular risk (Brunner et al., 1997). To maximize success, interventions need to involve behavioral and educational methods for the patient, training and cooperation by other members of the patient's household, support groups, and a long-term follow-up program (Carmody et al., 1982). They also need to address the reasons people do not change their diets, such as their low self-efficacy or readiness for change, strong taste preferences for high-fat foods, and difficulties having low-fat foods when not eating at home (McCann et al., 1995, 1996; Terry, Oakland, & Ankeny, 1991).

produced opposing results (Byers et al., 1987; Greenberg et al., 1994). On the basis of the early findings, some people began to take high doses of vitamin A, C, and E supplements. Nutritionists recommend against this, especially with vitamin A because it builds up in the body, and it is easy to overdose.

What people include in their diets is clearly related to their risk of developing several major chronic diseases. Other dietary problems that affect health arise from consuming too many calories. Experimental research with animals has shown that reducing calorie intake by 30% from standard nutritious diets decreases metabolism, slows the aging process, and increases longevity (Lane et al., 1996). Eating too much food can be unhealthful, as we are about to see.

WEIGHT CONTROL AND DIET

People in many cultures around the world are very "weight conscious." In the United States, individuals often start being concerned about their weight in childhood, particularly if they are overweight and are teased and excluded from social groups (Brownell, 1986b; DeBon, Klesges, Klesges, & Cohen, 1992). When children reach the teenage years, many become greatly preoccupied with their physical appearance and would like to change how they look (Conger & Petersen, 1984). They frequently express concerns about skin problems and wanting to have a better figure or more athletic body, to be taller or shorter, and to be the "right" weight. People with less-than-ideal bodies are often thought of as lazy and self-indulgent, and many of them wish or strive for bodies they are biologically unable to achieve (Brownell, 1991).

DESIRABLE AND UNDESIRABLE WEIGHTS

We judge the desirability of our weight with two criteria. One is attractiveness. Being the "wrong" weight often affects people's self-esteem, and American females provide a clear example. A study of overweight 10- to 16-year-old Caucasians found that girls' self-esteem declined sharply and consistently through those years, but boys' self-esteem declined only during the early years (Mendelson & White, 1985). Perhaps as overweight boys get older, some degree

of bulk is considered "manly." Another study surveyed teenagers and found that 63% of the girls and 16% of the boys were trying to *lose* weight, and 9% of the girls and 28% of the boys were trying to *gain* weight (Rosen & Gross, 1987). The greater concern among females than males about their weight—especially about being overweight—continues in adulthood (Forman et al., 1986). But cultural differences exist. Among overweight women, African-Americans are more satisfied with their bodies than whites are (Flynn & Fitzgibbon, 1998).

The other criterion for judging weight is healthfulness, based on data from studies of morbidity and mortality rates of men and women. Using such data, the Metropolitan Life Insurance Company developed a chart of healthful *desirable weights* with specific weight ranges for people of different sex, heights, and body types—that is, whether the frame is small, medium, or large. Table 8.1 presents these ranges and shows, for example, that a man with a medium frame who is 5'10" tall (with shoes) has a desirable weight range of 151–163 pounds, including an allowance for clothing. *Whether* individuals do anything about their weight and *what* they do can have important implications for their health.

Overweight and Obesity

No matter how fit we are, our bodies have some fat—and they should. Having fat is a problem only when we have too much. The question is, how much is too much? Determining how much fat a person's body has is not as easy as it may seem. Bulk or stockiness alone can be misleading since some stocky people simply have larger skeletal frames than others, or their bodies are more muscular. Until the mid-1990s, overweight was evaluated by the degree of departure from the weights given in Table 8.1. Today, these judgments are based on the *body mass index* (BMI): people are classified as **overweight** if their BMI exceeds 25, and **obese** if their BMI is greater than 30 (NCHS, 2000). Your BMI is easy to calculate: for American measurements, multiply your weight in pounds by 705 and divide *twice* by your height in inches (for metric measurements, simply divide your weight in kilograms twice by your height in meters). Most people have BMIs in the 20s. Neither the desirable weights nor the BMI measures the amount of body fat an individual has, but professionals can use complex methods that do (Perri, Nezu, & Viegener, 1992).

Table 8.1 *Desirable Weights from the* 1983 *Metropolitan Height and Weight Tables for Men and Women, Ages 25–59*

Height (in shoes)[a]		Weight in Pounds (in indoor clothing)[b]		
Feet	Inches	Small Frame	Medium Frame	Large Frame
		Men		
5	2	128–134	131–141	138–150
5	3	130–136	133–143	140–153
5	4	132–138	135–145	142–156
5	5	134–140	137–148	144–160
5	6	136–142	139–151	146–164
5	7	138–145	142–154	149–168
5	8	140–148	145–157	152–172
5	9	142–151	148–160	155–176
5	10	144–154	151–163	158–180
5	11	146–157	154–166	161–184
6	0	149–160	157–170	164–188
6	1	152–164	160–174	168–192
6	2	155–168	164–178	172–197
6	3	158–172	167–182	176–202
6	4	162–176	171–187	181–207
		Women		
4	10	102–111	109–121	118–131
4	11	103–113	111–123	120–134
5	0	104–115	113–126	122–137
5	1	106–118	115–129	125–140
5	2	108–121	118–132	128–143
5	3	111–124	121–135	131–147
5	4	114–127	124–138	134–151
5	5	117–130	127–141	137–155
5	6	120–133	130–144	140–159
5	7	123–136	133–147	143–163
5	8	126–139	136–150	146–167
5	9	129–142	139–153	149–170
5	10	132–145	142–156	152–173
5	11	135–148	145–159	155–176
6	0	138–151	148–162	158–179

Source: Metropolitan Life Foundation (1983).
[a]Shoes with 1-inch heels.
[b]Indoor clothing weighing 5 pounds for men and 3 pounds for women.

Sociocultural, Gender, and Age Differences in Weight Control

The prevalence of overly fat people varies with nationality, sociocultural factors, gender, and age. For example, the United States has a higher percentage of overweight and obese adults than Britain and Canada do (Millar & Stephens, 1987). Among Americans, more than half of adults are overweight and two-fifths of these are obese; one in eight children and adolescents are overweight or obese (NCHS, 2000). A higher percentage of men than women are overweight, but more women are obese. The percentage of women who are overweight or obese is higher for African Americans and Hispanics than for whites, and the percentage of overweight men is higher for Hispanics than for African Americans and whites. Americans get heavier throughout the early- and middle-adulthood years, with the percentage of overweight people peaking between 55 and 64 years of age (NCHS, 2000). And research has revealed a disturbing trend: among children and the population as a whole in the United States, the percentage who are overly fat has increased substantially during the last few decades (NCHS, 2000).

BECOMING OVERLY FAT

People add fat to their bodies by consuming more calories than they burn up through metabolism. Children who put on a lot of weight also eat much more fatty foods than others do (Robertson et al., 1999). The body stores excess calories as fat in *adipose tissue*, which consists of cells that vary in number and size (Logue, 1991). According to researcher Margaret Straw, the

> growth of adipose tissue throughout childhood and adolescence involves both an increase in cell size and in cell number. Thereafter, it appears that growth in adipose tissue is initially associated with an increase in cell size; if cell size becomes excessive, new adipose tissue is generated through an increase in the number of cells. (1983, p. 223)

There are two main reasons why adults tend to gain weight as they get older. First, people often gain weight periodically, such as around holidays, without taking it all off; the balance accumulates across years (Yanovski et al., 2000). Second, physical activity and metabolism decline with age (Smith, 1984). To maintain earlier weight levels, people need to take in fewer calories and exercise more as they get older. Both biological and psychosocial factors affect weight control.

Biological Factors in Weight Control

Because the metabolic rates of individuals can differ greatly, some thin people consume many more

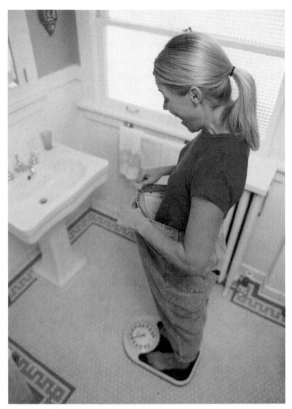

Losing weight is an important goal in many people's lives that brings great joy when it is clear that the effort worked.

calories than some heavy people do and still stay slim. Fat tissue is less metabolically active than lean tissue, "so fatness itself can directly lower metabolic rate if fat tissue begins to replace lean tissue" (Rodin, 1981, p. 362). This may be one of the reasons why many individuals who have become obese no longer overeat, as they did while they were gaining weight. Not all heavy people eat a great deal—indeed, studies have found that obese and normal-weight individuals do not differ in the amount or type of food they report having consumed recently, such as in the last 24 hours (Braitman, Adlin, & Stanton, 1985; Shah & Jeffery, 1991). It is possible, however, that heavy and normal-weight people differ in the accuracy of their reports. Studies of dietary intake with adult subjects have found that underreporting is very common and is more likely among heavy rather than normal-weight individuals, females than males, and people with little education (Klesges, Eck, & Ray, 1995; Lichtman et al., 1992).

Many people believe individuals become obese because of glandular problems. Although malfunctioning endocrine glands can cause extreme weight gains, this occurs in only a small percentage of obese people (Robinson & Lawler, 1977). Are other biological processes important in the development of obesity? Yes—heredity clearly plays a role (Insel & Roth, 1998). Researchers have identified defective genes in animals and humans that disrupt the balance between metabolism and energy intake (Barina, 1995; Lee et al., 1996; Wade, 1997; Zhang et al., 1994). Twin studies have shown that identical twins reared apart or together are much more alike in their degree of overweight than are same-sex fraternal twins (Allison et al., 1994; Stunkard, Foch, & Hrubec, 1986). Adoption studies have found that children's being overweight is much more strongly related to the weight of their biological parents than to that of their adoptive parents (Price, Cadoret, Stunkard, & Troughton, 1987; Stunkard et al., 1986). Relationships have also been noted between the fatness of parents and that of their offspring (Whitaker et al., 1997). Only about 7% of normal-weight children with normal-weight parents become obese by 30 years of age. But obesity in the child or parents increases this risk. For offspring of normal weight in childhood, having an obese parent doubles the risk of becoming obese. For offspring who are obese in childhood, about 38% of those with normal-weight parents and 73% of those with an obese parent are obese in young adulthood. These parent–child similarities may not be the result only of genetic factors—for instance, children learn many of their eating habits and physical activity patterns from their parents.

How does heredity affect our weight? Part of the answer seems to be described in **set-point theory,** which proposes that each person's body has a certain or "set" weight that it strives to maintain (Bennett & Gurin, 1982; Keesey, 1986; Keesey & Powley, 1975). The body tries to maintain its weight near the set-point by means of a thermostat-like physiological mechanism. When a person's weight departs from the set-point, the body takes corrective measures, such as by increasing or decreasing metabolism. According to the theory, people whose caloric intake is either drastically reduced or increased for a few months should show rapid corresponding weight changes initially, but the weight should then show slower changes and reach a limit. Studies have found that these predictions are correct and that people quickly return to their original weight when they can eat what they want again (Keys et al., 1950; Leibel, Rosenbaum, & Hirsch, 1995; Sims, 1974, 1976). But set-point theory is incomplete: it doesn't explain, for instance, why some people who lose a lot of weight manage to keep it off.

The mechanism controlling the set-point seems to involve the hypothalamus (Keesey, 1986; Keesey & Powley, 1975). Research with animals has shown that damage to specific parts of the hypothalamus causes weight to change and eventually level off, suggesting that a new set-point has been established. If the damage is in the *lateral* region of the hypothalamus, the new set-point is for a lower weight; damage to the *ventromedial* region leads to obesity. One way the hypothalamus might regulate body weight is by monitoring some aspect of fat cells. One study found, for instance, that after obese people lost weight, they began to produce large amounts of an enzyme that makes it easier to store fat in cells and gain weight (Kern, Ong, Saffari, & Carty, 1990). Moreover, the more obese the people were before losing weight, the more of this enzyme they produced. It may be that the loss of fat in cells triggers the hypothalamus to initiate enzyme production to maintain the set-point.

Another way the hypothalamus may affect the process of weight control is by regulating the level of insulin in the person's blood (Keesey & Powley, 1975). **Insulin** is a hormone that is produced by the pancreas, speeds the conversion of sugar (glucose) to fat, and promotes the storage of fat in adipose tissue (Rodin, 1981, 1985). Obese people tend to have high serum levels of insulin, which is called *hyperinsulinemia*. Elevations in serum insulin levels increase the person's sensations of hunger, perceived pleasantness of sweet tastes, and food consumption. Taken together, these findings indicate that weight gain results from a biopsychosocial process in which physiological factors interact with psychological and environmental factors (Rodin, 1985).

It seems likely that the setting and function of the set-point in regulating a person's weight depend on the number and size of fat cells in the body. Psychologist Kelly Brownell (1986b) has suggested that people whose weights are above the set-point may be able to reduce fairly readily until the fat cells reach their lower limit in *size*. The body weight at which this level is reached would depend on the *number* of fat cells in the body. Since the number of fat cells increases mainly in childhood and adolescence, the diets of

individuals during that time in the life span are likely to be very important. Obese children between 2 and 10 years of age have fat cells that are as large as those of adults (Knittle et al., 1981). As these children gain weight, they do so mainly by adding fat cells. Fat cell size for normal-weight children does not reach adult levels until age 12, and the number of their fat cells does not increase very much between 2 and 10 years of age.

Evidence indicates that the number of fat cells can increase, but *not* decrease (Brownell, 1982). Individuals who develop too many fat cells—a condition called *fat-cell hyperplasia*—may be doomed to a difficult struggle against a high set-point for the rest of their lives. When fat-cell-hyperplastic adults try to lose weight, their fat cells shrink and

> send out metabolic signals similar to those during food deprivation. As a result, bodily mechanisms respond as though the person were starving, resulting in, among other things, an increase in hunger and a decrease in basal metabolism so that energy stores (i.e., fat) are maintained more efficiently. (Buck, 1988, p. 467)

This suggests that the diets children eat may be critical in determining whether they become overly fat. It may be possible to help prevent obesity by encouraging children to exercise, eat in moderation, and consume nutritious diets that do not lead to hyperplasia (Brownell, 1986b). Once the person's set-point becomes established, however, changing it appears to be very difficult. Although some researchers have suggested that set-points may be changed through exercise, drugs, and other methods, there is little evidence for these possiblities (Brownell, 1986a).

Psychosocial Factors in Weight Control

Psychosocial factors are also involved in weight control. For one thing, many people claim to eat more when they are anxious or upset, and evidence indicates that stress can induce eating (Arnow, Kenardy, & Agras, 1992; Logue, 1991). Lifestyle is important, too. Regularly drinking a lot of alcohol adds calories to the diet and reduces the body's disposal of fat (Suter, Schutz, & Jequier, 1992; Tremblay et al., 1995). Watching television can affect weight control by decreasing people's physical activity and lowering the rate at which the body burns calories, and by presenting mainly low-nutrient, sweet foods in shows and commercials (Andersen et al., 1998; Gortmaker, Dietz, & Cheung, 1990; Story & Faulkner, 1990). A study compared obese and normal-weight children's metabolic rates while they simply rested and while they watched the show "The Wonder Years" (Klesges, Shuster, Klesges, & Werner, 1992). During the show, the children's metabolic rates dropped to *below* their resting rates—12% below for the normal-weight and 16% below for the obese subjects.

Another psychosocial factor in weight control is the person's sensitivity to food-related cues in the environment: obese people are more sensitive than nonobese people to certain cues (Schachter, 1971). For example, compared with the amount normal-weight people eat, obese individuals eat more when food tastes good, but eat less when it tastes bad. This stronger responsiveness to food cues appears to make obese individuals more susceptible to, say, the influence of a sales pitch when deciding whether to have a dessert. A study found that obese diners at a restaurant were more persuaded by a waitress's description or display of the dessert than nonobese diners (Herman, Olmstead, & Polivy, 1983). Because of this susceptibility to food-related cues, obese children may have difficulty controlling their eating at home. Studies examining family behaviors at mealtimes have shown that parents give more encouragement for eating and offer food more often to heavier children than to slimmer ones (Baranowski & Nader, 1985).

For many people, keeping their weight at a desired level is a struggle in which they constantly worry about what they eat and try to resist eating what they want. These people have been described as *restrained* eaters (Herman & Mack, 1975; Herman & Polivy, 1980; Ruderman, 1986). At the other end of the spectrum are *unrestrained* eaters who eat freely, as the desire strikes them. **Restraint theory** proposes that restrained eaters may develop abnormal eating patterns marked by vacillating between inhibited consumption, such as dieting, and overindulgence. According to this theory, the inhibited eating behavior of restrained eaters often becomes temporarily "disinhibited," or released, by certain events, and this produces a bout of overeating.

Research has supported the idea of disinhibition by comparing individuals assessed as restrained or unrestrained eaters by their responses to a questionnaire (Ruderman, 1986; Rutledge & Linden, 1998). One type of event that appears to disinhibit restrained eaters is the perception that they have already violated their diet, as might happen at a dinner party that begins with a fattening first course. After eating this course, restrained eaters may think, "I've blown it now—I might as well eat what I want." Dieting is an all-or-none thing for them, and simply *anticipating* violating their diet may sometimes be enough to lead restrained eaters to give up trying to inhibit their eating for the moment. Another type of event that leads restrained eaters to overindulge is experiencing negative emotional states, such as anxiety or depression. Last, social influence through modeling can affect the food consumption of both restrained and unrestrained eaters.

It is tempting to think that obese people are simply unrestrained eaters, but we currently have little evidence that obese and nonobese individuals differ in their food consumption. A very different view comes from nutrition researcher Barbara Rolls (1995), who presented evidence that obese people and normal-weight, restrained eaters share an insensitivity to the fat content of food. When yogurts that were secretly spiked with different amounts of fat were given to subjects to eat before lunch, male and female *normal-weight unrestrained* eaters ate *less* at lunch if the yogurt contained a lot of fat. But men and women who were *obese* or *normal-weight, restrained* eaters did not adjust their intake at lunch to compensate for the amount of fat in their yogurts. And for the obese individuals, being restrained or unrestrained eaters had no effect. How these effects lead to the development of obesity is still unclear.

Overweight and Health

In a study of overweight and normal-weight men and women, people were asked to rate their own health on a 10-point scale, where 1 equaled the "worst health" and 10 equaled the "best health" they could imagine (Laffrey, 1986). The ratings of the overweight and normal-weight individuals were about the same, averaging in the mid-7s. Are overweight and normal-weight people equally healthy?

To answer this question, we need to consider three factors, one of which is the *degree of overweight*. Research has clearly demonstrated that obesity is associated with high cholesterol levels and the development of hypertension, coronary heart disease, diabetes, and cancer (AHA, 2000; Calle et al., 1999; Chan et al., 1994; Ford, 1999; Jeffery, 1991, 1992; Must et al., 1999). The greater the severity of obesity, the greater the person's risk of developing and dying

Compared with normal-weight individuals, an obese person is at greater risk of developing heart disease and diabetes. And this young man's lunch won't help matters.

from one of these diseases. Thus, a person whose BMI is over 32 has a much greater risk of morbidity and mortality from, say, heart disease than someone whose BMI is 26. But the risk of dying from one of these diseases for someone who is 10–15 pounds overweight is almost as low as for someone at the desirable weight. One thing to keep in mind, however, is that people of ideal weight are not necessarily at low risk themselves—recall from the previous chapter that individuals who smoke cigarettes tend to weigh less than those who do not.

The second factor in the health risks of being heavy involves the *distribution of fat* on the body. Whereas heavy men's fat tends to collect in the abdominal region, heavy women have more of their fat on the thighs, hips, and buttocks (Brownell, 1986a). Since men have a higher prevalence of cardiovascular disorders than women, these and other health problems may be related to having bodies that are

"rounded in the middle." The results of a study of over 30,000 women support this possibility (Hartz, Rupley, & Rimm, 1984). Subjects whose *ratio of waist to hip girth*—that is, their waist measurements compared to their hip measurements—was large had a higher incidence of hypertension and diabetes than those whose ratio was small. Other studies with women and with men have also found higher rates of hypertension, diabetes, coronary heart disease, and mortality among people with higher, rather than lower, ratios of waist to hip girth (Folsom et al., 1993; Gillum, 1987a, 1987b; Welin et al., 1987). The reason for the role of fat distribution on health is unclear, but it may be that abdominal fat breaks down and is released into the bloodstream more readily than other fat.

The third factor in overweight as a health risk is *fitness*. Among heavy people, those who are physically active and fit have much lower rates of death and of heart disease and diabetes than those who are sedentary (Blair & Brodney, 1999).

Preventing Overweight

Being obese presents disadvantages to the person's health and social relationships in childhood and adulthood (Bray, 1984; Brownell, 1986b). Is it true, as many people believe, that children tend to outgrow weight problems, or that they will find it easy to lose weight when they are interested in dating? Probably neither belief is true for most children (Brownell, 1986b; Jeffery, 1998). Losing weight after becoming obese is not easy at any age, and this is one reason why it is important to try to prevent overweight.

Preventing overweight should begin in childhood (Brownell, 1986b; Jeffery, 1998). Beginning fairly early is important for two reasons. First, obesity in childhood is likely to continue into adult life (Serdula et al., 1993). As Figure 8–2 depicts, this likelihood depends on the age of the child—although only 14% of obese infants become obese adults, 70% of obese 10- to 13-year-olds do. Few normal-weight children become obese adults. Another reason to begin early is to prevent the excess development of fat cells, which occurs in childhood and adolescence. Obese adults who were fat in childhood have the double burden of dealing with bigger fat cells and more of them.

Most children will not require special preventive efforts to control their weight. Those who will need these efforts are likely either to have a family history of obesity or to have become overweight already (Jeffery, 1998). Efforts to help control their weight

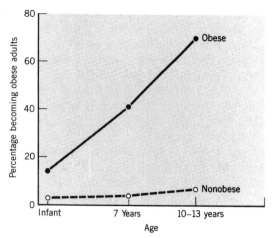

Figure 8–2 Percentage of obese and nonobese children who eventually become obese adults, as a function of age when weight status is assessed. (Data of Epstein, reported in Brownell, 1986b, p. 313.)

need to focus on improving the diets and physical activity of the children, and should involve their families in the program (Baranowski & Hearn, 1997; Jeffery, 1998). Health and physical education programs in schools provide excellent opportunities to promote healthful eating and exercise habits. Studies have shown, for example, that children who receive instruction on healthful diets begin to bring more healthful lunches to school and throw fewer healthful foods away (Striegel-Moore & Rodin, 1985; Wadden & Brownell, 1984). Children who are at risk of becoming obese on the basis of family history or current overweight can be identified and given special attention and training in dietary and exercise behavior. School programs for preventing obesity are most effective when they include a variety of training methods, involve cafeteria and educational facilities and staff, and enlist the cooperation of the parents (Striegel-Moore & Rodin, 1985).

Parents provide almost all the food that comes into the house and most of the food their children eat. They also model and encourage eating and physical activity patterns. Nutritionists and other researchers have identified several ways parents can help their children avoid becoming overly fat (Striegel-Moore & Rodin, 1985; Suitor & Hunter, 1980). These recommendations include:

● Encourage regular physical activity and restrict TV watching.

● Don't use unhealthful food rewards for eating a nonpreferred food (e.g., "You may have dessert if you eat your peas"); use praise as the reward instead.

● Decrease buying high-cholesterol and sugary foods of all kinds—have less of them in the house.

● Use fruits, nuts, and other healthful foods as regular desserts, and reserve rich cakes and other less healthful desserts for special occasions or once-a-week treats.

● Make sure the child eats a healthful breakfast (with few eggs) each day and does not have high-calorie snacks at night. Calories consumed early in the day tend to be used as fuel; metabolism generally decreases later in the day, and calories consumed at night often become fat.

● Monitor the child's BMI on a regular basis.

Childhood is probably the ideal time to establish activity and dietary habits to prevent individuals from becoming overly fat. Parents, schools, and the mass media can play important roles in helping people control their weight.

DIETING AND TREATMENTS TO LOSE WEIGHT

Many millions of people around the world are dieting on any given day of the year, especially in the spring when they are getting ready to bare their bodies in the summer. In the United States alone, nearly 44% of the women and 29% of the men are trying to lose weight (Serdula et al., 1999). Some individuals try to lose weight because they are concerned about the health risks of being overly fat: losing weight does in fact improve blood pressure and levels of lipids and lipoproteins (Datillo & Kris-Etherton, 1992; Linden & Chambers, 1994). But attractiveness motivates many people.

By American tastes, fatness is considered unattractive, particularly for females—and this confers important disadvantages for heavy people in social situations, such as dating. There is also a social stigma to being fat because many people *blame* heavy individuals for their condition, believing they simply lack willpower. Experiments by William DeJong (1980) had high school girls rate whether they thought they would like girls they did not know. The subjects gave lower ratings for an obese girl than for a normal-weight girl unless the obese girl described an acceptable reason for her weight, such as a "thyroid condition," or indicated that she had recently lost a good deal of weight. The social aspects of overweight can be distressing to those who see themselves as being too heavy, and this often motivates them to try to lose weight.

Most people try to reduce their weight on their own by "going on a diet." In the United States, only about 20% of people who are trying to lose weight follow official guidelines to reduce calories and get 2½ hours of exercise a week; 35–40% use a poor dieting strategy of consuming less fat rather than fewer calories (Serdula et al., 1999). Using ineffective methods may account for a paradoxical finding: the more that teenage girls try control their weight, the greater their increases in weight in the long run (Stice et al., 1999). Losing weight and keeping it off is difficult. Many people go on frequent diets, losing, say, 10% of their weight and gaining it right back. Kelly Brownell (1988) has described repeated cycles of substantial weight loss and gain as *yo-yo dieting*. Although some studies have found that people who diet repeatedly have a harder time losing weight in the future, other studies have not (Wing, 1992).

The best approach for losing weight is to do it gradually and make permanent lifestyle changes that the dieter and his or her family can accept and maintain. Several factors influence the likelihood that overweight people will lose weight and keep it off. They are more likely to succeed if they have a high degree of self-efficacy or confidence that they can do it, and if they have constructive social support from their families and others in their social network (Colletti & Brownell, 1983; Edell et al., 1987). Although being moderately dissatisfied with one's body can motivate weight loss efforts, people who are extremely dissatisfied with their bodies when they start dieting are less likely to succeed and may need counseling to overcome these feelings (Kiernan et al., 1998).

Although many overweight people succeed in making and sticking with the lifestyle changes needed to lose weight on their own, most do not (Rzewnicki & Forgays, 1987; Schachter, 1982). Many who do not succeed on their own feel they need help. Probably all of those who seek help have tried to reduce on their own at some time—perhaps numerous times—and either failed to reduce or could not maintain the new weight. What kinds of help do people seek, and what works?

"Beep-beep-beep...The number you are trying to reach, 173, has been changed. The new number is..."

Reprinted courtesy of Bunny Hoest.

Commercial and "Fad Diet" Plans

One kind of help millions of people try is the latest "miracle diet," which is often "guaranteed" to work in a short time. There never seems to be a shortage of these "crash" *fad diets*—many of which are not only ineffective, but are nutritionally unsound and often produce unpleasant and unhealthful side effects (Beck et al., 1990; Warshaw, 1992). Some fad diets prescribe a strict dietary regimen with virtually no deviations permitted—the "Scarsdale Diet" outlines specific meals to eat each day. Other fad diets have people eat certain types of food, such as only fruit, as in the "Beverly Hills diet," or foods that are high in protein and fat and low in carbohydrates and sugar, as in the "Atkins Diet." Several commercial plans sell low-calorie liquid or solid replacements for part or all of the person's diet, but provide little or no help in maintaining weight loss later. Little evidence exists for the success they claim (Rosenthal, 1992). No crash diet is a substitute for adopting a healthful lifestyle of exercise and moderately sized, balanced meals.

Exercise

Some people think that exercising is self-defeating when they try to control their weight because they associate exercising with large appetites (Suitor & Hunter, 1980). They have heard, for instance, that some football players eat enormous meals. But these players generally have huge bodies and they are trying to maintain their weight, not lose weight. For some positions in football, bulk is a great advantage.

Physical activity is an important component in controlling weight. One of its benefits is that it increases metabolism, thereby helping the body to burn off an increased number of calories. Unfortunately, dieters often fail to exercise as part of reducing because they notice that it takes a lot of exercise to use up a few hundred calories—for instance, they would have to jog about half an hour to burn off the 400 or so calories in a milkshake. But studies of dieting obese individuals have revealed a variety of benefits of exercise in weight control, and these advantages seem to accumulate over time. A benefit of exercise in the first few months of weight reduction is that it focuses the reduction mostly on body fat, while preserving lean tissue (Andersen et al., 1999). Over the next several months, combining exercise with reduced caloric intake leads to greater weight losses than dieting alone (Epstein, Wing, Penner, & Kress, 1985). After losing weight, continued physical activity—even frequent short bouts of walking instead of driving or climbing stairs instead of taking an elevator—helps in maintaining the reduced weight, and more vigorous exercise helps people lose even more (Andersen et al., 1999; Epstein, Wing, Valoski, & DeVos, 1988).

Behavioral and Cognitive Methods

People who try to lose weight usually find that changing their eating patterns is very hard to do. Why? A major reason is that they don't know how to control environmental conditions—antecedents and consequences—that maintain their eating patterns. Behavioral methods have been developed to help dieters gain the control they need. Richard Stuart (1967) conducted a pioneering study of the utility of behavioral techniques, such as self-monitoring and stimulus control, in helping several obese women lose weight over a 12-month period. The results were quite impressive: each of the eight women who stayed with the program lost weight fairly consistently throughout the year, losing from 26 to 47 pounds.

The dramatic success of Stuart's program prompted dozens of other researchers to study the usefulness of behavioral methods in weight control. The outcome of these studies suggests the following conclusions (Haddock, Shadish, Klesges, & Stein, 1994; Perri, Nezu, & Viegener, 1992; Wilson, 1984):

First, behavioral techniques are generally helpful in losing weight, but they do not work with all people. Second, behavioral programs have very low dropout rates, and people who complete a program lose an average of about 10% of their original weight in the first 4 months. Third, the more individuals weigh at the start of treatment and the longer the program, the more weight they lose. Fourth, behavioral methods are more effective in helping people lose weight than any other approach, except certain medical treatments. Fifth, a clear majority of individuals who complete a behavioral program for weight control maintain their lower weight for at least a year. Although most studies of behavioral programs have used adult dieters, research has shown that these techniques are also effective with children of various ages (Haddock, Shadish, Klesges, & Stein, 1994).

What techniques do behavioral programs for weight loss use? Although the specific techniques vary somewhat from one program to the next, they typically include the following components (Perri, Nezu, & Viegener, 1992; Stunkard & Berthold, 1985; Wilson, 1984):

- *Nutrition* and *exercise counseling.*
- *Self-monitoring* by keeping careful records of the foods eaten, when, where, with whom, and under what circumstances.
- *Stimulus control* techniques, such as shopping for food with a list, storing food out of sight, and eating at home in only one room.
- *Altering the act of eating*, for example, by chewing the food very thoroughly before swallowing and putting utensils down on the table between mouthfuls.
- *Behavioral contracting*, or setting up a system of rewards for sticking to the diet.

In addition, rewarding overweight individuals for *not engaging in sedentary activities*, such as watching TV or playing computer games, is very helpful in promoting weight loss (Epstein et al., 1995). Using portable computers to help dieters plan and monitor their physical activity and calorie intake can improve weight loss and subsequent lifestyle maintenance (Agras, 1987; Burnett, Taylor, & Agras, 1985). One behavioral approach that does *not* work and has been largely abandoned for treating weight problems involves using aversive strategies, such as pairing eating certain foods with unpleasant stimuli (Straw, 1983).

An important way to enhance the effectiveness of behavioral programs is to involve family and friends in the weight-reduction process, working as a team (Wing & Jeffery, 1999). Family-based behavioral programs were found highly effective in helping obese children and their parents lose weight together over a 10-year period (Epstein, Valoski, Wing, & McCurley, 1994). The interventions were most successful when they focused on weight loss in both the parents and children, included exercise in the program, and had the children and parents reward each other for diet and exercise behavior.

Cognitive methods have also been used in weight loss programs. In a method called *cognitive restructuring*, dieters learn how to counter pessimistic thoughts they have about dieting and their self-efficacy. For example, a person who thinks, "Everyone in my family has a weight problem. It's in my genes," would learn to counter this thought with, "That just makes it harder, not impossible. If I stick with this program, I will succeed" (Stunkard, 1987). Another method, called *problem-solving training*, is designed to teach

people strategies to help them deal with everyday difficulties they encounter in sticking to their diets (Perri, Nezu, & Viegener, 1992). Individuals often have difficulty sticking to a diet at family celebrations, when eating at restaurants, and when under stress, for instance. The skills learned in problem-solving training enable people to find solutions to these difficulties. Overweight people who can generate these kinds of solutions tend to lose more weight and have fewer lapses than do others (Drapkin, Wing, & Shiffman, 1995). (Go to ●.)

Self-Help Groups and Worksite Weight-Loss Programs

Although there are dozens of self-help organizations for weight control, *Weight Watchers* is the most widely known of these groups, with hundreds of thousands of people attending each week (Brownell, 1986a). The Weight Watchers approach uses several behavioral techniques, such as self-monitoring, along with nutritional information and group meetings for social support. Different self-help organizations have

CLINICAL METHODS AND ISSUES
Problem-Solving Training to Control Weight

The cognitive method called problem-solving training can help people deal with a variety of behavioral and emotional difficulties by teaching them how to generate solutions to specific problems in their lives (Sarafino, 2001). For example, when people try to follow a low calorie diet, they often have trouble eating healthfully when they eat outside their own households, such as at restaurants, work, or sporting events. Here are some common problems these dieters face and examples of solutions they might produce.

PROBLEM: *I eat vending machine and restaurant food too much. How can I curb this?*

SOLUTIONS: Prepare lunch and take it to work; eat with others who do the same. Take low calorie snacks with you to work, movies, sporting events, shopping malls, etc.

PROBLEM: *When I know I will be eating out, how can I choose a restaurant that will make it easier to stick to my diet?*

SOLUTIONS: Identify restaurants in advance that have healthy selections. Avoid going to all-you-can-eat buffet restaurants that have tempting high calorie selections.

PROBLEM: *When faced with a restaurant menu that includes high calorie foods, how can I restrict the calories I eat?*

SOLUTIONS: Learn about high and low calorie ingredients and preparation methods, such as frying versus grilling, and ask the waiter questions. Skim the menu to reject high calorie selections; read only low calorie options. If ordering a salad, ask for the dressing on the side; use only a little. If others are having dessert, either share one with another person or order fruit or sherbet. Ask about portion size; if too large, ask for smaller.

their own mix of methods to help people lose weight (Chesney, 1984; Perri, Nezu, & Viegener, 1992). Very little research has been done on the success of self-help groups because they have been "notoriously unwilling to permit external evaluation" of their effectiveness (Brownell, 1986a, p. 525). But dropout rates for self-help groups appear to be extremely high, being over 50% in some groups in the first 6 weeks alone (Stunkard, 1987).

Worksite weight-loss programs have been introduced and evaluated in a variety of businesses and industries. These programs generally used behavioral techniques, but were not very successful (Foreyt & Leavesley, 1991). High dropout rates and small weight losses have been common, suggesting that inadequate motivation is a major problem. Evidence indicates that these problems can be reduced with two approaches: gearing the program to the workers' stages of readiness to change and providing incentives for participation (Gomel, Oldenburg, Simpson, & Owen, 1993). An example of using incentives comes from three successful *weight-loss competitions* introduced in different businesses and industries (Brownell et al., 1984). In one competition, for instance, the presidents of banks issued challenges to each other's bank for a weight loss contest over a 3-month period. All participating employees from each bank made up a team, with each participant having a reasonable weight loss goal. The prize for the team that achieved the greatest percentage of its weight loss goal was a pool of money to which each participant contributed $5. The only help they received was a series of weekly manuals that gave information about such factors as nutrition, exercise, self-monitoring, stimulus control, and reinforcement. The outcome for the three competitions was impressive: only one of the 213 overweight or obese individuals dropped out of the contest, and the average weight loss was 12 pounds—about a pound a week. A follow-up of the bank employees 6 months later showed that the overweight and obese individuals kept off 80% of the weight they lost in the competition. Clearly, addressing the *motivation* of dieters is a useful approach.

Medically Supervised Approaches

Some approaches for losing weight involve medical procedures or require supervision by a physician. Using prescribed drugs is one such approach. Drugs can suppress appetite, as *amphetamines* and the combination of *fenfluramine* and *phentermine* (called

"fen-phen") do, or decrease the conversion of calories to fat, as *orlistat* does. No currently available drug is both effective and safe to use. For example, amphetamines produce psychological and, perhaps, physical dependence and fen-phen can cause a heart valve disease (Perri, Nezu, & Viegener, 1992; Wadden et al., 1998); orlistat produces only small weight reductions (Stolberg, 1999b). Because of the side effects all such drugs seem to have, new drugs are likely to be recommended only for people who are *obese*, some of whom may need to take them indefinitely (Stallone & Stunkard, 1991).

Another medical approach for losing weight involves placing the patient on a *very-low-calorie diet* (VLCD) regimen. VLCDs contain fewer than 800 calories per day—often only 500 or so (Agras, 1987; Perri, Nezu, & Viegener, 1992; Wilson, 1984). A VLCD can be unsafe to use if it is deficient in protein and potassium, but "protein sparing" VLCDs are safe if the patients do not have certain medical conditions, such as heart disease, and their health is monitored regularly. Although VLCDs produce rapid and substantial weight losses, they have unpleasant side effects, such as constipation and fatigue. Furthermore, relapse rates are high in the months following VLCDs. A study of obese patients revealed large weight losses during VLCD treatment, but most subjects regained the lost weight in the subsequent 3 years (Wadden, Stunkard, & Liebschutz, 1988). Some of the patients who relapsed sought additional treatment, which again helped. VLCDs are appropriate mainly for otherwise healthy obese patients who are more than 50 pounds overweight, have failed to control their weight with behavioral methods, and whose obesity poses an unusually high health risk (Agras, 1987).

The most drastic medical approaches for losing weight involve surgery, particularly to the stomach or intestines. In one surgical approach called *gastric restriction*, the size of the stomach is reduced by literally stapling part of it up; a less commonly used method is to remove part of the intestines to reduce the amount of nutrients absorbed from the digestive system. Although these approaches effectively reduce weight, they entail some surgical risk and may proudce unpleasant side effects—for example, some patients who have undergone gastric restriction surgery experience nausea, vomiting, and abdominal pain after eating. As a result, these methods are recommended only or patients who are more than 100% overweight and have failed to lose weight by less drastic means

(Hsu et al., 1998; Perri, Nezu, & Viegener, 1992). The surgical procedure called *liposuction*, in which adipose tissue is torn from the body and sucked out with a tube, is not really a weight reduction method—its function is strictly cosmetic. It is used for removing fat from specfic regions of the body, such as the thighs or abdomen. Although the procedure is usually safe, it can be fatal (Rao, Ely, & Hoffman, 1999).

We have considered methods for losing weight that range from adjusting one's diet and exercising to using surgical procedures. Choosing the most appropriate approaches to use requires *matching* the methods to people's weight problems and charac-teristics, such as their metabolic function, dieting history, and financial resources (Brownell & Wadden, 1991). Someone who is 10% overweight might be advised to use a structured self-dieting approach or a worksite program, but someone who is 100% overweight would probably need to use medically supervised approaches.

Relapse after Weight Loss

The problem of relapse after completing treatment to lose weight is similar to that which many people experience after receiving treatment to quit smok-ing, drinking, or using drugs (Brownell, Marlatt, Lichtenstein, & Wilson, 1986). The reasons for re-lapse often relate to certain types of situations, such as being upset (Grilo, Shiffman, & Wing, 1989; Jeffery, French, & Schmid, 1990). Although most individuals who lose weight in behavioral programs maintain their lower weight for at least a year without follow-up treatment programs, many others do not. And those who maintain their reduced weight for a few years stand a very good chance of maintaining that weight in subsequent years (McGuire et al., 1999). When considering weight gain in the years after losing weight, keep in mind that people gen-erally gain weight as they get older—1 or 2 pounds a year in middle-aged Americans, on average. A fair assessment of a weight loss program's success should also take into account *the weight dieters didn't gain* that other people do (Perri, Nezu, & Viegener, 1992).

Michael Perri and his colleagues (1988) demon-strated that follow-up treatment programs can be effective in reducing the relapse problem in weight control. In this study, obese men and women lost an average of 12.5 pounds in a behavioral program for dietary and exercise behaviors. The subjects were then randomly assigned to different follow-up treatment conditions that were balanced for degree of the subjects' overweight. Assessments 18 months later revealed that the average weight losses the subjects maintained was 10.6 pounds for those who received follow-up treatment and only 3.6 pounds for those who received no follow-up treatment. Analysis of the follow-up treatments revealed two critical components in their success: (1) frequent therapist meetings to deal with specific problems individuals were having in maintaining their weight and (2) social influences of other members of a treatment group. These findings are very encouraging and suggest that many obese individuals who have lost weight would benefit from having continued meetings with therapists, relapse "hot lines" to call, and support groups.

Most people who lose weight do not use effective ways to maintain the loss. If you wanted to lose weight and keep it off, what methods could you use? Here are some:

- When losing the weight, use behavioral tech-niques—such as self-monitoring and stimulus control—to diet and increase exercise. Choose a reasonable final weight goal, and plan to lose weight *gradually*, such as a pound a week or less. Weigh yourself each time you exercise.

- Reduce the fat content of your diet by substitut-ing other foods (carbohydrates have fewer calo-ries ounce-for-ounce and turn into body fat less readily).

- After reaching your weight goal, continue your lifestyle changes by using behavioral methods, such as keeping diet and exercise records, avoid-ing situations that prompt lapses, and rewarding good behavior.

- Recognize that maintaining your lower weight re-quires that the lifestyle changes be *permanent*. Oc-casional lapses are not a problem as long as you get back on track as soon as possible.

- Join a self-help or support group, especially if you find that you have too many lapses.

(Go to 🍎.)

ANOREXIA AND BULIMIA

Although gaining weight by overeating is a very com-mon problem with psychosocial relationships, it is

ASSESS YOURSELF
Your Weight Control Patterns

For each of the following questions, put a check mark in the preceding space if your answer is "yes."

_____ Do you watch your calorie intake more carefully than anyone else you know?

_____ Do you weigh less than the "desirable weight" range for your height and frame given in Table 8.1 on page 245?

_____ Do you think gaining a few pounds during a holiday season would be a terrible thing?

_____ Have you ever eaten so much so quickly that you felt like you had lost control of your eating?

_____ If yes, has this happened more than about 10 times in the past year?

_____ Have you ever eaten a lot and then tried to "purge" the food by using laxatives, diuretics, or self-induced vomiting?

_____ If yes, has this happened more than about 10 times in the past year?

_____ Have you felt a lot of emotional distress in recent months?

_____ Do you often eat fewer than two meals a day?

_____ Do you regularly exercise more than 10 hours a week to lose weight?

How many "yes" answers did you give? A high number suggests that you may have an eating disorder. If your number is: from 3 to 5, you may want to consider getting professional help, especially if your situation seems to be getting worse; 6 or more, you should seek help right away. You can find help through your college's counseling office or by contacting professional organizations, such as the American Psychological Association and the American Psychiatric Association, which are in Washington, DC. (_Sources:_ Based on material in Brownell, 1989; Davison & Neale, 1998; Logue, 1991.)

not a psychiatric disorder. In contrast, two relatively unusual eating problems—_anorexia nervosa_ and _bulimia nervosa_—are included as psychiatric disorders in the _Diagnostic and Statistical Manual of Mental Disorders_ (DSM-IV) of the American Psychiatric Association (1994). People with these two disorders use extreme ways to keep their weight down. Anorexia is illustrated in the following case study of a 19-year-old, 5'3" tall coed named Frances who had been 20 pounds overweight 6 years earlier. She

> weighed 83 lbs upon admission [to therapy]. She reported eating very little food each day (estimated to be less than 500 kcal). She exercised for at least 3 hours each day by attending aerobics classes and running. When she did consume a normal meal, she purged it via self-induced vomiting.... She never binged (i.e., ate large quantities of food). She was obsessed with fears of weight gain. (Williamson, Cubic, & Fuller, 1992, p. 367)

When she was younger, she had been teased by peers and repeatedly criticized by her mother for being

overweight. As Frances's case shows, **anorexia nervosa** is an eating disorder that involves a drastic reduction in food intake and an unhealthy loss of weight. This disorder is characterized by a weight loss of at least 25%, efforts to maintain body weight 15% below the normal weight for one's age and height, and an intense fear of becoming fat, which continues despite the extreme loss of weight (Agras, 1987; Logue, 1991). The starvation in anorexia may be so extreme as to cause or contribute to the person's death—for instance, by causing extremely low blood pressure, heart damage, or cardiac arrhythmias (due to low body levels of electrolytes, such as sodium or potassium).

It is difficult to know how prevalent eating disorders are. A study that compared women's medical records with returned surveys on eating disorders to the researchers found that many of those who did not return the survey did in fact have eating disorders (Beglin & Fairburn, 1992). Thus, existing prevalence data are likely to be underestimates. Anorexia nervosa occurs 10 or 15 times more frequently in females than males; its incidence increases during the adolescent years and probably declines in early adulthood (Hoek et al., 1995; Sokol & Gray, 1998). Studies done in North America and Europe have found that it afflicts about 1 of every 250 adolescent girls, is more prevalent in upper-class than lower-class individuals, and appears to have become more prevalent since the 1960s (Hoek et al., 1995; Lacey & Birtchnell, 1986; Sokol & Gray, 1998). Anorexia is especially common among dance students, models, and athletes who feel pressured to control their weight (French & Jeffery, 1994).

Bulimia nervosa is an eating disorder that is characterized by recurrent episodes of *binge eating*, generally followed by *purging* by self-induced vomiting, laxative use, or other means to prevent gaining weight (Lacey & Birtchnell, 1986; Logue, 1991; Sokol & Gray, 1998). This disorder can cause a wide range of medical problems, inlcuding inflammation of the digestive tract and cardiac problems, such as arrhythmias resulting from low levels of electrolytes. Bulimic individuals are aware that their eating pattern is abnormal, are fearful of having lost control of their eating, and tend to be depressed and self-critical after a bulimic episode.

Bulimia was not recognized as a distinct syndrome until the late 1970s. As a result, less is known about this disorder than about anorexia (Agras, 1987). Bulimia is far more prevalent among females than males and is more likely to occur in adolescence and early adulthood than at other times in the life span. Findings from studies of college students suggest that this disorder is more prevalent than anorexia nervosa, afflicting perhaps 1 to 3% of female adolescents (Agras, 1987; Logue, 1991; Sokol & Gray, 1998). Many individuals exhibit some bulimic behaviors, such as purging, but are not classified as bulimics because they engage in these behaviors infrequently.

Why People Become Anorexics and Bulimics

What causes the eccentric eating habits of anorexia and bulimia? The answer is still unclear, and researchers have suggested biological, psychological, and cultural factors that may be involved. There is evidence for genetic and physiological links to these disorders (Kaye, Klump, Frank, & Strober, 2000). For example, studies have examined the occurrence of anorexia and bulimia in twins and found that these disorders are far more likely to appear in *both* twin members if they are identical twins rather than

Anorexics tend to see themselves as "too fat" despite their thinness.

fraternal twins. Other research findings indicate that the functioning of neuroendocrine and neurotransmitter processes may be abnormal in eating-disordered individuals.

Cultural factors may provide the answer to two obvious questions about these eating disorders: Why is the prevalence of anorexia and bulimia so much greater among females, and why has it increased in recent years? Beauty plays a central role in the sex-role stereotype of women in many cultures, and Western cultures have witnessed recent changes in their ideals about female beauty (Striegel-Moore, 1997). These changes are evident in the body proportions of models and beauty pageant contestants. Years ago, the "ideally beautiful woman" had a figure that was more rounded, with larger bust and hip measurements. After 1960 or so, the ideal figure of a woman became much thinner, and the social pressures on women to be slender increased. As we saw earlier, females are more likely than males to wish they were thinner and to diet. These gender differences begin to show up by age 11 or so (Cohen, Brownell, & Felix, 1990). In social interactions with other children, parents, and teachers, girls more than boys are given the message: thin is better (Attie & Brooks-Gunn, 1987). And once the message is clear, they reach puberty, when girls add an average of over 20 pounds of fat to their bodies while boys add muscle. This is a no-win situation for adolescent girls. How do they deal with it?

When adolescents—especially females—start trying to control their weight, they typically adjust their diets in a normal manner. But the methods they use sometimes become more extreme, involving occasional fasting or purging. A study of over 1,700 15-year-old male and female high school students, for instance, revealed that about 13% of them had engaged in some form of purging behavior, with the rate for females being twice as high as that for males (Killen et al., 1986). Most of these purging behaviors occurred infrequently—on a monthly basis or less. The results of prospective studies indicate that individuals who become anorexic and bulimic typically start out dieting normally but have relatively strong concerns about their weight, and then begin using more extreme methods (French & Jeffery, 1994; Killen et al., 1994). African American girls have lower prevalence rates of eating disorders than white girls, party because they tend to be less concerned about their weight even when they are heavy (Abrams, Allen, & Gray, 1993). Dieters with strong weight concerns may come to rely more and more on fasting and purging because these methods keep weight off. Those who become bulimic develop an entrenched pattern of restrained eating and bingeing. Bulimics tend to binge after unpleasant experiences, particularly negative social interactions, which function as disinhibiting events (Steiger et al., 1999).

Why do these eating patterns become so compulsive? People who are extremely concerned about their weight tend to see themselves as round-faced and pudgy, even when others do not. Studies using ingenious apparatuses, such as special projectors, have shown that the great majority of women overestimate their size and generally perceive themselves to be one-fourth larger than they really are (Thompson, 1986). Although men make similar errors, they do so

to a much lesser degree—and, unlike women, many of these men may *want* to be larger. Body size overestimation is particularly pronounced among anorexics and bulimics. Among anorexics, for example, the idea that they are overweight persists long after they have become slim. When they are reduced to skin and bones, anorexics still claim to be "too fat" and greatly overestimate their size (Askevold, 1975; Crisp & Kalucy, 1974). Interventions delivered on the Internet or in person can reduce the risk of developing eating disorders in people who are very dissatisfied with their body shapes (Celio et al., 2000).

Treatments for Anorexia and Bulimia

Because anorexia nervosa involves a severe and health-threatening underweight condition, the first priority in treating this disorder is to restore the person's body weight and nutrition to as near normal as possible. This is often done in a hospital setting. Several approaches that include behavioral techniques and drug therapy are effective for putting weight on (Agras, 1987; Logue, 1991; Williamson, Cubic, & Fuller, 1992). But keeping the weight on is difficult; about half of previously treated anorexics continue to have eating problems and often show other social and emotional difficulties, such as depression. Treatments need to include cognitive methods to alter irrational thinking, such as the person's distorted body image, and follow-up efforts to address any continued desire to restrict food intake and various interpersonal and job-related problems.

The most effective treatments for bulimia nervosa combine behavioral and cognitive methods (Compas et al., 1998). These methods—such as self-monitoring, reinforcement, relaxation training, and cognitive restructuring—focus on reducing bingeing and purging behaviors (Agras, 1987). If a patient does not respond to these methods, *antidepressant drugs* may be added to elevate the person's mood (Compas et al., 1998). Treatment is less effective for bulimics who have very high initial rates of bingeing and purging and a history of substance abuse (Wilson et al., 1999). Is treatment more successful for bulimia than for anorexia? It is initially (Agras, 1987; Williamson, Cubic, & Fuller, 1992). But some studies of the long-term success of bulimia treatments have found fairly high relapse rates. For instance, a study with female bulimics compared treatments using behavioral methods only or both behavioral and cognitive methods with a control condition that used only self-monitoring (Thackwray, Smith, Bodfish, & Meyers, 1993). Follow-up assessments 6 months later revealed no bingeing or purging in 69% of the women who received the cognitive-behavioral treatment, 38% of those with the behavioral treatment, and 15% of the controls. The 31% relapse rate with cognitive-behavioral methods may be an understimate because there was no independent source to confirm the patients' reports of bingeing and purging.

We have discussed the problems people have in controlling their weight through adjustments in their diets. We have also seen that exercise can play an important role in reducing body fat and, thereby, can enhance people's health. The next section examines exercise as a means of becoming fit and keeping well.

EXERCISE

Sometimes it seems like a fitness boom has occurred in many nations. For instance, the proportion of Americans who exercise doubled in the 20 years after the early 1960s (Serfass & Gerberich, 1984). Joggers and bicyclists today can be seen on roads and paths in cities and out in the country, and fitness clubs have sprung up everywhere. But in the United States and most other industrialized countries, adults' lifestyles still include very little or irregular physical activity (Sallis & Owen, 1999; USBC, 1999). We've all heard that exercise is healthy. We will see why in this section. (Go to 💡.)

THE HEALTH EFFECTS OF EXERCISE

If you asked fitness-conscious people why they exercise, they would probably give a variety of reasons: "Exercising helps me keep my weight down," "I like it when I'm in shape—and so does my boyfriend," "It helps me unwind and relieves my tension," "Being in shape keeps me sharp on my job," "I don't get sick as often when I'm fit," and "It makes people's hearts stronger, so they live longer." These answers describe several psychosocial and physical health benefits of exercising and are, for the most part, correct.

Three psychosocial benefits of exercise have been studied extensively. First, research has shown that engaging in regular vigorous exercise is associated with lower feelings of *stress* and anxiety, as

we discussed in Chapter 5. Second, people who get involved in fitness programs report that their *work performance* and attitudes improve—they make fewer errors, for instance (Quick, Quick, Nelson, & Hurrell, 1997). Third, participating in regular exercise is linked to enhanced *self-concepts* of individuals, especially children (Dishman, 1986; Sallis & Owen, 1999). Self-concept enhancements may occur because individuals who exercise are better able to control their weight, maintain an attractive appearance, and engage successfully in physical activities and sports. These outcomes help people to feel a greater sense of esteem and to receive the many social advantages that accrue with being fit. But keep in mind that most studies of psychosocial benefits from exercise have used correlational or retrospective methods, making it difficult to determine cause-effect relationships. Some evidence suggests that part of the self-reported benefits may have resulted from a placebo effect of the subjects' expecting that psychosocial benefits would occur (Desharnais et al., 1993).

Of the many physiological effects that physical activity produces, one effect is especially intriguing: vigorous exercise seems to increase the body's production of *endorphins*, which are morphinelike chemical substances. Studies have shown that endorphin levels in the blood are higher after exercise than before (Carr et al., 1981). Some researchers claim that the euphoric "runner's high" that many individuals feel after a very vigorous aerobic workout results from high levels of endorphins reaching the brain. These researchers have also proposed that these higher endorphin levels may be responsible for decreases in both the stress and sensations of pain many people feel during or after vigorous exercise. But research has not confirmed these possibilities (Hopson, 1988; Sime, 1984).

Exercise can enhance many aspects of people's physical fitness throughout the life span. In the early childhood years, aerobic exercise improves agility and cardiovascular function (Alpert, Field, Goldstein, & Perry, 1990). What about the other end of the life span, when people generally show a gradual decline in their physical work capacity—as reflected in their muscle flexibility, strength, and endurance? This decline occurs partly because many individuals get less exercise as they get older. An 18-year longitudinal study examined the physical work capacity of men who were over 50 years of age at the start of the study and who engaged in aerobic exercise regularly (Kasch, Wallace,

Highlight on Issues

Types and Amounts of Healthful Exercise

All physical activities—even just fidgeting—use energy and burn calories. *Exercise* is a special class of physical activity in which people exert their bodies in a structured and repetitive way for the sake of health or body development. There are several types of exercise, each with its own form of activity and physical goals. Let's see what these types of exercise are and what pattern of activities experts recommend to benefit most people's health.

Isotonics, Isometrics, and Isokinetics

Isotonic, isometric, and isokinetic exercise differ in the types of activities and their effects. **Isotonic exercise** refers to a type of activity that builds strength *and* endurance by the person's moving a heavy object, exerting most of the muscle force in one direction. This type of exercise includes weight lifting and many calisthenics. In doing push-ups, for example, most of the exertion occurs in raising the body.

Isometric exercise builds mainly strength rather than endurance, and the person exerts muscle force against an *immovable* object. An example of an isometric exercise is the "chair lift": the person sits in a standard unupholstered chair, grasps the sides of the seat with both hands, and pulls upward, straining the arm muscles. The pulling doesn't move the seat. **Isokinetic exercise** builds strength *and* endurance by the person's exerting muscle force in more than one direction in the course of moving an object. An example would be in exerting substantial force to push forward and to pull it back. Isokinetic exercise typically requires special equipment, such as Nautilus machines.

Aerobics

The word *aerobic* literally means "with oxygen." What does oxygen have to do with exercise? When we exert ourselves in physical activity, the energy for it comes from the metabolic process of burning fatty acids and glucose in the presence of oxygen. Continuous exertion at high intensity over many minutes requires a great deal of oxygen. Being "in shape" means the person consumes a high *volume of oxygen* (VO$_2$) per heartbeat during physical exertion.

The term **aerobic exercise** refers to energetic physical activity that requires high levels of oxygen over an extended number of minutes, say, half an hour. Aerobic activities generally involve rhythmical actions that move the body over a distance or against gravity—as occurs in fast dancing, jogging, bicycling, swimming, or certain calisthenics. Performing aerobic activity with sufficient intensity and duration on a regular basis increases the body's ability to extract oxygen from the blood and burn fatty acids and glucose efficiently.

An Ideal Exercise Program for Health

How much and what kinds of exercise are best for fitness? To answer this question, we need to recognize that any specific program would depend on the individual's age, current health and physical capacity, goals, interests, and opportunities, such as whether facilities or partners are available (Insel & Roth, 1998). Almost all individuals need to begin with a moderate *starter program* and progress in a gradual manner toward fitness, and people who are elderly or less fit should progress more slowly than others. Starting gradually avoids muscle soreness and injury and allows the body to adapt to increasing demands, such as in the use of oxygen. Heavy exercise without sufficient oxygen simply causes the muscles to fatigue.

An ideal exercise program would involve about 3 hours of exercise a week divided into three to five sessions, each having three phases (Blair, Kohl, Gordon, & Paffenbarger, 1992; Insel & Roth, 1998):

1. *Warmup*. Each session should include two types of warmup activities: (1) stretching and flexibility exercises, for various major muscle groups, such as of the neck, back, shoulders, abdomen, and legs and (2) strength and endurance exercises, such as push-ups, pull-ups, and lifting.

2. *Aerobics*. The next 20 minutes or more involves rhythmical exercise of large muscle groups, performed vigorously enough to raise the heart (pulse) rate to a moderately high target range. The easiest way to estimate the target range for an adult is to use a formula based on the person's

(continued) HIGHLIGHT ON ISSUES

age: the *minimum* heart rate is 160 pulse beats per minute minus the person's age; the *maximum* is 200 minus age (La Place, 1984). Thus, 30-year-olds would maintain their heart rate between 130 and 170 beats per minute during aerobics.

3. *Cool-down.* The last few minutes of exercise should taper off in intensity to return the body to its normal state. These exercises can include calisthenics or walking.

Although this ideal seems fairly rigid, there is room for variation. Thus, individuals who exercise at the upper end of their target range can use fewer or shorter exercise periods each week. People can also tailor the program to their goals and interests by varying the exercises they perform during each phase and across sessions. For instance, they can vary the aerobics they do, jogging on one day, skipping rope on another, swimming on another, and so on. If they want to firm their abdomens, they can focus on appropriate activities during the warmup and cool-down phases.

Is the Ideal Necessary to Benefit Health?

Not all people can or will get the ideal amount and type of physical activity. Can they benefit from less? Absolutely, and the activity needn't be "exercise." Individuals can get substantial health and fitness benefits from just 30 minutes of daily moderate activity—such as walking briskly, taking a leisurely bicycle ride, or gardening—and this activity can occur in, say, 10-minute periods rather than all at once (Blair, Kohl, Gordon, & Paffenbarger, 1992). The closer to the ideal type and amount of activity one gets, the greater the benefits. But the most important thing for maintaining health is *not* to have an almost completely sedentary lifestyle.

& Van Camp, 1985). The work capacity of these men decreased only slightly across the 18 years, whereas individuals in the general population tend to show a 1–2% decrease per year. Also, the percentage of body fat and resting blood pressure of these men did not show the increases that usually occur during these years. This and other evidence clearly indicates that engaging in aerobic exercise curbs the usual decline in fitness that people experience as they get older (Buchner et al., 1992).

The physical benefits from regular exercise are reflected also in people's health and longevity (Sallis & Owen, 1999). Vigorous exercise produces the greatest gains, but even several brisk walks a month can benefit longevity (Kujala, Kaprio, Sarna, & Koskenvuo, 1998). The main health benefits of exercise relate to

People of all ages can benefit from exercise programs. These kindergartners are in a physical education class.

preventing cardiovascular problems and some forms of cancer (Blair, Kohl, Gordon, & Paffenbarger, 1992; Sallis & Owen, 1999). Many studies have demonstrated that individuals who regularly engage in vigorous physical activity are less likely to develop and die from coronary heart disease (CHD) than those who lead relatively sedentary lives (Powell, Thompson, Caspersen, & Kendrick, 1987). Although no experimental research has been done in which human subjects were randomly assigned to exercise and nonexercise conditions, research with animals and prospective studies with humans indicate that the link between physical activity and reduced risk of CHD is probably causal.

How does engaging in regular vigorous activity protect individuals against CHD? The role of exercise in reducing blood pressure is especially clear. Studies have shown that children and adults who are physically active have lower systolic and diastolic blood pressure than those who are not (Haskell, 1984; Hofman, Walter, Connelly, & Vaughn, 1987; Panico et al., 1987). Furthermore, prospective studies have found that people who are physically fit and active are less likely to develop hypertension than less-fit and inactive people (Blair, Kohl, Gordon, & Paffenbarger, 1992). The evidence regarding whether exercising by itself can decrease blood pressure in hypertensive patients was inconsistent in early studies (Siegel & Blumenthal, 1991). But more recent experimental research has shown that exercise lowers blood pressure in both hypertensive and normotensive people (Arroll & Beaglehole, 1992; Braith et al., 1994; Kokkinos et al., 1995; Pescatello, Fargo, Leach, & Scherzer, 1991). Exercise may also prevent CHD in two other ways: by reducing the occurrence of arrhythmic heartbeats and by decreasing LDL while increasing HDL serum cholesterol. Some evidence supports each of these possibilities (Blair, Kohl, Gordon, & Paffenbarger, 1992).

The risk of developing cancer has been linked to low physical activity; the evidence is fairly strong for colon cancer and more modest for other cancers, such as of the breast and prostate (Sallis & Owen, 1999). Although the reason for this link is unclear, part of it may involve the beneficial effect of both immediate and long-term exercise on the immune system. One study tested healthy, physically active 24- to 35-year-olds and 65- to 79-year-olds for the effects of a vigorous exercise session on immune function (Fiatarone et al., 1989). Natural killer cell number and

function were similar in both age groups before the session and increased substantially in both groups in response to the exercise.

Not all effects of exercise are beneficial—there can be hazards as well. One hazard occurs when people jog or bicycle in traffic, of course, risking a collision. But the most common problems that arise involve injury to bones or muscles from other kinds of accidents and from overstraining the body (Sallis & Owen, 1999). Many injuries happen to people who do not exercise regularly or are beginners. The main dangers to these people come from overtaxing their bodies and from unsafe exercise conditions, such as having improper shoes. Exercising too long in very hot weather can lead to heat exhaustion—with symptoms of dizziness, rapid and weak pulse, and headache—or a more severe condition called heat stroke, which can be fatal.

An infrequent but extermely serious hazard of exercise is in precipitating cardiac arrest. A study of autopsy reports for individuals who had died in association with exercising revealed that almost all these people died of cardiac arrest, and most of them had cardiovascular problems that existed prior to the attack (Northcote, Flannigan, & Ballantyne, 1986). Most of these problems could have been detected by medical screening, and the deaths of these people might have been avoided through medical counseling. Physicians and physical therapists can prescribe exercise programs for people with specific health problems, such as diabetes and CHD.

Another health hazard that relates to exercising is people's use of *anabolic steroids*—male hormones that build tissue—to increase muscle size and strength. Many more males than females use steroids, and most users are athletes (Strauss & Yesalis, 1991). Using steroids over an extended period has several negative health effects. It raises LDL and lowers HDL serum cholesterol and is related to liver and kidney tumors and to heart attacks and strokes. It also has a permanent masculinizing effect in women, increasing facial hair and lowering the voice, for instance. In males, it increases acne and balding and decreases the size and firmness of testes, at least temporarily. And adolescents who use steroids often share needles with others, putting each other at risk for HIV infection, and tend to use other drugs, too (DuRant et al., 1993). Tentative evidence suggests that continued steroid use may lead to psychological and physical dependence (Brower et al., 1990).

Conclusions regarding the health effects of exercise are fairly clear. Frequent physical activity, especially vigorous exercise, is psychologically and physically healthful, particularly for preventing heart disease. People who begin exercise programs should guard against overtaxing their bodies, exercise under safe conditions with proper skills, and have periodic medical examinations to determine whether any underlying risks exist. Although more people exercise today than was the case decades ago, most adults in industrialized countries do not get enough regular and energetic physical activity to gain substantial health benefits.

WHO GETS ENOUGH EXERCISE, WHO DOES NOT—AND WHY?

Physical activity varies across cultures. Probably most people around the world have lifestyles that provide regular, vigorous, and sustained activity naturally, without actually doing exercises. They commute to work by bicycle, for instance, or have jobs that involve energetic work, as farmers, laborers, and homemakers often do. These people can get very healthful amounts of physical activity if it occurs in at least three episodes a week, totaling about 3 hours (Blair, Kohl, Gordon, & Paffenbarger, 1992). But most people in the United States and other industrialized nations have relatively sedentary life circumstances. Many individuals who could be physically active in their normal lifestyles choose not to be—they may take rest breaks rather than sustaining an activity or opt to use a machine instead of doing a task manually. The high levels of physical activity of early childhood decline sharply; only half of American adolescents are vigorously active on a regular basis (Marcus et al., 2000). Because little is known about people's everyday physical activities, we will focus our discussion on factors associated with doing and not doing exercises.

Gender, Age, and Sociocultural Differences in Exercise

Overall demographic patterns give a portrait of who exercises in the United States. Men exercise more than women, and whites exercise more than blacks and Hispanics (USBC, 1999). People who exercise tend to be young and well-educated adults, members of upper socioeconomic groups, and individuals who have

participated in exercise in the past (Dishman, 1982, 1991). Similar patterns exist in other industrialized countries, such as Australia (Sallis & Owen, 1999). Another factor is age—as adults get older, most tend to

> disengage from participating in physical activities due less, it appears, to decrements in physiological functioning ability than to cultural and psychosocial factors which persuade them that vigorous exercise is not appropriate for the elderly. Sedentary social role models, distorted body image, exaggerated notions of risk, expectations of disapproval, fear of failure, misinformation, and limited previous involvement in physical activities all conspire to limit the elderly's desire to be active. (Vertinsky & Auman, 1988, p. 16)

These forces against exercise are particularly strong among many of today's elderly women. In contrast, elderly men engage in vigorous exercise more than men half their age (USBC, 1999). Women seem to learn from past sex-role experiences that men are more socially and physically suited to vigorous activity than females. Although both male and female older people tend to underrate their physical capabilities and exaggerate their health risks in performing energetic exercise after middle age, women are especially prone to these beliefs (Vertinsky & Auman, 1988; Woods & Birren, 1984). Health care workers and organizations for the elderly have many opportunities to dispel incorrect beliefs about health risks, change sex-role stereotypes regarding exercise, and encourage active lifestyles.

Reasons for Not Exercising

When individuals are asked why they don't exercise, the most common reason they give is that they cannot find the time (Dishman, 1991; Godin et al., 1992). Actually, of course, most people could have the time but choose to use it in other ways. People also report not exercising because they have no convenient place to do it or because the weather or other environmental conditions make it unpleasant or impossible.

Whether people exercise is also related to the amount of stress in their lives, social influences, and their beliefs. People who exercise regularly tend to skip sessions when they experience high levels of stress (Stetson et al., 1997). Social influences on exercise involve modeling, encouragement, and reinforcement by peers and family. Studies have found that adults who exercise tend to have spouses who encourage them to do so, and children and adolescents who exercise or engage in sports tend to have friends or family who also do so (Dishman, Sallis, & Orenstein, 1985; Gottlieb & Baker, 1986; Sallis et al., 1988). People's beliefs can influence exercising in at least two ways. First, individuals with high self-efficacy regarding their ability to exercise are more likely to do so than those with low self-efficacy (Clark, Patrick, Grembowski, & Durham, 1995; Wilcox & Storandt, 1996). Second, perceived susceptibility to illness can spur people to exercise. This was demonstrated in research in which individuals received information describing their level of fitness or indicating they might be susceptible to health problems that could be prevented through exercise (Godin, Desharnais, Jobin, & Cook, 1987; Wurtele & Maddux, 1987). Compared to people who did not get such information, those who did were more likely to start exercising.

People who do *not* exercise tend to have other risk factors for developing serious illnesses, such as by being overweight or smoking cigarettes. From the standpoint of performing health-protective behavior, people whose health would benefit most from physical activity seem to be the most resistant to starting or maintaining an exercise program. Quitting smoking may help: a study of smokers found that those who quit were more likely to start exercising than those who didn't (Perkins et al., 1993).

"SURE, JOGGING TAKES THE YEARS OFF · · · · I HAVEN'T FELT THIS RIDICULOUS SINCE I WAS 13."

Reprinted courtesy of Bunny Hoest.

PROMOTING EXERCISE BEHAVIOR

A person who spends time watching youngsters play is likely to have the impression that children are innately very active—running, jumping, and climbing—and that they do not need to be encouraged to exercise, as older individuals do. Some children seem to find physical activity naturally reinforcing (Epstein, Kilanowski, Consalvi, & Paluch, 1999). Although most children and adolescents are more active than adults, many other children are not active enough (Marcus et al., 2000). People of all ages could benefit from school, park, and worksite recreation programs and facilities to promote exercise.

To obtain the full health benefits of physical activity, people need to continue doing exercises or being very active in their normal lifestyles throughout their lives. Few people in industrialized societies achieve this ideal. Of individuals who are already exercising

regularly at any given time, about half will quit in the coming year (Dishman, Sallis, & Orenstein, 1985). Table 8.2 presents several strategies that are important in helping people start and continue exercising. These strategies can be applied by individuals who decide on their own to start or by organized interventions to promote exercise in target populations, such as schoolchildren, workers, or the elderly. Note two additional points. First, we can promote physical activity by giving rewards for increased exercising *and* for decreased sedentary behavior (Epstein, Saelens, & O'Brien, 1995). Second, physicians can increase physical activity markedly in sedentary patients by giving verbal and written advice on specific behaviors and goals (Swinburn et al., 1998).

Interventions with various populations have been successful in promoting exercise, particularly if they included behavioral methods to modify the antecedents and consequences of physical activity (Sallis & Owen, 1999). Interventions since the late 1980s that have included strategies like those in

Table 8.2 *Strategies to Promote Exercising*

- *Preassessment.* Before people begin an exercise program, they need to determine their purposes for exercising and the benefits they can expect. They should also assess their health status, preferably through a medical checkup.
- *Exercise selection.* The exercises included in the program should be tailored to meet the health needs of the individual and his or her interests and purposes, such as firming up certain parts of the body. People are more likely to stick with the program if it includes exercises that they enjoy doing.
- *Exercise conditions.* Before people start an exercise program, they should determine when and where they will exercise and arrange to get any equipment they will need. Some people seem to adhere to a program if they pick a fixed time for exercising and refuse to schedule anything else at that time; others can be more flexible and still make sure to exercise about every other day. The exercise conditions should be safe and convenient.
- *Goals.* Most people adhere to a program more closely if they write out a specific sequence of goals and consequences for exercise behavior in a behavioral contract. The goals should be graduated, beginning at a modest level. They should also be measurable— as body weight or number of push-ups would be—rather than vague, such as "to feel good."
- *Consequences.* Exercise should lead to reinforcement. Some individuals may need tangible reinforcers to maintain their exercise behavior in the early stages of the program. After these people get in shape, many will find that the enjoyment of exercise and the physical benefits are sufficient rewards.
- *Social influence.* People are more likely to start and stick with an exercise program if these efforts have the support and encouragement of family and friends. Exercising with a partner or in groups sometimes enhances people's motivation to continue in a program.
- *Record keeping.* People can enhance their motivation to exercise by keeping records of their weight and performance. Seeing on paper how far they have progressed can be very reinforcing.

Sources: Dishman, Sallis, & Orenstein, 1985; Oldridge, 1984; Sallis & Owen, 1999; Serfass & Gerberich, 1984.

Table 8.2 have reported higher rates of exercise adherence and fewer dropouts than earlier programs (Marcus et al., 2000). Two other strategies appear to increase success. First, interventions that provide contact by telephone to assess progress and provide advice when there are problems are more successful than those that do not (Marcus et al., 2000). Second, an important factor in people's starting and sticking with an exercise routine is their *readiness* to do so, in terms of the stages of change model (see Chapter 6). People who are at the contemplation stage—that is, those who are considering the change seriously—are more likely to start exercising and to exercise vigorously once they do than are people at the precontemplation stage (Armstrong, Sallis, Hovell, & Hofstetter, 1992). Interventions that are tailored to the motivational readiness of individuals to exercise are more effective than standard, nontailored programs (Marcus et al., 1998).

SAFETY

Unsafe conditions threaten people's health in virtually all environments, such as in traffic, at home, on the job, and at the beach. These conditions produce huge numbers of illnesses, injuries, and deaths each year. In most cases, these health problems could have been avoided if the victim or other people had used reasonable safety precautions. Sometimes people don't know how to prevent injury—as is often the case for elderly individuals who become injured when they fall— but safety training can reduce these injuries (Tinetti et al., 1994). Let's see what is known about the hazards people face and how to help people live safer lives.

ACCIDENTS

Each day in the United States, over 150,000 injuries occur that lead to restricted activity or require medical attention (USBC, 1999). Some of these injuries are serious enough to cause long-term disability or death. More than 86,000 Americans die each year from unintentional injuries in accidents (USBC, 1999). By far the most frequent of these accidental fatalities involve traffic mishaps—followed by falls, poisonings, fires, and drownings. More than 5,000 people die in accidents at their jobs each year, and thousands of other workers are seriously injured (NCHS, 2000). The industries with the highest mortality rates include construction and transportation, and industries with the highest injury rates are transportation, construction, manufacturing, agriculture and fishing, and mining. Government data reveal that accidental injury is:

- The fifth most frequent cause of death in the American population as a whole.
- The leading cause of death of individuals under age 45.
- Responsible for nearly 40% of all deaths of children 1 to 14 years of age (USBC, 1999).

Another way to see the relative impact of injury versus disease on life is to estimate the years of life lost by the victims of these causes of death. We could, for instance, use the age of 65 as a standard, subtract the age of death of each person who dies earlier, and then total all the years lost to injuries separately from those lost to disease. Calculations like these reveal that the total number of years lost from the combination of unintentional and intentional (that is, homicide or suicide) injuries in the United States is about the same as from the combination of heart disease, cancer, and stroke—the three most frequent causes of death in America (USDHHS, 1995). Over 60% of all injury deaths are unintentional.

How can accidental injuries be prevented? In discussing this question, we will focus on injuries in traffic mishaps for two reasons: (1) they account for about half of all accidental deaths and (2) researchers have done many studies on methods to prevent traffic injuries. The death rates for motor vehicle accidents in the United States increase dramatically during adolescence, as depicted in Figure 8–3, and the rate of deaths from traffic mishaps among 15- to 24-year-olds is over twice as high for males as for females (NCHS, 2000). Because of the high rates of traffic fatalities in adolescence, special safe-driving programs have been directed toward teenagers. One approach has involved providing driver training in high schools, and early quasi-experimental research showed that students who take driver education courses subsequently have fewer accidents than those who do not. But later studies revealed that the course itself was *not* the cause of this relationship; for some reason, students who elect to take driver education simply drive less than those who do not (Robertson, 1986). Similarly, driver education for adults—for example, as a condition for employment or in response to traffic violations—also seems to have little effect on accidents.

Other ways to reduce traffic accidents have been more effective than driver training. One approach capitalizes on research findings regarding drivers' perceptual and reaction abilities, with the goal of reducing their errors and enhancing their reaction time. Public

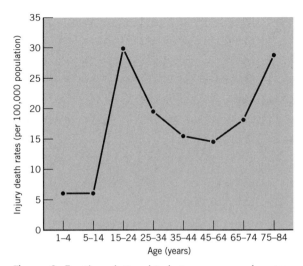

Figure 8–3   The relationship between age and motor-vehicle-injury death rates in the United States. (Data from NCHS, 2000, Table 45.) Note, however, that the dramatic increase during adolescence primarily reflects the deaths of individuals who are *occupants* of motor vehicles; much of the upswing in old age reflects deaths of individuals who are *pedestrians* (Cataldo et al., 1986).

health researcher Leon Robertson has described two examples:

> An extra brake light mounted in the center of the vehicle above the trunk resulted in a 50% reduction in rear-end collisions when the front vehicle was braking, compared to randomly assigned control cars in the same fleets.
> Stripes across a road at an exponentially decreasing distance creates the illusion of acceleration when crossing at a constant speed. ...Installation of such stripes at high speed approaches to traffic circles in England resulted in an average 66% reduction in crashes at such sites. (1986, pp. 22–23)

Findings such as these have led to changes in automobile design and highway markings, which should reduce traffic injuries. Another approach that is quite effective in reducing traffic deaths is not very popular with teenagers; it involves raising the legal driving age (Robertson, 1986).

Injuries and deaths can also be prevented if drivers and passengers will use protective equipment, such as seat belts in cars and helmets when riding motorcycles or bicycles (Latimer & Lave, 1987; Robertson, 1986; Waller, 1987). After seat belts were installed as standard equipment in cars, few people opted to use them. As a result, researchers began to study methods to promote the use of protective equipment in cars. Some of these studies were conducted to improve car safety for children by providing instruction and information to parents through hospitals and pediatricians. These programs have had mixed success (Cataldo et al., 1986; Christophersen, 1984). A successful hospital-based program provided computer-assisted video instruction on using an infant safety seat to mothers before leaving the hospital after giving birth (Hletko, Robin, Hletko, & Stone, 1987). A parking lot attendant at the hospital subsequently assessed the use of a safety seat when the mother brought the baby back for a checkup 4 months later. Many more of these mothers than untrained mothers had their infants correctly restrained. Interventions that target the parents are more successful when there are strong consequences for the parents' behavior—reinforcement for safety action or punishment for inaction (Tremblay & Peterson, 1999).

Some programs to increase children's traffic safety have been directed at the child, rather than the parent. One program presented a 2-week passenger safety curriculum to children in several preschools, using a theme character called "Bucklebear" (Chang, Dillman, Leonard, & English, 1985). The children in several other preschools served as a control group who were matched to the experimental subjects for their prior seat belt use. Follow-up observations in the preschool parking lots 3 weeks after the program was completed revealed that over 44% of the "Bucklebear" children and only about 22% of the control children were using seat belts. Other programs have focused on children's use of bicycle helmets or car safety restraints; some included incentives for the parents, such as discounts to buy helmets (Tremblay & Peterson, 1999). After one of these programs, children in the community increased helmet use markedly and had fewer head injuries over the next several years.

Fewer than 15% of Americans were using seat belts by the early 1980s, despite public health announcements and other programs to promote this behavior (Latimer & Lave, 1987). As a result, many states began to pass laws requiring adults and children to use protective equipment in cars. Seat belt and safety seat use generally increased sharply and traffic fatalities decreased after these laws went into effect (Latimer & Lave, 1987; Robertson, 1986; Wagenaar & Webster, 1986; Waller, 1987). But the behaviors regressed after a while, and probably less than half of the people were complying with the laws by the time a year had passed. Although such laws are helpful, they may not be sufficient.

ENVIRONMENTAL HAZARDS

A 1987 newspaper poll in New Jersey asked people, "Do you use sunscreen in the summer?" One young

Parents can teach their children to use sunscreen.

man answered, "No. I don't use anything—never have, never will," and a young woman said, "Never, because the sun's not too hot in New Jersey." Another young woman said she uses only the weakest sunscreen because, "I want to have a gorgeous tan." Ever since the French fashion designer Coco Chanel made tanning fashionable, people in many parts of the world have come to believe tans are attractive and healthful. This belief develops by early adolescence (Broadstock, Borland, & Gason, 1992).

Today we know that excessive exposure to the sun's ultraviolet rays makes the skin age and can cause skin cancers, particularly in people who are fair skinned and burn easily (Harrison, MacLennan, Speare, & Wronski, 1994). Keep in mind that sunlamps and sunbeds have the same effect, and the more exposure to them the greater the chance of getting cancer (Westerdahl et al., 1994). Although most cases of skin cancer can be easily treated and cured, others cannot, especially if they are discovered late (ACS, 2000). Dermatologists and other health care practitioners

recognize that most people will not stay out of the sun and that many strive for a "healthy" and attractive tan. As a result, these practitioners recommend that most people use sunscreens when exposed to the sun for more than, say, an hour or so. A study of adult California sunbathers found that those who use sunscreens tend to be females rather than males and know about skin cancer risks (Keesling & Friedman, 1987). Research on message framing in interventions found that people are influenced more to use sunscreen by gain-framed messages ("Using sunscreen increases your chances of maintaining healthy, young-looking skin") than by loss-framed messages, which might state that not using sunscreen can cause cancer and prematurely aged skin (Detweiler et al., 1999).

Ultraviolet radiation is only one of many environmental hazards people need to guard against. Many harmful chemicals and gases exist in people's households, worksites, and general communities. Table 8.3 describes some of these hazards. People who work with hazardous materials need to know what the

Table 8.3   *Some Hazardous Chemicals and Gases That Can Appear in Households, Worksites, and Communities*

Household Hazards

People's homes contain various chemicals, such as pesticides and cleaning solvents, that are health hazards if they are accessible to children or used without adequate ventilation. Two other hazards are:

- *Lead* poisoning, which presents a serious health problem for developing embryos and children and can damage their nervous system and impair intelligence and hearing (Harvey, 1984). Children may ingest lead in many ways, such as by mouthing objects painted with lead-based paints, drinking water from a plumbing system with poorly soldered lead joints, or drinking acidic beverages from lead-glazed ceramics. Pregnant women who ingest leaded water or beverages may pass the substance on to their developing babies.
- *Radon*, a radioactive odorless gas that can cause lung cancer with long-term exposure, especially in people who smoke. This gas may be present at high levels in millions of homes throughout the United States (Leary, 1998). Because radon enters the house from the ground, the usual way for reducing radon pollution is to ventilate the basement.

Worksite Hazards

Millions of people have jobs that can bring them in contact with hazardous substances, some of which are toxic or carcinogenic (Anderson, 1982; Baker, 1988; Clever & Omenn, 1988; Levy, 1985; USDHHS, 1985b).

- *Asbestos* is a substance that has been used in buildings and equipment as a fire retardant. People who have regular contact with it risk developing lung cancer.
- *Benzine* exposure at high levels and over time is linked to bone marrow cancer; *vinyl chloride*, with liver cancer; *aromatic amines*, with bladder cancer; and *cadmium*, with prostate cancer.

Community Hazards

The air, water, and ground have become polluted with harmful chemicals and gases in communities in the United States and around the world. This pollution can harm people directly or by getting into the foods they eat.

- *Chemical waste* from industry and other sources can contain toxic substances, such as cyanide, benzine, and lead (Holusha, 1991). The accidental, massive release of cyanide gas at a Union Carbide plant in Bhopal, India, killed thousands of people.
- *Radiation* gets into the environment from nuclear power, hospital, military, and industrial sources. Exposure at high levels or for extended periods causes cancer, as seen after the massive radiation release in 1986 at the Soviet nuclear power plant in Chernobyl (Kolata, 1992a).

substances are, what dangers they pose, and how to use them safely. Some states in America have enacted "Right to Know" laws that require (1) employers to notify and train employees regarding the safe use of hazardous materials and (2) community agencies to provide information about the exposure of residents to hazardous materials. If people know that a danger exists, they can try to take protective action (for example, by drinking bottled water), become involved in community change, and notify their physician so that appropriate tests can be done periodically as secondary prevention (Winett, King, & Altman, 1989).

People are becoming increasingly concerned about the chemicals and gases that pervade our lives.

They should be vigilant—but they should also be aware of three things. First, not every chemical or gas is harmful. Second, exposure to toxic or carcinogenic substances poses little risk when the contact is infrequent and the dosage is small (Ames & Gold, 1990; Cohen & Ellwein, 1990). Third, some harmful substances may have benefits that outweigh their dangers. For example, chlorinating water has all but erased many of the waterborne infections that once threatened enormous numbers of lives. But chlorinated water often has very small amounts of the carcinogen *chloroform* in it. Given these circumstances, the benefits of chlorinating appear to outweight the risks.

SUMMARY

In addition to water, food contains five types of chemical components: carbohydrates, lipids or "fats," proteins, vitamins, and minerals. People can get all the nutrients and fiber they need by eating diets that include grains, fruits, vegetables, milk products, and meats and fish. Until recently, the trend in American diets was toward consuming more and more sugar, animal fats, and animal proteins, while consuming less and less fiber. People's food preferences are determined by biological and psychosocial factors.

Diet is associated with the development of atherosclerosis, hypertension, and cancer. Cholesterol is the main dietary culprit in atherosclerosis. Whether plaques form in our blood vessels depends on the presence of three types of lipoproteins: low-density lipoprotein, very-low-density lipoprotein, and high-density lipoprotein. Genetic factors and the foods people eat determine serum cholesterol levels. Although Americans have been reducing their intake of cholesterol, they still consume far too much. Intervention programs can be effective in helping people reduce dietary cholesterol substantially. High blood pressure can result from consuming too much sodium. Diets high in fat and low in fiber increase people's risk of cancer, especially cancer of the colon.

Many people are very conscious of and concerned about their weight. Most concerns among Americans are with being too fat, rather than too thin, particularly among females. We can determine whether individuals are too heavy by comparing their weights against the desirable weights given in standard tables or by calculating their body mass index (BMI). People are classified as overweight if their BMI exceeds 25; they are considered obese if their BMI is more than 30. People become

fat because they consume more calories than they burn up through metabolism. Excess calories are stored as fat in adipose tissue, which contains cells that can increase in size and number, especially in childhood and adolescence. Heredity plays a role in weight control, probably by affecting the set-point for body weight. Psychosocial factors also affect weight control. Restraint theory proposes that individuals who struggle constantly to keep their weight down develop abnormal eating patterns of inhibition and disinhibition.

Obesity is associated with the development of hypertension, coronary heart disease, and diabetes. These health risks depend on the person's fitness and amount and location of fat tissue. Risks decrease with fitness and increase as the degree of obesity increases and when fat is concentrated in the abdominal region, rather than mostly in the thighs, hips, and buttocks. Prevention of overweight should begin in childhood to avoid fat-cell hyperplasia. Schools and parents can play important roles in this effort.

Most heavy people try to reduce their weight on their own by going on a diet. Those who are not able to lose weight on their own often seek help, such as through self-help groups and weight-loss programs. Behavioral and cognitive methods are more effective than other approaches. In relatively extreme cases, drastic procedures with medical supervision may be warranted; these procedures include placing the patient on a very-low-calorie diet, using appetite-suppressing drugs, or performing surgery. Although most people who lose weight in cognitive-behavioral programs keep most of that weight off, others do not; relapse can be reduced if the programs make use of frequent follow-up meetings with weight-control therapists and social influences of other members in a treatment group.

Anorexia nervosa is an eating disorder that results in an unhealthy and extreme loss of weight. Bulimia nervosa is an eating disorder that involves recurrent episodes of binge eating and purging. Both of these disorders occur mainly in adolescence and early adulthood and are much more prevalent in females than in males. Treatment is more difficult and less successful for anorexia than for bulimia.

More people are exercising today than they were years ago. Three types of exercise are isotonic, isometric, and isokinetic. Aerobic exercise refers to energetic physical activity that involves rhythmical movement of large muscle groups and requires high levels of oxygen over a period of half an hour or so. A healthful program of exercise would include a warmup phase, an aerobic exercise phase, and a cool-down phase. Engaging regularly in vigorous exercise increases people's life span and protects them against coronary heart disease, partly because it reduces blood pressure. People who exercise tend to be young and well-educated adults from the upper social classes. Individuals whose health would benefit most from physical activity seem to be the most resistant to starting and maintaining exercising.

Tens of thousands of people die each year in accidents involving traffic mishaps, falls, drowning, fire, and poisoning. Death rates for motor vehicle accidents increase dramatically during adolescence. People also need to guard against many environmental hazards, including excessive exposure to sunlight and harmful chemicals and gases.

KEY TERMS

lipoproteins	high-density lipoprotein	insulin	isotonic exercise
low-density lipoprotein	overweight	restraint theory	isometric exercise
very-low-density lipoprotein	obese	anorexia nervosa	isokinetic exercise
	set-point theory	bulimia nervosa	aerobic exercise

PART IV

BECOMING ILL AND GETTING MEDICAL TREATMENT

9

USING HEALTH SERVICES

PROLOGUE

Jo's life had just undergone major changes—she had been promoted by her employer and relocated to a new town with her two children. Then she noticed that a mole had developed on her shoulder. Uncertain whether the mole was a sign of something serious, and harried by her current pressures, she decided to wait before doing anything about it. Then, soon after she found a new family physician, her youngest child became ill with the flu. Jo made an appointment for 10-year-old Mary with Dr. Armstrong and thought, "If I get a chance, I'll mention the mole to the doctor when we go, and have him look at it." But she wondered if he would be like their last physician, who would sweep into the examining room, hurriedly ask very specific short-answer questions, dominate the conversation, and rush on to the next patient.

Fortunately, Dr. Armstrong was not like their last doctor. He started the visit by chatting a little with Mary to learn more about her and to establish a friendly relationship. Then he asked her about her health problem, did some physical tests, and discussed with her and Jo what they needed to do to treat the illness. At the end of that discussion, he switched the focus to Jo, asking about her job and general life situation to assess possible risk factors. When he asked, "How has your health been recently?" she anxiously told him about the mole, which he inspected. He told her that it looked harmless—as most moles are. He added, "People who have a mole should inspect it periodically, once a month or so. If it changes color, bleeds, grows, or changes in any other way please have me examine it without delay. Some moles develop into a skin cancer called melanoma, which can be treated effectively if we catch it early. I'll give you some information about moles before you leave."

Jo left the office very much relieved that the doctor had examined the mole and pronounced it harmless. She also noted that if the mole had been the beginnings of melanoma, they would have caught it early. She felt secure in having found a competent and caring physician whom she and her children could talk to easily and trust.

With this chapter, our main focus in this book begins to *shift from primary to secondary prevention* efforts. Most health care systems engage chiefly in secondary and tertiary care, providing treatment to stop or reverse a problem or to retard damage it might cause and rehabilitate the person. In this chapter, we will see that the relationship formed between the patient and the health care *practitioner*, or health professional, can influence the actions they take in primary, secondary, and tertiary prevention. The importance of this relationship will become clear as we discuss the kinds of health services available to people, how patients decide when to use these services, and why some patients use health services effectively whereas others do not. As we examine these topics, you will find answers to questions you may have about people's use of health services. How do people decide they are sick and may need medical attention? Why do some individuals seek health care more readily than others do? How can patients influence their health care? Do people follow medical advice—and if not, why don't they comply?

TYPES OF HEALTH SERVICES

Systems of medical care delivery and management are complex in most societies, particularly in industri-alized nations like the United States, where the medical system consists of an enormous variety of health services. To see the complex nature of health care systems, we will consider the specialized functions of health care workers, compare office-based and inpatient treatment, and contrast the American medical system with systems in other countries.

SPECIALIZED FUNCTIONS OF PRACTITIONERS

Medical care systems have staffs of health care workers who differ greatly in their roles and specialties. The American system, for instance, employs millions of professionals, including physicians of many types—general practitioners, pediatricians, cardiologists, neurosurgeons, dermatologists, gynecologists, psychiatrists, and so on—as well as nurses, dentists, optometrists, respiratory therapists, physical therapists, medical social workers, and dietitians, to name only a small number. Each type of practitioner provides a different type of health service, using specialized knowledge and skills.

Because each of these services involves an enormous amount of knowledge and skill that grows and changes very rapidly, individual practitioners cannot perform the services of several specialties simultaneously with a high degree of skill. The advantage in organizing the health care system into specialties is that patients can receive the greatest expertise available for each aspect of the treatment of each health problem. But this great advantage is not without drawbacks. For instance, the many professionals who provide care for a particular individual do not always communicate with each other effectively, so that the physician in charge of the treatment may not have a full picture of the person's condition or progress. Also, because many practitioners work with a patient very briefly—performing just a few medical tests, for example—the contact these practitioners have with patients is often impersonal.

OFFICE-BASED AND INPATIENT TREATMENT

When we get sick and seek professional treatment, the first place we usually go is to our family physician at his or her office. This practitioner can treat the illness, refer us to a specialist for treatment, or arrange for hospitalization.

People with serious illnesses who require medical attention either on a continuous basis or with complex equipment or procedures generally receive treatment as inpatients in hospitals and nursing homes. *Hospitals* are the most complex medical facilities in medical care systems, employing highly sophisticated equipment and skilled practitioners from almost all specialty areas. As a result, they can provide a wide variety of services, ranging from emergency care, to diagnostic testing, to curative treatment, to rehabilitation and social services. Many hospitals also offer health promotion facilities, such as wellness centers and weight loss programs. Some hospitals have specialized missions, such as in providing care for children or for certain health problems—cancer, eye diseases, or orthopedic problems, for instance.

Nursing homes provide care for individuals who need relatively long-term medical and personal care, particularly if the patients or their families cannot provide this care (Shanas & Maddox, 1985; USBC, 1999; Vladeck, 1983). The large majority of patients in nursing homes are handicapped or frail, elderly individuals who often need help in day-to-day activities such as dressing and bathing themselves. The average nursing home in the United States is a moderately sized facility, having about 100 beds. But because there are so many nursing homes, and patients stay there for fairly long periods of time, on any given day nursing homes serve many more individuals than hospitals do. Nursing homes vary in the degree of skilled nursing and rehabilitative services they are prepared to provide. Although most American nursing homes provide high-quality care, many others do not and have been cited for having unsanitary conditions, abusing patients, and failing to follow doctors' instructions for giving drugs (Tolchin, 1988).

People with serious health problems in many nations have been relying less and less on inpatient services in recent years, using *outpatient* or *home health care* instead (Shanas & Maddox, 1985; NCHS, 2000; USBC, 1999). After 1980 in the United States, hospital admissions declined sharply, and the number of outpatient visits doubled. The shift away from inpatient care has occurred because of the fast-rising costs of hospital and nursing home services and because technological advances have made it possible to maintain medical treatment with outpatients. An example of a widely used technological device that provides treatment on an outpatient basis is the *pacemaker*, which sends electrical pulses to regulate heartbeat. Many individuals with pacemakers can even transmit electrocardiograms by telephone to their physicians' offices. Another device is a pocket-sized pump that can deliver precise amounts of medication on a specific schedule.

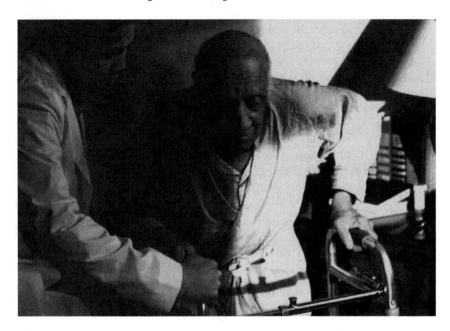

Most patients in nursing homes are elderly individuals who need long-term medical and personal care.

Clients who use home care usually begin their treatment on an inpatient basis, but are then discharged in the care of a home health care service.

Outpatient care offers some advantages over inpatient care. For one thing, home care is likely to be less expensive. Also, people usually prefer being at home, and can often return to work or school while receiving outpatient treatment. But for some patients—particularly the elderly—home health care can present problems if they lack needed help from family or friends and do not have means of transportation to make periodic visits to their physicians (Shanas & Maddox, 1985).

THE AMERICAN HEALTH CARE SYSTEM

When most Americans get sick and need treatment, their health insurance pays for most of the costs. Employers provide insurance for most working people. Many other people are covered under governmental insurance programs: *Medicare* for the elderly and *Medicaid* for low-income people. But 16% of Americans are not insured (USBC, 1999). This percentage has been increasing in recent years, and is much higher for Hispanics and blacks than whites. These people can't afford to get sick.

Several decades ago, private-practice physicians gave all office-based medical treatment in the United States, and each charged a fee for each service. American health insurance now structures medical care within two broad options: fee-for-service and managed-care programs. People who opt for *fee-for-service* programs can choose their physicians, and the insurance pays most (often, 80%) of incurred charges. Practitioners who treat fee-for-service patients generally must accept the amount of payment insurance plans specify. The amount is often lower than the practitioner requests; because Medicaid plans usually pay very low amounts, members often have difficulty finding a practitioner who will provide treatment. *Managed-care* programs place important restrictions on their members' choices and services. Most managed-care and fee-for-service programs charge annual fees members or their employers pay; fees are lower in managed-care plans. Over half of employed Americans opt for managed-care programs; Medicare began offering managed-care programs in the late 1990s (Luft, 1998; USBC, 1999).

The most common type of managed-care plan is the *health-maintenance organization* (HMO), in which members are entitled to use the services of any affiliated physician or hospital with little or no additional charges (CU, 1999b; Miller & Luft, 1994; USBC, 1999). Some affiliated physicians practice in HMO clinics, but others have their own offices; some are salaried employees of the HMO, and others receive payment based on the number of clients they see or the specific procedures they perform. If necessary, the primary care physician can arrange for the patient to be referred to a specialist or admitted to a hospital. The HMO pays for all treatments it arranges or recommends and negotiates with specific hospitals and physicians for discounted fee-for-service rates. Some HMOs provide financial incentives to their physicians for cost-saving behaviors, such as seeing a large number of clients per hour or sending a small number of patients to hospitals. HMOs that use these kinds of incentives may encourage less-than-optimal care. Another type of managed-care plan—called the *preferred provider organization* (PPO)—is very similar to some HMOs. Each PPO consists of a network of affiliated physicians and hospitals that have agreed to discount their usual charges; members may go to any affiliated physician or hospital.

Is the medical care provided by HMOs as good as that given by private physicians? There are some important problems in arriving at a clear answer to this question. For one thing, HMOs vary greatly in their policies and structures, which change frequently. Also, the research comparing HMO and private-physician care has used quasi-experimental methods, and most of the HMOs studied have been large, well-established plans, rather than newer, developing ones. Findings from research comparing fee-for-service with HMO plans indicates that patients in HMOs (CU, 1999b; Miller & Luft, 1994):

- Are less likely to be admitted to a hospital, and when admitted, they are likely to leave sooner.

- Use more preventive examinations and procedures.

- Often face major obstacles getting treatment they need (HMOs vary in willingness to approve procedures), but medical care is comparable for most patients otherwise.

- Report being somewhat less satisfied with the care they received but much more satisfied with the costs to them.

But some research has revealed worse health outcomes for chronically ill elderly and poor patients in American HMO plans than in fee-for-service plans (Ware et al., 1996). And consumer organizations have found substantial variations in the quality of HMO plans and recommend that people choose plans carefully (CU, 1999b). People can seek ratings of HMOs

and answers to critical questions, such as whether the health plan pays for emergency care received in other countries or without the plan's OK and allows physicians to refer members to specialists freely.

Some people argue that physicians in large HMOs are less concerned with satisfying their clients because the HMO pays their salaries, not the patients. Managed-care plans are owned privately, and mergers are producing huge, centralized organizations that may not be responsive to clients' needs. These circumstances may undermine patients' trust in their physicians and medical care (Mechanic, 1998). Americans receive medical care that is among the very finest in the world. But the health care system has important flaws. Its costs are skyrocketing, it is not accessible to the many people who have inadequate or no insurance, and it is so complex and offers so many managed-care options that deciding to use these services can be intimidating to some people. It also distributes care unequally, even among people who are insured: of people hospitalized for heart disease, those with Medicaid insurance are far less likely to receive widely used but expensive procedures, such as bypass surgery, than those with private insurance (Wenneker, Weissman, & Epstein, 1990). Do other countries have health care systems that have solved these problems?

HEALTH CARE SYSTEMS IN OTHER COUNTRIES

Canada, Japan, and most European countries have adopted health care systems that incorporate national health insurance programs for all of their citizens (Schmidt & Dlugosch, 1991). The health care they provide is excellent and usually less complicated to use than America's. People in poorer countries generally have little or no coverage, and the ability to pay for service or private insurance is increasing as a device to ration medical care, even in richer nations (WHO, 1999c).

How are the health care systems with national health insurance programs structured and financed? Each one is different—for instance, some systems provide insurance through the government, but others require employers to provide it; in some systems most physicians are employed by the government, but in others most doctors are privately employed. Let's look at the Canadian system as an example. It has the following features (CU, 1992):

- The Canadian system provides coverage for everyone in the nation, financed through payroll taxes. Each province pays its citizens' medical bills and determines its own policies, such as what types of care will be covered. In addition to office-based and hospital care, most provinces cover prescription drugs for people over age 65, long-term care, and mental health services. Private insurance is available for services not covered.

- Canadian physicians are typically employed privately and practice in their own offices. Patients may choose any doctor they wish.

- The fees physicians charge are determined by the province in negotiation with the medical association.

Compared with the American health care system, other systems are far less expensive in terms of costs per citizen and the percentage of each country's gross domestic product spent on health care (NCHS, 2000). Because of steadily increasing costs in most nations, efforts are being made around the world to slow these increases (WHO, 1999c). Funding problems in some countries, such as Britain, have sometimes led to long waits for care and the inability to get needed treatment (Lyall, 2000).

In any health care system, a critical step in seeking medical attention is finding a regular physician to contact when we are sick. He or she can either cure our illness or help us find other help within the system. Now, suppose someone who has a regular physician develops some symptoms—say, nausea and a moderately high fever. Will the person go to the doctor? An important step in using health services involves deciding when we are sick enough to require medical attention in the first place. This is the topic of the next section.

PERCEIVING AND INTERPRETING SYMPTOMS

If you came down with a case of strep throat as a child, chances are the symptoms you experienced were obvious to you and your parents. You had a very sore throat, fever, and headache, for instance. Your physician asked about your symptoms, took your temperature and did some tests, and prescribed a curative course of action. From experiences of this type, you learned that symptoms accompany illness—and when they go away, you are well again. You also learned that certain symptoms reliably signal certain illnesses, and that some symptoms are more serious than others. As an adult, you decide whether to visit your physician on the basis of the symptoms you perceive and what they mean to you.

PERCEIVING SYMPTOMS

Perceiving symptoms of illness is more complicated than it may seem. It is true that we perceive internal states on the basis of physical sensations, and we are more likely to notice strong sensations than weak ones. But we do not assess our internal states very accurately. For example, people's estimates of their own heart rate, breathing function, and degree of nasal congestion correlate poorly with physiological measures of these states (Pennebaker, 1983; Rietveld & Brosschot, 1999). Individuals also have trouble perceiving external symptoms, such as whether a mole-like skin lesion is melanoma (Miles & Meehan, 1995). Partly because of people's low degree of accuracy in assessing signs of illness, the point at which people recognize a symptom can differ from one individual to the next and within the same person from one time to the next. Furthermore, people do not always notice a symptom—even a strong one—when it is there, and sometimes they may perceive a symptom that has no actual physical basis. Let's see what factors affect our perception of symptoms.

Individual Differences

"He's such a big baby; he notices every little ache and pain," you may have heard someone say. Why do some individuals report more symptoms than others do? One reason is that some people simply *have* more symptoms than others, of course. Another possibility is that people could differ in the sensations they experience from the same symptom, such as a specific intensity of a painful stimulus. But research has cast doubt on this possibility. For instance, studies testing large numbers of normal individuals with stimuli of different temperatures have found that people seem to have a uniform threshold at which heat becomes painful—"almost all persons begin to feel pain when the tissue temperature rises to a level between 44°C and 46°C" (Guyton, 1985, p. 302). On the other hand, individuals differ in the degree of pain they will tolerate before doing something about it, such as taking medication (Karoly, 1985; Melzack & Wall, 1982).

Some individuals seem to pay more attention to their internal states than others do (Pennebaker, 1983). They show a heightened awareness of or sensitivity to their body sensations. As a result, these people notice changes more quickly than individuals who tend to focus their attention on external happenings. But this does not mean internally focused individuals' perceptions of internal changes are more *accurate*—indeed, research has found that they are more likely than externally focused people to overestimate changes in their bodily functions, such as heart rate (Pennebaker, 1983). Other research has shown that among patients who seek medical treatment for symptoms, those who are internally focused tend to have less severe illness and perceive their recovery as slower than those who pay less attention to their internal states (Miller, Brody, & Summerton, 1987). These findings suggest that many internally focused individuals may pay *too much* attention to their internal states and, in so doing, magnify departures from normal bodily sensations.

Competing Environmental Stimuli

You may have heard anecdotes about athletes who were unaware of a major injury they had suffered during a competition until after the sporting event was over—*then* it hurt! The extent to which people pay attention to internal stimuli at any given time depends partly on the nature or degree of environmental stimuli present at that time.

When the environment contains a great deal of sensory information or is exciting, people become less likely to notice internal sensations. People are far more likely to report sensations or physical symptoms when the external environment is boring or lacks information than when the environment captures their attention (Pennebaker, 1983). For instance, when watching a movie, they are more likely to notice an itch or a tickle in their throats during boring parts. Also, people who hold boring jobs or live alone tend to report more physical symptoms and use more aspirin and sleeping pills than those who hold interesting jobs or live with other people.

Psychosocial Influences

Because people are not very accurate in assessing their actual internal physical states, their percep-

tion of body sensations can be heavily influenced by cognitive, social, and emotional factors (Rietveld & Brosschot, 1999; Suls, Martin, & Leventhal, 1997). One way researchers have demonstrated the role of cognitive factors in symptom perception is in the effects of *placebos*, which are inert substances or sham treatments (Melzack & Wall, 1982; Roberts, 1995). For example, people who receive a placebo "drug" to reduce their pain, not knowing the drug is inert, often report that it relieves their symptoms or sensations.

Another demonstration of the role of cognitive factors in symptom perception focused on the symptoms women experience just before the onset of menstrual periods. Diane Ruble (1977) gave women a physiological "test" that she falsely described as accurately pinpointing the timing of their next menstruation. Using these false test results, she told randomly selected women either that they were within a couple of days of begining menstruation or that their menstruation was a week or more away. In fact, the beginning of menstruation was an average of about a week away for women in both conditions. The women then filled out a questionnaire that asked about current premenstrual symptoms. The women who were told they were near menstruation reported more premenstrual symptoms—such as water retention and pain—than the other women. These findings indicate that the premenstrual symptoms women experience may result not only from the physiological changes that occur in their bodies but from their beliefs, too.

The combined roles of cognitive, social, and emotional factors in symptom perception can be seen in two interesting phenomena. The first is called *medical student's disease*. As medical students learn about the symptoms of various diseases, more than two-thirds of them come to believe incorrectly that they have contracted one of these illnesses at one time or another (Mechanic, 1972). The second phenomenon, called *mass psychogenic illness* involves widespread symptom perception among a large group of individuals, even though tests indicate that their symptoms have no medical basis either in their bodies or in the environment, such as from toxic substances. Michael Colligan and his associates (1979) have described a case of mass psychogenic illness that began one summer morning at an electronics plant in a Midwestern city. A female production worker became faint, and another female worker who came to her aid also fainted. Soon, many other workers began reporting dizziness, headache, nausea, and difficulty breathing; 20 workers were taken to the hospital; and the building was evacuated. Two similar episodes occurred days later after the plant reopened. Medical and environmental tests after each episode revealed no abnormalities that could account for the symptoms the workers experienced.

Why do such phenomena occur? Researchers have described several reasons (Colligan et al., 1979; Mechanic, 1972; Suls, Martin, & Leventhal, 1997). The symptoms in medical student's disease and mass psychogenic illness often involve common physical sensations, such as headache or dizziness, that are vague and very subjective in nature. Cognitive factors come into play when the person exaggerates these sensations and attaches to them more importance than they warrant. Modeling is a social factor that undoubtedly contributes to the contagion in mass psychogenic illness; and the symptoms experienced in medical student's disease often seem to be modeled after those of a patient the students have seen. An important emotional factor in these phenomena is stress—that is, medical student's disease and mass psychogenic illness tend to occur when people have been experiencing high levels of anxiety, heavy workloads, or disturbing interpersonal conflicts. In some cases, stress may cause or exaggerate the sensations individuals perceive, as when nausea or headache are the symptoms the person notices. Research has shown that people report heightened symptoms when they experience negative emotional states, particularly anxiety (Rietveld & Brosschot, 1999; Watson & Pennebaker, 1989).

Sociocultural Differences

People in different cultures seem to differ in their perceptions of and reactions to illness symptoms—for instance, displaying much more distress and disability to pain in some cultures than in others (Young & Zane, 1995). These differences may result from cultural norms for reinforcing stoical versus distressed and disabled behaviors when in pain. We can consider three research findings. First, people of Asian cultures report more physical symptoms with psychological bases than people of other cultures (Chun, Enomoto, & Sue, 1996). Second, a study compared disability in individuals with long-term low back pain conditions in six different countries (Sanders et al., 1992). American pain patients reported the greatest overall impairment, such as of their work and social ac-

tivities. Italians and New Zealanders reported the second-largest impairments, followed by Japanese, Colombian, and Mexican pain patients. These differences did not result from differences in the severity or duration of the subjects' pain conditions. Third, of heart attack patients in the United States, black individuals experience symptoms that are less typical than those of whites and delay getting treatment longer (Lee et al., 1999).

In summary, people's perception of a symptom depends on the strength of the underlying physical sensation, their tendency to pay attention to their internal states, the degree to which external stimuli compete for their attention, and a variety of cognitive, social, and emotional processes. What individuals *do* when they perceive symptoms is the topic of the next section.

INTERPRETING AND RESPONDING TO SYMPTOMS

Psychiatrist George Engel (1980) described the case of a 55-year-old man whom he called Mr. Glover, who suffered his second heart attack 6 months after his first. He was at work, alone at his desk, when he experienced general discomfort, pressure over his chest, and pain down his left arm.

> The similarity of those symptoms to those of his heart attack six months earlier immediately came to mind ... but he dismissed this in favor of "fatigue," "gas," "muscle strain," and, finally, "emotional tension." But the negation itself, *"not another heart attack,"* leaves no doubt that the idea "heart attack" was very much in his mind despite his apparent denial. Behaviorally, he alternated between sitting quietly to "let it pass," pacing about the office "to work it off," and taking Alka-Seltzer. (p. 539)

When Mr. Glover's boss noticed his strange behavior and sick appearance, she convinced him to let her take him to the hospital.

People's prior experiences affect their interpretation of and response to the symptoms they perceive. The knowledge individuals extract from their experiences plays an important role in their decisions about what the symptoms reflect and whether they warrant professional attention. Probably most often, this knowledge helps people make appropriate judgments. A study found, for instance, that one of the strongest factors in mothers' correct decisions to seek medical care for their children is prior experience—that is, whether the child or a relative had a similar problem in the past (Turk, Litt, Salovey, & Walker, 1985). But sometimes people's prior experiences and expectations can lead them to incorrect interpretations of their symptoms. For example, many elderly individuals assume tiredness and weakness are symptoms of old age rather than signs of illness (Leventhal & Prohaska, 1986; Prohaska, Keller, Leventhal, & Leventhal, 1987). And people who notice symptoms while under long-term, intense stress may attribute the symptoms to their stress reaction (Cameron, Leventhal, & Leventhal, 1995). Although these interpretations may sometimes be correct, they may also lead people to ignore symptoms that do, in fact, need treatment.

In the case of Mr. Glover, his prior experience did not help him interpret and respond to the symptoms appropriately. His reaction to the classic heart attack symptoms he was having was governed by emotion, probably elicited by the memory of his earlier attack. Although fear can motivate a person toward health behavior, it can also motivate maladaptive avoidance behavior. As we saw in Chapter 6, *conflict theory* proposes that stress can interfere with rational decision-making (Janis, 1984; Janis & Mann, 1977). In Mr. Glover's case, he perceived severe risks in both seeking and not seeking medical care. He tried to deny the meaning of the symptoms, but that didn't seem to work, and the real meaning was still on his mind. As conflict theory predicts in these circumstances, he used a *hypervigilant* coping pattern: he believed he was fast running out of time and began to search frantically for a solution, as when he tried sitting quietly, pacing, and taking Alka-Seltzer.

Mr. Glover finally decided to go to the hospital after his boss persuaded him that his symptoms needed treatment. Before people decide to seek medical attention for their symptoms, they typically get advice from friends, relatives, or coworkers (Croyle & Barger, 1993; Suls, Martin, & Leventhal, 1997). These advisers form a **lay referral system,** an informal network of nonpractitioners who provide their own information and interpretations regarding the person's symptoms (Freidson, 1961). People in the lay referral system provide information or advice when the person requests it, or even if he or she simply looks sick or mentions the symptoms.

Close family or friends are generally the first people consulted for lay referral, and they might:

- Help interpret a symptom—such as, "Jim and his sister Lynn both had rashes like that. They were just allergic to a new soap their mother had bought."
- Give advice about seeking medical attention—as in, "MaryLou had a dizzy spell like the one you just had, and it was a mild stroke. You'd better call your doctor."
- Recommend a remedy—such as, "A little chicken soup, some aspirin, and bed rest, and you'll be fine in no time."
- Recommend consulting another lay referral person—as in, "Pat had the same problem. You should give him a call."

Although the lay referral system often provides good advice, laypersons are, of course, far more likely than practitioners to recommend actions that worsen the condition or delay the person's use of appropriate and needed treatment. (Go to 🔖.)

USING AND MISUSING HEALTH SERVICES

The pharmacist is often the first health professional that people consult when they have a health problem. A customer might ask, "My hands get these red patches that peel, and hand creams don't do any good. Do you have anything that'll help?" When pharmacists suggest an over-the-counter remedy, they usually recommend that the person see a physician if it doesn't work.

Most prospective patients clearly try hard to avoid contacting their physicians. But despite these avoidance efforts, Americans consult their doctors' offices either in person or by telephone $1\frac{1}{2}$ billion times a year—about six contacts per person—for medical advice or treatment (NCHS, 2000). What are the most frequent *acute* and *chronic* conditions discussed in these contacts? The acute conditions are flu, common cold, fractures or dislocations, sprains or strains, wounds, and ear infections; the chronic conditions are hypertension, orthopedic problems, arthritis, diabetes, asthma, and heart disease. Of course, these illnesses are not evenly distributed over the

FOCUS ON RESEARCH
People's Ideas about Illness

Do you believe that germs cause disease, that all diseases have noticeable symptoms, or that we are cured when the symptoms disappear? From direct experience and the things we read and hear about illnesses throughout our lives, we develop ideas and expectations about disease. Some of these ideas are correct, and some are not. We use this information to construct *cognitive representations* or **commonsense models** of different illnesses (Croyle & Barger, 1993; Lau & Hartman, 1983; Leventhal, Leventhal, & Contrada, 1998). These models can affect our health-related behavior and seem to involve four basic components of how people think about disease:

1. *Illness identity*, which consists of the name and symptoms of the disease.
2. *Causes and underlying pathology* are ideas concerning how one gets the disease ("I got a cold because a girl sneezed her germs in my face.") and what physiological events occur with it. Some of these ideas may be correct, but others are not. People's amount of education, social class, and cultural background influence their ideas about the causes of illness (Kaden, McCarter, Johnson, & Ferencz, 1985; Perez-Stable et al., 1992).
3. *Time line*, which involves prognosis ideas, such as how long the disease takes to appear and lasts. A letter to newspaper columnist Ann Landers (1992) provides an example of an incorrect time line: a person who developed symptoms of salmonella 30 minutes after eating chicken on an airplane believed the airline chicken caused the illness, not knowing that salmonella symptoms take more than 24 hours to appear.
4. *Consequences*, which involve ideas about the seriousness, effects, and outcomes of an illness. Many people mistakenly believe, for instance, that the diagnosis of breast cancer is a death sentence, that the disease is always painful, and that the woman must lose the breast.

People use many types of information in constructing ideas about illnesses—they seem to use illness *prevalence* in judging its seriousness, for instance. John Jemmott and his colleagues reported a series of studies showing that people tend to believe rare diseases are more serious than common ones (Jemmott, Croyle, & Ditto, 1988; Jemmott, Ditto, & Croyle, 1986). In the first of these studies, the researchers recruited college students and had them fill out questionnaires and undergo several medical tests, such as for blood pressure and eyesight. One of these tests, called the "Thioamine Acetylase Saliva Reaction Test," was false and purportedly assessed an enzyme deficiency that could lead to a disorder of the pancreas. Each student was shown the results of the test, indicating that he or she had the deficiency, and told either that the deficiency was rare or that it was prevalent. The students then completed a questionnaire that included items asking them to rate the seriousness of various diseases, including "thioamine acetylase deficiency." (The subjects were then debriefed immediately so they would understand that they were not ill, the disease was fictitious, and the test results were fabricated.) Those students who were told that the deficiency was rare rated it as being more serious than those who were told the deficiency was prevalent.

Commonsense models of illness are important for at least two reasons. First, people with incorrect ideas may fail to adopt healthful behaviors to prevent illness or not seek treatment or follow their physician's recommendations if they do. Second, people's ideas about an illness they develop, such as arthritis, can affect their psychological adjustment to it (Schiaffino, Shawaryn, & Blum, 1998).

People with health problems often consult pharmacists for over-the-counter remedies before seeing their physician.

American population—and as you might expect, some segments of the population who become ill are more likely to use health services than are others.

WHO USES HEALTH SERVICES?

Public health researchers have outlined several demographic and sociocultural factors that are related to the use of health services in America. These relationships probably are similar in most industrialized countries.

Age and Gender

One factor in using health services is *age*. In general, young children and the elderly have contact with physicians more often each year than adolescents and young adults do (NCHS, 2000). Young children visit physicians for general checkups and vaccinations, and they develop a variety of infectious childhood diseases. As we saw in Chapter 2, children's immune systems are relatively weak at birth, but develop rapidly in the early years. Physician contacts decline in late childhood and remain relatively infrequent in early adulthood, but increase in the middle-age and elderly years as the incidence of chronic diseases rises.

Figure 9–1 depicts how physician contacts vary with age and with another important factor, the patient's *gender*. Women have a higher rate of physician contacts than men (NCHS, 2000). This gender difference begins to appear during adolescence.

Although much of women's higher rates of physician contacts in early adulthood results from the medical care they require in pregnancy, the difference remains even when physician visits for pregnancy and childbirth are not counted (Reddy, Fleming, & Adesso,

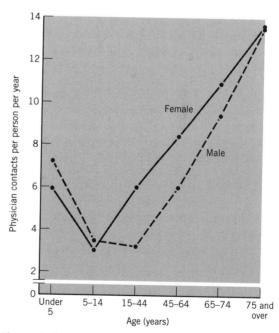

Figure 9–1 Average number of physician contacts (in person and by telephone) per person per year as a function of age and gender. (Data from NCHS, 2000, Table 75, for 1996.)

1992; Verbrugge, 1980, 1985). The reasons for gender differences in using medical care are unclear, but there are several possible explanations. One obvious explanation is that women may simply develop more illnesses that require medical attention: they show higher rates of medical drug use and illness from acute conditions, such as respiratory infections, and from nonfatal chronic diseases, such as arthritis and migraine headache. Another reason is that men are more hesitant to admit having symptoms and to seek medical care for the symptoms they experience. In a study that asked men and women about recent experiences of various symptoms, women reported more of almost all symptoms, including ones that had no medical confirmation (Kroenke & Spitzer, 1998). Gender differences in reporting and, perhaps, perceiving symptoms probably reflects sex-role stereotypes; that is, American society encourages men more than women to ignore pain and to be tough and independent.

Sociocultural Factors in Using Health Services

The United States Department of Health and Human Services conducts periodic large-scale surveys to determine usage rates of health services by different segments of the American population. The results of recent surveys lead to two important conclusions about sociocultural differences in usage (NCHS, 2000). First, the percentage of people who seek medical care at a physician's office or by telephone increases with family income. Second, African Americans and other individuals with low family incomes are far more likely than whites and others with higher incomes to use outpatient clinics and hospital emergency rooms for medical care. This is probably because disadvantaged people are less likely to have regular physicians (Flack et al., 1995). Although there is clearly a gap between social classes in utilization of health services in America, it has narrowed since the mid-1960s, when the government introduced Medicare and Medicaid insurance programs for the elderly and poor, respectively. These programs account for much of the 25% increase in physician visits that occurred between 1968 and 1972 (USDHHS, 1985a).

Despite the help these programs provide, the costs American patients must bear for medical treatment can still be substantial because public and private insurance programs generally do not cover all the expenses. Some kinds of treatment are excluded, and patients typically must pay part of the costs for those treatments that are covered. These circumstances are especially difficult for the poor because they tend to become sick more often and require longer hospital stays (Penn et al., 1995; UDSHHS, 1995). Worldwide, a lack of knowledge about prevention and poor access to health counseling and preventive services contributes to the high illness rates of low-income people (WHO, 1999c).

Although medical insurance can help many low-income people get the treatment they need, there are reasons besides the expense of medical care for the gap between social classes and cultural groups in using health services (Flack et al., 1995; Penn et al., 1995; Rundall & Wheeler, 1979; Young & Zane, 1995). For one thing, individuals from the lower classes tend to perceive themselves as being less susceptible to illness than those from the higher classes do. As a result, low-income people are less likely to seek out preventive care. Second, people with low incomes and from minority groups are less likely to have regular sources of health care than others are. Often this situation develops because low-income regions are less able to attract physicians to provide health services there. In addition, people in the lower classes and from minority groups may feel less welcomed by and trustful of the health care system than other individuals. Third, in many countries language can be a barrier to health care for immigrants if they do not speak the dominant language and no translators are available. These and many other factors tend to reduce the likelihood that low-income individuals will use health services for preventive care and when they are ill. Because low-income people have greater health problems and poorer health habits, public health efforts need to break down cultural barriers that impede the use of health care and prevention services by providing community health education programs and formal training in self-health care specifically for low-income persons (Crandall & Duncan, 1981).

The title of this section is Who Uses Health Services? To answer this question, we can construct two portraits—one of the users and one of the nonusers of these services. The users of health services tend to be young children, women, and elderly individuals from the higher social classes. The nonusers are likely to be members of the lower classes and minority groups, particularly those who are males in adolescence and early adulthood. But almost all people use health services at some time, and many upper-class individuals fail to get medical treatment when they should. Thus, although these portraits give us an image of *who* uses health services, they do not provide a full explanation of *why*.

WHY PEOPLE USE, DON'T USE, AND DELAY USING HEALTH SERVICES

Health psychologists and others who study health care have discovered many factors that influence whether and when individuals are likely to seek medical care. Some of these factors involve people's ideas and beliefs about treating illness.

Ideas, Beliefs, and Using Health Services

An ailing man who was considering whether to seek treatment thought, "Remember how the medicine Buddy's doctor gave him made him sicker? I don't trust doctors." Patients sometimes develop health problems as a *result* of medical treatment, and these problems are called **iatrogenic conditions.** The condition can result either from a practitioner's error or as a normal side effect or risk of the treatment, as may occur when people undergo surgery or begin to take a new medication. In Buddy's case, the medication he received caused an allergic reaction. Tens of thousands of people are killed each year in the United States alone as a result of medical errors in the hospital and adverse effects of drugs, either from pharmacists' errors or interactions of drugs with other substances patients consume (Gerlin, 1999; Stolberg, 1999a). Positive and negative stories we hear about the treatment patients received may influence our decisions to use medical services.

Not trusting practitioners can stop people from seeking the care they need; we will consider two issues of trust. First, individuals may avoid getting care because they worry about the confidentiality of information they disclose to or is found by their practitioners. For instance, a study found that most American adolescents have health concerns they want to keep private from their parents, and one-fourth said they would forgo treatment if their parents could find out about it (Cheng, Savageau, Sattler, & DeWitt, 1993). Many gay men and women avoid medical care because of concerns about confidentiality or fears of physician reaction to their sexual orientation (Mann, 1996). Second, minority group members have heard stories, some of which are true, of discriminatory practices and atrocities carried out by medical personnel against them (Dula, 1994). One true story is that physicians in the United States falsely told black men with syphilis that they were being treated and that the disease was "bad blood." This was done so that a research project, called the Tuskegee Syphilis Study, could chart the effects of untreated syphilis, which include blindness, brain damage, and death.

The Health Belief Model and Seeking Medical Care

In Chapter 6, we examined the role of health beliefs in taking preventive action, such as adopting healthful habits. We saw that the *health belief model* provides a useful framework for explaining why people do and do not practice health-related behaviors. How does the health belief model apply to people's seeking medical care when they notice symptoms?

According to the health belief model (refer back to Figure 6–2), symptoms initiate a decision-making process about seeking medical care. Part of this process involves assessing the *perceived threat* suggested by the symptoms (Becker & Rosenstock, 1984; Rosenstock & Kirscht, 1979). How much threat individuals perceive depends mainly on three factors. One factor is *cues to action*, which arouse concern. The cues can include the symptoms themselves, advice sick people receive in lay referral, and information from the mass media, such as descriptions of cancer symptoms. Two other factors, *perceived susceptibility* and *perceived seriousness*, modify the concern aroused by the cues: the threat people feel intensifies with increases in the perceived susceptibility to the particular illness and the perceived seriousness of the physical and social consequences of contracting the disease.

The health belief model also proposes that individuals assess whether the *perceived benefits* of getting treatment outweigh the *perceived barriers* to doing so. People assess the benefits of seeking care mainly on the basis of their beliefs about the effectiveness of treatment. People who believe treatment can cure the symptoms or arrest the progression of the illness are more likely to seek medical care than those who believe otherwise. In assessing the barriers to medical care, people bring in many beliefs, such as whether the treatment will have unpleasant side effects and will be costly, painful, and difficult to obtain. The assessed sum of benefits and barriers combines with the perceived threat to determine the likelihood of seeking care. People who feel threatened by their symptoms and believe the benefits of receiving treatment outweigh the barriers are likely to visit a practitioner. But individuals who do not feel threatened or assess that the barriers are too strong are likely to decide to delay treatment or avoid it altogether.

The results of research suggest that the factors described by the health belief model do influence people's decisions of whether and how soon to use health services (Becker & Rosenstock, 1984; Rosenstock & Kirscht, 1979). For example, studies of people with cancer symptoms have found that those who are aware of the symptoms of cancer *and* believe cancer cannot be treated effectively or cured are likely to delay seeking medical care much longer than individuals who know the symptoms *but* believe treatment can be successful (Antonovsky & Hartman, 1974). However, some studies have found only a weak relationship between factors in the health belief model and people's likelihood of using health services, which suggests that other variables are also important in decisions to seek treatment (Harris & Guten, 1979; Langlie, 1977).

Social and Emotional Factors and Seeking Medical Care

Earlier, we considered the case of Mr. Glover, who delayed medical treatment for clear symptoms of a heart attack and saw that social and emotional factors can play important roles in people's decisions about seeking treatment for their symptoms.

Strong emotional reactions to symptoms sometimes impede people's use of health services. Individuals may perceive a disease, such as cancer, to be so serious that they avoid medical attention for their symptoms because of the extreme anxiety and fear their perceptions generate. As a result, the threat these individuals perceive does not increase their likelihood of using health services, but may decrease it. Interviews with hundreds of adults, for instance, revealed that many associate great physical pain with the cancer and its treatment, and 18% of these people said they might be reluctant to seek medical care for cancer symptoms because of their fear of the pain (Levin, Cleeland, & Dar, 1985). Expectations of pain probably play a role in people's fear of dental care, too—about 5% of Americans are so fearful that they avoid all kinds of dental treatment (Gatchel, 1980). People may also avoid medical care if they fear embarrassment, such as when adults have problems of bladder control.

Social factors influence people's tendencies to seek medical care for their symptoms. For example, many men believe getting medical care is a sign of weakness, violating their social role for being strong. But social factors can also encourage people to seek care, such as through the process of lay referral. According to sociologist Irving Zola (1973), three types of "social triggers" can prompt people to seek treatment. One of these social triggers is *perceived interference* of the symptoms with individuals' interpersonal relations or activities. For example, a man with an ulcer experienced pain when he would consume certain foods and beverages, such as beer. One day after one of these painful episodes, he decided to seek treatment, saying, "If you can't drink beer with friends, what the hell" (Zola, 1973, p. 684). Similarly, symptoms that interfere with work may spur a person to seek care. An *interpersonal crisis* can also serve as a trigger, particularly if the person uses medical treatment as a means of resolving or escaping the crisis. Zola described an example of a woman who was having serious problems with her relatives while she was on vacation. She decided to enter a hospital and have a benign cyst removed so that her relatives would "stop bothering" her. The third type of social trigger is called *sanctioning*, in which someone asks or insists that an ill person have his or her symptoms treated. For instance, a man who had been having problems with his vision for a while finally went to a doctor after his wife prodded him to do so. Sometimes overt prodding isn't even necessary—sick individuals who simply believe significant others want them to seek treatment are more likely to do so than those who believe others think they should wait (Timko, 1987).

Stages in Delaying Medical Care

When symptoms of a potentially serious illness develop, seeking treatment promptly is imperative. **Treatment delay** refers to the time that elapses between when a person first notices a symptom and when he or she enters medical care. In medical emergencies, such as severe injury or a heart attack, people often seek help in a matter of minutes or hours, as Mr. Glover did. Some drugs for treating heart attacks can prevent myocardial damage if administered within, say, an hour or so after the attack begins. What determines how long people wait?

On the basis of extensive interviews with patients at a clinic, researchers discovered that treatment

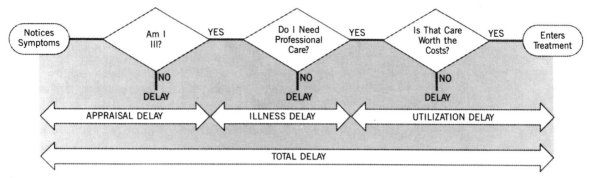

Figure 9–2 Treatment delay is conceptualized as having three stages: appraisal delay, illness delay, and utilization delay. (From Safer, Tharps, Jackson, & Leventhal, 1979, Figure 1.)

delay occurs as a sequence of three stages (Safer, Tharps, Jackson, & Leventhal, 1979). As the diagram in Figure 9–2 illustrates, the three stages are:

1. *Appraisal delay*—the time a person takes to interpret a symptom as an indication of illness.

2. *Illness delay*—the time taken between recognizing one is ill and deciding to seek medical attention.

3. *Utilization delay*—the time after deciding to seek medical care until actually going in to use that health service.

The patients' reasons for delaying treatment revealed that different factors were important for different stages of delay. During *appraisal delay*, the sensory experience of a symptom had the greatest impact on delay—for instance, patients recognized a symptom

as an indication of illness more quickly if they experienced severe pain or bleeding than if they did not.

In the *illness delay* stage, thoughts about the symptom had the greatest impact. Thus, individuals decided to seek medical attention more quickly if the symptom was new rather than very familiar and if they didn't think much about the symptom and its implications. During *utilization delay*, perceptions of benefits and barriers were important—delay was shortest for those people who were less concerned about the cost of treatment, had severe pain, and felt that their symptoms could be cured. In addition, the researchers found that having a major nonillness problem or life event, such as a marriage or divorce, was an important factor that increased the *total* treatment delay.

How long did these people wait before going in for medical care after first noticing a symptom? For half of these patients, treatment delay was about a week or less, but many of the others waited 2 months or more. Some of these people may have delayed a long time because they were not experiencing pain. As we just discussed, *not having pain* is a major factor in delaying. This factor is potentially very important because pain is *not* a major symptom of many very serious diseases, such as hypertension. Pain is also not one of the main warning signs of cancer. Most people who notice a warning sign of cancer wait at least a month before visiting a physician, and between 35 and 50% delay for more than 3 months (Antonovsky & Hartman, 1974). People need to know what the symptoms of serious diseases are and realize that some illnesses do not have the signs people often rely on in deciding whether to seek medical care.

"You called me just in time. Another day or two, and you would have been up and around."

© 1991; Reprinted courtesy of Bunny Hoest and *Parade* Magazine.

USING ALTERNATIVE MEDICINE TREATMENTS

When Elena feels a cold coming on, she takes echinacea, an herb that is extracted from a plant. Many people in various parts of the world, including industrialized nations, choose to use therapies physicians think are unconventional, such as massage or herbal methods, either instead of or in addition to medical care (CU, 2000; Eisenberg et al., 1998). These therapies are classified as **alternative medicine** (or *holistic* or *complementary* medicine) treatments because they use methods that seem inconsistent with the biomedical model, and most have little or no scientific evidence for their effectiveness. Although these methods are viewed as unconventional by medical societies in developed nations, they are often widely used, traditional treatments in other countries, such as China, Puerto Rico, and Haiti (Belluck, 1996; Bezkor & Lee, 1999).

Because alternative medicine methods are quite varied and have little in common with each other, it's difficult to characterize them (Bezkor & Lee, 1999). Instead, we'll look at several examples. Some frequently used alternative treatments in the United States are: *relaxation techniques*, *herbal therapy*, *massage*, *spinal manipulation* (chiropractic), and *high-dose vitamins* (CU, 2000; Eisenberg et al., 1998). Other methods include *folk healing* (using herbs, rituals to invoke spirits, or both), *energy healing* (using magnets to modify energy flow), *hypnosis*, *acupuncture*, and *aroma therapy*. Some methods require the services of a practitioner, and others can be used without supervision. Patients often use alternative treatments without telling their physicians.

Who uses alternative medicine? Probably most people around the world who use them learned to do so through their religious or cultural backgrounds. Individuals in the United States who use alternative medicine tend to be well educated, have beliefs and values that are consistent with the method's rationale, and have troublesome symptoms, such as pain or stress, that have not improved with standard medical care (Astin, 1998; CU, 2000; Vecchio, 1994). A large-scale survey of thousands of North Americans regarding illness treatments in the prior 2 years found that most were satisfied with the medical care they received and, if they had tried alternative methods, had gotten better results from medical treatment for almost all illnesses (CU, 2000). Over one-third of the respondents reported having used alternative methods.

Most of these methods were not very successful, having helped the people "feel much better" in only 10–30% of cases, depending on the illness and method used. (Although there was no control group, a placebo would probably have gotten similar ratings.) Two alternative treatments, chiropractic and deep-tissue massage, were particularly successful for back pain.

Some alternative medicine treatments have been tested in careful experiments. At various points in this book, you will find evidence for the utility of relaxation techniques, deep-tissue massage, and biofeedback in treating pain and other chronic conditions, such as asthma and diabetes. Although spinal manipulation appears to be useful for treating back pain, it is not effective with tension headache (Bove & Nilsson, 1998). Many herbal remedies are not very effective and some have serious side effects (CU, 1999a), but a few have good evidence of success, such as in treating irritable bowel syndrome (Bensoussan et al, 1998). Some alternative methods have value, but others clearly do not. People who want to use an alternative medicine treatment should look for independent information on its effectiveness and side effects and discuss it with their physicians.

MISUSING HEALTH SERVICES

In a sense, delaying medical care and using alternative treatments without informing physicians are misuses of health services, but a more obvious *misuse* is *overuse*—that is, using health services repeatedly when there is no need. People in the general population commonly refer to patients who overuse medical care as "hypochondriacs" and think these people are either malingering or imagining symptoms, so that the illness is "all in their heads."

But this common view is inaccurate. Although some individuals do imagine symptoms and some malinger to get various benefits of the sick role, *hypochondriacs* tend to interpret real but benign bodily sensations as symptoms of illness (Barsky & Klerman, 1983). They may decide, for example, that their gastric pains are signs of a serious disease rather than the results of eating spicy foods or amplify minor sensations, such as muscle soreness or twinges, and perceive them as very painful. Because of these characteristics, psychologists and psychiatrists use the term **hypochondriasis** to refer to the tendency of individuals to worry excessively about their own health, monitor their bodily sensations closely, make frequent unfounded medical complaints, and believe they are ill despite reassurances by physicians that they are not (Barsky & Klerman, 1983; Costa & McCrae, 1985; Kellner, 1985, 1987).

Paul Costa and Robert McCrae (1980, 1985) have demonstrated an important link between hypochondriasis and emotional maladjustment, or *neuroticism*, which they defined as

> a broad dimension of normal personality that encompasses a variety of specific traits, including self consciousness, inability to inhibit cravings, and vulnerability to stress as well as the tendency to experience anxiety, hostility, and depression. (1985, p. 21)

These researchers tested about 1,000 normal adults, using two self-report scales: (1) the Cornell Medical Index to assess the subjects' "somatic complaints," that is, medical conditions or symptoms, and (2) the Emotional Stability Scale to measure neuroticism. The subjects were in generally good health and ranged in age from under 20 to over 90. Analysis of the questionnaire responses showed that somatic complaints increased with neuroticism—individuals who scored high on neuroticism reported two to three times as many somatic complaints as those who scored low on neuroticism.

Does this association mean that neuroticism causes more complaints, or that having many illnesses causes neuroticism? Although either causal direction is possible, some of the clearest research findings suggest that "neuroticism appears to lead to complaints" (Costa & McCrae, 1985, p. 23). For example, two prospective studies with hundreds of patients found that people who scored high on neuroticism or hypochondriasis were more likely than those who scored low to report unfounded symptoms at a later time (Feldman et al, 1999; Wielgosz et al., 1984). The symptoms in the Wielgosz study were episodes of chest pain—or *angina*—with minimal or no coronary disease, which was determined by a test (*coronary angiography*) that measures the degree to which coronary arteries are constricted. Other researchers have found similar links between angina and sensitivity to body sensations (Davies et al., 1993).

Many people believe hypochondriasis increases in old age. Costa and McCrae (1980, 1985) have presented evidence that this belief is incorrect. For one thing, neuroticism does not increase with age. Second, although older individuals have more somatic

complaints and use health services more than younger adults do, the greater somatic complaints of the elderly are mainly related to *real* problems—sensory, cardiovascular, and genitourinary conditions, which are known to increase in old age. If elderly people were prone to hypochondriasis, we would expect them to report more complaints with regard to other body systems, too. But they do not. This indicates that the elderly use health services more than younger individuals simply because they are less healthy. The proportion of people who are hypochondriacs appears to be no higher in old age than in earlier adult periods.

One other issue should be discussed: sometimes people may have real health problems that medical technology cannot yet confirm. A clear and increasingly frequent example is a condition called *chronic fatigue syndrome* (CFS). The main symptom of CFS is persistent, unexplained severe fatigue for a period of several months, but other symptoms can include frequent infections and headaches (Johnson, DeLuca, & Natelson, 1999). Not long ago physicians incorrectly thought this condition was an extended form of mononucleosis, which is caused by the Epstein-Barr virus. Although some research findings suggest that other viral agents or immune system disorders may cause CFS, the evidence is not yet clear. Because there are no medical tests to detect CFS, diagnosis is based on ruling out all other diseases, and many doctors believe the condition is basically a psychiatric disorder. But it seems likely that these doctors are wrong. Studies that have tried to link CFS with psychological disorders have produced mostly inconsistent results (Johnson, DeLuca, & Natelson, 1999).

To summarize, there is an enormous variety of reasons why people use, don't use, overuse, and delay using health services. These reasons include the nature of the symptoms people perceive, the health beliefs they hold, and social and emotional factors. Another factor that affects people's decisions about using health services is the quality of the relationships they have with their physicians, as we are about to see.

THE PATIENT–PRACTITIONER RELATIONSHIP

A woman who had been receiving treatment for cancer at a clinic on a regular basis began to procrastinate about going in for periodic examinations and care. When her family asked why she had not gone in on schedule, she replied, "They gave me a new doctor, and he's not very nice. He treats me like a number, and I feel uncomfortable talking to him—he talks down to me when I ask him questions." Many patients have stories about negative experiences with practitioners, and these experiences can lead people to delay or stop getting the medical attention they need. These stories often involve the practitioner's hurried manner, insensitivity, lack of responsiveness, failure to explain the medical problem or the treatment, or unwillingness to involve the client in planning the treatment. Problems like these are likely to be aggravated if the client and practitioner have very different cultural backgrounds (Young & Zane, 1995).

PATIENT PREFERENCES FOR PARTICIPATION IN MEDICAL CARE

When people visit physicians about health problems, do they just want to be "cured" or do they also want to know about the illnesses and how to treat them? How involved do they want to be in decisions and activities in their treatment? Physicians often misjudge their patients' answers to these kinds of questions (Kindelan & Kent, 1987). Correctly judging the amount and type of participation people prefer can be important—patient–practitioner relationships depend to

"Hi! I'm Carl, and I'll be your doctor for today!"

Reprinted courtesy of Bunny Hoest.
When the general practitioner changes from one visit to the next, patients may have a difficult time establishing a good relationship with a physician.

some extent on the compatibility between what the patient wants and what the practitioner provides.

People differ in the participation they want—although almost all want to know what their illnesses are and how to treat them, some want more details about the illnesses, self-administration of treatment, and involvement in decisions than others do (Krantz, Baum, & Wideman, 1980). Research has revealed interesting things about clients' participation preferences. For one thing, age differences exist: compared with younger adults, elderly people are less likely to seek information about their illnesses from medical staff and more likely to want health professionals to make health-related decisions for them (Turk-Charles, Meyerowitz, & Gatz, 1997; Woodward & Wallston, 1987). Also, it appears that receiving the desired amount and type of participation enhances individuals' adjustment to and satisfaction with medical treatment (Auerbach, Martelli, & Mercuri, 1983; Martelli, Auerbach, Alexander, & Mercuri, 1987). And patients who report that they usually want or take an active role in their treatment tend to adjust to their recovery periods better and recover faster than those who prefer an inactive role (Brody et al., 1989; Mahler & Kulik, 1991).

Just as people differ in the information and involvement they want regarding their health, practitioners differ in the participation they are inclined to provide. Some doctors are more inclined than others to share their authority and decision-making even among colleagues (Eisenberg, Kitz, & Webber, 1983). What happens in the patient–practitioner relationship when the person wants a different level of participation from what the practitioner is willing to give? The outcome of a large-scale survey of patients and physicians suggests two conclusions (Haug & Lavin, 1981). First, although both the patients and the physicians express the attitude that clients should participate in activities and decisions pertaining to their health, neither the patients nor the physicians behave in this way very often. Second, when a distinct mismatch between the client's and the physician's preference occurs, discomfort and conflict can result and lead to a switch in doctors. The results of other research also indicate that mismatches in participation preferences can increase the stress patients experience during unpleasant medical procedures (Auerbach, Martelli, & Mercuri, 1983; Miller & Mangan, 1983). In deciding how much information and involvement to provide each client, practitioners clearly need to assess and consider how much the person wants. (Go to .)

THE PRACTITIONER'S BEHAVIOR AND STYLE

Imagine this test: you recently completed medical training and have just started a position in a clinic as a general practitioner. Your next patient this morning is waiting in an examination room, which you are preparing to enter. Your task will be to decide which one of more of the more than 1,300 disease entities known to medicine this person has (Mentzer & Snyder, 1982). Or maybe the person has no physical problem at all. You have 20 minutes.

Diagnosing and treating health problems are difficult tasks, which different physicians undertake with their own behaviors and styles of interacting with patients. Patrick Byrne and Barrie Long (1976) identified different styles of interacting by analyzing about 2,500 tape-recorded medical consultations with physicians in several countries, including England, Ireland,

---

HIGHLIGHT ON ISSUES
Fighting for Your Life

Not all victims of serious diseases who are getting medical care receive the most effective treatments available (Kolata, 1992b). Although this situation sometimes occurs because a doctor is overworked or not competent, it's more likely to result from physicians' difficulty keeping up with rapid advances in medical knowledge and their reluctance to switch from a procedure that works reasonably well to one that may work better. What can people do to get the best possible treatment?

Patients and people close to them can join the fight for their lives by taking an active interest in their illnesses and health care (CU, 1995b; Gipson, Liskevych, & Swillinger, 1996; Laszlo, 1987). Let's consider a hypothetical case of a man named Morry who has a serious illness, such as heart disease or cancer. Once he receives the diagnosis, he and his family can swing into action. They can:

- Get information about the disease and the usual courses of treatment. Information is readily available on the Internet and in books they can purchase in bookstores or use through public, college, and medical school libraries.
- Make a list of questions to ask for each meeting with physicians working on his case. If possible, Morry should have a relative or friend accompany him to discussions with physicians. One of them should take notes, and they should ask to know all possible treatment options and determine what each treatment involves, what the risks are, and the likelihood

of success. Be sure all uncertainties are cleared up before leaving each meeting.

- Broaden the sources of information. Major organizations—such as the American Heart Association and the American Cancer Society—have Internet sites and toll-free phone numbers to get information about support groups, treatment methods, and physicians who specialize in treating the illness. At least one of the physicians Morry consults regarding treatment options should be certified in the specialty and, preferably, on staff at a major university or teaching hospital. Many people consult only the original physician on their case, and this is a mistake.

- Use reputable information sources to find out about very new medical procedures (and even some risky experimental ones). Even though many newer approaches may provide the most effective treatment, not all physicians know about them or feel comfortable about recommending them.

Individuals with any serious illness can join the fight for their lives in these ways. When patients and people close to them take an active interest in their health care, they can play an informed role in discussions and negotiations with their physicians toward making decisions. Patients who do this can be satisfied that they are getting the best treatment available and feel a sense of efficacy in themselves and in their physicians.

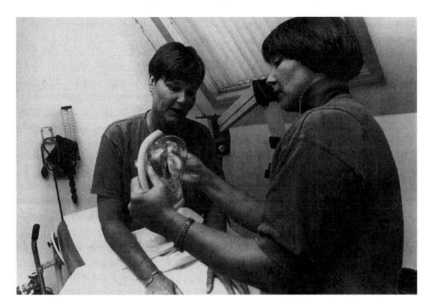

Patients tend to prefer a physician who gives clear explanations about illnesses and treatments, encourages them to ask questions, and conveys a feeling of concern for them.

Australia, and Holland. Each physician tended to use a consistent style for all clients treated. Most of the styles were classified as **doctor-centered,** in which the physician asked questions that required only brief answers—generally "yes" or "no"—and focused mainly on the first problem the person mentioned. These physicians tended to ignore attempts by patients to discuss other problems. Doctor-centered physicians seemed to be intent on establishing a link between the initial problem and some organic disorder, without being sidetracked. In contrast, physicians who used a **patient-centered** style took less controlling roles. They tended to ask open-ended questions, such as, "Can you describe the situations when the pain occurs?" that allow a patient to relate more information and introduce new facts that may be pertinent. They also tended to avoid using medical jargon and to allow clients to participate in some of the decision making.

The patient–practitioner relationship depends on the ability of the two participants to communicate with each other. But physicians sometimes impede communication by using *medical jargon* or technical terms. For example, telling hypertensive patients to "reduce sodium intake" is an accurate recommendation, but will they know what it means? Some people will know exactly what sodium is, others won't have any idea, and others will think it only means table salt, not realizing that there are other sources of dietary sodium. Studies have found that most patients, particularly those from lower-class backgrounds, fail

to understand many of the terms their physicians use—such terms as "mucus," "sutures," and "glucose," for instance (DiMatteo & DiNicola, 1982; McKinlay, 1975). Although jargon is useful for accuracy and for communicating among medical professionals, practitioners who use medical and technical terms in talking with clients without explaining the terms or checking comprehension can create confusion, incorrect ideas, and dissatisfaction in them.

John McKinlay (1975) assessed lower-class women's understanding of 13 terms their physicians used with them in a maternity ward. Although over two-thirds of the women understood the terms "breech" and "navel," almost none understood "protein" and "umbilicus"—and on the average, each of the 13 words was understood by only about 39% of the patients. McKinlay also had the physicians indicate for each word whether they thought "average lower-working-class women" would understand the term. The physicians expected even *less* comprehension than the clients showed, yet they used these terms often with these women.

Why would physicians use terms with a patient when they do not expect the person to understand? Sometimes they may do this "out of habit," that is, the terms are so familiar to them that they forget the client is less medically sophisticated. Or they may feel—perhaps in a patronizing way—that the person "doesn't need to know." Other reasons for using jargon may involve their perceptions of what would benefit the patient or the medical staff (DiMatteo & DiNicola,

1982; McKinlay, 1975). How might using jargon benefit the client? Sometimes physicians may feel that the person is better off not knowing exactly what the disease or its treatment may entail; knowing may produce too much stress or interfere with treatment, they may think. And how may using jargon with a patient benefit the medical staff? For one thing, using medical terms without explanations keeps interactions between the client and practitioners short. It may also reduce the chances that the client will react emotionally to the information, or ask questions about the treatment, or discover if errors have been made. Finally, using "big words" the client does not understand elevates the status of practitioners.

First and foremost, people prefer to have a practitioner they think is competent. But there are other factors that are important in the patient–practitioner relationship, too—especially the *sensitivity, warmth,* and *concern* the person perceives in the practitioner's behavior. People prefer and evaluate highly dentists and physicians who seem friendly and interested in them as persons, show empathy for their feelings, project a feeling of reassurance, and present a calm and competent image (Corah et al., 1988; DiMatteo, Linn, Chang, & Cope, 1985; Hall, Milburn, Roter, & Daltroy, 1998). In contrast, practitioners who seem emotionally neutral are often evaluated less positively, perhaps because they appear detached and unconcerned. People assess these characteristics not just by the words the practitioner says, but by his or her body language—facial expressions, eye contact, and body positions (DiMatteo, 1985; DiMatteo, Friedman, & Taranta, 1979; Thompson, 1984). With regard to body positions, for instance, Americans tend to perceive a person who stands or sits a moderate distance away, leans toward them, gestures and nods, and has a relaxed posture as being relatively warm and friendly.

The behavior and style of practitioners can have important implications for them and their patients. Research has shown that people tend to express greater satisfaction for physicians who give them a chance to talk, take the time to listen, give clear explanations about illnesses and treatments, and project a feeling of concern and reassurance than for doctors who do not (Feletti, Firman, & Sanson-Fisher, 1986). The greater satisfaction these patients feel may translate into a higher likelihood that they will keep appointments with their doctors. A study found that physicians who were more sensitive to others' emotions had fewer cancellations of appointments that were not rescheduled than doctors who were less sensitive (DiMatteo, Hays, & Prince, 1986).

Perhaps the most important implication of physicians' styles relates to the diagnostic information they receive from their patients. Physicians vary greatly in their ability to elicit significant diagnostic information from their clients (Marvel, Epstein, Flowers, & Beckman, 1999; Roter & Hall, 1987). Physicians who ask more open- and closed-ended questions, allow clients to give a full answer, give more information about the cause and prognosis of the illness, and discuss more details about prevention and treatment receive more diagnostic facts from their clients than doctors who do less of these things. The additional facts doctors receive are not trivial ones, but ones other physicians judge to be important in diagnosing the person's illness. The first complaint or detail the client gives is often not the most significant one, and getting a full statement of the client's concerns takes only several additional seconds. Findings like these have led medical schools to introduce programs to educate future physicians regarding interviewing skills and psychosocial factors in treating patients—Harvard's "New Pathway" program is an example (CU, 1995b; Winefield, 1992). (Go to 🍎.)

THE PATIENT'S BEHAVIOR AND STYLE

It takes two to tango, as the saying goes. Although the practitioner's behavior plays an important role in the relationship he or she forms with a patient, the client's behavior and style are important, too. Physicians reported in a survey, for instance, that patients sometimes do things that can be very troubling or unsettling for a doctor (Smith & Zimny, 1988). Some of these behaviors include:

- Expressing criticism or anger toward the physician.
- Ignoring or not listening to what the doctor is trying to say.
- Insisting on laboratory tests, medications, or procedures the physician thinks are unnecessary.
- Requesting that the doctor certify something, such as a disability, the physician thinks is untrue.
- Making sexually suggestive remarks or behaviors toward the physician.

ASSESS YOURSELF
Do You Know Medical Terms' Meanings?

The following ten medical terms were used in McKinlay's (1975) study of patients' understanding of medical jargon, which is described in the text. Match the terms with the definitions given below: in the space preceding each term, place the number for the corresponding definition.

_____ antibiotic   _____ mucus

_____ breech   _____ protein

_____ enamel   _____ purgative

_____ glucose   _____ suture

_____ membrane   _____ umbilicus

1. The rump or back part.
2. A small scar on the abdomen; the navel.
3. A substance that makes up plant and animal tissue.

4. A simple sugar that the body manufactures from ingested food.
5. A joining together of separated tissue or bone, or a device to achieve this joining.
6. A sheet of tissue that covers or lines a body organ.
7. An agent that works against bacterial infections.
8. A hard, glossy coating or surface.
9. A substance or procedure that causes a cleansing of a body organ, as occurs in a bowel movement.
10. A secretion of body tissues.

Check your answers against the key below. Did you get them all correct? Would you have known as many of the definitions if they weren't given? Would your friends—especially ones who have not gone to college—know the terms?

Answers, in order:

7, 1, 8, 4, 6, 10, 3, 9, 5, 2

If behaviors such as these lead to a breakdown in the relationship between the patient and practitioner, the quality of the medical care the client receives may suffer.

The potential for people to bring malpractice suits against practitioners can also affect their relationship, making physicians wary of patients and less satisfied with their careers (Kolata, 1990; Pear, 1990). These suits are stressful, emotionally devastating experiences for clients and physicians alike, regardless of who wins. Patients who have poor relationships with their physicians are more likely to file malpractice suits than those who do not. These suits usually claim incompetence or negligence in the physician's treatment, but they sometimes allege that the doctor did not communicate important information to the client.

Do patients do things that impair patient–practitioner communication? Yes. For one thing, they may not give signs of any distress they are feeling about their conditions or treatment (Roter & Ewart,1992). On the other hand, people who are high in neuroticism may convey too much concern and seem less credible and less in need of medical care (Ellington & Wiebe, 1999). Sometimes clients also describe their symptoms in unclear or misleading ways. As an example, two women who had developed the same condition, _hyperopia_ (farsightedness), went to their physicians for medical care (Zola, 1973). In response to the practitioner's question, "What seems to be the trouble?" one client simply said, "I can't see to thread a needle or read the paper." The other patient answered, "I have a constant headache and my eyes seem to get all red and burny." Each patient's manner or focus in describing her problem was different, and neither expanded the description with significant facts when asked if she had anything to add.

Why do patients describe their symptoms for the same health problem so differently? One reason may lie in the way they perceive or interpret different symptoms. As we saw earlier, people differ in the attention they pay to internal states and the degree to which they associate different sensations with health problems. Also, individuals form different commonsense models of illness. When reporting symptoms to a doctor, people may describe only or mainly those problems they think are important, based on their own notions (Bishop & Converse, 1986). Lastly, clients may try either to emphasize or to downplay a symptom they believe may reflect a serious illness. For example, people high in hypochondriasis may try to maximize the physician's attention to a sensation they are worried about, whereas other patients may describe a worrisome symptom very casually or offhandedly in the hope that the doctor will agree that "it's nothing."

Another communication problem can occur in medical situations when patients cannot describe their symptoms in terms the doctor can clearly understand. This often occurs when the person either is very young or lacks a good command of the practitioner's primary language. The United States, for example, has always had large numbers of immigrants from many parts of the world who do not speak English well. Their English descriptions of their problems are likely to be inaccurate and incomplete (Giachello & Arrom, 1997). They are also unlikely to understand fully what their illnesses are or what they need to do to treat them.

What can be done to improve communication between patients and practitioners? Physicians' interviewing skills can be enhanced with training programs that teach how and when to summarize information, ask questions, and check for comprehension (Roter & Hall, 1989). Researchers have also found that a simple approach can improve clients' communication: while patients wait for their visits, have them fill out a form that has them list any symptoms and questions they have and encourages them to ask questions when they see the doctor (Thompson, Nanni, & Schwankovsky, 1990).

One thing to keep in mind with respect to the way patient–practitioner relationships develop is that practitioners don't always get feedback regarding their work. For example, although a patient may visit the doctor again if symptoms persist or if the illness is serious or long term, physicians cannot be certain that *not* hearing from a person means a diagnosis was correct or the treatment was effective. And as we are about to see, practitioners usually cannot be sure to what extent a client is following the medical *regimen*— the treatment program or lifestyle change—they recommended.

COMPLIANCE: ADHERING TO MEDICAL ADVICE

"Now don't tell the doctor, but I don't always take my medicine when I'm supposed to," Amy whispered to a friend in her physician's waiting room. People don't always *adhere to*, or *comply with*, their practitioner's advice. **Adherence** and **compliance** are terms that refer to the degree to which patients carry out the behaviors and treatments their practitioners recommend. Most researchers have used these terms interchangeably, and we will, too. But *adherence* is a more satisfactory term because the dictionary definition of the word *compliance*—"giving in to a request or demand" or "acquiescence"—suggests that the practitioner uses an authoritarian style and that the person obeys reluctantly (DiMatteo & DiNicola, 1982; Turk & Meichenbaum, 1991). The remainder of this chapter examines the extent to which clients fail to follow medical advice, why they do and do not comply, and what can be done to increase their adherence.

EXTENT OF THE NONADHERENCE PROBLEM

How widespread is the problem of noncompliance? Answering this question is actually more difficult than it may seem (Cluss & Epstein, 1985; Turk & Meichenbaum, 1991). First of all, failures to adhere may occur for many different types of medical advice. For instance, patients may fail to take medication as directed, not show up for appointments, skip or stop doing rehabilitation exercises, or "cheat a little" in following specific diet or other lifestyle changes advised by practitioners. Second, people can violate each of these types of advice in many different ways. In failing to take their medication as directed, for example, they might omit some doses, use a drug for the wrong reasons, take medication in the wrong amount or at the wrong time, or discontinue the drug before the prescribed course of therapy ends. Finally, there is the problem of determining whether a person has or has not complied. What is the most accurate and practical way to assess compliance?

Researchers assess patient adherence to medical recommendations in several different ways, and each way has advantages and disadvantages (Cluss & Epstein, 1985; Rand & Weeks, 1998; Turk & Meichenbaum, 1991). One of the easiest approaches for measuring compliance is to *ask a practitioner* who works with the client to estimate it. As it turns out, however, practitioners do not really know; they generally overestimate their patients' compliance and are poor at estimating which clients adhere better than others. Another simple approach is to

Table 9.1 *Objective Methods for Assessing Adherence to Using Medication*

- *Pill or quantity accounting*, in which the remaining medication is measured, such as by counting the number of pills left. This is compared against the quantity that should be left at that point in treatment if the patient has been following the directions correctly. Of course, this method does not reveal whether the person used the medication at the right times, and patients who expect an accounting and want to conceal their noncompliance can discard some of the contents.
- *Medication-recording dispensers* contain mechanical or electromechanical recording devices that can count and record the time when the dispenser is used. Although this approach is expensive to implement, it assesses compliance accurately as long as the patient does not deliberately create a ruse. If patients know about the device and want to avoid taking the medicine, they can operate the dispenser at the right time and discard the drug.
- *Biochemical tests*, such as of the patient's blood or urine. This approach can assess whether medication was used recently, but usually cannot determine how much or when, and it can be very time-consuming and expensive to implement.

ask the patient. But people tend to overreport their adherence, perhaps because they know they should "follow the doctor's orders." These two methods are very subjective and open to various forms of bias, including lying and wishful thinking. As a result, researchers who use these approaches today usually supplement them with reports of family members or medical personnel and with other methods that are more objective. Table 9.1 describes three relatively objective approaches for assessing adherence to using medication.

Despite the complexities in assessing adherence, we can provide some general answers to the question we started with: How widespread is the problem of noncompliance? Speaking in very broad terms, the average rate of noncompliance to medical advice is about 40%, that is, *two of every five patients fail to adhere* reasonably closely to their regimens (DiMatteo, 1985; Rand & Weeks, 1998). Conversely, the overall rate of *adherence* is about 60%. Adherence varies considerably, depending on the type of medical advice, the duration of the recommended regimen, and whether its purpose is to prevent an illness from occurring or to treat or cure an illness that has developed. An overview of the findings of research on compliance indicates the following conclusions (Cluss & Epstein, 1985; Sackett & Snow, 1979):

- The average adherence rate for taking medicine to treat acute illnesses with short-term treatment regimens is about 78%; for chronic illnesses with long-term regimens, the rate drops to about 54%.
- The average adherence rate for taking medicine to prevent illness is roughly 60% for both short-term and long-term regimens.
- Patients' adherence to scheduled appointments with a practitioner is much higher if the client

initiated the appointment than if the practitioner did.

- Adherence to recommended changes in lifestyle, such as stopping smoking or altering one's diet, is generally quite variable and often very low.

But keep in mind two things about these conclusions. First, the percentages given may *overestimate* adherence because most studies have included in their samples only people who agreed to participate (Cluss & Epstein, 1985). It seems likely that people who do not participate may differ in important ways from those who do, such as by having lower health motivation. Second, the adherence rates cited do not reflect the *range* of noncompliance: some patients adhere exactly to a medical regimen, others do not comply at all, and probably most adhere to some degree.

WHY PATIENTS DO AND DO NOT ADHERE TO MEDICAL ADVICE

We have seen that practitioners do not generally know how well their clients adhere to medical advice. What do physicians think when they learn their patients have not followed their advice? They are concerned about the effects of noncompliance on the person's health, of course, and they tend to place most of the "blame" on the patients—their "uncooperative" personalities, inability to understand the advice, or difficult life situations (Davis, 1966). But studies have shown that both the practitioners and their patients influence adherence (DiMatteo & DiNicola, 1982; Ley, 1982). We will see that a person's degree of adherence depends on characteristics of (1) the *illness or regimen*, (2) the *person*, and (3) the *interactions* between the practitioner and patient.

FRANK & ERNEST® by Bob Thaves

Reprinted by permission of United Feature Syndicate, Inc.

Medical Regimens and Illness Characteristics

The medical regimens practitioners advise can differ in many ways, such as in their complexity, duration, cost, side effects, and the degree to which they require changes in the patient's habits. Let's see how each of these factors relates to compliance.

Some regimens require clients to *change long-standing habits*—for example, to begin and maintain exercising regularly, reduce the calories or certain components in their diets, stop smoking cigarettes, or cut down on drinking alcoholic beverages. We have seen in previous chapters that these changes can be very difficult for people to make. Recommendations by physicians can induce many patients to make changes in such habits, particularly if the individuals are at high risk for serious illness (Dolecek et al., 1986; Pederson, 1982). But studies have consistently found that people are much less likely to adhere to medical advice for changes in personal habits than to advice for taking medication (Haynes, 1976; Burke, Dunbar-Jacobs, & Hill, 1997).

Some treatment regimens are more *complex* than others—such as by requiring the person to take two or more drugs, each with its own special instructions: "Take one of these pills after meals, and two of these other pills at bedtime, and one of these other pills every 8 hours." As you might expect, the greater the number of drugs and the more complex the medication schedule and dosage, the greater the likelihood the person will make an error, thereby failing to adhere to the regimen (Haynes, 1976; Kirscht & Rosenstock, 1979). Regimens also become difficult if they have the

patient do a variety of complicated tasks, as, for example, individuals suffering from chronic *kidney disease* must do (Finn & Alcorn, 1986; NKF, 2000; Swigonski, 1987). Many of these patients must:

- Undergo *hemodialysis*, in which the blood is shunted from an artery to a filtering apparatus and returned to a vein. This procedure generally takes 4 to 6 hours three times a week, during which time the person may either sleep or engage in a sedentary activity, such as reading.
- Take large quantities of medication and vitamins—sometimes involving dozens of pills a day—while also strictly limiting fluid intake.
- Severely restrict their dietary intake of *sodium*, mainly salt; *potassium* and *phosphorus*, which are found in many fruits and vegetables; and *protein*, especially meats and dairy products.

In general, the more a client is required to do, the more likely compliance will suffer (Kirscht & Rosenstock, 1979).

Many people believe the duration, expense, and side effects of a medical regimen are major factors in people's adherence to their practitioner's advice. Studies have confirmed the role of *duration*—compliance tends to decline over time (Parrish, 1986; Varni & Babani, 1986). Short-term regimens are usually prescribed for acute illnesses and show beneficial effects fairly quickly and dramatically, but long-term regimens usually apply to chronic health problems and have slower and less obvious beneficial effects. Do the *expense* and *side effects* of treatment also affect adherence? Some studies have found that the expense and side effects distinguish between patients who comply and those who do not, but other studies have not confirmed these findings (DiMatteo & DiNicola, 1982; Haynes, 1976). It may be that treatment expense may not prevent most people from adhering because they have sufficient incomes or insurance to pay for it or feel the benefits of the treatment are essential despite the cost. Similarly, most drugs do not have noticeable or worrisome side effects. But what happens, for instance, when individuals cannot afford their medicine or its side effects do become a problem? Some patients may reduce the dosage of the drug or discontinue using it entirely. The expense and side effects of treatment can impair adherence for some people (Murdaugh, 1998).

We might expect that individuals who have health problems that could disable them or threaten their lives would be more likely to adhere to their treatment regimens than people with less serious illnesses. Whether this idea is correct seems to depend on whose perspective of the severity of the health problem we consider—the practitioner's or the patient's. When comparisons are based on illness severity judged by *physicians*, clients with serious illnesses are no more likely to adhere than those with milder health problems (Becker & Rosenstock, 1984; Haynes, 1976). Perhaps this is because many very serious health problems, such as hypertension and atherosclerosis, have no symptoms that worry people greatly or interfere with their functioning; on the other hand, many less serious illnesses do have such symptoms. In contrast, when comparisons are based on illness severity judged by *patients* who have the health problem, clients who rate their illness as relatively serious generally show better adherence to their treatment regimens than those who perceive their illness to be less severe (Becker & Rosenstock, 1984).

Age, Gender, and Sociocultural Factors

Most early studies of adherence found little or no association between compliance in general and clients' specific personal and demographic characteristics, such as their age, gender, social class, race, and religion (Cluss & Epstein, 1985; Haynes, 1976). Does this mean these factors never affect compliance? Probably not. For one thing, although each of these factors is not *by itself* strongly related to adherence, when they are *joined*—for example, gender plus age plus social class—their combination shows a stronger association to compliance (Korsch, Fine, & Negrete, 1978). What's more, some of these factors may be related to adherence in some circumstances but not others.

Consider the factor of *age*, which seems to affect adherence in different ways, depending on the ages of the subjects and types of illness. For example, studies have found that:

- For childhood cancer patients, problems in adherence to specific care procedures, such as using antibiotics correctly, were greater for younger than for older children (Manne et al., 1993). Although the parents mainly controlled these procedures, the child's age made a difference.

- Among child and adolescent diabetics, adolescents were less adherent to their special diets than children (Johnson et al., 1992).

- For adult arthritis patients, 47% of 55–84-year-olds and only 28% of 34–54-year-olds made no medication errors in several weeks of monitoring; middle-aged people with very busy lives made the most errors (Park et al., 1999).

Children become increasingly responsible for their own medical treatment as they get older (La Greca & Stone, 1985). Adolescents may be less likely than individuals from other age groups to comply with long-term treatments that single them out or make them different from peers. And the elderly are more likely than other age groups to suffer from visual, hearing, and cognitive impairments that may lead to noncompliance (Murdaugh, 1998).

Gender and *sociocultural* influences on adherence may also depend on specific circumstances. For instance, women's concern about controlling their weight appears to interfere with using medication to control their blood sugar (Polonsky et al., 1994). And some cultural groups may have beliefs or customs that undermine adherence. As an example, among American Indians, the idea "of taking something all the time, like an antihypertensive drug, is foreign to some cultures where 'cure' is inherent to the healing process, thus making medications that must be taken continuously appear ineffective" (Baines, 1992).

Psychosocial Aspects of the Patient

We saw earlier that the seriousness of an illness and the costs of its treatment can affect compliance, depending on the point of view of the patient. Perceived seriousness and perceived costs and benefits are two psychosocial factors that should have a familiar ring by now—we have examined them more than once before as components in the *health belief model*. The health belief model components are as important in explaining why people do and do not adhere to medical advice as they are in explaining other health-related behaviors, such as whether people are likely to adopt health behaviors or use health services (Becker, 1979; Becker & Rosenstock, 1984; Rosenstock & Kirscht, 1979). Thus, a patient who feels threatened by an illness and believes the benefits of the recommended regimen outweigh the barriers is likely to adhere to his or her practitioner's advice. But individuals who do not feel threatened by the health problem or assess that the barriers of the regimen outweigh the benefits are unlikely to comply.

Some researchers have pointed out that noncompliance is often *deliberate* and based on *valid reasons*, regardless of whether the reasons are medically sound (Kaplan & Simon, 1990; Turk & Meichenbaum, 1991). This is called **rational nonadherence.** How can nonadherence to medical advice be rational? Patients may be acting rationally when they fail to take medication as directed because they:

- Have reason to believe the medication isn't helping.
- Feel that its side effects are very unpleasant, worrisome, or seriously reducing the quality of their lives.
- Are confused about when to take it, or how much.
- Don't have the money to buy the next refill.
- Want to "see if the illness is still there" when they withdraw the medication.

These are not unreasonable reasons—and sometimes the clients may be medically correct in not adhering, such as when they experience serious or unexpected side effects. A study of arthritis patients found that most instances of nonadherence were for unintentional reasons, such as forgetting; the most common *intentional* reasons for not taking medication were the side effects and the cost (Lorish, Richards, & Brown, 1989).

Patients' adherence to medical advice is often affected by *cognitive and emotional* factors operating at the time they receive the recommendations. Table 9.2 summarizes the findings of research on these factors. For people to comply with a treatment regimen,

Table 9.2 *Cognitive and Emotional Factors in Patients' Recall of Information from Physicians*

1. Patients forget much of what the doctor tells them.
2. Instructions and advice are more likely to be forgotten than other information.
3. The more a patient is told, the greater the proportion he or she will forget.
4. Patients will remember: (a) what they are told first and (b) what they consider most important.
5. More intelligent patients do not remember more than less intelligent patients.
6. Older patients remember just as much as younger ones.
7. Moderately anxious patients recall more of what they are told than highly anxious patients or patients who are not anxious.
8. The more medical knowledge a patient has, the more he or she will recall.

Source: Cassata, cited in DiMatteo & DiNicola (1982, p. 45).

they must be cognitively and emotionally able to understand and remember what they are to do. The directions they receive are often complex and given at a time when they may not be listening as carefully as they should. Even when health information is given in writing, most adult patients may not understand it if it is written much above the fifth-grade reading level (Estey, Musseau, & Keehn, 1994).

Another psychosocial factor that is associated with adherence is *social support*. Generally speaking, people who feel they receive the comfort, caring, and help they need from other individuals or groups are more likely to follow medical advice than clients who have less social support (DiMatteo & DiNicola, 1982). This support can come from the patient's family, friends, or support groups, such as the many organizations to help people deal with specific illnesses. The support patients receive seems to be most beneficial to regimen adherence when it specifically involves help and encouragement in caring for the health problem (Carmody et al., 1982; Stanton, 1987). But for some people, such as kidney disease patients who must restrict fluid intake, social relationships can sometimes lead to nonadherence (Swigonski, 1987). This may happen because social gatherings often occur with food and beverages present—in meetings for lunch, dinner, drinks, or just a cup of coffee, for instance. Some evidence indicates that individuals who are low in conscientiousness are more likely to be led astray by social support than people who are high in conscientiousness (Moran, Christensen, & Lawton, 1997).

PATIENT–PRACTITIONER INTERACTIONS

The word "doctor" comes from the Latin *docere*, which means "to teach." Two features of good teaching involve explaining information in a clear and organized fashion and assessing whether the learner has learned or understands. Some medical practitioners are good teachers, and others are not:

> for example, there are documented cases of men consuming contraceptive drugs intended for their wives. The idea may be amusing, but the fact of an unwanted child was not. (Hunt & MacLeod, 1979, p. 315)

This example illustrates that physicians do not always make sure the patient understands what they have said. Successful communication in patient–practitioner interactions is essential if the client is to adhere to the advice.

Communicating with Patients

If your physician told you to "take one pill every 6 hours," does that mean you should wake up in the middle of each night to take one? Or would it be OK simply to take four pills a day, equally spaced during your waking hours? Would you ask? Sometimes the information people get from practitioners is not very clear. You might argue that the advice *was* clear: every 6 hours, on the dot. But practitioners need to anticipate unspoken questions—saying, for instance, "You'll need to wake up to take one because the infection may recur if the medicine wears off." If practitioners don't do this, patients usually answer these questions themselves, often incorrectly.

Many people leave their doctors' offices not knowing how to follow their treatment regimens. Bonnie Svarstad (1976) conducted a study in which she interviewed patients at a community health center, recorded their actual verbal interactions with their physicians, and checked their medication containers a week later. This study revealed four findings. First, the patients' knowledge about their treatment was seriously deficient—for example, half of the clients did not know how long they should continue taking their medication, and about one-fifth of them did not know the purpose of or how often to take the prescribed drugs. Second, an important reason for the patients' poor knowledge was that the physicians often did not provide the needed information. For most prescriptions, for example, the physicians failed to give explicit instructions on how regularly or how often to

use the medication; some drugs were not discussed at all during the visit. Third, the clients asked very few questions during the visits. Fourth, the more explicit the doctors' directions, the more the people complied, which Svarstad measured by pill counts at the patients' homes about a week later. Today, many pharmacies provide instructions.

Physicians spend very little time giving information to patients during a visit. Howard Waitzkin and John Stoeckle (1976) recorded the interactions between hundreds of clients and their physicians in office and hospital visits. They found that during these visits, which lasted an average of about 20 minutes, the physicians spent only about 1 minute, or 5% of the time, communicating information to the individuals about their illnesses or treatment. Interestingly, the physicians themselves reported a very different picture of their interactions: when asked how much time they spent giving information, the doctors gave estimates that were several times higher than the records showed. Other researchers have conducted similar studies and found doctors spending somewhat more time communicating with their clients. Averaging across these studies, it appears that doctors spend perhaps 10% of the time in consultations giving patients information (DiMatteo, 1985).

A person's adherence to medical advice depends on the practitioner's communicating information. Good communication takes time and is much more likely to occur when the practitioner's style is more patient-centered than doctor-centered.

Adherence and the Patient–Practitioner Relationship

As we have seen, people generally prefer medical care that involves a patient-centered style. Research has shown that individuals who have good relationships with their physicians are more likely to adhere to the medical advice they give (DiMatteo, 1985; Garrity, 1981; Ley, 1982).

Barbara Korsch and her colleagues have examined the link between patients' satisfaction with pediatric care and compliance (Francis, Korsch, & Morris, 1969; Freemon, Negrete, Davis, & Korsch, 1971; Korsch, Gozzi, & Francis, 1968). The researchers interviewed several hundred mothers at a walk-in clinic immediately after they left the doctor's office. Although most mothers reported being at least moderately satisfied with the visits, nearly one-fifth said they did not receive clear statements of what was wrong with their children, and about half did not know what caused the illnesses. The most common complaint of the mothers was that the physician did not seem to respond warmly or sympathetically to their anxiety about their children. One mother, for instance, felt the doctor did not pay attention to her concern that the convulsions her child experienced might damage his brain. Then, a week or two after the medical consultation, the researchers visited the mothers to determine their adherence with the recommended regimens. This assessment was done through the mothers' reports and, when possible, through pill counts or contacts with the pharmacy. The results revealed that those mothers who were very satisfied with the physician's warmth, concern, and communication of information were three times more likely to adhere closely to the regimens than those who were dissatisfied. It may be that doctors who succeed in fostering compliance are those who use patient-centered styles.

To summarize, the reasons why patients do and do not adhere to medical advice include characteristics of the illness and regimen, the clients and practitioners, and the way these people interrelate or communicate. While reading this material, you may have thought, "Couldn't many of the circumstances that lead to nonadherence be changed to enhance compliance?" The next section examines this question.

INCREASING PATIENT ADHERENCE

Implicit in our interest in enhancing adherence is the assumption that doing so is important—that it would benefit the person's health. How important is adherence to the patient's health? If it is very important, should health care workers aim for each client to comply perfectly to his or her regimen, or would a lesser degree of adherence be acceptable? We will address these questions briefly before considering ways to increase compliance.

Noncompliance and Health Outcomes

By not adhering to regimens recommended by their physicians, people increase their risk of developing health problems they don't already have or of prolonging or worsening their current illnesses. Estimates suggest that 20% of hospital admissions probably result from patients' noncompliance with medication regimens (Ley, 1982). Prospective studies of people with serious illnesses have shown that individuals who adhered poorly to their medical regimens were much more likely to die during a 2-year follow-up

period than people who adhered well. One study, for example, found higher mortality rates in heart disease patients who adhered poorly to taking a drug to prevent arrhythmia (Irvine et al., 1999); another study found higher death rates among kidney disease patients who adhered poorly to dialysis treatments (Kimmel et al., 1998). Research with HIV patients has shown that even occasional deviations from the regimen allows the virus to rebound, giving it a chance to develop drug resistance (Catz et al., 2000).

But failing to follow a practitioner's orders exactly is not always detrimental to the client's health. One reason is that some treatments are harmful and have side effects that produce iatrogenic conditions. Patients should notify their physicians when a treatment causes problems. Another reason is that doctors sometimes prescribe unnecessary drugs or other procedures with nonmedical goals in mind, such as to avoid risking malpractice suits. Of course, in the great majority of cases, the doctor's recommendations are correct and are in the client's best interests. Yet even when medically sound advice is given, some people who follow their doctors' orders closely show little benefit from the treatment, whereas other individuals who are much less compliant show substantial improvements in their health (Cluss & Epstein, 1985; Hayes et al., 1994).

The importance of following medical advice closely seems to depend on the particular health problem and the treatment prescribed. For hypertensive patients, for instance, consuming 80% of the medication prescribed to reduce their blood pressure is probably the minimum level of compliance needed to treat hypertension effectively. For other health problems, however, "an 80% rate of compliance may be unnecessary" (Epstein & Cluss, 1982, p. 952). And so, following the usual regimen of penicillin for treating rheumatic fever at only a 50% rate may be sufficiently effective. Unhealthful noncompliance might therefore be defined as "the point below which the desired preventive or therapeutic result is unlikely to be achieved with the medication prescribed" (Parrish, 1986, p. 456). Unfortunately, however, compliance cutoff points still need to be established for individual illnesses and treatments.

Although more research is needed to determine compliance cutoff points, two things should be clear. First, *perfect* adherence may not be necessary in many cases. Second, the current adherence levels of clients are very far from perfect. We can enhance adherence by improving communication skills of physicians and applying psychosocial methods with patients.

Improving Physicians' Communication Skills

Probably most physicians in the past who have dealt with the compliance problem at all did so after the fact. Rather than trying to prevent noncompliance, they tried to correct it if and when they learned about it. How did they try to correct it? A study examined this question and found that the first step physicians used when a client failed to adhere was to give a "thorough explanation of the regimen and repeat it so that the patient understands" (Davis, 1966). As we have seen, explaining the regimen and making sure the person understands can prevent noncompliance in the first place.

Getting practitioners to improve their style of communicating with patients is not necessarily difficult to accomplish. One study presented a brief program to instruct physicians at a hospital clinic about the kinds of reasons hypertensive people have for not adhering to their regimens and about ways to detect and improve low compliance (Inui, Yourtee, & Williamson, 1976). Compared to doctors in a control group, the physicians who received the program subsequently spent more time giving information during patient visits—and, more importantly, their clients showed more knowledge about their regimens and illnesses, greater adherence in taking medications, and better blood pressure control. Oftentimes such changes in physician behavior last indefinitely (Roter & Hall, 1989). (Go to .)

Improving Psychosocial Factors in Patients

Other approaches to promote adherence focus on modifying psychosocial factors in the patient. One method that seems to be effective at least for short-term regimens is to have the person state explicitly that he or she will comply. An experiment by James Kulik and Patricia Carlino (1987) demonstrated this in a pediatric setting with the parents of children who were suffering from acute infections. The researchers randomly assigned the subjects to two groups: parents in the experimental group were simply asked by the physician, "Will you promise me you'll give all the doses?" and all agreed; parents in the control condition were not asked for this commitment. When the patients returned for a follow-up visit about 10 days later, their recovery was medically evaluated and compliance was assessed both by interviewing the parents and by analyzing the

---

CLINICAL METHODS AND ISSUES

How to Present Medical Information

Because patients often misunderstand or forget medical recommendations, practitioners are also learning specific techniques for presenting medical information. Several methods are particularly effective (Ley, 1982; Parrish, 1986; Schraa & Dirks, 1982). These methods include:

- Simplifying verbal instructions by using clear and straightforward language and sentences, without condescending.

- Using specific and concrete statements—such as, "You should walk a mile a day for the first week, and 2 miles after that," instead of, "You should get daily exercise."

- Breaking down a complicated or long-term regimen

into smaller segments. The patient might begin the regimen by doing only part of it and then adding to it later. Or the regimen might involve a series of smaller goals that the client believes he or she can achieve.

- Emphasizing key information by stating why it is important and offering it early in the presentation.

- Using simple, written instructions.

- Having the patient repeat instructions or state them in his or her own words.

These techniques appear to be more effective in improving compliance with short-term regimens than with long-term regimens (Haynes, 1982).

children's urine. Compared with the control group, those in the experimental condition showed higher compliance rates and greater recovery from their illnesses.

Social and motivational forces in a patient's life can have important effects on adherence, particularly when the regimen is long term or requires lifestyle changes. One approach that makes use of social and motivational factors is for the practitioner or client to recruit constructive sources of *social support* (Jenkins, 1979; Peck & King, 1985). Family and friends who are committed to the regimen can promote compliance by having positive attitudes about the treatment activities and making sure they occur. Patients who receive encouragement, praise, reminders, and assistance in carrying out the regimen are more likely to comply than those who do not. Effective social support can also come from self-help groups, patient groups, and organizations established to help with specific health problems. These groups can give information and assistance, provide a sense of comfort and belongingness, and bolster the person's sense of esteem. Practitioners can help patients make contact with appropriate groups.

Several *behavioral methods* are also effective in enhancing patients' motivation to adhere to their treatment regimens (Burke, Dunbar-Jacob, & Hill, 1997; Epstein & Cluss, 1982; Haynes, 1982; Jenkins, 1979; Roter et al., 1998). These methods include:

● *Tailoring the regimen*, in which activities in the treatment are designed to be compatible with the patient's habits and rituals. For example, taking a pill at home at breakfast or while preparing for bed is easier to do and remember for most people than taking it in the middle of the day.

● *Providing prompts and reminders*, which serve as cues to perform recommended activities. These cues can include reminder phone calls for appointments or notes posted at home that remind the client to exercise. Innovative drug packaging can also help—for instance, some drugs today come in dispensers with dated compartments or built-in reminder alarms.

● *Self-monitoring*, in which the patient keeps a written record of regimen activities, such as the foods eaten each day.

● *Behavioral contracting*, whereby the practitioner and client negotiate a series of treatment activities and goals in writing and specify rewards the patient will receive for succeeding.

A major advantage of these methods is that the client can become actively involved in their design and execution (Turk & Meichenbaum, 1991). Furthermore, the patient can carry them out alone or with the aid of the practitioner, family, or friends.

The procedures we have examined for increasing patient compliance often involve the practitioner in much more constructive interactions with the person than just giving brief instructions. Although some of these methods are easy to incorporate into existing ways of interacting with clients, others are complicated and time-consuming to arrange and involve skills that are outside the expertise of most medical workers. When people have treatment regimens that are difficult for them to adhere to, interventions based on the methods we've discussed can enhance the patients' treatment compliance and, thereby, their health. These interventions can occur in nonmedical settings, such as at the person's school or workplace.

SUMMARY

Health care systems for the delivery and management of medical care are complex, involving professionals with a wide variety of specialized functions who provide inpatient and office-based treatment. Inpatient treatment for people with serious illnesses occurs in hospitals; nursing homes provide care primarily for elderly individuals who need long-term medical and personal care. Practitioners give office-based treatment in private practice and in prepaid group plans, such as health-maintenance organizations. Although the health care systems in many countries provide insurance for all citizens, the American system does not.

People decide they are sick and in need of medical attention mainly on the basis of the symptoms they perceive. The point at which people notice a symptom differs from one individual to the next and within the same person from one time to another. Some people seem to pay closer attention to their internal states than other individuals do and are, therefore, more likely to notice changes in physical sensations and to perceive these sensations as symptoms. External stimuli in the environment can interfere with or mask people's attention to internal sensations. Because people generally do not assess their internal states very accurately, psychosocial factors can have a strong influence on the perception of symptoms and may produce two interesting phenomena: medical student's disease and mass psychogenic illness. People's commonsense models of different illnesses influence their health-related behaviors. A commonsense model consists of information about the illness identity and its causes and underlying pathology, time line, and consequences.

Many factors affect how individuals interpret and respond to the symptoms they perceive. The knowledge people extract from their experience with symptoms generally helps them to make appropriate decisions about seeking medical attention. Sometimes people's prior experiences and their emotions, such as intense fear or anxiety, can lead them to interpret their symptoms incorrectly and delay seeking care. Before individuals decide to seek medical attention, they typically get advice from their lay referral system, which consists of relatives, friends, and coworkers.

Young children and the elderly use health services more than adolescents and young adults do, and women use more medical drugs and have higher rates of illness from acute and nonfatal chronic illnesses than men do. When Americans from the lower social classes are sick, they are less likely to contact physicians at their offices and more likely to use outpatient clinics and emergency rooms, probably because they do not have a regular physician. This class difference is especially troubling because individuals from the lower classes have higher rates of health problems and poorer health habits than those from higher classes.

The health belief model has been useful in helping to explain why people use, don't use, and delay using health services. People's ideas about iatrogenic conditions may also affect whether they decide to seek medical care. Treatment delay appears to involve three stages—appraisal delay, illness delay, and utilization delay—and each is affected by different factors. Many individuals wait several months before seeking attention for symptoms of serious illnesses, such as cancer. In contrast, some people overuse health services. Hypochondriasis involves the tendency for a person to interpret real but benign bodily sensations as symptoms of illness despite reassurances by a doctor that they are harmless. This tendency is linked to emotional maladjustment, but it is not more common in old age than at other ages. Many people supplement medical care with alternative medicine treatments.

People generally express high levels of satisfaction with the care they receive from physicians who communicate with a patient-centered rather than a doctor-centered style. Patient-centered physicians tend to ask open-ended questions, avoid using medical jargon or technical terms, and allow clients to participate in some of the decision making regarding the treatment of their illness. These doctors are also likely to project feelings of concern and reassurance and to give clear explanations about illnesses and treatments. Of course, patients vary in their behaviors and styles, too, and may impair communication with their doctors because of the way they describe their symptoms.

Patient compliance with or adherence to medical advice varies greatly; noncompliance is very common. About two of every five clients fail to adhere reasonably closely to the medical regimens their doctors prescribe. Individuals tend to be less compliant for long-term regimens to treat chronic diseases than for short-term regimens to treat acute illnesses, and they are particularly unlikely to adhere to recommendations to change long-standing habits. Also, the more complicated the regimen, the more likely adherence will suffer. Adherence is affected by various psychosocial factors, including rational nonadherence decisions and the patient's health beliefs, social support, and cognitive and emotional conditions when receiving medical advice. Many people leave their doctors' offices not knowing how to follow the prescribed regimens. Patients are more likely to adhere closely to their regimens when their practitioners are patient-centered and explain their illnesses and treatments clearly. Behavioral and communication-enhancing methods can help to improve people's adherence to medical advice.

KEY TERMS

lay referral system	treatment delay	doctor-centered	compliance
commonsense models	alternative medicine	patient-centered	rational nonadherence
iatrogenic conditions	hypochondriasis	adherence	

10

IN THE HOSPITAL: THE SETTING, PROCEDURES, AND EFFECTS ON PATIENTS

PROLOGUE

"I had a fast-growing conviction that a hospital was no place for a person who was seriously ill," a patient once wrote. This patient was Norman Cousins, former editor of *Saturday Review*, whom we described in Chapter 1 as having developed and recovered from a typically incurable and painful crippling disease. His symptoms began with a fever and general achiness—the kinds of sensations we usually associate with minor illnesses. Within a week, however, his condition worsened, and he began to have difficulty moving his neck, legs, arms, and hands. He was soon hospitalized for the diagnostic tests that pinpointed his disease: ankylosis spondylitis.

What experiences did Cousins have that led to his negative view of hospitals? One example he described is:

> I was astounded when four technicians from four different departments took four separate and substantial blood samples on the same day. That the hospital didn't take the trouble to coordinate the tests, using one blood specimen, seemed to me inexplicable and irresponsible. When the technicians came the second day to fill their containers with blood for processing in separate laboratories, I turned them away and had a sign posted on my door saying that I would give just one specimen every three days and that I expected the different departments to draw from it for their individual needs. (Cousins, 1985, pp. 55–56)

He also criticized other hospital practices, such as awakening patients from sleep to carry out regular routines. In his view, sleep in the hospital is an "uncommon blessing" that should not be interrupted casually.

Few people enjoy being hospitalized, even under the best of circumstances. Although many people probably have more positive feelings about their hospital experiences than those Cousins had, some have even worse impressions. We have all heard stories of mistakes being made or other situations that produced more serious health problems than those with which the patient was admitted to the hospital. This chapter focuses on the experience of being hospitalized. First we examine the hospital—its history, setting, and procedures—as well as the roles and points of view of the hospital staff. Then we consider what being hospitalized is like from the perspective of patients, and what can be done to assess and provide help for their psychological needs. As we study these topics, we will consider important questions that are of great concern to patients, their families, and practitioners. For instance, hospital personnel have difficult jobs—what impact does this have on them? How do people adjust to being hospitalized? What special needs do children have as patients, and how can hospitals and parents help? How can practitioners reduce the stress individuals experience with unpleasant, painful, and surgical procedures?

THE HOSPITAL—ITS HISTORY, SETTING, AND PROCEDURES

Hospitals in industrialized countries around the world are typically large institutions with separate wards or buildings for different kinds of health problems and treatment procedures. These institutions have changed in their long history, and so have people's attitudes about them. People in the United States today are more likely than people years ago to view hospitals as places to go to get well rather than to die, even though most Americans are in hospitals when they die (Easterbrook, 1987). Let's see how hospitals began and evolved.

HOW THE HOSPITAL EVOLVED

Special places to care for the ill did not always exist. One of the earliest roots of this approach can be seen in the ancient Greeks' establishment of temples where sick people would pray and receive cures or advice from the god Aesculapius (Anderson & Gevitz, 1983). But the idea of having special facilities to house and treat the sick probably began with the Roman military, who established separate barracks for their ill and disabled soldiers.

The first institutions established to care for the sick were associated with Christian monasteries and had a broad charitable purpose—that of helping the less fortunate members of society. As a result, these facilities housed not only sick people, but also orphans, the poor, and even travelers who needed lodging. One of the earliest of these hospitals, the Hôtel-Dieu of Lyons in present-day France, was established in A.D. 542 (Anderson & Gevitz, 1983). The charitable purposes of hospitals in Western Europe continued with little change until the 18th and 19th centuries, when these institutions became more specialized in two ways.

> First, the conventional approach of lumping all types of dependents into the same facility was gradually discarded as hospitals became repositories for the poor sick. Not all of the medically incapacitated were admitted, though—only the "worthy poor," i.e., those lower class individuals adjudged by administrators and sponsors to be potentially useful citizens capable of making a contribution to the commonweal. Others, namely the aged, the very young, the physically handicapped, and the mentally deficient ... were confined to abysmally kept poorhouses, irrespective of whether they were in need of medical attention. The second change was that hospitals became more medically specialized. Wards were established for different illness categories.... By keeping patients with the same or seemingly related ailments together, one could readily make far more detailed comparisons and thus advance learning. (Anderson & Gevitz, 1983, p. 307)

The American colonies used similar approaches to those used in Europe for the care of the sick. In 1751,

Pennsylvania Hospital opened in Philadelphia as the first institution in the colonies devoted exclusively to treating disease. It was built as a result of a citizens' campaign led by Benjamin Franklin.

Until the 20th century, hospitals had always had a well-deserved bad reputation as places that gave miserable care and ministered exclusively to poor people, who often died from infections they did not have when they entered. Sick people from the upper and middle classes were treated at home. But this situation quickly changed with advances in medical knowledge and technology in the late 1800s. In 1873, there were only 178 hospitals in the United States; in 1909, there were over 4,300, and the increase in the number of hospital beds was seven times that which would be expected on the basis of population growth alone (Anderson & Gevitz, 1983). American hospitals in the early 20th century gained a much more positive reputation and were attracting patients from all social classes. Nowadays, the nation's hospitals admit over 31 million people as inpatients each year (USBC, 1999).

Hospitals today involve a wider variety of functions than ever before. They provide services to inpatients and outpatients to cure disease and repair injury, prevent illness, conduct diagnostic tests, and aid people's rehabilitation and life situations after being discharged. They are also involved in conducting research and teaching current and future medical personnel. To carry out these complex and varied functions, hospitals require organized hierarchies of personnel with specific roles and lines of authority.

THE ORGANIZATION AND FUNCTIONING OF HOSPITALS

The organizational structure of hospitals in the United States differs from structures used in most other countries. At the top of the structure is a board of trustees, whose members are generally upper-level business and professional people from the community (Anderson & Gevitz, 1983; APA, 1998). Most boards limit their role mainly to long range planning and fund-raising. At the next level of authority, the chain of command splits into two parallel lines of responsibility. The hospital *administrators* are mainly in charge of the day-to-day business of the institution, such as in purchasing equipment and supplies, keeping records and accounts, and providing food and maintenance

Typical of hospitals prior to the 20th century, this women's ward had many beds close together in a huge room.

services. These functions often affect the medical care patients receive. The *medical staff* are responsible for patient care. Each of these two lines has its own hierarchy of authority. We will focus on the medical staff.

The head of the medical staff is a physician who usually has the title "Medical Director" or "Chief of Staff." The next level of authority consists of the staff (or "attending") physicians. In the majority of American hospitals, most staff physicians are not actually employed or paid by the institution. They are employed in private practice or affiliated with a private clinic or group health plan, and they provide services at the hospital for their clients from these sources (Anderson & Gevitz, 1983; APA, 1998). Those doctors who are in private practice get paid for their hospital services by billing each of their patients; the remaining doctors are paid salaries by their employers. To become a staff physician, a doctor must receive *admission privileges*, generally by applying to a committee of physicians at the hospital. As a condition for granting privileges, most hospitals require staff physicians to do certain tasks, such as teaching or providing emergency or clinic service. The main exception to this system of staff physicians occurs at "teaching hospitals," which are affiliated with medical schools. Although teaching hospitals grant admission privileges, they also have large staffs of doctors whom they em-

ploy; these doctors include (1) *residents*, who are recent medical school graduates, and (2) full-fledged physicians, whose duties include supervising the residents.

Nurses form the next rung in the hierarchy of medical staff in hospitals. Although many physicians think of nurses as their assistants, nurses are actually salaried employees of the hospitals who have two functions: caring for patients and managing the wards (Aiken, 1983). Because the former function is medical and the latter is administrative, nurses may receive directives from physicians and administrators. Sometimes the orders nurses receive from these two sources are incompatible and cause conflict, such as when a physician orders an action that the administration has banned as a cost-cutting measure. Nurses also experience conflicts and difficulties from the discrepancy between their high level of training and low involvement in medical decision making (Aiken, 1983; Easterbrook, 1987). Nurses are, of course, as important as doctors to a patient's recovery, and they spend more time with the person, often explaining medical regimens and procedures when physicians do not.

The medical staff also includes a great variety of allied health workers, such as physical therapists, respiratory therapists, laboratory technicians, pharmacists' assistants, and dietitians (Ginzberg, 1983).

ASSESS YOURSELF

Who's Who in Physician Care

The medical staffs in hospitals contain a great variety of specialized personnel. If you were hospitalized, chances are you'd receive care from at least two of the ten types of medical specialists listed below. Do you know what their specialty areas of illness or treatment are? For this matching task, write the number for each specialty area in the space preceding the corresponding type of specialist. Then use the answer key to find out how many you matched correctly.

_____ Anesthesiologist   _____ Gastroenterologist

_____ Cardiologist   _____ Hematologist

_____ Neurologist   _____ Otolaryngologist

_____ Orthopedist   _____ Proctologist

_____ Oncologist   _____ Radiologist

Specialty areas: **1.** Cancer; **2.** Blood; **3.** Nervous system; **4.** Colon and rectum; **5.** Painkilling drugs; **6.** Ear, nose, and throat; **7.** Bones and joints; **8.** X rays; **9.** Heart; **10.** Digestive system.

Answers, in order:

5,9,10,2,3,7,1,6,4,8

These workers often have less authority than nurses. At the bottom of the medical staff hierarchy are orderlies and other workers whose roles require less advanced skills than those of the allied health workers. (Go to 🍎.)

ROLES, GOALS, AND COMMUNICATION

Picture this scene: as the ambulance crew wheels the victim of an automobile accident into the emergency room, the medical staff swings into action. Their specific actions and roles are dictated by the presenting health problems of the patient and would be different if the person had suffered serious burns in a fire or experienced symptoms of a heart attack, for instance. Quick assessments and decisions need to be made regarding tests to perform, medications to administer, and procedures to apply to control the damage, stabilize the person's body functions, and set the stage for recovery. Nurses and orderlies know the usual procedures for patients with the presenting problems and begin to perform their roles without specific instruction—for example, a nurse may prepare to take a blood sample and an orderly may wheel a piece of equipment into place. The physician is, of course, in charge and either conducts needed actions directly or orders others to do them.

Coordinating Patient Care

Years ago, the typical hospital patient received services from a small team of physicians and nurses who worked side by side in close communication throughout the person's stay (Benoliel, 1977). This situation rarely exists today. Instead, assessment and treatment procedures for a hospitalized person involve a wide array of personnel who have different specialties and carry out their roles separately, often with little contact with each other and with the patient. The danger in the current approach is that the patient's care can become *fragmented*, or uncoordinated, with seemingly no one in charge. Hospitals attempt to minimize this danger by giving a particular staff position, usually a nurse, responsibility for coordinating the care of each patient in a ward (Aiken, 1983; Benoliel, 1977; Kneut, 1982). But *direct* communication—say, between the patient's physician and physical therapist—is best. It uses more of a team approach, leaves less opportunity for errors, and provides important information and feedback to each team member.

Health Hazards in Hospitals

Communication among medical personnel is also important because hospitals contain many health hazards for personnel and patients. These hazards include chemicals that are used in treatment and various other hospital procedures (Clever & Omenn, 1988; USDHHS, 1985b). One substance, called *ethylene oxide*, for example, is widely used as a sterilizing agent for medical supplies and equipment. Long-term high-level exposure to this chemical has been linked with the development of several forms of cancer. Hospitals need to maintain good channels of communication to protect their workers from high exposure to such chemicals when equipment is malfunctioning or improperly designed. Hospitals also need to protect patients from unsafe exposure to various substances used in their treatment.

Another hazard in hospitals is the potential exposure of personnel and patients to disease-causing microorganisms (Clever & LeGuyader, 1995; Yoffe, 1999). As we saw earlier, hospitals prior to the 20th century were places where infection spread quickly and widely, and patients often died of diseases they did not have when they entered. Although the spreading of infection in hospitals has been reduced, it has not been eliminated. About 5% of patients in American hospitals—over 1½ million people each year—acquire a **nosocomial infection,** an infection that a patient contracts while in the hospital setting, and 20,000 of these people die from these infections (Yoffe, 1999). To combat this problem, national guidelines for hospital infection control have been developed and widely adopted. According to these guidelines, each hospital should have an Infection Control Committee headed by an epidemiologist to establish policies to control the spread of disease. Furthermore, the medical staff should include an Infection Control Nurse (ICN) with experience in a clinical setting and training in epidemiology and infectious diseases. The ICN has the most direct role in curbing the spread of disease, being responsible for detecting and recording instances of nosocomial infections and taking measures to prevent them.

Hospitals have attempted to reduce nosocomial infections by establishing regulations regarding such issues as when medical workers must wash their hands or wear masks. But hospital personnel often break these rules, and physicians in intensive care may be the worst offenders (Yoffe, 1999). Bertram Raven and Robert Haley (1982) surveyed about 8,000 nurses, ICNs, and epidemiologists at hundreds of hospitals in the United States to determine whether medical workers adhere to infection control regulations and what is done when they do not. Physicians were

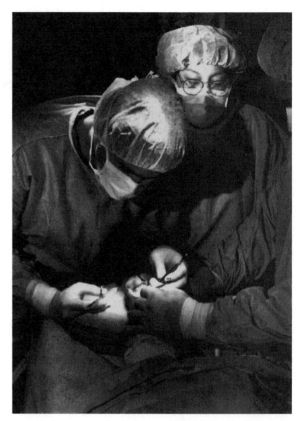

Hospitals try to reduce the spread of infection by establishing rules about medical staff wearing clean masks, clothing, and gloves.

considerably less likely to comply than were nurses and laboratory technicians. The ICNs were also asked how often they would "say something to a staff member" who violated infection control rules, such as by entering a strict isolation area without putting on a mask or by discarding an unprotected syringe in a waste basket. Their responses indicated that ICNs usually correct nurses and technicians, but they are much less likely to correct physicians.

Although nosocomial infection continues to be a serious problem in hospitals, role relationships among medical personnel seem to impair the communication needed to reduce the spread of disease. In general, personnel feel much less comfortable giving advice or corrective feedback to an individual whose status is higher, rather than equal to or lower, than their own. Hospitals need to find constructive ways to enable a staff member at a lower level of the medical staff hierarchy to give feedback to individuals at higher levels regarding their nonadherence to infection control regulations.

THE IMPACT OF THE "BOTTOM LINE"

The costs of hospital services have probably always been high. The Medicare system in the United States today probably helps contain medical costs, but it made the situation worse when it was first introduced because its procedures encouraged overcharging, keeping patients in the hospital, and performing many tests and procedures. In those days, maintaining a hospital's financial solvency was a relatively easy job for administrators.

This situation in America soon changed when Medicare adopted a payment method called the *prospective-payment system* (PPS) (APA, 1998; Lave, 1989). With the PPS approach, health problems are classified into "diagnostic-related groups," and a hospital that is treating a person who has a particular health problem receives a predetermined fixed fee. This fee reflects the average cost of treating individuals in the corresponding diagnostic-related group, based on past recovery rates for similar people. If the patient's condition does not respond to the treatment as readily as expected and requires extra care, the hospital usually bears the cost beyond the PPS allowance. But if the patient's condition responds better than expected, the hospital keeps the excess payment. The combination of the spiraling costs of medical care and hospital administrators' concern for the "bottom line" has led to changes in hospital procedures.

How have hospital procedures changed? Although some American hospitals focus on treating patients who require long-term care, the great majority were established to treat people quickly and discharge them in good health (Lawrence & Gaus, 1983; USDHHS, 1985a). Most hospitals keep patients for an average of less than 30 days, and are classified as *short-stay hospitals*. As Figure 10–1 depicts, the rate at which short-stay hospitals admit and discharge patients increased from 1970 to 1980, when the average length of stay was about a week. Since 1980, both admissions and lengths of stay have declined sharply. These decreases reflect three important changes. First, people are having more procedures done on an outpatient basis. Second, medical procedures are becoming increasingly efficient. For example, new surgical methods for correcting orthopedic injuries

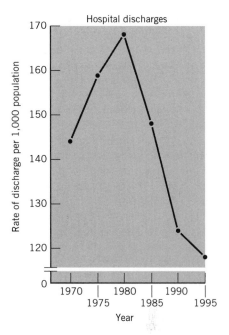

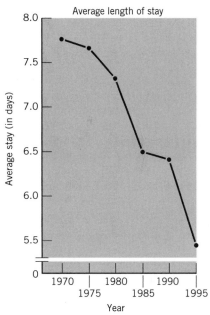

Figure 10–1 United States hospital utilization from 1970 to 1995, as indicated by patient discharge rate and average length of stay at non-Federal "short-stay" hospitals. (Pre-1980 data from USDHHS, 1985a, Figure 30; later data from USBC, 1999, Table 207. Note that a change in research methodology beginning in 1988 may be responsible for part of any differences seen between earlier and later data.)

entail little or no cutting of healthy tissue, so that recovery time and pain are greatly diminished. And emergency room diagnoses are being made more quickly with the aid of new, accurate tests, such as for heart attacks (Puleo et al., 1994). Third, patients are being released at earlier stages of recovery, so that a larger part of their recovery time is spent at home while receiving care as outpatients. Although there is some concern that people are being released too quickly from hospitals, for the most part patients have not been harmed by the PPS procedures (Kahn et al., 1990; Lave, 1989; Rogers et al., 1990).

People typically prefer being released from the hospital as early as possible. Being hospitalized is in many ways a negative experience—financially, physically, socially, and emotionally. The next section considers the impact on the patient of being hospitalized.

BEING HOSPITALIZED

Although being sick is unpleasant and being seriously ill is worse, being hospitalized adds many other negative aspects to a person's sick-role experience: It drastically disrupts the individual's lifestyle, involves a high degree of dependency on others, and presents many events that can be extremely distressing. The unpleasantness may begin at admission, such as when a clerk in an American hospital asks questions about the patient's ability to pay for the medical services. As this example suggests, part of the unpleasantness of being hospitalized relates to the interactions between the patient and the hospital staff.

RELATIONS WITH THE HOSPITAL STAFF

Imagine that you have just been admitted to a hospital. How should you behave toward the staff if you don't get the care or information you want? Patients typically enter the hospital with a clear social role—that of being dependent for their very lives on the medical staff, who have most of the knowledge, authority, and power in their relationship (CU, 1995b; Rodin & Janis, 1979; Taylor, 1979). The patient is a stranger in the hospital community and is likely to be unfamiliar with its structure, procedures, and terminology. These conditions often make the person feel uneasy in an already worrisome situation.

Anxiety is probably the most common and pervasive emotion of hospitalized people (Newman, 1984a). If their health problems have not yet been identified, they worry about what the problems are, what the outcomes will be, and how the illnesses will influence their lives. If the diagnoses have been made, they worry about many other matters, such as what the treatment will be like and the degree to which it will be successful. Many of the worries patients have stem from uncertainties that result from a lack of information. Although the lack of information may occur because tests have not yet been completed, frequently it occurs because no one has taken the time to inform the person (CU, 1995b). One hospital patient, for example, gave the following description of experiences with a physician:

> He'll say well, we'll talk about it next time. And next time he'll talk fast, he out-talks you—and rushes out of the room and then when he's out of the room you think, well, I was supposed to ask him what he's going to do about my medicine ... you run in the hall and he has disappeared that fast. (Tagliacozzo & Mauksch, 1972, p. 177)

Hospitals are busy places, but the limited time of medical personnel is only one reason for their failure to provide the information patients may need. Practitioners sometimes withhold information or disguise it with jargon because they expect the person will misunderstand it or be alarmed by it (McKinlay, 1975).

Many patients react to not being informed by their doctors by gathering information from other patients, asking orderlies and nurses, and eavesdropping. As one patient put it:

> Well, I ask the nurses about the blood pressure and if they don't tell me, I go to my chart and look at it. It's six of one and half-a-dozen of the other. When the doctor comes by, I listen to him. I get some information from him when he's speaking about me to the students, although he doesn't know he's giving it to me. (McKinlay, 1975, p. 9)

People are resourceful, but the information they receive in these indirect ways may be incorrect or misleading. If so, the beliefs these individuals develop may impair compliance with the advice of the medical staff or lead to unnecessary emotional suffering. Thus, withholding information may produce, rather than prevent, misunderstandings and alarm in patients.

Another common characteristic of the way practitioners interact with patients is called **depersonalization,** or treating the patient as though he or she were either not present or not a person. Sociologist Erving Goffman referred to this characteristic as "nonperson treatment"—the patient is treated like "a possession someone has left behind" (1961. pp. 341–342). A psychologist has described the following example of depersonalization from his own experience as a patient for an eye injury. The physician

abruptly terminated his conversation with me as soon as I lay down on the operating table. Although I had no sedative, or anesthesia, he acted as if I were no longer conscious, directing all his questions to a friend of mine—questions such as, What's his name?, What occupation is he in?. . . As I lay there, these two men were speaking about me as if I were not there at all. The moment I got off the table and was no longer a cut to be stitched, the surgeon resumed his conversation with me, and existence was conferred upon me again. (Zimbardo, 1970, p. 298)

Why do practitioners treat patients as nonpersons? One reason, according to Goffman (1961), is that practitioners want to distance themselves from the fact that the body they are treating belongs to a thinking and worried person—a person who can observe what is going on, ask questions, and behave in ways that can interfere with their work. He contrasted this situation with that of a mechanic who repairs a car or appliance in a shop without the owner present. The implication of Goffman's view is that medical workers try to save themselves and the patient a lot of trouble, awkwardness, and anxiety by acting as if the person had dropped off the defective body at the hospital for repair and would pick it up when it was ready.

There are also many emotional factors that lead hospital workers to treat patients in a depersonalized manner. Hospital jobs can be very hectic, particularly when many emergencies punctuate the day. Furthermore, practitioners' jobs entail heavy responsibilities and, sometimes, risks to their own health, as when they work with hazardous chemicals or patients with serious contagious illnesses (Clever & Omenn, 1988; O'Donnell et al., 1987). Quite literally, the activities and decisions of hospital workers have life-or-death implications for their patients and themselves. These features can create high levels of stress, which may lead workers to give less personalized care. Some-

times practitioners who are under prolonged stress may even begin to blame patients for their health problems, thinking, for instance, "You wouldn't have this illness if you had taken care of yourself and not smoked" (Maslach & Jackson, 1982). Last, practitioners need ways to protect themselves emotionally when a patient takes a turn for the worse or dies (Benoliel, 1977; Kneut, 1982). The death of a patient can be a crushing experience. Depersonalization probably helps practitioners be relatively detached and less emotionally affected when death occurs.

Some hospitals in the United States and other countries are changing the look and feel of their wards, using recommendations of an organization called Program Planetree (CU, 1995b). Wards have rooms with homelike furnishings and libraries with medical and health information, and the staff work as a team with a nurse-coordinator for each patient.(Go to 🌿.)

SICK-ROLE BEHAVIOR IN THE HOSPITAL

Relations between patients and practitioners in the hospital are affected not only by the behavior of the medical staff, but by the patient's behavior, too. A hospital presents an unfamiliar and strange environment that requires psychological and social adjustments that most patients have difficulty making. They must get used to a lack of privacy, strict rules and time schedules, having their activities restricted, having little control over events around them, and being dependent on others. These things complicate their psychosocial transition to the sick role (Kasl & Cobb, 1966b). How are patients supposed to behave in the hospital?

When patients enter the hospital, they have ideas about how they should behave. Judith Lorber (1975) studied these ideas and the sick-role behavior of over 100 patients, mostly over 40 years of age, who entered a hospital for elective surgeries ranging from routine to very serious. In interviews at the start and end of the hospital stays, the patients indicated their degree of agreement or disagreement with several statements, such as: "The best thing to do in the hospital is to keep quiet and do what you're told," "I cooperate best as a patient when I know the reason for what I have to do," and "When I'm sick, I expect to be pampered and catered to." Their responses indicated whether they thought patients should be *active* or *passive*: agreement with the first of these items and disagreement with

FOCUS ON RESEARCH

Burnout among Health Care Professionals

Hour after hour, day after day, people who work with people who are suffering and distressed must cope with the stress these encounters produce. All jobs have stressful conditions of some kind, such as heavy workloads, deadlines, and interpersonal conflicts. But workers in certain professions—for example, police work, social work, and health care—have the added emotional burden of working continuously in emotionally charged situations that involve feelings of anxiety, fear, embarrassment, and hostility. This burden makes the risk of "burnout" greater in these professions than in most others. **Burnout** is a state of psychosocial and physical exhaustion that results from chronic exposure to high levels of stress with little personal control (McGuigan, 1999; McKnight & Glass, 1995; Parker & Kulik, 1995). Workers who experience burnout tend to show low levels of job satisfaction and high levels of absenteeism, job turnover, and alcohol and drug abuse.

What psychological characteristics contribute to burnout in workers? Christina Maslach and Susan Jackson (1982) have developed the Maslach Burnout Inventory (MBI) and used it in research with health care workers. This treatment assesses three psychosocial components of burnout:

1. *Emotional exhaustion*—the feeling of being drained of emotional resources and being unable to help others on a psychological level. People who feel this way are likely to agree with the MBI item, "Working with people all day is really a strain for me."
2. *Depersonalization*—a lack of personal regard for others, as shown by treating people as objects, having little concern for and sensitivity to their needs, and developing callous attitudes toward them. Workers with this characteristic tend to agree with the statement, "I worry that this job is hardening me emotionally."
3. *Perceived inadequacy of professional accomplishment*—the feeling of falling short of personal expectations for work performance. Workers who feel this way are likely to *disagree* with the MBI item, "I feel I'm

positively influencing other people's lives through my work."

Maslach and Jackson administered the MBI to a large sample of workers in a variety of helping professions and to separate samples of nurses and physicians.

This research produced several important findings. First, the nurses, physicians, and workers in various helping professions reported fairly similar, high levels of emotional exhaustion. Second, differences were found among occupations for the two other components of burnout: the nurses showed the lowest degree of depersonalization and the physicians reported the least dissatisfaction with their sense of accomplishment in their work. The researchers suggested that the low degree of depersonalization among nurses may reflect a sex difference in empathy toward people since the females consistently showed less depersonalization than the males in the helping professions sample, and almost all the nurses but few of the physicians were females. The relatively high sense of accomplishment among doctors may be the result of such factors as their high pay and status in the medical staff hierarchy. Finally, Maslach and Jackson found that the more time health care workers spent in direct care of patients, the greater was their risk of emotional exhaustion. For instance, physicians who spent almost all their time in direct care reported greater emotional exhaustion than those who spent some of their time in teaching or administrative duties.

What can hospitals do to help health care workers avoid or cope with burnout? We can describe two things. First, hospitals can provide opportunities for workers to mix direct care for patients and other tasks in their daily activities whenever possible. Second, hospitals can help establish support groups for their health care workers. Meetings of these groups can provide training in stress-management and coping methods, like those we discussed in Chapter 5. Health care workers who receive such training and periodic booster sessions experience much less burnout than individuals without such training (Rowe, 1999).

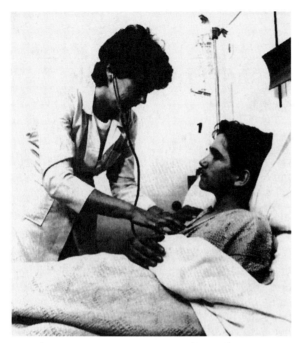

"Good patients" are cooperative, calm, and attentive in discussions with the medical staff.

the second two, for example, would indicate that they believe patients should be passive, or "conforming." One finding of this study was that people who had passive beliefs when they entered were less likely than those with active beliefs to argue with the staff and complain about minor discomforts.

Another purpose of this study was to examine the reactions of the medical staff to the patients' sick-role behaviors. At the end of each patient's stay, the medical staff rated the individual as a "good patient," "average patient," or "problem patient." They were also asked to provide verbal descriptions of the person's behavior and their reactions when the behavior occurred. In general, individuals rated as *good patients* were those who behaved passively, being cooperative, uncomplaining, and stoical; those rated as *problem patients* were seen as uncooperative, constantly complaining, overemotional, and dependent. An example problem patient was a 74-year-old man who had had his gallbladder removed and had had postoperative psychological and medical complications. He

was labeled a problem patient by the surgeon, resident, intern, and day staff nurse. In the questionnaire, the resident said the patient's uncoop-

erativeness made it difficult to perform routine procedures on him. The surgeon wrote that the patient was "lachrymose, combative, and generally impossible"... the surgeon added that the patient had called him names, lied, and generally carried on. (Lorber, 1975, p. 218)

An important consequence of poor patient–practitioner relationships is that the patient is less likely to adhere to medical recommendations, as we saw in Chapter 9.

But the opposite behavior of patients—being overly passive or too considerate—can present problems, too. One very sick person "didn't want to bother" the nurses, even when she should have. As a result, the nurses' routines were disrupted by having to check on her status very frequently to make sure she was all right. Patients who are too passive in the hospital may fail to take active roles in their recovery, thereby limiting their rehabilitation (Taylor, 1979). Ideal relationships between patients and practitioners foster mutual involvement in the treatment process.

Severe medical conditions can make patients' difficult behavior understandable, and so the staff in Lorber's study distinguished between two types of problem patients. One type consists of individuals who are very seriously ill, having severe complications or poor prognoses. Although these patients show problem behaviors and require a lot of attention, the staff often forgives their behavior because of their medical conditions. The second type consists of people who are not seriously ill but take up more time and attention than is warranted by their conditions—they frequently argue, complain, or fail to cooperate with the staff. According to psychologist Shelley Taylor (1979), patients who are not seriously ill may behave disruptively in reaction to being angry at their loss of freedoms and control. For instance, a patient may not be allowed to walk for a while because of a leg injury, or watch television late because it would disturb other patients, or have visitors at certain times because their presence might make the work of the medical staff more difficult. People's angry responses to being controlled or believing their freedom is threatened are called **reactance** (Brehm, 1966).

How does the hospital staff deal with problem patients? In many cases, hospital workers respond in a pleasant manner—by providing reassurance or explanations, for example (Lorber, 1975). In other cases, the response is not so positive. Staff members sometimes

"WE'LL HAVE YOU OUT OF HERE IN NO TIME, MR. LOCKHORN···THE NURSES HAVE HAD IT WITH YOU."   Reprinted courtesy of Bunny Hoest.

scold patients, or begin to ignore their problem behavior, or respond less quickly to their calls for attention. In addition, hospital personnel often deal with problem patients by administering sedatives and, in highly problematic cases, even by arranging for premature discharge.

Fortunately, the large majority of patients are not problem patients (Lorber, 1975). Most hospitalized people try to be considerate, recognizing that medical workers have difficult jobs. Other individuals behave as "good patients" because they are wary of the consequences of being disliked by the staff. These people do not want to appear to be "troublemakers," by being too demanding or too dependent. They may think an angered staff may "refuse to answer your bell" or "refuse to make your bed," for instance. As a result, these patients may anxiously watch the clock when their medication does not arrive on time, rather than reminding the nurse (Tagliacozzo & Mauksch, 1972).

The sick-role behavior of hospitalized individuals is affected by many factors in addition to the seriousness of their illnesses, their ideas about how they should behave, and their reactions to their restricted freedoms. As we have seen before, social interactions in a medical setting involve a "two-way street" in which both the patient's and the practitioner's behavior are important. Patients respond differently to medical staff who grumble or frown when asked to do something than to staff who carry out requests cheerfully and seem to want to help (Tagliacozzo & Mauksch, 1972). Finally, sick-role behavior depends on how well patients cope with their medical condi-

tions and the medical treatment procedures they experience in the hospital.

EMOTIONAL ADJUSTMENT IN THE HOSPITAL

Imagine you are in your 30s, waiting in your hospital room for surgery to remove the large tumor you have seen in X rays that is growing in your lung. Then imagine that the operation goes badly, not all of the tumor could be removed, and the radiation and chemotherapy treatments over the next several weeks leave you weak and nauseated for days at a time. This was the real experience of Fitzhugh Mullan, which he described in his 1983 book called *Vital Signs*. Being hospitalized with a serious illness or injury produces enormous stress and anxiety.

Hospitalized people must cope with their emotions, and they tend to adjust gradually. For example, most surgical patients experience anxiety levels that are especially high when they are admitted, remain quite high prior to the operation, and then decline steadily during the week or two after surgery (Newman, 1984a). But sometimes the anxiety levels of patients increase with time, as happened with a 25-year-old man who had suffered serious burns over 30% of his body:

> In his third postburn week he became increasingly uncooperative and demanding. He complained of pain despite adequate analgesia, to the point that

he would not let anyone near him for dressing changes. ... The staff reacted angrily to his conduct, which in turn led to a perpetuation and increase in his complaints and demands. In a series of brief interviews the motivation for his conduct was elucidated. He had a very exaggerated view of the nature of his injury, expecting it would render him a cripple for life and unable to support himself or his family. He feared discharge and the subsequent demands of his family. (Steiner & Clark, 1977, p. 138)

The way a patient adjusts to his or her health problem and treatment in the hospital depends on many factors, such as the person's age or gender and characteristics of the illness or injury (Moos, 1982). For instance, young adults often have more difficulty coping with serious illnesses than older individuals do. Also, men tend to be more distressed than women by illnesses that reduce their vigor and physical abilities, but women often have an especially difficult time adjusting to disfigurement, such as facial injuries or losing one of their breasts.

COPING PROCESSES IN HOSPITAL PATIENTS

How would you try to cope with the stress and anxiety of being hospitalized? You can get an indication of the answer by turning back to page 135 in Chapter 5, where you assessed your tendency to use coping processes to achieve two main goals: to alter the problem causing the stress and to regulate the emotional response to the problem. Some of the situations that produce stress in the hospital can be altered by the patient's taking action, such as by asking for medication to reduce pain or by reading information about his or her health problem. Because these actions can reduce the demands of the stressor or expand the person's resources for dealing with it, they are examples of *problem-focused coping*.

Patients in the hospital experience many stressors they believe they cannot change. In some cases these beliefs are correct, as when a person whose spinal cord was severed in an accident must cope with not being able to walk. But in other cases they are incorrect, as when a patient does not realize that it may be possible to use another medication if the current one produces discomfort or other side effects. People who believe they can do nothing to

change a stressor usually try to cope with their emotions and the situation by using methods classified as *emotion-focused coping*. Patients may try to regulate their emotions by denying unpleasant facts, performing distracting activities, or seeking social support, for example. Research has consistently shown that social support aids people's recovery from and adjustment to illness (Kulik & Mahler, 1989; Wallston, Alagna, DeVellis, & DeVellis, 1983).

Cognitive Processes in Coping

One cognitive process many patients engage in after becoming ill or injured is attributing *blame*—trying to answer the question, "Who's at fault for my condition?" They often grapple with this issue while in the hospital. Some people blame mainly themselves, others blame someone else, and others attribute their conditions to luck or God's will. Does the way people attribute blame affect their success in coping with their conditions? We might expect, for instance, that people who blame themselves would have intense feelings of guilt and self-recrimination and, therefore, have more difficulty adjusting to their conditions than those who blame someone else. On the other hand, blaming someone else may induce intense feelings of anger and bitterness, which would impair adjustment.

Research has examined this issue and found that the more blame for a traumatic event that individuals attribute to themselves or other people, the poorer their adjustment tends to be (Downey, Silver, & Wortman, 1990). The findings of several other studies suggest that poor adjustment may be more strongly related to blaming others than to self-blame (Bulman & Wortman, 1977; Kiecolt-Glaser & Williams, 1987; Taylor, Lichtman, & Wood, 1984). Although it is unclear why adjustment is so difficult when patients blame someone else, the reason may be that these people feel an added sense of injustice if the person they blame did not suffer severe consequences, too. These feelings are reflected in such statements as, "I'm paralyzed, but the driver only broke his leg," or, "I can't walk now, but the guy who shot me is now walking free" (Bulman & Wortman, 1977, p. 360).

One thing to keep in mind about the cognitive processes used in ascribing blame is that they can be quite convoluted or disturbed, as in

a case in which a young man bought gasoline from a service station owned by his father-in-law. He used the gasoline to set himself on fire at the service station. He attributed all the blame for the incident to his father-in-law, saying he acted as he did because his father-in-law had said disparaging things about him. (Kiecolt-Glaser & Williams, 1987, p. 191)

This example raises a question for researchers: Should reasonable and unreasonable attributions of blame be examined separately for their relation to adjustment? Last, we must keep in mind that all this research on the role of blame has been correlational. Thus, it may be that variations in both blame and adjustment are caused by some other factor.

Another cognitive process that patients engage in involves the assessment of their personal control. Patients enter the hospital with the expectation of losing some degree of personal control, either from the effects of the illness itself or from being dependent on the actions of the medical staff. Hospital environments encourage patients to believe their involvement in the treatment process is irrelevant—that they are *helpless*. Patients often express this feeling, saying, "When you are really sick, you are at the mercy of the hospital staff," or, "Trying to change things is futile and won't get you anywhere" (Tagliacozzo & Mauksch, 1972). Those people who feel this way are likely to behave like "good patients" (Taylor, 1979). Some patients enter the hospital feeling quite helpless right from the start, but others try to exert control and fail. Through repeated failures in exerting control, many people learn to be helpless in the hospital, eventually making no effort to initiate changes when control is actually possible. One study found, for instance, that patients' helplessness and feelings of depression increased with time in the hospital, even as their health improved (Raps, Peterson, Jonas, & Seligman, 1982).

The connections among "good patient" behavior, helplessness, and depression can be seen in the case of a 50-year-old divorced man who had suffered burns over 40% of his body. When he returned to the hospital 6 months later for a follow-up visit, his hands were still stiff, and he was having many psychological problems. He had moved in with his very supportive daughter and son-in-law

in hopes that he would be able to take care of repair work that needed doing around the house. When it became clear that he was not able to do any of these things to his satisfaction, he became

increasingly depressed. . . . On reviewing his case it turned out that he had indeed been a very "good" patient, quiet and cooperative. He never asked any questions about the details or the implications of his illness. (Steiner & Clark, 1977, p. 139)

This case is consistent with the view of some researchers that a "so-called 'good patient' is often actually in a state of helplessness" (Taylor, 1979, p. 171), which may eventually lead to feelings of depression.

Helping Patients Cope

Suppose you were having surgery with *full anesthesia.* Would it make any difference to your recovery if *during surgery* someone said to you, "How quickly you recover from your operation depends on you," and gave suggestions of things you should do to speed recovery? Perhaps. An experiment found that anesthetized patients who received this kind of information recovered more quickly and had fewer complications than control patients who got no suggestions during their operations (Evans & Richardson, 1988). These results and those of other studies indicate that people hear and understand at least broad meanings while anesthetized, even though they cannot say what they heard (Bennett, 1989). This is important for two reasons: (1) medical staff often make negative or disparaging remarks during surgery and (2) it may be possible to help surgical patients cope by giving them constructive suggestions while they are anesthetized.

An effective way to help hospitalized people cope is to provide psychological counseling during their stays. Walter Gruen (1975) gave brief counseling sessions to heart attack patients almost every day during the 3 weeks or so that they were in the hospital. Compared with a control group, the subjects who received the counseling spent fewer days in intensive care and in the hospital, had fewer heart complications and less psychological depression during their stays, and showed fewer signs of anxiety problems when contacted about 4 months after discharge.

A circumstance in the hospital that may help a patient adjust to his or her illness and impending treatment is sharing a room with a person who is recovering after undergoing a similar medical procedure. James Kulik and Heike Mahler (1987a) conducted an experiment with 46- to 69-year-old male patients who were scheduled for coronary bypass surgery. Upon admission, each man was assigned a roommate, based on room availability, for the 2 days prior to surgery. About half of them shared rooms with men who were also awaiting operations, and the remaining patients shared rooms with men who had already had operations and were recovering. Assessments were made of the men's anxiety the evening before their surgeries, physical activity during the week after the operation, and speed of recovery. The results showed that compared to the men who had preoperative roommates, those with roommates who had already undergone surgery were far less anxious before their operation, engaged in much more physical activity after surgery, and were able to leave the hospital an average of 1.4 days sooner.

Although patients entering a hospital for surgery typically prefer having roommates who are already recovering from surgery, honoring such requests would be logistically very difficult (Kulik & Mahler, 1987a). In addition, we don't yet know *why* the type of roommate affects patients' adjustment. The findings of two studies may provide an answer. First, when patients have multiple roommates, they spend more time talking to roommates with a similar surgery status and health problem than to other roommates (Moore, Kulik, & Mahler, 1998). Second, having presurgery patients share a room may increase the anxiety of both individuals by some form of "emotional contagion" (Kulik, Moore, & Mahler, 1993). Perhaps presurgery patients try to alleviate their anxiety by talking to a similar roommate, but the information they share makes things worse for both.

PREPARING PATIENTS FOR STRESSFUL MEDICAL PROCEDURES

Preparing people psychologically for surgery has important implications for their recovery: among patients with similar medical conditions, the more anxiety they feel before surgery, the more difficult their adjustment and recovery are likely to be after surgery. People with high preoperative anxiety tend to report more pain, use more medication for pain, stay in the hospital longer, and report more anxiety and depression during their recovery than patients with less preoperative fear (Anderson & Masur, 1983; Johnson, 1983). What can psychologists do to reduce the stress people experience in conjunction with medical procedures?

Psychological Preparation for Surgery

Although several methods seem to be useful in helping people cope with impending surgery, the most effective of these approaches are those that enhance patients' sense of *control* over the situation or the recovery process (Anderson & Masur, 1983; Mathews & Ridgeway, 1984; Thompson, 1981). These approaches are generally designed to give the person one or more of the following types of control:

- *Behavioral control*—being able to reduce discomfort or promote recovery during or after the medical procedure by performing certain actions, such as special breathing or coughing exercises.
- *Cognitive control*—knowing how to focus on the benefits of the medical procedure and not its unpleasant aspects.
- *Informational control*—gaining knowledge about the events and/or sensations to expect during or after the medical procedure.

Patients can acquire the knowledge for these types of control in many ways, such as through discussion with practitioners, reading, listening to tape recordings, or watching film or video recordings.

An example of an approach to enhance *cognitive control* comes from an experiment with individuals who were in the hospital to undergo major *elective* surgeries that typically have favorable prognoses (Langer, Janis, & Wolfer, 1975). The researchers assigned the people to groups on a random basis, but also tried to equate the groups for several characteristics, such as age, sex, and seriousness of the operation. One of the groups received training in cognitive control that pointed out how paying attention to negative aspects of an experience increases stress and taught them to focus on the positive aspects of their impending surgery when feeling distressed by the surgical experience. A comparison group spent an equal amount of time with a psychologist, but they only engaged in general conversation about the hospital experience. The records and nurses' ratings on the surgical ward revealed important benefits of training in cognitive control: the patients who received this training showed greater reductions in preoperative stress behavior, less postoperative stress, and fewer requests for medication after surgery than the comparison subjects.

Several other studies have demonstrated beneficial effects of enhancing surgical patients' *informational* and *behavioral control* (Anderson, 1987; Andrew, 1970; Johnson, Rice, Fuller, & Endress, 1978; Johnston & Vogele, 1993). In one of these experiments, Erling Anderson randomly assigned to three groups 60 adult male cardiac patients who were scheduled for coronary bypass surgery. One group had a general conversation with the researcher and received the *standard preparation* of the hospital, in which the patient and a nurse discussed two pamphlets that outlined the procedures related to the upcoming surgery. A second group received the standard preparation plus training in *informational control* that gave procedural and sensory information in two ways. These subjects (1) watched a videotape called "Living Proof," which presents interviews with recovered bypass patients and follows a patient from admission through various preoperative tests and exercises, preparation for surgery, recovery, and discharge; and (2) were given an audiotape, describing sensations they might experience, that they could play in their rooms. The third group received training in both *informational and behavioral control.* They had the same preoperative training as the informational control group, but were also taught how to perform various behaviors, such as coughing exercises and ways to turn in bed, that they would need to do after the operation.

To assess the effects of these methods of psychological preparation on the patients' adjustment and recovery, Anderson had the patients fill out a questionnaire (the State–Trait Anxiety Inventory) to measure their distress at three times: when they were admitted, the evening before surgery, and 1 week after the operation. As Figure 10–2 depicts, anxiety levels in the three groups were almost identical on admission, but then diverged after the different preparation methods were conducted. Both types of psychological preparation reduced the patients' anxiety substantially before and after the operation. Assessments were also made of the subjects' use of pain medication and length of stay in the hospital, but the three groups did not differ on these measures. Finally, the patients' blood pressures were monitored closely because dangerous levels of acute hypertension occur very commonly during the first 12 hours following bypass surgery. For this critical measure, psychological preparation had a very beneficial effect. Of the patients who received the standard preparation, 75% developed acute hypertension and required medication to dilate their blood vessels. In contrast, only 45% of subjects in the informational control group and 40%

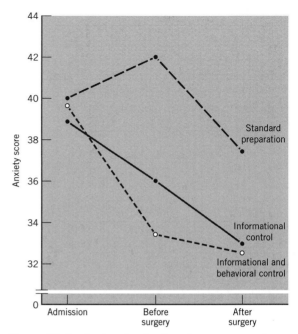

Figure 10–2   Anxiety levels of cardiac surgery patients as a function of the psychological preparation they received. Anxiety was measured by the State-Trait Anxiety Inventory at three times: on admission, the evening before surgery, and 1 week after the operation. (Adapted from Anderson, 1987, Figure 1.)

of those in the informational and behavioral control group had episodes of acute hypertension.

Similar benefits accrue with videotapes showing the hospital experiences of patients with comparable surgeries. For instance, men and women awaiting hip replacement who saw a videotape of a prior hip surgery patient subsequently showed less anxiety, lower serum cortisol levels, fewer instances of acute hypertension during the surgery, and less pain medication use than comparable patients without the videotape (Doering et al., (2000). Although psychological preparations that increase patients' sense of control when awaiting operations have obvious value, the materials and instructions must be clear and straightforward. Unclear information can lead to misconceptions and anxiety, producing more harm than good (Wallace, 1986). Patients may need to discuss the information with medical and psychological staff. Of course, surgery is only one of many types of stressful medical procedures that may occur in the hospital, and patients often dread experiencing each of them.

Psychological Preparations for Nonsurgical Procedures

How would you like to be awake while a physician inserts a thin, hollow tube called a *catheter* into one of your blood vessels, gently threads it toward your heart, and then injects dye through the catheter? This is a procedure called *cardiac catheterization*, which is used with people who show signs of cardiovascular disorders, such as damage to a major blood vessel or heart valve. The dye enables practitioners to see the damage with the aid of X-ray or other radiological devices. By using this procedure, physicians can determine whether to recommend other medical procedures, such as bypass or open-heart surgery. A patient undergoing cardiac catheterization receives tranquilizing medication and a local anesthetic for the area where the tube enters the body. This procedure is typically not painful, but it is quite unpleasant and produces strange and frightening sensations, such as "hot flashes" when dye is injected into the heart.

How might patients and hospital staff benefit by the use of psychological preparations for people undergoing cardiac catheterization? Preparing them for unpleasant medical procedures should help to reduce patients' anxiety and disruptive behavior during the procedures, for example, and their general level of stress prior to surgery. Philip Kendall and his associates (1979) examined the effects of psychological preparation for cardiac catheterization on the anxiety experienced by male patients, about two-thirds of whom had undergone the procedure at least a year earlier. The subjects were randomly assigned to four groups. One group received training in *cognitive control* methods from a therapist, learning how to recognize signs of their own anxiety and ways to cope when these signs occur. Another group received preparation to enhance their *informational control*, learning about the procedures and sensations to expect through printed materials and discussions with therapists. Two other groups served as comparison (control) conditions. Analyses of the patients' self-reports and of hospital staff ratings showed that both the cognitive and the informational control preparations effectively reduced patients' anxiety; subjects who received these preparations experienced less anxiety than those in the two comparison groups before and during catheterization.

As you may have surmised, the catheterization procedure requires that the patient be inactive. There are no actions the person can take to make the process occur more smoothly or pleasantly—that is, the patient has little or no behavioral control. This is true of many but not all aversive medical procedures. One medical procedure in which patients can perform useful actions is called an *endoscopy*, which is used in diagnosing ulcers and other disorders of the digestive tract. The most aversive aspect of an endoscopic examination is that a long, flexible, fiber-optic tube, almost half an inch in diameter, must be passed through the patient's mouth and down to the stomach and intestine. This tube remains in the digestive tract, transmitting images of the lining, for about 15 to 30 minutes. During this procedure, the person is awake, but has received tranquilizing medication, and the throat has been swabbed with a local anesthetic.

In an experiment with patients who had never undergone an endoscopy before, Jean Johnson and Howard Leventhal (1974) provided psychological preparation to enhance the behavioral and informational control the subjects could use during the procedure. Training for behavioral control included teaching the subjects helpful ways to breathe and swallow while the throat is swabbed and the tube is inserted. For informational control, descriptions were given of the procedures and sensations people could expect during the examination. Some patients received instruction for one type of control (either behavioral informational), some had both types of preparation, and others served as a comparison group, receiving no psychological preparation. All patients, however, received a standard explanation of the endoscopic procedure from a physician. The researchers found that subjects in the comparison group tended to show more emotional behavior and gagging during the procedure than those who received psychological preparation, particularly if this preparation included instruction for both informational and behavioral control.

In summary, psychological preparation can enhance patients' sense of control and adjustment to nonsurgical medical procedures. Generally speaking, when these procedures offer little opportunity for the person to take helpful action, psychological preparation to promote informational and cognitive control may be especially effective. But when patients will undergo procedures in which they can take direct action to facilitate the process and reduce their own discomfort, preparation should usually include approaches to enhance behavioral control. (Go to ☝.)

Highlight on Issues

Lamaze Training as a Method of Psychological Preparation for a Medical Procedure

During much of the 20th century, Americans generally accepted two ideas about childbirth: (1) the mother will experience intense and prolonged pain unless she is given tranquilizing and pain-reducing drugs, and (2) the use of drugs is best for the mother and her baby. But these beliefs have changed since the 1960s for two reasons. First, drugs given to the mother during childbirth pass through the placenta and can have unwanted effects, such as reducing oxygen flow to the fetus and impairing motor control in the newborn's first days (Feldman, 2000). Second, anthropologists have reported that women in cultures where childbirth is regarded as an easy and open process have shorter and less complicated labors than women in cultures where birth is regarded as fearful and private (Mead & Newton, 1967). Could it be that part of the difficulty many American mothers have in childbirth is the result of the inadequate psychological preparation they receive?

Because of these considerations, many prospective parents opt for preparation involving "natural childbirth" methods, such as **Lamaze training.** Natural childbirth methods generally involve three components: preparation, participation, and minimal medication (Parfitt, 1977). Birth is essentially a process in which the muscles of the uterus contract in a rhythmical pattern to push the baby out. A fearful woman is likely to tighten her muscles, which then act against the natural muscular contractions and make labor more painful. A main purpose of natural childbirth methods is to prepare the woman to be more relaxed and better able to control her breathing and muscular activity to help in the process at each stage.

Margaret Wideman and Jerome Singer (1984) have analyzed Lamaze training and described the psy-chological mechanisms it includes. In addition to the social support women in Lamaze training get from the baby's father and the people in the training meetings, the method is designed to enhance the mother's sense of control. Lamaze training includes features that promote

- Informational control, such as by providing descriptions of the physiological processes in birth and the procedures and sensations to expect during labor and delivery.
- Behavioral control, for example, through instruction and practice in muscle relaxation and special breathing techniques.
- Cognitive control, such as by teaching the woman to stare at an object in the room or to concentrate on images or phrases during the childbirth process.

American hospitals generally cooperate with the procedures the method describes, such as having the father present.

Is Lamaze preparation beneficial? Although the results of studies suggest that it is, the evidence is not yet very clear (Feldman, 2000; Wideman & Singer, 1984). Women who receive Lamaze training use less painkilling medication during delivery and are less anxious about the birth procedure than those who do not; but these studies have used quasi-experimental designs and self-report methods. Part of the difficulty in interpreting these findings is that women who choose natural childbirth are different from those who do not—for example, they tend to be from higher social classes and report lower anxiety levels even before receiving the training.

Coping Styles and Psychological Preparation

People use many different styles in coping with stress, as we discussed in Chapter 5. When faced with stressful medical procedures, for instance, some individuals tend to cope by using *avoidance* strategies to minimize the impact of the situation. They may deny that a threat exists; refuse to seek or attend to threatening information, perhaps saying, "I don't want to know", or suppress unpleasant thoughts. In contrast, other individuals tend to use *attention* or "vigilant" strategies, seeking detailed information about the situation (Newman, 1984a). Some studies have found that patients who use avoidance strategies often show better emotional adjustment to medical procedures, such as blood donation or dental surgery, than those who use attention strategies (Kaloupek, White, & Wrong, 1984; Kiyak, Vitaliano, & Crinean, 1988). If this is so, how do people who use avoidance strategies react to psychological preparations that enhance their control?

Researchers have examined this question by using approaches to enhance informational control with patients who were classified as using avoidance or attention styles. Suzanne Miller and Charles Mangan (1983) conducted one of these studies with women who were scheduled to undergo an unpleasant but painless diagnostic test for gynecological cancer. The women were classified as using avoidance or attention styles on the basis of their responses in a questionnaire. By random assignment, half of the avoidance subjects (called "blunters") and the attention subjects ("monitors") received extensive information regarding the procedures and sensations they would experience during the examination; the remaining subjects got very little information about the examination. Measures of the patients' distress were taken at three times: before receiving the information, after getting the information but before the examination, and after the examination. Figure 10–3 presents the results of this research, using the patients' pulse rates as the measure of distress. These findings indicate that monitors who receive very little information and blunters who receive extensive information react negatively to the amount of information they receive, as shown by their continued high pulse rates after the examination.

Other research has confirmed these findings and shown that psychological preparation for medical procedures is most effective when its content is matched to the needs of the person (Carpenter, Gatchel, & Hasegawa, 1994; Litt, Nye, & Shafer, 1995; Ludwick-Rosenthal & Neufeld, 1993). In addition, the number of times people see the information seems to affect the amount of stress they experience. In one study, patients awaiting endoscopic examinations filled out a questionnaire that assessed their coping styles and then watched a videotape that showed the procedures and sensations they could expect during their own endoscopies (Shipley, Butt, Horwitz, & Farbry, 1978). Some subjects watched the informational tape only once, and others viewed it three times. A comparison group watched an irrelevant tape. Measures of the

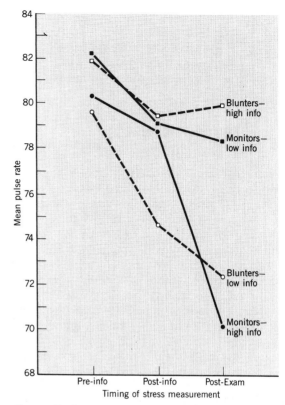

Figure 10–3 Effects of extensive information versus little information regarding an impending medical examination on the stress experienced by patients who use avoidance coping strategies (the "blunters") or attention strategies (the "monitors"). Pulse rate, the measure of stress, was taken for each subject at three times: before receiving the information, after the information, and after the examination. High pulse rate indicates more distress. (From Miller & Mangan, 1983, Figure 7.)

patients' anxiety during their endoscopies included heart rate and questionnaire assessments by the patients and practitioners after the examinations. The study found that *avoidance copers* who saw the informational tape only once experienced more anxiety than those who saw it three times and those who watched the irrelevant tape. Of the *attention copers*, those who watched the irrelevant tape experienced the most anxiety, and those who viewed the informational tape three times had the least anxiety.

The benefits of psychological preparations for medical procedures seem to depend on the patients' coping styles, and it may be that different preparations are more helpful for people using avoidance strategies than for those using attention strategies. Although being exposed to information about impending medical procedures more than once appears to help all patients, it may be particularly beneficial to those who tend to cope by using avoidance strategies.

WHEN THE HOSPITALIZED PATIENT IS A CHILD

About 2.2 million individuals who are admitted to short-stay hospitals in the United States each year are under 15 years of age, and most of these children are under 5 years old (USBC, 1999). We have seen that adults become distressed by pain and illness, think hospitals are big and frightening places, and become anxious when undergoing unpleasant or painful medical procedures. So do children, but their level of psychosocial development may make some aspects of the hospital experience particularly difficult for them. For one thing, children are less able than adults to influence and understand what is happening to them. Children at young ages may also feel abandoned or unloved by being without their families, and some may even believe that they were put in the hospital as punishment for misbehavior. What special adjustments do children need to make when they are hospitalized, and how well do they cope? Answers to these questions depend partly on the child's age.

Hospitalization in the Early Years of Childhood

The experience of being hospitalized is distressing for children of all ages, but the reasons for their distress tend to change as they get older (La Greca & Stone, 1985; Sarafino, 1986). For children in toddlerhood and the preschool years—who are rarely inactive when healthy—a hospital experience that involves being immobilized can be very stressful. These children may protest loudly and struggle against medically necessary devices that restrain their movement (Smith & Autman, 1985). But the most salient source of stress of young children in the hospital is being separated from their parents.

Separation distress is the normal reaction of being upset and crying that young children exhibit when they are separated from their parents, particularly in unfamiliar surroundings (Ainsworth, 1973, 1979). Late in the first year of life, most infants begin showing

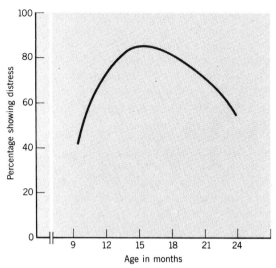

Figure 10–4 Illustration of children's tendency to exhibit separation distress when tested with short-term separations at different ages. (From Sarafino & Armstrong, 1986, Figure 5.3.) The graph represents approximate percentages at each age, averaged across cultures—for example, the reaction occurs in about 90% of American working-class infants and 70–80% of Guatemalan babies at 15 months (Super, 1981).

this reaction, even in everyday short separations of a few minutes or hours. As Figure 10–4 illustrates, the tendency of children to show distress in situations of short-term separation peaks at roughly 15 months of age. This is true of children from a wide variety of cultures around the world. After that age, the percentage of children showing distress with short-term separations declines universally (Super, 1981). Being hospitalized can involve prolonged periods of separation, with little parent–child contact for days, weeks, or longer. How well do toddlers and preschool-age children cope with long-term separation?

Prolonged separation produces dramatic and, perhaps, long-lasting reactions in young children. During hospitalization, children's conduct often regresses sharply, reverting back to forms of behavior they may have used at younger ages. Thus, they may become less sociable and start wetting the bed and having temper tantrums again (Ramsey, 1982). John Bowlby (1969, 1973) has described the behavioral and psychological consequences that unfold during the first weeks of prolonged separation. The initial reaction is one of *protest*, in which the child displays excessive crying, calling, and searching for his or her parents, typically the mother. Following this period, the child reacts with *despair*, usually reflected in reduced activity, withdrawal, and apparent hopelessness. If the separation is quite long or permanent, such as if the parents died, the last period, *detachment*, begins. The child's behavior is "back to normal", but if the parents return, the child seems to reject them, no longer seeking interaction or contact with them.

After a prolonged or difficult stay in the hospital, young children often display anxious behavior at home. They may continue their regressive behaviors, begin having nightmares, or become very clinging and unwilling to let their mothers out of their sight. One child named Sara, for instance, had attended nursery school and was becoming quite independent for her age before having a difficult hospital experience that included receiving 22 injections in just 2 days. After she returned home, she was highly anxious. Her mother reported:

> She follows me everywhere! I can't even go to the bathroom alone. She wakes up screaming five or six times at night, shaking and crying, "The nurses are giving me shots! I can't run away! They're tying me down"... and when I approach her, she backs away and shakes like a hurt puppy! (Ramsey, 1982, p. 332)

Sara's hospital experience was very traumatic. Subsequently, she seemed to be afraid that if she were separated from her mother, she would again be left alone and unprotected.

Preschoolers do not yet think very logically and, as a result, may have many misconceptions about their health problems and why things happen in the hospital (Eiser, 1985; Ramsey, 1982; Smith & Autman, 1985). They may, for example, believe their illnesses or the treatments they receive are punishments for having been bad. These ideas probably come from two sources: (1) young children's general belief that breaking rules leads to inevitable punishment and (2) adults' statements that link disobedience with getting sick or injured. Adults say, for instance, "You'll catch cold if you don't wear your coat," "You'll fall and hurt yourself if you climb trees," or "You'll get an upset stomach if you eat too much candy." Some adults even threaten children with going to the doctor or having an operation if they continue to disobey (Eiser, 1985). In the hospital, young children sometimes become worried when they see other patients with disfigurements, such as an amputation or extensive scars. They may

think one of these conditions may happen to themselves in the hospital.

Hospitalized School-Age Children

Advances in school-age children's psychosocial development enable them to cope with some aspects of hospitalization better than younger patients can. For instance, although prolonged separation from their parents can be difficult for older children, they can usually tolerate it more easily than preschoolers can. The cognitive ability of school-age children progresses rapidly, but they sometimes retain earlier misconceptions about their illnesses or develop new ones. An older child's incorrect ideas can be seen in a nursing student's report about a 10-year-old hemophiliac patient:

> When I asked him what happened when he bled, he said, "Oh ... there's a hemophiliac bug eating his way in and out of my blood vessels, and that's what makes me bleed." And when asked what caused his disease, he answered, "Well, it's 'cause I ate too much candy after my mom told me not to." (Ramsey, 1982, pp. 335–336).

Clearly, the idea that illness is a punishment can continue long after early childhood.

Four aspects of hospitalization seem to become increasingly difficult for children as they get older (Ramsey, 1982; Smith & Autman, 1985). One aspect involves feelings of personal control. As children get older and their greater cognitive and social abilities strengthen their sense of control, the limited independence and influence they experience in the hospital may become very irritating and distressing. Second, school-age children's increased cognitive abilities allow them to think about and worry about the outcomes of their illness or treatment, such as whether they will be physically harmed or even die. Third, being away from friends and schoolmates can lead to feelings of loneliness, boredom, and concern about losing friends or status in their social groups. Fourth, as children get older—particularly when they are entering puberty—they tend to become more embarrassed by exposing their bodies to strangers or needing help with "private" activities, such as toileting.

Studies conducted in industrialized nations in the 1950s revealed that most children who were hospitalized were very poorly prepared for the experience (Eiser, 1985). Most children were either told nothing about why they were there, or received only vague reasons, or learned why by overhearing others'

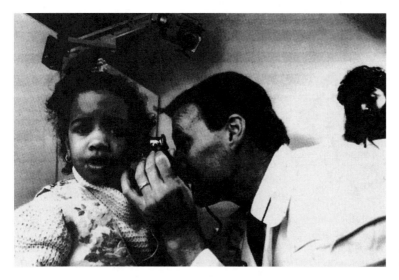

Medical procedures and equipment are often very frightening to young children.

conversations. This situation has changed since then, and children today are much better prepared for stays in the hospital. A survey in the United States, for example, found that the large majority of hospitals in the late 1990s provided the kinds of preparation we have described for children who will undergo surgery or other major procedures (O'Byrne, Peterson, & Saldana, 1997). (Go to 🏃.)

Helping Children Cope with Being Hospitalized

When a child is admitted to the hospital, one or both parents (or another very familiar adult) should accompany and remain with the child at least until he or she is settled into the room. Many parents stay much longer, taking advantage of opportunities hospitals provide today for a parent to "room-in" with the child, especially when the patient is very young or very seriously ill (Olivet, 1982). American pediatric hospitals typically have rooming-in options (Melamed & Bush, 1985).

What kinds of psychological preparation can hospitals provide for children? American hospitals use several approaches (O'Byrne, Peterson, & Saldana, 1997). Printed leaflets, narrative presentations, and tours describing hospital routines and medical procedures are among the most commonly used methods. Another method involves using puppets in a play activity to demonstrate medical procedures, such as inducing anesthesia or taking an X ray. This approach

may be especially appropriate for preschoolers and younger school age children. Two other commonly used approaches involve training in coping skills and relaxation, using methods like those we examined in Chapter 5.

One last approach hospitals often use with children uses a video or film presentation. This method was evaluated in an experiment by Barbara Melamed and Lawrence Siegel (1975) with 4- to 12-year-old children who were in the hospital for elective surgery, such as for hernias or tonsillectomies. The children were assigned to two groups, matching for age, sex, race, and type of operation. One group saw a film that was relevant to having surgery, and the other group saw a film about a boy who goes on a nature trip in the country. The relevant film, entitled "Ethan Has an Operation," portrays the hospital experience of a 7-year-old boy,

> showing various events that most children encounter when hospitalized for elective surgery from the time of admission to time of discharge including the child's orientation to the hospital ward and medical personnel such as the surgeon and anesthesiologist; having a blood test and exposure to standard hospital equipment; separation from the mother, and scenes in the operating and recovery rooms. In addition to explanations of the hospital procedures provided by the medical staff, various scenes are narrated by the child, who describes his feelings and concerns. (Melamed & Siegel, 1975, p. 514)

CLINICAL METHODS AND ISSUES

Preparing Children for Impending Hospitalization

Ideally, psychological preparation should begin before the child enters the hospital, if at all possible. Research has shown that children cope better with medical procedures if their parents give them information about their illnesses and treatment and try to allay their fears than if the parents do not (Melamed & Bush, 1985). Hospitals can initiate this process by discussing it with the parents and providing materials and services. Medical and psychological staff can inform parents about several ways to help their child cope with an impending hospital stay (Sarafino, 1986). Parents can:

- Explain the reason for the stay and what it will be like.
- Give the child opportunities to ask questions, answering them carefully and in a way he or she can understand.

- Read with the child a children's book that describes a child's hospital experience.
- Take the child to the hospital and explain some of the hospital routines, such as what to do about going to the bathroom and how he or she will be awakened in the morning and have breakfast in bed.
- Describe when the parents will be with the child.
- Maintain a calm and confident manner, thereby conveying the message that there is no need to be very frightened.

Parents should try not to appear agitated and anxious about the child's medical treatment because they can transmit their fear. Children of outwardly anxious parents do not cope as well with medical procedures as those with parents who are relatively calm (Bush, Melamed, Sheras, & Greenbaum, 1986; Melamed & Bush, 1985).

Although Ethan exhibits visible apprehension initially, he overcomes his fear and has the operation without serious distress.

The researchers assessed the emotional adjustment of the children in the two groups the evening before surgery and at a follow-up visit about 3 weeks after the operation with three types of measures: the children's hand sweating, questionnaire self-reports of fear, and ratings of their emotional behavior by trained observers. The results with all three measures revealed that the children who saw the film about Ethan's operation experienced less anxiety before and after surgery than those who saw the irrelevant film. Several studies have found similar benefits in reducing children's medical fears with video presentations (Eiser, 1985; Miller & Green, 1984). What's more, video preparations for surgery are cost-effective: a study of children in the hospital for elective surgery found that those who received video preparation recovered more quickly than those who did not. The savings from being released from the hospital sooner amounted to

several times the cost of providing the preparation (Pinto & Hollandsworth, 1989).

Although most children benefit from information about impending medical procedures presented by any of the methods we have considered, not all children do—and some are actually made *more* anxious by the preparation. Studies have shown that the effects of the preparation depend on its timing and on the child's age, coping style, and previous medical experience (Dahlquist et al., 1986; Melamed & Bush, 1985; Melamed, Dearborn, & Hermecz, 1983; Miller & Green, 1984). More specifically, children younger than age 7 or so seem to profit from information presented shortly before the medical procedure, whereas older children are more likely to benefit from information presented several days before. In addition, young children more so than older ones may be made more anxious by information if they have had prior difficult experiences with medical procedures. Also, some evidence indicates that children who tend to use avoidance strategies to cope with stressful events probably derive less benefit from information about medical procedures than those who use attention strategies.

Hospitals and medical workers usually try to make a child's stay as pleasant as they can. Pediatric nurses, for instance, receive training in the special needs of children and ways to introduce tests and equipment in a nonthreatening manner (Ramsey, 1982). When preparing to take the child's blood pressure with a sphygmomanometer, for example, the nurse might demonstrate its use on someone else and say, "When I squeeze this ball, the thing on the arm just becomes tight, like a belt. It doesn't hurt—it just gets tight. ... Now when I'm done, I make it get loose and take it off." Often when a young child undergoes stressful procedures, such as drawing blood, a parent is present. Although most techniques parents use to help reduce the child's distress don't work very well, one that does involves distracting attention from the procedure—for instance, by saying, "Look at this nice picture" (Manne et al., 1992, 1994). Hospital pediatric wards also arrange for children to play together when possible and try to have entertainment, such as a clown show, for their patients. For most hospitalized children who have positive health outcomes today, the stress of their hospital experience tends to be temporary and does not seem to produce serious long-term emotional problems (La Greca & Stone, 1985).

People of all ages can have difficulty coping with hospitalization and medical procedures. Psychological interventions can help promote positive emotional adjustment among patients and reduce the psychological problems that may be associated with their medical conditions.

HOW HEALTH PSYCHOLOGISTS ASSIST HOSPITALIZED PATIENTS

Some patients in hospitals have illnesses that result partly from psychosocial factors, such as Type A behavior or alcohol abuse, and some individuals develop psychosocial problems because of their illnesses, hospitalizations, or treatment regimens. In the former case, health psychologists are interested in correcting the factors that produced the disease to help these patients recover and prevent recurrences of their illnesses. In the latter case, health psychologists

try to help clients cope with their illnesses, treatment regimens, possible disabilities or deformities, and, for terminal conditions, with impending death.

The potential importance of the help psychologists provide can be seen in research findings on psychological characteristics among people with cardiovascular disease. Depression is an important characteristic: compared with people who are not depressed, those who are very depressed show slower recovery and are much more likely to develop subsequent cardiac problems (Carney et al., 1988; Tennen, Eberhardt, & Affleck, 1999). Pessimism is also important: compared with optimistic people, coronary bypass patients who have a very pessimistic outlook are more likely to be hospitalized again for coronary problems in subsequent months (Scheier et al., 1999).

The number of psychologists working in hospitals in the United States and their role in treatment programs for patients have expanded greatly since the 1970s (APA, 1998; Enright et al., 1990; Sweet, 1991). Psychologists

- Consult with patients' specialists, such as cardiologists, neurologists, and pediatricians, to provide diagnostic and counseling services.

- Assess clients' needs for and provide psychological preparation to cope with surgery and other stressful procedures.

- Help patients adhere to medication and treatment regimens in the hospital.

- Provide behavioral programs for improving clients' self-care skills and compliance with medical and lifestyle regimens after discharge.

- Assist in rehabilitation processes, such as by promoting adherence to physical therapy, helping family members adjust to a patient's condition, and helping clients decide on new careers, if needed.

Let's look at how health psychologists assist patients, beginning with determining who needs and wants help.

INITIAL STEPS IN HELPING

Patients who need psychological help generally don't request it themselves—the request usually comes from a physician or nurse who has noticed signs of a psychological, social, or intellectual problem (Huszti & Walker, 1991). This is not an ideal situation, since most medical staff are not trained to identify signs of distress or behavioral problems. A study found that physicians are not very good at recognizing emotional problems in their clients—they tend to judge that such problems exist if they think the patient has a severe medical illness and is dissatisfied with the present treatment (Jones, Mabe, & Riley, 1989). A brief training seminar does not improve their judgments (Deshields, Carmin, Ross, & Mannen, 1995).

After the psychologist receives the request to see a patient, he or she then consults the person who made the request and reviews the client's medical record. The next step involves interviewing the patient and/or relevant family members to arrive at an impression of what the problem is and its history and status (Sweet, 1991). Sometimes the resulting impression is sufficient for the psychologist to decide how to help, but frequently more information is needed and can be obtained by administering psychological tests.

TESTS FOR PSYCHOLOGICAL ASSESSMENT OF MEDICAL PATIENTS

Psychologists have developed hundreds of instruments to assess a wide variety of psychological characteristics of people. The tests the psychologist administers depend on the type of illness or problem the client seems to have (Derogatis, Fleming, Sudler, & DellaPietra, 1995; Sweet, 1991). For example, patients with serious head injuries and behavioral signs of neurological problems are especially likely to be assessed with tests of intelligence, academic skills, and specific perceptual and motor functions. Clients who will need to change existing or planned careers may be tested for vocational interests and abilities. Some of the most widely used instruments with hospital patients assess their psychosocial needs and problems (Piotrowski & Lubin, 1990). We will describe a few of these instruments.

The Minnesota Multiphasic Personality Inventory

One approach psychological tests use for assessing the needs and problems of individuals is to ask them questions about themselves to reveal aspects of their personalities. The most widely used personality test is the **Minnesota Multiphasic Personality Inventory** (MMPI), which was developed in the 1930s and updated in the 1980s as the MMPI-2 (Butcher et al., 1989; Hathaway & McKinley, 1967; Sweet, 1991). This test has the person respond in a true-false format to about 500 statements, such as, "I would rather win than lose a game" and "I am worried about sex matters." The items in the test cover a great variety of topics.

Although the MMPI was developed to characterize the personalities that underlie or correspond with specific psychiatric disorders, portions of the test can supply important information about the emotional adjustment of medical patients. The instrument contains ten scales, each of which assesses features of psychiatric conditions and personality traits. Three of these scales are especially relevant toward providing psychological help for medical patients. These scales are:

- *Hypochondriasis*, which assesses people's preoccupation with and complaints about their physical health.
- *Depression*, which measures people's feelings of unhappiness, pessimism, and hopelessness.
- *Hysteria*, which assesses people's tendency to cope with problems by using avoidance strategies and developing physical symptoms.

The scores individuals obtain on these scales can suggest significant issues for the therapist to explore further. For one thing, individuals who score high on these three scales are prone to developing psychophysiological disorders, such as ulcers and chronic headaches (Gilberstadt & Duker, 1965). Also, patients with serious illnesses, such as cancer or heart disease, may fail to comply with their treatment regimens because of intense feelings of depression, which might be revealed by their scores on the depression scale of the MMPI (Green, 1985).

The MMPI can be usefully applied in psychological treatment in medical settings, but it has two important drawbacks: it takes about 1½ hours to complete, and it measures many traits that are not pertinent to the treatment of most medical patients.

Specialized Tests for Medical Patients

In recent years, psychologists have developed new tests that are specifically designed to assess psychological characteristics associated with physical illness. These tests include instruments that we considered in Chapters 3 and 4, which measure people's stress and their Type A and Type B behavior patterns—two characteristics that are associated with heart disease, for instance. As we saw in Chapter 5, psychological methods can be applied effectively to reduce people's stress and modify their Type A behavior, thereby lowering their risk of heart attack. We turn now to a discussion of other psychological tests that were designed specifically for medical populations.

The **Millon Behavioral Health Inventory** (MBHI) is a self-report questionnaire that was developed to assess specific psychosocial factors and decision-making issues that are known to be relevant for medical patients (Green, 1985; Millon, Green, & Meagher, 1982). It consists of 150 true-false items that provide information regarding the client's

- *Basic coping style*, or the way the person tends to approach difficult life situations and interact with other people.
- *Psychogenic attitude*, which includes assessments of the patient's experience of stress, tendency toward helplessness and hopelessness, social support, and hypochondriacal tendencies.

The MBHI also attempts to assess the client's reaction to his or her illness and predict difficulties with the treatment regimen. Although the MBHI is being used in medical settings, such as in pain treatment centers and cancer units, and it should prove to be a valuable tool, more research is needed to establish its utility. Some evidence for its usefulness in medical settings has been found (Gatchel et al., 1986).

The **Psychosocial Adjustment to Illness Scale** (PAIS) is another psychological test designed specifically for use with medical patients (Derogatis, 1977, 1986). The PAIS consists of just 46 items, and the person responds to each item on a 4-point scale, such as "not at all," "mildly," "moderately," or "markedly." This test is available in two forms—one that patients can fill out on their own and one that is administered by an interviewer. It was designed to assess seven psychosocial characteristics of the client's life, each of which has been associated with adjustment to medical illness. Table 10.1 outlines these characteristics. The results of several studies appear to confirm the ability of the PAIS to measure adjustment problems accurately in patients with a variety of serious illnesses, such as

Table 10.1 *Patients' Psychosocial Characteristics Assessed by the Psychosocial Adjustment to Illness Scale (PAIS)*

- *Health care orientation*—The nature of the patient's attitudes about health care in general, views regarding health care professionals, and expectancies about his or her health problem and its treatment.
- *Vocational environment*—the impact of the health problem on such issues as the person's vocational performance and satisfaction.
- *Domestic environment*—difficulties the health problem will present for the client and his or her family in the home environment.
- *Sexual relationships*—modifications in sexual activity as a result of the health problem.
- *Extended family relationships*—disruptions in relationships between the patient and family members outside of his or her immediate family.
- *Social environment*—the impact of the health problem on the client's socializing and leisure time activities.
- *Psychological distress*—the effect of the health problem on such factors as the patient's self-esteem and feelings of depression, anxiety, and hostility.

kidney disease, hypertension, and cancer (Derogatis, 1986).

In summary, psychologists have developed instruments specifically for the purpose of assessing the psychological needs and problems of medical patients. These tests and those yet to be developed offer considerable promise for aiding health psychologists and other health care workers in promoting the health and adjustment of their patients.

PROMOTING PATIENTS' HEALTH AND ADJUSTMENT

Once health psychologists determine the nature and extent of the client's difficulty, they decide which specific therapeutic techniques should be applied to address it. As we have seen in previous chapters and will see ahead, behavioral and cognitive methods have been applied with some success—sometimes with great success—in many primary, secondary, and tertiary prevention efforts. These techniques are useful in helping people improve their eating and exercise habits, stop smoking and curb their drinking, and reduce the stress and other negative emotional states they experience (Parker, 1995; Sarafino, 2001; Turk & Salovey, 1995).

Many hospitalized people develop severe psychosocial problems, particularly if their illnesses or injuries continue to be life threatening or leave them disfigured or handicapped. These individuals and their families often need help to overcome feelings of depression and counseling to anticipate and plan for the difficulties they are likely to experience. As nurse-educator Catherine Norris has noted:

> When someone says, "I never really got over my operation," it means that that person has not accomplished the formidable tasks of convalescence. These include reassessment of one's goals in life, reintegration of a changed body image, working out feelings about dependence and independence, and coping with heightened emotional reactions and role failure, as well as making physical adaptations. (1990, p. 47)

Several psychological approaches are helpful in dealing with patients' psychosocial problems. These approaches often involve group-discussion and cognitive-behavioral therapy to identify, examine, and replace negative thought patterns with more constructive ones (Davison & Neale, 1998; Turk & Salovey, 1995).

The approaches health psychologists currently use in promoting patients' health and adjustment sometimes have important limitations, particularly in their continued effectiveness over long periods of time and in preventing relapse, such as in health-related lifestyle changes. Health psychologists are working to enhance their effectiveness in helping clients by improving the techniques they use, but they must also continue to develop stronger relationships with medical professionals, such as by expanding their knowledge of the language and rules of hospital settings (Huszti & Walker, 1991). More and more, medical and psychological staff are working together to improve these relationships for the benefit of their patients.

SUMMARY

The huge hospitals of today evolved from institutions in Europe that were established to give help to people with various needs—the sick, the poor, orphans, and even travelers who needed lodging. By the 19th century, hospitals became separate from poorhouses, but still provided health care only to people who were poor. Well-to-do individuals received better care at home. In the early 20th century, hospitals gained a much better reputation and began to attract patients from all social classes.

The hospital medical staff has a typical hierarchy of authority with physicians at the top, followed by nurses and various allied health workers. The specialization and variety of hospital personnel can lead to fragmented health care. Good communication among hospital personnel not only improves the treatment patients receive but can help protect patients and health care workers from potential hazards in the hospital, such as from toxic substances and nosocomial infection. The system of payment for medical care in the United States has led to decreases in hospital admissions and the length of time patients stay there.

Being hospitalized is unpleasant because of the disruptions it produces in the patients' lifestyles, the high degree of dependency patients have on others, the experience of aversive medical procedures, and the many worries patients have about their conditions, treatment, and futures. Many of these worries develop because patients do not always receive the information they need. Sometimes the treatment people receive is characterized by depersonalization. Working in emotionally charged situations with heavy workloads can lead to burnout among health care professionals, especially those who spend almost all of their time providing direct care to clients.

Some patients enter the hospital with the idea that the sick role involves being passive. These people are generally described by hospital staff as "good patients," being relatively cooperative, uncomplaining, and stoical. Other clients believe they should be more active in their sick-role behavior. Some of these people are described as "problem patients," showing little cooperation, voicing many complaints, and being very dependent and emotional. When problem patients are very seriously ill, their difficult behavior is usually understandable to the medical staff. But other problem patients take up more time and attention than their conditions seem to warrant, and may display angry reactance behavior in response to having their freedoms or control curtailed.

Patients engage in problem-focused and emotion-focused coping techniques to adjust to the stress and anxiety that they experience in the hospital. Some of their anxiety stems from their impending surgery and from nonsurgical medical procedures, such as cardiac catheterization and endoscopy. High levels of anxiety before surgery, for instance, appear to impair people's physical recovery after the operation. Reducing the anxiety connected with medical procedures can be accomplished through methods of psychological preparation that provide clients with behavioral, cognitive, and informational control. Lamaze training for childbirth seems to provide these kinds of preparation.

Although most patients benefit from methods of psychological preparation that enhance control, some benefit more than others. One factor that seems to affect the success of these methods is whether the patient's coping style tends toward avoidance rather than attention strategies. Children's separation distress in the hospital can be reduced if parents visit often or room in.

Children can also benefit from psychological preparation for medical procedures, but the success of providing children with information depends on its timing and on their ages, coping styles, and previous medical experience.

The role of psychologists in the overall treatment effort for hospitalized people has increased in recent years, particularly in preparing clients for surgery and other medical procedures, helping them adjust to their medical conditions, and enhancing their adherence to treatment regimens after discharge. To identify the needs and problems of patients, psychologists use personality tests, such as the Minnesota Multiphasic Personality Inventory, and instruments developed specifically for use with medical clients, such as the Millon Behavioral Health Inventory and the Psychosocial Adjustment to Illness Scale.

KEY TERMS

nosocomial infection
depersonalization
burnout

reactance
Lamaze training
separation distress

Minnesota Multiphasic
  Personality Inventory
Millon Behavioral
  Health Inventory

Psychosocial Adjustment
  to Illness Scale

PART V

PHYSICAL SYMPTOMS: PAIN AND DISCOMFORT

11

THE NATURE AND SYMPTOMS OF PAIN

PROLOGUE

"Wouldn't it be wonderful never to experience pain," many people have thought when they or others they have known were suffering. Pain hurts, and people typically dislike it and try to avoid it. But being able to sense pain is critical to our survival—without it, how would we know when we are injured? We could have a sprained ankle or an ulcer, for instance, without realizing it, and not seek treatment. And how would we know we are about to be injured, such as when we approach a hot flame without seeing it? Pain serves as a signal to take protective action.

Are there people who do not feel pain? Yes—several disorders can reduce or eliminate the ability to sense pain. People with a condition called *congenital insensitivity to pain*, which is present from birth, may report only a "tingling" or "itching" sensation when seriously injured. A young woman with this disorder

> seemed normal in every way, except that she had never felt pain. As a child she had bitten off the tip of her tongue while chewing food, and had suffered third-degree burns after kneeling on a hot radiator to look out of a window. When examined by a psychologist . . . in the laboratory, she reported . . . no pain when parts of her body were subjected to strong electric shock, to hot water at temperatures that usually produce reports of burning pain, or to a prolonged ice-bath. Equally astonishing was the fact that she showed no changes in blood pressure, heart rate, or respiration when these stimuli were presented. Furthermore, she could not remember ever sneezing or coughing, the gag reflex could be elicited only with great difficulty, and the cornea reflexes (to protect the eyes) were absent. (Melzack, quoted in Bakal, 1979, p. 141)

This disorder contributed to her death at the age of 29. People with congenital insensitivity to pain often die young because injuries or illnesses, such as acute appendicitis, go unnoticed (Chapman, 1984; Manfredi et al., 1981).

Health psychologists study pain because it influences whether individuals seek and comply with medical treatment and because being in pain can be very stressful, particularly when it is intense or enduring. In this chapter we examine the nature and symptoms of pain, and the effects it has on its victims when it is severe. As we consider these topics, you will find answers to questions you may have about pain. What is pain, and what is the physical basis for it? Can people feel pain when there is no underlying physical disorder? Do psychosocial factors affect our experience of pain? Since pain is a subjective experience, how do psychologists assess how much pain a person feels?

WHAT IS PAIN?

Pain is the sensory and emotional experience of discomfort, which is usually associated with actual or threatened tissue damage or irritation (Sanders, 1985). Virtually all people experience pain and at all ages—from the pains of birth for mother and baby, to those of colic and teething in infancy, to those of injury and illness in childhood and adulthood. Some pain becomes chronic, as with arthritis, problems of the lower back, migraine headache, or cancer.

People's experience with pain is important for several reasons. For one thing, no medical complaint is more common than pain. According to researcher Paul Karoly, pain is the "most pervasive symptom in medical practice, the most frequently stated 'cause' of disability, and the single most compelling force underlying an individual's choice to seek or avoid medical care" (1985, p. 461). As we saw in Chapter 9, people are more likely to seek medical treatment without delay if they feel pain. Also, severe and prolonged pain can come to dominate the lives of its victims, impairing their general functioning, ability to work, social relationships, and emotional adjustment. Last, pain has enormous social and economic effects on all societies of the world. In the United States at any given time, a third or more people suffer from one or more continuous or recurrent painful conditions that require medical care, and tens of millions of these people are partially or completely disabled by their conditions (Sanders, 1985; Von Korff, Dworkin, & Le Resche, 1990). Americans spend tens of billions of dollars each year on pain-related expenses, such as for treatment, loss of income, disability payments, and litigation.

THE QUALITIES AND DIMENSIONS OF PAIN

Our sensations of pain can be quite varied and have many different qualities. We might describe some pains as "sharp" and others as "dull," for example—and sharp pains can have either a stabbing or pricking feel. Some pains involve a burning sensation, and others have a cramping, itching, or aching feel. And some pains are throbbing, or constant, or shooting, or pervasive, or localized. Often the feelings we experience depend on the kinds of irritation or damage that has occurred and the location. For instance, when damage occurs deep within the body, individuals usually report feeling a "dull" or "aching" pain; but damage produced by a brief noxious event to the skin is often described as "sharp" (McClintic, 1985; Schiffman, 1996).

The painful conditions people experience also differ in how the pain originates and how long it lasts. We will consider two dimensions that describe these differences, beginning with the degree to which the origin of the pain can be traced to tissue damage.

Organic Versus Psychogenic Pain

People who suffer physical injuries, such as a serious burn, experience pain that is clearly linked to tissue damage. When discomfort is caused mainly by tissue damage, it is described as *organic pain*. For other pains, no tissue damage appears to exist—at least, medical examinations fail to find an organic basis. The discomfort involved in these pains seems to result primarily from psychological processes. For this reason, this type of discomfort is described as *psychogenic pain*. I once witnessed an extreme example of psychogenic

pain in a schizophrenic man: he claimed—and *really* looked like—he was "feeling" stings from being "shot by enemy agents with ray guns."

Not long ago, researchers considered organic and psychogenic pain to be separate entities, with psychogenic pain not involving "real" sensations. As pain researcher Donald Bakal has noted, a practitioner's reference to pain as "psychogenic"

> was taken to mean "due to psychological causes," which implied that the patient was "imagining" his pain or that it was not really pain simply because an organic basis could not be found. Psychogenic pain is not experienced differently, however, from that arising from physical disease or injury. Psychogenic and organic pain both hurt. (1979, p. 167)

Researchers now recognize that virtually all pain experiences involve an interplay of both physiological and psychological factors. As a result, the dimension of pain involving organic and psychogenic causes is viewed as a continuum rather than a dichotomy. Different pain experiences simply involve different mixtures of organic and psychogenic factors. A mixture of these factors seems clear in the findings that many people with tissue damage experience little or no pain, others without damage report severe pain, and the role of psychological factors in people's pain increases when the condition is long lasting (Turk & Okifuji, 1999). When people experience chronic pain with no detectable physical basis, psychiatrists diagnose the condition as a *pain disorder* (classified within *somatoform disorders*) and often assume the origin is mainly psychogenic (Davison & Neale, 1998). Keep in mind, however, that failing to find a physical basis for someone's pain does not necessarily mean there is none. Unfortunately, many health care workers still think pain that has no demonstrated physical basis is purely psychogenic, and their patients struggle to prove that "the pain isn't just in my head, Doc" (Karoly, 1985).

Acute Versus Chronic Pain

Experiencing pain either continuously or frequently over a period of many months or years is different from having occasional and isolated short-term bouts with pain. The length of experience an individual has had

By permission of Johnny Hart and Creators Syndicate, Inc.

with a painful condition is an important dimension in describing his or her pain.

Most of the painful conditions people experience are temporary—the pain arrives and then subsides in a matter of minutes, days, or even weeks, often with the aid of painkillers or other treatments prescribed by a physician. If a similar painful condition occurs in the future, it is not connected in a direct way to the earlier experience. This is the case for most everyday headaches, for instance, and for the pain typically produced by such conditions as toothaches, muscle strains, accidental wounds, and surgeries.

Acute pain refers to the discomfort people experience with temporary painful conditions that last less than 6 months or so (Chapman, 1991; Turk, Meichenbaum, & Genest, 1983). Patients with acute pain often have higher than normal levels of anxiety while the pain exists, but their distress subsides as their conditions improve and their pain decreases (Fordyce & Steger, 1979).

When a painful condition lasts for more than a few months, it is called *chronic*. People with chronic pain continue to have high levels of anxiety and tend to develop feelings of hopelessness and helplessness because various medical treatments have not helped. Pain interferes with their daily activities, goals, and sleep (Affleck et al., 1998), and it can come to dominate their lives. These effects can be seen in the following passage:

Pain patients frequently say that could stand their pain much better if they could only get a good night's sleep.... They feel worn down, worn out, exhausted. They find themselves getting more and more irritable with their families, they have fewer and fewer friends, and fewer and fewer interests. Gradually, as time goes by, the boundaries of their world seem to shrink. They become more and more preoccupied with their pain, less and less interested in the world around them. Their world begins to center around home, doctor's office, and pharmacy. (Sternbach, quoted in Bakal, 1979, p. 165)

Although pain itself can interfere with sleep, intrusive thoughts and worry before getting to sleep may be a more important factor (Smith et al., 2000). Another problem of people with chronic pain is that many leave their jobs for emotional and physical reasons and must live on reduced incomes at the same time that their medical bills are piling up. The experience of pain is very different when the condition is chronic than when it is acute.

The effects of chronic pain also depend on whether the underlying condition is *benign* (harmless) or is *malignant* (injurious) and worsening and whether the discomfort exists *continuously* or occurs in frequent and intense *episodes*. Using these factors, Dennis Turk, Donald Meichenbaum, and Myles Genest (1983) have described three types of chronic pain:

1. **Chronic-recurrent pain** stems from benign causes and is characterized by repeated and intense episodes of pain separated by periods without pain. Two examples of chronic-recurrent pain are migraine headaches and tension-type (muscle-contraction) headaches; another example is *myofascial pain*, a syndrome that typically involves shooting or radiating, but dull, pain in the muscles and connective tissue of the head and neck, and sometimes the back (Hare & Milano, 1985; Turk, Meichenbaum, & Genest, 1983).

2. **Chronic-intractable-benign pain** refers to discomfort that is typically present all of the time, with varying levels of intensity, and is not related to an underlying malignant condition. Chronic low back pain often has this pattern.

3. **Chronic-progressive pain** is characterized by continuous discomfort, is associated with a malignant condition, and becomes increasingly intense as the underlying condition worsens. Two of the most prominent malignant conditions that frequently produce chronic-progressive pain are rheumatoid arthritis and cancer.

As we shall see later in this chapter and in the next one, the type of pain people experience influences their psychosocial adjustment and the treatment they receive to control their discomfort. (Go to 💡.)

PERCEIVING PAIN

Of the several perceptual senses the human body uses, the sense of pain has three important and unique properties (Chapman, 1984; Melzack & Wall, 1982). First, although nerve fibers in the body sense and send signals of tissue damage, the receptor cells for pain are different from those of other perceptual systems, such as vision. Whereas the visual system contains specific receptor cells that transmit only messages about a particular type of stimulation—light—there are no *specific* receptor cells in the body that transmit *only* information about pain. Second, the body senses pain in response to many types of noxious stimuli, such as physical pressure, lacerations, and intense heat or cold. Third, the perception of pain almost always includes a strong emotional component. As we are about to see, perceiving pain involves a complex interplay of physiological and psychological processes.

The Physiology of Pain Perception

To describe the physiology of perceiving pain, we will trace the bodily reaction to tissue damage, as when the body receives a cut or burn. The noxious stimulation instantly triggers chemical activity at the site of injury, releasing chemicals called **algogenic substances** that exist naturally in the tissue (Chapman, 1984). These chemicals—which include *serotonin*, *histamine*, and *bradykinin*—promote immune system activity, cause inflammation at the injured site, and activate endings of nerve fibers in the damaged region, signaling injury.

The signal of injury is transmitted by afferent neurons of the peripheral nervous system to the spinal cord, which carries the signal to the brain. The afferent nerve endings in a damaged region of the body that respond to pain stimuli and signal injury are called **nociceptors** (AMA, 1989; Chapman, 1984; Tortora & Grabowski, 2000). These fibers

> have no special structure for detecting injury; they are simply free nerve endings. They may be found in skin, blood vessels, subcutaneous tissue, muscle, ... joints, and other structures, When activated, these end organs, like other receptors, generate impulses that are transmitted along peripheral fibers to the central nervous system. (Chapman, 1984, p. 1261)

Pain signals are carried by afferent peripheral fibers of two types: A-delta and C fibers. A-*delta fibers* are coated with myelin, a fatty substance that enables neurons to transmit impulses very quickly. These fibers are associated with sharp, well-localized, and distinct pain experiences. C *fibers* transmit impulses more slowly—because they are not coated with myelin—and seem to be involved in experiences of diffuse dull, burning, or aching pain sensations (Chapman, 1984; Melzack & Wall, 1982; Tortora & Grabowski, 2000).

Signals from A-delta and C fibers follow different paths when they reach the brain (Bloom, Lazerson, & Hofstadter, 1985; Guyton, 1985). A-delta signals, which reflect sharp pain, pass through specific areas of the thalamus on their way to motor and sensory areas of the cerebral cortex (refer back to Figures 2–3 and 2–4 on pages 37 and 38. This suggests that signals of sharp pain receive special attention in our sensory awareness, probably so that we can respond to them quickly. On the other hand, C fiber signals, which reflect burning or aching pain, terminate mainly in the

HIGHLIGHT ON ISSUES

Acute Pain in Burn Patients

Almost every day we hear or read about people being seriously burned, such as in a fire or through scalding. Each year in the United States, over 2 million individuals become victims of burn injuries that require medical attention (AMA, 1989). Those burned badly enough to require hospitalization number about 70,000, many of whom are children. These people suffer acute pain both from their injuries and from the treatment procedures that must be performed.

Medical workers describe the severity of a burn on the basis of its location and with two measures of its damage (AMA, 1989). One measure estimates the amount of skin *area* affected in terms of the percentage of the body surface burned; the other assesses the *depth* of the burn, expressed in three "degrees":

1. *First-degree burns* involve damage restricted to the epidermis, or outermost layer of skin. The skin turns red, but does not blister—as, for example, in most cases of sunburn.

2. *Second-degree burns* are those that include damage to the dermis, the layer below the epidermis. These burns are quite painful, often form blisters, and can result from scalding and fire.

3. *Third-degree burns* destroy the epidermis and dermis down to the underlying layer of fat, and may extend to the muscle and bone. These burns usually result from fire. Because the nerve endings are generally damaged in third-degree burns, there is generally no pain sensation in these regions initially.

Practitioners assess the depth of a burn by its appearance and the sensitivity of the region to pain.

Hospital treatment for patients with severe burns progresses through three phases (AMA, 1989; Wernick, 1983). The first few days after the burn is called the *emergency phase*, during which medical staff assess the severity of the burn and work to maintain the patient's body functions and defenses, such as in preventing infection and keeping a balance of fluids and electrolytes. The *acute phase* extends from the end of the emergency phase until the burned area is covered with new skin. This process can take from several days to several months, depending on the severity of the burn. The pain is constant during most or all of this phase, particularly when nerve endings begin to regenerate in third-degree burns. Suffering is generally

> greatest during "tankings," in which the patient is lowered on a stretcher into a large tub. The old dressings are removed and the patient is gently scrubbed to remove encrusted medication. Debridement, which is usually necessary during the early weeks of hospitalization, involves the vigorous cutting away of dead tissue in burned areas. The process, which may last for more than an hour and involve several people working on different parts of the body simultaneously, ends when fresh medication and new dressings are applied. (Wernick, 1983, p. 196)

These and many other painful medical procedures occur very frequently, and burn patients must also do exercises for physical or occupational therapy. Last, the *rehabilitation phase* begins at about the time of discharge from the hospital and continues until the scar tissue has matured. Although the pain has now subsided, itching in the healed area (which should not be scratched) can be a source of discomfort, as can using devices and doing exercises to prevent scarring and contractures (skin shrinkage that can restrict the person's range of motion).

Analgesic medication is the main approach for controlling acute pain in the hospital (Kanner, 1986). But psychological approaches can also help burn patients cope with their pain so that they need less medication. Robert Wernick (1983) used a program of psychological preparation with adult severe-burn patients. This preparation was designed to enhance the patients' sense of informational, behavioral, and cognitive control over their discomfort, especially with regard to the tanking and debridement procedures. Although these patients were not specifically asked to reduce their use of drugs, they subsequently requested much less medication than patients in a comparison (control) group who received the standard hospital preparation. Similar preparation methods have also been successful with children (Tarnowski, Rasnake, & Drabman,1987).

brainstem and lower portions of the forebrain, such as the limbic system, thalamus, and hypothalamus. The remaining C fiber impulses spread to many areas of the brain by connecting with a diffuse network of neurons. Signals of dull pain are less likely to command our immediate attention than those of sharp pain, but are more likely to affect our mood, general emotional state, and motivation.

So far, the description we have given of physiological reactions to tissue damage makes it seem as though the process of perceiving pain is rather straightforward. But it actually isn't. One phenomenon that complicates the picture is that pains originating from internal organs are often perceived as coming from other parts of the body, usually near the surface of the skin. This is called **referred pain** (AMA, 1989; McClintic, 1985; Tortora & Grabowski, 2000). The pain people often feel in a heart attack provides one of the most widely known examples of this phenomenon: the pain is referred to the shoulders, pectoral area of the chest, and arms. Other examples of referred pain include:

- Pain perceived to be in the shoulder that results from inflammation of the diaphragm.
- Pain in the upper back originating in the stomach.
- Pain in the ear or in the wrong area of the mouth that results from a toothache.

Referred pain results when sensory impulses from an internal organ and the skin use the same pathway in the spinal cord (AMA, 1989; Tortora & Grabowski, 2000). Because people are more familiar with sensations from the skin than from internal organs, they tend to perceive the spinal cord impulses as coming from the skin. Another issue that complicates our understanding of pain perception is that people feel pains that have no detectable physical basis, as the next section discusses.

Pain Without Detectable Body Damage

Some pains people experience are quite mysterious, since they occur with no detectable "reason"—for instance, no noxious stimulus is present. Most of these pain experiences belong to one of three syndromes: neuralgia, causalgia, and phantom limb pain. These syndromes often begin with tissue damage, such as from an injury, but the pain (1) persists long after healing is complete, (2) may spread and increase in inten-

sity, and (3) may become stronger than the pain experienced with the initial damage (AMA, 1989; Melzack & Wall, 1982).

Neuralgia is an extremely painful syndrome in which the patient experiences recurrent episodes of intense shooting or stabbing pain along the course of a nerve (AMA, 1989; Chapman, 1984; Melzack & Wall, 1982). In one form of this syndrome, called *trigeminal neuralgia*, excruciating spasms of pain occur along the trigeminal nerve that projects throughout the face. Episodes of neuralgia occur very suddenly and without any apparent cause. Curiously, attacks of neuralgia can be provoked more readily by innocuous stimuli than by noxious ones. For instance, drawing a cotton ball across the skin can trigger an attack, but a pin prick does not.

Another mysterious pain syndrome is *causalgia*, which is characterized by recurrent episodes of severe burning pain (AMA, 1989; Melzack & Wall, 1982; Weisenberg, 1977). A patient with causalgia might report, for instance, that the pain feels "like my arm is pressed against a hot stove." In this syndrome, the pain feels as though it originates in a region of the body where the patient had at some earlier time been seriously wounded, such as by a gunshot or stabbing. Curiously, only a small minority of severely wounded patients develop causalgia—but for those who do, the pain persists long after the wound has healed and damaged nerves have regenerated. Episodes of causalgia often occur spontaneously and

> may take minutes or hours to subside, but may occur repeatedly each day for years after the injury. The frequency and intensity of the spontaneous pain-attacks may increase over the years, and the pain may even spread to distant areas of the body. (Melzack, quoted in Bakal, 1979, p. 142)

Like neuralgia, attacks of causalgia can be triggered by minor stimuli, such as a gentle touch or a puff of air.

Phantom limb pain is an especially puzzling phenomenon because the patient—an amputee or someone whose peripheral nervous system is irreparably damaged—feels pain in a limb that either is no longer there or has no functioning nerves (AMA, 1989; Chapman, 1984; Melzack, 1997). After an amputation, for instance, most patients claim to have sensations of their limb still being there—such as by feeling it "move"—and most of these individuals report feeling pain, too. Phantom limb pain generally persists for months or years, can be quite severe, and sometimes resembles the pain produced by the injury that required the amputation. Although the pain tends to decrease over time, it sometimes gets worse (Bakal, 1979). Individuals with phantom limb pain may experience either recurrent or continuous pain and may describe it as shooting, burning, or cramping. For example, many patients who feel pain in a phantom hand report sensing that the hand is tightly clenched and its fingernails are digging into the palm (Melzack, 1997).

Why do people feel pain when no noxious stimulation is present? Perhaps the answer relates to the neural damage that precedes the development of causalgia and phantom limb pain—and perhaps even neuralgia involves neural damage, albeit of a less obvious nature, such as from infection (Hare & Milano, 1985). But then why is it that the large majority of patients who suffer obvious neural damage do not develop these curious pain syndromes? Although the puzzle is far from being solved, the explanation will almost surely involve both physiological and psychological factors.

The Role of the "Meaning" of Pain

Some people evidently like pain—at least under some, usually sexual, circumstances—and are described as *masochists*. For them, the meaning of pain seems to be different from what it is for most people. Some psychologists believe individuals may come to like pain through classical conditioning, that is, by participating in or viewing activities that associate pain with pleasure in a sexual context (Wincze, 1977). Most of the evidence for the view that the meaning of pain can change by its association with pleasure comes from research with animals. For example, Ivan Pavlov (1927) demonstrated that the dogs' negative reaction to aversive stimuli, such as electric shocks or skin pricks, changed if the stimuli repeatedly preceded presentation of food. Eventually, the dogs would try to approach the aversive stimuli, which now signaled that food, not danger, was coming.

Physician Henry Beecher (1956) described a dramatic example of how the meaning of pain affects people's experience of it. During World War II, he had examined soldiers who had recently been very seriously wounded and were in a field hospital for treatment. Of these men, only 49% claimed to be in "moderate" or "severe" pain and only 32% requested medication when asked if they "wanted something to relieve it." Some years later, Beecher conducted a similar examination—this time with civilian men who had just undergone surgery. Although the surgical wounds were in the same body regions as those of the soldiers, the soldiers' wounds had been more extensive. Nevertheless, 75% of the civilians claimed to be in "moderate" or "severe" pain and 83% requested medication. (The painkillers used for the soldiers and civilians were narcotics.)

Why did the soldiers—who had more extensive wounds—perceive less pain than the civilians? Beecher described the meaning the injuries had for the soldiers, who

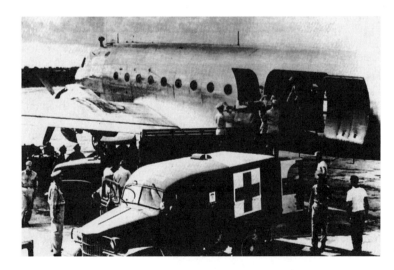

For many wounded soldiers, their pain seemed to be reduced by the knowledge that they were going home.

had been subjected to almost uninterrupted fire for weeks. Notable in this group of soldiers was their optimistic, even cheerful, state of mind. . . . They thought the war was over for them and that they would soon be well enough to be sent home. It is not difficult to understand their relief on being delivered from this area of danger. The battlefield wound marked the end of disaster for them. (1956, p. 1069)

For the civilian surgical patients, however, the wound marked the *start* of a personal disaster and their condition represented a major disruption in their lives.

We discussed in Chapter 9 how people's perceptions of body sensations are influenced by cognitive, social, and emotional factors—for instance, that they are less likely to notice pain when they are distracted by competing environmental stimuli, such as while participating in competitive sports. Psychological factors play an important role in perceiving pain, and theories of pain need to take these factors into account.

THEORIES OF PAIN

You have probably seen demonstrations in which hypnotized people were instructed that they would not feel pain—they were then stuck by a pin and did not react. When people under hypnosis do not react to noxious stimulation, do they still perceive the pain—only "it doesn't matter" to them? Similarly, do patients who seem relaxed while under the influence of painkillers actually perceive their pain? Some theories of pain would answer "yes" to these questions (Karoly, 1985). Let's look at two of these theories as we begin to examine how to explain pain perception.

EARLY THEORIES OF PAIN

In the early 1900s, the dominant theories of pain took a very mechanistic view of pain perception. They proposed that if an appropriate stimulus activates a receptor, the signal travels to the spinal cord and then the brain, and sensation results (Melzack & Wall, 1965, 1982; Schneider & Tarshis, 1975; Weisenberg, 1977). *Specificity theory* argued, for example, that the body has a separate sensory system for perceiving pain—just as it does for hearing and vision. This system was thought to contain its own special receptors for de-

tecting pain stimuli, its own peripheral nerves and pathway to the brain, and its own area of the brain for processing pain signals. But this structure is not correct.

Another view of pain, called *pattern theory*, proposed that there is no separate system for perceiving pain, and the receptors for pain are shared with other senses, such as of touch. According to this view, people feel pain when certain patterns of neural activity occur, such as when appropriate types of activity reach excessively high levels in the brain. These patterns occur only with intense stimulation. Because strong and mild stimuli of the same sense modality produce different patterns of neural activity, being hit hard feels painful, but being caressed does not.

None of the early theories adequately explained pain perception (Melzack & Wall, 1982). Pattern theory has been criticized because it requires that the stimuli triggering pain must be intense. Thus, it cannot account for the fact that innocuous stimuli can trigger episodes of causalgia and neuralgia. Perhaps the most serious problem with the early theories is that they do not attempt to explain why the experience of pain is affected by psychological factors, such as the person's ideas about the meaning of pain, beliefs about the likelihood of pain, and attention to (or distraction from) noxious events. Partly because these theories overlook the role of psychological factors, they incorrectly predict that a person must feel just as much pain when hypnotized as when not hypnotized, even though he or she does not show it. Research findings indicate that people who are instructed not to feel pain actually do feel less pain when deeply hypnotized than when in the normal waking state (Hilgard & Hilgard, 1983). (Go to 🔍.)

THE GATE-CONTROL THEORY OF PAIN

In the 1960s, Ronald Melzack and Patrick Wall (1965, 1982) introduced the **gate-control theory** of pain perception. This theory integrated useful conceptions from earlier theories and improved on them in several ways, particularly by describing a physiological mechanism by which psychological factors can affect people's experience of pain. As a result, the gate-control theory can account for many phenomena in pain perception that have vexed earlier theories. For instance, it does not have to predict that hypnotized people must feel noxious stimulation (Karoly,1985).

FOCUS ON RESEARCH

Inducing Pain in Laboratory Research

To conduct an experiment dealing with pain, researchers sometimes need to create a physically painful situation for human participants. How can they accomplish this in a standard way without harming the people? Several approaches have been used safely; two of the more common methods are the *cold-pressor procedure* and the *muscle-ischemia procedure* (Turk, Meichenbaum, & Genest, 1983). Let's look at these two methods and research that has used them.

The Cold-Pressor Procedure

The cold-pressor procedure basically involves immersing the person's hand and forearm in ice water for a few minutes. A special apparatus is used, like the one illustrated in Figure 11F–1, so that the researcher can maintain a standard procedure across all people they test. The apparatus consists of an armrest mounted on an ice chest filled with water, which is maintained at a temperature of 2°C (35.6° F). Water at this temperature produces a continuous pain that subjects describe as "aching" or "crushing." A pump circulates the water to prevent it from warming in local areas around the arm.

Before using the apparatus, the person's arm is immersed in a bucket of room-temperature water for 1 minute. The researcher also explains the cold-pressor procedure, solicits questions, and indicates that some temporary discoloration of the arm is common. When the procedure is over and the person's arm is removed from the apparatus, the researcher notes that the discomfort will decrease rapidly but that it sometimes increases first for a short while (Turk, Meichenbaum, & Genest, 1983). When using this procedure, the person's pain may be assessed in several ways, such as by self-ratings or by the length of time he or she is willing to endure the discomfort.

An experiment by Michel Girodo and Douglas Wood (1979) used the cold-pressor procedure to examine the role of coping methods on pain perception. The subjects were randomly assigned to several conditions, with each person undergoing the cold-pressor procedure twice. Before the second procedure, subjects in different groups received different types of training for coping with pain. We will focus on two groups. One group was trained to cope by making positive *self-statements*; they were taught a list of 20 statements, such as, "No matter how cold it gets, I can handle it," and "It's not the worst thing that can happen." For the other group, training involved the same self-statements, but they also received an *explanation* of how using these statements can enhance their personal control and help them cope with the pain. Immediately after each cold-pressor procedure,

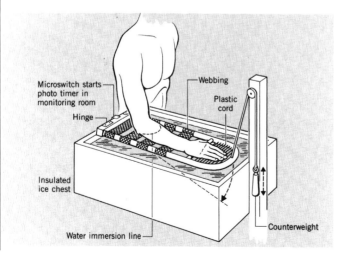

Microswitch starts
photo timer in
monitoring room

Hinge

Insulated
ice chest

Water immersion line

Webbing

Plastic
cord

Counterweight

Figure 11F-1   Apparatus for the cold-pressor procedure.

the subjects rated their experience of pain on an 11-point scale, ranging from "no pain felt" to "worst pain ever felt." Comparing data from the first to the second procedure revealed that the pain ratings *decreased* for subjects who received the explanation for making the statements and *increased* for those who did not receive the explanation. These results suggest that people's beliefs about the purpose of using self-statements may affect their experience of pain.

The Muscle-Ischemia Procedure

The condition of *ischemia*—or insufficient blood flow—is an important stimulus for the experience of pain when circulation is blocked in internal organs (AMA, 1989). The pain people experience in a heart attack, for instance, results from poor blood flow in the blood vessels to the heart muscle.

The muscle-ischemia procedure for inducing pain involves reducing blood flow to the muscles of the arm. This is accomplished by wrapping the cuff of a sphygmomanometer (blood pressure testing device) around the arm, inflating it, and maintaining the pressure at a high level—240 mm Hg (Turk, Meichenbaum, & Genest, 1983). This pressure produces pain without causing damage and can be applied safely for 50 minutes or so. Before the procedure begins, the arm is raised over the subjects's head for 1 minute to drain excess venous blood. The researcher also informs the person that the procedure is safe and harmless, but that it is uncomfortable and may produce temporary numbness, throbbing, changes in arm temperature, and discoloration of the arm and hand. When the cuff is being removed, the researcher informs the person that the discomfort will continue for a short while before subsiding. The person then raises the arm over his or her head (sometimes with the aid of the other arm) to allow blood flow to return gradually and comfortably—a process taking 3 to 5 minutes. As with the cold-pressor procedure, measures of muscle-ischemia pain can include self-ratings and endurance.

Another way to measure muscle-ischemia pain involves a variation of the procedure we described; that is, the cuff is inflated only to the point when the subject first reports discomfort. This approach

assesses the individual's pain *threshold*. Researchers used this approach to examine the effects of laughter and relaxation experiences on discomfort thresholds (Cogan, Cogan, Waltz, & McCue, 1987). The researchers randomly assigned people to four conditions, each involving a different type of experience immediately preceding assessment of discomfort. The *laughter* group listened to a comedy recording by Lily Tomlin, and every subject did in fact laugh out loud; the *relaxation* group listened to a tape designed to induce progressive muscle relaxation; the *narrative* group listened to a tape of a lecture on ethics and sociology; and a control group did not listen to any recording. The pain thresholds, or cuff pressures at which subjects reported discomfort, were more than 50% higher for individuals in the laughter and relaxation groups than for those in the narrative and control groups.

Using muscle-ischemia, cold-pressor, and other procedures to induce pain, researchers have found almost no correlation in the thresholds for different types of pain *within* individuals (Janal, Glusman, Kuhl, & Clark, 1994). This suggests that most people cannot be characterized as "stoical" or "sensitive" to pain in general.

Pain Research and Ethical Standards

When conducting any kind of research with human participants, psychologists are obliged to follow the ethical standards set forth by the American Psychological Association (separate guidelines apply for animal studies). Some of the standards are especially pertinent for research with aversive stimuli. First of all, researchers should make certain that any aversive stimulus they use is not actually harmful. In addition, all participants should:

- Be informed of any features of the study that might affect their willingness to participate.
- Receive clear answers to their questions.
- Be allowed to choose freely, and without undue influence, whether to participate and whether to quit at any point.

If a participant is a child, researchers should also obtain consent from an appropriate guardian, usually a parent.

The Gating Mechanism

At the heart of the gate-control theory is a neural "gate" that can be opened or closed in varying degrees, thereby modulating incoming pain signals before they reach the brain. The theory proposes that the *gating mechanism* is located in the spinal cord—more specifically, in the *substantia gelatinosa* of the *dorsal horns*, which are part of the *gray matter* that runs the lenth of the core of the spinal cord. Figure 11–1 depicts how the gate-control process works. You can see in both diagrams of the figure that signals of noxious stimulation enter the gating mechanism (substantia gelatinosa) of the spinal cord from *pain fibers* (A-delta and C fibers). After these signals pass through the gating mechanism, they activate *transmission cells*, which send impulses to the brain. When the output of signals from the transmission cells reaches a critical level, the person perceives pain; the greater the output beyond this level, the greater the pain intensity.

The two diagrams in the figure outline how the gating mechanism controls the output of impulses by the transmission cells. When pain signals enter the spinal cord and the gate is open, the transmission cells send impulses freely; but to the extent that the gate is closed, the output of the transmission cells is inhibited. What controls the opening and closing of the gate? The gate-control theory proposes that three factors are involved:

1. *The amount of activity in the pain fibers.* Activity in these fibers tends to open the gate. The stronger the noxious stimulation, the more active the pain fibers.

2. *The amount of activity in other peripheral fibers.* Some peripheral fibers, called A-beta fibers, carry information about harmless stimuli or mild irritation, such as touching, rubbing, or lightly scratching the skin. Activity in A-beta fibers tends to close the gate, inhibiting the perception of pain when noxious stimulation exists. This would explain why gently massaging or applying heat to sore muscles decreases the pain.

3. *Messages that descend from the brain.* Neurons in the brainstem and cortex have efferent pathways to

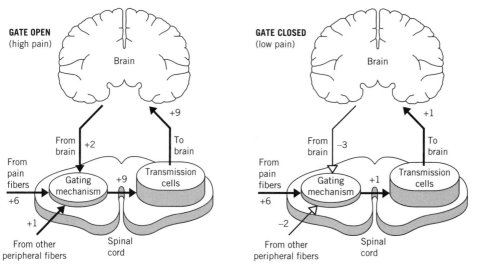

Figure 11–1   Two diagrams to illustrate gate-control theory predictions when strong pain signals arrive from *pain fibers* (A-delta and C) at the spinal cord, along with signals from other *peripheral fibers* (A-beta) and the *brain*. The diagram on the left depicts what conditions might exist when the gate is *open*, and the person feels strong pain; the one on the right shows a scenario when the gate is *closed*, and the person feels little pain. The thick arrows indicate "stimulation" conditions that tend to open the gate and send pain signals through, and the thin ones indicate the opposite, "inhibition," effect. The numbers that accompany each arrow represent hypothetical values for the degrees of pain *stimulation* (positive numbers) or *inhibition* (negative numbers). Pain signals enter the spinal cord and pass through a gating mechanism before activating transmission cells, which send impulses to the brain. (From information in Melzack & Wall, 1965, 1982.)

the spinal cord, and the impulses they send can open or close the gate. The effects of some brain processes, such as those in anxiety or excitement, probably have a general impact, opening or closing the gate for *all* inputs from *any* areas of the body. But the impact of other brain processes may be very specific, applying to only some inputs from certain parts of the body. The idea that brain impulses influence the gating mechanism helps to explain why people who are hypnotized or distracted by competing environmental stimuli may not notice the pain of an injury.

The theory proposes that the gating mechanism responds to the combined effects of these three factors. As Melzack and Wall have stated, "The degree to which the gate increases or decreases sensory transmission is determined by the relative activity in large-diameter (A-beta) and small-diameter (A-delta and C) fibers and by descending influences from the brain" (1982, p. 222). Table 11.1 presents a variety of conditions in people's lives that seem to open or close the gate. For instance, anxiety and boredom are conditions that tend to open the gate, and positive emotions and distraction tend to close it.

Evidence on the Gate-Control Theory

The gate-control theory has stimulated a great deal of research and has received strong support from the findings of many, but not all, of these studies (Melzack & Wall, 1982; Winters, 1985). One study, for instance, confirmed the prediction from gate-control theory that impulses from the brain can inhibit the perception of pain. David Reynolds (1969) conducted this study with rats as subjects. He first implanted an electrode in the midbrain portion of each rat's brainstem, varying the exact location from one rat to the next. Then he made sure they could feel pain by applying a clamp to their tails—and all reacted. Several days later, he tested whether stimulation through the electrode would block pain. While providing continuous, mild electrical stimulation, he again applied the clamp. Although most of the subjects did show a pain reaction, those with electrodes in a particular region of the midbrain—the **periaqueductal gray** area—did not. The electrical stimulation had produced a state of not being able to feel pain, or *analgesia*, in these rats. Then Reynolds used these few rats for a dramatic demonstration: he performed abdominal surgery on them while they were awake and with only the analgesia produced through

Table 11.1 *Conditions That Can Open or Close the Pain Gate*

Conditions That Open the Gate
- Physical conditions
  Extent of the injury
  Inappropriate activity level
- Emotional conditions
  Anxiety or worry
  Tension
  Depression
- Mental conditions
  Focusing on the pain
  Boredom; little involvement in life activities

Conditions That Close the Gate
- Physical conditions
  Medication
  Counterstimulation (e.g., heat or massage)
- Emotional conditions
  Positive emotions (e.g., happiness or optimism)
  Relaxation
  Rest
- Mental conditions
  Intense concentration or distraction
  Involvement and interest in life activities

Source: Based on material by Karol et al., cited in Turk, Meichenbaum, & Genest (1983).

electrode stimulation. Subsequent studies by other researchers have confirmed that stimulation to the periaqueductal gray area can induce analgesia in animals and in humans. Moreover, they have determined that morphine works as a painkiller by activating the brainstem to send impulses down the spinal cord (Chapman, 1984; Melzack & Wall, 1982; Winters, 1985).

Other research findings have disconfirmed some details of the theory. But, as one reviewer has noted:

> Regardless of the specific wiring diagrams involved, the gate-control theory of pain has been the most influential and important current theory of pain perception. It ties together many of the puzzling aspects of pain perception and control.... It has generated new interest in pain perception, stimulating a multidisciplinary view of pain for research and treatment. It has been able to demonstrate the tremendous importance of psychological variables. (Weisenberg, 1977, p. 1012).

The gate-control theory clearly takes a biopsychosocial perspective in explaining how people perceive pain. You will see many features of this theory as you read the material in the next section.

BIOPSYCHOSOCIAL ASPECTS OF PAIN

Why does electrical stimulation to the periaqueductal gray area of the brainstem produce analgesia? The search for an answer to this question played an important part in major discoveries about the neurochemical bases of pain. We will begin this section by examining some of these discoveries and seeing that the neurochemical substances that underlie acute pain are linked to psychosocial processes. Then we will consider how psychosocial factors are related to the experience of chronic pain.

NEUROCHEMICAL TRANSMISSION AND INHIBITION OF PAIN

The phenomenon whereby stimulation to the brainstem produces insensitivity to pain has been given the name **stimulation-produced analgesia** (SPA). To understand how SPA occurs, we need to see how transmission cells are activated to send pain signals to the brain. This activation is triggered by a neurotransmitter called *substance* P that is secreted by pain fibers and crosses the synapse to the transmission cells (Chapman, 1984; Tortora & Grabowski, 2000). SPA occurs when another chemical blocks the pain fibers' release of substance P. Let's see how this happens and what this other chemical is.

What Stimulating the Periaqueductal Gray Area Does

Electrical stimulation to the periaqueductal gray area starts a neurochemical chain reaction that seems to take the course shown in Figure 11–2. The impulse travels down the brainstem to the spinal cord, where the neurotransmitter *serotonin* activates nerve cells called "inhibitory interneurons." Impulses in these interneurons then cause the release of the neurotransmitter *endorphin* at the synapse with pain fibers; endorphin inhibits these fibers from releasing substance P (Tortora & Grabowski, 2000; Winters, 1985). Endorphin is a chemical belonging to a class of opiatelike substances called **endogenous opioids** that the body produces naturally; *enkephalin* is another of these chemicals. (*Endogenous* means "developing from within," and *oid* is a suffix meaning "resembling.")

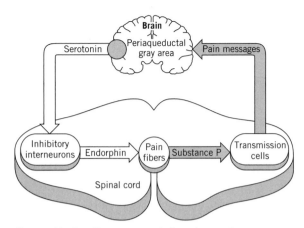

Figure 11–2 Illustration of the chain of activity involved in SPA. Stimulation to the periaqueductal gray area of the brain starts a sequence of electrochemical reactions, eventually leading to inhibition (shown by shaded arrows) of the pain fibers' release of substance P, thereby reducing pain messages from the transmission cells to the brain.

Endogenous opioids and opiates (morphine and heroin) appear to function in much the same way in reducing pain (Snyder, 1977; Winters, 1985). Many neurons in the central nervous system have receptors that are sensitive to both opiates and opioids and allow these chemicals to bind to them. Evidence now indicates that people with chronic pain have diminished levels of endogenous opioids in their blood, which may partly explain why their pain gets worse and why they are highly sensitive to acute pain (Bruehl, McCubbin, & Harden, 1999).

How Opiates and Opioids Work

Researchers have studied the action of opiates and endogenous opioids by using the drug *naloxone*, which acts in opposition to opiates and opioids and prevents them from working as painkillers (Schiffman, 1996; Winters, 1985). In fact, physicians administer naloxone to counteract the effects of heroin in addicts who have taken an overdose of the narcotic. In studying the action of opioids, researchers have examined whether these chemicals are involved in the phenomenon of SPA and found that naloxone blocks the analgesic effects of electrical stimulation to the periaqueductal gray area. One study, for instance, found that when animals received naloxone prior to brainstem stimulation, they continued to feel pain—they felt a noxious stimulus and reacted strongly. But if they did not receive naloxone, analgesia occurred, and they did not react to the noxious stimulus (Akil, Mayer, & Liebeskind, 1976). Furthermore, research with humans found that injecting naloxone in patients who have undergone tooth extractions increases their pain (Levine, Gordon, & Fields, 1978). These findings indicate that endogenous opioids are involved in producing SPA.

The body clearly contains its own natural painkilling substances, but the mechanisms by which they reduce pain are more complicated than they once appeared. For one thing, studies have found that naloxone does not always block SPA; the effect of naloxone may depend on exactly where the electrode delivers stimulation in the periaqueductal gray area (Cannon, Prieto, Lee, & Liebeskind, 1982). As Melzack and Wall have noted:

> It soon became apparent that there was not one but several descending control systems, and that some are sensitive to naloxone and others are not. Furthermore, a host of non-opioid transmitters—such as noradrenalin, acetylcholine and dopamine—are also involved in analgesia. . . . The role of endorphins and enkephalins—despite their undoubted existence—is becoming more hazy. They play a role in pain and analgesia, but the nature of that role is poorly understood. It is possible that they are involved in sudden stress or sudden injury to prevent the animal or person from being overwhelmed by pain, but there is little evidence that they play a role beyond that. (1982, p. 174)

Part of the reason for questioning the extent to which endogenous opioids influence pain is that research on these chemicals has focused mainly on their role in momentary pain that generally lasts only seconds or minutes. Some research findings suggest that neurotransmitters may have different effects for momentary pain than for pain lasting for an hour or more (Melzack & Wall, 1982).

Furthermore, when morphine is given to control pain, tolerance to the drug occurs quickly for momentary pain but does *not* seem to occur for longer-lasting acute pain and for chronic severe pain, such as that experienced by some cancer patients. These patients, for example, "show little evidence of tolerance to

morphine," so that "the same dose maintains its effectiveness" during months or years of use (Melzack & Wall, 1982, p. 176). Just why these differences in tolerance occur is unclear.

Although researchers do not have a full understanding of the mechanisms by which endogenous opioids work, it seems clear that having internal pain-relieving chemicals serves an adaptive function. It enables people to regulate the pain they experience to some extent so that they can attend to other matters, such as taking immediate action to survive serious injuries. Pain activates this analgesic system (Winters, 1985). But most of the time, high levels of endogenous opioid activity are not needed and would be maladaptive since chronic analgesia would undermine the value of pain as a warning signal. And people can use cognitive coping processes, such as diverting the attention, to supplement the use of endogenous opioids (Bruehl et al., 1996). Perhaps because pain and emotions are closely linked, studies have found that psychological stress can trigger endogenous opioid activity (Bloom, Lazerson, & Hofstadter, 1985; Winters, 1985). The release of endogenous opioids in times of stress may help to explain how injured athletes in competition and soldiers on the battlefield continue to function with little or no perception of pain. The connection between stress, coping, and opioid activity points up the interplay between biological and psychosocial factors in people's experience of pain. (Go to 💡.)

PERSONAL AND SOCIAL EXPERIENCES AND PAIN

Imagine this scene: little Stevie is a year old and is in the pediatrician's office to receive a standard immunization shot, as he has done before. As the physician approaches with the needle, Stevie starts to cry and tries to kick the doctor. He is reacting in anticipation of pain—something he learned through *classical conditioning* when he had received vaccinations before.

Learning and Pain

We learn to associate pain with antecedent cues and its consequences, especially if the pain is severe and repeated, as it usually is with chronic pain (Martin, Milech, & Nathan, 1993). Many individuals who suffer from migraine headaches, for example, often can tell

HIGHLIGHT ON ISSUES

Placebos and Pain

You have probably heard of physicians prescribing a medicine that actually consisted of "sugar pills" when they could not find a physical cause for a patient's complaints or did not know of any medication that would help. You may also have heard that this treatment sometimes works—the patient claims the symptoms are reduced. An inert substance or procedure that produces an effect is called a *placebo*. Studies have shown that placebos can often be effective in treating a wide variety of ailments, including coughs, nausea, and hypertension, at least on a temporary basis (Agras, 1984; Roberts, 1995; Sobel, 1990).

Placebos can also be effective in treating pain (Melzack & Wall, 1982). They do not always work, but they seem to produce substantial relief in about half as many patients as do real drugs, such as aspirin or morphine. The effect of placebos depends on the patient's belief that they will work—for instance, they are more effective:

- With large doses—such as more capsules or larger ones—than with smaller doses.
- When injected than when taken orally.
- When the practitioner indicates explicitly and strongly that they will work.

Unfortunately, however, the effectiveness of placebos in treating pain tends to decline with repeated use.

Why do placebos reduce pain? One explanation is that the patient's expectation that the treatment will work triggers the release of endogenous opioids in the body, thereby inhibiting the transmission of pain signals (Fields & Levine, 1984). An experiment with dental patients who had had impacted wisdom teeth removed found evidence that this is the case (Levine, Gordon, & Fields, 1978). Patients who volunteered to participate in the study all received nitrous oxide anesthetic at the start of surgery, an injection 2 hours later, and another injection 3 hours after that. All subjects were told the substance in each injection might increase, decrease, or have no effect on the pain. These injections contained either naloxone or a placebo and were randomly assigned, using the following pattern: one group of subjects got the placebo as their first injection, and naloxone as their second; another group got naloxone first and the placebo second; and a third group received placebos for both. The researchers used a double-blind procedure so that neither the subject nor the practitioner knew which substance was injected.

To determine the effects of these treatments, the researchers had the subjects rate the intensity of their pain several times during the study. The results revealed two important findings: first, the patients reported much more pain when given naloxone than when given the placebo. Second, of the subjects who got the placebo first and then naloxone, those who reported pain relief with the placebo reported increased pain with the naloxone, but those who did not respond to the placebo showed no change in their pain with the naloxone. Because the effects of naloxone occurred mainly among subjects who had gotten relief from the placebo, these findings suggest that placebos relieve pain by activating endogenous opioids. The role of opioids in the placebo effect of relieving pain has been confirmed by other researchers, using the cold-pressor procedure to induce pain (Bandura et al., 1987).

The effects of placebos are fascinating and important, but they also present major ethical dilemmas for practitioners. Is it appropriate to use placebo drugs or procedures to treat symptoms and illnesses—and if so, when and under what circumstances?

when headaches are on the way because they experience symptoms, such as dizziness, that precede the pain. These symptoms become conditioned stimuli that tend to produce distress, a conditioned response, and may heighten the perception of pain when it arrives. Also, words or concepts that describe the pain people have experienced can become conditioned stimuli and produce conditioned responses. A study of people who do and do not have migraine headaches measured their physiological arousal in response to pain-related words, such as "throbbing," "sickening," "stabbing," "scalding," and "itching"

(Jamner & Tursky, 1987). Migraine sufferers displayed much stronger physiological reactions to these words—especially the words that described their own experience with pain—than those without migraines did. Other findings indicate that people who suffer from chronic pain, such as headaches, show lower discomfort thresholds for pain and nonpain stimuli than others do (Ukestad & Wittrock, 1996). Perhaps they learn to notice and react more strongly to low levels of discomfort.

Learning also influences the way people behave when they are in pain. People in pain behave in characteristic ways—they may moan, grimace, or limp, for instance. These actions are called **pain behaviors,** and they can be classified into four types (Turk, Wack, & Kerns, 1985):

- *Facial or audible expression of distress,* as when people clench their teeth, moan, or grimace.
- *Distorted ambulation or posture,* such as moving in a guarded or protective fashion, stooping while walking, or rubbing or holding the painful area.
- *Negative affect,* such as being irritable.
- *Avoidance of activity,* as when people lie down frequently during the day, stay home from work, or refrain from motor or strenuous behavior.

Pain behaviors are a part of the sick role, and people in pain may begin to exaggerate these behaviors because, they think, "No one believes me" (Hendler, 1984). Regardless of why the behaviors start, they are often strengthened or maintained by reinforcement in *operant conditioning,* as Wilbert Fordyce has pointed out (1976; Fordyce & Steger, 1979). When pain persists and becomes chronic, these behaviors often become part of the person's habits and lifestyle. People with entrenched patterns of pain behavior usually feel powerless to change.

How are pain behaviors reinforced? Although being sick or in pain is unpleasant, it sometimes has benefits, or "secondary gains." Someone who is in pain may be relieved of certain chores around the house or of going to work, for instance. Also, when a person has a painful condition that flares up in certain circumstances, such as when lifting heavy objects, he or she may begin to avoid these activities. In both of these situations, pain behavior is reinforced if the person does not like doing these activities in the first place: getting out of doing them is rewarding. Another way pain behavior and

other sick-role behaviors may be reinforced is if the person receives disability payments. Studies of injured or ill patients who differ in the financial compensation they receive have found that those with greater compensation tend to remain hospitalized and miss work longer, report more chronic pain, and show less success from pain treatments (Chapman, 1991; Ciccone, Just, & Bandilla, 1999; Rohling, Binder, & Langhinrichsen-Rohling, 1995). Part of these differences probably reflects a willingness of those receiving compensation to take more time to recover and try to prevent a relapse. Many pain patients who receive disability compensation show substantial emotional and behavioral improvements from pain rehabilitation programs (Trabin, Rader, & Cummings, 1987).

Social Processes and Pain

People who suffer with pain also receive attention, care, and affection from family and friends, which can provide social reinforcement for pain behavior. Researchers have demonstrated this relationship with both child and adult patients. Karen Gil and her colleagues (1988) conducted a study of parents' reactions to the pain behavior of their children who had a chronic skin disorder with severe itching that should not be scratched since it can cause peeling and infection. The researchers videotaped the behavior of each child and his or her parent in the child's hospital room. As you might expect, the parents paid attention to the scratching, perhaps because of the harm it can do. But what effect did the attention have? An analysis revealed that parent attention appeared to *increase* the children's scratching, rather than decrease it, and paying attention to the children when they were *not* scratching seemed to reduce their scratching behavior.

Research has examined how family members' reactions affect pain behavior. Studies have used questionnaires to assess how patients' pain behaviors relate to their receipt of social rewards, such as being able to avoid disliked social activities or getting from their spouses solicitous care, that is, high levels of help and attention (Ciccone, Just, & Bandilla, 1999; Flor, Kerns, & Truck, 1987). Receiving higher levels of social reward was associated with patients reporting more pain and showing more disability and less activity, such as in visiting friends or going shopping. In other research, patients with chronic pain reported their perc_____ of their spouses' solicitousness regarding their pain behavior (Block, Kremer, & Gaylor, 1980). The patients were also interviewed individually in two meetings in which they were aware of being observed through a one-way mirror and who was observing. In one interview, the observer was the patient's spouse; in the other, the observer was a hospital employee. The results showed that the degree of pain the patients described in each interview depended on two factors: (1) whether the spouse or the employee was observing and (2) whether the patient thought the spouse was solicitous. Patients who felt their spouses were solicitous reported *more* pain when their spouses watched than when the employee did. In contrast, patients who felt their spouses were not solicitous reported *less* pain when their spouses watched than when the employee did.

Research findings on parents' and spouses' reactions to chronic pain behavior and the social climate within the family system illustrate how each family member's behavior impacts on the behavior of the others (Flor, Kerns, & Turk, 1987; Kerns & Weiss, 1994; Romano, Turner, & Jensen, 1997). When families lack cohesion or the members are highly solicitous to pain behavior without encouraging the patient to become active, they are likely to promote sick-role behavior. These conditions can develop into a vicious circle—for example, solicitousness may lead to more pain behavior, which elicits more solicitousness, and so on. Showing care and concern when people are in pain is, of course, important and constructive. But the patient's diminished activity may then lead to physical deterioration, such as through muscle atrophy, and lead to progressively more pain and less activity. These social processes in the family system of pain patients are gradual and insidious—they tend to increase the patients' dependency and decrease their self-efficacy and self-esteem. Self-efficacy is important because people who believe they cannot control their pain very well experience more pain and use more medication than those who believe they can control it (Turk, 1996).

Gender, Sociocultural Factors, and Pain

Studies have found gender and sociocultural differences in the experience of pain. Men and women appear to differ in the types of pain they experience and reactions to pain. Women have higher incidence rates of pain from arthritis, migraine headache, myofacial

neuralgia, and causalgia, but men have a greater incidence of back pain and cardiac pain (Bodnar, 1998). Women tend to report more than men that pain interfered with their daily activities (Lester, Lefebvre, & Keefe, 1994). Surveys of adults in different countries who suffer from chronic low back pain revealed greater work and social impairments among Americans, followed by Italians and New Zealanders, and then by Japanese, Colombian, and Mexican individuals (Sanders et al., 1992). Research on the pain experienced after dental surgery by people from different ethnic groups in the United States found that blacks reported more pain than people of European, Asian, or Hispanic backgrounds, and women in each group reported more pain than men (Faucett, Gordon, & Levine, 1994). The reasons for these gender and sociocultural differences are not clear, but they may include differences in the social support and financial consequences these people receive for being sick.

EMOTIONS, COPING PROCESSES, AND PAIN

People in chronic pain experience high levels of anger, fear, and sadness (Fernandez, Clark, & Rudick-Davis, 1998). Pain and emotion are intimately linked, and cognitive processes mediate this link. In a study of these relationships, Gerry Kent (1985) had dental patients fill out a brief dental anxiety scale while waiting for their appointments. Then they rated the pain they expected in their visits. After the appointment, the patients rated the pain they actually experienced, and rated it again by mail 3 months later. The results revealed that anxiety played a role in their expectations of pain and in their memories of it 3 months later. The patients with high dental anxiety expected *and* later remembered four times as much pain as they experienced. In contrast, the low-anxiety patients expected and remembered less than twice as much pain as they experienced. These findings suggest that high-anxiety patients' memories of pain are determined more by what they expect than by what they feel.

Does Emotion Affect Pain?

A study of emotion and pain compared the anxiety and stress levels of children who suffered from migraine headache with those of their best friends, and then had the migraine sufferers keep diaries of

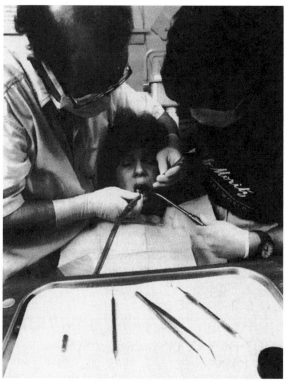

Pain is an important factor in making dental patients feel uneasy about going to the dentist.

their headaches over the next 4 months. Although the scores on tests of anxiety and stress were about the same for the two groups and were within the normal range, migraine sufferers with high levels of anxiety had more frequent and severe headaches than those with lower anxiety (Cooper, Bawden, Camfield, & Camfield, 1987). Other investigations using self-report methods have found that migraine and muscle-contraction headaches tend to occur after periods of heightened stress and that Type A individuals have more frequent chronic headaches than others do (Köhler & Haimerl, 1990; Wittrock & Myers, 1998; Woods et al., 1984). These studies clearly indicate that stress and headache are related. Has any research shown that stress causes headaches?

Convincing evidence that stress can cause headaches comes from a study with adults who suffered from either chronic headache or only occasional headaches (Gannon, Haynes, Cuevas, & Chavez, 1987). Before testing a subject, researchers attached sensors to the person's body to take several physiological measurements, such as of heart rate and electrical activity of muscles. A researcher also told the subjects that they "might or might not" experience headache pain in the procedures and that they would rate their perception of pain several times during the study. After sitting quietly for 15 minutes, they were given a stressful task—calculating arithmetic problems, such as 349 + 229, every 15 seconds for an hour—and told that a buzzer would sound if their performance fell below a norm. Actually, the buzzer sounded periodically regardless of their performance. Then the subjects sat quietly for 10 minutes. How did they react to these conditions? More than two-thirds of the chronic headache sufferers and only one-fourth of the occasional sufferers reported developing headaches during the stress task. Ratings of headache pain increased throughout the stress condition, and decreased later while they sat quietly. The headaches tended to resemble tension-type headaches and be preceded by sustained physiological arousal. These are important findings that indicate that stress can cause headaches.

Emotions are also related to other kinds of pain, but whether emotions cause the pain is still in question. Research has demonstrated, for instance, that the amount of pain people with sickle cell disease report increases with the amount of stress they experience each day and with increases in stress during the preceding 2 days (Porter et al., 2000). But although people with recurrent low back pain report higher levels of anxiety and tension than pain-free control subjects do, these mood states do not worsen in the day or so preceding pain attacks (Feuerstein, Carter, & Papciak, 1987). Feelings of depression appear to result from pain people with chronic discomfort experience on previous days, and lead to pain on subsequent days (Feldman, Downey, & Schaffer-Neitz, 1999). Pain is itself very stressful, and many people with chronic pain consider their discomfort—the actual pain and the physical limitations it produces—to be the most prominent stressor in their lives (Turk, Rudy, & Vitaliano, 1987). Health psychologists with pain patients often try to assess h with their pain. (Go to 🏃.)

Coping with Pain

Part of the stress that
rience stems from
have little person

CLINICAL METHODS AND ISSUES
Assessing Difficulty Coping with Pain

One way a psychologist can evaluate coping difficulties of pain patients is to assess their emotional adjustment with psychological tests, particularly the Minnesota Multiphasic Personality Inventory (MMPI). As we saw in Chapter 10, this test contains several scales, three of which are especially relevant for medical patients. These three scales assess: *hypochondriasis*, the tendency toward being preoccupied with physical symptoms and health; *depression*, feelings of unhappiness, pessimism, and hopelessness; and *hysteria*, the tendency to cope with problems by developing physical symptoms and using avoidance methods, such as denial. Because the MMPI is given and scored in a standardized manner and has been administered to large samples of people, norms exist that allow psychologists to compare an individual's scores on the different scales with those of the general population. For instance, a score of 70 or above on any scale occurs in less than 5% of the population and is considered extreme and clinically significant (Anastasi, 1982). Psychologists generally refer to hypochondriasis, depression, and hysteria as the *neurotic triad* because clients with neurotic disorders often have high scores on these three scales. By combining information from psychological tests and other sources, such as interviews, psychologists can identify and help patients who are having difficulty coping with the stress of pain conditions.

from avoiding activities they believe can trigger an attack or make it worse. As a result, they tend to deal with their stress by using emotion-focused coping strategies. That is, rather than trying to alter the problem itself, they try to regulate their emotional responses to it. Some of the more common coping methods adults and children with chronic pain use include hoping or praying the pain will get better someday and diverting their attention, such as by counting numbers or running a song through their heads (Gil, Wilson, & Edens, 1997; Keefe & Dolan, 1986). These approaches are not very effective in reducing chronic pain.

How effectively do people cope with pain? Studies that tested pain patients with the MMPI have found some fairly consistent outcomes (Cox, Chapman, & Black, 1978; Rappaport, McAnulty, Waggoner, & Brantley, 1987; Rosen, Grubman, Bevins, & Frymoyer, 1987). These outcomes lead to three conclusions. First, individuals who suffer from various types of chronic pain, such as severe headache and low back pain, show a characteristic MMPI profile with extremely high scores on hypochondriasis, depression, and hysteria—the neurotic triad scales, as Figure 11–3 ⟨illu⟩strates. But their scores on the seven other MMPI ⟨ten⟩d to be well within the normal range. ⟨This p⟩attern appears to hold regardless of ⟨whether it⟩ has a known organic source. In

other words, people whose pain might be classified as psychogenic by a physician tend to show similar problems of adjustment on the MMPI as those whose pain has a clear organic basis. Third, individuals with acute

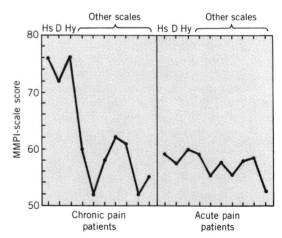

Figure 11–3 Illustration of MMPI profiles comparing chronic pain and acute pain patients: chronic pain patients typically show abnormally high scores (70 or above) on the "neurotic triad" scales (Hs = hypochondriasis, D = depression, Hy = hysteria), but not on the seven other MMPI scales. These data were averaged across mean scores presented in two studies (Cox, Chapman, & Black, 1978; Rosen, Grubman, Bevins, & Frymoyer, 1987).

pain, such as patients recovering from injuries, sometimes have moderately elevated scores on the neurotic triad scales, but these scores and those for the remaining MMPI scales are generally well within the normal range. These findings make sense and reflect the differential psychological impact of pain that patients expect will end soon versus pain they fear will never end. Keep in mind also that people with chronic-recurrent pain conditions show worse psychological symptoms during pain episodes than during pain-free periods (Holroyd, France, Nash, & Hursey, 1993).

It is clear that being in frequent, severe discomfort is related to having high scores on the MMPI neurotic triad scales, but does chronic pain cause maladjustment? One school of thought is that the causal sequence may be the other way around—that is, chronic pain may be a symptom of a psychological disorder, such as depression, that preceded the pain syndrome (Blumer & Heilbronn, 1982). But most current evidence points in the other direction—indicating, for instance, that people in chronic pain become depressed because of the stress they experience without being able to change their situations (Anderson et al., 1985; Turk & Holzman, 1986). They develop a sense of helplessness, which leads to depression. One type of evidence indicating that pain leads to depression is that people whose pain has ended show substantial reductions in various measures of psychological disturbance (Melzack & Wall, 1982).

Of course, this does not mean psychological factors cannot lead to physical pain—for instance, we've seen that stress can cause headaches. One study examined this issue prospectively for 8 years and found support for both causal directions (Magni, Moreschi, Rigatti-Luchini, & Merskey, 1994). People who are depressed are somewhat more likely than others to develop a chronic pain condition in the future, and people with chronic pain are much more likely than others to become depressed. Pain and maladjustment involve interactive processes, with each feeding on the other over time, but chronic pain is more likely to lead to maladjustment than the other way around. Also keep in mind that not all patients with severe chronic pain become maladjusted—many adapt to their conditions much better than others do (Klapow et al., 1993; Linton et al., 1994). Coping well with chronic pain is a struggle that unfolds over time, as this arthritis patient noted:

Over time I've figured out that I can do things to bring on the pain and things that could limit it. I also figured out that my flares won't last forever, although while they're happening it seems like forever. It took quite a while to figure that out. (Tennen & Affleck, 1997, p. 274).

To summarize, the process by which people perceive pain involves a complex chain of physiological and neurochemical events. These events can be affected by psychosocial processes, such as people's beliefs about whether a drug will reduce their discomfort. Pain also affects and can be influenced by people's learning, cognition, social experiences, and emotion. Although people can indicate through their behavior that they are feeling pain, the pain they perceive is actually a private and subjective experience. How can researchers and clinicians who work with patients who have painful symptoms assess the level and type of pain these individuals perceive? We turn now to answering this question.

ASSESSING PEOPLE'S PAIN

Researchers and clinicians have developed a variety of techniques for assessing people's pain. Although virtually all these methods can be applied both in research and in treating pain patients, some techniques are used more often in research, whereas others are used mostly to supplement a detailed medical history in clinical practice. In either setting, it is advisable to use two or more different measurement techniques to enhance the accuracy of the assessment (Bradley, 1994). We will organize our discussion of techniques for measuring people's pain by classifying them into three groups: self-report methods, behavioral assessment approaches, and psychophysiological measures.

SELF-REPORT METHODS

Perhaps the most obvious approach to measuring people's pain is to ask them to describe their discomfort, either in their own words or by filling out a rating scale or questionnaire. In treating a patient's pain, health care workers ask where the pain is, what it feels like, how strong it is, and when it tends to occur. With chronic pain patients, medical and psychological professionals often incorporate this kind of questioning within the structure of a clinical interview.

Interview Methods in Assessing Pain

To treat chronic pain effectively, professionals need more information than just a description of the pain. Interviews with the patient and key others, such as family members and coworkers, provide a rich source of background information in the early phases of treatment (Chapman, 1991; Karoly, 1985; Turk, Meichenbaum, & Genest, 1983). These discussions ordinarily focus on such issues as:

● The history of the pain problem, including when it started, how it progressed, and what approaches have been used for controlling it.

● The patient's emotional adjustment, currently and before the pain syndrome began.

● The patient's lifestyle—recreational interests, exercise patterns, diet, and so on—before the pain condition began.

● The pain syndrome's impact on the patient's current lifestyle, interpersonal relations, and work.

● The social context of pain episodes, such as happenings in the family before an attack and how family members respond when the pain occurs.

● Factors that seem to trigger attacks or make them worse.

● How the patient typically tries to cope with the pain.

The information obtained in these interviews can also be supplemented by having the patient and key others fill out questionnaires (Turk, Meichenbaum, & Genest, 1983).

Pain Rating Scales and Diaries

One of the most direct, simple, and commonly used ways to assess pain is to have individuals rate some aspect of their discomfort on a scale (Chapman et al., 1985; Karoly, 1985; Turk & Okifuji, 1999). This approach is used very often to measure how strong the pain is, and three different types of scales for rating pain intensity are illustrated in Figure 11–4. One type is the *visual analog scale*, which has people rate their pain by marking a point on a line that has labels only at each end. This type of scale is very easy for people to use and can be used with children as young as 5 years of age (Karoly, 1985). The *box scale* has individuals choose one number from a series of numbers that represent levels of pain within a specified range. The *verbal*

VISUAL ANALOG SCALE

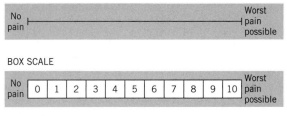

BOX SCALE

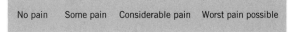

VERBAL RATING SCALE

No pain   Some pain   Considerable pain   Worst pain possible

Figure 11–4   Illustrations of the visual analog, box, and verbal rating scales. Example instructions are as follows: *visual analog scale*—"Mark a point on the line to show how strong your pain is"; *box scale*—"Rate the level of your pain by circling one number on the scale, where 0 means 'no pain' and 10 means 'worst pain possible'"; *verbal rating scale*—"Circle the one phrase that best describes your pain." The labels and number of choices on a scale can be different from those shown here.

rating scale has people describe their pain by choosing a word or phrase from several that are given.

Because rating scales are so easy and quick to use, people can rate their pain frequently. Averaging these ratings across time gives a more accurate picture of the pain the person generally experiences than individual ratings do (Jensen & McFarland, 1993). Repeated ratings can also reveal how the pain changed over time, such as during everyday activities or during the course of an experiment. Chronic pain patients, for example, could rate their pain on index cards each waking hour of each day (Turk, Meichenbaum, & Genest, 1983). They would do this for, say, 2 weeks, also indicating whenever they take pain medication. Before starting this procedure, they would learn what to say if someone sees them filling out the card and asks what they are doing, ways to remind themselves to do each hourly rating, and what to do if they forget. One use of repeated ratings is in showing the ebbs and flows of pain intensity that patients often experience. For instance, one patient's wife

> believed that her husband was experiencing incapacitating and severe pain every waking hour of his life. This belief contributed to her preventing him from participating in any but the simplest chores around the house. Their social life had deteriorated, and the couple had grown increasingly

PAIN DIARY for _Ed_

Date: _3-5-97_   Did you change your medication today? If yes, describe _____ _No_ _____

Pain Rating Scale: No pain | 0 | 1 | 2 | 3 | 4 | 5 | Unbearable pain

Time	Pain rating and body location.	Activity at start of pain.	What medicine did you take, and how much?	Pain rating after 1 or 2 hours.	Comments and other problems.
8:30 pm	4/lower back	Leaned over to turn on bath water	Aspirin (2)	3—helped a little	Could stand up and walk better
11:00pm	2/lower back, dull ache	Lying flat on back in bed	Ibuprofen (Motrin) (2)	1—helped	Couldn't sleep at first; got to sleep by 1:00

Figure 11–5 A pain diary. The chronic pain patient keeps a daily record of important information about pain episodes.

depressed over the course of 4 years. Upon hearing that her husband experienced only moderate pain most of the time, that he indeed felt capable of various tasks, and that he actually resented his wife's efforts at pampering him, she was helped to alter her behavior. (Turk, Meichenbaum, & Genest, 1983, pp. 218–219)

Repeated ratings during each day may also reveal patterns in the timing of severe pain. Is the pain most severe in the evening, or on certain days? If so, are there aspects of the environment that may be responsible and, perhaps, changeable?

Pain ratings can also be used in a *pain diary*, which is a detailed record of a person's pain experiences. As Figure 11–5 illustrates, the pain diary a patient keeps would include pain ratings and information about the time and circumstances of pain episodes, any medications taken, and comments about each episode. (Go to 🍎.)

Pain Questionnaires

Pain is only partly described by the intensity of the discomfort people feel—the experience of pain has many qualities and dimensions. Ronald Melzack began to recognize the multidimensional nature of pain through his interactions with pain patients. He de-

scribed in an interview how this realization emerged from talks he had with a woman who suffered from phantom limb pain. She

would describe burning pains that were like a red-hot poker being shoved through her toes and her ankle. She would cry out from the pain in her legs. Of course, there were no legs. Well, that made me realize the utter subjectivity of pain—no objective physical measure is very likely to capture that.... I began to write down the words she used to describe her pain. I realized that the words describing the *emotional-motivational* component of her pain—"exhausting, sickening, terrifying, punishing"—were very different from those for the *sensory* component—"shooting, scalding, splitting, cramping." Later I came to see there was also an *evaluative* component, such as "it's unbearable" or "it's annoying." I wrote down the words other patients used, too, but I didn't know what to do with them. (Warga, 1987, p. 53, italics added)

Melzack determined that pain involves three broad dimensions—*affective* (emotional-motivational), *sensory*, and *evaluative*—by conducting a study in which subjects sorted over 100 pain-related words into separate groups of their own making (Melzack & Torgerson, 1971).

ASSESS YOURSELF

Describing Your Pain

Use the questionnaire in Figure 11A–1 to assess an acute or chronic pain you have experienced. Try to choose a painful condition that you either currently have, had recently, or remember vividly from the past. If the pain you assess is not current, answer the questions as if it is. Do this now.

Figure 11A-1 The McGill Pain Questionnaire. (Source: Melzack, 1975.)

Ronald Melzack (1975) developed this questionnaire and described its scoring system, which is too complex to do here. You can get a sense of the pain you assessed in two ways: (1) Review the answers you chose—for instance, questions 2 and 3 of Part 4 tell you its range of intensity. (2) Refer back to your answers as you read the description of the McGill Pain Questionnaire in the text.

Part 1. Where Is Your Pain?

Please mark on the drawing below, the areas where you feel pain. Put E if external, or I if internal, near the areas which you mark. Put EI if both external and internal.

Part 2. What Does Your Pain Feel Like?

Some of the words below describe your present pain. Circle ONLY those words that best describe it. Leave out any category that is not suitable. Use only a single word in each appropriate category–the one that applies best.

1	2	3	4
Flickering	Jumping	Pricking	Sharp
Quivering	Flashing	Boring	Cutting
Pulsing	Shooting	Drilling	Lacerating
Throbbing		Stabbing	
Beating		Lancinating	
Pounding			

5	6	7	8
Pinching	Tugging	Hot	Tingling
Pressing	Pulling	Burning	Itchy
Gnawing	Wrenching	Scalding	Smarting
Cramping		Searing	Stinging
Crushing			

9	10	11	12
Dull	Tender	Tiring	Sickening
Sore	Taut	Exhausting	Suffocating
Hurting	Rasping		
Aching	Splitting		
Heavy			

13	14	15	16
Fearful	Punishing	Wretched	Annoying
Frightful	Grueling	Blinding	Troublesome
Terrifying	Cruel		Miserable
	Vicious		Intense
	Killing		Unbearable

17	18	19	20
Spreading	Tight	Cool	Nagging
Radiating	Numb	Cold	Nauseating
Penetrating	Drawing	Freezing	Agonizing
Piercing	Squeezing		Dreadful
	Tearing		Torturing

Part 3. How Does Your Pain Change With Time?

1. Which word or words would you use to describe the pattern of your pain?

1	2	3
Continuous	Rhythmic	Brief
Steady	Periodic	Momentary
Constant	Intermittent	Transient

2. What kind of things relieve your pain?

3. What kind of things increase your pain?

Part 4. How Strong Is Your Pain?

People agree that the following 5 words represent pain of increasing intensity. They are:

1	2	3	4	5
Mild	Discomforting	Distressing	Horrible	Excruciating

To answer each question below, write the number of the most appropriate word in the space beside the question.

1. Which word describes your pain right now? _____
2. Which word describes it at its worst? _____
3. Which word describes it when it is least? _____
4. Which word describes the worst toothache you ever had? _____
5. Which word describes the worst headache you ever had? _____
6. Which word describes the worst stomach-ache you ever had? _____

Melzack's research also indicated that each of the three dimensions consisted of subclasses. For instance, the sensory dimension included a subclass with the words "hot," "burning," "scalding," and "searing"—words relating to temperature. Notice that these four words connote increasingly hot temperatures, with searing being the hottest. Similarly, the affective dimension included a subclass of three words relating to fear: "fearful," "frightful," "terrifying." Then, by determining the degree of pain reflected by each word, Melzack (1975)—a professor at McGill University—was able to construct an instrument to measure pain. This test is called the **McGill Pain Questionnaire** (MPQ), which you filled out in the Assess Yourself exercise.

Part 2 of the MPQ presents a list of descriptive words, separated into a total of 20 subclasses. The test instructs the person to select from each subclass the best word to describe his or her pain. Each word in each class has an assigned value based on the degree of pain it reflects. Let's look, for instance, at subclass 7, which ranges from "hot" to "searing." Selecting "searing" would contribute the highest number of points from this subclass to the person's pain score ("hot" would contribute the lowest number). The sum of these points across the 20 subclasses is called the *pain rating index*. Part 4 of the MPQ contains a series of verbal rating scales; the one that rates "your pain right now" yields a separate score called the *present pain intensity*.

The MPQ appears to have many strengths as an instrument for assessing chronic pain, both for research and for clinical purposes. For one thing, research has generally confirmed that the experience of pain is multidimensional, involving between two and four dimensions (Brennan, Barrett, & Garretson, 1987). Also, individuals with similar pain syndromes tend to choose the same patterns of words to describe their pain. But people suffering from very different types of pain—for example, toothache, arthritis, cancer, and phantom limb pain—choose different patterns of words in the MPQ to describe their different pain experiences (Melzack & Wall, 1982). The main limitation of the MPQ is that it requires a fairly strong English vocabulary (Chapman et al., 1985; Karoly, 1985). For instance, it includes a few words, such as "taut" and "lancinating," that many people may not know. Moreover, sometimes respondents must make very fine distinctions between words, as with "throbbing," "beating," and "pounding." Even if an interviewer

is present to define the words, the MPQ may be of limited use with people who have poor English skills and children under about 12 years of age.

The MPQ is the best-known and most widely used pain questionnaire, but others have been developed more recently. One of these, the *Multidimensional Pain Inventory*, accurately assesses people's pain and its psychosocial effects (Kerns, Turk, & Rudy, 1985; Lousberg et al., 1997).

BEHAVIORAL ASSESSMENT APPROACHES

Because people tend to exhibit pain behaviors when they are in discomfort, it should be possible to assess their pain by observing their behavior. A person is likely to show different types and patterns of behavior if the pain is intense as compared to moderate, if it involves a headache as opposed to low back pain, and if chronic pain is recurrent than if it is intractable. Psychologists have developed procedures for assessing pain behavior in two types of situations: in *everyday activities* and in *structured clinical sessions*.

Assessing Pain Behavior in Structured Clinical Sessions

Procedures are available whereby health care workers can assess the pain behavior of patients in structured sessions that are usually conducted in hospital settings. They are structured by the specific pain behaviors to be assessed and the tasks the patient is asked to perform. One approach of this kind has been developed into a pain assessment instrument—the UAB *Pain Behavior Scale*—for use by nurses during their standard routines, such as in early morning rounds (Richards, Nepomuceno, Riles, & Suer, 1982). The nurse has the patient perform several activities and rates each of 10 behaviors, such as the patient's mobility and use of medication, on a 3-point scale: "none," "occasional," and "frequent." These ratings are converted into numerical values and summed for a total score.

Some studies using structured clinical sessions have focused on assessing discomfort in individuals suffering from low back pain (Follick, Ahern, & Aberger, 1985; Keefe & Block, 1982; Kleinke & Spangler, 1988; Öhlund et al., 1994). Each investigation had patients perform a standard set of activities. In the study by Chris Kleinke and Arthur Spangler, for example, the people were asked to walk, pick up an object on the floor, remove their shoes while sitting, and perform several exercises, such as trunk rotations, toe touching, and sit-ups. Patients in each investigation were videotaped, and trained assessors rated their performance for several pain behaviors, such as guarded movement, rubbing the pain area, grimacing, and sighing. These studies have shown that pain behaviors can be assessed easily and reliably and that behavioral assessments correlate well with patients' self-ratings of pain.

Assessing Pain Behavior in Everyday Activities

How does the pain patient behave in everyday activities, especially at home? Does the person spend much time in bed, complain of discomfort a lot, seek help frequently in moving, or walk with a limp most of the time? How much of these behaviors does the person exhibit? Behavioral assessments of everyday activities like these can be made.

Family members or key others in the patient's life are usually the best people to make these everyday assessments of pain behavior. These people must, of course, be willing to help and be trained to make careful observations and keep accurate records. Researcher Wilbert Fordyce (1976) has recommended a procedure whereby the assessor—say, the client's spouse—compiles a list of five to ten behaviors that generally signal when the patient is in pain. Then the spouse is trained to watch for these behaviors, to keep track of the amount of time the patient exhibits them, and to monitor how people, including the assessor, react to the client's pain behavior. This procedure is useful not only in assessing the patient's pain experiences but in determining their impact on his or her life and the social context that may maintain pain behaviors.

Other researchers have described several modifications or supplements to Fordyce's procedure (Turk, Meichenbaum, & Genest, 1983). For one thing, the assessor—usually the patient's spouse—may fill out a rating scale periodically to measure the intensity of the pain, as reflected by the client's behavior. Also, the spouse may keep a pain diary about the patient's severe pain episodes, recording the date and time, as well as where the episode occurred, such as in the car or at home in bed. Then the spouse describes what he or she:

This woman's pain behavior can be used in assessing her discomfort.

- Noticed as behaviors that suggested the patient was in pain.
- Thought and felt during the episode.
- Did in order to help, along with a rating of the action's effectiveness, ranging on a scale from "did not help at all" to "seemed to stop the pain completely."

These supplemental procedures provide additional data that can be of value in dealing with interpersonal issues that influence the pain experience.

PSYCHOPHYSIOLOGICAL MEASURES

Another approach for assessing pain involves taking measurements of physiological activity, since pain has both sensory and emotional components that can produce changes in bodily functions. *Psychophysiology* is the study of mental or emotional processes as reflected by changes they produce in physiological activity (Lykken, 1987).

One psychophysiological measure researchers have used for assessing pain uses an apparatus called an *electromyograph* (EMG) to measure the electrical activity in muscles, which reflects their tension. Because *muscle tension* is associated with various pain states, such as headaches and low back pain, we might expect EMG recordings to be different between pain patients and pain-free controls. Studies have compared EMG recordings of headache and low back pain patients while *not* in pain with recordings of pain-free subjects and have generally not confirmed this expectation (Blanchard & Andrasik, 1985; Chapman et al., 1985). But the findings of other research suggest that differences between pain patients and controls may exist when the subjects' muscles are active (Chapman et al., 1985). And headache patients show different EMG patterns when they have headaches than when they do not (Blanchard & Andrasik, 1985). More research is needed to verify that EMG measurements provide a useful measure of pain.

Researchers have also attempted to assess people's pain with measures of *autonomic activity*, such as of heart rate and skin conductance. A study by John Dowling (1983) used these two measures of autonomic activity on college students before, during, and after they underwent a cold-pressor procedure. Before the procedure, measurements of skin conductance and heart rate were taken during a *warning* period, as the subjects awaited a signal to immerse the hand in the ice-cold water; after the procedure, measurements were taken during a *resting* period, when the students knew they would not experience further pain. The results showed that autonomic activity during *both* the warning period and immersion correlated moderately with the length of time the subjects left their hands in the water. Finding that pain tolerance correlated with autonomic activity during the warning period is interesting and illustrates a limitation to this measure of pain—that is, changes in autonomic activity readily occur in the absence of the sensation of pain. Although some measures of autonomic activity may be useful in assessing the emotional component of pain, they are not likely to be useful beyond that role (Chapman et al., 1985).

The last psychophysiological measure of pain we will consider involves the electrical activity of the brain, as measured by an *electroencephalograph* (EEG).

When a person's sensory system detects a stimulus, such as a clicking sound from earphones, the signal to the brain produces a change in EEG voltage. Electrical changes produced by stimuli are called *evoked potentials* and show up in EEG recordings as sharp surges or peaks in the graph. Pain stimuli produce evoked potentials that vary in magnitude—the amplitudes of the surges increase with the intensity of the stimuli, decrease when subjects take analgesics, and correlate with people's subjective reports of pain (Chapman et al., 1985).

Even though psychophysiological measures provide objective assessments of bodily changes that occur in response to pain, these changes may also be affected by other factors, such as attention, diet, and stress. In clinical situations, measures of muscle tension, autonomic activity, and evoked potential are probably best used as supplements to self-report and behavioral assessment approaches (Chapman et al., 1985).

PAIN IN CHILDREN

We have focused in this chapter mainly on the experience of pain by adults, and we have mentioned many different types of discomfort and pain syndromes. Virtually every pain condition we have considered afflicts children, too (Lavigne, Schulein, & Hahn, 1986b; McGrath & Hillier, 1996). Children suffer acute pain from illnesses and injury, often being victims of burns and fractures, for instance. They also experience pain associated with chronic diseases, such as arthritis and cancer, and suffer from painful conditions that do not have known physical bases—conditions such as recurrent abdominal pain, causalgia, and migraine and muscle-contraction headache. Indeed, some children suffer from a curious painful condition—unique to their age group—that involves pain deep in the arms or legs but not near a joint. The condition is sometimes called "growing pains," which may be a misnomer because it is most prevalent among 8- to 12-year-olds, a time when growth is relatively slow for children (Lavigne, Schulein, & Hahn, 1986).

Although less is known about the pain people experience in childhood than at other times in their lives, much research since the early 1980s has focused on children's pain (Jeans, 1983; McGrath & Hillier, 1996). Prior to that time, some practitioners believed that babies feel relatively little pain because their nervous systems are immaturely developed and their reactions to pain often differ from those of older individuals. As a result, minor surgery, such as circumcision, was commonly done on infants with little or no anesthesia. But this situation changed rapidly as a result of new research. Let's see what is known today about pain in children.

PAIN AND CHILDREN'S SENSORY AND COGNITIVE DEVELOPMENT

Although the issue of whether babies are as sensitive as adults to pain is not yet resolved, one thing is clear: newborn babies feel pain. The fact that they typically cry when slapped on the rump if they do not start to breathe after birth certainly suggests that they feel pain. Is clearer evidence available?

Better evidence that young babies perceive pain comes from studies with newborns as they underwent noxious medical procedures, such as when the foot is pierced to draw a blood sample. One of these studies found that babies' reactions to the noxious stimulus included a "pain" facial expression: they had their eyes squeezed, brows contracted, tongue taut, and mouth open (Grunau & Craig, 1987). This pattern is comparable to the expression adults display when in pain. Another study found that the pattern of newborns' crying varied with the intensity of the noxious procedure they experienced (Porter, Miller, & Marshall, 1986). Highly noxious procedures elicited cries with certain characteristics, such as relatively high-pitched peak tones, that adults judged as indicating "urgency."

One difficulty young children have in expressing their experience of pain is that their language abilities are very limited. Toddlers may know the word "hurt," but they do not usually have many other words to describe their pain (McGrath & Hillier, 1996; Mills, 1989). Instead of telling adults of their pain, they may display other pain behaviors, such as crying, rubbing the affected area, or clenching their jaws. Mary Ellen Jeans (1983) interviewed 5- to 13-year-old children to determine their knowledge about pain. When asked to describe pain, the 5-year-olds used only an average of 5 different adjectives in their descriptions. But the children's use of different adjectives increased with age, with the 13-year-olds using an average of 26. The strategies the children gave for coping with pain also changed as they got older. Children under age 10 reported physical strategies, such as rubbing the painful area, almost exclusively. In contrast, the 13-year-olds cited more varied strategies, and 35% of their descriptions reflected psychological coping strategies, such as distracting their attention.

ASSESSING PAIN IN CHILDREN

When a patient has symptoms that include pain, the physician usually needs to know its location, intensity, quality, duration, and temporal patterning. This

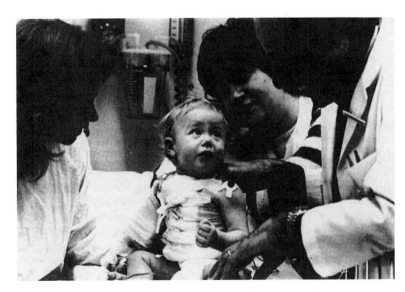

Very young children in acute pain do not have sufficient language to express what they are feeling and need special efforts to reduce their distress.

information helps in making an accurate diagnosis. Although children's ability to provide this information is limited, especially if they are young, researchers have developed measures that use self-report, behavioral, and physiological methods (Bush & DeLuca, in press; McGrath & Hillier, 1996). Effectively interviewing children requires considerable skill in developing rapport with them, asking the right questions in ways they can understand, and knowing what their answers mean.

What kinds of self-report methods are available to assess children's pain? One approach uses rating scales to describe the intensity of their pain (McGrath & Hillier, 1996). Children as young as 5 years of age can understand and use visual analog scales correctly and reliably. They can also use verbal rating scales if the choices are labeled in ways they can understand, such as with faces indicating graded degrees of distress. Other approaches are designed to measure multiple dimensions of child and adolescent pain experiences (Bush & DeLuca, in press). Two of these questionnaires that are commonly used are the Pediatric Pain Questionnaire (Varni & Thompson, 1986) and the Children's Comprehensive Pain Questionnaire (McGrath & Hillier, 1996). These instruments assess the pain itself and its psychosocial effects, such as how the child and family reacted to the pain. Adults may help the children fill out portions of the questionnaires when they lack needed language skills.

Behavioral and physiological assessment approaches also provide valuable ways to measure children's pain, especially in early childhood (Bush & DeLuca, in press; McGrath & Hillier, 1996. The most obvious behavioral approach simply involves having the child or parents report the child's pain behaviors in pain diaries. Other behavioral assessments can use structured clinical sessions in which health care workers rate or record the occurrence of pain behavior. Methods for physiological assessment are like those we considered earlier.

Children's pain experiences are affected by a variety of psychosocial factors, particularly the social environment in which pain occurs (Bush & DeLuca, in press). Parents serve as models and agents of reinforcement for the pain behavior of their children. But little is known about the personality and family characteristics of children that may contribute to the intensity and frequency of their pain. Most studies on pain have focused on adult subjects, not on children, and the studies conducted with children have generally produced unclear results because they were often poorly designed and carried out (Jeans, 1983; Lavigne, Schulein, & Hahn, 1986). Now that researchers have methods to assess children's pain, they can do the kind of high-quality research that is needed.

SUMMARY

Although pain is typically unpleasant, it is a critical sense for survival because it warns us of actual or threatened tissue damage. It is the most frequent medical complaint of patients and the most commonly stated reason for disability. Pain includes both sensory and emotional components, and it has many different qualities. Sometimes it feels sharp and localized, other times it's dull and pervasive, sometimes it has a burning sensation, and other times it has a cramping or aching feeling.

Pain experiences also vary along a continuum, ranging from those that are mostly organic in origin to those that are mostly psychogenic. Virtually all pain experiences involve an interplay of both physiological and psychological processes, but the mixture of organic and psychogenic factors varies. Most painful experiences involve acute pain, which eventually disappears. They may last just a moment or as long as a few months, as with a very serious burn. Other pain conditions last for more than a few months, and are described as chronic. Long-lasting pain can be classified as chronic-recurrent, chronic-intractable-benign, and chronic-progressive pain.

The body's tissues contain algogenic substances that are released at the site where an injury occurs, thereby activating nociceptors, which are afferent free nerve endings. Pain signals are carried toward the central nervous system by two types of afferent peripheral fibers: (1) A-delta fibers carry signals of sharp and well-localized pain rapidly through the thalamus to motor and sensory areas of the cortex. These signals probably receive special attention in our sensory awareness, permitting a quick response. (2) C fibers carry information about dull and diffuse pain. These signals travel relatively slowly and terminate mainly in the brainstem and lower portions of the forebrain.

The process of pain perception involves three curious and fascinating phenomena. The first is called referred pain, whereby pain originating from internal organs is perceived as coming from other parts of the body. The second involves pain with no detectable physical basis. Neuralgia, causalgia, and phantom limb pain are syndromes that involve intense pain even though no noxious stimulus is present. Third, the meaning of pain affects people's experience of it. Individuals for whom pain means a personal disaster is almost over and better things are coming seem to perceive less pain than do people with similar wounds who believe the personal disaster is just beginning.

The gate-control theory of pain proposes that neural signals of pain pass through a gate that can modulate the signals before they reach the brain. The degree to which the gate is open or closed depends on three factors: the amount of activity in the pain fibers, the amount of activity in other peripheral fibers, and messages that descend from the brain. This theory allows for the influence of psychological factors in pain perception. The phenomenon of stimulation-produced analgesia supports this theory, demonstrating that stimulation to the periaqueductal gray area of the brainstem can block the sensation of noxious stimulation elsewhere in the body. The findings of research with a drug called naloxone indicate that this phenomenon depends on the action of endogenous opioids—a class of neurochemicals that includes endor-

phin and enkephalin. The effect of placebos in reducing pain also depends on opioids.

Psychological processes play an important role in the experience of pain. People in pain generally display pain behaviors, such as moaning, guarded movement, or avoidance of activity. These behaviors are often reinforced—for instance, when they result in the person being relieved of doing disliked activities or receiving special attention, care, and affection. Pain and stress are intimately linked: pain is stressful, and stress can produce pain—at least headache pain. People often have difficult times coping with chronic pain, which can lead to psychological maladjustment.

A person's pain can be assessed in several ways. Self-report methods include interviews, rating scales, and pain questionnaires. The McGill Pain Questionnaire assesses three dimensions of pain: affective, sensory, and evaluative. Behavioral assessment approaches can measure pain in the person's everyday activities and in structured clinical sessions. Psychophysiological measures of pain assess muscle tension, autonomic activity, and evoked potentials of the brain. Children can perceive pain when they are born. Methods to assess pain and its psychosocial effects in children have been developed, but methods that require strong language skills may be difficult to use because of children's limited language development.

KEY TERMS

pain	chronic-progressive pain	gate-control theory	endogenous opioids
acute pain	algogenic substances	periaqueductal gray	pain behaviors
chronic-recurrent pain	nociceptors	stimulation-produced	McGill Pain Questionnaire
chronic-intractable-benign pain	referred pain	analgesia	

12

MANAGING AND CONTROLLING CLINICAL PAIN

"Ouch! My foot hurts," the little girl cried as she tried to walk. The nurse responded quickly, saying, "I'm sorry it hurts. Show me where it hurts. . . . Let's get some exercise some other time." This 3-year-old girl was a patient who had had a difficult life. She was in her tenth month of hospitalization after receiving second- and third-degree burns to her legs and buttocks from having been immersed in scaldingly hot water. There was some evidence that the burn had been deliberately inflicted, and that she was a victim of child abuse.

After all these months this little girl's discomfort was not over. She still needed physical therapy and operations for plastic surgery, and she still had to wear uncomfortable knee-extension splints to prevent contractures. But her therapy was not going well. What had become clear was that the hospital staff was inadvertently reinforcing her pain behavior by comforting her and allowing her to avoid disliked activities. James Varni and Karen Thompson have described how this situation was not in the child's long-term best interests, having disrupted her physical, social, and emotional rehabilitation:

> Physical therapy was essentially terminated because of the patient's interfering pain behaviors. Two patterns emerged when the patient was placed in her bedroom in the crib with knee extension splints on. First, the child would struggle until she had removed the splints, resulting in further contractures and the need for additional plastic surgery. Second, if she failed to remove the splints, her crying would intensify to the point of screaming. At times she would fall asleep, exhausted, and continue sobbing well into the naptime hour. Other times, she would continue screaming until, in consideration of the other children, the nursing staff would remove her to a separate room for the reminder of the hour. (1986, p. 382)

Her rehabilitation and interactions with adults and other children were being limited because of her behavior, and she was clearly not coping well with her situation.

What can be done to help patients who, like this girl, have developed chronic pain behaviors that interfere with their rehabilitation? We will examine in this chapter how she was helped and what methods are effective in reversing chronic pain behaviors. We will also discuss a variety of techniques and programs for treating and helping patients control the pain experience. As we study these issues, we will try to answer other questions you may have about dealing with pain. Do effective treatments for acute pain also work with chronic pain? What role do drugs have in treating pain, and how can patients decrease drug use? Do such methods as hypnosis and acupuncture really work in reducing pain? What are pain clinics, and are they effective in treating pain?

CLINICAL PAIN

Not all of our pain experiences receive professional treatment, and not all of them require it. The term **clinical pain** refers to any pain that receives or requires professional treatment. The pain may be either acute or chronic and may result from known or unknown causes (Sanders, 1985). Clinical pain calls for treatment in and of itself, and not only because it may be a symptom of a progressive disease, such as arthritis or cancer. Relieving pain is important for humanitarian reasons, of course—and doing so also produces medical and psychosocial benefits for the patient (Chapman, 1984). Let's look at medical and psychosocial issues that are associated with controlling clinical pain, beginning with acute pain.

ACUTE CLINICAL PAIN

By using techniques to prevent or relieve acute pain, practitioners make medical procedures go more smoothly, reduce patients' stress and anxiety, and help them recover more quickly. Much of the acute pain people experience in today's world has little survival value (Chapman, 1984). What survival value would there be in feeling the pain as a dentist drills a tooth or a surgeon removes an appendix? How would people's survival be enhanced by feeling the intense pain that accompanies normal healing while resting in a hospital during the days after surgery?

When competent medical care is available, these pains are not useful. Yet during recovery after surgery in the United States, at least half of patients experience higher-than-necessary pain (Chapman, 1984; Williams, 1996). The level of pain varies, depending on the type of surgery involved and a variety of psychosocial factors, such as the patients' past medical experiences, anxiety prior to the operations, and knowledge about the sensations they can expect. Inadequately reduced postoperative pain can cause abnormal physiological reactions that can lead to medical complications and even death. For instance, inadequately relieved pain and muscle spasms that may arise from abdominal and chest surgery can prevent patients from breathing deeply and coughing, thereby allowing bacterial infections to take hold in the lungs and cause pneumonia (Chapman, 1984).

CHRONIC CLINICAL PAIN

When pain persists and becomes chronic, patients begin to perceive its nature differently. Although in the acute phase the pain was very aversive, they expected it to end and did not see it as a permanent part of their lives. As the pain persists, they tend to become discouraged and angry and are likely to seek the opinions of many other physicians. This can be constructive. But when this is not successful, and as patients come to see less and less connection between their discomfort and any known or treatable disorder, increasing hopelessness and despair may lead them to resort to consulting quacks (Chapman, 1984).

The transition from acute to chronic pain is a critical time when many of these patients develop feelings of helplessness and psychological disorders, such as depression, especially if the pain is disabling (Epping-Jordan et al., 1998; Gatchel, 1996). The neurotic triad—hypochondriasis, depression, and hysteria—often becomes a dominant aspect of their personalities (Gatchel, 1996; Rosen, Grubman, Bevins, & Frymoyer, 1987). These changes typically parallel alterations in the patients' lifestyles, employment status, and family lives—as the following letter from a wife to her husband's therapist reflects:

> perhaps if I could explain my husband's attitudes it might help you understand his problems.... The questionnaire you gave him to complete and send back became a tremendous ordeal for him. Why, I'll never know, because the questions were simple, but in the state of mind he is in, everything gets to be a chore.... Since his back operation five years ago he has become increasingly impatient and progressively slower with no ambition at all to even try to help himself. He had made himself an invalid and it has become very difficult for me or my family to tolerate his constant complaining. He blames me, blames our two sons, who he says don't help him around the house when in fact he does little or nothing to help himself. He does exactly the same things day after day with projects he starts and never completes and always because of his health.... To dwell on his illness is what he wants and only that he will do, believe me. He needs psychiatry of some kind. (Flor & Turk, 1985, p. 268)...

A study of people who had suffered for years with severe chronic-recurrent and chronic-intractable-benign pain found that about half had considered suicide because of their conditions (Hitchcock, Ferrell, & McCaffery, 1994). Chronic pain often creates a broad array of long-term psychosocial problems and impaired interrelationships, which distinguish its victims from those of acute pain (Weir et al. 1994).

Individuals who receive treatment for their pain after it has progressed and become chronic tend to exhibit certain physical and psychosocial symptoms that characterize a "chronic pain syndrome." According to psychologist Steven Sanders (1985), these symptoms include:

● Associated tissue damage or irritation, which may be minor or major.

● Persistent pain complaints and other pain behaviors, such as grimacing or guarded movement, when in discomfort.

- Disrupted daily activity patterns, characterized either by a general reduction or by recurrent large fluctuations.

- Disrupted social, marital, employment, and recreational activities.

- Excessive use of drugs or repeated use of surgical procedures to relieve pain.

- Disturbed sleep patterns.

- Increased anxiety and depression.

Chronic pain patients usually exhibit the first two symptoms and at least one of the remaining ones. Generally speaking, the more symptoms the patient presents, the greater the impact the pain has had and the greater the maladjustment it has produced.

Because of the differences between acute pain and chronic pain in their duration and the effects they have on their victims, these conditions usually require different treatment methods. Health care professionals need to distinguish between acute and chronic pain conditions and provide the most appropriate pain relief techniques for the patient's needs (Gatchel, 1996). Failing to do so can make the condition worse. Keeping this caution in mind, we will turn our attention for the remainder of this chapter to the many medical, psychological, and physical techniques available to help control patients' pain.

MEDICAL TREATMENTS FOR PAIN

A few centuries ago, peasants in Western cultures commonly treated pain by piercing the affected area of the body with a "vigorous" twig of a tree, believing that the twig would absorb the pain from the body (Turk, Meichenbaum, & Genest, 1983). Then, to prevent anyone from getting the pain from that twig, they buried it deep in the ground. Other early practices for controlling pain were not so farfetched, but they were crudely applied, even by physicians. In 19th-century America, alcoholic beverages and "medicines" laced with opium were readily available (Critchlow, 1986; Kett, 1977). Many people used these substances to alleviate pain, and physicians commonly employed them as anesthetics for surgery before the mid-1800s, when ether was introduced. Today when patients suffer from pain, physicians try to reduce the discomfort in two ways—chemically and surgically.

Readily available elixirs in 19th-century America often contained such substances as opium and cocaine.

SURGICAL METHODS FOR TREATING PAIN

Treating chronic pain with surgical methods is a relatively radical approach, and some surgical procedures are more useful than others. In some procedures, the surgery removes or disconnects portions of the peripheral nervous system or the spinal cord, thereby preventing pain signals from reaching the brain. These are extreme procedures—and if they are successful, they produce numbness and, sometimes, paralysis in the region of the body served by the affected nerves. But these procedures seldom provide long-term relief from the pain, which is often replaced after some days or months by pain and other sensations that are worse than the original condition (Hare & Milano, 1985; Melzack & Wall, 1982). Because of the poor prospects of permanent relief and the risks involved in these surgical procedures, they are rarely used today.

Other surgical procedures for relieving pain do not remove or disconnect nerve fibers and are much more successful. One example is the *synovectomy*, a technique whereby a surgeon removes membranes that become inflamed in arthritic joints (AMA, 1989; Anderson et al., 1985). Another example is *spinal fusion*, a procedure that joins two or more adjacent vertebrae to treat severe back pain (AMA, 1989). Surgery procedures are commonly used in the United States to treat back pain, but there is little evidence that they produce better long-term pain reduction than nonsurgical methods, and they are used at a far lower rate in other developed countries, such as Denmark and England (Cherkin et al., 1994; Volinn, Turczyn, & Loeser, 1994). Surgery for chronic skeletal pain conditions is most appropriate when the person is severely disabled and nonsurgical treatment methods have failed. Physicians and patients usually prefer other medical approaches, such as chemical methods.

CHEMICAL METHODS FOR TREATING PAIN

Although medical research has led to many advances in treating pain since the 1800s, this progress has been slow. The field of medicine has been much more concerned with developing methods for curing disease than with reducing pain (Melzack & Wall, 1982). In the early 1990s, the United States Agency for Health Care Policy and Research recommended that medical practitioners (1) have patients rate their pain periodically on a scale and (2) keep patients as pain-free as possible, using drugs, relaxation methods, and other approaches (Leary, 1992). Doing so leads to faster recovery. Let's look at the use of chemical methods for treating acute and chronic pain. (Go to 💡.)

Using Chemicals for Acute Pain

Many pharmaceuticals are very effective for relieving acute pain, such as after surgery. Physicians choose the specific drug and dosage by considering many factors, such as how intense the pain is and its location and cause. Do practitioners use these chemicals effectively, giving as much pain relief as they safely can? The degree to which they do depends on characteristics of the drug, the patients, and sociocultural factors. In some countries, such as in Latin America, using narcotics for pain relief is extremely rare (DePalma, 1996). Other cultures have become much more accepting of narcotic pain control.

About half of American hospital patients in pain are *undermedicated*, and those who receive too little pain relief tend to be children and minority group members, even when compared against other patients with the same medical condition (Bush & DeLuca, in press; Cleeland et al., 1994; Ng, Dimsdale, Shragg, & Deutsch, 1996). For instance, when the patient is a child, practitioners tend to administer

painkillers less frequently, give doses below the recommended level, and discontinue it earlier, especially if the drug is a narcotic. The reasons for these age and sociocultural differences are unclear. In the case of children, it may be that practitioners believe children feel less pain than adults or are more likely to become addicted to a drug (Bush, Holmbeck, & Cockrell, 1989). Or children may simply request less medication, perhaps because they dislike injections or taking pills more than adults do. Similar reasons may explain the ethnic differences.

The conventional ways for administering painkilling chemicals involve giving injections or pills, and these are given under one of two arrangements: a prescribed schedule or "as needed" (called PRN for the Latin *pro re nata*) by the patient. But two other methods are available today (Chapman, 1984; Zeltzer, Bush, Chen, & Riveral, 1997). In one of these methods—called an *epidural block*—practitioners inject narcotics or local anesthetics epidurally, that is, near the membrane that surrounds the spinal cord. These chemicals then prevent pain signals from being transmitted to the brain. The second technique is called *patient-controlled analgesia*. This procedure allows the patient to determine how much painkiller, such as morphine, he or she needs, and get it without delay. The patient simply pushes a button to activate a computerized pump that dispenses a preset dose of the chemical through a needle that remains inserted continuously. Practitioners monitor the patient's use of the drug and set limits on the rate and amount of its use.

Do patients abuse the opportunity to control their use of narcotics for pain control? Current evidence suggests that the risk of abuse is low for most patients, at least under certain circumstances. A study by Marc Citron and his colleagues (1986) examined this issue with hospitalized men with severe cancer pain. They were placed on a patient-controlled analgesia procedure for a little over 2 days, on average. A physician preset for each patient the dosage of morphine the pump would deliver and a lockout time, that is, the interval after a dose when no more morphine would be available. The average lockout time was about 30 minutes. The results revealed that the patients' rate of morphine use *declined* over time rather than increased, being used far more heavily in the first few hours than it was later. During the first 4 hours, the subjects took about one dose per hour, on average, consuming morphine at a rate of 4 milligrams

Highlight on Issues
Types of Pain-Relieving Chemicals

The most common medical approaches for treating pain today involve the use of various chemicals, some of which are used mainly in hospitals. Four types of chemicals are commonly used in treating pain (Winters, 1985; Zeltzer, Bush, Chen, & Riveral, 1997).

1. *Peripherally active analgesics* make up one type of pain-relieving chemical. As the name implies, these drugs reduce pain by their action in the peripheral nervous system, such as by inhibiting the synthesis of neurochemicals that sensitize nociceptors to algogenic substances released at the site of tissue damage. These analgesics include *aspirin*, *acetaminophen* (brand names Tylenol and Datril), and *ibuprofen* (Advil and Motrin). Aspirin was first manufactured in the late 1800s and is by far the best-known and most widely used drug in this class; Americans take many billions each year. Aspirin is a remarkable drug, being a very effective analgesic for mild-to-moderate pain, while also reducing fever and inflammation. Using aspirin on an occasional basis has no adverse effects, but heavy use can irritate the stomach lining. Peripherally acting analgesics provide substantial pain relief for many pain conditions, especially arthritis and other conditions that involve inflammation.

2. *Centrally acting analgesics* are narcotics (opioids) that bind to opiate receptors in the central nervous system and inhibit nociceptor transmission or alter the perception of pain stimuli. These drugs are derived either directly from the opium poppy—as are codeine and morphine—or synthetically, such as heroin, methadone, and the brand name drugs Percodan and Demerol. Narcotics are highly effective in reducing severe pain, and they are far more potent and fast-acting when administered by injection than orally. The chief reservation physicians and patients have in using narcotics for pain relief is the potential these drugs have for producing tolerance, in which the individual requires increasingly large doses, and for causing addiction. But narcotics can be used for acute pain without this concern because these effects are not likely to develop until several days of use. If physical dependence develops with long-term use, methadone can be used to wean the person off of the narcotic.

3. *Local anesthetics*, such as novocaine, lidocaine, and bupivacaine, make up the third category of chemicals for relieving pain. Although local anesthetics can be applied topically, they are much more potent when injected at the site where the pain originates, as a dentist does before drilling or pulling a tooth. These chemicals work by blocking nerve cells in the region from generating impulses—and they often continue to relieve pain for hours or days after the chemical action has worn off (Hare & Milano, 1985). Long-term use of currently available local anesthetics is not recommended because of their serious side effects (Melzack & Wall, 1982).

4. *Indirectly acting drugs* affect nonpain conditions, such as emotions, that produce or contribute to pain. These drugs include sedatives, tranquilizers, and antidepressants. *Sedatives*, such as barbiturates, and *tranquilizers*, such as diazepam (Valium), are depressants—they depress bodily functions by decreasing the transmission of impulses throughout the central nervous system. Although depressants reduce anxiety and help patients sleep, they do not relieve pain and can produce psychological and physical dependence with long-term use. Drugs classed as *antidepressants* reduce psychological depression and appear to increase the effects of analgesics in relieving pain.

an hour. But their use dropped sharply after the initial high use—for the remainder of the 2 days, their rate of morphine use was less than 40% of the earlier-rate. These patients were free to take much more medication, but they did not. Similar results have been found with male and female adolescent patients following surgery (Tyler, 1990). But there is a caution in using patient-controlled analgesia with patients who are relatively young, have high levels of anxiety, or have low levels of social support. They tend to use more of the drug than other acute pain patients do (Gil et al., 1990).

Using Chemicals for Chronic Pain

When a patient is dying, practitioners generally view options for pain relief differently from those when a person has chronic pain from a nonterminal illness. Many health care practitioners have long advocated using narcotics for the relief of severe pain in cancer patients, and narcotic analgesics are commonly prescribed when these patients are dying (Foley, 1985). In some cases of cancer, severe pain becomes chronic as the disease progresses. Despite guidelines to treat clinical pain more aggressively, a large percentage of American cancer patients receive inadequate analgesic drugs (Cleeland et al., 1994). Why? Part of the reason is that cancer patients—especially older, less educated ones—often fear they will become addicted if the drug is a narcotic and believe that "good" patients don't complain (Ward et al., 1993). Practitioners need to discuss these issues with their patients and correct misconceptions.

Should narcotics be used in treating chronic non-cancer pain? Research has shown that narcotics are effective in treating a variety of chronic pain conditions (Jadad et al., 1992). For example, researchers tested the utility of drug therapy, combining methadone and an antidepressant, over a 2-year period for men and women patients with severe phantom limb pain (Urban et al., 1986). The subjects reported having had the pain syndrome for an average of 5 years, being in pain almost constantly, having limited their lifestyles because of it, and having used a wide variety of treatments for pain relief in the past, including narcotics. They began the drug therapy as hospital inpatients, reported at discharge that their pain had been reduced by about two thirds, and maintained this level of pain reduction throughout the next 2 years with very low daily doses of each drug.

These findings are very important and indicate that narcotics in low doses can provide effective pain relief without requiring progressively larger doses or leading to addiction. Because of a growing body of similar findings, American practitioners are using narcotics more than in the past for patients who are severely disabled by their chronic pain conditions, such as rheumatoid arthritis and severe back injury (Hoffman, 1993; Turk, Brody, & Okifuji, 1994). But increases in using narcotics for chronic pain are occurring cautiously for at least three reasons. First, the findings we have described need to be confirmed with a greater variety of subjects and types of pain conditions. Despite the low risk that drug abuse appears to have for most pain patients, it probably poses a high risk for *some* patients. Second, studies need to determine specifically how taking daily doses of narcotics alters patients' lives and functioning. Third, researchers need to find out why tolerance and addiction to narcotics are less likely when they are taken for pain relief. Is it because the doses are so small, for instance, or that the practitioners monitor and set limits on the drug use? Or is it that the patients believe they may lose their painkillers if they use them too much?

Although future research findings may lead to a wider application of narcotics for pain sufferers—particularly some who suffer disabling chronic-intractable-benign pain—it seems unlikely that these drugs will prove to be a valuable component of treatment for the vast majority of chronic pain patients. And even though the widely used nonnarcotic chemicals we described earlier can help in relieving chronic pain, health professionals often prefer not to rely on them for long-term pain control for two reasons. First, drugs often have undesirable side effects and can lead to psychological and, sometimes, physical dependence. Second, chemical methods are usually not sufficient for controlling pain by themselves. Other approaches are also needed—as physician Ronald Kanner has noted, "There is no *single* answer to pain" (1986, p. 2113).

The need for other approaches in helping pain patients can be seen in the findings of research on three issues. First, studies of coping patterns have found that chronic headache patients tend to use maladaptive ways of coping with everyday stressors more than do nonheadache control subjects (Mosley et al., 1990). Second, arthritis patients with high feelings of helplessness before drug treatment begins report poorer treatment success in reducing pain and disability than do comparable low-helplessness patients (Nicassio et al., 1993). Third, *placebo* drugs seem to affect patients' reports of pain. Research has investigated the effectiveness of various drugs—analgesics, tranquilizers, and chemicals that constrict blood vessels—in treating migraine and muscle contraction headache, using double-blind procedures and giving some subjects placebos (Andrasik, Blake, & McCarran, 1986; Feuerstein & Gainer, 1982). These studies have shown that although many headache patients claim to experience substantial relief when taking one drug or another, so do many who take the placebo. Because placebo effects result from psychological processes, we might expect that treatments using psychological methods might also relieve pain. As we saw in Chapter 11 when considering the gate-control theory of pain, separating physiological and psychosocial aspects of a person's pain experience is artificial.

Because psychosocial factors are so important in people's experience of chronic pain, many medical practitioners treat pain patients by joining forces with psychologists and other health care professionals, such as social workers and physical and occupational therapists. When introducing a team approach to chronic pain patients, physicians need to describe the rationale for it and the functions each professional can provide. As psychologists Roy Cameron and Larry Shepel have noted, for instance,

> pain patients might balk at the suggestion that they see a psychologist. They typically believe, generally quite correctly, that their problems have a physical basis. Hence, the relevance of a psychological consultation may not be evident to the patient. The meaning of the referral also may be unclear. The patient may infer that the physician making the referral believes the problem to be somehow less than real, or believes the patient to be seriously maladjusted psychologically. Patients who interpret the referral this way are likely to be guarded with the psychologist. (1986, p. 242)

The physician should state clearly that (1) he or she realizes the patient is "obviously living in a great deal of pain," (2) patients can help themselves control their pain by working with these other professionals, and (3) the physician will be an active part of the team.

To summarize, medical treatments of pain focus mainly on using chemical approaches to reduce discomfort. For chronic pain patients, these approaches can be enhanced when combined with pain control methods that other health care professions provide. Physicians usually want to minimize the use of medication by their patients, especially when drugs would be taken on a long-term basis. Reducing the patient's drug consumption is one of the goals in using other methods of pain control with pain patients.

BEHAVIORAL AND COGNITIVE METHODS FOR TREATING PAIN

Gate-control theory changed the way many health care workers conceptualize pain by proposing that pain can be controlled not only by biochemical methods that alter sensory input directly, but by modifying motivational and cognitive processes, too. This more complex view of pain provided the rationale for psychologists to develop techniques to help patients (1) *cope more effectively* with the pain and other stressors they experience and (2) *reduce their reliance on drugs* for pain control. Some approaches psychologists developed involve behavioral and cognitive methods, and we will examine three of these approaches in this section. The first approach focuses on changing patients' pain behavior through techniques of operant conditioning.

THE OPERANT APPROACH

At the start of this chapter, we considered the case of a 3-year-old girl whose pain behaviors hampered her rehabilitation after she suffered severe burns months earlier. The help therapists provided was successful. It used an *operant approach*, in which therapists apply operant conditioning techniques to modify patients' behavior.

The approach the therapists used in changing this girl's behavior involved extinction procedures for her pain behavior and reinforcement for appropriate, or "well," behavior (Varni, Jay, Masek, & Thompson, 1986; Varni & Thompson, 1986). Observations of the child's social environment revealed that the hospital staff reinforced her pain behaviors—crying, complaining of pain, resisting the nurse's efforts to put her splints on, and so forth—by giving attention to those behaviors and allowing her to avoid uncomfortable or disliked activities, such as physical therapy. To change this situation, the therapists instructed the hospital staff to:

● Ignore the pain behaviors they paid attention to in the past.

● Provide rewards for compliant behavior—telling her, for instance, "If you don't cry while I put your splints on, you can have some cookies when I'm finished," or, "If you do this exercise, we can play a game."

● Praise her if she helps in putting on the splints, sleeps through naptime, goes for a period of time without complaining, or does an exercise.

Changing the consequences of her behavior in these ways had a dramatic effect: her pain behaviors decreased sharply, and she began to comply with requests to do exercises, make positive comments about her accomplishments, and assist in putting on her splints.

The operant approach to treating pain can be adapted for use with individuals of all ages, in hospitals and at home—and elements of the operant approach can be introduced before pain behavior becomes chronic. But treatment programs using this approach are usually applied with patients whose chronic pain has already produced serious difficulties in their lives. These programs typically have two main goals: the first is to reduce the patient's reliance on medication. This can be achieved with the patient's approval, using a technique described by Wilbert Fordyce (1976). One feature of this technique is that the medication is given on a fixed schedule, such as every 4 hours, rather than whenever the patient requests it. This makes receiving the painkiller independent of requesting it, thereby eliminating any reinforcing effect the drug may have on that pain behavior. In addition, the medication is mixed with flavored syrup to mask its taste. Then, over a period of several weeks, the dosage of medication in this "pain cocktail" is gradually reduced until the syrup contains little or no drugs.

The second goal of the operant approach is to reduce the disability that generally accompanies chronic pain conditions. This is accomplished by altering the consequences for behavior so that they promote "well" behavior and discourage pain behavior, as we just saw in the program with the young burn

patient. The chief feature of this approach is that the therapist trains people in the patient's social environment to monitor and keep a record of pain behaviors, try not to reinforce them, and systematically reward physical activity. The reinforcers may be of any kind—attention, praise and smiles, candy, money, or the opportunity to watch TV, for example—and may be formalized within a behavioral contract (Fordyce, 1976; Roberts, 1986). The therapist periodically reviews the record of pain behavior to determine whether changes in the program are needed.

Is the operant approach effective? Studies have shown that operant techniques can successfully decrease patients' pain reports and medication use and increase their activity levels (Morley, Eccleston, & Williams, 1999; Roberts, 1986; Turk, Rudy, & Sorkin, 1992). Although these findings are promising, some limitations should be mentioned. First, after the operant intervention ends and rewards are discontinued, some patients revert to their old pattern of inactivity and pain behavior. Second, not all chronic pain patients are likely to benefit from the operant approach. For one thing, the goals of this approach seem more appropriate for patients with chronic-recurrent or chronic-intractable-benign pain than for those with chronic-progressive pain, such as in cancer patients. Also, patients are less likely to show behavioral improvements if they or people in their social environment are unwilling to participate and if they receive disability compensation (Fordyce, 1976). Despite these limitations, it seems clear that the operant approach can be a very useful component in treatment programs for many acute and chronic pain patients.

RELAXATION AND BIOFEEDBACK

Many people experience chronic episodes of pain that result from underlying physiological processes, and these processes are often triggered by stress. If these patients could control their stress or the physiological processes that cause pain, they should be able to decrease the frequency or intensity of discomfort they experience. Headache provides a good example of the way stress and physiological arousal may influence pain. The classic view of how headaches occur is that migraine headaches result from the dilation of arteries surrounding the brain, and tension headaches result from persistent contraction of muscles of the scalp, neck, and shoulders

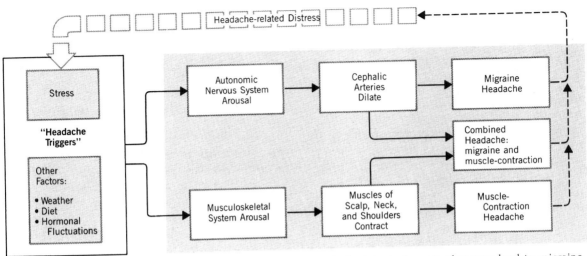

Figure 12–1 "Headache triggers" (stress and other factors) and physiological events that may lead to migraine, muscle-contraction (tension-type), and combined headache. (Adapted from Andrasik, 1986, Figure 13.1.)

(AMA, 1989). Other theories of headache have focused on events occurring in the brain, but studies of migraine and tension headache sufferers have found evidence supporting the classic view (Lipchik et al., 1996; McGrady, Wauquier, McNeil, & Gerard, 1994). Figure 12–1 diagrams how stress may be involved in the classic model. If stress causes arteries surrounding the brain to dilate, migraine headaches develop; but if stress causes muscles of the scalp, neck, and shoulders to contract, tension-type (muscle-contraction) headaches result.

Because of the connection of stress and physiological processes in producing pain, therapists have applied the methods of progressive muscle relaxation and biofeedback in helping people control their pain. These treatments are usually conducted in weekly sessions that span about 2 or 3 months (see, for example, Blanchard et al., 1986). We saw in Chapter 5 that individuals using the technique of *progressive muscle relaxation* focus their attention on specific muscle groups while alternately tightening and relaxing these muscles. People who receive training in relaxation to control pain are urged to use this technique to reduce feelings of stress, particularly if they feel pain episodes coming on. Figure 12–1 shows why reducing stress might be effective in controlling headache pain.

In *biofeedback* procedures, people learn to exert voluntary control over a bodily function, such as heart rate, by monitoring its status with information from electronic devices (Sarafino, 2001). Of the many physi-

ological processes people can learn to control through biofeedback, two have received particular attention in the treatment of pain. One of these processes is muscle activity and is used to treat tension-type (muscle-contraction) headaches. Patients learn to control the tension of specific muscle groups—such as those in the forehead or neck—by receiving biofeedback from an electromyograph (EMG) device, which measures electrical activity in those muscles. The other process is used for migraine headaches by focusing on the constriction and dilation of arteries—such as in the head or fingers—which can be measured indirectly on the basis of the temperature of the skin in that body area. Patients learn to control arterial dilation through temperature biofeedback—as the arteries dilate and contain more blood, the region becomes warmer. Therapists urge patients who learn to control muscle tension or arterial dilation to practice this skill at home and use it when they feel pain episodes beginning—doing so greatly improves treatment success (Gauthier, Côté, & French, 1994). Figure 12–1 shows why using one or the other of these biofeedback skills might reduce headache pain.

Do progressive muscle relaxation and biofeedback procedures help in relieving pain? Yes, they do. This broad conclusion comes from reviews and meta-analyses of studies that examined the effectiveness of these procedures (Andrasik, Blake, & McCarran, 1986; Blanchard, 1987; Bogaards & ter Kuile, 1994;

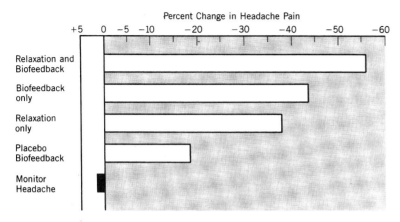

Figure 12–2 Percentage of change in headache pain, pretreatment to posttreatment, across many studies with patients suffering from chronic *muscle-contraction* (tension-type) headaches. Treatments consisted of EMG biofeedback, or relaxation, or EMG biofeedback and relaxation combined. Control conditions consisted of placebo biofeedback or simply monitoring headache pain. (Data from Holroyd & Penzien, 1985, Table IV.)

Chapman, 1991; Holroyd & Penzien, 1985; Morley, Eccleston, & Williams, 1999; Sarafino & Goehring, 2000). But several points need to be made to clarify this conclusion. First, although studies have demonstrated that relaxation and biofeedback treatments can help alleviate many types of pain, such as arthritic, phantom limb, and low back pain, the large majority of studies testing these treatments have focused on headache pain. For migraine headache, treatment combining relaxation and biofeedback is as effective as treatment with a drug that prevents arterial dilation, and using all three components is even more successful (Holroyd et al., 1995; Holroyd & Penzien, 1990).

Second, progressive muscle relaxation and biofeedback treatments are about equally effective in relieving headache pain—relaxation is somewhat more effective with migraine headache, and biofeedback is somewhat more effective with tension-type (muscle-contraction) headache (Andrasik, Blake, & McCarran, 1986; Holroyd & Penzien, 1985). Studies have examined the success of these procedures by assessing whether the patients' daily records at the end of treatment showed decreases in the headache pain (its frequency, intensity, and duration) and by comparing the headache pain of patients who received these treatments with those who were in control groups. In one type of control group, the subjects receive no training but monitor their headache pain with daily records. In another type of control condition, subjects keep records and receive a placebo treatment, such as by taking sham medication or by receiving biofeedback sessions that give false feedback about changes in the subjects' bodily functions.

Generally speaking, treatment with relaxation or biofeedback is about twice as effective in relieving pain as placebo conditions, which are more effective than just monitoring headache pain. Figure 12–2 depicts these effects for tension-type (muscle-contraction) headache sufferers, averaged across subjects in many studies.

Third, the graph in Figure 12–2 suggests that tension-type headache sufferers get slightly more pain relief with biofeedback than with progressive muscle relaxation treatment, and that they seem to gain even more relief when these treatments are combined. This may be the case and may be important for clinical purposes, but these differences are not reliable because patients vary greatly in the amount of benefit they get from these treatments. For instance, among subjects who received relaxation treatment only, the percentage by which their pain improved ranged from 17 to 94%; among those who had the combined treatment, improvements ranged from 29 to 88% (Holroyd & Penzien, 1985). This variability is important: it reflects that many patients—especially middle-aged and elderly ones—seem to gain relatively little relief with these treatments (Blanchard & Andrasik, 1985; Holroyd & Penzien, 1985). Since biofeedback treatment is relatively expensive to conduct, being able to predict who will benefit from it most would be useful. Some evidence suggests, for example, that most children and those individuals of all ages who show certain psychophysiological patterns, such as a high correlation between their pain and EMG levels, may be better candidates for biofeedback treatment than other people (Keefe & Gil, 1985; Sarafino & Goehring, 2000).

Fourth, although the pain relief patients experience with progressive muscle relaxation or biofeedback treatment may result from the specific skills they have learned for controlling physiological processes, other psychological factors also seem to play a role. Consider, for instance, that placebo conditions often produce more relief than simply monitoring headache pain (Andrasik, 1986). Why is this? Patients' thoughts, beliefs, and spontaneous cognitive strategies probably account for the success of placebo conditions and contribute to part of the success of relaxation and biofeedback treatments in controlling pain (Turk, Meichenbaum, & Genest, 1983).

Progressive muscle relaxation and biofeedback techniques are very helpful in controlling the discomfort many chronic pain patients experience, but these treatments do not provide all the pain relief most patients need. Because chronic pain involves a complex interplay of sensory and psychosocial factors, therapists generally use these techniques along with several other approaches, especially cognitive therapies that address the thought patterns that occur when people experience pain. (Go to 🔖.)

COGNITIVE METHODS

What do people think about when they experience pain? In an acute pain situation, some people focus on the ordeal and how uncomfortable and miserable they are, but others do not (Turk & Rudy, 1986). For example, researchers asked children and adolescents what they think about when getting an injection at their dentist's office (Brown, O'Keeffe, Sanders, & Baker, 1986). Over 80% of the subjects reported thoughts that focused on negative emotions and pain, such as, "This hurts, I hate shots," "I'm scared," and "My heart is pounding and I feel shaky." One-fourth of the subjects had thoughts of escaping or avoiding the situation, as in, "I want to run away." Thoughts like these focus the person's attention on the unpleasant aspects of the experience and make the pain worse (Keefe et al., 1994; Turk & Rudy, 1986).

Not all people who experience acute pain focus on the ordeal and discomfort; many use cognitive strategies to modify their experience. For instance, by 10 years of age, many children report that they try to cope with pain in a dental situation by thinking about something else or by saying to themselves such things as, "It's not so bad," or, "Be brave" (Brown, O'Keeffe, Sanders, & Baker, 1986). But even when children

know ways to cope with pain and recommend them for others to use, they don't necessarily use those skills themselves (Peterson, Crowson, Saldana, & Holdridge, 1999). Although coping skills tend to improve as children get older, many patients in adulthood still exaggerate the fearful aspects of the painful medical procedures they experience (Chaves & Brown, 1987).

How do people cope with chronic pain? Some approaches they use involve *active coping*, in which they try to keep functioning by ignoring their pain or keeping busy with an interesting activity. Other approaches involve *passive coping*, such as taking to bed or curtailing social activities. For many chronic pain patients, a vicious circle develops in which passive coping leads to feelings of helplessness and depression, which leads to more passive coping, and so on (Smith & Wallston, 1992). Family and friends influence people's coping patterns by reinforcing some behaviors, but not others (Menefee, Haythornthwaite, Clark, & Koenig, 1996). The impact of chronic pain also depends on they way patients view their conditions (Jensen et al., 1999; Williams & Keefe, 1991). Those who believe their pain will last a very long time, is a sign of a disabling injury, and has unknown causes tend to show more pain behaviors and cope poorly, thinking the worst about their conditions and feeling that active coping strategies will not work. On the other hand, patients who believe that they understand the nature of their pain and that their conditions will improve tend to use active coping strategies. Those who cope well are more likely to return to work despite their pain (Linton & Buer, 1995).

To help people cope effectively with pain, medical and psychological practitioners need to assess and address their patients' beliefs. Cognitive techniques for treating pain involve active coping strategies, and many of these methods are, in fact, quite effective in helping people cope with pain. These techniques can be classified into three basic types: *distraction*, *imagery*, and *redefinition* (Fernandez, 1986; McCaul & Malott, 1984). We will examine these methods and consider their usefulness for people with acute and chronic pain.

Distraction

At your dentist's office, do the examination rooms have colorful pictures or large windows with nice views on all the walls that a patient can see while in

FOCUS ON RESEARCH

How Durable Are the Effects of Relaxation and Biofeedback Treatments for Pain?

After a patient completes the treatment for chronic pain, how long do the effects of the treatment last? Do the effects wear off in a few weeks or months? This is an issue of great importance in health psychology. As we saw in earlier chapters, psychological interventions do not always last, such as in cases of alcohol abuse, and relapse often occurs. Edward Blanchard, Frank Andrasik, and their associates have addressed this issue by conducting a 5-year follow-up investigation on chronic headache patients who completed training for either progressive muscle relaxation or for both relaxation and biofeedback (Blanchard et al., 1986; Blanchard, Andrasik, et al., 1987; Blanchard, Appelbaum, et al., 1987).

The subjects in this research were adult patients who had suffered an average of 18 years either from muscle-contraction (tension-type) headache or from "vascular" headache, which includes both migraine and combined (migraine plus tension-type) headache. All patients received relaxation training in ten sessions, spanning 8 weeks. Those patients whose headache pain had not improved by at least 60% were offered additional treatment with biofeedback. All subjects had an audiotape to guide their practice of relaxation, and the vascular patients who received training in temperature biofeedback were given a temperature-monitoring device to use at home. The subjects kept daily "headache diaries" with four ratings each day of their headache pain. Psychological assessment before the treatment and again a few months after treatment revealed that the subjects' feeling of depression and anxiety decreased substantially (Blanchard et al., 1986).

Of the subjects who completed the treatment and continued to be available for the study, the researchers attempted to follow only those whose headache pain had been improved by at least 50% at the end of treatment. During the first 6 months after treatment, these 38 subjects continued to keep daily headache diaries, were interviewed by a therapist monthly, and received treatment booster sessions at these interviews if they desired them. Thereafter, each patient who continued in the

study met with a therapist yearly and was paid for participating.

A major difficulty in doing longitudinal research is that the number of original subjects who are available and willing to participate declines over time. At the time of the last annual follow-up, only 21 patients (9 muscle-contraction and 12 vascular) could be located and agreed to participate. To assess the treatment's continued success, the researchers used the ratings these subjects made during each of seven 4-week periods: pretreatment, post treatment, and years 1 through 5 in the follow-up. As Figure 12F–1 shows, the treatment effects were quite durable for the patients who continued in the study.

What about the 17 patients who did not continue through the 5-year follow-up—were their treatments durable? Although there is no way of knowing for sure, there is reason to believe they were (Blanchard, Andrasik, et al., 1987; Blanchard, Appelbaum, et al.,

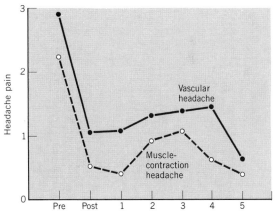

Figure 12F–1 Averaged ratings of headache pain for muscle-contraction (tension-type) and vascular (migraine and combined) headache patients who successfully completed treatment and continued to participate in the follow-up. The graphs depict these ratings at pretreatment, posttreatment, and follow-up years 1 through 5. (Data from Blanchard, Appelbaum, et al., 1987, Table 1.)

1987). Most of these patients simply could not be located, but five were contacted and did not indicate that they were having pain problems when they declined to participate. Moreover, most of those who dropped out during the 5 years had reported very successful pain relief in the last follow-up they had

completed, which suggests that they dropped out for reasons other than a relapse in pain. Findings of several other follow-up studies confirm that completing relaxation training or both relaxation and biofeedback training provides durable headache relief for at least 2 years (Blanchard, 1987).

---

the dental chair? My dentist's rooms do, and I use the pictures and windows to distract my attention when I feel the need. **Distraction** is the technique of focusing on a nonpainful stimulus in the immediate environment to divert one's attention from discomfort (Fernandez, 1986). We can be distracted from pain in many ways, such as by looking at a picture, listening to someone's voice, singing a song, counting ceiling tiles, playing a video game, or doing mathematics problems.

Not all distraction attempts are likely to work in relieving pain. Research on acute pain has shown that these strategies are more effective if the pain is mild or moderate than if it is strong (McCaul & Malott, 1984). Three aspects of the distraction task seem to affect how well it works. One aspect is the amount of attention the task requires. Experiments with college students have used the cold-pressor procedure and varied the amount of attention the distraction task required (Christenfeld, 1997; McCaul, Monson, & Maki, 1992). The distraction tasks were neutral (neither pleasant nor unpleasant) and involved watching and reacting to numbers or colored lights on a panel or screen. High-distraction tasks required frequent or complex reactions to the stimuli. The results indicate that the effect of the amount of attention distraction tasks require depends on *when* the subjects rate the pain. If they rate the pain while the arm is in the cold water or right after removing it, the amount of attention does not influence the ratings. But if ratings of the pain they experienced are taken several minutes later, the ratings are lower if they had a high-distraction task during the pain.

The second factor that seems to affect whether distraction relieves pain is the extent to which the task is interesting or engrossing. Researchers compared the pain and coping behavior of 10-year-old children when receiving immunization injections under three conditions: standard care, application of a local

anesthetic, or distraction (Cohen, Blount et al., 1999). The distraction task was engrossing: it involved watching a movie of the child's choice and answering a nurse's questions, such as "Which one is the good guy?" The children showed less distress and better coping under the distraction condition than under the standard care or anesthetic conditions.

The third factor in whether a distraction technique relieves pain is whether it seems credible to the person. A study demonstrated this by having college students undergo the cold-pressor procedure while listening to distracting stimuli through earphones (Melzack, Weisz, & Sprague, 1963). During the cold-pressor test, the students in one condition listened to a clearly noticeable sound, such as music, after having been told that they could control its volume and that dentists had found that loud sound helps reduce pain. Students in another condition got similar instructions, but they tried to listen for a low-intensity "hum" that really didn't exist. The subjects who heard the noticeable sound kept their hands in the cold water longer than those who listened for the hum.

Why was the nonexistent hum less effective than the sound in helping the subjects tolerate pain? Since there was no sound, the subjects probably didn't believe the technique would work. Because of the role that credibility can play in using distraction methods, therapists may need to help patients understand how these techniques can work. One therapist described the following approach for doing this:

> First, I ask the patient to be aware of the sensations in his thighs as he sits in his chair. I note that those sensations are real, and they have a physical basis, but they are not normally experienced because other things occupy his attention. Then I suggest that he think of a TV set: he could block out the channel 9 signal by tuning in channel 11; the channel 9 signal is still there, but not being tuned in. I suggest that while his pain signals are real, he can

learn to "tune them out."...A number of pain patients have reported that they frequently think of the TV metaphor when experiencing pain and take appropriate action to "tune out." (Cameron, quoted in Turk, Meichenbaum, & Genest, 1983, p. 284)

By providing plausible explanations for a recommended technique, therapists can increase its effectiveness and the likelihood that the patient will use it.

Distraction strategies are useful for reducing acute pain, such as that experienced in some medical or dental procedures, and they can also provide relief for chronic pain patients in some circumstances (McCaul & Malott, 1984). Singing a song or staring intently at a stimulus can divert the person's attention for a short while—and this may be a great help, such as for an arthritis sufferer who experiences heightened pain when climbing stairs. People who want to use distraction for moderate levels of continuous pain may get longer-lasting relief by engaging in an extended engrossing activity, such as watching a movie or reading a book.

Imagery

Sometimes when children are about to receive injections, their parents will say something like, "It'll be easier if you think about something nice, like the fun things we did at the park." **Nonpain imagery**—sometimes called *guided imagery*—is a strategy whereby the person tries to alleviate discomfort by conjuring up a mental scene that is unrelated to or incompatible with the pain (Fernandez, 1986). The most common type of imagery people use involves scenes that are pleasant to them—they think of "something nice." This scene might involve being at the beach or in the country, for instance. Therapists usually encourage, or "guide," the person to include aspects of different senses: vision, hearing, taste, smell, and touch. As an example, the scene at the beach could include the sight and smell of the ocean water, the sound of the waves, and the warm, grainy feel of the sand. Other types of imagery for controlling pain are not necessarily pleasant—they can involve such themes as having an argument with someone or replacing the feeling of pain with another sensation, such as a tingling feeling. The person generally tries to keep the imagined event in mind as long as possible.

The imagery technique is in many ways like distraction. The main difference is that imagery is based on the person's imagination rather than on real objects or events in the environment. As a result, individuals who use imagery do not have to depend on the environment to provide a suitably distracting stimulus. They can develop one or more scenes that work reliably, which they "carry" around in their heads. They can then call one of these scenes up for pain relief whenever they need it. Imagery seems to work best when it attracts high levels of the person's attention or involvement, and it is likely to work better with mild or moderate pain than with strong pain (McCaul & Malott, 1984; Turk, Meichenbaum, & Genest, 1983). Although imagery clearly helps in reducing acute pain, the extent of this technique's usefulness with longer-lasting pain episodes is unclear. One limitation with using imagery in pain control is that some individuals are less adept in imagining scenes than others (Melzack & Wall, 1982).

Redefinition

The third type of cognitive strategy for reducing discomfort is **pain redefinition,** in which the person substitutes constructive or realistic thoughts about the pain experience for ones that arouse feelings of threat or harm (Fernandez, 1986; McCaul & Malott, 1984). Therapists can help people redefine their pain experiences in several ways. One approach involves teaching clients to engage in an internal dialogue, using positive self-statements. There are basically two kinds of self-statements for controlling pain (Fernandez, 1986): *coping statements* emphasize the person's ability to tolerate the discomfort, as when people say to themselves, "It hurts, but you're in control," or, "Be brave—you can take it", *reinterpretative statements* are designed to negate the unpleasant aspects of the discomfort, as when people think, "It's not so bad," "It's not the worst thing that could happen," or, "It hurts, but think of the benefits of this experience." This last statement can be particularly appropriate when undergoing painful medical procedures.

Two other methods can help people redefine their pain experiences. First, therapists can provide information about the sensations to expect in medical procedures, thereby reducing the pain that patients experience when undergoing these procedures (Anderson & Masur, 1983). The information therapists provide can also help clients remember more accurately the amount of pain they experienced in these procedures in the past and how well they coped (Chen, Zeltzer, Craske, & Katz, 1999). Since many patients exaggerate the discomfort they will feel and misre-member past pain experiences, providing realistic in-formation helps them redefine the experiences before they occur. Second, therapists can help individuals see that some of their beliefs are illogical and are mak-ing the discomfort worse. (Go to 🌳.)

The Value of Cognitive Strategies in Controlling Pain

Studies have found that cognitive strategies effec-tively reduce acute pain (Fernandez & Turk, 1989;

Manne et al., 1994). Distraction and imagery seem to be particularly useful with mild or moderate pain, and redefinition appears to be more effective with strong pain (McCaul & Malott, 1984). How helpful are cogni-tive methods for treating chronic pain? The answer is likely to depend on many factors, such as the sever-ity of the pain, the type of illness, and the methods used. Redefinition may be more effective in relieving chronic pain than distraction is. A study compared these two techniques in reducing the chronic pain of patients who were receiving physical rehabilitation for a variety of medical problems, including arthritis,

CLINICAL METHODS AND ISSUES
Guiding a Client to Pain Redefinition

The following dialogue illustrates how a clinical health psychologist can guide a client with illogical beliefs toward pain redefinition. "Mrs. D," a 56-year-old patient, worried that her chronic-recurrent head pain was actually caused by a tumor, which repeated neurological tests had failed to reveal. The therapist suggested that they examine those thoughts, and she replied:

MRS. D: Yes, I know they're not true but I cannot help it.

THERAPIST: You don't think you have control over your thoughts?

MRS. D: Yes, they just come to me.

T: Well, let's come back to the idea that your thoughts are automatic. First, let's break down your flood of negative thoughts and look at each part sep-arately. Do you really think that you have a tumor?

MRS. D: I don't know. I guess not (pause) but it's hard not to worry about it. My head hurts so bad.

T: Yes, I know. So how do you convince yourself that you don't have a tumor or something else seri-ously wrong?

MRS. D: Well, as you know I've been examined many times by the best neurologists around. They say I'm OK. Also, my pain always goes away and I've never had any other neurological problems. My only problem is the pain. But, it's hard to

remember these facts when my pain is so awful.

T: It's much easier to be positive about your condition when you're not suffering. Nevertheless, ratio-nally, you really are convinced that there's noth-ing seriously wrong.

MRS. D: I guess so. If only I could remember that when my pain starts coming on.

T: So the goal of our work today could be to figure out a strategy to increase the likelihood that you'll remember the positive thoughts during a pain episode.

MRS. D: Yes, that sounds good.

T: Let's start by generating a list of accurate state-ments about your pain. Then we can talk about ways you can cue yourself to remember the list when you begin to feel pain. You already men-tioned a couple of beliefs about your pain; that is, that there's nothing seriously wrong, that the pain always goes away, and that, other than the pain, you feel pretty healthy. Can you think of other accurate and positive thoughts? (Holzman, Turk, & Kerns, 1986, pp. 45–46)

In this example, the therapist helped the client exam-ine the logic of her thought patterns and generate a list of ideas she believed that were incompatible with her irrational fears. They later rehearsed these beliefs so that she could use them as self-statements when pain episodes occurred.

amputation, and spinal cord injury (Rybstein-Blinchik, 1979). Although both techniques were effective, patients who received redefinition training reported less pain and exhibited less pain behavior than those who were trained in distraction.

Because each behavioral and cognitive strategy we have considered can be helpful in treating clinical pain, programs to help chronic pain sufferers control their pain generally combine different types of methods. In one study, for instance, arthritis sufferers received a 5-week pain control program that included training in distraction, imagery, and redefinition (O'Leary, Shoor, Lorig, & Holman, 1988). The program gave special emphasis to having the patients use these techniques in specific painful activities, such as carrying groceries, climbing stairs, and mopping floors. A control group simply received a self-help book for arthritis sufferers. Assessments before and after the program revealed that it was very effective. The control group showed little or no improvement during that time period. In contrast, the treated group reported having less pain, greater self-efficacy, less depression, and improved sleep patterns.

Another study used a program that combined imagery, redefinition, and progressive muscle relaxation training to treat chronic low back pain patients (Turner, 1982). Some subjects received this program, others received a program of only relaxation training, and a third group served as controls. Compared with the control subjects, the patients in both programs reported much less pain, depression, and disability by the end of treatment, and these improvements were similar for the people in both programs. A follow-up on the patients in the two programs more than $1\frac{1}{2}$ years later revealed that the benefits of the treatments were maintained, as measured by the subjects' ratings of pain and reports of health care use. But the patients who received the program combining cognitive strategies and relaxation also showed a marked improvement in their employment, working 60% more hours per week than those who had the program of relaxation only.

Programs combining behavioral and cognitive methods are at least as effective as chemical methods in reducing chronic tension-type headaches (Holroyd et al., 1991). What's more, a review of research and a meta-analysis have shown that cognitive-behavioral programs are effective in treating chronic pain conditions, such as headache, arthritis, and low back pain, but programs with only behavioral methods

may sometimes be sufficient (Compas et al., 1998; Morley, Eccleston, & Williams, 1999). It is clear that several behavioral and cognitive methods are effective in helping people control acute and chronic pain. These methods include operant techniques, progressive muscle relaxation and biofeedback, and the cognitive strategies of distraction, imagery, and redefinition. Behavioral and cognitive methods are often most helpful when used in combination. (Go to 🍎.)

HYPNOSIS AND INSIGHT-ORIENTED PSYCHOTHERAPY

You may have noticed that the behavioral and cognitive methods we just described for relieving pain sound familiar—and they should. For the most part, they involve psychological procedures derived from the stress reduction techniques we considered in Chapter 5. Because people's experiences of pain include an emotional component and are stressful, and because behavioral and cognitive methods are effective in reducing stress, psychologists have adapted these techniques to help people control their pain. Other psychological approaches have also been applied to relieve pain. These approaches include hypnosis and insight therapy.

HYPNOSIS AS A TREATMENT FOR PAIN

In the mid-1800s, before ether was discovered, dramatic reports began to appear of physicians performing major surgery on individuals, using hypnosis as the sole method of analgesia (Bakal, 1979; Barber, 1986). In one such case of a woman with breast cancer, a surgeon made an incision halfway across her chest and removed the tumor as well as several enlarged glands in her armpit. During the procedure, the woman conversed with the surgeon and showed no signs of feeling pain. Another physician reported having done hundreds of major surgeries with hypnosis as the only analgesic, and argued that the patients experienced no pain. Were all of these operations ꝑ less? Probably not—although many patients ꝺ feel no pain, some showed other pain beh᷍ as facial expressions, suggesting they ꞏ ing their agony (Bakal, 1979). Neve does appear to reduce the inter

ASSESS YOURSELF

Would Behavioral or Cognitive Methods Help *Your* Pain?

For each of the following questions about your recent experiences relating to pain, put a check mark in the preceding space if your answer is "yes."

_____ Have you been experiencing strong pain three or more days a week for more than a month?

_____ Do you take painkillers four or more days a week?

_____ Do you often take painkillers to prevent pain before it begins?

_____ Has your pain been getting worse?

_____ Have you cancelled or avoided making social plans in the past month because you thought your pain would interfere with them?

_____ Do you ever drink alcohol to relieve your pain or the stress it produces?

_____ Have you seen more than three physicians about your pain?

_____ Are you afraid of performing physical activ-

ities, feeling they could elicit or aggravate your pain condition?

_____ Has your pain caused you to feel depressed and helpless for more than a couple of weeks or so?

_____ Do family or friends either seem annoyed by your pain or often ask how your pain is doing?

If you have been suffering from pain but have not yet seen a physician about it, see one soon. If you have seen your physician about the pain repeatedly but the treatments have not worked, consider supplementing your medical therapy with behavioral and cognitive approaches, especially if you answered "yes" to three or more of the above questions. If you answered "yes" to five or more questions, consider getting help from a *multidisciplinary pain clinic*, as described toward the end of this chapter. (*Source*: Based on material in Tunks and Bellissimo, 1991.)

some individuals experience (Hilgard & Hilgard, 1983; Zeltzer, Bush, Chen, & Williams, 1997).

How and why does hypnosis reduce pain? First of all, we should note that hypnosis is not effective for all people—in fact, it produces a high degree of analgesia in only a minority of individuals (Hilgard & Hilgard, 1983; Melzack & Wall, 1982). People vary in their ability to be hypnotized, and those who can be hypnotized very easily and deeply seem to gain more pain relief from hypnosis than those who are less hypnotically susceptible (DeBenedittis, Panerai, & Villamira, 1989; Spanos, Perlini, & Robertson, 1989). The mechanisms underlying the pain relief that some individuals get from hypnosis are not clear. Part of the mechanism may involve the deep relaxation people experience when hypnotized—as we saw earlier, relaxation can help relieve pain. Cognitive factors also seem to be ~~~ved (Barber, 1986; Turk, Meichenbaum, & Genest,

1983). Hypnosis often produces states of heightened attention to internal images and inattention to environmental stimuli. For instance, while under hypnosis, people may experience "positive" hallucinations, in which they perceive objects and events that are not really there, or "negative" hallucinations, in which they fail to perceive things they ordinarily would. Because hypnosis may produce analgesia somewhat like placebos do, researchers have looked for neurophysiological mechanisms that may underlie hypnotic pain relief. Although research has apparently disconfirmed the role of endorphins, findings for other neurochemicals seem more promising (Barber, 1986; DeBenedittis, Panerai, & Villamira, 1989).

Hypnosis is a dramatic and unusual phenomenon. When it produces analgesia, it can do so very quickly and substantially. What's more, patients who experience hypnotic analgesia sometimes do not even believe they were hypnotized, perhaps because they have unrealistic ideas about what it feels like to be hypnotized. One person, for example, underwent a normally painful dental procedure with only hypnosis as an anesthetic. He claimed to the dentist that he was not hypnotized "because I can't be hypnotized" and that the reason he did not feel pain was that "you didn't do anything to me that would hurt" (Barber, 1986).

In some cases these patients' claims that they were not hypnotized may actually be right. According to researcher Theodore Barber (1982), laboratory research on acute pain, induced by cold-pressor or muscle-ischemia procedures, has found that:

- Hypnosis can reduce pain.
- When hypnotized, the people who gain the most pain relief from suggestions of analgesia tend to be those who are highly responsive to other suggestions, such as that their arm is becoming light.
- Whether under hypnosis or not, individuals who are told to try not to feel pain tend to use distraction and redefinition techniques.
- Contrary to the common myths about hypnosis, people usually show as much pain reduction using cognitive strategies, such as imagery and redefinition, as they do under hypnosis.

It may be that some patients who were supposedly hypnotized actually were not, and they may have applied cognitive strategies to reduce the pain.

Can hypnosis also help relieve chronic pain? Although some research has found that hypnosis can relieve chronic headache, low back pain, and cancer pain, almost all these studies either lacked appropriate control groups or simply provided descriptions of individual cases (Barber, 1986; Melzack & Wall, 1982). As a result, there is little clear evidence that hypnosis provides any better relief for chronic pain than a placebo drug or sham treatment would. The success of hypnosis with acute pain suggests that it might be effective with chronic pain, but better research is needed to demonstrate this clearly. Even if this research is eventually done and confirms its usefulness, hypnosis is likely to be most effective when used along with other therapy techniques, such as behavioral and cognitive methods, rather than as the sole treatment approach (Barber, 1986).

INSIGHT THERAPY FOR PAIN

We saw in Chapter 7 that *insight therapy* focuses on helping people discover the roots of their problems, especially when they involve underlying motivations (Davison & Neale, 1998). The assumption is that an awareness of motivations can help individuals control their behavior and emotions. In the case of chronic pain patients, the insights often relate to the feelings these patients and their families have about the pain condition, the way they deal with pain behaviors, and the changes that have developed in the interpersonal relationships of these people. Insight therapy can be used in individual treatment and in groups.

One insight-oriented approach involves showing patients how their pain behavior is part of "pain games" they play with other people (Szasz, cited in Bakal, 1979). In these games, individuals with chronic pain seem to take on roles in which they continually seek to confirm their identities as suffering persons, maintain their dependent lifestyles, and receive various secondary gains, such as attention and sympathy. These patients are probably not aware of what is actually happening in these games, and the purpose of this psychotherapeutic approach is to make them aware. The assumption is that once patients gain an insight into how their behavior patterns are affecting their lives, they can give up the games if they want to and are shown how. Studies with chronic pain patients have found that treatment programs that include an insight-oriented component can help reduce pain, but the specific value of insight as part of the programs was not assessed (Turk, Meichenbaum, & Genest, 1983).

Conducting psychotherapy for chronic pain patients within a group format rather than individually has several advantages. Table 12.1 describes some of these advantages in helping patients cope with their pain and disability. The pain group provides a forum for talking about their worst fears and conflicts to people who share these concerns and understand. Patients often say, "I'm afraid the pain will get worse," "I was beginning to believe I was imagining the pain," and "I can't do things because of the pain, and I feel guilty, helpless, frustrated, and angry" (Hendler, 1984). Patients in the group may answer, for instance, "You hurt whether you go shopping or not; so the choice isn't between having pain or not, it's a choice between whether you go shopping or stay home!" (Gentry &

Table 12.1 *Advantages of Group Psychotherapy Over Individual Therapy in Treating Pain*

1. *Efficiency.* Although each patient has unique problems, chronic pain sufferers also face common difficulties, such as depression and addiction to medication. As a result, they often need similar types of advice and information. Group meetings use the therapist's time more efficiently.
2. *Reduced isolation.* Chronic pain sufferers are typically isolated from extended social contact. This situation can lead to a sense of alienation, which involves feelings of being different from others and of anger and suspicion toward them. Group meetings can help to overcome these feelings.
3. *Credible feedback for patients.* Pain patients often resist feedback or advice from therapists, saying such things as, "You don't know what it's like to live with pain 24 hours a day!" In their eyes, the type of feedback other patients can give may be more believable.
4. *A new reference group for patients.* Patients in a pain group develop new social networks of individuals who are comparable to themselves and who can provide social pressure to conform to the realities and constructive "rules" of living with pain and physical limitations.
5. *A different perspective for the therapist.* Watching the patient relate to other individuals in a group provides the therapist with certain kinds of information that may aid in identifying specific problems therapy should address, such as maladaptive coping styles.

Source: Based on Gentry & Owens (1986).

Owens, 1986). These people can say things to each other that others could not, without seeming cruel. Group members can also disconfirm each other's misconceptions, share their own ways for managing pain on a day-to-day basis, give each other hope and social support, and detect and confront each others' pain games.

Insight-oriented approaches can also help chronic pain patients and their families understand the problems they experience in their relationships within the family system (Flor & Turk, 1985; Kerns & Payne, 1996). For instance, when a spouse suffers from chronic pain, both spouses experience feelings of frustration, anger, helplessness, and guilt that they often do not communicate openly to each other. These feelings can result from changes in their roles, general style of communication, and sexual relationship. The following excerpt shows how a therapist was able to help a pain patient, John Cox, and his wife gain insights about their feelings and behavior. The three of them were discussing a pain episode John had had while he watched TV with his wife, and the therapist asked the wife how she reacted when she realized he was in pain:

MRS. COX: I really felt sorry for John, but I didn't know what to do. I just tried to watch the show and not say anything to him. At those times I feel...so helpless.

T: Mr. Cox, it sounds as if your wife tried to avoid talking about your pain. She sounds sort of helpless and frustrated....How did you feel about her response?

MR. COX: I think I got kind of mad at her because she seemed to be ignoring me, not really caring how I was feeling.

T: Mr. Cox, what do you think she should have done at that time?

MR. COX: I don't really know.

T: Mr. Cox, do you think there was anything she could have done to make you feel better?

MR. COX: Not really.

T: ...Perhaps at such times ignoring your pain may be the most she can do....

MR. COX: Perhaps.

T: Perhaps?

MR. COX: Well maybe she did know how I was feeling, but I felt upset that she didn't tell me. (Turk, Meichenbaum, & Genest, 1983, pp. 244–245)

Insights such as these help family members understand each others' feelings and points of view, and this understanding can help to break down the longstanding confusion and conflicts that have developed over time. Improvements in family relationships can enable the therapist to enhance the cooperation of each member in the treatment process (Kerns & Payne, 1996).

In summary, hypnosis and insight-oriented therapies offer promising techniques in the treatment of chronic pain. Although both approaches can probably enhance the success of pain control programs for many patients, there is currently little experimental research to confirm this belief. Thus far in our discussion of methods for reducing pain we have considered a variety of medical and psychological techniques. In the next section, we will see how physical therapy and certain skin stimulation methods can also play important roles in controlling pain.

PHYSICAL AND STIMULATION THERAPIES FOR PAIN

Anthropologists and medical historians have noted that most, if not all, cultures in recorded history have learned that people can "fight pain with pain" (Melzack & Wall, 1982). One pain can cancel another—a brief or moderate pain can cancel a longer-lasting or stronger one. For example, you might reduce the pain of an injection by pressing your thumbnail into your forefinger as the shot is given. Reducing one pain by creating another is called **counter-irritation.** People in ancient cultures developed a counter-irritation procedure called *cupping* to relieve headaches, backaches, and arthritic pain. In this procedure, one or more heated glass cups are inverted and pressed on the skin. As the air in the cup cools, it creates a vacuum, causing the skin to be bruised as it is drawn up into the cup. This method is still used in some parts of the world today (Melzack & Wall, 1982).

The principle of counter-irritation is the basis for present-day stimulation therapies for reducing pain. After examining these pain control methods, we will discuss the important role other physical approaches can play in reducing pain.

STIMULATION THERAPIES

Why does counter-irritation relieve pain? One reason is that people actively distract their attention from the stronger pain to the milder one. Another explanation comes from gate-control theory. Recall that activity in the peripheral fibers that carry signals about mildly irritating stimuli tends to close the gate, thereby inhibiting the transmission cells from sending pain signals to the brain. Counter-irritation, such as massaging a sore muscle, activates these peripheral fibers, and this may close the gate and soothe the pain.

This gate-control view of how counter-irritation works led to the development of a pain control technique called **transcutaneous electrical nerve stimulation** (TENS). This technique involves placing electrodes on the skin near where the patient feels pain and stimulating that area with mild electric current, which is supplied by a small portable device. TENS can be effective in reducing acute muscular and postoperative pain in most patients (Chapman, 1984; Hare & Milano, 1985). In a dramatic example of its effec-

tiveness, a 9-year-old boy began receiving TENS while still unconscious after kidney surgery. When he awoke, the hospital staff asked repeatedly if he felt pain in his belly, and he said, "No, it doesn't hurt." The startling thing about this example is that he did not even realize the surgery already occurred—after the surgeon left the room, the boy talked

> casually with the others in the room. When asked whether there was anything he feared, he began to cry and confessed his terror of the expected operation that would remove his kidney. His surprised nurse tried to reassure him that the surgery had already been done, and that there was nothing to worry about. He refused to believe her. "But don't you remember?" she contended. "That's why they put you to sleep this morning—so they could do the operation." The little boy looked very threatened. "It's not true!" he shouted, "It's not true!" when asked why it couldn't be true, he asserted confidently. "Because I haven't got any bandages." We asked him to feel his belly, since his hands were outside of the bedclothes. When he did, an expression of astonishment came over his face. (Chapman, 1984, p. 1265)

Now he claimed to feel pain and began to cry.

TENS has also been used in treating chronic pain, but its success has been mixed. When TENS does relieve discomfort for some chronic conditions, such as phantom limb pain, its effects are often short-lived (Hare & Milano, 1985; Zeltzer, Bush, Chen, & Williams, 1997). But for patients with arthritis, TENS often produces substantial and long-lasting pain relief (Johnson, 1984; Minor & Sanford, 1993). Moreover, for other chronic pain conditions, such as certain forms of neuralgia, TENS sometimes produces long-lasting pain relief in patients who have gotten little or no relief from various others methods (Melzack & Wall, 1982).

Another stimulation therapy that is used today for reducing pain is **acupuncture,** a technique in which fine metal needles are inserted under the skin at special locations and then twirled or electrically charged to create stimulation. Acupuncture has been used in China for at least the past 2,000 years and was originally based on the idea that pain occurs when the life forces of yin and yang are out of balance (Bakal, 1979; CU, 1994a; Melzack & Wall, 1982). Although acupuncturists do not necessarily believe this rationale any longer, many, but not all, still

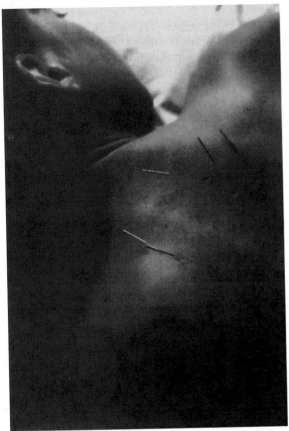

Acupuncture can be effective in reducing pain in some individuals.

determine the placement of the needles on the basis of charts that show hundreds of insertion points on the body. These acupuncturists believe that stimulation at several specific points relieves pain in associated parts of the body. On the nose and ear, for example, certain points are associated with the small intestine, whereas other points are associated with the kidney, or heart, or abdomen.

Does acupuncture work? Its ability to produce high levels of analgesia for acute pain in some individuals has been clearly and dramatically demonstrated—for instance, surgeons have performed major surgery on patients with only acupuncture anesthesia. But research findings point to several conclusions about its effects and its limitations (Bakal, 1979; Chapman, 1984; Melzack & Wall, 1982):

- Even in China, physicians perform only a small percentage (less than 10%) of surgeries with

acupuncture analgesia, and these operations are straightforward ones with little likelihood of complications. Patients must volunteer for the procedure, and then their physicians select appropriate candidates very carefully and make sure these patients are well indoctrinated.

- Acupuncture is rarely effective for surgical patients in Western cultures.
- Laboratory studies have shown that acupuncture produces only mild analgesia in most people.
- The degree of analgesia acupuncture produces depends on the intensity of the stimulation, and not on its being applied at the exact points described on acupuncture charts.
- Pain patients who benefit most from acupuncture tend to be those who are also easily and deeply hypnotizable.

Acupuncture does *not* provide long-term relief for most chronic pain patients, but some evidence indicates that it is useful in treating headache and low back pain (Mayer, 2000; Zeltzer, Bush, Chen, & Williams, 1997).

It is tempting to conclude from these findings that acupuncture works simply through suggestion or distraction effects, but this seems unlikely because the technique also produces analgesia in animals, such as monkeys and mice (Melzack & Wall, 1982). Psychological factors cannot provide a full explanation. Gate-control theory provides two plausible reasons for the effects of acupuncture: stimulation from the needles may close the gate by activating peripheral fibers or the release of opioids, such as endorphins (Bakal, 1979; Zeltzer, Bush, Chen, & Williams, 1997). TENS and acupuncture can be useful in programs for treating pain, and so can several methods of physical therapy.

PHYSICAL THERAPY

Physical therapy is an important rehabilitation component for many medical conditions—for instance, after injury or surgery, patients perform exercises to enhance muscular strength and tissue flexibility to restore their range of motion. Physical therapists have a variety of techniques they can incorporate into individualized treatment programs to help patients who suffer from acute and chronic pain conditions. Exercise is a common feature in these programs

(Hare & Milano, 1985; Zeltzer, Bush, Chen, & Williams, 1997).

The therapist and patient generally plan the program together, setting daily or weekly goals that promote very gradual but steady progress. The progress is tailored to the patient's needs, being fast enough to promote a feeling of accomplishment but slow enough to prevent overexertion, reinjury, or failure. In cases of acute injury, such as serious damage to the knee joint, the exercise program might span a year or two. The rationale for using exercise to control pain depends on the type of health problem the patient has—with arthritis, for instance, exercise helps by maintaining the flexibility of the joints and preventing them from becoming deformed (Minor & Sanford, 1993). Other approaches in physical therapy, such as massage, traction, and applying heat or cold to the painful area of the body, seem to provide temporary pain relief (Tunks & Bellissimo, 1991). The spinal manipulation treatment people get from *chiroproactic* and *osteopathic* specialists, especially for neck and lower back pain, is not generally considered to be physical therapy, but it appears to relieve back pain (Bove & Nilsson, 1998; Andersson et al., 1999).

Physical therapy programs are widely used in treating two highly prevalent chronic pain conditions, arthritis and low back pain (Hare & Milano, 1985; Minor & Sanford, 1993; Moffet et al., 1999). For both of these conditions, exercise is probably the most important physical therapy approach for achieving long-term pain relief. Research with low back pain patients, for instance, has shown that programs that gradually increase aerobic and back-strengthening exercise produce substantial improvements after the first month or two in self-reports of pain and ability to perform physical activities, such as standing and lifting weights (Alaranta et al., 1994; Manniche et al., 1988; Moffet et al., 1999).

Sometimes physical therapy is combined with behavioral methods in treating chronic pain to gain the benefits of each approach, and treatments for low back pain provide a good example again. A study by Richard Heinrich and his colleagues (1985) compared the benefits from physical therapy with those of a program of behavioral and cognitive methods for adults with chronic low back pain. Both therapy programs met for 10 weeks for 2 hours each week. Assessments of pain and of physical and psychosocial functioning taken prior to, at the end of, and 6 months after

Physical therapy not only promotes rehabilitation for this patient suffering from an arm injury but may also help in reducing her pain.

the program revealed two main findings. First, during the programs both groups experienced similar reductions in pain, which they maintained in the following months. Second, each group showed improvements that were specific to the programs they received: at the end of the programs and at follow-up, subjects in the physical therapy group showed better physical functioning, and those in the behavioral-cognitive group showed better psychosocial adjustment. These findings suggest that chronic pain patients might benefit from receiving both types of treatment. Other research has found that low back pain patients show less pain behavior, disability, and self-reported pain with both physical and behavioral-cognitive therapy than with either approach alone (Turner, Clancy, McQuade, & Cardenas, 1990).

In this chapter we have described many different types of treatment, including medical, psychological, and physical therapies, and we have seen that each method can help to alleviate clinical pain. Some methods seem to be more effective than others, especially for particular pain conditions. Typically, no single approach is sufficient by itself. Therefore, specialists who provide treatment in pain clinics often apply several methods in combination. (Go to 🔦.)

PAIN CLINICS

Before the 1970s, if a person's pain lingered, and physicians could not determine its cause or find a remedy for the discomfort, that patient was left with virtually no reasonable treatment alternatives. In desperation, such people often tried extreme medical approaches that could lead to drug addiction or irreversible nerve damage, or they may have turned to charlatans. Although many people with chronic pain still use ill-conceived, desperate measures to gain relief from their discomfort, effective alternatives are available today, as we have seen. Effective pain control treatments can now be obtained through **pain clinics** (or *pain centers*), which are institutions or organizations that have been developed specifically for the treatment of chronic pain conditions.

The concept of having special institutions for treating pain originated with John Bonica, an anesthesiologist who founded the first pain clinic at the University of Washington Medical School (Fordyce, 1976; Melzack & Wall, 1982). Soon other professionals followed suit, and by the late 1990s there were perhaps a thousand pain clinics in the United States alone (Turk & Stacey, 2000). The structure, methods, and quality of pain clinics vary widely. Many pain clinics are private organizations, whereas others are affiliated with medical schools, university departments of behavioral medicine, and hospitals. Many provide inpatient treatment, and others focus on outpatient care; and many incorporate a variety of treatment methods, whereas others provide basically one approach, such as acupuncture, hypnosis, biofeedback, or TENS (Follick, Ahern, Attanasio, & Riley, 1985; Kanner, 1986; Turk & Stacey, 2000). Pain centers that have been accredited by the Commission on Accreditation of Rehabilitation Facilities in Tucson, Arizona,

typically offer high-quality treatment (Chapman, 1991).

MULTIDISCIPLINARY PROGRAMS

A theme that has appeared more than once in this chapter is that no single method for treating chronic pain is likely to succeed. In fact, one physician has advised avoiding clinics that focus on applying a single approach, such as biofeedback or nerve block methods (Kanner, 1986). *Multidisciplinary pain clinics* (or *centers*)—those that combine and integrate several effective approaches—are likely to succeed for the largest percentage of patients and provide the greatest pain relief for each individual. Clinics that use multidisciplinary programs generally use assessment and treatment procedures for each patient that involve medical, psychosocial, physical therapy, occupational therapy, and vocational factors and approaches (Follick, Ahern, Attanasio, & Riley, 1985; Turk & Stacey, 2000).

Assessment procedures are used in determining the factors that are contributing to the patient's condition, identifying the specific problems to address in the program, and customizing the program to match the needs of the patient (Chapman, 1991; Turk & Stacey, 2000). Although the goals and objectives of different multidisciplinary programs vary, they typically include:

● Reducing the patient's experience of pain.
● Improving physical and lifestyle functioning.
● Decreasing or eliminating drug intake.
● Enhancing social support and family life.
● Reducing the patient's use of medical services.

Multidisciplinary programs generally integrate specific treatment components to achieve each goal (Follick, Ahern, Attanasio, & Riley, 1985). These programs include, for example, procedures to decrease the patient's reliance on medication and physical exercises to increase the person's strength, endurance, flexibility, and range of motion. They provide counseling to improve family relationships and to enable the patient to find full-time employment when possible. And they offer a range of psychological services to reduce the experience of pain, decrease pain behavior, and improve the patient's psychological adjustment to the pain condition.

HIGHLIGHT ON ISSUES
Physical Activity and Back Pain

The spine has an intricate structure, with each of its many sections of bone, called *vertebrae*, being cushioned from adjacent sections by rubbery *disks* of connective tissue. Each vertebra is connected to adjacent ones by antler-shaped *facet joints* that enable the vertebrae to pivot against one another (Tortora & Grabowski, 2000). But the spine depends on the muscles of the back and abdomen for support, without which it would just topple over. When all these muscles are strong and in good working order, they balance each other's action and keep the body's weight centered on the spine. But when these muscles are weak or the back muscles are under excessive or prolonged tension—sometimes due to emotional stress—back problems tend to occur.

A 10-year longitudinal study of men and women found evidence suggesting that low back pain progresses over time through a vicious circle: poor muscle function may lead to low back disorders, which lead to poorer muscle function, and so on (Leino, Aro, & Hasan, 1987). Although back pain can arise from such conditions as arthritis and ruptured disks, this is not typical—medical examinations fail to find underlying physical causes in the large majority of back cases (Chapman, 1984; Deyo, Cherkin, Conrad, & Volinn, 1991). Most backaches seem to arise from muscle or ligament strains, lack of proper exercise, and normal wear and tear on facet joints. These problems tend to increase with age for many reasons—for instance, people's muscular conditioning usually declines as they get older, the effects of wear and tear accumulate, and the disks gradually dry out and provide less cushioning for the vertebrae.

People whose jobs require frequent heavy lifting are more likely than other workers to develop low back pain (Kelsey & Hochberg, 1988). Exercise can help protect people from back problems, but it needs to consist of *proper* activities. People who do the wrong kinds of exercises do not get this protection, and those who overexert themselves can precipitate back pain.

What kinds of physical activity can help protect against back problems? Proper exercise involves a program of back-strengthening and stretching activities, along with abdominal exercises. Many different exercises are available for these purposes, and Figure 12H-1 presents a few easy ones. What should people do when they develop backaches? Medical advice in the past called for getting lots of bed rest and taking aspirin. But this advice has changed as a result of new research (Deyo, Cherkin, Conrad, & Volinn, 1991; USDHHS, 1994). Most backaches resolve themselves in a few days or weeks with or without medical attention. Physicians today recommend that the person *become active as soon as possible*—walking and exercising cautiously—even if it hurts a little. People with back pain should consult their doctor when the pain is:

- Linked to a known injury, such as from a fall.
- Severe enough to disable the sufferer and awaken him or her at night.
- Not relieved by changing position or lying down.
- Accompanied by nausea, fever, difficulty or pain in urinating, loss of bladder or bowel control, numbness or weakness in a leg or foot, or pain that shoots down the leg.

Figure 12H–1 Six stretching and strengthening exercises to protect from low back pain.

EVALUATING THE SUCCESS OF PAIN CLINICS

How effective are multidisciplinary pain clinics? To answer this question, we'll start by examining the procedures and results of two pain programs. Each program (1) was conducted by a hospital-affiliated pain clinic, (2) provided treatment on an inpatient basis for 4 weeks with weekends off, (3) treated several patients at a time with a variety of treatment techniques, and (4) had staff to provide medical, psychological, physical, and occupational therapy.

The first of these programs took place at the Miller-Dwan Hospital Pain Control Center in Minnesota (Cinciripini & Floreen, 1982). The patients were men and women who had suffered intractable pain from known injuries or diseases, such as arthritis, for at least a year and were unemployed because of their pain conditions. All subjects received the full program, which consisted of a medication reduction procedure, physical therapy, relaxation and biofeedback training, self-monitoring, behavioral contracting, cognitive-behavioral group therapy, and family involvement and training. The researchers assessed the patients' behavior and functioning at the start and at the end of the program, and in follow-ups 6 and 12 months after. By the end of this program, the patients' activity levels had increased and their pain experiences, pain behaviors, and drug use had decreased sharply—indeed, 90% of the patients were now free of analgesic medication. The subjects who participated in the follow-up assessments reported that they continued to be active, and about half were employed. Moreover, their pain continued to diminish: before treatment their average pain rating was 4.6 on a 10-point scale; by the end of the program it was 2.2, and after a year it was 1.2.

The second program was conducted at the University of Nebraska Pain Management Center (Guck, Skultety, Meilman, & Dowd, 1985). This study compared a *treatment group* that completed the program with a *control group* that met all the criteria for acceptance into the program but declined to participate solely because they lacked insurance coverage. The two groups were similar in age, gender composition, marital status, employment status, educational level, use of drugs, length of pain history, and prior hospitalization history. The treatment program included a medication reduction procedure, physical therapy, relaxation and biofeedback training, group and individual therapy, family therapy, and vocational counseling. Follow-up assessments comparing the treatment and control subjects 1 to 5 years later revealed impressive outcomes: the treatment group reported experiencing far less pain, less evidence of depression, and less interference from pain in various activities, such as household chores, socializing, sexual relations, exercise, and sleep. Almost two-thirds of the treatment group and only one-fifth of the controls were employed, and far fewer treatment subjects used painkilling drugs.

Meta-analyses of dozens of studies have shown that people suffering with chronic pain who receive treatment at multidisciplinary pain centers report much less subsequent pain and are far more likely to return to work than individuals who have standard pain treatment (Cutler et al., 1994; Flor, Fydrich, & Turk, 1992). What's more, the cost of the treatment is only a small fraction of the medical and disability payments patients would receive for a year (Stieg & Turk, 1988). Of course, not all pain patients benefit from this treatment, but most do. Programs that provide medical, psychosocial, physical, and occupational therapy can improve chronic pain patients' psychological and physical functioning and reduce their pain behavior, and drug use. The relationships that develop between patient and therapist may be important to the success of the program. One study found that patients' hostility and depression may impair the relationships they develop with their physical therapists (Burns et al., 1999).

SUMMARY

Pain that receives or requires professional attention is called clinical pain. Practitioners try to reduce acute clinical pain for humanitarian reasons and for practical reasons, such as to enable medical procedures to be carried out smoothly, reduce patients' stress, and help patients recover quickly and without complications. Relieving chronic pain is important because of the severe and pervasive impact it can have on almost every aspect of patients' lives. Although the medical treatment for pain may involve surgery if all other methods have failed, it usually involves pharmaceuticals selected from four types: peripherally acting analgesics; centrally acting analgesics; local anesthetics; and indirectly acting drugs, such as sedatives, tranquilizers, and antidepressants. These chemical methods are used extensively for relieving acute pain; they can be administered in several ways, such as by epidural block or patient-controlled analgesia. Health care professionals usually try not to rely on chemical methods for reducing chronic pain.

One of the main goals of behavioral and cognitive methods for treating chronic pain is to reduce the patient's drug consumption. The operant approach focuses on reducing pain behaviors through extinction procedures and increasing other behavior through reinforcement. Therapists apply progressive muscle relaxation and biofeedback to reduce the stress and muscle tension that can cause or aggravate patients' pain experiences. Research has shown that relaxation and biofeedback training produce effective and long-lasting relief for many chronic pain patients. Cognitive techniques focus on changing thought patterns that increase the intensity or frequency of pain experiences. Distraction and nonpain imagery methods appear to be effective chiefly for mild or moderate acute pain or for brief episodes of heightened chronic pain. Pain redefinition can involve clarifying what a pain experience will be like, using positive self-statements, and correcting faulty beliefs and logic. Redefinition can help reduce strong pain and chronic pain.

Hypnosis seems to relieve pain to the extent that the person can be deeply hypnotized; it provides a high degree of analgesia in only a minority of individuals. In general, people can reduce their pain as effectively with cognitive strategies in the waking state as with hypnosis. Insight psychotherapies help people achieve an understanding of the roots of their problems. For pain patients, this may involve making them aware of what is happening in the pain games they play or of how others feel about their pain conditions.

Counter-irritation is a procedure whereby a brief or moderate pain cancels a longer-lasting or stronger one. A pain control technique that is based on this procedure is called transcutaneous electrical nerve stimulation, in which mild electrical stimulation is applied to the skin at the painful region. This technique helps relieve acute pain and some types of chronic pain. Acupuncture is an ancient Asian procedure for reducing pain; it produces high levels of analgesia for acute pain in some patients, but not in most. Although it does not provide long-term relief for most chronic pain patients, it appears useful in treating headache and low back pain. Physical therapy includes such approaches as exercise, massage, traction, and the application of heat and cold to painful regions. Spinal manipulation techniques appear to reduce headache and low back pain. Proper exercise can protect individuals from low back pain.

Pain clinics are institutions developed specifically for treating chronic pain. Although some of these clinics focus on applying essentially one technique, such as hypnosis or biofeedback, the complex nature of chronic pain usually requires treatment that integrates medical, psychosocial, physical, and occupational therapy. Multidisciplinary pain clinics provide highly effective and long-lasting pain relief, while also rehabilitating patients physically, psychologically, socially, and vocationally.

KEY TERMS

clinical pain	pain redefinition	transcutaneous electrical	acupuncture
distraction	counter-irritation	nerve stimulation	pain clinics
nonpain imagery			

PART VI

CHRONIC AND LIFE-THREATENING HEALTH PROBLEMS

13

SERIOUS AND DISABLING CHRONIC ILLNESSES: CAUSES, MANAGEMENT, AND COPING

Adjusting to a Chronic Illness

Initial Reactions to Having
a Chronic Condition

Influences on Coping with
a Health Crisis

The Coping Process

Impacts of Different Chronic Conditions

Asthma

Epilepsy

Nervous System Injuries

Diabetes

Arthritis

Alzheimer's Disease

Psychosocial Interventions for People with Chronic Conditions

Educational, Social Support, and
Behavioral Methods

Relaxation and Biofeedback

Cognitive Methods

Insight and Family Therapy

PROLOGUE

"It's not fair," 12-year-old Joe complained. "Why can't I eat the stuff I like? Other kids can. Why do I have to check my blood every day and take shots? Nobody else has to do that." He voiced these complaints as he left the emergency room after suffering severe stomach cramps because he was not adhering to his medical regimen. Hospital tests recently determined that Joe has diabetes, and he was not adjusting well to the regimen his physician instructed him to follow. His parents tried to explain that not following the regimen could have serious health consequences, but Joe thought, "I'll do some of the things they say I should do, and that'll be enough. I feel fine—so those problems won't happen to me." When his noncompliance led to his being rushed to the hospital with severe abdominal pain and difficulty breathing, he finally believed the warnings he received, and he began to adhere closely to his regimen.

Different individuals react differently to developing a chronic illness. Their reactions depend on many factors, such as their coping skills and personalities, the social support they have, the nature and consequences of their illnesses, and the impact of the illnesses on their daily functioning. At the very least, having a chronic condition entails frequent impositions on the patients and their families. Chronically ill people may suffer periodic episodes of feeling poorly and need to have regular medical checkups, restrict their diets or other aspects of their lifestyles, or administer daily treatment, for instance. Many chronic conditions entail more than just impositions— they produce frequent pain or lead to disability or even death. Although the prospect of developing a chronic health problem is unappealing, most of us will develop at least one of these illnesses in our lifetimes, and one of them, such as cancer or cardiovascular disease, will probably take our lives.

This chapter and the next focus mainly on *tertiary prevention* for chronic illness— to retard its progression, prevent disability, and rehabilitate the person, physically and psychologically. We examine how people react to and cope with chronic health problems and what can be done to help these people cope effectively. In contrast to the next chapter, which deals with illnesses that have high rates of mortality and on processes relating to dying and death, the present chapter concentrates on health problems that are less likely to result in death but often lead to disability. This chapter begins by discussing people's reactions to having a chronic condition, then examines the experiences and needs of individuals living with various health problems, and ends by considering psychosocial interventions to enhance patients' long-term adaptation to their conditions. These discussions address many questions that are of great concern to patients, to their families and friends, and probably to you. How do individuals react after their initial shock of learning that they have a chronic illness? What kinds of health problems usually involve the most difficult adjustments for people? How do patients' chronic conditions impact on their families? What can families, friends, and therapists do to help chronically ill people adapt effectively to their conditions?

ADJUSTING TO A CHRONIC ILLNESS

"I felt like I'd been hit in the stomach by a sledgehammer"—this is how many patients describe their first reaction upon learning that they have a disabling or life-threatening illness. Questions without immediate answers flash through their minds: Is the diagnosis right and, if so, what can we do about it? Will I be disabled, disfigured, or in pain? Will I die? How soon will these consequences happen? What will happen to my family? Do I have adequate medical and life insurance? Learning of a chronic health problem usually comes as a great shock, and this is often the first reaction individuals experience when the physician tells them the diagnosis.

INITIAL REACTIONS TO HAVING A CHRONIC CONDITION

By observing patients in rehabilitation and health settings, Franklin Shontz (1975) has described a sequence of reactions people tend to exhibit following the diagnosis of a serious illness. This sequence of reactions is:

1. Shock—an emergency response, marked by three characteristics: (a) being stunned or bewildered, (b) behaving in an automatic fashion, and (c) feeling detached from the situation, that is, feeling like being an observer rather than a participant in the events that occur. The shock may last only a short while or may continue for weeks, occurs to some degree in any crisis situation people experience, and it is likely to be most pronounced when the crisis comes without warning.

2. Encounter—a phase that is marked by disorganized thinking and feelings of loss, grief, helplessness, despair, and being overwhelmed by reality.

3. Retreat—a phase in which people tend to use avoidance strategies, such as denying either the existence of the health problem or its implications. But then reality begins to intrude: the symptoms remain or get worse, additional diagnoses confirm the original one, and it becomes clear that adjustments need to be made.

Using retreat as a "base of operation," patients tend to contact reality a little at a time until they reach some form of adjustment to the health problem and its implications.

Do all individuals react in the ways Shontz has described when they are faced with such crises as being diagnosed with a serious illness? No, but probably most do. For instance, when faced with a crisis, most people react with shock initially, but other individuals may be "cool and collected," while others may be "paralyzed" with anxiety or may become "hysterical" (Silver & Wortman, 1980). Similarly, although many people with serious illnesses feel extremely helpless and overwhelmed after the initial shock, others do not. And many patients do not rely heavily on avoidance strategies to cope with the stress caused by having a health problem.

People who use denial and other avoidance strategies do so to control their emotional responses to a stressor, especially when they believe they can do nothing to change the situation (Croyle & Ditto, 1990; Lazarus, 1983). But the usefulness of this approach has limits. Although using avoidance strategies often provides psychological benefits early in the process of coping with health problems, excessive avoidance can soon become maladaptive to patients' physical and psychological well-being (Suls & Fletcher, 1985). For example, when hospitalized people receive information about their conditions and future risk factors, those individuals who use avoidance strategies heavily gain less information about their conditions than those who use these strategies to a lesser degree (Shaw, Cohen, Doyle, & Palesky, 1985). Patients often need to make major decisions about their immediate treatment. How can they make these decisions rationally if they fail to take in the information practitioners present? Later, they may need to take action to promote their recovery, reduce the likelihood of future health problems, and adjust their lifestyles, social relationships, and means of employment. What factors influence how people cope with their health problems? The next section provides some answers to this question.

INFLUENCES ON COPING WITH A HEALTH CRISIS

Healthy people tend to take their health for granted. They expect to be able to carry out their daily activities and social roles from one day to the next without substantial disruptions due to illness. When a serious illness or injury occurs, their everyday life activities are disrupted. Regardless of whether the condition is temporary or chronic, the first phases in coping with it are similar. But there is an important difference: in contrast to the short-term disruptions that temporary illnesses cause, chronic health problems usually require that patients and their families make permanent behavioral, social, and emotional adjustments.

When people learn that they have a serious chronic illness, the diagnosis quickly changes the way they view themselves and their lives. The plans they had for tomorrow and for the next days, weeks, and years may be affected. Major plans and minor ones may change: Did they plan to go on a trip this weekend? They may change their minds now. Did they plan to complete a college education, or enter a specific career field, or get married and have children, or move to a new community when they retire? Some of these ideas for the future may evaporate after the diagnosis. As psychologists Frances Cohen and Richard Lazarus have noted, because the idea of

> being healthy, able, and having a normal physique is central to most people's image and evaluation, becoming ill can be a shock to a person's sense of security and to his or her self-image. Not only does it threaten the customary view of oneself, but it further underscores that one is indeed vulnerable ... and that one's life may be changed in major respects. As a result, adjustment to an illness or injury which is life-threatening or potentially disabling may require considerable coping effort. (1979, p. 218)

Potentially disabling or life-threatening conditions leave patients and their families with many uncertainties. Often no one can tell for certain exactly what the course of the illness will be.

Why do some individuals cope differently from others after learning they have a chronic health problem? Rudolf Moos (1982; Moos & Schaefer, 1986) has proposed the **crisis theory,** which describes factors that influence how people adjust during a crisis, such as having an illness. Figure 13–1 presents his conceptual model, showing that the outcome of the crisis—or the adjustment the person makes—depends on the coping process, which depends on three contributing influences: *illness-related* factors, *background and personal* factors, and *physical and social environmental* factors. We will look at these contributing influences, and then see how they affect the coping process the patient uses.

Illness-Related Factors

Some health problems present a greater threat to the person than others do—they may be more disabling, disfiguring, painful, or life-threatening, for example. As you might expect, the greater the threats patients perceive for any of these factors, the more difficulty they are likely to have coping with their conditions (Cohen & Lazarus, 1979; Diamond, 1983; Moos, 1982). Adjusting to being disfigured can be extremely difficult, particularly when it involves the person's face. Many individuals whose faces are badly scarred withdraw from social encounters, sometimes completely. Often people who see the disfigurement react awkwardly, and some show feelings of revulsion. Even children react more negatively to people's facial disfigurements than to injuries to other parts of the body, such as when people are crippled or missing a limb (Richardson, Goodman, Hastorf, & Dornbusch, 1961).

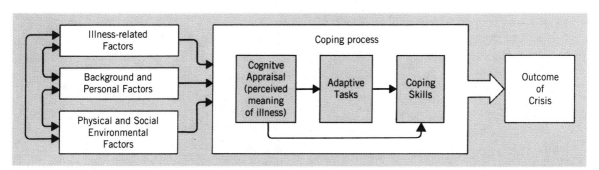

Figure 13–1 A diagram of crisis theory's description of factors and the coping process patients use in the first phases of adjusting psychologically to a serious illness. Arrows denote the flow of effects. (Adapted from Moos, 1982, Figure 1.)

Patients also have difficulty coping with illness-related factors that involve annoying or embarrassing changes in bodily functioning or that draw attention to their conditions (Bekkers et al., 1995; Diamond, 1983; Norris, 1990). People with some illnesses, for instance, may need artificial devices for excreting fecal or urinary wastes. These devices may be noticeable either visibly or by their odors, and many patients have exaggerated impressions of the social impact such devices have. Other chronically ill people must treat their conditions with ointments that may have odors or equipment that is visible or makes noise. Still others may experience periodic seizures or muscle spasms that can be embarrassing. Many people with chronic illnesses feel self-conscious about their health problems—or even stigmatized by them—and want to hide them from others (Scambler, 1984).

Various other aspects of treatment regimens can make adjustment very difficult, too. Some treatments are painful or involve medications that produce serious side effects—either by leading to additional health problems or by interfering with the patient's daily functioning, such as by making the person immobile or drowsy. Other regimens may have treatment schedules and time commitments that make it difficult for the person to find or hold a job. Some regimens require patients and their families to make substantial changes in their lifestyles, which they might resent and fail to carry out. Each of these factors can impair people's adjustment to chronic health problems.

Background and Personal Factors

People who cope well with chronic health problems have the psychological and behavioral resources to "resolve the chronicity or 'long-termness' of the situation, balance hope against despair, and find purpose and quality in life" (Diamond, 1983, p. 683). Often, these people have hardy or resilient personalities that allow them to see a good side in difficult situations (Pollock, Christian, & Sands, 1991). As an example, a 16-year-old boy named Ralfie, whose body had wasted away to 50 pounds from a rare spinal-muscular disease, stated:

> When I take a bath and look at myself naked, I think, "God Jesus." I'm disappointed when it comes to my body, but when it comes to my inside, my personality, my sense of humor, I'm proud of the way I am. I think I'm a nicer person. The girls always

tell me, "You're very special. You're different than the other guys." (Hurley, 1987, p. 34)

People with chronic diseases who are like Ralfie can often find purpose and quality in their lives, maintain their self-esteem, and resist feeling helpless and hopeless.

The ways individuals cope with chronic health problems also depend on many other background and personal factors, such as their age, gender, social class, philosophical or religious commitments, emotional maturity, and self-esteem (Moos & Schaefer, 1986). With respect to gender differences, for instance, men are more likely than women to be "threatened by the decreases in ambition, vigor, and physical prowess that often result from serious illness because, by comparison with women, they are confident in the stability of their physical abilities and bodily functioning" (Moos, 1982, p. 132). Having a chronic illness often means that the individual must take on a dependent and passive role for a long period of time. For men, this can be especially difficult since it is inconsistent with the assertive and independent roles they generally occupy in most societies of the world.

The timing of a health problem in the person's life span also affects the impact on him or her. In the case of very young children, their limited cognitive abilities prevent them from understanding fully the nature of their illnesses, the treatment regimens they must follow, and the long-term implications of their conditions (Bibace & Walsh, 1979; Burbach & Peterson, 1986). Their concerns are likely to focus on any restrictions that are imposed on their lifestyles and activities, the frightening medical procedures they experience, and possible separations from their parents. As children get older and their comprehension improves, they may be able to participate in making some decisions about their treatment. Adolescents can understand information about their illnesses and treatment, but their needing to be like and feel accepted by their peers can lead to difficulties in coping with their health problems (La Greca & Stone, 1985). Because of these motivations, adolescents may deny important aspects of their conditions and neglect their medical care to avoid appearing different from their friends.

In adulthood, too, the difficulties individuals have in coping with chronic health problems change with age (Mages & Mendelsohn, 1979; Moos, 1982). When people develop disabling or life-threatening illnesses or injuries in early adulthood, they tend to resent not having had the chance to develop their lives in the direction they planned—to get married, to have children, or to enter a particular career. In contrast, middle-aged patients may have problems adjusting to the disruption of established roles and lifestyles and to being unable to finish tasks they have started, such as building up a business. In old age, people who develop chronic illnesses may resent not being able to enjoy the leisure they feel they earned in their lifetimes of work and self-sacrifice.

Another personal factor that affects how people cope with chronic health problems is their degree of self-blame for their condition. People who believe they are personally responsible for developing a chronic illness and its symptoms tend to cope poorly with their condition, showing higher levels of depression in subsequent months than patients with less self-blame (Schiaffino, Shawaryn, & Blum, 1998). People's beliefs about the causes, effects, and treatments of their illnesses are often wrong and can affect their adjustment to a health problem.

Physical and Social Environmental Factors

Many physical and social features of our environments can affect the way we adjust to chronic health problems (Moos, 1982). The physical aspects of a hospital environment, for instance, are usually very dull and confining for patients, thereby depressing their general morale and mood. For some individuals, the home environment may not be much better. Many patients have difficulty getting around their houses or performing self-help tasks, such as buttoning clothes or opening food containers, and lack special equipment or tools that can help them do these tasks and be more self-sufficient. These people's adjustment to their health problems can be impaired as long as these situations persist.

The patient's social environment functions as a system, with the behavior of each person affecting the others (Kerns & Weiss, 1994; Revenson, 1994). The presence of social support, for example, generally helps patients and their families and friends cope with their illnesses. Individuals who live alone and have few friends or who have poor relationships with the people they live with tend to adjust poorly to chronic health conditions (Gentry & Kobasa, 1984; Wallston, Alagna, DeVellis, & DeVellis, 1983). But it is also true that sometimes people in a patient's social network may undermine effective coping by providing bad

Sources of social support for patients usually involve their families, but also include friends and people from support groups and religious organizations.

examples or poor advice (Suls, 1982). The degree to which each member of the social system adjusts in constructive ways to the illness affects the adjustment of the others.

The primary source of social support for children and most adults who are ill typically comes from their immediate families (Cantor & Little, 1985; Miller & Cafasso, 1992). People in old age whose spouses are either deceased or unable to help are likely to receive support mainly from their children, but also from siblings, friends, and neighbors. At almost any age, patients may join *support groups* for people with specific medical problems. These groups can provide informational and emotional support.

As Figure 13–1 depicts, crisis theory's three contributing influences are interrelated and can modify each other. The patient's social class or cultural background, for instance, may affect his or her self-consciousness about or access to special devices and equipment to promote self-sufficiency. These contributing factors combine to influence the coping process the person uses to deal with the crisis.

THE COPING PROCESS

Crisis theory proposes that coping begins with the patient's *cognitive appraisal* of the meaning or significance of the health problem to his or her life. The outcome of this appraisal leads the individual to formulate an array of *adaptive tasks* and to apply various *coping skills* to deal with these tasks. Let's see what these tasks and skills are.

The Tasks and Skills of Coping

According to Moos (1982), people who are ill need to address two types of adaptive tasks in the coping process:

- *Tasks related to the illness or treatment*, which involve learning to (1) cope with the symptoms or disability the health problem causes, (2) adjust to the hospital environment and medical procedures needed to treat the problem, and (3) develop and maintain good relationships with their practitioners.

- *Tasks related to general psychosocial functioning*, which involve striving to (1) control negative feelings and retain a positive outlook for the future, (2) maintain a satisfactory self-image and sense of competence, (3) preserve good relationships with family and friends, and (4) prepare for an uncertain future.

These tasks can be very difficult for patients, particularly when their health problems may lead to disability, disfigurement, or death. Still, many people with poor prognoses for their health manage to adapt successfully and make the most of their new life circumstances.

Crisis theory proposes that patients encounter these adaptive tasks in any health problem they experience. But the relative importance or salience of each task for each illness or injury depends on the nature of the condition and the patient's personality and environmental circumstances (Moos, 1982). A person who becomes blind may have little physical discomfort, but may experience difficulty maintaining a job or social relations. A woman who has a mastectomy may need to focus on adapting to her new self-image. A professional athlete, construction worker, or other physically active individual is likely to experience more difficulty adapting to a wheelchair than a more sedentary person. Family members must make

similar adjustments, and these individuals are critically important in helping patients achieve each goal. Patients are likely to adapt well to a chronic condition if their family members participate actively in their treatment regimens, encourage them to be self sufficient, and respond to their needs in a caring and sensitive manner.

What coping skills do patients and their families employ to deal with these adaptive tasks? Table 13.1 describes several useful strategies that they commonly use. Each of these skills can help in achieving the goals of adaptive tasks and in leading to a positive outcome of the crisis. Is one approach best? Generally speaking, although moderate or temporary use of any specific skill can be beneficial, using any single skill exclusively may undermine the coping process (Moos, 1982). Some coping skills may be more appropriate for dealing with some tasks than with others. As a result, people generally use these skills selectively, often in combination. For instance, seeking information may help patients deal with the symptoms, and setting reasonable goals may help them do exercises

Table 13.1 *Coping Strategies for Chronic Health Problems*

- *Denying or minimizing* the seriousness of the situation. As we have seen, this approach can be beneficial in the early phases of adjusting to a health problem. Patients may benefit from this approach by using it selectively to put aside their emotions temporarily, thereby saving them from feeling overwhelmed and giving them time to organize other personal coping resources.
- *Seeking information* about the health problem and treatment procedures.
- *Learning to provide one's own medical care* such as self-administering insulin shots. With this approach, patients gain a sense of control and personal effectiveness with respect to their conditions.
- *Setting concrete, limited goals* such as in exercising or in going to shows or social gatherings, and maintaining regular routines as well as possible. By doing this, patients and their families have things to look forward to and opportunities to achieve goals they consider meaningful.
- *Recruiting instrumental and emotional support* from family, friends, and practitioners by expressing needs and feelings.
- *Considering possible future events* and stressful circumstances in order to know what lies ahead and to be prepared for unexpected difficulties.
- *Gaining a manageable perspective* on the health problem and its treatment by finding a long-term "purpose" or "meaning" for the experience. Patients often do this by applying religious beliefs or by recognizing how they have been changed in positive ways by the experience.

Source: Based on Moos (1982).

and reduce their incapacitation. Individuals who have adjusted successfully to each phase of the crises are ready to deal effectively with subsequent phases in their adjustment to their health problems.

Long-Term Adaptation to Chronic Health Problems

Chronic disorders last for a very long time—and patients and their families need to adapt to the illnesses and whether they worsen, stay the same, or improve over time. The term **adaptation** refers to the process of making changes in order to adjust constructively to life's circumstances. For chronically ill individuals and their families, the adaptive changes they make can enhance their quality of life by promoting their effective physical, psychological, and social functioning (Cohen & Lazarus, 1983; Diamond, 1983). What does "quality of life" mean? **Quality of life** refers to the degree of excellence people appraise their lives to contain. People around the world appraise excellence with similar criteria, such as performing daily activities, energy or discomfort, positive and negative feelings, personal control, interpersonal relations, pleasant activities, personal and intellectual growth, and material possessions (Gill & Feinstein, 1994; Power et al., 1999).

Individuals who show effective long-term adaptation to chronic illness often have psychological resources that enable them to apply appropriate coping strategies to deal with the problems they face. When chronically ill people can expect to live for many years, they need to make many decisions, such as career selections, that involve examining their options based on realistic assessments of their conditions. People who continue to rely heavily on avoidance coping strategies, such as denial, are less likely to adapt effectively than those who use strategies that allow them to consider their situations more carefully and objectively (Suls & Fletcher, 1985).

To summarize, most people tend to react to becoming seriously ill with shock, followed by a period of disorganized thinking and feelings of loss and helplessness. Avoidance strategies, such as denial, constitute one of several types of coping skills patients use to deal with the adaptive tasks they identify through the process of cognitive appraisal. The importance of each adaptive task depends on the person's personality, the physical and social environment, and the specific chronic health problem to which he or she must adjust.

IMPACTS OF DIFFERENT CHRONIC CONDITIONS

What is it like to live with a chronic health problem? To some extent, the answer depends on the illness. Beginning with this section, we will consider the impact of specific chronic medical conditions and treatments on patients and their families. The particular health problems we will examine were selected to illustrate disorders of different body systems and widely different adjustment difficulties. Some of the health problems tend to develop at much earlier ages than others; some require much more complex treatment regimens than others; and some produce more pain and disability than others. People who are disabled by illness are more likely than others to adjust poorly to their condition and become clinically depressed (Williamson, 2000). At the end of the chapter, we will consider psychosocial approaches to help chronically ill people adapt to their condition.

Although the medical problems we will discuss here include some that can be life-threatening, none of these chronic conditions is among the most deadly illnesses people around the world develop—particularly heart disease, cancer, stroke, and AIDS, which we will examine in the next chapter. We will use a *life-span perspective* to order the health problems in this chapter: illnesses that generally begin in childhood will be presented first, and illnesses that usually begin in old age will be considered last. As we have seen, the impact of a health problem and the way people cope with it depend partly on the patient's age. We will start by considering the impact of asthma, a chronic respiratory disorder that generally begins in the early childhood years.

ASTHMA

We all experience respiratory disorders at one time or another. If we are fortunate, these disorders are limited to occasional bouts with winter colds and the flu. But millions of people are not so fortunate—they suffer from chronic respiratory problems. In some cases, these problems involve constant breathing impairments that vary in intensity from one day to the next. In other cases, the victims breathe normally most of the time but suffer recurrent episodes of impaired breathing. Some chronic respiratory illnesses, such as *emphysema*, result largely from environmental causes, such as cigarette smoking. Others do not. Some chronic respiratory disorders become severe enough to disable their victims and may even claim their lives. This can happen with *asthma*.

What Is Asthma?

Imagine being at home reading one evening and noticing that a slight whistling, wheezing sound starts to accompany each breath you take. Soon the sound becomes louder and your breathing becomes labored. You try opening your mouth to breathe, but very little air goes in or out. When your chest begins to contract from the effort and your heart pounds rapidly, you are quite frightened and worry, "Will my next gasp for air be my last?" This is what a major asthma attack is like. Victims of extreme attacks may begin to turn blue and look as if they are about to die, and some do die.

Asthma is a respiratory disorder involving recurrent episodes of impaired breathing when the airways become obstructed. This disease in very prevalent around the world; in the United States alone, about 17 million people—6% of the population—suffer from asthma (ALA, 2000). Prevalence rates are much higher for children than adults. Although the disorder may emerge at any age, it is most likely to develop by age 5 in children and between the ages of 30 and 40 among adults (AAFA, 2000). Fortunately, most childhood cases of asthma become less severe over time (Burg & Ingall, 1985), and 25 to 50% of the children who develop asthma no longer have symptoms by the time they reach adulthood (Cluss & Fireman, 1985; Eiser, 1985). Each year, over 5,400 asthmatics in the United States die from asthma attacks; the death rates from attacks have increased since 1980 and are higher among African Americans than white individuals (ALA, 2000). Because African Americans have lower incomes than whites and are less likely to have regular physicians, they tend to use hospital emergency rooms as their main source of treatment for asthma and seek help mainly when attacks are severe.

Asthma is a leading cause of short-term disability in the United States (Weiss, Gergen, & Hodgson, 1992). Each year, it results in millions of restricted-activity days in which patients either remain in bed or are unable to carry out their usual major activities, such as going to work or school. In childhood alone, asthma results in:

- 28 million restricted-activity days a year
- 28 million physician visits, making it the tenth most frequent reason
- 200,000 hospitalizations, which have increased sharply since the 1970s (ALA, 2000)

Asthma is clearly a major health problem. Let's see what causes asthma attacks.

The Physiology, Causes, and Effects of Asthma

Asthma episodes typically begin when the immune system is activated to react in an allergic manner, producing antibodies that cause the bronchial tubes and other affected body tissues to release a chemical called *histamine*. This chemical causes irritation to those tissues. In an asthma attack, these events cause the bronchial tubes to become obstructed as their smooth muscles become inflamed, develop spasms, and produce mucus (AAFA, 2000; Evans, 1990). These events last, perhaps, an hour or two and can lead to tissue damage, thereby increasing the likelihood of more frequent and severe future attacks. For some asthmatics, airway inflammation becomes constant.

What causes asthma attacks to happen? We do not have a full answer to this question, but we do know that attacks usually occur in the presence of certain conditions, called *triggers* (Evans, 1990). Asthma triggers can include *personal factors*, such as having a respiratory infection or feelings of anger or anxiety; *environmental conditions*, such as air pollution, pollen, or cold temperature; and *physical activities*, such as strenuous exercise (Janson-Bjerklie, Carrieri, & Hudes, 1986; Sarafino & Goldfedder, 1995). The triggers that lead to attacks are different for different asthmatics, and some individuals have attacks only when two or more triggers occur at the same time (Evans, 1990). The main triggers for many asthmatics are allergens—substances, such as pollens or molds, that are known to cause allergic reactions. But other asthmatics do not have any known allergies, and other factors, such as physical exercise or cold air, are the main triggers for them. Tests for allergic reactions usually jecting a small amount of the allergen and checking to see if the skin in that inflamed.

Researchers demonstrated the important role of immune processes in the development of allergic reactions with a study involving transplanted bone marrow, the tissue that produces white blood cells (Agosti et al., 1988). The subjects were cancer patients who needed the transplants as part of their treatment. Each subject and donor was given skin tests with 17 allergen extracts—including house dust, cat hair, penicillin, mites, and ragweed—before the transplant and one year after. In some of the pretransplant tests, the donor showed a positive allergic reaction but the patient did not. When tested again a year later, the subjects now showed reactions in 44.5% of the tests. In other pretransplant tests, neither the donor nor the patient showed an allergic reaction. This situation served as a control condition—and a year later the subjects showed reactions in only 3% of these tests. These findings indicate that bone marrow contains allergen-specific antibodies and that the donors' allergies were passed on to the patients. This research also produced evidence of asthma being transmitted from donors to people who previously had no history of asthma.

What causes the condition of asthma to develop? Twin studies and other genetic research have shown that heredity clearly plays a role in determining whether individuals develop asthma (Sarafino, 2000). Research has also found evidence linking genetic factors to the severity of the condition and some of the specific triggers that are involved (Sarafino & Goldfedder, 1995). Other important factors include the person's history of respiratory infection and exposure to cigarette smoke. Individuals who contract serious viral infections in infancy or early childhood are more likely to develop asthma than individuals who do not (Li & O'Connell, 1987; Sarafino & Dillon, 1998). Children are more likely to develop asthma if their parents smoke (Hu, Persky, Flay, & Richardson, 1997). It may be that infections and smoke damage the respiratory system, making it highly sensitive to certain triggering conditions.

Medical Regimens for Asthma

Medical approaches provide the cornerstone of treatment for asthma (AAFA, 2000; Cluss & Fireman, 1985; Evans, 1990). Asthma regimens consist of three components, the first being to *avoid known triggers* of attacks. The second component involves medication. To treat an acute attack, patients mainly use *bronchodilators*, which open up constricted airways. To prevent attacks, patients can use *anti-inflammatories*, such as inhaled or oral corticosteroids and cromolyn, which reduce bronchial inflammation or block the release of histamine and other chemicals that cause inflammation. Steroids that are inhaled in low doses have little risk of undesirable side effects, but those taken orally or in large doses can have serious side effects, such as rapid heartbeat and decreased bone density, and are usually reserved for people with severe asthma and used sparingly. Inhaled steroids are usually applied three or four times a day.

The third component of asthma regimens involves *exercise*. In the past, physicians advised many asthmatics to avoid exercise because it could induce an attack (Stockton, 1988). But it now appears that the less these people exercise, the worse their conditions get. Many physicians today recommend treatment regimens that carefully combine fitness training and the use of medication. Asthma's potential for producing disability and, sometimes, death makes it important that patients adhere to their regimens. Although adhering to asthma regimens reduces attacks and incidents of wheezing, many asthmatics fail to take medication to prevent attacks and use medication during an attack incorrectly (Cluss & Fireman, 1985).

Psychosocial Factors in Asthma

We saw in Chapter 4 that psychosocial factors, including stress, can produce or aggravate an asthmatic episode. Many people with asthma report that the triggers of their attacks often involve their emotional states, such as being worried, angry, or excited (Janson-Bjerklie, Carrieri, & Hudes, 1986). Experimental research has shown that emotional arousal, such as when watching an exciting movie, can trigger attacks in some children (Miller & Wood, 1994).

Studies have also found that *suggestion* can induce symptoms in some asthmatics. In one study, researchers had asthmatics inhale several doses of a placebo solution, with each succeeding dose labeled as containing an increasingly strong level of an allergen (Luparello, Lyons, Bleecker, & McFadden, 1968). Nearly half of the subjects developed symptoms, either as full asthmatic attacks or as spasms of the bronchial muscles. Another study confirmed the effect of suggestion, but also showed that the asthmatic reaction could be negated if the subjects were first given another placebo that was described as a new asthma drug (Butler & Steptoe, 1986). In other words, the first suggestion blocked the second one. Other studies have shown that false feedback indicating that the airways are becoming obstructed increases breathlessness in people with asthma (Rietveld & Brosschot, 1999). Although there is little question that psychosocial factors can influence asthma attacks, we do not know how these factors work and which asthmatics are more affected by them. It is possible that psychosocial factors make asthmatics more sensitive to allergens or other conditions that trigger their attacks.

Asthma attacks are frightening for the patient and family alike, and frequent episodes are costly to the family and disrupt these people's lives and functioning (Cluss & Fireman, 1985). Living with this disorder adds to the stress that asthmatics and their families experience, and studies have found that asthma is sometimes related to maladjustment in patients and their families (Werry, 1986). This relationship probably involves two causal directions: (1) living with asthma sometimes leads to emotional problems and (2) maladjustment in the family increases asthmatic episodes. Some asthmatics are chronically short of breath and have frequent attacks, and others have long attack-free periods. The psychosocial impact of asthma is likely to depend on how severe and disabling the condition is. In the next section, we will examine what it is like to live with epilepsy, which is a disorder of the brain that produces recurrent seizures.

EPILEPSY

Epilepsy is a condition marked by recurrent, sudden seizures that result from electrical disturbances of the cerebral cortex (EFA, 2000; Fraser, 1999). Although the seizures epileptics experience can vary greatly, the two most common types are the:

- *Grand mal (or "tonic-clonic") attack*, which is the most severe form and entails two phases. It begins with a very brief "tonic" phase, in which the person loses consciousness and body is rigid. It then progresses to a longer "clonic" phase that lasts 2 or 3 minutes and includes muscle spasms and twitching. The body may then relax until the person awakens soon. Sometimes before a grand mal attack epileptics experience an *aura*, which consists of unexplained sounds, smells, or other sensations.

- *Petit mal (or "absence")* ished consciousnes stares blankly for a few seconds, and ing. When the epis sumes whatever h not even being aw tit mal attacks occur mainly ... ally disappear by adulthood.

Estimates of the prevalence of epilepsy vary somewhat, but it afflicts about 1% of people worldwide (Tortora & Grabowski, 2000). There are probably over 2 million cases of epilepsy in the United States, perhaps half of which are undiagnosed and untreated (Eichenwald, 1987; Hauser & Hesdorffer, 1990). Over 100,000 new cases are diagnosed each year. Although the condition can develop at any age, the great majority of epileptics experience their first seizures by 20 years of age (Seidenberg & Berent, 1992). What causes epilepsy? Sometimes physicians find a specific neurological defect that is the cause of an epileptic's disorder, but usually they do not (Hauser & Hesdorffer, 1990). Risk factors for developing epilepsy include a strong family history of the condition, severe head injury, infections of the central nervous system, and stroke. Most people with epilepsy eventually become seizure-free for at least 5 years. (Go to 💡.)

Medical Regimens for Epilepsy

Anticonvulsant drugs provide the main medical treatment for epilepsy (EFA, 2000; Fraser, 1999). These medications must be taken regularly to maintain the most effective serum concentrations throughout the day and can have undesirable side effects, such as facial hair in women, and blurred vision and nausea if the dose is too high. A promising new treatment involves using an implanted device that delivers stimulation to the vagal nerve (Fraser, 1999). Epileptics whose seizures result from clear neurological defects may have the option of surgical treatment if they have frequent, severe attacks and other treatments do not work or cause problematic side effects. Neuropsychologists conduct tests to pinpoint the affected area of the brain and minimize cognitive and motor impairments the surgery might produce (DeAngelis, 1990). After surgery, as many as 80% of patients become seizure-free in the next few years (Fraser, 1999). But undergoing surgery without

HIGHLIGHT ON ISSUES
What to Do for a Seizure

People react negatively to seeing a grand mal attack for many reasons, one of which may be that they don't know what to do to help. Actually, there is little one *can* do other than to remain calm and try to protect the epileptic from injury as he or she falls or flails about during the tonic or clonic phases. If you witness a seizure, the following five actions are recommended (Eichenwald, 1987; EFA, 2000):

1. Prevent injury from falls or flailing. Break the fall if possible and provide a cushion, such as a coat, between the person's head and the ground.

2. Do *not* put anything in the person's mouth. Many people believe they must put a spoon or other object in the mouth to prevent the epileptic from swallowing his or her tongue, which actually can-

not happen. Loosen tight clothing around the neck. Turn the person on his or her side so that saliva does not obstruct breathing.

3. Do *not* restrain the person. If you believe the epileptic could be injured while flailing near a hard object, try to move the object.

4. If the person does not come out of the attack in about 5 minutes, call an ambulance.

5. After the person wakes up, describe what happened and see if he or she needs help when ready to leave. Epileptics are often disoriented after an attack. For the most part, the role of the bystander requires calm and composed caring and common sense.

---

becoming seizure-free may lead to subsequent psychosocial difficulties, such as heightened anxiety and depression (Rose, Derry, & McLachlan, 1995).

Psychosocial Factors in Epilepsy

Because individuals who are having epileptic episodes lose control of their behavior and "act strange," their condition stigmatizes them among people who do not understand it (Scambler, 1984). This stigma is clear in the experience of a college freshman named Kurt when he witnessed a severe epileptic attack for the first time:

In the center of my college dining hall, a young man who worked in the kitchen had collapsed in a convulsion. Four students quickly piled on top of him. His arms and legs jerked violently and, in the process of trying to hold him down, the students seemed to be smothering him. The young man's face, twisted and red, made him appear to be in great pain and, somehow, inhuman. Yet I could see myself in his place—I had just found out that I had epilepsy.

I did not want to say anything, but I thought the four students, in their panic, might kill the young man. So I told the largest of them, who

by then had a headlock on the kitchen worker, to let go. The student brushed off my concern and seemed irritated that I should bother him at such a time. I paused, then repeated my statement in louder tones. The student was angry. "Look, kid, I'm a pre-med. I know what I'm doing. What makes you think you know so much?" I opened my mouth, but no words came out. Instead, I walked to a corner and leaned against a wall. As the young man's convulsions grew more violent, I whispered an apology to him and began to cry.

Just four weeks before, back home in Dallas, a neurologist had diagnosed my epilepsy. The doctor warned me—and so did members of my family soon afterward—that if I did not keep my epilepsy a secret, people would fear me and I would be subject to discrimination. (Eichenwald, 1987, p. 30)

Long ago, many people believed that individuals with the condition were possessed by the devil. Although few people in advanced societies today shun victims of epilepsy, witnessing an attack may still arouse feelings of fear and aversion.

Aside from the reactions their attacks produce in people, what other problems do epileptics face as a result of their illness? Having strong seizures, especially with a loss of consciousness, is sometimes associated with important cognitive and motor impairments that can limit eligibility for certain activities and jobs, such as those that involve high memory loads or danger from heights or machinery (Fraser, 1999). An example of the discrimination epileptics sometimes experience comes from the case of Kurt, the freshman we just discussed. Because of his condition, he was dismissed from the prestigious college he attended. As it turned out, however, he was reinstated after the United States Department of Health and Human Services advised him that dismissal on the basis of a handicapping condition is discriminatory. He graduated in 1983.

Epilepsy seems to be related to psychosocial processes in two ways. First, some evidence suggests that emotional arousal, such as of anxiety, may increase the likelihood or severity of epileptic episodes (Goldstein, 1990). Second, epileptics and their families sometimes adjust poorly to the disorder, especially if episodes are frequent and severe (Fraser, 1999; Hauser & Hesdorffer, 1990). Emotional difficulties, such as with anxiety or depression, often lead clients to drop out of rehabilitation programs. Many of the adjustment problems that epileptics face can be reduced through counseling when the diagnosis is made and through the work of support groups.

NERVOUS SYSTEM INJURIES

A woman named Leslie who suffered a *brain injury* in a car accident awoke after 17 days in a coma with, as she put it, the "mentality of a cantankerous 13-year-old." Upon awakening she bit and pinched her physical therapist because, in her words,

> I didn't know who I was, what happened to me. All of a sudden you wake up in this bed one day and these people are hurting you, bending your leg and such. And you think it's a dream or a nightmare of some kind. (Leonard, 1990, p. 49)

This was the start of her long recovery. Many thousands of people in the United States suffer injuries to the brain or spinal cord each year, leaving them debilitated for life. Neuropsychologists and health psychologists play important roles in assessing these patients' impairments and helping them adapt to their conditions (Bleiberg, Ciulla, & Katz, 1991). In this section, we will focus on the impact of having a spinal cord injury.

Prior to the 1940s, medical practitioners knew almost nothing about treating people who suffered a severe injury to the spinal cord (Hendrick, 1985). In World War I, 80% of the soldiers who received such injuries died within 2 weeks. People who survived severe spinal cord injuries had a poor prognosis for their future health, which was characterized by major health complications and a short life span. As a result, patients and practitioners had a defeatist attitude, and little attempt was made toward rehabilitation. But in World War II, England established special medical units to develop and provide comprehensive care and rehabilitation for people with spinal cord injuries. These medical units served as a model for others to be developed in countries around the world.

The Prevalence, Causes, and Physical Effects of Spinal Cord Injuries

The term **spinal cord injury** refers to neurological damage in the spine that results in the loss of motor control, sensation, and reflexes in associated body areas. The damage may be caused by disease or by an injury that compresses, tears, or severs the cord (Hendrick, 1985; NSCIA, 2000). When the cord is badly torn or severed, the damage is permanent because little or no nerve tissue will regenerate; but if the cord is compressed or has an abrasion, some function may be recovered when the pressure is removed or healing occurs. As we saw in Chapter 2, the degree to which the person's function is impaired depends on the amount of damage and its location. If the cord is completely severed in the neck region, *quadriplegia* results. Actor Christopher Reeve's horse-riding accident left him quadriplegic. If a lower portion is severed, *paraplegia* results. If the cord is not completely severed, partial function remains.

Millions of people around the world are living with spinal cord injuries; in the United States, there are more than 250,000 people with this affliction, and about 8,000 new cases occur each year (Bleiberg, Ciulla, & Katz, 1991; NSCIA, 2000). About half of these people suffer neck injuries and are quadriplegics. The great majority of Americans who receive spinal cord injuries are males, and most of them are between 10 and 30 years of age at the time. The most common cause is automobile and motorcycle accidents, and the remainder result mainly from falls, sporting activities, and wounds, such as from a gunshot or stabbing.

The physical effects patients experience after spinal cord injuries change over time and progress through two stages:

1. *Short-term effects.* The immediate physiological reaction is called "spinal shock," which usually lasts between a few days and 3 months (Hendrick, 1985; Nash & Smith, 1982). In spinal shock, neural function is devastated either by the cord being severed or by inflammation at the site of lesser damage. The result is that the body cannot regulate blood pressure, temperature, respiration, and bladder and bowel function. Medical personnel must intervene to control these functions. Usually, the shorter the period of spinal shock, the better the prognosis of recovery.

2. *Long-term effects.* The full extent of spinal cord damage may not be clear for some time, and long-term predictions are difficult to make during the first 6 months or so (Hendrick, 1985). If the cord is not severed, considerable functional recovery may occur over a long period of time. If the cord is severed, some autonomic functions will recover, but other functions will not. People who survive severe damage to the higher regions of the cord are typically fully paralyzed and unable to breathe without a respirator.

Actor Christopher Reeve has resumed an active life after a horse-riding accident rendered him quadriplegic.

The initial care these patients receive typically focuses on their medical needs, with little or no attention to their psychological reactions (Brucker, 1983). They receive very little information about their prognosis because it is so hard to predict, and medical staff want to avoid the depression their speculations might produce. Once the condition of these individuals has stabilized, the process of rehabilitation begins. Almost all spinal cord injury patients enter rehabilitation expecting to regain total function and are not prepared to cope with the reality of permanent functional losses. A major goal for psychologists at this time is to help these people adjust to the demands and limitations of the rehabilitation process (Bleiberg, Ciulla, & Katz, 1991).

Physical Rehabilitation

The process of physical rehabilitation for people with spinal cord injuries is geared toward helping them (1) regain as much physical function as the neurological damage will allow and (2) become as independent in their functioning as possible (Brucker, 1983). This process focuses initially on training the patients to develop bladder and bowel control and on assisting them in moving paralyzed limbs to maintain their range of motion (Hendrick, 1985). Although many of these people will eventually be able to control their bladder functions, others will not and will need to use catheters or other devices. Hygienic bladder care is extremely important because a common cause of death in these patients after the spinal shock period is kidney failure from repeated infections (Hendrick, 1985; NSCIA, 2000).

The next phase of rehabilitation extends the focus of physical therapy toward maintaining and improving the function of muscles over which the person has some control (Hendrick, 1985). For example, quadriplegics receive special attention toward improving respiration; paraplegics do exercises to strengthen the upper body. When some neural connection to affected parts of the body remains, therapy with biofeedback to "reeducate" the muscles in those areas appears to help some, but not all, patients (Klose et al., 1993). The last phase of physical rehabilitation extends the therapy as much as possible to include activities of daily living. Those patients who have regained sufficient function learn how to perform self-care activities independently and to use devices to compensate for permanent physical losses.

Some devices today are highly sophisticated and use computers, allowing paralyzed individuals to turn on lights, answer the telephone, and operate computer keyboards with voice commands.

Psychosocial Aspects of Spinal Cord Injury

People with spinal cord injuries face a long life ahead—85% of those who live through the first day are still alive 10 years later, and many survive 30 to 50 years after the injury (NSCIA, 2000). Most victims who were employed prior to the injury are working again within a year or so (Heinemann, 1999). The victims' main challenges after spinal cord injury are to make the most of their remaining abilities and lead as full a life as possible. This can be very difficult for many with spinal cord injuries because they often suffer from chronic pain conditions as a complication of the injury and lack the resources to help them live and function independently (Mariano, 1992; Tate, Maynard, & Forchheimer, 1993).

What can health care workers, family, and friends do to help? A lot depends on the way they respond to the person's condition. John Adams and Erich Lindemann (1974) described and contrasted case studies of two young men, 17 and 18 years of age, who had suffered spinal cord injuries that rendered them quadriplegic. One adapted successfully, and the other did not. The patient who adapted well was able to accept the injury and abandon the part of his self-concept that was associated with his being a fine athlete. He then turned his energies toward academic pursuits and eventually became a history teacher. He also coached a local basketball team from his wheelchair. The other patient provides a striking contrast. He was never able to accept the injury or the permanence of his condition. He became extremely withdrawn and depressed—at one point he was spending "much time in bed with the curtains drawn and frequently with the sheet over his head". A few years later, he was readmitted to the hospital after taking an overdose of medication. At last contact, he was living at home, still clinging to the hope that he would walk again.

Why did these young men adapt so differently to their similar physical conditions? Adams and Lindemann noted the strikingly different ways these patients' families and friends responded to their condition. In the case of the patient who adapted well to his condition, his parents and friends also accepted his paralysis and provided an environment in which he could redefine his self-concept. For instance, his parents installed ramps in their home and widened doorways to accommodate a wheelchair. The other patient's family and friends were not able to accept his condition or provide the support he needed to help him adapt.

Family and friends can also help by providing social support without being overprotective and "taking over" when the patient has difficulty performing self-help tasks. Having a disabled individual in the household increases the stress of all family members. They need to make many adjustments in daily living and, while doing so, try not to make the person feel like a burden. If the patient is a husband or wife, his or her spouse faces very difficult adjustments (Hendrick, 1985). Role changes occur immediately—at least for a while, and perhaps permanently. The healthy spouse, with or without the help of other family members, must suddenly take on full responsibility for providing the family's income, maintaining the household, caring for the children, and caring for the disabled person. Sexual problems brought on by the patient's injury may become a major source of stress in the marital relationship.

Many people believe that all individuals who become paralyzed below the waist lose all sexual function and interest. This belief is not correct (Brucker, 1983; NSCIA, 2000). Males usually lose their fertility. But although they initially lose the ability to have an erection, they often regain it to some degree. Females generally retain their fertility after paralysis, and about half become able to achieve orgasm. The most serious barriers to sexual function in people with spinal cord injuries appear to be psychosocial rather than physical. These patients and their sexual partners can overcome many of these barriers through counseling and education, such as in ways to position themselves during sex acts and to heighten the degree of stimulation they achieve.

Disabled people also experience many unpleasant thoughts about themselves, their future, their relations with other people in general, and physical barriers in society (Eisenberg, 1984). They find that many places they once liked to go to are inaccessible by wheelchair, for example. Furthermore, people in general act strangely toward them—staring, or quickly averting their eyes, or behaving awkwardly or uncomfortably in their presence. These experiences tend to reduce the self-esteem of disabled people, many of whom have heightened levels of depression and drug and alcohol use (Heinemann, 1999). Adapting to becoming disabled takes time, and a couple of years may pass before many individuals with spinal cord injuries report improvements in their adjustment and quality of life (Krause & Crewe, 1991).

DIABETES

"Too much of a good thing is wonderful," the late actress Mae West once said. Although her rule might possibly apply for some good things, glucose in the blood is not one of them. The body needs glucose to fuel metabolic processes, but too much of it in the blood over a long period of time—a condition called *hyperglycemia*—is the mark of *diabetes mellitus*. The body normally controls blood sugar levels with the hormone *insulin*, which the pancreas produces. In the disorder of diabetes, however, abnormal levels of glucose accumulate in the blood because the pancreas does not produce sufficient insulin (ADA, 2000; Guare, Myers, & Marrero, 1999; Kilo & Williamson, 1987).

Diabetes is a prevalent illness around the world; it is among the most common chronic conditions in the United States, with over 10 million currently diagnosed cases and over 5 million people who are not aware that they have the disorder (ADA, 2000; USBC, 1999). Prevalence rates for diagnosed diabetes increase with age throughout the life span, being many times higher among middle-aged and elderly adults than among children and adolescents. Furthermore, this age difference is widening—prevalence rates of diabetes in the United States have increased fairly steadily for many years among middle-aged and older people, but not among younger individuals, as Figure 13–2 shows. Women from Hispanic, African, and Native American groups are at especially high risk of dying from diabetes (USDHHS, 1995).

The Types and Causes of Diabetes

Diabetes is not a single disease—it occurs in two major patterns that require different kinds of treatment and may have somewhat different causes. The two forms of diabetes are:

- **Type 1 diabetes** (sometimes called *insulin-dependent diabetes mellitus*) typically develops in childhood or adolescence and accounts for only 5 to 10% of diabetes cases. In this form of diabetes,

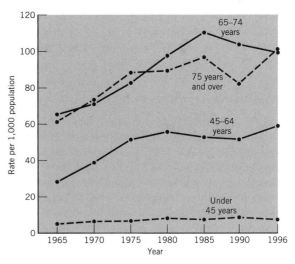

Figure 13–2 Prevalence rates of diagnosed diabetes in the United States from 1965 to 1996 as a function of age. (1965–1980 data from USDHHS, 1985a, Figure 17; 1985 data from USBC, 1989, Table 172; 1990 data from USBC, 1994, Table 206; 1996 data from USBC, 1999, Table 232.)

autoimmune processes have destroyed cells of the pancreas that normally produce insulin, and people afflicted with it require insulin injections to prevent acute and very serious complications (ADA, 2000; Guare, Myers, & Marrero, 1999; Kilo & Williamson, 1987). An acute complication that occurs without insulin in type 1 diabetes is called *ketoacidosis*, in which high levels of fatty acids in the blood lead to kidney malfunctions, thereby causing wastes to accumulate and poison the body. The symptoms of ketoacidosis generally begin with chronic thirst and urination, followed by an acute episode of nausea, vomiting, abdominal pain, and labored breathing. About one-third of type 1 cases are diagnosed after these symptoms appear. If left untreated, ketoacidosis can lead to coma and death in a matter of days or weeks.

- **Type 2 diabetes** (sometimes called *non-insulin-dependent diabetes mellitus*) is very prevalent, accounting for the vast majority of diabetes cases. In this form of diabetes, the pancreas produces at least some insulin, and treatment often does not require insulin injections. Most, but not all, people with type 2 diabetes can manage their glucose levels by carefully following special diets and taking medication (ADA, 2000; Guare, Myers, & Marrero, 1999). Although type

2 diabetes can develop at any age, it usually appears after the age of 40. Most type 2 patients are very overweight, and many produce substantial amounts of insulin—sometimes more than normal—but their bodies seem to "resist" the glucose-controlling action of insulin (Chan et al., 1994; Kohrt et al., 1993). Normal-weight type 2 patients seem to produce reduced levels of insulin. In either case, hyperglycemia results.

What causes the pancreas to reduce its production of insulin? Although the causes are not well understood, twin studies have demonstrated that genetic factors are involved in both type 1 and type 2 diabetes (ADA, 2000; Guare, Myers, & Marrero, 1999; Kilo & Williamson, 1987). Most diabetics probably inherit some form of susceptibility to the effects of environmental conditions that could affect insulin production. In type 1, one environmental condition seems to involve a viral infection that stimulates the immune system to attack pancreas cells (Conrad et al., 1994). For type 2, evidence exists for three possible conditions: diets high in fat and sugar, stress, and an overproduction of a protein that impairs the metabolism of sugars and carbohydrates (Maddux et al., 1995; Surwit, 1993). At this time, however, the nature of people's susceptibility to diabetes and the environmental conditions involved are not clear. (Go to ✎.)

Health Implications of Diabetes

Diabetes can be a direct cause of death; in the United States it claims over 60,000 lives each year (USBC, 1999). Many of these deaths result from acute complications that can be prevented by appropriate medical care. Few diabetics die of acute complications if they follow the recommended medical regimens for controlling glucose levels (Santiago, 1984).

But the deaths that are caused directly by diabetes constitute only part of the serious health effects of this disease (ADA, 2000; Crofford, 1995; Kilo & Williamson, 1987). Diabetes is implicated in the development of a variety of disabling health problems and contributes indirectly to about 100,000 deaths each year. One health problem diabetes can lead to is *neuropathy*, or nerve disease. High blood glucose levels appear to cause chemical reactions that can destroy the myelin sheath that insulates nerve fibers. When this occurs in peripheral fibers, such as in the feet, the person may lose sensation in the affected area or have abnormal sensations, such as chronic pain. If the damage occurs in autonomic nerves, the symptoms may include chronic dizziness, urinary incontinence, and sexual impotence (in males).

Diabetes can also lead to the development of other serious health problems. Physicians Charles Kilo and Joseph Williamson have noted that compared to individuals who are not diabetic, people who have diabetes are:

ASSESS YOURSELF
Do You Have Diabetes?

About half of the people who have diabetes don't know it. To tell if you might have this disorder, put a check mark in the space preceding each of the following warning signs that are true for you.

_____ Very frequent urination.
_____ Frequent excessive thirst.
_____ Often hungry, even after eating.
_____ Unexplained large weight loss.
_____ Chronically tired.
_____ Occasional blurry vision.

_____ Wounds heal very slowly.
_____ Tingling or numbness in your feet.
_____ Waist measurement greater than half your height.

If you check three or more of these signs, see your doctor—one or two signs alone may not mean anything is wrong. But the more signs you checked, the greater the chance that you have diabetes. (*Source:* Based on *Signs and Symptoms of Diabetes* distributed by the American Diabetes Association.)

- 6.8 times more likely to become blind
- 11.3 times more likely to develop kidney disease
- 29.9 times more likely to get gangrene
- 4.6 times more likely to develop heart disease
- 5.4 times more likely to have a stroke (1987, p. 54)

The way diabetes contributes to these health problems is through its effects on the vascular system (Guare, Myers, & Marrero, 1999; Kilo & Williamson, 1987). High levels of glucose in the blood lead to a thickening of arterial walls as a result of atherosclerosis. This can occur in large blood vessels, such as those in the legs and near the heart, causing gangrene in a limb or heart disease. It can also occur in small blood vessels and capillaries, such as those in the eyes, kidneys, and brain. Eye disease that results from diabetes can be treated effectively if caught early (Javitt et al., 1994).

The long-term health risks of diabetes are extremely serious, and patients and their families worry about them greatly (Holmes, 1986; Wilkinson, 1987). They worry about the possibilities of, for instance, dying prematurely, becoming blind, losing a limb if gangrene cannot be controlled, and being unable to perform sexually.

Medical Regimens for Diabetes

Ideally, the treatment for diabetes would enable the body to perform or simulate the normal biochemical activities for processing and maintaining normal levels of glucose. Normal and diabetic serum glucose levels in the hours after eating are shown in Figure 13–3. Medical regimens available today compensate for these differences, but they do not enable the body to function exactly as it normally does, such as in continuously monitoring the need for insulin and secreting this hormone in precisely needed bursts. Physicians generally prescribe somewhat different regimens for type 1 and type 2 patients and tailor the treatment for individual needs (Guare, Myers, & Marrero, 1999).

The main approach for treating diabetes entails a balancing act with medication, diet, and regular exercise under medical supervision. Can diabetics reduce their long-term health risks by keeping their blood glucose levels within the normal range? Yes, these risks can be markedly reduced—with complications occurring much later and far less often—if diabetics receive

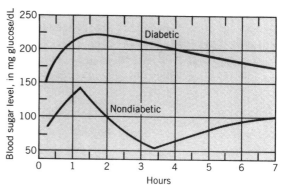

Figure 13–3   Serum levels of glucose for nondiabetics and unmedicated diabetic individuals in the hours after consuming glucose. The data come from a standardized procedure in which subjects consume a specified amount of glucose per kilogram of body weight. (From Holum, 1994, Figure 26.4.)

intensive medical care and control their blood glucose levels by carefully following prescribed treatment regimens (Crofford, 1995; Santiago, 1984; Wang, Lau, & Chalmers, 1993). But the *full extent* of the reduced risk is unclear because long-term complications of diabetes take many years or decades to develop, and many diabetics with good blood glucose control are not always able to keep their glucose levels consistently in the normal range. Regimens for treating diabetes today allow patients to have better control over their blood sugar than in the past, but these new methods are still not perfect. And many diabetics who have regimens that could provide good control over their blood glucose do not adhere to them closely.

Do Diabetics Adhere to their Regimens?

Noncompliance with the treatment regimen is a major problem in managing diabetes. According to researchers who have reviewed studies on this issue, the most thorough survey of patients' adherence to diabetes regimens found that:

- 58% administered the wrong dose of insulin.
- 77% tested their glucose levels incorrectly or interpreted the results "in a manner likely to be detrimental to their treatment."
- 75% did not eat the prescribed foods.
- 75% did not eat with sufficient regularity. (Wing, Epstein, Nowalk, & Lamparski, 1986, p. 78).

People with diabetes generally do *try* to adhere to their regimens, but they do not always succeed. One reason some fail may be that they rely on symptoms they perceive, such as dizziness or emotional states, to assess their glucose levels (Cox et al., 1993; Diamond, Massey, & Covey, 1989). Although many diabetics can make crude estimates of their actual glucose levels on the basis of perceived symptoms, these judgments are usually not very accurate.

Research with type 1 diabetics, ranging from about 12 years of age to old age, found that they have more difficulty following dietary and exercise advice than the more "medical" aspects of their regimens—testing their glucose levels and taking their insulin on time (Glasgow, McCaul, & Schafer, 1986, 1987). The patients' self-reports indicated they had complied fairly closely with their insulin and testing regimens. However, self-report data can be misleading. In two studies, for instance, researchers secretly inserted memory chips in blood glucose testing devices of adult and adolescent diabetics but also had the subjects keep records of their testing (Mazze et al., 1984; Wilson & Endres, 1986). The results showed that many subjects' records were inaccurate—at least according to the memory chips' records. The records did *not* contain data for some tests the subjects had done and *did* contain data for tests that they did not actually perform. (Go to 💡.)

Psychosocial Factors in Diabetes Care

A 60-year-old diabetic named Beth had not been able to get her glucose levels under control (Holt, 1995). Part of the problem was that she was mentally retarded but able to live on her own, and she didn't understand how to plan her diet. A home-care nurse discovered an approach to help: they made up recipe cards for each meal, with pictures of its foods and a shopping list. Because there were cards for breakfast, lunch, dinner, and snacks, Beth could choose the meal she wanted, shop for it, and follow the recipe to make it. And she succeeded in doing so. Not understanding how to interpret glucose test results and adjust the regimen accordingly is a very common problem even among nonretarded diabetics (Patrick, Gill et al., 1994).

We saw in Chapter 9 that compliance to medical recommendations tends to be low when the regimen is complex, must be followed for a long time, requires changes in the person's lifestyle, and is designed to prevent rather than cure illness. Treatment regimens for diabetes have all of these characteristics. In addition, psychosocial factors in patients' lives are related to compliance. Two of these factors are social support and self-efficacy. A study of type 2 diabetics found that their self-reports of adherence to dietary, exercise, and glucose testing aspects of their regimens increased with their perceived social support (Wilson et al., 1986). But the role of social support is unclear because it was not related to actual glucose control, as measured by analysis of blood samples. Other research has shown that diabetics' self-efficacy for being able to follow the diabetes regimen is related to their self-reports of subsequent adherence and their actual glucose control (Kavanaugh, Gooley, & Wilson, 1993; Skelly et al., 1995).

Coping processes are also important in diabetes care. Stress impairs blood sugar control in many diabetics (Kramer, Ledolter, Manos, & Bayless, 2000), especially those who have sedentary lifestyles (Aikens, Aikens, Wallander, & Hunt, 1997). The effects of stress may occur in two ways. First, when people are under stress, the adrenal glands release epinephrine and cortisol into the bloodstream (Surwit, Feinglos, & Scovern, 1983). *Epinephrine* causes the pancreas to decrease insulin production; *cortisol* causes the liver to increase glucose production and body tissues to decrease their use of glucose. These biochemical reactions to stress clearly worsen the glucose regulation problems of diabetics. Second, stress can affect blood glucose levels indirectly by reducing adherence to diabetes regimens (Goldston, Kovacs, Obrosky, & Iyengar, 1995). Many diabetics do not cope well with their condition and suffer from severe depression (Kovacs, 1997). The more that the condition interferes with their daily activities and reduces their feelings of personal control, the more depressed they feel (Talbot et al., 1999).

People's everyday lives present many circumstances that make it difficult to adhere to diabetes regimens (Glasgow, McCaul, & Schafer, 1986). Diabetics may feel that testing their glucose levels at work or school is embarrassing, or forget to take their testing materials with them, or have difficulty getting up on weekend mornings to take their injections on time, or make mistakes in judgments about what they can eat, for example. Four other issues can be important. First, because some temporary weight gain tends to occur when diabetics get their glucose under control, many female patients, in an effort to control their weight,

HIGHLIGHT ON ISSUES
Self-Managing Diabetes

Managing diabetes requires self-care activities that focus mainly on four components: self-monitoring of blood glucose, taking insulin or other medication, diet, and exercise.

Self-Monitoring Blood Glucose

Patients estimate the sugar content of their blood by testing either their urine or, more accurately, the blood itself (ADA, 2000; Kilo & Williamson, 1987). To test the blood, a diabetic pricks his or her finger to get a drop of blood, puts the blood on a chemically treated strip of paper that changes color in reaction to glucose, and inserts the strip into a small meter that displays a digital glucose reading. Although this procedure may sound simple, it requires some accuracy: the reading it gives depends on fairly careful timing of activities. Treatment regimens usually require type 2 diabetics to monitor blood glucose once a day and type 1 patients to do it four times: before each meal and at bedtime.

Taking Insulin and Oral Medication

In the early 1920s, a physician named Frederick Banting devised a method that made it possible to extract insulin from the pancreas glands of slaughtered pigs and cattle, which are the chief sources of insulin for treating diabetes today. Over the years, refinements have been made to the insulin extracted, and forms of the hormone are available that last for different lengths of time. Diabetics who need to take insulin should inject it three times a day, but most opt for twice—morning and evening—which is less effective (Guare, Myers, & Marrero, 1999; Kilo & Williamson, 1987). Some diabetics are able to use a device called an insulin pump that can be implanted in the body and delivers small amounts of insulin continuously, with extra doses at mealtimes.

One of the difficulties in using insulin is knowing how much to inject—taking too much may be as dangerous as taking too little. Using too much insulin can produce *hypoglycemia*, the condition of having too little sugar in blood. Severe hypoglycemia

can cause insulin shock, in which the person lapses into a coma (Kilo & Williamson, 1987). When hypoglycemia is less severe, it can markedly impair cognitive and emotional functioning, making the person excited, irritable, confused, and, sometimes, violent (Holmes, 1986). Diabetics dread these episodes, and so do their families (Wilkinson, 1987). With careful training, people with diabetes can reduce these episodes by adjusting their insulin doses accurately to keep glucose levels within the normal range.

Many diabetics use drugs to control their blood glucose levels. Different types of chemicals work in different ways—for instance, some drugs increase insulin production in functioning pancreatic cells whereas others reduce the liver's production of glucose (Kilo & Williamson, 1987). Physicians typically do periodic blood tests in these patients because these drugs sometimes become less effective in controlling glucose levels over time.

Diet and Exercise

The diets physicians recommend for diabetics are designed to accomplish four things: (1) reduce the intake of foods that contain sugar and some other carbohydrates that lead to high blood glucose levels, (2) reduce cholesterol consumption, (3) achieve and maintain a healthy body weight, and (4) maintain a balanced intake of nutrients (ADA, 2000; Kilo & Williamson, 1987). Patients who take insulin must also maintain consistency in the timing of their meals and, usually, in their calorie intake each day. Once they take their insulin, they generally need to eat within a range of time thereafter to prevent an episode of hypoglycemia.

Because physical activity burns up glucose as fuel, exercise is another important part of the treatment of diabetes. Research has shown that engaging in physical activity after meals inhibits glucose production by the liver and increases glucose use by the muscles (Zinman, 1984). Regular exercise also complements dietary efforts to reduce body weight and maintain overall fitness. But unplanned vigorous (continued)   # HIGHLIGHT ON ISSUES

activity can cause an episode of hypoglycemia. People with diabetes who engage in vigorous activity should eat a sufficient number of calories to last through the event or carry packets of medication to adjust their blood sugar quickly (Kilo & Williamson, 1987).

Following a regimen to treat diabetes is difficult, but the risks of not doing so are very serious. It takes a good deal of planning, strong efforts to maintain the routine with only occasional departures, and the confidence of patients and their families that they can do it.

---

fail to take their insulin (Polonsky et al., 1994). Second, a regimen's dietary recommendations may be incompatible with the food habits of patients in certain ethnic groups (Raymond & D'Eramo-Melkus, 1993). Third, diabetics often feel frustrated when they "didn't cheat," but their glucose control is off target for some other reason, such as being under stress. Fourth, because diabetes is not a painful condition, patients may not feel that following the regimen closely is critical (Kilo & Williamson, 1987).

One other psychosocial situation that can lead to noncompliance is when the patient and the physician have different goals of treatment. A study demonstrated this by having doctors and the parents of diabetic children serve as subjects and asking them to assess hypothetical glucose test profiles (Marteau, Johnston, Baum, & Bloch, 1987). The researchers presented the subjects with several different test results, including one each reflecting a normal glucose level, hypoglycemia, and three degrees of hyperglycemia. The doctors were asked to pick the one profile they would be "happiest to see" for a child at their clinic; the parents were asked to pick the one they would be "happiest to see" for *their* own child. The results showed that the vast majority of physicians, but only about half of the parents, chose the profile reflecting the normal glucose level. More than a third of the parents chose either the mild or the moderate *hyperglycemic* profile. This suggests that the main focus of doctors is on preventing long-term complications from developing. In comparison, parents seem to be more interested in preventing *hypoglycemic* episodes and in promoting they day-to-day well-being and activity of their children. Not surprisingly, the children's actual glucose levels more closely matched the goals of their parents than those of physicians. Because much smaller deviations from normal blood sugar levels result in symptoms of hypoglycemia than in those of hyperglycemia, parents and diabetics may choose to err on the side of higher glucose levels (Varni & Babani, 1986).

When the Diabetic Is a Child or Adolescent

Most parents of diabetic children cope well with the disease (Eiser, 1985). Many family stressors remain, however, and stem from having to deal with occasional diabetic crises, take the child in for periodic medical examinations, give the glucose tests and injections, and make dietary adjustments, either by making special meals for the patient or by modifying the whole family's diet. Parents also worry more than their diabetic children about future health complications.

Diabetic children younger than, say, 8 or 10 years of age have little knowledge or understanding about their conditions, possible long-term health problems, and why aspects of their regimens are necessary (Eiser, 1985). They also do not see themselves as being very different from other children. The things that set diabetic children apart from others are their rigid eating patterns and dietary restrictions, their need to balance their intake of food carefully in relation to exercise, and, of course, the glucose monitoring and insulin injections. These are aspects children dislike most about having diabetes. Most of these activities can be done at home or privately.

Maintaining the diabetes treatment regimen during childhood is essentially the parents' responsibility. When can children do some of the treatment activities on their own? Children's cognitive and motor abilities allow most of them to learn to select appropriate foods by 8 years of age, give themselves injections by 9 or 10, and perform glucose testing by 12 (Eiser, 1985). Moreover, adolescent and preadolescent diabetics generally think children are able to manage their own diabetes care at around 12 years of age. Parents tend to agree—and as adolescence approaches, they allow their children more and more responsibility for managing the diabetes regimen. But research has shown that the quality of diabetes care is often lower in adolescence than in the preadolescent years (Anderson et al., 1990; Bond, Aiken, & Somerville, 1992; Johnson et al., 1990). Compliance with glucose monitoring and diet declines with age in adolescence; blood sugar control also decreases. Diabetics experience many compliance conflicts—for example, they may want to adhere to their regimens but friends suggest nonadherent activities, such as drinking. Although adolescents can generate solutions that would enable them to adhere, they are likely to succumb to peer pressure (Thomas, Peterson, & Goldstein, 1997). Noncompliance is probably not the only reason for decreased glucose control in adolescence: hormonal changes may make controlling blood glucose more difficult (Eiser, 1985).

By the time children with diabetes reach adolescence, they have the cognitive abilities to understand the disease and its long-term implications. Instead of feeling confident in their futures—as other teenagers do—they may see cloudy and vulnerable lives ahead, and feel angry and cheated (Holmes, 1986). Teenagers' adherence to their diabetes regimens is relatively high among those who have high levels of self-esteem and social competence and have good relations with their parents (Hanson, Henggeler, & Burghen, 1987; Jacobson et al., 1994; Miller-Johnson et al., 1994). Teens who feel less sure of themselves may neglect their self-care activities partly because they may feel a greater need to avoid appearing different from their peers.

ARTHRITIS

Before developing a severe case of arthritis, Ron had been active in athletics for most of his 50 years of life, having played and coached college football and become an avid golfer and tennis player (McIlwain, Silverfield, Burnette, & Bruce, 1991). In the last 5 years, playing golf and tennis became increasingly difficult because of pain in his knee and hip, and he eventually stopped playing completely. After 2 months of treatment with medication and exercise for this musculoskeletal disorder, he was able to resume these activities without severe pain.

Musculoskeletal disorders affecting the body's muscles, joints, and connective tissues near the joints are classified as *rheumatic diseases*, which include over

100 conditions that cause pain, stiffness, or inflammation (Lee & Abramson, 1999). Rheumatic diseases that affect mainly the joints are called **arthritis.** Disorders of the bones and joints have probably always plagued humans and almost all other animals—archaeologists have found evidence of arthritis in the fossil bones of dinosaurs and prehistoric bears, for instance (Achterberg-Lawlis, 1988). By far the most common rheumatic condition is osteoarthritis—which afflicts over 20 million Americans—followed by fibromyalgia, rheumatoid arthritis, and gout (AF, 2000).

The Types and Causes of Rheumatic Diseases

Osteoarthritis is a disease in which the joints degenerate, mainly as a result of wear and tear (AF, 2000; AMA, 1989). People's risk of developing this condition increases with age and body weight and is associated with certain occupations in which particular joints are subjected to repeated heavy use (Kelsey & Hochberg, 1988). For instance, weavers and cotton pickers often develop osteoarthritis of the hands, whereas ballet dancers tend to have the condition in their feet.

Fibromyalgia produces pain and stiffness mainly in the muscles and other soft tissue (AF, 2000; Lee & Abramson, 1999). *Gout* can affect any of the body's joints, but is most common in the big toe. In this disease, the body produces more uric acid than the kidneys can process, and the excess acid circulates in the blood and leaves crystalline deposits at the joints (AF, 2000; AMA, 1989). *Rheumatoid arthritis* is a disease that involves extreme inflammation of joint tissues and also affects the heart, blood vessels, and lungs when it reaches advanced stages (AF, 2000; AMA, 1989). It is potentially the most serious arthritic condition, being the most crippling and painful type. It often spreads to all of the body's joints. Although the mechanisms that lead to rheumatoid arthritis are unclear, they seem to involve an autoimmune response that attacks the tissues and bones of the joints (Lee & Abramson, 1999; Benjamini, Sunshine, & Leskowitz, 1996).

An estimated 43 million Americans suffer from a rheumatic disease (AF, 2000). Each rheumatic disease appears to have its own pattern of causes, including genetic factors and viral infections (McIlwain, Silverfield, Burnette, & Bruce, 1991). Although arthritis can appear at any age, it becomes far more prevalent as people get older. As Figure 13–4 depicts,

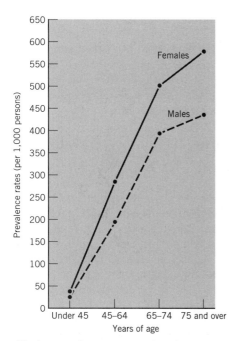

Figure 13–4 Prevalence rates of arthritis per 1,000 males and females in the United States at each age range. (Data from USBC, 1999, Table 232.)

arthritis afflicts nearly half of Americans over 65 years of age and occurs more often among females than males. But three points should be made about the data in the figure. First, these data probably underestimate the actual number of people who have the disorder because mild cases often do not come to the attention of health agencies (Kelsey & Hochberg, 1988). Second, the figure does not show that, whereas females are much more likely than males to develop osteoarthritis, fibromyalgia, and rheumatoid arthritis, males are far more likely to develop gout (AF, 2000). Third, about 285,000 American children have arthritis; 50,000 have *juvenile rheumatoid arthritis*. An encouraging point about juvenile rheumatoid arthritis is that most patients do *not* suffer serious disability in their adult lives; for many, the disorder disappears in several years (AMA, 1989; Burg & Ingall, 1985).

The Effects and Treatment of Arthritis

Arthritis is a leading cause of disability around the world. Any type of arthritis can disable its victims on a short-term or long-term basis. Of the major chronic diseases that afflict people in the United States, arthritis is the leader each year in causing

people to cut down on their usual activities and is second, behind heart disease, in causing work disability (AF, 2000). Elderly people have more functional limitations from osteoarthritis of the knee than from most other chronic illnesses (Guccione et al., 1994).

In the case of rheumatoid arthritis, some patients experience only mild episodes of inflammation and pain in a few joints; others, however, suffer intense pain in many joints, often showing the following progression:

- The lubricating fluid leaks out of the joints, usually in the knees, ankles, shoulders, elbows, and wrists.

- Cartilage is destroyed and joint function is reduced.

- The conversion of organic matter into minerals for bones decreases near the joints.

- Bone erosions take place near the joints.

- Joints become dislocated and sometimes fused, producing deformities. (Anderson et al., 1985)

Some of the people whose rheumatoid arthritis progresses to the later stages show associated damage to other organ systems, developing vascular or heart valve diseases, for example.

What treatments can be used in managing the pain and functional impairment of arthritis? People with arthritis typically take some form of pain-relieving medication, especially aspirin and other drugs, such as ibuprofen, that reduce inflammation (AMA, 1989; Lee & Abramson, 1999; McIlwain, Silverfield, Burnette, & Bruce, 1991). For relatively severe cases, two types of medication may be prescribed. *Steroids* are fast-acting drugs that tend to reduce inflammation, stiffness, and swelling in a matter of hours. *Gold compounds* are salts that are soluble in liquid. Although most patients who are treated with gold get at least moderate relief, it usually takes weeks or months for them to notice improvements, and the action of this drug is not well understood. But using gold compounds and certain kinds of steroids for a long time can have serious side effects, such as gastrointestinal problems and kidney damage. In extreme cases when other medical approaches have not helped, surgeons replace affected joints with artificial ones.

Other approaches for managing arthritic pain and impairment involve maintaining proper body weight

Physical therapy for a patient with arthritic hands can involve enjoyable activities that exercise the affected joints.

and, especially for people with gout, limiting certain foods and alcohol (McIlwain, Silverfield, Burnette, & Bruce, 1991). Physical therapy is very important and includes exercise, applying heat or cold, and using devices to prevent joint damage and assist patients in performing daily activities (Lee & Abramson, 1999; Minor & Sanford, 1993). For example, a 58-year-old woman with rheumatoid arthritis whose hand pain and weakness made lifting heavy pots, opening jars, and doing other household tasks difficult received the following physical therapy components:

● *Exercises* to increase hand strength and range of motion.

● *Splints*, which she wore on her left or right hand on alternating nights to reduce pain and swelling in her wrists and fingers.

● *Advice on devices* that can make daily activities easier, such as a cart to transport things, purses that hang from the shoulder instead of the hand, and handles with large diameters. (Philips, 1989)

Many arthritis sufferers supplement medical care with alternative medicine methods, such as acupuncture and herbal therapy, especially if they are dissatisfied with medical procedures (Vecchio, 1994).

Studies of compliance for medical treatment regimens have shown that people with arthritis adhere closely to recommendations for the more powerful

drugs, but not for milder ones, such as aspirin, and they adhere less closely with physical therapy than with taking medication (Anderson et al., 1985). Many patients dislike physical therapy, seeing its negative aspects, rather than its positive ones (Jensen & Lorish, 1994). They feel, for instance, that exercising is boring and its value is not obvious.

Psychosocial Factors in Arthritis

Any chronic pain condition is distressing for the patients and their families, and the distress is worse if the pain is severe and frequent. If the pain is disabling, the condition produces a great deal of stress for patients and their families. Some research has linked stress to rheumatoid arthritis flare-ups, but the effects seem complex: one study found, for instance, that daily hassles were associated with increased pain, but major life events were associated with decreased pain (Potter & Zautra, 1997).

People with severe rheumatoid arthritis experience at least some pain virtually every day, and on many days it is intense (Affleck, Tennen, Urrows, & Higgins, 1991). This pain can interfere in many everyday activities: as one patient stated,

> There are times when I'm downright miserable, like when I can't even pick up a pot off the stove. Every once in a while, I have to miss work for a week or two because I simply can't keep my knee in a position to drive a car. (Tennen & Affleck, 1997, p. 264)

People with severe arthritis are much more likely to feel helpless and seriously depressed than those with milder conditions (Anderson et al., 1985). One study, for instance, examined over 200 patients' disability and feelings of helplessness about their conditions over a 1-year period (Nicassio et al., 1985). Their self-reports showed that their feelings of helplessness correlated with changes in their ability to perform daily activities, such as dressing, turning faucets on and off, and getting in and out of a car. Other studies have confirmed the link between arthritis severity and feelings of helplessness and found that these feelings lead to maladjustment and depression (Nicassio et al., 1993; Parker et al., 1991; Smith & Wallston, 1992; Smith, Peck, & Ward, 1990; Zautra et al., 1995).

Of course, not all individuals with severe arthritis experience serious emotional difficulties. Some arthritic people with severe pain feel a greater sense of personal control over their conditions than others do, and this difference relates to their emotional adjustment. In a study examining this relationship, researchers interviewed adults with rheumatoid arthritis regarding their mood states and their perceptions of personal control over their illness (Affleck, Tennen, Pfeiffer, & Fifield, 1987). These interviews revealed three main findings. First, the subjects generally thought their practitioners had greater control over the *course* of the disease than they did themselves. Second, of the patients who had relatively active symptoms, those who believed they could control their *daily symptoms* reported less mood disturbance than those who did not. Third, the subjects who saw themselves as *active partners* in decisions about their medical care and treatment showed better adjustment to their illness. These findings are also important because people with arthritis who understand their treatment and believe it can help are more likely to adhere closely to their medical regimens than those individuals who do not (Jette, 1984).

What impact does the arthritis condition have on the psychological status of the patient's family? The severity of the disease by itself seems to have little impact. Spouses of arthritis patients seem to adapt similarly to different levels of disease severity—the feelings of distress or depression they report relate mainly to their perceptions of the quality of the marriage and of social support (Manne & Zautra, 1990). But the impact of arthritis severity appears to depend on social support: as severity increases, spouses who perceive little social support in their lives report *more* depression, while spouses with high levels of social support report *less* depression (Revenson & Majerovitz, 1991).

ALZHEIMER'S DISEASE

For a long time, Martha, the wife of 75-year-old Alfred, denied her husband was sick, making excuses for his forgetful and odd behavior. Then

> one evening, they were out dining with friends. During the meal, Alfred refused to remove his overcoat and wouldn't talk to anyone. Instead, he clanged his fork on his plate, put his napkin in his soup, and tried to eat his salad with his knife. When Martha whispered to him to put down his silverware, he yelled at her. She burst into tears. Finally, one of the male dinner guests led Alfred from the table, leaving a humiliated, mortified wife to confront a reality that could no longer be ignored: Alfred had Alzheimer's disease. (McCahon, 1991, p. 44)

Dementia is a term that refers to a progressive loss of cognitive functions that often occurs in old age. By far, the most common form of dementia is **Alzheimer's disease,** a brain disorder characterized by a deterioration of attention, memory, and personality. Figure 13–5 illustrates the cognitive deficits of an Alzheimer victim. An estimated 4 million Americans have Alzheimer's disease, and the proportion of those afflicted increases with age: whereas probably 3% of individuals ages 65 to 74 have the disease, 19% of people 75 to 84 years of age and 47% of those 85 and older

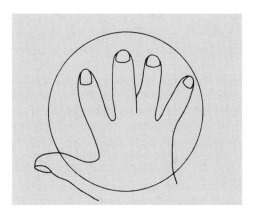
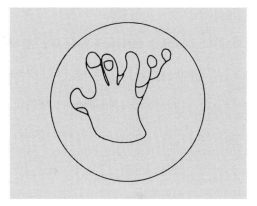

Figure 13–5   Illustration of cognitive deficits in Alzheimer's disease. A graphic artist with this disorder was asked to copy the drawing of a hand shown on the left. The hand he drew was much smaller and had distortions in spatial relationships, misplaced fingernails, and an incorrect number of fingers.

have it (ADEAR, 2000; Haley, 1998). Some individuals show symptoms of the disease in their 40s (Gruetzner, 1992).

The cognitive functions of people with Alzheimer's disease do not disappear all at once. Perhaps the most critical functions to go at first are *attention* and *memory*. Peter Vitaliano and his colleagues (1986) conducted a 2-year follow-up study of Alzheimer victims with mild impairment and found that their main deficits initially were in their attentive and memory abilities. The extent of these deficits was strongly associated with the degree of their impairment 2 years later. As the disease progresses over several years, the effects of the disorder become more pronounced (Haley, 1998). Personality changes often emerge, with the victims becoming less spontaneous and more apathetic and withdrawn. Self-care deteriorates, and behavior problems appear, as when these individuals wander and become lost. At some point, they may become frequently disoriented with regard to time, their location, and their identity. These declines develop faster if the patients suffer a severe loss of language or have a history of alcohol abuse or of neurological disorders, such as from a stroke or Parkinson's disease (Bracco et al., 1994; Teri, Hughes, & Larson, 1990).

The Causes and Treatment of Alzheimer's Disease

What causes Alzheimer's disease? The most promising answer seems to involve a characteristic that differentiates the brains of Alzheimer victims from those of other elderly individuals: Alzheimer brains contain extensive *lesions*, consisting of gnarled and tangled nerve fibers and of a protein, called *beta-amyloid*, the body produces (ADEAR, 2000, Larson, Kukull, & Katzman, 1992). Evidence now indicates that genetic defects may cause these large deposits to occur. For instance, one study examined stored tissue samples from many members of a family across three generations (Murrell, Farlow, Ghetti, & Benson, 1991). All members with the genetic defect also had Alzheimer's disease, and no member who did not have the defect had the disease. And a likely gene involved in early onset of the disease has been identified (Levy-Lahad et al., 1995). Two other findings are also important. First, one study found that people with the brain lesions that characterize the disease are far more likely to develop Alzheimer symptoms if they have had strokes, even fairly mild ones, than if they have not

(Snowdon et al., 1997). Second, research has found a link between the development of Alzheimer's disease and prior head injury (Larson, Kukull, & Katzman, 1992). It seems likely that this disease can result from several types of genetic defects and environmental factors.

Diagnosis of Alzheimer's disease should be made at specialized centers, is based mainly on tests of mental ability and physiological signs, and is nearly 90% accurate, as compared with autopsy findings of brain structure (ADEAR, 2000; Haley, 1998). Other diagnostic methods are being developed that use brain scans and eye tests (Reiman et al., 1996; Scinto et al., 1994). No treatment exists yet to prevent or stop the progression of Alzheimer's disease.

Psychosocial Effects of Alzheimer's Disease

Most victims of Alzheimer's disease live at home and receive care from their spouses or adult children (Gruetzner, 1992; Haley, 1998). In the early stages of the disease, family members and others may be able to help maximize the person's functioning, such as by marking objects clearly and giving social support. But many families either don't know or deny that the person has Alzheimer's disease. As patients lose more and more of their cognitive function, their inability to do simple tasks and remember everyday things becomes very frustrating and often leads to feelings of helplessness, which may account for their high rates of depression (Migliorelli et al., 1995).

Alzheimer patients' behavior becomes increasingly problematic as the disease progresses, producing great stress in the family. People with this disease may, for instance, accuse a family member of hiding things they cannot find, develop sleep disturbances and stay awake most of the night, get lost after wandering out of the house, lose control of their bowels and bladder, or become bedridden (Gruetzner, 1992; Haley, 1998). The demands in caring for Alzheimer patients can become physically and emotionally overwhelming, particularly when the caregivers are elderly spouses in failing health or grown children who have many career and family pressures of their own. The stress these caregivers experience is likely to affect their own health. Studies comparing caregivers with control subjects have found that caregivers have lower immune function, more days of illness, greater risk of hypertension, and higher mortality rates (Kiecolt-Glaser et al., 1991; Schulz &

Beach, 1999; Shaw et al., 1999; Vedhara et al., 1999). Some evidence suggests that the health effects are worse in caregivers with low levels of social support and high distress from dementia-related behaviors. The emotional and physical effects on Alzheimer caregivers appear similar in different cultures, such as in America and China (Patterson et al., 1998).

In the Alzheimer's case we saw earlier, Martha provided care for Alfred at home for a few years until his condition got too difficult for her to handle (McCahon, 1991). On the urging of their son, she placed Alfred in a nursing home but felt "defeated, inadequate, and guilty" for doing so. Although she loved her husband and visited him almost every day, she eventually developed psychological problems because watching him deteriorate and realizing that he had, in effect, died years ago was so stressful. She wished she could visit less often, but felt guilty at the prospect. Alzheimer's patients usually need care for 5 to 10 years of decline (Haley, 1998). Their families often feel that watching the person deteriorate over several years is unbearable—like watching an endless funeral. The slow deterioration, severe dementia-related behavior problems, and knowledge that it will only end when the patient dies generally makes Alzheimer's disease more difficult for families to adapt to than the other chronic illnesses we considered.

We have examined in this chapter what it is like to live with each of a wide variety of chronic health problems. Some of these disorders begin earlier in the life span than others, some are more visible to people than are others, some involve more difficult treatment regimens than others, and some are more painful, disabling, or life-threatening than others. Each of these differences is important in determining patients' and their families' adaptation to the health problems and the psychosocial help they may need from professionals.

PSYCHOSOCIAL INTERVENTIONS FOR PEOPLE WITH CHRONIC CONDITIONS

Before people actually experience specific chronic illnesses in their families, they usually have some ideas about how serious the health problems are. How do they feel about an illness after someone in the family develops it? Is it worse than they expected, or not as bad, or about the same? The answers to these questions should have a bearing on how well the family adjusts to health problems. One study had parents whose children had either diabetes, asthma, epilepsy, or no chronic illness rate how serious each of the three health problems would be if their children were to develop it or had it now (Marteau & Johnston, 1986). The ratings revealed two interesting findings: (1) the lowest ratings of seriousness the parents gave were for the health problems their own children had and (2) parents whose children did not have chronic illnesses rated each of the health problems as being very serious. These findings indicate that parents who live with chronic illnesses in their children tend to have less negative views of the health problems than parents whose children do not have those illnesses. People are frightened by the prospects of health problems, but most families adjust fairly well if a child develops a chronic illness (Cadman, Rosenbaum, Boyle, & Offord, 1991).

As we have seen, not all people adjust well to chronic health conditions. The types of adjustment problems that commonly develop with chronic conditions are outlined in Table 13.2. The problems patients and their families experience depend on many factors, such as how visible, painful, disabling, or life-threatening the illness is. Another factor is the patient's age (O'Dougherty & Brown, 1990). In the early childhood years, victims of chronic illness may become excessively dependent if the parents are overprotective, such as by not allowing an epileptic child to play in a wading pool with careful supervision. In later childhood and adolescence, chronically ill individuals may experience school failure because of absences and peer criticism or rejection because of the illness. These events can impair the development of friendships, self-confidence, and self-esteem. Adults who develop a chronic condition may have difficulties

Table 13.2 *Types of Adjustment Problems in Chronic Illness*

- *Physical*—being unable to cope with disability or pain.
- *Vocational*—having difficulty revising educational and career plans or finding a new job.
- *Self-concept*—being unable to accept one's changed body image, self-esteem, and level of achievement or competence.
- *Social*—having difficulty with losing enjoyable activities or finding new ones and coping with changed relationships with family, friends, and sexual partners.
- *Emotional*—experiencing high levels of denial, anxiety, or depression.
- *Compliance*—failing to adhere to the rehabilitation regimen.

if their illness leads them to stop working or change jobs, alter their parenting role, or change or stop their sexual relations.

Ideally, intervention programs to help individuals with chronic health problems involve interdisciplinary teams of professionals—physicians, nurses, psychologists, physical and occupational therapists, vocational counselors, social workers, and recreational therapists—working in an integrated manner toward the overall goals of rehabilitation (Bleiberg, Ciulla, & Katz, 1991). Psychologists contribute to this process by helping each client cope with the psychosocial implications of his or her medical condition and by using behavioral and cognitive principles to enhance the person's participation in and adherence to the therapeutic regimen. We'll consider many useful psychosocial approaches, most of which can be used either with individuals or in groups and for a variety of illnesses.

EDUCATIONAL, SOCIAL SUPPORT, AND BEHAVIORAL METHODS

The first thing chronically ill people and their families need to help them adapt to a health problem is correct *information* about the disease and its prognosis and treatment. Part of the problem Martha had dealing with Alfred's Alzheimer's disease is that she was led to believe that he would "be a vegetable" in a matter of months. But Alfred's deterioration went on for years, as it does for most Alzheimer victims. She needed better information and might also have benefited from community services for Alzheimer families. For instance, many American communities have *respite centers* where Alzheimer patients can get occasional day care and temporary overnight care, giving the family a break from the caregiving burden (Gruetzner, 1992).

Effective systems of social support are also important for patients' and their families' adaptation to chronic health problems. People with chronic medical conditions usually receive this support from family or friends, but it can also come from *support groups* that offer patients and family information and opportunities to meet with people who are in the same boat. For example, support groups for Alzheimer families help by providing information, giving sensitive emotional support, and sharing members' own experiences and ways of dealing with everyday problems and difficult decisions, such as whether to place the patient in a nursing home (Gruetzner, 1992; Kapust

& Weintraub, 1984). Information about the availability of support groups in specific geographical areas can be obtained through physicians, local community service agencies, or national organizations for any particular illness. Virtually all national organizations now have websites, and newspapers often print announcements of support group meetings.

Training and education programs to promote correct self-care procedures are very important in helping patients and their families adapt to the illness. These programs can be provided by professionals in medical settings or by trained laypersons, such as in support groups. For example, the Arthritis Self-Management Program (Lorig et al., 1998) was designed to help arthritis sufferers cope with their illness and comply with their treatment. It is now offered in several countries by the Arthritis Foundation. The program involves six weekly group meetings in which individuals with arthritis receive training in:

- Exercising, including which exercises to do and exactly how to do them.
- Protecting their joints, such as through changing the way they lift heavy objects.
- Relaxation techniques to control stress.
- Appropriate diets for their illness.
- Self-monitoring and behavioral contracting to promote their complying with regimen activities.

The program is often conducted by a layperson who has arthritis. Programs like this one do appear to help arthritis patients to reduce pain and enhance their health status (CAH, 1999; Hirano, Laurent, & Lorig, 1994; Lorig et al., 1998). What's more, in the first year alone, the savings in health care costs is more than seven times the cost of providing such programs for arthritis patients (Cronan, Groessl, & Kaplan, 1997). Similar programs have been developed for other illnesses, such as asthma (CAH, 1999).

Psychosocial factors are often involved in patients' failing to adhere to their medical regimens for managing chronic conditions. In Chapter 9, we discussed methods that can enhance adherence. Some methods involve improving the way practitioners present information about the procedures and the importance of following the treatment. Other approaches use *behavioral methods*, such as tailoring the regimen to make it as compatible as possible with the person's habits, using prompts and reminders, having patients keep records of their self-care activities, and providing a system of rewards through the method of behavioral contracting. Various behavioral approaches can help improve compliance with different aspects of diabetes regimens, for instance (Goodall & Halford, 1991; Wing, Epstein, Nowalk, & Lamparski, 1986). As an example, a program used self-monitoring and behavioral contracting methods for 8 weeks to improve regimen adherence in three noncompliant 16- to 18-year-old type 1 diabetes patients: Kathy, Tom, and Kim (Schafer, Glasgow, & McCaul, 1982). Adherence and glucose control improved greatly in both Kathy and Tom. Kim's self-care did not improve, probably because she came from a family with severe marital and family problems, and therapy had failed to resolve their conflicts. Family problems can have an overriding influence and undermine efforts to improve compliance with medical recommendations.

Another example of using behavioral methods to enhance compliance with medical regimens involves the physical rehabilitation process for individuals with spinal cord injuries. Reinforcement techniques are very effective in improving these patients' performance of therapeutically beneficial behaviors (Brucker, 1983). These behaviors include:

- Increasing daily fluid intake to prevent urinary tract infections.
- Changing one's sitting or lying position frequently to reduce the occurrence of bedsores.
- Using orthopedic devices to improve limb functioning.
- Performing exercises to increase strength and endurance.

Reinforcement can be given, for instance, by praising the client for each measurable improvement, such as in arm strength, and periodically updating the person's graph that charts these improvements.

RELAXATION AND BIOFEEDBACK

We have seen that stress and anxiety can aggravate some chronic conditions, such as by decreasing diabetics' ability to metabolize glucose and by triggering or worsening asthma attacks. Psychologists use stress management techniques—especially *progressive muscle relaxation* and *biofeedback*—to help patients

control these psychosocial factors and the underlying body processes (Parker, 1995).

These approaches are useful for several chronic conditions. For instance, relaxation training can help diabetic patients manage their stress and their blood glucose levels (Surwit, Feinglos, & Scovern, 1983; Wing, Epstein, Nowalk, & Lamparski, 1986). People with epilepsy can benefit from both relaxation and biofeedback training. In using relaxation, epileptics are taught to recognize sensations and events that are associated with attacks and to apply relaxation techniques when those situations occur. In using biofeedback, epileptics receive training with feedback from an electroencephalograph (EEG) device, which measures electrical brain activity (Goldstein, 1990). Although not all patients benefit from this approach, many do. Unfortunately, there is no good way yet to determine in advance who will benefit from using biofeedback to reduce seizures and who will not. Epileptics who receive biofeedback therapy usually require many hours of costly training with a psychologist or other highly trained individual, using expensive equipment and computer analyses. (Go to 🍇.)

COGNITIVE METHODS

An 18-year-old diabetic girl entered psychotherapy because of difficulty coping with her condition. The therapy revealed that her difficulties were based on incorrect beliefs that she now could not attend college, "would constantly look drunk and crazy," and would be a social outcast (Roback, 1984). Her therapy helped her disconfirm this belief and see that she could pursue her life goals much as she had planned before learning of her condition. *Cognitive methods* can help people change their feelings and thought processes (Davison & Neale, 1998, Sarafino, 2001). One cognitive approach is *cognitive restructuring*, whereby individuals or groups discuss incorrect thoughts and beliefs and learn ways to cope better by thinking more constructively or realistically.

We have seen that many chronically ill people and their families experience strong feelings of helplessness, hopelessness, and depression. In the case of Alzheimer's disease, research has found that elderly caregivers are two to five times more likely to suffer severe levels of depression than other elders (Neundorfer, 1991). Their depression is related to the degree of stress or burden they perceive in their caregiving role, such as from the patient's memory

CLINICAL METHODS AND ISSUES
Treating Asthma with Biofeedback and Relaxation

Psychosocial intervention for asthma provides a good example of how biofeedback and relaxation can help. In using *biofeedback* with asthmatics, an apparatus gives feedback regarding airflow in breathing so that the asthma patient can learn to control the diameter of the bronchial airways (Sarafino, 1997). One way to measure airflow has the person breathe through a device that varies the air pressure and assesses airway resistance to these variations: the greater the resistance, the poorer the airflow. The feedback tells the person when changes occur; it can be presented as corresponding numbers on a gauge or as differ-

ent levels of (1) brightness of a light or (2) pitch or loudness of tones. Although airflow improvements are slight initially, feedback over several training sessions helps the person make them stronger, eventually enabling the person to increase airflow when an attack begins. Training in *progressive muscle relaxation* is used to help the person reduce the role of tension in either initiating an asthma attack or making it worse if one occurs. Studies have generally found that these methods are effective and provide useful supplements to medical treatments for asthma (Sarafino, 1997).

and behavioral problems. Many people who are disabled or have chronic pain also become severely depressed, often because of their restricted daily activities (Talbot et al., 1999). Cognitive approaches can help people identify distorted thoughts ("I never get to do anything I like anymore"), replace those thoughts with more accurate ones, and learn how to increase their ability to perform activities, such as by scheduling them in reasonable amounts. Cognitive methods are very effective in treating depression (Sarafino, 2001). (Go to 🏃.)

INSIGHT AND FAMILY THERAPY

Insight therapy is designed to help people gain an understanding of the roots of their feelings and problems (Davison & Neale, 1998). This approach is especially useful in helping patients deal with their anxieties and changed self-concepts or relationships with family and friends (Bleiberg, Ciulla, & Katz, 1991). As an example, one hospitalized quadriplegic man who became difficult to deal with each night revealed in group therapy that he felt very vulnerable and helpless at nighttime, which frightened him. By learning in the group that other patients had similar feelings, be began to feel better able to deal with his disability and the day-to-day problems it created (Eisenberg,

1984). Insight therapy has also been used in helping chronically ill people deal with sexual difficulties and understand the thoughts, needs, and problems their friends and family members face.

Family therapy typically has the family meet as a group and draws on cognitive, behavioral, and insight-oriented methods to examine and change patterns of interaction among family members (Davison & Neale, 1998; Kerns, 1995; Patterson & Garwick, 1994). A family with a chronically ill member might meet to review household and medical-regimen responsibilities, discuss grievances, and plan ways to alter daily routines. If the patient is a child, they may discuss, for instance:

- Jealousies siblings may feel if the patient seems to be getting more or special attention.

- Activities the chronically ill person can engage in successfully to build his or her feelings of competence and self-esteem.

- How to tell friends and relatives about the illness so they will understand what it is, the limitations it imposes on the patient, and what to do if an episode occurs.

- How and when the ill person could take responsibility for or improve self-care.

FOCUS ON RESEARCH

Cognitive-Behavioral Approaches in Managing Arthritis

Jerry Parker and his colleagues (1988) studied the effects of a program of cognitive and behavioral techniques in helping arthritis patients manage their condition. The researchers randomly assigned 83 subjects from a Veterans Administration hospital to three groups. The *intervention* group received an intensive program of cognitive and behavioral techniques during a 1-week stay at the hospital and subsequently met together periodically in support group sessions. The patients received training in relaxation, pain redefinition, and distraction techniques and discussed their pain behavior and family dynamics and communication.

The two other groups got no psychosocial intervention. A *placebo* group received an educational program of films and written materials on arthritis during a 1-week hospital stay and met subsequently in support groups, but no cognitive or behavioral methods were discussed. This group got as much time and attention as the intervention group did. The *control* group received the standard care for people with arthritis and was not asked to spend a week in the hospital or to attend support group meetings.

All subjects completed a variety of psychosocial measures and had their disease status evaluated by medical personnel at the start of the study and again after 6 and 12 months. At the last assessment, the intervention subjects were asked to rate the extent to which they continued to practice each of the techniques they were taught. The data across the 12 months revealed three findings: first, the patients' disease status worsened, as one would expect for this disease. Second, the groups did not differ in their reports of pain and helplessness at 6 and 12 months. But third, those intervention subjects who reported a high degree of adherence to the cognitive-behavioral methods reported substantially less pain and helplessness than the placebo and control subjects. These results suggest that long-term *adherence* may be critical for chronically ill people to benefit from cognitive-behavioral interventions.

Parents and their ill children often do not communicate about sharing responsibilities for the patients' care (Anderson et al., 1990). As a result, each person incorrectly assumes someone else is taking care of a task.

Sometimes a patient's *recovery* can present family problems. For example, a husband whose wife's epilepsy was greatly improved with surgery "felt secure when his wife with epilepsy was dependent on him" but became uncomfortable when she could function on her own and take advantage of new opportunities (DeAngelis, 1990). Family therapy can help to uncover and resolve anxieties that develop when the family dynamics and modes of interaction change in either a positive or negative direction.

In summary, psychosocial intervention can apply many approaches to address many different adjustment problems that chronically ill people and their families face. In most cases, using more than one approach provides the optimal help these people need.

SUMMARY

The initial reactions of individuals when diagnosed with chronic illnesses tend to follow three phases: (1) shock, in which they are bewildered and behave in an automatic fashion; (2) encounter, characterized by feeling overwhelmed and helpless; and (3) retreat, which often involves avoidance coping strategies, such as denial. Avoidance coping is likely if people believe they can do nothing to change the situation.

Crisis theory provides a model that describes how patients adjust to learning they have chronic health problems. According to this model, their adjustment depends on the coping processes they use, which, in turn, depend on illness-related, background and personal, and physical and social environmental factors. Patients begin the coping process with a cognitive appraisal of the meaning or significance of the health problem to their lives. This appraisal leads to their formulating adaptive tasks, such as adjusting to their symptoms or maintaining positive relations with family or friends, and applying various coping skills to deal with these tasks. These coping skills include denying or minimizing the implications of their conditions, learning how to provide their own treatment, maintaining regular routines as well as possible, and discussing the future. Long-term adaptation to chronic health problems occurs when the patient and his or her family make adjustments that enhance the patient's quality of life by promoting effective physical, psychological, and social functioning.

Some chronic conditions usually begin early in the life span, and asthma is one of them. Asthma is a respiratory disorder that produces periodic attacks of extremely labored breathing. Attacks are generally triggered by certain circumstances. For many asthmatics, the triggers are allergens, such as pollen. Other asthma triggers include respiratory infections, weather conditions, air pollution, and emotions, such as stress and anger. Although asthma is treated mainly with medication to prevent and combat attacks, exercise and psychosocial methods can also be useful.

Epilepsy is a disorder in which electrical disturbances in the brain produce seizures that vary in intensity. In tonic-clonic attacks, the epileptic loses consciousness and exhibits muscle spasms. Sometimes specific neurological defects are identified as causing the disorder. Drugs provide the main form of treatment, but sometimes surgery and biofeedback are useful. Spinal cord injuries often occur in adolescence or early adulthood, are generally caused by accidents, and render the person paraplegic or quadriplegic. Rehabilitation programs are geared toward helping these individuals regain as much physical function and independence as possible.

Other chronic health problems are more likely to begin in middle adulthood and old age than at other times in the life span. One of those chronic diseases is diabetes, in which the blood contains high levels of glucose. Some people with this disorder have type 1 diabetes and must inject insulin daily to prevent very serious acute and long-term health complications. But the vast majority of diabetics have type 2 diabetes, and most of them can use medication and diet to control their blood sugar.

Disorders that affect the joints and connective tissues are called rheumatic diseases. Some rheumatic diseases produce painful inflammation and stiffness of the joints; they are called arthritis. The four most common rheumatic diseases are osteoarthritis, fibromyalgia, rheumatoid arthritis, and gout. Although each of these diseases can lead to disability, rheumatoid arthritis is usually the most crippling and painful of the four. Treatment is mainly through drugs, but also includes physical therapy and maintaining proper body weight.

Alzheimer's disease involves a progressive deterioration of the person's cognitive functions, beginning with attention and memory. Since there is no effective treatment for this disorder, therapy focuses on maximizing the patient's functioning and helping the family cope.

Many chronically ill people and their families have difficulty adjusting to the health problem and its medical regimen. They can be helped with psychosocial interventions that involve education, support services, behavioral methods, relaxation and biofeedback, cognitive methods, insight therapy, and family therapy.

KEY TERMS

crisis theory	asthma	type 1 diabetes	arthritis
adaptation	epilepsy	type 2 diabetes	Alzheimer's disease
quality of life	spinal cord injury		

14

HEART DISEASE, STROKE, CANCER, AND AIDS: CAUSES, MANAGEMENT, AND COPING

PROLOGUE

Deep down, in the "wishing" part of his mind, Jack thought he was immortal. Oh, he acknowledged that he'd die someday, but that day would *forever* be a long way off, he believed. He lived his life accordingly, even though he had almost every known major risk factor for heart disease. He was 30 pounds overweight, ate high-cholesterol food with abandon, smoked two packs of cigarettes a day, got little exercise, experienced a lot of anger that he had trouble expressing, and had a father who had died of a heart attack at the age of 48. Jack had felt especially invulnerable 2 years ago on his 49th birthday, almost believing that, because he had lived past his father's age of death, the grim reaper would somehow never find him.

Jack's beliefs were jolted a couple of months ago—he had a heart attack that put him in the hospital for 3 weeks, including a week in the coronary care unit. He was stunned at first. "This can't be happening to *me*," he thought. Soon it sank in that it *was* happening to him, and he felt anger and a sense of grief and helplessness. He was not prepared for this. He tried to deny and minimize the problem, but his physical weakness made it clear to him that he is, after all, vulnerable. Although this realization was depressing to him for a while, he had always taken pride in his "fighting spirit." A month later Jack announced, "I'm gonna change my life," and he did! He gave up smoking, changed his diet, and started an exercise program. Just as important, he gradually changed his outlook on life. He now realizes how much the people in his life mean to him and how important he is to them, and he is actively working to get closer to them.

The majority of deaths in developed countries result from three chronic diseases: heart disease, cancer, and stroke (WHO, 1999c). In the United States, the death *rate* for heart disease has declined by half since 1970, but it is still the number-one killer by far; cancer is second, and stroke is third (NCHS, 2000; USBC, 1999). People know these are the leading causes of death—and for many patients and their families, being diagnosed with one of these diseases *means* death. AIDS emerged in the 1980s as a major killer, and public attention has focused on how it is spread, the large numbers of people infected with the virus, and the huge numbers of AIDS victims who die each year around the world. These four high-mortality illnesses are the focus of this chapter.

Although many people deal with having high-mortality chronic illnesses in positive and constructive ways, not all do. In this chapter we will examine how patients and their families react to and cope with health problems that have a high likelihood of taking their lives. We will also see the psychosocial adjustments these people make when the illnesses are terminal. As we study these difficult circumstances, we will consider many important issues and try to provide answers to questions you may have. What is it like to live with heart disease, stroke, cancer, or AIDS? How do these illnesses affect the patient's functioning, and what treatment regimens do they entail? What special problems exist when the victim is a child? What can be done to help terminally ill people and their loved ones cope?

COPING WITH AND ADAPTING TO HIGH-MORTALITY ILLNESS

Many healthy individuals who wonder how much longer they are likely to live look up the statistical life expectancy for people their age and gender and probably adjust that figure on the basis of the longevity of other people in their families. But estimates of a person's life expectancy are very imprecise, and this is true even for people with health conditions that seriously threaten their lives. Public opinion aside, having a high-mortality disease—even cancer or AIDS—does not usually mean a person will die in a matter of a few weeks or months. Many cancer patients, for instance, survive for 10 or 20 years before the disease takes their lives, and some are totally cured. Still, no one can tell for sure what the course of the disease will be, and these individuals and their families must adapt to this uncertainty.

ADAPTING WHILE THE PROSPECTS SEEM GOOD

Since none of us knows for sure what lies ahead for us, we all live with some degree of uncertainty. But for patients with high-mortality illnesses, the uncertainty for them and their families is more real and urgent. Even though they may have good prospects for the future, either in the short run or more permanently, the diagnosis changes them.

Mortality is the main issue of concern to patients in the first few months of convalescence with a seriously life-threatening illness. During this time, patients often show optimistic attitudes, hope they will be cured, but begin to view their plans for the future more tentatively (Moos, 1982; Weisman, 1979). They also tend to switch from using mainly avoidance coping strategies to using active problem-focused approaches. Jack, the man we described who had had a heart attack, showed these adjustments when he changed his lifestyle and his outlook regarding the people in his life. Lifestyle changes are typically part of the rehabilitation programs people with heart disease, stroke, cancer, and AIDS are asked to follow. Self-help and support groups that interact either in group meetings or online are available for patients with these illnesses to discuss and get advice about specific problems and stressors in their daily lives (Davison, Pennebaker, & Dickerson, 2000). As a patient's recovery progresses, he or she is able to return more and more to a regular routine, often gaining great satisfaction by once again being able to do simple household or self-help activities.

Having activities to occupy the day is important to convalescing people, particularly those with chronic high-mortality health problems. These activities give them some respite from thinking about their conditions. Patients often try to isolate the diseases from the rest of their lives by focusing on other things, such as preparing to do projects around the house or to

return to work. Sometimes these plans and preparations can lead to problems, however, if patients overestimate what they can do. For example, a patient named Clay who had suffered a serious stroke described how he started making plans the "glorious day" he left the hospital—projects to do,

> museums and galleries to visit, friends I had wanted to meet for lunch. It was not until several days later that I realized I simply couldn't do them. I didn't have the mental or physical strength, and I sank into depression. (Dahlberg, 1977, p. 124)

Patients need to be encouraged to develop reasonable plans and to carry them out, especially with regard to going back to work or getting training to enter a new job, if necessary.

Sometimes the helplessness that chronically ill people feel and the nurturance their families give lead to a cycle of continued dependence that persists when the patients are able to begin doing things for themselves. This was starting to happen with Clay after his stroke, and his wife realized it. So she gradually

> started asking him to do certain things, leaving things undone which were previously his domain, acting indecisively, and leaving decisions up to him. At first he was surprised, and then did what was needed. He gradually took over more and more, giving up his "stroke personality." (Dahlberg, 1977, p. 128)

Gentle nudges by family members, like those from Clay's wife, can help patients become more self-sufficient, thereby making them feel useful and bolstering their self-esteem.

In the process of adapting to high-mortality illnesses over a long period of time, some individuals make helpful cognitive adjustments. By interviewing women who had had surgery for breast cancer a few years earlier, researchers found that these adjustments center on three themes (Taylor, 1983; Taylor, Lichtman, & Wood, 1984). First, patients may find *meaning* in their illness experiences, either by determining why the illnesses happened or by rethinking their attitudes and priorities. One woman said, for instance,

> I have much more enjoyment each day, each moment. I am not so worried about what is or isn't or what I wish I had. All those things you get entangled with don't seem to be part of my life right now. (Taylor, 1983, p. 1163)

Second, some individuals gain a *sense of control* over their illnesses, such as by engaging in activities that reduce their risk of their conditions getting worse or increase their knowledge about their care. A spouse said of his wife:

> She got books, she got pamphlets, she studied, she talked to cancer patients, she found out everything that was happening to her, and she fought it. She went to war with it. She calls it taking in her covered wagons and surrounding it. (1983, p. 1164)

Third, some patients *restore their self-esteem*, often by comparing themselves with less fortunate people. For example, a married woman compared herself with others who may be dating and having to tell the man about the cancer.

These cognitive adjustments seem to promote adaptation and probably help patients achieve or, in some cases, exceed their previous levels of psychosocial functioning. But many individuals, perhaps one-half, do not achieve these adjustments (Thompson, 1998).

ADAPTING IN A RECURRENCE OR RELAPSE

One thing that makes high-mortality diseases so dangerous is that the deadly medical conditions they produce have high rates of recurrence or relapse. Among stroke victims, for instance, 30 to 40% develop another stroke within 5 years (Flinn, Dalsing, & White, 1986). Patients correctly recognize their heightened vulnerability and worry about it, and so do their families. Convalescing individuals tend to be very watchful for symptoms and changes in their conditions even if they are optimistic about their health.

A recurrence or relapse of the condition presents another crisis for patients and their families, which may be harder to cope with than the first (Moos, 1982; Weisman, 1979). They rightly perceive this event as a bad sign—it typically indicates that the prognosis is now worse than before, since additional damage has occurred. Patients focus again on the illness, trying to forestall deterioration in their general functioning and quality of life. They undergo a new round of hospitalization, medical procedures, and, perhaps, surgery. Patients and their families go through the kinds of coping processes they experienced in the original bout, but they are likely to be less hopeful than they were before.

Living with any high-mortality disease can be quite stressful, but each disease creates a pattern of stresses that is unique. We turn now to considering how people adapt to living with specific high-mortality health problems, starting with heart disease.

HEART DISEASE

Coronary heart disease refers to illnesses that result from the narrowing and blocking of the coronary arteries, which enmesh the heart and supply it with oxygen-rich blood. As we saw in Chapter 2, blood vessels become narrowed as plaque builds up in the condition called *atherosclerosis*. Blockage can occur if a clot of plaque or blood platelets develops and gets lodged in an artery, preventing blood flow.

Brief reductions of oxygenated blood to the heart can produce painful cramps, called **angina pectoris,** in the chest and arm, back, or neck (AMA, 1989). This is most likely during exercise or stress, and little or no permanent damage occurs if the blockage ends quickly. But if reduced blood supply is severe or prolonged, part of the muscle tissue of the heart (myocardium) may be destroyed—a condition called **myocardial infarction,** or "heart attack." Table 14.1 describes common symptoms of a heart attack. Many people with heart disease develop *congestive heart failure*, which has three permanent features: the heart is enlarged, the pumping capacity is reduced, and the person becomes short of breath with little exertion. Heart disease is prevalent in developed countries. In the United States, each year about 1.1 million Americans suffer a heart attack; more than a

Table 14.1 *Symptoms of a Heart Attack*

Many victims delay going to the hospital for hours because they don't know the symptoms of a heart attack, which are:

- Uncomfortable pressure, fullness, squeezing, or pain in the center of the chest that lasts for more than a few minutes.
- Pain spreading to the shoulders, neck, or arms.
- Chest discomfort with lightheadedness, fainting, sweating, nausea, or shortness of breath.

Not all of these symptoms always happen in a heart attack—if some start to occur, the person should get medical care immediately. Prompt treatment can often prevent serious myocardial damage.

Source: AHA (2000).

third of the victims die, usually before they reach a hospital (AHA, 2000). About half of heart attack victims take 2 hours or longer to get medical help.

The prognosis for a patient after a myocardial infarction depends on several factors, especially the extent of arterial damage and the condition of the heart's ventricles (Langosch, 1984). If the ventricles are functioning well, the survival rates after 10 years are 97% when the damage involves one coronary blood vessel, 79% when it involves two vessels, and 66% for three vessels. But if ventricular functioning is impaired, these survival rates drop to 85%, 58%, and 40%, respectively.

WHO IS AT RISK OF HEART DISEASE, AND WHY?

Several demographic, lifestyle, and physiological characteristics are associated with developing heart disease.

Age, Gender, and Sociocultural Risk Factors

The prevalence rates for heart disease increase as people get older, particularly after about 45 years of age. In the years prior to old age, far more men than women develop and die from heart disease (AHA, 2000). Even though women are less likely than men to have heart attacks, they are more likely to die from them if they have them. The link between heart disease and sociocultural factors can be seen in the death rate data for different ethnic groups in the United States: Among both men and women, heart disease death rates are two to three times higher for blacks than for Asian Americans, with the rates for whites, Native Americans, and Hispanics being intermediate (NCHS, 2000). Interestingly, a study of death rates around 1990 in New York City revealed that blacks who were born in the Southern United States had far higher mortality rates from cardiovascular disease than those born in the North, whose death rates were similar to those of whites (Fang, Madhavan, & Alderman, 1996). And cross-cultural research has found that men and women in Russia have extremely high death rates from cardiovascular disease, while the French and Japanese have very low rates (AHA, 1995). These findings suggest an important role of lifestyle in heart disease.

Lifestyle and Biological Risk Factors

Part of the reason for age, sex, and sociocultural differences in risk of heart disease lies in biological and lifestyle variations. For example, *hypertension*—the condition of having high blood pressure consistently over an extended period of time—is a major risk factor for heart disease (AHA, 2000). Nearly one-fourth of adult Americans are hypertensive (NCHS, 2000). High blood pressure has no overt symptoms, but its presence indicates that the heart is working harder than normal. When this continues over a long period of time, the heart becomes enlarged and has more and more difficulty meeting the demands of the body. High blood pressure also increases the development of atherosclerosis, causing blood vessels to become narrowed and less elastic. This increases the risk of a blood clot or piece of plaque becoming lodged in an artery and causing a myocardial infarction. Prevalence rates for hypertension increase with age, and are higher in males than females and in black than white Americans (NCHS, 2000).

Several other lifestyle and biological risk factors are important in heart disease (AHA, 2000). They include:

- Family history of heart disease
- Cigarette smoking
- High blood pressure
- High LDL and low HDL cholesterol levels
- Physical inactivity
- Diabetes
- Obesity
- Stress

People who stop smoking and reduce their cholesterol intake and blood pressure have half the risk of dying of heart disease (Jousilahti et al., 1995). In Chapter 4 we saw that *stress* plays an important role in the development of heart disease, particularly through its connection to the Type A behavior pattern and hypertension. Chronic stress, anger, and hostility appear to contribute to people's high blood pressure (Ewart, 1991a).

Negative Emotions and Heart Disease

Prospective studies have shown that men and women who experience chronic high levels of hostility, depression, or anxiety are more likely than others to develop heart disease and hypertension (Weidner & Mueller, 1999). The link between negative emotions and heart disease involves two avenues. First, people tend to have less healthful lifestyles when they experience negative emotions. Second, negative emotions have physiological effects that promote heart disease. Some of the clearest physiological links have been shown among people with the Type A behavior pattern. When in stressful situations. Type A individuals—particularly those who experience frequent high levels of anger and hostility—often show high physiological *reactivity*, which includes increased blood pressure, catecholamine, and corticosteroid levels (Smith, 1992).

Type A people chronically produce high levels of catecholamines and corticosteroids, especially when under stress (Pope & Smith, 1991; Suarez et al., 1991). Chronic high levels of these hormones in the blood can damage the heart and blood vessels. Evidence now suggests that epinephrine (a catecholamine) increases the formation of platelet clots in the blood, which can block arteries and cause a heart attack (Markovitz & Matthews, 1991). Although heart attacks can happen at any time in any 24-hour day, they are most likely to occur on Mondays, at least for working people, and in the morning hours from 6 to 11 A.M.; they are least likely to occur during sleep at night (Muller et al., 1987; Somers, Dyken, Mark, & Abboud, 1993; Willich et al., 1994). The increased risk in the morning hours probably occurs because dreaming shortly before awakening and becoming active after awakening increase blood pressure and catecholamines, which increase platelet clotting.

MEDICAL TREATMENT AND REHABILITATION OF CARDIAC PATIENTS

Heart attack treatment follows a sequence from emergency care to a program of rehabilitation.

Initial Treatment for Heart Attack

When heart attack victims enter the hospital, they receive emergency medical treatment to prevent or limit damage to the myocardium. Part of this treatment generally involves using *clot-dissolving medication* to free blocked arteries. Most patients are then placed in *coronary care units*, where medical staff can monitor their physiological functioning closely. The risk of another attack is high during the first few days.

Medical assessments indicate whether certain other procedures are also needed. One procedure is called *balloon angioplasty*, in which a tiny balloon is inserted in the blocked artery and inflated to open the blood vessel (Rey, 1999). A metal mesh *stent* is then placed permanently at the site to keep the vessel open. Another procedure—called *bypass surgery*—entails replacing the diseased section of artery with a healthy vessel taken from another part of the person's body.

As you might expect, most cardiac patients experience extremely high levels of anxiety in the first day or two of coronary care. Many of these people cope with this crisis through *denial*, and those who use denial tend to be less anxious in the first few days than those who do not (Froese, Hackett, Cassem, & Silverberg, 1974). Regardless of whether cardiac patients use denial, their anxiety levels soon start to decline. After a few days, the anxiety levels of those who do and do not use denial are about the same, but still higher than normal. These fairly high anxiety levels tend to persist for the remainder of their hospital stays (Cay, Philip, & Dugard, 1972; Froese, Hackett, Cassem, & Silverberg, 1974). The cardiac patients with the greatest difficulty coping are not necessarily the ones who are the most seriously ill—instead, they tend to be those who were experiencing distress and social problems before the heart attack.

Excessive anxiety, depression, or denial can impair recovery, and psychological intervention may be needed (Erdman, 1990). For example, some patients may deny they had a heart attack and insist on leaving the hospital too early. Many patients anticipate psychosocial problems ahead, particularly in relation to their work. A program for rehabilitation generally begins after the first week, when cardiac patients are transferred to a general ward.

Rehabilitation of Cardiac Patients

Rehabilitation programs for heart attack patients are designed to promote recovery and reduce risk factors for having another attack (Erdman, 1990). These programs provide patients with information on such topics as lifestyle changes and restrictions they should follow, medications to take, and symptoms to expect. Many patients will experience recurrent angina pectoris episodes for many months or even years after discharge (Langosch, 1984; Rey, 1999). These episodes can be very frightening to them and their families.

Sometimes the chest pain requires medical attention, but the patients do not seem to suffer tissue damage, and they often can simply take medication to control it. For some patients, the pain can be quite severe and even disabling (Rey, 1999; Wielgosz et al., 1984). Medical tests often reveal no physical basis for the pain—that is, there is no substantial artery blockage or ventricle impairment—but the pain persists (Ketterer et al., 1996).

To reduce the likelihood of another infarction, most cardiac patients receive advice on lifestyle changes, such as to:

- Quit smoking
- Lose weight
- Exercise
- Reduce dietary fat and cholesterol
- Reduce high alcohol consumption

Because stress and hostility are linked to heart disease, these patients often receive training in stress management, too (Langosch, 1984). Many heart attack victims who make healthful changes in their lifestyles and attitudes live longer than comparable people who have not had infarctions.

Some cardiac patients find it easy to adhere to their rehabilitation programs; others do not, and may resent the restrictions their conditions impose. One man said of his doctor's advice: "If he tells you that you cannot walk upstairs, he is telling you that you are weak, that you are no longer strong. He has taken something away from you . . . your pride." (Tagliacozzo & Mauksch, 1972, p. 178). In addition, coronary patients with low self-efficacy for carrying out their medical regimens and who perceive little social support in their lives show less adherence to their regimens and slower recovery than those who have high levels of social support (Bastone & Kerns, 1995; Fontana, Kerns, Rosenberg, & Colonese, 1989; Friis & Taff, 1986).

Exercise is a very important aspect of rehabilitation programs for cardiac patients. A program of physical activity needs to be introduced gradually and tailored to each person's physical condition. It often begins in the hospital with supervised short-distance walking. In the following weeks, the physical activities become more and more vigorous and long-lasting, and are likely to include long-distance walking, calisthenics, and often jogging, bicycling, or swim-

ming. Cardiac patients who adhere to their exercise programs gain substantial relevant benefits (Miller, Balady, & Fletcher, 1997). First, they reduce their risk of death in the next few years by 20 to 25% and their symptoms of angina pectoris and congestive heart failure. Second, they reduce their physical risk factors for a subsequent heart attack, such as blood pressure and cholesterol levels. Third, they reduce psychosocial risk factors, such as levels of negative emotion and cardiovascular reactivity to stress, and improve their self-concepts.

Unfortunately, many cardiac patients never begin an exercise program and about 50% of those who do discontinue them within the first 6 months (Dishman, 1982; Dishman, Sallis, & Orenstein, 1985). People who drop out of exercise programs are likely to be those who smoke cigarettes, work in blue-collar occupations, and begin the programs with poorer cardiovascular function, higher body weight, more sedentary lifestyles, and greater anxiety and depression (Blumenthal et al., 1982; Dishman, 1981; Oldridge & Spencer, 1985). Compliance is likely to be higher if the rehabilitation program provides a special place, like a wellness center, for the patients to exercise, instead of having them exercise on their own.

Cardiac patients may also have a difficult time making other lifestyle changes, particularly in their diets and in stopping smoking. Dietary changes to reduce fat and cholesterol are often hard to make because they have an impact on family life (Croog, 1983). With respect to stopping smoking, studies have found that only perhaps 30 to 40% of individuals who suffer myocardial infarctions quit or substantially reduce their smoking (Ockene et al., 1985; Rigotti, Singer, Mulley, & Thibault, 1991). Those who continue to smoke are in many ways like those who do not exercise. That is, compared to patients who quit, those who do not quit tend to be more anxious, come from lower occupational and educational groups, smoke more heavily, and have fewer negative attitudes about smoking.

THE PSYCHOSOCIAL IMPACT OF HEART DISEASE

"Is it OK for me to drive a car, do chores around the house, or lift heavy things?" heart attack patients often ask their doctors, fearing that overexertion could bring on new attacks (Erdman, 1990). The extent of

The treadmill test is used in assessing the ability of heart patients to engage in strenuous exercise.

patients' disability is likely to affect how well they and their families adjust to their conditions.

Being able to work has a special meaning to individuals who suffer from chronic health problems. People who have suffered heart attacks, for instance, often view returning to work as an important sign that they are recovering (Croog, 1983). Advice about returning to work depends on how severe the heart condition is and the physical requirements of the job (Rey, 1999). In the past, most individuals were advised to wait about 60 days before returning to work if the condition was not very severe. But jobs in industrialized countries have become less physically demanding (Rey, 1999). Research has found that most cardiac patients can resume working about 2 weeks earlier without increasing their risk of another

cardiac episode (Dennis et al., 1988). Physicians often advise people with heart disease to cut back on the amount of physical effort and stress they experience on the job. Following this advice may mean finding a new job, which may be difficult to do, particularly for people over age 50 or so. Patients who are near retirement age may simply leave the work force if they can. Nevertheless, most cardiac patients do go back to work, often with jobs that require less productivity or shorter hours than they previously had worked. Studies have found that roughly 80% of cardiac victims who were previously employed return to some type and amount of work within the year following the heart attack (Doehrman, 1977; Shanfield, 1990). Compared to individuals who do not return to work, those who do return tend to be younger, in better physical condition, better educated, and employed in white-collar jobs. Delaying or failing to go back to work is often associated with having long-lasting emotional distress and depression.

Sometimes cardiac patients' work restrictions cause them to experience interpersonal problems with coworkers and heightened work stress. Sociologist Sydney Croog has described the case of a man who returned to his clerical job after a heart attack, but occasionally felt mild chest pain and shortness of breath. Although his coworkers were sympathetic at first and complied with his requests to lift heavy boxes, they started to resent these chores, as shown in this man's experience when asking

> a fellow worker to lift a box for him. The response comes, "Why don't you go ahead and drop dead, you lazy son-of-a-bitch!"
>
> The solutions are limited for this 55-year-old man. Transferring to another department is not possible, as the company is a small one. Leaving for another job is not possible for many reasons. . . . So picking up the heavy boxes seems like the easiest solution—but for how long can he continue? What will be the eventual effects on his heart? (1983, pp. 300–301)

Going back to work usually contributes to the long-term well-being of a cardiac victim. But as this example illustrates, the work situation can also create problems that may impair the person's physical and psychosocial condition.

Cardiac illness and family relationships are closely interrelated. Studies have found that cardiac patients with strong social support recover faster and survive longer than those with less support (Berkman, 1995; Reifman, 1995). For many heart patients, family difficulties—such as quarreling over financial or sexual problems—existed prior to the infarction, and these difficulties often become worse (Croog & Fitzgerald, 1978; Swan, Carmelli, & Rosenman, 1986). The illness adds to the original difficulties, such as by making the financial and sexual problems worse. What also seems to happen in these families is that a "cycle of guilt and blame" tends to develop (Croog, 1983). For example, a husband who suffers a myocardial infarction may blame his wife or children for his condition, and they may agree and feel guilty. But even when harmonious relations exist before the attack, the illness adds to the stress of all members of the family. One marital difficulty that may arise after a heart attack relates to sexual activity, which often never returns to the level that existed prior to the attack (Krantz & Deckel, 1983; Michela, 1987). Either or both spouses may fear that having sex could precipitate another attack, even though this risk is very low, especially if the patient exercises regularly (Muller et al., 1996). The marital satisfaction of both partners generally benefits by having little or no sex initially and then increasing its frequency gradually, with the advice of the patient's doctor (Michela, 1987).

Families have an enormous impact on the process of cardiac rehabilitation: patients adjust better, adhere more closely to their regimens, and recover sooner if their efforts receive family encouragement (Kaplan & Toshima, 1990; Krantz & Deckel, 1983). But the danger exists that families will promote *cardiac invalidism*, in which people with heart disease become increasingly dependent and helpless. The beliefs a spouse has about the patient's physical capabilities can aid or retard rehabilitation. A study of this process examined the beliefs that wives held about their husbands' physical abilities several weeks after these men had suffered myocardial infarctions (Taylor et al., cited in Bandura, 1986). Each wife evaluated her husband's cardiac and physical ability before and after one of three conditions: she either *observed* him perform vigorously on a treadmill, *participated* on the treadmill herself after watching him perform, or was *uninvolved* in the treadmill situation. The wives who participated on the treadmill after watching their husbands perform raised their assessments of their husbands' physical abilities, but the others continued to give low assessments, even after receiving medical counseling to the

contrary. By seeing and personally experiencing the physical feats the cardiac patient can perform, family members can provide more effective encouragement for the person to become increasingly active.

What are the long-term emotional consequences of heart disease? After having a heart attack, most patients have higher-than-normal levels of anxiety and depression during the first weeks or months, but their distress tends to decline during the next year or two (Carney, Freedland, Rich, & Jaffe, 1995; Doehrman, 1977). Most eventually adjust fairly well, especially if they have high levels of social support (Holahan, Moos, Holahan, & Brennan, 1997). But if very high levels of anxiety and depression continue beyond a few months, these emotions become signs of poor adaptation and tend to be linked to decreased compliance with the cardiac regimen and deterioration in the person's physical condition. Patients with severe depression or anxiety in the weeks after a heart attack are much more likely to suffer subsequent cardiac problems, such as arrhythmias, or to die in the next year than those who are less distressed (Carney et al., 1988; Frasure-Smith et al., 1999; Moser & Dracup, 1996). Similarly, patients who, after undergoing a successful angioplasty, feel optimistic about the future and have a strong sense of personal control and self-esteem are less likely than others to suffer a heart attack or require bypass surgery or another angioplasty in the next several months (Helgeson & Fritz, 1999).

PSYCHOSOCIAL INTERVENTIONS FOR HEART DISEASE

Interventions to enhance people's recovery from and long-term adaptation to having heart disease have used several different approaches. One approach used technological devices: researchers equipped cardiac patients with electrocardiogram (ECG, or "EKG") monitors to transmit analyses of their heart function to a hospital nurse by telephone on a periodic schedule and whenever they felt certain symptoms (Follick et al., 1988). If an analysis indicated medical action was needed, the nurse dispatched a rescue squad and instructed the patient to take a drug. Compared with people who received the standard cardiac care, those with the ECG system were far less depressed during the next several months.

Other approaches have used programs in which patients received health and regimen education, psychosocial counseling, or both to improve their compliance with the cardiac regimen, enhance their adjustment to the illness, and reduce their risk of future cardiac problems. Two meta-analyses have been conducted with data from many interventions using these approaches (Dusseldorp et al., 1999; Linden, Stossel, & Maurice, 1996). In most interventions nurses or physicians provided the education and counseling. Analyses comparing patients who received usual medical care with those who had the interventions revealed four important findings. First, the interventions produced substantial reductions in mortality and recurrence of heart problems in the subsequent year or two. Second, the programs successfully reduced several risk factors, improving blood pressure, cholesterol levels, body weight, eating habits, exercise, and smoking. Third, the interventions did *not* improve patients' anxiety or depression. Fourth, compared with programs that were not successful in reducing risk factors, those that were successful were more effective in reducing mortality and heart problems.

Why weren't programs with psychosocial counseling successful in reducing patients' anxiety and depression? The answer may be that counseling in most programs was given by medical personnel, not professionals trained in psychological methods. Therapy with psychologists using behavioral and cognitive methods is highly effective in reducing people's depression and anxiety (Sarafino, 2001). Two examples can be given in which psychological counseling improved emotional adjustment in cardiac victims. One intervention provided patients with information about their conditions and treatment, training in relaxation to reduce stress, and counseling for their fears and anxieties while they were still in the hospital (Oldenburg, Perkins, & Andrews, 1985). Individuals who received this program showed far better psychosocial adjustment during the next year than those who received standard care. In another intervention, hospitalized patients who received counseling showed reduced anxiety and depression (Gruen, 1975).

Interventions by psychologists to help cardiac patients cope with stress can have additional benefits. One study found that stress management reduced the daily number of angina pectoris attacks by nearly 40% compared against attacks of clients who received standard medical care (Bundy, Carroll, Wallace, & Nagle, 1994). Other research has shown that stress

management can reduce patients' Type A behavior and lower blood pressure. As we saw in Chapter 5, these approaches can effectively reduce coronary risk (Friedman et al., 1986; Powell et al., 1984). All these benefits suggest that training to help patients anticipate and manage stressful situations can be a useful component in cardiac rehabilitation programs.

In a now-famous intervention, Dean Ornish and his colleagues (1990) developed and tested a multicomponent program of dietary, exercise, and stress management approaches for cardiac rehabilitation. The patients who volunteered to participate were randomly assigned to receive either the program or standard medical care. The program had the people eat a mainly vegetarian diet, eliminate caffeine and restrict alcohol consumption, stop smoking, get moderate exercise regularly, meet regularly as support groups, and use stress management techniques, including relaxation and meditation. Medical assessments were made at the start of the study and at the end of a year. Comparisons of the two groups showed that the atherosclerosis and reports of chest pain worsened for the subjects who received standard medical care but improved for those in the intervention program. Although the results don't indicate which features of the program worked, they show that changes in lifestyle can unclog arteries. Other studies have not only confirmed these findings but found that intensive reduction of lifestyle risk factors reduces subsequent cardiac problems and hospitalizations (Haskell et al., 1994; Ornish et al., 1998; Superko & Krauss, 1994).

To summarize, recovery after a heart attack presents difficult physical and psychosocial challenges for patients and their families. Cardiac rehabilitation programs require individuals to adhere to regimens of exercise, diet, medication, and stress management. These programs can reverse the disease process. The long-term impact of heart disease often involves emotional, vocational, and marital problems that may require therapeutic interventions to enhance adaptation.

STROKE

Sitting at the breakfast table, Neil began to feel faint and weak, his vision dimmed, and the right side of his body became numb and tingly. As he realized he was having a stroke, he tried to say so, but the words

Table 14.2 *Symptoms of Stroke*

Individuals who experience any of the following warning signs of a stroke should see a physician immediately.

- Sudden weakness or numbness of the face, arm, or leg (typically on one side of the body).
- Sudden dimness or loss of vision (usually in only one eye).
- Loss of speech, or trouble talking or understanding speech.
- Sudden, unexplained, severe headache.
- Unexplained dizziness, unsteadiness, or sudden fall, especially if this occurs with any of the above symptoms.

Source: AHA (2000).

would not come out. Soon he lost consciousness. As Table 14.2 shows, these are common symptoms of a **stroke**—a condition in which damage occurs in some area of the brain when the blood supply to that area is disrupted, depriving it of oxygen. Stroke is a leading cause of death worldwide (WHO, 1999c); in the United States each year, 600,000 new or recurrent strokes occur and claim about 160,000 lives (AHA, 2000; USBC, 1999).

CAUSES, EFFECTS, AND REHABILITATION OF STROKE

The disruption in blood supply that causes strokes occurs in two ways (AHA, 2000; AMA, 1989). In some cases, damage results from an *infarction* when the blood supply in a cerebral artery is sharply reduced or cut off, either when a blood clot (a *thrombus*) forms or a piece of plaque (an *embolus*) becomes lodged in that area of the artery. In other cases, damage results from a *hemorrhage*, in which a blood vessel ruptures and bleeds into the brain. A stroke caused by a hemorrhage generally occurs rapidly and causes the person to lose consciousness; most of the damage it produces happens in a few minutes. In contrast, a stroke caused by an infarction tends to occur more slowly, and the person is less likely to lose consciousness. Strokes from hemorrhages occur much less frequently but are much more likely to cause extensive damage and death than those from infarctions (AHA, 2000; AMA, 1989).

Age, Gender, and Sociocultural Risk Factors for Stroke

The incidence of stroke is very low prior to the middle-age years and increases sharply after 55 years of age,

doubling in each successive decade (AHA, 2000). Men are more likely than women to develop a stroke and die from it. We can see a role of sociocultural factors in death rate data for different ethnic groups in the United States: among both men and women, death rates from stroke are about twice as high for blacks as for whites and Asian, Hispanic, and Native Americans (NCHS, 2000).

As in heart disease, part of the reason for age, sex, and sociocultural differences in the risk of stroke lies in biological and lifestyle variations. For example, high blood pressure is a risk factor for stroke, and the prevalence rates for hypertension increase with age and are higher in males than females and in black than white Americans (NCHS, 2000).

Lifestyle and Biological Risk Factors for Stroke

Several lifestyle and biological factors can increase the risk of a person having a stroke, and some of them can be changed or treated (AHA, 2000). These risk factors are:

- High blood pressure.
- Cigarette smoking.
- Heart disease, diabetes, and their risk factors, such as obesity and physical inactivity.
- Family history of stroke.
- High red blood cell count, which makes the blood thicker and more likely to form clots.
- "Mini-strokes" called *transient ischemic attacks* that may occur one or more times before a full stroke.

Negative emotions also appear to be involved: prospective studies have found that people who are depressed are more likely than others to develop a stroke and die from one in the next two decades (Everson, Roberts, Goldberg, & Kaplan, 1998; Jonas & Mussolino, 2000). Many of the risk factors for a stroke are the same as those for heart disease. As a result, people who have had strokes are usually asked to make similar lifestyle changes to those of people who have had heart attacks: lose weight, stop smoking, exercise, and reduce dietary fat and cholesterol.

Stroke Effects and Rehabilitation

Strokes vary in severity. People who survive moderate or severe strokes generally suffer some degree of motor, sensory, cognitive, or speech impairment as a result of the brain damage. If enough cells are affected, the functions controlled by the damaged area of the brain can be severely disrupted. The extent and type of impairment stroke patients suffer and their medical treatment—drugs and surgery—can vary greatly, depending on the amount and location of damage (AHA, 2000). Getting immediate treatment is critical because clot-dissolving drugs can limit the damage from a stroke. The following discussion applies to strokes that produce at least moderately severe damage.

Although the initial deficits stroke victims experience can be permanent, these people often show considerable improvement over time. Medical treatment and physical, occupational, and speech therapy can help patients regain some of the functions they lost. Some evidence suggests that younger stroke patients may show somewhat better recovery than older ones, and the functional impairments caused by hemorrhages are more easily overcome than those caused by infarction (Hier, 1986). Hemorrhages often impair functioning partly by creating pressure on neurons. If that pressure is relieved by the blood being reabsorbed by the body, the person may gradually recover some of the lost functioning.

Stroke is one of the most disabling chronic illnesses (AHA, 2000; Guccione et al., 1994). The most common deficits stroke patients experience involve motor action (Diller, 1999; Newman, 1984b). For these patients, some degree of paralysis occurs immediately, and the person usually cannot move the arm and leg on one side of the body. Which side becomes paralyzed depends on which side of the brain is damaged: the left hemisphere of the brain controls movement of the right side of the body and the right hemisphere controls movement on the left side. As a result, the paralysis occurs on the side of the body opposite to the hemisphere that sustained damage in the stroke. Because of the paralysis, these patients often cannot walk, dress themselves, or perform many usual self-help activities. Most of the gains these people show in the first month appear to happen spontaneously (AHA, 2000). Although most patients will be able to get around on their own and perform self-care, such as bathing and dressing, after 6 months without formal rehabilitation, engaging in rehabilitation activities reduces their disability (Diller, 1999). Biofeedback and physical therapy methods are effective treatments for improving motor functioning in stroke victims

(Moreland & Thompson, 1994). For complex sequences of behavior, many patients can benefit from constructing and practicing verbal instructions (O'Callaghan & Couvadelli, 1998). For instance, to transfer from a wheelchair to a bed, the person might say, "I position the wheelchair facing the bed; perpendicular to it," "Next, I put on the brakes," and so on.

Other common deficits many stroke patients face involve cognitive functions—language, learning, memory, and perception. The specific type of impairment they have depends on which side of the brain was damaged. In most people, the left hemisphere contains the areas that handle language processes, including speech and writing (Tortora & Grabowski, 2000). Thus, damage on the left side often causes language and learning deficits. A common language disorder in stroke patients is *aphasia*, which is marked by difficulty in understanding or using words. There are two kinds of aphasia: *receptive aphasia* refers to a difficulty in understanding verbal information; *expressive aphasia* involves a problem in producing language, even though the person can make the component sounds. For example, the individual may not be able to differentiate between two verbalized words, such as "coal" and "cold." Or the patient may have difficulty remembering a sequence of things he or she is told to do—such as, "Touch your right ear with your left hand, and touch your left eyebrow with your right hand."

What deficits are associated with damage on the right side of the brain? The right hemisphere usually processes visual imagery, emotions, and the perception of patterns, such as melodies (Tortora & Grabowski, 2000). As a result, visual disorders are common with right-brain damage (Diller, 1999). In the disorder called *visual neglect*, patients fail to process information on the left side of the normal visual field. For example, they may not notice food on the left side of a tray, items on the left side of a menu, or a minus sign in an arithmetic task (see Figure 14–1). This problem also impairs their ability to perceive distances correctly and causes them to bump into objects or doorframes on the left side of the visual field, making them accident-prone. Sometimes patients with this disorder feel they are "going crazy" when they hear someone speaking but cannot see the person because he or she is standing in the left side of the visual field. The discrepancy between what they hear and what they see makes them wonder if they are hallucinating.

$$7 \quad 6 \quad 28 \quad 31 \quad 96 \quad 74$$
$$+4 \quad -2 \quad +11 \quad -10 \quad -29 \quad +18$$
$$11 \quad 8 \quad 39 \quad 41 \quad 125 \quad 92$$

Figure 14–1 An illustration of arithmetic errors (circled items) a stroke patient with a visual disorder might make at the start of rehabilitation. In this case, the patient fails to scan to the left and assumes all of the problems involve addition. Rehabilitation can help patients overcome this deficit.

The specific location of damage in the brain also can determine emotional disorders that stroke patients may show. Some studies have found associations between (1) specific left-hemisphere damage and patients' degree of depression and (2) specific right-hemisphere damage and patients' ability to interpret and express affect (Bleiberg, 1986; Newman, 1984b). An example of an emotional disorder some stroke patients have is called *emotional lability*, which can occur in varying degrees (AHA, 2000; Bleiberg, 1986). Some people with this disorder may laugh or cry with little or no provocation, realizing and being surprised by the discrepancy; others with milder disorders may display the appropriate emotion, but at excessive levels, such as sobbing when thinking mildly sad thoughts. In other emotional disorders, stroke patients may be unable to interpret other people's emotions correctly and may react oddly to them. (Go to 🌳.)

PSYCHOSOCIAL ASPECTS OF STROKE

Recovery from a severe stroke is a long and arduous process. The initial physical and cognitive deficits are extremely frightening, but many patients are heartened by early gains in their functioning. Although patients with all chronic illnesses often rely on avoidance strategies to cope during the early phases of convalescence, denial seems to be more common among patients who have had strokes than those with heart disease or cancer (Krantz & Deckel, 1983). Stroke patients who continue to deny their current or possible future limitations often retard their progress in rehabilitation. Instead, they need a balance of reality and hope: stroke patients who feel a sense of control over their condition at the end of the first month show better recovery months later than others do (Johnston, Morrison, MacWalter, & Partridge, 1999).

When a stroke produces physical or cognitive deficits, the emotional adjustments can be very difficult. Stroke patients are very prone to depression (Bleiberg, 1986; Krantz & Deckel, 1983; Newman, 1984b). Those who are depressed in the first weeks remain in the hospital much longer and show less

CLINICAL METHODS AND ISSUES
Stroke Rehabilitation for Visual Neglect

Like people in general, stroke patients with visual neglect initially take for granted that what they see reflects the full size of their normal visual field. Because they think they see the whole field, they first need to have their visual deficits clearly demonstrated. One way psychologists can do this involves placing paper money on a

    table in front of the patient. The large bills are purposely put on the impaired side. The patient is asked to pick up all of the money on the table. Naturally, a large sum of money remains on the table after the patient says that he or she has

completed the task. Having the patient turn his or her head to see all the money that was left on the table is one way to begin to teach the patient that . . . this difficulty can be overcome by turning the head. (Gordon & Diller, 1983, p. 119)

Rehabilitation then proceeds from very simple tasks, such as turning the head to track squares in a ceiling, to more difficult ones, such as tracking objects that move from the right to the left side of the visual field, so that the patient turns the head automatically (Diller, 1999). The therapist can provide cues before the response and reinforcement when it occurs.

improvement from the rehabilitation program before they leave (Tennen, Eberhardt, & Affleck, 1999). As patients see the gains in recovery slowing down and begin to realize the extent of their impairment, they may feel hopeless and helpless. At this point, the more severe their condition, the stronger the depression they develop (Diller, 1999). Intervention with cognitive-behavioral therapy is effective in treating depression (Sarafino, 2001).

Although stroke usually afflicts individuals who are beyond retirement age, many of its victims are employed when the illness occurs and suffer impairments that prevent them from returning to work. The results of follow-up studies suggest that less than half of patients who were working prior to the stroke return to work within 6 months, often at reduced hours (Diller, 1999). Some stroke victims who do not return to work are old enough to retire early with pensions, but others must leave the work force under less favorable circumstances, which can be financially and emotionally trying.

The impairments produced by stroke have important social effects on patients and their families, particularly when the patients are severely paralyzed or have aphasia (Evans et al., 1992; Newman, 1984b). Some families adjust to the patient's condition reasonably well, as in the following case:

> Mrs. M. had always taken charge of bookkeeping and running the family. When her husband had a stroke, she adapted very well to his aphasia, inventing ways to communicate with him. When he developed cancer five years later, she helped him keep track of his medications by putting them in little cups at the beginning of the day, with coded instructions on how many to take and when to take them. In this way, Mr. M., who worried that he hadn't taken his medication, could keep track of it when she wasn't there. (Gervasio, 1986, p. 115)

But other families do not adjust well to the changing role relationships, and marital harmony often declines. In addition, social contacts and leisure activities with friends also drop off for both the stroke patient and his or her spouse (Newman, 1984b). Although the decrease in social and leisure activities worsens with the extent of the victim's disability, it is often substantial even when the person has made a good recovery. Family therapy and support groups can help stroke patients and their

families adapt, but these approaches often need to address practical problems, such as not having transportation, before trying to resolve interpersonal problems (Evans et al., 1992; Krantz & Deckel, 1983).

In summary, stroke is a high-mortality illness that involves neurological damage as a result of disrupted blood flow to the brain. Survivors of stroke often suffer substantial physical and cognitive impairments, but medical treatment and physical, occupational, and speech therapy can help these people regain many of their lost abilities. The more severe the remaining deficits after rehabilitation, the more likely patients are to experience psychosocial problems.

CANCER

Cancer is probably the disease most people fear most—the word "cancer" itself scares many people, and they often overestimate the deaths that cancer causes (Burish, Meyerowitz, Carey, & Morrow, 1987). Receiving mammogram results indicating possible breast cancer can leave some women with high levels of anxiety months after further tests disconfirm the suspicion (Lerman et al., 1991). But most women's distress from false-positive cancer tests is not very severe or long-lasting (Wardle et al., 1993).

Most practitioners recognize how people feel about cancer and are reluctant to discuss the disease and its effects with their patients. In a study some years ago of cancer victims who had begun radiation treatment, most reported that their physicians had not told them they had cancer (Peck, 1972). Some even claimed their doctors said the conditions were benign—such as a wart—but 80% of the subjects said they knew it was cancer anyway. Doctors in the United States today are far more likely than in the past to share the bad news about serious medical conditions with their patients, but some probably still withhold distressing information about patients' diagnoses and prognoses (Blaney, 1985; Laszlo, 1987; Shuchman & Wilkes, 1989).

THE PREVALENCE AND TYPES OF CANCER

A basic characteristic of life and growth is that body cells reproduce in an orderly and controlled fashion. Scientists know what the normal pattern of tissue growth looks like. Irregularities in this process can cause unrestricted cell growth, usually forming a tumor called a *neoplasm* (AMA, 1989; Tortora & Grabowski, 2000). Although we know little about the process that maintains the proper number of different types of cells in the body, researchers have discovered an enzyme that exists mainly in tumor cells and may cause these cells to overproduce (Counter, Hirte, Bacchetti, & Harley, 1994). Some neoplasms are harmless, or benign, but others are malignant.

Cancer is a disease of the cells and is characterized by unrestricted cell proliferation that usually forms a malignant neoplasm. There are many varieties of cancer, and the large majority are classified into four types based on the kind of tissue in which it develops (Tortora & Grabowski, 2000; Williams, 1990). These four types of cancer are:

- *Carcinomas*, which are malignant neoplasms of the skin cells and cells lining many body organs, such as the digestive, respiratory, and reproductive tracts. About 85% of human cancers are carcinomas.

- *Lymphomas*, or cancers of the lymphatic system.

- *Sarcomas*, which are malignant neoplasms of the muscle, bone, or connective tissue.

- *Leukemias*, or cancers of the blood-forming organs, such as the bone marrow, that lead to an extreme proliferation of white blood cells.

An important characteristic of cancer cells is that they do not adhere to each other as strongly as normal cells do (Laszlo, 1987; Williams, 1990). As a result, they may separate and spread to other parts of the body through the blood or lymph systems. This migration is called *metastasis*, as is the new neoplasm (plural is *metastases*).

Cancer is a leading cause of death worldwide (WHO, 1999c). In the United States, it is the second most frequent cause of death, and its mortality rates increased dramatically in the second half of the 20th century (NCHS, 2000; USBC, 1999). These increases may be due in part to the decline in deaths from heart disease during the same period. The data on American cancer mortality and morbidity are sobering: each year cancer takes more than 560,000 lives, and over 1.2 million new cases are diagnosed (ACS, 2000). About 60% of these newly diagnosed people can expect to live at least 5 years—most of these people will be *cured*

having virtually the same life expectancy as someone who never had the disease. Although cancer can strike any area of the body, as Figure 14–2 shows, almost all of the increase in cancer death rates since 1950 is from neoplasms in one body site: the lung.

THE SITES, EFFECTS, AND CAUSES OF CANCER

What are the physical effects of cancer, and how does it kill? Cancer progresses by enlarging and spreading to different sites; its growth at each site interferes with normal development and functioning. As the disease progresses, it can produce pain, often because the tumor creates pressure on normal tissue and nerves or blocks the flow of body fluids (Melzack & Wall, 1982). Substantial pain afflicts 40% of cancer victims in intermediate stages of the disease and 70 to 90% of those with advanced cancer (Foley, 1985; Greenwald, Bonica, & Bergner, 1987; Ward et al., 1993). The disease leads to death in direct and indirect ways. In the direct route, the cancer spreads over time to a vital organ, such as the brain, liver, or lungs; it then competes for and takes most of the nutrients the organ tissues need to survive, thereby causing the organ to fail. Cancer kills indirectly in two ways: the disease itself weakens the victims, and both the disease and the treatment can impair the patient's appetite and ability to fight infection (Laszlo, 1987).

Prognosis and Causes of Cancer

The prognosis for cancer depends on how early it is detected and its location (ACS, 2000; Williams, 1990). Table 14.3 describes cancers of common sites, listed in order of their yearly incidence in the United States.

We have seen in earlier chapters that cancer is caused by the interplay of genetic and environmental factors, and that stress can promote the development and progression of the disease. Environmental factors include smoking tobacco, diet, ultraviolet radiation, and household and worksite chemical hazards, among others. Some research has also found a link between certain viral infections and the development of some cancers, such as in the cervix and in the liver (Tortora & Grabowski, 2000; Williams, 1990). In cervical cancer, viral transmission probably occurs during intercourse. Because not all women who are exposed to the viruses develop cancer, it seems likely that

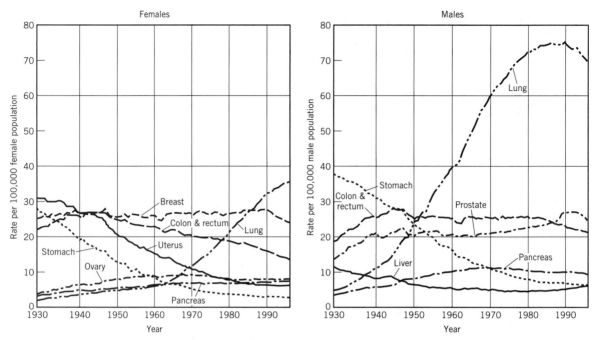

Figure 14–2 Age-adjusted death rates for selected cancer sites per 100,000 females and males in the United States between 1930 and 1995. (From ACS, 2000.) Notice two things: First, mortality rates for most forms of cancer have either declined or remained fairly constant; lung cancer is the dramatic exception. Second, the increases in lung cancer deaths for males and females correspond to gender differences in the prevalence of cigarette smoking.

the effects of the infections depend on or combine with genetic and environmental factors to produce the disease.

Age, Gender, and Sociocultural Factors in Cancer

The risk of developing cancer typically increases with age, especially from the middle-age years onward. For all types of cancer combined, incidence rates for the disease quadruple from 40 to 80 years of age (Mor et al., 1985). Taking age into account, the incidence rates of cancer in the United States are much higher for males than females (NCHS, 2000). After skin cancer, the most common newly diagnosed malignancies are prostate cancer for men and breast cancer for women (ACS, 2000). The link between cancer and sociocultural factors can be seen in the death rate data for different ethnic groups in the United States. Cancer incidence and death rates are about twice as high for blacks as for Asian, Hispanic, and Native Americans, with the rates for whites being

intermediate (ACS, 2000). Although the cancer incidence rates are not so discrepant for blacks and whites, survival rates are much lower in blacks partly because their diagnoses occur later (Meyerowitz, Richardson, Hudson, & Leedham, 1998). There are also national differences in cancer prevalence— for instance, lung cancer is far more common in England than in Nigeria, and stomach cancer is far more common in Japan than in Uganda (AMA, 1989).

DIAGNOSING AND TREATING CANCER

People can increase the likelihood of early rather than late detection of certain cancers by knowing the warning signs of cancer and having or doing regular examinations, which are listed in Table 14.4.

The process for diagnosing cancer can involve three medical procedures (AMA, 1989; Laszlo, 1987; Nguyen et al., 1994). First, *blood* or *urine tests* are useful for suggesting the presence of cancer by revealing telltale signs, such as unusual levels of certain hormones

Table 14.3 *Common Cancer Sites and Facts of the United States*

- *Skin cancer.* With over 1,000,000 cases diagnosed in the skin each year, it is the organ with the highest cancer incidence by far in the United States. The vast majority of these cancers are *basal cell* and *squamous cell carcinomas*, and cure is almost assured with early detection. But about 5% of skin cancers are *melanomas*, which form in the pigment-carrying skin cells and are more serious because they metastasize quickly. Still, 88% of melanoma patients survive at least 5 years.
- *Prostate cancer.* Today, 180,000 diagnoses are made of neoplasms of the prostate gland in the male reproductive system each year. The 5-year survival rate for prostate cancer is about 93% and increases to 100% if detected in its early stages; 68% of all cases survive 10 years. These rates are unclear because diagnosis usually occurs after the men are over 65 years of age.
- *Breast cancer.* The incidence of breast cancer is about 175,000 cases a year. Early detection permits over 97% of breast cancer patients to survive at least 5 years, but this rate drops to 77% if the cancer has begun to spread; 69% of all cases survive 10 years.
- *Lung cancer.* Nearly 172,000 new cases of lung cancer are diagnosed annually, and the incidence is far greater among males than among females, probably because of men's higher smoking rates in the past. The 5-year survival rate is only 14% overall and 50% if the disease is discovered while still localized. In lung cancer, neoplasms tend to metastasize while still small, and, for this reason, they generally have already spread by the time they are discovered.
- *Colorectal cancer.* Neoplasms of the colon or rectum account for over 129,000 cancer diagnoses each year. The 5-year survival rates are about 62% overall and 91% when detected early (only 37% of cases) in recommended tests; 55% of all cases survive 10 years.
- *Uterine and cervical cancer.* Neoplasms of the uterus or cervix of the female reproductive system can be either *invasive*, which have an incidence of about 50,000 cases a year, or precancerous *carcinomas in situ*, which are discovered very early with Pap tests and are usually fully curable. For invasive cases detected early, the 5-year survival rate is 91% for cervical and 96% for uterine cancer.

Source: ACS (2000).

Table 14.4 *Early Cancer Detection: Examinations and Warning Signs*

Examinations

Physician- or self-administered examinations are available for early detection of the following cancer sites:

- Breast
- Skin
- Colon or rectum
- Testes
- Prostate
- Uterus or cervix

Warning Signs of Cancer: "CAUTION"

If you have any of the following signs, see your doctor soon. Notice that the first letters spell "caution."

- **C**hange in bowel or bladder habits.
- **A** sore that does not heal.
- **U**nusual bleeding or discharge.
- **T**hickening or lump in the breast or elsewhere.
- **I**ndigestion or difficulty swallowing.
- **O**bvious change in a wart or mole.
- **N**agging cough or hoarseness.

Sources: ACS (1989, 2000).

or enzymes. Second, *radiological imaging*, through X ray and other techniques, allows physicians to see the structure of internal organs and whether a tumor exists. Third, in a *biopsy* a physician takes out a small piece of suspicious tissue and has it analyzed. Even when the tissue is deep within the abdomen, it can generally be removed with minor surgical procedures and a local anesthetic.

The ideal goal of cancer treatment is to cure the disease—to free the person from it forever. This ideal is possible when all the neoplasms are found and eliminated (Guyton, 1985; Laszlo, 1987). If not all of the cancer was eliminated, the patient's symptoms may disappear for a time—or "go into remission"— only to return at a later date. Sometimes physicians can be reasonably certain that all of the cancer was removed, but often they cannot be sure. This is why they use the individual's survival for at least 5 years as a gauge of a treatment's success. There are basically three types of treatment for cancer—surgery, radiation, and chemotherapy—that may be used singly or in combination. When choosing the treatment components, patients and practitioners consider many factors, such as the size and site of the neoplasm, whether it has metastasized, and how the treatment will affect the patient's quality of life. One factor that seems to affect the treatment choice, sometimes inappropriately, is the patient's age: younger victims (under age 60) are more likely than older ones to receive radiation or chemotherapy in their treatment for cancers with similar stages and sites of neoplasms (Mor et al., 1985).

From a medical standpoint, *surgery* is frequently the preferred treatment for eliminating a neoplasm, such as in breast or colorectal cancer (Laszlo, 1987; Williams, 1990). If the cancer is localized, surgery often can be completely effective by itself; if the cancer

While the patient lies on a table in a large apparatus in the background, a radiological image of his brain appears on the monitor.

has spread, surgery may be useful in removing large clusters of cancerous cells, leaving the remainder for radiation or chemotherapy treatment. Sometimes the surgeon removes large portions of tissue near the neoplasm because of the possibility that the cancer has spread to those areas, too. In patients with colorectal cancer, for example, the surgeon may remove a long section of the colon even though the neoplasm seems to be restricted to a small area. But the practice of removing large amounts of nearby tissue is changing, particularly in the treatment of breast cancer: a *mastectomy*—the removal of the entire breast—is not necessary in many, if not most, cases (ACS, 2000; Jacobson et al., 1995). Instead, a woman may choose to have a *lumpectomy*, in which just the tumor is removed, followed by radiation treatment.

Radiation in high doses alters body cells in such a way that they are either destroyed or cannot reproduce (Holum, 1994). In treating cancer, radiation is used in two ways (Laszlo, 1987; McNaull, 1984). One approach, *external beam therapy*, involves directing a beam of intense radiation at the malignant tissue for a period of seconds or minutes. This is the most commonly used method and the one most people

picture when the term "radiation therapy" is used. External beam therapy is usually given several times in a week, and may be continued for up to several weeks. The second approach is called *internal radiation therapy* and involves placing a radioactive substance inside the body, near or into the tumor, by surgery or injection. Although radiation therapy is painless, it can have problematic side effects, depending on the area of the body radiated and the dose. Because radiation affects both healthy and malignant cells, the affected area may suffer irritation, burns, or hair loss, for example. The person may experience nausea, vomiting, loss of appetite, sterility, and reduced bone marrow function, particularly if the radiated area is large or is in the abdomen. In the day or two before undergoing radiation treatment, individuals often worry about these side effects and report heightened anxiety, similar to that of people awaiting surgery (Andersen, Karlsson, Anderson, & Tewfik, 1984).

In *chemotherapy*, patients receive powerful drugs, usually orally or by injection, that circulate through the body to kill cells that divide very rapidly (Laszlo, 1987; Williams, 1990). The intended targets, of course, are cancerous cells, most of which reproduce rapidly. Some forms of cancer respond more readily than others to the drugs currently available; cancer of the testicles and some types of leukemia are very responsive, but cancers of the brain and pancreas are not. One problem with chemotherapy is that the drugs also kill certain types of normal cells that divide rapidly—for example, cells of the bone marrow, mouth and intestinal lining, and hair follicles, especially those of the scalp. Some programs of chemotherapy continue for a long time and can have several very adverse side effects, including reduced immunity to infection, sores in the mouth, hair loss, nausea and vomiting, and damage to internal organs (ACS, 2000, AMA, 1989; Williams, 1990).

For many patients, two side effects of cancer treatment are especially difficult. First, most people who undergo repeated radiation or chemotherapy experience severe and long-lasting fatigue that often gets worse after the treatment ends (Cella et al., 1998; Jacobsen & Stein, 1999). Second, chemotherapy often produces periods of nausea and vomiting during and soon after each treatment; these periods can be so aversive and prolonged that patients have discontinued treatment, knowing that doing so could shorten their lives (Carey & Burish, 1988). Moreover, after a few treatments, some patients who are about to receive the drug begin vomiting before it is given—they have developed *anticipatory nausea*. They may even become nauseated and throw up when they arrive at the hospital or while thinking about the upcoming treatment at home the night before.

Anticipatory nausea appears to develop in about 25 to 50% of chemotherapy patients who have received the treatment repeatedly (Andrykowski, 1990; Carey & Burish, 1988). These patients seem to learn this reaction through classical conditioning, whereby the drug itself is the unconditioned stimulus that reflexively produces the unconditioned response of nausea. Through association, other related events, such as seeing the hospital or thinking about the procedure, become conditioned stimuli and can elicit nausea in the absence of the drug (Bovbjerg et al., 1992; Jacobsen et al., 1995). Anticipatory nausea is more likely to develop in people who, before treatments start, expect they will become nauseated than in those who do not expect nausea (Montgomery et al., 1998). Using relaxation techniques can help to reduce the nausea (Compas et al., 1998).

Cancer treatment not only can be unpleasant, it can be complex and demanding. Most cancer patients must also take medications at home, and many must return to their clinics frequently for laboratory tests, keep diaries of their food intake, or adhere to dietary and other changes in living habits. Because of these conditions, we might expect cancer patients to show poor compliance with their treatment regimens. Studies of adherence to cancer regimens have produced mixed findings (Levy, 1985; Nehemkis & Gerber, 1986; Richardson et al., 1987; Tebbi et al., 1986). Although most adults seem to adhere well to cancer regimens, adolescents and minority group individuals from the lower classes do not. Adherence to medical regimens depends on and influences psychosocial factors in patients' lives. (Go to 🔍.)

THE PSYCHOSOCIAL IMPACT OF CANCER

Like all chronic illnesses, cancer involves a series of threats and difficulties that change, often getting worse over time. Cancer creates unique stresses for patients and their families. These patients have a disease they recognize as a "real killer," and one that can lead to intense pain, disability, and disfigurement. The treatment decisions they make are complex—having to balance health benefits against distressing side effects, such as toxic reactions or disfigurement—and can lead to adjustment problems if the outcomes are not as expected (Stanton et al., 1998).

Even among patients who go into remission and adapt well during the first months or years, the threat of a recurrence looms—and if the disease flares up, some individuals are psychologically paralyzed by their fear (Mages & Mendelsohn, 1979). In addition, some patients experience medical procedures that, for them, can be more aversive than the disease itself. How well patients adapt to having cancer can have medical consequences and affect the progression of the disease. Those who have high levels of hopelessness and depression do not survive as long as others do (Watson et al., 1999). Cancer patients who experience high levels of stress and do not cope well show poor immune system activity, and some evidence suggests that cancers worsen more quickly if immune functions are impaired (Kiecolt-Glaser & Glaser, 1986; Levy et al., 1985; Redd et al., 1991).

Given all of the stress associated with having cancer, most patients show a remarkable amount

FOCUS ON RESEARCH

Chemotherapy and Learned Food Aversions

When people with cancer begin chemotherapy, many experience a loss of appetite that can lead to excessive weight loss. This can create problems in their medical treatment and in their home lives. Families of patients who are not eating well become concerned about this situation, and eating may involve a constant battle, with the patients feeling hounded to eat (Nevidjon, 1984). Cancer patients who receive chemotherapy or radiation therapy often report that they develop a distaste for some foods they once liked. Coming to dislike foods they previously liked a lot, such as chocolate desserts or a steak, can be demoralizing to cancer victims, who may feel that their quality of life has suffered enough.

Why do these patients come to dislike foods they had liked? Since chemotherapy produces nausea and vomiting in many people, these symptoms may become associated with one or more foods they ingest before or after the symptoms occur. A **learned food aversion** is a phenomenon in which a food becomes distasteful because the individual associates it with symptoms of illness or physical discomfort. Researchers studied learned food aversions in 76 adult cancer patients who had no other physical conditions, such as diabetes, that might relate to their food preferences (Mattes, Arnold, & Boraas, 1987a, 1987b). During the hour preceding their first treatment, the patients were interviewed to determine their medical histories, the foods they had consumed during the prior 24 hours, their ratings of recently eaten foods, and any food aversions they already had. They took home a form on which they listed and rated all foods eaten during the 24 hours after the treatment.

At the next scheduled visit and at other visits during the next 6 months of treatment, the subjects reported food preference information and any side effects they experienced from the treatment. The results revealed several interesting findings. First, 55% of the patients developed aversions to foods consumed within the 24 hours preceding and following treatments. Second, many of these aversions formed after only one treatment, and subsequent treatments produced fewer and fewer new dislikes. Third, the amount of time (up to 24 hours) between eating the food and receiving the treatment did not affect whether an aversion would develop. Fourth, compared with individuals whose side effects did not include vomiting, subjects who vomited developed more learned food aversions, but receiving drugs to prevent vomiting did not help prevent aversions from forming. Fifth, the aversions generally lasted less than a month and included many of the foods the patients previously ate frequently and liked a great deal.

Can something be done to prevent cancer patients from learning to dislike foods they normally eat? One promising approach involves having a patient consume a strongly flavored, unfamiliar food between his or her last meal and the chemotherapy treatment. Why? The purpose is to create a scapegoat—that is, to direct the learning process to this new food and allow *it* to become disliked, instead of foods in the patient's normal diet. Research has shown that this approach works for many adult and child cancer patients (Broberg & Bernstein, 1987; Mattes, Arnold, & Boraas, 1987b). Individuals who form aversions to the scapegoat foods are much less likely to develop dislikes to foods in normal diets.

of resilience and adapt fairly well (van't Spijker, Trijsburg, & Duivenvoorden, 1997). Even among hospitalized cancer patients, studies have generally found that less than half show significant emotional difficulties, and most of these involve relatively transient problems—chiefly anxiety and depressed mood—that are usually responsive to psychological therapy (Burish, Meyerowitz, Carey, & Morrow, 1987).

This incidence of emotional problems may seem high, but keep in mind that hospitalization itself elevates emotional difficulties and the patients may have been highly anxious or depressed before the illness. Psychologists often consider it "normal" for cancer patients to have some elevations in depression and anxiety. Given the life circumstances of these patients, our deciding when these reactions are appropriate and when they are dysfunctional is likely to be difficult and based on arbitrary criteria.

Although adaptation to cancer can be very difficult for patients during the first several months and when their conditions worsen, their ability to adjust to their illnesses appears to improve with time during remission or after a cure (Burish, Meyerowitz, Carey, & Morrow, 1987; Glanz & Lerman, 1992). By 2 years or so, their psychosocial functioning stabilizes at levels similar to those they had prior to the diagnosis. One study had breast cancer patients and women from the general population fill out questionnaires assessing their psychosocial adjustment (Craig, Comstock, & Geiser, 1974). All cancer victims had been diagnosed and treated more than 9 months before the study. The patients and the other women showed very similar levels of depression, happiness, optimism for the future, and perceived health.

The adaptation of people with cancer depends on many aspects of their illnesses and psychosocial situations. For example, the emotional adjustment cancer victims achieve depends on their ages and physical conditions—those who are middle-aged or physically impaired seem to fare worse than those who are older or less impaired (Vinokur, Threatt, Vinokur-Kaplan, & Satariano, 1990). Patients who become most severely depressed tend to be those who are physically disabled by the disease or in pain (Burish, Meyerowitz, Carey, & Morrow, 1987; Spiegel, Sands, & Koopman, 1994). The site of the cancer is also important, and its impact often depends on the patient's age and gender. Cancer in some sites relates to sexual function, physically and psychologically, particularly for prostate and testicular cancer in men and for breast and gynecological cancer in women. Men with prostate cancer often become impotent and experience urinary incontinence; testicular cancer renders the man sterile. The effect of age can be seen in the cases of two testicular cancer victims, a middle-aged married man with grown children and a younger man who had begun a career and developed a strong relationship with a woman 2 years before the diagnosis. The younger man was more distressed because his sterility

> meant that he could never have children of his own and, perhaps unrealistically, raised doubts about a future marriage and his sexual competence. . . . The older man, in contrast, was relatively little affected

by his disease. Though he too had to face the issue of a potentially shortened life span, he had long since established a stable and satisfying adult existence and was securely embedded in a supportive social network. (Mages & Mendelsohn, 1979, p. 277)

A similar pattern of concerns affects women of different ages with cancer of the breast, cervix, and uterus (Andersen, Woods, & Copeland, 1997; Glanz & Lerman, 1992; Spencer et al., 1999). Their difficulties may be compounded if cancer or its treatment disfigures their bodies or alters their physical ability to function sexually, but breast-conserving surgery reduces disfigurement and adjustment problems (Moyer, 1997). Keep in mind, however, that sexual problems do not occur only among patients with cancers in sex-related organs. Many patients with cancers in other sites may also experience sexual problems as a result of their medical regimens, such as when chemotherapy causes fatigue (Burish, Meyerowitz, Carey, & Morrow, 1987; Redd et al., 1991).

Many cancer patients experience psychosocial problems that stem from changes in their relationships with family members and friends. Patients who perceive little social support and negative behaviors from significant people tend to have adjustment problems in part because they do not feel others want to talk about the cancer experience (Lepore & Helgeson, 1998; Manne, 1999). Although patients may withdraw from social contact because they feel socially awkward or embarrassed by their conditions, two other reasons are probably more common (Bloom, Kang, & Romano, 1991). First, patients' physical conditions and treatment may interfere with their seeing friends and family. Second, people may begin to avoid the patient. Although this sometimes occurs as a result of fear and ignorance, such as when people believe cancer is contagious, other reasons are often involved. For example, friends and family may experience conflicts between wanting to be cheerful and optimistic with the patient, while at the same time feeling very sad and personally vulnerable in his or her presence (Wortman & Dunkel-Schetter, 1979). They may also worry that they will "break down," or "betray their feelings," or "say the wrong thing" in front of the patient. When these people and the patient do get together, everyone may behave awkwardly.

PSYCHOSOCIAL INTERVENTIONS FOR CANCER

Psychosocial approaches for helping individuals cope with their cancers can begin in the diagnostic interview with the physician (Roberts et al., 1994). The physician can promote positive adaptation to the illness by discussing the diagnosis while the patient is alert with a spouse or other significant person present, expressing concern and giving the people some time to react emotionally and compose themselves, and then presenting information about the prognosis and treatment options. Medical personnel can also help by providing information on ways to manage the disease and difficult aspects of treatment and advice on improving the patient's diet and physical activity (Helgeson, Cohen, Schulz, & Yasko, 1999; Pinto, Eakin, & Maruyama, 2000).

Several types of psychosocial interventions have been applied successfully to improve cancer patients' adjustment to their illnesses and quality of life (Meyer & Mark, 1995). Some programs have been applied to reduce patients' nausea from chemotherapy (Carey & Burish, 1988). Two approaches with particularly strong support are relaxation training and systematic desensitization. For example, one study found that training patients to use progressive muscle relaxation and imagery before and during chemotherapy sessions sharply reduced the development of nausea after the first session (Burish & Jenkins, 1992). Another study showed that systematic desensitization can help people who have already developed anticipatory nausea (Morrow et al., 1992). Patients used relaxation techniques while they imagined increasingly difficult scenes relating to chemotherapy, such as driving to the clinic or entering the waiting room. These individuals reported much less nausea and vomiting in subsequent chemotherapy sessions. Not all patients benefit from these techniques, partly because they don't believe psychosocial approaches will help (Carey & Burish, 1988).

Other interventions have had broader focuses and shown that psychosocial methods not only enhance patients' adjustment to cancer, but may improve their survival, too. In one study, psychological and immunological assessments were made on cancer patients before serving in one of two research conditions, after serving in the condition, and 6 months later (Fawzy, Cousins et al., 1990; Fawzy, Kemeny et al., 1990). Subjects in the intervention met in groups for 1½ hours in each of 6 weeks to discuss their concerns and problems and to learn health-promotion activities, positive coping strategies, and stress management techniques. Subjects in the control condition received no psychosocial intervention. The results at the 6-month assessment revealed that the intervention subjects had better immune function and reported more vigor, better coping behavior, and less depression than the controls. A follow-up 6 years later revealed that 29% of the controls and only 9% of the intervention subjects had died (Fawzy et al., 1993).

Another study assessed the survival of cancer patients after a year-long intervention in which they attended weekly group meetings that were led by

The social support of the cancer patient in the foreground is evident from his friends' having shaved their heads to help him feel more comfortable about losing his hair as a result of chemotherapy.

therapists who had cancers that were in remission (Spiegel, Bloom, Kraemer, & Gottheil, 1989). The meetings enabled the patients to discuss their feelings and coping strategies and to learn self-hypnosis to manage pain. Compared with a control group, the patients who received the psychosocial intervention lived nearly 18 months longer during a 10-year follow-up period. Although interventions that have improved survival are encouraging, two similar efforts were not successful, and we don't yet know why (Cunningham et al., 1998; Edelman, Lemon, Bell, & Kidman, 1999). If psychosocial methods can, in fact, enhance survival, they may do so by improving immune function and reducing physiological stress reactions (Andersen et al., 1998; Cruess et al., 2000).

Because of the social problems cancer patients face, they and their families may benefit from family therapy and attending support groups that include education and group discussion (Helgeson & Cohen, 1996; Tovian, 1991). In one study, cancer patients in a support group received counseling sessions, training in relaxation, and information about diet, exercise, and their illnesses (Cain et al., 1986). Subsequent comparisons with control subjects revealed that those in the support group were less depressed and anxious, had fewer sexual problems, and participated more in leisure activities. (Go to 💡.)

CHILDHOOD CANCER

Cancer strikes tens of thousands of children around the world each year. In the United States, *leukemia* is the most common form of cancer in childhood, with 2,300 new cases annually (ACS, 2000; Laszlo, 1987; Williams, 1990). Improved treatment methods have improved the 5-year survival rate for childhood leukemia from 53% to 78% since 1975. Chemotherapy is the main form of treatment, but radiation may be used to prevent the disease from developing in the brain. These treatments produce much the same side effects in children as they do in adults, including chronic nausea and vomiting. Losing their hair can be a very traumatic and embarrassing experience to most children and teenagers even though it does grow back eventually (Spinetta, 1982). If a child receives treatment and a relapse does not occur in the first 5 years after diagnosis, the chances are very high that the leukemia will never recur (Laszlo, 1987).

The treatment program for leukemia begins on an inpatient basis with an "induction" phase, in which the patients receive combinations of drugs in high doses to produce a full remission (Eiser, 1985; Williams, 1990). Because of the high risk of relapse without continued treatment during the next 3 years, the program continues with a "maintenance" phase on an

HIGHLIGHT ON ISSUES
Can Patients "Will Away" Their Cancer?

The mind is a powerful instrument, and what people think can affect their health. How powerful is this instrument? Could cancer patients use it to recruit the soldiers of the immune system to seek and destroy malignant cells? The notion that the mind could do this forms the basis of a controversial approach for helping cancer patients control their disease.

O. Carl Simonton developed a therapy program in which patients receive group counseling and training in muscle relaxation while also receiving medical treatment (Simonton & Simonton, 1975; see also Scarf, 1980). The main feature of the program is an "imaging" exercise in which the patients imagine that they can see their white blood cells attack and destroy cancer cells. One patient, for instance, imagined her white cells were sharks that would chase her cancer cells (small fish) "and then pounce upon them, rending them to bits with their long, jagged teeth and destroying them" (Scarf, 1980, p. 40).

Does this therapy program work? Little or no evidence exists to support the notion that the imaging exercise helps in curing cancer (Blaney, 1985; Laszlo, 1987). But other aspects of the program are quite promising. As adjuncts to medical treatment, counseling and relaxation can benefit patients' psychosocial adjustment, which is likely to enhance their immune function, improve their quality of life, increase their self-efficacy and resilience, help them become more involved in their treatment, and encourage them to maintain a "fighting spirit."

outpatient basis. During this time, patients receive chemotherapy, weekly or biweekly blood tests, and frequent bone marrow examinations to check for the presence of cancer cells. One procedure—called a *bone marrow aspiration*—is extremely painful. It involves inserting a large needle into the child's hip bone, and then suctioning out a sample of marrow. The whole procedure is painful, but the most excruciating pain occurs as the marrow is withdrawn. Although painkilling drugs help somewhat, the patients still feel intense pain. Research has found that children's pain and distress in this procedure can be reduced with psychological methods, such as showing them a film of a child coping realistically and teaching them to use techniques to distract their attention from the pain (Jay, Elliot, Katz, & Siegel, 1987; Reeb & Bush, 1996).

What are the psychosocial effects of having cancer on children and their families? In an overall sense, the effects are like those with adult patients. The initial trauma is extremely difficult, but the child's and family's adjustment tends to improve over time (Eiser, 1985; Koocher, O'Malley, Gogan, & Foster, 1980). Two factors that are important in children's psychosocial adaptation to cancer are the age at the onset of the disease and the time since the diagnosis. The earlier the diagnoses and treatment occurred in the children's lives and the longer the patients survive in remission, the better their long-term adjustment tends to be. Another psychosocial issue in childhood cancer is that these patients often lag behind other children in academic skills, particularly during the first few years of school (Allen & Zigler, 1986; Eiser, 1985). These deficits probably result from their missing many school days and the psychosocial and physical effects of their medical treatment.

AIDS

Acquired immune deficiency syndrome—AIDS—is a very different high-mortality chronic illness from the others we have discussed in at least three ways. First, AIDS is a new disease and was virtually unknown before 1980. Second, it is an infectious disease that is caused by a virus (HIV) and is spread through the shared contact of blood and semen. Third, in the United States, the number deaths from AIDS in each of the last several years is only a small fraction of the number who have died of stroke, the third most deadly

illness. What's more, AIDS is a worldwide epidemic, its annual mortality statistics are skyrocketing, many millions of people are already infected with the virus, and the large majority of these people will probably die as a result of AIDS. Most of these people are heterosexuals who do not use drugs but live in developing countries with high rates of unsafe sex (Johnson & Laga, 1990).

RISK FACTORS, EFFECTS, AND TREATMENT OF AIDS

The risk factors for AIDS involve ways by which an infected person's blood or semen contacts the body fluid of an uninfected person. This contact almost always occurs in one of three main ways:

- Sexual activity that exposes each person's body fluids to the other's. Exposure is more likely if the genital area has wounds or inflammation from a sexually transmitted disease (Peterman, 1990).
- Sharing contaminated syringes in drug use.
- Birth by an infected mother.

We saw in Chapter 6 that public health efforts have reduced these risks, especially among gay men and drug users in technologically advanced countries. But many people around the world still engage in risky behavior.

Age, Gender, and Sociocultural Factors in AIDS

The likelihood of becoming infected and developing AIDS depends on the person's age, gender, and sociocultural background. Worldwide, there are 33.6 million people living with HIV/AIDS; 17.6 million are men, 14.8 million are women, and 1.2 million are children (WHO, 1999a). In the United States, the rate of HIV infection is much higher among 20- to 45-year-old adults than other age groups and about three times higher in men than women; males have constituted over 80% of all AIDS cases since the epidemic began (CDC, 2000). AIDS death rate data reveal sociocultural differences: for American males and females, the death rates are about three times higher for blacks than Hispanics, whose rates are far higher than for whites; Asian and Native Americans have low AIDS death rates (NCHS, 2000). Hispanic AIDS data reflect infections mainly among those of Puerto Rican descent (Flack et al.,

1995). The largest concentrations of HIV infection in the world today are in sub-Saharan Africa, Southeast Asia, and Latin America (WHO, 1999a).

From HIV Infection to AIDS

When HIV infection occurs, several years may pass before the person's immune function is impaired—mainly from reduced numbers of helper T cells—and symptoms appear (Benjamini, Sunshine, & Leskowitz, 1996). During the period before symptoms emerge, the virus appears to hide in the person's lymph tissue, multiplying there and battling the immune system (Cole & Kemeny, 1997; Pantaleo et al., 1993).

The diagnosis of AIDS is made only once the victim's condition has reached a certain criterion. Before 1993, the criterion required that the person have contracted one of several opportunistic diseases associated with the loss of immune function. These illnesses include *Pneumocystis carinii pneumonia* and *Kaposi's sarcoma*, a previously rare form of cancer. In 1993, the U.S. Centers for Disease Control changed the criterion to involve a low level of helper T cells (also called CD4 cells) in the person's blood. Years before reaching either of these criteria, however, the victim may have learned from a blood test that he or she was infected with HIV. There is now an accurate method to test a person's "viral load," an assessment of the number of viral particles in a blood sample, that reflects the amount of HIV in the body.

Between the time of infection and the AIDS diagnosis, the victim's immune system begins to falter, producing a variety of recurrent symptoms, such as spiking fever, night sweats, diarrhea, fatigue, and swollen lymph glands. Prior to this stage, called AIDS-*related complex* (ARC), the only way individuals with HIV can tell they are infected is by having a blood test. If the diagnosis comes after symptoms appear, the immune system is already severely weakened and struggles to fight repeated bouts of opportunistic diseases.

Medical Treatment for People with HIV/AIDS

Most, but not all, opportunistic diseases in AIDS can be medically treated effectively, such as with antibiotics, but sometimes victims become hypersensitive, or allergic, to the medications, and no therapy is available that their bodies will tolerate. For patients whose immune systems continue to falter, the prognosis is poor (Osborn, 1988; Tross & Hirsch, 1988). Their

bodies become severely weakened, and they gradually waste away. Many AIDS patients develop a brain disorder when the HIV invades the central nervous system. This invasion causes the brain to deteriorate—a condition called *encephalopathy*. These patients gradually lose their cognitive functions, become disoriented and confused, and may also become mute and have seizures. Eventually, they lapse into comas.

The main treatment for AIDS uses drugs *called antiretroviral agents*. From the mid-1980s to the mid-1990s the main drug was AZT (*azidothymidine*, or *zidovudine*), which slows HIV reproduction in the early stages and prolongs survival, but does not cure the disease (Hamilton et al., 1992; Osborn, 1988). By the mid-1990s, new antiretroviral drugs appeared; some, called *protease inhibitors*, interfere with HIV reproduction and dramatically reduce the viral load in many, but not all, HIV-infected individuals (ATIS, 2000). Antiretroviral drug regimens may not work for all strains of HIV and usually involve a combination of drugs taken on a complex schedule that must be adhered to strictly. If a regimen fails, another set of similar drugs may work. Although these drugs have maintained low viral loads in many patients, it is too early to tell what the long-term effects will be. Even if the drugs are successful, the treatment is expensive ($15,000 a year) and can have serious side effects. Many people who use antiretroviral drugs do not adhere to the regimen well enough because of its complexity and side effects (Catz et al., 2000; Chesney et al., 1999). The cost makes treatment unavailable for the large majority of AIDS patients around the world.

AIDS has been fatal to virtually all of its victims; most die within 3 years of the AIDS diagnosis (Cole & Kemeny, 1997). A small minority of patients survive more than 3 years, and some are still living and active many years after the diagnosis (Gavzer, 1988). Why do some individuals survive so much longer than most others? The answer seems to involve biological and psychosocial differences between those who do and those who do not continue to survive. For one thing, researchers have discovered genetically driven processes that modulate the body's production of proteins and enzymes that slow down or speed up HIV progression (Hendel et al., 1999). Also, HIV victims who have high reactivity to stress and cope poorly show poorer immune function and faster progression of the disease than others do (Cole & Kemeny, 1997). Because AIDS is a new disease, most of the knowledge that exists about patients' treatment and survival is tentative. A new and hopeful finding has emerged: a study found with several subjects that starting antiviral treatment very soon after infection and having brief interruptions once the virus was controlled enabled the body to develop immune defenses to fight the infection without further treatment (Rosenberg et al., 2000). If these effects are replicated with large numbers of subjects, the challenge will be in getting people to be tested early.

THE PSYCHOSOCIAL IMPACT OF AIDS

Every epidemic arouses fear—but when so little is known about the disease except that it is so deadly, people tend to react in extreme ways to protect themselves and the people they love. In 1983, a young man in San Francisco who was diagnosed with AIDS told his housemates of his condition. Soon after, he arrived home one evening and found that the door locks had been changed. He knocked, but no one answered. A few days later, he found that everything in his room had been thrown out—clothes, bed linens, toothbrush, books, curtains, carpeting, and even the wallpaper (Gavzer, 1988). The American news media in the mid-1980s had frequent stories of AIDS patients being fired from their jobs, children with AIDS not being allowed to attend school, families with an AIDS patient being driven from their homes, and health care workers refusing to treat AIDS patients.

Although stories like these have declined in the last two decades, AIDS still arouses fear and discrimination in many people the United States and around the world (Herek, 1999; Herek & Capitanio, 1999). Many Americans still believe that AIDS patients are being punished by God for their misbehavior, and in some developing nations, people with HIV continue to be shunned by neighbors and medical workers, and a woman was beaten to death for revealing her illness. Some irrationality is likely to continue, even among people who are well informed. A medical editor who attended a session for AIDS volunteers wrote about meeting her first AIDS patient, a man named Tom who had been reduced to "skin and bones" by his illness:

> I felt an overwhelming anxiety, which peaked and diminished often throughout the presentation. I had to control it. . . . Part of me wanted to hug this man; part of me wanted to leave. Can you be compassionate from a distance? (Kaufman, 1988, p. 31)

If people recognize and discuss the irrationality of

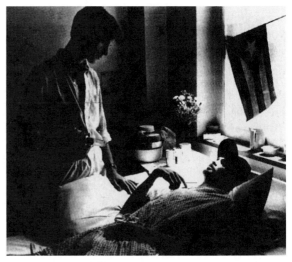

An AIDS patient talking to a nurse.

their feelings, they can overcome them. Of course, AIDS patients realize the fears other people have of them and must cope with people treating them "like a leper."

Because of the fears about AIDS, and because the disease is often associated with homosexuality and drug abuse in industrialized countries, AIDS patients and their families—which includes lovers—often feel stigmatized (Flaskerud, 1988; Herek, 1999). One of the first questions they consider is, "Should I tell anyone—and if so, who?" Many with HIV infections don't even tell their immediate family (Simoni et al., 1995). They worry that family, friends, neighbors, and coworkers will reject them. This may lead to their being secretive and withdrawn, thereby cutting off the social support they will need as the disease progresses. For some families, learning of the AIDS diagnosis comes at the same time they first learn that the patient—their child or spouse—is gay, or bisexual, or a drug user. Moreover, spouses or lovers fear that the patient has already infected them, too. All these factors fuel the stigma associated with the disease, which has three health effects. First, some societies have resisted acknowledging the disease, thereby allowing it to spread. Second, the stigma leads some people to delay being tested for HIV and getting care and to avoid telling partners if they are infected (Chesney & Smith, 1999). Third, the progression of people's HIV disease appears to slow after they disclose their illness to others (Sherman, Bonanno, Wiener, & Battles, 2000). Recall from Chapter 4 that discussing traumatic experiences seems to improve people's health.

People's adaptation to HIV and AIDS depends on their access to effective treatment. Using effective antiretroviral agents after many months of less effective care reduces patients' distress, and these reductions seem to result mainly from decreases in physical symptoms and limitations (Rabkin et al., 2000). But uncertainties regarding the future success of the drugs and new decisions for a "second life" can create stress. For people who do not have access to effective treatment, adjustment varies; most eventually adapt well to their conditions (Pugh et al., 1994; Rotheram-Borus, Murphy, Reid, & Colman, 1996). For instance, a victim who had begun to experience some joy as his anxiety faded said: "This forces you to investigate what you really want your life to be. ... What's there to be afraid of now? I live with my greatest fear all the time." (Hall, 1990, p. 1).

Other people with HIV don't fare as well. Some fear they will be abandoned by those they love and suffer pain, debilitation, and disfigurement (Flaskerud, 1988). Others suffer the loss of loved ones to AIDS. The cycles of AIDS-related diseases can arouse feelings of hopelessness and helplessness. Depression may become very severe, especially among those patients who try to cope mainly with avoidance strategies, believe their illness is punishment for past wrongdoings, and have been rejected by people they care about (Maj, 1990; Nichols & Santelli, 1990; Sikkema et al., 2000). Preventing and treating emotional distress is important because depressed HIV patients subsequently show faster disease progression and shorter survival than those who are not depressed (Ironson et al., 1994; Mayne et al., 1996; Patterson et al., 1996).

PSYCHOSOCIAL INTERVENTIONS FOR AIDS

Psychosocial efforts for AIDS need to begin when patients are tested for HIV (Sheridan, 1991). These individuals usually decide to get tested because they believe they could have the virus. They need carefully presented information to help reduce anxiety during the time before getting the results. Those who test HIV-positive will need counseling regarding the illness, treatment, and the many organizations and support groups available today to help AIDS patients and their families cope. Interventions for individuals with

and without access to effective antiretroviral treatment need to focus in different issues. Because antiretroviral regimens are complex and must be strictly followed, interventions for people taking the drugs must monitor and promote adherence (Chesney et al., 1999).

Many people with HIV and AIDS need psychosocial interventions for other problems, including emotional distress, pain management, and sleep disorders (Sikkema & Kelly, 1996). So far, most interventions have focused on using stress management training, exercise, and cognitive therapy to promote adaptation and reduce anxiety and depression among patients who did not have effective antiretroviral drugs. These interventions can help HIV-positive patients when begun in the early stages of HIV infection or long after. Research by Michael Antoni and his colleagues (1990, 1991) recruited gay men who did not know their HIV status and randomly assigned them to intervention and control groups. Intervention began weeks before HIV testing and consisted of aerobic exercise, relaxation training, and group meetings that included cognitive restructuring methods to modify self-defeating beliefs. Psychological and immunological assessments were made at various points in the weeks before and after notification of the HIV test results. For individuals who tested positive, those who had received the intervention subsequently showed substantially less anxiety and depression and much stronger immune function, and these benefits increased with the amount of relaxation practice they did. Other studies have found that similar interventions also enhance immune function and reduce anxiety and depression for people with advanced levels of HIV or AIDS (Antoni et al., 2000; Lutgendorf et al., 1997; Maj, 1990).

In this chapter, we have examined what it is like to live with and adapt to four very different high-mortality health problems. Each of these diseases can disable its victims and progress to the point that the patients and their loved ones are aware that the disease is terminal and death is imminent.

ADAPTING TO A TERMINAL ILLNESS

When people talk about the hypothetical prospects of dying, you will often hear them say, "I hope I go quickly and without pain." Some people might argue that there are no good ways to die, but almost everyone would agree that a slow and painful death is the worst way. By definition, a terminal illness entails a slow death. The patient typically suffers a progressive deterioration in the feeling of well-being and ability to function and may also experience chronic pain. Although dying from a terminal illness generally takes several weeks, it sometimes takes as little as a few days or as long as several months (Hinton, 1984). One factor that affects how people adapt to a terminal illness is the age of the victim.

THE PATIENT'S AGE

"Tragic" and "untimely" are words people often use to describe a young person's terminal illness or death. One feature that distinguishes between timely and untimely deaths is whether death is "appropriate" to the person's age (Weisman, 1976). Death is more appropriate at 80 years of age than at 20. Let's consider how people adapt to terminal illness at different times in the life span.

A Terminally Ill Child

What does "dying" mean? Death is a very abstract concept and, as such, it is not well understood by young children (Lonetto, 1980; Speece & Brent, 1984). Prior to about 5 years of age, children think death is like living in another place and the person can come back. They may also believe people can avoid death. For instance, a child might conceive of death as a monster and argue that "you won't die if you run faster than the monster or trick it." By about 8 years of age, most children understand that death happens to everyone, is final, and involves the absence of bodily functions.

Most children at early ages have some experience with dying—for instance, in the death of a close person, such as a grandparent or neighbor, or of a pet. Dying is not an easy topic for many adults to discuss, and they usually try to spare children the realities of death, saying that the dead person "has gone away," or "is in heaven, with Jesus," or "is only sleeping" (Koch, 1977; Sarafino, 1986). When a child has a terminal illness, parents sometimes decide not to tell him or her so that the child will have less emotional suffering. But dying school-age children seem to realize their illnesses are extremely serious even when they are not told, and they exhibit far greater anxiety than seriously ill children who are not dying (Spinetta, 1974).

Terminally ill children's awareness that they are dying develops gradually. At first, these children recognize that they are very ill but believe they will recover. Later, they realize that they are continuously ill and will not get better, and then, when they learn of the death of a peer, especially one with a similar illness, they surmise that they are, in fact, dying, too (Bluebond-Langner, 1977). Child specialists today generally believe children should know as much about their illnesses as they can comprehend. Because preschool-age children do not understand the meaning of death, there is little need to discuss death with them; the important thing is to allay their concerns about separation from their parents. With older children, an open, honest, and sensitive approach seems to reduce their anxiety and maintain a trusting relationship with their parents (La Greca & Stone, 1985).

A Terminally Ill Adolescent or Young Adult

Although some adolescents and young adults, particularly those of the lower classes, think their odds of dying at a young age are fairly high, they envision their deaths as being sudden and violent (Kastenbaum & Costa, 1977). If they develop terminal illnesses at this time of life, they realize how unlikely dying at their ages is and feel angry about the "senselessness" and "injustice" of it and about not having a chance to develop their lives. As one dying college student put it, "Now a perfectly good person with an awful lot to give is going to die. A young person is going die. His death is going to be senseless" (Shneidman, 1977, p. 77).

This young man was having a very difficult time coping with his impending death, and his shouting and quarrelsome behavior were creating problems on the hospital ward. Edwin Shneidman, a therapist whom the patient's physician called in, described taking on this case because he felt that the boy

> was in for a rough time, and with his own defenses and alienating behavior, he might turn people away from him and have an unnecessarily psychologically painful death. I began to see him almost every day, alone, just he and I. It developed that he was an only child, his father was dead, and his relationship with his mother for the past several years could be characterized as a running verbal hostile fight. The content of our sessions grew more serious as he became increasingly

ill. He sobered and matured enormously in a matter of weeks. (1977, p. 75)

During this time this young man's relationship with his mother became very close, and he noted, "I have let her love me. I have let her be a mother. She has been so beautiful. I get more comfort from her than anybody else" (p. 76).

Having a terminal illness seems especially untimely when victims have young children. This condition is a threat to the family unit, and the patients feel guilty at not being able to care for their children and cheated out of the joys of seeing them develop. Because death at this point in the life span is so untimely, young adults seem to experience more anger and emotional distress when they have life-threatening illnesses than older individuals do (Leventhal, Leventhal, & Van Nguyen, 1985).

Terminal Illness in Middle-Aged and Older Adults

As people develop beyond the early adulthood years, the likelihood of contracting a high-mortality chronic illness—especially heart disease, cancer, or stroke—increases sharply. Although dying may not be easy at any point in the life span, it seems to become less difficult as people progress from middle age to old age. Studies have found, for instance, that adults become less and less afraid of death as they get older (Bengston, Cuellar, & Ragan, 1977; Kalish & Reynolds, 1976). Why is this?

Researcher Richard Kalish (1985) has outlined several reasons why the elderly have an easier time than younger individuals in facing impending death. As people get older, developing a terminal illness becomes less unexpected, less of a shock. The elderly know their remaining years are few, they realize that they will probably die of a chronic illness, and they think and talk more about poor health and death than most younger people do. Most of their peers and many relatives are suffering from declining health or have died. They often have made financial preparations, and some have even made plans or given instructions regarding the terminal care they would prefer and their funeral arrangements. In addition, older individuals have had longer pasts than younger people, which have allowed them the time to achieve more. People who review their pasts and believe they have accomplished important things and lived good lives tend to

have less difficulty adapting to terminal illnesses than those who do not (Mages & Mendelsohn, 1979).

PSYCHOSOCIAL ADJUSTMENTS TO TERMINAL ILLNESS

As we have seen, most people with life-threatening chronic illnesses manage to adapt reasonably well to their conditions over time after the initial crises, and so do the closest people in their lives. But when their conditions worsen and progress to a terminal phase, new crises emerge that require intense coping efforts.

How People Cope with Terminal Illness

How do terminally ill people and their families cope, and what types of stress do they experience? The principal coping mechanism people use during the phase of terminal illness is denial (Hackett & Weisman, 1985; Hinton, 1984). As we saw in Chapter 5, emotion-focused coping is especially useful when the individuals cannot do anything to change their situations. Unfortunately, when people mutually avoid facing the imminent death, they may not discuss with each other how they feel or have any way to "say their good-byes."

Psychiatrist John Hinton (1984) has described three types of stress terminal patients experience. First, they must cope with the physical effects of their worsening conditions, such as pain, difficulty breathing, sleeplessness, or loss of bowel control. Second, their conditions severely alter their styles of living, restricting their activity and making them highly dependent on others. Perhaps two-thirds of dying people are restricted in their activities during the last 3 months of their lives, and one-fifth of these patients are confined to bed. Third, they typically realize that the end of their lives is near, even when they are not told so. If they are in a hospital, they may think about never going home again or no longer being able to experience the intimacy they used to have with those they love.

Thinking about someone who is dying typically arouses feelings of sadness in people. According to Hinton (1984), healthy individuals who are unaccustomed to serious illness or the declining abilities of age may not realize how well many terminally ill people come to face and accept dying. He has noted similarities between people who are dying and those with diminished lives—such as the frail, disabled, or bereaved: they can still get pleasure from their lives despite earlier thoughts that such circumstances would be unbearable. The quality of life for such persons can be fairly good if they have

a sense of fulfillment; that sense depends on the individual's own values. People may derive their greatest satisfaction from their past family life, their career or the children they are leaving behind. . . . Some have the sense that they need struggle no longer and they can now find peace or believe that their life is now reasonably complete. There may be the conviction that they will rejoin a loved person in immortal existence. . . . With good care many people do achieve a positive acceptance of dying and have a peaceful death. (p. 245)

Individuals who are most likely to adapt to dying with the least amount of anger or depression are those who are in little pain, receive sensitive and caring social support, feel satisfied with their lives, and have a history of coping well with life's problems and crises (Carey, 1975; Hinton, 1984; Kalish, 1985). Often, patients adapt better than their loved ones. For instance, spouses of dying people often experience increased health problems, depression, and memory difficulties (Howell, 1986). Support groups and family therapy can be of great help to dying individuals and their families.

Does Adapting to Dying Happen in "Stages"?

"Time changes things," people say. Since time passes in the process of dying from a terminal illness, we might expect that patients' reactions would change as they come to terms with their impending deaths. Do these changes occur in a predictable pattern, as a series of stages?

On the basis of interviews with over 200 terminally ill people, Elisabeth Kübler-Ross (1969) proposed that people's adjustment to dying usually follows a predictable pattern, passing through a sequence of *five stages*. Table 14.5 outlines these stages. Not all the patients she interviewed showed this pattern—a few, for example, continued to deny that they were dying to the very last. But the pattern of adjustments seemed sufficiently regular for Kübler-Ross to propose that coping in most dying people begins with denial and advances through the stages in order.

Table 14.5 *Kübler-Ross's Stages of Adjustment to Dying*

1. *Denial.* The first reaction to the prognosis of death involves refusing to believe it is true. Terminally ill patients say, "No, it can't be true," or "There must be some mistake," or "The lab reports must have gotten mixed up." Denial can be a valuable first reaction by giving patients time to mobilize other coping strategies and motivation to get second opinions. According to Kübler-Ross, denial soon fades in most patients and is replaced by anger.

2. *Anger.* The patients now realize, "Oh, yes, it is me, it was not a mistake," and are outraged and irate, asking, "Why me?" or, "Why couldn't it have been that miserable no-good guy down the street?" They resent others who are healthy and may show their anger in outbursts toward almost anyone—nurses, doctors, and family.

3. *Bargaining.* At this point, patients try to change their circumstances by offering to "make a deal." Most of the bargains they try to negotiate are with God, for example, thinking, "Oh, God, I promise to be a better person if you'll just make me well."

4. *Depression.* When bargaining no longer helps and patients feel their time is running out, hopelessness and depression set in. They grieve for things they had in the past and for things they will miss in the future. According to Kübler-Ross, even though depression is painful and may last for a prolonged period, it is helpful because part of the grieving process involves becoming detached from the things in the patient's world. Being detached enables the last stage—acceptance—to occur.

5. *Acceptance.* Patients who live long enough may reach the last stage in which they are no longer depressed, but feel a quiet calm and readiness for death.

Source: Kübler-Ross (1969).

Do Kübler-Ross's stages correctly reflect the emotional reactions most dying patients experience as they cope with terminal illnesses? Although many people believe most individuals adjust to dying with a predictable and orderly sequence of coping reactions, the evidence from subsequent research does not support this belief (Hinton, 1984; Kalish, 1985; Silver & Wortman, 1980; Zisook, Peterkin, Shuchter, & Bardone, 1995). An overview of this evidence indicates that some terminal patients do follow an orderly and predictable sequence of adjustment, but most people's emotions and coping patterns fluctuate back and forth. Some people may go through a specific stage, such as anger, more than once during their adjustment; others experience more than one emotional reaction simultaneously; and some seem to skip stages. And some evidence indicates that people who achieve and "acceptance" of their impending death die much sooner than those who do not reach this stage (Reed et al., 1994).

Despite these shortcomings, Kübler-Ross's work has had many positive effects. For one thing, it has been influential in stimulating people's awareness and discussion of the dying process and the needs of terminal patients. It has also led to important and very beneficial changes in the care and treatment of dying people, thereby improving the quality of the last weeks and days of their lives.

THE QUALITY OF LIFE IN DEATH

The medical community and patients' families face one dilemma after another in trying to do what's best for a dying person. Medical technology has made it possible to keep some patients alive only in a legal sense, and societies have begun to question whether these people are alive in a humane sense. The news media describe patients lying in comas for years, dependent on life-support systems to stay alive, but with virtually no likelihood of recovery. An artificial respirator can make a person breathe, and other devices can keep the heart going. The vast majority of American physicians favor withdrawing life-support systems from hopelessly ill or irreversibly comatose individuals if the patients or their families request it (Shogren, 1988). In most of the United States, a person who anticipates these circumstances may issue a "living will" that instructs practitioners not to use extraordinary life-support measures.

A principal issue that enters into people's judgments about maintaining life support is the patient's quality of life. This is actually an issue that is relevant to all terminally ill people, not just the extreme cases. What kind of medical and psychological care do dying patients need? Who should be responsible for that care, and where should it be given? These are the main issues we consider in this section. (Go to 🍎.)

MEDICAL AND PSYCHOLOGICAL CARE OF DYING PATIENTS

The terminal phase of care begins when medical judgment indicates that the patient's condition is worsening and no treatment is available to reverse or arrest the progress toward death (AMA, 1989; Benoliel, 1977). At this point, medical treatment is mainly *palliative*, that is, it focuses on reducing pain and discomfort. This phase of treatment can be very distressing not only to the patients and their fami-

lies, but to medical personnel, who entered the medical field to save lives. Terminally ill people in the United States can request that the specific instruction, "Do Not Resuscitate," be entered on their hospital charts. If they begin to die—for instance, if the person's heart stops beating—the medical staff is not to interfere.

Individuals who work with dying people on a daily basis must come to grips with the feelings of failure and loss they experience when patients die (Benoliel, 1977; Maguire, 1985). In an effort to protect themselves from this pain and to perform efficiently in their heavy work loads, medical staff often distance themselves psychologically from terminally ill people. By doing this, doctors and nurses avoid dealing with the psychological problems these patients are having. How do staff members distance themselves? They may simply not ask about the person's feelings or adjustment, or they may provide false reassurance, saying, "I'm sure you'll feel better soon," when they believe otherwise. The staff may also use selective attention, as illustrated in the following interaction:

SURGEON: Well, how are you today?

PATIENT: (dying of breast cancer): I'm very worried about what is happening to me. I'm beginning to think I'm not going to get better this time. The pain in my hip is getting worse.

SURGEON: Tell me more about this pain in your hip. (Maguire, 1985, p. 1711)

Although this patient mentioned both physical and psychological difficulties, the physician followed up only on the physical one. This may lead the patient to conclude that it is not appropriate to discuss psychological problems with medical staff.

Should terminally ill adults be told they are dying? This is a controversial question, and medical personnel often face the dilemma of believing people have the right to know and being instructed by the patient's family not to tell (Maguire, 1985). Some physicians and psychiatrists take the view that the issue of whether to tell the patient is moot, since terminally ill people generally realize they are dying and that the prognosis should be given to the patient and family together (Weisman, 1977; White, 1977). In this view, practitioners should be "compassionately candid" for medical reasons, to give the person the right to choose or refuse treatments, and to encourage the patient and family to be prepared psychologically

ASSESS YOURSELF

Your Living Will Choices

Fill out the *Health Care Living Will and Proxy* below, indicating what your wishes would be if you were unable to make decisions about your medical treatment, such as if you were in a coma. What specific treatments would you *want* or *not want* to receive? Whom would you choose as your agent or "proxy" in making decisions if you were unable to make them? This person should be an adult who is familiar with your personal and health care views—someone you would trust to make the decisions you would make.

If this were a legal document, you and two witnesses would need to sign it. Some living wills are much more complicated than this one, having the person make dozens of choices regarding many different medical procedures that might be considered in very different scenarios. One concern in being so specific is that knowledge about treatments can change: suppose evidence on a treatment's effectiveness changes between the time a patient rejects it in the will and the scenario actually occurs? What then?

HEALTH CARE LIVING WILL AND PROXY

TO MY FAMILY, PHYSICIANS, AND OTHER CONCERNED PARTIES:

I, _____ (the *principal*), being of sound mind, make the following advance directives to be carried out if I become unable to make or communicate decisions about my medical treatment.

LIVING WILL
I request the withdrawal or withholding of life-sustaining procedures,consistent with my desire that I be permitted to die naturally if the situation occurs that I am either (1) near death with no reasonable likelihood of recovery or (2) in a coma or vegetative state and my physicians believe that there is no significant possibility of my ever regaining consciousness or higher functions of my brain. Under these circumstances, I specifically:

    1. *DO NOT* want the following treatments I have *initialed*.
        • Cardiac resuscitation _____
        • Artificial respiration _____
        • Artificial feeding or fluids _____
        • Other (specify) _____

    2. *DO* want the following conditions I have *initialed*.
        • Medication to relieve pain _____
        • To die at home, if possible _____
        • Other (specify) _____

PROXY
I designate here (1) a *first proxy*, _____
(name), to make decisions in accordance with the wishes and conditions specified above, or as he or she otherwise knows, and (2) a *second proxy*, _____ (name), as a substitute if the first proxy is unable, unwilling, or unavailable to act as my health care proxy.

and legally. Other physicians note that some patients would prefer not to know, and these wishes should take precedence (AMA, 1989). To follow this approach, physicians need to probe sensitively to assess the person's wishes. Those who prefer not to know may be given the option of having their families handle all decisions (Blackhall et al., 1995).

Although many people are able to approach death with a feeling of acceptance and peacefulness, others become very troubled. What can be done to help dying patients cope? In some cases, hospitals may provide individual psychotherapy for those individuals who are clearly having difficulty (Shneidman, 1977). Health care workers may also be able to provide information about support groups that have developed specifically to improve the quality of life for people with terminal illnesses. In addition, professionally led group therapy can help terminal patients face their impending deaths with less anxiety and depression and a greater sense of control over their remaining periods of life (Levy, 1983).

A PLACE TO DIE—HOSPITAL, HOME, OR HOSPICE?

Most people in developed nations die in hospitals or nursing homes (Hays, Gold, Flint, & Winer, 1999). Although hospitals can provide a great deal of expertise, technical equipment, and efficient caregiving, they are usually not "psychologically comfortable" places for people. The environment there is unfamiliar, and often it is mechanical and impersonal. Patients have little control over their daily routine and activities, and they lack access to such things as photo albums or musical recordings, for example, that they have relied on in the past for enjoyment and to enrich their experiences. Moreover, most of the people there are strangers, not family or friends. As a result, many terminally ill people would rather die at home, and many do. Is this a reasonable alternative?

Home Care for the Dying Patient

Whether home care is a reasonable alternative for a dying person depends on his or her condition and the quality of care available at home. Although few terminal patients require prolonged, complex care, some do and may be better off at a hospital (AMA, 1989; Garfield, 1978). Can patients receive good terminal care at home? Yes, they can. Studies have found that terminally ill people who have regular contact at home with a medical team and whose family members are trained receive very good care (Malkin, 1976; Zimmer, Juncker, & McCusker, 1985). Unfortunately, many dying patients may not have the option of home care because they lack family members who are able to provide the care they need or financial resources that may be required.

Caring for a terminally ill person at home can be a very physically and emotionally exhausting experience (Hinton, 1984). There may be only one individual at home who can provide the care, and all of the burden falls on that person's shoulders. If the patient requires continuous attention, the life of that one caretaker may become limited to coping with the dying person's needs. This may go on for weeks or, sometimes, months. Even when there is more than one person available to help, their lives are to some extent restricted by the needs of the patient. Some terminally ill people are bedridden and need to be fed and bathed, for instance. Despite these hardships, many people who have cared for dying persons at home claim it is extremely rewarding to know they have done everything they could to make the last days or weeks as pleasant as possible for someone they love.

Hospice Care for the Dying Patient

Is it possible to combine the strengths of a professional support system with the warm and loving care one can get at home, thereby helping terminal patients die comfortably and with dignity? This question led to the development of the concept of **hospice care,** which involves a medical and social support system to provide an enriched quality of life—through physical, psychosocial, and spiritual care—for terminally ill people and their families (Cioppa, 1984; HFA, 2000; Insel & Roth, 1998). In hospice care, the staff consists of a medically supervised team of professionals and volunteers. Much of the physical care the staff provides is designed to reduce discomfort and pain, often with the use of drugs.

The hospice care approach originated in Great Britain, largely through the efforts of physician Cicely Saunders, who was originally trained as a nurse and social worker (Saunders, 1977; Torrens, 1985). After working at a hospice in Ireland, she founded St. Christopher's Hospice near London in 1967. Originally, hospices were designed as separate institutions for the purpose of caring for dying patients on an inpatient basis. But as the philosophy of hospice care spread to the United States and Canada, the organizational structure for delivering this care began to broaden. Hospice services in North America are available today both at *home* and at hundreds of *inpatient facilities*, many of which are housed in hospitals or nursing homes. When home hospice care is used, services are provided on a part-time, regularly scheduled basis and staff are available on-call 24 hours a day, 7 days a week (Cioppa, 1984).

Inpatient facilities generally try to make the environment as much like home as possible, often including a kitchen and family room area. If the facility is in a hospital, existing policies are adjusted to satisfy the goals of the program. These adjustments often provide for flexible visiting hours and regulations, freedom to wear one's own clothes, family members to prepare and share meals with alcoholic beverages, psychological and spiritual counseling, and assistance in completing unfinished business (Cioppa, 1984).

In the hospice care approach, the patient and his or her family are considered to be the "unit of care." What this means is that all of these people actively participate to develop a plan for the care of the whole unit (Cioppa, 1984). Cicely Saunders (1986) has outlined several "essential elements" in the hospice approach, some of which deal with psychosocial issues.

First, people who are dying should be in a *place of choice* as they end their lives. They and their families should decide whether that place should be at home or in an inpatient setting. Most people prefer to be at home (Hays, Gold, Flint, & Winer, 1999). Second, the care given during the terminal phase should enable patients to *maximize their potential*, so that they perform to the limits of their physical, cognitive, and social potential, particularly as active members of their families. Third, the care should *address all family members' needs*, which may involve resolving interpersonal discord and feelings of anxiety, guilt, and depression. Fourth, *follow-up care* is available for family members to receive help through and after the period of bereavement.

Does hospice care help patients and their families cope better with the dying process than conventional care does? The testimonials from patients and family members are massive and glowing, describing the programs as enormously supportive and enriching. And a study found that the quality of life is better with inpatient hospice care than standard hospital care (Viney et al., 1994). Evidence from the small number of carefully controlled studies of inpatient hospice and conventional care suggests that both provide similar pain control and daily activities, but hospice patients show less anxiety and greater satisfaction with their care (Torrens, 1985).

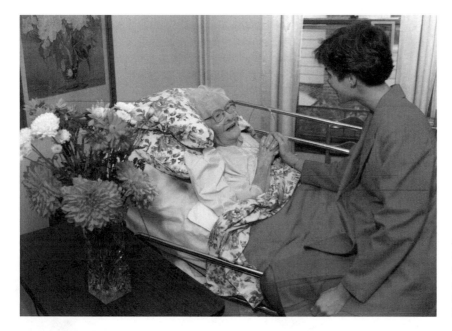

A hospice nurse attends a terminally ill patient. Hospice care can be given at home or in inpatient facilities that look more like a home than a hospital.

THE SURVIVORS: AND LIFE GOES ON

Whether a person dies suddenly and unexpectedly or with warning over a long period of time, there are survivors who must then come to terms with the death and eventually pick up the pieces of their lives. The state of having lost someone through death is called *bereavement*. Feelings of *grief* and the expression of these feelings in *mourning* characterize this state.

People adapt to their bereavement in their own individual ways. This process takes time, usually at least a year, but it does not seem to follow any particular pattern or stages, and there is no good rule of thumb to predict how long it will take (Joyce, 1984; Silver & Wortman, 1980; Zisook, Peterkin, Shuchter, & Bardone, 1995). Each grieving person needs to adjust at his or her own pace, and urgings to "start living again" may be both insensitive and unproductive when they occur early in the adjustment process. A longitudinal study of individuals whose spouses succumbed to serious illnesses revealed that their psychological distress was similar before and soon after the death, remained high for about a year, and was greater for middle-aged than elderly individuals (Hays, Kasl, & Jacobs, 1994). Several types of psychosocial interventions, such as individual therapy and support groups, can help people adjust to their losses (Zisook, Peterkin, Shuchter, & Bardone, 1995).

The AIDS epidemic has revealed two important issues about bereavement in gay individuals. First, many experience long series of bereavements within a few years, without time to complete their mourning between deaths. This has happened to many gay men in big cities who have experienced multiple losses—often losing long-term partners and most of their friends—to AIDS. Coping with terminal illness repeatedly takes a severe emotional toll, and each death adds to the toll with increased demoralization, sleep problems, and stress reactions (Martin, 1988; Martin & Dean, 1993). Second, gay individuals who have lost their lovers receive less social support from others, such as bosses and coworkers, than heterosexuals do. For example, a man who was troubled by his partner's death and performing below par at work reported that his getting little understanding from his boss "makes me feel depressed, angry, and used. ... I really loved him and I do miss him" (Moskowitz, Folkman, Collette, & Vittinghoff, 1996, p. 49). Most people in the larger society probably do not realize that gay couples' relationships can be so strong and loving.

Some people think coming to terms with the loss of someone we love means we forget that person—he or she no longer means anything to us. This is not so. People who eventually adapt to the loss may feel recurrent moments or periods of sadness years later, especially on anniversaries or other significant dates (Joyce, 1984). A mother who lost her infant child years ago wrote:

> My mind does not mourn yesterday
> It mourns today
> The images that pass before my eyes
> Do not recall the infant son
> But see you running through my house
> A teenage child in search of food and gym shoes and maybe me.
> I do not mourn you for what you were,
> But for what can't be ...
> (Anonymous, cited in Silver & Wortman, 1980, p. 337)

The death of a child is one of the most tragic events that can happen to a family, and parents often experience grief for many years after the loss (Knapp, 1987).

When a parent dies, the surviving children need special attention and understanding. Often the surviving parent is so caught up in his or her own shock and grief that the children's emotional needs are not adequately addressed. Many surviving parents say little about the death and exclude their children from the mourning process. It is not unusual for children to show little sense of loss or outward grief when a close family member dies (Koch, 1977; Sarafino, 1986). Young children do not understand fully what death is, and this may account for their seeming lack of concern. Older children may be so confused and shocked by the tragedy that they are simply numbed emotionally. Their outward calmness should not be mistaken as a sign that they do not love the dead person. Sometimes their grief comes out later, and sometimes it happens privately.

During the first weeks after the death of a spouse, the surviving husband or wife usually receives a great deal of attention from friends and relatives. But soon this changes, and the bereaved person may feel isolated in efforts to organize his or her life and make decisions alone. A widow or widower must gradually become involved again in work and leisure activities, in maintaining old friendships and developing new ones, and, perhaps, in finding a new mate. One man described his experience as a widower in the following way:

> Having to "date" in the early 40s, or older, and after long years of marriage is, for many, an unnerving experience. I suggest there is something even worse—not getting out and having companionship.
>
> How the widower chooses to begin his new social and sex life depends, of course, on his personality, his philosophy, and the sort of companionship he wants. Some widowers prefer to join Parents Without Partners, where they are sure to meet people with common interests. Like the majority of widowers, I had friends and relatives who put forward suggestions and invited me to dinner parties. I found most of these either tedious or

painful. One night . . . however I did meet a beautiful woman. She was a widow, with one child. . . . We are a complete household again and throughout the home there once again is the sound of laughter, of music and, best of all, the rich sound of meaningful conversation between children and their parents. (Lindeman, 1976, pp. 285–286)

Of course, not all stories of people's coping with the loss of someone they love have happy endings. Some bereaved individuals never adjust to the loss. But with the help and support of others and a determined drive on their own part, most people can build a new and once-again enriching life. The social support bereaved people need can come from family and friends, but support groups may be especially helpful.

SUMMARY

People with a high-mortality illness do not know for sure what the course of their disease will be or if or when they will die from it. But their lives are threatened, and they and their families must adapt to living with uncertainty. Convalescing people tend to be optimistic about their future health, but watchful for symptoms and changes in their conditions. Families can help patients adapt by encouraging them to develop reasonable plans and to carry them out, rather than encouraging helplessness and dependence. In adapting to illness over a long period of time, patients make cognitive adjustments by finding meaning in their illness experiences, gaining a sense of control over their illnesses, and restoring their self-esteem. A recurrence or relapse of the condition creates a new, and often very difficult, crisis.

Most deaths in developed countries result from three chronic diseases: heart disease, cancer, and stroke. Coronary heart disease may show up in an episode of angina pectoris or of myocardial infarction. The prevalence rate for heart disease is greater in men than in women and increases with age. Cardiac rehabilitation involves the use of medication, a program of exercise, stress management, and changes in diet and other aspects of lifestyle, especially if the person smokes, drinks too much, or is overweight. Many heart patients fail to comply with the exercise programs and lifestyle changes. Most cardiac patients who were employed before the illness eventually return to work, often in less demanding jobs. Some people with heart disease need special interventions to enhance adaptation.

A stroke can cause damage to the brain through either an infarction or a hemorrhage. Depending on the amount and location of neurological damage, patients may suffer motor and cognitive deficits. Some impairments recover with time and rehabilitation, but others are permanent. Deficits may involve motor action, aphasia, visual disorders, and emotional disorders. Stroke patients are very prone to depression.

Although there are many varieties of cancer, most can be classified into four types: carcinomas, lymphomas, sarcomas, and leukemias. Untreated neoplasms eventually metastasize and spread to other parts of the body. The most common sites of cancer are the skin, prostate gland, breast, lungs, colon or rectum, and uterus or cervix. Medical treatment consists of surgery, radiation, and chemotherapy, each of which has important drawbacks. Chemotherapy, in particular, causes nausea and vomiting that is associated with learned food aversions. Despite the great stress cancer victims experience, most show a remarkable ability to adapt with time during remission or after a cure. Some, however, become very depressed and withdraw from social contact, but usually benefit from psychosocial interventions. Leukemia is the most common form of cancer in childhood.

AIDS is caused by HIV infection, which impairs the immune system, leaving the victims subject to opportunistic diseases. Most people with AIDS die within 3 years of that diagnosis if they do not receive effective antiretroviral treatment. Because AIDS is an infectious disease, many people have reacted to its outbreak with alarm and discrimination, making adaptation all the more difficult. Psychosocial intervention can reduce anxiety and depression and enhance immune function.

If and when a chronic condition deteriorates and no cure is likely, the illness is considered terminal. One factor that affects how people adapt to terminal illness is the age of the patient. Adults see the death of a young person as particularly tragic and untimely. Young children have little understanding of the meaning of death; by about 8 years of age, children's understanding is fairly complete. Adolescents and young adults react to their impending deaths with very strong feelings of anger and emotional distress. As adults get older, they become less fearful of death. Dying people may react to their conditions with denial, anger, bargaining, depression, and acceptance. The hospice care approach provides physical, psychosocial, and spiritual care for dying patients and their families during the terminal phase and in bereavement.

KEY TERMS

angina pectoris
myocardial infarction
stroke

cancer
learned food aversion

acquired immune
   deficiency syndrome

hospice care

PART VII

LOOKING TO THE FUTURE

15

WHAT'S AHEAD FOR HEALTH PSYCHOLOGY?

Goals for Health Psychology
Enhancing Efforts to Prevent Illness
Improving Efforts for Helping
 Patients Cope
Documenting the Efficacy and
 Cost-Benefit Ratio of Care
Enhancing Psychologists' Acceptance
 in Medical Settings

Careers and Training in Health Psychology
Career Opportunities
Training Programs

Issues and Controversies for the Future
Environment, Health, and Psychology
Quality of Life
Ethical Decisions in Medical Care

Future Focuses in Health Psychology
Life-Span Health and Illness
Sociocultural Factors in Health
Gender Differences and Women's
 Health Issues

Factors Affecting Health Psychology's Future

"Oh, this looks very good," the palm reader said as she studied Marty's hand. She explained: "Your life line is very long, which usually means you will have a long and prosperous life. At first I thought this break here in the line meant you might have a serious health problem in your 50s, but these lines here at your wrist suggest otherwise. You'll have a long and healthy life!" Marty was relieved. He had come to have his fortune told rather than being tested for HIV. He knew that his past behavior put him at risk for HIV infection, but he couldn't bring himself to reveal this to the palm reader. Unreasoned behavior is not uncommon when people are very anxious.

Predicting the future is always a chancy enterprise. Still, because the field of health psychology is at an early stage in its development, many people wonder what the field and its goals will be like in the future. This chapter will try to predict what's ahead for health psychology, and our crystal ball will involve the views of noted researchers and trends that seem clear in recent research. As we consider what the crystal ball suggests, we will try to answer questions you may have about the field's prospects. What role will future health psychologists play in medical care? Are career opportunities and training programs for health psychologists likely to expand? How will the field's goals, issues, and perspectives change? What factors will affect the success and direction of health psychology in the coming years?

GOALS FOR HEALTH PSYCHOLOGY

Health and health care systems around the world have changed dramatically over the last several decades. People in most parts of the world today are living longer and are more likely to develop chronic illnesses than ever before. Many current health problems result from or are aggravated by people's long-standing habits, such as smoking cigarettes and coping poorly with stress, that medical professionals lack sufficient skills and time to change. The field of health psychology has made enormous advances, generating new knowledge and applying information gained from many disciplines to supplement medical efforts in promoting health. Let's look at some major goals that lie ahead for health psychology.

ENHANCING EFFORTS TO PREVENT ILLNESS

We have seen that efforts to prevent health problems should try to reduce unhealthful behaviors. These efforts can be directed toward health-protective activity while the person is well, when symptoms appear, or once an illness is identified and treatment starts.

Health-related behaviors that become features of people's lifestyles have received a great deal of attention in health psychology. Many of the health problems people develop result at least partly from lifestyle behaviors, and efforts have been directed toward preventing these behaviors from developing and changing unhealthful behaviors that have already developed. Unhealthful lifestyles seem to be harder to change than to prevent (Wright & Friedman, 1991). We have seen that psychologists' efforts to change lifestyle behaviors, such as smoking, exercising, and eating habits, have focused mainly on cognitive and behavioral approaches. Although these approaches are often very effective in producing initial changes, the behaviors frequently revert back to the unhealthful patterns after the interventions end. Relapse is a critical problem that researchers are working to reduce, and it will certainly be an important focus for health psychology in the future.

Once people notice symptoms or are diagnosed with serious health conditions, they often—but by no means always—engage in symptom-based and sick-role behaviors to protect their health. For instance, they may go to physicians, take medication, or even follow medical advice that involves changing their lifestyles. Researchers have identified many psychosocial factors that influence whether people will seek health care and adhere to medical regimens. We know, for example, that individuals often decide to reject or delay seeking medical attention because they don't know the symptoms of serious diseases, such as cancer or diabetes. And people are less likely to adhere to medical advice if the regimens involve complex or long-term behavioral changes and if their physicians do not seem caring or explain the illnesses and treatment clearly. Although we know some methods to reduce these problems, these methods often require extra time or effort that medical professionals are just beginning to incorporate into their practices. Health psychologists in the future will continue their search for ways to improve patients' use of health care services and adherence to medical regimens.

Since the mid-1980s, advances of two types have occurred that may influence future efforts to prevent illness. First, new theories have appeared that attempt to explain why people do or do not change unhealthful behaviors, building on the knowledge gained from earlier theories, especially the health belief model. The *stages of change model*, which outlines a series of stages in people's readiness to change health-related behaviors, is an example. This and other theories are beginning to generate important research that will undoubtedly contribute to our understanding of ways to promote healthier lifestyles. Second, Internet sites are being developed to provide medical information and two-way video and audio communication to individuals in numerous countries and inaccessible areas. One such site provides diagnostic and treatment services and advice on lifestyle changes (PRPO, 2000).

One other issue relating to future efforts in health promotion should be mentioned: it is possible for people to become *overly concerned* with preventing illness (Becker, 1990; Brownell, 1991). This issue can take two forms. First, individuals may struggle to achieve impossible goals that require overriding strong biological forces, as often happens when obese adults set their sights on having slim, athletic bodies. Second, some healthy people become obsessive in trying to adhere to too many restrictions, worrying if they occasionally have a piece of cheesecake or fail to exercise. As statesman-philosopher Benjamin Franklin noted, "Nothing is more fatal to health than an over care of it" (Brownell, 1991, p. 308). Future health promotion efforts need to identify and emphasize the most important risk factors that people can change.

IMPROVING EFFORTS FOR HELPING PATIENTS COPE

Major advances have been made in using psychosocial methods to help people cope with various difficulties in their lives. Stress management programs are being applied widely with nonpatient populations, such as in worksite wellness programs, to help prevent illness.

People with serious medical conditions often must cope with pain, anxiety and fear, and depression. Psychosocial interventions are being applied more and more widely with patients in pain clinics, hospitals, and other medical settings. Years ago, the main function of psychologists in medical settings involved administering and interpreting tests of patients' emotional and cognitive functioning (Wright & Friedman, 1991). But this situation has changed, and psychologists are focusing much more on a broader array of activities, such as training medical students and interns and applying interventions to help patients cope with illnesses and medical treatment. The future is likely to see the role of health psychologists expand substantially in hospitals and outpatient rehabilitation programs for people with chronic health problems, such as heart disease and nervous system injuries (Frank, Gluck, & Buckelew, 1990).

DOCUMENTING THE EFFICACY AND COST–BENEFIT RATIO OF CARE

Should health care organizations and employers provide psychosocial interventions to prevent illness and help patients cope? Perhaps most people would answer, "Yes, because it's the humane thing to do." But with today's spiraling medical costs, the answer is more commonly based on two factors: the intervention's *efficacy*, or degree to which it accomplishes what is needed, and its *cost–benefit ratio*, or the extent to which providing the intervention saves more money in the long run than it costs (Graham et al., 1998; Kaplan, 1989). These bottom-line issues often are weighed heavily in deciding whether to offer wellness programs or psychosocial interventions at work and in medical settings.

Health psychologists recognize the importance of documenting the efficacy of approaches they use, and they do careful research to compare different approaches against each other and control groups. But psychologists are not accustomed to calculating the financial costs and benefits of interventions and seldom do these analyses. Often the costs of providing an intervention are easily assessed, but the full benefits are not. At a worksite, for instance, what benefits of a wellness program could you assess in dollars to compare with the costs of running it? You might assess worker absenteeism or medical insurance claims, but these variables would reflect only part of the benefits. They wouldn't reflect other important financial gains, such as in workers' improved job satisfaction and resulting increases in productivity. In medical settings, measuring the benefits of psychosocial interventions can be easier—for example, you could assign dollar values to the reduced time intervention patients spend recovering in the hospital and compare these data against the cost of the program.

Many psychosocial interventions for promoting health and helping patients cope have the potential for producing far more financial benefits than costs (Cummings, 1991). More and more evidence is becoming available to document these effects (Friedman, Sobel et al., 1995). We considered research in Chapter 10 showing, for example, that hospital patients who receive help in coping with medical procedures recover more quickly and use less medication than those who don't receive such help. Other studies have shown that the financial savings are far greater than the costs of providing advice to reduce drinking (Fleming et al., 2000) and psychosocial and educational interventions to help pregnant women stop smoking and other patients manage their pain, arthritis, and asthma (Cronan, Groessl, & Kaplan, 1997; Liljas & Lahdensuo, 1997; Stieg & Turk, 1988; Windsor et al., 1993). Although most psychosocial methods with documented efficacy have not yet been subjected to cost–benefit analyses, health psychologists in the future will probably give much more attention to these analyses than they have in the past. They will also need to develop more effective methods to help people change unhealthful lifestyles—particularly with regard to using tobacco, eating healthful diets, and exercising—and demonstrate that the benefits of these methods outweigh the costs.

ENHANCING PSYCHOLOGISTS' ACCEPTANCE IN MEDICAL SETTINGS

A woman wrote an article in the late 1980s and described her experience when she developed breast cancer. Her physicians advised her to get treatment from a variety of medical professionals but

> at no point did anyone in the medical fraternity recommend that I see a mental health professional to help me cope with the emotional impact of breast cancer. Perhaps they didn't realize that breast cancer had an emotional impact. But I did. So, I went to see a psychologist, ironically the one specialist not covered by my insurance. It was worth the cash out of pocket. (Kaufman, cited in Cummings, 1991, p. 119)

Although gaining acceptance by the medical profession has progressed steadily since the 1980s, it continues to be a major challenge for health psychology.

Part of the difficulty health psychologists have faced in gaining acceptance in medical settings stems from their past role and training. Before 1970, psychological services were usually seen as tangential to the medical needs of most patients, and psychologists had little or no training in physiological systems, medical illnesses and treatments, and the organization and protocols of hospitals. But these conditions have been changing quickly. Today, health psychologists are receiving the training they need to work effectively in medical settings. And more and more physicians are coming to recognize the importance of psychosocial factors in their patients' health, adherence to treatment regimens, and rehabilitation. They also realize that they do not have the skills or time to address many of these factors.

Initial relations between medical staff and health psychologists still tend to be strained in some settings, particularly when one function of the psychologist may be to teach physicians and interns the "people skills" that are important for interviewing patients and communicating with them effectively. This kind of training may get a mixed reception, especially from some medical staff who feel these skills are not part of medicine (Christensen & Levinson, 1991). Even after medical and psychological staff have collaborated for a long time and seen that a biopsychosocial approach to health care can benefit patients, be intellectually stimulating, and lead to developing new techniques, their different styles and points of view can lead to conflicts (McDaniel & Campbell, 1986). For example, psychologists generally want to talk directly with the attending physician to describe subtle and complex issues relating to a patient's treatment plan, but medical specialists typically communicate with each other

> through notes in the hospital chart, which follow a particular pattern, showing the person who referred the case, the reason for the referral, the consultant's observation of the patient, the tests performed, the results of the tests, the conclusions reached, and the recommendations for the patient's care. (Huszti & Walker, 1991)

Differences like these can be resolved, enabling future relations between medical and psychological staff to become increasingly integrated. Physicians who have called upon the services of psychologists in hospitals appear to be satisfied with the outcome, but would like their patients to receive more follow-up services after being discharged (Huszti & Walker, 1991).

What about patients—how do they feel about receiving psychological services? Their view is likely to depend on the way the physician and psychologist introduce these services. If a patient thinks the services are offered because his or her physician thinks he or she is "crazy" or that the problem "is all in your head," the patient is likely to have negative attitudes and fail to cooperate. People are more likely to view psychosocial interventions positively if the services are introduced as part of a standard "team approach" with a biopsychosocial orientation. (Go to 🌳.)

CAREERS AND TRAINING IN HEALTH PSYCHOLOGY

Most health psychologists follow one of two career categories: those who work mainly in clinical capacities with patients and those who work mainly in academic or research capacities (Altman & Cahn, 1987; Sweet, Rozensky, & Tovian, 1991). Many health psychologists have careers that combine these areas, being involved in both clinical and academic or research activities, and some do administrative work, such as in governmental agencies or programs to promote health.

CAREER OPPORTUNITIES

The opportunities for careers in health psychology in the United States have been good, especially in health care settings—hospitals and clinics (DeAngelis, 1995). For example, the number of psychologists working in health care more than doubled from about 20,000 in 1974 to over 45,000 in 1985 (Enright et al., 1990). Some states have passed laws enabling psychologists to obtain full staff status in hospitals, giving them the same privileges as physicians. Psychologists have traditionally held lesser status levels with little influence on hospital policy (Rozensky, 1991). Other states are considering similar laws. What the job market will be in the future for health psychologists is hard to predict, but career opportunities in a variety of settings will probably continue to grow.

CLINICAL METHODS AND ISSUES
Psychologists in the Primary Care Team

In the late 1990s, some American managed-care programs, such as HMOs, began to include psychologists as members of the medical care team (D. Bruns, personal communication, September 1, 1998). Why? Program administrators came to realize that psychological factors, such as stress and emotional problems, play a pivotal role in the symptoms most patients present in their health care visits. The psychologists interview these patients and provide help, such as with brief counseling or training in stress and pain management.

Besides hospitals, where else do health psychologists work? Some of the more prominent sites are:

- Colleges and universities
- Medical schools
- Health maintenance organizations
- Rehabilitation centers
- Pain centers
- Private practice and consultancy offices

Sometimes job descriptions for these settings are broad, making eligible even professionals from nonpsychology fields, such as nursing, public health, or social work. Although this can increase the competition for those jobs, broad job descriptions can increase the number of opportunities for psychologists, too.

TRAINING PROGRAMS

What kind of training is available and necessary in health psychology? Training is offered at three educational levels: *undergraduate* courses in health psychology or behavioral medicine, *graduate* programs, and *postdoctoral* programs. Because health psychologists typically hold doctoral degrees, dozens of graduate programs now exist in the United States and other countries specifically for that training. Postdoctoral programs are available in health psychology or behavioral medicine, particularly for people with doctoral degrees that did not focus on the relationship between health and psychology.

Graduate and postdoctoral training programs in health psychology are quite diverse (Altman & Green, 1988; Belar, 1988, 1991). Some are highly interdisciplinary programs that are designed solely for this field. They often specialize in training students either for research careers or for direct clinical service to patients. Other programs provide graduate training in traditional psychology areas, such as clinical or social psychology, and contain special tracks or emphases relating to health. Common to all these programs is a solid grounding in psychology, along with training in research methods, biopsychosocial processes in health and disease, and health care terminology and organization. Programs that educate students for direct clinical service to patients generally include medical courses, such as in physiology and pharmacology. The future may see greater standardization of health

psychology training programs in the United States and around the world, as some professionals have recommended (Methorst, Jansen, & Kerkhof, 1991).

Information about graduate and postdoctoral training programs in health psychology can be obtained by contacting the following professional organizations:

- American Psychological Association, Division of Health Psychology, 750 First Street N.E., Washington, DC 20002-4242.
  WebPage: http://www.health-psych.org
- Society of Behavioral Medicine, 7600 Terrace Avenue, Suite 203, Middleton, WI 53562.
  WebPage: http://www.sbmweb.org

ISSUES AND CONTROVERSIES FOR THE FUTURE

Findings from research and clinical experience will enable health psychologists to help societies resolve important issues and controversies in the future. We will look at several examples, beginning with the impact of environmental conditions on health and psychology.

ENVIRONMENT, HEALTH, AND PSYCHOLOGY

Each of the varied environments in which people live around the world contains conditions that have the potential to harm the health and psychological status of its inhabitants. We read and hear in the news media that the environment is becoming increasingly polluted with toxic substances, which may be released accidently or deliberately into the air, ground, or bodies of water. The environments in which people live are also becoming more crowded and noisy. What effects do these conditions have? How can we reduce harmful environmental conditions? Some answers use a public health approach: because cigarette smoke pollutes the air and can lead to illnesses in those who breathe it, some psychologists have called for governmental control of tobacco products (Kaplan, Orleans, Perkins, & Pierce, 1995).

Many toxic environmental pollutants are produced as byproducts either of manufacturing or of generating energy. For instance, some manufacturing industries produce highly toxic cyanide or mercury as byproducts, which have made their ways into the environment. Power plants and automobiles generate energy along with potentially harmful byproducts, such as sulfur dioxide, carbon monoxide, and nuclear radiation. What direct effects on health does long-term exposure to low levels of these pollutants have? How stressful is it to live or work in contaminated environments, and how much does this stress affect health? How much does the stress of crowding and noise affect health? Health psychologists can help in efforts to answer these questions and find ways to change behaviors that produce these problems (Weinman, 1990). Although we have some information on these questions, much more research will be needed in the future before we can provide accurate answers.

QUALITY OF LIFE

People's *quality of life* has become a significant issue in medical care because (1) it is reduced by becoming sick and by staying sick and (2) it is an important consideration in prevention efforts before and after an illness occurs. Efforts to maintain people's good health also maintain their quality of life, and efforts to help patients recover quickly and fully lessen the negative impact of the illness on their lives. For people who are ill, their quality of life enters into decisions about the medical and psychological treatment they will receive. Are they in pain? If so, what type of painkilling medication should they get, and how much? If they're distressed, what psychosocial methods are likely to improve their emotional status?

Life-or-death medical decisions are often heavily influenced by appraisals of patients' current and future quality of life. Current quality of life is especially important if there is virtually no hope of the patient's recovery. In such cases, the views of the patient, family, and medical staff are likely to come down to a judgment of whether living in the current state is better than not living at all. Future quality of life is important in medical decisions that can enable the patient to survive, but will leave him or her with seriously impaired physical, psychological, and social capacities. For example, the family of an elderly man with a disabling cardiovascular condition felt he would be better off not living

> if he was just going to be a vegetable. They said his whole life revolved around working in his yard and playing bridge; these were the things in life that gave him joy. Now the doctors were not giving any hope that he would ever get back to what he was before; the best that could be hoped for was that he would be able to sit in a wheelchair. They said they didn't want that for him, and . . . he wouldn't want that for himself either. (Degner & Beaton, 1987, p. 64)

Decisions to withhold heroic medical efforts clearly involve humane concerns, but financial considerations are important, too (Spurgeon, Broome, Earll, & Harris, 1990). Heroic medical efforts and aftercare are extremely expensive. With the enormous pressures to contain the cost of health care, are these expenses always justified even when the resulting quality of life will be poor?

Making medical and psychological decisions based on a patient's current or future quality of life is difficult, partly because researchers need to determine the best ways to measure it. One approach that some people favor for making these decisions uses a scale called *quality-adjusted life years* (QALYs, pronounced "KWAL-eez"). To calculate the QALYs for a medical treatment, we would assess how long a person is likely to live after receiving the treatment, multiply each year by its quality of life, and total these data (Bradley, 1993; Kaplan, 1994). Using QALYs, we could rank the value of different treatments for a particular person or in general, perhaps even taking the cost per QALY into account, and decide whether to provide the treatment. At the heart of this approach is the measurement of quality of life. Although there are dozens of questionnaires to assess quality of life, the qualities they measure vary widely (Gill & Feinstein, 1995; Wilson & Cleary, 1995). Which should we use? Health psychologists will play an important role in resolving measurement problems and how best to use quality of life assessments in making treatment decisions.

ETHICAL DECISIONS IN MEDICAL CARE

Suppose you were an obstetrician delivering a baby when you realized that complications you see developing will surely kill the baby and, maybe, the mother, too. Suppose also that the mother flatly refuses a Caesarean delivery for religious reasons. What do you do? The typical medical response is to seek an immediate court order to override her decision. The decisions made in this case and the quality of life decisions we just considered all involve ethical issues. Many hospitals today have *bioethics committees* to discuss ethical issues in health care, make policy, and recommend action regarding specific cases. The ethical issues these committees consider often involve the patient's right to choose treatments, to withhold or withdraw treatment, or to die (Bouton, 1990). We will examine two other important issues: the role of technology in medical decisions and the role of physicians in helping patients die.

Technology and Medical Decisions

The technological advances we have seen in our lives over the past few decades have been quite remarkable. Many of these advances have been in medical technology, and they have sometimes raised important ethical questions.

One of these technological advances is a computer program called APACHE III that calculates the odds that individual patients will die in intensive care or after they leave it (Seligmann & Sulavik, 1992). Why might this be a problem? Decisions about continuing to provide intensive care treatment are made every day, based on the likelihood that it will help the patient survive. The alternative decision is to transfer the person to a regular hospital ward. These decisions are based on physicians' broad estimates, such as, "Her chances look bleak." With the computer program, physicians can get precise estimates of the person's odds of dying if he or she continues in intensive care, say 42%, versus if he or she is transferred, say 78%. In this example, transferring the patient would greatly increase the odds that he or she would die. The comparison helps in making the decision. The ethical problems relate to how these numbers will be used. Should physicians tell families these numbers? Will physicians and families weigh these data too heavily in their decisions? Will hospitals release these data to insurance companies, which could then decide to limit coverage when scores drop below some level? Health psychologists can play a role in some of these decisions, especially those relating to families having and using these data (Weinman, 1990).

Other ethical dilemmas arise in deciding whether to provide an organ transplant for patients. Nearly 20,000 transplants are done each year in the United States (USBC, 1999). Health psychologists help medical practitioners to select candidates who are best able to benefit from the surgery and the scarce organs because these people are able to cope with the stress and behave appropriately to maintain their health with the new organ. To help make these decisions, psychologists screen potential candidates—some patients will be clearly up to the task, and some will not, such as candidates for liver transplant who have not been able to control their drinking. Others will be in between and may benefit from interventions of behavioral contracting and therapy to help them cope better (Olbrisch, 1996).

Advances in genetics technology may also present ethical problems. For instance, geneticists are now able to identify individuals who are likely to develop serious diseases, such as cystic fibrosis and some forms of cancer, and may soon be able to identify individuals who are vulnerable to environmental causes of cancer and heart disease (Detjen, 1991; Lerman, Audrain, & Croyle, 1994). Who should be tested for these risks, and who should have access to the results? Insurance companies would like this information, and some are already turning down applicants for insurance on the basis of known family histories of certain diseases.

Assisted Suicide and Euthanasia

Some people with serious illnesses come to the decision that they want to end their lives. Should physicians help them in their wishes? This is a very controversial issue for society in general and in the medical community. Among physicians, some feel they should not help because of certain beliefs they hold, such as that life is sacred or that medical workers should only save lives and not take them. Other physicians feel they should participate in this act if the patient is actually beyond all help and the decision was not made because of psychological depression that could be reduced (Wanzer et al., 1989). Depressed people who want to end their lives may change their minds if the depression is relieved (Zisook, Peterkin, Shuchter, & Bardone, 1995).

Some physicians have helped patients end their lives in two ways (Meier et al., 1998; Wanzer et al., 1989). In *assisted suicide* the patient takes the final act, but the physician knowingly prescribes the needed drugs or describes the methods and doses required. Because of the legal consequences for physicians who help people take their lives, a book called *Final Exit* was published in 1991 describing the procedures physicians would recommend. In *euthanasia* the physician (or someone else) takes the final act, usually by administering a drug that ends the life. Laws permit euthanasia in the Netherlands and physician-assisted suicide in Oregon under certain circumstances. When societies decide that it is acceptable for physicians to help a patient end his or her life, laws should require that psychologists assess the person's emotional status, ability to make sound decisions, and likelihood of benefiting from psychosocial intervention (Clay, 1997). (Go to 🍎.)

FUTURE FOCUSES IN HEALTH PSYCHOLOGY

The research that contributes to our knowledge in health psychology comes from many different fields. But early studies gave a relatively narrow view of the biopsychosocial processes involved in health and illness because of the people researchers tended to recruit as subjects: they often were 18- to 60-year-old white American males—for example, in studies of Type A behavior. Two reasons for this focus are that these subjects were readily

ASSESS YOURSELF
Some Ethical Dilemmas: What Do You Think?

Each of the following cases describes a decision involving an ethical dilemma that is related to health. Circle the Y for "yes" or the N for "no" preceding each case to indicate whether you agree with the decision.

Y N A 47-year-old woman developed cirrhosis of the liver as a result of long-term alcoholism. She promised to stop drinking if she could receive a liver transplant. Her request was denied because of likely future drinking.

Y N An overweight, chain-smoking, sedentary 51-year-old man with high blood pressure had his first heart attack 7 years ago. His request for a heart transplant was denied because of continuing risk factors.

Y N A 28-year-old married woman with a hereditary crippling disease that is eventually fatal decided to become pregnant, knowing that there was a 50% chance that she would pass on the disease to her baby and she would not consider having an abortion.

Y N A 37-year-old executive was told by his boss that he would have to pay half of the costs of his employer-provided health insurance if he did not quit smoking and lower his cholesterol.

Y N An obese 20-year-old woman who refused to try to lose weight was expelled from nursing school, despite having good grades and clinical evaluations, because it was said she would "set a poor example for patients."

Y N A 24-year-old man was denied employment as a bank clerk because he was overweight and smoked cigarettes.

Y N A 30-year-old woman was denied a promotion to a job that involved working in an area with gases that could harm an embryo if she were to become pregnant.

Y N A year after a boy developed leukemia, the company that provided his family's health insurance quadrupled their premium.

These dilemmas are all based on real examples from the news media. Because they all involve controversies, there is no key to the "right" answers. But you might want to ask friends or classmates what they think.

available and some researchers incorrectly believed that the findings with these people would easily generalize to other populations. In the 1980s, studies began to broaden their focus to include subjects representing a wider range of people. This trend will surely continue in the future.

LIFE-SPAN HEALTH AND ILLNESS

We have seen that the health problems people have and the extent to which they use health services change with age. Very young and elderly individuals use health services more than others do, and the elderly are much more likely to have chronic health problems than younger people are.

From Conception to Adolescence

Children's prenatal environments have a major effect on their health. Enormous numbers of babies are born each year with illnesses or defects that develop because of prenatal exposure to harmful conditions or chemicals, particularly when mothers use alcohol, drugs, or tobacco during pregnancy. The health problems these babies develop can last for years or for life. Health psychologists are studying ways to improve babies' prenatal environments, such as by educating and counseling prospective parents (Weinman, 1990). Although these approaches help, we need to find more effective ways to prevent these health problems from developing.

Childhood and adolescence are important periods in the life span because many health beliefs and habits form during these years. But very little research has examined how these beliefs and habits develop (Weinman, 1990). We do know that efforts to promote health should be introduced early, before unhealthful beliefs and habits develop. Early childhood is clearly the time to intervene for some behaviors, such as for proper diets, exercise, dental care, and seat belt use. In later childhood, interventions should focus on preventing accidents, cigarette and drug use, and unsafe sex. We saw in Chapter 7, for example, that programs to prevent children from starting to smoke cigarettes have had some success. We have also seen that behaviors that put people at high risk for AIDS can be changed substantially, thereby reducing their risk. Efforts to prevent the spread of HIV need to be intensified and applied worldwide. To design more effective health promotion programs, we will need to focus more research—especially longitudinal studies—on how health behaviors form and change in childhood and adolescence.

Adulthood and Old Age

By the time people reach adulthood, most health-related values and behaviors are ingrained and difficult to change. People's lifestyles during the early adulthood and middle-age years tend to continue and affect whether or when they will develop major chronic illnesses, particularly heart disease and cancer. The earlier people change unhealthful behaviors, the lower their health risks are likely to be. In addition, prolonged emotional difficulties, particularly depression, are linked to future illness, such as heart disease. Among elderly people equated for initial physical health, those who are depressed show sharper physical declines, such as in walking speed, over the next few years than nondepressed elders do (Penninx et al., 1998).

People in most areas of the world are living longer, and the proportion of elderly individuals is increasing. As the world population ages, the proportion of individuals with disabling or life-threatening illnesses will surely grow, thereby requiring more health services and psychosocial interventions. In the United States, for example, an unusually high birth rate after World War II created a very large generation of people called "Baby Boomers," who now are swelling the ranks of the middle-aged. How will health care systems around the world respond to the added loads? This potential makes it even more crucial that we find ways to prevent or change risky lifestyles, particularly with regard to diet, exercise, and substance use. We will also need to improve ways to help families cope with the difficulties of caring for elderly relatives. The number of studies dealing with health issues in old age published each year has increased since 1980 and will continue to be a major focus of health psychologists in the future.

SOCIOCULTURAL FACTORS IN HEALTH

Sociocultural differences in the United States and around the world are related to health and health behavior. For instance, Americans from the lower social classes and from black and Hispanic minority groups tend to have poorer health and health habits than whites and those from higher classes. These differences have been clear for a long time. Although researchers have begun to investigate why these differences exist and what can be done to reduce them, our knowledge on these issues is not yet very specific. For example, we don't know how cultural customs and socioeconomic factors shape the everyday lives of different ethnic groups (Anderson & Armstead, 1995; Kaplan, 1995). And so we tend to make broad conclusions, as when we say people in a minority group "live in environments that do not encourage the practice of health-protective behavior." Health psychology must give greater emphasis to sociocultural issues so that we can provide specific and useful solutions in the future.

Cross-cultural research also needs more emphasis. We have spotty information about cultural differences in lifestyles, perceiving symptoms of illness, and using health services, but most research on these differences is old and very incomplete. The study of health psychology outside North America is advancing slowly, even in Europe (Schmidt & Dlugosch, 1991; Stone, 1991). In the poorer nations of the world, where infectious diseases and malnutrition are often rampant, one in ten children under the age of 5 die each year (WHO, 1999c). The number of people infected with HIV in Africa and other developing areas of the world is astounding and growing rapidly. The countries with the most urgent need to change behavioral risk factors have not yet recognized that principles of health psychology can help promote public health. In addition, health psychologists need to conduct research to determine how to adapt the principles that work in the United States and other industrialized countries to the needs of other cultures.

GENDER DIFFERENCES AND WOMEN'S HEALTH ISSUES

Health issues relating to women and gender differences were also neglected in health psychology research until the 1980s (Blechman, 1983; Matthews et al., 1997). Since that time, studies have begun to examine health issues that are specific to women, such as menstrual problems and reactions to breast cancer. Research has also studied differences between males and females in a wide variety of characteristics, such as reactions to stress, Type A and B behavior patterns, risk of AIDS and of heart disease, weight regulation, and tobacco and alcohol use. On the issue of breast cancer, for instance, researchers have shown that mammography screening markedly reduces breast cancer mortality and that certain types of programs are more effective than others in promoting women's screening use (Kerlikowske et al., 1995; Rimer, 1994).

Gender-related research has become a main focus of health psychology today and for the future. This research is making clearer the uniqueness of women and men in their health and health-protective behaviors and the special interventions they are likely to need to promote their health.

FACTORS AFFECTING HEALTH PSYCHOLOGY'S FUTURE

The picture of health psychology's future that we have considered is based on trends and needs that seem clear today. But trends and needs can change, and the prospects for our discipline will depend on forces and events in society, medical fields, and psychology (Pattishall, 1989; Weinman, 1990). What factors are likely to affect the role and direction of health psychology in the future?

Some factors are likely to have a broad impact on health psychology, affecting the amount and type of research, clinical intervention, and health promotion activities that we do. One of these factors is monetary: How much financial support will there be for these activities? During hard economic times, cutbacks in governmental and private funding may reduce this support. But there is another side to this coin—health care costs around the world are increasing, and many health experts believe that two of the best ways to decrease these costs involve improving people's health behaviors and helping those individuals who become ill to recover quickly. Research findings have enabled health psychologists to help reduce costs in both of these ways. Funding will also depend on how health insurance and services are structured. Health care systems are changing rapidly in many countries. The changes that emerge will probably continue or strengthen support for psychosocial interventions with favorable research evidence regarding their cost–benefit ratios.

Another factor that can have a broad impact on health psychology's future is education and training in this discipline (Weinman, 1990). Undergraduate courses in health psychology can reach students from various nonpsychology fields, such as nursing, pre-med, and sociology. Students who have a positive view of the role and success of health psychology are likely to promote its research, application, and interdisciplinary contacts in the future. If these students go into medical fields, they are likely to be receptive to learning about psychosocial methods by which they and health psychologists can promote the health of their patients. These circumstances can enhance acceptance of health psychologists in medical settings.

Developments in medicine will also influence the future of health psychology (Weinman, 1990). New and growing health problems generally require psychosocial interventions to reduce people's risk factors for these illnesses and help patients and their families cope. This can be seen clearly in the role of health psychology in addressing these kinds of issues in AIDS and Alzheimer's disease, for instance. Health psychologists often have an important role to play when new medical treatments are found, particularly if these treatments are unpleasant or if they may impair the patient's quality of life.

As you can see, many factors can affect the future of health psychology. The field has made dramatic and rapid advances in its short history, but we still have much to learn. Although we sometimes head in the wrong direction, we can take heart and humor from the following perspective:

> Life is a test,
> It is only a test.
> If this were your actual life,
> You would have been given better instructions!
> (Anonymous, cited in Pattishall, 1989, p. 47)

SUMMARY

Major changes have occurred in health and health care systems around the world in the past several decades. People are living longer today and are more likely to develop chronic illnesses that result from or are aggravated by their long-standing health habits. Health psychology has made major advances in helping to prevent or change these behaviors. The field has also developed effective psychosocial methods to help patients and their families cope with chronic illnesses. For many of the interventions health psychologists use, research has demonstrated favorable cost–benefit ratios. These successes have helped to promote the acceptance of health psychologists in medical settings.

Career opportunities for health psychologists have expanded rapidly, and the employment outlook for the future continues to look good. The availability of training in health psychology has grown at the undergraduate, graduate, and postgraduate levels. This training is solidly based in psychology and includes a substantial amount of information on biopsychosocial processes in health and illness and on medical terminology and procedures.

Health psychology has begun to address important health issues and controversies that societies will need to resolve in the future. These issues and controversies include the impact of environmental pollutants on people's health and psychological status, patients' quality of life, and ethical decisions in medical care. Some ethical questions relate to the use of technological advances in health care and whether physicians should participate, through assisted suicide or euthanasia, in helping hopelessly ill patients end their lives. Health psychology has also begun to focus its attention on life-span, sociocultural, and gender issues in health. Forces and events in society, medicine, and psychology will affect the future role and direction of health psychology.

GLOSSARY

abstinence-violation effect A cognitive process whereby a relapse occurs when people feel guilt and reduced self-efficacy if they experience a lapse in efforts to change their behavior.

acquired immune deficiency syndrome (AIDS) An infectious disease that disables the immune system. Individuals with AIDS are susceptible to a variety of life-threatening diseases.

acupuncture A pain-control technique in which fine metal needles are inserted under the skin at certain locations and then activated.

acute pain The discomfort patients experience with temporary medical conditions, lasting less than about 6 months.

adaptation The changes people undergo in making positive adjustments to circumstances in their lives.

addiction The condition of physical and psychological dependence on using a substance.

adherence The degree to which patients follow the medical recommendations of practitioners. Also called *compliance.*

adoption studies Research with subjects adopted at very early ages, comparing their characteristics with corresponding traits of their adoptive and natural parents to assess the influence of heredity.

adrenal glands Endocrine glands that secrete several hormones, such as cortisol, epinephrine, and norepinephrine, that are involved in stress reactions.

aerobic exercise (air-OH-bik) Sustained and energetic physical activity in which the body uses high volumes of oxygen over many minutes.

alarm reaction The first stage in the general adaptation syndrome when the body's resources are mobilized.

alcoholics People who drink alcohol heavily and are addicted to it.

algogenic substances (al-go-JEN-ik) Chemicals released at the site of tissue damage that cause inflammation and signal injury.

alternative medicine Unconventional treatments that seem inconsistent with the biomedical model; usually have little scientific evidence for their effectiveness.

Alzheimer's disease A chronic and progressive brain disorder marked by a loss of cognitive functions, such as memory.

angina pectoris (an-JEYE-nah, or AN-ji-nah, PEK-to-ris) A condition marked by chest pain that generally results from a brief or incomplete blockage of the blood supply to heart tissue.

anorexia nervosa (an-or-EX-ee-ah ner-VOE-sah) An eating disorder marked by self-starvation and an extreme and unhealthy loss of weight.

antibodies Protein molecules created to protect against specific antigens in body fluids.

antibody-mediated immunity The immune process that employs antibodies to attack antigens while they are still in body fluids and before they have invaded the cells.

antigen Any substance that can trigger the immune system to respond.

arteriosclerosis (ar-TEER-ee-o-skleh-ROE-sis) A condition in which fatty patches have accumulated to and hardened on artery walls, thereby reducing the elasticity of these walls.

arthritis A category of painful and potentially disabling chronic conditions that involve inflammation of the joints.

asthma A psychophysiological disorder of the respiratory system in which bronchial inflammation and spasms lead to episodes of difficult breathing.

atherosclerosis (ATH-eh-roe-skleh-ROE-sis) The condition in which fatty patches (plaques) form on artery walls.

attribution The process by which people attempt to judge or explain events or their own or others' behavior.

autonomic nervous system A division of the peripheral nervous system that carries messages between the central nervous system and the internal organs. It has two parts: the sympathetic and parasympathetic nervous systems.

aversion strategies Methods that use unpleasant stimuli to discourage undesirable behaviors.

B cells Lymphocytes that lead to the formation of antibodies.

behavioral control A form of personal control involving the ability to reduce the impact of a stressor by taking concrete action.

behavioral medicine An interdisciplinary field introduced in the early 1970s to study the relationships between behavior and health.

behavioral methods Psychological techniques that use mainly operant and classical conditioning principles to change behavior.

biobehavioral model   The theory that people who smoke come to depend on nicotine to regulate their cognitive and emotional states in coping processes.

biofeedback   A process by which individuals can acquire voluntary control over a physiological function by monitoring its status.

biomedical model   The view that illness results from physical causes, such as infection or injury; psychosocial processes are not viewed as causal factors.

biopsychosocial model   The view that health and illness involve the interplay of biological, psychological, and social factors in people's lives.

blood pressure   The force of the blood against the inner walls of the arteries.

brainstem   The lowest portion of the brain, located at the top of the spinal cord, consisting of the midbrain, reticular system, pons, and medulla.

buffering hypothesis   The view that the health benefits of social support come from its reducing the negative health effects of high stress levels.

bulimia nervosa   (buh-LIM-ee-ah ner-VOE-sah) An eating disorder marked by repeated binge eating, usually followed by purging.

burnout   An emotional and behavioral impairment resulting from exposure to high levels of occupational stress.

cancer   A class of malignant diseases in which cells proliferate in an unrestricted manner, usually forming a tumor.

carbon monoxide   A gas that is a constituent of cigarette smoke.

carcinogens   Chemical or physical agents that can cause cancer.

cardiovascular system   A network of organs that circulates blood to supply oxygen and nutrients to the body's cells and removes wastes and other substances.

case study   A nonexperimental method in which a researcher uses interviews, past records, and current observations to construct a biography of a single subject.

catecholamines   (kat-eh-KOL-a-meenz) A class of hormones, including epinephrine and norepinephrine, secreted by the adrenal glands.

cell-mediated immunity   The immune process that operates at the cellular level, using T cells to attack infected cells.

central nervous system   That part of the nervous system consisting of the brain and spinal cord.

cerebellum   (ser-uh-BEL-um) A large portion of the brain that coordinates motor activities and maintains body balance.

cerebrum   (ser-EE-brum) The upper and largest portion of the human brain. It has primary control over motor and mental activity.

chromosomes   Threadlike structures in the nucleus of each cell that contain genes that carry hereditary information.

chronic diseases   Illnesses that persist and generally get worse over a long period of time.

chronic-intractable-benign pain   Long-term continuous, but variable, discomfort stemming from benign causes.

chronic-progressive pain   Long-term continuous discomfort that worsens as the underlying malignant condition progresses.

chronic-recurrent pain   Long-term repeated and intense episodes of discomfort stemming from benign causes.

clinical pain   Any pain symptoms that receive or require professional treatment.

cognitive appraisal   The mental process people use in assessing whether a demand is threatening and what resources are available to meet the demand.

cognitive control   A form of personal control involving the ability to reduce the impact of a stressor by using thought processes.

cognitive methods   Psychological techniques that focus on changing people's feelings and thought processes.

cognitive restructuring   A therapeutic process for replacing thoughts that provoke stress with ones that do not.

cognitive therapy   A cognitive restructuring approach that has clients test hypotheses about maladaptive beliefs they hold about events in their lives.

cohort effect   The influence of different subjects having been born and raised in different eras.

commonsense models   Cognitive representations people develop regarding specific illnesses.

compliance   See *adherence*.

conflict theory   An explanation of health-related behavior that includes both rational and emotional factors.

coping   The process by which people try to manage the stress they experience.

coronary heart disease (CHD)   A class of illnesses that result when a narrowing or blockage of the coronary arteries restricts the blood supply to the heart muscle (myocardium).

correlation coefficient   A statistic that reflects the degree and direction of relationship between two variables; it can range from +1.00, through .00, to −1.00.

correlational studies   Nonexperimental research conducted to determine the degree and direction of relationship between variables.

corticosteroids   (cor-ti-koe-STEH-royds) A class of hormones, including cortisol, secreted by the adrenal glands.

counter-irritation   A technique whereby one pain is reduced by creating another one.

crisis theory   A model describing the factors that affect people's adjustment to having serious illnesses. The theory proposes that coping processes are influenced by three types of factors: illness-related, background and personal, and physical and social environmental.

cross-sectional approach   Method of studying developmental trends by observing different groups of subjects of different ages within a relatively short period of time.

daily hassles   Everyday annoyances or unpleasant events.

decisional control   A form of personal control involving the ability to reduce the impact of a stressor by choosing between alternative courses of action.

depersonalization   A behavioral style of some practitioners that involves treating a patient as if he or she were not there or not a person.

depressants   Drugs that induce relaxation and sleep.

detoxification   The process of getting an addicted individual safely through withdrawal after discontinuing the use of a substance.

dietary diseases   Illnesses that result from poor nutrition.

digestive system   The network of organs that processes ingested food by breaking it down for the body's use and excreting the remains.

direct effects hypothesis   The view that the health benefits of social support accrue regardless of whether people experience high or low levels of stress.

distraction   A pain management technique in which people divert their focus to nonpain stimuli in the environment.

doctor-centered   The behavioral style of some physicians in which interactions with patients are highly controlled by the practitioner and focus on the symptoms or treatment rather than the person.

double-blind   An experimental procedure whereby neither the subject nor the researcher knows which research treatment the subject is receiving.

emetic drug   (eh-MEH-tik) A chemical that induces nausea when a person drinks alcohol.

emotion-focused coping   Approaches people use for managing stress that are aimed at regulating their emotional responses.

endocrine system   An array of glands that secrete hormones into the bloodstream.

endogenous opioids   (en-DAH-je-nus OH-pee-oydz) Opiatelike substances the body produces naturally that reduce the sensation of pain.

enzymes   (EN-zymz) Substances that increase the speed of chemical reactions in cells.

epidemic   The situation in which the occurrence of a health problem has increased rapidly.

epilepsy   A chronic condition of the nervous system that produces recurrent seizures.

essential hypertension   Persistent high blood pressure with no known organic cause.

experiment   A controlled study in which variables are manipulated and observed to assess cause–effect relationships.

extinction   In operant conditioning, a process by which a previously reinforced behavior no longer receives reinforcement, making it less likely to occur in the future.

gate-control theory   An explanation of pain perception that proposes that a neural gate in the spinal cord can modulate incoming pain signals. The opening and closing of the gate is influenced by messages that descend from the brain and by the amount of activity in pain fibers and in other peripheral fibers.

general adaptation syndrome (GAS)   The sequence of physiological reactions to prolonged and intense stress. The sequence consists of the alarm reaction, the stage of resistance, and the stage of exhaustion.

genetic counseling   A service whereby prospective and expectant parents may get information regarding their risks of giving birth to children with genetic defects.

hallucinogens   (ha-LOO-sin-a-jins) Drugs that can produce perceptual and cognitive distortions.

hardiness   An array of personality characteristics that enables individuals to withstand stress and not succumb to its negative health effects.

health   A positive state of physical, mental, and social well-being that changes in degree over time.

health behavior   Any behavior people perform with the intention of promoting or maintaining well-being regardless of the state of their health.

health belief model   An explanation of people's health-related behavior based on their perception of the threat of illness or injury and the pros and cons of taking action.

health psychology   A field of psychology introduced in the late 1970s to examine the causes of illnesses and to study ways to promote and maintain health, prevent and treat illness, and improve the health care system.

high-density lipoprotein (HDL) A cholesterol-carrying protein that is associated with decreased cholesterol deposits in blood vessels.

hormones Chemical substances secreted by endocrine glands that affect body functions and behavior.

hospice care A philosophy and procedure for enriching the quality of life of terminally ill patients and their families.

hypertension The condition of persistent high blood pressure.

hypochondriasis (hy-poe-kon-DRY-uhsis) The tendency of some individuals to be excessively concerned and vigilant regarding their health and body sensations.

hypothalamus A part of the forebrain that contains control centers for many body functions, such as eating, drinking, and sexual activity.

iatrogenic conditions (eye-a-tro-JEN-ik) Health problems that develop as a result of medical treatment.

illness/wellness continuum A model that describes health and sickness as overlapping concepts that vary in degree, rather than being separate categories.

immune system The organs and structures that protect the body against harmful substances or agents, such as bacteria and viruses.

incidence The number of *new* cases reported during a given period of time, such as the previous year.

infectious diseases Illnesses caused by the body being invaded by microorganisms, such as bacteria or viruses.

inflammatory bowel disease A psychophysiological disorder involving wounds in the large or small intestine.

informational control A form of personal control involving the ability to reduce the impact of a stressor by acquiring knowledge about impending events.

insulin A hormone secreted by the pancreas that speeds the conversion of blood sugar to fat.

irritable bowel syndrome A digestive system disease with symptoms of pain, diarrhea, and constipation but no evidence of organic disorder.

isokinetic exercise (eye-so-kin-EH-tic) A type of activity that involves exerting muscle force in more than one direction while moving an object.

isometric exercise (eye-so-MET-rik) A type of activity that involves exerting muscle force against an object that does not move.

isotonic exercise (eye-so-TAH-nik) A type of activity that involves exerting most of the muscle force in one direction.

Lamaze training An educational and procedural program for natural childbirth that involves preparation, participation, and minimal medication.

lay referral system An informal network of individuals who provide advice or information regarding a person's symptoms and health.

learned food aversion A phenomenon in which a food becomes disliked as a result of being associated with symptoms of illness.

learned helplessness A condition of apathy or inactivity that results from repeated experiences with unavoidable stress.

life events Major occurrences in people's lives that require some degree of psychological adjustment.

life-span perspective The viewpoint that considers the individual's prior development, current level of development, and likely development in the future.

limbic system A set of structures in the forebrain that seems to play a role in emotional expression.

lipids (LIH-pidz) Fatty materials, such as the cholesterol found in blood.

lipoproteins (LIP-oh-pro-teenz or LY-po-pro-teenz) Proteins that transport cholesterol in the blood.

locus of control A generalized belief people have about the causes of events in their lives—whether the causes are within or outside their control.

longitudinal approach Method of studying developmental changes in the same subjects by making repeated observations over a long period of time.

low-density lipoprotein (LDL) A cholesterol-carrying protein that is associated with increased cholesterol deposits in blood vessels.

lymphocytes (LIM-foe-sites) Various types of white blood cells that have several important functions in the body's immune response.

McGill Pain Questionnaire (MPQ) A self-report instrument for assessing people's pain.

medulla (meh-DULL-ah) A part of the brainstem that contains control centers for such vital functions as breathing and heartbeat rate.

meta-analysis A statistical technique that combines the results from earlier studies to generate an overview of those findings.

metabolism The chemical reactions of the body's cells that synthesize new cell material, regulate body processes, and create energy.

methadone A chemical agent used in treating narcotic addiction that blocks the euphoric effects of opiates.

midbrain A portion of the brainstem that plays an important role in vision, hearing, and muscle movement.

migraine headache Recurrent head pain that results from the constriction and dilation of blood vessels in the head.

Million Behavioral Health Inventory (MBHI) A test that assesses several relevant characteristics of medical patients, such as their basic coping styles and hypochondriacal tendencies.

mind/body problem The issue in psychology and philosophy regarding the relationship between processes and functions of the mind and those of the body.

Minnesota Multiphasic Personality Inventory (MMPI) A lengthy test that assesses a variety of psychological problems, such as hypochondriasis, depression, and hysteria.

modeling Learning by watching the behavior of other people.

morbidity The condition of illness, injury, or disability.

mortality Death, usually with reference to large populations.

motivated reasoning Cognitive process whereby people's desires or preferences influence their decisions about the validity and utility of new information.

myocardial infarction (my-oh-KAR-dee-al in-FARK-shun) Damage to the heart muscle (myocardium) that results from severe or prolonged blockage of blood supply to the tissue. Commonly called a *heart attack*.

narcotics Drugs that relieve pain, act as sedatives, and may produce euphoria. These substances are also called *opiates* and usually lead to addiction with continued use.

neurons Specialized cells that provide for communication within the nervous system.

neurotransmitter A chemical involved in the transmission of impulses across the synapse from one neuron to another.

nicotine A chemical in cigarette smoke that appears to produce physical dependence.

nicotine regulation model An explanation of continued cigarette smoking based on the body's dependence on nicotine.

nociceptors (noe-see-SEP-torz) Afferent nerve endings that respond to pain stimuli in the damaged region of the body.

nonpain imagery A pain management method that involves picturing a mental scene that is unrelated to or incompatible with feeling discomfort.

nosocomial infection (noe-soe-KOE-mee-al) An infection a patient acquires while in the hospital.

obese The weight classification of individuals whose *body mass index* exceeds a value of 30 as a result of excess fat (formerly based on weight more than 20% over the desirable range).

overweight The weight classification of individuals whose *body mass index* exceeds a value of 25 as a result of excess fat (formerly based on weight 10–20% over the desirable range).

pain Sensory and emotional discomfort, usually related to actual or threatened tissue damage.

pain behaviors Characteristic ways people behave when they are in pain.

pain clinics Centers specializing in the treatment of chronic pain.

pain redefinition A pain management technique in which thoughts about pain that arouse a sense of threat are replaced with other thoughts that are more constructive or realistic.

parasympathetic nervous system A division of the autonomic nervous system that helps the body conserve energy and restore the normal body state after arousal.

passive smoking Breathing the smoke in the environment from someone else's cigarette or other smoking product.

patient-centered The behavioral style of some physicians in which their interactions encourage patients to share information and participate in medical decisions.

periaqueductal gray (per-ee-ak-weh-DUK-tal) A region of the midbrain that plays a major role in the perception of and reaction to pain stimuli.

peripheral nervous system The network of nerve fibers that carry messages between the central nervous system and the skin, skeletal muscles, and internal organs. This network has two parts: the somatic and autonomic nervous systems.

personal control The feeling people have that they can make decisions and take action to produce favorable events and avoid unfavorable ones.

personality Cognitive, affective, or behavioral predispositions of people in different situations and over time.

phagocytes (FAG-oh-sites) Certain types of white blood cells that engulf and ingest any kind of invading particles.

physical dependence A state in which the body has become accustomed to the presence of a substance in its physiological functioning.

pituitary gland An endocrine gland that has connections to the brain and secretes hormones that stimulate other endocrine glands to secrete.

placebo An inactive substance or procedure that may cause a change in an individual's behavior or health.

polygraph An electromechanical device that assesses the body's arousal by measuring and recording several physiological indexes, such as blood pressure and respiration rate, simultaneously.

pons A portion of the brainstem involved in the control of eye movements and facial expressions.

prevalence   The total number of cases existing at a given moment in time.

primary appraisal   The cognitive process people use in assessing the meaning of an event or situation for their well-being.

primary prevention   Actions undertaken to avoid health problems before they occur.

problem drinkers   People who are psychologically dependent on alcohol and drink heavily.

problem-focused coping   Approaches people use for managing stress aimed at reducing the discrepancy between their resources and the demands of the situation.

problem-solving training   A cognitive-behavioral approach that trains clients in strategies to identify and deal with life circumstances that require action based on careful decision-making processes.

progressive muscle relaxation   A stress reduction technique in which people are trained to alternate between tightening and relaxing specific muscle groups.

prospective approach   A research strategy whereby characteristics of subjects are measured and later examined for their relationships to future conditions, such as health problems.

psychological dependence   A state in which a person feels compelled to use a substance for the pleasant effect it produces.

psychoneuroimmunology   (psy-ko-noo-roe-ih-myu-NOL-oh-jee) A field of study focusing on relationships between psychosocial processes and nervous, endocrine, and immune system functioning.

psychophysiological disorders   Physical symptoms or illnesses resulting from some combination of psychosocial and physiological processes.

Psychosocial Adjustment to Illness Scale (PAIS)   A test of several psychosocial aspects of a patient's life that are related to adjustment to medical illness.

psychosomatic medicine   A field introduced in the 1930s to study the relationships between people's symptoms of illness and their emotions.

punishment   A process by which a consequence of an operant behavior suppresses that response.

quality of life   Individuals' appraisals of the degree to which their lives contain features that they find satisfying or meaningful.

quasi-experimental studies   Nonexperimental research in which subjects are categorized or separated into two or more groups on the basis of existing characteristics and then compared regarding other variables.

rational-emotive therapy (RET)   A cognitive restructuring approach for replacing irrational thought patterns that provoke stress with thought patterns that are more realistic.

rational nonadherence   Noncompliance with medical regimens for valid, but not necessarily medically beneficial, reasons.

reactance   People's angry responses to restrictions on their freedom of action or choice.

reactivity   The physiological component of the response to stress.

referred pain   The experience of discomfort as coming from an area of the body other than where the injury exists.

reinforcement   A process whereby a consequence of an operant response strengthens or maintains that behavior.

relapse   Regressing to the full-blown pattern of an unwanted behavior after beginning to change it.

respiratory system   A network of organs that supply oxygen for metabolism and expel carbon dioxide.

restraint theory   An explanation of eating regulation that proposes that people who constantly try to resist eating what they want tend to develop abnormal eating patterns in which they vacillate between inhibited and disinhibited consumption.

reticular system   A portion of the brainstem that contains control centers for sleep, arousal, and attention.

retrospective approach   A research strategy whereby the histories of subjects are examined for their relationships to recent conditions, such as health problems.

risk factors   Characteristics or conditions that occur more often among individuals who develop particular diseases or injuries than among those who do not.

secondary appraisal   The cognitive process people use in assessing the resources they have to meet demands.

secondary prevention   Actions undertaken to identify or treat a health problem early with the aim of arresting or reversing the condition.

self-efficacy   People's belief that they can succeed at something they want to do.

self-management strategies   Methods used in helping people gain control over the conditions in their environment that encourage undesirable behaviors.

separation distress   Emotional upset often shown by infants and young children when separated from their primary caretakers, typically their parents.

set-point theory   An explanation of weight regulation that proposes that each person has a "set" physiologically based weight level that the body strives to maintain.

single-subject designs   Research approaches in which a variable is observed in one individual during two or more research conditions.

social network   A person's linkages with other people, as assessed by various qualitative and quantitative measures of social contacts.

social support   The perceived comfort, caring, esteem, or help an individual receives from other people or groups.

sociocultural   Relating to or involving social and cultural features or processes.

somatic nervous system   A division of the peripheral nervous system that transmits sensory and motor impulses.

spinal cord   The major neural pathway that carries impulses between the brain and the peripheral nervous system.

spinal cord injury   Neurological damage in the spine that impairs motor and sensory function.

stage of exhaustion   The third stage in the general adaptation syndrome, when the body's energy reserves are severely depleted.

stage of resistance   The second stage in the general adaptation syndrome, when the body tries to adapt to the stressor.

stages of change model   A theory of intentional behavior that describes people's readiness to change with five potential stages: precontemplation, contemplation, preparation, action, and maintenance.

stimulants   Drugs that activate the nervous system, producing physiological and psychological arousal.

stimulation-produced analgesia (SPA)   A phenomenon whereby stimulation to the brainstem causes insensitivity to pain.

strain   The psychological and physiological response to a stressor.

stress   The condition that results when person–environment transactions lead the individual to perceive a discrepancy between the demands of a situation and his or her resources.

stress-inoculation training   A cognitive-behavioral approach for stress management that teaches people a variety of skills for alleviating stress and achieving personal goals.

stressors   Events or circumstances a person perceives as threatening or harmful.

stroke   A condition involving brain damage that results from a disruption in the blood supply to that area of the brain.

substance abuse   The prolonged overuse of a substance, involving a clear pattern of pathological use and heightened social and occupational problems.

sudden death   The abrupt death from cardiac dysfunction of a person who seemed healthy.

sympathetic nervous system   A division of the autonomic nervous system that enables the body to mobilize and expend energy during physical and emotional arousal.

system   A continuously changing entity that consists of constantly interrelated components.

systematic desensitization   A classical conditioning technique for reducing fear or anxiety by replacing it with a calm response.

tars   Tiny particles in cigarette smoke.

T cells   A class of lymphocytes; some attack antigens directly, and some work to regulate other immune functions.

temperaments   Basic personality characteristics or dispositions that individuals show right from birth, allowing many of them to be classified broadly as "easy" or "difficult."

tension-type headache   Recurrent head pain that results from persistent muscle tension in the head and neck. Also called *muscle-contraction* headache.

tertiary prevention   Actions undertaken to contain or slow the progress of damage from a serious or established health problem.

thalamus   A structure in the forebrain that serves as a relay station for sensory impulses to and commands from the cerebrum.

theory   A tentative explanation of phenomena.

theory of planned behavior   An explanation of people's health-related behavior. Their behavior depends on their intention, which is based on their attitudes regarding the behavior and beliefs about the subjective norm and behavioral control.

time management   Methods for managing stress that involve organizing one's time.

tolerance   A gradual decrease in the body's response to a drug, thereby requiring larger and larger doses to achieve the same effect.

transactions   The continuous interplay and adjustments of the person and environment.

transcutaneous electrical nerve stimulation (TENS) (tranz-kyu-TAIN-ee-us) A counter-irritation pain control technique that involves electrically stimulating an area near where the patient feels pain.

treatment delay   The elapsed time between noticing a symptom and getting medical care.

twin studies   Research to assess the influence of heredity in determining a characteristic by focusing on differences between identical and fraternal twins.

type 1 diabetes   The health problem of having chronically elevated blood sugar levels because the pancreas produces little or no insulin. People with type 1 diabetes typically require daily insulin supplements. Formerly called *insulin-dependent diabetes mellitus* (IDDM).

type 2 diabetes The health problem of having chronically elevated blood sugar levels even though the pancreas does produce at least some insulin. Most people with type 2 diabetes can manage their conditions without insulin supplements. Formerly called *non-insulin-dependent diabetes mellitus* (NIDDM).

Type A behavior pattern A behavioral or emotional style characterized by high levels of competitiveness, time urgency, and anger or hostility.

Type B behavior pattern A behavioral or emotional style characterized by low levels of competitiveness, time urgency, and anger or hostility.

ulcers A psychophysiological disorder involving wounds to the stomach or upper section of the small intestine.

variable A measurable characteristic of people, objects, or events that may change in quantity or quality.

very-low-density lipoproteins (VLDL) A cholesterol-carrying protein that is associated with increased deposits of cholesterol in blood vessels.

withdrawal Physical and psychological symptoms that occur when people stop taking a substance on which the body has become physically dependent.

REFERENCES*

AAFA (Asthma and Allergy Foundation of America) (2000). *Educational/materials: Answers.* Retrieved (3-17-2000) from http://www.aafa.org.

AANP (American Academy of Nurse Practitioners) (2000). *What is a nurse practitioner?* Retrieved (9-20-2000) from http://www.aanp.org.

AAPA (American Academy of Physician Assistants) (2000). *PA education.* Retrieved (3-4-2000) from http://www.aapa.org.

AARON , J., ZAGLUL, H., & EMERY, R. E. (1999). Posttraumatic stress disorder in children following acute physical injury. *Journal of Pediatric Psychology, 24,* 335–343.

ABELE, A., & BREHM, W. (1993). Mood effects of exercise versus sports games: Findings and implications for well-being and health. In S. MAES, H. LEVENTHAL, & M. JOHNSTON (Eds.), *International review of health psychology* (Vol. 2). New York: Wiley.

ABRAMS, D. B., NIAURA, R. S., CAREY, K. B., MONTI, P. M., & BINKOFF, J. A. (1986). Understanding relapse and recovery in alcohol abuse. *Annals of Behavioral Medicine, 8* (2–3), 27–32.

ABRAMS, K. K., ALLEN, L., GRAY, J. J. (1993). Disordered eating attitudes and behaviors, psychological adjustment, and ethnic identity: A comparison of black and white female college students. *International Journal of Eating Disorders, 14,* 49–57.

ABRAMSON, L. Y., SELIGMAN, M. E. P., & TEASDALE, J. D. (1978). Learned helplessness in humans: Critique and reformulation. *Journal of Abnormal Psychology, 87,* 49–74.

ACEVEDO, H. F., TONG, J. Y., & HARTSOCK, R. J. (1995). Human chorionic gonadotropin-beta subunit gene expression in cultured human fetal cells different types and origins. *Cancer, 76,* 1467–1475.

ACHTERBERG-LAWLIS, J. (1988). Musculoskeletal disorders. In E. A. BLECHMAN & K. D. BROWNELL (Eds.), *Handbook of behavioral medicine for women.* New York: Pergamon.

ACS (American Cancer Society) (1989). *Cancer facts and figures—1989.* Atlanta: Author.

ACS (American Cancer Society) (1996). *Cancer facts and figures—1996.* Atlanta: Author.

ACS (American Cancer Society) (2000). *Cancer facts and figures—1999.* Retrieved (3-7-2000) from http://www.cancer.org.

ADA (American Diabetes Association) (2000). *Diabetes Info* (Type 1 diabetes; Type 2 diabetes; Diabetes facts and figures). Retrieved (3-24-2000) from http://www.diabetes.org.

ADAMS, A., OCKENE, J. K., WHEELER, E. V., & HURLEY, T. G. (1998). Alcohol counseling: Physicians will do it. *Journal of General Internal Medicine, 13,* 692–698.

ADAMS, J. E., & LINDEMANN, E. (1974). Coping with long-term disability. In G. V. COELHO, D. A. HAMBURG, & J. E. ADAMS (Eds.), *Coping and adaptation.* New York: Basic Books.

ADEAR (Alzheimer's Disease Education and Referral Center) (2000). *Alzheimer's disease fact sheet.* Retrieved (3-17-2000) from http://www.alzheimers.org.

ADER, R. (1997). The role of conditioning in pharmacotherapy. In A. HARRINGTON (Ed.), *The placebo effect.* Cambridge: Harvard University Press.

ADER, R., & COHEN, N. (1975). Behaviorally conditioned immunosuppression. *Psychosomatic Medicine, 37,* 333–340.

ADER, R., & COHEN, N. (1982). Behaviorally conditioned immunosuppression and murine systemic lupus erythematosus. *Science, 215,* 1534–1536.

ADER, R., & COHEN, N. (1985). CNS-immune system interactions: Conditioning phenomena. *Behavioral and Brain Sciences, 8,* 379–395.

ADESSO, V. J. (1985). Cognitive factors in alcohol and drug use. In M. GALIZIO & S. A. MAISTO (Eds.), *Determinants of substance abuse: Biological, psychological, and environmental factors.* New York: Plenum.

ADietA (American Dietetic Association) (2000). *Becoming a registered dietitian.* Retrieved (3-3-2000) from http://www.eatright.org.

ADLER, N. E., BOYCE, T., CHESNEY, M. A., COHEN, S., FOLKMAN, S., KAHN, R. L., & SYME, S. L. (1994). Socioeconomic status and health: The challenge of the gradient. *American Psychologist, 49,* 15–24.

ADLER, N. E., & STONE, G. C. (1979). Social science perspectives on the health system. In G. C. STONE, F. COHEN, & N. E. ADLER (Eds.), *Health psychology—A handbook.* San Francisco: Jossey-Bass.

AF (Arthritis Foundation) (2000). *Fact sheets (Arthritis fact sheet; Arthritis types and prevalence; and Gout fact sheet).* Retrieved (3-17-2000) from http://www.arthritis.org.

AFFLECK, G., TENNEN, H., PFEIFFER, C., & FIFIELD, J. (1987). Appraisals of control and predictability in adapting to a chronic disease. *Journal of Personality and Social Psychology, 53,* 273–279.

AFFLECK, G., TENNEN, H., URROWS, S., & HIGGINS, P. (1991). Individual differences in the day-to-day experience of chronic pain: A prospective daily study of rheumatoid arthritis patients. *Health Psychology, 10,* 419–426.

*Authorship for references with more than ten authors is cited with this format: first four authors followed by et al.

AFFLECK, G., TENNEN, H., URROWS, S., HIGGINS, P., ABELES, M., HALL, C., KAROLY, P., & NEWTON, C. (1998). Fibromyalgia and women's pursuit of personal goals: A daily process analysis. *Health Psychology*, 17, 40–47.

AGOSTI, J. M., SPRENGER, J. D., LUM, L. G., WITHERSPOON, R. P., FISHER, L. D., STORB, R., & HENDERSON, W. R. (1988). Transfer of allergen-specific IgE-mediated hypersensitivity with allogenic bone marrow transplantation. *New England Journal of Medicine*, 319, 1623–1628.

AGRAS, W. S. (1984). The behavioral treatment of somatic disorders. In W. D. GENTRY (Ed.), *Handbook of behavioral medicine*. New York: Guilford.

AGRAS, W. S. (1987). *Eating disorders: Management of obesity, bulimia, and anorexia nervosa*. New York: Pergamon.

AHA (American Heart Association) (1994). *Heart and stroke facts*. Dallas, TX: Author.

AHA (American Heart Association) (1995). *Heart and stroke facts: 1996 statistical supplement*. Dallas, TX: Author.

AHA (American Heart Association) (2000). *Heart and stroke A–Z guide*. Retrieved (3-7-2000) from http://www.americanheart.org.

AIKEN, L. H. (1983). Nurses. In D. MECHANIC (Ed.), *Handbook of health, health care, and the health professions*. New York: Free Press.

AIKENS, K. S., AIKENS, J. E., WALLANDER, J. L., & HUNT, S. (1997). Daily activity level buffers stress-glycemia associations in older sedentary NIDDM patients. *Journal of Behavioral Medicine*, 20, 379–390.

AINSWORTH, M. D. S. (1973). The development of infant-mother attachment. In B. M. CALDWELL & H. N. RICCIUTI (Eds.), *Review of child development research* (Vol. 3). Chicago: University of Chicago Press.

AINSWORTH, M. D. S. (1979). Infant-mother attachment. *American Psychologist*, 34, 932–937.

AJZEN, I. (1985). From intentions to actions: A theory of planned behavior. In J. KUHL & J. BECKMAN (Eds.), *Action control: From cognition to behavior* (pp. 11–39). New York: Springer Verlag.

AJZEN, I., & FISHBEIN, M. (1980). *Understanding attitudes and predicting social behavior*. Englewood Cliffs, NJ: Prentice-Hall.

AKIL, H., MAYER, D. J., & LIEBESKIND, J. C. (1976). Antagonism of stimulation-produced analgesia by naloxone, a narcotic antagonist. *Science*, 191, 961–962.

ALA (American Lung Association) (2000). *Diseases A–Z* (*Trends in: asthma, chronic bronchitis and emphysema, pneumonia and influenza, and tuberculosis*). Retrieved (3-7-2000) from http://www.lungusa.org.

ALAGNA, S. W., & REDDY, D. M. (1984). Predictors of proficient technique and successful lesion detection in breast self-examination. *Health Psychology*, 3, 113–127.

ALARANTA, H., RYTÖKOSKI, U., RISSANEN, A., TALO, S., RÖNNEMAA, T., PUUKKA, P., KARPPI, S.-L., VIDEMAN, T., KALLIO, V., & SLÄTIS, P. (1994). Intensive physical and psychosocial training program for patients with chronic low back pain: A controlled clinical trial. *Spine*, 19, 1339–1349.

ALDERMAN, M. H. (1984). Worksite treatment of hypertension. In J. D. MATARAZZO, S. M. WEISS, J. A. HERD, N. E. MILLER, & S. M. WEISS (Eds.), *Behavioral health: A handbook of health enhancement and disease prevention*. New York: Wiley.

ALDWIN, C. M., & BRUSTROM, J. (1997). Theories of coping with chronic stress: Illustrations from the health psychology and aging literatures. In B. H. GOTTLIEB (Ed.), *Coping with chronic stress*. New York: Plenum.

ALEXANDER, F. (1950). *Psychosomatic medicine: Its principles and applications*. New York: Norton.

ALEXANDER, J. A. (1984). Blood pressure and obesity. In J. D. MATARAZZO, S. M. WEISS, J. A. HERD, N. E. MILLER, & S. M. WEISS (Eds.), *Behavioral health: A handbook of health enhancement and disease prevention*. New York: Wiley.

ALEXY, B. B. (1991). Factors associated with participation and nonparticipation in a workplace wellness center. *Research in Nursing & Health*, 14, 33–40.

ALLAN, R., & SCHEIDT, S. (1990). Life style: Its effect and modification for the prevention of sudden cardiac death. In J. B. KOSTIS & M. SANDERS (Eds.), *The prevention of sudden cardiac death*. New York: Wiley.

ALLEN, L., & ZIGLER, E. (1986). Psychosocial adjustment of seriously ill children. *Journal of the American Academy of Child Psychiatry*, 25, 708–712.

ALLISON, D. B., HESHKA, S., NEALE, M. C., LYKKEN, D. T., & HEYMSFIELD, S. B. (1994). A genetic analysis of relative weight among 4,020 twin pairs, with an emphasis on sex effects. *Health Psychology*, 13, 362–365.

ALPERT, B., FIELD, T., GOLDSTEIN, S., & PERRY, S. (1990). Aerobics enhances cardiovascular fitness and agility in preschoolers. *Health Psychology*, 9, 48–56.

ALTMAN, D. G., & CAHN, J. (1987). Employment options for health psychologists. In G. C. STONE, S. M. WEISS, J. D. MATARAZZO, N. E. MILLER, J. RODIN, C. D. BELAR, M. J. FOLLICK, & J. E. SINGER (Eds.), *Health psychology: A discipline and a profession*. Chicago: University of Chicago Press.

ALTMAN, D. G., & GREEN, L. W. (1988). Area review: Education and training in behavioral medicine. *Annals of Behavioral Medicine*, 10, 4–7.

ALTMAN, D. G., WHEELIS, A. Y., MCFARLANE, M., LEE, H., & FORTMANN, S. P. (1999). The relationship between tobacco access and use among adolescents: A four community study. *Social Science & Medicine*, 48, 759–775.

AMA (American Medical Association) (1989). *The American Medical Association encyclopedia of medicine.* New York: Random House.

American Psychiatric Association (1994). *Diagnostic and statistical manual of mental disorders* (4th ed.). Washington, DC: Author.

AMES, B. N., & GOLD, L. S. (1990). Too many rodent carcinogens: Mitogenisis increases mutogenesis. *Science,* 249, 970–971.

AMOS, C. I., HUNTER, S. M., ZINKGRAF, S. A., MINER, M. H., & BERENSON, G. S. (1987). Characterization of a comprehensive Type A measure for children in a biracial community: The Bogalusa Heart Study. *Journal of Behavioral Medicine,* 10, 425–439.

ANASTASI, A. (1982). *Psychological testing* (5th ed.). New York: Macmillan.

ANDERSEN, B. L., FARRAR, W. B., GOLDEN-KREUTZ, D., KUTZ, L. A., MACCALLUM, R., COURTNEY, M. E., & GLASER, R. (1998). Stress and immune responses after surgical treatment for regional breast cancer. *Journal of the American Cancer Institute,* 90, 30–36.

ANDERSEN, B. L., KARLSSON, J. A., ANDERSON, B., & TEWFIK, H. H. (1984). Anxiety and cancer treatment: Response to stressful radiotherapy. *Health Psychology,* 3, 535–551.

ANDERSEN, B. L., WOODS, X. A., & COPELAND, L. J. (1997). Sexual self-schema and sexual morbidity among gynecological cancer survivors. *Journal of Consulting and Clinical Psychology,* 65, 221–229.

ANDERSEN, R. E., CRESPO, C. J., BARTLETT, S. J., CHESKIN, L. J., & PRATT, M. (1998). Relationship of physical activity and television watching with body weight and level of fatness among children: Results from the Third National Health and Nutrition Survey. *Journal of the American Medical Association,* 279, 938–942.

ANDERSEN, R. E., WADDEN, T. A., BARTLETT, S. J., ZEMEL, B., VERDE, T. J., & FRANCKOWIAK, S. C. (1999). Effects of lifestyle activity vs structured aerobic exercise in obese women: A randomized trial. *Journal of the American Medical Association,* 281, 335–340.

ANDERSON, A. (1982, July). Neurotoxic follies. *Psychology Today,* pp. 30–42.

ANDERSON, B. J., AUSLANDER, W. F., JUNG, K. C., MILLER, J. P., & SANTIAGO, J. V. (1990). Assessing family sharing of diabetes responsibilities. *Journal of Pediatric Psychology,* 15, 477–492.

ANDERSON, E. A. (1987). Preoperative preparation for cardiac surgery facilitates recovery, reduces psychological distress, and reduces the incidence of acute postoperative hypertension. *Journal of Consulting and Clinical Psychology,* 55, 513–520.

ANDERSON, K. O., BRADLEY, L. A., YOUNG, L. D., McDANIEL, L. K., & WISE, C. M. (1985). Rheumatoid arthritis: Review of psychological factors related to etiology, effects, and treatment. *Psychological Bulletin,* 98, 358–387.

ANDERSON, K. O., & MASUR, F. T. (1983). Psychological preparation for invasive medical and dental procedures. *Journal of Behavioral Medicine,* 6, 1–40.

ANDERSON, L. A., JANES, G. R., & JENKINS, C. (1998). Implementing preventive services: To what extent can we change provider performance in ambulatory care? A review of the screening, immunization, and counseling literature. *Annals of Behavioral Medicine,* 20, 161–167.

ANDERSON, N. B., & ARMSTEAD, C. A. (1995). Toward understanding the association of socioeconomic status and health: A new challenge for the biopsychosocial approach. *Psychosomatic Medicine,* 57, 213–225.

ANDERSON, O. W., & GEVITZ, N. (1983). The general hospital: A social and historical perspective. In D. MECHANIC (Ed.), *Handbook of health, health care, and the health professions.* New York: Free Press.

ANDERSSON, G. B. J., LUCENTE, T., DAVIS, A. M., KAPPLER, R. E., LIPTON, J. A., & LEURGANS, S. (1999). A comparison of osteopathic spinal manipulation with standard care for patients with low back pain. *New England Journal of Medicine,* 341, 1426–1431.

ANDRASIK, F. (1986). Relaxation and biofeedback for chronic headaches. In A. D. HOLZMAN & D. C. TURK (Eds.), *Pain management: A handbook of psychological treatment approaches.* New York: Pergamon.

ANDRASIK, F., BLAKE, D. D., & McCARRAN, M. S. (1986). A biobehavioral analysis of pediatric headache. In N. A. KRASNEGOR, J. D. ARASTEH, & M. F. CATALDO (Eds.), *Child health behavior: A behavioral pediatrics perspective.* New York: Wiley.

ANDREW, J. M. (1970). Recovery from surgery with and without preparatory instruction for three coping styles. *Journal of Personality and Social Psychology,* 15, 223–226.

ANDRYKOWSKI, M. A. (1990). The role of anxiety in the development of anticipatory nausea in cancer chemotherapy: A review and synthesis. *Psychosomatic Medicine,* 52, 458–475.

ANTONI, M. H. (1987). Neuroendocrine influences in psychoimmunology and neoplasia: A review. *Psychology and Health,* 1, 3–24.

ANTONI, M. H., BAGGETT, L., IRONSON, G., LaPERRIERE, A., AUGUST, S., KLIMAS, N., SCHNEIDERMAN, N., & FLETCHER, M. A. (1991). Cognitive-behavioral stress management intervention buffers distress responses and immunologic changes following notification of HIV-1 seropositivity. *Journal of Consulting and Clinical Psychology,* 59, 906–915.

ANTONI, M. H., CRUESS, D. G., CRUESS, S., LUTGENDORF, S., KUMAR, M., IRONSON, G., KLIMAS, N., FLETCHER, M. A., &

SCHNEIDERMAN, N. (2000). Cognitive-behavioral stress management intervention effects on anxiety, 24-hr urinary norepinephrine output, and T-cytotoxic/suppressor cells over time among symptomatic HIV-infected gay men. *Journal of Consulting and Clinical Psychology, 68,* 31–45.

ANTONI, M. H., SCHNEIDERMAN, N., FLETCHER, M. A., GOLDSTEIN, D. A., IRONSON, G., & LAPERRIERE, A. (1990). Psychoneuroimmunology and HIV-1. *Journal of Consulting and Clinical Psychology, 58,* 38–49.

ANTONOVSKY, A. (1979). *Health, stress, and coping.* San Francisco: Jossey-Bass.

ANTONOVSKY, A. (1987). *Unraveling the mystery of health: How people manage stress and stay well.* San Francisco: Jossey-Bass.

ANTONOVSKY, A., & HARTMAN, H. (1974). Delay in the detection of cancer: A review of the literature. *Health Education Monographs, 2,* 98–128.

ANTONUCCI, T. C. (1985). Personal characteristics, social support, and social behavior. In R. H. BINSTOCK & E. SHANAS (Eds.), *Handbook of aging and the social sciences* (2nd ed.). New York: Van Nostrand-Reinhold.

ANTONUCCIO, D. O., & LICHTENSTEIN, E. (1980). Peer modeling influences on smoking behavior of heavy and light smokers. *Addictive Behaviors, 5,* 299–306.

AOTA (American Occupational Therapy Association) (2000). *About us.* Retrieved (3-4-2000) from http://www.aota.org.

APA (American Psychological Association: Practice Directorate) (1998). *Practicing psychology in hospitals and other health care facilities.* Washington: Author.

APTA (American Physical Therapy Association) (2000). APTA *background sheet* 1999. Retrieved (3-4-2000) from http://www.apta.org.

ARMSTRONG, C. A., SALLIS, J. F., HOVELL, M. F., & HOFSTETTER, C. R. (1992, March). *Predicting exercise adoption: A stages of change analysis.* Paper presented at the meeting of the Society of Behavioral Medicine, New York.

ARNOW, B., KENARDY, J., & AGRAS, W. S. (1992). Binge eating among the obese. *Journal of Behavioral Medicine, 15,* 155–170.

ARROLL, B., & BEAGLEHOLE, R. (1992). Does physical activity lower blood pressure: A critical review of the clinical trials. *Journal of Clinical Epidemiology, 45,* 439–447.

ARY, D. V., & BIGLAN, A. (1988). Longitudinal changes in adolescent cigarette smoking behavior: Onset and cessation. *Journal of Behavioral Medicine, 11,* 361–382.

ARY, D. V., BIGLAN, A., GLASGOW, R., ZOREF, L., et al. (1990). The efficacy of social-influence prevention programs versus "standard care": Are new initiatives needed? *Journal of Behavioral Medicine, 13,* 281–296.

ASHBURN, S. S. (1986). Biophysical development of the toddler and the preschooler. In C. S. SCHUSTER & S. S. ASHBURN (Eds.), *The process of human development: A holistic life-span approach* (2nd ed.). Boston: Little, Brown.

ASHLEY, M. J., & RANKIN, J. G. (1988). A public health approach to the prevention of alcohol-related health problems. *Annual Review of Public Health, 9,* 233–271.

ASHTON, H., & STEPNEY, R. (1982). *Smoking: Psychology and pharmacology.* London: Tavistock.

ASKEVOLD, F. (1975). Measuring body image. *Psychotherapy and Psychosomatics, 26,* 71–77.

ASTIN, J. A. (1998). Why patients use alternative medicine: Results of a national study. *Journal of the American Medical Association, 279,* 1548–1553.

ATIS (HIV/AIDS Treatment Information Service). (2000). *Guidelines for the use of antiretroviral agents in HIV-infected adults and adolescents.* Retrieved (8-14-2000) from http://www.hivatis.org.

ATKINS, E., SOLOMON, L. J., WORDEN, J. K., & FOSTER, R. S. (1991). Relative effectiveness of methods of breast self-examination. *Journal of Behavioral Medicine, 14,* 357–367.

ATTANASIO, V., ANDRASIK, F., BURKE, E. J., BLAKE, D. D., KABELA, E., & McCARRAN, M. S. (1985). Clinical issues in utilizing biofeedback with children. *Clinical Biofeedback and Health, 8,* 134–141.

ATTIE, I., & BROOKS-GUNN, J. (1987). Weight concerns as chronic stressors in women. In R. C. BARNETT, L. BIENER, & G. K. BARUCH (Eds.), *Gender and Stress.* New York: Free Press.

AUDRAIN, J., RIMER, B., CELLA, D., STEFANEK, M., GARBER, J., PENNANEN, M., HELZLSOUER, K., VOGEL, V., LIN, T. H., & LERMAN, C. (1999). The impact of a brief coping skills intervention on adherence to breast self-examination among first-degree relatives of newly diagnosed breast cancer patients. *Psycho-Oncology, 8,* 220–229.

AUERBACH, S. M., MARTELLI, M. F., & MERCURI, L. G. (1983). Anxiety, information, interpersonal impacts, and adjustment to a stressful health care situation. *Journal of Personality and Social Psychology, 44,* 1284–1296.

AVERILL, J. R. (1973). Personal control over aversive stimuli and its relationship to stress. *Psychological Bulletin, 80,* 286–303.

AZAR, B. (1994, November). Eating fat: Why does the brain say, "Ahhh"? *American Psychological Association Monitor,* p. 20.

BABYAK, M., BLUMENTHAL, J. A., HERMAN, S., KHATRI, P., DORAISWAMY, M., MOORE, K., CRAIGHEAD, W. E., BALDEWICZ, T. T., & KRISHNAN, K. R. (2000). Exercise treatment for major depression: Maintenance of therapeutic benefit at 10 months. *Psychosomatic Medicine, 62,* 633–638.

BAER, J. S., HOLT, C. S., & LICHTENSTEIN, E. (1986). Self-efficacy and smoking reexamined: Construct validity and clinical utility. *Journal of Consulting and Clinical Psychology, 54,* 846–852.

BAER, P. E., GARMEZY, L. B., McLAUGHLIN, R. J., POKORNY, A. D., & WERNICK, M. J. (1987). Stress, coping, family conflict, and adolescent alcohol use. *Journal of Behavioral Medicine, 10,* 449–466.

BAGOZZI, R. P. (1981). Attitudes, intentions, and behavior: A test of some key hypotheses. *Journal of Personality and Social Psychology, 41,* 606–627.

BAINES, D. R. (1992). Issues in cultural sensitivity: Examples from the Indian peoples. In D. M. BECKER, D. R. HILL, J. S. JACKSON, D. M. LEVINE, F. A. STILLMAN, & S. M. WEISS (Eds.), *Health behavior research in minority populations: Access, design, and implementation.* Bethesda, MD: National Heart, Lung, and Blood Institute.

BAKAL, D. A. (1979). *Psychology and medicine: Psychological dimensions of health and illness.* New York: Springer.

BAKER, E. L. (1988). Organic solvent neurotoxicity. *Annual Review of Public Health, 9,* 223–232.

BAKER, R. (1989, January 29). The cholesterol thing. *New York Times,* p. A31.

BALL, J. F. (1976–1977). Widow's grief: The impact of age and mode of health. *Omega, 7,* 307–333.

BANDURA, A. (1965a). Influence of model's reinforcement contingencies on the acquisition of imitative responses. *Journal of Personality and Social Psychology, 1,* 589–595.

BANDURA, A. (1965b). Vicarious processes: A case of no-trial learning. In L. BERKOWITZ (Ed.), *Advances in experimental social psychology* (Vol. 2). New York: Academic Press.

BANDURA, A. (1969). *Principles of behavior modification.* New York: Holt, Rinehart & Winston.

BANDURA, A. (1977). Self-efficacy: Toward a unifying theory of behavioral change. *Psychological Review, 84,* 191–215.

BANDURA, A. (1986). *Social foundations of thought and action: A social cognitive theory.* Englewood Cliffs, NJ: Prentice-Hall.

BANDURA, A., O'LEARY, A., TAYLOR, C. B., GAUTHIER, J., & GOSSARD, D. (1987). Perceived self-efficacy and pain control: Opioid and nonopioid mechanisms. *Journal of Personality and Social Psychology, 53,* 563–571.

BANDURA, A., REESE, L., & ADAMS, N. E. (1982). Microanalysis of action and fear arousal as a function of differential levels of perceived self-efficacy. *Journal of Personality and Social Psychology, 43,* 5–21.

BANDURA, A., TAYLOR, C. B., WILLIAMS, S. L., MEFFORD, I. N., & BARCHAS, J. D. (1985). Catecholamine secretion as a function of perceived coping self-efficacy. *Journal of Consulting and Clinical Psychology, 53,* 406–414.

BANKS, S. M., SALOVEY, P., GREENER, S., ROTHMAN, A. J., MOYER, A., BEAUVAIS, J., & EPPEL, E. (1995). The effects of message framing on mammography utilization. *Health Psychology, 14,* 178–184.

BARANOWSKI, T., & HEARN, M. D. (1997). Health behavior interventions with families. In D. S. GOCHMAN (Ed.), *Handbook of health behavior research IV: Relevance for professionals and issues for the future* (pp. 303–323). New York: Plenum.

BARANOWSKI, T., & NADER, P. R. (1985). Family health behavior. In D. C. TURK & R. D. KERNS (Eds.), *Health, illness, and families: A life-span perspective.* New York: Wiley.

BARBER, J. (1986). Hypnotic analgesia. In A. D. HOLZMAN & D. C. TURK (Eds.), *Pain management: A handbook of psychological treatment approaches.* New York: Pergamon.

BARBER, T. X. (1982). Hypnosuggestive procedures in the treatment of clinical pain: Implications for theories of hypnosis and suggestive therapy. In T. MILLON, C. J. GREEN, & R. B. MEAGHER (Eds.), *Handbook of clinical health psychology.* New York: Plenum.

BARDO, M. T., & RISNER, M. E. (1985). Biochemical substrates of drug abuse. In M. GALIZIO & S. A. MAISTO (Eds.), *Determinants of substance abuse: Biological, psychological, and environmental factors.* New York: Plenum.

BAREFOOT, J. C., DAHLSTROM, W. G., & WILLIAMS, R. B. (1983). Hostility, CHD incidence and total mortality: A 25-year follow-up study of 255 physicians. *Psychosomatic Medicine, 45,* 559–563.

BARINA, M. (1995). "Obese" protein slims mice. *Science, 269,* 475–476.

BARNES, V. A., TREIBER, F. A., TURNER, R., DAVIS, H., & STRONG, W. B. (1999). Acute effects of transcendental meditation on hemodynamic functioning in middle-aged adults. *Psychosomatic Medicine, 61,* 525–531.

BARON, R. A. (1986). *Behavior in organizations: Understanding and managing the human side of work* (2nd ed.). Boston: Allyn & Bacon.

BARRETT, R. J. (1985). Behavioral approaches to individual differences in substance abuse. In M. GALIZIO & S. A. MAISTO (Eds.), *Determinants of substance abuse: Biological, psychological, and environmental factors.* New York: Plenum.

BARSKY, A. J., & KLERMAN, G. L. (1983). Overview: Hypochondriasis, bodily complaints, and somatic styles. *American Journal of Psychiatry, 140,* 273–283.

BARTON, J., CHASSIN, L., PRESSON, C. C., & SHERMAN, S. J. (1982). Social image factors as motivators of smoking initiation in early and middle adolescence. *Child Development, 53,* 1499–1511.

BASTONE, E. C., & KERNS, R. D. (1995). Effects of self-efficacy and perceived social support on recovery-related behaviors after coronary artery bypass graft surgery. *Annals of Behavioral Medicine, 17,* 324–330.

BAUM, A. (1988, April). Disasters, natural & otherwise. *Psychology Today,* pp. 56–60.

BAUM, A. (1990). Stress, intrusive imagery, and chronic distress. *Health Psychology, 9,* 653–675.

BAUM, A. (1994). Behavioral, biological, and environmental interactions in disease processes. In S. J. BLUMENTHAL, K. MATTHEWS, & S. M. WEISS (Eds.), *New research frontiers in behavioral medicine: Proceedings of the national conference*. Washington: U.S. Government Printing Office.

BAUM, A., AIELLO, J. R., & CALESNICK, L. E. (1978). Crowding and personal control: Social density and the development of learned helplessness. *Journal of Personality and Social Psychology, 36*, 1000–1011.

BAUM, A., & GATCHEL, R. J. (1981). Cognitive determinants of reaction to uncontrollable events: Development of reactance and learned helplessness. *Journal of Personality and Social Psychology, 40*, 1078–1089.

BAUM, A., GRUNBERG, N. E., & SINGER, J. E. (1982). The use of physiological and neuroendocrinological measurements in the study of stress. *Health Psychology, 1*, 217–236.

BAUMANN, L.J., & LEVENTHAL, H. (1985). "I can tell when my blood pressure is up, can't I?" *Health Psychology, 4*, 203–218.

BEACH, D. L., & MAYER, J. A. (1990). The effects of social demand on breast self-examination self-report. *Journal of Behavioral Medicine, 13*, 195–205.

BEAN-BAYOG, M. (1991). Alcoholics anonymous. In D. A. CIRAULO & R. I. SHADER (Eds.), *Clinical manual of chemical dependence*. Washington, DC: American Psychiatric Press.

BECK, A. T. (1976). *Cognitive therapy and the emotional disorders*. New York: International Universities Press.

BECK, A. T., FREEMAN, A., & ASSOCIATES. (1990). *Cognitive therapy of personality disorders*. New York: Guilford.

BECK, A. T., & SHAW, B. F. (1977). Cognitive approaches to depression. In A. ELLIS & R. GRIEGER (Eds.), *Handbook of rational-emotive therapy*. New York: Springer.

BECK, M., SPRINGEN, K., BEACHY, L., HAGER, M., & BUCKLEY, L. (1990, April 30). The losing formula. *Newsweek*, pp. 52–58.

BECK, R., & FERNANDEZ, E. (1998). Cognitive-behavioral therapy in the treatment of anger: A meta-analysis. *Cognitive Therapy and Research, 22*, 63–74.

BECKER, M. H. (1979). Understanding patient compliance: The contributions of attitudes and other psychosocial factors. In S. J. COHEN (Ed.), *New directions in patient compliance*. Lexington, MA: Heath.

BECKER, M. H. (1990). In hot pursuit of health promotion: Some admonitions. In S. M. WEISS, J. E. FIELDING, & A. BAUM (Eds.), *Perspectives in behavioral medicine: Health at work*. Hillsdale, NJ: Erlbaum.

BECKER, M. H., MAIMAN, L. A., KIRSCHT, J. P., HAEFNER, D. P., & DRACHMAN, R. H. (1977). The health belief model and prediction of dietary compliance: A field experiment. *Journal of Health and Social Behavior, 18*, 348–366.

BECKER, M. H., & ROSENSTOCK, I. M. (1984). Compliance with medical advice. In A. STEPTOE & A. MATHEWS (Eds.), *Health care and human behaviour*. London: Academic Press.

BEECHER, H. K. (1956). Relationship of significance of wound to pain experienced. *Journal of the American Medical Association, 161*, 1609–1613.

BEGLEY, S. (1994, February 7). One pill makes you larger, and one pill makes you small. *Newsweek*, pp. 36–40.

BEGLIN, S. J., & FAIRBURN, C. G. (1992). Women who choose not to participate in surveys on eating disorders. *International Journal of Eating Disorders, 12*, 113–116.

BEKKERS, M. J. T. M., VAN KNIPPENBERG, F. C. E., VAN DEN BORNE, H. W., POEN, H., BERGSMA, J., & VANBERGEHENEGOUWEN, G. P. (1995). Psychosocial adaptation to stoma surgery: A review. *Journal of Behavioral Medicine, 18*, 1–31.

BELAR, C. D. (1988). Education in behavioral medicine: Perspectives from psychology. *Annals of Behavioral Medicine, 10*, 11–14.

BELAR, C. D. (1991). Issues in training clinical health psychologists. In M. A. JANSEN & J. WEINMAN (Eds.), *The international development of health psychology*. Chur, Switzerland: Harwood.

BELAR, C. D. (1997). Clinical health psychology: A specialty for the 21st century. *Health Psychology, 16*, 411–416.

BELLOC, N. B., & BRESLOW, L. (1972). Relationship of physical health status and health practices. *Preventive Medicine, 1*, 409–421.

BELLUCK, P. (1996, May 9). Mingling two worlds of medicine. *New York Times*, pp. B1, 4.

BENGSTON, V. L., CUELLAR, J. B., & RAGAN, P. K. (1977). Stratum contrasts and similarities in attitudes toward death. *Journal of Gerontology, 32*, 76–88.

BENIGHT, C. C., ANTONI, M. H., KILBOURN, K., IRONSON, G., KUMAR, M. A., FLETCHER, M. A., REDWINE, L., BAUM, A., & SCHNEIDERMAN, N. (1997). Coping self-efficacy buffers psychological and physiological disturbances in HIV-infected men following a natural disaster. *Health Psychology, 16*, 248–255.

BENJAMINI, S., SUNSHINE, G., & LESKOWITZ, S. (1996). *Immunology: A short course* (3rd ed.). New York: Wiley.

BENNETT, H. L. (1989, Fall/Winter). Report of the First International Symposium on Memory and Awareness in Anaesthesia. *Health Psychologist*, pp. 3–4.

BENNETT, W., & GURIN, J. (1982). *The dieter's dilemma: Eating less and weighing more*. New York: Basic Books.

BENNETT, W. I. (1987, December 13). Monitoring drugs for the aged. *New York Times Magazine*, pp. 73–74.

BENOLIEL, J. Q. (1977). Nurses and the human experience of dying. In H. FEIFEL (Ed.), *New meanings of death*. New York: McGraw-Hill.

BENSCHOP, R. J., GEENEN, R., MILLS, P. J., NALIBOFF, B. D. et al. (1998). Cardiovascular and immune responses to acute psychological stress in young and old women. *Psychosomatic Medicine, 60,* 290–296.

BENSON, H. (1984). The relaxation response and stress. In J. D. MATARAZZO, S. M. WEISS, J. A. HERD, N. E. MILLER, & S. M. WEISS (Eds.), *Behavioral health: A handbook of health enhancement and disease prevention.* New York: Wiley.

BENSON, H. (1991). Mind/body interactions including Tibetan studies. In THE DALAI LAMA, H. BENSON, R. A. F. THURMAN, H. E. GARDNER, & D. GOLEMAN (Eds.), *Mindscience: An East-West dialogue.* Boston: Wisdom.

BENSON, H., MALHOTRA, M. S., GOLDMAN, R. F., JACOBS, G. D., & HOPKINS, P. J. (1990). Three case reports of the metabolic and electroencephalographic changes during advanced Buddhist meditation techniques. *Behavioral Medicine, 16,* 90–94.

BENSOUSSAN, A., TALLEY, N. J., HING, M., MENZIES, R., GUO, A., & NGU, M. (1998). Treatment of irritable bowel syndrome with Chinese herbal medicine: A randomized controlled trial. *Journal of the American Medical Association, 280,* 1585–1589.

BENTLER, P. M., & SPECKART, G. (1979). Models of attitude-behavior relations. *Psychological Review, 86,* 452–464.

BERGMAN, L. R., & MAGNUSSON, D. (1986). Type A behavior: A longitudinal study from childhood to adulthood. *Psychosomatic Medicine, 48,* 134–142.

BERKMAN, L. F. (1995). The role of social relations in health promotion. *Psychosomatic Medicine, 57,* 245–254.

BERKMAN, L. F., & SYME, S. L. (1979). Social networks, host resistance, and mortality: A nine-year follow-up study of Alameda County residents. *American Journal of Epidemiology, 109,* 186–204.

BERTALANFFY, L. VON (1968). *General systems theory.* New York: Braziller.

BEST, D. L., DAVIS, S. W., VAZ, R. M., & KAISER, M. (1996). Testicular cancer education: A comparison of teaching methods. *American Journal of Health Behavior, 20,* 229–241.

BEST, J. A., THOMSON, S. J., SANTI, S. M., SMITH, E. A., & BROWN, K. S. (1988). Preventing cigarette smoking among school children. *Annual Review of Psychology, 9,* 161–201.

BEZKOR, M. F., & LEE, M. H. M. (1999). Alternative medicine and its relationship to rehabilitation. In M. G. EISENBERG, R. L. GLUECKAUF, & H. H. ZARETSKY (Eds.), *Medical aspects of disability: A handbook for the rehabilitation professional* (2nd ed., pp. 587–597). New York: Springer.

BIBACE, R., & WALSH, M. E. (1979). Developmental stages in children's conceptions of illness. In G. C. STONE, F. COHEN, & N. E. ADLER (Eds.), *Health psychology—A handbook.* San Francisco: Jossey-Bass.

BIENER, L., GLANZ, K., McLERRAN, D., SORENSEN, G., THOMPSON, B., BASEN-ENGQUIST, K., LINNAN, L., & VARNES, J. (1999). Impact of the Working Well Trial on the worksite smoking and nutrition environment. *Health Education and Behavior, 26,* 478–494.

BIGLAN, A., McCONNELL, S., SEVERSON, H. H., BAVRY, J., & ARY, D. (1984). A situational analysis of adolescent smoking. *Journal of Behavioral Medicine, 7,* 109–114.

BIGLAN, A., SEVERSON, H., ARY, D., FALLER, C., GALLISON, C., THOMPSON, R., GLASGOW, R., & LICHTENSTEIN, E. (1987). Do smoking prevention programs really work? Attrition and the internal and external validity of an evaluation of a refusal skills training program. *Journal of Behavioral Medicine, 10,* 159–171.

BILLINGS, A. G., & MOOS, R. H. (1981). The role of coping responses and social resources in attenuating the stress of life events. *Journal of Behavioral Medicine, 4,* 139–157.

BIONDI, M., & PANCHERI, P. (1995). Clinical research strategies in psychoimmunology: A review of 46 human research studies (1972–1992). In B. LEONARD & K. MILLER (Eds.), *Stress, the immune system and psychiatry.* New York: Wiley.

BIRREN, J. E., & ZARIT, J. M. (1985). Concepts of health, behavior, and aging. In J. E. BIRREN & J. LIVINGSTON (Eds.), *Cognition, stress, and aging.* Englewood Cliffs, NJ: Prentice-Hall.

BISHOP, G. D., & CONVERSE, S. A. (1986). Illness representations: A prototype approach. *Health Psychology, 5,* 95–114.

BLACK, F. L. (1992). Why did they die? *Science, 258,* 1739–1740.

BLACKBURN, H., LUEPKER, R., KLINE, F. G., BRACHT, N., CARLAW, R., JACOBS, D., MITTELMARK, M., STAUFFER, L., & TAYLOR, H. L. (1984). The Minnesota Heart Health Program: A research and demonstration project in cardiovascular disease prevention. In J. D. MATARAZZO, S. M. WEISS, J. A. HERD, N. E. MILLER, & S. M. WEISS (Eds.), *Behavioral health: A handbook of health enhancement and disease prevention.* New York: Wiley.

BLACKHALL, L. J., MURPHY, S. T., FRANK, G., MICHEL, V., & AZEN, S. (1995). Ethnicity and attitudes toward patient autonomy. *Journal of the American Medical Association, 274,* 820–825.

BLAIR, S. N., & BRODNEY, S. (1999). Effects of physical inactivity and obesity on morbidity and mortality: Current evidence and research issues. *Medicine and Science in Sports and Exercise, 31*(Suppl.), S646–S662.

BLAIR, S. N., KOHL, H. W., GORDON, N. F., & PAFFENBARGER, R. S. (1992). How much physical activity is good for health? *Annual review of public health, 13,* 99–126.

BLAKESLEE, S. (1994, April). Black smokers' higher risk of cancer may be genetic. *New York Times,* p. C14.

BLAKEY, R., & BAKER, R. (1980). An exposure approach to alcohol abuse. *Behaviour Research and Therapy*, 18, 319–325.

BLANCHARD, E. B. (1987). Long-term effects of behavioral treatment of chronic headache. *Behavior Therapy*, 18, 375–385.

BLANCHARD, E. B., & ANDRASIK, F. (1985). *Management of chronic headaches: A psychological approach*. New York: Pergamon.

BLANCHARD, E. B., ANDRASIK, F., APPELBAUM, K. A., EVANS, D. D., MYERS, P., & BARRON, K. D. (1986). Three studies of the psychologic changes in chronic headache patients associated with biofeedback and relaxation therapies. *Psychosomatic Medicine*, 48, 73–83.

BLANCHARD, E. B., ANDRASIK, F., GUARNIERI, P., NEFF, D. F., & RODICHOK, L. D. (1987). Two-, three-, and four-year follow-up on the self-regulatory treatment of chronic headache. *Journal of Consulting and Clinical Psychology*, 55, 257–259.

BLANCHARD, E. B., APPELBAUM, K. A., GUARNIERI, P., MORRILL, B., & DENTINGER, M. P. (1987). Five year prospective follow-up on the treatment of chronic headache with biofeedback and/or relaxation. *Headache*, 27, 580–583.

BLANCHARD, E. B., MCCOY, G. C., WITTROCK, D., MUSSO, A., GERARDI, R. J., & PANGBURN, L. (1988). A controlled comparison of thermal biofeedback and relaxation training in the treatment of essential hypertension: II. Effects on cardiovascular reactivity. *Health Psychology*, 7, 19–33.

BLAND, S. H., O'LEARY, E. S., FARINARO, E., JOSSA, F., KROGH, V., VIOLANTI, J. M., & TREVISAN, M. (1997). Social network disturbances and psychological distress following earthquake evacuations. *Journal of Nervous and Mental Disease*, 185, 188–194.

BLAND, S. H., O'LEARY, E. S., FARINARO, E., JOSSA, F., & TREVISAN, M. (1996). Long-term psychological effects of natural disasters. *Psychosomatic Medicine*, 58, 18–24.

BLANEY, P. H. (1985). Psychological considerations in cancer. In N. SCHNEIDERMAN & J. T. TAPP (Eds.), *Behavioral medicine: The biopsychosocial approach*. Hillsdale, NJ: Erlbaum.

BLANTON, H., & GERRARD, M. (1997). Effect of sexual motivation on men's risk perception for sexually transmitted disease: There must be 50 ways to justify a lover. *Health Psychology*, 16, 374–379.

BLECHMAN, E. (1983). Behavioral medicine and women's health issues: Responding to the challenges of biological events. *Behavioral Medicine Update*, 5, 7–10.

BLEIBERG, J. (1986). Psychological and neuropsychological factors in stroke management. In P. E. KAPLAN & L. J. CERULLO (Eds.), *Stroke rehabilitation*. Boston: Butterworth.

BLEIBERG, J., CIULLA, R., & KATZ, B. I. (1991). Psychological components of rehabilitation programs for brain-injured and spinal-cord-injured patients. In J. J. SWEET, R. H. ROZENSKY, & S. M. TOVIAN (Eds.), *Handbook of clinical psychology in medical settings*. New York: Plenum.

BLOCK, A. R., KREMER, E., & GAYLOR, M. (1980). Behavioral treatment of chronic pain: The spouse as a discriminative cue for pain behavior. *Pain*, 9, 243–252.

BLOCK, J. H. (1983). Differential premises arising from differential socialization of the sexes: Some conjectures. *Child Development*, 54, 1335–1354.

BLOOM, F. E., LAZERSON, A., & HOFSTADTER, L. (1985). *Brain, mind, and behavior*. New York: Freeman.

BLOOM, J. R., KANG, S. H., & ROMANO, P. (1991). Cancer and stress: The effect of social support as a resource. In C. L. COOPER & M. WATSON (Eds.), *Cancer and stress: Psychological, biological and coping studies*. Chichester: Wiley.

BLOOM, J. W., KALTENBORN, W. T., PAOLETTI, P., CAMILLI, A., & LEBOWITZ, M. D. (1987). Respiratory effects of non-tobacco cigarettes. *British Medical Journal*, 295, 1516–1518.

BLUEBOND-LANGNER, M. (1977). Meanings of death to children. In H. FEIFEL (Ed.), *New meanings of death*. New York: McGraw-Hill.

BLUMENTHAL, J. A., & MCCUBBIN, J. A. (1987). Physical exercise as stress management. In A. BAUM & J. E. SINGER (Eds.), *Handbook of psychology and health* (Vol. 5). Hillsdale, NJ: Erlbaum.

BLUMENTHAL, J. A., WILLIAMS, R. S., NEEDELS, T. L., & WALLACE, A. G. (1982). Psychological changes accompany aerobic exercise in healthy middle-aged adults. *Psychosomatic Medicine*, 44, 529–536.

BLUMENTHAL, J. A., WILLIAMS, R. S., WALLACE, A. G., WILLIAMS, R. B., & NEEDLES, T. L. (1982). Physiological and psychological variables predict compliance to prescribed exercise therapy in patients recovering from myocardial infarction. *Psychosomatic Medicine*, 44, 519–527.

BLUMER, D., & HEILBRONN, M. (1982). Chronic pain as a variant of depressive disease: The pain-prone disorder. *Journal of Nervous and Mental Disease*, 170, 381–406.

BODMER, W. F., BAILEY, C. J., BODMER, J., BUSSEY, H. J. R., et al. (1987). Localization of the gene for familial adenomatous polyposis on chromosome 5. *Nature*, 328, 614–616.

BODNAR, R. J. (1998). Pain. In E. A. BLECHMAN & K. D. BROWNELL (Eds.), *Behavioral medicine and women: A comprehensive handbook* (pp. 695–699). New York: Guilford.

BOFFEY, P. M. (1987, April 16). Gains against cancer since 1950 are overstated, Congress is told. *New York Times*, pp. A1, B10.

BOGAARDS, M. C., & TER KUILE, M. M. (1994). Treatment of recurrent tension headache: A meta-analytic review. *Clinical Journal of Pain*, 10, 174–190.

Bohm, L. C., & Rodin, J. (1985). Aging and the family. In D. C. Turk & R. D. Kerns (Eds.), *Health, illness, and families: A life-span perspective*. New York: Wiley.

Bond, G. G., Aiken, L. S., & Somerville, S. C. (1992). The health belief model and adolescents with insulin-dependent diabetes mellitus. *Health Psychology, 11*, 190–198.

Booth-Kewley, S., & Friedman, H. S. (1987). Psychological predictors of heart disease: A quantitative review. *Psychological Bulletin, 101*, 343–362.

Borysenko, J. (1984). Stress, coping, and the immune system. In J. D. Matarazzo, S. M. Weiss, J. A. Herd, N. E. Miller, & S. M. Weiss (Eds.), *Behavioral health: A handbook of health enhancement and disease prevention*. New York: Wiley.

Boscarino, J. A. (1997). Diseases among men 20 years after exposure to severe stress: Implications for clinical research and medical care. *Psychosomatic Medicine, 59*, 605–614.

Bosma, H., Peter, R., Siegrist, J., & Marmot, M. (1998). Two alternative job stress models and the risk of coronary heart disease. *American Journal of Public Health, 88*, 68–74.

Botvin, G. J., & Epstein, J. A. (1999). Preventing cigarette smoking among children and adolescents. In D. F. Seidman & L. S. Covey (Eds.), *Helping the hard-core smoker: A clinician's guide* (pp. 51–71). Mahwah, NJ: Erlbaum.

Botvin, G. J., Renick, N. L., & Baker, E. (1983). The effects of scheduling format and booster sessions on a broad-spectrum psychosocial approach to smoking prevention. *Journal of Behavioral Medicine, 6*, 359–379.

Botvin, G. J., & Wills, T. A. (1985). Personal and social skills training: Cognitive-behavioral approaches to substance abuse prevention. In C. S. Bell & R. Battjes (Eds.), *Prevention research: Deterring drug abuse among children and adolescents* (NIDA Research Monograph 63). Washington, DC: U.S. Government Printing Office.

Bouton, K. (1990, August 5). Painful decisions: The role of the medical ethicist. *New York Times Magazine*, pp. 22–25, 53, 65.

Bovbjerg, D. H., Redd, W. H., Jacobsen, P. B., Manne, S. L., et al. (1992). An experimental analysis of classically conditioned nausea during cancer chemotherapy. *Psychosomatic Medicine, 54*, 623–637.

Bovbjerg, V. E., McCann, B. S., Retzlaff, B. M., Walden, C. E., & Knopp, R. H. (1999). Effect of cholesterol-lowering diets on indices of depression and hostility. *Annals of Behavioral Medicine, 21*, 98–101.

Bove, G. & Nilsson, N. (1998). Spinal manipulation in the treatment of episodic tension-type headache. *Journal of the American Medical Association, 280*, 1576–1579.

Bowen, A. M., & Trotter, R. (1995). HIV risk in intravenous drug users and crack cocaine smokers: Predicting stage of change for condom use. *Journal of Consulting and Clinical Psychology, 63*, 238–248.

Bowlby, J. (1969). *Attachment and loss. Vol. 1: Attachment*. New York: Basic Books.

Bowlby, J. (1973). *Attachment and loss. Vol. 2: Separation*. New York: Basic Books.

Bracco, L., Gallato, R., Grigoletto, F., Lippi, A., et al. (1994). Factors affecting the course and survival in Alzheimer's disease. *Archives of Neurology, 51*, 1213–1219.

Bradford, L. P. (1986). Can you survive retirement? In R. H. Moos (Ed.), *Coping with life crises: An integrated approach*. New York: Plenum.

Bradley, G. W. (1993). *Disease, diagnosis, & decisions*. New York: Wiley.

Bradley, L. A. (1994). Pain measurement in arthritis. *Arthritis Care and Research, 6*, 178–186.

Braith, R. W., Pollock, M. L., Lowenthal, D. T., Graves, J. E., & Limacher, M. C. (1994). Moderate- and high-intensity exercise lowers blood pressure in normotensive subjects 60 to 79 years of age. *American Journal of Cardiology, 73*, 1124–1128.

Braitman, L. E., Adlin, E. V., & Stanton, J. L. (1985). Obesity and caloric intake: The National Health and Nutrition Examination Survey of 1971–1975 (HANES I). *Journal of Chronic Diseases, 9*, 727–732.

Brandon, T. H., Collins, B. N., Juliano, L. M., & Lazev, A. B. (2000). Preventing relapse among former smokers: A comparison of minimal interventions through telephone and mail. *Journal of Consulting and Clinical Psychology, 68*, 103–113.

Brandon, T. H., Zelman, D. C., & Baker, T. B. (1987). Effects of maintenance sessions on smoking relapse: Delaying the inevitable? *Journal of Consulting and Clinical Psychology, 55*, 780–782.

Brandsma, J. M., Maultsby, M. C., & Welsh, R. J. (1980). *Outpatient treatment of alcoholism: A review and comparative study*. Baltimore: University Park Press.

Braveman, N. S. (1987). Immunity and aging: Immunologic and behavioral perspectives. In M. W. Riley, J. D. Matarazzo, & A. Baum (Eds.), *Perspectives in behavioral medicine: The aging dimension*. Hillsdale, NJ: Erlbaum.

Bray, G. A. (1984). The role of weight control in health promotion and disease prevention. In J. D. Matarazzo, S. M. Weiss, J. A. Herd, N. E. Miller, & S. M. Weiss (Eds.), *Behavioral health: A handbook of health enhancement and disease prevention*. New York: Wiley.

Brehm, J. W. (1966). *A theory of psychological reactance*. New York: Academic Press.

Brennan, A. F., Barrett, C. L., & Garretson, H. D. (1987). The utility of McGill Pain Questionnaire subscales for discriminating psychological disorder in chronic pain patients. *Psychology and Health*, 1, 257–272.

BRESLOW, L. (1983). The potential of health promotion. In D. MECHANIC (Ed.), *Handbook of health, health care, and the health professions*. New York: Free Press.

BRESLOW, L., & SOMERS, A. R. (1977). The lifetime health-monitoring program. *New England Journal of Medicine*, 296, 601–608.

BRISTOL, J. B., EMMETT, P. M., HEATON, K. W., & WILLIAMSON, R. C. N. (1985). Sugar, fat, and the risk of colorectal cancer. *British Medical Journal*, 291, 1467–1470.

BROADHEAD, W. E., KAPLAN, B. H., JAMES, S. A., WAGNER, E. H., SCHOENBACH, V. J., GRIMSON, R., HEYDEN, S., TIBBLIN, G., & GEHLBACH, S. H. (1983). The epidemiologic evidence for a relationship between social support and health. *American Journal of Epidemiology*, 117, 521–537.

BROADSTOCK, M., BORLAND, R., & GASON, R. (1992). Effects of suntan on judgements of healthiness and attractiveness by adolescents. *Journal of Applied Social Psychology*, 22, 157–172.

BROBERG, D. J., & BERNSTEIN, I. L. (1987). Candy as a scapegoat in the prevention of food aversions in children receiving chemotherapy. *Cancer*, 60, 2344–2347.

BRODY, D. S., MILLER, S. M., LERMAN, C. E., SMITH, D. G., & CAPUTO, G. C. (1989). Patient perception on involvement in medical care: Relationship to illness attitudes and outcomes. *Journal of General Internal Medicine*, 4, 506–511.

BROMAN, C. L. (1993). Social relationships and health-related behavior. *Journal of Behavioral Medicine*, 16, 335–350.

BRONDOLO, E., ROSEN, R. C., KOTSIS, J. B., & SCHWARTZ, J. E. (1999). Relationship of physical symptoms and mood to perceived and actual blood pressure in hypertensive men: A repeated-measures design. *Psychosomatic Medicine*, 61, 311–318.

BROOK, J. S., WHITEMAN, M., GORDON, A. S., & COHEN, P. (1986). Dynamics of childhood and adolescent personality traits and adolescent drug use. *Developmental Psychology*, 22, 403–414.

BROWER, K. J., ELIOPULOS, G. A., BLOW, F. C., CATLIN, D. H., & BERESFORD, T. P. (1990). Evidence for physical and psychological dependence on anabolic steroids in eight weight lifters. *American Journal of Psychiatry*, 147, 510–512.

BROWN, J. M., O'KEEFFE, J., SANDERS, S. H., & BAKER, B. (1986). Developmental changes in children's cognition to stressful and painful situations. *Journal of Pediatric Psychology*, 11, 343–357.

BROWNELL, K. D. (1982). Obesity: Understanding and treating a serious, prevalent, and refractory disorder. *Journal of Consulting and Clinical Psychology*, 50, 820–840.

BROWNELL, K. D. (1986a). Public health approaches to obesity and its management. *Annual Review of Public Health*, 7, 521–533.

BROWNELL, K. D. (1986b). Social and behavioral aspects of obesity in children. In N. A. KRASNEGOR, J. D. ARASTEH, & M. F. CATALDO (Eds.), *Child health behavior: A behavioral pediatrics perspective*. New York: Wiley.

BROWNELL, K. D. (1988, January). Yo-yo dieting. *Psychology Today*, pp. 20–23.

BROWNELL, K. D. (1989, June). When and how to diet. *Psychology Today*, pp. 40–46.

BROWNELL, K. D. (1991). Personal responsibility and control over our bodies: When expectation exceeds reality. *Health Psychology*, 10, 303–310.

BROWNELL, K. D., COHEN, R. Y., STUNKARD, A. J., FELIX, M. R. J., & COOLEY, N. B. (1984). Weight loss competitions at the work site: Impact on weight, morale and cost-effectiveness. *American Journal of Public Health*, 74, 1283–1285.

BROWNELL, K. D., MARLATT, G. A., LICHTENSTEIN, E., & WILSON, G. T. (1986). Understanding and preventing relapse. *American Psychologist*, 41, 765–782.

BROWNELL, K. D., & WADDEN, T. A. (1991). The heterogeneity of obesity: Fitting treatments to individuals. *Behavior Therapy*, 22, 153–177.

BRUBAKER, R. G., & WICKERSHAM, D. (1990). Encouraging the practice of testicular self-examination: A field application of the theory of reasoned action. *Health Psychology*, 9, 154–163.

BRUCKER, B. S. (1983). Spinal cord injuries. In T. G. BURISH & L. A. BRADLEY (Eds.), *Coping with chronic disease: Research and applications*. New York: Academic Press.

BRUEHL, S., CARLSON, C. R., WILSON, J. F., NORTON, J. A., COLCLOUGH, G., BRADY, M. J., SHERMAN, J. J., & McCUBBIN, J. A. (1996). Psychological coping with acute pain: An examination of the role of endogeneous opioid mechanisms. *Journal of Behavioral Medicine*, 19, 129–141.

BRUEHL, S., McCUBBIN, J. A., & HARDEN, R. N. (1999). Theoretical review: Altered pain regulatory systems in chronic pain. *Neuroscience and Biobehavioral Reviews*, 23, 877–890.

BRUHN, J. G., & PHILLIPS, B. U. (1987). A developmental basis for social support. *Journal of Behavioral Medicine*, 10, 213–229.

BRUNNER, E., WHITE, I., THOROGOOD, M., BRISTOW, A., CURLE, D., & MARMOT, M. (1997). Can dietary interventions change diet and cardiovascular risk factors? A meta-analysis of randomized controlled trials. *American Journal of Public Health*, 87, 1415–1422.

BRUVOLD, W. H. (1993). A meta-analysis of adolescent smoking prevention programs. *American Journal of Public Health*, 83, 872–880.

BRYER, K. B. (1986). The Amish way of death: A study of family support systems. In R. H. Moos (Ed.), *Coping with life crises: An integrated approach*. New York: Plenum.

BUCHNER, D. M., BERESFORD, S. A. A., LARSON, E. B., LaCROIX, A. Z., & WAGNER, E. H. (1992). Effects of physical activity on health status in older adults II: Intervention studies. *Annual Review of Public Health*, 13, 469–488.

BUCK, R. (1988). *Human motivation and emotion* (2nd ed.). New York: Wiley.

BUDZYNSKI, T. H., STOYVA, J. M., ADLER, C. S., & MULLANEY, D. J. (1973). EMG biofeedback and tension headache: A controlled outcome study. *Psychosomatic Medicine*, 35, 484–496.

BULCOURF, B. B., UNROD, M. E., & ADAMS, S. G. (1996, March). *Daily stress and upper respiratory illness*. Paper presented at the meeting of the Society of Behavioral Medicine in Washington.

BULLOCK, K. D., REED, R. J., & GRANT, I. (1992). Reduced mortality risk in alcoholics who achieve long-term abstinence. *Journal of the American Medical Association*, 267, 668–672.

BULMAN, R. J., & WORTMAN, C. B. (1977). Attributions of blame and coping in the "real world": Severe accident victims react to their lot. *Journal of Personality and Social Psychology*, 35, 351–363.

BUNDY, C., CARROLL, D., WALLACE, L., & NAGLE, R. (1994). Psychological treatment of chronic stable angina pectoris. *Psychology and Health*, 10, 69–77.

BURBACH, D. J., & PETERSON, L. (1986). Children's concepts of physical illness: A review and critique of the cognitive-developmental literature. *Health Psychology*, 5, 307–325.

BURG, I. N., & INGALL, C. G. (1985). The immune system. In L. L. HAYMAN & E. M. SPORING (Eds.), *Handbook of pediatric nursing*. New York: Wiley.

BURG, M. M., & SEEMAN, T. E. (1994). Families and health: The negative side of social ties. *Annals of Behavioral Medicine*, 16, 109–115.

BURISH, T. G., & JENKINS, R. A. (1992). Effectiveness of biofeedback and relaxation training in reducing the side effects of cancer chemotherapy. *Health Psychology*, 11, 17–23.

BURISH, T. G., MEYEROWITZ, B. E., CAREY, M. P., & MORROW, G. R. (1987). The stressful effects of cancer in adults. In A. BAUM & J. E. SINGER (Eds.), *Handbook of psychology and health* (Vol. 5). New York: Erlbaum.

BURKE, L. E., DUNBAR-JACOB, J. M., & HILL, M. N. (1997). Compliance with cardiovascular disease prevention strategies: A review of the research. *Annals of Behavioral Medicine*, 19, 239–263.

BURNETT, K. F., TAYLOR, C. B., & AGRAS, W. S. (1985). Ambulatory computer-assisted therapy for obesity: A new frontier for behavior therapy. *Journal of Consulting and Clinical Psychology*, 53, 698–703.

BURNS, E. M., & ARNOLD, L. E. (1990). Biological aspects of stress: Effects on the developing brain. In L. E. ARNOLD (Ed.), *Childhood stress*. New York: Wiley.

BURNS, J. W., HIGDON, L. J., MULLEN, J. T., LANSKY, D., & WEI, J. M. (1999). Relationships among patient hostility, anger expression, depression, and the working alliance in a work hardening program. *Annals of Behavioral Medicine*, 21, 77–82.

BURNSIDE, I. G., TOBIAS, H. S., & BURSILL, D. (1982). Electromyographic feedback in the remobilization of stroke patients: A controlled trial. *Archives of Physical Medicine and Rehabilitation*, 63, 217–222.

BURROUGHS, B. R., & DIETERLE, P. (1985). The respiratory system. In L. L. HAYMAN & E. M. SPORING (Eds.), *Handbook of pediatric nursing*. New York: Wiley.

BUSH, J. P., & DeLUCA, C. J. (in press). The biopsychosocial construct of pain: Developmental considerations and implications for clinical practice. *Journal of Psychological Practice*.

BUSH, J. P., HOLMBECK, G. N., & COCKRELL, J. L. (1989). Patterns of PRN analgesic drug administration in children following elective surgery. *Journal of Pediatric Psychology*, 14, 433–448.

BUSH, J. P., MELAMED, B. G., SHERAS, P. L., & GREENBAUM, P. E. (1986). Mother-child patterns of coping with anticipatory medical stress. *Health Psychology*, 5, 137–157.

BUSJAHN, A., FAULHABER, H.-D., FREIER, K., & LUFT, F. C. (1999). Genetic and environmental influences on coping styles: A twin study. *Psychosomatic Medicine*, 61, 469–475.

BUSS, A. H., & PLOMIN, R. (1975). *A temperamental theory of personality development*. New York: Wiley.

BUSS, A. H., & PLOMIN, R. (1986). The EAS approach to temperament. In R. PLOMIN & J. DUNN (Eds.), *The study of temperament: Changes, continuities and challenges*. Hillsdale, NJ: Erlbaum.

BUSS, A. R. (1973). An extension of developmental models that separate ontogenetic changes and cohort differences. *Psychological Bulletin*, 80, 466–479.

BUTCHER, J. N., DAHLSTROM, W. G., GRAHAM, J. R., TELLEGEN, A., & KRAEMER, B. (1989). *Minnesota Multiphasic Personality Inventory-2: Manual for administration and scoring*. Minneapolis: University Minnesota Press.

BUTLER, C., & STEPTOE, A. (1986). Placebo responses: An experimental study of psychophysiological processes in asthmatic volunteers. *British Journal of Clinical Psychology*, 25, 173–183.

BYERS, T. E., GRAHAM, S., HAUGHEY, B. P., MARSHALL, J. R., & SWANSON, M. K. (1987). Diet and lung cancer risk: Findings from the Western New York Diet Study. *American Journal of Epidemiology, 125,* 351–363.

BYRNE, D. G., & ROSENMAN, R. H. (1986). The Type A behaviour pattern as a precursor to stressful life-events: A confluence of coronary risks. *British Journal of Medical Psychology, 59,* 75–82.

BYRNE, P. S., & LONG, B. E. L. (1976). *Doctors talking to patients.* London: Her Majesty's Stationery Office.

CACIOPPO, J. T., PETTY, R. E., & MARSHALL-GOODELL, B. (1985). Physical, social, and inferential elements of psychophysiological measurement. In P. KAROLY (Ed.), *Measurement strategies in health psychology.* New York: Wiley.

CACIOPPO, J. T., POEHLMANN, K. M., KIECOLT-GLASER, J. K., MALARKEY, W. B., BURLESON, M. H., BERNTSON, G. G., & GLASER, R. (1998). Cellular immune responses to acute stress in female caregivers of dementia patients and matched controls. *Health Psychology, 17,* 182–189.

CADDY, G. R., & BLOCK, T. (1985). Individual differences in response to treatment. In M. GALIZIO & S. A. MAISTO (Eds.), *Determinants of substance abuse: Biological, psychological, and environmental factors.* New York: Plenum.

CADMAN, D., ROSENBAUM, P., BOYLE, M., & OFFORD, D. R. (1991). Children with chronic illness: Family and parent demographic characteristics and psychosocial adjustment. *Pediatrics, 87,* 884–889.

CAGGIULA, A. R., EPSTEIN, L. H., SIEGEL, S., VEZINA, P., & BOVBJERG, D. (1992, March). *The role of conditioning in chronic drug effects: Implications for theories of drug abuse and therapeutic drug efficacy:* Symposium conducted at the meeting of the Society of Behavioral Medicine, New York.

CAGGIULA, A. W., CHRISTAKIS, G., FARRAND, M., HULLEY, S. B., JOHNSON, R., LASSER, N. L., STAMLER, J., & WIDDOWSON, G. (1981). The Multiple Risk Intervention Trial (MRFIT): IV. Intervention on blood lipids. *Preventive Medicine, 10,* 443–475.

CAH (Center for the Advancement of Health) (1999). *Patients as effective collaborators in managing chronic conditions.* New York: Millibank Memorial Fund.

CAHILL, L., PRINS, B., WEBER, M., & McGAUGH, J. L. (1994). β-adrenergic activation and memory for emotional events. *Nature, 371,* 702–704.

CAIN, E. N., KOHORN, E. I., QUINLAN, D. M., LATIMER, K., & SCHWARTZ, P. E. (1986). Psychosocial benefits of a cancer support group. *Cancer, 57,* 183–189.

CALHOUN, D. A., MUTINGA, M. L., COLLINS, A. S., WYSS, J. M., & OPARIL, S. (1993). Normotensive blacks have heightened sympathetic response to cold pressor test. *Hypertension, 22,* 801–805.

CALHOUN, K. S., & BURNETTE, M. M. (1983). Etiology and treatment of menstrual disorders. *Behavioral Medicine Update, 5*(4), 21–26.

CALIFANO, J. A. (1979). *Healthy people: The Surgeon General's report on health promotion and disease prevention.* Washington, DC: U.S. Government Printing Office.

CALLAHAN, E. J. (1980). Alternative strategies in the treatment of narcotic addiction: A review. In W. R. MILLER (Ed.), *The addictive behaviors: Treatment of alcoholism, drug abuse, smoking, and obesity.* New York: Pergamon.

CALLE, E. E., THUN, M. J., PETRELLI, J. M., RODRÍGUEZ, C., & HEATH, C. W. (1999). Body-mass index and mortality in a prospective cohort of U.S. adults. *New England Journal of Medicine, 341,* 1097–1105.

CAMERON, L., LEVENTHAL, E. A., & LEVENTHAL, H. (1995). Seeking medical care in response to symptoms and life stress. *Psychosomatic Medicine, 57,* 1–11.

CAMERON, R., & SHEPEL, L. F. (1986). The process of psychological consultation in pain management. In A. D. HOLZMAN & D. C. TURK (Eds.), *Pain management: A handbook of psychological treatment approaches.* New York: Pergamon.

CAMPBELL, T., & CHANG, B. (1981). Health care of the Chinese in America. In G. HENDERSON & M. PRIMEAUX (Eds.), *Transcultural health care.* Menlo Park, CA: Addison-Wesley.

CANNON, J. T., PRIETO, G. J., LEE, A., & LIEBESKIND, J. C. (1982). Evidence for opioid and non-opioid forms of stimulation-produced analgesia in the rat. *Brain Research, 243,* 315–321.

CANNON, W. B. (1929). *Bodily changes in pain, hunger, fear and rage* (2nd ed.). New York: Appleton.

CANNON, W. B. (1942). Voodoo death. *American Anthropologist, 44,* 169–181.

CANTOR, M., & LITTLE, V. (1985). Aging and social care. In R. H. BINSTOCK & E. SHANAS (Eds.), *Handbook of aging and the social sciences.* New York: Van Nostrand-Reinhold.

CAPLAN, R. D., COBB, S., & FRENCH, J. R. P. (1975). Relationships of cessation of smoking with job stress, personality, and social support. *Journal of Applied Psychology, 60,* 211–219.

CARELS, R. A., BLUMENTHAL, J. A., & SHERWOOD, A. (1998). Effect of satisfaction with social support on blood pressure in normotensive and borderline hypertensive men and women. *International Journal of Behavioral Medicine, 5,* 76–85.

CAREY, M. P. (1999). Prevention of HIV infection through sexual behavior change: Progress report focusing on downstream, midstream, and upstream strategies. *American Journal of Health Promotion, 14,* 104–111.

CAREY, M. P., BRAATEN, L. S., MAISTO, S. A., GLEASON, J. R., FORSYTH, A. D., DURANT, L. E., & JAWORSKI, B. C. (2000). Using information, motivational enhancement, and skills training to reduce risk of HIV infection for low-income urban women: A second randomized clinical trial. *Health Psychology, 19,* 3–11.

CAREY, M. P., & BURISH, T. G. (1988). Etiology and treatment of the psychological side effects associated with cancer chemotherapy: A critical review and discussion. *Psychological Bulletin*, 104, 307–325.

CAREY, M. P., KALRA, D. L., CAREY, K. B., HALPERIN, S., & RICHARDS, C. S. (1993). Stress and unaided smoking cessation: A prospective investigation. *Journal of Consulting and Clinical Psychology*, 61, 831–838.

CAREY, M. P., MORRISON-BEEDY, D., & JOHNSON, B. T. (1998). The HIV-Knowledge Questionnaire. In C. M. DAVIS, W. L. YARBER, R. BAUSERMAN, G. SCHREER, & S. L. DAVIS (Eds.), *Handbook of sexually related measures* (pp. 313–315). Thousand Oaks, CA: Sage.

CAREY, R. G. (1975). Living until death: A program of service and research for the terminally ill. In E. KÜBLER-ROSS (Ed.), *Death: The final stage of growth*. Englewood Cliffs, NJ: Prentice-Hall.

CAREY, W. B., & McDEVITT, S. C. (1978). Stability and change in individual temperament diagnoses from infancy to early childhood. *Journal of the American Academy of Child Psychiatry*, 17, 331–337.

CARLSON, C. R., & HOYLE, R. H. (1993). Efficacy of abbreviated muscle relaxation training: A quantitative review of behavioral medicine research. *Journal of Consulting and Clinical Psychology*, 61, 1059–1067.

CARMARGO, C. A., VRANIZAN, K. M., THORESEN, C. E., & WOOD, P. D. (1986). Type A behavior pattern and alcohol intake in middle-aged men. *Psychosomatic Medicine*, 48, 575–581.

CARMELLI, D., DAME, A., SWAN, G., & ROSENMAN, R. (1991). Long-term changes in Type A behavior: A 27-year follow-up of the Western Collaborative Group Study. *Journal of Behavioral Medicine*, 14, 593–606.

CARMELLI, D., ROSENMAN, R. H., & CHESNEY, M. A. (1987). Stability of the Type A Structured Interview and related questionnaires in a 10-year follow-up of an adult cohort of twins. *Journal of Behavioral Medicine*, 10, 513–525.

CARMODY, T. P., FEY, S. G., PIERCE, D. K., CONNOR, W. E., & MATARAZZO, J. D. (1982). Behavioral treatment of hyperlipidemia: Techniques, results, and future directions. *Journal of Behavioral Medicine*, 5, 91–116.

CARNEY, R. M., FREEDLAND, K. E., RICH, M. W., & JAFFE, A. S. (1995). Depression as a risk factor for cardiac events in established coronary heart disease: A review of possible mechanisms. *Annals of Behavioral Medicine*, 17, 142–149.

CARNEY, R. M., RICH, M. W., FREEDLAND, K. E., SAINI, J., TEVELDE, A., SIMEONE, C., & CLARK, K. (1988). Major depressive disorder predicts cardiac events in patients with coronary artery disease. *Psychosomatic Medicine*, 50, 627–633.

CARPENTER, D. J., GATCHEL, R. J., & HASEGAWA, T. (1994). Effectiveness of a videotaped behavioral intervention for dental anxiety: The role of gender and need for information. *Behavioral Medicine*, 20, 123–132.

CARR, D. B., BULLEN, B. A., SKRINAR, G. S., ARNOLD, M. A., ROSENBLATT, M., BEITINS, I. Z., MARTIN, J. B., & McARTHUR, J. W. (1981). Physical conditioning facilitates the exercise-induced secretion of beta-endorphin and beta-lipotropin in women. *New England Journal of Medicine*, 305, 560–563.

CARRUTHERS, M. (1983). Instrumental stress tests. In H. SELYE (Ed.), *Selye's guide to stress research* (Vol. 2). New York: Van Nostrand Reinhold.

CARVER, C. S., COLEMAN, A. E., & GLASS, D. C. (1976). The coronary-prone behavior pattern and the suppression of fatigue on a treadmill test. *Journal of Personality and Social Psychology*, 33, 460–466.

CARVER, C. S., DeGREGORIO, E., & GILLIS, R. (1981). Challenge and Type A behavior among intercollegiate football players. *Journal of Sport Psychology*, 3, 140–148.

CARVER, C. S., DIAMOND, E. L., & HUMPHRIES, C. (1985). Coronary prone behavior. In N. SCHNEIDERMAN & J. T. TAPP (Eds.), *Behavioral medicine: The biopsychosocial approach*. Hillsdale, NJ: Erlbaum.

CASTRO, F. G., COTA, M. K., & VEGA, S. C. (1999). Health promotion in Latino populations: A sociocultural model for program planning, development, and evaluation. In R. M. HUFF & M. V. KLINE (Eds.), *Promoting health in multicultural populations: A handbook for practitioners* (pp. 137–168). Thousand Oaks, CA: Sage.

CASTRO, F. G., NEWCOMB, M. D., McCREARY, C., & BAEZCONDE-GARBANATI, L. (1989). Cigarette smokers do more than just smoke cigarettes. *Health Psychology*, 8, 107–129.

CATALDO, M. F., DERSHEWITZ, R. A., WILSON, M., CHRISTOPHERSEN, E. R., FINNEY, J. W., FAWCETT, S. B., & SEEKINS, T. (1986). Childhood injury control. In N. A. KRASNEGOR, J. D. ARASTEH, & M. F. CATALDO (Eds.), *Child health behavior: A behavioral pediatrics perspective*. New York: Wiley.

CATANIA, J. A., COATES, T. J., STALL, R., BYE, L., et al. (1991). Changes in condom use among homosexual men in San Francisco. *Health Psychology*, 10, 190–199.

CATTANACH, L., & RODIN, J. (1988). Psychological components of the stress process in bulimia. *International Journal of Eating Disorders*, 7, 75–88.

CATZ, S. L., KELLY, J. A., BOGART, L. M., BENOTSCH, E. G., & McAULIFFE, T. L. (2000). Patterns, correlates, and barriers to medication adherence among persons prescribed new treatments for HIV disease. *Health Psychology*, 19, 124–133.

CAY, E. L., VETTER, N., PHILIP, A. E., & DUGARD, P. (1972). Psychosocial status during recovery from an acute heart attack. *Journal of Psychosomatic Research*, 16, 425–435.

CDC (Centers for Disease Control and Prevention, U.S. Public Health Service) (2000). HIV/AIDS *prevention— Basic statistics*. Retrieved (2-28-2000) from http://www.cdc.gov.

CELIO, A. A., WINZELBERG, A. J., WILFLEY, D. E., EPPSTEIN-HERALD, D., SPRINGER, E. A., DEV, P., & TAYLOR, C. B. (2000). Reducing risk factors for eating disorders: Comparison of an Internet- and classroom-delivered psychoeducational program. *Health Psychology, 68,* 650–657.

CELLA, D., PETERMAN, A., PASSIK, S., JACOBSEN, P., & BREITBART, W. (1998). Progress toward guidelines for the management of fatigue. *Oncology, 12,* 369–377.

CEPEDA-BENITO, A. (1993). Meta-analytical review of the efficacy of nicotine chewing gum in smoking treatment programs. *Journal of Consulting and Clinical Psychology, 61,* 822–830.

CHAMBLESS, D. L., & GILLIS, M. M. (1993). Cognitive therapy of anxiety disorders. *Journal of Consulting and Clinical Psychology, 61,* 248–260.

CHAMPION, V. L. (1990). Breast self-examination in women 35 and older: A prospective study. *Journal of Behavioral Medicine, 13,* 523–538.

CHAN, J. M., RIMM, E. B., COLDITZ, G. A., STAMPFER, M. J., & WILLETT, W. C. (1994). Obesity, fat distribution, and weight gain as risk factors for clinical diabetes in men. *Diabetes Care, 17,* 961–969.

CHANDRA, R. K. (1991). Interactions between early nutrition and the immune system. In D. J. P. BARKER (Chair, Ciba Foundation Symposium, No. 156), *The childhood environment and adult disease.* New York: Wiley.

CHANEY, E. F. (1989). Social skills training. In R. K. HESTER & W. R. MILLER (Eds.), *Handbook of alcoholism treatment approaches: Effective alternatives.* New York: Pergamon.

CHANEY, E. F., O'LEARY, M. R., & MARLATT, G. A. (1978). Skill training with alcoholics. *Journal of Consulting and Clinical Psychology, 46,* 1092–1104.

CHANG, A., DILLMAN, A. S., LEONARD, E., & ENGLISH, P. (1985). Teaching car passenger safety to preschool children. *Pediatrics, 76,* 425–428.

CHAPMAN, C. R. (1984). New directions in the understanding and management of pain. *Social Science and Medicine, 19,* 1261–1277.

CHAPMAN, C. R., CASEY, K. L., DUBNER, R., FOLEY, K. M., GRACELY, R. H., & READING, A. E. (1985). Pain measurement: An overview. *Pain, 22,* 1–31.

CHAPMAN, S. L. (1991). Chronic pain: Psychological assessment and treatment. In J. J. SWEET, R. H. ROZENSKY, & S. M. TOVIAN (Eds.), *Handbook of clinical psychology in medical settings.* New York: Plenum.

CHAPMAN, S. L., & BRENA, S. F. (1985). Pain and society. *Annals of Behavioral Medicine, 7(3),* 21–24.

CHASSIN, L., PRESSON, C. C., PITTS, S. C., & SHERMAN, S. J. (2000). The natural history of cigarette smoking from adolescence to adulthood in a Midwestern community sample: Multiple trajectories and their psychosocial correlates. *Health Psychology, 19,* 223–231.

CHASSIN, L., PRESSON, C. C., SHERMAN, S. J., & EDWARDS, D. A. (1991). Four pathways to young-adult smoking status: Adolescent social-psychological antecedents in a Midwestern community sample. *Health Psychology, 10,* 409–418.

CHAVES, J. F., & BROWN, J. M. (1987). Spontaneous cognitive strategies for the control of clinical pain and stress. *Journal of Behavioral Medicine, 10,* 263–276.

CHEN, E., ZELTZER, L. K., CRASKE, M. G., & KATZ, E. R. (1999). Alteration of memory in the reduction of children's distress during repeated aversive medical procedures. *Journal of Consulting and Clinical Psychology, 67,* 481–490.

CHEN, K., SCHEIER, L. M., & KANDEL, D. B. (1996). Effects of chronic cocaine use on physical health: A prospective study in a general population sample. *Drug and Alcohol Dependence, 43,* 23–37.

CHEN, Y., CHEN, C.-F., RILEY, D. J., ALLRED, D. C., CHEN, P.-H., VON HOFF, D., OSBORNE, C. K., & LEE, W.-H. (1995). Aberrant subcellular localization of BRCA1 in breast cancer. *Science, 270,* 789–791.

CHENG, T. L., SAVAGEAU, J. A., SATTLER, A. L., & DEWITT, T. G. (1993). Confidentiality in health care: A survey of knowledge, perceptions, and attitudes among high school students. *Journal of the American Medical Association, 269,* 1404–1407.

CHERKIN, D. C., DEYO, R. A., LOESER, J. D., BUSH, T., & WADDELL, G. (1994). An international comparison of back surgery rates. *Spine, 19,* 1201–1206.

CHESNEY, M. A. (1984). Behavior modification and health enhancement. In J. D. MATARAZZO, S. M. WEISS, J. A. HERD, N. E. MILLER, & S. M. WEISS (Eds.), *Behavioral health: A handbook of health enhancement and disease prevention.* New York: Wiley.

CHESNEY, M. A., EAGLESTON, J. R., & ROSENMAN, R. H. (1980). The Type A Structured Interview: A behavioral assessment in the rough. *Journal of Behavioral Assessment, 2,* 255–272.

CHESNEY, M. A., FRAUTSCHI, N. M., & ROSENMAN, R. H. (1985). Modifying Type A behavior. In J. C. ROSEN & L. J. SOLOMON (Eds.), *Prevention in health psychology.* Hanover, NH: University Press of New England.

CHESNEY, M. A., ICKOVICS, J., HECHT, F. M., SIKIPA, G., & RABKIN, J. (1999). Adherence: A necessity for successful HIV combination tharapy. *AIDS, 13*(Suppl. A), S271–S278.

CHESNEY, M. A., & SMITH, A. W. (1999). Critical delays in HIV testing and care. *American Behavioral Scientist, 42,* 1162–1174.

CHILCOAT, H. D., DISHION, T. J., & ANTHONY, J. C. (1995). Parent monitoring and the incidence of drug sampling in urban elementary school children. *American Journal of Epidemiology, 141,* 25–31.

CHILDRESS, A. R. (1996, March). *Cue reactivity and drug craving.* Paper presented at the meeting of the Society of Behavioral Medicine, Washington, DC.

CHOU, C.-P., MONTGOMERY, S., PENTZ, M. A., ROHRBACH, L. A., JOHNSON, C. A., FLAY, B. R., & MACKINNON, D. P. (1998). Effects of a community-based prevention program on decreasing drug use in high-risk adolescents. *American Journal of Public Health, 88,* 944–948.

CHRISMAN, N. J., & KLEINMAN, A. (1983). Popular health care, social networks, and cultural meanings: The orientation of medical anthropology. In D. MECHANIC (Ed.), *Handbook of health, health care, and the health professions.* New York: Free Press.

CHRISTENFELD, N. (1997). Memory for pain and the delayed effects of distraction. *Health Psychology, 16,* 327–330.

CHRISTENFELD, N., GERIN, W., LINDEN, W., SANDERS, M., MATHUR, J., DEICH, J. D., & PICKERING, T. G. (1997). Social support effects on cardiovascular reactivity: Is a stranger as effective as a friend? *Psychosomatic Medicine, 59,* 388–398.

CHRISTENSEN, A. J., EDWARDS, D. L., WIEBE, J. S., BENOTSCH, E. G., McKELVEY, L., ANDREWS, M., & LUBAROFF, D. M. (1996). Effect of verbal self-disclosure on natural killer cell activity: Moderating influence of cynical hostility. *Psychosomatic Medicine, 58,* 150–155.

CHRISTENSEN, A. J., MORAN, P. J., & WEIBE, J. S. (1999). Assessment of irrational health beliefs: Relation to health practices and medical regimen adherence. *Health Psychology, 18,* 169–176.

CHRISTENSEN, A. J., & SMITH, T. W. (1995). Personality and patient adherence: Correlates of the five-factor model in renal dialysis. *Journal of Behavioral Medicine, 18,* 305–313.

CHRISTENSEN, J., & LEVINSON, W. (1991). Implementing a behavioral medicine program in an internal medicine residency: A description of curriculum content, resources and barriers encountered. In M. A. JANSEN & J. WEINMAN (Eds.), *The international development of health psychology.* Chur, Switzerland: Harwood.

CHRISTOPHERSEN, E. R. (1984). Preventing injuries to children: A behavioral approach to child passenger safety. In J. D. MATARAZZO, S. M. WEISS, J. A. HERD, N. E. MILLER, & S. M. WEISS (Eds.), *Behavioral health: A handbook of health enhancement and disease prevention.* New York: Wiley.

CHUN, C.-A., ENOMOTO, K., & SUE, S. (1996). Health care issues among Asian Americans: Implications of soma-tization. In P. M. KATO & T. MANN (Eds.), *Handbook of diversity issues in health psychology* (pp. 347–365). New York: Plenum.

CIARANELLO, R. D. (1983). Neurochemical aspects of stress. In N. GARMEZY & M. RUTTER (Eds.), *Stress, coping, and development in children.* New York: McGraw-Hill.

CICCONE, D., JUST, N., & BANDILLA, E. B. (1999). A comparison of economic and social reward in patients with chronic nonmalignant back pain. *Psychosomatic Medicine, 61,* 552–563.

CINCIRIPINI, P. M., CINCIRIPINI, L. G., WALLFISCH, A., HAQUE, W., & VAN VUNAKIS, H. (1996). Behavior therapy and the transdermal nicotine patch: Effects on cessation outcome, affect, and coping. *Journal of Consulting and Clinical Psychology, 64,* 314–323.

CINCIRIPINI, P. M., & FLOREEN, A. (1982). An evaluation of a behavioral program for chronic pain. *Journal of Behavioral Medicine, 5,* 375–389.

CINCIRIPINI, P. M., LAPITSKY, L., SEAY, S., WALLFISCH, A., KITCHENS, K., & VAN VUNAKIS, H. (1995). The effects of smoking schedules on cessation outcome: Can we improve on common methods of gradual and abrupt nicotine withdrawal? *Journal of Consulting and Clinical Psychology, 63,* 388–399.

CIOPPA, A. L. (1984). Hospice care. In S. N. McINTIRE & A. L. CIOPPA (Eds.), *Nursing care: A developmental approach.* New York: Wiley.

CIRAULO, D. A., & RENNER, J. A. (1991). Alcoholism. In D. A. CIRAULO & R. I. SHADER (Eds.), *Clinical manual of chemical dependence.* Washington, DC: American Psychiatric Press.

CIRAULO, D. A., & SHADER, R. I. (Eds.) (1991). *Clinical manual of chemical dependence.* Washington, DC: American Psychiatric Press.

CITRON, M. L., JOHNSTON-EARLY, A., BOYER, M., KRASNOW, S. H., HOOD, M., & COHEN, M. H. (1986). Patient-controlled analgesia for severe cancer pain. *Archives of Internal Medicine, 146,* 734–736.

CLARK, D. O., PATRICK, D. L., GREMBOWSKI, D., & DURHAM, M. L. (1995). Socioeconomic status and exercise self-efficacy in late life. *Journal of Behavioral Medicine, 18,* 355–376.

CLARK, R., ANDERSON, N. B., CLARK, V. R., & WILLIAMS, D. R. (1999). Racism as a stressor for African Americans. *American Psychologist, 54,* 805–816.

CLARKE, V. A., & SAVAGE, S. A. (1999). Breast self-examination training: A brief review. *Cancer Nursing, 22,* 320–326.

CLARKSON, T. B., MANUCK, S. B., & KAPLAN, J. R. (1986). Potential role of cardiovascular reactivity in atherogenesis. In K. A. MATTHEWS, S. M. WEISS, T. DETRE, T. M. DEMBROSKI, B. FALKNER, S. B. MANUCK, & R. B. WILLIAMS

(Eds.), *Handbook of stress, reactivity, and cardiovascular disease*. New York: Wiley.

CLAY, R. A. (1997, April). Is assisted suicide ever a rational choice? *American Psychological Association Monitor*, pp. 1, 43.

CLEELAND, C. S., GONIN, R., HATFIELD, A. K., EDMONSON, J. H., BLUM, R. H., STEWART, J. A., & PANDYA, K. J. (1994). Pain and its treatment in outpatients with metastatic cancer. *New England Journal of Medicine, 330,* 592–596.

CLEVER, L. H., & LEGUYADER, Y. (1995). Infectious health risks for health care workers. *Annual Review of Public Health, 16,* 141–164.

CLEVER, L. H., & OMENN, G. S. (1988). Hazards for health care workers. *Annual Review of Public Health, 9,* 273–303.

CLUSS, P. A., & EPSTEIN, L. H. (1985). The measurement of medical compliance in the treatment of disease. In P. KAROLY (Ed.), *Measurement strategies in health psychology*. New York: Wiley.

CLUSS, P. A., & FIREMAN, P. (1985). Recent trends in asthma research. *Annals of Behavioral Medicine, 7(4),* 11–16.

COATES, T. J. (1990). Strategies for modifying sexual behavior for primary and secondary prevention of HIV disease. *Journal of Consulting and Clinical Psychology, 58,* 57–69.

COBB, S. (1976). Social support as a moderator of stress. *Psychosomatic Medicine, 38,* 300–314.

COBB, S., & ROSE, R. M. (1973). Hypertension, peptic ulcer, and diabetes in air traffic controllers. *Journal of the American Medical Association, 224,* 489–492.

CODDINGTON, R. D. (1972a). The significance of life events as etiological factors in the diseases of children—I: A survey of professional workers. *Journal of Psychosomatic Research, 16,* 7–18.

CODDINGTON, R. D. (1972b). The significance of life events as etiological factors in the diseases of children—II: A study of a normal population. *Journal of Psychosomatic Research, 16,* 205–213.

COGAN, R., COGAN, D., WALTZ, W., & McCUE, M. (1987). Effects of laughter and relaxation on discomfort thresholds. *Journal of Behavioral Medicine, 10,* 139–144.

COHEN, F., KEARNEY, K. A., ZEGANS, L. S., KEMENY, M. E., NEUHAUS, J. M., & STITES, D. P. (1999). Differrent immune system changes with acute and persistent stress for optimists vs pessimists. *Brain, Behavior, and Immunity, 13,* 155–174.

COHEN, F., & LAZARUS, R. S. (1979). Coping with the stresses of illness. In G. C. STONE, F. COHEN, & N. E. ADLER (Eds.), *Health psychology—A handbook*. San Francisco: Jossey-Bass.

COHEN, F., & LAZARUS, R. S. (1983). Coping and adaptation in health and illness. In D. MECHANIC (Ed.), *Handbook of health, health care, and the health professions*. New York: Free Press.

COHEN, L. L., BLOUNT, R. L., COHEN, R. J., SCHAEN, E. R., & ZAFF, J. F. (1999). Comparative study of distraction versus topical anesthesia for pediatric pain management during immunizations. *Health Psychology, 18,* 591–598.

COHEN, R. Y., BROWNELL, K. D., & FELIX, M. R. J. (1990). Age and sex differences in health habits and beliefs of schoolchildren. *Health Psychology, 9,* 208–224.

COHEN, S., EVANS, G. W., STOKOLS, D., & KRANTZ, D. S. (1986). *Behavior, health, and environmental stress*. New York: Plenum.

COHEN, S., FRANK, E., DOYLE, W. J., SKONER, D. P., RABIN, B. S., & GWALTNEY, J. M. (1998). Types of stressors that increase susceptibility to the common cold in healthy adults. *Health Psychology, 17,* 214–223.

COHEN, S., KAMARCK, T., & MERMELSTEIN, R. (1983). A global measure of perceived stress. *Journal of Health and Social Behavior, 24,* 385–396.

COHEN, S., & LICHTENSTEIN, E. (1990). Perceived stress, quitting smoking, and smoking relapse. *Health Psychology, 9,* 466–478.

COHEN, S., LICHTENSTEIN, E., PROCHASKA, J. O., ROSSI, J. S., et al. (1989). Debunking myths about self-quitting: Evidence from 10 prospective studies of persons who attempt to quit smoking by themselves. *American Psychologist, 44,* 1355–1365.

COHEN, S., & McKAY, G. (1984). Social support, stress and the buffering hypothesis: A theoretical analysis. In A. BAUM, S. E. TAYLOR, & J. E. SINGER (Eds.), *Handbook of psychology and health*. Hillsdale, NJ: Erlbaum.

COHEN, S., & RODRIGUEZ, M. S. (1995). Pathways linking affective disturbances and physical disorders. *Health Psychology, 14,* 374–380.

COHEN, S., & SPACAPAN, S. (1978). The aftereffects of stress: An attentional interpretation. *Environmental Psychology and Nonverbal Behavior, 3,* 43–57.

COHEN, S., TYRELL, D. A. J., RUSSELL, M. A. H., JARVIS, M. J., & SMITH, A. P. (1993). Smoking, alcohol consumption, and susceptibility to the common cold. *American Journal of Public Health, 83,* 1277–1283.

COHEN, S., TYRRELL, D. A. J., & SMITH, A. P. (1991). Psychological stress and susceptibility to the common cold. *New England Journal of Medicine, 325,* 606–612.

COHEN, S., & WILLS, T. A. (1985). Stress, social support, and the buffering hypothesis. *Psychological Bulletin, 98,* 310–357.

COHEN, S. M., & ELLWEIN, L. B. (1990). Cell proliferation in carcinogenesis. *Science, 249,* 1007–1011.

COHEN, W. S. (1985). Health promotion in the workplace: A prescription for good health. *American Psychologist, 40,* 213–216.

COHN, L. D., MACFARLANE, S., YANEZ, C., & IMAI, W. K. (1995). Risk-perception: Differences between adolescents and adults. *Health Psychology*, 14, 217–222.

COLF, S. W., & KEMENY, M. E. (1997). Psychobiology of HIV infection. *Critical Reviews in Neurobiology*, 11, 289–321.

COLERICK, E. J. (1985). Stamina in later life. *Social Science and Medicine*, 21, 997–1006.

COLLETTI, G., & BROWNELL, K. D. (1983). The physical and emotional benefits of social support: Application to obesity, smoking, and alcoholism. In M. HERSEN, R. M. EISLER, & P. M. MILLER (Eds.), *Progress in behavior modification*. New York: Academic Press.

COLLIGAN, M. J., URTES, M., WISSEMAN, C., ROSENSTEEL, R. E., ANANIA, T. L., & HORNUNG, R. W. (1979). An investigation of apparent mass psychogenic illness in an electronics plant. *Journal of Behavioral Medicine*, 2, 297–309.

COLLINS, A., & FRANKENHAEUSER, M. (1978). Stress responses in male and female engineering students. *Journal of Human Stress*, 4, 43–48.

COLLINS, G. (1987, April 29). Keeping fit wasn't easy in 1837, either. *New York Times*, pp. C1, 12.

COMPAS, B. E., HAAGA, D. A. F., KEEFE, F. J., LEITENBERG, H., & WILLIAMS, D. A. (1998). Sampling of empirically supported psychological treatments from health psychology: Smoking, chronic pain, cancer, and bulimia nervosa. *Journal of Consulting and Clinical Psychology*, 66, 89–112.

COMPAS, B. E., WORSHAM, N. L., EY, S., & HOWELL, D. C. (1996). When mom or dad has cancer: II. Coping, cognitive appraisals, and psychological distress in children of cancer patients. *Health Psychology*, 15, 167–175.

CONEL, J. L. (1939–1963). *The postnatal development of the human cerebral cortex* (Vols. 1–7). Cambridge, MA: Harvard University Press.

CONGER, J. J., & PETERSEN, A. C. (1984). *Adolescence and youth: Psychological development in a changing world* (3rd ed.). New York: Harper & Row.

CONNELL, C. M., & D'AUGELLI, A. R. (1990). The contribution of personality characteristics to the relationship between social support and perceived physical health. *Health Psychology*, 9, 192–207.

CONRAD, B., WEIDMANN, E., TRUCCO, G., RUDERT, W. A., BEHBOO, R., RICORDI, C., RODRIQUEZ-RILO, H., FINEGOLD, D., & TRUCCO, M. (1994). Evidence for superantigen involvement in insulin-dependent diabetes mellitus aetiology. *Nature*, 371, 351–355.

CONRAD, K. M., FLAY, B. R., & HILL, D. (1992). Why children start smoking cigarettes: Predictors of onset *British Journal of Addiction*, 87, 1711–1724.

CONSTABLE, J. F., & RUSSELL, D. W. (1986). The effect of social support and the work environment upon burnout among nurses. *Journal of Human Stress*, 12, 20–26.

CONTRADA, R. J. (1989). Type A behavior, personality hardiness, and cardiovascular responses to stress. *Journal of Personality and Social Psychology*, 57, 895–903.

CONTRADA, R. J., & KRANTZ, D. S. (1988). Stress, reactivity, and Type A behavior: Current status and future directions. *Annals of Behavioral Medicine*, 10, 64–70.

CONTRADA, R. J., KRANTZ, D. S., & HILL, D. R. (1988). Type A behavior, emotion, and psychophysiologic reactivity: Psychological and biological interactions. In B. K. HOUSTON & C. R. SNYDER (Eds.), *Type A behavior pattern: Research, theory, and intervention*. New York: Wiley.

CONWAY, T. L., VICKERS, R. R., WARD, H. W., & RAHE, R. H. (1981). Occupational stress and variation in cigarette, coffee, and alcohol consumption. *Journal of Health and Social Behavior*, 22, 155–165.

COOK, P. S., PETERSEN, R. C., & MOORE, D. T. (1990). *Alcohol, tobacco, and other drugs may harm the unborn*. Rockville, MD: U.S. Department of Health and Human Services.

COOK, W. W., & MEDLEY, D. M. (1954). Proposed hostility and pharisaic-virtue scores for the MMPI. *Journal of Applied Psychology*, 38, 414–418.

COOPER, K. H. (1988). *Controlling cholesterol*. New York: Bantam.

COOPER, M. L., & ORCUTT, H. K. (2000). Alcohol use, condom use, and partner type among heterosexual adolescents and young adults. *Journal of Studies on Alcohol*, 61, 413–419.

COOPER, M. L., PEIRCE, R. S., & HUSELID, R. F. (1994). Substance use and sexual risk taking among black adolescents and white adolescents. *Health Psychology*, 13, 251–262.

COOPER, P. J., BAWDEN, H. N., CAMFIELD, P. R., & CAMFIELD, C. S. (1987). Anxiety and life events in childhood migraine. *Pediatrics*, 79, 999–1004.

COOPER, S. (1987). The fetal alcohol syndrome. *Journal of Child Psychology and Psychiatry*, 28, 223–227.

CORAH, N. L., O'SHEA, R. M., BISSELL, G. D., THINES, T. J., & MENDOLA, P. (1988). The dentist-patient relationship: Perceived dentist behaviors that reduce patient anxiety and increase satisfaction. *Journal of the American Dental Association*, 116, 73–76.

COSTA, P. T., & MCCRAE, R. R. (1980). Somatic complaints in males as a function of age and neuroticism: A longitudinal analysis. *Journal of Behavioral Medicine*, 3, 245–257.

COSTA, P. T., & MCCRAE, R. R. (1985). Hypochondriasis, neuroticism, and aging. *American Psychologist*, 40, 19–28.

COTTINGTON, E. M., & HOUSE, J. S. (1987). Occupational stress and health: A multivariate relationship. In A. BAUM & J. E. SINGER (Eds.), *Handbook of psychology and health* (Vol. 5). Hillsdale, NJ: Erlbaum.

COUNTER, C. M., HIRTE, H. W., BACCHETTI, S., & HARLEY. C. B. (1994). Telomerase activity in human ovarian carcinoma. *Proceedings of the National Academy of Sciences, 91,* 2900–2904.

COUSINS, N. (1979). *Anatomy of an illness.* New York: Norton.

COUSINS, N. (1985). Anatomy of an illness (as perceived by the patient). In A. MONAT & R. S. LAZARUS (Eds.), *Stress and coping: An anthology* (2nd ed). New York: Columbia University Press.

COX, D. J., GONDER-FREDERICK, L., ANTOUN, B., CRYER, P. E., & CLARKE, W. L. (1993). Preceived symptoms in the recognition of hypoglycemia. *Diabetes Care, 16,* 519–527.

COX, G. B., CHAPMAN, C. R., & BLACK, R. G. (1978). The MMPI and chronic pain: The diagnosis of psychogenic pain. *Journal of Behavioral Medicine, 1,* 437–443.

COX, W. M. (1985). Personality correlates of substance abuse. In M. GALIZIO & S. A. MAISTO (Eds.), *Determinants of substance abuse: Biological, psychological, and environmental factors.* New York: Plenum.

COYNE, J. C., & HOLROYD, K. (1982). Stress, coping, and illness: A transactional perspective. In T. MILLON, C. GREEN, & R. MEAGHER (Eds.), *Handbook of clinical health psychology.* New York: Plenum.

CRAIG, T. G., COMSTOCK, G. W., & GEISER, P. B. (1974). The quality of survival in breast cancer: A case-control comparison. *Cancer, 33,* 1451–1457.

CRAMER, P. (2000). Defense mechanisms in psychology today: Further processes for adaptation. *American Psychologist, 55,* 637–646.

CRANDALL, L. A., & DUNCAN, R. P. (1981). Attitudinal and situational factors in the use of physician services by low-income persons. *Journal of Health and Social Behavior, 22,* 64–77.

CRAUN, A. M., & DEFFENBACHER, J. L. (1987). The effects of information, behavioral rehearsal, and prompting on breast self-exams. *Journal of Behavioral Medicine, 10,* 351–365.

CRUESS, D. G., ANTONI, M. H., McGREGOR, B. A., KILBOURN, K. M., BOYERS, A. E., ALFIERI, S. M., CARVER, C. S., & KUMAR, M. (2000). Cognitive-behavioral stress management reduces serum cortisol by enhancing benefit finding among women being treated for early stage breast cancer. *Psychosomatic Medicine, 62,* 304–308.

CRIQUI, M. H., & RINGEL, B. L. (1994). Does diet or alcohol explain the French paradox? *Lancet, 344,* 1719–1723.

CRISP, A. H., & KALUCY, R. S. (1974). Aspects of the perceptual disorder in anorexia nervosa. *British Journal of Medical Psychology, 47,* 349–361.

CRITCHLOW, B. (1986). The powers of John Barleycorn: Beliefs about the effects of alcohol on social behavior. *American Psychologist, 41,* 751–764.

CROFFORD, O. B. (1995). Diabetes control and complications. *Annual Review of Medicine, 46,* 267–279.

CRONAN, T. A., GROESSL, E., & KAPLAN, R. M. (1997). The effects of social support and education interventions on health care costs. *Arthritis Care and Research, 10,* 99–110.

CROOG, S. H. (1983). Recovery and rehabilitation of heart patients: Psychosocial aspects. In D. S. KRANTZ, A. BAUM, & J. E. SINGER (Eds.), *Handbook of psychology and health* (Vol. 3). Hillsdale, NJ: Erlbaum.

CROOG, S. H., & FITZGERALD, E. F. (1978). Subjective stress and serious illness of a spouse: Wives of heart patients. *Journal of Health and Social Behavior, 19,* 166–178.

CROYLE, R. T., & BARGER, S. D. (1993). Illness cognition. In S. MAES, H. LEVENTHAL, & M. JOHNSTON (Eds.), *International review of health psychology* (Vol. 2). New York: Wiley.

CROYLE, R. T., & DITTO, P. H. (1990). Illness cognition and behavior: An experimental approach. *Journal of Behavioral Medicine, 13,* 31–52.

CU (Consumers Union) (1992, September). Health care in crisis: The search for solutions. *Consumer Reports,* pp. 579–592.

CU (Consumers Union) (1994a, January). Acupuncture. *Consumer Reports,* pp. 54–59.

CU (Consumers Union) (1994b, September). Taking vitamins: Can they prevent disease? *Consumer Reports,* pp. 561–564.

CU (Consumers Union) (1995a, November). Herbal roulette. *Consumer Reports,* pp. 698–705.

CU (Consumers Union) (1995b, February). How is your doctor treating you? *Consumer Reports,* pp. 81–88.

CU (Consumers Union). (1998a, August). Checkups: Are you getting what you need? *Consumer Reports,* pp. 17–19.

CU (Consumers Union). (1998b, October). Cholesterol drugs: Should you be taking one? *Consumer Reports,* pp. 54–55.

CU (Consumers Union). (1999a, March). Herbal Rx: The promise and pitfalls. *Consumer Reports,* pp. 44–48.

CU (Consumers Union). (1999b, August). How does your HMO stack up? *Consumer Reports,* pp. 23–29.

CU (Consumers Union). (2000, May). The mainstreaming of alternative medicine. *Consumer Reports,* pp. 17–25.

CUMMINGS, N. A. (1991). Arguments for the financial efficacy of psychological services in health care settings. In J. J. SWEET, R. H. ROZENSKY, & S. M. TOVIAN (Eds.), *Handbook of clinical psychology in medical settings.* New York: Plenum.

CUNNINGHAM, A. J., EDMONDS, C. V. I., JENKINS, G. P., POLLACK, H., LOCKWOOD, G. A., & WARR, D. (1998). A randomized controlled trial of the effects of group psychological therapy on survival in women with metastatic breast cancer. *Psycho-Oncology, 7,* 508–517.

CUNNINGHAM, C. L. (1998). Drug conditioning and drug-seeking behavior. In W. O'DONAHUE (Ed.), *Learning and behavior therapy* (pp. 518–544). Boston: Allyn & Bacon.

CURRY, S. J., & EMMONS, K. M. (1994). Theoretical models for predicting and improving compliance with breast cancer screening. *Annals of Behavioral Medicine, 16,* 302–316.

CURRY, S. J., & MCBRIDE, C. M. (1994). Relapse prevention for smoking cessation: Review and evaluation of concepts and interventions. *Annual Review of Public Health, 15,* 345–366.

CURRY, S. J., TAPLIN, S. H., ANDERMAN, C., BARLOW, W. E., & MCBRIDE, C. (1993). A randomized trial of the impact of risk assessment and feedback on participation in mammography screening. *Preventive Medicine, 22,* 350–360.

CURRY, S., WAGNER, E. H., & GROTHAUS, L. C. (1990). Intrinsic and extrinsic motivation for smoking cessation. *Journal of Consulting and Clinical Psychology, 58,* 310–316.

CUTLER, R. B., FISHBAIN, D. A., ROSOMOFF, H. L., ABDEL-MOTY, E., KHALIL, T. M., & ROSOMOFF, R. S. (1994). Does non-surgical pain center treatment of chronic pain return patients to work?: A review and meta-analysis of the literature. *Spine, 19,* 643–652.

CUTRONA, C. E. (1986). Behavioral manifestations of social support: A microanalytic investigation. *Journal of Personality and Social Psychology, 51,* 201–208.

CUTRONA, C. E., & RUSSELL, D. W. (1990). Type of social support and specific stress: Toward a theory of optimal matching. In B. A SARASON, I. G. SARASON, & G. R. PIERCE (Eds.), *Social support: An interactional view.* New York: Wiley.

CUTRONA, C. E., & TROUTMAN, B. R. (1986). Social support, infant temperament, and parenting self-efficacy: A mediational model of postpartum depression. *Child Development, 57,* 1507–1518.

DAHLBERG, C. C. (1977, June). Stroke. *Psychology Today,* pp. 121–128.

DAHLQUIST, L. M., GIL, K. M., ARMSTRONG, F. D., DELAWYER, D. D., GREENE, P., & WUORI, D. (1986). Preparing children for medical examinations: The importance of previous medical experience. *Health Psychology, 5,* 249–259.

DALESSIO, D. J. (1994). Diagnosing the severe headache. *Neurology, 44* (Suppl. 3), S6–12.

DATILLO, A. M., & KRIS-ETHERTON, P. M. (1992). Effects of weight reduction on blood lipids and lipoproteins: A meta-analysis. *American Journal of Clinical Nutrition, 56,* 320–328.

DAVIDSON, R. S. (1985). Behavioral medicine and alcoholism. In N. SCHNEIDERMAN & J. T. TAPP (Eds.), *Behavioral medicine: The biopsychosocial approach.* Hillsdale, NJ: Erlbaum.

DAVIES, R. F., LINDEN, W., HABIBI, H., KLINKE, P., et al., (1993). Relative importance of psychologic traits and severity of ischemia in causing angina during treadmill exercise. *Journal of the American College of Cardiology, 21,* 331–336.

DAVIS, M. C., MATTHEWS, K. A., & TWAMLEY, E. W. (1999). Is life more difficult on Mars or Venus? A meta-analytic review of sex differences in major and minor life events. *Annals of Behavioral Medicine, 21,* 83–97.

DAVIS, M. S. (1966). Variations in patients' compliance with doctors' orders: Analysis of congruence between survey responses and results of empirical investigations. *Journal of Medical Education, 41,* 1037–1048.

DAVISON, G. C., & NEALE, J. M. (1998). *Abnormal psychology* (7th ed.). New York: Wiley.

DAVISON, K. P., PENNEBAKER, J. W., & DICKERSON, S. S. (2000). Who talks? The social psychology of illness suport groups. *American Psychologist, 55,* 205–217.

DEANGELIS, T. (1990, October). Psychologists involved with epilepsy treatment. *American Psychological Association Monitor,* p. 24.

DEANGELIS, T. (1995, October). Primary-care collaborations growing. *American Psychological Association Monitor,* p. 22.

DEARDORFF, W. W. (1996). Board certification: What do you mean you're not board certified? *Health Psychologist, 18*(3), 10–11.

DEBENEDITTIS, G., PANERAI, A. A., & VILLAMIRA, M. A. (1989). Effects of hypnotic analgesia and hypnotizability on experimental ischemic pain. *International Journal of Clinical and Experimental Hypnosis, 35,* 55–69.

DEBON, M. W., KLESGES, R. C., KLESGES, L. M., & COHEN, R. (1992, March). *Dieting exposure and knowledge of first, third, and fifth graders.* Paper presented at the meeting of the Society of Behavioral Medicine, New York.

DEGNER, L. F., & BEATON, J. I. (1987). *Life-death decisions in health care.* New York: Hemisphere.

DEJONG, W. (1980). The stigma of obesity: The consequences of naive assumptions concerning the causes of physical deviance. *Journal of Health and Social Behavior, 21,* 75–87.

DEJONG, W., & HINGSON, R. (1998). Strategies to reduce driving under the influence of alcohol. *Annual Reviews, 19,* 359–378.

DELAHANTY, D. L., DOUGALL, A. L., HAWKEN, L., TRAKOWSKI, J. H., SCHMITZ, J. B., JENKINS, F. J., & BAUM, A. (1996). Time course of natural killer cell activity and lymphocyte proliferation in response to two acute stressors in healthy men. *Health Psychology, 15,* 48–55.

DELONGIS, A., COYNE, J. C., DAKOF, G., FOLKMAN, S., & LAZARUS, R. S. (1982). Relationship to daily hassles, uplifts, and major life events to health status. *Health Psychology, 1,* 119–136.

DENISSENKO, M. F., PAO, A., TANG, M.-S., & PFEIFER, G. P. (1996). Preferential formation of benzo[a]pyrene adducts at lung cancer mutational hotspots in P53. *Science, 274,* 430–432.

DENNIS, C., HOUSTON-MILLER, N., SCHWARTZ, R. G., AHN, D. K., KRAEMER, H. C., GOSSARD, D., JUNEAU, M., TAYLOR, C. B., & DEBUSK, R. F. (1988). Early return to work after uncomplicated myocardial infarction: Results of a randomized trial. *Journal of the American Medical Association, 260,* 214–220.

DENTON, D., WEISINGER, R., MUNDY, N. I., WICKINGS, E. J., et al. (1995). The effect of increased salt intake on blood pressure of chimpanzees. *Nature Medicine, 1,* 1009–1016.

DEPALMA, A. (1996, June 19). In Mexico, pain relief is a medical and political issue. *New York Times,* p. A6.

DEROGATIS, L. R. (1977). *Psychological Adjustment to Illness Scale.* Baltimore: Clinical Psychometric Research.

DEROGATIS, L. R. (1986). The Psychological Adjustment to Illness Scale (PAIS). *Journal of Psychosomatic Research, 30,* 77–91.

DEROGATIS, L. R., FLEMING, M. P., SUDLER, N. C., & DELLAPIETRA, L. (1995). Psychological assessment. In P. M. NICASSIO & T. W. SMITH (Eds.), *Managing chronic illness: A biopsychosocial perspective.* Washington, DC: American Psychological Association.

DESCARTES, R. (1664). *Traite de l'Homme.* Paris: Angot.

DESHARNAIS, R., JOBIN, J., CÔTÉ, C., LÉVESQUE, L., & GODIN, G. (1993). Aerobic exercise and the placebo effect: A controlled study. *Psychosomatic Medicine, 55,* 149–154.

DESHIELDS, T., CARMIN, C., ROSS, L., & MANNEN, K. (1995, March). *Diagnosis of psychological disorders in primary care patients by medicine residents.* Paper presented at the meeting of the Society of Behavioral Medicine, San Diego.

DES JARLAIS, D. C., & FRIEDMAN, S. R. (1988). The psychology of preventing AIDS among intravenous drug users: A social learning conceptualization. *American Psychologist, 43,* 865–870.

DES JARLAIS, D. C., FRIEDMAN, S. R., & CASRIEL, C. (1990). Target groups for preventing AIDS among intravenous drug users: 2. The "hard" data studies. *Journal of Consulting and Clinical Psychology, 58,* 50–56.

DES JARLAIS, D. C., FRIEDMAN, S. R., CASRIEL, C., & KOTT, A. (1987). AIDS and preventing initiation into intravenous (IV) drug use. *Psychology and Health, 1,* 179–194.

DETJEN, J. (1991, November 10). Will genetics revolution mark some as victims? *Philadelphia Inquirer,* pp. A1, 18.

DETWEILER, J. B., BEDEL, B. T., SALOVEY, P., PRONIN, E., & ROTHMAN, A. J. (1999). Message framing and sunscreen use: Gain-framed messages motivate beach goers. *Health Psychology, 18,* 189–196.

DEVINS, G. M., BINIK, Y. M., HOLLOMBY, D. J., BARRÉ, P. E., & GUTTMANN, R. D. (1981). Helplessness and depression in end-stage renal disease. *Journal of Abnormal Psychology, 90,* 531–545.

DEYO, R. A., CHERKIN, D., CONRAD, D., & VOLINN, E. (1991). Cost, controversy, crisis: Low back pain and the health of the public. *Annual Review of Public Health, 12,* 141–156.

DIAMOND, E. L. (1982). The role of anger and hostility in essential hypertension and coronary heart disease. *Psychological Bulletin, 92,* 410–433.

DIAMOND, E. L., MASSEY, K. L., & COVEY, D. (1989). Symptom awareness and blood glucose estimation in diabetic adults. *Health Psychology, 8,* 15–26.

DIAMOND, E. L., SCHNEIDERMAN, N., SCHWARTZ, D., SMITH, J. C., VORP, R., & PASIN, R. D. (1984). Harassment, hostility, and Type A as determinants of cardiovascular reactivity during competition. *Journal of Behavioral Medicine, 7,* 171–189.

DIAMOND, M. (1983). Social adaptation of the chronically ill. In D. MECHANIC (Ed.), *Handbook of health, health care, and the health professions,* New York: Free Press.

DICLEMENTE, C. C., PROCHASKA, J. O., FAIRHURST, S. K., VELICER, W. F., VELASQUEZ, M. M., & ROSSI, J. S. (1991). The process of smoking cessation: An analysis of precontemplation, contemplation, and preparation stages of change. *Journal of Consulting and Clinical Psychology, 59,* 295–304.

DICLEMENTE, C. C., PROCHASKA, J. O., & GILBERTINI, M. (1985). Self-efficacy and the stages of self-change of smoking. *Cognitive Therapy and Research, 9,* 181–200.

DICLEMENTE, R. J., ZORN, J., & TEMOSHOK, L. (1987). The association of gender, ethnicity, and length of residence in the Bay Area to adolescents' knowledge and attitudes about acquired immune deficiency syndrome. *Journal of Applied Social Psychology, 17,* 216–230.

DIEHR, P., KOEPSELL, T., CHEADLE, A., PSATY, B. M., WAGNER, E., & CURRY, S. (1993). Do communities differ in health behaviors? *Journal of Clinical Epidemiology, 46,* 1141–1149.

DIFRANZA, J. R., & LEW, R. A. (1995). Effect of maternal cigarette smoking on pregnancy complications and sudden infant death syndrome. *Journal of Family Practice, 40,* 385–394.

DIJKSTRA, A., DE VRIES, H., ROIJACKERS, J., & VAN BREUKELEN, G. (1998). Tailored interventions to communicate stage-matched information to smokers in different motivational stages. *Journal of Consulting and Clinical Psychology, 66,* 549–557.

DILLER, L. (1999). Hemiplegia. In M. G. EISENBERG, R. L. GLUECKAUF, & H. H. ZARETSKY (Eds.), *Medical aspects of disability: A handbook for the rehabilitation professional* (2nd ed., pp. 528–547). New York: Springer.

DIMATTEO, M. R. (1985). Physician-patient communication: Promoting a positive health care setting. In J. C.

Rosen & L. J. Solomon (Eds.), *Prevention in health psychology*. Hanover, NH: University Press of New England.

DiMatteo, M. R., & DiNicola, D. D. (1982). *Achieving patient compliance: The psychology of the medical practitioner's role*. New York: Pergamon.

DiMatteo, M. R., Friedman, H. S., & Taranta, A. (1979). Sensitivity to bodily nonverbal communication as a factor in practitioner-patient rapport. *Journal of Nonverbal Behavior, 4*, 18–26.

DiMatteo, M. R., Hays, R. D., & Prince, L. M. (1986). Relationship of physicians' nonverbal communication skill to patient satisfaction, appointment noncompliance, and physician workload. *Health Psychology, 5*, 581–594.

DiMatteo, M. R., Linn, L. S., Chang, B. L., & Cope, D. W. (1985). Affect and neutrality in physician behavior: A study of patients' values and satisfaction. *Journal of Behavioral Medicine, 8*, 397–409.

Dimsdale, J. E., Alpert, B. S., & Schneiderman, N. (1986). Exercise as a modulator of cardiovascular reactivity. In K. A. Matthews, S. M. Weiss, T. Detre, T. M. Dembroski, B. Falkner, S. B. Manuck, & R. B. Williams (Eds.), *Handbook of stress, reactivity, and cardiovascular disease*. New York: Wiley.

Dinh, K. T., Sarason, I. G., Peterson, A. V., & Onstad, L. E. (1995). Children's perception of smokers and nonsmokers: A longitudinal study. *Health Psychology, 14*, 32–40.

DISC (Writing group for the DISC Collaborative Research Group) (1995). Efficacy and safety of lowering dietary intake of fat and cholesterol in children with elevated low-density lipoprotein cholesterol: The Dietary Intervention Study in Children (DISC). *Journal of the American Medical Association, 273*, 1429–1435.

Dishman, R. K. (1981). Biologic influences on exercise adherence. *Research Quarterly for Exercise and Sport, 52*, 143–159.

Dishman, R. K. (1982). Compliance/adherence in health-related exercise. *Health Psychology, 1*, 237–267.

Dishman, R. K. (1986). Mental health. In V. Seefeldt (Ed.), *Physical activity and well-being*. Reston, VA: American Alliance for Health, Physical Education, Recreation, and Dance.

Dishman, R. K. (1991). Increasing and maintaining exercise and physical activity. *Behavior Therapy, 22*, 345–378.

Dishman, R. K., Sallis, J. F., & Orenstein, D. R. (1985). The determinants of physical activity and exercise. *Public Health Reports, 100*, 158–171.

Distefan, J. M., Gilpin, E. A., Sargent, J. D., & Pierce, J. P. (1999). Do movie stars encourage adolescents to start smoking? Evidence from California. *Preventive Medicine, 28*, 1–11.

Ditto, B. (1993). Familial influences on heart rate, blood pressure, and self-report anxiety responses to stress: Results from 100 twin pairs. *Psychophysiology, 30*, 635–645.

Doehrman, S. R. (1977). Psycho-social aspects of recovery from coronary heart disease: A review. *Social Science and Medicine, 11*, 199–218.

Doering, S., Katzlberger, F., Rumpold, G., Roessler, S. et al. (2000). Videotape preparation of patients before hip replacement surgery reduces stress. *Psychosomatic Medicine, 62*, 365–373.

Doherty, K., Militello, F. S., Kinnunen, T., & Garvey, A. J. (1996). Nicotine gum dose and weight gain after smoking cessation. *Journal of Consulting and Clinical Psychology, 64*, 799–807.

Dohrenwend, B. S., & Dohrenwend, B. P. (1981). Life stress and illness: Formulation of the issues. In B. S. Dohrenwend & B. P. Dohrenwend (Eds.), *Stressful life events and their contexts*. New York: Prodist.

Dohrenwend, B. S., Krasnoff, L., Askenasy, A. R., & Dohrenwend, B. P. (1978). Exemplification of a method for scaling life events: The PERI Life Events Scale. *Journal of Health and Social Behavior, 19*, 205–229.

Dolecek, T. A., Milas, N. C., Van Horn, L. V., Farrand, M. E., Gorder, D. D., Duchene, A. G., Dyer, J. R., Stone, P. A., & Randall, B. L. (1986). A long-term nutrition experience: Lipid responses and dietary adherence patterns in the Multiple Risk Factor Intervention Trial. *Journal of the American Dietetic Association, 86*, 752–758.

Dolinski, D., Gromski, W., & Zawisza, E. (1987). Unrealistic pessimism. *Journal of Social Psychology. 127*, 511–516.

Donnerstein, E., & Wilson, D. W. (1976). Effects of noise and perceived control on ongoing and subsequent aggressive behavior. *Journal of Personality and Social Psychology, 34*, 774–781.

Donny, E. C., Caggiula, A. R., Mielke, M. M., Jacobs, K. S., Rose, C., & Sved, A. F. (1998). Acquisition of nicotine self-administration in rats: The effects of dose, feeding schedule, and drug contingency. *Psychopharmacology, 136*, 83–90.

Dorman, S. M., & Rienzo, B. A. (1988). College students' knowledge of AIDS. *Health Values, 12*(4), 33–38.

Dowling, J. (1983). Autonomic measures and behavioral indices of pain sensitivity. *Pain, 16*, 193–200.

Downey, G., Silver, R. C., & Wortman, C. B. (1990). Reconsidering the attribution-adjustment relation following a major negative event: Coping with the loss of a child. *Journal of Personality and Social Psychology, 59*, 925–940.

Drapkin, R. G., Wing, R. R., & Shiffman, S. (1995). Responses to hypothetical high risk situations: Do the predict weight loss in a behavioral treatment program or the context of dietary lapses? *Health Psychology, 14,* 427–434.

DRUMMOND, D. C., & GLAUTIER, S. (1994). A controlled trial of cue exposure treatment in alcohol dependence. *Journal of Consulting and Clinical Psychology, 62,* 809–817.

DULA, A. (1994). African American suspicion of the health-care system is justified: What do we do about it? *Cambridge Quarterly of Healthcare Ethics, 3,* 347–357.

DUNCAN, S. C., STRYCKER, L. A., & DUNCAN, T. E. (1999). Exploring associations in developmental trends of adolescent substance use and risky sexual behavior in a high-risk population. *Journal of Behavioral Medicine, 22,* 21–34.

DUNKEL-SCHETTER, C., & BENNETT, T. L. (1990). Differentiating the cognitive and behavioral aspects of social support. In B. R. SARASON, I. G. SARASON, & G. R. PIERCE (Eds.), *Social support: An interactional view.* New York: Wiley.

DUNN, A. J. (1995). Psychoneuroimmunology: Introduction and general perspectives. In B. LEONARD & K. MILLER (Eds.), *Stress, the immune system and psychiatry.* New York: Wiley.

DUNN, M. E., & GOLDMAN, M. S. (1998). Age and drinking-related differences in the memory organization of alcohol expectancies in 3rd-, 6th-, 9th-, and 12th-grade children. *Journal of Consulting and Clinical Psychology, 66,* 579–585.

DURANT, R. H., RICKERT, V. I., ASHWORTH, C. S., NEWMAN, C., & SLAVENS, G. (1993). Use of multiple drugs among adolescents who use anabolic steroids. *New England Journal of Medicine, 328,* 922–926.

DUSSELDORP, E., VAN ELDEREN, T., MAES, S., MEULMAN, J., & KRAAIJ, V. (1999). A meta-analysis of psychoeducational programs for coronary heart disease patients. *Health Psychology, 18,* 506–519.

DWECK, C. S., DAVIDSON, W., NELSON, S., & ENNA, B. (1978). Sex differences in learned helplessness: II. The contingencies of evaluative feedback in the classroom, and III. An experimental analysis. *Developmental Psychology, 14,* 268–276.

DWECK, C. S., & ELLIOTT, E. S. (1983). Achievement motivation. In P. H. MUSSEN (Ed.), *Handbook of child psychology* (4th ed., Vol. 4). New York: Wiley.

DWECK, C. S., & REPUCCI, N. D. (1973). Learned helplessness and reinforcement responsibility in children. *Journal of Personality and Social Psychology, 25,* 109–116.

D'ZURILLA, T. J. (1988). Problem-solving therapies. In K. S. DOBSON (Ed.), *Handbook of cognitive–behavioral therapies.* New York: Guilford.

EARLE, T. L., LINDEN, W., & WEINBERG, J. (1999). Differential effects of harassment on cardiovascular and salivary cortisol stress reactivity and recovery in women and men. *Journal of Psychosomatic Research, 46,* 124–141.

EASTERBROOK, G. (1987, January 26). The revolution. *Newsweek,* pp. 40–74.

EDELL, B. H., EDINGTON, S., HERD, B., O'BRIEN, R. M., & WITKIN, G. (1987). Self-efficacy and self-motivation as predictors of weight loss. *Addictive Behaviors, 12,* 63–66.

EDELMAN, S., LEMON, J. BELL, D. R., & KIDMAN, A. D. (1999). Effects of group CBT on the survival time of patients with metastatic breast cancer. *Psycho-Oncology, 8,* 474–481.

EDELSTEIN, L. (1984). *Maternal bereavement: Coping with the unexpected death of a child.* New York: Praeger.

EFA (Epilepsy Foundation of America) (2000). *Information & education* (*Seizure recognition + first aid; Medicines for epilepsy*). Retrieved (3-17-2000) from http://www.efa.org.

EICHENWALD, K. (1987, January 11). Braving epilepsy's storm. *New York Times Magazine,* pp. 30–36.

EISENBERG, D. M., DAVIS, R. B., ETTNER, S. L., APPEL, S., WILKEY, S., VAN ROMPAY, M., & KESSLER, R. C. (1998). Trends in alternative medicine use in the United States, 1990–1997: Results of a follow-up national survey. *Journal of the American Medical Association, 280,* 1569–1575.

EISENBERG, J. M., KITZ, D. S., & WEBBER, R. A. (1983). Development of attitudes about sharing decision-making: A comparison of medical and surgical residents. *Journal of Health and Social Behavior, 24,* 85–90.

EISENBERG, M. G. (1984). Spinal cord injuries. In H. B. ROBACK (Ed.), *Helping patients and their families cope with medical problems.* San Francisco: Jossey-Bass.

EISER, C. (1985). *The psychology of childhood illness.* New York: Springer-Verlag.

EITEL, P., K, & FRIEND, R. (1999). Reducing denial and sexual risk behaviors in college students: A comparison of a cognitive and a motivational approach. *Annals of Behavioral Medicine, 21,* 12–19.

ELIOPOULOS, C., KLEIN, J., PHAN, M. K., KNIE, B., GREENWALD, M., CHITAYAT, D., & KOREN, G. (1994). Hair concentrations of nicotine and cotinine in women and their newborn infants. *Journal of the American Medical Association, 271,* 621–623.

ELLINGTON, L., & WIEBE, D. J. (1999). Neuroticism, symptom presentation, and medical decision making. *Health Psychology, 18,* 634–643.

ELLIS, A. (1962). *Reason and emotion in psychotherapy.* New York: Lyle Stuart.

ELLIS, A. (1977). The basic clinical theory of rational-emotive therapy. In A. Ellis & R. GRIEGER (Eds.), *Handbook of rational-emotive therapy.* New York: Springer.

ELLIS, A. (1987). The impossibility of achieving consistently good mental health. *American Psychologist, 42,* 364–375.

EMERY, A. E. H., & PULLEN, I. M. (1986). A contemporary approach to genetic counseling. In M. J. CHRISTIE & P. G. MELLETT (Eds.), *The psychosomatic approach: Contemporary practice of whole-person care.* New York: Wiley.

EMMONS, K., LINNAN, L. A., SHADEL, W. G., MARCUS, B., & ABRAMS, D. B. (1999). The Working Healthy Project: A worksite health-promotion trial targeting physical activity, diet, and smoking. *Journal of Occupational and Environmental Medicine, 41,* 545–555.

EMRICK, C. D., & HANSEN, J. (1983). Assertions regarding effectiveness of treatment for alcoholism. *American Psychologist, 38,* 1078–1088.

ENGEL, G. L. (1977). The need for a new medical model: A challenge for biomedicine. *Science, 196,* 129–136.

ENGEL, G. L. (1980). The clinical application of the biopsychosocial model. *American Journal of Psychiatry, 137,* 535–544.

ENGEL, G. L., REICHSMAN, R., & SEGAL, H. L. (1956). A study of an infant with a gastric fistula: I. Behavior and the rate of total hydrochloric acid secretion. *Psychosomatic Medicine, 18,* 374–398.

ENGELS, G. I., GARNEFSKI, N., & DIEKSTRA, R. F. W. (1993). Efficacy of rational-emotive therapy: A quantitative analysis. *Journal of Consulting and Clinical Psychology, 61,* 1083–1090.

ENGSTROM, D. (1984). A psychological perspective of prevention in alcoholism. In J. D. MATARAZZO, S. M. WEISS, J. A. HERD, N. E. MILLER, & S. M. WEISS (Eds.), *Behavioral health: A handbook of health enhancement and disease prevention.* New York: Wiley.

ENRIGHT, M. F., RESNICK, R., DELEON, P. H., SCIARA, A. D., & TANNEY. F. (1990). The practice of psychology in hospital settings. *American Psychologist, 45,* 1059–1065.

EPDET (Expert Panel on Detection, Evaluation, and Treatment of High Blood Cholesterol in Adults) (2001). Executive summary of the Third Report of the National Cholesterol Education Program (NCEP) Expert Panel on Detection, Evalution, and Treatment of High Blood Cholesterol in Adults (Adult Treatment Panel III). *Journal of the American Medical Association, 285,* 2486–2497.

EPPING-JORDAN, J. E., WAHLGREN, D. R., WILLIAMS, R. A., PRUITT, S. D., SLATER, M. A., PATTERSON, T. L., GRANT, I., WEBSTER, J. S., & ATKINSON, J. H. (1998). Transition to chronic pain in men with low back pain: Predictive relationships among pain intensity, disability, and depressive symptoms. *Health Psychology, 17,* 421–427.

EPSTEIN, J. A., BOTVIN, G. J., & DIAZ, T. (1999). Social influence and psychological determinants of smoking among inner-city adolescents. *Journal of Child & Adolescent Substance Abuse, 8,* 1–19.

EPSTEIN, L. H., & CLUSS, P. A. (1982). A behavioral medicine perspective on adherence to long-term medical regimens. *Journal of Consulting and Clinical Psychology, 50,* 950–971.

EPSTEIN, L. H., & JENNINGS, J. R. (1986). Smoking, stress, cardiovascular reactivity, and coronary heart disease. In K. A. MATTHEWS, S. M. WEISS, T. DETRE, T. M. DEMBROSKI, B. FALKNER, S. B. MANUCK, & R. B. WILLIAMS (Eds.), *Handbook of stress, reactivity, and cardiovascular disease.* New York: Wiley.

EPSTEIN, L. H., KILANOWSKI, C. K., CONSALVI, A. R., & PALUCH, R. A. (1999). Reinforcing value of physical activity as a determinant of child activity level. *Health Psychology, 18,* 599–603.

EPSTEIN, L. H., SAELENS, B. E., & O'BRIEN, J. G. (1995). Effects of reinforcing increases in active behavior versus decreases in sedentary behavior for obese children. *International Journal of Behavioral Medicine, 2,* 41–50.

EPSTEIN, L. H., VALOSKI, A., VARA, L. S., McCURLEY, J., WISNIEWSKI, L., KALARCHIAN, M. A., KLEIN, K. R., & SHRAGER, L. R. (1995). Effects of decreasing sedentary behavior and increasing activity on weight change in obese children. *Health Psychology, 14,* 109–115.

EPSTEIN, L. H., VALOSKI, A., WING, R. R., & McCURLEY, J. (1994). Ten-year outcomes of behavioral family-based treatment for childhood obesity. *Health Psychology, 13,* 373–383.

EPSTEIN, L. H., WING, R. R., PENNER, B. C., & KRESS, M. J. (1985). Effect of diet and controlled exercise on weight loss in obese children. *Journal of Pediatrics, 107,* 358–361.

EPSTEIN, L. H., WING, R. R., VALOSKI, A., & DeVOS, D. (1988). Long-term relationship between weight and aerobic-fitness change in children. *Health Psychology, 7,* 47–53.

ERDMAN, R. A. M. (1990). Myocardial infarction and cardiac rehabilitation. In A. A. KAPTEIN, H. M. VAN DER PLOEG, B. GARSSEN, P. J. G. SCHREURS, & R. BEUNDERMAN (Eds.), *Behavioural medicine: Psychological treatment of somatic disorders.* Chichester: Wiley.

ERIKSEN, M. P., LEMAISTRE, C. A., & NEWELL, G. R. (1988). Health hazards of passive smoking. *Annual Review of Public Health, 9,* 47–70.

ERIKSSON, P. S., PERFILIEVA, E., BJORK-ERIKSSON, T., ALBORN, A. M., NORDBORG, C., PETERSON, D. A., & GAGE, F. H. (1998). Neurogenesis in the adult human hippocampus. *Nature Medicine, 4,* 1313–1317.

ESTERLING, B. A., ANTONI, M. H., FLETCHER, M. A., MARGULIES, S., & SCHNEIDERMAN, N. (1994). Emotional disclosure through writing or speaking modulates latent Epstein-Barr virus antibody titers. *Journal of Consulting and Clinical Psychology, 62,* 130–140.

ESTERLING, B. A., KIECOLT-GLASER, J. K., & GLASER, R. (1996). Psychosocial modulation of cytokine-induced natural killer cell activity in older adults. *Psychosomatic Medicine, 58*, 264–272.

ESTEY, A., MUSSEAU, A., & KEEHN, L. (1994). Patient's understanding of health information: A multihospital comparison. *Patient Education and Counseling, 24*, 73–78.

EUROPEAN COLLABORATIVE STUDY (1991). Children born to women with HIV-1 infection: Natural history and risk of transmission. *Lancet, 337*, 253–260.

EVANS, C., & RICHARDSON, P. H. (1988). Improved recovery and reduced postoperative stay after therapeutic suggestions during general anaesthesia. *Lancet, 332*, 491–493.

EVANS, F. J. (1987). Hypnosis. In R. J. CORSINI (Ed.), *Concise encyclopedia of psychology.* New York: Wiley.

EVANS, R. (1990, August/September). What you should know about childhood asthma. *Asthma and Allergy Advance* (reprint), pp. 1–4.

EVANS, R. I. (1976). Smoking in children: Developing a social psychological strategy of deterrence. *Preventive Medicine, 5*, 122–127.

EVANS, R. I. (1984). A social inoculation strategy to deter smoking in adolescents. In J. D. MATARAZZO, S. M. WEISS, J. A. HERD, N. E. MILLER, & S. M. WEISS (Eds.), *Behavioral health: A handbook of health enhancement and disease prevention.* New York: Wiley.

EVANS, R. I., ROZELLE, R. M., MITTELMARK, M. B., HANSEN, W. B., BANE, A. L., & HAVIS, J. (1978). Deterring the onset of smoking in children: Knowledge of immediate physiological effects and coping with peer pressure, media pressure, and parent modeling. *Journal of Applied Social Psychology, 8*, 126–135.

EVANS, R. L., HENDRICKS, R. D., HASELKORN, J. K., BISHOP, D. S., & BALDWIN, D. (1992). The family's role in stroke rehabilitation: A review of the literature. *American Journal of Physical Medicine & Rehabilitation, 71*, 135–139.

EVERSON, S. A., GOLDBERG, D. E., KAPLAN, G. A., COHEN, R. D., PUKKALA, E., TUOMILEHTO, J., & SALONEN, J. T. (1996). Hopelessness and risk of mortality and incidence of myocardial infarction and cancer. *Psychosomatic Medicine, 58*, 113–121.

EVERSON, S. A., KAPLAN, G. A., GOLDBERG, D. E., LAKKA, T. A., SIVENIUS, J., & SALONEN, J. T. (1999). Anger expression and incident stroke: Prospective evidence from the Kuopio Ischemic Heart Disease Study. *Stroke, 30*, 523–528.

EVERSON, S. A., LYNCH, J. W., CHESNEY, M. A., KAPLAN, G. A., GOLDBERG, D. E., SHADE, S. B., COHEN, R. D., SALONEN, R., & SALONEN, J. T. (1997). Interaction of workplace demands and cardiovascular reactivity in progression of carotid atherosclerosis: Population based study. *British Medical Journal, 314*, 553–558.

EVERSON, S. A., MCKEY, B. S., & LOVALLO, W. R. (1995). Effect of trait hostility on cardiovascular responses to harassment in young men. *International Journal of Behavioral Medicine, 2*, 172–191.

EVERSON, S. A., ROBERTS, R. E., GOLDBERG, D. E., & KAPLAN, G. A. (1998). Depressive symptoms and increased risk of stroke mortality over a 29-year period. *Archives of Internal Medicine, 158*, 1133–1138.

EWART, C. K. (1991a). Familial transmission of essential hypertension: Genes, environments, and chronic anger. *Annals of Behavioral Medicine, 13*, 40–47.

EWART, C. K. (1991b). Social action theory for a public health psychology. *American Psychologist, 46*, 931–946.

FACCHINI, F., CHEN, Y.-D. I., & REAVEN, G. M. (1994). Light-to-moderate alcohol intake is associated with enhanced insulin sensitivity. *Diabetes Care, 17*, 115–119.

FALKNER, B., & LIGHT, K. C. (1986). The interactive effects of stress and dietary sodium on cardiovascular reactivity. In K. A. MATTHEWS, S. M. WEISS, T. DETRE, T. M. DEMBROSKI, B. FALKNER, S. B. MANUCK, & R. B. WILLIAMS (Eds.), *Handbook of stress, reactivity, and cardiovascular disease.* New York: Wiley.

FANG, J., MADHAVAN, S., & ALDERMAN, M. H. (1996). The association between birthplace and mortality from cardiovascular causes among black and white residents of New York City. *New England Journal of Medicine, 335*, 1545–1551.

FARKAS, A. J. (1999). When does cigarette fading increase the likelihood of future cessation? *Annals of Behavioral Medicine, 21*, 71–76.

FARKAS, A. J., DISTEFAN, J. M., CHOI, W. S., GILPIN, E. A., & PIERCE, J. P. (1999). Does parental smoking cessation discourage adolescent smoking? *Preventive Medicine, 28*, 213–218.

FARQUHAR, J. W., MACCOBY, N., & SOLOMON, D. S. (1984). Community applications of behavioral medicine. In W. D. GENTRY (Ed.), *Handbook of behavioral medicine.* New York: Guilford.

FARQUHAR, J. W., MACCOBY, N., WOOD, P. D. ALEXANDER, J. K., et al. (1977, June 4). Community education for cardiovascular health. *Lancet*, 1192–1195.

FATHALLA, M. F. (1990). Relationship between contraceptive technology and HIV transmission: An overview. In N. J. ALEXANDER, H. L. GABELNICK, & J. M. SPIELER (Eds.), *Heterosexual transmission of AIDS.* New York: Wiley-Liss.

FAUCETT, J., GORDON, N., & LEVINE, J. (1994). Differences in postoperative pain severity among four ethnic groups. *Journal of Pain and Symptom Management, 9*, 383–389.

FAWZY, F. I., COUSINS, N. FAWZY, N. W., KEMENY, M. E., ELASHOFF, R., & MORTON, D. (1990). A structured psychiatric intervention for cancer patients: I. Changes over time in methods of coping and affective disturbance. *Archives of General Psychiatry, 47,* 720–725.

FAWZY, F. I., FAWZY, N. W., HYUN, C. S., ELASHOFF, R., GUTHRIE, D., FAHEY, J. L., & MORTON, D. L. (1993). Effects of an early structured psychiatric intervention, coping, and affective state on recurrence and survival 6 years later. *Archives of General Psychiatry, 50,* 681–689.

FAWZY, F. I., KEMENY, M. E., FAWZY, N. W., ELASHOFF, R., MORTON, D., COUSINS, N., & FAHEY, J. L. (1990). A structured psychiatric intervention for cancer patients: II. Changes over time in immunological measures. *Archives of General Psychiatry, 47,* 729–735.

FELDMAN, M., & RICHARDSON, C. T. (1986). Role of thought, sight, smell, and taste of food in the cephalic phase of gastric acid secretion in humans. *Gastroenterology, 90,* 428–433.

FELDMAN, P. J., COHEN, S., DOYLE, E. J., SKONER, D. P., & GWALTNEY, J. M. (1999). The impact of personality on the reporting of unfounded symptoms and illness. *Journal of Personality and Social Psychology, 77,* 370–378.

FELDMAN, R. S. (2000). *Development across the life span* (2nd ed.). Upper Saddle River, NJ: Prentice Hall.

FELDMAN, S. I., DOWNEY, G., & SCHAFFER-NEITZ, R. (1999). Pain, negative mood, and perceived support in chronic pain patients: A daily diary study of people with reflex sympathetic dystrophy syndrome. *Journal of Consulting and Clinical Psychology, 67,* 776–785.

FELETTI, G., FIRMAN, D., & SANSON-FISHER, R. (1986). Patient satisfaction with primary-care consultations. *Journal of Behavioral Medicine, 9,* 389–399.

FERNANDEZ, E. (1986). A classification system of cognitive coping strategies for pain. *Pain, 26,* 141–151.

FERNANDEZ, E., CLARK, T. S., & RUDICK-DAVIS, D. (1998). A framework for conceptualizing and assessment of affective disturbance in pain. In A. R. BLOCK, E. F. KREMER, & E. FERNANDEZ (Eds.), *Handbook of pain syndromes: Biopsychosocial perspectives* (pp. 123–147). Mahwah, NJ: Erlbaum.

FERNANDEZ, E., & TURK, D. C. (1989). The utility of cognitive coping strategies for altering pain perception: A meta-analysis. *Pain, 38,* 123–135.

FEUERSTEIN, M., CARTER, R. L., & PAPCIAK, A. S. (1987). A prospective analysis of stress and fatigue in recurrent low back pain. *Pain, 31,* 333–344.

FEUERSTEIN, M., & GAINER, J. (1982). Chronic headache: Etiology and management. In D. M. DOLEYS, R. L. MEREDITH, & A. R. CIMINERO (Eds.), *Behavioral medicine: Assessment and treatment strategies.* New York: Plenum.

FIATARONE, M. A., MORLEY, J. E., BLOOM, E. T., BENTON, D., SOLOMON, G. F., & MAKINODAN, T. (1989). The effect of exercise on natural killer cell activity in young and old subjects. *Journal of Gerontology: Medical Sciences, 44,* M37-45.

FIELD, T. M. (1996). Touch therapies across the life span. In P. M. KATO & T. MANN (Ed.), *Handbook of diversity issues in health psychology.* New York: Plenum.

FIELD, T. M. (1998). Massage therapy effects. *American Psychologist, 53,* 1270–1281.

FIELDING, J. E. (1990). The challenges of work-place health promotion. In S. M. WEISS, J. E. FIELDING, & A. BAUM (Eds.), *Perspectives in behavioral medicine: Health at work.* Hillsdale, NJ: Erlbaum.

FIELDING, J. E. (1991). Smoking control at the workplace. *Annual Review of Public Health, 12,* 209–234.

FIELDING, J. E., & PISERCHIA, P. V. (1989). Frequency of worksite health promotion activities. *American Journal of Public Health, 79,* 16–20.

FIELDS, H. L., & LEVINE, J. D. (1984). Placebo analgesia—A role for endorphins? *Trends in Neurosciences, 7,* 271–273.

FILSINGER, E. E. (1987). Social class. In R. J. CORSINI (Ed.), *Concise encyclopedia of psychology.* New York: Wiley.

FINN, P. E., & ALCORN, J. D. (1986). Noncompliance to hemodialysis dietary regimens: Literature review and treatment recommendations. *Rehabilitation Psychology, 31,* 67–78.

FINNEY, J. W., & MOOS, R. H. (1997). Psychosocial treatments for alcohol use disorders. In P. E. NATHAN & J. M. GORMAN (Eds.), *A guide to treatments that work* (pp. 156–166). New York: Oxford University Press.

FIORE, M. C., JORENBY, D. E., & BAKER, T. B. (1997). Smoking cessation: Principles and practice based upon the AHCPR Guideline, 1996. *Annals of Behavioral Medicine, 19,* 213–219.

FIORE, M. C., NEWCOMB, P., & MCBRIDE, P. (1993). Natural history and epidemiology of tobacco use and addiction. In C. T. ORLEANS & J. SLADE (Eds.), *Nicotine addiction: Principles and management.* New York: Oxford University Press.

FIORE, M. C., SMITH, S. S., JORENBY, D. E., & BAKER, T. B. (1994). The effectiveness of the nicotine patch for smoking cessation: A meta-analysis. *Journal of the American Medical Association, 271,* 1940–1947.

FISHER, E. B., LICHTENSTEIN, E., & HAIRE-JOSHU, D. (1993). Multiple determinants of tobacco use and cessation. In C. T. ORLEANS & J. SLADE (Eds.), *Nicotine addiction: Principles and management.* Oxford University Press.

FISHER, J. D., FISHER, W. A., MISOVICH, S. H., KIMBLE, D. L., & MALLOY, T. E. (1996). Changing AIDS risk behavior: Effects of an intervention emphasizing AIDS risk reduction information, motivation, and behavioral skills in a college student population. *Health Psychology, 15,* 114–123.

FISKE, D. W., & MADDI, S. R. (1961). A conceptual framework. In D. W. FISKE & S. R. MADDI (Eds.), *Functions of varied experience.* Homewood, IL: Dorsey.

FLACK, J. M., AMARO, H., JENKINS, W., KUNITZ, S., LEVY,

J., MIXON, M., & YU, E. (1995). Panel I: Epidemiology of minority health. *Health Psychology, 14*, 592–600.

FLASKERUD, J. H. (1988). AIDS: Psychosocial aspects. *Health Values, 12*(4), 44–52.

FLAY, B. R. (1985). Psychosocial approaches to smoking prevention: A review of findings. *Health Psychology, 4*, 449–488.

FLAY, B. R. (1987). Mass media and smoking cessation: A critical review. *American Journal of Public Health, 77*, 153–160.

FLAY, B. R., HU, F. B., & RICHARDSON, J. (1998). Psychosocial predictors of different stages of cigarette smoking among high school students. *Preventive Medicine, 27*, A9-A18.

FLAY, B. R., KOEPKE, D., THOMSON, S. J., SANTI, S., BEST, A., & BROWN, K. S. (1989). Six-year follow-up of the first Waterloo school smoking prevention trial. *American Journal of Public Health, 79*, 1371–1376.

FLAY, B. R., RYAN, K. B., BEST, J. A., BROWN, K. S., KERSELL, M. W., d'AVERNAS, J. R., & ZANNA, M. P. (1985). Are social-psychological smoking prevention programs effective? The Waterloo Study. *Journal of Behavioral Medicine, 8*, 37–59.

FLEMING, I., BAUM, A., DAVIDSON, L. M., RECTANUS, E., & McARDLE, S. (1987). Chronic stress as a factor in physiologic reactivity to challenge. *Health Psychology, 6*, 221–237.

FLEMING, M. F., MUNDT, M. P., FRENCH, M. T., MANWELL, L. B., STAUFFACHER, E. A., & BARRY, K. L. (2000). Benefit-cost analysis of brief physician advice with problem drinkers in primary care settings. *Medical Care, 38*, 7–18.

FLEMING, R., BAUM, A., GISRIEL, M. M., & GATCHEL, R. J. (1982). Mediating influences of social support on stress at Three Mile Island. *Journal of Human Stress, 8*, 14–22.

FLINN, W. R., DALSING, M. C., & WHITE, J. V. (1986). Carotid endarterectomy: Indications, technique, and results. In P. E. KAPLAN & L. J. CERULLO (Eds.), *Stroke rehabilitation*. Boston: Butterworth.

FLOR, H., FYDRICH, T., & TURK, D. C. (1992). Efficacy of multidiciplinary pain treatment centers: A meta-analytic review. *Pain, 49*, 221–230.

FLOR, H., KERNS, R. D., & TURK, D. C. (1987). The role of spouse reinforcement, perceived pain, and activity levels of chronic pain patients. *Journal of Psychosomatic Research, 31*, 251–259.

FLOR, H., & TURK, D. C. (1985). Chronic illness in an adult family member: Pain as a prototype. In D. C. TURK & R. D. KERNS (Eds.), *Health, illness, and families: A life-span perspective*. New York: Wiley.

FLYNN, K. J., & FITZGIBBON, M. (1998). Body images and obesity risk among black females: A review of the literature. *Annals of Behavioral Medicine, 20*, 13–24.

FOA, E. B. (1998). Rape and posttraumatic stress disorder. In E. A. BLECHMAN & K. D. BROWNELL (Eds.), *Behavioral medicine and women: A comprehensive handbook*. New York: Guilford.

FOGEL, E. R. (1987). Biofeedback-assisted musculoskeletal therapy and neuromuscular reeducation. In M. S. SCHWARTZ (Ed.), *Biofeedback: A practitioner's guide*. New York: Guilford.

FOLEY, K. M. (1985). The medical treatment of cancer pain. *New England Journal of Medicine, 313*, 84–95.

FOLKMAN, S., & LAZARUS, R. S. (1988). Coping as a mediator of emotion. *Journal of Personality and Social Psychology, 54*, 466–475.

FOLKMAN, S., LAZARUS, R. S., DUNKEL-SCHETTER, C., DeLONGIS, A., & GRUEN, R. J. (1986). Dynamics of a stressful encounter: Cognitive appraisal, coping, and encounter outcomes. *Journal of Personality and Social Psychology, 50*, 992–1003.

FOLKMAN, S., LAZARUS, R. S., PIMLEY, S., & NOVACEK, J. (1987). Age differences in stress and coping processes. *Psychology and Aging, 2*, 171–184.

FOLLICK, M. J., AHERN, D. K., & ABERGER, E. W. (1985). Development of an audiovisual taxonomy of pain behavior: Reliability and discriminant validity. *Health Psychology, 4*, 555–568.

FOLLICK, M. J., AHERN, D. K., ATTANASIO, V., & RILEY, J. F. (1985). Chronic pain programs: Current aims, strategies, and needs. *Annals of Behavioral Medicine, 7*(3), 17–20.

FOLLICK, M. J., GORKIN, L., SMITH, T. W., CAPONE, R. J., VISCO, J., & STABLEIN, D. (1988). Quality of life post-myocardial infarction: Effects of a transtelephonic coronary intervention system. *Health Psychology, 7*, 169–182.

FOLSOM, A. R., KAYE, S. A., SELLERS, T. A., HONG, C.-P., CERHAN, J. R., POTTER, J. D., & PRINEAS, R. J. (1993). Body fat distribution and 5-year risk of death in older women. *Journal of the American Medical Association, 269*, 483–487.

FONTANA, A. F., KERNS, R. D., ROSENBERG, R. L., & COLONESE, K. L. (1989). Support, stress, and recovery from coronary heart disease: A longitudinal causal mode. *Health Psychology, 8*, 175–193.

FORD, E. S. (1999). Body mass index and colon cancer in a national sample of adult US men and women. *American Journal of Epidemiology, 150*, 190–398.

FORDYCE, W. E. (1976). *Behavioral methods for chronic pain and illness*. St. Louis: Mosby.

FORDYCE, W. E. & STEGER, J. C. (1979). Behavioral management of chronic pain. In O. F. POMERLEAU & J. P. BRADY (Eds.), *Behavioral medicine: Theory and practice*.

FOREM, J. (1974). *Transcendental meditation*. New York: Dutton.

FOREYT, J. P., & LEAVESLEY, G. (1991). Behavioral treatment of obesite at the work site. In S. M. WEISS, J. E. FIELDING, & A. BAUM (Eds.), *Perspectives in behavioral medicine: Health at work*. Hillsdale, NJ: Earlbaum.

FOREYT, J. P., SCOTT, L. W., MITCHELL, R. E., & GOTTO, A. M. (1979). Plasma lipid changes in the normal population following behavioral treatment. *Journal of Consulting and Clinical Psychology, 47*, 440–452.

FORMAN, M. R., TROWBRIDGE, F. L., GENTRY, E. M., MARKS, J. S., & HOGELIN, G. C. (1986). Overweight adults in the United States: The behavioral risk factor surveys. *American Journal of Clinical Nutrition, 44*, 410–416.

FORTMANN, S. P., WINKLEBY, M. A., FLORA, J. A., HASKELL, W. L., & TAYLOR, C. B. (1990). Effect of long-term community health education on blood pressure and hypertension control: The Stanford Five City Project. *American Journal of Epidemiology, 132*, 629–646.

FOX, B. H. (1978). Premorbid psychological factors as related to cancer incidence. *Journal of Behavioral Medicine, 1*, 45–133.

FOX, D. K., HOPKINS, B. L., & ANGER, W. K. (1987). The long-term effects of a token economy on safety performance in open-pit mining. *Journal of Applied Behavior Analysis, 20*, 215–224.

FRADKIN, B., & FIRESTONE, P. (1986). Premenstrual tension, expectancy, and mother-child relations. *Journal of Behavioral Medicine, 9*, 245–259.

FRANCE, C., & DITTO, B. (1988). Caffeine effects on several indices of cardiovascular activity at rest and during stress. *Journal of Behavioral Medicine, 11*, 473–482.

FRANCIS, V., KORSCH, B. M., & MORRIS, M. J. (1969). Gaps in doctor-patient communication. *New England Journal of Medicine, 280*, 535–540.

FRANK, E., WINKLEBY, M. A., ALTMAN, D. G., ROCKHILL, B., & FORTMANN, S. P. (1991). Predictors of physicians' smoking cessation advice. *Journal of the American Medical Association, 266*, 3139–3144.

FRANK, R. G., GLUCK, J. P., & BUCKELEW, S. P. (1990). Rehabilitation: Psychology's greatest opportunity. *American Psychologist, 45*, 757–761.

FRANKENHAEUSER, M. (1986). A psychobiological framework for research on human stress and coping. In M. H. APPLEY & R. TRUMBULL (Eds.), *Dynamics of stress: Physiological, psychological, and social perspectives*. New York: Plenum.

FRANKISH, J., & LINDEN, W. (1991). Is response adaptation a threat to the high-low reactor distinction among female college students? *Health Psychology, 10*, 224–227.

FRASER, R. T. (1999). Epilepsy. In M. G. EISENBERG, R. L. GLUECKAUF, & H. H. ZARETSKY (Eds.), *Medical aspects of disability: A handbook for the rehabilitation professional* (2nd ed., pp. 225–244). New York: Springer.

FRASURE-SMITH, N., LESPERANCE, F., JUNEAU, M., TALAJIC, M., & BOURASSA, M. G. (1999). Gender, depression, and one-year prognosis after myocardial infarction. *Psychosomatic Medicine, 61*, 26–37.

FREDRIKSON, M., & MATTHEWS, K. A. (1990). Cardiovascular responses to behavioral stress and hypertension: A meta-analytic review. *Annals of Behavioral Medicine, 12*, 30–39.

FREELS, S. A., WARNECKE, R. B., PARSONS, J. A., JOHNSON, T. P., FLAY, B. R., & MORENA, O. F. (1999). Characteristics associated with exposure to and participation in a televised smoking cessation intervention program for women with high school or less education. *Preventive Medicine, 28*, 579–588.

FREEMAN, A. (1990). Cognitive therapy. In A. S. BELLACK & M, HERSEN (Eds.), *Handbook of comparative treatments for adult disorders*. New York: Wiley.

FREEMON, B., NEGRETE, V. F., DAVIS, M., & KORSCH, B. M. (1971). Gaps in doctor-patient communication: Doctor-patient interaction analysis. *Pediatric Research, 5*, 298–311.

FREIDSON, E. (1961). *Patients' views of medical practice*. New York: Russell Sage Foundation.

FRENCH, S. A., & JEFFERY, R. W. (1994). Consequences of dieting to lose weight: Effects on physical and mental health. *Health Psychology, 13*, 195–212.

FRIEDMAN, H. S., & BOOTH-KEWLEY, S. (1987). The "disease-prone" personality. *American Psychologist, 42*, 539–555.

FRIEDMAN, H. S., TUCKER, J. S., & REISE, S. P. (1995). Personality dimensions and measures potentially relevant to health: A focus on hostility. *Annals of Behavioral Medicine, 17*, 245–253.

FRIEDMAN, H. S., TUCKER, J. S., SCHWARTZ, J. E., TOMLINSON-KEASEY, C., WINGARD, D. L., & CRIQUI, M. H. (1995). Psychosocial and behavioral predictors of longevity. The aging and death of the "Termites." *American Psychologist, 50*, 69–78.

FRIEDMAN, L. A., & KIMBALL, A. W. (1986). Coronary heart disease mortality and alcohol consumption in Framingham. *American Journal of Epidemiology, 124*, 481–489.

FRIEDMAN, M. (1996). *Type A behavior: Its diagnosis and treatment*. New York: Plenum.

FRIEDMAN, M., & ROSENMAN, R. H. (1974). *Type A behavior and your heart*. New York: Knopf.

FRIEDMAN, M., THORESEN, C. E., GILL, J. J., ULMER, D., et al. (1986). Alteration of Type A behavior and its effect on cardiac recurrences in post myocardial infarction patients: Summary results of the Recurrent Coronary

Prevention Project. *American Heart Journal*, 112, 653–665.

FRIEDMAN, R., SOBEL, D., MYERS, P., CAUDILL, M., & BENSON, H. (1995). Behavioral medicine, clinical health psychology, and cost offset. *Health Psychology*, 14, 509–518.

FRIIS, R., & TAFF, G. A. (1986). Social support and social networks, and coronary heart disease and rehabilitation. *Journal of Cardiopulmonary Rehabilitation*, 6, 132–147.

FROESE, A., HACKETT, T. P., CASSEM, N. H., & SILVERBERG, E. L. (1974). Trajectories of anxiety and depression in denying and nondenying acute myocardial infarction patients during hospitalization. *Journal of Psychosomatic Research*, 18, 413–420.

FULLERTON, J. T., KRITZ-SILVERSTEIN, D., SADLER, G. R., & BARRETT-CONNOR, E. (1996). Mammography usage in a community-based sample of older women. *Annals of Behavioral Medicine*, 18, 67–72.

FULLILOVE, M. T., FULLILOVE, R. E., HAYNES, K., & GROSS, S. (1990). Black women and AIDS prevention: A view towards understanding the gender rules. *Journal of Sex Research*, 27, 47–64.

FUNK, S. C. (1992). Hardiness: A review of theory and research. *Health Psychology*, 11, 335–345.

FUTTERMAN, A. D., KEMENY, M. E., SHAPIRO, D., & FAHEY, J. L. (1994). Immunological and physiological changes associated with induced positive and negative mood. *Psychosomatic Medicine*, 56, 499–511.

GALAVOTTI, C., CABRAL, R. J., LANSKY, A., GRIMLEY, D. M., RILEY, G. E., & PROCHASKA, J. O. (1995). Validation of measures of condom and other contraceptive use among women at high risk for HIV infection and unintended pregnancy. *Health Psychology*, 14, 570–578.

GANNON, L. R., HAYNES, S. N., CUEVAS, J., & CHAVEZ, R. (1987). Psychophysiological correlates of induced headaches. *Journal of Behavioral Medicine*, 10, 411–423.

GARFIELD, C. (1978). *Psychosocial care of the dying patient*. New York: McGraw-Hill.

GARMEZY, N. (1983). Stressors of childhood. In N. GARMEZY & M. RUTTER (Eds.), *Stress, coping, and development in children*, New York: McGraw-Hill.

GARRITY, T. F. (1981). Medical compliance and the clinician-patient relationship: A review. *Social Science and Medicine*, 15, 215–222.

GARRITY, T. F., & MARX, M. B. (1979). Critical life events and coronary disease. In W. D. GENTRY & R. B. WILLIAMS (Eds.), *Psychological aspects of myocardial infarction and coronary care* (2nd ed.). St. Louis: Mosby.

GATCHEL, R. J. (1980). Effectiveness of two procedures for reducing dental fear: Group-administered desensitization and group education and discussion. *Journal of the American Dental Association*, 101, 634–638.

GATCHEL, R. J. (1996). Psychological disorders and chronic pain: Cause-and-effect relationships. In R. J. GATCHEL & D. C. TURK (Eds.), *Psychological approaches to pain management: A practitioner's handbook* (pp. 33–52). New York: Guilford.

GATCHEL, R. J., MAYER, T. G., CAPRA, P., DIAMOND, P., & BARNETT, J. (1986). Millon Behavioral Health Inventory: Its utility in predicting physical function in low back pain patients. *Archives of Physical Medicine and Rehabilitation*, 67, 878–882.

GAUTHIER, J., CÔTÉ, G., & FRENCH, D. (1994). The role of home practice in the thermal biofeedback treatment of migraine headache. *Journal of Consulting and Clinical Psychology*, 62, 180–184.

GAVZER, B. (1988, September 18). Why do some people survive AIDS? *Parade*, pp. 4–7.

GAZIANO, J. M., BURING, J. E., BRESLOW, J. L., GOLDHABER, S. Z., ROSNER, B., VANDENBURGH, M., WILLETT, W., & HENNEKENS, C. H. (1993). Moderate alcohol intake, increased levels of high-density lipoprotein and its subfractions, and decreased risk of myocardial infarction. *New England Journal of Medicine*, 329, 1829–1834.

GENTRY, W. D. (1984). Behavioral medicine: A new research paradigm. In W. D. GENTRY (Ed.), *Handbook of behavioral medicine*. New York: Guilford.

GENTRY, W. D., & KOBASA, S. C. O. (1984). Social and psychological resources mediating stress-illness relationships in humans. In W. D. GENTRY (Ed.), *Handbook of behavioral medicine*. New York: Guilford.

GENTRY, W. D., & OWENS, D. (1986). Pain groups. In A. D. HOLZMAN & D. C. TURK (Eds.), *Pain management: A handbook of psychological treatment approaches*. New York: Pergamon.

GERACE, R. A., & VORP, R. (1985). Epidemiology and behavior. In N. SCHNEIDERMAN & J. T. TAPP (Eds.), *Behavioral medicine: The biopsychosocial approach*. Hillsdale, NJ: Erlbaum.

GERLIN, A. (1999, September 12). Health care's deadly secret: Accidents routinely happen. *Philadelphia Inquirer*, pp. A1, A20.

GERVASIO, A. H. (1986). Family relationships and compliance. In K. E. GERBER & A. M. NEHEMKIS (Eds.), *Compliance: The dilemma of the chronically ill*. New York: Springer.

GIACHELLO, A. L., & ARROM, J. O. (1997). Health service access and utilization among adolecsent minorities. In D. K. WILSON, J. R. RODRIGUE, & W. C. TAYLOR (Eds.), *Health-promoting and health-compromising behaviors among minority adolescents* (pp. 303–320). Washington: American Psychological Association.

GIANG, D. W., GOODMAN, A. D., SCHIFFER, R. B., MATTSON, D. H., PETRIE, M., COHEN, N., & ADER, R. (1996). Conditioning of cyclophosphamide-induced leukopenia in humans. *Journal of Neuropsychiatry and Clinical Neurosciences*, 8, 194–201.

GIBBONS, F. X., McGOVERN, P. G., & LANDO, H. A. (1991). Relapse and risk perception among members of a smoking cessation clinic. *Health Psychology*, 10, 42–45.

GIDRON, Y., DAVIDSON, K., & BATA, I. (1999). The short-term effects of a hostility-reduction intervention on male coronary heart disease patients. *Health Psychology*, 18, 416–420.

GIL, K. M., GINSBERG, B., MUIR, M., SYKES, D., & WILLIAMS, D. A. (1990). Patient-controlled analgesia in postoperative pain: The relation of psychological factors to pain and analgesic use. *Clinical Journal of Pain*, 6, 137–142.

GIL, K. M. KEEFE, F. J., SAMPSON, H. A., McCASKILL, C. C., RODIN, J., & CRISSON, J. E. (1988). Direct observation of scratching behavior in children with atopic dermatitis. *Behavior Therapy*, 19, 213–227.

GIL. K. M., WILSON, J. J., & EDENS, J. L. (1997). The stability of pain coping strategies in young children, adolescents, and adults with sickle cell disease over an 18-month period. *Clinical Journal of Pain*, 13, 110–115.

GILBERSTADT, H., & DUKER, J. (1965). *A handbook for clinical and actuarial MMPI interpretation*. Philadelphia: Saunders.

GILBERT, D. G., & SPIELBERGER, C. D. (1987). Effects of smoking on heart rate, anxiety, and feelings of success during social interaction. *Journal of Behavioral Medicine*, 10, 629–638.

GILL, T. M., & FEINSTEIN, A. R. (1994). A critical appraisal of the quality of quality-of-life measurements. *Journal of the American Medical Association*, 272, 619–626.

GILLUM, R. F. (1987a). The association of body fat distribution with hypertension, hypertensive heart disease, coronary heart disease, diabetes and cardiovascular risk factors in men and women aged 18–79 years. *Journal of Chronic Diseases*, 40, 421–428.

GILLUM, R. F. (1987b). The association of the ratio of waist to hip girth with blood pressure, serum cholesterol and serum uric acid in children and youths aged 6–17 years. *Journal of Chronic Diseases*, 40, 413–420.

GINZBERG, E. (1983), Allied health resources. In D. MECHANIC (Ed.), *Handbook of health, health care, and the health professions*. New York: Free Press.

GIOVANUCCI, E., RIMM, E. B., COLDITZ, G. A., STAMPFER, M. J., ASCHERIO, A., CHUTE, C. C., & WILLETT, W. C. (1993). A prospective study of dietary fat and risk of prostate cancer. *Journal of the National Cancer Institute*, 85, 1571–1579.

GIPSON, M., LISKEVYCH, T., & SWILLINGER, E. (1996). *Managing your health care: Making the most of your medical resources*. Ventura, CA: Pathfinder.

GIRODO, M., & WOOD, D. (1979). Talking yourself out of pain: The importance of believing that you can. *Cognitive Therapy and Research*, 3, 23–33.

GLADIS, M. M., MICHELA, J. L., WALTER, H. J., & VAUGHAN, R. D. (1992). High school students' perceptions of AIDS risk: Realistic appraisal or motivated denial? *Health Psychology*, 11, 307–316.

GLANZ, K., & LERMAN, C. (1992). Psychosocial impact of breast cancer: A critical review. *Annals of Behavioral Medicine*, 14, 204–212.

GLASER, R., THORN, B. E., TARR, K. L., KIECOLT-GLASER, J. K., & D' AMBROSIO, S. M. (1985). Effects of stress on methyltransferase synthesis: An important DNA repair enzyme. *Health Psychology*, 4, 403–412.

GLASGOW, R. E., KLESGES, R. C., MIZES, J. S., & PECHACEK, T. F. (1985). Quitting smoking: Strategies used and variables associated with success in a stop-smoking contest. *Journal of Consulting and Clinical Psychology*, 53, 905–912.

GLASGOW, R. E., & LICHTENSTEIN, E. (1987). Long-term effects of behavioral smoking cessation interventions. *Behavior Therapy*, 18, 297–324.

GLASGOW, R. E., McCAUL, K. D., & SCHAFER, L. C. (1986). Barriers to regimen adherence among persons with insulin-dependent diabetes. *Journal of Behavioral Medicine*, 9, 65–77.

GLASGOW, R. E., McCAUL, K. D., & SCHAFER, L. C. (1987). Self-care behaviors and glycemic control in Type I diabetes. *Journal of Chronic Diseases*, 40, 399–412.

GLASS, D. C. (1977). *Behavior patterns, stress, and coronary heart disease*. Hillsdale, NJ: Erlbaum.

GLASS, D. C., KRAKOFF, L. R., CONTRADA, R., HILTON, W. F., KEHOE, K., MANNUCCI, E. G., COLLINS, C., SNOW, B., & ELTING, E. (1980). Effect of harassment and competition upon cardiovascular and plasma catecholamine responses in Type A and Type B individuals. *Psychophysiology*, 17, 453–463.

GLYNN, L. M., CHRISTENFELD, N., & GERIN, W. (1999). Gender, social support, and cardiovascular responses to stress. *Psychosomatic Medicine*, 61, 234–242.

GLYNN, S. M., GRUDER, C. L., & JEGERSKI, J. A. (1986). Effects of biochemical validation of self-reported cigarette smoking on treatment success and on misreporting abstinence. *Health Psychology*, 5, 125–136.

GODIN, G., DESHARNAIS, R., JOBIN, J., & COOK, J. (1987). The impact of physical fitness and health-age appraisal upon exercise intentions and behavior. *Journal of Behavioral Medicine*, 10, 241–250.

GODIN, G., DESHARNAIS, R., VALOIS, P., LEPAGE, L., JOBIN, J., & BRADET, R. (1992, March). *Perceived barriers to exercise among different populations*. Paper presented at the meeting of the Society of Behavioral Medicine, New York.

GODIN, G., VALOIS, P., SHEPHARD, R. J., & DESHARNAIS, R. (1987). Prediction of leisuretime exercise behavior: A path analysis (LISREL V) model. *Journal of Behavioral Medicine*, 10, 145–158.

GOFFMAN, E. (1961). *Asylums*. Garden City, NY: Doubleday.

GOLD, R. S., & SKINNER, M. J. (1996). Judging a book by its cover: Gay men's use of perceptible characteristics to infer antibody status. *International Journal of STD & AIDS*, 7, 39–43.

GOLD, R. S., SKINNER, M. J., & HINCHY, J. (1999). Gay men's stereotypes about who is HIV-infected: A further study. *International Journal of STD & AIDS*, 10, 1–6.

GOLDBERG, C. (1998, September 11). Little drop in college binge drinking. *New York Times*, p. A14.

GOLDBERG, E. L., & COMSTOCK, G. W. (1980). Epidemiology of life events: Frequency in general populations. *American Journal of Epidemiology*, 111, 736–752.

GOLDING, J. F., & CORNISH, A. M. (1987). Personality and lifestyle in medical students: Psychopharmacological aspects. *Psychology and Health*, 1, 287–301.

GOLDMAN, M. S. (1983). Cognitive impairment in chronic alcoholics. *American Psychologist*, 38, 1045–1054.

GOLDSTEIN, I. B., JAMNER, L. D., & SHAPIRO, D. (1992). Ambulatory blood pressure and heart rate in healthy male paramedics during a workday and a nonworkday. *Health Psychology*, 11, 48–54.

GOLDSTEIN, L. H. (1990). Behavioural and cognitive-behavioural treatments for epilepsy: A progress review. *British Journal of Clinical Psychology*, 29, 257–269.

GOLDSTON, D. B., KOVACS, M., OBROSKY, D. S., & IYENGAR, S. (1995). A longitudinal study of life events and metabolic control among youths with insulin-dependent diabetes mellitus. *Health Psychology*, 14, 409–414.

GOLDWATER, B. C., & COLLIS, M. L. (1985). Psychologic effects of cardiovascular conditioning: A controlled experiment. *Psychosomatic Medicine*, 47, 174–181.

GOMEL, M., OLDENBURG, B., SIMPSON, J. M., & OWEN, N. (1993). Work-site cardiovascular risk reduction: A randomized trial of health risk assessment, education, counseling, and incentives. *American Journal of Public Health*, 83, 1231–1238.

GOODALL, T. A., & HALFORD, W. K. (1991). Self-management of diabetes mellitus: A critical review. *Health Psychology*, 10, 1–8.

GORDER, D. D., DOLECEK, T. A., COLEMAN, G. G., TILLOTSON, J. L., BROWN, H. B., LENZ-LITZOW, K., BARTSCH, G. E., & GRANDITS, G. (1986). Dietary intake in the Multiple Risk Factor Intervention Trial (MRFIT): Nutrient and food group changes over 6 years. *Journal of the American Dietetic Association*, 86, 744–751.

GORDON, C. M., & CAREY, M. P. (1996). Alcohol's effects on requisites for sexual risk reduction in men: An initial experimental investigation. *Health Psychology*, 15, 56–60.

GORDON, W. A., & DILLER, L. (1983). Stroke: Coping with a cognitive deficit. In T. G. BURISH & L. A. BRADLEY (Eds.), *Coping with chronic disease: Research and applications*. New York: Academic Press.

GORTMAKER, S. L., DIETZ, W. H., & CHEUNG, L. W. Y. (1990). Inactivity, diet, and the fattening of America. *Journal of the American Dietetic Association*, 90, 1247–1252, 1255.

GORTMAKER, S. L., ECKENRODE, J., & GORE, S. (1982). Stress and the utilization of health services: A time series and cross-sectional analysis. *Journal of Health and Social Behavior*, 23, 25–38.

GOTTLIEB, B. H. (1997). Conceptual and measurement issues in the study of coping with chronic stress. In B. H. GOTTLIEB (Ed.), *Coping with chronic stress*. New York: Plenum.

GOTTLIEB, N. H. (1983). The effect of health beliefs on the smoking behavior of college women. *Journal of American College Health*, 31, 214–221.

GOTTLIEB, N. H., & BAKER, J. A. (1986). The relative influence of health beliefs, parental and peer behaviors and exercise program participation on smoking, alcohol use and physical activity. *Social Science and Medicine*, 22, 915–927.

GOTTLIEB, N. H., & GREEN, L. W. (1987). Ethnicity and lifestyle health risk: Some possible mechanisms. *American Journal of Health Promotion*, 2, 37–45, 51.

GRAHAM, J. D., CORSO, P. S., MORRIS, J. M., SEGUI-GOMEZ, M., & WEINSTEIN, M. C. (1998). Evaluating the cost-effectiveness of clinical and public health measures. *Annual Review of Public Health*, 19, 125–152.

GRANT, J. C. B. (1972). *An atlas of anatomy*. Baltimore: Williams & Wilkins.

GRAZIANO, A. M., DEGIOVANNI, I. S., & GARCIA, K. A. (1979). Behavioral treatment of children's fears: A review. *Psychological Bulletin*, 86, 804–830.

GREEN, C. J. (1985). The use of psychodiagnostic questionnaires in predicting risk factors and health outcomes. In P. KAROLY (Ed.), *Measurement strategies in health psychology*. New York: Wiley.

GREEN, P. J., & SULS, J. (1996). The effects of caffeine on ambulatory blood pressure, heart rate, and mood in coffee drinkers. *Journal of Behavioral Medicine*, 19, 111–128.

GREENBERG, E. R., BARON, J. A., TOSTESON, T. D., FREEMAN, D. H., et al. (1994). A clinical trial of antioxidant vitamins to prevent colorectal adenoma. *New England Journal of Medicine*, 331, 141–147.

GREENFIELD, D. (1985). Nutritional basis of health and disease. In N. SCHNEIDERMAN & J. T. TAPP (Eds.), *Behavioral medicine: The biopsychosocial approach*. Hillsdale, NJ: Erlbaum.

GREENGLASS, E. R., & NOGUCHI, K. (1996, August). *Longevity, gender and health: A psychocultural perspective*. Paper presented at the meeting of the International Society of Health Psychology in Montreal.

GREENWALD, H. P., BONICA, J. J., & BERGNER, M. (1987). The prevalence of pain in four cancers. *Cancer, 60*, 2563–2569.

GRIFFIN, K. W., BOTVIN, G. J., DOYLE, M. M., DIAZ, T., & EPSTEIN, J. A. (1999). A six-year follow-up study of determinants of heavy cigarette smoking among high-school seniors. *Journal of Behavioral Medicine, 22*, 271–284.

GRILO, C. M., SHIFFMAN, S., & WING, R. R. (1989). Relapse crises and coping among dieters. *Journal of Consulting and Clinical Psychology, 57*, 488–495.

GRITZ, E. R., CARR, C. R., & MARCUS, A. C. (1991). The tobacco withdrawal syndrome in unaided quitters. *British Journal of Addiction, 86*, 57–69.

GROB, G. N. (1983). Disease and environment in American history. In D. MECHANIC (Ed.), *Handbook of health, health care, and the health professions*. New York: Free Press.

GROBBEE, D. E., RIMM, E. B., GIOVANNUCCI, E., COLDITZ, G., STAMPFER, M., & WILLETT, W. (1990). Coffee, caffeine, and cardiovascular disease in men. *New England Journal of Medicine, 323*, 1026–1032.

GRØNBÆK, M., BECKER, U., JOHANSEN, D., GOTTSCHAU, A., SCHNOHR, P., HEIN, H. O., JENSEN, G., & SØRENSEN, T. I. A. (2000). Type of alcohol consumed and mortality from all causes, coronary heart disease, and cancer. *Annals of Internal Medicine, 133*, 411–419.

GROSECLOSE, S. L., WEINSTEIN, B., JONES, T. S., VALLEROY, L. A., FEHRS, L. J., & KASSLER, W. J. (1995). Impact of increased legal access to needles and syringes on practices of injecting-drug users and police officers—Connecticut, 1992–1993. *Journal of Acquired Immune Deficiency Syndromes and Human Retrovirology, 10*, 82–89.

GROSSBART, T. A. (1982, February). Bringing peace to embattled skin. *Psychology Today*, pp. 55–60.

GRUBE, J. W., & WALLACK, L. (1994). Television beer advertising and drinking knowledge, beliefs, and intentions among schoolchildren. *American Journal of Public Health, 84*, 254–259.

GRUEN, W. (1975). Effects of brief psychotherapy during the hospitalization period on the recovery process in heart attacks. *Journal of Consulting and Clinical Psychology, 43*, 223–232.

GRUETZNER, H. (1992). *Alzheimer's: A caregiver's guide and sourcebook*. New York: Wiley.

GRUNAU, R. V. E., & CRAIG, K. D. (1987). Pain expression in neonates: Facial action and cry. *Pain, 28*, 395–410.

GRUNBERG, N. E. (1991). Cigarette smoking at work. In S. M. WEISS, J. E. FIELDING, & A. BAUM (Eds.), *Perspectives in behavioral medicine: Health at work*. Hillsdale, NJ: Erlbaum.

GRUNBERG, N. E., & BOWEN, D. J. (1985). Coping with the sequelae of smoking cessation. *Journal of Cardiopulmonary Rehabilitation, 5*, 285–289.

GUARE, J. C., MYERS, G. A., & MARRERO, D. G. (1999). Diabetes mellitus. In M. G. EISENBERG, R. L. GLUECKAUF, R. L., & H. H. ZARETSKY (Eds.), *Medical aspects of disability: A handbook for the rehabilitation professional* (2nd ed., pp. 205–224). New York: Springer.

GUCCIONE, A. A., FELSON, D. T., ANDERSON, J. J., ANTHONY, J. M., ZHANG, Y., WILSON, P. W. F., KELLY-HAYES, M., WOLF, P. A., KREGER, B. E., & KANNEL, W. B. (1994). The effects of specific medical conditions on the functional limitations of elders in the Framingham Study. *American Journal of Public Health, 84*, 351–358.

GUCK, T. P., SKULTETY, F. M., MEILMAN, P. W., & DOWD, E. T. (1985). Multidisciplinary pain center follow-up study: Evaluation with a no-treatment control group. *Pain, 21*, 295–306.

GUMP, B. B., & MATTHEWS, K. A. (1999). Do background stressors influence reactivity to and recovery from acute stressors? *Journal of Applied Social Psychology, 29*, 469–494.

GUYLL, M., & CONTRADA, R. J. (1998). Trait hostility and ambulatory cardiovascular activity: Responses to social interaction. *Health Psychology, 17*, 30–39.

GUYTON, A. C. (1985). *Anatomy and physiology*. Philadelphia: Saunders.

HAAGA, D. A. F., & DAVISON, G. C. (1993). An appraisal of rational-emotive therapy. *Journal of Consulting and Clinical Psychology, 61*, 215–220.

HAAPANEN, A., KOSKENVUO, M., KAPRIO, J., KESÄNIEMI, Y. A., & HEIKKILÄ, K. (1989). Carotid arteriosclerosis in identical twins discordant for cigarette smoking. *Circulation, 80*, 10–16.

HAAS, F., & HAAS, S. S. (1990). *The chronic bronchitis and emphysema handbook*. New York: Wiley.

HACKETT, T. P., & WEISMAN, A. D. (1985). Reactions to the imminence of death. In A. MONAT & R. S. LAZARUS (Eds.), *Stress and coping: An anthology* (2nd ed.). New York: Columbia University Press.

HADDOCK, C. K., SHADISH, W. R., KLESGES, R. C., & STEIN, R. J. (1994). Treatments for childhood and adolescent obesity. *Annals of Behavioral Medicine, 16*, 235–244.

HAFEN, B. Q. (1981). *Nutrition, food, and weight control*. Boston: Allyn & Bacon.

HALEY, W. E. (1998). Alzheimer's disease: A general review. In E. A. BLECHMAN & K. D. BROWNELL (Eds.), *Behavioral medicine and women: A comprehensive handbook* (pp. 546–550). New York: Guilford.

HALKITIS, P. N., & WILTON, L. (1999, Fall). Optimism and HIV treatment advances: The impact on sexual risk-taking among gay men. *The Health Psychologist, 21*, 10–12.

HALL, J. A., MILBURN, M. A., ROTER, D. L., & DALTROY, L. H. (1998). Why are sicker patients less satisfied with their medical care? Tests of two explanatory models. *Health Psychology, 17,*70–75.

HALL, S. M., RUGG, D., TUNSTALL, C., & JONES, R. T. (1984). Preventing relapse to cigarette smoking by behavioral skill training. *Journal of Consulting and Clinical Psychology, 52,* 372–382.

HALL, T. (1990, June 17). After AIDS diagnosis, some embrace life. *New York Times,* pp. 1, 20.

HALPERN, D. F., & COREN, S. (1991). Handedness and life span. *New England Journal of Medicine, 324,* 998.

HAMILTON, J. D., HARTIGAN, P. M., SIMBERKOFF, M. S., DAY, P. L., et al. (1992). A controlled trial of early versus late treatment with zidovudine in symptomatic human immunodeficiency virus infection: Results of the Veterans Affairs Cooperative Study. *New England Journal of Medicine, 326,* 437–443.

HAMMOND, S, K., SORENSON, G., YOUNGSTROM, R., & OCKENE, J. K. (1995). Occupational exposure to environmental tobacco smoke. *Journal of the American Medical Association, 274,* 956–960.

HANSEN, W. B., GRAHAM, J. W., SOBEL, J. L., SHELTON, D. R., FLAY, B. R., & JOHNSON, C. A. (1987). The consistency of peer and parent influences on tobacco, alcohol, and marijuana use among young adolescents. *Journal of Behavioral Medicine, 10,* 559–579.

HANSEN, W. B., RAYNOR, A. E., & WOLKENSTEIN, B. H. (1991). Perceived personal immunity to the consequences of drinking alcohol: The relationship between behavior and perception. *Journal of Behavioral Medicine, 14,* 205–224.

HANSON, C. L., HENGGELER, S. W., & BURGHEN, G. A. (1987). Social competence and parental support as mediators of the link between stress and metabolic control in adolescents with insulin-dependent diabetes mellitus. *Journal of Consulting and Clinical Psychology, 55,* 529–533.

HARBURG, E., ERFURT, J. C., HAUENSTEIN, L. S., CHAPE, C., SCHULL, W. J., & SCHORK, M. A. (1973). Socio-ecological stress, suppressed hostility, skin color, and black-white male blood pressure: Detroit. *Psychosomatic Medicine, 35,* 276–296.

HARE, B. D., & MILANO, R. A. (1985). Chronic pain: Perspectives on physical assessment and treatment. *Annals of Behavioral Medicine, 7*(3), 6–10.

HARLAN, W. R. (1984). Rationale for intervention on blood pressure in childhood and adolescence. In J. D. MATARAZZO, S. M. WEISS, J. A. HERD, N. E. MILLER, & S. M. WEISS (Eds.), *Behavioral health: A handbook of health enhancement and disease prevention.* New York: Wiley.

HARLEY, H. G., BROOK, J. D., RUNDLE, S. A., CROW, S., REARDON, W., BUCKLER, A. J., HARPER, P. S., HOUSEMAN, D. E., & SHAW, D. J. (1992). Expansion of an unstable DNA region and phenotypic variation in myotonic dystrophy. *Nature, 355,* 545–546.

HARRIS, D. M., & GUTEN, S. (1979). Health-protective behavior: An exploratory study. *Journal of Health and Social Behavior, 20,* 17–29.

HARRIS, J. R., PEDERSON, N. L., MCCLEARN, G. E., PLOMIN, R., & NESSELROADE, J. R. (1992). Age differences in genetic and environmental influences for health from the Swedish Adoption/Twin Study of Aging. *Journal of Gerontology, 47,* P213–220.

HARRISON, S. L., MACLENNAN, R., SPEARE, R., & WRONSKI, I. (1994). Sun exposure and melanocytic naevi in young Australian children. *Lancet, 1994,* 1529–1532.

HART, W. (1987). *The art of living: Vipassana meditation.* New York: HarperCollins.

HARTER, S. (1983). Developmental perspectives on the self-system. In P. H. MUSSEN (Ed.), *Handbook of child psychology* (4th ed., Vol. 4). New York: Wiley.

HARTUP, W. W. (1983). Peer relations. In P. H. MUSSEN (Ed.), *Handbook of child psychology* (4th ed., Vol. 4). New York: Wiley.

HARTZ, A. J., RUPLEY, D. C., & RIMM, A. A. (1984). The association of girth measurements with disease in 32, 856 women. *American Journal of Epidemiology, 119,* 71–80.

HARVEY, P. G. (1984). Lead and children's health—Recent research and future questions. *Journal of Child Psychology and Psychiatry, 25,* 517–522.

HASKELL, W. L. (1984). Overview: Health benefits of exercise. In J. D. MATARAZZO, S. M. WEISS, J. A. HERD, N. E. MILLER, & S. M. WEISS (Eds.), *Behavioral health: A handbook of health enhancement and disease prevention.* New York: Wiley.

HASKELL, W. L., ALDERMAN, E. L., FAIR, J. M., MARON, D. J., et al. (1994). Effects of intensive multiple risk factor reduction on coronary atherosclerosis and clinical cardiac events in men and women with coronary artery disease: The Standford Coronary Risk Intervention Project (SCRIP). *Circulation, 89,* 975–990.

HATCH, J. P., GATCHEL., R. J., & HARRINGTON, R. (1982). Biofeedback: Clinical applications in medicine. In R. J. Gatchel, A. Baum, & J. E. Singer (Eds.), *Handbook of psychology and health* (Vol. 1). Hillsdale, NJ: Erlbaum.

HATHAWAY, S. R., & MCKINLEY, J. C. (1967). *The Minnesota Multiphasic Personality Inventory Manual.* New York: Psychological Corporation.

HAUG, M. R., & LAVIN, B. (1981). Practitioner or patient— Who's in charge? *Journal of Health and Social Behavior, 22,* 212–229.

HAUSER, W. A., & HESDORFFER, D. C. (1990). *Facts about epilepsy.* Landover, MD: Epilepsy Foundation of America.

HAY, D., & OKEN, D. (1985). The psychological stresses of intensive care unit nursing. In A. MONAT &

R. S. LAZARUS (Eds.), *Stress and coping* (2nd ed.). New York: Columbia University Press.

HAYES, R. D., KRAVITZ, R. L., MAZEL, R. M., SHERBOURNE, C. D., DIMATTEO, M. R., ROGERS, W. H., & GREENFIELD, S. (1994). The impact of patient adherence on health outcomes for patients with chronic disease in the Medical Outcomes Study. Journal of *Behavioral Medicine*, 17, 347–360.

HAYNES, R. B. (1976). A critical review of the "determinants" of patient compliance with therapeutic regimens. In D. L. SACKETT & R. B. HAYNES (Eds.), *Compliance with therapeutic regimens.* Baltimore: Johns Hopkins University Press.

HAYNES, R. B. (1982). Improving patient compliance: An empirical review. In R. B. STUART (Ed.), *Adherence, compliance, and generalization in behavioral medicine.* New York: Brunner/Mazel.

HAYNES, S. G., LEVINE, S., SCOTCH, N., FEINLEIB, M., & KANNEL, W. B. (1978). The relationship of psychosocial factors to coronary heart disease in the Framingham Study: I. Methods and risk factors. *American Journal of Epidemiology*, 107, 362–383.

HAYNES, S. G., & MATTHEWS, K. A. (1988). Review and methodological critique of recent studies on Type A behavior and cardiovascular disease. *Annals of Behavioral Medicine*, 10, 47–59.

HAYS, J. C., GOLD, D. T., FLINT, E. P., & WINER, E. P. (1999). Patient preference for place of death: A qualitative approach. In B. DE VRIES (Ed.), *End of life issues: Interdisciplinary and multidimensional perspectives* (pp. 3–21). New York: Springer.

HAYS, J. C., KASL, S. V., & JACOBS, J. C. (1994). The course of psychological distress following threatened and actual conjugal bereavement. *Psychological Medicine*, 24, 917–927.

HEARN, M. D., BARANOWSKI, T., BARANOWSKI, J., DOYLE, C., SMITH, M., LIN, L. S., & RESNICOW, K. (1998). Environmental influences on dietary behavior among children: Availability and accessibility of fruits and vegetables enable consumption. *Journal of Health Education*, 29, 26–32.

HEBB, D. O. (1955). Drives and the C. N. S. (conceptual nervous system). *Psychological Review*, 62, 243–254.

HEINEMANN, A. W. (1999). Spinal cord injury. In M. G. EISENBERG, R. L. GLUECKAUF, & H. H. ZARETSKY (Eds.), *Medical aspects of disability: A handbook for the rehabilitation professional* (2nd ed., pp. 499–527). New York: Springer.

HEINRICH, R. L., COHEN, M. J., NALIBOFF, B. D., COLLINS, G. A., & BONNEBAKKER, A. D. (1985). Comparing physical and behavior therapy for chronic low back pain on physical abilities, psychological distress, and patients' perceptions. *Journal of Behavioral Medicine*, 8, 61–78.

HEITZMANN, C. A., & KAPLAN, R. M. (1988). Assessment of methods for measuring social support. *Health Psychology*, 7, 75–109.

HELGESON, V. S., & COHEN, S. (1996). Social support and adjustment to cancer: Reconciling descriptive, correlational, and intervention research. *Health Psychology*, 15, 135–148.

HELGESON, V. S., COHEN, S., SCHULZ, R. & YASKO, J. (1999). Education and peer discussion group interventions and adjustment to breast cancer. *Archives of General Psychiatry*, 56, 340–347.

HELGESON, V. S., & FRITZ, H. L. (1999). Cognitive adaptation as a predictor of new coronary events after percutaneous transluminal coronary angioplasty. *Psychosomatic Medicine*, 61, 488–495.

HELLER, K., PRICE, R. H., & HOGG, J. R. (1990). The role of social support in community and clinical interventions. In B. R. SARASON, I. G. SARASON, & G. R. PIERCE (Eds.), *Social support: An interactional view.* New York: Wiley.

HELLHAMMER, D. K., BUCHTAL, J., GUTBERLET, I., & KIRSCHBAUM, C. (1997). Social hierarchy and adrenocortical stress reactivity in men. *Psychoneuroendocrinology*, 22, 643–650.

HENDEL, H., CAILLAT-ZUCMAN, S., LEBUANEC, H., CARRINGTON, M. et al. (1999). New class I and II HLA alleles strongly associated with opposite patterns of progression to AIDS. *Journal of Immunology*, 162, 6942–6946.

HENDERSON, D. K., FAHEY, B. J., WILLY, M., SCHMITT, J. M., CAREY, K., KOZIOL, D. E., LANE, H. C., FEDIO, J., & SAAH, A. J. (1990). Risk for occupational transmission of human immunodeficiency virus type 1 (HIV-1) associated with clinical exposures: A prospective evaluation. *Annals of Internal Medicine*, 113, 740–746.

HENDERSON, G., & PRIMEAUX, M. (1981). Religious beliefs and healing. In G. HENDERSON & M. PRIMEAUX (Eds.), *Transcultural health care.* Menlo Park, CA: Addison-Wesley.

HENDLER, N. H. (1984). Chronic pain. In H. B. ROBACK (Eds.), *Helping patients and their families cope with medical problems.* San Francisco: Jossey-Bass.

HENDRICK, S. S. (1985). Spinal cord injury and neuromuscular reeducation. In N. SCHEIDERMAN & J. T. TAPP (Eds.), *Behavioral medicine: The biopsychosocial approach.* Hillsdale, NJ: Erlbaum.

HENNINGFIELD, J. E., COHEN, C., & PICKWORTH, W. B. (1993). Psychopharmacology of nicotine. In C. T. ORLEANS & J. SLADE (Eds.), *Nicotine addiction: Principles and management.* New York: Oxford University Press.

HENRY, J. H., LIU, Y.-Y., NADRA, W. E., QIAN, C.-G., MORMEDE, P., LEMAIRE, V., ELY, D., & HENDLEY, E. D. (1993). Psychosocial stress can induce chronic hypertension in normotensive strains of rats. *Hypertension*, 21, 714–723.

HEPBURN, C. G., LOUGHLIN, C. A., & BARLING, J. (1997). Coping with chronic work stress. In B. H. GOTILIEB (Ed.), *Coping with chronic stress*. New York: Plenum.

HERBERT, T. B., & COHEN, S. (1993). Stress and immunity in humans: A meta-analytic review. *Psychosomatic Medicine, 55,* 364–379.

HERD, J. A., & WEISS, S. M. (1984). Overview of hypertension: Its treatment and prevention. In J. D. MATARAZZO, S. M. WEISS, J. A. HERD, N. E. MILLER, & S. M. WEISS (Eds.), *Behavioral health: A handbook of health enhancement and disease prevention*. New York: Wiley.

HEREK, G. M. (1999). AIDS and stigma. *American Behavioral Scientist, 42,* 1106–1116.

HEREK, G. M., & CAPITANIO, J. P. (1999). AIDS stigma and sexual prejudice. *American Behavioral Scientist, 42,* 1130–1147.

HEREK, G. M., & GLUNT, E. K. (1988). An epidemic of stigma: Public reactions to AIDS. *American Psychologist, 43,* 886–891.

HERMAN, C. P., & MACK, D. (1975). Restrained and unrestrained eating. *Journal of Personality, 43,* 647–660.

HERMAN, C. P., OLMSTEAD, M. P., & POLIVY, J. (1983). Obesity, externality, and susceptibility to social influence: An integrated analysis. *Journal of Personality and Social Psychology, 45,* 926–934.

HERMAN, C. P., & POLIVY, J. (1980). Restrained eating. In A. J. STUNKARD (Ed.), *Obesity*. Philadelphia: Saunders.

HERNANDEZ, J. T., & SMITH, F. J. (1990). Inconsistencies and misperceptions putting college students at risk of HIV infection. *Journal of Adolescent Health Care, 11,* 295–297.

HERSHEY, G. K. K., FRIEDRICH, M. F., ESSWEIN, L. A. THOMAS, M. L., & CHATLIA, T. A. (1997). The association of atopy with a gain-of-function mutation in the (alpha) subunit of the interluken-4 receptor. *New England Journal of Medicine, 337,* 1720–1725.

HESTER, R. K., & DELANEY, H. D. (1997). Behavioral self-control program for Windows: Results of a controlled clinical trial. *Journal of Consulting and Clinical Psychology, 65,* 686–693.

HESTER, R. K., & MILLER, W. R. (1989). Self-control training. In R. K. HESTER & W. R. MILLER (Eds.), *Handbook of alcoholism treatment approaches: Effective alternatives*. New York: Pergamon.

HFA (Hospice Foundation of America) (2000). *What is hospice?* Retrieved (3-23-2000) from http://www. hospice-foundation. org.

HIER, D. B. (1986). Recovery from behavioral deficits after stroke. In P. E. KAPLAN & L. J. CERULLO (Eds.), *Stroke rehabilitation*. Boston: Butterworth.

HIGGINS, S. T., WONG, C. J., BADGER, G. J., OGDEN, D. E. H., & DANTONA, R. L. (2000). Contingent reinforcement increases cocaine abstinence during outpatient treatment and 1 year follow-up. *Journal of Consulting and Clinical Psychology, 68,* 64–72.

HILGARD, E. R. (1967). Individual differences in hypnotizability. In J. E. GORDON (Ed.), *Handbook of clinical and experimental hypnosis*. New York: Macmillan.

HILGARD, E. R., & HILGARD, J. R. (1983). *Hypnosis in the relief of pain* (rev. ed.). Los Altos, CA: Kaufmann.

HINTON, J. (1984). Coping with terminal illness. In R. FITZPATRICK, J. HINTON, S. NEWMAN, G. SCAMBLER, & J. THOMPSON (Eds.), *The experience of illness*. London: Tavistock.

HIRANO, P. C., LAURENT, D. D., & LORIG, K. (1994). Arthritis patient education studies, 1987-1991: A review of the literature. *Patient Education and Counseling, 24,* 9–54.

HIROTO, D. S., & SELIGMAN, M. E. P. (1975). Generality of learned helplessness in man. *Journal of Personality and Social Psychology, 31,* 311–327.

HITCHCOCK, L. S., FERRELL, B. R., & McCAFFERY, M. (1994). The experience of chronic nonmalignant pain. *Journal of Pain and Symptom Management, 9,* 312–318.

HLETKO, P. J., ROBIN, S. S., HLETKO, J. D., & STONE, M. (1987). Infant safety seat use: Reaching the hard to reach. *American Journal of Diseases in Children, 141,* 1301–1304.

HOBFOLL, S. E. (1989). Conservation of resources: A new attempt at conceptualizing stress. *American Psychologist, 44,* 513–524.

HODGINS, D. C., EL-GUEBALY, N., & ARMSTRONG, S. (1995). Prospective and retrospective reports of mood states before relapse to substance abuse. *Journal of Consulting and Clinical Psychology, 63,* 400–407.

HODGINS, D. C., LEIGH, G., MILNE, R., & GERRISH, R. (1997). Drinking goal selection in behavioral self-management of chronic alcoholics. *Addictive Behaviors, 22,* 247–255.

HOEK, H. W., BARTELDS, A. I. M., BOSVELD, J. J. F., VANDER GRAAF, Y., LIMPENS, V. E. L., MAIWALD, M., & SPAAIJ, C. J. K. (1995). Impact of urbanization on detection rates of eating disorders. *American Journal of Psychiatry, 152,* 1272–1278.

HOELSCHER, T. J., LICHSTEIN, K. L., & ROSENTHAL, T. L. (1986). Home relaxation practice in hypertension treatment: Objective assessment and compliance induction. *Journal of Consulting and Clinical Psychology, 54,* 217–221.

HOFFMAN, M. (1993, June 28). Killing the pain. *Philadelphia Inquirer*, pp. C1, 4.

HOFMAN, A., WALTER, H. J., CONNELLY, P. A., & VAUGHN, R. D. (1987). Blood pressure and physical fitness in children. *Hypertension, 9,* 188–191.

HOLAHAN, C. J., & MOOS, R. H. (1985). Life stress and health: Personality, coping, and family support in stress resistance. *Journal of Personality and Social Psychology, 49,* 739–747.

HOLAHAN, C. J., & MOOS, R. H. (1986). Personality, coping,

and family resources in stress resistance: A longitudinal analysis. *Journal of Personality and Social Psychology*, 51, 389–395.

HOLAHAN, C. J., MOOS, R. H., HOLAHAN, C. K., & BRENNAN, P. L. (1997). Social context, coping strategies, and depressive symptoms: An expanded model with cardiac patients. *Journal of Personality and Social Psychology*, 72, 918–928.

HOLAHAN, C. K., HOLAHAN, C. J., & BELK, S. S. (1984). Adjustment in aging: The roles of life stress, hassles, and self-efficacy. *Health Psychology*, 3, 315–328.

HOLDEN, C. (1980). Love Canal residents under stress. *Science*, 208, 1242–1244.

HOLLON, S. D., SHELTON, R. C., & DAVIS, D. D. (1993). Cognitive therapy for depression: Conceptual issues and clinical efficacy. *Journal of Consulting and Clinical Psychology*, 61, 270–275.

HOLMES, D. M. (1986). The person and diabetes in psychosocial context. *Diabetes Care*, 9, 194–206.

HOLMES, D. S. (1984). Meditation and somatic arousal reduction. *American Psychologist*, 39, 1–10.

HOLMES, D. S. (1993). Aerobic fitness and the response to psychological stress. In P. SERAGANIAN (Ed.), *Exercise psychology: The influence of physical exercise on psychological processes*. New York: Wiley.

HOLMES, T. H., & MASUDA, M. (1974). Life change and illness susceptibility. In B. S. DOHRENWEND & B. P. DOHRENWEND (Eds.), *Stressful life events: Their nature and effects*. New York: Wiley.

HOLMES, T. H., & RAHE, R. H. (1967). The Social Readjustment Rating Scale. *Journal of Psychosomatic Research*, 11, 213–218.

HOLROYD, K. A., FRANCE, J. L., CORDINGLEY, G. E., ROKICKI, L. A., KVAAL, S. A., LIPCHIK, G. L., & McCOOL, H. R. (1995). Enhancing the effectiveness of relaxation-thermal biofeedback training with propranolol hydrochloride. *Journal of Consulting and Clinical Psychology*, 63, 327–330.

HOLROYD, K. A., FRANCE, J. L., NASH, J. M., & HURSEY, K. G. (1993). Pain state as artifact in the psychological assessment of recurrent headache sufferers. *Pain*, 53, 229–235.

HOLROYD, K. A., NASH, J. M., PINGEL, J. D., CORDINGLEY, G. E., & JEROME, A. (1991). A comparison of pharmacological (amitriptyline HCL) and nonpharmacological (cognitive-behavioral) therapies for chronic tension headaches. *Journal of Consulting and Clinical Psychology*, 59, 387–393.

HOLROYD, K. A., & PENZIEN, D. B. (1985). Client variables and the behavioral treatment of recurrent tension headache: A meta-analytic review. *Journal of Behavioral Medicine*, 9, 515–536.

HOLROYD, K. A., & PENZIEN, D. B. (1990). Pharmacological versus non-pharmacological prophylaxis of recurrent migraine headache: A meta-analytic review of clinical trials. *Pain*, 42, 1–13.

HOLT, J. (1995, December). Motivating Beth. *American Journal of Nursing*, 95, pp. 60, 62.

HOLTZMAN, D., LOWRY, R., KANN, L., COLLINS, J. L., & KOLBE, L. J. (1994). Changes in HIV-related information sources, instruction, knowledge, and behaviors among US high school students, 1989 and 1990. *American Journal of Public Health*, 84, 388–393.

HOLUM, J. R. (1994). *Fundamentals of general, organic, and biological chemistry* (5th ed.). New York: Wiley.

HOLUSHA, J. (1991, October 13). The nation's polluters—Who emits what, and where. *New York Times*, p. 10.

HOLZMAN, A. D., TURK, D. C., & KERNS, R. D. (1986). The cognitive-behavioral approach to the management of chronic pain. In A. D. HOLZMAN & D. C. TURK (Eds.), *Pain management: A handbook of psychological treatment approaches*. New York: Pergamon.

HONIG, A. S. (1987). Stress and coping in children. In H. E. FITZGERALD & M. G. WALRAVEN (Eds.), *Annual editions: Human development 87/88*. Guilford, CT: Dushkin.

HOPKINS, P. N. (1992). Effects of dietary cholesterol on serum cholesterol: A meta-analysis and review. *American Journal of Clinical Nutrition*, 55, 1060–1070.

HOPSON, J. L. (1988, July/August). A pleasurable chemistry. *Psychology Today*, pp. 29–30, 32–33.

HORN, J. C., & MEER, J. (1987, May). The vintage years. *Psychology Today*, pp. 76–84, 89–90.

HOSOI, J., MURPHY, G. F., EGAN, C. L., LERNER, E. A., GRABBE, S., ASAHINA, A., & GRANSTEIN, R. D. (1993). Regulation of Langerhans cell function by nerves containing calcitonin gene-related peptide. *Nature*, 363, 159–163.

HOSSACK, K. F., & LEFF, N. B. (1987). Influence of education and work history on patient perception of cardiovascular risk factors. *Journal of Cardiopulmonary Rehabilitation*, 7, 540–546.

HOUGH, R. L., FAIRBANK, D. T., & GARCIA, A. M. (1976). Problems in the ratio measurement of life stress. *Journal of Health and Social Behavior*, 17, 70–82.

HOUSE, J. S. (1984). Barriers to work stress: I. Social support. In W. D. GENTRY, H. BENSON, & C. DE WOLFF (Eds.), *Behavioral medicine: Work, stress, and health*. The Hague: Martinus Nijhoff.

HOUSE, J. S., ROBBINS, C., & METZNER, H. L. (1982). The association of social relationships and activities with mortality: Prospective evidence from the Tecumseh Community Health Study. *American Journal of Epidemiology*, 116, 123–140.

HOUSTON, B. K. (1986). Psychological variables and cardiovascular and neuroendocrine reactivity. In K. A. MATTHEWS, S. M. WEISS, T. DETRE, T. M. DEMBROSKI, B.

FALKNER, S. B. MANUCK, & R. B. WILLIAMS (Eds.), *Handbook of stress, reactivity, and cardiovascular disease*. New York: Wiley.

HOUSTON, B. K., & VAVAK, C. R. (1991). Cynical hostility: Developmental factors, psychosocial correlates, and health behaviors. *Health Psychology*, 10, 9–17.

HOWARD, G., WAGENKNECHT, L. E., BURKE, G. L., DIEZ-ROUX, A., EVANS, G. W., MCGOVERN, P., NIETO, F. J., & TELL, G. S. (1998). Cigarette smoking and progression of atherosclerosis: The Atherosclerosis Risk in Communities (ARIC) Study. *Journal of the American Medical Association*, 279, 119–224.

HOWARD, J. H., RECHNITZER, P. A., CUNNINGHAM, D. A., & DONNER, A. P. (1986). Change in Type A behavior a year after retirement. *The Gerontologist*, 26, 643–649.

HOWELL, D. (1986). The impact of terminal illness on the spouse. *Journal of Palliative Care*, 2, 22–30.

HSU, L. K. G., BENOTTI, P. N., DWYER, J., ROBERTS, S. B., SALTZMAN, E., SHIKORA, S., ROLLS, B. J., & RAND, W. (1998). Nonsurgical factors that influence the outcome of bariatric surgery: A review. *Psychosomatic Medicine*, 60, 338–346.

HU, F. B., PERSKY, V., FLAY, B. R., & RICHARDSON, J. (1997). An epidemiological study of asthma prevalence and related factors among young adults. *Journal of Asthma*, 34, 67–76.

HUFFMAN, L. C., & DEL CARMEN, R. (1990). Prenatal stress. In L. E. ARNOLD (Ed.), *Childhood stress*. New York: Wiley.

HUGHES, J. R. (1986). Genetics of smoking: A brief review. *Behavior Therapy*, 17, 335–345.

HULL, J. G., & BOND, C. F. (1986). Social and behavioral consequences of alcohol consumption and expectancy: A meta-analysis. *Psychological Bulletin*, 99, 347–360.

HULL, J. G., VAN TREUREN, R. R., & VIRNELLI, S. (1987). Hardiness and health: A critique and alternative approach. *Journal of Personality and Social Psychology*, 53, 518–530.

HULL, J. G., YOUNG, R. D., & JOURILES, E. (1986). Applications of the self-awareness model of alcohol consumption: Predicting patterns of use and abuse. *Journal of Personality and Social Psychology*, 51, 790–796.

HUMBLE, C., CROFT, J., GERBER, A., CASPER, M., HAMES, C. G., & TYROLER, H. A. (1990). Passive smoking and 20-year cardiovascular disease mortality among nonsmoking wives, Evans County, Georgia. *American Journal of Public Health*, 80, 599–601.

HUNT, E. B., & MACLEOD, C. M. (1979). Cognition and information processing in patient and physician. In G. C. STONE, F. COHEN, & N. E. ADLER (Eds.), *Health psychology: A handbook*. San Francisco: Jossey-Bass.

HUNT, W. A., & MATARAZZO, J. D. (1982). Changing smoking behavior: A critique. In R. J. GATCHEL, A. BAUM, & J. E.

SINGER (Eds.), *Handbook of psychology and health* (Vol. 1). Hillsdale, NJ: Erlbaum.

HUNT, W. A., MATARAZZO, J. D., WEISS, S. M., & GENTRY, W. D. (1979). Associative learning, habit, and health behavior. *Journal of Behavioral Medicine*, 2, 111–124.

HURLEY, D. (1987, August). A sound mind in an unsound body. *Psychology Today*, pp. 34–43.

HUSSUSSIAN, C. J., STRUEWING, J. P., GOLDSTEIN, A. M., HIGGINS, P. A. T., ALLY, D. S., SHEAHAN, M. D., CLARK, W. H., TUCKER, M. A., & DRACOPOLI, N. C. (1994). Germline p16 mutations in familial melanoma. *Nature Genetics*, 8, 15–21.

HUSTON, A. C. (1983). Sex-typing. In P. H. MUSSEN (Ed.), *Handbook of child psychology* (4th ed., Vol. 4). New York: Wiley.

HUSZTI, H. C., & WALKER, C. E. (1991). Critical issues on consultation and liaison. In J. J. SWEET, R. H. ROZENSKY, & S. M. TOVIAN (Eds.), *Handbook of clinical psychology in medical settings*. New York: Plenum.

HYSON, M. C. (1983). Going to the doctor: A developmental study of stress and coping. *Journal of Child Psychology and Psychiatry*, 24, 247–259.

IHGSC (International Human Genome Sequencing Consortium) (2001). Initial sequencing and analysis of the human genome. *Nature*, 409, 860–921.

ILFELD, F. W. (1980). Coping styles of Chicago adults: Description. *Journal of Human Stress*, 6, 2–10.

INSEL, P. M., & ROTH, W. T. (1998). *Core concepts in health* (8th ed.). Mountain View, CA: Mayfield.

INUI, T. S., YOURTEE, E. L., & WILLIAMSON, J. W. (1976). Improved outcomes in hypertension after physician tutorials. *Annals of Internal Medicine*, 84, 646–651.

IRONSON, G., FRIEDMAN, A., KLIMAS, N., ANTONI, M., FLETCHER, M. A., LAPERRIERE, A., SIMONEAU, J., & SCHNEIDERMAN, N. (1994). Distress, denial, and low adherence to behavioral interventions predict faster disease progression in gay men infected with human immunodeficiency virus. *International Journal of Behavioral Medicine*, 1, 90–105.

IRONSON, G., TAYLOR, C. B., BOLTWOOD, M., BARTZOKIS, T., DENNIS, C., CHESNEY, M., SPITZER, S., & SEGALL, G. M. (1992). Effects of anger on left ventricular ejection fraction in coronary artery disease. *American Journal of Cardiology*, 70, 281–285.

IRVIN, J. E., BOWERS, C. A., DUNN, M. E., & WANG, M. C. (1999). Efficacy of relapse prevention: A meta-analytic review. *Journal of Consulting and Clinical Psychology*, 67, 563–570.

IRVINE, J., BAKER, B., SMITH, J., JANDCIU, S., PAQUETTE, M., CAIRNS, J., CONNOLLY, S., ROBERTS, R., GENT, M., & DORIAN, P. (1999). Poor adherence to placebo or amiodarone therapy predicts mortality: Results from the CAMIAT study. *Psychosomatic Medicine*, 61, 566–575.

IRWIN, M., MASCOVICH, A., GILLIN, J. C., WILLOUGHBY, R., PIKE, J., & SMITH, T. L. (1994). Partial sleep deprivation reduces natural killer cell activity in humans. *Psychosomatic Medicine*, 56, 493–498.

ISRAEL, B. A., SCHULZ, A. J., PARKER, E. A., & BECKER, A. B. (1998). Review of community-based research: Assessing partnership approaches to improve public health. *Annual Review of Public Health*, 19, 173–202.

IZARD, C. E. (1979). Emotions as motivations: An evolutionary developmental perspective. In H. E. HOWE & R. A. DIENSTBIER (Eds.), *Nebraska Symposium on Motivation 1978* (Vol. 27). Lincoln, NE: University of Nebraska Press.

IZARD, C. E., HEMBREE, E. A., DOUGHERTY, L. M., & SPIZZIRRI, C. C. (1983). Changes in facial expressions of 2- to 19-month-old infants following acute pain. *Developmental Psychology*, 19, 418–426.

JACCARD, J., & TURRISI, R. (1987). Cognitive processes and individual differences in judgments relevant to drunk driving. *Journal of Personality and Social Psychology*, 53, 135–145.

JACOB, R. G., & CHESNEY, M. A. (1986). Psychological and behavioral methods to reduce cardiovascular reactivity. In K. A. MATTHEWS, S. M. WEISS, T. DETRE, T. M. DEMBROSKI, B. FALKNER, S. B. MANUCK, & R. B. WILLIAMS (Eds.), *Handbook of stress, reactivity, and cardiovascular disease*. New York: Wiley.

JACOBSEN, P. B., BOVBJERG, D. H., SCHWARTZ, M. D., HUDIS, C. A., GILEWSKI, T. A., & NORTON, L. (1995). Conditioned emotional distress in women receiving chemotherapy for breast cancer. *Journal of Consulting and Clinical Psychology*, 63, 108–114.

JACOBSEN, P. B., & STEIN, K. (1999). Is fatigue a long-term side effect of breast cancer treatment? *Cancer Control*, 6, 256–263.

JACOBSEN, P. B., WIDOWS, M. R., HANN, D. M., ANDRYKOWSKI, M. A., KRONISH, L. E., & FILEDS, K. K. (1998). Posttraumatic stress disorder symptoms after bone marrow transplantation for breast cancer. *Psychosomatic Medicine*, 60, 366–371.

JACOBSON, A. M., HAUSER, S. T., LAVORI, P., WILLETT, J. B., COLE, C. F., WOLFSDORE, J. I., DUMONT, R. H., & WERTLIEB, D. (1994). Family environment and glycemic control: A four-year prospective study of children and adolescents with insulin-dependent diabetes mellitus. *Psychosomatic Medicine*, 56, 401–409.

JACOBSON, E. J. (1938). *Progressive relaxation*. Chicago: University of Chicago Press.

JACOBSON, J. A., DANFORTH, D. N., COWAN, K. H., D'ANGELO, T., STEINBERG, S. M., PIERCE, L., LIPPMAN, M. E., LICHTER, A. S., GLATSTEIN, E., & OKUNIEFF, P. (1995). Ten-year results of a comparison of conservation with mastectomy in the treatment of stage I and II breast cancer. *New England Journal of Medicine*, 332, 907–911.

JADAD, A. R., CARROLL, D., GLYNN, C. J., MOORE, R. A., & MCQUAY, H. J. (1992). Morphine responsiveness of chronic pain: Double-blind randomised crossover study with patient-controlled anesthesia. *Lancet*, 339, 1367–1371.

JAMES, G. D., YEE, L. S., HARSHFIELD, G. A., BLANK, S. G., & PICKERING, T. G. (1986). The influence of happiness, anger, and anxiety on the blood pressure of borderline hypertensives. *Psychosomatic Medicine*, 48, 502–508.

JAMES, S. A., LACROIX, A. Z., KLEINBAUM, D. G., & STROGATZ, D. S. (1984). John Henryism and blood pressure among black men. II. The role of occupational stressors. *Journal of Behavioral Medicine*, 7, 259–274.

JAMNER, L. D., SHAPIRO, D., & JARVIK, M. E. (1999). Nicotine reduces the frequency of anger reports in smokers and nonsmokers with high but not low hostility: An ambulatory study. *Experimental and Clinical Psychopharmacology*, 7, 454–463.

JAMNER, L. D., & TURSKY, B. (1987). Syndrome-specific descriptor profiling: A psychophysiological and psychophysical approach. *Health Psychology*, 6, 417–430.

JANAL, M. N., GLUSMAN, M., KUHL, J. P., & CLARK, W. C. (1994). On the absence of correlation between responses to noxious heat, cold, electrical, and ischemic stimulation. *Pain*, 403–411.

JANIS, I. L. (1958). *Psychological stress*. New York: Wiley.

JANIS, I. L. (1967). Effects of fear arousal on attitude change: Recent developments in theory and experimental research. In L. BERKOWITZ (Ed.), *Advances in experimental social psychology* (Vol. 3). New York: Academic Press.

JANIS, I. L. (1984). The patient as decision maker. In W. D. GENTRY (Ed.), *Handbook of behavioral medicine*. New York: Guilford.

JANIS, I. L., & MANN, L. (1977). *Decision making: A psychological analysis of conflict, choice, and commitment*. New York: Free Press.

JANSON-BJERKLIE, S., CARRIERI, V. K., & HUDES, M. (1986). The sensations of pulmonary dyspnea. *Nursing Research*, 35, 154–159.

JARET, P. (1986, June). Our immune system: The wars within. *National Geographic*, 169, 702–735.

JARET, P. (1994, July). Viruses. *National Geographic*, 186, 58–91.

JARVIK, M. E., & HENNINGFIELD, J. E. (1993). Pharmacological adjuncts for the treatment of tobacco dependence. In C. T. ORLEANS & J. SLADE (Eds.), *Nicotine addiction: Principles and management*. New York: Oxford University Press.

JAVITT, J. C., AIELLO, L. P., CHIANG, Y., FERRIS, F. L., CANNER, J. K., & GREENFIELD, S. (1994). Preventive eye care in people with diabetes is cost-saving to the federal government. *Diabetes Care, 17,* 909–917.

JAY, S. M., ELLIOTT, C. H., KATZ, E., & SIEGEL, S. E. (1987). Cognitive-behavioral and pharmacologic interventions for children's distress during painful medical procedures. *Journal of Consulting and Clinical Psychology, 55,* 860–865.

JEANS, M. E. (1983). Pain in children—A neglected area. In P. FIRESTONE, P. J. MCGRATH, & W. FELDMAN (Eds.), *Advances in behavioral medicine for children and adolescents.* Hillsdale, NJ: Erlbaum.

JEFFERY, R. W. (1991). Weight management and hypertension. *Annals of Behavioral Medicine, 13,* 18–22.

JEFFERY, R. W. (1992). Is obesity a risk factor for cardiovascular disease? *Annals of Behavioral Medicine, 14,* 109–112.

JEFFERY, R. W. (1998). Prevention of obesity. In G. A. BRAY, C. BOUCHARD, & W. P. T. JAMES (Eds.), *Handbook of obesity* (pp. 819–829). New York: Marcel Dekker.

JEFFERY, R. W., FRENCH, S. A., & SCHMID, T. L. (1990). Attributions for dietary failures: Problems reported by participants in the Hypertension Prevention Trial. *Health Psychology, 9,* 315–329.

JEFFERY, R. W., HENNRIKUS, D. J., LANDO, H. A., MURRAY, D. M., & LIU, J. W. (2000). Reconciling conflicting findings regarding postcessation weight concerns and success in smoking cessation. *Health Psychology, 19,* 242–246.

JEMMOTT, J. B., CROYLE, R. T., & DITTO, P. H. (1988). Commonsense epidemiology: Self-based judgments from laypersons and physicians. *Health Psychology, 7,* 55–73.

JEMMOTT, J. B., DITTO, P. H., & CROYLE, R. T. (1986). Judging health status: Effects of perceived prevalence and personal relevance. *Journal of Personality and Social Psychology, 50,* 899–905.

JEMMOTT, J. B., JEMMOTT, L. S., & FONG, G. T. (1999). Abstinence and safer sex HIV risk-reduction interventions for African American adolescents: A randomized controlled trial. *Journal of the American Medical Association, 279,* 1529–1536.

JEMMOTT, J. B., & LOCKE, S. E. (1984). Psychosocial factors, immunologic mediation, and human susceptibility to infectious diseases: How much do we know? *Psychological Bulletin, 95,* 78–108.

JENKINS, C. D. (1979). An approach to the diagnosis and treatment of problems of health related behaviour. *International Journal of Health Education, 22*(Suppl. 2), 1–24.

JENKINS, C. D., ZYZANSKI, S. J., & ROSENMAN, R. H. (1979). *The Jenkins Activity Survey for Health Prediction.* New York: The Psychological Corporation.

JENKINS, L. S., & GORTNER, S. R. (1998). Correlates of self-efficacy expectations and prediction of walking behavior in cardiac surgery elders. *Annals of Behavioral Medicine 20,* 99–103.

JENNINGS, G., NELSON, L., NESTEL, P., ESLER, M., KORNER, P., BURTON, D., & BAZELMANS, J. (1986). The effects of changes in physical activity on major cardiovascular risk factors, hemodynamics, sympathetic function, and glucose utilization in man: A controlled study of four levels of activity. *Circulation, 73,* 30–40.

JENSEN, G. M., & LORISH, C. D. (1994). Promoting patient cooperation with exercise programs. *Arthritis Care and Research, 7,* 181–189.

JENSEN, M. P., & MCFARLAND, C. A. (1993). Increasing the reliability and validity of pain intensity measurement in chronic pain patients. *Pain, 55,* 195–203.

JENSEN, M. P., ROMANO, J. M., TURNER, J. A., GOOD, A. B., & WALD, L. H. (1999). Patient beliefs predict patient functioning: Further support for a cognitive-behavioral model of chronic pain. *Pain, 81,* 95–104.

JESSOR, R. (1984). Adolescent development and behavioral health. In J. D. MATARAZZO, S. M. WEISS, J. A. HERD, N. E. MILLER, & S. M. WEISS (Eds.), *Behavioral health: A handbook of health enhancement and disease prevention.* New York: Wiley.

JETTE, A. M. (1984). Understanding and enhancing patient cooperation with arthritis treatments. In G. K. RIGGS & E. P. GALL (Eds.), *Rheumatic diseases: Rehabilitation and management.* Boston: Butterworth.

JOHNSON, A. M., & LAGA, M. (1990). Heterosexual transmission of HIV. In N. J. ALEXANDER, H. L. GABELNICK, & J. M. SPIELER (Eds.), *Heterosexual transmission of AIDS.* New York: Wiley-Liss.

JOHNSON, B. G. (1984). Biofeedback, transcutaneous electrical nerve stimulation, acupuncture, and hypnosis. In G. K. RIGGS & E. P. GALL (Eds.), *Rheumatic diseases: Rehabilitation and management.* Boston: Butterworth.

JOHNSON, C. A., HANSEN, W. B., COLLINS, L. M., & GRAHAM, J. W. (1986). High-school smoking prevention: Results of a three-year longitudinal study. *Journal of Behavioral Medicine, 9,* 439–452.

JOHNSON, J. E. (1983). Psychological interventions and coping with surgery. In A. BAUM, S. E. TAYLOR, & J. E. SINGER (Eds.), *Handbook of psychology and health* (Vol. 4). Hillsdale, NJ: Erlbaum.

JOHNSON, J. E., & LEVENTHAL, H. (1974). Effects of accurate expectations and behavioral instructions on reactions during a noxious medical examination. *Journal of Personality and Social Psychology, 29,* 710–718.

JOHNSON, J. E., RICE, V. H., FULLER, S. S., & ENDRESS, M. P. (1978). Sensory information, instruction in a coping strategy, and recovery from surgery. *Research in Nursing and Health, 1,* 4–17.

JOHNSON, J. H. (1986). *Life events as stressors in childhood and adolescence.* Newbury Park, CA: Sage.

JOHNSON, K., ANDERSON, N. B., BASTIDA, E., KRAMER, B. J.,

WILLIAMS, D., & WONG, M. (1995). Panel II. Macrosocial and environmental influences on minority health. Health Psychology, 14, 601–612.

JOHNSON, S. B. (1985). The family and the child with chronic illness. In D. C. TURK & R. D. KERNS (Eds.), Health, illness, and families: A life-span perspective. New York: Wiley.

JOHNSON, S. B., FREUND, A., SILVERSTEIN, J., HANSEN, C. A., & MALONE, J. (1990). Adherence-health status relationships in childhood diabetes. Health Psychology, 9, 606–631.

JOHNSON, S. B., KELLY, M., HENRETTA, J. C., CUNNINGHAM, W. R., TOMER, A., & SILVERSTEIN, J. H. (1992). A longitudinal analysis of adherence and health status in childhood diabetes. Journal of Pediatric Psychology, 17, 537–553.

JOHNSON, S. K., DeLUCA, J., & NATELSON, B. H. (1999). Chronic fatigue syndrome: Reviewing the research findings. Annals of Behavioral Medicine, 21, 258–271.

JOHNSTON, D. W. (1992). The management of stress in the prevention of coronary heart disease. In S. MAES, H. LEVENTHAL, & M. JOHNSTON (Eds.), International review of health psychology (Vol. 1). New York: Wiley.

JOHNSTON, L. D., O'MALLEY, P. M., & BACHMAN, J. G. (2000). Monitoring the Future: National survey results on drug use from the Monitoring the Future Study, 1975–1999. Volume I: Secondary school students. (NIH Publication No. 00–4802). Bethesda, MD: National Institute on Drug Abuse.

JOHNSTON, M., MORRISON, V., MacWALTER, R., & PARTRIDGE, C. (1999). Perceived control, coping and recovery from disability following stroke. Psychology and Health, 14, 181–192.

JOHNSTON, M., & VÖGELE, C. (1993). Benefits of psychological preparation for surgery: A meta-analysis. Annals of Behavioral Medicine, 15, 245–256.

JOHNSTON-BROOKS, C. H., LEWIS, M. A., EVANS, G. W., & WHALEN, C. K. (1998). Chronic stress and illness in children. Psychosomatic Medicine, 60, 597–603.

JONAS, B. S., & MUSSOLINO, M. E. (2000). Symptoms of depression as a prospective risk factor for stroke. Psychosomatic Medicine, 62, 463–471.

JONES, L. R., MABE, P. A., & RILEY, W. T. (1989). Physician interpretation of illness behavior. International Journal of Psychiatry in Medicine, 19, 237–248.

JORGENSEN, R. S., FRANKOWSKI, J. J., & CAREY, M. P. (1999). Sense of coherence, negative life events, and appraisal of physical health. Personality and Individual Differences, 27, 1079–1089.

JOSE, W. S., & ANDERSON, D. R. (1990). Control Data's Stay-Well Program: A health cost management strategy. In S. M. WEISS, J. E. FIELDING, & A. BAUM (Eds.), Perspectives in behavioral medicine: Health at work: Hillsdale, NJ: Erlbaum.

JOSEPH, J. G., MONTGOMERY, S. B., EMMONS, C., KESSLER, R. C., OSTROW, D. G., WORTMAN, C. B., O'BRIEN, K., ELLER, M., & ESHLEMAN, S. (1987). Magnitude and determinants of behavioral risk reduction: Longitudinal analysis of a cohort at risk for AIDS. Psychology and Health, 1, 73–96.

JOUSILAHTI, P., VARTIAINEN, E., TUOMILEHTO, J., PEKKANEN, J., & PUSKA, P. (1995). Effect of risk factors and changes in risk factors on coronary mortality in three cohorts of middle-aged people in Eastern Finland. American Journal of Epidemiology, 141, 50–60.

JOYCE, C. (1984, November). A time for grieving. Psychology Today, pp. 42–46.

KABAT-ZINN, J. (1982). An outpatient program in behavioral medicine for chronic pain patients based on the practice of mindfulness meditation: Theoretical considerations and preliminary results. General Hospital Psychiatry, 4, 33–47.

KABAT-ZINN, J., LIPWORTH, L., & BURNEY, R. (1985). The clinical use of mindfulness meditation for the self-regulation of chronic pain. Journal of Behavioral Medicine, 8, 163–190.

KABAT-ZINN, J., MASSION, A. O., HEBERT, J. R., ROSENBAUM, E. (1998). Meditation. In J. C. HOLLAND (Ed.), Textbook on Psycho-oncology. Oxford: Oxford University press.

KADEN, G. G., McCARTER, R. J., JOHNSON, S. F., & FERENCZ, C. (1985). Physician-patient communication: Understanding congenital heart disease. American Journal of Diseases in Children, 139, 995–999.

KAHN, K. L., KEELER, E. B., SHERWOOD, M. J., ROGERS, W. H., DRAPER, D., BENTOW, S. S., REINISCH, E. J., RUBENSTEIN, L. V., KOSECOFF, J., & BROOK, R. H. (1990). Comparing outcomes of care before and after implementation of the DRG-based prospective payment system. Journal of the American Medical Association, 264, 1984–1988.

KALICHMAN, S. C. (1998). Preventing AIDS: A sourcebook for behavioral interventions. Mahwah, NJ: Erlbaum.

KALICHMAN, S. C., CAREY, M. P., & JOHNSON, B. T. (1996). Prevention of sexually transmitted HIV infection: A meta-analytic review of the behavioral outcome literature. Annals of Behavioral Medicine, 18, 6–15.

KALICHMAN, S. C., & COLEY, B. (1995). Context framing to enhance HIV-antibody-testing messages targeted at African American women. Health Psychology, 14, 247–254.

KALICHMAN, S. C., KELLY, J. A., HUNTER, T. L., MURPHY, D. A., & TYLER, R. (1993). Culturally tailored HIV-AIDS risk-reduction messages targeted to African-American urban women: Impact on risk sensitization and risk reduction. Journal of Consulting and Clinical Psychology, 61, 291–295.

KALICHMAN, S. C., & NACHIMSON, D. (1999). Self-efficacy and disclosure of HIV-positive serostatus to sex partners. Health Psychology, 18, 281–287.

KALICHMAN, S. C., ROMPA, D., & COLEY, B. (1996). Experimental component analysis of a behavioral HIV-AIDS prevention intervention for inner-city women. *Journal of Consulting and Clinical Psychology, 64,* 687–693.

KALISH, R. A. (1985). The social context of death and dying. In R. H. BINSTOCK & E. SHANAS (Eds.), *Handbook of aging and the social sciences.* New York: Van Nostrand-Reinhold.

KALISH, R. A., & REYNOLDS, D. K. (1976). *Death and ethnicity: A psychocultural study.* Los Angeles: University of Southern California Press.

KALOUPEK, D. G., WHITE, H., & WONG, M. (1984). Multiple assessment of coping strategies used by volunteer blood donors: Implications for preparatory training. *Journal of Behavioral Medicine, 7,* 35–60.

KAMARCK, T. W., & LICHTENSTEIN, E. (1985). Current trends in clinic-based smoking control. *Annals of Behavioral Medicine, 7*(2), 19–23.

KAMARCK, T. W., MANUCK, S. B., & JENNINGS, J. R. (1990). Social support reduces cardiovascular reactivity to psychological challenge: A laboratory model. *Psychosomatic Medicine, 52,* 42–58.

KAMEN, L. P., & SELIGMAN, M. E. P. (1989). Explanatory style and health. In M. JOHNSTON & T. MARTEAU (Eds.), *Applications in health psychology.* New Brunswick, NJ: Transaction.

KANDEL, D. (1974). Inter- and intragenerational influences of adolescent marijuana use. *Journal of Social Issues, 30,* 107–135.

KANDEL, D., & FAUST, R. (1975). Sequence and stages in patterns of adolescent drug use. *Archives of General Psychiatry, 32,* 923–932.

KANDEL, D. B., WU, P., & DAVIES, M. (1994). Maternal smoking during pregancy and smoking by adolescent daughters. *American Journal of Public Health, 84,* 1407–1413.

KANNER, A. D., COYNE, J. C., SCHAEFER, C., & LAZARUS, R. S. (1981). Comparison of two modes of stress measurement: Daily hassles and uplifts versus major life events. *Journal of Behavioral Medicine, 4,* 1–39.

KANNER, R. (1986). Pain management. *Journal of the American Medical Association, 256,* 2110–2114.

KAPLAN, G. A. (1995). Where do shared pathways lead? Some reflections on a research agenda. *Psychosomatic Medicine, 57,* 208–212.

KAPLAN, N. M. (1986). Dietary aspects of the treatment of hypertension. *Annual Review of Public Health, 7,* 503–519.

KAPLAN, R. M. (1989). Health outcome models for policy analysis. *Health Psychology, 8,* 723–735.

KAPLAN, R. M. (1994). The Ziggy theorem: Toward an outcomes-focused health psychology. *Health Psychology, 13,* 451–460.

KAPLAN, R. M., ATKINS, C. J., & REINSCH, S. (1984). Specific efficacy expectations mediate exercise compliance in patients with COPD, *Health Psychology, 3,* 223–242.

KAPLAN, R. M., ORLEANS, C. T., PERKINS, K. A., & PIERCE, J. P. (1995). Marshalling the evidence for greater regulation and control of tobacco products: A call for action. *Annals of Behavioral Medicine, 17,* 3–14.

KAPLAN, R. M., PATTERSON, T. L., KERNER, D., GRANT, I. et al. (1997). Social support: Cause or consequence of poor health outcomes in men with HIV infection? In G. R. PIERCE, B. LAKEY, I. G. SARASON, & B. R. SARASON (Eds.), *Sourcebook for social support and personality.* New York: Plenum.

KAPLAN, R. M., & SIMON, H. J. (1990). Compliance in medical care: Reconsideration of self-predictions. *Annals of Behavioral Medicine, 12,* 66–71.

KAPLAN, R. M., & TOSHIMA, M. T. (1990). The functional effects of social relationships on chronic illnesses and disability. In B. R. SARASON, I. G. SARASON, & G. R. PIERCE (Eds.), *Social support: An interactional view.* New York: Wiley.

KAPUST, L. R., & WEINTRAUB, S. (1984). Living with a family member suffering from Alzheimer's disease. In H. B. ROBACK (Ed.), *Helping patients and their families cope with medical problems.* San Francisco: Jossey-Bass.

KARLBERG, L., KRAKAU, I., & UNDEN, A.-L. (1998). Type A behavior intervention in primary health care reduces hostility and time pressure: A study in Sweden. *Social Science and Medinine, 46,* 397–402.

KARLIN, R. A., EPSTEIN, Y. M., & AIELLO, J. R. (1978). A setting-specific analysis of crowding. In A. BAUM & Y. M. EPSTEIN (Eds.), *Human response to crowding.* Hillsdale, NJ: Erlbaum.

KAROLY, P. (1985). The assessment of pain: Concepts and procedures. In P. KAROLY (Ed.), *Measurement strategies in health psychology.* New York: Wiley.

KASCH, F. W., WALLACE, J. P., & VAN CAMP, S. P. (1985). Effects of 18 years of endurance exercise on the physical work capacity of older men. *Journal of Cardiopulmonary Rehabilitation, 5,* 308–312.

KASL, S. V., & COBB, S. (1966a). Health behavior, illness behavior, and sick role behavior: I. Health and illness behavior. *Archives of Environmental Health, 12,* 246–266.

KASL, S. V., & COBB, S. (1966b). Health behavior, illness behavior, and sick role behavior: II. Sick role behavior. *Archives of Environmental Health, 12,* 531–541.

KASTENBAUM, R., & COSTA, P. T. (1977). Psychological perspectives on death. *Annual Review of Psychology, 28,* 225–249.

KAUFMAN, B. (1988). A distant compassion. *Health Values, 12*(4), 31–32.

KAVANAUGH, D. J., GOOLEY, S., & WILSON, P. H. (1993). Prediction of adherence and control in diabetes. *Journal of Behavioral Medicine, 16,* 509–522.

KAWACHI, I., COLDITZ, G. A., STAMPFER, M. J., WILLETT, W. C., MANSON, J. E., ROSNER, B., SPEIZER, F. E., & HENNEKENS,

C. H. (1993). Smoking cessation and decreased risk of stroke in women. *Journal of the American Medical Association*, 269, 232–236.

KAWACHI, I., COLDITZ, G. A., & STONE, C. B. (1994). Does coffee drinking increase the risk of coronary heart disease? Results from a meta-analysis. *British Heart Journal*, 72, 269–275.

KAYE, W. H., KLUMP, K. L., FRANK, G. K. W., & STROBER, M. (2000). Anorexia and bulimia nervosa. *Annual Review of Medicine*, 51, 299–313.

KEEFE, F. J., & BLOCK, A. R. (1982). Development of an observation method for assessing pain behavior in chronic low back pain patients. *Behavior Therapy*, 13, 363–375.

KEEFE, F. J., & DOLAN, E. (1986). Pain behavior and pain coping strategies in low back pain and myofascial pain dysfunction syndrome patients. *Pain*, 24, 49–56.

KEEFE, F. J., & GIL, K. M. (1985). Recent advances in the behavioral assessment and treatment of chronic pain. *Annals of Behavioral Medicine*, 7(3), 11–16.

KEEFE, F. J., HAUCK, E. R., EGERT, J., RIMER, B., & KORNGUTH, P. (1994). Mammography pain and discomfort: A cognitive-behavioral perspective. *Pain*, 56, 247–260.

KEESEY, R. E. (1986). A set point theory of obesity. In K. D. BROWNELL & J. P. FOREYT (Eds.), *The physiology, psychology, and treatment of the eating disorders*. New York: Basic Books.

KEESEY, R. E., & POWLEY, T. L. (1975). Hypothalamic regulation of body weight. *American Scientist*, 63, 558–565.

KEESLING, B., & FRIEDMAN, H. S. (1987). Psychosocial factors in sunbathing and sunscreen use. *Health Psychology*, 6, 477–493.

KELLNER, R. (1985). Functional somatic symptoms and hypochondriasis: A survey of empirical studies. *Archives of General Psychiatry*, 42, 821–833.

KELLNER, R. (1987). Hypochondriasis and somatization. *Journal of the American Medical Association*, 258, 2718–2722.

KELLY, J. A., KALICHMAN, S. C. (1998). Reinforcement value of unsafe sex as a predictor of condom use and continued HIV/AIDS risk behavior among gay and bisexual men. *Health Psychology*, 17, 328–335.

KELLY, J. A., KALICHMAN, S. C., KAUTH, M. R., KILGORE, H. G., HOOD, H. V., CAMPOS, P. E., RAO, S. M., BRASFIELD, T. L., & ST. LAWRENCE, J. S. (1991). Situational factors associated with AIDS risk behavior lapses and coping strategies used by gay men who successfully avoid lapses. *American Journal of Public Health*, 81, 1335–1338.

KELLY, J. A., MURPHY, D. A., SIKKEMA, K. J., McAULIFFE, T. L., et al. (1997). Randomized, controlled, community-level HIV-prevention intervention for sexual-risk behaviour among homosexual men in US cities. *Lancet*, 350, 1500–1505.

KELLY, J. A., SIKKEMA, K. J., WINETT, R. A., SOLOMON, L. J., ROFFMAN, R. A., HECKMAN, T. G., STEVENSON, L. Y., PERRY, M. J., NORMAN, A. D., & DESIDERATO, L. J. (1995). Factors predicting continued high-risk behavior among gay men in small cities: Psychological, behavioral, and demographic characteristics related to unsafe sex. *Journal of Consulting and Clinical Psychology*, 63, 101–107.

KELSEY, J. L., & HOCHBERG, M. C. (1988). Epidemiology of chronic musculoskeletal disorders. *Annual Review of Public Health*, 9, 379–401.

KEMPE, C. H. (1976). Child abuse and neglect. In N. B. TALBOT (Ed.), *Raising children in modern America: Problems and prospective solutions*. Boston: Little, Brown.

KENDALL, P. C., WILLIAMS, L., PECHACEK, T. F., GRAHAM, L. E., SHISSLAK, C., & HERZOFF, N. (1979). Cognitive-behavioral and patient education interventions in cardiac catheterization procedures: The Palo Alto Medical Psychology Project. *Journal of Consulting and Clinical Psychology*, 47, 49–58.

KENNEDY, S., KIECOLT-GLASER, J. K., & GLASER, R. (1990). Social support, stress, and the immune system. In B. R. SARASON, I. G. SARASON, & G. R. PIERCE (Eds.), *Social support: An interactional view*. New York: Wiley.

KENT, G. (1985). Memory of dental pain. *Pain*, 21, 187–194.

KERLIKOWSKE, K., GRADY, D., RUBIN, S. M., SANDROCK, C., & ERNSTER, V. L. (1995). Efficacy of screening mammography: A meta-analysis. *Journal of the American Medical Association*, 273, 149–154.

KERN, P. A., ONG, J. M., SAFFARI, B., & CARTY, J. (1990). The effects of weight loss on the activity and expression on adipose-tissue lipoprotein lipase in very obese humans. *New England Journal of Medicine*, 322, 1053–1059.

KERNS, R. D. (1995). Family assessment and intervention. In P. M. NICASSIO & T. W. SMITH (Eds.), *Managing chronic illness: A biopsychosocial perspective*. Washington, DC: American Psychological Association.

KERNS, R. D., & PAYNE, A. (1996). Treating families of chronic pain patients. In R. J. GATCHEL & D. C. TURK (Eds.), *Psychological approaches to pain management: A practitioner's handbook* (pp. 283–304). New York: Guilford.

KERNS, R. D., TURK, D. C., & RUDY, T. E. (1985). The West Haven-Yale Multidimensional Pain Inventory. *Pain*, 23, 345–356.

KERNS, R. D., & WEISS, L. H. (1994). Family influences on the course of chronic illness: A cognitive-behavioral transactional model. *Annals of Behavioral Medicine*, 16, 116–121.

KETT, J. F. (1977). *Rites of passage: Adolescence in America 1790 to present*. New York: Basic Books.

KETTERER, M. W., BRYMER, J., RHOADS, K., KRAFT, P., KENYON, L., FOLEY, B., LOVALLO, W. R., & VOIGHT, C. J. (1996). Emotional distress among males with "syndrome X." *Journal of Behavioral Medicine*, 19, 455–466.

KEYS, A., BROZEK, J., HENSCHEL, A., MICKELSEN, O., & TAYLOR, H. L. (1950). *The biology of human starvation.* Minneapolis: University of Minnesota Press.

KHAW, K., & BARRETT-CONNOR, E. (1986). Family history of heart attack: A modifiable risk factor? *Circulation, 74,* 239–244.

KIECOLT-GLASER, J. K., DURA, J. R., SPEICHER, C. E., TRASK, O. J., & GLASER, R. (1991) Spousal caregivers of dementia victims: Longitudinal changes in immunity and health. *Psychosomatic Medicine, 53,* 345–362.

KIECOLT-GLASER, J. K., FISHER, L. D., OGROCKI, P., STOUT, J. C., SPEICHER, C. E., & GLASER, R. (1987). Marital quality, marital disruption, and immune function. *Psychosomatic Medicine, 49,* 13–34.

KIECOLT-GLASER, J. K., GARNER, W., SPEICHER, C., PENN, G. M., HOLLIDAY, J., & GLASER, R. (1984). Psychosocial modifiers of immunocompetence in medical students. *Psychosomatic Medicine, 46,* 7–14.

KIECOLT-GLASER, J. K., & GLASER, R. (1986). Psychological influences on immunity. *Psychosomatics, 27,* 621–624.

KIECOLT-GLASER, J. K., & GLASER, R. (1995). Psychoneuroimmunology and health consequences: Data and shared mechanisms. *Psychosomatic Medicine, 57,* 269–274.

KIECOLT-GLASER, J. K., STEPHENS, R. E., LIPETZ, P. D., SPEICHER, C. E., & GLASER, R. (1985). Distress and DNA repair in human lymphocytes. *Journal of Behavioral Medicine, 8,* 311–320.

KIECOLT-GLASER, J. K., & WILLIAMS, D. A. (1987). Self-blame, compliance, and distress among burn patients. *Journal of Personality and Social Psychology, 53,* 187–193.

KIERNAN, M., KING, A. C., KRAEMER, H. C., STEFANICK, M. L., & KILLEN, J. D. (1998). Characteristics of successful and unsuccessful dieters: An application of signal detection methodology. *Annals of Behavioral Medicine, 20,* 1–6.

KILLEN, J. D., & FORTMANN, S. P. (1994). Craving is associated with smoking relapse: Findings from three prospective studies. *Experimental and Clinical Psychopharmacology, 5,* 137–142.

KILLEN, J. D., ROBINSON, T. N., HAYDEL, K. F., HAYWARD, C., WILSON, D. M., HAMMER, L. D., LITT, I. F., & TAYLOR, C. B. (1997). Prospective study of risk factors for the initiation of cigarette smoking. *Journal of Consulting and Clinical Psychology, 65,* 1011–1016.

KILLEN, J. D., TAYLOR, C. B., HAYWARD, C., WILSON, D. M., et al. (1994). Pursuit of thinness and onset of eating disorder symptoms in a community sample of adolescent girls: A three-year prospective analysis. *International Journal of Eating Disorders, 16,* 227–238.

KILLEN, J. D., TAYLOR, C. B., TELCH, M. J., SAYLOR, K. E., MARON, D. J., & ROBINSON, T. N. (1986). Self-induced vomiting and laxative and diuretic use among teenagers. *Journal of the American Medical Society, 255,* 1447–1449.

KILO, C., & WILLIAMSON, J. R. (1987). *Diabetes: The facts that let you regain control of your life.* New York: Wiley.

KILPATRICK, D. G., ACIERNO, R., SAUNDERS, B., RESNICK, H. S., BEST, C. L., & SCHNURR, P. P. (2000). Risk factors for adolescent substance abuse and dependence: Data from a national sample. *Journal of Consulting and Clinical Psychology, 68,* 19–30.

KIMMEL, P. L., PETERSON, R. A., WEIHS, K. L., SIMMENS, S. J., ALLEYNE, S., CRUZ, I., & VEIS, J. H. (1998). Psychosocial factors, behavioral compliance and survival in urban hemodialysis patients. *Kidney International, 54,* 245–254.

KINDELAN, K., & KENT, G. (1987). Concordance between patients' information preferences and general practitioners' perceptions. *Psychology and Health, 1,* 399–409.

KING, L. A., & MINER, K. N. (2000). Writing about the perceived benefits of traumatic events: Implications for physical health. *Personality and Social Psychology Bulletin, 26,* 220–230.

KIRSCHBAUM, D., & HELLHAMMER, D. (1999). Noise and stress—Salivary cortisol as a noninvasive measure of allostatic load. *Noise and Health, 4,* 57–65.

KIRSCHBAUM, D., WOST, S., & HELLHAMMER, D. (1992). Consistent sex differences in cortisol responses to psychological stress. *Psychosomatic Medicine, 54,* 648–657.

KIRSCHT, J. P. (1983). Preventive health behavior: A review of research and issues. *Health Psychology, 2,* 277–301.

KIRSCHT, J. P., & ROSENSTOCK, I. M. (1979). Patients' problems in following recommendations of health experts. In G. C. Stone, F. Cohen, & N. E. Adler (Eds.), *Health psychology—A handbook.* San Francisco: Jossey-Bass.

KIVLAHAN, D. R., MARLATT, G. A., FROMME, K., COPPEL, D. B., & WILLIAMS, E. (1990). Secondary prevention with college drinkers: Evaluation of an alcohol skills training program. *Journal of Consulting and Clinical Psychology, 58,* 805–810.

KIYAK, H. A., VITALIANO, P. P., & CRINEAN, J. (1988). Patients' expectations as predictors of orthognathic surgery outcomes. *Health Psychology, 7,* 251–268.

KLAG, M. J., WHELTON, P. K., CORESH, J., GRIM, C. E., & KULLER, L. H. (1991). The association of skin color with blood pressure in US black with low socioeconomic status. *Journal of the American Medical Association, 265,* 599–602.

KLAPOW, J. C., SLATER, M. A., PATTERSON, T. L., DOCTOR, J. N., ATKINSON, J. H., & GARFIN, S. R. (1993). An empirical evaluation of multidimensional clinical outcome in chronic low back pain patients. *Pain, 55,* 107–118.

KLEINKE, C. L., & SPANGLER, A. S. (1988). Psychometric analysis of the audiovisual taxonomy for assessing pain behavior in chronic back-pain patients. *Journal of Behavioral Medicine, 11,* 83–94.

KLEPP, K.-I., KELDER, S. H., & PERRY, C. L. (1995). Alcohol and marijuana use among adolescents: Long-term outcomes of the Class of 1989 Study. *Annals of Behavioral Medicine, 17,* 19–24.

KLESGES, R. C., BENOWITZ, N. L., & MEYERS, A. W. (1991). Behavioral and biobehavioral aspects of smoking and smoking cessation: The problem of postcessation weight gain. *Behavior Therapy, 22,* 179–199.

KLESGES, R. C., ECK, L. H., & RAY, J. W. (1995). Who underreports dietary intake in a dietary recall? Evidence from the Second National Health and Nutrition Examination Survey. *Journal of Consulting and Clinical Psychology, 63,* 438–444.

KLESGES, R. C., HADDOCK, C. K., LANDO, H, & TALCOTT, G. W. (1999). Efficacy of forced smoking cessation and an adjunctive behavioral treatment on long-term smoking rates. *Journal of Consulting and Clinical Psychology, 67,* 952–958.

KLESGES, R. C., SHUSTER, M. L., KLESGES, L. M., & WERNER, K. (1992, March). *The effects of television viewing on metabolic rate in normal weight and obese children.* Paper presented at the meeting of the Society of Behavioral Medicine, New York.

KLESGES, R. C., WARD, K. D., RAY, J. W., CUTTER, G., JACOBS, D. R., & WAGENKNECHT, L. E. (1998). The prospective relationships between smoking and weight in a young, biracial cohort: The Coronary Artery Risk Development in Young Adults Study. *Journal of Consulting and Clinical Psychology, 66,* 987–993.

KLESGES, R. C., WINDERS, S. E., MEYERS, A. W., ECK, L. H., WARD, K. D., HULTQUIST, C. M., RAY, J. W., & SHADISH, W. R. (1997). How much weight gain occurs following smoking cessation? A comparison of weight gain using both continuous and point prevalence abstinence. *Journal of Consulting and Clinical Psychology, 65,* 286–291.

KLESGES, R. C., ZBIKOWSKI, S. M., LANDO, H. A., HADDOCK, C. K., TALCOTT, G. W., & ROBINSON, L. A. (1998). The relationship between smoking and body weight in a population of young military personnel. *Health Psychology, 17,* 454–458.

KLOHN, L. S., & ROGERS, R. W. (1991). Dimensions of the severity of a health threat: The persuasive effects of visibility, time of onset, and rate of onset on young women's intentions to prevent osteoporosis. *Health Psychology, 10,* 323–329.

KLOSE, K. J., NEEDHAM, B. M., SCHMIDT, D., BROTON, J. G., & GREEN, B. A. (1993). An assessment of the contribution of electromyographic biofeedback as an adjunct therapy in the physical training of spinal cord injured persons. *Archives of Physical Medicine and Rehabilitation, 74,* 453–456.

KNAPP, R. J. (1987, July). When a child dies. *Psychology Today,* pp. 60–67.

KNEUT, C. M. (1982). Legal, ethical, and moral considerations in pediatric nursing. In M. J. SMITH, J. A. GOODMAN, N. L. RAMSEY, & S. B. PASTERNACK (Eds.), *Child and family: Concepts of nursing practice.* New York: McGraw-Hill.

KNITTLE, J., MERRITT, R. J., DIXON-SHANIES, D., GINSBERG-FELLNER, F., TIMMERS, K. I., & KATZ, D. P. (1981). Childhood obesity. In R. M. Suskind (Ed.), *Textbook of pediatric nutrition.* New York: Raven Press.

KNOX, S. S., SIEGMUND, K. D., WEIDNER, G., ELLISON, R. C., ADELMAN, A., & PATON, C. (1998). Hostility, social support, and coronary heart disease in the National Heart, Lung, and Blood Institute Family Heart Study. *American Journal of Cardiology, 82,* 1192–1196.

KOBASA, S. C. (1979). Stressful life events, personality, and health: An inquiry into hardiness. *Journal of Personality and Social Psychology, 37,* 1–11.

KOBASA, S. C. O. (1986). How much stress can you survive? In M. G. WALRAVEN & H. E. FITZGERALD (Eds.), *Annual editions: Human development 86/87.* Guilford, CT: Dushkin.

KOBASA, S. C., & MADDI, S. R. (1977). Existential personality theory. In R. CORSINI (Ed.), *Current personality theories.* Itasca, IL: Peacock.

KOBASA, S. C., MADDI, S. R., & PUCCETTI, M. C. (1982). Personality and exercise as buffers in the stress-illness relationship. *Journal of Behavioral Medicine, 5,* 391–404.

KOBASA, S. C. O., MADDI, S. R., PUCCETTI, M. C., & ZOLA, M. A. (1985). Effectiveness of hardiness, exercise and social support as resources against illness. *Journal of Psychosomatic Research, 29,* 525–533.

KOCH, J. (1977, August). When children meet death. *Psychology Today,* pp. 64–66, 79–80.

KÖHLER, T., & HAIMERL, C. (1990). Daily stress as a trigger of migraine attacks: Results of thirteen single-subject studies. *Journal of Consulting and Clinical Psychology, 58,* 870–872.

KOHRT, W. M., KIRWAN, J. P., STATEN, M. A., BOUREY, R. E., KING, D. S., & HOLLOSZY, J. O. (1993). Insulin resistance in aging is related to abdominal obesity. *Diabetes. 42,* 273–281.

KOKKINOS, P. F., NARAYAN, P., COLLERAN, J. A., PITTARAS, A., NOTARGIACOMO, A., REDA, D., & PAPADEMETRIOU, V. (1995). Effects of regular exercise on blood pressure and left ventricular hypertrophy in African-American men with severe hypertension. *New England Journal of Medicine, 333,* 1462–1467.

KOLATA, G. (1990, February 20). Wariness is replacing trust between health and patient. *New York Times,* pp. A1, D15.

KOLATA, G. (1992a, September 3). A cancer legacy from Chernobyl. *New York Times,* p. A9.

KOLATA, G. (1992b, May 10). Confronting new ideas, doctors often hold on to the old. *New York Times*, p. E6.

KOLBE, L. J., GREEN, L. FOREYT, J., DARNELL, L., et al. (1986). Appropriate functions of health education in schools: Improving health and cognitive performance. In N. A. KRASNEGOR, J. D. ARASTEH, & M. F. CATALDO (Eds.), *Child health behavior*: A *behavioral pediatrics perspective*. New York: Wiley.

KOLBE, L. J., & IVERSON, D. C. (1984). Comprehensive school health education programs. In J. D. MATARAZZO, S. M. WEISS, J. A. HERD, N. E. MILLER, & S. M. WEISS (Eds.), *Behavioral health: A handbook of health enhancement and disease prevention*. New York: Wiley.

KOOCHER, G. P., O'MALLEY, J. E., GOGAN, J. L., & FOSTER, D. J. (1980). Psychological adjustment among pediatric cancer survivors. *Journal of Child Psychology and Psychiatry*, 21, 163–173.

KOP, W. J. (1999). Chronic and acute psychological risk factors for clinical manifestations of coronary artery disease. *Psychosomatic Medicine*, 61, 476–487.

KORSCH, B. M., FINE, R. N., & NEGRETE, V. F. (1978). Noncompliance in children with renal transplants. *Pediatrics*, 61, 872–876.

KORSCH, B. M., GOZZI, E. K., & FRANCIS, V. (1968). Gaps in doctor-patient communication: I. Doctor-patient interaction and patient satisfaction. *Pediatrics*, 42, 855–871.

KOSTEN, T. R., JACOBS, S. C., & KASL, S. V. (1985). Terminal illness, bereavement, and the family. In D. C. TURK & R. D. KERNS (Eds.), *Health, illness, and families: A life-span perspective*. New York: Wiley.

KOVACS, M. (1997). Depression in patients with diabetes. *Contemporary Internal Medicine*, 9, 53–58.

KOZLOWSKI, L. T. (1984). Pharmacological approaches to smoking modification. In J. D. MATARAZZO, S. M. WEISS, J. A. HERD, N. E. MILLER, & S. M. WEISS (Eds.), *Behavioral health: A handbook of health enhancement and disease prevention*. New York: Wiley.

KRAJICK, K. (1988, May). Private passions and public health. *Psychology Today*, pp. 50–58.

KRAMER, J. R., LEDOLTER, J., MANOS, G. N., & BAYLESS, M. L. (2000). Stress and metabolic control in diabetes mellitus: Methodological issues and an illustrative analysis. *Annals of Behavioral Medicine*, 22, 17–28.

KRANTZ, D. S., BAUM, A., & WIDEMAN, M. V. (1980). Assessment for preferences for self-treatment and information in health care. *Journal of Personality and Social Psychology*, 39, 977–990.

KRANTZ, D. S., & DECKEL, A. W. (1983). Coping with coronary heart disease and stroke. In T. G. BURISH & L. A. BRADLEY (Eds.), *Coping with chronic disease: Research and applications*. New York: Academic Press.

KRANTZ, D. S., & DUREL, L. A. (1983). Psychobiological substrates of the Type A behavior pattern. *Health Psychology*, 2, 393–411.

KRANTZ, D. S., DUREL, L. A., DAVIA, J. E., SHAFFER, R. T., ARABIAN, J. M., DEMBROSKI, T. M., & MACDOUGALL, J. M. (1982). Propranolol medication among coronary patients: Relationship to Type A behavior and cariovascular response. *Journal of Human Stress*, 8, 4–12.

KRANTZ, D. S., LUNDBERG, U., & FRANKENHAEUSER, M. (1987). Stress and Type A behavior: Interactions between environmental and biological factors. In A. BAUM & J. E. SINGER (Eds.), *Handbook of psychology and health* (Vol. 5). Hillsdale, NJ: Erlbaum.

KRANZLER, H. R., & ANTON, R. F. (1994). Implications of recent neuropsychopharmacologic research for understanding the etiology and development of alcoholism. *Journal of Consulting and Clinical Psychology*, 62, 1116–1126.

KRAUSE, J. S., & CREWE, N. M. (1991). Chronologic age, time since injury, and time of measurement: Effect on adjustment after spinal cord injury. *Archives of Physical Medicine and Rehabilitation*, 72, 91–100.

KREUTER, M. W., & STRECHER, V. J. (1995). Changing inaccurate perceptions of health risk: Results from a randomized trial. *Health Psychology*, 14, 56–63.

KREUTER, M. W., STRECHER, V. J. & GLASSMAN, B. (1999). One size does not fit all: The case for tailoring print materials. *Annals of Behavioral Medicine*, 21, 276–283.

KRIEG, A. M., YI, A.-K., MATSON, S., WALDSCHMIDT, T. J., BISHOP, G. A., TEASDALE, R., KORETZKY, G. A., & KLINMAN, D. M. (1995). CpG motifs in bacterial DNA trigger direct B-cell activation. *Nature*, 374, 546–549.

KROENKE, K., & SPITZER, R. L. (1998). Gender differences in the reporting of physical and somatoform symptoms. *Psychosomatic Medicine*, 60, 150–155.

KU, L., SONENSTEIN, F. L., & PLECK, J. H. (1993). Young men's risk behaviors for HIV infection and sexually transmitted diseases, 1988 through 1991. *American Journal of Public Health*, 83, 1609–1615.

KÜBLER-ROSS, E. (1969). *On death and dying*. New York: Macmillan.

KUDIELKA, B. M., HELLHAMMER, J., HELLHAMMER, D. H., WOLF, O. T., PIRKE, K.-M., VARADI, E., PILZ, J., & KIRSCHBAUM, C. (1998). Sex differences in endocrine and psychological responses to psychosocial stress in healthy elderly subjects and the impact of a 2-week dehydroepiandrosterone treatment. *Journal of Clinical Endocrinology and Metabolism*, 83, 1756–1761.

KUJALA, U. M., KAPRIO, J., SARNA, S., & KOSKENVUO, M. (1998). Relationship of leisuretime physical activity and.mortality: The Finish twin cohort. *Journal of the American Medical Association*, 279, 440–444.

KULIK, J. A., & CARLINO, P. (1987). The effect of verbal

commitment and treatment choice on medication compliance in a pediatric setting. *Journal of Behavioral Medicine, 10,* 367–376.

KULIK, J. A., & MAHLER, H. I. M. (1987a). Effects of preoperative roommate assignment on preoperative anxiety and recovery from coronary-bypass surgery. *Health Psychology, 6,* 525–543.

KULIK, J. A., & MAHLER, H. I. M. (1987b). Health status, perceptions of risk, and prevention interest for health and nonhealth problems. *Health Psychology, 6,* 15–27.

KULIK, J. A., & MAHLER, H. I. M. (1989). Social support and recovery from surgery. Health Psychology, *8,* 221–238.

KULIK, J. A., MOORE, P. J., & MAHLER, H. I. M. (1993). Stress and affiliation: Hospital roommate effects on preoperative anxiety and social interaction. *Health Psychology, 12,* 118–124.

KUNDA, Z. (1990). The case for motivated reasoning. *Psychological Bulletin, 108,* 480–498.

KUSAKA, Y., KONDOU, H., & MORIMOTO, K. (1992). Healthy lifestyles are associated with higher natural killer cell activity. *Preventive Medicine, 21,* 602–615.

LABARBA, R. C. (1984). Prenatal and neonatal influences on behavioral health development. In J. D. MATARAZZO, S. M. WEISS, J. A. HERD, N. E. MILLER, & S. M. WEISS (Eds.), *Behavioral health: A handbook of health enhancement and disease prevention.* New York: Wiley.

LACEY, J. H., & BIRTCHNELL, S. A. (1986). Abnormal eating behavior. In M. J. CHRISTIE & P. G. MELLETT (Eds.), *Thepsychosomatic approach: Contemporary practice of wholeperson care.* New York: Wiley.

LACHMAN, M. E. (1986). Personal control in later life: Stability, change, and cognitive correlates. In M. M. BALTES & P. B. BALTES (Ed.), *The psychology of control and aging.* Hillsdale, NJ: Erlbaum.

LACROIX, A. Z., LANG, J., SCHERR, P., WALLACE, R. B., CORNONI-HUNTLEY, J., BERKMAN, L., CURB, D., EVANS, D., & HENNEKENS, C. H. (1991). Smoking and mortality among older men and women in three communities. *New England Journal of Medicine, 324,* 1619–1625.

LAFFREY, S. C. (1986). Normal and overweight adults: Perceived weight and health behavior characteristics. *Nursing Research, 35,* 173–177.

LAFORGE, R. G., WILLEY, C., PROCHASKA, J. O., & LEVESQUE, D. A. (1995, March). *Naturalistic evidence for a synergistic effect of nicotine patch with a stage matched smoking cessation intervention.* Paper presented at the meeting of the Society of Behavioral Medicine, San Diego.

LAGRECA, A. M., & STONE, W. L. (1985). Behavioral pediatrics. In N. SCHNEIDERMAN & J. T. TAPP (Eds.), *Behavioral medicine: The biopsychosocial approach.* Hillsdale, NJ: Erlbaum.

LAKEIN, A. (1973). *How to get control of your time and life.* New York: New American Library.

LANDERS, A. (1992, August 9). Was it airline food that cut short a passenger's trip of a lifetime? *Philadelphia Inquirer,* p. L3.

LANDO, H. A. (1993). Formal quit smoking treatments. In C. T. ORLEANS & J. SLADE (Eds.), *Nicotine addiction: Principles and management.* New York: Oxford University Press.

LANE, M. A., BAER, D. J., RUMPLER, W. V., WEINDRUCH, R., INGRAM, D. K., TILMONT, E. M., CUTLER, R. G., & ROTH, G. S. (1996). Calorie restriction lowers body temperature in rhesus minkeys, consistent with a postulated anti-aging mechanism in rodents. *Proceedings of the National Academy of Sciences, 93,* 4159–4164.

LANG, A. R., & MARLATT, G. A. (1982). Problem drinking: A social learning perspective. In R. J. GATCHEL, A. BAUM, & J. E. SINGER (Eds.), *Handbook of psychology and health* (Vol. 1). Hillsdale, NJ: Erlbaum.

LANGER, E. J. (1975). The illusion of control. *Journal of Personality and Social Psychology, 32,* 311–328.

LANGER, E. J., JANIS, I. L., & WOLFER, J. A. (1975). Reduction of psychological stress in surgical patients. *Journal of Experimental Social Psychology, 11,* 155–165.

LANGER, E. J., & RODIN, J. (1976). The effects of choice and enhanced personal responsibility for the aged: A field experiment in an institutional setting. *Journal of Personality and Social Psychology, 34,* 191–198.

LANGLIE, J. K. (1977). Social networks, health beliefs, and preventive health behavior. *Journal of Health and Social Behavior, 18,* 244–260.

LANGOSCH, W. (1984). Behavioural interventions in cardiac rehabilitation. In A. STEPTOE & A. MATHEWS (Eds.), *Health care and human behaviour.* London: Academic Press.

LAPLACE, J. (1984). *Health* (4th ed.). Englewood Cliffs, NJ: Prentice-Hall.

LARKIN, K. T., KNOWLTON, G. E., & D'ALESSANDRI, R. (1990). Predicting treatment outcome to progressive relaxation training in essential hypertensive patients. *Journal of Behavioral Medicine, 13,* 605–618.

LARKIN, K. T., & ZAYFERT, C. (1996). Anger management training with mild essential hypertensive patients. *Journal of Behavioral Medicine, 19,* 415–433.

LAROCCO, J. M., HOUSE, J. S., & FRENCH, J. R. P. (1980). Social support, occupational stress, and health. *Journal of Health and Social Behavior, 21,* 202–218.

LARSON, E. B., KUKULL, W. A., & KATZMAN, R. L. (1992). Cognitive impairment: Dementia and Alzheimer's disease. *Annual Review of Public Health, 13,* 431–449.

LASATER, T., ABRAMS, D., ARTZ, L., BEAUDIN, P., CABRERA, L., ELDER, J., FERREIRA, A., KNISLEY, P., PETERSON, G.,

RODRIGUES, A., ROSENBERG, P., SNOW, R., & CARLTON, R. (1984). Lay volunteer delivery of a community-based cardiovascular risk factor change program: The Pawtucket experiment. In J. D. MATARAZZO, S. M. WEISS, J. A. HERD, N. E. MILLER, & S. M. WEISS (Eds.), *Behavioral health: A handbook of health enhancement and disease prevention*. New York: Wiley.

LASZLO, J. (1987). *Understanding cancer*. New York: Harper & Row.

LATIMER, E. A., & LAVE, L. B. (1987). Initial effects of the New York State auto safety belt law. *American Journal of Public Health, 77*, 183–186.

LAU, R. R., & HARTMAN, K. A. (1983). Common sense representations of common illnesses. *Health Psychology, 2*, 167–185.

LAU, R. R., HARTMAN, K. A., & WARE, J. E. (1986). Health as a value: Methodological and theoretical considerations. *Health Psychology, 5*, 25–43.

LAU, R., KANE, R., BERRY, S., WARE, J., & ROY, D. (1980). Channeling health: A review of the evaluation of televised health campaigns. *Health Education Quarterly, 7*, 56–89.

LAVE, J. R. (1989). The effect of the Medicare prospective payment system. *Annual Review of Public Health, 10*, 141–161.

LAVIGNE, J. V., SCHULEIN, M. J., & HAHN, Y. S. (1986). Psychological aspects of painful medical conditions in children. II. Personality factors, family characteristics and treatment. *Pain, 27*, 147–169.

LAW, M. R., FROST, C. D., & WALD, N. J. (1991). Analysis of data from trials of salt reduction. *British Medical Journal, 302*, 819–824.

LAW, M., & WALD, N. (1999). Why heart disease mortality is low in France: The time lag explanation. *British Medical Journal, 318*, 1471–1480.

LAWLER, K. A., ALLEN, M. T., CRITCHER, E. C., & STANDARD, B. A. (1981). The relationship of physiological responses to the coronary-prone behavior pattern in children. *Journal of Behavioral Medicine, 4*, 203–216.

LAWRENCE, D. B., & GAUS, C. R. (1983). Long-term care: Financing and policy issues. In D. MECHANIC (Ed.), *Handbook of health, health care, and the health professions*. New York: Free Press.

LAZARUS, A. A. (1971). *Behavior therapy and beyond*. New York: McGraw-Hill.

LAZARUS, R. S. (1983). The costs and benefits of denial. In S. BRESNITZ (Ed.), *Denial of stress*. New York: International Universities Press.

LAZARUS, R. S. (1987). Coping. In R. J. CORSINI (Ed.), *Concise encyclopedia of psychology*. New York: Wiley.

LAZARUS, R. S. (1999). *Stress and emotion: A new synthesis*. New York: Springer.

LAZARUS, R. S., & DELONGIS, A. (1983). Psychological stress and coping in aging. *American Psychologist, 38*, 245–254.

LAZARUS, R. S., & FOLKMAN, S. (1984a). Coping and adaptation. In W. D. GENTRY (Ed.), *Handbook of behavioral medicine*. New York: Guilford.

LAZARUS, R. S., & FOLKMAN, S. (1984b). *Stress, appraisal, and coping*. New York: Springer.

LAZARUS, R. S., & LAUNIER, R. (1978). Stress-related transactions between person and environment. In L. A. PERVIN & M. LEWIS (Eds.), *Perspectives in interactional psychology*. New York: Plenum.

LEAHEY, T. H. (1987). *A history of psychology: Main currents in psychological thought* (2nd ed.). Englewood Cliffs, NJ: Prentice-Hall.

LEAKE, R., FRIEND, R., & WADHWA, N. (1999). Improving adjustment to chronic illness through strategic self-presentation: An experimental study on a renal dialysis unit. *Health Psychology, 18*, 54–62.

LEARY, W. E. (1992, March 6). U.S. urges doctors to fight surgical pain (and myths). *New York Times*, pp. A1, 17.

LEARY, W. E. (1995, September 20). Report endorses needle exchanges as AIDS strategy. *New York Times*, pp. A1, B10.

LEARY, W. E. (1998, February 20). Research ties radon to as many as 21,800 deaths each year. *New York Times*, p. A13.

LEE, C. (1989). Perceptions of immunity to disease in adult smokers. *Journal of Behavioral Medicine, 12*, 267–277.

LEE, G.-H., PROENCA, R., MONTEZ, J. M., CARROLL, K. M., DARVISHZADEH, J. G., LEE, J. I., & FRIEDMAN, J. M. (1996). Abnormal splicing of the leptin receptor in *diabetic* mice. *Nature, 379*, 632–635.

LEE, H., BAHLER, R., TAYLOR, A., ALONZO, A., & ZELLER, R. A. (1999). Clinical symptoms of myocardial infarction and delayed treatment-seeking behavior in Blacks and Whites. *Journal of Applied Biobehavioral Research, 3*, 135–159.

LEE, S. H., & ABRAMSON, S. B. (1999). Rheumatic diseases. In M. G. EISENBERG, R. L. GLUECKAUF, & H. H. ZARETSKY (Eds.), *Medical aspects of disability: A handbook for the rehabilitation professional* (2nd ed., pp. 472–498). New York: Springer.

LEE, W.-H., MORTON, R. A., EPSTEIN, J. I., BROOKS, J. D., CAMPBELL, P. A., BOVA, G. S., HSIEH, W.-S., ISAACS, W. B., & NELSON, W. G. (1994). Cytidine methylation of regulatory sequences near the π class glutathione S-transferase gene accompanies human prostatic carcinogenesis. *Proceedings of the National Academy of Sciences USA, 91*, 11733–11737.

LEFFERT, N., & PETERSEN, A. C. (1998). Healthy adolescent development: Risks and opportunities. In P. M. KATO & T. MANN (Eds.), *Handbook of diversity issues in health psychology* (pp. 117–140). New York: Plenum.

LEGRADY, D., DYER, A. R., SHEKELLE, R. B., STAMLER, J., LIU, K., PAUL, O., LEPPER, M., & SHRYOCK, A. M. (1987).

Coffee consumption and mortality in the Chicago Western Electric Company Study. *American Journal of Epidemiology*, 126, 803–812.

LEIBEL, R. L., ROSENBLUM, M., & HIRSCH, J. (1995). Changes in energy expenditure resulting from altered body weight. *New England Journal of Medicine*, 332, 621–628.

LEIGH, B. C. (1990). The relationship of substance use during sex to high-risk sexual behavior. *Journal of Sex Research*, 27, 199–213.

LEIGH, B. C., MORRISON, D. M., TROCKI, K., & TEMPLE, M. T. (1994). Sexual behavior of American adolescents: Results from a U.S. national survey. *Journal of Adolescent Health*, 15, 117–125.

LEINO, P., ARO, S., & HASAN, J. (1987). Trunk muscle function and low back disorders: A ten-year follow-up study. *Journal of Chronic Diseases*, 40, 289–296.

LEKANDER, M., FÜRST, C. J., ROTSTEIN, S. BLOMGREN, H., & FREDRIKSON, M. (1995). Anticipatory immune changes in women treated with chemotherapy for ovarian cancer. *International Journal of Behavioral Medicine*, 2, 1–12.

LENNEBERG, E. H. (1967). *Biological foundations of language.* New York: Wiley.

LEONARD, B. E. (1995). Stress and the immune system: Immunological aspects of depressive illness. In B. E. LEONARD & K. MILLER (Eds.), *Stress, the immune system and psychiatry.* New York: Wiley.

LEONARD, E. A. (1990, April 9). How the brain recovers. *Newsweek*, pp. 48–50.

LEPORE, S. J. (1995). Cynicism, social support, and cardiovascular reactivity. *Health Psychology*, 14, 210–216.

LEPORE, S. J. (1997). Social-environmental influences on the chronic stress process. In B. H. GOTTLIEB (Ed.), *Coping with chronic stress.* New York: Plenum.

LEPORE, S. J., ALLEN, K. A. M., EVANS, G. W. (1993). Social support lowers cardiovascular reactivity to an acute stressor. *Psychosomatic Medicine*, 55, 518–524.

LEPORE, S. J., & HELGESON, V. S. (1998). Social constraints, intrusive thoughts, and mental health after prostate cancer. *Journal of Social and Clinical Psychology*, 17, 89–106.

LEPORE, S. J., MILES, H. J., & LEVY, J. S. (1997). Relation of chronic and episodic stressors to psychological distress, reactivity, and health problems. *International Journal of Behavioral Medicine*, 4, 39–59.

LERMAN, C., AUDRAIN, J., & CROYLE, R. T. (1994). DNA-testing for heritable breast cancer risks: Lessons from traditional genetic counseling. *Annals of Behavioral Medicine*, 16, 327–333.

LERMAN, C., CAPORASO, N. E., AUDRAIN, J., MAIN, D., BOWMAN, E. D., LOCKSHIN, B., BOYD, N. R., & SHIELDS, P. G. (1999). Evidence suggesting the role of specific genetic factors in cigarette smoking. *Health Psychology*, 18, 14–20.

LERMAN, C., CAPORASO, N. E., MAIN, D., AUDRAIN, J., BOYD, N. R., BOWMAN, E. D., & SHIELDS, P. G. (1998). Depression and self-medication with nicotine: The modifying influence of the dopamine D4 receptor gene. *Health Psychology*, 17, 56–62.

LERMAN, C., HUGHES, C., TROCK, B. J., MYERS, R. E. et al., (1999). Genetic testing in families with heredity non-polyposis colon cancer. *Journal of the American Medical Association*, 17, 1618–1622.

LERMAN, C., NAROD, S., SCHULMAN, K., HUGHES, C. et al. (1996). BRAC1 testing in families with hereditary breast-ovarian cancer: A prospective study of patient decision making and outcomes. *Journal of the American Medical Association*, 275, 1885–1892.

LERMAN, C., TROCK, B., RIMER, B. K., BOYCE, A., JEPSON, C., & ENGSTROM, P. F. (1991). Psychological and behavioral implications of abnormal mammograms. *Annals of Internal Medicine*, 114, 657–661.

LESTER, N., LEFEBVRE, J. C., & KEEFE, F. J. (1994). Pain in young adults: I. Relationship to gender and family history. *Clinical Journal of Pain*, 10, 282–289.

LEVENSON, R. W. (1986). Alcohol, reactivity, and the heart: Implications for coronary health and disease. In K. A. MATTHEWS, S. M. WEISS, T. DETRE, T. M. DEMBROSKI, B. FALKNER, S. B. MANUCK, & R. B. WILLIAMS (Eds.), *Handbook of stress, reactivity, and cardiovascular disease.* New York: Wiley.

LEVENSTEIN, S., ACKERMAN, S., KIECOLT-GLASER, J. K., & DUBOIS, A. (1999). Stress and peptic ulcer disease. *Journal of the American Medical Association*, 281, 10–11.

LEVENTHAL, E. A., & PROHASKA, T. R. (1986). Age, symptom interpretation, and health behavior. *Journal of the American Geriatrics Society*, 34, 185–191.

LEVENTHAL, H., & CLEARY, P. D. (1980). The smoking problem: A review of research and theory in behavioral risk modification. *Psychological Bulletin*, 88, 370–405.

LEVENTHAL, H., LEVENTHAL, E. A., & CONTRADA, R. J. (1998). Self regulation, health, and behavior: A perceptual-cognitive approach. *Psychology & Health*, 13, 717–733.

LEVENTHAL, H., LEVENTHAL, E. A., & VAN NGUYEN, T. (1985). Reactions of families to illness: Theoretical models and perspectives. In D. C. Turk & R. D. Kerns (Eds.), *Health, illness, and families: A life-span perspective.* New York: Wiley.

LEVENTHAL, H., PROHASKA, T. R., & HIRSCHMAN, R. S. (1985). Preventive health behavior across the life span. In J. C. ROSEN & L. J. SOLOMON (Eds.), *Prevention in health psychology.* Hanover, NH: University Press of New England.

LEVIN, D. N., CLEELAND, C. S., & DAR, R. (1985). Public attitudes toward cancer pain. *Cancer*, 56, 2337–2339.

LEVINE, J. D., GORDON, N. C., & FIELDS, H. L. (1978, September 23). The mechanism of placebo analgesia. *Lancet*, 654–657.

LEVINE, M. A., GROSSMAN, R. S., DARDEN, P. M., JACKSON, S. M., et al. (1992). Dietary counseling of hypercholesterolemic patients by internal medicine residents. *Journal of General Internal Medicine, 7,* 511–516.

LEVY, R. L., CAIN, K. C., JARRETT, M., & HEITKEMPER, M. M. (1997). The relationship between daily stress and gastrointestinal symptoms in women with irritable bowel syndrome. *Journal of Behavioral Medicine, 20,* 177–193.

LEVY, S. M. (1983). The process of death and dying: Behavioral and social factors. In T. G. BURISH & L. A. BRADLEY (Eds.), *Coping with chronic disease: Research and applications.* New York: Academic Press.

LEVY, S. M. (1985). *Behavior and cancer.* San Francisco: Jossey-Bass.

LEVY, S. M., & HEIDEN, L. (1991). Depression, distress, and immunity: Risk factors for infectious disease. *Stress Medicine, 7,* 45–51.

LEVY, S. M., HERBERMAN, R. B., MALUISH, A. M., SCHLIEN, B., & LIPPMAN, M. (1985). Prognostic risk assessment in primary breast cancer by behavioral and immunological parameters. *Health Psychology, 4,* 99–113.

LEVY, S. M., HERBERMAN, R. B., WHITESIDE, T., SANZO, K., LEE, J., & KIRKWOOD, J. (1990). Perceived social support and tumor estrogen/progesterone receptor status as predictors of natural killer cell activity in breast cancer patients. *Psychosomatic Medicine, 52,* 73–85.

LEVY-LAHAD, E., WASCO, W., POORKAJ, P., ROMANO, D. M., et al. (1995). Candidate gene for the chromosome 1 familial Alzheimer's disease locus. *Science, 269,* 973–977.

LEWIN, K. (1935). *A dynamic theory of personality.* New York: McGraw-Hill.

LEWINSOHN, P. M., MERMELSTEIN, R. M., ALEXANDER, C., & MACPHILLAMY, D. J. (1985). The Unpleasant Events Schedule: A scale for the measurement of aversive events. *Journal of Clinical Psychology, 41,* 483–498.

LEY, P. (1982). Satisfaction, compliance, and communication. *British Journal of Clinical Psychology, 21,* 241–254.

LI, J. T. C., & O'CONNELL, E. J. (1987). Viral infections and asthma. *Annals of Allergy, 59,* 321–331.

LICHSTEIN, K. L. (1988). *Clinical relaxation strategies.* New York: Wiley.

LICHTENSTEIN, E., HOLLIS, J. F., SEVERSON, H. H., STEVENS, V. J., VOGT, T. M., GLASGOW, R. E., & ANDREWS, J. A. (1996). Tobacco cessation interventions in health care settings: Rationale, model, outcomes. *Addictive Behaviors, 21,* 709–720.

LICHTENSTEIN, E., & MERMELSTEIN, R. J. (1984). Review of approaches to smoking treatment: Behavior modification strategies. In J. D. MATARAZZO, S. M. WEISS, J. A. HERD, N. E. MILLER, & S. M. WEISS (Eds.), *Behavioral health: A handbook of health enhancement and disease prevention.* New York: Wiley.

LICHTENSTEIN, E., WEISS, S. M., HITCHCOCK, J. L., LEVETON, L. B., O'CONNELL, K. A., & PROCHASKA, J. O. (1986). Task Force 3: Patterns of smoking relapse. *Health Psychology, 5,* (Supplement), 29–40.

LICHTENSTEIN, P., HOLM, N. V., VERKASALO, P. K., ILIADOU, A., KAPRIO, J., KOSKENVUO, M., PUKKALA, E., SKYTTHE, A., & HEMMINKI, K. (2000). Environmental and heritable factors in the causation of cancer—Analyses of cohorts of twins from Sweden, Denmark, and Finland. *New England Journal of Medicine, 343,* 78–85.

LICHTMAN, S. W., PISARSKA, K., BERMAN, E. R., PESTONE, M., DOWLING, H., OFFENBACHER, E., WEISEL, H., HESHKA, S., MATTHEWS, D. E., & HEYMSFIELD, S. B. (1992). Discrepancy between self-reported and actual caloric intake and exercise in obese subjects. *New England Journal of Medicine, 327,* 1893–1898.

LILJAS, B., & LAHDENSUO, A. (1997). Is asthma self-management cost-effective? *Patient Education and Counseling, 32,* S97–S104.

LIN, E. H., & PETERSON, C. (1990). Pessimistic explanatory style and response to illness. *Behavior Research and Therapy, 28,* 243–248.

LINDEMAN, B. (1976). Widower, heal thyself. In R. H. MOOS (Ed.), *Human adaptation: Coping with life crises.* Lexington, MA: Heath.

LINDEN, W., & CHAMBERS, L. (1994). Clinical effectiveness of non-drug treatment for hypertension: A meta-analysis. *Annals of Behavioral Medicine, 16,* 35–45.

LINDEN, W., STOSSEL, C., & MAURICE, J. (1996). Psychosocial interventions for patients with coronary artery disease. *Archives of Internal Medicine, 156,* 745–752.

LINDENBERG, C. S., ALEXANDER, E. M., GENDROP, S. C., NENCIOLI, M., & WILLIAMS, D. G. (1991). A review of the literature on cocaine abuse in pregnancy. *Nursing Research, 40,* 69–75.

LINTON, S. J., ALTHOFF, B., MELIN, L., LUNDIN, A., BODIN, L., MÄGI, A., LINDSTROM, K., & LIHAGEN, T. (1994). Psychological factors related to health, back pain, and dysfunction. *Journal of Occupational Rehabilitation, 4,* 1–10.

LINTON, S. J., & BUER, N. (1995). Working despite pain: Factors associated with work attendance versus dysfunction. *International Journal of Behavioral Medicine, 2,* 252–262.

LIPCHIK, G. L., HOLROYD, K. A., TALBOT, F., GREER, M., MCCOOL, H. R., & BEARE, D. (1996, March). *Central and peripheral mechanisms in recurrent headache II: Replication and extension.* Paper presented at the meetings of the Society of Behavioral Medicine, Washington, DC.

LIPOWSKI, Z. J. (1986). What does the word "psychosomatic" really mean? A historical and semantic inquiry. In M. J. CHRISTIE & P. G. MELLETT (Eds.), *The psychosomatic approach: Contemporary practice and wholeperson care.* New York: Wiley.

LIPTON, R. B., SILBERSTEIN, S. D., & STEWART, W. F. (1994). An update on the epidemiology of migraine. *Headache, 34,* 319–328.

LITT, M. D., NYE, C., & SHAFER, D. (1995). Preparation for oral surgery: Evaluating elements of coping. *Journal of Behavioral Medicine, 18,* 435–459.

LITTLE, R. E. (1998). Public health in Central and Eastern Europe and the role of environmental pollution. *Annual Review of Public Health, 19,* 153–172.

LIVERMORE, B. (1991, December). What reflexology can do for you. *Self,* p. 50.

LOGUE, A. W. (1991). *The psychology of eating and drinking: An introduction* (2nd ed.). New York: Freeman.

LOLLIS, C. M., JOHNSON, E. H., ANTONI, M. H., & HINKLE, Y. (1996). Characteristics of African-Americans with multiple risk factors associated with HIV/AIDS. *Journal of Behavioral Medicine, 19,* 55–71.

LOMBARDO, T., & CARRENO, L. (1987). Relationship of Type A behavior pattern in smokers to carbon monoxide exposure and smoking topography. *Health Psychology, 6,* 445–452.

LONETTO, R. (1980). *Children's conceptions of death.* New York: Springer.

LONG, R. T., LAMONT, J. H., WHIPPLE, B., BANDLER, L., BLOM, G. E., BURGIN, L., & JESSNER, L. (1958). A psychosomatic study of allergic and emotional factors in children with asthma. *American Journal of Psychiatry, 114,* 890–899.

LORBER, J. (1975). Good patients and problem patients: Conformity and deviance in a general hospital. *Journal of Health and Social Behavior, 16,* 213–225.

LORIG, K., GONZÁLEZ, V. M., LAURENT, D. D., MORGAN, L., & LARIS, B. A. (1998). Arthritis Self-Management Program variations: Three studies. *Arthritis Care and Research, 11,* 448–454.

LORISH, C. D., RICHARDS, B., & BROWN, S. (1989). Missed medication doses in rheumatic arthritis patients: Intentional and unintentional reasons. *Arthritis Care and Research, 2,* 3–9.

LOUSBERG, R., SCHMIDT, A. J. M., GROENMAN, N. H., VENDRIG, L., & DIJKMAN-CAES, C. I. M. (1997). Validating the MPI-DLV using experience sampling data. *Journal of Behavioral Medicine, 20,* 195–206.

LOVALLO, W. R. (1997). *Stress and health: Biological and psychological interactions.* Thousand Oaks, CA: Sage.

LOVALLO, W. R., AL'ABSI, M., PINCOMB, G. A., EVERSON, S. A., SUNG, B. H., PASSEY, R. B., & WILSON, M. F. (1996). Caffeine and behavioral stress effects on blood pressure in borderline hypertensive Caucasian men. *Health Psychology, 15,* 11–17.

LOVALLO, W. R., PINCOMB, G. A., SUNG, B. H., EVERSON, S. A., PASSEY, R. B., & WILSON, M. F. (1991). Hypertension risk and caffeine's effect on cardiovascular activity during mental stress in young men. *Health Psychology, 10,* 236–243.

LOWRY, R., HOLTZMAN, D., TRUMAN, B. I., KANN, L., COLLINS, J. L., & KOLBE, L. J. (1994). Substance use and HIV-related sexual behaviors among US high school students: Are they related? *American Journal of Public Health, 84,* 1116–1120.

LUCINI, D., COVACCI, G., MILANI, R., MELA, G. S., MALLIANI, A., & PAGANI, M. (1997). A controlled study of the effects of mental relaxation on autonomic excitatory responses in healthy subjects. *Psychosomatic Medicine, 59,* 541–552.

LUDWICK-ROSENTHAL, R., & NEUFELD, R. W. J. (1993). Preparation for undergoing an invasive medical procedure: Interacting effects of information and coping style. *Journal of Consulting and Clinical Psychology, 61,* 156–164.

LUECKEN, L. J., SUAREZ, E. C., KUHN, C. M., BAREFOOT, R. B., BLUMENTHAL, J. A., SIEGLER, I. C., & WILLIAMS, R. B. (1997). Stress in employed women: Impact of marital status and children at home on neurohormone output and home strain. *Psychosomatic Medicine, 59,* 352–359.

LUFT, H. S. (1998). Medicare and managed care. *Annual Review of Public Health, 19,* 459–475.

LUND, A. K., & KEGELES, S. S. (1984). Rewards and adolescent health behavior. *Health Psychology, 3,* 351–369.

LUNDBERG, U. (1986). Stress and Type A behavior in children. *Journal of the American Academy of Child Psychiatry, 25,* 771–778.

LUNDBERG, U. (1999). Coping with stress: Neuroendocrine reactions and implications for health. *Noise and Health, 4,* 67–74.

LUNDBERG, U. DOHNS, I. E., MELIN, B., SANDSJÖ, L., PALMERUD, G., EKSTRÖM, M., & PARR, D. (1999). Psychophysiological stress responses, muscle tension, and neck shoulder pain among supermarket cashiers. *Journal of Occupational Health Psychology, 4,* 245–255.

LUNDBERG, U., & FRANKENHAEUSER, M. (1999). Stress and workload in men and women in high-ranking positions. *Journal of Occupational Health Psychology, 4,* 142–151.

LUNDIN, R. W. (1987). Locus of control. In R. J. CORSINI (Ed.), *Concise encyclopedia of psychology.* New York: Wiley.

LUPARELLO, T. J., LYONS, H. A., BLEECKER, E. R., & McFADDEN, E. R. (1968). Influences of suggestion on airway reactivity in asthmatic subjects. *Psychosomatic Medicine, 30,* 819–825.

LUTGENDORF, S. K., ANTONI, M. H., IRONSON, G., KLIMAS, N., KUMAR, M., STARR, K., McCABE, P., CLEVEN, K., FLETCHER, M. A., & SCHNEIDERMAN, N. (1997). Cognitive-behavioral stress management decreases dysphoric mood and herpes simplex virus-type 2 antibody titers in symptomatic HIV-seropositive gay men. *Journal of Consulting and Clinical Psychology, 65,* 31–43.

LYALL, S. (2000, February 10). In Britain's health service, sick itself, cancer care is dismal. *New York Times*, pp. A1, A20.

LYKKEN, D. T. (1987). Psychophysiology. In R. J. CORSINI (Ed.), *Concise encyclopedia of psychology*. New York: Wiley.

LYNAM, D. R., MILICH, R., ZIMMERMAN, R., NOVAK, S. P., LOGAN, T. K., MARTIN, C., LEUKEFELD, C., & CLAYTON, R. (1999). Project DARE: No effects at 10-year follow-up. *Journal of Consulting and Clinical Psychology, 67*, 590–593.

LYNCH, J. J. (1990). The broken heart: The psychobiology of human contact. In R. ORNSTEIN & C. SWENCIONIS (Eds.), *The healing brain: A scientific reader*. New York: Guilford.

LYNCH, J. W., EVERSON, S. A., KAPLAN, G. A., SALONEN, R., SALONEN, J. T. (1998). Does low socioeconomic status potentiate the effects of heightened cardiovascular responses to stress on the progression of carotid atherosclerosis? *American Journal of Public Health, 88*, 389–394.

MACDONALD, T. K., MACDONALD, G., ZANNA, M. P., & FONG, G. T. (2000). Alcohol, sexual arousal, and intentions to use condoms in young men: Applying alcohol myopia theory to risky sexual behavior. *Health Psychology, 19*, 290–298.

MACKAY, C., & COX, T. (1978). Stress at work. In T. Cox (Ed.), *Stress*. Baltimore: University Park Press.

MADDI, S. R. (1998). Hardiness. In E. A. BLECHMAN & K. D. BROWNELL (Eds.), *Behavioral medicine and women: A comprehensive handbook*. New York: Guilford.

MADDUX, B. A., SBRACCIA, P., KUMAKURA, S., SASSON, S., et al. (1995). Membrane glycoprotein PC-1 and insulin resistance in non-insulin-dependent diabetes mellitus. *Nature, 373*, 448–451.

MADDUX, J. E., ROBERTS, M. C., SLEDDEN, E. A., & WRIGHT, L. (1986). Developmental issues in child health psychology. *American Psychologist, 41*, 25–34.

MAGES, N. L., & MENDELSOHN, G. A. (1979). Effects of cancer on patients' lives: A personological approach. In G. C. STONE, F. COHEN, & N. E. ADLER (Eds.), *Health psychology—A handbook*. San Francisco: Jossey-Bass.

MAGNI, G., MORESCHI, C., RIGATTI-LUCHINI, S., & MERSKEY, H. (1994). Prospective study on the relationship between depressive symptoms and chronic musculoskeletal pain. *Pain, 56*, 289–297.

MAGUIRE, P. (1985). Barriers to psychological care of the dying. *British Medical Journal, 291*, 1711–1713.

MAHLER, H. I. M., & KULIK, J. A. (1991). Health care involvement preferences and social-emotional recovery of male coronary-artery-bypass patients. *Health Psychology, 10*, 399–408.

MAIER, S. F., WATKINS, L. R., & FLESHNER, M. (1994). Psychoneuroimmunology: The interface between behavior, brain, and immunity. *American Psychologist, 49*, 1004–1017.

MAI, M. (1990). Psychiatric aspects of HIV-1 infection and AIDS. *Psychological Medicine, 20*, 547–563.

MAJOR, B., RICHARDS, C., COOPER, M. L., COZZARELLI, C., & ZUBEK, J. (1998). Personal resilience, cognitive appraisals, and coping: An integrative model of adjustment to abortion. *Journal of Personality and Social Psychology, 74*, 735–752.

MALKIN, S. (1976). Care of the terminally ill. *Canadian Medical Association Journal, 115*, 129–130.

MALKOFF, S. B., MULDOON, M. F., ZEIGLER, Z. R., & MANUCK, S. B. (1993). Blood platelet responsivity to acute mental stress. *Psychosomatic Medicine, 55*, 477–482.

MANFREDI, M., BINI, G., CRUCCU, G., ACCORNERO, N., BERADELLI, A., & MEDOLAGO, L. (1981). Congenital absence of pain. *Archives on Neurology, 38*, 507–511.

MANN, T. (1996). Why do we need a health psychology of gender or sexual orientation? In P. M. KATO & T. MANN (Eds.), *Handbook of diversity issues in health psychology* (pp. 187–198). New York: Plenum.

MANNE, S. L. (1999). Intrusive thoughts and psychological distress among cancer patients: The role of spouse avoidance and criticism. *Journal of Consulting and Clinical Psychology, 67*, 539–546.

MANNE, S. L., BAKEMAN, R., JACOBSEN, P. B., GORFINKLE, K., BERNSTEIN, D., & REDD, W. H. (1992). Adult-child interaction during invasive medical procedures. *Health Psychology, 11*, 241–249.

MANNE, S. L., BAKEMAN, R., JACOBSEN, P. B., GORFINKLE, K., & REDD, W. H. (1994). An analysis of a behaviroal intervention for children undergoing venipuncture. *Health Psychology, 13*, 556–566.

MANNE, S. L., JACOBSEN, P. B., GORFINKLE, K., GERSTEIN, F., & REDD, W. H. (1993). Treatment adherence difficulties among children with cancer: The role of parenting style. *Journal of Pediatric Psychology, 18*, 47–62.

MANNE, S. L., & ZAUTRA, A. J. (1990). Couples coping with chronic illness: Women with rheumatoid arthritis and their healthy husbands. *Journal of Behavioral Medicine, 13*, 327–342.

MANNICHE, C., HESSELSOE, G., BENTZEN, L., CHRISTENSEN, I., & LUNDBERG, E. (1988). Clinical trial of intensive muscle training for chronic low back pain. *Lancet, 332*, 1473–1476.

MANUCK, S. B. (1994). Cardiovascular reactivity in cardiovascular disease: "Once more unto the breach." *International Journal of Behavioral Medicine, 1*, 4–31.

MANUCK, S. B., MARSLAND, A. L., KAPLAN, J. R., & WILLIAMS, J. K. (1995). The pathogenicity of behavior and its neuroendocrine mediation: An example from coronary artery disease. *Psychosomatic Medicine, 57*, 275–283.

MANUCK, S. B., KAPLAN, J. R., ADAMS, M. R., & CLARKSON, T. B. (1988). Effects of stress and the sympathetic nervous system on coronary artery atherosclerosis in the cynomolgus macaque. *American Heart Journal*, 116, 328–333.

MARCUS, B. H., BOCK, B. C., PINTO, B. M., FORSYTH, L. H., ROBERTS, M. B., & TRAFICANTE, R. M. (1998). Efficacy of an individualized, motivationally-tailored physical activity intervention. *Annals of Behavioral Medicine*, 20, 174–180.

MARCUS, B. H, DUBBERT, P. M., FORSYTH, L. H., McKENZIE, T. L., STONE, E. J., DUNN, A. L., & BLAIR, S. N. (2000). Physical activity behavior change: Issues in adoption and maintenance. *Health Psychology*, 19, 32–41.

MARGOLIS, L. H., McLEROY, K. R., RUNYAN, C. W., & KAPLAN, B. H. (1983). Type A behavior: An ecological approach. *Journal of Behavioral Medicine*, 6, 245–258.

MARIANO, A. J. (1992). Chronic pain and spinal cord injury. *Journal of Clinical Pain*, 8, 87–92.

MARKOVITZ, J. H., & MATTHEWS, K. A. (1991). Platelets and coronary heart disease: Potential psychophysiologic mechanisms: *Psychosomatic Medicine*, 53, 643–668.

MARKOVITZ, J. H., MATTHEWS, K. A., KISS, J., & SMITHERMAN, T. C. (1996). Effects of hostility on platelet reactivity to psychological stress in coronary heart disease patients and healthy controls. *Psychosomatic Medicine*, 58, 143–149.

MARKS, G., RICHARDSON, J. L., GRAHAM, J. W., & LEVINE, A. (1986). Role of health locus of control beliefs and expectations of treatment efficacy in adjustment to cancer. *Journal of Personality and Social Psychology*, 51, 443–450.

MARKS, G., RICHARDSON, J. L., & MALDONADO, N. (1991). Self-disclosure of HIV infection to sexual partners. *American Journal of Public Health*, 81, 1321–1323.

MARLATT, G. A. (1983). The controlled-drinking controversy: A commentary. *American Psychologist*, 38, 1097–1110.

MARLATT, G. A., BAER, J. S., KIVLAHAN, D. R., DIMEFF, L. A., LARIMER, M. E., QUIGLEY, L. A., SOMERS, J. M., & WILLIAMS, E. (1998). Screening and brief intervention for high-risk college student drinkers: Results from a 2-year follow-up assessment. *Journal of Consulting and Clinical Psychology*, 66, 604–616.

MARLATT, G. A., & GORDON, J. R. (1980). Determinants of relapse: Implications for the maintenance of behavior change. In P. O. Davidson & S. M. Davidson (Eds.), *Behavioral medicine: Changing health lifestyles*. New York: Brunner/Mazel.

MARLATT, G. A., KOSTURN, C. F., & LANG, A. R. (1975). Provocation to anger and opportunity for retaliation as determinants of alcohol consumption in social drinkers. *Journal of Abnormal Psychology*, 84, 652–659.

MARMOT, M. G., KOGEVINAS, M., & ELSTON, M. A. (1987). Social/economic status and disease. *Annual Review of Public Health*, 8, 111–135.

MARON, D., J., FAZIO, S., & LINTON, M. F. (2000). Current perspectives on statins. *Circulation*, 101, 207.

MARON, D. J., & FORTMANN, S. P. (1987). Nicotine yield and measures of cigarette smoke exposure in a large population: Are lower-yield cigarettes safer? *American Journal of Public Health*, 77, 546–549.

MARSLAND, A. L., MANUCK, S. B., FAZZARI, T. V., STEWART, C. J., & RABIN, B. S. (1995). Stability of individual differences in cellular immune responses to acute psychological stress. *Psychosomatic Medicine*, 57, 295–298.

MARTEAU, T. M., & JOHNSTON, M. (1986). Determinants of beliefs about illness: A study of parents of children with diabetes, asthma, epilepsy, and no chronic illness. *Journal of Psychosomatic Research*, 30, 673–683.

MARTEAU, T. M., JOHNSTON, M., BAUM, J. D., & BLOCH, S. (1987). Goals of treatment in diabetes: A comparison of doctors and parents of children with diabetes. *Journal of Behavioral Medicine*, 10, 33–48.

MARTELLI, M. F., AUERBACH, S. M., ALEXANDER, J., & MERCURI, L. G. (1987). Stress management in the health care setting: Matching interventions with patient coping styles. *Journal of Consulting and Clinical Psychology*, 55, 201–207.

MARTIN, J. E., & DUBBERT, P. M. (1985). Exercise in hypertension. *Annals of Behavioral Medicine*, 7(1), 13–18.

MARTIN, J. L. (1988). Psychological consequences of AIDS-related bereavement among gay men. *Journal of Consulting and Clinical Psychology*, 56, 856–862.

MARTIN, J. L. (1990). Drug use and unprotected anal intercourse among gay men. *Health Psychology*, 9, 450–465.

MARTIN, J. L., & DEAN, L. (1993). Effects of AIDS-related bereavement and HIV-related illness on psychological distress among gay men: A 7-year longitudinal study, 1985–1991. *Journal of Consulting and Clinical Psychology*, 61, 94–103.

MARTIN, P. R., MILECH, D., & NATHAN, P. R. (1993). Towards a functional model of chronic headaches: Investigation of antecedents and consequences. *Headache*, 33, 461–470.

MARTIN, P. R., & SENEVIRATNE, H. M. (1997). Effects of food deprivation and a stressor on head pain. *Health Psychology*, 16, 310–318.

MARTIN, R., DAVIS, G. M. BARON, R. S., SULS, J., & BLANCHARD, E. B. (1994). Specificity in social support: Perceptions of helpful and unhelpful provider behaviors among irritable bowel, headache, and cancer patients. *Health Psychology*, 13, 432–439.

MARTINEZ, F. D., WRIGHT, A. L., TAUSSIG, L. M., & THE GROUP HEALTH MEDICAL ASSOCIATES (1994). The effect of paternal smoking on the birthweight of newborns whose mothers did not smoke. *American Journal of Public Health*, 84, 1489–1491.

MARVEL, M. K., EPSTEIN, R. M., FLOWERS, K., & BECKMAN, H. B. (1999). Soliciting the patient's agenda: Have we improved? *Journal of the American Medical Association, 281,* 283–287.

MARX, M. H., & HILLIX, W. A. (1963). *Systems and theories in psychology.* New York: McGraw-Hill.

MASLACH, C., & JACKSON, S. E. (1982). Burnout in health professions: A social psychological analysis. In G. S. SANDERS & J. SULS (Eds.), *Social psychology of health and illness.* Hillsdale, NJ: Erlbaum.

MASON, J. W. (1975). A historical view of the stress field. *Journal of Human Stress, 1,* 22–36.

MATARAZZO, J. D. (1982). Behavioral health's challenge to academic, scientific, and professional psychology. *American Psychologist, 37,* 1–14.

MATHEWS, A., & RIDGEWAY, V. (1984). Psychological preparation for surgery. In A. STEPTOE & A. MATHEWS (Eds.), *Health care and human behaviour.* London: Academic Press.

MATICKA-TYNDALE, E. (1991). Sexual scripts and AIDS prevention: Variations in adherence to safer-sex guidelines by heterosexual adolescents. *Journal of Sex Research, 28,* 45–66.

MATTES, R. D., ARNOLD, C., & BORAAS, M. (1987a). Learned food aversions among cancer chemotherapy patients. *Cancer, 60,* 2576–2580.

MATTES, R. D., ARNOLD, C., & BORAAS, M. (1987b). Management of learned food aversions in cancer patients receiving chemotherapy. *Cancer Treatment Reports, 71,* 1071–1078.

MATTHEWS, K. A. (1982). Psychological perspectives on the Type A behavior pattern. *Psychological Bulletin, 91,* 293–323.

MATTHEWS, K. A. (1986). Summary, conclusions, and implications. In K. A. MATTHEWS, S. M. WEISS, T. DETRE, T. M. DEMBROSKI, B. FALKNER, S. B. MANUCK, & R. B. WILLIAMS (Eds.), *Handbook of stress, reactivity, and cardiovascular disease.* New York: Wiley.

MATTHEWS, K. A. (1988). Coronary heart disease and Type A behaviors: Update on and alternative to the Booth-Kewley and Friedman (1987) quantitative review. *Psychological Bulletin, 104,* 373–380.

MATTHEWS, K. A., & ANGULO, J. (1980). Measurement of the Type A behavior pattern in children: Assessment of children's competitiveness, impatience-anger, and aggression. *Child Development, 51,* 466–475.

MATTHEWS, K. A., & JENNINGS, J. R. (1984). Cardiovascular responses of boys exhibiting the Type A behavior pattern. *Psychosomatic Medicine, 46,* 484–497.

MATTHEWS, K. A., OWENS, J. F., KULLER, L. H., SUTTON-TYRRELL, K., LASSILA, H. C., & WOLFSON, S. K. (1998). Stress-induced pulse pressure change predicts women's carotid atherosclerosis. *Stroke, 29,* 1525–1530.

MATTHEWS, K. A., ROSENMAN, R. H., DEMBROSKI, T. M., HARRIS, E. L., & MACDOUGALL, J. M. (1984). Familial resemblance in components of the Type A behavior pattern: A re-analysis of the California Type A Twin Study. *Psychosomatic Medicine, 46,* 512–522.

MATTHEWS, K. A., SHUMAKER, S. A., BOWEN, D. J., LANGER, R. D., HUNT, J. R., KAPLAN, R. M., KLESGES, R. C., & RITENBAUGH, C. (1997). Women's Health-Initiative: Why now? What is it? What's new? *American Psychologist, 52,* 101–116.

MATTHEWS, K. A., & WOODALL, K. L. (1988). Childhood origins of overt Type A behaviors and cardiovascular reactivity to behavioral stressors. *Annals of Behavioral Medicine, 10,* 71–77.

MATTSON, M. E., POLLACK, E. S., & CULLEN, J. W. (1987). What are the odds that smoking will kill you? *American Journal of Public Health, 77,* 425–431.

MAUDE-GRIFFIN, P. M., HOHENSTEIN, J. M., HUMFLEET, G. L., REILLY, P. M., TUSEL, D. J., & HALL, S. M. (1998). Superior efficacy of congnitive-behavioral therapy for urban crack cocaine abusers: Main and matching effects. *Journal of Consulting and Clinical Psychology, 66,* 832–836.

MAYER, D. J. (2000). Acupuncture: An evidence-based review of the clinical literature. *Annual Review of Medicine, 51,* 49–63.

MAYER, W. (1983). Alcohol abuse and alcoholism: The psychologist's role in prevention, research, and treatment. *American Psychologist, 38,* 1116–1121.

MAYNE, T. J., VITTINGHOFF, E., BARRETT, D. C., CHESNEY, M. A., & COATES, T. J. (1996, March). *Depressive affect and HIV survival.* Paper presented at the meeting of the Society of Behavioral Medicine in Washington, DC.

MAYS, V. M., & COCHRAN, S. D. (1988). Issues in the perception of AIDS risk and risk reduction activities by black and Hispanic/Latina women. *American Psychologist, 43,* 949–957.

MAZZE, R. S., SHAMOON, H., PASMANTIER, R., LUCIDO, D., MURPHY, J., HARTMANN, K., KUYKENDALL, V., & LOPATIN, W. (1984). Reliability of blood glucose monitoring by patients with diabetes mellitus. *American Journal of Medicine, 77,* 211–217.

MCADOO, W. G., WEINBERGER, M. H., MILLER, J. Z., FEINBERG, N. S., & GRIM, C. E. (1990). Race and gender influence hemodynamic responses to psychological and physical stimuli. *Journal of Hypertension, 8,* 961–967.

MCALLISTER-SISTILLI, C. G., CAGGIULA, A. R., KNOPF, S., ROSE, C. A., MILLER, A. L., & DONNY, E. C. (1998). The effects of nicotine on the immune system. *Psychoneuroendocrinology, 23,* 175–187.

McAuley, E., Talbot, H.-M., & Martinez, S. (1999). Manipulating self-efficacy in the exercise environment in women: Influences on affective responses. *Health Psychology*, 18, 288–294.

McCahon, C. P. (1991). Why did Martha want her husband to deteriorate? *Nursing*, 21(4), 44–46.

McCann, B. S., Bovbjerg, V. E., Brief, D. J., Turner, C., Follette, W. C., Fitzpatrick, V., Dowdy, A, Retzlaff, B., Walden, C. E., & Knopp, R. H. (1995). Relationship of self-efficacy to cholesterol lowering and dietary change in hyperlipidemia. *Annals of Behavioral Medicine*, 17, 221–226.

McCann, B. S., Bovbjerg, V. E., Curry, S. J., Retzlaff, B. M., Walden, C. E., & Knopp, R. H. (1996). Predicting participation in a dietary intervention to lower cholesterol among individuals with hyperlipidemia. *Health Psychology*, 15, 61–63.

McCarty, D. (1985). Environmental factors in substance abuse: The microsetting. In M. Galizio & S. A. Maisto (Eds.), *Determinants of substance abuse: Biological, psychological, and environmental factors*. New York: Plenum.

McCaul, K. D., & Malott, J. M. (1984). Distraction and coping with pain. *Psychological Bulletin*, 95, 516–533.

McCaul, K. D., Monson, N., & Maki, R. H. (1992). Does distraction reduce pain-produced distress among college students? *Health Psychology*, 11, 210–217.

McClearn, G. E. (1968). Behavioral genetics: An overview. *Merrill-Palmer Quarterly*, 14, 9–14.

McClellan, A. T., Arndt, I. O., Metzger, D. S., Woody, G. E., & O'Brien, C. P. (1993). The effects of psychosocial services in substance abuse treatment. *Journal of the American Medical Association*, 269, 1953–1959.

McClintic, J. R. (1985). *Physiology of the human body* (3rd ed.). New York: Wiley.

McConnell, S., Biglan, A., & Severson, H. H. (1984). Adolescents' compliance with self-monitoring and physiological assessment of smoking in natural environments. *Journal of Behavioral Medicine*, 7, 115–122.

McCoy, S. B., Gibbons, F. X., Reis, T. J., Gerrard, M., Luus, C. A. E., & Von Wald Sufka, A. (1992). Perceptions of smoking risk as a function of smoking status. *Journal of Behavioral Medicine*, 15, 469–488.

McCrady, B. S. (1988). Alcoholism. In E. A. Blechman & K. D. Brownell (Eds.), *Handbook of behavioral medicine for women*. New York: Pergamon.

McCrady, B. S., & Irvine, S. (1989). Self-help groups. In R. K. Hester & W. R. Miller (Eds.), *Handbook of alcoholism treatment approaches: Effective alternatives*. New York: Pergamon.

McDaniel, S., & Campbell, T. L. (1986). Physicians and family therapists: The risk of collaboration. *Family Systems Medicine*, 4, 4–8.

McEwen, B. S., & Stellar, E. (1993). Stress and the individual: Mechanisms leading to disease. *Archives of Internal Medicine*, 153, 2093–2101.

McFarlane, A. H., Norman, G. R., Streiner, D. L., & Roy, R. G. (1983). The process of social stress: Stable, reciprocal, and mediating relationships. *Journal of Health and Social Behavior*, 24, 160–173.

McFarlane, A. H., Norman, G. R., Streiner, D. L., Roy, R., & Scott, D. J. (1980). A longitudinal study of the influence of the psychosocial environment on health status: A preliminary report. *Journal of Health and Social Behavior*, 21, 124–133.

McGehee, D. S., Heath, M. J. S., Gelber, S., Devay, P., & Role, L. W. (1995). Nicotine enhancement of fast excitatory transmission in CNS by presynaptic receptors. *Science*, 269, 1692–1696.

McGinnis, J. M. (1994). The role of behavioral research in national health policy. In J. A. Blumenthal, K. Matthews, & S. M. Weiss (Eds.), *New frontiers in behavioral medicine: Proceedings of the national conference*. Washington, DC: National Institutes of Health.

McGinnis, J. M., & Lee, P. R. (1995). Healthy People 2000 at mid decade. *Journal of the American Medical Association*, 273, 1123–1129.

McGinnis, J. M., Shopland, D., & Brown, C. (1987). Tobacco and health: Trends in smoking and smokeless tobacco consumption in the United States. *Annual Review of Public Health*, 8, 441–467.

McGrady, A., Conran, P., Dickey, D., Garman, D., Farris, E., & Schumann-Brzezinski, C. (1992). The effects of biofeedback-assisted relaxation on cell-mediated immunity, cortisol, and white blood cell count in healthy adult subjects. *Journal of Behavioral Medicine*, 15, 343–354.

McGrady, A., & Higgins, J. T. (1990). Effect of repeated measurements of blood pressure in essential hypertension: Role of anxiety. *Journal of Behavioral Medicine*, 13, 93–101.

McGrady, A., Wauquier, A., McNeil, A., & Gerard, G. (1994). Effect of biofeedback-assisted relaxation on migraine headache and changes in cerebral blood flow velocity in the middle cerebral artery. *Headache*, 34, 424–428.

McGrath, P. A., & Hillier, L. M. (1996). Controlling children's pain. In R. J. Gatchel & D. C. Turk (Eds.), *Psychological approaches to pain management: A practitioner's handbook* (pp. 331–370). New York: Guilford.

McGuigan, F. J. (1999). *Encyclopedia of stress*. Boston: Allyn & Bacon.

McGuire, F. L. (1982). Treatment of the drinking driver. *Health Psychology*, 1, 137–152.

McGuire, M. T., Wing, R. R., Klem, M. L., Lang, W., & Hill, J. O. (1999). What predicts weight regain in a group of successful weight losers? *Journal of Consulting and Clinical Psychology*, 67, 177–185.

MCILWAIN, H. H., SILVERFIELD, J. C., BURNETTE, M. C., & BRUCE, D. F. (1991). *Winning with arthritis*. New York: Wiley.

MCKENNA, M. C., ZEVON, M. A., CORN, B., & ROUNDS, J. (1999). Psychosocial factors and the development of breast cancer: A meta-analysis. *Health Psychology*, 18, 520–531.

MCKINLAY, J. B. (1975). Who is really ignorant—Physician or patient? *Journal of Health and Social Behavior*, 16, 3–11.

MCKNIGHT, J. D., & GLASS, D. C. (1995). Perceptions of control, burnout, and depressive symptomatology: A replication and extension. *Journal of Consulting and Clinical Psychology*, 63, 490–494.

MCNAULL, F. W. (1984). Radiation therapy. In S. N. MCINTIRE & A. L. CIOPPA (Eds.), *Cancer nursing: A developmental approach*. New York: Wiley.

MDBDF (March of Dimes Birth Defects Foundation) (2000). *National perinatal statistics*. Retrieved (3-23-2000) from http://www.modimes.org.

MEAD, M., & NEWTON, N. (1967). Cultural patterning of perinatal behavior. In S. A. RICHARDSON & A. F. GUTTMACHER (Eds.), *Childbearing: Its social and psychological aspects*. Baltimore: Williams & Wilkins.

MECHANIC, D. (1972). Social psychologic factors affecting the presentation of bodily complaints. *New England Journal of Medicine*, 286, 1132–1139.

MECHANIC, D. (1979). The stability of health and illness behavior: Results from a 16-year follow-up. *American Journal of Public Health*, 69, 1142–1145.

MECHANIC, D. (1998). The functions and limitations of trust in the provision of medical care. *Journal of Health Politics, Policy and Law*, 23, 661–686.

MEICHENBAUM, D., & CAMERON, R. (1983). Stress inoculation training: Toward a general paradigm for training coping skills. In D. MEICHENBAUM & M. E. JAREMKO (Eds.), *Stress reduction and prevention*. New York: Plenum.

MEICHENBAUM, D., & DEFFENBACHER, J. L. (1988). Stress inoculation training. *Counseling Psychologist*, 16, 69–90.

MEICHENBAUM, D., & TURK, D. (1982). Stress, coping, and disease: A cognitive-behavioral perspective. In R. W. J. NEUFIELD (Ed.), *Psychological stress and psychopathology*. New York: McGraw-Hill.

MEIER, D. E., EMMONS, C.-A., WALLENSTEIN, S., QUILL, T., MORRISON, R. S., & CASSEL, C. K. (1998). A national survey of physician-assisted suicide and euthanasia in the United States. *New England Journal of Medicine*, 338, 1193–1201.

MELAMED, B. G., & BUSH, J. P. (1985). Family factors in children with acute illness. In D. C. TURK & R. D. KERNS (Eds.), *Health, illness, and families: A life-span approach*. New York: Wiley.

MELAMED, B. G., DEARBORN, M., & HERMECZ, D. A. (1983). Necessary conditions for surgery preparation: Age and previous experience. *Psychosomatic Medicine*, 45, 517–525.

MELAMED, B. G., & SIEGEL, L. J. (1975). Reduction of anxiety in children facing hospitalization and surgery by use of filmed modeling. *Journal of Consulting and Clinical Psychology*, 43, 511–521.

MELIN, B., LUNDBERG, U., SODERLUND, J., & GRANQVIST, M. (1999). Psychological and physiological stress reactions of male and female assembly workers: A comparison between two different forms of work organization. *Journal of Organizational Behavior*, 20, 47–61.

MELZACK, R (1975). The McGill Pain Questionnaire: Major properties and scoring methods. *Pain*, 1, 277–299.

MELZACK, R. (1997). Phantom limbs. *Scientific American*, 7 (1, Special issue), 84–91.

MELZACK, R., & TORGERSON, W. S. (1971). On the language of pain. *Anesthesiology*, 34, 50–59.

MELZACK, R., & WALL, P. D. (1965). Pain mechanisms: A new theory. *Science*, 150, 971–979.

MELZACK, R., & WALL, P. D. (1982). *The challenge of pain*. New York: Basic Books.

MELZACK, R., WEISZ, A. Z., & SPRAGUE, L. T. (1963). Strategems for controlling pain: Contributions of auditory stimulation and suggestion. *Experimental Neurology*, 8, 239–247.

MENDELSON, B. K., & WHITE, D. R. (1985). Development of self-body-esteem in overweight youngsters. *Developmental Psychology*, 21, 90–96.

MENEFEE, L. A., HAYTHORNTHWAITE, J. A., CLARK, M. R., & KOENIG, T. (1996, March). *The effect of social responses on pain coping strategies*. Paper presented at the meeting of the Society of Behavioral Medicine, Washington, DC.

MENKES, M. S., MATTHEWS, K. A., KRANTZ, D. S., LUNDBERG, U., MEAD, L. A., QAQISH, B., & LIANG, K.-Y. (1989). Cardiovascular reactivity to the cold pressor test as a predictor of hypertension. *Hypertension*, 14, 524–530.

MENTZER, S. J., & SNYDER, M. L. (1982). The doctor and the patient: A psychological perspective. In G. S. SANDERS & J. SULS (Eds.), *Social psychology of health and illness*. Hillsdale, NJ: Erlbaum.

MEREDITH, H. V. (1978). *Human body growth in the first ten years of life*. Columbia, SC: The State Printing Company.

METHORST, G. J., JANSEN, M. A., & KERKHOF, A. J. F. M. (1991). Training in health psychology: An international look. In M. A. JANSEN & J. WEINMAN (Eds.), *The international development of health psychology*. Chur, Switzerland: Harwood.

METROPOLITAN LIFE FOUNDATION (1983). 1983 Metropolitan Height and Weight Tables. *Statistical Bulletin*, 64(1), 2–9.

MEYER, A. J., NASH, J. D., McALISTER, A. L., MACCOBY, N., & FARQUHAR, J. W. (1980). Skills training in a cardiovascular health education campaign. *Journal of Consulting and Clinical Psychology*, 48, 129–142.

MEYER, T. J., & MARK, M. M. (1995). Effects of psychosocial interventions with adult cancer patients: A meta-analysis of randomized experiments. *Health Psychology*, 14, 101–108.

MEYEROWITZ, B. E. (1983). Postmastectomy coping strategies and quality of life. *Health Psychology*, 2, 117–132.

MEYEROWITZ, B. E., RICHARDSON, J., HUDSON, S., & LEEDHAM, B. (1998). Ethnicity and cancer outcomes: Behavioral and psychosocial considerations. *Psychological Bulletin*, 123, 47–70.

MICHELA, J. L. (1987). Interpersonal and individual impacts of a husband's heart attack. In A. BAUM & J. E. SINGER (Eds.), *Handbook of psychology and health* (Vol. 5). Hillsdale, NJ: Erlbaum.

MIGLIORELLI, R., TESON, A., SABE, L., PETRACCHI, M., LEIGUARDA. R., & STARKSTEIN, S. E. (1995). Prefalence and correlates of dysthymia and major depression among patients with Alzheimer's disease. *American Journal of Psychiatry*, 152, 37–44.

MILES, F., & MEEHAN, J. W. (1995). Visual discrimination of pigmented skin lesions. *Health Psychology*, 14, 171–177.

MILLAR, W. J., & STEPHENS, T. (1987). The prevalence of overweight and obesity in Britain, Canada, and the United States. *American Journal of Public Health*, 77, 38–41.

MILLER, B., & CAFASSO, L. (1992). Gender differences in caregiving: Fact or artifact? *Gerontologist*, 32, 498–507.

MILLER, B. C., & SOLLIE, D. L. (1986). Normal stresses during the transition to parenthood. In R. H. Moos (Ed.), *Coping with life crises: An integrated approach*. New York: Plenum.

MILLER, B. D., & WOOD, B. L. (1994). Psychophysiologic reactivity in asthmatic children: A cholinergically mediated confluence of pathways. *Journal of the American Academy of Child and Adolescent Psychiatry*, 33, 1236–1245.

MILLER, N. E. (1959). Liberalization of basic S-R concepts: Extensions to conflict behavior, motivation, and social learning. In S. KOCH (Ed.), *Psychology: A study of a science* (Vol. 2). New York: McGraw-Hill.

MILLER, N. E. (1978). Biofeedback and visceral learning. *Annual Review of Psychology*, 29, 373–404.

MILLER, R. H. & LUFT, H. S. (1994). Managed care plans: Characteristics, growth, and premium performance. *Annual Review of Public Health*, 15, 437–459.

MILLER, S. B., TURNER, J. R., SHERWOOD, A., BROWNLEY, K. A., HINDERLITER, A. L., & LIGHT, K. C. (1995). Parental history of hypertension and cardiovascular response to stress in black and white men. *International Journal of Behavioral Medicine*, 2, 339–357.

MILLER, S. M. (1979). Controllability and human stress: Method, evidence and theory. *Behaviour Research and Therapy*, 17, 287–304.

MILLER, S. M., BRODY, D. S., & SUMMERTON, J. (1987). Styles of coping with threat: Implications for health. *Journal of Personality and Social Psychology*, 54, 142–148.

MILLER, S. M., & GREEN, M. L. (1984). Coping with stress and frustration: Origins, nature, and development. In M. LEWIS & C. SAARNI (Eds.), *Origins of behavior* (Vol. 5). New York: Plenum.

MILLER, S. M., & MANGAN, C. E. (1983). Interacting effects of information and coping style in adapting to gynecologic stress: Should the doctor tell all? *Journal of Personality and Social Psychology*, 45, 223–236.

MILLER, T. D., BALADY, G. J., & FLETCHER, G. F. (1997). Exercise and its role in the prevention and rehabilitation of cardiovascular disease. *Annals of Behavioral Medicine*, 19, 220–229.

MILLER, W. R. (1989a). Increasing motivation for change. In R. K. HESTER & W. R. MILLER (Eds.), *Handbook of alcoholism treatment approaches: Effective alternatives*. New York: Pergamon.

MILLER, W. R. (1989b). Matching individuals with interventions. In R. K. HESTER & W. R. MILLER (Eds.), *Handbook of alcoholism treatment approaches: Effective alternatives*. New York: Pergamon.

MILLER, W. R., & HESTER, R. K. (1980). Treating the problem drinker: Modern approaches. In W. R. MILLER (Ed.), *The addictive behaviors: Treatment of alcoholism, drug abuse, smoking, and obesity*. New York: Pergamon.

MILLER, W. R., & HESTER, R. K. (1985). Inpatient alcoholism treatment: Who benefits? *American Psychologist*, 41, 794–805.

MILLER, W. R., MEYERS, R. J., & TONIGAN, J. S. (1999). Engaging the unmotivated in treatment for alcohol problems: A comparison of three strategies for intervention through family members. *Journal of Consulting and Clinical Psychology*, 67, 688–697.

MILLER-JOHNSON, S., EMERY, R. E., MARVIN, R. S., CLARKE, W., LOVINGER, R., & MARTIN, M. (1994). Parent-child relationships and the management of insulin-dependent diabetes mellitus. *Journal of Consulting and Clinical Psychology*, 62, 603–610.

MILLON, T., GREEN, C., & MEAGHER, R. (1982). *Millon Behavioral Health Inventory Manual*. Minneapolis: National Computer Systems.

MILLS, N. M. (1989). Pain behaviors in infants and toddlers. *Journal of Pain and Symptom Management*, 4, 184–190.

MINOR, M. A., & SANFORD, M. K. (1993). Physical interventions in the management of pain in arthritis. *Arthritis Care and Research*, 6, 197–206.

MISOVICH, S. J., FISHER, J. D., & FISHER, W. A. (1997). Close relationships and elevated HIV risk behavior: Evidence and possible underlying psychological processes. *Review of General Psychology*, 1, 72–107.

MITCHELL, J. C. (Ed.) (1969). *Social networks in urban situations*. Manchester, England: Manchester University Press.

MITTLEMAN, M. A., MACLURE, M., SHERWOOD, J. B., MULRY, R. P., TOFLER, G. H., JACOBS, S. C., & FRIEDMAN, R. (1995). Triggering of acute episodes of myocardial infarction onset by episodes of anger. *Circulation*, 92, 1720–1725.

MITTLEMAN, M. A., MINTZER, D., MACLURE, M., TOFLER, G. H., SHERWOOD, J. B., & MULLER, J. E. (1999). Triggering of myocardial infarction by cocaine. *Circulation*, 99, 2737–2741.

MIZOGUCHI, H., O'SHEA, J. J., LONGO, D. L., LOEFFLER, C. M., McVICAR, D. W., & OCHOA, A. C. (1992). Alterations in signal transduction molecules in T lymphocytes from tumor-bearing mice. *Science*, 258, 1795–1798.

MOFFET, J. K., TORGERSON, D., BELL-SYER, S., JACKSON, D., LLEWLYN-PHILLIPS, H., FARRIN, A., & BARBER, J. (1999). Randomized controlled trial of exercies for low back pain: Clinical outcomes, costs, and preferences. *British Medical Journal*, 319, 279–283.

MÖLLER, J., HALLQVIST, J., DIDERICHSEN, F., THEORELL, T., REUTERWALL, C., & AHLBOM, A. (1999). Do eposodes of anger trigger myocardial infarction? A case-crossover analysis in the Stockholm Heart Epidemiology Program (SHEEP). *Psychosomatic Medicine*, 61, 842–849.

MONTGOMERY, G. H., TOMOYASU, N., BOVBJERG, D. H., ANDRYKOWSKI, M. A., CURRIE, V. E., JACOBSEN, P. B., & REDD, W. H. (1998). Patients' pretreatment expectations of chemotherapy-related nausea are an independent predictor of anticipatory nausea. *Annals of Behavioral Medicine*, 20, 104–109.

MONTI, P. M., ROHSENOW. D. J., RUBONIS, A. V., NAIURA, R. S., SIROTA, A. D., COLBY, S. M., GODDARD, P., & ABRAMS, D. B. (1993). Cue exposure with coping skills treatment for male alcoholics: A preliminary investigation. *Journal of Consulting and Clinical Psychology*, 61, 1011–1019.

MOORE, M. L. (1983). *Realities of childbearing* (2nd ed.). Philadelphia: Saunders.

MOORE, P. J., KULIK, J. A., & MAHLER, H. I. M. (1998). Stress and multiple potential affiliates: Does misery choose miserable company? *Journal of Applied Biobehavioral Research*, 3, 81–95.

MOORE, S. M., BARLING, N. R., & HOOD, B. (1998). Predicting testicular and breast self-examination behaviour: A test of the theory of reasoned action. *Behaviour Change*, 15, 41–49.

MOOS, R. H. (1982). Coping with acute health crises. In T. MILLON, C. GREEN, & R. MEAGHER (Eds.), *Handbook of clinical health psychology*. New York: Plenum.

MOOS, R. H., & SCHAEFER, J. A. (1986). Life transitions and crises: A conceptual overview. In R. H. MOOS (Ed.), *Coping with life crises: An integrated approach*. New York: Plenum.

MOR, V., MASTERSON-ALLEN, S., GOLDBERG, R. J., CUMMINGS, F. J., GLICKSMAN, A. S., & FRETWELL, M. D. (1985). Relationships between age at diagnosis and treatments received by cancer patients. *Journal of the American Geriatrics Society*, 33, 585–589.

MORAN, P. M., CHRISTENSEN, A. J., & LAWTON, W. J. (1997). Social support and conscientiousness in hemodialysis adherence. *Annals of Behavioral Medicine*, 19, 333–338.

MORELAND, J., & THOMPSON, M. A. (1994). Efficacy of electromyographic biofeedback compared with conventional physical therapy for upper-extremity function in patients following stroke: A research overview and meta-analysis. *Physical Therapy*, 74, 534–547.

MORLEY, S., ECCLESTON, C., & WILLIAMS, A. (1999). Systematic review and meta-analysis of randomized controlled trials of cognitive behaviour tharapy and behaviour therapy for chronic pain in adults, excluding headache. *Pain*, 80, 1–13.

MORRIS, R. J., & KRATOCHWILL, T. R. (1983). *Treating children's fears and phobias: A behavioral approach*. New York: Pergamon.

MORROW, G. R., ASBURY, R., HAMMON, S., DOBKIN, P., CARUSO, L., PANDYA, K., & ROSENTHAL, S. (1992). Comparing the effectiveness of behavioral treatment for chemotherapy-induced nausea and vomiting when administered by oncologists, oncology nurses, and clinical psychologists. *Health Psychology*, 11, 250–256.

MOSER, D. K., & DRACUP, K. (1996). Is anxiety early after myocardial infarction associated with subsequent ischemic and arrhythmic events? *Psychosomatic Medicine*, 58, 395–401.

MOSKOWITZ, J. T., FOLKMAN, S., COLLETTE, L., & VITTINGHOFF, E. (1996). Coping and mood during AIDS-related caregiving and bereavement. *Annals of Behavioral Medicine*, 18, 49–57.

MOSLEY, T. H., PENZIEN, D. B., JOHNSON, C. A., WITTROCK, D., RUBMAN, S., PAYNE, T. J., & HOLROYD, K. A. (1990, April). *Coping with stress in headache sufferers and noheadache controls*. Paper presented at the meeting of the Society of Behavioral Medicine, Chicago.

MOSS, G. E., DIELMAN, T. E., CAMPANELLI, P. C., LEECH, S. L., HARLAN, W. R., VAN HARRISON, R., & HORVATH, W. J. (1986). Demographic correlates of SI assessments of Type A behavior. *Psychosomatic Medicine*, 48, 564–574.

MOYER, A. (1997). Psychosocial outcomes of breast-conserving surgery versus mastectomy: A meta-analytic review. *Health Psychology, 16,* 284–298.

MULDOON, M. F., & MANUCK, S. B. (1992). Health through cholesterol reduction: Are there unforeseen risks? *Annals of Behavioral Medicine, 14,* 101–108.

MULDOON, M. F., MANUCK, S. B., & MATTHEWS, K. A. (1990). Lowering cholesterol concentrations and mortality: A quantitative review of primary prevention trials. *British Medical Journal, 301,* 309–314.

MULLAN, F. (1983). *Vital signs: A young doctor's struggle with cancer.* New York: Farrar, Straus, & Giroux.

MULLER, J. E., LUDMER, P. L., WILLICH, S. N., TOFLER, G. H., AYLMER, G., KLANGOS, I., & STONE, P. H. (1987). Circadian variation in the frequency of sudden cardiac death. *Circulation, 75,* 131–138.

MULLER, J. E., MITTLEMAN, M. A., MACLURE, M., SHERWOOD, J. B., et al. (1996). Triggering myocardial infarction by sexual activity: Low absolute risk and prevention by regular physical exertion. *Journal of the American Medical Association, 275,* 1405–1409.

MURDAUGH, C. L. (1998). Problems with adherence in the elderly. In S. A. SHUMAKER, E. B. SCHRON, J. K. OKENE, & W. L. MCBEE (Eds.), *The handbook of health behavior change* (2nd ed., pp. 357–376). New York: Springer.

MURPHY, L. B. (1974). Coping, vulnerability, and resilience in childhood. In G. V. COELHO, D. A. HAMBURG, & J. E. ADAMS (Eds.), *Coping and adaptation.* New York: Basic Books.

MURRAY, D. M., DAVIS-HEARN, M., GOLDMAN, A. I., PIRIE, P., & LUEPKER, R. V. (1988). Four- and five-year follow-up results from four seventh-grade smoking prevention strategies. *Journal of Behavioral Medicine, 11,* 395–405.

MURRAY, D. M., PIRIE, P., LEUPKER, R. V., & PALLONEN, U. (1989). Five- and six-year follow-up results from four seventh-grade smoking prevention strategies. *Journal of Behavioral Medicine, 12,* 207–218.

MURRAY, D. M., RICHARDS, P. S., LUEPKER, R. V., & JOHNSON, C. A. (1987). The prevention of cigarette smoking in children: Two- and three-year follow-up comparisons of four prevention strategies. *Journal of Behavioral Medicine, 10,* 595–611.

MURRAY, M., SWAN, A. V., JOHNSON, M. R. D., & BEWLEY, B. R. (1983). Some factors associated with increased risk of smoking by children. *Journal of Child Psychology and Psychiatry, 24,* 223–232.

MURRAY, P., LIDDELL, A., & DONOHUE, J. (1989). A longitudinal study of the contribution of dental experience to dental anxiety in children between 9 and 12 years of age. *Journal of Behavioral Medicine, 12,* 309–320.

MURRELL, J., FARLOW, M., GHETTI, B., & BENSON, M. D. (1991). A mutation in the amyloid precursor protein associated with hereditary Alzheimer's disease. *Science, 254,* 97–99.

MUSCAT, J. E., HARRIS, R. E., HALEY, N. J., & WYNDER, E. L. (1991). Cigarette smoking and plasma cholesterol. *American Heart Journal, 121,* 121–141.

MUST, A., SPADANO, J., COAKLEY, E. H., FIELD, A. E., COLDITZ, G., & DIETZ, W. H. (1999). The disease burden associated with overweight and obesity. *Journal of the American Medical Association, 282,* 1523–1529.

MYERS, H. F., KAGAWA-SINGER, M., KUMANYIKA, S. K., LEX, B. W., & MARKIDES, K. S. (1995). Panel III: Behavioral risk factors related to chronic diseases in ethnic minorities. *Health Psychology, 14,* 613–621.

NADITCH, M. P. (1984). The Stay Well Program. In J. D. MATARAZZO, S. M. WEISS, J. A. HERD, N. E. MILLER, & S. M. WEISS (Eds.), *Behavioral health: A handbook of health enhancement and disease prevention.* New York: Wiley.

NASH, S. S., & SMITH, M. J. (1982). Perception and coordination. In M. J. SMITH, J. A. GOODMAN, N. L. RAMSEY, & S. B. PASTERNACK (Eds.), *Child and family: Concepts in nursing practice.* New York: McGraw-Hill.

NASW (National Association of Social Workers) (2000). *Social work careers.* Retrieved (3-4-2000) from http://www.naswdc.org.

NATHAN, P. (1984). Johnson & Johnson's Live for Life: A comprehensive positive lifestyle change program. In J. D. MATARAZZO, S. M. WEISS, J. A. HERD, N. E. MILLER, & S. M. WEISS (Eds.), *Behavioral health: A handbook of health enhancement and disease prevention.* New York: Wiley.

NATHAN, P. E. (1985). Prevention of alcoholism: A history of failure. In J. C. ROSEN & L. J. SOLOMON (Eds.), *Prevention in health psychology.* Hanover, NH: University Press of New England.

NATHAN, P. E. (1986). Outcomes of treatment for alcoholism: Current data. *Annals of Behavioral Medicine, 8(2-3),* 40–46.

NAVARRO, A. M., SENN, K. L., McNICHOLAS, L. J., KAPLAN, R. M., ROPPÉ, B., & CAMPO, M. C. (1998). *Por La Vita* model intervention enhances use of cancer screening tests among Latinas. *American Journal of Preventive Medicine, 15,* 32–41.

NCADI (National Clearinghouse for Alcohol and Drug Information) (2000). *Drugs of abuse.* Retrieved (3-23-2000) from http://www.samhsa.gov.

NCHS (National Center for Health Statistics) (2000) *Health, United States, 1999.* Retrieved (3-21-2000) from http://www.cdc.gov/nchs.

NEGRI, E., LA VECCHIA, C., D'AVANZO, B., NOBILI, A., et al. (1994). Acute myocardial infarction: Association with time since stopping smoking in Italy. *Journal of Epidemiology and Community Health, 48,* 129–133.

NEHEMKIS, A. M., & GERBER, K. E. (1986). Compliance and the quality of survival. In K. E. GERBER & A. M. NEHEMKIS (Eds.), *Compliance: The dilemma of the chronically ill*. New York: Springer.

NEIGHBORS, C. J., O'LEARY, A., & LABOUVIE, E. (1999). Domestically violent and nonviolent male inmates' responses to their partners' requests for condom use: Testing a social-information processing model. *Health Psychology, 18*, 427–431.

NEUGARTEN, B. L., & NEUGARTEN, D. A. (1987, May). The changing meanings of age. *Psychology Today*, pp. 29–33.

NEUNDORFER, M. M. (1991). Coping and health outcomes in spouse caregivers of persons with dementia. *Nursing Research, 40*, 260–265.

NEVIDJON, B. M. (1984). Chemotherapy. In S. N. MCINTIRE & A. L. CIOPPA (Eds.), *Cancer nursing: A developmental approach*. New York: Wiley.

NEWCOMB, M. D., & BENTLER, P. M. (1986). Cocaine use among adolescents: Longitudinal associations with social context, psychopathology, and use of other substances. *Addictive Behaviors, 11*, 263–273.

NEWCOMB, M. D., MADDAHIAN, E., & BENTLER, P. M. (1986). Risk factors for drug use among adolescents: Concurrent and longitudinal analyses. *American Journal of Public Health, 76*, 525–531.

NEWCOMB, P. A., WEISS, N. S., STORER, B. E., SCHOLES, D., YOUNG, B. E., & VOIGT, L. F. (1991). Breast self-examination in relation to the occurrence of advanced breast cancer. *Journal of the National Cancer Institute, 83*, 260–265.

NEWLIN, D. B., & THOMSON, J. B. (1991). Chronic tolerance and sensitization to alcohol in sons of alcoholics. *Alcoholism: Clinical and experimental research, 15*, 399–405.

NEWMAN, M. G., & STONE, A. A. (1996). Does humor moderate the effects of experimentally-induced stress? *Annals of Behavioral Medicine, 18*, 101–109.

NEWMAN, S. (1984a). Anxiety, hospitalization, and surgery. In R. FITZPATRICK, J. HINTON, S. NEWMAN, G. SCAMBLER, & J. THOMPSON (Eds.), *The experience of illness*. London: Tavistock.

NEWMAN, S. (1984b). The psychological consequences of cerebrovascular accident and head injury. In R. FITZPATRICK, J. HINTON, S. NEWMAN, G. SCAMBLER, & J. THOMPSON (Eds.), *The experience of illness*. London: Tavistock.

NEZU, A. M., NEZU, C. M., & PERRI, M. G. (1989). *Problem-solving therapy for depression: Theory, research, and clinical guidelines*. New York: Wiley.

NG, B., DIMSDALE, J. E., SHRAGG, P., & DEUTSCH, R. (1996). Ethnic differences in analgesic consumption for post-operative pain. *Psychosomatic Medicine, 58*, 125–129.

NGUYEN, M., WATANABE, H., BUDSON, A. E., RICHIE, J. P.,

HAYES, D. F., & FOLKMAN, J. (1994). Elevated levels of an angiogenic peptide, basic fibroblast factor, in the urine of patients with a wide spectrum of cancers. *Journal of the National Cancer Institute, 86*, 356–361.

NIAAA (National Institute on Alcohol Abuse and Alcoholism) (1993). *Alcohol and health* (8th Special Report to the U.S. Congress; Publication No. 94-3699). Washington, DC: U.S. Government Printing Office.

NICASSIO, P. M., RADOJEVIC, V., WEISMAN, M. H., CULBERTSON, A. L., LEWIS, C., & CLEMMEY, P. (1993). The role of helplessness in the response to disease-modifying drugs in rheumatoid arthritis. *Journal of Rheumatology, 20*, 1114–1120.

NICASSIO, P. M., WALLSTON, K. A., CALLAHAN, L. F., HERBERT, M., & PINCUS, T. (1985). The measurement of helplessness in rheumatoid arthritis: The development of the Arthritis Helplessness Index. *Journal of Rheumatology, 12*, 462–467.

NICHOLS, R. S., & SANTELLI, J. (1990, March). *The AIDS patient: Extreme elevation of MMPI scales*. Paper presented at the meeting of the Eastern Psychological Association, Philadelphia.

NIDES, M. A., RAKOS, R. F., GONZALES, D., MURRAY, R. P., et al., (1995). Predictors of initial smoking cessation and relapse through the first 2 years of the Lung Health Study. *Journal of Consulting and Clinical Psychology, 63*, 60–69.

NKF (National Kidney Foundation) (2000). *About kidney disease*. Retrieved (3-20-2000) from http://www.kidney.org.

NLN (National League of Nursing) (2000). *About NLN*. Retrieved (3-4-2000) from http://www.nln.org.

NORMAN, P., CONNER, M., & BELL, R. (1999). The theory of planned behavior and smoking cessation. *Health Psychology, 18*, 89–94.

NORRIS, C. M. (1990). The work of getting well. *American Journal of Nursing, 90*, 47–50.

NORTHCOTE, R. J., FLANNIGAN, C., & BALLANTYNE, D. (1986). Sudden death and vigorous exercise—A study of 60 deaths associated with squash. *British Heart Journal, 55*, 198–203.

NOVACO, R. W. (1975). *Anger control: The development and evaluation of an experimental treatment*. Lexington, MA: Heath.

NOVACO, R. W. (1978). Anger and coping with stress: Cognitive behavioral interventions. In J. P. FOREYT & D. P. RATHJEN (Eds.), *Cognitive behavior therapy: Research and application*. New York: Plenum.

NOWACK, K. M. (1989). Coping style, cognitive hardiness, and health status. *Journal of Behavioral Medicine, 12*, 145–158.

NSCIA (National Spinal Cord Injury Association) (2000). *Fact Sheets (#1, #2, and #3)*. Retrieved (3-24-2000) from http://www.spinalcord.org.

NYSTUL, M. S. (1987). Transcendental meditation. In R. J. CORSINI (Ed.), *Concise encyclopedia of psychology*. New York: Wiley.

O'BRIEN, C. P. (1996). Recent developments in the pharmacotherapy of substance abuse. *Journal of Consulting and Clinical Psychology, 64*, 677–686.

O'BYRNE, K. K., PETERSON, L., & SALDANA, L. (1997). Survey of pediatric hospitals' preparation programs: Evidence for the impact of health psychology research. *Health Psychology, 16*, 147–154.

O'CALLAGHAN, M. E., & COUVADELLI, B. (1998). Use of self-instructional strategies with three neurologically impaired adults. *Cognitive Therapy and Research, 22*, 91–107.

OCKENE, I. S., HEBERT, J. R., OCKENE, J. K., SAPERIA, G. M., STANEK, E., NICOLOSI, R., MERRIAM, P. A., & HURLEY, T. G. (1999). Effect of physician-delivered nutrition counseling training and an office support program on saturated fat intake, weight, and serum lipid measurements in a hyperlipidemic population: Worcester Area Trial for Counseling in Hyperlipidemia (WATCH). *Archives of Internal Medicine, 159*, 725–731.

OCKENE, J. K., ADAMS, A., HURLEY, T. G., WHEELER, E. V., & HEBERT, J. R. (1999). Brief physician- and nurse practitioner-delivered counseling for high-risk drinkers. *Archives of Internal Medicine, 159*, 2198–2205.

OCKENE, J. K., EMMONS, K. M., MERMELSTEIN, R. J., PERKINS, K. A., BONOLLO, D. S., VOORHEES, C. C., & HOLLIS, J. F. (2000). Relapse and maintenance issues for smoking cessation. *Health Psychology, 19*, 17–31.

OCKENE, J. K., HOSMER, D., RIPPE, J., WILLIAMS, J., GOLDBERG, R. J., DECOSIMO, D., MAHER, P. M., & DALEN, J. E. (1985). Factors affecting cigarette smoking status in patients with ischemic heart disease. *Journal of Chronic Diseases, 38*, 985–994.

OCKENE, J. K., KRISTELLER, J., GOLDBERG, R., AMICK, T. L., PEKOW, P. S., HOSMER, D., QUIRK, M., & KALAN, K. (1991). Increasing the efficacy of physician-delivered smoking interventions. *Journal of General Internal Medicine, 6*, 1–8.

OCKENE, J. K., KRISTELLER, J. L., PBERT, L., HEBERT, J. R., LUIPPOLD, R., GOLDBERG, R. J., LANDON, J., & KALAN, K. (1994). The Physician-Delivered Smoking Intervention Project: Can short-term interventions produce long-term effects for a general outpatient population? *Health Psychology, 13*, 278–281.

O'DONNELL, L., O'DONNELL, C. R., PLECK, J. H., SNAREY, J., & ROSE, R. M. (1987). Psychosocial responses of hospital workers to acquired immune deficiency syndrome (AIDS). *Journal of Applied Social Psychology, 17*, 269–285.

O'DOUGHERTY, M., & BROWN, R. T. (1990). The stress of childhood illness. In L. E. ARNOLD (Ed.), *Childhood stress*. New York: Wiley.

ÖHLUND, C., LINDSTROM, I., ARESKOUG, B., EEK, C., PETERSON, L.-E., & NACHEMSON, A. (1994). Pain behavior in industrial subacute low back pain: Part I. Reliability: Consurrent and predictive validity of pain behavior assessments. *Pain, 58*, 201–209.

OLAFSSON, O., & SVENSSON, P. (1986). Unemployment-related lifestyle changes and health disturbances in adolescents and children in the Western countries. *Social Science and Medicine, 22*, 1105–1113.

OLBRISCH, M. E. (1996). Picking winners and grooming the dark horse: Psychologists evaluate and treat organ transplant patients. *Health Psychologist, 18*(1), 10–11.

OLDENBURG, B. (1994). Promotion of health: Integrating the clinical and public health approaches. In S. MAES, H. LEVENTHAL, & M. JOHNSTON (Eds.), *International review of health psychology* (Vol. 3). New York: Wiley.

OLDENBURG, B., PERKINS, R. J., & ANDREWS, G. (1985). Controlled trial of psychological intervention in myocardial infarction. *Journal of Consulting and Clinical Psychology, 53*, 852–859.

OLDRIDGE, N. B. (1984). Adherence to adult exercise fitness programs. In J. D. MATARAZZO, S. M. WEISS, J. A. HERD, N. E. MILLER, & S. M. WEISS (Eds.), *Behavioral health: A handbook of health enhancement and disease prevention*. New York: Wiley.

OLDRIDGE, N. B., & SPENCER, J. (1985). Exercise habits and perceptions before and after graduation of dropout from supervised cardiac exercise rehabilitation. *Journal of Cardiopulmonary Rehabilitation, 5*, 313–319.

O'LEARY, A., SHOOR, S., LORIG, K., & HOLMAN, H. R. (1988). Cognitive-behavioral treatment for rheumatoid arthritis. *Health Psychology, 7*, 527–544.

OLFF, M., BROSSCHOT, J. F., GODAERT, G., BENSCHOP, R. J., BALLIEUX, R. E., HEIJNEN, C. J., DE SMET, M. B. M., & URSIN, H. (1995). Modulatory effects of defense and coping on stress-induced changes in endocrine and immune parameters. *International Journal of Behavioral Medicine, 2*, 85–103.

OLIVET, L. W. (1982). Basic needs of the hospitalized child. In M. J. SMITH, J. A. GOODMAN, N. L. RAMSEY, & S. B. PASTERNACK (Eds.), *Child and family: Concepts of nursing practice*. New York: McGraw-Hill.

OLSHANSKY, S. J., CARNES, B. A., & CASSEL, C. (1990). In search of Methuselah: Estimating the upper limits to human longevity. *Science, 250*, 634–640.

ORFUTT, C, & LACROIX, J. M. (1988). Type A behavior pattern and symptom reports: A prospective investigation. *Journal of Behavioral Medicine, 11*, 227–237.

ORNE, M. T. (1989). On the construct of hypnosis: How its definition affects research and its clinical application. In G. D. BURROWS & L. DENNERSTEIN (Eds.), *Handbook of hypnosis and psychosomatic medicine*. Amsterdam: Elsevier.

ORNISH, D., BROWN, S. E., SCHERWITZ, L. W., BILLINGS, J. H., ARMSTRONG, W. T., PORTS, T. A., MCLANAHAN, S. M., KIRKEEIDE, R. L., BRAND, R. J., & GOULD, K. L. (1990). Can lifestyle changes reverse coronary heart disease: The Lifestyle Heart Trial. *Lancet*, 336, 129–133.

ORNISH, D., SHERWITZ, L. W., BILLINGS, J. H., GOULD, K. L., et al. (1998). Can intensive lifestyle changes reverse coronary heart disease? Four-year follow-up of the Lifestyle Heart Trial. *Journal of the American Medical Association*, 280, 2001–2007.

O'ROURKE, D. F., HOUSTON, B. K., HARRIS, J. K., & SNYDER, C. R. (1988). The Type A behavior pattern: Summary, conclusions, and implications. In B. K. HOUSTON & C. R. SNYDER (Eds.), *Type A behavior pattern: Research, theory, and intervention*. New York: Wiley.

OSBORN, J. E. (1988). The AIDS epidemic: Six years. *Annual Review of Public Health*, 9, 551–583.

OSSIP-KLEIN, D. J., BIGELOW, G., PARKER, S. R., CURRY, S., HALL, S., & KIRKLAND, S. (1986). Task Force 1: Classification and assessment of smoking behavior. *Health Psychology*, 5(Supplement), 3–11.

OSTROVE, J. M., FELDMAN, P., & ADLER, N. E. (1999). Relations among socioeconomic status indicators and health for African-Americans and whites. *Journal of Health Psychology*, 4, 451–463.

OUIMETTE, P. C., FINNEY, J. W., & MOOS, R. H. (1997). Twelve-step and cognitive-behavioral treatment for substance abuse: A comparison of treatment effectiveness. *Journal of Consulting and Clinical Psychology*, 65, 230–240.

PALLONEN, U. E., MURRAY, D. M., SCHMID, L., PIRIE, P., LUEPKER, R. V. (1990). Patterns of self-initiated smoking cessation among young adults. *Health Psychology*, 9, 418–426.

PANDINA, R. J. (1986). Methods, problems, and trends in studies of adolescent drinking practices. *Annals of Behavioral medicine*, 8(2–3), 20–26.

PANICO, S., CELENTANO, E., KROGH, V., JOSSA, F., FARINARO, E., TREVISAN, M., & MANCINI, M. (1987). Physical activity and its relationship to blood pressure in school children. *Journal of Chronic Diseases*, 40, 925–930.

PANTALEO, G., GRAZIOSI, C., DEMAREST, J. F., BUTINI, L., MONTRONI, M., FOX, C. H., ORENSTEIN, J. M., KOTLER, D. P., & FAUCI, A. S. (1993). HIV infection is active and progressive in lymphoid tissue during the clinically latent stage of the disease. *Nature*, 362, 355–358.

PAOLETTI, P., CAMILLI, A. E., HOLBERG, C. J., & LEBOWITZ, M. D. (1985). Respiratory effects in relation to estimated tar exposure from current and cumulative cigarette consumption. *Chest*, 88, 849–855.

PARCEL, G. S., BRUHN, J. G., & CERRETO, M. C. (1986). Longitudinal analysis of health and safety behaviors among school children. *Psychological Reports*, 59, 265–266.

PARFITT, R. R. (1977). *The birth primer*. Philadelphia: Running Press.

PARK, D. C., HERTZOG, C., LEVENTHAL, H., MORRELL, R. W., LEVENTHAL, E., BIRCHMORE, D., MARTIN, M., & BENNETT, J. (1999). Medication adherence in rheumatoid arthritis patients: Older is wiser. *Journal of the American Geriatric Society*, 47, 172–183.

PARKER, J. C. (1995). Stress management. In P. M. NICASSIO & T. W. SMITH (Eds.), *Managing chronic illness: A biopsychosocial perspective*. Washington, DC: American Psychological Association.

PARKER, J. C., FRANK, R. G., BECK, N. C., SMARR, K. L., BUESCHER, K. L., PHILLIPS, L. R., SMITH, E. I., ANDERSON, S. K., & WALKER, S. E. (1988). Pain management in rheumatoid arthritis patients: A cognitive-behavioral approach. *Arthritis and Rheumatism*, 31, 593–601.

PARKER, J. C., SMARR, K. L., WALKER, S. E., HAGGLUND, K. J., ANDERSON, S. K., HEWETT, J. E., BRIDGES, A. J., & CALDWELL, C. W. (1991). Biopsychosocial parameters of disease activity in rheumatoid arthritis. *Arthritis Care and Research*, 4, 73–80.

PARKER, P. A., & KULIK, J. A. (1995). Burnout, self-and supervisor-rated job performance, and absenteeism among nurses. *Journal of Behavioral Medicine*, 18, 581–599.

PARKER, S. R. (1985). Future directions in behavioral research related to lung diseases. *Annals of Behavioral Medicine*, 7(4), 21–25.

PARRISH, J. M. (1986). Parent compliance with medical and behavioral recommendations. In N. A. KRASNEGOR, J. D. ARASTEH, & M. F. CATALDO (Eds.), *Child health behavior: A behavioral pediatrics perspective*. New York: Wiley.

PARROTT, A. C. (1999). Does cigarette smoking *cause* stress? *American Psychologist*, 54, 817–820.

PARSONS, O. A. (1986). Alcoholics' neuropsychological impairment: Current findings and conclusions. *Annals of Behavioral Medicine*, 8(2–3), 13–19.

PARSONS, T. (1951). *The social system*. New York: Free Press.

PARSONS, T. (1964). *Social structure and personality*. London: Collier-Macmillan & Co.

PASSER, M. W. (1982). Psychological stress in youth sports. In R. A. MAGILL, M. J. ASH, & F. L. SMOLL (Eds.), *Children in sport* (2nd ed.). Champaign, IL: Human Kinetics.

PATERSON, R. J., & NEUFELD, R. W. J. (1987). Clear danger: Situational determinants of the appraisal of threat. *Psychological Bulletin*, 101, 404–416.

PATRICK, A. W., GILL, G. V., MACFARLANE, I. A., CULLEN, A., POWER, E., & WALLYMAHMED, M. (1994). Home glucose monitoring in type 2 diabetes: Is it a waste of time? *Diabetic Medicine*, 11, 62–65.

PATRICK, K., SALLIS, J. F., LONG, B., CALFAS, K. J., WOOTEN, W., HEATH, G., & PRATT, M. (1994). A new tool for encouraging activity: Project PACE. *Physician and Sportsmedicine*, 22(11), 45–55.

PATTERSON, J. M., & GARWICK, A. W. (1994). The impact of chronic illness on families: A family systems perspective. *Annals of Behavioral Medicine, 16,* 131–142.

PATTERSON, S. M., MATTHEWS, K. A., ALLEN, M. T., & OWENS, J. F. (1995). Stress-induced hemoconcentration of blood cells and lipids in healthy women during acute psychological stress. *Health Psychology, 14,* 319–324.

PATTERSON, S. M., ZAKOWSKI, S. G., HALL, M. H., COHEN, L., WOLLMAN, K., & BAUM, A. (1994). Psychological stress and platelet activation: Differences in platelet reactivity in healthy men during active and passive stressors. *Health Psychology, 13,* 34–38.

PATTERSON, T. L., SEMPLE, S. J., SHAW, W. S., YU, E., HE, Y., ZHANG, M. Y., WU, W., & GRANT, I. (1998). The cultural context of caregiving: A comparison of Alzheimer's caregivers in Shanghai, China and San Diego, California. *Psychological Medicine, 28,* 1071–1084.

PATTERSON, T. L., SHAW, W. S., SEMPLE, S. J., CHERNER, M., et al. (1996). Relationship of psychosocial factors to HIV disease progression. *Annals of Behavioral Medicine, 18,* 30–39.

PATTISHALL, E. G. (1989). The development of behavioral medicine: Historical models. *Annals of Behavioral Medicine, 11,* 43–48.

PAVLOV, I. P. (1927). *Conditioned reflexes.* New York: Oxford University Press.

PAYNE, R. L., & JONES, J. G. (1987). Measurement and methodological issues in social support. In S. V. KASL & C. L. COOPER (Eds.), *Stress and health: Issues in research methodology.* New York: Wiley.

PEAR, R. (1990, September 23). Insurers reducing malpractice fees for doctors in U.S. *New York Times,* pp. A1, 26.

PEARLIN, L. I., & SCHOOLER, C. (1978). The structure of coping. *Journal of Health and Social Behavior, 19,* 2–21.

PECHACEK, T. F., FOX, B. H., MURRAY, D. M., & LUEPKER, R. V. (1984). Review of techniques for measurement of smoking behavior. In J. D. MATARAZZO, S. M. WEISS, J. A. HERD, N. E. MILLER, & S. M. WEISS (Eds.), *Behavioral health: A handbook of health enhancement and disease prevention.* New York: Wiley.

PECHACEK, T. F., MURRAY, D. M., LUEPKER, R. V., MITTELMARK, M. B., JOHNSON, C. A., & SHUTZ, J. M. (1984). Measurement of adolescent smoking behavior: Rationale and methods. *Journal of Behavioral Medicine, 7,* 123–140.

PECK, A. (1972). Emotional reactions to having cancer. *American Journal of Roentgenology, Radium Therapy, and Nuclear Medicine, 114,* 591–599.

PECK, C. L., & KING, N. J. (1985). Compliance and the doctor-patient relationship. *Drugs, 30,* 78–84.

PEDERSEN, N. L., LICHTENSTEIN, P., PLOMIN, R., DeFAIRE, U., McCLEARN, G. E., & MATTHEWS, K. A. (1989). Genetic and environmental influences for Type A-like measures and related traits: A study of twins reared apart and twins reared together. *Psychosomatic Medicine, 51,* 428–440.

PEDERSON, L. L. (1982). Compliance with physician advice to quit smoking: A review of the literature. *Preventive Medicine, 11,* 71–84.

PEELE, S. (1984). The cultural context of psychological approaches to alcoholism: Can we control the effects of alcohol? *American Psychologist, 39,* 1337–1351.

PEIRCE, R. S., FRONE, M. R., RUSSELL, M., & COOPER, M. L. (1996). Financial stress, social support, and alcohol involvement: A longitudinal test of the buffering hypothesis in a general population survey. *Health Psychology, 15,* 38–47.

PEIRCE, R. S., FRONE, M. R., RUSSELL, M., COOPER, M. L., & MUDAR, P. (2000). A longitudinal model of social contact, social support, depression, and alcohol use. *Health Psychology, 19,* 28–38.

PENN, A., & SNYDER, C. A. (1993). Inhalation of sidestream cigarette smoke accelerates development of arteriosclerotic placques. *Circulation, 88*(Part 1), 1820–1825.

PENN, N. E., KAR, S., KRAMER, J., SKINNER, J., & ZAMBRANA, R. E. (1995). Panel VI: Ethnic minorities, health care systems, and behavior. *Health Psychology, 14,* 641–646.

PENNEBAKER, J. W. (1983). Accuracy of symptom perception. In A. BAUM, S. E. TAYLOR, & J. SINGER (Eds.), *Handbook of psychology and health* (Vol. 4). Hillsdale, NJ: Erlbaum.

PENNEBAKER, J. W. (1990). *Opening up: The healing power of confiding in others.* New York: William Morrow.

PENNEBAKER, J. W. (1997). Writing about emotional experiences as a therapeutic process. *Psychological Science, 8,* 162–166.

PENNEBAKER, J. W., & WATSON, D. (1988). Blood pressure estimation and beliefs among normotensives and hypertensives. *Health Psychology, 7,* 309–328.

PENNINX, B. W. J. H., GURALNIK, J. M., FERRUCCI, L., SIMONSICK, E. M., DEEG, D. J. H., & WALLACE, R. B. (1998). Depressive symptoms and physical decline in community-dwelling older persons. *Journal of the American Medical Association, 279,* 1720–1726.

PEREZ-STABLE, E. J., SABOGAL, F., OTERO-SABOGAL, R., HIATT, R. A., & McPHEE, S. J. (1992). Misconceptions about cancer among Latinos and Anglos. *Journal of the American Medical Association, 268,* 3219–3223.

PERINI, C., NIL, R., BOLLI, P., BÄTTIG, K., & BÜHLER, F. R. (1993). Ischemic ECG changes are found more often in asymptomatic men with coronary prone behaviour pattern. *Journal of Psychosomatic Research, 37,* 355–360.

PERKINS, K. A. (1985). The synergistic effect of smoking and serum cholesterol on coronary heart disease. *Health Psychology, 4,* 337–360.

PERKINS, K. A. (1994). Issues in the prevention of

weight gain after smoking cessation. *Annals of Behavioral Medicine, 16,* 46–52.

PERKINS, K. A., LEVINE, M., MARCUS, M., SHIFFMAN, S., D'AMICO, D., D., MILLER, A., KEINS, A., ASHCOM, J., & BROGE, M. (2000). Tobacco withdrawal in women and menstrual cycle phase. *Journal of Consulting and Clinical Psychology, 68,* 176–180.

PERKINS, K. A., ROHAY, J., MEILAHN, E. N., WING, R. R., MATTHEWS, K. A., & KULLER, L. H. (1993). Diet, alcohol, and physical activity as a function of smoking status in middle-aged women. *Health Psychology, 12,* 410–415.

PERRI, M. G., MCALLISTER, D. A., GANGE, J. J., JORDAN, R. C., MCADOO, W. G., & NEZU, A. M. (1988). Effects of four maintenance programs on the long-term management of obesity. *Journal of Consulting and Clinical Psychology, 56,* 529–534.

PERRI, M. G., NEZU, A. M., & VIEGENER, B. J. (1992): *Improving the long-term management of obesity.* New York: Wiley.

PERZ, C. A., DICLEMENTE, C. C., & CARBONARI, J. P. (1996). Doing the right thing at the right time? The interaction of stages and processes of change in successful smoking cessation. *Health Psychology, 15,* 462–468.

PESCATELLO, L. S., FARGO, A. E., LEACH, C. N., & SCHERZER, H. H. (1991). Short-term effect of dynamic exercise on arterial blood pressure. *Circulation, 83,* 1557–1561.

PETERMAN, T. A. (1990). Facilitators of HIV transmission during sexual contact. In N. J. ALEXANDER, H. L. GABELNICK, & J. M. SPIELER (Eds.), *Heterosexual transmission of AIDS.* New York: Wiley-Liss.

PETERSON, J. L., & MARIN, G. (1988). Issues in the prevention of AIDS among black and Hispanic men. *American Psychologist, 43,* 871–877.

PETERSON, L., CROWSON, J., SALDANA, L., & HOLDRIDGE, S. (1999). Of needles and skinned knees: Children's coping with medical procedures and minor injuries for self and other. *Health Psychology, 18,* 197–200.

PETRAITIS, J., FLAY, B. R., MILLER, T. Q., TORPY, E. J., & GREINER, B. (1998). Illicit substance use among adolescents: A matrix of prospective predictors. *Substance Use and Misuse, 33,* 2561–2604.

PETRY, N. M., MARTIN, B., COONEY, J. L., & KRANZLER, H. R. (2000). Give them prizes, and they will come: Contingency management for treatment of alcohol dependence. *Journal of Consulting and Clinical Psychology, 68,* 250–257.

PETTICREW, M., FRASER, J. M., & REGAN, M. F. (1999). Adverse life-events and risk of breast cancer: A meta-analysis. *British Journal of Health Psychology, 4,* 1–17.

PEVELER, R. C., & JOHNSTON, D. W. (1986). Subjective and cognitive effects of relaxation. *Behaviour Research and Therapy, 24,* 413–419.

PHARES, E. J. (1984). *Introduction to personality.* Columbus, OH: Merrill.

PHARES, E. J. (1987). Locus of control. In R. J. CORSINI (Eds.), *Concise encyclopedia of psychology.* New York: Wiley.

PHILIPS, C. A. (1989). Rehabilitation of the patient with rheumatoid hand involvement. *Physical Therapy, 69,* 1091–1098.

PIANEZZA, M. L., SELLERS, E. M., & TYNDALE, R. F. (1998). Nicotine metabolism defect reduces smoking. *Nature, 393,* 750.

PIASECKI, T. M., KENFORD, S. L., SMITH, S. S., FIORE, M. C., & BAKER, T. B. (1997). Listening to nicotine: Negative affect and the smoking withdrawal conundrum. *Psychological Science, 8,* 184–189.

PIERCE, J. P., & GILPIN, E. A. (1995). A historical analysis of tobacco marketing and the uptake of smoking by youth in the United States: 1890–1977. *Health Psychology, 14,* 500–508.

PIETTE, J. D., BARNETT, P. G., & MOOS, R. H. (1998). First-time admissions with alcohol-related medical problems: A 10-year follow-up of a national sample of alcoholic patients. *Journal of Studies on Alcohol, 59,* 89–96.

PIKE, J. L., SMITH, T. L., HAUGER, R. L., NICASSIO, P. M., PATTERSON, T. L., MCCLINTIC, T. L., COSTLOW, C., & IRWIN, M. R. (1997). Chronic life stress alters sympathetic, neuroendocrine, and immune responsivity to an acute psychological stressor in humans. *Psychomatic Medicine, 59,* 447–457.

PILISUK, M. (1982). Delivery of social support: The social inoculation. *American Journal of Orthopsychiatry, 52,* 20–31.

PILLITTERI, A. (1981). *Child health nursing: Care of the growing family* (2nd ed.). Boston: Little, Brown.

PINES, M (1979, January). Superkids. *Psychology Today,* pp. 53–63.

PINTO, B. M., EAKIN, E., & MARUYAMA, N. C. (2000). Health behavior changes after a cancer diagnosis: What do we know and where do we go from here? *Annals of Behavioral Medicine, 22,* 38–52.

PINTO, R. P., & HOLLANDSWORTH, J. G. (1989). Using videotape modeling to prepare children psychologically for surgery: Influence of parents and costs versus benefits of providing preparation services. *Health Psychology, 8,* 79–95.

PIOTROWSKI, C., & LUBIN, B. (1990). Assessment practices of health psychologists: Survey of APA Division 38 clinicians. *Professional Psychology: Research and Practice, 21,* 99–106.

PLACE, M. (1984). Hypnosis and the child. *Journal of Child Psychology and Psychiatry, 25,* 339–347.

PMRG (Project Match Research Group) (1998). Matching alcholism treatments to client heterogeneity: Treatment main effects and matching effects on drinking during treatment. *Journal of Studies on Alcohol, 59,* 631–639.

POLLOCK, S. E., CHRISTIAN, B. J., & SANDS, D. (1991). Responses to chronic illness: Analysis of psychological and physiological adaptation. *Nursing Research, 39,* 300–304.

POLONSKY, W. H., ANDERSON, B. J., LOHRER, P. A., APONTE, J. E., JACOBSON, A. M., & COLE, C. F. (1994). Insulin omission in women with IDDM. *Diabetes Care, 17,* 1178–1185.

POMERLEAU, O. F., COLLINS, A. C., SHIFFMAN, S., & POMERLEAU, C. S. (1993). Why some people smoke and others do not: New perspectives. *Journal of Consulting and Clinical Psychology, 61,* 723–731.

POMERLEAU, O. F., & POMERLEAU, C. S. (1989). A biobehavioral perspective on smoking. In T. NEY & A. GALE (Eds.), *Smoking and human behavior.* New York: Wiley.

POPE, M. K., & SMITH, T. W. (1991). Cortisol excretion in high and low cynically hostile men. *Psychosomatic Medicine, 53,* 386–392.

PORGES, S. W. (1992). Vagal tone: A physiological marker of stress vulnerability. *Pediatrics, 90,* 498–504.

PORGES, S. W. (1995). Cardiac vagal tone: A physiological index of stress. *Neuroscience and Behavioral Reviews, 19,* 225–233.

PORTER, F. L., MILLER, R. H., & MARSHALL, R. E. (1986). Neonatal pain cries: Effects of circumcision on acoustic features and perceived urgency. *Child Development, 57,* 790–802.

PORTER, L. S., GIL, K. M., CARSON, J., ANTHONY, K. K., & READY, J. (2000). The role of stress and mood in sickle cell disease pain. *Journal of Health Psychology, 5,* 53–63.

POTHMANN, R., FRANKENBERG, S. V., MÜLLER, B., SARTORY, G., & HELLMEIER, W. (1994). Epidemiology of headache in children and adolescents: Evidence of high prevalence of migraine among girls under 10. *International Journal of Behavioral Medicine, 1,* 76–89.

POTTER, P. T., & ZAUTRA, A. J. (1997). Stressful life events' effects on rheumatoid arthritis disease activity. *Journal of Consulting and Clinical Psychology, 65,* 319–323.

POWCH, I. G., & HOUSTON, B. K. (1996). Hostility, anger-in, and cardiovascular reactivity in white women. *Health Psychology, 15,* 200–208.

POWELL, K. E., THOMPSON, P. D., CASPERSEN, C. J., & KENDRICK, J. S. (1987). Physical activity and the incidence of coronary heart disease. *Annual Review of Public Health, 8,* 253–287.

POWELL, L. H. (1984). The Type A behavior pattern: An update on conceptual, assessment, and intervention research. *Behavioral Medicine Update, 6*(4), 7–10.

POWELL, L. H. (1987). Issues in the measurement of the Type A behaviour pattern. In S. V. KASL & C. L. COOPER (Eds.), *Stress and health: Issues in research methodology.* Chichester, England: Wiley.

POWELL, L. H., & FRIEDMAN, M. (1986). Alteration of Type A behaviour in coronary patients. In M. J. CHRISTIE & P. G. MELLETT (Eds.), *The psychosomatic approach: Contemporary practice of whole-person care.* New York: Wiley.

POWELL, L. H., FRIDMAN, M., THORESEN C. E., GILL, J. J., & ULMER, D. K. (1984). Can the Type A behavior pattern be altered after myocardial infraction? A second year report from the Recurrent Coronary Prevention Project. *Psychosomatic Medicine, 46,* 293–313.

POWER, M., BULLINGER, M., HARPER, A., and the World Health Organization Quality of Life Group (1999). The World Health Organization WHOQOL-100: Tests of the universality of quality of life in 15 different cultural groups worldwide. *Health Psychology, 18,* 495–505.

PRESCOTT, C. A., & KENDLER, K. S. (1999). Genetic and environmental contributions to alcohol abuse and dependence in a population-based sample of male twins. *American Journal of Psychiatry, 156,* 34–40.

PRICE, R. A., CADORET, R. J., STUNKARD, A. J., & TROUGHTON, E. (1987). Genetic contributions to human fatness: An adoption study. *American Journal of Psychiatry, 144,* 1003–1008.

PRIEST, R. G. (1986). Benzodiazepines: The search for tranquililty. In M. J. CHRISTIE & P. G. MELLETT (Eds.), *The psychosomatic approach: Contemporary practice of wholeperson care.* New York: Wiley.

PROCHASKA, J. O., & DiCLEMENTE, C. C. (1984). *The transtheoretical approach: Crossing traditional boundaries of therapy.* Homewood, IL: Dow Jones/Irwin.

PROCHASKA, J. O., DiCLEMENTE, C. C., & NORCROSS, J. C. (1992). In search of how people change: Applications to addictive behaviors. *American Psychologist, 47,* 1102–1114.

PROHASKA, T. R., KELLER, M. L., LEVENTHAL, E. A., & LEVENTHAL, H. (1987). Impact of symptoms and aging attribution emotions and coping. *Health Psychology, 6,* 495–514.

PRPO (Pacific Regional Program Office) (2000). *E-Health.* Retrieved (8-18-2000) from http://akamai.tamc.amedd.army.mil.

PUGH, K., RICCIO, M., JADRESIC, D., BURGESS, A. P., BALDEWEG, T., CATALAN, J., LOVETT, E., HAWKINS, D. A., GRUZELIER, J., & THOMPSON, C. (1994). A longitudinal study of the neuropsychiatric consequences of HIV-1 infection in gay men. II. Psychological and health status at baseline and at 12-month follow-up. *Psychological Medicine, 24,* 897–904.

PULEO, P. R., MEYER, D., WATHEN, C., TAWA, C. B., et al. (1994). Use of rapid assay of subforms of creatine kinase MB to diagnose or rule out acute myocardial infarction. *New England Journal of Medicine, 331,* 561–566.

PURCELL, K., WEISS, J., & HAHN, W. (1972). Certain psychosomatic disorders. In B. B. WOLMAN (Ed.), *Manual of child psychopathology.* New York: McGraw-Hill.

QUADAGNO, D. M., DIXON, L. A., DENNEY, N. W., & BUCK, H. W. (1986). Postpartum moods in men and women. *American Journal of Obstetrics and Gynecology, 154,* 1018–1023.

QUAY, H. C., & LaGRECA, A. M. (1986). Disorders of anxiety, withdrawal, and dysphoria. In H. C. QUAY & J. S. WERRY (Eds.), *Psychopathological disorders of childhood* (3rd ed.) New York: Wiley.

QUICK, J. C. (1999). Occupational health psychology: Historical roots and future directions. *Health Psychology, 18,* 82–88.

QUICK, J. C., QUICK, J. D., NELSON, D. L., & HURRELL, J. J. (1997). *Preventive stress management in organizations.* Washington, DC: American Psychological Association.

QUINLAN, K. B., & McCAUL, K. D. (2000). Matched and mismatched interventions with young adult smokers: Testing a stage theory. *Health Psychology, 19,* 165–171.

QUITTNER, A. L., ESPELAGE, D. L., OPIPARI, L. C., CARTER, B., EID, N., & EIGEN, H. (1998). Role strain in couples with and without a child with a chronic illness: Associations with marital satisfaction, intimacy, and daily mood. *Health Psychology, 17,* 112–124.

RABKIN, J. G., FERRANDO, S. J., SHU-HSING, L., SEWELL, M., & McELHINEY, M. (2000). Psychological effects of HAART: A 2-year study. *Psychosomatic Medicine, 62,* 413–422.

RADECKI, S. E., & BRUNTON, S. A. (1992). Health promotion/disease prevention in family practice residency trainig: Results of a national survey. *Family Medicine, 24,* 534–534.

RAGLAND, D. R., & BRAND, R. J. (1988). Type A behavior and mortality from coronary heart disease. *New England Journal of Medicine, 318,* 65–69.

RAHE, R. H. (1974). The pathway between subjects' recent life changes and their near-future illness reports: Representative results and methodological issues. In B. S. Dohrenwend & B. P. Dohrenwend (Ed.), *Stressful life events: Their nature and effects.* New York: Wiley.

RAHE, R. H. (1987). Recent life changes, emotions, and behaviors in coronary heart disease. In A. BAUM & J. E. SINGER (Eds.), *Handbook of psychology and health* (Vol. 5). Hillsdale, NJ: Erlbaum.

RAHE, R. H., & ARTHUR, R. J. (1978). Life change and illness studies: Past history and future directions. *Journal of Human Stress, 4,* 3–15.

RÄIKKÖNEN, K., MATTHEWS, K. A., FLORY, J. D., OWENS, J. F., & GUMP, B. B. (1999). Effects of optimism, pessimism, and trait anxiety on ambulatory blood pressure and meed during everyday life. *Journal of Personality and Social Psychology, 76,* 104–113.

RAKOWSKI, W., DUBE, C. E., MARCUS, B. H., PROCHASKA, J. O., VELICER, W. F., & ABRAMS, D. B. (1992). Assessing elements of women's decisions about mammography. *Health Psychology, 11,* 111–118.

RAMSEY, N. L. (1982). Effects of hospitalization on the child and family. In M. J. SMITH, J. A. GOODMAN, N. L. RAMSEY, & S. B. PASTERNACK (Eds.), *Child and family: Concepts of nursing practice.* New York: McGraw-Hill.

RAND, C. S., & WEEKS, K. (1998). Measuring adherence with medication regimens in clinical care research. In S. A. SHUMAKER, E. B. SCHRON, J. L., OCKENE, & W. L. McBEE (Eds.), *The handbook of health behavior change* (2nd ed., pp. 114–132). New York: Springer.

RAO, R. B., ELY, S. F., & HOFFMAN, R. S. (1999). Deaths related to liposuction. *New England Journal of Medicine, 340,* 1471–1475.

RAPHAEL, B. G. (1999). Hematological disorders. In M. G. EISENBERG, R. L., GLUECKAUF, & H. H. ZARETSKY (Eds.), *Medical aspects of disability: A handbook for the rehabilitation professional.* New York: Springer.

RAPHAEL, K. G., CLOITRE, M., & DOHRENWEND, B. P. (1991). Problems of recall and misclassification with checklist methods of measuring stressful life events. *Health Psychology, 10,* 62–74.

RAPPAPORT, N. B., McANULTY, D. P., WAGGONER, C. D., & BRANTLEY, P. J. (1987). Cluster analysis of Minnesota Multiphasic Personality Inventory (MMPI) profiles in a chronic headache population. *Journal of Behavioral Medicine, 10,* 49–60.

RAPS, C. S., PETERSON, C., JONAS, M., & SELIGMAN, M. E. P. (1982). Patient behavior in hospitals: Helplessness, reactance, or both? *Journal of Personality and Social Psychology, 42,* 1036–1041.

RATLIFF-CRAIN, J., & BAUM, A. (1990). Individual differences and health: Gender, Coping, and stress. In H. S. FRIEDMAN (Ed.), *Personality and disease,* New York: Wiley.

RAVEN, B. H. & HALEY, R. W. (1982). Social influence and compliance of hospital nurses with infection control policies. In J. R. EISER (Ed.), *Social psychology and behavioral medicine,* New York: Wiley.

RAYMOND, N. R., D'ERAMO-MELKUS, G. (1993). Non-insulin-dependent diabetes and obesity in the black and Hispanic population: Culturally sensitive management. *Diabetes Educator, 19,* 313–317.

REDD, W. H., SILBERFARB, P. M., ANDERSEN, B. L., ANDRYKOWSKI, M. A. et al. (1991). Physiologic and psychobehavioral research in oncology. *Cancer, 67,* 813–822.

REDDY, D, M., FLEMING, R., & ADESSO, V. J. (1992). Gender and health. In S. MAES, H. LEVENTHAL, & M. JOHNSTON (Eds.), *International review of health psychology* (Vol. 1). New York: Wiley.

REEB, R. N., & BUSH, J. P. (1996). Preprocedural psychological preparation in pediatric oncology: A process-oriented intervention study. *Children's Health Care, 25,* 265–279.

REED, G. M., KEMENY, M. E., TAYLOR, S. E., WANG, H.-Y., & VISSCHER, B. R. (1994). Realistic acceptance as a predictor of decreased survival time in gay men with AIDS. *Health Psychology, 13,* 299–307.

REIFMAN, A. (1995). Social relationships, recovery from illness, and survival: A literature review. *Annals of Behavioral Medicine, 17,* 124–131.

REIMAN, E. M., CASELLU, R. J., YUN, L. S., CHEN, K., BANDY, D., MINOSHIMA, SL, THIBODEAU, S. N., & OSBORNE, D. (1996). Preclinical evidence of Alzheimer's disease in persons homozygous for the ϵ 4 allele for apolipoprotein E. *New England Journal of Medicine, 334,* 752–758.

REINIS, S., & GOLDMAN, J. M. (1980). *The development of the brain: Biological and functional perspectives.* Springfield, IL: Charles C. Thomas.

REISCH, L. M., WIEHL, L. G., & TINSLEY, B. J. (1994, August). *Health locus of control and health-related behaviors—A meta-analytic review.* Paper presented at the meeting of the American Psychological Association in Los Angeles.

REKER, G. T., & WONG, P. T. P. (1985). Personal optimism, physical and mental health. In J. E. BIRREN & J. LIVINGSTON (Eds.), *Cognition, stress, and aging.* Englewood Cliffs, NJ: Prentice-Hall.

RETCHIN, S. M., WELLS, J. A., VALLERON, A.-J., & ALBRECHT, G. L. (1992). Health behavior changes in the United States, the United Kingdom, and France. *Journal of General Internal Medicine, 7,* 615–622.

REVENSON, T. A. (1994). Social support and marital coping with chronic illness. *Annals of Behavioral Medicine, 16,* 122–130.

REVENSON, T. A., & MAJEROVITZ, S. D. (1991). The effects of chronic illness on the spouse: Social resources as stress buffers. *Arthritis Care and Research, 4,* 63–72.

REY, M. J. (1999). Cardiovascular disorders. In M. G. EISENBERG, R. L. GLUECKAUF, & H. H. ZARETSKY (Eds.), *Medical aspects of disability: A handbook for the rehabilitation professional* (pp. 154–184). New York: Springer.

REYNOLDS, D. V. (1969). Surgery in the rat during electrical anesthesia induced by focal brain stimulation. *Science, 164,* 444–445.

RHOADES, R., & PFLANZER, R. (1996). *Human physiology* (3rd ed.). Fort Worth: Saunders.

RIBISL, K. M., WINKLEBY, M. A., FORTMANN, S. P., & FLORA, J. A. (1998). The interplay of socioeconomic status and ethnicity on Hispanic and White men's cardiovascular disease risk and health communication patterns. *Health Education Research, 13,* 407–417.

RICHARDS, J. S., NEPOMUCENO, C., RILES, M., & SUER, Z. (1982). Assessing pain behavior: The UAB Pain Behavior Scale. *Pain, 14,* 393–398.

RICHARDSON, J. L., MARKS, G., JOHNSON, C. A., GRAHAM, J. W., CHAN, K. K., SELSER, J. N., KISHBAUGH, C., BARRANDAY, Y., & LEVINE, A. M. (1987). Path model of multidimensional compliance with cancer therapy. *Health Psychology, 6,* 183–207.

RICHARDSON, S. A., GOODMAN, N., HASTORF, A. H., & DORNBUSCH, S. M. (1961). Cultural uniformity in reaction to physical disabilities. *American Sociological Review, 26,* 241–247.

RIETVELD, S., & BROSSCHOT, J. F. (1999). Current perspectives on symptom perception in asthma: A biomedical and psychological review. *International Journal of Behavioral Medicine, 6,* 120–134.

RIGOTTI, N. A., SINGER, D. E., MULLEY, A. G., & THIBAULT, G. E. (1991). Smoking cessation following admission to a coronary care unit. *Journal of General Internal Medicine, 6,* 305–311.

RIMER, B. K. (1994). Mammography use in the U.S.: Trends and the impact of interventions. *Annals of Behavioral Medicine, 16,* 317–326.

RIMER, B. K. (1998). Interventions to enhance cancer screening: A brief review of what works and what is on the horizon. *Cancer, 83,* 1770–1774.

RIMER, B. K., CONAWAY, M., LYNA, P., GLASSMAN, B., YARNALL, K. S. H., LIPKUS, I., & BARBER, T. (1999). The impact of tailored interventions on a community health center population. *Patient Education and Counseling, 37,* 125–140.

RIMM, D. C., & MASTERS, J. C. (1979). *Behavior therapy: Techniques and empirical findings* (2nd ed.). New York: Academic Press.

RIMM, E. B., GIOVANNUCCI, E. L., WILLETT, W. C., COLDITZ, G. A., ASCHERIO, A., ROSNER, B., & STAMPFER, M. J. (1991). Prospective study of alcohol consumption and risk of coronary disease. *Lancet, 338,* 464–468.

RISSER, N. L., & BELCHER, D. W. (1990). Adding spirometry, carbon monoxide, and pulmonary symptom results to smoking cessation counseling: A randomized trial. *Journal of General Internal Medicine, 5,* 16–22.

ROBACK, H. B. (1984). Introduction: The emergence of disease-management groups. In H. B. ROBACK (Ed.), *Helping patients and their families cope with medical problems.* San Francisco: Jossey-Bass.

ROBBINS, L. (1994). Precipitating factors in migraine: A retrospective review of 494 patients. *Headache, 34,* 214–216.

ROBERTS, A. H. (1986). The operant approach to the management of pain and excess disability. In A. D. HOLZMAN & D. C. TURK (Eds.), *Pain management: A handbook of psychological treatment approaches.* New York: Pergamon.

ROBERTS, A. H. (1995). The powerful placebo revisited: Magnitude of nonspecific effects. *Mind/Body Medicine*, 1, 35–43.

ROBERTS, C. S., COX, C. E., REINTGEN, D. S., BAILE, W. F., & GILBERTINI, M. (1994). Influence of physician communication on newly diagnosed breast patients' psychologic adjustment and decision-making. *Cancer*, 74, 336–341.

ROBERTSON, L. S. (1986). Behavioral and environmental interventions for reducing motor vehicle trauma. *Annual Review of Public Health*, 7, 13–34.

ROBERTSON, S. M., CULLEN, D. W., BARANOWSKI, J., BARANOWSKI, T., HU, S., & deMOOR, C. (1999). Factors related to adiposity among children aged 3 to 7 years. *Journal of the American Dietetic Association*, 99, 938–943.

ROBINS, C. J., & HAYES, A. M. (1993). An appraisal of cognitive therapy. *Journal of Consulting and Clinical Psychology*, 61, 205–214.

ROBINSON, B., & THURNHER, M. (1986). Taking care of aged parents: A family cycle transition. In R. H. Moos (Ed.), *Coping with life crises: An integrated approach*. New York: Plenum.

ROBINSON, C. H., & LAWLER, M. R. (1977). *Normal and therapeutic nutrition* (15th ed.). New York: Macmillan.

ROBINSON, L. A., & KLESGES, R. C. (1997). Ethnic and gender differences in risk factors for smoking onset. *Health Psychology*, 16, 499–505.

RODENHUIS, S., VANDE WETERING, M. L., MOOR, W. J., EVERS, S. G., VAN ZANDWIJK, N., & BOS, J. L. (1987). Mutational activation of the K-ras oncogene. *New England Journal of Medicine*. 317, 929–935.

RODIN, J. (1981). Current status of the internal-external hypothesis for obesity: What went wrong? *American Psychologist*, 36, 361–372.

RODIN, J. (1985). Insulin levels, hunger, and food intake: An example of feedback loops in body weight regulation. *Health Psychology*, 4, 1–24.

RODIN, J. (1986). Health, control, and aging. In M. M. BALTES & P. B. BALTES (Eds.), *The psychology of control and aging*. Hillsdale, NJ: Erlbaum.

RODIN, J. (1987a). personal control throughout the life course. In R. P. ABELES (Ed.), *Lifespan perspectives and social psychology*. Hillsdale, NJ: Erlbaum.

RODIN, J., & BAUM, A. (1978). Crowding and helplessness: Potential consequences of density and loss of control. In A. BAUM & Y. M. EPSTEIN (Eds.), *Human response to crowding*. Hillsdale, NJ: Erlbaum.

RODIN, J., & JANIS, I. L. (1979). The social power of healthcare practitioners as agents of change. *Journal of Social Issues*, 35, 60–81.

RODIN, J., & LANGER, E. J. (1977). Long-term effects of a control-relevant intervention with the institutionalized aged. *Journal of Personality and Social Psychology*, 35, 897–902.

RODRIGUE, J. R., TERCYAK, K. P., & LESCANO, C. M. (1997). Health promotion in minority adolescents: Emphasis on sexually transmitted diseases and the human immunodeficiency virus. In D. K. WILSON, J. R. RODRIGUE, & W. C. TAYLOR (Eds.), *Health-promoting and health-compromising behaviors among minority adolescents* (pp. 87–105). Washington, DC: American Psychological Association.

ROGENTINE, G. N., VAN KAMMEN, D. P., FOX, B. H., DOCHERTY, J. P., ROSENBLATT, J. E., BOYD, S. C., & BUNNEY, W. E. (1979). Psychological factors in the prognosis of malignant melanoma: A prospective study. *Psychosomatic Medicine*, 41, 647–655.

ROGERS, W. H., DRAPER, D., KAHN, K. L., KEELER, E. B., RUBENSTEIN, L. V., KOSECOFF, J., & BROOK, R. H. (1990). Quality of care before and after implementation of the DRG-based prospective payment system. *Journal of the American Medical Association*, 264, 1989–1994.

ROHLING, M. L., BINDER, L. M., & LANGHINRICHSEN-ROHLING, J. (1995). A meta-analytic review of the association between financial compensation and the experience and treatment of chronic pain. *Health Psychology*, 14, 537–547.

ROLLS, B. J. (1995). Carbohydrates, fats, and satiety. *American Journal of Clinical Nutrition*, 61(Suppl.), 960S–967S.

ROMANO, J. M., TURNER, J. A., & JENSEN, M. P. (1997). The family environment in chronic pain patients: Comparison to controls and relationship to patient functioning. *Journal of Clinical Psychology in Medical Settings*, 4, 383–395.

RONA, R. J., ANGELICO, F., ANTONINI, R., ARCA, M., et al. (1985). Plasma cholesterol response to a change in dietary fat intake: A collaborative twin study. *Journal of Chronic Diseases*, 38, 927–934.

ROSE, J. S., CHASSIN, L., PRESSON, C. C., & SHERMAN, S. J. (1996). Prospective predictors of quit attempts and smoking cessation in young adults. *Health Psychology*, 15, 261–268.

ROSE, K. J., DERRY, P. A., & McLACHLAN, R. S. (1995). Patient expectations and postoperative depression, anxiety, and psychosocial adjustment after temporal lobectomy: A prospective study. *International Journal of Behavioral Medicine*, 2, 27–40.

ROSE, R. J. (1986). Familial influences on cardiovascular reactivity to stress. In K. A. MATTHEWS, S. M. WEISS, T. DETRE, T. M. DEMBROSKI, B. FALKNER, S. B. MANUCK, & R. B. WILLIAMS (Eds.), *Handbook of stress, reactivity, and cardiovascular disease*. New York: Wiley.

ROSELLA, J. D. (1994). Testicular cancer health education: An integrative review. *Journal of Advanced Nursing, 20*, 666–671.

ROSEN, J. C., & GROSS, J. (1987). Prevalence of weight reducing and weight gaining in adolescent boys and girls. *Health Psychology, 6*, 131–147.

ROSEN, J. C., GRUBMAN, J. A., BEVINS, T., & FRYMOYER, J. W. (1987). Musculoskeletal status and disability of MMPI profile subgroups among patients with low back pain. *Health Psychology, 6*, 581–598.

ROSENBERG, E. S., ALTFELD, M., POON, S. H., PHILLIPS, M. N., WILKES, B. M., ELDRIDGE, R. L., ROBBINS, G. K., D'AQUILA, T., GOULDER, P. J. R., & WALKER, B. D. (2000). Immune control of HIV-1 after early treatment of acute infection. *Nature, 407*, 523–526.

ROSENHAN, D. L., & SELIGMAN, M. E. P. (1984). *Abnormal psychology*. New York: Norton.

ROSENMAN, R. H. (1978). The interview method of assessment of the coronary-prone behavior pattern. In T. M. DEMBROSKI, S. M. WEISS, J. L. SHIELDS, S. G. HAYNES, & M. FEINLEIB (Eds.), *Coronary-prone behavior*. New York: Springer-Verlag.

ROSENMAN, R. H., BRAND, R. J., JENKINS, C. D., FRIEDMAN, M., STRAUS, R., & WURM, M. (1975). Coronary heart disease in the Western Collaborative Group Study: Final follow-up experience of 8½ years. *Journal of the American Medical Association, 233*, 872–877.

ROSENMAN, R. H., BRAND, R. J., SHOLTZ, R. I., & FRIEDMAN, M. (1976). Multivariate prediction of coronary heart disease during 8.5 year follow-up in the Western Collaborative Group Study. *American Journal of Cardiology, 37*, 903–910.

ROSENMAN, R. H., SWAN, G. E., & CARMELLI, D. (1988). Definition, assessment, and evolution of the Type A behavior pattern. In B. K. HOUSTON & C. R. SNYDER (Eds.), *Type A behavior pattern: Research, theory, and intervention*. New York: Wiley.

ROSENSTOCK, I. M. (1966). Why people use health services. *Millbank Memorial Fund Quarterly, 44*, 94–127.

ROSENSTOCK, I. M., & KIRSCHT, J. P. (1979). Why people seek health care. In G. C. STONE, F. COHEN, & N. E. ADLER (Eds.), *Health psychology—A handbook*. San Francisco: Jossey-Bass.

ROSENTHAL, E. (1992, November 24). Commercial diets lack proof of their long-term success. *New York Times*, pp. A1, C11.

ROSKIES, E. (1983). Stress management for Type A individuals. In D. MEICHENBAUM & M. E. JAREMKO (Eds.), *Stress reduction and prevention*. New York: Plenum.

ROSKIES, E., KEARNEY, H., SPEVACK, M., SURKIS, A., COHEN, C., & GILMAN, S. (1979). Generalizability and durability of treatment effects in an intervention program for coronary-prone (Type A) managers. *Journal of Behavioral Medicine, 2*, 195–207.

ROSKIES, E., SERAGANIAN, P., OSEASOHN, R., HANLEY, J. A., COLLU, R., MARTIN, N., & SMILGA, C. (1986). The Montreal Type A Intervention Project: Major findings. *Health Psychology, 5*, 45–69.

ROSKIES, E., SPEVACK, M., SURKIS, A., COHEN, C., & GILMAN, S. (1978). Changing the coronary-prone (Type A) behavior pattern in a nonclinical population. *Journal of Behavioral Medicine, 1*, 201–216.

ROSS, R., & GLOMSET, J. A. (1976a). The pathogenesis of atherosclerosis (first of two parts.). *New England Journal of Medicine, 295*, 369–377.

ROSS, R., & GLOMSET, J. A. (1976b). The pathogenesis of atherosclerosis (second of two parts). *New England Journal of Medicine, 295*, 420–425.

ROTER, D. L., & EWART, C. K. (1992). Emotional inhibition in essential hypertension: Obstacle to communication during medical visits? *Health Psychology, 11*, 163–169.

ROTER, D. L., & HALL, J. A. (1987). Physicians' interviewing styles and medical information obtained from patients. *Journal of General Internal Medicine, 2*, 325–329.

ROTER, D. L., & HALL, J. A. (1989). Studies of doctor-patient interaction. *Annual Review of Public Health, 10*, 163–180.

ROTER, D. L., HALL, J. A., MERSICA, R., NORDSTROM, B., CRETIN, D., & SVARSTAD, B. (1998). Effectiveness of interventions to improve patient compliance: A meta-analysis. *Medical Care, 36*, 1138–1161.

ROTH, D. L., & HOLMES, D. S. (1985). Influence of physical fitness in determining the impact of stressful life events on physical and psychologic health. *Psychosomatic Medicine, 47*, 164–173.

ROTHERAM-BORUS, M. J., MURPHY, D. A., REID, H. M., & COLEMAN, C. L. (1996). Correlates of emotional distress among HIV+ youths: Health status, stress, and personal resources. *Annals of Behavioral Medicine, 18*, 16–23.

ROTHMAN, A. J., & SALOVEY, P. (1997). Shaping perceptions to motivate healthy behavior: The role of message framing. *Psychological Bulletin, 121*, 3–19.

ROTTER, J. B. (1966). Generalized expectancies for the internal versus external control of reinforcement. *Psychological Monographs, 90*(1), 1–28.

ROWBOTHAM, M. C., & LOWENSTEIN, D. H. (1990). Neurologic consequences of cocaine use. *Annual Review of Medicine, 41*, 417–422.

ROWE, M. M. (1999). Teaching health-care providers coping: Results of a two-year study. *Journal of Behavioral Medicine, 22*, 511–527.

ROZENSKY, R. H. (1991). Psychologists, politics, and hospitals. In J. J. SWEET, R. H. ROZENSKY, & S. M. TOVIAN (Eds.), *Handbook of clinical psychology in medical settings*. New York: Plenum.

Rozin, P. (1989). The role of learning in the acquisition of food preferences by humans. In R. Shepherd (Ed.), *Handbook of the psychophysiology of human eating.* Chichester: Wiley.

Rozlog, L. A., Kiecolt-Glaser, J. K., Marucha, P. T., Sheridan, J. F., & Glaser, R. (1999). Stress and immunity: Implications for viral disease and wound healing. *Journal of Periodontology, 70,* 786–792.

Rubin, J. Z., Provenzano, F. J., & Luria, Z. (1974). The eye of the beholder: Parents' views on sex of newborns. *American Journal of Orthopsychiatry, 44,* 512–519.

Ruble, D. N. (1977). Premenstrual symptoms. A reinterpretation. *Science, 197,* 291–292.

Ruderman, A. J. (1986). Dietary restraint: A theoretical and empirical review. *Psychological Bulletin, 99,* 247–262.

Rundall, T. G., & Wheeler, J. R. C. (1979). The effect of income on use of preventive care: An evaluation of alternative explanations. *Journal of Health and Social Behavior, 20,* 397–406.

Runyan, C. W. (1985). Health assessment and public policy within a public health framework. In P. Karoly (Ed.), *Measurement strategies in health psychology.* New York: Wiley.

Rutledge, T., & Linden, W. (1998). To eat or not to eat: Affective and physiological mechanisms in the stress-eating relationship. *Journal of Behavioral Medicine, 21,* 221–240.

Rutter, M. (1983). Stress, coping, and development: Some issues and some questions. In N. Garmezy & M. Rutter (Eds.), *Stress, coping, and development in children.* New York: McGraw-Hill.

Ryan, R. S., & Travis, J. W. (1981). *The wellness workbook.* Berkeley, CA: Ten Speed Press.

Rybstein-Blinchik, E. (1979). Effects of different congnitive strategies on chronic pain experience. *Journal of Behavioral Medicine, 2,* 93–101.

Rychtarik, R. G., Connors, G. J., Whitney, R. B., McGillicuddy, N. B., Fitterling, J. M., & Wirtz, P. W. (2000). Treatment settings for persons with alcoholism: Evidence for matching clients to inpatient versus outpatient care. *Journal of Consulting and Clinical Psychology, 68,* 277–289.

Rzewnicki, R, & Forgays, D. G. (1987). Recidivism and self-cure of smoking and obesity: An attempt to replicate. *American Psychologist, 42,* 97–100.

Saab, P. G., Llabre, M. M., Schneiderman, N., Hurwitz, B. E., McDonald, P. G., Evans, J., Wohlgemuth, W., Hayashi, P., & Klein, B. (1997). Influence of ethnicity and gender on cardiovascular responses to active coping and inhibitory-passive coping challenges. *Psychosomatic Medicine, 59,* 434–446.

Sabbioni, M. E. E. (1991). Cancer and stress: A possible role for psychoneuroimmunology in cancer research? In C. L. Watson & M. Watson (Eds.), *Cancer and stress: Psychological, biological, and coping studies.* New York: Wiley.

Sabol, S. Z., Nelson, M. L., Fisher, C., Gunzerath, L., et al. (1999). A genetic association for cigarette smoking behavior. *Health Psychology, 18,* 7–13.

Sacco, R. L., Elkind, M., Boden-Albala, B., Lin, I.-F., Kargman, D. E., Hauser, W. A., Shea, S., & Paik, M. C. (1999). The protective effect of moderate alcohol consumption on ischemic stroke. *Journal of the American Medical Association, 281,* 53–60.

Sackett, D. L., & Snow, J. C. (1979). The magnitude of compliance and noncompliance. In R. B. Haynes, D. W. Taylor, & D. L. Sackett (Eds.), *Compliance in health care.* Baltimore: Johns Hopkins University Press.

Sacks, D. A., & Koppes, R. H. (1986). Blood transfusion and Jehovah's Witnesses: Medical and legal issues in obstetrics and gynecology. *American Journal of Obstetrics and Gynecology. 154,* 483–486.

Safer, M. A., Tharps, Q. J., Jackson, T. C., & Leventhal, H. (1979). Determinants of three stages of delay in seeking care at a medical clinic. *Medical Care, 17,* 11–29.

Sallis, J. F., & Owen, N. (1999). *Physical activity and behavioral medicine.* Thousand Oaks, CA: Sage.

Sallis, J. F., Patterson, T. L., Buono, M. J., Atkins, C. J., & Nader, P. R. (1988). Aggregation of physical activity habits in Mexican-American and Anglo families. *Journal of Behavioral Medicine, 11,* 31–41.

Sallis, J. F., Trevorrow, T. R., Johnson, C. C., Hovell, M. F., & Kaplan, R. M. (1987). Worksite stress management: A comparison of programs. *Psychology and Health, 1,* 237–255.

Salonen, J. T., Heinonen, O. P., Kottke, T. E., & Puska, P. (1981). Change in health behaviour in relation to estimated coronary heart disease risk during a community-based cardiovascular disease prevention programme. *International Journal of Epidemiology, 10,* 343–354.

Salovey, P., Schneider, T. R., & Apanovitch, A. M. (in press). Message framing in the prevention and early detection of illness. In J. P. Dillard & M. Pfau (Eds.), *The persuasion handbook: Theory and practice.* Thousand Oaks, CA: Sage.

Salvaggio, A., Periti, M., Miano, L., & Zambelli, C. (1990). Association between habitual coffee consumption and blood pressure levels. *Journal of Hypertension, 8,* 585–590.

SAMHSA (Substance Abuse and Mental Health Services Administration) (1999). *Fact sheet: 1998 national household survey on drug abuse.* Retrieved (3-23-2000) from http://www. samhsa. gov.

Sandberg, G. G., & Marlatt, G. A. (1991). Relapse prevention. In D. A. Ciraulo & R. I. Shader (Eds.), *Clinical manual of chemical dependence* Washington, DC: American Psychiatric Press.

SANDERS, J. D., SMITH, T. W., & ALEXANDER, J. F. (1991). Type A behavior and marital interaction: Hostile-dominant responses during conflict. *Journal of Behavioral Medicine,* 14, 567–580.

SANDERS, S. H. (1985). Chronic pain: Conceptualization and epidemiology. *Annals of Behavioral Medicine,* 7(3), 3–5.

SANDERS, S. H., BRENA, S. F., SPIER, C. J., BELTRUTTI, D., McCONNELL, H., & QUINTERO, O. (1992). Chronic low back pain patients around the world: Cross-cultural similarities and differences. *Journal of Clinical Pain,* 8, 317–323.

SANDLER, I. N., & GUENTHER, R. T. (1985). Assessment of life stress events. In P. KAROLY (Ed.), *Measurement strategies in health psychology.* New York: Wiley.

SANSON-FISHER, R. (1993). Primary and secondary prevention of cancer: Opportunities for behavioural scientists. In S. MAES, H. LEVENTHAL, & M. JOHNSTON (Eds.), *Interdisciplinary review of health psychology* (Vol. 2). New York: Wiley.

SANTIAGO, J. V. (1984). Effect of treatment on the long term complications of IDDM. *Behavioral Medicine Update,* 6(1), 26–31.

SAPON-SHEVIN, M. (1980). Teaching cooperation in early childhood settings. In G. CARTLEDGE & J. F. MILBURN (Eds.), *Teaching social skills to children: Innovative approaches.* New York: Pergamon.

SARAFINO, E. P. (1986). *The fears of childhood: A guide to recognizing and reducing fearful states in children.* New York: Human Sciences Press.

SARAFINO, E. P. (1987a). Personal space. In R. J. CORSINI (Ed.), *Concise encyclopedia of psychology.* New York: Wiley.

SARAFINO, E. P. (1987b). Rewards and intrinsic interest. In R. J. CORSINI (Ed.), *Concise encyclopedia of psychology.* New York: Wiley.

SARAFINO, E. P. (1988). Undergraduate health psychology courses. *Health Psychologist,* 10(3), 2.

SARAFINO, E. P. (1997). *Behavioral treatments for asthma: Biofeedback-, respondent-, and rrelaxation-based approaches.* Lewiston, NY: Edwin Mellon Press.

SARAFINO, E. P. (2000). Connections among parent and child atopic illnesses. *Pediatric Allergy and Immunology,* 11, 80–86.

SARAFINO, E. P. (2001). *Behavior modification: Principles of behavior change* (2nd ed.). Mountain View, CA: Mayfield.

SARAFINO, E. P., & ARMSTRONG, J. W. (1986). *Child and adolescent development* (2nd ed.). St. Paul, MN: West.

SARAFINO, E. P., & DILLON, J. M. (1998). Relationships among respiratory infections, triggers of attacks, and asthma severity in children. *Journal of Asthma,* 35, 497–504.

SARAFINO, E. P., & EWING, M. (1999). The Hassles Assessment Scale for Students in College: Measuring the frequency and unpleasantness of and dwelling on stressful events. *Journal of American College Health,* 48, 75–83.

SARAFINO, E. P., & GOEHRING, P. (2000). Age comparisons in acquiring biofeedback control and success in reducing headache pain. *Annals of Behavioral Medicine,* 22, 10–16.

SARAFINO, E. P., & GOLDFEDDER, J. (1995). Genetic factors in the presence, severity, and triggers of asthma. *Archives of Disease in Childhood,* 73, 112–116.

SARAFINO, E. P., GROFF, A., & DEPAULO, D. J. (2000). *The Scale of Information Processing Diligence: Development and psychometric evaluation.* Manuscript submitted for publication.

SARASON, I. G., JOHNSON, J. H., & SIEGEL, J. M. (1978). Assessing the impact of life changes: Development of the Life Experiences Survey. *Journal of Consulting and Clinical Psychology,* 46, 932–946.

SARASON, I. G., LEVINE, H. M., BASHAM, R. B., & SARASON, B. R. (1983). Assessing social support: The Social Support Questionnaire. *Journal of Personality and Social Psychology,* 44, 127–139.

SARASON, I. G., & SARASON, B. R. (1984). *Abnormal psychology* (4th ed.). Englewood Cliffs, NJ: Prentice-Hall.

SARASON, I. G., SARASON, B. R., POTTER, E. H., & ANTONI, M. H. (1985). Life events, social support, and illness. *Psychosomatic Medicine,* 47, 156–163.

SASTRE, M. T. M., MULLET, E., & SORUM, P. C. (1999). Relationship between cigarette dose and perceived risk of lung cancer. *Preventive Medicine,* 28, 566–571.

SAUNDERS, C. (1977). Dying they live: St. Christopher's Hospice. In H. FEIFEL (Ed.), *New meanings of death.* New York: McGraw-Hill.

SAUNDERS, C. (1986). A philosophy of terminal care. In M. J. CHRISTIE & P. G. MELLETT (Eds.), *The psychosomatic approach: Contemporary practice of whole-person care.* New York: Wiley.

SCAMBLER, G. (1984). Perceiving and coping with stigmatizing illness. In R. FITZPATRICK, J. HINTON, S. NEWMAN, G. SCAMBLER, & J. THOMPSON (Eds.), *The experience of illness.* London: Tavistock.

SCANLAN, J. M., VITALIANO, P. P., OCHS, H., SAVAGE, M. V., & BORSON, S. (1998). CD4 and CD8 counts are associated with interactions of gender and psychosocial stress. *Psychosomatic Medicine,* 60, 644–653.

SCARF, M. (1980, September). Images that heal: A doubtful idea whose time has come. *Psychology Today,* pp. 33–46.

SCARR, S., & KIDD, K. K. (1983). Developmental behavior genetics. In P. H. MUSSEN (Ed.), *Handbook of child psychology* (4th ed., Vol. 2). New York: Wiley.

SCHACHTER, S. (1971). Some extraordinary facts about obese humans and rats. *American Psychologist,* 26, 129–144.

SCHACHTER, S. (1980). Urinary pH and the psychology of nicotine addiction. In P. O. DAVIDSON & S. M. DAVIDSON (Eds.), *Behavioral medicine: Changing health lifestyles*. New York: Brunner/Mazel.

SCHACHTER, S. (1982). Recidivism and self cure of smoking and obesity. *American Psychologist, 37*, 436–444.

SCHACHTER, S., SILVERSTEIN, B., KOZLOWSKI, L. T., PERLICK, D., HERMAN, C. P., & LIEBLING, B. (1977). Studies of the interaction of psychological and pharmacological determinants of smoking. *Journal of Experimental Psychology: General, 106*, 3–40.

SCHACHTER, S., & SINGER, J. E. (1962). Cognitive, social, and physiological determinants of emotional state. *Psychological Review, 69*, 379–399.

SCHAEFER, C., COYNE, J. C., & LAZARUS, R. S. (1981). The health-related functions of social support. *Journal of Behavioral Medicine, 4*, 381–406.

SCHAFER, L. C., GLASGOW, R. E., & McCAUL, K. D. (1982). Increasing the adherence of diabetic adolescents. *Journal of Behavioral Medicine, 5*, 353–362.

SCHAIE, K. W. (1965). A general model for the study of developmental problems. *Psychological Bulletin, 64*, 92–107.

SCHEIER, L. M., & BOTVIN, G. J. (1997). Expectancies as mediators of the effects of social influences and alcohol knowledge on adolescent alcohol use: A prospective analysis. *Psychology of Addictive Behaviors, 11*, 48–64.

SCHEIER, M. F., & BRIDGES, M. W. (1995). Person variables and health: Personality predispositions and acute psychological states as shared determinants for disease. *Psychosomatic Medicine, 57*, 255–268.

SCHEIER, M. F., & CARVER, C. S. (in press). Adapting to cancer: The importance of hope and purpose. In A. BAUM & B. L. ANDERSON (Eds.), *Psychosocial interventions for cancer*. Washington, DC: American Psychological Association.

SCHEIER, M. F., CARVER, C. S., & BRIDGES, M. W. (2000). Optimism, pessimism, and psychological well-being. In E. C. CHANG (Ed.), *Optimism and pessimism: Implications for Theory, Research and Practice*. Washington, DC: American Psychological Association.

SCHEIER, M. F., MATTHEWS, K. A., OWENS, J. F., SCHULZ, R., BRIDGES, M. W., MAGOVERN, G. J., & CARVER, C. S. (1999). Optimism and rehospitalization after coronary artery bypass graft surgery. *Archives of Internal Medicine, 159*, 829–835.

SCHERER, K. R. (1986). Voice, stress, and emotion. In M. H. APPLEY & R. TRUMBULL (Eds.), *Dynamics of stress: Physiological, psychological, and social perspectives*. New York: Plenum.

SCHIAFFINO, K. M., SHAWARYN, M. A., & BLUM, D. (1998). Examining the impact of illness representations on psychological adjustment to chronic illnesses. *Health Psychology, 17*, 262–268.

SCHIFFMAN, H. R. (1996). *Sensation and perception: An integrated approach* (4th ed.). New York: Wiley.

SCHIFTER, D. E., & AJZEN, I. (1985). Intention, perceived control, and weight loss: An application of the theory of planned behavior. *Journal of Personality and Social Psychology, 45*, 843–851.

SCHINKE, S. (1996). Behavioral approaches to illness prevention for Native Americans. In P. M. KATO & T. MANN (Eds.), *Handbook of diversity issues in health psychology* (pp. 367–387). New York: Plenum.

SCHMIDT, L. R., & DLUGOSCH, G. E. (1991). Health psychology within the European health care systems. In M. A. JANSEN & J. WEINMAN (Eds.), *The international development of health psychology*. Chur, Switzerland: Harwood.

SCHMIEDER, R., FRIEDRICH, G., NEUS, H., RUDEL, H., & VON EIFF, A. W. (1983). The influence of beta-blockers on cardiovascular reactivity and Type A behavior pattern in hypertensives. *Psychosomatic Medicine, 45*, 417–423.

SCHNALL, P. L., PIEPER, C., SCHWARTZ, J. E., KARASEK, R. A., SCHLUSSEL, Y., DEVEREUX, R. B., GANAU, A., ALDERMAN, M., WARREN, K., & PICKERING, T. G. (1990). The relationship between "job strain," workplace diastolic blood pressure, and left ventricular mass index: Results of a case-control study. *Journal of the American Medical Association, 263*, 1929–1935.

SCHNALL, P. L., SCHWARTZ, J. E., LANDSBERGIS, P. A., WARREN, K., & PICKERING, T. G. (1998). A longitudinal study of job strain and ambulatory blood pressure: Results from a three-year follow-up. *Psychosomatic Medicine, 60*, 697–706.

SCHNEIDER, A. M., & TARSHIS, B. (1975). *An introduction to physiological psychology*. New York: Random House.

SCHNEIDERMAN, N., & HAMMER, D. (1985). Behavioral medicine approaches to cardiovascular disorders. In N. SCHNEIDERMAN & J. T. TAPP (Eds.), *Behavioral medicine: The biopsychosocial approach*. Hillsdale, NJ: Erlbaum.

SCHOENBORN, C. A. (1993). The Alameda Study—25 years later. In S. MAES, H. LEVENTHAL, & M. JOHNSTON (Eds.), *International review of health psychology* (Vol. 2). New York: Wiley.

SCHRAA, J. C., & DIRKS, J. F. (1982). Improving patient recall and comprehension of the treatment regimen. *Journal of Asthma, 19*, 159–162.

SCHUCKIT, M. A. (1985). Genetics and the risk for alcoholism. *Journal of the American Medical Association, 254*, 2614–2617.

SCHUCKIT, M. A. (1996). Recent developments in the pharmacotherapy of alcohol dependence. *Journal of Consulting and Clinical Psychology, 64*, 669–676.

SCHUCKIT, M. A., DAEPPEN, J.-B., DANKO, G. P., TRUPP, M. L., SMITH, T. L., LI, T.-K. HESSELBROCK, V. M., & BUCHOLZ, K. K. (1999). Clinical implications for four drugs of the

DSM-IV distinction between substance dependence with and without a physiological component. *American Journal of Psychiatry*, 156, 41–49.

SCHULZ, R. (1976). Effects of control and predictability on the physical and psychological well-being of the institutionalized aged. *Journal of Personality and Social Psychology*, 33, 563–573.

SCHULZ, R., & BEACH, S. R. (1999). Caregiving as a risk factor for mortality: The Caregiver Effects Study. *Journal of the American Medical Association*, 282, 2215–2219.

SCHULZ, R., & HANUSA, B. H. (1978). Long-term effects of control and predictability-enhancing interventions: Findings and ethical issues. *Journal of Personality and Social Psychology*, 36, 1194–1201.

SCHUNK, D. H., & CARBONARI, J. P. (1984). Self-efficacy models. In J. D. MATARAZZO, S. M. WELSS, J. A. HERD, N. E. MILLER, & S. M. WELSS (Eds.), *Behavioral health: A handbook of health enhancement and disease prevention*. New York: Wiley.

SCHUSTER, C. R., & KILBEY, M. M. (1992). Prevention of drug abuse. In J. M. LAST & R. B. WALLACE (Eds.), *Maxcy-Rosenau-Last public health and preventive medicine* (13th ed.). Norwalk, CT: Appleton & Lange.

SCHUSTER, C. S. (1986). Biophysical development of the adolescent. In C. L. SCHUSTER & S. S. ASHBURN (Eds.), *The process of human development: A holistic life-span approach*. Boston: Little, Brown.

SCHUTZ, H. G., & DIAZ-KNAUF, K. V. (1989). The role of the mass media in influencing eating. In R. SHEPHERD (Ed.), *Handbook of the psychophysiology of human eating*. Chichester: Wiley.

SCHWARTZ, G. E. (1982). Testing the biopsychosocial model: The ultimate challenge facing behavioral medicine? *Journal of Consulting and Clinical Psychology*, 50, 1040–1053.

SCHWARTZ, M. D., TAYLOR, K. L., WILLARD, K. S., SIEGEL, J. E., LAMDAN, R. M., & MORAN, K. (1999). Distress, personality, and mammography utilization among women with a family history of breast cancer. *Health Psychology*, 18, 327–332.

SCHWARTZ, R. H., HAYDEN, G. F., GETSON, P. R., & DiPAOLA, A. (1986). Drinking patterns and social consequences: A study of middle-class adolescents in two private pediatric practices. *Pediatrics*, 77, 139–143.

SCHWARTZ, S. P., & BLANCHARD, E. B. (1990). Inflammatory bowel disease: A review of the psychological assessment and treatment literature. *Annals of Behavioral Medicine*, 12, 95–105.

SCINTO, L. F. M., DAFFNER, K. R., DRESSLER, D., RANSIL, B. I., RENTZ, D., WEINTRAUB, S., MESAULAM, M., & POTTER, H. (1994). A potential noninvasive neurobiological test for Alzheimer's disease. *Science*, 266, 1051–1053.

SEARS, S. J., & MILBURN, J. (1990). School-age stress. In L. E. ARNOLD (Ed.), *Childhood stress*. New York: Wiley.

SEEMAN, M., & SEEMAN, T. E. (1983). Health behavior and personal autonomy: A longitudinal study of the sense of control in illness. *Journal of Health and Social Behavior*, 24, 144–160.

SEEMAN, T. E., & McEWEN, B. S. (1996). Impact of social environment characteristics on neuroendocrine regulation. *Psychosomatic Medicine*, 58, 459–471.

SEEMAN, T. E., SINGER, B. H., ROWE, J. W., HORWITZ, R. I., & McEWEN, B. S. (1997). Price of adaptation—allostatic load and its health consequences. *Archives of Internal Medicine*, 157, 2259–2268.

SEIDENBERG, M., & BERENT, S. (1992). Childhood epilepsy and the role of psychology. *American Psychologist*, 47, 1130–1133.

SELF, C. A., & ROGERS, R. W. (1990). Coping with threats to health: Effects of persuasive appeals on depressed, normal, and antisocial personalities. *Journal of Behavioral Medicine*, 13, 343–357.

SELIGMAN, M. E. P. (1975). *Helplessness: On depression, development, and death*. San Francisco: Freeman.

SELIGMANN, J., & SULAVIK, C. (1992, April 27). Software for hard issues. *Newsweek*, p. 55.

SELYE, H. (1956). *The stress of life*. New York: McGraw-Hill.

SELYE, H. (1974). *Stress without distress*. Philadelphia: Lippincott.

SELYE, H. (1976). *Stress in health and disease*. Reading, MA: Butterworth.

SELYE, H. (1985). History and present status of the stress concept. In A. MONAT & R. S. LAZARUS (Eds.), *Stress and coping* (2nd ed.). New York: Columbia University Press.

SERAGANIAN, P., ROSKIES, E., HANLEY, J. A., OSEASOHN, R., & COLLU, R. (1987). Failure to alter psychophysiological reactivity in Type A men with physical exercise and stress management programs. *Psychology and Health*, 1, 195–213.

SERDULA, M. K., IVERY, D., COATES, R. J., FREEDMAN, D. S., WILLIAMSON, D. F., & BYERS, T. (1993). Do obese children become obese adults? A review of the literature. *Preventive Medicine*, 22, 167–177.

SERDULA, M. K., MOKDAD, A. H., WILLIAMSON, D. F., GALUSKA, D. A., MENDLEIN, J. M., & HEATH, G. W. (1999). Prevalence of attempting weight loss and strategies for controlling weight. *Journal of the American Medical Association*, 282, 1353–1358.

SERFASS, R. C., & GERBERICH, S. G. (1984). Exercise for optimal health: Strategies and motivational considerations. *Preventive Medicine*, 13, 79–99.

SEVERSON, H. H. (1993). Smokeless tobacco: Risks, epidemiology, and cessation. In C. T. ORLEANS & J. SLADE

(Eds.), *Nicotine addiction: Principles and management.* New York: Oxford University Press.

SHADEL, W. G., & MERMELSTEIN, R. (1993). Cigarette smoking under stress: The role of coping expectancies among smokers in a clinic-based smoking cessation program. *Health Psychology, 12,* 443–450.

SHADEL, W. G., SHIFFMAN, S., NIAURA, R., NICHTER, R., NICHTER, M., & ABRAMS, D. B. (2000). Current models of nicotine dependence: What is known and what is needed to advance understanding of tobacco etiology among youth. *Drug and Alcohol Dependence, 59* (Suppl.), S9–S22.

SHAH, M., & JEFFERY, R. W. (1991). Is obesity due to overeating and inactivity, or to a defective metabolic rate? A review. *Annals of Behavioral Medicine, 13,* 73–81.

SHAIN, R. N., PIPER, J. M., NEWTON, E. R., PERDUE, S. T., RAMOS, R., CHAMPION, J. D., & GUERRA, F. A. (1999). A randomized, controlled trial of a behavioral intervention to prevent sexually transmitted disease among minority women. *New England Journal of Medicine. 340,* 93–100.

SHANAS, E., & MADDOX, G. L. (1985). Health, health resources, and the utilization of care. In R. H. BINSTOCK & E. SHANAS (Eds.), *Handbook of aging and the social sciences.* New York: Van Nostrand-Reinhold.

SHANFIELD, S. B. (1990). Return to work after an acute myocardial infarction: A review. *Heart & Lung, 19,* 109–117.

SHAPIRO, A. P., KRANTZ, D. S., & GRIM, C. E. (1986). Pharmacologic agents as modulators of stress. In K. A. MATTHEWS, S. M. WEISS, T. DETRE, T. M. DEMBROSKI, B. FALKNER, S. B. MANUCK, & R. B. WILLIAMS (Eds.), *Handbook of stress, reactivity, and cardiovascular disease.* New York: Wiley.

SHAPIRO, D, & GOLDSTEIN, I. B. (1982). Biobehavioral perspectives on hypertension. *Journal of Consulting and Clinical Psychology, 50,* 841–858.

SHAPIRO, S. L., SCHWARTZ, G. E., & BONNER, G. (1998). Effects of mindfulness-based stress reduction on medical and premedical students. *Journal of Behavioral Medicine, 21,* 581–599.

SHAW, R. E., COHEN, F., DOYLE, B., & PALESKKY, J. (1985). The impact of denial and repressive style on information gain and rehabilitation outcomes in myocardial infarction patients. *Psychosomatic Medicine, 47,* 262–273.

SHAW, W. S., PATTERSON, T. L., ZIEGLER, M. G., DIMSDALE, J. E., SEMPLE, S. J., & GRANT, I. (1999). Accelerated risk of hypertensive blood pressure recordings among Alzheimer caregivers. *Journal of Psychosomatic Research, 46,* 215–227.

SHEKELLE, R. B., HULLEY, S. B., NEATON, J. D., BILLINGS, J. H., BORHANI, N. O., GERACE, T. A., JACOBS, D. R., LASSER, N. L., MITTELMARK, M. B., & STAMLER, J. (1985). The MRFIT Behavior Pattern Study: II. Type A behavior and incidence of coronary heart disease. *American Journal of Epidemiology, 122,* 559–570.

SHEPPERD, S. L., SOLOMON, L. J., ATKINS, E., FOSTER, R. S., & FRANKOWSKI, B. (1990). Determinants of breast self-examination among women of lower income and lower education. *Journal of Behavioral Medicine, 13,* 359–371.

SHERIDAN, K. (1991). Psychosocial services for persons with human immunodeficiency virus disease. In J. J. SWEET, R. H. ROZENSKY, & S. M. TOVIAN (Eds.), *Handbook of clinical psychology in medical settings.* New York: Plenum.

SHERIF, M., & SHERIF, C. W. (1953). *Groups in harmony and tension.* New York: Harper.

SHERMAN, B. F., BONANNO, G. A., WIENER, L. S., & BATTLES, H. B. (2000). When children tell their friends they have AIDS: Possible consequences for psychological well-being and disease progression. *Psychosomatic Medicine, 62,* 238–247.

SHERMAN, J. J., CARLSON, C. R., McCUBBIN, J. A., & WILSON, J. F. (1997). Effects of stretch-based progressive relaxation training on the secretion of salivary immunoglobulin A in orofacial pain patients. *Journal of Orofacial Pain, 11,* 115–124.

SHERWOOD, A., GIRDLER, S. S., BRADDON, E. E., WEST, S. G., BROWNLEY, K. A., HINDERLITER, A. L., & LIGHT, K. C. (1997). Ten-year stability of cardiovascular responses to laboratory stressors. *Psychophysiology, 34,* 185–191.

SHERWOOD, A., MAY, C. W., SIEGEL, W. C., & BLUMENTHAL, J. A. (1995). Ethnic differences in hemodynamic responses to stress in hypertensive men and women. *American Journal of Hypertension, 8,* 552–557.

SHERWOOD, A., & TURNER, J. R. (1995). Hemodynamic responses during psychological stress: Implications for studying disease processes. *International Journal of Behavioral Medicine, 2,* 193–218.

SHIFFMAN, S. (1986). A cluster-analytic classification of smoking relapse episodes. *Addictive Behaviors, 11,* 295–307.

SHIFFMAN, S. (1993). Smoking cessation treatment: Any progress? *Journal of Consulting and Clinical Psychology, 61,* 718–722.

SHIFFMAN, S., BALABANIS, M. H., PATY, J. A., ENGBERG, J., GWALTNEY, C. J., LIU, K. S., GNYS, M., HICKCOX, M., & PATON, S. M. (2000). Dynamic effects of self-efficacy on smoking lapse and relapse. *Health Psychology, 19,* 315–323.

SHIFFMAN. S., FISHER, L. B., ZETTLER-SEGAL, M., & BENOWITZ, N. L. (1990). Nicotine exposure among nondependent smokers. *Archives of General Psychiatry, 47,* 333–336.

SHIFFMAN, S., HICKCOX, M., PATY, J. A., GNYS, M., KASSEL, J. D., & RICHARDS, T. J. (1996). Progression from a smoking lapse to relapse: Prediction from abstinence violation effects, nicotine dependence, and lapse characteristics. *Journal of Consulting and Clinical Psychology, 64,* 993–1002.

SHIFFMAN, S., PATY, J. A., GNYS, M., KASSEL, J. D., & ELASH, C. (1995). Nicotine withdrawal in chippers and regular smokers: Subjective and cognitive effects. *Health Psychology, 14,* 301–309.

SHIFFMAN, S., & STONE, A. A. (1998). Introduction to the special section: Ecological momentary assessment in health psychology. *Health Psychology, 17,* 3–5.

SHIPLEY, R. H., BUTT, J. H., HORWITZ, B., & FARBRY, J. E. (1978). Preparation for a stressful medical procedure: Effect of amount of stimulus preexposure and coping style. *Journal of Consulting and Clinical Psychology, 46,* 499–507.

SHNEIDMAN, E. S. (1977). The college student and death. In H. FEIFEL (Ed.), *New meanings of death.* New York: McGraw-Hill.

SHOGREN, E. (1988, June 3). Physicians favor death with "dignity." *Philadelphia Inquirer,* p. D14.

SHONTZ, F. C. (1975). *The psychological aspects of physical illness and disability.* New York: Macmillan.

SHOPLAND, D. R., & BROWN, C. (1985). Changes in cigarette smoking prevalence in the U.S.: 1955 to 1983. *Annals of Behavioral Medicine, 7*(2), 5–8.

SHOPLAND, D. R., & BURNS, D. M. (1993). Medical and public health implications of tobacco addiction. In C. T. ORLEANS & J. SLADE (Eds.), *Nicotine addiction: Principles and management.* New York: Oxford University Press.

SHUCHMAN, M., & WILKES, M. (1986, September 28). Challenging the annual physical. *The New York Times Magazine,* pp. 36–40.

SHUCHMAN, M., & WILKES, M. S. (1989, February 12). Asking—And telling. *The New York Times Magazine,* pp. 45–46.

SHUPE, D. R. (1985). Perceived control, helplessness, and choice: Their relationship to health and aging. In J. E. BIRREN & J. LIVINGSTON (Eds.), *Cognition, stress, and aging.* Englewood Cliffs, NJ: Prentice-Hall.

SIEGEL, L. J., & PETERSON, L. (1980). Stress reduction in young dental patients through coping skills and sensory information. *Journal of Consulting and Clinical Psychology, 48,* 785–787.

SIEGEL, W. C., & BLUMENTHAL, J. A. (1991). The role of exercise in the prevention and treatment of hypertension. *Annals of Behavioral Medicine, 13,* 23–30.

SIEGLER, I. C., FEAGANES, J. R., & RIMER, B. K. (1995). Predictors of adoption of mammography in women under age 50. *Annals of Behavioral Medicine, 14,* 274–278.

SIEGMAN, A. W. (1993). Cardiovascular consequences of expressing, experiencing, and repressing anger. *Journal of Behavioral Medicine, 16,* 539–569.

SIKKEMA, K. J. (1998). HIV prevention. In E. A. BLECHMAN & K. D. BROWNELL (Eds.), *Behavioral medicine and women: A comprehensive handbook* (pp. 198–202). New York: Guilford.

SIKKEMA, K. J., KALICHMAN, S. C., HOFFMANN, R., KOOB, J. J., KELLY, J. A., & HECKMAN, T. G. (2000). Coping strategies and emotional wellbeing among HIV-infected men and women experiencing AIDS-related bereavement. *AIDS Care, 12,* 613–624.

SIKKEMA, K. J., & KELLY, J. A. (1996). Behavioral medicine interventions can improve the quality-of-life and health of persons with HIV disease. *Annals of Behavioral Medicine, 18,* 40–48.

SIKKEMA, K. J., KELLY, J. A., WINETT, R. A., SOLOMON, L. J., et al. (2000). Outcomes of a randomized community-level HIF prevention intervention for women living in 18 low-income housing developments. *American Journal of Public Health, 90,* 57–63.

SILVER, R. L., & WORTMAN, C. B. (1980). Coping with undesirable life events. In J. GARBER & M. E. P. SELIGMAN (Eds.), *Human helplessness: Theory and applications.* New York: Academic Press.

SILVERMAN, K., WONG, C. J., UMBRICHT-SCHNEIDER, A., MONTOYA, I. D., SCHUSTER, C. R., & PRESTON, K. L. (1998). Broad beneficial effects of cocaine abstinence reinforcement among methadone patients. *Journal of Consulting and Clinical Psychology, 66,* 811–824.

SIME, W. E. (1984). Psychological benefits of exercise training in the healthy individual. In J. D. MATARAZZO, S. M. WEISS, J. A. HERD, N. E. MILLER, & S. M. WEISS (Eds.), *Behavioral health: A handbook of health enhancement and disease prevention.* New York: Wiley.

SIMONI, J. M., MASON, H. R. C., MARKS, G., RUIZ, M. S., REED, D., & RICHARDSON, J. L. (1995). Women's self-disclosure of HIV infection: Rates, reasons, and reactions. *Journal of Consulting and Clinical Psychology, 63,* 474–478.

SIMONTON, O. C., & SIMONTON, S. S. (1975). Belief systems and the management of emotional aspects of malignancy. *Journal of Transpersonal Psychology, 7,* 29–47.

SIMS, E. A. H. (1974). Studies in human hyperphagia. In G. A. BRAY & J. E. BETHUNE (Eds.), *Treatment and management of obesity.* New York: Harper & Row.

SIMS, E. A. H. (1976). Experimental obesity, dietary-induced thermogenesis, and their clinical implications. *Clinics in Endocrinology and Metabolism, 5,* 377–395.

SINGER, J. E., & DAVIDSON, L. M. (1986). Specificity and stress research. In M. H. APPLEY & R. TRUMBULL (Eds.), *Dynamics of stress: Physiological, psychological, and social perspectives.* New York: Plenum.

SISSON, R. W., & AZRIN, N. H. (1986). Family-member involvement to initiate and promote treatment of problem drinkers. *Journal of Behavior Therapy and Experimental Psychiatry*, 17, 15–21.

SKELLY, A. H., MARSHALL, J. R., HAUGHEY, B. P., DAVIS, P. J., & DUNFORD, R. G. (1995). Self-efficacy and confidence in outcomes as determinants of self-care practices in inner-city, African-American women with non-insulin-dependent diabetes. *Diabetes Educator*, 21, 38–46.

SKELTON, M., & DOMINIAN, J. (1973). Psychological stress in wives of patients with myocardial infarction. *British Medical Journal*, 2, 101–103.

SKINNER, C. S., CAMPBELL, M. K., RIMER, B. K., CURRY, S., & PROCHASKA, J. O. (1999). How effective is tailored print communication? *Annals of Behavioral Medicine*, 21, 290–298.

SKLAR, L. S., & ANISMAN, H.(1981). Stress and cancer. *Psychological Bulletin*, 89, 369–406.

SKOLNICK, A. S. (1986). *The psychology of human development*. San Diego: Harcourt Brace Jovanovich.

SMART, C. R. (1994). Highlights of the evidence of benefit for women aged 40–49 years from the 14-year follow-up of the Breast Cancer Detection Demonstration Project. *Cancer*, 74, 296–300.

SMART, J. L. (1991). Critical periods in brain development. In D. J. P. BARKER (Chair, Ciba Foundation Symposium, No. 156), *The childhood environment and adult disease*. New York: Wiley.

SMITH, C. A., & WALLSTON, K. A. (1992). Adaptation in patients with chronic rheumatoid arthritis: Application of a general model. *Health Psychology*, 11, 151–162.

SMITH, C. E., FERNENGEL, K., HOLCORFT, C., GERALD, K., & MARIEN, L. (1994). Meta-analysis of the associations between social support and health outcomes. *Annals of Behavioral Medicine*, 16, 352–362.

SMITH, E. L. (1984). Special considerations in developing exercise programs for the older adult. In J. D. MATARAZZO, S. M. WEISS, J. A. HERD, N. E. MILLER, & S. M. WEISS (Eds.), *Behavioral health: A handbook of health enhancement and disease prevention*. New York: Wiley.

SMITH, G. S., & KRAUS, J. F. (1988). Alcohol and residential, recreational, and occupational injuries: A review of the epidemiologic evidence. *Annual Review of Public Health*, 9, 99–121.

SMITH, J. B., & AUTMAN, S. H. (1985). The experience of hospitalization. In L. L. Hayman & E. M. Sporing (Eds.), *Handbook of pediatric nursing*. New York: Wiley.

SMITH, M. T., PERLIS, M. L., SMITH, M. S., GILES, D. E., & CARMODY, T. P. (2000). Sleep quality and presleep arousal in chronic pain. *Journal of Behavioral Medicine*, 23, 1–13.

SMITH, R. C., & ZIMNY, G. H. (1988). Physicians' emotional reactions to patients. *Psychosomatics*, 29, 392–397.

SMITH, T. W. (1992). Hostility and health: Current status of a psychosomatic hypothesis. *Health Psychology*, 11, 139–150.

SMITH, T. W., & ANDERSON, N. B. (1986). Models of personality and disease: An interactional approach to Type A behavior and cardiovascular risk. *Journal of Personality and Social Psychology*, 50, 1166–1173.

SMITH, T. W., & GALLO, L. C. (1999). Hostility and cardiovascular reactivity during marital interaction. *Psychosomatic Medicine*, 61, 436–445.

SMITH, T. W., GALLO, L. C., GOBLE, L., NGU, L. Q., & STARK, K. A. (1998). Agency, communion, and cardiovascular reactivity during marital interaction. *Health Psychology*, 17, 537–545.

SMITH, T. W., PECK, J. R., & WARD, J. R. (1990). Helplessness and depression in rheumatoid arthritis. *Health Psychology*, 9, 377–389.

SMITH, T. W., TURNER, C. W., FORD, M. H., HUNT, S. C., BARLOW, G. K., STULTS, B. M., & WILLIAMS, R. R. (1987). Blood pressure reactivity in adult male twins. *Health Psychology*, 6, 209–220.

SMYTH, J. M., STONE, A. A., HUREWITZ, A., & KAELL, A. (1999). Effects of writing about stressful experiences on symptom reduction in patients with asthma or rheumatoid arthritis. *Journal of the American Medical Association*, 281, 1304–1309.

SNOW, L. F. (1981). Folk medical beliefs and their implications for care of patients: A review based on studies among black Americans. In G. Henderson & M. Primeaux (Eds.), *Transcultural health care*. Menlo Park, CA: Addison-Wesley.

SNOWDON, D. A., GREINER, L. H., MORTIMER, J. A., RILEY, K. P., GREINER, P. A., & MARKESBERY, W. R. (1997). Brain infarction and the clinical expression of Alzheimer disease. *Journal of the American Medical Association*, 277, 813–817.

SNUSTAD, D. P., & SIMMONS, M. J. (2000). *Principles of genetics* (2nd ed.). New York: Wiley.

SNYDER, S. H. (1977). Opiate receptors and internal opiates. *Scientific American*, 236, 44–56.

SOBEL, D. S. (1990). The placebo effect: Using the body's own healing mechanisms. In R. ORNSTEIN & C. SWENCIONIS (Eds.), *The healing brain: A scientific reader*. New York: Guilford.

SOBEL, L. C., SOBEL, M. B., TONEATTO, T., & LEO, G. I. (1993). What triggers the resolution of alcohol problems without treatment? *Alcoholism: Clinical and Experimental Research*, 17, 217–224.

SOKOL, M. S., & GRAY, N. S. (1998). Anorexia nervosa. In E. A. BLECHMAN & K. D. BROWNELL (Eds.), *Behavioral medicine & women: A comprehensive handbook* (pp. 350–357). New York: Guilford.

SOLÉ-LERIS, A. (1986). *Tranquility and insight*. Boston: Shambhala.

SOLOMON, L. J., FLYNN, B. S., WORDEN, J. K., MICKEY, R. M., SKELLY, J. M., GELLER, B. M., PELUSO, N. W., & WEBSTER, J. A. (1998). Assessment of self-reward strategies for maintenance of breast self-examination. *Journal of Behavioral Medicine, 21,* 83–102.

SOMERS, V. K., DYKEN, M. E., MARK, A. L., & ABBOUD, F. M. (1993). Sympathetic-nerve activity during sleep in normal subjects. *New England Journal of Medicine, 328,* 303–307.

SORENSEN, G., JACOBS, D. R., PIRIE, P., FOLSOM, A., LUEPKER, R., & GILLUM, R. (1987). Relationships among Type A behavior, employment experiences, and gender: The Minnesota Heart Survey. *Journal of Behavioral Medicine, 10,* 323–336.

SORENSEN, G., PECHACEK, T., & PALLONEN, U. (1986). Occupational and worksite norms and attitudes about smoking cessation. *American Journal of Public Health, 76,* 544–549.

SOUTHARD, D. R., COATES, T. J., KOLODNER, K., PARKER, F. C., PADGETT, N. E., & KENNEDY, H. L. (1986). Relationship between mood and blood pressure in the natural environment: An adolescent population. *Health Psychology, 5,* 469–480.

SPANOS, N. P., PERLINI, A. H., & ROBERTSON, L. A. (1989). Hypnosis, suggestion, and placebo in the reduction of experimental pain. *Journal of Abnormal Psychology, 98,* 285–293.

SPECTER, M. (1996, March 31). 10 years later, through fear, Chernobyl still kills in Belarus. *New York Times,* pp. 1, 6.

SPEECE, M. W., & BRENT, S. B. (1984). Children's understanding of death: A review of three components of a death concept. *Child Development, 55,* 1671–1686.

SPEISMAN, J. C., LAZARUS, R. S., MORDKOFF, A., & DAVISON, L. (1964). Experimental demonstration of stress based on ego-defense theory. *Journal of Abnormal and Social Psychology, 68,* 367–380.

SPENCE, J. D., BARNETT, P. A., LINDEN, W., RAMSDEN, V., & TAENZER, P. (1999). Recommendations on stress management. *Canadian Medical Association Journal, 160*(9 Suppl.), S46–S50.

SPENCER, S. M., LEHMAN, J. M., WYNINGS, C., ARENA, P., CARVER, C. S., ANTONI, M. H., DERHAGOPIAN, R. P., & LOVE, N. (1999). Concerns about breast cancer and relations to psychosocial well-being in a multiethnic sample of early-stage patients. *Health Psychology, 18,* 159–168.

SPIEGEL, D., BLOOM, J. R., KRAEMER, H. C., & GOTTHEIL, E. (1989). Effect of psychosocial treatment on survival of patients with metastic breast cancer. *Lancet, 334,* 888–891.

SPIEGEL, D., SANDS, S., & KOOPMAN, C. (1994). Pain and depression in patients with cancer. *Cancer, 74,* 2570–2578.

SPIGA, R. (1986). Social interaction and cardiovascular response of boys exhibiting the coronary-prone behavior pattern. *Journal of Pediatric Psychology, 11,* 59–69.

SPINETTA, J. J. (1974). The dying child's awareness of death: A review. *Psychological Bulletin, 81,* 256–260.

SPINETTA, J. J. (1982). Behavioral and psychological research in childhood cancer. *Cancer, 50,* 1939–1943.

SPURGEON, P., BROOME, A., EARLL, L., & HARRIS, B. (1990). Health psychology in a broader context. In P. BENNETT, J. WEINMAN, & P. SPURGEON (Eds.), *Current developments in health psychology.* Chur, Switzerland: Harwood.

STACY, A. W. (1997). Memory activation and expectancy as prospective mediators of alcohol and marijuana use. *Journal of Abnormal Psychology, 106,* 61–73.

STACY, A. W., BENTLER, P. M., & FLAY, B. R. (1994). Attitudes and health behavior in diverse populations: Drunk driving, alcohol use, binge eating, marihuana use, and cigarette use. *Health Psychology, 13,* 73–85.

STALL, R. D., COATES, T. J., & HOFF, C. (1988). Behavioral risk reduction for HIV infection among gay and bisexual men: A review of results from the United States. *American Psychologist, 43,* 878–885.

STALLONE, D. D., & STUNKARD, A. J. (1991). The regulation of body weight: Evidence and clinical implications. *Annals of Behavioral Medicine, 13,* 220–230.

STAMLER, J., STAMLER, R., NEATON, J. D., WENTWORTH, D., DAVIGLUS, M. L., GARSIDE, D., DYER, A. R., LIU, K., & GREENLAND, P. (1999). Low risk-factor profile and long-term cardiovascular and noncardiovascular mortality and life expectancy. *Journal of the American Medical Association, 282,* 2012–2018.

STAMLER, J., WENTWORTH, D., & NEATON, J. D., et al. (1986). Is relationship between serum cholesterol and risk of premature death from coronary heart disease continuous and graded? Findings in 356,222 primary screenees of the Multiple Risk Factor Intervention Trial (MRFIT). *Journal of the American Medical Association, 256,* 2823–2828.

STAMLER, R., STAMLER, J., GOSCH, F. C., CIVINELLI, J., FISHMAN, J., McKEEVER, P., McDONALD, A., & DYER, A. R. (1989). Primary prevention of hypertension by nutritional-hygienic means: Final report of a radomized, controlled trial. *Journal of the Americal Medical Association, 262,* 1801–1807.

STANTON, A. L. (1987). Determinants of adherence to medical regimens by hypertensive patients. *Journal of Behavioral Medicine, 10,* 377–394.

STANTON, A. L., ESTES, M. A., ESTES, N. C., CAMERON, C. L., DANOFF-BURG, S., & IRVING, L. M. (1998). Treatment decision making and adjustment to breast cancer: A longitudinal study. *Journal of Consulting and Clinical Psychology, 66,* 313–322.

STEIGER, H., GAUVIN, L., JABALPURWALA, S., SÉGUIN, J. R., & STOTLAND, S. (1999). Hypersensitivity to social interaction in bulimic syndromes: Relationship to binge eating. *Journal of Consulting and Clinical Psychology,* 67, 765–775.

STEIN, J. A., NEWCOMB, M. D., & BENTLER, P. M. (1987). An 8-year study of multiple influences on drug use and drug use consequences. *Journal of Personality and Social Psychology,* 53, 1094–1105.

STEIN, J. H., KEEVIL, J. G., WIEBE, D. A., AESCHLIMANN, S., & FOLTS, J. D. (1999). Purple grape juice improves endothelial function and reduces the susceptibility of LDL cholesterol to oxidation in patients with coronary artery disease. *Circulation,* 100, 1050–1055.

STEINBERG, L. (1985). Early temperamental antecedents of adult Type A behaviors. *Developmental Psychology,* 21, 1171–1180.

STEINER, H., & CLARK, W. R. (1977). Psychiatric complications of burned adults: A classification. *Journal of Trauma,* 17, 134–143.

STEPHENS, R. S., ROFFMAN, R. A., & SIMPSON, E. E. (1994). Treating adult marijuana dependence: A test of the relapse prevention model. *Journal of Consulting and Clinical Psychology,* 62, 92–99.

STEPTOE, A., CROPLEY, M., & JOEKES, K. (2000). Task demands and the pressures of everyday life: Associations between cardiovasclar reactivity and work blood pressure and heart rate. *Health Psychology,* 19, 46–54.

STEPTOE, A., WARDLE, J., VINCK, J., TUOMISTO, M., HOLTE, A., & WICHSTRØM, L. (1994). Personality and attitudinal correlated of healthy and unhealthy lifestyles in young adults. *Psychology and Health,* 9, 331–343.

STERNBERG, E. M., & GOLD, P. W. (1997). The mind–body interaction in disease. *Scientific American,* 7(Special Issue, No. 1), 8–15.

STETSON, B. A., RAHN, J. M., DUBBERT, P. M., WILNER, B. I., & MERCURY, M. G. (1997). Prospective evaluation of the effects of stress on exercise adherence in community-residing women. *Health Psychology,* 16, 515–520.

STEWART, W. F., SHECHTER, A., & LIPTON, R. B. (1994). Migraine heterogeneity: Disability, pain intensity, and attack frequency and duration. *Neurology,* 44(Suppl. 4), S24–39.

STEWART, W. F., SHECHTER, A., & RASMUSSEN, B. K. (1994). Migraine prevalence: A review of population-based studies. *Neurology,* 44(Suppl. 4), S17–23.

STICE, E., CAMERON, R. P., KILLEN, J. D., HAYWARD, C., & TAYLOR, C. B. (1999). Naturalistic weight-reduction efforts prospectively predict growth in relative weight and onset of obesity among female adolescents. *Journal of Consulting and Clinical Psychology,* 67, 967–974.

STEIG, R. L., & TURK, D. C. (1988). Chronic pain syndrome: Demonstrating the cost-benefit of treatment. *Clinical Journal of Pain,* 4, 58–63.

ST. JEOR, S. T., SUTNICK, M. R., & SCOTT, B. J. (1988). Nutrition. In E. A. BLECHMAN & K. D. BROWNELL (Eds.), *Handbook of behavioral medicine for women.* New York: Pergamon.

ST. LAWRENCE, J. S., BRASFIELD, T. L., JEFFERSON, K. W., ALLEYNE, E., O'BANNON, R. E., & SHIRLEY, A. (1995). Cognitive-behavioral intervention to reduce African American adolescents' risk for HIV infection. *Journal of Consulting and Clinical Psychology,* 63, 221–237.

ST. LAWRENCE, J. S., JEFFERSON, K. W., ALLEYNE, E., & BRASFIELD, T. L. (1995). Comparison of education versus behavioral skills training interventions in lowering sexual HIV-risk behavior of substance-dependent adolescents. *Journal of Consulting and Clinical Psychology,* 63, 154–157.

STOCKTON, W. (1988, March 7). Fresh research tells asthmatics to stay active. *New York Times,* p. C9.

STOCKWELL, T., & TOWN, C. (1989). Anxiety and stress management. In R. K. HESTER & W. R. MILLER (Eds.), *Handbook of alcoholism treatment approaches: Effective alternatives.* New York: Pergamon.

STOLBERG, S. G. (1998, August 2). Superbugs. *The New York Times Magazine,* pp. 42–47.

STOLBERG, S. G. (1999a, June 3). The boom in medications brings rise in fatal risks. *New York Times,* pp. A1, A24.

STOLBERG, S. G. (1999b, April 27). F. D. A. approves fat-blocking anti-obesity drug. *New York Times,* pp. A1, A19.

STONE, A. A., & NEALE, J. M. (1984). New measure of daily coping: Development and preliminary results. *Journal of Personality and Social Psychology,* 46, 892–906.

STONE, A. A., NEALE, J. M., COX, D.S., NAPOLI, A., VALDIMARSDOTTIR, H., & KENNEDY-MOORE, E. (1994). Daily events are associated with a secretory immune response to an oral antigen in men. *Health Psychology,* 13, 440–446.

STONE, G. C. (1979). Health and the health system: A historical overview and conceptual framework. In G. C. STONE, F. COHEN, & N. E. ADLER (Eds.), *Health psychology— A handbook.* San Francisco: Jossey-Bass.

STONE, G. C. (1991). An international review of the emergence and development of health psychology. In M. A. JANSEN & J. WEINMAN (Eds.), *The international development of health psychology.* Chur, Switzerland: Harwood.

STORY, M., & FAULKNER, P. (1990). The prime time diet: A content analysis of eating behavior and food messages in television program content and commercials. *American Journal of Public Health,* 80, 738–740.

STRAUSS, L. M., SOLOMON, L. J., COSTANZA, M. C., WORDEN, J. K., & FOSTER, R. S. (1987). Breast self-examination practices and attitudes of women with and without a history of breast cancer. *Journal of Behavioral Medicine,* 10, 337–350.

STRAUSS, R. H., & YESALIS, C. E. (1991). Anabolic steroids in the athlete. *Annual Review of Medicine,* 42, 449–457.

STRAW, M. K. (1983). Coping with obesity. In T. G. BURISH & L. A. BRADLEY (Eds.), *Coping with chronic disease: Research and applications*. New York: Academic Press.

STRECHER, V. J., KREUTER, M. W., & KOBRIN, S. C. (1995). Do cigarette smokers have unrealistic perceptions of their heart attack, cancer, and stroke risks? *Journal of Behavioral Medicine*, 18, 45–54.

STRICKLAND, B. R. (1978). Internal-external expectancies and health-related behaviors. *Journal of Consulting and Clinical Psychology*, 6, 1192–1211.

STRIEGEL-MOORE, R. H. (1997). Risk factors for eating disorders. *Annals of the New York Academy of Sciences*, 817, 98–109.

STRIEGEL-MOORE, R., & RODIN, J. (1985). Prevention of obesity. In J. C. ROSEN & L. J. SOLOMON (Eds.), *Prevention in health psychology*. Hanover, NH: University Press of New England.

STRONG, J. P., MALCOM, G. T., MCMAHAN, C. A., TRACY, R. E., NEWMAN, W. P., HERDERICK, E. E., & CORNHILL, J. F. (1999). Prevalence and extent of atherosclerosis in adolescents and young adults: Implications for prevention from the Pathobiological Determinants of Atherosclerosis in Youth Study. *Journal of the American Medical Association*, 281, 727–735.

STUART, R. B. (1967). Behavioral control of overeating. *Behavior Research and Therapy*, 5, 357–365.

STUNKARD, A. J. (1987). Conservative treatments for obesity. *American Journal of Clinical Nutrition*, 45, 1142–1154.

STUNKARD, A. J., & BERTHOLD, H. C. (1985). What is behavior therapy? A very short description of behavioral weight control. *American Journal of Clinical Nutrition*, 41, 821–823.

STUNKARD, A. J., FELIX, M. R. J., & COHEN, R. Y. (1985). Mobilizing a community to promote health: The Pennsylvania County Health Improvement Program (CHIP). In J. C. ROSEN & L. J. SOLOMON (Eds.), *Prevention in health psychology*. Hanover, NH: University Press of New England.

STUNKARD, A. J., FOCH, T. T., & HRUBEC, Z. (1986). A twin study of human obesity. *Journal of the American Medical Association*, 256, 51–54.

STUNKARD, A. J., SORENSEN, T. I. A., HANIS, C., TEASDALE, T. W., CHAKRABORTY, R., SCHULL, W. J., & SCHULSINGER, F. (1986). An adoption study of human obesity. *New England Journal of Medicine*, 314, 193–198.

STURGES, J. W., & ROGERS, R. W. (1996). Preventive health psychology from a developmental perspective: An extension of protection motivation theory. *Health Psychology*, 15, 158–166.

SUAREZ, E. C., BATES, M. P., & HARRALSON, T. L. (1998). The relation of hostility to lipids and lipoproteins in women: Evidence for the role of antagonistic hostility. *Annals of Behavioral Medicine*, 20, 59–63.

SUAREZ, E. C., KUHN, C. M., SCHANBERG, S. M., WILLIAMS, R. B., & ZIMMERMAN, E. A. (1998). Neuroendocrine, cardiovascular, and emotional responses of hostile men: The role of interpersonal challenge. *Psychosomatic Medicine*, 60, 78–88.

SUAREZ, E. C., WILLIAMS, R. B., KUHN, C. M., ZIMMERMAN, E. H., & SCHANBERG, S. M. (1991). Biobehavioral basis of coronary-prone behavior in middle-aged men. Part II: Serum cholesterol, the Type A behavior pattern, and hostility as interactive modulators of physiological reactivity. *Psychosomatic Medicine*, 53, 528–537.

SUAREZ, M., RAFFAELLI, M., & O'LEARY, A. (1996). Use of folk healing practices by HIV-infected Hispanics living in the Unites States. *AIDS Care*, 8, 683–690.

SUEDFELD, P. (1990). Restricted environmental stimulation and smoking cessation: A 15-year progress report. *International Journal of the Addictions*, 25, 861–888.

SUEDFELD, P., & IKARD, F. F. (1974). Use of sensory deprivation in facilitating the reduction of cigarette smoking. *Journal of Consulting and Clinical Psychology*, 42, 888–895.

SUINN, R. M. (1982). Intervention with Type A behavior. *Journal of Consulting and Clinical Psychology*, 50, 933–949.

SUITOR, C. W., & HUNTER, M. F. (1980). *Nutrition: Principles and application in health promotion*. Philadelphia: Lippincott.

SULLIVAN, J. M. (1991). Salt sensitivity: Definition, conception, methodology, and long-term issues. *Hypertension*, 17(Supplement I), 161–168.

SULS, J. (1982). Social support, interpersonal relations, and health: Benefits and liabilities. In G. S. SANDERS & J. SULS (Eds.), *Social psychology of health and illness*. Hillsdale, NJ: Erlbaum.

SULS, J. (1984). Levels of analysis and efforts to modify adolescent health behavior: A commentary on Lund and Kegeles. *Health Psychology*, 3, 371–375.

SULS, J., & FLETCHER, B. (1985). The relative efficacy of avoidant and nonavoidant coping strategies: A meta-analysis. *Health Psychology*, 4, 249–288.

SULS, J., MARTIN, R., & LEVENTHAL, H. (1997). Social comparison, lay referral, and the decision to seek medical care. In B. P. BUUNK & F. X. GIBBONS (Eds.), *Health, coping, and well-being: Perspectives from social comparison theory* (pp. 195–226). Mahwah, NJ: Erlbaum.

SULS, J., & MULLEN, B. (1981). Life change and psychological distress: The role of perceived control and desirability. *Journal of Applied Social Psychology*, 11, 379–389.

SULS, J., & SANDERS, G. S. (1988). Type A behavior as a general risk factor for physical disorder. *Journal of Behavioral Medicine*, 11, 210–226.

SULS, J., SANDERS, G. S., & LABRECQUE, M. S. (1986). Attempting to control blood pressure without systematic instruction: When advice is counterproductive. *Journal of Behavioral Medicine*, 9, 567–576.

SULS, J., & SWAIN, A. (1993). Use of meta-analysis in health psychology. In S. MAES, H. LEVENTHAL, & M. JOHNSTON (Eds.), *International review of health psychology* (Vol. 2). New York: Wiley.

SULS, J., WAN, C. K., & BLANCHARD, E. B. (1994). A multilevel data-analytic approach for evaluation of relationships between daily life stressors and symptomatology: Patients with irritable bowel syndrome. *Health Psychology*, 13, 103–113.

SULS, J., WAN, C. K., & COSTA, P. T. (1995). Relationship of trait anger to resting blood pressure: A meta-analysis. *Health Psychology*, 14, 444–456.

SUPER, C. N. (1981). Cross-cultural research on infancy. In H. C. TRANDIS & A. HERON (Eds.), *Handbook of cross-cultural psychology: Developmental psychology* (Vol. 4). Boston: Allyn & Bacon.

SUPERKO, H. R., & KRAUSS, R. M. (1994). Coronary artery disease regression: Convincing evidence for the benefit of aggressive lipoprotein management. *Circulation*, 90, 1056–1069.

SURWIT, R. S. (1993). Of mice and men: Behavioral medicine in the study of type II diabetes. *Annals of Behavioral Medicine*, 15, 227–235.

SURWIT, R. S., FEINGLOS, M. N., & SCOVERN, A. W. (1983). Diabetes and behavior: A paradigm for health psychology. *American Psychologist*, 38, 255–262.

SUSSER, M., HOPPER, K., & RICHMAN, R. (1983). Society, culture, and health. In D. MECHANIC (Ed.), *Handbook of health, health care, and the health professions*. New York: Free Press.

SUTER, P. O., SCHUTZ, Y., & JEQUIER, E. (1992). The effect of ethanol on fat storage in healthy subjects. *New England Journal of Medicine*, 326, 983–987.

SUTTON, S., & HALLETT, R. (1988). Understanding the effects of fear-arousing communications: The role of cognitive factors and the amount of fear aroused. *Journal of Behavioral Medicine*, 11, 353–360.

SUTTON, S., McVEY, D., & GLANZ, A. (1999). A comparative test of the theory of reasoned action and the theory of planned behavior in the prediction of condom use intentions in a national sample of English young people. *Health Psychology*, 18, 72–81.

SUTTON, S. R. (1982). Fear-arousing communications: A critical examination of theory and research. In J. R. EISER (Ed.), *Social psychology and behavioral medicine*. New York: Wiley.

SVARSTAD, B. (1976). Physician-patient communication and patient conformity with medical advice. In D. MECHANIC (Ed.), *The growth of bureaucratic medicine*. New York: Wiley.

SWAN, G. E., CARMELLI, D., & ROSENMAN, R. H. (1986). Spouse-pair similarity on the California Psychological Inventory with reference to husband's coronary heart disease. *Psychosomatic Medicine*, 48, 172–186.

SWEET, J. J. (1991). Psychological evaluation and testing services in medical settings. In J. J. SWEET, R. H. ROZENSKY, & S. M. TOVIAN (Eds.), *Handbook of clinical psychology in medical settings*. New York: Plenum.

SWEET, J. J., ROZENSKY, R. H., & TOVIAN, S. M. (1991). Clinical psychology in medical settings: Past and present. In J. J. SWEET, R. H. ROZENSKY, & S. M. TOVIAN (Eds.), *Handbook of clinical psychology in medical settings*. New York: Plenum.

SWIGONSKI, M. E. (1987). *Bio-psycho-social factors affecting coping and compliance with the hemodialysis treatment regimen*. University Microfilms International. (Order No. 8803518).

SWINBURN, B. A., WALTER, L. G., ARROL, B., TILYARD, M. W., & RUSSELL, D. G. (1998). The Green Prescription Study: A randomized controlled trial of written exercise advice provided by general practitioners. *American Journal of Public Health*, 88, 288–291.

SYME, S. L. (1984). Sociocultural factors and disease etiology. In W. D. GENTRY (Ed.), *Handbook of behavioral medicine*. New York: Guilford.

TAGLIACOZZO, D. L., & MAUKSCH, H. O. (1972). The patient's view of the patient's role. In E. G. JACO (Ed.), *Patients, physicians, and illness* (2nd ed.). New York: Free Press.

TALBOT, F., NOUWEN, A., GINGRAS, J., BÉLANGER, A., & AUDET, J. (1999). Relations of diabetes intrusiveness and personal control to symptoms of depression among adults with diabetes. *Health Psychology*, 18, 537–542.

TALLMER, J., SCHERWITZ, L., CHESNEY, M., HECKER, M., HUNKELER, E., SERWITZ, J., & HUGHES, G. (1990). Selection, training, and quality control of Type A interviewers in a prospective study of young adults. *Journal of Behavioral Medicine*, 13, 449–466.

TANNER, J. M. (1970). Physical growth. In P. H. MUSSEN (Ed.), *Carmichael's manual of child psychology* (3rd ed.). New York: Wiley.

TANNER, J. M. (1978). *Foetus into man*. Cambridge, MA: Harvard University Press.

TAPP, J. T. (1985). Multisystems interventions in disease. In N. SCHNEIDERMAN & J. T. TAPP (Eds.), *Behavioral medicine: The biopsychosocial approach*. Hillsdale, NJ: Erlbaum.

TARNOWSKI, K. J., RASNAKE, L. K., & DRABMAN, R. S. (1987). Behavioral assessment and treatment of pediatric burn injuries: A review. *Behavior Therapy*, 18, 417–441.

TATE, D. G., MAYNARD, F., & FORCHHEIMER, M. (1993). Predictors of psychologic distress one year after spinal cord injury. *American Journal of Physical Medicine and Rehabilitation*, 72, 272–275.

TAYLOR, R. L., LAM, D. J., ROPPEL, C. E., & BARTER, J. T. (1984). Friends can be good medicine: Excursion into mental health promotion. *Community Mental Health Journal, 20,* 294–303.

TAYLOR, S. E. (1979). Hospital patient behavior: Reactance, helplessness, or control? *Journal of Social Issues, 35,* 156–184.

TAYLOR, S. E. (1983). Adjustment to threatening events: A theory of cognitive adaptation. *American Psychologist, 38,* 1161–1173.

TAYLOR, S. E., LICHTMAN, R. R., & WOOD, J. V. (1984). Attributions, beliefs about control, and adjustment to breast cancer. *Journal of Personality and Social Psychology, 46,* 489–502.

TEBBI, C. K., CUMMINGS, K.M., ZEVON, M. A., SMITH, L., RICHARDS, M., & MALLON, J. (1986). Compliance of pediatric and adolescent cancer patients. *Cancer, 58,* 1179–1184.

TELL, G. S., POLAK, J. F., WARD, B. J., KITTNER, S. J., et al. (1994). Relation of smoking with carotid artery wall thickness and stenosis in older adults: The Cardiovascular Health Study. *Circulation, 90,* 2905–2908.

TEMOSHOK, L. (1990). On attempting to articulate the biopsychosocial model: Psychological-psychophysiological homeostasis. In H. S. FRIEDMAN (Ed.), *Personality and disease.* New York: Wiley.

TEMOSHOK, L., & DREHER, H. (1992). *The Type C connection: The behavioral links to cancer and your health.* New York: Random House.

TENNEN, H., & AFFLECK, G. (1997). Social comparison as a coping process: A critical review and application to chronic pain disorders. In B. P. BUUNK & F. X. GIBBONS (Eds.), *Health, coping, and well-being: Perspectives from social comparison theory* (pp. 263–298). Mahwah, NJ: Erlbaum.

TENNEN, H., AFFLECK, G., ARMELI, S., & CARNEY, M. A. (2000). A daily process approach to coping: Linking theory, research, and practice. *American Psychologist, 55,* 626–636.

TENNEN, H., EBERHARDT, T. L., & AFFLECK, G. (1999). Depression research methodologies at the social-clinical interface: Still hazy after all these years. *Journal of Social and Clinical Psychology, 18,* 121–159.

TENNES, K., & KREYE, M. (1985). Children's adrenocortical responses to classroom activities and tests in elementary school. *Psychosomatic Medicine, 47,* 451–460.

TERI, L., HUGHES, J. P., & LARSON, E. B. (1990). Cognitive deterioration in Alzheimer's disease: Behavioral and health factors. *Journal of Gerontology: Psychological Sciences, 45,* P58–63.

TERRY, R. D., OAKLAND, M. J., & ANKENY, K. (1991). Factors associated with adoption of dietary behavior to reduce heart disease risk among males. *Journal of Nutrition Education, 23,* 154–160.

THACKWRAY, D. E., SMITH, M. C., BODFISH, J. W., & MEYERS, A. W. (1993). A comparison of behavioral and cognitive-behavioral interventions for bulimia nervosa. *Journal of Consulting and Clinical Psychology, 61,* 639–645.

THELEN, M. H., FRY, R. A., FEHRENBACH, P. A., & FRAUTSCHI, N. M. (1979). Therapeutic videotape and film modeling: A review. *Psychological Bulletin, 86,* 701–720.

THEORELL, T., & RAHE, R. H. (1975). Life change events, ballistocardiography, and coronary death. *Journal of Human Stress, 1,* 18–24.

THOITS, P. A. (1982). Conceptual, methodological, and theoretical problems in studying social support as a buffer against life stress. *Journal of Health and Social Behavior, 23,* 145–159.

THOMAS, A., CHESS, S., & BIRCH, H. G. (1970, August). The origin of personality. *Scientific American,* pp. 102–109.

THOMAS, A. M., PETERSON, L., & GOLDSTEIN, D. (1997). Problem solving and diabetes regimen adherence by children and adolescents with IDDM in social pressure situations: A reflection of normal development. *Journal of Pediatric Psychology, 22,* 541–561.

THOMPSON, J. (1984). Communicating with patients. In R. FITZPATRICK, J. HINTON, S. NEWMAN, G. SCAMBLER, & J. THOMPSON (Eds.), *The experience of illness.* London: Tavistock.

THOMPSON, J. K. (1986, April). Larger than life. *Psychology Today,* pp. 38–44.

THOMPSON, S. C. (1981). Will it hurt less if I can control it? A complex answer to a simple question. *Psychological Bulletin, 90,* 89–101.

THOMPSON, S. C. (1998). Blockades to finding meaning and control. In J. H. HARVEY (Ed.), *Perspectives on loss: A sourcebook* (pp. 21–34). Philadelphia: Brunner/Mazel.

THOMPSON, S. C., KENT, D. R., THOMAS, C., & VRUNGOS, S. (1999). Real and illusory control over exposure to HIV in college students and gay men. *Journal of Applied Social Psychology, 29,* 1128–1150.

THOMPSON, S. C., & KYLE, D. J. (in press). The role of perceived control in coping with the losses associated with chronic illness. In J. H. HARVEY & E. D. MILLER (Eds.), *Loss and trauma: General and close relationship perspectives.* Philadelphia: Bruner/Mazel.

THOMPSON, S. C., NANNI, C., & SCHWANKOVSKY, L. (1990). Patient-oriented interventions to improve communication in a medical office visit. *Health Psychology, 9,* 390–404.

THORESEN, C. E. (1984). Overview. In J. D. MATARAZZO, S. M. WEISS, J. A. HERD, N. E. MILLER, & S. M. WEISS (Eds.), *Behavioral health: A handbook of health enhancement and disease prevention.* New York: Wiley.

THORESEN, C. E., FRIEDMAN, M., POWELL, L. H., GILL, J. J., & ULMER, D. K. (1985). Altering the Type A behavior pattern in postinfarction patients. *Journal of Cardiopulmonary Rehabilitation*, 5, 258–266.

THORESEN, C. E., & PATTILLO, J. R. (1988). Exploring the Type A behavior pattern in children and adolescents. In B. K. HOUSTON & C. R. SNYDER (Eds.), *Type A behavior pattern: Research, theory, and intervention*. New York: Wiley.

THORNDIKE, A. N., RIGOTTI, N. A., STAFFORD, R. S., & SINGER, D. E. (1998). National patterns in the treatment of smokers by physicians. *Journal of the American Medical Association*, 279, 604–608.

THUN, M. J., DAY-LALLY, C. A., CALLE, E. E., FLANDERS, W. D., & HEATH, C. W. (1995). Excess mortality among cigarette smokers: Changes in a 20-year interval. *American Journal of Public Health*, 85, 1223–1230.

THUN, M. J., PETO, R., LOPEZ, A. D., MONACO, J. H., HENLEY, S. J., HEATH, C. W., & DOLL, R. (1997). Alcohol consumption and mortality among middle-aged and elderly U.S. adults. *New England Journal of Medicine*, 337, 1705–1714.

TIMKO, C. (1987). Seeking medical care for a breast cancer symptom: Determinants of intentions to engage in prompt or delay behavior. *Health Psychology*, 6, 305–328.

TIMS, F. M., FLETCHER, B. W., & HUBBARD, R. L. (1991). Treatment outcomes for drug abuse clients. In R. W. PICKENS, C. G. LEUKEFELD, & C. R. SCHUSTER (Eds.), *Improving drug abuse treatment*. Rockville, MD: National Institute on Drug Abuse.

TINETTI, M. E., BAKER, D. I., McAVAY, G., CLAUS, E. B., GARRETT, P., GOTTSCHALK, M., KOCH, M. L., TRAINOR, K., & HORWITZ, R. I. (1994). A multifactorial intervention to reduce the risk of falling among elderly people living in the community. *New England Journal of Medicine*, 331, 821–827.

TOLCHIN, M. (1988, December 2). U.S. study faults nursing home care over medications. *New York Times*, pp. A1, B7.

TOMAKA, J. BLASCOVICH, J., KIBLER, J., & ERNST, J. M. (1997). Cognitive and physiological antecedents to threat and challenge appraisal. *Journal of Personality and Social Psychology*, 73, 63–72.

TOMKINS, S. (1966). Psychological model for smoking behavior. *American Journal of Public Health*, 56(12, Supplement), 17–20.

TOMKINS, S. (1968). A modified model of smoking behavior. In E. F. BORGATTA & R. R. EVANS (Eds.), *Smoking, health and behavior*. Chicago: Aldine.

TORRENS, P. R. (1985). Hospice care: What have we learned? *Annual Review of Public Health*, 6, 65–83.

TORRES, G., & HOROWITZ, J. M. (1999). Drugs of abuse and brain gene expression. *Psychosomatic Medicine*, 61, 630–650.

TORTORA, G. J., & GRABOWSKI, S. R. (2000). *Principles of anatomy and physiology* (9th ed.). New York: Wiley.

TOTMAN, R. (1982). Psychosomatic theories. In J. R. EISER (Ed.), *Social psychology and behavioral medicine*. New York: Wiley.

TOVIAN, S. M. (1991). Integration of clinical psychology into adult and pediatric oncology programs. In J. J. SWEET, R. H. ROZENSKY, & S. M. TOVIAN (Eds.), *Handbook of clinical psychology in medical settings*. New York: Plenum.

TRABIN, T., RADER, C., & CUMMINGS, C. (1987). A comparison of pain management outcomes for disability compensation and non-compensation patients. *Psychology and Health*, 1, 341–351.

TRAPP, B. D., PETERSON, J., RANSOHOFF, R. M., RUDICK, R., MORK, S., & BO, L. (1998). Axonal transection in the lesions of multiple sclerosis. *New England Journal of Medicine*, 338, 278–285.

TRAUE, H. C., & KOSARZ, P. (1999). Everyday stress and Crohn's disease activity: A time series analysis of 20 single cases. *International Journal of Behavioral Medicine*, 6, 101–119.

TREMBLAY, A., WOUTERS, E., WENKER, M., ST-PIERRE, S., BOUCHARD, C., & DESPRÉS, J.-P. (1995). Alcohol and a high-fat diet: A combination favoring overfeeding. *American Journal of Clinical Nutrition*, 62, 639–644.

TREMBLAY, G. C., & PETERSON, L. (1999). Prevention of childhood injury: Clinical and public health policy challenges. *Clinical Psychology Review*, 19, 415–434.

TROSS, S. & HIRSCH, D. A. (1988). Psychological distress and neuropsychological complications of HIV infection and AIDS. *American Psychologist*, 43, 929–934.

TRUMBULL, R., & APPLEY, M. H. (1986). A conceptual model for examination of stress dynamics. In M. H. APPLEY & R. TRUMBULL (Eds.), *Dynamics of stress: Physiological, psychological, and social perspectives*. New York: Plenum.

TSC (Trenton State College) (1992). *Alcohol & drug education program*. Trenton, NJ: Author.

TUCKER, J. S., FRIEDMAN, H. S., WINGARD, D. L., & SCHWARTZ, J. E. (1996). Marital history at midlife as a predictor of longevity: Alternative explanations to the protective effect of marriage. *Health Psychology*, 15, 94–101.

TUNKS, E., & BELLISSIMO, A. (1991). *Behavioral medicine: Concepts and procedures*. New York: Pergamon.

TURK, D. C. (1996). Biopsychosocial perspective on chronic pain. In ROBERT J. GATCHEL & D. C. TURK (Eds.), *Psychological approaches to pain management: A practitioner's handbook* (pp. 3–32). New York: Guilford.

TURK, D. C., BRODY, M. C., & OKIFUJI, E. A. (1994). Physicians' attitudes and practices regarding the long-term prescribing of opioids for non-cancer pain. *Pain*, 59, 201–208.

TURK, D. C., & HOLZMAN, A. D. (1986). Commonalities among psychological approaches in the treatment of chronic pain: Specifying the meta-constructs. In A. D. HOLZMAN & D. C. TURK (Eds.), *Pain management: A handbook of psychological treatment approaches.* New York: Pergamon.

TURK, D. C., LITT, M. D., SALOVEY, P., & WALKER J. (1985). Seeking urgent pediatric treatment: Factors contributing to frequency, delay, and appropriateness. *Health Psychology,* 4, 43–59.

TURK, D. C., & MEICHENBAUM, D. (1991). Adherence to self-care regimens: The patient's perspective. In J. J. SWEET, R. H. ROSENSKY, & S. M. TOVIAN (Eds.), *Handbook of clinical psychology in medical settings.* New York: Plenum.

TURK, D. C., MEICHENBAUM, D., & GENEST, M. (1983). *Pain and behavioral medicine: A cognitive-behavioral perspective.* New York: Guilford.

TURK, D. C., & OKIFUJI, A. (1999). Assessment of patients' reporting of pain: An integrated perspective. *Lancet,* 353, 1784–1788.

TURK, D. C., & RUDY, T. E. (1986). Assessment of cognitive factors in chronic pain: A worthwhile enterprise? *Journal of Consulting and Clinical Psychology,* 54, 760–768.

TURK, D. C., RUDY, T. E., & SALOVEY, P. (1984). Health protection: Attitudes and behaviors of LPNs, teachers, and college students. *Health Psychology,* 3, 189–210.

TURK, D. C., RUDY, T. E., & SORKIN, B. A. (1992). Chronic pain: Behavioral conceptualizations and interventions. In S. M. TURNER, K. S. CALHOUN, & H. E. ADAMS (Eds.), *Handbook of clinical behavior therapy* (2nd ed.). New York: Wiley.

TURK, D. C., & SALOVEY, P. (1995). Cognitive-behavioral treatment of illness behavior. In P. M. NICASSIO & T. W. SMITH (Eds.), *Managing chronic illness: A biopsychosocial perspective.* Washington, DC: American Psychological Association.

TURK, D. C., & STACEY, B. R. (2000). Multidisciplinary pain centers in the treatment of chronic back pain. In J. W. FRYMOYER, T. B. DUCKER, N. M. HADLER, J. P. KOSTUIK, J. N. WEINSTEIN, & T. S. WHITCLOUD (Eds.), *The adult spine: Principles and practice* (2nd ed.). Philadelphia: Lippincott Williams & Wilkins.

TURK, D. C., WACK, J. T., & KERNS, R. D. (1985). An empirical examination of the "pain-behavior" construct. *Journal of Behavioral Medicine,* 8, 119–130.

TURK-CHARLES, S., MEYEROWITZ, B. E., & GATZ, M. (1997). Age differences in information-seeking among cancer patients. *International Journal of Aging and Human Development,* 45, 85–98.

TURKKAN, J. S., McCAUL, M. E., & STITZER, M. L. (1989). Psychophysiological effects of alcohol-related stimuli: II. Enhancement with alcohol availability. *Alcoholism: Clinical and Experimental Research,* 13, 392–398.

TURNER, J. A. (1982). Comparison of group progressive-relaxation training and cognitive-behavioral group therapy for chronic low back pain. *Journal of Consulting and Clinical Psychology,* 50, 757–765.

TURNER, J. A., CLANCY, S., McQUADE, K. J., & CARDENAS, D. D. (1990). Effectiveness of behavioral therapy for chronic low back pain: A component analysis. *Journal of Consulting and Clinical Psychology,* 58, 573–579.

TURNER, J. A., CLANCY, S., & VITALIANO, P. P. (1987). Relationships of stress, appraisal and coping, to chronic low back pain. *Behavior Research and Therapy,* 25, 281–288.

TURNER, J. R., & HEWITT, J. K. (1992). Twin studies of cardiovascular response to psychological challenge: A review and suggested future directions. *Annals of Behavioral Medicine,* 14, 12–20.

TURNER, J. R., WARD, M. M., GELLMAN, M. D., JOHNSTON, D. W., LIGHT, K. C., & VAN DOORNEN, L. J. P. (1994). The relationship between laboratory and ambulatory cardiovascular activity: Current evidence and future directions. *Annals of Behavioral Medicine,* 16, 12–23.

TYLER, D. C. (1990). Patient-controlled analgesia in adolescents. *Journal of Adolescent Health Care,* 11, 154–158.

UCHINO, B. N., & GARVEY, T. S. (1997). The availability of social support reduces cardiovascular reactivity to acute psychological stress. *Journal of Behavioral Medicine,* 20, 15–27.

UCHINO, B. N., HOLT-LUNSTAD, J., UNO, D., BETANCOURT, R., & GARVEY, T. S. (1999). Social support and age-related differences in cardiovascular function: An examination of potential mediators. *Annals of Behavioral Medicine,* 21, 135–142.

UKESTAD, L. K., & WITTROCK, D. A. (1996). Pain perception and coping in female tension headache sufferers and headache-free controls. *Health Psychology,* 15, 65–68.

URBAN, B. J., FRANCE, R. D., STEINBERGER, E. K., SCOTT, D. L., & MALTBIE, A. A. (1986). Long-term use of narcotic/antidepressant medication in the management of phantom limb pain. *Pain,* 24, 191–196.

USBC (United States Bureau of the Census) (1971). *Statistical Abstract of the United States: 1971.* (92nd ed.). Washington, DC: U.S. Government Printing Office.

USBC (United States Bureau of the Census) (1989). *Statistical Abstracts of the United States: 1988* (108th ed.). Washington, DC: U.S. Government Printing Office.

USBC (United States Bureau of the Census) (1991). *Statistical Abstracts of the United States: 1991* (111th ed.). Washington, DC: U.S. Government Printing Office.

USBC (United States Bureau of the Census) (1994). *Statistical Abstracts of the United States: 1993* (113th ed.). Washington, DC: U.S. Government Printing Office.

USBC (United States Bureau of the Census) (1995). *Statistical Abstracts of the United States: 1994* (114th ed.). Washington, DC: U.S. Government Printing Office.

USBC (United States Bureau of the Census) (1999). *Statistical Abstracts of the United States: 1998* (118th ed.). Retrieved (2-28-2000) from http://www.census.gov.

USDA (United States Department of Agriculture) (1995). *Nutrition and your health: Dietary guidelines for Americans* (4th ed.). Washington, DC: U.S. Government Printing Office.

USDA (United States Department of Agriculture) (1999). *America's eating habits: Changes and consequences.* Retrieved (3-24-2000) from http://www.usda.gov.

USDHHS (United States Department of Health and Human Services) (1981). *Medicines and you* (Publication No. NIH 81-2140). Washington, DC: U.S. Government Printing Office.

USDHHS (United States Department of Health and Human Services) (1982). *Changes in mortality among the elderly: United States, 1940–78* (Publication No. PHS 82-1406). Washington, DC: U.S. Government Printing Office.

USDHHS (United States Department of Health and Human Services) (1985a). *Charting the nation's health: Trends since 1960* (Publication No. PHS 85-1251). Washington, DC: U.S. Government Printing Office.

USDHHS (United States Department of Health and Human Services) (1985b). *NIOSH pocket guide to chemical hazards* (Publication No. DHEW 85-114). Washington, DC: U.S. Government Printing Office.

USDHHS (United States Department of Health and Human Services) (1986a). *Clinical opportunities for smoking intervention: A guide for the busy physician* (Publication No. NIH 86-2178). Washington, DC: U.S. Government Printing Office.

USDHHS (United States Department of Health and Human Services) (1986b). *Health status of the disadvantaged: Chartbook 1986* (Publication No. HRS-P-DV86-2). Washington, DC: U.S. Government Printing Office.

USDHHS (United States Department of Health and Human Services) (1986c). *The health consequences of involuntary smoking: A report of the Surgeon General* (Publication No. CDC 87-8398). Washington, DC: U.S. Government Printing Office.

USDHHS (United States Department of Health and Human Services) (1987). *Vital statistics of the United States, 1984: Life tables* (Publication No. PHS 87-1104). Washington, DC: U.S. Government Printing Office.

USDHHS (United States Department of Health and Human Services) (1989). *Reducing the health consequences of smoking: 25 years of progress. A report of the Surgeon General* (DHHS Publication No. CDC 89-8411). Rockville, MD: Office on Smoking and Health.

USDHHS (United States Department of Health and Human Services) (1990). *Alcohol and health* (Publication No. ADM 90-1656). Rockville, MD: National Institute on Alcohol Abuse and Alcoholism.

USDHHS (United States Department of Health and Human Services) (1994). *Acute low back pain problems in adults: Assessment and treatment.* (Quick reference guide for clinicians: Number 14). Washington, DC: U.S. Government Printing Office.

USDHHS (United States Department of Health and Human Services) (1995). *Health United States: 1994* (Publication No. PHS 95-1232). Washington, DC: U.S. Government Printing Office.

VALOIS, R. F., ADAMS, K. G., & KAMMERMANN, S. K. (1996). One-year evaluation results from CableQuit: A community cable television smoking cessation pilot program. *Journal of Behavioral Medicine, 19,* 479–499.

VAN ECK, M. M., & NICOLSON, N. A. (1994). Perceived stress and salivary cortisol in daily life. *Annals of Behavioral Medicine, 16,* 221–227.

VAN EGEREN, L. F., SNIDERMAN, L. D., & ROGGELIN, M. S. (1982). Competitive two-person interactions of Type-A and Type-B individuals. *Journal of Behavioral Medicine, 5,* 55–56.

VAN GRIENSVEN, G. J. P., DE VROOME, E. M. M., GOUDSMIT, J., & COUTINHO, R. E. (1989). Changes in sexual behaviour and the fall in incidence of HIV infection among homosexual men. *British Medical Journal, 298,* 218–221.

VAN'T SPIJKER, A., TRIJSBURG, R. W., & DUIVENVOORDEN, H. J. (1997). Psychological sequelae of cancer diagnosis: A meta-analytic review of 58 studies after 1980. *Psychosomatic Medicine, 59,* 280–293.

VARNI, J. W., & BABANI, L. (1986). Long-term adherence to health care regimens in pediatric chronic disorders. In N. A. KRASNEGOR, J. D. ARASTEH, & M. F. CATALDO (Eds.), *Child health behavior: A behavioral pediatrics perspective.* New York: Wiley.

VARNI, J. W., JAY, S. M., MASEK, B. J., & THOMPSON, K. L. (1986). Cognitive-behavioral assessment and management of pediatric pain. In A. D. HOLZMAN & D. C. TURK (Eds.), *Pain management: A handbook of psychological treatment approaches.* New York: Pergamon.

VARNI, J. W., & THOMPSON, K. L. (1986). Biobehavioral assessment and management of pediatric pain. In N. A. KRASNEGOR, J. D. ARASTEH, & M. F. CATALDO (Eds.), *Child health behavior: A behavioral pediatrics perspective.* New York: Wiley.

VECCHIO, P. C. (1994). Attitudes to alternative medicine by rheumatology outpatient attenders. *Journal of Rheumatology, 21,* 147–147.

VEDHARA, K., COX, N. K. M., WILCOCK, G. K., PERKS, P., HUNT, M., ANDERSON, S., LIGHTMAN, S. L., & SHANKS, N. M.

(1999). Chronic stress in elderly carers of dementia patients and antibody response to influenza vaccination. *Lancet, 353,* 627–631.

VEIT, R., BRODY, S., & RAU, H. (1997). Four-year stability of cardiovascular reactivity to psychological stress. *Journal of Behavioral Medicine, 20,* 447–460.

VELICER, W. F., PROCHASKA, J. O., FAVA, J. L., LAFORGE, R. G., & ROSSI, J. S. (1999). Interactive versus noninteractive interventions and dose-response relationships for stage-matched smoking cessation programs in a managed care setting. *Health Psychology, 18,* 21–28.

VENER, A. M., & KRUPKA, L. R. (1990). AIDS knowledge and attitudes revisited (1987-1989). *American Biology Teacher, 52,* 461–466.

VENN, J. R., & SHORT, J. G. (1973). Vicarious classical conditioning of emotional responses in nursery school children. *Journal of Personality and Social Psychology, 28,* 249–255.

VERBRUGGE, L. M. (1980). Sex differences in complaints and diagnoses. *Journal of Behavioral Medicine, 3,* 327–355.

VERBRUGGE, L. M. (1985). Gender and health: An update on hypotheses and evidence. *Journal of Health and Social Behavior, 26,* 156–182.

VERRIER, R. L., DESILVA, R. A., & LOWN, B. (1983). Psychological factors in cardiac arrhythmias and sudden death. In D. S. KRANTZ, A. BAUM, & J. E. SINGER (Eds.), *Handbook of psychology and health* (Vol. 3). Hillsdale, NJ: Erlbaum.

VERTINSKY, P., & AUMAN, J. T. (1988). Elderly women's barriers to exercise, Part I: Perceived risks. *Health Values, 12*(4), 13–19.

VINEY, L. L., WALKER, B. M., ROBERTSON, T., LILLEY, B., & EWAN, C. (1994). Dying in palliative care units and in hospital: A comparison of the quality of life of terminal cancer patients. *Journal of Consulting and Clinical Psychology, 62,* 157–164.

VINOKUR, A. D., THREATT, B. A., VINOKUR-KAPLAN, D., & SATARIANO, W. A. (1990). The process of recovery from breast cancer for younger and older patients: Changes during the first year. *Cancer, 65,* 1242–1254.

VISINTAINER, P. F., & MATTHEWS, K. A. (1987). Stability of overt Type A behaviors in children: Results from a two- and five-year longitudinal study. *Child Development, 58,* 1586–1591.

VITALIANO, P. P., RUSSO, J., BAILEY, S. L., YOUNG, H. M., & MCCANN, B. S. (1993). Psychosocial factors associated with cardiovascular reactivity in older adults. *Psychosomatic Medicine, 55,* 164–177.

VITALIANO, P. P., RUSSO, J., BREEN, A. R., VITIELLO, M. V., & PRINZ, P. N. (1986). Functional decline in the early stages of Alzheimer's disease. *Journal of Psychology and Aging, 1,* 41–46.

VITALIANO, P. P., RUSSO, J., & NIAURA, R. (1995). Plasma lipids

and their relationships with psychosocial factors in older adults. *Journal of Gerontology, 50B,* P18–24.

VLADECK, B. C. (1983). Nursing homes. In D. MECHANIC (Ed.), *Handbook of health, health care, and the health professions.* New York: Free Press.

VOLINN, E., TURCZYN, K. M., & LOESER, J. D. (1994). Patterns of low back pain hospitalizations: Implications for the treatment of low back pain in an era of health care reform. *Clinical Journal of Pain, 10,* 64–70.

VON KORFF, M., DWORKIN, S. F., & LE RESCHE, L. (1990). Graded chronic pain status: An epidemiologic evaluation. *Pain, 40,* 279–291.

WADDEN, T. A., & ANDERTON, C. H. (1982). The clinical use of hypnosis. *Psychological Bulletin, 91,* 215–243.

WADDEN, T. A., BERKOWITZ, R. I., SILVESTRY, F., VOGT, R. A., ST. JOHN SUTTON, M. G., STUNKARD, A. J., FOSTER, G. D., & ABER, J. L. (1998). The fen-phen finale: A study of weight loss and valvular heart disease. *Obesity Research, 6,* 278–284.

WADDEN, T. A., & BROWNELL, K. D. (1984). The development and modification of dietary practices in individuals, groups, and large populations. In J. D. MATARAZZO, S. M. WEISS, J. A. HERD, N. E. MILLER, & S. M. WEISS (Eds.), *Behavioral health: A handbook of health enhancement and disease prevention.* New York: Wiley.

WADDEN, T. A., STUNKARD, A. J., & LIEBSCHUTZ, J. (1988). Three-year follow-up of the treatment of obesity by very low calorie diet, behavior therapy, and their combination. *Journal of Consulting and Clinical Psychology, 56,* 925–928.

WADE, N. (1997, June 24). Genetic cause found for some cases of human obesity. *New York Times,* p. C3.

WAGENAAR, A. C., & WEBSTER, D. W. (1986). Preventing injuries to children through compulsory automobile safety seat use. *Pediatrics, 78,* 662–672.

WAITZKIN, H., & STOECKLE, J. D. (1976). Information control and the micropolitics of health care: Summary of an ongoing research project. *Social Science and Medicine, 10,* 263–276.

WALLACE, L. M. (1986). Communication variables in the design of pre-surgical preparatory information. *British Journal of Clinical Psychology, 25,* 111–118.

WALLER, J. A. (1987). Injury: Conceptual shifts and preventive implications. *Annual Review of Public Health, 8,* 21–49.

WALLERSTEIN, J. S. (1983). Children of divorce: Stress and developmental tasks. In N. GARMEZY & M. RUTTER (Eds.), *Stress, coping, and development in children.* New York: McGraw-Hill.

WALLERSTEIN, J. S. (1986). Children and divorce: The psychological tasks of the child. In R. H. MOOS (Ed.), *Coping with life crises: An integrated approach.* New York: Plenum.

WALLSTON, B. S., ALAGNA, S. W., DEVELLIS, B. M., & DEVELLIS, R. F. (1983). Social support and physical illness. *Health Psychology, 2,* 367–391.

WALLSTON, K. A. (1993). Health psychology in the USA. In S. MAES, H. LEVENTHAL, & M. JOHNSTON (Eds.), *International review of health psychology* (Vol. 2). Chichester, UK: Wiley.

WALLSTON, K. A., & WALLSTON, B. S. (1982). Who is responsible for your health? The construct of health locus of control. In G. S. SANDERS & J. SULS (Eds.), *Social psychology of health and illness.* Hillsdale, NJ: Erlbaum.

WALLSTON, K. A., WALLSTON, B. S., & DEVELLIS, R. (1978). Development of the Multidimensional Health Locus of Control (MHLC) Scales. *Health Education Monographs, 6,* 161–170.

WALTER, H. J., HOFMAN, A., CONNELLY, P. A., BARRETT, L. T., & KOST, K. L. (1985). Primary prevention of chronic disease in children: Changes in risk factors after one year of intervention. *American Journal of Epidemiology, 122,* 772–781.

WANG, P. H., LAU, J. & CHALMERS, T. C. (1993). Meta-analysis of effects of intensive blood-glucose control on late complications of type I diabetes. *Lancet, 341,* 1306–1309.

WANG, Y., CORR, J. G., THALER, H. T., TAO, Y., FAIR, W. R., & HESTON, W. D. W. (1995). Decreased growth of established human prostate LNCaP tumors in nude mice fed a low-fat diet. *Journal of the National Cancer Institute, 87,* 1456–1462.

WANZER, S. H., FEDERMAN, D. D., ADELSTEIN, S. J., CASSEL, C. K., et al. (1989). The physician's responsibility toward hopelessly ill patients: A second look. *New England Journal of Medicine, 320,* 844–849.

WARD, S. E., GOLDBERG, N., MILLER-MCCAULRY, V., MUELLER, C., NOLAN, A., PAWLIK-PLANK, D., ROBBINS, A., STORMOEN, D., & WEISSMAN, D. E. (1993). Patient-related barriers to management of cancer pain. *Pain, 52,* 319–324.

WARDLE, F. J., COLLINS, W., PERNET, A. L., WHITEHEAD, M. I., BOURNE, T. H., & CAMPBELL, S. (1993). Psychological impact of screening for familial ovarian cancer. *Journal of the National Cancer Institute, 85,* 653–657.

WARE, J. E., BAYLISS, M. S., ROGERS, W. H., KOSINSKI, M., & TARLOV, A. R. (1996). Differences in 4-year health outcomes for elderly and poor, chronically ill patients treated in HMO and fee-for-service systems: Results from the Medical Outcomes Study. *Journal of the American Medical Association, 276,* 1039–1047.

WARGA, C. (1987, August). Pain's gatekeeper. *Psychology Today,* pp. 50–56.

WARSHAW, R. (1992, March 8). Fat chance. *Philadelphia Inquirer Magazine,* pp. 26–31.

WATSON, D., & PENNEBAKER, J. W. (1989). Health complaints, stress, and distress: Exploring the central role of negative affectivity. *Psychological Review, 96,* 234–254.

WATSON, M., HAVILAND, J. S., GREER, S., DAVIDSON, J., & BLISS, J. M. (1999). Influence of psychological response on survival in breast cancer: A population-based cohort study. *Lancet, 354,* 1331–1336.

WATSON, M., & RAMIREZ, A. (1991). Psychological factors in cancer prognosis. In C. L. COOPER & M. WATSON (Eds.), *Cancer and stress: Psychological, biological, and coping studies.* New York: Wiley.

WEIDNER, G., CONNOR, S. L., HOLLIS, J. F., & CONNOR, W. E. (1992). Improvements in hostility and depression in relation to dietary change and cholesterol lowering: The Family Heart Study. *Annals of Internal Medicine, 117,* 820–823.

WEIDNER, G., KOHLMANN, C.-W., DOTZAUER, E., & BURNS, L. R. (1996). The effect of academic stress on health behaviors in young adults. *Anxiety, Stress, and Coping, 9,* 123–133.

WEIDNER, G., & MATTHEWS, K. A. (1978). Reported physical symptoms elicited by unpredictable events and the Type A coronary-prone behavior pattern. *Journal of Personality and Social Psychology, 36,* 1213–1220.

WEIDNER, G., & MESSINA, C. R. (1998). Cardiovascular reactivity to mental stress. In K. ORTH-GOMER, M. CHESNEY, & N. K. WEGNER (Ed.), *Women, stress, and heart disease.* Mahwah, NJ: Erlbaum.

WEIDNER, G., & MUELLER, H. (1999). Emotions and heart disease. In M. B. GOLDMAN & M. C. HATCH (Eds.), *Women and health* (pp. 789–797). San Diego: Academic Press.

WEINBERGER, M., HINER, S. L., & TIERNEY, W. M. (1987). In support of hassles as a measure of stress in predicting health outcomes. *Journal of Behavioral Medicine, 10,* 19–31.

WEINER, H. (1977). *Psychobiology and human disease.* New York: Elsevier.

WEINHARDT, L. S., CAREY, M. P., JOHNSON, B. T., & BICKHAM, N. L. (1999). Effects of HIV counseling and testing on sexual risk behavior: Meta-analytic review of published research, 1985–1997. *American Journal of Public Health, 89,* 1397–1405.

WEINMAN, J. (1990). Health psychology: Progress, perspectives and prospects. In P. BENNETT, J. WEINMAN, & P. SPURGEON (Eds.), *Current developments in health psychology.* Chur, Switzerland: Harwood.

WEINSTEIN, N. D. (1982). Unrealistic optimism about susceptibility to health problems. *Journal of Behavioral Medicine, 5,* 441–460.

WEINSTEIN, N. D. (1987). Unrealistic optimism about susceptibility to health problems: Conclusions from a community-wide sample. *Journal of Behavioral Medicine, 10,* 481–500.

WEINSTEIN, N. D. (1988). The precaution adoption process. *Health Psychology*, 7, 355–386.

WEINSTEIN, N. D. (2000). Perceived probability, perceived severity, and health-protective behavior. *Health Psychology*, 19, 65–74.

WEINSTEIN, N. D., & KLEIN, W. M. (1995). Resistance of personal risk perceptions to debiasing interventions. *Health Psychology*, 14, 132–140.

WEIR, R., BROWNE, G., ROBERTS, J., TUNKS, E., & GAFNI, A. (1994). The Meaning of Illness Questionnaire: Further evidence for its reliability and validity. *Pain*, 58, 377–386.

WEISENBERG, M. (1977). Pain and pain control. *Psychological Bulletin*, 84, 1008–1044.

WEISMAN, A. D. (1976). Coping with untimely death. In R. H. MOOS (Ed.), *Human adaptation: Coping with life crises*. Lexington, MA: Heath.

WEISMAN, A. D. (1977). The psychiatrist and the inexorable. In H. FEIFEL (Ed.), *New meanings of death*. New York: McGraw-Hill.

WEISMAN, A. D. (1979). *Coping with cancer*. New York: McGraw-Hill.

WEISS, G. L., LARSEN, D. L., & BAKER, W. K. (1996). The development of health protective behaviors among college students. *Journal of Behavioral Medicine*, 19, 143–161.

WEISS, K. B., GERGEN, P. J., & HODGSON, T. A. (1992). An economic evaluation of asthma in the United States. *New England Journal of Medicine*, 326, 862–866.

WEISS, R. (1997, November). Aging: New answers to old questions. *National Geographic*, 192, 2–31.

WEISS, S. M. (1984). Health hazard/health risk appraisals. In J. D. MATARAZZO, S. M. WEISS, J. A. HERD, N. E. MILLER, & S. M. WEISS (Eds.), *Behavioral health: A handbook of health enhancement and disease prevention*. New York: Wiley.

WELIN, L., SVÄRDSUDD, K., WILHELMSEN, L., LARSSON, B., & TIBBLIN, G. (1987). Analysis of risk factors for stroke in a cohort of men born in 1913. *New England Journal of Medicine*, 317, 521–526.

WENNEKER, M. B., WEISSMAN, J. S., & EPSTEIN, A. M. (1990). The association of payer with utilization of cardiac procedures in Massachusetts. *Journal of the American Medical Association*, 264, 1255–1260.

WERNER, E. E. (1987). Resilient children. In H. E. FITZGERALD & M. G. WALRAVEN (Eds.), *Annual editions: Human development 87/88*. Guilford, CT: Dushkin.

WERNER, E. E., & SMITH, R. S. (1982). *Vulnerable but invincible: A study of resilient children*. New York: McGraw-Hill.

WERNICK, R. I. (1983). Stress inoculation in the management of clinical pain: Applications to burn pain. In D. MEICHENBAUM & M. E. JAREMKO (Eds.), *Stress reduction and prevention*. New York: Plenum.

WERRY, J. S. (1986). Physical illness, symptoms, and allied disorders. In H. C. QUAY & J. S. WERRY (Eds.), *Psychopathological disorders of childhood* (3rd ed.). New York: Wiley.

WEST, S. G., LIGHT, K. C., HINDERLITER, A. L., STANWYCK, C. L., BRAGDON, E. E., & BROWNLEY, K. A. (1999). Potassium supplementation induces beneficial cardiovascular changes during rest and stress in salt sensitive individuals. *Health Psychology*, 18, 229–240.

WESTERDAHL, J., OLSSON, H., MÄSBÄCK, A., INGVAR, C., JONSSON, N., BRANDT, L., JÖNSSÖN, P.-E., & MOLLER, T. (1994). Use of sunbeds or sunlamps and malignant melanoma in Southern Sweden. *American Journal of Epidemiology*, 140, 691–699.

WETTER, D. W., FIORE, M. C., BAKER, T. B., & YOUNG, T. B. (1995). Tobacco withdrawal and nicotine replacement influence objective measures of sleep. *Journal of Consulting and Clinical Psychology*, 63, 658–667.

WETTER, D. W., KENFORD, S. L., SMITH, S. S., FIORE, M. C., JORENBY, D. E., & BAKER, T. B. (1999). Gender differences in smoking cessation. *Journal of Consulting and Clinical Psychology*, 67, 555–562.

WHALEN, C K., HENKER, B., O'NEIL, R., HOLLINGSHEAD, J., HOLMAN, A., & MOORE, B. (1994). Optimism in children's judgements of health and environmental risks. *Health Psychology*, 13, 319–325.

WHITAKER, R. C., WRIGHT, J. A., PEPE, M. S., SEIDEL, K. D., & DIETZ, W. H. (1997). Predicting obesity in young adulthood from childhood and parental obesity. *New England Journal of Medicine*, 337, 869–873.

WHITE, L. P. (1977). Death and the physician: Mortus vivos docent. In H. FEIFE (Ed.), *New meanings of death*. New York: McGraw-Hill.

WHITEHEAD, A. S., GALLAGHER, P., MILLS, J. L., KIRKE, P. N., BURKE, H., MOLLOY, A. M., WEIR, D. G., SHIELDS, D. C., & SCOTT, J. M. (1995). A genetic defect in 5,10 methylenetetrahydrofolate reductase in neural tube defects. *Quarterly Journal of Medicine*, 88, 763–766.

WHITEHEAD, W. E. (1986). Pediatric gastrointestinal disorders. In N. A. KRASNEGOR, J. D. ARASTEH, & M. F. CATALDO (Eds.), *Child health behavior: A behavioral pediatrics perspective*. New York: Wiley.

WHITEHEAD, W. E., BUSCH, C. M., HELLER, B. R., & COSTA, P. T. (1986). Social learning influences on menstrual symptoms and illness behavior. *Health Psychology*, 5, 13–23.

WHO (World Health Organization) (1998). *Tobacco epidemic: Health dimensions*. Retrieved (2-28-2000) from http://www.who.org.

WHO (World Health Organization) (1999a). AIDS *epidemic update*. Retrieved (2-28-2000) from http://www.who.org.

WHO (World Health Organization) (1999b, December 3). *Weekly epidemiological record*. Retrieved (2-28-2000) from http://www.who.org.

WHO (World Health Organization) (1999c). *World health report*. Retrieved (2-28-2000) from http:// www.who.org.

WIDEMAN, M. V., & SINGER, J. E. (1984). The role of psychological mechanisms in preparation for childbirth. *American Psychologist*, 39, 1357–1371.

WIEBE, D. J., & McCALLUM, D. M. (1986). Health practices and hardiness as mediators in the stress-illness relationship. *Health Psychology*, 5, 425–438.

WIELGOSZ, A. T., FLETCHER, R. H., McCANTS, C. B., McKINNIS, R. A., HANEY, T. L., & WILLIAMS, R. B. (1984). Unimproved chest pain in patients with minimal or no coronary disease: A behavioral phenomenon. *American Heart Journal*, 108, 67–72.

WIENS, A. N., & MENUSTIK, C. E. (1983). Treatment outcome and patient characteristics in an aversion therapy program for alcoholism. *American Psychologist*, 38, 1089–1096.

WILCOX, S., & STORANDT, M. (1996). Relations among age, exercise, and psychological variables in a community sample of women. *Health Psychology*, 15, 110–113.

WILCOX, V. L., KASL, S. V., & BERKMAN, L. F. (1994). Social support and physical disability in older people after hospitalization: A prospective study. *Health Psychology*, 13, 170–179.

WILKINSON, G. (1987). The influence of psychiatric, psychological and social factors on the control of insulin-dependent diabetes mellitus. *Journal of Psychosomatic Research*, 31, 277–286.

WILLIAMS, C. J. (1990). *Cancer biology and management: An introduction*. New York: Wiley.

WILLIAMS, D. A. (1996). Acute pain management. In R. J. GATCHEL & D. C. TURK (Eds.), *Psychological approaches to pain management: a practitioner's handbook* (pp. 55–77). New York: Guilford.

WILLIAMS, D. A., & KEEFE, F. J. (1991). Pain beliefs and the use of cognitive-behavioral coping strategies. *Pain*, 46, 185–190.

WILLIAMS, D. R., & RUCKER, T. (1996). Socioeconomic status and the health of racial minority populations. In P. M. KATO & T. MANN (Eds.), *Handbook of diversity issues in health psychology* (pp. 407–423). New York: Plenum.

WILLIAMS, P. G., WIEBE, D. J., & SMITH, T. W. (1992). Coping processes as mediators of the relationship between hardiness and health. *Journal of Behavioral Medicine*, 15, 237–255.

WILLIAMS, R. (1989, January/February). The trusting heart. *Psychology Today*, pp. 36–42.

WILLIAMS, R. B., & BAREFOOT, J. C. (1988). Coronary-prone behavior: The emerging role of the hostility complex. In B. K. HOUSTON & C. R. SNYDER (Eds.), *Type A behavior pattern: Research, theory, and intervention*, New York: Wiley.

WILLIAMS, R. B., HANEY T. L., LEE, K. L., KONG, Y.-H., BLUMENTHAL, J. A., & WHALEN, R. E. (1980). Type A behavior, hostility, and coronary atherosclerosis. *Psychosomatic Medicine*, 42, 539–549.

WILLIAMS, R. B., SUAREZ, E. C., KUHN, C. M., ZIMMERMAN, E. A., & SCHANBERG, S. M. (1991). Biobehavioral basis of coronary-prone behavior in middle-aged men. Part I: Evidence for chronic SNS activation in Type As. *Psychosomatic Medicine*, 53, 517–527.

WILLIAMSON, D. A., CUBIC, B. A., & FULLER, R. D. (1992). Eating disorders. In S. E. TURNER, K. S. CALHOUN, & H. E. ADAMS (Eds.), *Handbook of clinical behavior therapy* (2nd ed.). New York: Wiley.

WILLIAMSON, D. F., MADANS, J., ANDA, R. F., KLEINMAN, J. C., GIOVINO, G. A., & BYERS, T. (1991). Smoking cessation and severity of weight gain in a national cohort. *New England Journal of Medicine*, 324, 739–745.

WILLIAMSON, G. M. (2000). Extending the activity restriction model of depressed affect: Evidence from a sample of breast cancer patients. *Health Psychology*, 19, 339–347.

WILLICH, S. N., LÖWEL, H., LEWIS, M., HÖRMANN, A., ARNTZ, H.-R., & KEIL, U. (1994). Weekly variation of acute myocardial infarction: Increased Monday risk in the working population. *Circulation*, 90, 87–93.

WILLIS, L., THOMAS, P., GARRY, P. J., & GOODWIN, J. S. (1987). A prospective study of response to stressful life events in initially healthy elders. *Journal of Gerontology*, 42, 627–630.

WILLS, T. A. (1984). Supportive functions of interpersonal relationships. In S. Cohen & L. SYME (EDS.), *Social support and health*. New York: Academic Press.

WILLS, T. A. (1986). Stress and coping in early adolescence: Relationships to substance use in urban school samples. *Health Psychology*, 5, 503–529.

WILSON, D. K., HOLMES, S. D., ARHEART, K., & ALPERT, B. S. (1995). Cardiovascular reactivity in black and white siblings versus matched controls. *Annals of Behavioral Medicine*, 17, 207–212.

WILSON, D. K., KLIEWER, W., BAYER, L., JONES, D., WELLEFORD, A., HEINEY, M., & SICA, D. A. (1999). The influence of gender and emotional versus instrumental support on cardiovascular reactivity in African-American adolescents. *Annals of Behavioral Medicine*, 21, 235–243.

WILSON, D. K., SICA, D. A., & MILLER, S. B. (1999). Effects of potassium on blood pressure in salt-sensitive and salt-resistant black adolescents. *Hypertension*, 34, 181–186.

WILSON, D. P., & ENDRES, R. K. (1986). Compliance with blood glucose monitoring in children with type 1 diabetes mellitus. *Behavioral Pediatrics*, 108, 1022–1024.

WILSON, G. T. (1984). Weight control treatments. In

J. D. Matarazzo, S. M. Weiss, J. A. Herd, N. E. Miller, & S. M. Weiss (Eds.), *Behavioral health: A handbook of health enhancement and disease prevention*. New York: Wiley.

Wilson, G. T., Loeb, K. L., Walsh, B. T., Labouvie, E., Petkova, E., Liu, X., & Waternaux, C. (1999). Psychological versus pharmacological treatments for bulimia nervosa: Predictors and processes of change. *Journal of Consulting and Clinical Psychology, 67,* 451–459.

Wilson, I. B., & Cleary, P. D. (1995). Linking clinical variables with health-related quality of life. *Journal of the American Medical Association, 273,* 59–65.

Wilson, W., Ary, D. V., Biglan, A., Glasgow, R. E., Toobert, D. J., & Campbell, D. R. (1986). Psychosocial predictors of self-care behaviors (compliance) and glycemic control in non-insulin-dependent diabetes mellitus. *Diabetes Care, 9,* 614–622.

Wincze, J. P. (1977). Sexual deviance and dysfunction. In D. C. Rimm & J. W. Somervill (Eds.), *Abnormal psychology*. New York: Academic Press.

Windsor, R. A., Lowe, J. B., Perkins, L. L., Smith-Yoder, D., Artz, L., Crawford, M., Amburgy, K., & Boyd, N. R. (1993). Health education for pregnant smokers: Its behavioral impact and cost benefit. *American Journal of Public Health, 83,* 201–206.

Winefield, H. R. (1992). Doctor-patient communication: An interpersonal helping process. In S. Maes, H. Leventhal, & M. Johnston (Eds.), *International review of health psychology* (Vol. 1). New York: Wiley.

Winett, R. A., King, A. C., & Altman, D. G. (1989). *Health psychology and public health: An integrative approach*. New York: Pergamon.

Wing, R. R. (1992). Weight cycling in humans: a review of the literature. *Annals of Behavioral Medicine, 14,* 113–119.

Wing, R. R., Epstein, L. H., Nowalk, M. P., & Lamparski, D. M. (1986). Behavioral self-regulation in the treatment of patients with diabetes mellitus. *Psychological Bulletin, 99,* 78–89.

Wing, R. R., & Jeffery, R. W. (1999). Benefits of recruiting participants with friends and increasing social support for weight loss and maintenance. *Journal of Consulting and Clinical Psychology, 67,* 132–138.

Wing, R. R., Nowalk, M. P., & Guare, J. C. (1998). Diabetes mellitus. In E. A. Blechman & K. D. Brownell (Eds.), *Handbook of behavioral medicine for women*. New York: Pergamon.

Winikoff, B. (1983). Nutritional patterns, social choices, and health. In D. Mechanic (Ed.), *Handbook of health, health care, and the health professions*. New York: Free Press.

Winkleby, M. A., Flora, J. A., & Kraemer, H. C. (1994). A community-based heart disease intervention: Predictors of change. *American Journal of Public Health, 84,* 767–772.

Winters, R. (1985). Behavioral approaches to pain. In N. Schneiderman & J. T. Tapp (Eds.), *Behavioral medicine: The biopsychosocial approach*. Hillsdale, NJ: Erlbaum.

Witryol, S. L. (1971). Incentives and learning in children. In H. W. Reese (Eds.), *Advances in child development and behavior* (Vol. 6). New York: Academic Press.

Wittrock, D. A., & Myers, T. C. (1998). The comparison of individuals with recurrent tension-type headache and headache-free controls in physiological response, appraisal, and coping with stressors: A review of the literature. *Annals of Behavioral Medicine, 20,* 118–134.

Wolf, S., & Wolff, H. G. (1947). *Human gastric function* (2nd ed.). New York: Oxford University Press.

Wolk, A., Bergstrom, R., Hunter, D., Willett, W., Ljung, H., Holmberg, L., Bergkvist, L., Bruce, A., & Adami, H. O. (1998). A prospective study of association of monounsaturated fat and other types of fat with risk of breast cancer. *Archives of Internal Medicine, 158,* 41–45.

Wolpe, J. (1958). *Psychotherapy by reciprocal inhibition*. Stanford, CA: Stanford University Press.

Wolpe, J. (1973). *The practice of behavior therapy* (2nd ed.). New York: Pergamon.

Woods, A. M., & Birren, J. E. (1984). Late adulthood and aging. In J. D. Matarazzo, S. M. Weiss, J. A. Herd, N. E. Miller, & S. M. Weiss (Eds.), *Behavioral health: A handbook of health enhancement and disease prevention*. New York: Wiley.

Woods, P. J., & Burns, J. (1984). Type A behavior and illness in general. *Journal of Behavioral Medicine, 7,* 411–415.

Woods, P. J., Morgan, B. T., Day, B. W., Jefferson, T., & Harris, C. (1984). Findings on a relationship between Type A behavior and headaches. *Journal of Behavioral Medicine, 7,* 277–286.

Woodward, N. J., & Wallston, B. S. (1987). Age and health care beliefs: Self-efficacy as a mediator of low desire for control. *Psychology and Aging, 2,* 3–8.

Wooster, R., Bignell, G., Lancaster, J., Swift, S., et al. (1995). Identification of the breast cancer susceptibility gene BRCA2. *Nature, 378,* 789–792.

Wortman, C. B. (1975). Some determinants of perceived control. *Journal of Personality and Social Psychology, 31,* 282–294.

Wortman, C. B., & Dunkel-Schetter, C. (1979). Interpersonal relationships and cancer: A theoretical analysis. *Journal of Social Issues, 35,* 120–155.

Wortman, C. B., & Dunkel-Schetter, C. (1987). Conceptual and methodological issues in the study of social support. In A. Baum & J. E. Singer (Eds.), *Handbook of psychology and health* (Vol. 5). Hillsdale, NJ: Erlbaum.

Wright, L. (1988). The Type A behavior pattern and coronary artery disease. *American Psychologist, 43,* 2–14.

WRIGHT, L., & FRIEDMAN, A. G. (1991). Challenge of the future: Psychologists in medical settings. In J. J. SWEET, R. H. ROZENSKY, & S. M. TOVIAN (Eds.), *Handbook of clinical psychology in medical settings*. New York: Plenum.

WRIGHT, R. J., RODRIGUEZ, M., & COHEN, S. (1998). Review of psychosocial stress and asthma: An integrated biopsychosocial approach. *Thorax, 53*, 1066–1074.

WULFERT, E., WAN, C. K., & BACKUS, C. A. (1996). Gaymen's safer sex behavior: An integration of three models. *Journal of Behavioral Medicine, 19*, 345–366.

WURTELE, S. K., & MADDUX, J. E. (1987). Relative contributions of protection motivation theory components in predicting exercise intentions and behavior. *Health Psychology, 6*, 453–466.

YANOVSKI, J. A., YANOVSKI, S. Z., SOVIK, K. N., NGUYEN, T. T., O'NEIL, P. M., & SEBRING, N. G. (2000). A prospective study of holiday weight gain. *New England Journal of Medicine, 342*, 861–867.

YARNOLD, P. R., BRYANT, F. B., & GRIMM, L. G. (1987). Comparing the long and short forms of the student version of the Jenkins Activity Survey. *Journal of Behavioral Medicine, 10*, 75–90.

YEATON, W. H., SMITH, D., & ROGERS, K. (1990). Evaluating understanding of popular press reports of health research. *Health Education Quarterly, 72*, 223–234.

YEE, B. W. K., CASTRO, F. G., HAMMOND, W. R., JOHN, R., WYATT, G. E., & YUNG, B. R. (1995). Panel IV: Risk-taking and abusive behaviors among ethnic minorities. *Health Psychology, 14*, 622–631.

YOFFE, E. (1999, November 9). Doctors are reminded, "Wash up!" *New York Times*, pp. F1, F9.

YOUNG, K., & ZANE, N. (1995). Ethnocultural influences in evaluation and management. In P. M. NICASSIO & T. W. SMITH (Eds.), *Managing chronic illness: A biopsychosocial perspective*. Washington, DC: American Psychological Association.

ZARSKI, J. J. (1984). Hassles and health: A replication. *Health Psychology, 3*, 243–251.

ZAUTRA, A. J., BURLESON, M. H., SMITH, C. A., BLALOCK, S. J., WALLSTON, K. A., DEVELLIS, R. F., DEVELLIS, B. M., &

SMITH, T. W. (1995). Arthritis and perceptions of quality of life: An examination of positive and negative affect in rheumatoid arthritis patients. *Health Psychology, 14*, 399–408.

ZAUTRA, A. J., OKUN, M. A., ROBINSON, S. E., LEE, D., ROTH, S. H., & EMMANUAL, J. (1989). Life stress and lymphocyte alterations among patients with rheumatoid arthritis. *Health Psychology, 8*, 1–14.

ZELTZER, L. K., BUSH, J. P., CHEN, E., & RIVERAL, A. (1997). A psychobiologic approach to pediatric pain: Part II: Prevention and treatment. *Current Problems in Pediatrics, 27*, 264–284.

ZHANG, Y., PROENCA, R., MAFFEI, M., BARONE, M., LEOPOLD, L., & FRIEDMAN, J. M. (1994). Positional cloning of the mouse obese gene and its human homologue. *Nature, 372*, 425–432.

ZHU, S.-H., STRECH, V., BALABANIS, M., ROSBROOK, B., SADLER, G., & PIERCE, J. P. (1996). Telephone counseling for smoking cessation: Effects of single-session and multiple-session interventions. *Journal of Counseling and Clinical Psychology, 64*, 202–211.

ZIMBARDO, P. G. (1970). The human choice: Individuation, reason, and order versus deindividuation, impulse, and chaos. In W. J. ARNOLD & D. LEVINE (Eds.), *Nebraska symposium on motivation, 1969*. Lincoln, NE: University of Nebraska Press.

ZIMMER, J. G., JUNCKER, A. G., & MCCUSKER, J. (1985). A randomized controlled study of a home health care team. *American Journal of Public Health, 75*, 134–141.

ZINMAN, B. (1984). Diabetes mellitus and exercise. *Behavioral Medicine Update, 6*(1), 22–25.

ZISOOK, S., PETERKIN, J. J., SHUCHTER, S. R., & BARDONE, A. (1995). Death, dying, and bereavement. In P. M. NICASSIO & T. M. SMITH (Eds.), *Managing chronic illness: A biopsychosocial perspective*. Washington, DC: American Psychological Association.

ZOLA, I. K. (1973). Pathways to the doctor—From person to patient. *Social Science and Medicine, 7*, 677–689.

ZUCKER, R. A., & GOMBERG, E. S. L. (1986). Etiology of alcoholism reconsidered: The case for a biopsychosocial process. *American Psychologist, 41*, 783–793.

CREDITS

PHOTOS

Chapter 1
Page 6: Corbis-Bettmann. Page 8: John Verano, National Museum of Natural History; courtesy Smithsonian Institution. Page 9: From R. Melzack and P. Wall (1965). "Pain mechanisms: A new theory." *Science*, 150, 971–979. Reproduced with permission. Page 18 (top): Reprinted with special permission of King Features Syndicate. Page 18 (bottom): Paul Trummer/The Image Bank.

Chapter 2
Page 47: Courtesy Peggy Simsarian Striegel. Page 65: From N. Cushing, *The Pituitary Body and Its Disorders*.

Chapter 3
Page 72: Tom Kelly/The Mercury. Page 77: Mark Antman/The Image Works. Page 83: N. R. Rowan/The Image Works. Page 86: Jim Mahoney/The Image Works. Page 88: Courtesy Lafayette Instrument Company. Page 92: Reprinted with special permission of King Features Syndicate.

Chapter 4
Page 99: Comstock, Inc. Page 108: Michael Dwyer/Stock, Boston. Page 112: Reprinted with special permission of King Features Syndicate. Page 125: From F. Andrasik, D. D. Blake, & M. S. McCarran (1986).

Chapter 5
Page 136: Reprinted with special permission of King Features Syndicate. Page 141: Michael Heron/Woodfin Camp & Associates. Page 142: Richard Reinhold/EKM-Nepenthe. Page 149: David Powers/Stock, Boston.

Chapter 6
Page 166: Henley & Savage/The Stock Market. Page 171: Reprinted courtesy of Bunny Hoest. Page 183: Bruce Ayres/Tony Stone Images/New York, Inc. Page 192: Robert Kalman/The Image Works. Page 198: Tony Michaels/The Image Works.

Chapter 7
Page 213: Courtesy The American Cancer Society. Page 219: Corbis-Bettmann. Page 221: Larry Gatz/The Image Bank. Page 232: Joseph Sohm; ChromoSohm Inc./Corbis Images.

Chapter 8
Page 238: Bruce Ayres/Stone. Page 240: Reprinted by permission of Tribune Media Services. Page 246: PhotoDisc. Page 249: Robert E. Daemmrich/Stone. Page 251: Reprinted courtesy of Bunny Hoest. Page 257: Richard T. Nowitz/Corbis Images. Page 261: Bob Daemmrich/The Image Works. Page 264: Reprinted courtesy of Bunny Hoest. Page 267: Joe McBride/Stone.

Chapter 9
Page 276: Bruce Ayres/Stone. Page 283: Martha Tabor/Working Images Photographs. Page 290: © 1991. Reprinted courtesy of Bunny Hoest. Page 292: Gale Zucker/Stock, Boston. Page 297: FRANK & ERNEST reprinted by permission of United Feature Syndicate, Inc.

Chapter 10
Page 308: Culver Pictures, Inc. Page 310: Bob Daemmrich/Stock, Boston. Page 315: Billy Barnes. Page 316: Reprinted courtesy of Bunny Hoest. Page 326: Griffin/The Image Works.

Chapter 11
Page 338: Reproduced by permission of Johnny Hart and Creators Syndicate, Inc. Page 342: Bettman Archives/Corbis Images. Page 353: Tim Barnwell/Stock, Boston. Page 360: Robert Brenner/PhotoEdit. Page 362: Richard Wood/The Picture Cube.

Chapter 12
Page 368: Courtesy The New York Historical Society. Page 386: Kindra Clineff/Stone. Page 387: Terry Vine/Stone.

Chapter 13
Page 400: Jim Whitmer/Stock, Boston. Page 408: Richard Ellis/The Image Works. Page 418: Terry Vine/Stone.

Chapter 14
Page 434: David J. Sams/Stock, Boston. Page 444: Comstock, Inc. Page 448: © Houston Chronicle. Page 452:

A. Reininger/Woodfin Camp & Associates. Page 460: Al Campanie/The Image Works.

FIGURES AND TABLES

Figure 2–2: Drawings from E. H. Lenneberg (1967, Figure 4.6). *Biological foundations of language.* Copyright © 1967 by John Wiley & Sons, Inc.; reprinted by permission of the publisher. Drawings based on photographs from J. L. Conel (1939–1963). *The postnatal development of the human cerebral cortex* (Vols. 1–7). Reproduced by permission of Harvard University Press.

Figure 2H–1: From J. C. B. Grant (1972). *An atlas of anatomy.* Copyright © 1972 by Williams & Wilkins Co.

Table 3.1: From T. Holmes & R. Rahe (1967). The Social Readjustment Rating Scale. *Journal of Psychosomatic Research*, 11, 213–218.

Table 3A.1: Adapted from E. P. Sarafino & M. Ewing (1999). The Hassles Assessment Scale for Students in College: Measuring the frequency and unpleasantness of and dwelling on stressful events. *Journal of American College Health*, 48, 75–83. Reprinted by permission of the author.

Figure 4–5: From F. Andrasik, D. D. Blake, & M. S. McCarran (1986). A biobehavioral analysis of pediatric headache. In N. A. Krasnegor, J. D. Arasteh, & M. F. Cataldo (Eds.), *Child health behavior: A behavioral pediatrics perspective.* Copyright © 1986 by John Wiley & Sons, Inc.

Table 5.5: From R. W. Novaco (1978). Anger and coping with stress: Cognitive and behavioral interventions. In J. P. Foreyt & D. P. Rathjen (Eds.), *Cognitive behavior therapy: Research and application.* Copyright © 1978 by Plenum Press.

Figure 6–2: Adapted from M. H. Becker & I. M. Rosenstock (1984). Compliance with medical advice. In A. Steptoe & A. Mathews (Eds.), *Health care and human behavior.* Copyright © 1984 by Academic Press.

Table 8.1: From Metropolitan Life Foundation (1983). 1983 Metropolitan Height and Weight Tables. *Statistical Bulletin*, 64(1), 2–9. Courtesy of the Metropolitan Life Insurance Co.

Figure 9–2: From M. A. Safer, Q. J. Tharps, T. C. Jackson, & H. Leventhal (1979). Determinants of three stages of delay in seeking care at a medical clinic. *Medical Care*, 17, 11–29.

Figure 10–2: Adapted from E. A. Anderson (1987). Preoperative preparation for cardiac surgery facilitates recovery, reduces psychological distress, and reduces the incidence of acute postoperative hypertension. *Journal of Consulting and Clinical Psychology*, 55, 513–520. Copyright © 1987 by the American Psychological Association; adapted by permission of the author.

Figure 10–3: From S. M. Miller & C. E. Mangan (1983). Interacting effects of information and coping style in adapting to gynecologic stress: Should the doctor tell all? *Journal of Personality and Social Psychology*, 45, 223–236. Copyright © 1983 by the American Psychological Association; reprinted by permission of the author.

Figure 10–4: From E. P. Sarafino & J. W. Armstrong (1986). *Child and adolescent development* (2nd ed.). St. Paul, MN: West Publishing Co. Copyright © 1986 by Edward P. Sarafino and James W. Armstrong; reprinted by permission of the authors.

Figure 11A–1: From R. Melzack (1975). The McGill Pain Questionnaire: Major properties and scoring methods. *Pain*, 1, 277–299. Copyright © 1975 by Elsevier Science Publishers.

Figure 12–1: Adapted from F. Andrasik (1986). Relaxation and biofeedback for chronic headaches. In A. D. Holzman & D. C. Turk (Eds.), *Pain management: A handbook of psychological treatment approaches.* Copyright © 1986 by Pergamon Press PLC.

Figure 13–1: Adapted from R. H. Moos (1982). Coping with acute health crises. In T. Millon, C. Green, & R. Meagher (Eds.), *Handbook of clinical health psychology.* Copyright © 1982 by Plenum Press.

Figure 13–3: From J. R. Holum (1994). *Fundamentals of general, organic, and biological chemistry* (5th ed.). Copyright © 1994 by John Wiley & Sons, Inc.; reprinted by permission of the publisher.

Figure 14–1: From American Cancer Society (2000). *Cancer facts and figures—1999.* Retrieved (3-7-2000) from http://www.cancer.org. Reproduced with permission of the American Cancer Society.

SUBJECT INDEX

Conditioning:
classical, 14, 147–148
and immune functions,
123
operant, 14, 172, 222, 372–373
Conflict theory, 181–182, 480
Contracting, behavioral, 216, 228,
252.
Control. See Personal control
Control Data's "Stay Well" program,
194
Control groups, 26
Conversion hysteria, 13
Coping:
with chronic illness, 397–402
with chronic pain, 353–355
developing methods, 138–139
emotion-focused, 135, 136
functions of, 135–136
future role of health psychology,
469
gender differences, 139–140
glossary definition, 480
with high-mortality illness,
428–430
vs. managing, 134
methods of, 136–138
in old age, 139
overview, 134
problem attention vs. avoidance,
138
problem-focused, 135–136
skills and strategies, 136–138
sociocultural differences, 139–140
strategies for hospitalized
children, 326–328
with stress, 133–140
with stressful medical procedures,
322–324
with terminal illness, 455–456
Coronary heart disease (CHD):
age differences, 431
biological risk factors, 431
and exercise benefits, 262
gender differences, 431
glossary definition, 480
initial medical treatment, 432
lifestyle risk factors, 431
and negative emotions, 431–432
overview, 430–431
patient rehabilitation, 432–433
psychosocial impact, 433–435

psychosocial interventions,
435–436
reducing stress-related risk,
155–158
risk factors, 431–432
and smoking, 210–211
sociocultural differences, 431
and stress, 119, 128–129
and Type A behavior pattern,
115–116, 157
Correlation coefficient, 27–28, 480
Correlational studies, 27–28, 481
Corticosteroids, 88, 119, 120, 129,
481
Corticotropin-releasing factor, 43
Cortisol, 44, 62, 88, 120
Cost–benefit ratio, 469–470
Counter-irritation, 385, 481
Cousins, Norman, 13
Crisis theory, 398, 481
Cross-sectional approach, 29–30, 481
Cue exposure, 229

D

Daily hassles, 92, 93, 481
Darwin, Charles, 63
Death and dying. See also Terminal
illness
causes of death, 7
effect of smoking, 208, 209
medical care, 457, 459
psychological care, 457, 459
quality of life, 457–460
stages of adjustment, 456–457
and stress, 83, 84
and survivors, 461–462
Decisional control, 105–106, 481
Defense mechanisms, 138, 181
Degenerative illness, 7. See also
High-mortality illness
Dendrites, 34–35
Densensitization, systematic,
147–148
Deoxyribonucleic acid (DNA), 63
Depersonalization, 313, 481
Depressants, 231, 370, 481
Depression, 13, 79–80, 110
Descartes, Rene, 9
Detoxification, 226–227, 481
Diabetes mellitus:
causes of, 410–411

in children and adolescents,
415–416
health implications, 411–412
medical regimens, 412
overview, 410
and pancreas, 44
patient adherence to regimen,
412–413
psychosocial factors, 413, 415
self-managing, 414–415
types of, 410–411
Diastolic pressure, 53
Diencephalon, 36, 37
Dietary diseases, 5, 481
Dieting, 250–255
Dietitians, 22
Diets. See Food; Nutrition
Digestive system:
disorders, 48, 123–124
glossary definition, 481
illustrated, 46
overview, 44
step-by-step journey, 46–48
Diphtheria, 5, 6
Direct effects hypothesis, 104, 481
Disability, and stress, 83, 84
Diseases. See also Illnes
autoimmune, 61
dietary, 5
infectious, 5–6
Distraction, 376, 378–379, 481
Disulfiram, 229
Dizygotic (DZ) twins, 30–31
DNA (deoxyribonucleic acid), 63
Doctor-centered style, 292, 481
Doctors. See Patient-practitioner
relationships
Dominant genes, 63
Double-blind procedure, 26, 481
Drug abuse:
age differences, 230, 231–232
characteristics of drug abusers,
230–231
health issues, 232
overview, 230
preventing and stopping, 232–233
problems related to, 203
relapses, 233
treating, 233
Drugs:
for acute pain, 369, 370, 371
for chronic pain, 370, 371–372

AUTHOR INDEX